D1032877

THE WORKS

OF

HUBERT HOWE BANCROFT.

THE WORKS

OF

HUBERT HOWE BANCROFT.

VOLUME XX.

HISTORY OF CALIFORNIA.

VOL. III. 1825–1840.

SAN FRANCISCO:

A. L. BANCROFT & COMPANY, PUBLISHERS.

1885.

CONTENTS OF THIS VOLUME.

CHAPTER I.

A TERRITORY OF THE MEXICAN REPUBLIC.

1825.

CHAPTER II.

ECHEANDÍA'S RULE—POLITICAL AFFAIRS.

1826–1830.

CHAPTER III.

ECHEANDÍA AND HERRERA—FINANCE—THE SOLIS REVOLT.

1826–1830.

CHAPTER IV.

ECHEANDÍA AND THE PADRES—MISSION AND INDIAN AFFAIRS.

1826-1830.

CHAPTER V.

ECHEANDÍA'S RULE—MARITIME AND COMMERCIAL AFFAIRS.

1826-1830.

CHAPTER VI.

OVERLAND—SMITH AND PATTIE—FOREIGNERS.

1826-1830.

CHAPTER VII.

RULE AND OVERTHROW OF VICTORIA.

1831.

CHAPTER VIII.

AN INTERREGNUM—ECHEANDÍA AND ZAMORANO.

1832.

CHAPTER IX.

FIGUEROA'S RULE—HÍJAR AND PADRÉS COLONY.

1833-1834.

CHAPTER X.

FIGUEROA, CASTRO, AND GUTIERREZ—THE COLONY.

1834–1835.

CHAPTER XI.

MISSIONS AND SECULARIZATION.

1831–1833.

CHAPTER XII.

MISSION AND INDIAN AFFAIRS.

1834–1835.

CHAPTER XIII.

MARITIME, COMMERCIAL, AND FINANCIAL AFFAIRS.

1831–1835.

CHAPTER XIV.

PIONEERS AND FOREIGN RELATIONS.

1831–1835.

CHAPTER XV.

CHAPTER XVI.

CHAPTER XVII.

CHAPTER XVIII.

SAN DIEGO PLAN—ALVARADO AND CARRILLO.

1837.

CHAPTER XIX.

DON JUAN BAUTISTA AND DON CARLOS.

1838.

CHAPTER XX.

ALVARADO'S RULE—POLITICAL EVENTS.

1839–1840.

CHAPTER XXI.

LOCAL ANNALS OF SAN DIEGO DISTRICT.

1831–1840.

CHAPTER XXII.

LOCAL ANNALS OF LOS ANGELES DISTRICT.

1831–1840.

CHAPTER XXIII.

LOCAL ANNALS OF SANTA BARBARA DISTRICT.

1831–1840.

CHAPTER XXIV.

LOCAL ANNALS OF MONTEREY DISTRICT.

1831-1840.

PAGE

CHAPTER XXV.

LOCAL ANNALS OF SAN FRANCISCO DISTRICT.

1831-1840.

HISTORY OF CALIFORNIA.

CHAPTER I.

A TERRITORY OF THE MEXICAN REPUBLIC.

1825.

RATIFICATION OF THE FEDERAL CONSTITUTION—JUNTA DE CALIFORNIAS IN
MEXICO—COMPAÑÍA ASIÁTICO-MEXICANA—SESSIONS OF THE DIPUTA-
CION—ECHEANDÍA APPOINTED GOVERNOR—TRANSFER OF THE OFFICE
AT SAN DIEGO—BIOGRAPHY OF DON LUIS ARGÜELLO—ECHEANDÍA'S
COMPANIONS—PACHECO, ZAMORANO, AND RAMIREZ—HERRERA AS COM-
ISARIO DE HACIENDA—THE MISSIONS—THE PADRES REFUSE ALLEGIANCE
TO THE REPUBLIC—THE DIPUTACION ON SECULARIZATION—PADRE DU-
RAN AS PRESIDENT—MISSION SUPPLIES AND FINANCE—VESSELS ON THE
COAST—SURRENDER OF THE 'ASIA' AND ' CONSTANTE '—MORRELL'S VISIT
AND BOOK—COMMERCE—FOREIGN RESIDENTS—A RAINY SEASON.

IN the preceding volume I have completed the annals of California as a province of Spain and of the
Mexican empire to the year 1824. In the present
volume I continue its history as a territory and department of the Mexican republic to 1840. But while
1825–40 are the chronological limits assigned, it has
been found inconvenient, as already explained, to make
the subdivisions of time and topics agree exactly.
Local annals have been continued in an earlier volume
to 1830; herein they are completed for another decade,
and the regular thread of political history is followed
to 1840; but the institutional history for 1836–40,
including some important phases of foreign relations, is
necessarily left for the first six chapters of volume iv.
The leading features here presented are the develop-

ment of republicanism, the downfall of the missions, revolutionary movements, the first overland explorations, growth of foreign influence, the up-building of commercial industry, and the complicated series of political and sectional controversies. At the end of the volume I continue alphabetically the biographical register of pioneers begun in volume ii.

Early in 1825 Governor Argüello received the federal constitution of the Mexican republic adopted by congress October 4, 1824, and addressed to the states and territories on the 6th. It is not necessary to analyze this document here. By it Alta California became a territory, lacking the population for a state; entitled to a diputado in congress, but without the forty thousand inhabitants requisite to give him a vote; yet capable of being erected into a state by act of congress. This organic law made no provision for the government of the territories; and I know not exactly what authority the president had for appointing a governor and allowing the diputacion to subsist; or what authority congress had to make laws on the subject; or further, on what authority the two Californias were immediately united in one territory, or at least put under one governor. The constitution was similar to that of the United States of America.[1]

Before noting the reception of the constitution in the north, it is well to glance at subsequent acts of the national government in behalf of California down to the end of 1825—and briefly, for in Mexico but slight

[1] *Mexico, Constitucion Federal de los Estados Unidos Mexicanos, sancionada por el Congreso General Constituyente el 4 de Octubre de 1824.* Mexico, 1824, 16mo, 3 l. xviii. 62 p. 21. 3 p.; with at the end the following: *Mexico, Acta Constitutiva de la Federacion Mexicana. 31 de Enero, 1824.* Mexico, 1824. 16mo, 12 p. There are other editions of both documents. In the *Acta* the division into states and territories had been different, the two Californias being one territory. There is no evidence that the *Acta* reached California before the constitution. Among the signers of the constitution there appears no diputado for Alta California, though Baja California was represented by Manuel Ortiz de la Torre. Gov. Argüello understood Cal. as a territory to be attached to the state of Mexico. *Dept Rec.,* MS., i. 120; *Dept St. Pap. Ang.,* MS., i. 82-4.

attention was paid to this distant frontier, either in this or any other year. The first president did well enough, however, at the beginning, for he not only appointed a ruler, with a superintendent of territorial finances, but he sent troops, arms, supplies, and even a little money. I have noticed the lack of any constitutional provision for territorial government; but to aid the president in this respect a special board, or council, the 'junta de fomento de Californias,' was organized.[2]

In a note I have given the titles of this junta's reports. Ex-governor Sola was a member, though not a very prominent one. None of the plans ever attained to the dignity of law, but each had an influence

[2] This junta was dissolved at the end of 1827. It had ten members, in whom there were frequent changes, the following list including all that served in the order of their appointment: Mariano Bonilla, Pablo V. Sola, José Ign. Ormaechea, Mariano Dominguez, Tomás Salgado, Francisco de P. Tamariz, Manuel Ibarra, Francisco Cortina, Ignacio Cubas, Juan J. Espinosa de los Monteros, José Mariano Almanza, Francisco Fagoaga, Alejo García Conde, Cárlos M. Bustamante, Servando Mier, Isidro Icaza, Diego García Conde, Pedro Cárdenas, Juan Francisco Azcárate, Tomás Suria, sec'y, Crecenio Suarez, sec'y.

The various reports of this body were printed in Mexico, 1827, under the following title: *Junta de Fomento de Californias—Coleccion de los principales trabajos en que se ha ocupado le Junta nombrada para meditar y proponer al Supremo Gobierno los medios mas necesarios para promover el progreso de la cultura y civilizacion de los territorios de la Alta y de la Baja California. Año de 1827.* This collection includes the following documents: *Dictámen que dió la Junta, etc., sobre las instrucciones que para el Gefe superior Político.* Dated Jan. 3, 1825. 16 pages, 8vo; *Plan para el Arreglo de las Misiones de los territorios de la Alta y de la Baja California.* April 6, 1825, 11 p.; *Plan de Colonizacion Estrangera* (subtitle—*Reglamento á que debe sujetarse la colonizacion, etc.*), dated April 24, 1825, 8 p., with a diagram; *Plan de Colonizacion de Nacionales para los territorios, etc.* (subtitle—*Reglamento para la colonizacion por familias de los Estados Federados de México, en los territorios de Californias*), dated May 30, 1825, 18 p., 3 sheets, with a diagram; *Plan Político Mercantil para el mas pronto Fomento de las Californias,* including 1st, Correspondence Feb.–July 1825; 2d, *Proyecto para el Establecimiento de una compañía de comercio directo con el Asia y mar Pacífico, cuyo punta céntrico debe ser Monterey, capital de la Alta California, la cual será conocida baja el nombre de Compañía Asiático-Mexicana, Protectora del Fomento de la Peninsula de Californias.* Presented to the president by its author, Francisco de Paula Tamariz, Dec. 14, 1825, 14 p.; 3d, *Proyecto de Reglamento en Grande para el Establecimiento de la Compañia Asiático-Mexicana.* Dec. 14, 1825, 18 p. (numbered 24); *Iniciativa de Ley que propone la Junta para el mejor arreglo del gobierno de los territorios de Californias.* Dated May 12, 1827; including a *Subdivision de los territorios de la Alta y de la Baja California en cuatro distritos,* of June 26, 1826; and the final brief report of the junta announcing the close of its labors on Aug. 31, 1827. 44 p.

And finally—*Lista de los asuntos comprendidos en este libro.* 1 leaf.

on legislation in behalf of California. Several of the reports, or parts of the same, relating to special topics of government, colonization, and mission policy, will require notice elsewhere, and may therefore be briefly disposed of here.

Unfortunately the instructions to Governor Eche-andía, on which the junta reported January 3, 1825, are not extant. In the suggestions made, especial importance is attached to the obtaining of accurate information about the country, its people, and its productions; and it is evident from the allusions to Viz-caino, Venegas, the *Sutil y Mexicana*, Humboldt's works, etc., that the members had no idea of the fresh and complete sources of information accessible in the form of missionary and other official reports. There is also a noticeable confusion between the two Califor-nias. Great circumspection and careful instructions were recommended on the mission problem and Indian policy, subjects which must be treated with much delicacy to avoid trouble until a radical reform could be effected by means of definite laws. The junta expressed some very wise views, and showed a clear appreciation of the difficulties to be overcome, leaving, however, the ways and means of overcoming them mostly to a subsequent report of April 6th, which will be noticed in another chapter. In the matter of distributing lands, it was thought that the governor should confine his immediate attention to investigation and reports on the actual condition of the territories. The subject of foreign relations was believed to require serious consideration, with particular reference to possible encroachments of Russians and Americans on the north. There was yet some doubt whether the boundary of the forty-second parallel had been recognized by Mexico, but it was necessary at all hazards to prevent any passing of that line; and in this connection a naval force for the upper coast was recommended as of urgent necessity. Particularly was the attention of the government called to the prospective importance of the northern province, both by reason of its varied products and of its frontier position.[3]

The plan of April 21st for foreign colonization may be disposed of, since I have no space to give the document in full, with the remark that it was utilized by the government in preparing the regulations of 1828, in which many of its twenty-eight articles were more or less fully embodied.[4] To a great extent the same remark may be applied to the plan of May 30th for national colonization or settlement by Mexicans. But this plan contained certain elements intended for the special benefit of the Californias, and therefore not included in the general regulations which applied to all Mexican territory. It was proposed not only to grant lands to Mexican colonists, but to pay the expenses of their journey, a daily ration and monthly sum of three or four dollars to each family for three years, besides furnishing live-stock and tools; or in case the settler were not a farmer, he was to receive expenses of the journey, necessary tools, a house lot, and rations for one year. This aid it was thought might be furnished without burden to the treasury, by utilizing the accumulations of mission capital. It was deemed desirable to favor settlements on the coast islands; and to set apart one of them as a penal colony, not for Mexico, but for California.[5]

Another scheme of the junta, though pertaining to commerce, may as well be mentioned here, since it never went into practical effect. It was a politico-mercantile plan for the organization of a Compañía

---

[3] Jan. 6, 1825, José Argüello wrote to Captain Guerra from Guadalajara that a board had been established in Mexico to make regulations for Cal. *Guerra, Doc.*, MS., vi. 97. The *dictámen*, so far as it relates to Indian policy, is incidentally quoted by Manuel Castañares in an address of March 30, 1844, to Congress. *Castañares, Col. Doc.*, 12, 14, 50. Both Alvarado, *Hist. Cal.*, MS., i. 122–3, 233–6, and Vallejo, *Hist. Cal.*, MS., i. 299–300, speak of Sola as the leading spirit of the junta, which devised many liberal and enthusiastic measures without the slightest idea as to where the money was to come from. 'Fifty years later,' says Alvarado, 'in the hands of energetic men backed by coin, some of these plans might have proved successful.'

[4] See chap. ii. this vol. for reglamento of 1828.

[5] There are several other items, but as the recommendations were never adopted, it seems unnecessary to notice them.

Asiático-Mexicana, protective of Californian industrial development. Monterey was to be a grand commercial centre; and not only was California to be saved from all possibility of foreign aggression, but the whole trade of the Pacific was to be wrested from American and English hands. The author of the project, Tamariz, aimed at a revival of the old Philippine trade, with vastly augmented facilities and profits; and he pictured California in glowing colors as a veritable paradise abounding in all good things, and better fitted than any other spot on earth for its grand destiny. "Fortunate the Californians in the midst of the promised land; happy the provinces that adjoin that land; lucky even the hemisphere that contains it," writes the enthusiastic Mexican in substance page after page. The scheme was a grand one on paper— too grand to go any further; for though approved by the famous junta, and favored apparently by president, cabinet, and congress, it was never heard of so far as I know after 1827.[6]

In addition to the acts of the president and junta de fomento, there is nothing to be noted bearing on my present topic, beyond a few minor routine communications of the ministers in the different departments, in one of which the Californians were showered with flattery, even if they got no more substantial tokens of attention.[7]

[6] The reglamento is copied in full by Vallejo in his *Hist. Cal.*, MS., i. 300–10, from an original formerly in the possession of David Spence. The company is also mentioned in *Castañares, Col. Doc.*, 50. It seems useless to give the details of such a plan; some of the leading points are as follows: Capital, $4,000,000 in 2,000 shares, 50 of which were to be taken by the Mexican government, and 50 reserved for Cal. until she was able to pay for them. Term of existence, 10 years. The president of Mexico to preside at meetings. The company to have privileges in the matter of paying duties; to be preferred as sellers and buyers; to have a monopoly of fisheries and pearl-diving against foreigners; but had to bring settlers free to Cal., aid in the suppression of smuggling, etc.

[7] Californians are lovers of order and justice, 'compensating with these virtues for the influence which in other communities would be the effect of law and authority.' 'They have always shown a strong attachment to the supreme powers, and given constant evidence with ardent fidelity that they are, and glory in being, excellent Mexicans; and their *benemérito gefe político* Argüello answers in his last communications for good order and strict administration

On receipt of the constitution, Argüello at once summoned the diputados to assemble. The rivers were so swollen by the rains that the southern members could not come; but on the 26th of March the four Castros, with the president and secretary, met to ratify the new organic law of the nation. The document was read by Secretary Torre, and the oath was taken by governor and diputados. Then the constitution was read again in the plaza, and Argüello administered the oath to the garrison drawn up under arms, and to the assembled citizens of all classes. A salute of artillery, and the usual shouts of acclamation, with ringing of bells, repeated for three days, marked the act; but for the first time on such an occasion there was no mass, or sermon, or other religious ceremony, for Prefect Sarría declined to sanction republicanism. On the 28th of March Argüello forwarded copies of the constitution to the different presidios and pueblos, at each of which it was ratified with appropriate ceremonies before the end of May. At San Francisco Padre Esténega conducted the customary religious services, though it is not certain that he took the oath. At San Diego, as at Monterey, the padres refused to take any part in the ratification. At other places there is no record respecting the friars' action. Thus California become formally a territory of the Mexican republic.[8]

of justice, even in their actual condition.' *Mexico, Mem. Justicia,* 1826, p. 6. General information on finances of California, and relief sent from Mexico in 1824–5, in *Mexico, Mem. Hacienda,* 1826, p. 27. Aug. 6th, Minister Alaman orders gefe político to report on the suspension of the assembly, and to propose an administrative system. *Sup. Govt St. Pap.,* MS., iii. 9.

[8] I shall have more to say on the action of the friars. Action of the diputacion March 26th, in *Leg. Rec.,* MS., i. 41–3. March 28th, Argüello sends out the new constitution to be ratified, and orders all copies of the old Spanish constitution to be collected. *Dept Rec.,* MS., i. 116; *St. Pap., Sac.,* MS., xiv. 37. Apr. 22d, constitution received at S. Francisco, and will be published on Sunday. *St. Pap., Sac.,* MS., xix. 36. May 1st, comandante describes the ceremony, which took place Apr. 24th. The troops after three days were permitted to amuse themselves, $2 being given to each private and $3 to each corporal. *Id.,* xiv. 41–2. April 30th, swearing of allegiance at Los Angeles, where, on petition of the citizens, the ayuntamiento, with the approval of the diputados, Palomares and Carri.lo, set at liberty a prisoner, Juan José Higuera. Original record in *Doc. Hist. Cal.,* MS., iv. 739, 745. May 1st, Comandante Ruiz

A final meeting of the diputacion was held April 7th, when the majority were in favor of punishing recalcitrant friars by taking from them the management of the mission temporalities,[9] and then on May 2d the sessions were suspended by the governor, until new instructions could be obtained from national authorities. His reason for this action was that the term for which the body had been organized according to the Spanish constitution had now expired, and the new constitution made no provision for a territorial diputacion.[10]

General Miñon, appointed the year before to be ruler of California, did not accept the position, so that in January 1825 a new appointment had to be made.[11]

The choice fell upon Lieutenant-colonel José María Echeandía, an officer said to have been director of a college of engineers in Mexico. His appointment as gefe político superior and comandante general militar of both Californias was perhaps dated the 31st of January.[12]   In June he sailed from San Blas to Lo-

describes the ratification at S. Diego, where not only the Franciscans but apparently the Dominican padre Menendez, who chanced to be present, refused to assist. *Estudillo, Doc.*, MS., i. 209.   May 10th, certificate of ayuntamiento to the taking of the oath at San José, and to the three days of bull-fighting and other diversions that followed. *S. José, Arch.*, MS., vii. 22; *Dept St. Pap.* MS., i. 116–17.   I find no record of the event at Sta Bárbara. Dec. 4, 1826, the governor sends copies of the constitution and acta constitutiva to be circulated among the escoltas and padres. *Dept St. Pap., Ben. Mil.*, MS., lvii. 23.

[9] *Leg. Rec.*, MS., i. 41–6.   More of this topic when I come to speak of the missions. From *Doc. Hist. Cal.*, MS., iv. 725, it would appear that at a session held early in this year the office of comisionado for the pueblos was restored.

[10] May 2d, Argüello to comandantes and prefect. *Dept Rec.*, MS., i. 119. May 22d, Argüello to ayuntamiento of Los Angeles on same subject. *Dept St. Pap., Angeles*, MS., i. 82.   June 3d, comandante of S. Francisco has published the order. *St. Pap., Sac.*, MS., xiv. 36.

[11] As early as April it was known in Cal. that Miñon would not come.   With his successor Argüello at that time expected 60 artillerymen.   Apr. 11th, Argüello to P. Duran. *Arch. Sta B.*, MS., xii. 321–2.

[12] His instructions seem to have been issued on that date, *St. Pap., Miss. and Colon.*, MS., ii. 42, and it was on Feb. 1st that his appointment was announced by Minister Pedraza in a letter to Argüello. *Sup. Govt St. Pap.*, MS., iii. 3. Feb. 28th, Echeandía to Herrera, announcing his appointment with a salary of $3,000. *Dept St. Pap.*, MS., ii. 1.   The fact that he was director of the college of military engineers in Mexico rests on the statements of Valle, *Lo Pasado*, MS., 1, and Ord, *Ocurrencias*, MS., 42–3, but is probably accurate.

reto on the schooner *Nieves.* Possibly he had come
up from Acapulco on the *Morelos,* which was at San
Blas at the time en route for Monterey; but I think
not, though some of his officers came on that vessel
and joined him there.[13] He remained at Loreto from
June 22d until October, reorganizing peninsular affairs, issuing a reglamento, and appointing a sub gefe
político.[14] He finally set out for Monterey by land
on October 4th, but, worn out by the hardships of the
route, soon despatched to Argüello an order to meet
him at San Diego, where he arrived late in October.[15]

Meanwhile Argüello first heard of Echeandía's
appointment on July 4th by a letter from the latter
dated June 25th, and announcing his arrival at
Loreto en route for the capital. Later in the month,
probably by the *Morelos,* came the official notice
from Mexico.[16] The order to meet his successor at
San Diego came about the 26th, on which date
Argüello replied that the state of his health would
not permit him to make the journey so rapidly as was
ordered, but he would come slowly.[17] Two days later he
sailed on a schooner for San Diego,[18] where he turned
over his office in November. Though Argüello was
doubtless displeased at this innovation on his own

[13] In April–May he was at Tepic, and had some trouble about collecting
pay and supplies for his troops. *St. Pap., Sac.,* MS., x. 27–9. He also asked to
be relieved of the military command. *Sup. Govt St. Pap.,* MS., iii. 4. June 7th
he was at Tepic, expecting to sail on the *Morelos,* a new name for the old *San
Cárlos. Guerra, Doc.,* MS., vi. 139. For trip on the *Nieves,* see Pacheco's
testimony in *Herrera, Causa,* MS., p. 67–8; *St. Pap. Sac.,* MS., x. 31. Echeandía's statement in 1827 was that he sailed from S. Blas June 12th, and reached
Loreto in 10 days. *Dept Rec.,* MS., v. 103. June 25th he wrote to Argülleo
from Loreto. *Dept St. Pap.,* MS., i. 120–1.

[14] See *Hist. North Mexican States,* ii., this series.

[15] In July he sent up to S. Diego for mules. *Arch. Arzob.,* MS., iv. pt ii. 150.
Oct. 4th, started. *Dept St. Pap., Ben. Mil.,* MS., lvii. 3. Oct. 18th, sent
order to Argüello to come south. *Guerra, Doc.,* MS., iv. 161–2. Oct. 31st,
writes from S. Diego. *Dept St. Pap.,* MS., i. 74; *Dept Rec.,* MS., ii. 6.

[16] July 4th, Argüello to comandantes with purport of Echeandía's letter.
Dept St. Pap., MS., i. 120–1. July 22d 3d 8th, Argüello had received official
intelligence. *Id., Ben. Mil.,* MS., liv. 9; *Dept. Rec.,* MS., i. 230; ii. 37. Oct.
1st, Argüello expected his successor soon, and had made preparations for his
reception, being uncertain whether he would come by sea or land. *Guerra,
Doc.,* MS., iv. 159.

[17] Oct. 26th, Argüello to Guerra. *Guerra, Doc.,* MS., iv. 161–2.

[18] *Dept St. Pap.,* MS., i. 80.

personal comfort and on the old customs, and though
the people of Monterey liked not the new governor's
disposition to fix his residence in the south, yet I find
no contemporary evidence of controversy or of contemplated resistance. The records, however, are far
from complete, and both Alvarado and Vallejo credit
Argüello with a patriotic refusal to listen to the counsels of Montereyans and the troops who urged him to
take advantage of Echeandía's arbitrary order and
proclaim revolt.[19] It is not unlikely that there was
some clashing of opinion when the two officers met;
but there is no record on the subject. Echeandía had
remained at San Diego at first because exhausted by
his journey; and he continued to reside there chiefly
because he deemed the climate favorable to his health,
but also that as ruler of both Californias he might be
nearer Loreto, and because he found nothing in his
instructions which absolutely required him to live at
Monterey.[20] No transfer of the capital was made;

[19] *Vallejo, Hist. Cal.*, MS., ii. 48–51; *Alvarado, Hist. Cal.*, MS., ii. 105–9.
Vallejo states that the padres took advantage of the excitement in the north
to create a prejudice against Echeandía. Both imply that there was a sharp
correspondence before Argüello went south, which is impossible; and that one
cause of the excitement was the transfer of the custom-house to S. Diego,
when no such change was made. I suppose that both writers greatly exaggerate the popular feeling, looking at it through the colored glasses of memory, respecting later dissensions between the north and south.

[20] Doubtless the persuasions of the southerners had also an influence; and
J. J. Vallejo, *Reminis.*, MS., 87–9, implies that a certain lady of S. Diego had
more influence than all the rest. General mention of Echeandía's arrival
without additional details, or blunders worthy of notice, in *Machado, Tiempos Pasados*, MS., 21, 23; *Amador, Memorias*, MS., 85; *Ord, Ocurrencias*,
MS., 19–20; *Lugo, Vida*, MS., 12–13; *Avila, Cosas de Cal.*, MS., 25; *Petit-
Thouars, Voy.*, ii. 90; *Mofras, Explor.*, i. 293.
    The version of one author, who has made claims to be an accurate histo-
rian, is worth a record here. I allude to that given in *Willson's Mexico and
its Religion*, 148–50. 'The new republic was at peace, and the surplus soldiery
had to be got rid of. It was not safe to disband them at home, where they
might take to the roads and become successful robbers; but 1,500 of the worst
were selected for a distant expedition, the conquest of the far-off territory of
California. And then a general was found who was in all respects worthy of
his soldiery. He was pre-eminently the greatest coward in the Mexican
army—so great a coward that he subsequently, without striking a blow, surrendered a fort, with a garrison of 500 men, unconditionally, to a party of 50
foreigners. Such was the great General Echandrea, the Mexican conqueror
of California; and such was the army that he led to the conquest of unarmed
priests and an unarmed province.' 'Had there been 50 resolute persons to
oppose them, this valiant army would have absconded, and California would
have remained an appanage of the crown of Spain,' etc. 'When the prefect

but very soon the people of the south chose to take that view of the governor's residence among them, and were not a little elated at the honor.[21]

Although Ex-governor Argüello remained in California, resuming his former position as comandante of San Francisco; yet as he was never again prominent in public affairs, and as he died within the limits of this decade, on March 27, 1830, it seems best to append here his biography.[22] Don Luis was the first

of the missions was shipped off to Manilla the war was at an end.' Comments on this rubbish are unnecessary.

[21] As early as Nov. 9th, Sepúlveda from Los Angeles congratulates Echeandía on his arrival, and is glad that he will make San Diego his capital. 'You may count on this dismembered ayuntamiento and on all under my command.' *Los Angeles, Arch.*, MS., i. 2, 3.

[22] Luis Antonio Argüello, son of D. José Diarío Argüello, then alférez of the Sta Bárbara company, and Doña Ignacia Moraga, was born at San Francisco presidio June 21, 1784, and was christened the next day, his godparents being Lieut. Moraga and wife. *S. Francisco, Lib. Mis.*, MS., 20. He entered the military service as cadet of the S. Francisco company on Sept. 6, 1799, and was promoted to be alférez of the same company on Dec. 22, 1800. *St. Pap. Sac.*, MS., xi. 5; *Vallejo, Doc.*, MS., xv. 94; *Gacetas de Mex.*, x. 240. This same year he petitioned for license to marry Doña Rafaela Sal; but as the petition had to go to the viceroy and king, it was not until 1807 that the permission was received, and even then burdened with the condition that the wife should have no claim on the montepío fund at her husband's death, unless he were killed on the field of battle. The wife died at S. Francisco, Feb. 6, 1814. *Prov. St. Pap.*, MS., xix. 40, 196–7; *Prov. Rec.*, MS., ix. 101. She is said to have been remarkable for the kindness of her disposition and for her influence over her somewhat erratic husband. *Amador, Mem.*, MS., 121; *Lorenzana, Mem. de la Beata*, MS., 3.

On March 10, 1806, Don Luis was promoted to the lieutenancy, and in August his father turned over to him the command of the company. *Prov. St. Pap., Ben. Mil.*, MS., xxxvii. 3, 15. According to his *hoja de servicios* at the end of 1816, beside the routine of garrison duty, he had been engaged in two expeditions, one in pursuit of fugitive neophytes, and the other to explore new regions among the gentiles. *Vallejo, Doc.*, MS., xv. 94. He was recommended for promotion by Gov. Sola, July 8, 1817; was commissioned Oct. 30th, and was recognized as captain of the company from April 1, 1818. *Prov. St. Pap.*, MS., xx. 194; *Prov. Rec.*, MS., ix. 196; *Vallejo, Doc.*, MS., xvi. 48; *S. Francisco, Cuentas*, MS., i.–vi.

About 1818 Capt. Argüello made a boat voyage up the Sacramento River; in 1821 he made an expedition to the far north, up the Sacramento Valley, beyond what is now Red Bluff, and back over the coast mountains, to S. Rafael; and in 1822 he accompanied Canónigo Fernandez and Prefect Payeras on a trip to Bodega and Ross. Meanwhile he had married, in 1819, Doña Soledad, daughter of Sergeant José Dolores Ortega, who brought him as a dowry of somewhat doubtful cash value her father's arrears of pay due from the royal treasury.

Argüello was elected acting governor on or about Nov. 11, 1822, *Arch. Arzob.*, MS., iv. pt i. 96; *St. Pap., Sac.*, MS., xi. 6, and took possession of the office on the day of Sola's departure, on or about Nov. 22d. The events of his rule have been already given. His office of governor being only provisional, he still retained nominally the command of San Francisco. After he resigned rule at

hijo del país called upon to rule California, and he
filled most creditably a position which was by no
means free from difficulties. Had the rival candidate,
José de la Guerra, been chosen, it is hard to point out
in what way he could have ruled more wisely. Argüello's education was in some respects deficient, being
simply what his father could give him in his presidio
home; but in every position which he occupied he
showed much practical common sense if no extraordinary ability. He was much less strict than his
father, or than most of the old Spanish officers, in his
regard for the letter of national law; he was sometimes
reproved when comandante for his concessions to foreigners, and especially to the Russians; and when he
became governor, he still continued his innovations in

S. Diego in Nov. 1825, I think he remained for some time in the south with
his brother, Don Santiago. On April 15, 1826, Echeandía ordered his pay as
comandante to cease, the reason not being explained. *Dept Rec.*, MS., iv. 31.
On May 20th Echeandía ordered him to S. Francisco to take command of his
company. *Id.*, v. 46. Aug. 8, 1827, the minister of war was informed that
Argüello claimed the commission of lieutentant-colonel that had been given
him by Iturbide. *Id.*, v. 128. Oct. 7, 1828, Echeandía relieved Argüello
of his command in consideration of ill health; and on Nov. 20th he was ordered to Monterey 'for the good of the service.' *Id.*, vi. 109, 138. His purchase of the *Rover*, his enterprise in the China trade, and the resulting lawsuits with Capt. Cooper, the only notable events of his later life, are noticed
in other chapters.

Argüello's military record down to the end of 1828 gives him 29 years, 3
months, and 27 days of service, with an addition of 11 years and 11 days for
campaigns. Echeandía appends the following notes: 'Courage, proved;
ability, more than average; military conduct, indifferent; health, broken;
loyalty, supposed faithful. His services merit all consideration, but his conduct is now loose, doubtless from excessive drinking. He was suspended
from command for reasons presented to the supreme government on Feb.
15, 1828.' *St. Pap.*, *Sac.*, MS., xi. 5–7. He died at San Francisco on March
27, 1830, at 1:30 A. M., at the age of 46 years, and was interred in the mission
cemetery next day by P. Esténega. *S. Francisco*, *Lib. Mision*, MS., 73–4;
Vallejo, *Doc.*, MS., xx. 165. Mariano Estrada was the executor of the estate,
S. José, *Arch.*, MS., i. 36, which five years after his death was in debt to the
missions to the extent of over $1,000. *Dept. St. Pap.*, *Ben. Com. and Treas.*,
MS., iii. 76–7; *S. Francisco*, *Cuentas*, MS., v. 1. To his widow, Doña Soledad, was left the rancho of Las Pulgas, and notwithstanding the depredations
of lawyers and squatters, she was in easy circumstances until her death in
1874. None of the sons of Don Luis ever acquired any prominence in public life.
The Californian writers, almost without exception, speak in the highest terms
of Argüello's honesty, ability, and kindness of heart: See *Alvarado*, *Hist.
Cal.*, MS., ii. 102–4; *Vallejo*, *Hist. Cal.*, MS., i. 327–30; ii. 42–3; *Osio*, *Hist. Cal.*
MS., 5–21, 57; *Amador*, *Mem.*, MS., 81–3; *Castro*, *Rel.*, MS., 13–14; *Avila*,
Cosas, MS., 22; *Romero*, *Mem.*, MS., 10; *Machado*, *Lo Pasado*, MS., 21; *Spence's
Notes*, MS., 14; *Hayes' Em. Notes*, MS., 505; *Sta Bárbara Press*, Oct. 24, 1874;
S. Diego Union, Oct. 29, 1874.

that respect; but his disregard for law was always in the interest of his province and people, and no selfish or unworthy action is recorded against him. After his accession to the chief command, he had some enemies—notably José María Estudillo, José Joaquin de la Torre, and José Antonio Carrillo; but none of these were Californians of the best class. With the people, and especially with his soldiers, he was always popular, by reason of his kindness, liberality, and affability. If he came into somewhat more bitter controversy with the friars than had his predecessors, it was due to the times and circumstances rather than to the man. In person he was tall, stout, and attractive, with ruddy complexion and jet-black hair. He was a jovial companion, a *bon vivant*, so far as a man could be so in this poverty-stricken province, free with his money, in fact a spendthrift, and always in debt. His peculiarities of temperament led him into an increasing fondness for wine and aguardiente; and his drinking habits doubtless broke down his health, and hastened his death in middle life.

There were embarked on the *Nieves*, in June, from San Blas, besides Echeandía, Alférez Romualdo Pacheco and Alférez Agustin V. Zamorano, both engineer officers, and probably from the college of which Echeandía had been director, the former coming as aide-de-camp and the latter as secretary to the governor; also Alférez José María Ramirez, a cavalry officer, whose position at this time under Echeandía is not apparent; Alférez Patricio Estrada, in command of a detachment of about forty infantry of the battalion known as Fijo de Hidalgo;[23] and also probably a fifth alférez, Juan José Rocha, though it is possible that he came on to Monterey by the *Morelos*. Of Estrada and

---

[23] In 1833 this body of men was spoken of as the piquete del 2° batallon permanente, consisting of 1 sergeant, 3 trumpeters, 3 drummers, 1 corporal of fusileers, 1 corporal of artillery, 9 grenadiers and chasseurs, and 16 fusileers—34 in all. *Dept St. Pap., Ben. Mil.*, MS., lxxvi. 31.

his men, though they remained ten years in the country, hardly anything is known; but Zamorano, Pacheco, Rocha, and Ramirez were somewhat prominent in later annals.[24]

All those mentioned are supposed to have stopped with Echeandía at Loreto, and to have accompanied him to San Diego by land, though it is possible that there were some exceptions; but another passenger on the *Morelos*, which had sailed from Acapulco on March 25th, and had probably brought some of the officers named as far as San Blas,[25] was José María Herrera, who, being sent as comisario subalterno de hacienda to administer the territorial finances, did not stop at Loreto, but came on to Monterey, where he arrived July 27th, and took possession of his office August 3d, relieving Mariano Estrada, who had held a similar position under a different title by authority of the diputacion. Herrera was subordinate to the comisario general de occidente at Arizpe, and in financial matters he was largely independent of Echeandía. He brought with him a *memoria* of goods worth $22,-379, and $22,000 in silver;[26] but there was no provision made for the back pay of the troops; and Herrera refused to comply with Echeandía's order to pay the soldiers for three months in advance, because such an act was not allowed in his instructions, the funds were insufficient, and it would not be wise to put so much money into the hands of the troops.[27] Beyond some

[24] Pacheco's first important service was rendered this year, when he escorted Lieut.-col. Romero to the Colorado on his way to Sonora; explored two routes to the river; and perhaps made some preparations for permanently opening one of the routes. See vol. ii. p. 507 et seq., this work.

[25] *Dept Rec.*, MS., v. 103; *Herrera, Causa*, MS., 67.

[26] *Mexico, Mem. Relaciones*, 1826, p. 32; *Mexico, Mem. Hacienda*, 1826, p. 27, and annexes, 9, 25. Two hundred boxes of manufactured tobacco seem to have been also sent, worth $23,863; and there was an order on the comisario de occidente for $12,000, which does not seem to have been paid at this time. A small part of the $22,000 was perhaps spent at Loreto. With reference to the tobacco, Huish, *Narrative*, 426, says that the government, by way of paying up arrears of 11 years at S. Francisco, sent a brig with a cargo of paper cigars to be issued to the troops in place of dollars; but as Martinez observed, cigars would not satisfy the families, and the compromise was refused!

[27] Sept. 1st, Echeandía's order to Herrera. *Dept. Rec.*, MS., ii. 2. Oct.

minor correspondence on routine aspects of the department, and a slight clashing between the new comisario and the habilitados, there was nothing in connection with Herrera's administration during this year that requires notice.[28]

Herrera, however, was not the only official who arrived on the *Morelos* in July 1825. The vessel brought also to California Lieutenant Miguel Gonzalez in command of a detachment of artillerymen, who was immediately made a captain, and became comandante de armas at Monterey by virtue of his rank. There also came, probably in this vessel, and certainly about this time, three more alféreces, or sub-lieutenants, Antonio Nieto, Rodrigo del Pliego, and José Perez del Campo, the first being in command of a small body of infantry sent as a guard to eighteen convicts condemned to presidio life in California for various offences. With few exceptions, the new-comers, whether officers, soldiers, or convicts, were Mexicans of a class by no means desirable as citizens.[29]

15th, Herrera to Argüello, explaining his reasons for not obeying, and alluding to other communications. *Dept St. Pap.*, MS., i. 105. It is likely that Echeandía gave the order in the interest of his own popularity, knowing that it could not be obeyed.

[28] Oct. 10th, Lieut Estrada speaks of complaints of Echeandía through the comandante of Monterey, and calls for a statement of charges for supplies. Oct. 31st, Herrera is willing to furnish the account, though there are some mission items of supplies to escoltas that cannot be included yet. *Vallejo, Doc.*, MS., i. 98. Nov. 17th, the habilitado of Sta Bárbara objects to the comisario exacting accounts of the mission supplies, etc. He says the company will pay its own debts if the funds due it are supplied. *Dept St. Pap., Ben. Com. and Treas.*, MS., i. 6. Dec. 6th, Herrera says that public creditors are many and resources small. The government expects him to make a just distribution of the small revenue he controls; and he will make to the public a respectful statement of his administration. *Guerra, Doc.*, MS., vi. 148–9.

General mention of Herrera's appointment and arrival. See *Mexico, Mem. Hacienda*, 1826, p. 27, by which it appears that he was appointed on Feb. 8th; *Dept St. Pap.*, MS., iii. 209–10; *Leg. Rec.*, MS., i. 282–3; *Dept St. Pap., Ben. Com. and Treas.*, MS., i. 12; *St. Pap., Sac.*, MS., xiv. 2. He is called comisario subalterno, comisario sub-principal, comisario provisional, administrador sub-principal, comisario de guerra, sub-comisario, treasurer, superintendent of customs, etc.

[29] The number of the soldiers, both artillery and infantry, is not recorded. Vallejo, *Hist. Cal.*, MS., ii. 62–6, and Alvarado, *Hist. Cal.*, MS., ii. 110–14, confound this arrival of convicts with the later ones of 1830. A list of the 18 convicts who started is given in *St. Pap., Sac.*, MS., x. 20–2, and of the 17 who arrived, in *Dept St. Pap., Ben. Mil.*, MS., lvii. 3, besides mention of several of the number in *Id.*, li. 2–3. Eight or nine came with definite sen-

Prefect Sarría, as we have seen, declined to swear allegiance to the federal constitution or to sanction republicanism either as friar, prelate, or vicar. He left each of the friars free to decide for himself, and refused to issue instructions on the subject. There can be no doubt, however, that the question had been thoroughly discussed by the padres, and a definite understanding reached, during the many months in which the formal declaration of the republic in California had been only a question of time. Yet that the agreement had not been entirely unanimous is

tences, while the rest were simply banished to California. The former were mostly the companions of Vicente Gomez, 'el capador,' a fiend in human form, thief and assassin, who is said never to have spared nor failed to torture any man, woman, or child of Spanish blood that fell into his hands, but who, in consideration of his services to the 'cause of independence,' was simply sent to California subject to the orders of the comandante general. It is not quite certain that he came to Monterey with the rest, since there are indications that he came to S. Diego with Echeandía, or at least about the same time. He was soon sent overland to Sonora, perhaps in the hope that he would be killed by the Indians, where he arrived in March 1826, after narrowly escaping death at the hands of the Yumas. After having been employed by Gen. Figueroa on various commissions, he was sent back, and on the way he was killed by Alf. José María Ramirez at S. Vicente, Lower California, in a personal quarrel, probably in September 1827. *Dept St. Pap., Ben. Mil.*, MS., lvii. 21; *Dept Rec.*, MS., v. 96–7, 130.

One of the companions of Gomez bore the illustrious name of Fernando Cortés, 'de muy mala fama en toda la república,' but of whose Californian experience nothing is known. Another was Joaquin Solis, 'principal agente de Gomez, de muy mala conducta, voz general ser ladron,' who acquired fame as leader of a revolt in 1829, described in chap. iii. of this volume, as did also in lesser degree in the same affair another companion, Antonio Ávila, condemned to death for murders and robberies in Puebla, but pardoned on condition of exile to California. Another of the band was Francisco Badillo, sentenced to 10 years of presidio work in chains, or to be shot without hesitation or formality should he venture to move from the spot where he might be put to work. In 1835, the time having expired, Badillo was set at liberty, but remained in the country. *Dept St. Pap., Ben. Mil.*, MS., lxxvi. 20–2. In 1833 he had been charged with a new robbery. *Id.*, lxxiv. 44. He was married in 1830 to his mistress at Sta Bárbara. *Carrillo (José), Doc. Hist. Cal.*, MS., 26. He at one time kept a monte bank at Sta Bárbara, and Manuel Castro once found him concealed under the table, and stealthily reaching out to steal his own money, merely, as he said, to keep in practice! After a long career as cattle-thief, he was finally lynched about 1860, his body with that of his son being found one morning hanging to a tree with the feet very near the ground. A little granddaughter wept bitterly because the cruel Americans allowed her grandpapa to die when a little earth under his feet would have saved him! Another son known as Six-toed Pete escaped across the frontier. *Alvarado, Hist. Cal.*, MS., ii. 251–3; *Streeter's Recol.*, MS., 159–63.

Other members of this band of convicts were for the most part ordinary thieves and vagabonds, of whose life in California nothing is known, a few also not being named here by reason of their good behavior and respectable connections.

indicated by Padre Esténega's participation in the religious services at San Francisco as well as by ocurrences of a later date. Sarría defended his action in letters to the governor.[30] Anterior obligation to the king of Spain was the ground on which he based his refusal, with special reference to the fact that the new constitution required him to take up arms and resist invasion by a foreign power, including Spain. Thus he might have to resist the king himself at the head of his army, in a province which was justly a part of his dominion, which would be to disobey the divine law and teachings of the saints. He foresaw the objection that his previous oath to independence under Iturbide had required the same opposition to Spain; but he answered it by claiming that before Spain was not under her primitive government, the king was deprived of liberty, and religion was threatened; that under the plan of Iguala, Fernando VII. was to be called to the throne, with some chance of Spanish approval; and moreover, that the previous oath had not only been ordered by his diocesan, but had been formally decided on by a majority of the friars, including the prefect.

On the 7th of April the diputacion took up the matter. Francisco Castro urged immediate steps to learn at once who of the padres would follow the example of their prelate in refusing allegiance. He also proposed that such as took this course should be

[30] Feb. 11, 1825. 'My Venerable Sir and Master: After reflecting on the oath we are ordered to take to the federal constitution of the United Mexican States, for which oath you have designated next Sunday, 13th inst., I have decided that I cannot do it without violating what I owe to anterior obligations of justice and fidelity; and this I announce to you, though not without much and very grave regret on my part, since I would like so far as possible to give an example of submission as I have done up to this time; but I cannot, the decision of my conscience opposing. For the same reason I shall not use my influence that the other padres take the oath, nor that they sanction it with mass, te deum, etc., as ordered in your communication of the 3d. I understand that we are threatened with expatriation; but I will pass through all, though with tears at leaving my beloved flock. That which I took up for God, I will always leave if it be necessary for the same God, to whom I have prayed, etc. In other things very much at your service,' etc. *Arch. Arzob.*, MS., iv. pt ii. 135-6. Also letters of March 30th and April 14th, in *Id.*, 137-9.

deprived of all control over the temporalities of their respective missions, which should be intrusted to administrators. Argüello opposed the measure, because it would result in the padres abandoning spiritual as well as temporal interests, and also because it would be impossible to find competent administrators. Don Francisco zealously defended his proposition, and even wished to hold Argüello personally responsible to the country for any harm that might result from leaving the recalcitrant friars in charge of public property. All three of the Castros, that is, all the rest of the members, were of the same opinion, though Don Antonio was somewhat doubtful about the religious aspects of the case. Thus the vote remained on the records; but the only result that I find was the issuing of an order to the comandantes that each padre must be required to state in writing whether he would take the oath or not.[31]

In April Padre Narciso Duran assumed the presidency of the missions, an office that since the death of Señan had been held by Sarría in addition to that of prefect.[32] Duran also refused to take the oath, not, as he said, from any "disaffection to the independence," nor for any "odious passion," for indeed he believed independence to interest Spain more than America—that is, that Spain was better off without Mexico. But he was tired of taking so many oaths during the past few years, when oaths seemed to have become mere playthings. "I offer," he writes, "an oath of fidelity to do nothing against the established government, and if this be not accepted, I am resigned to the penalty of expatriation, which the constitution

---

[31] *Leg. Rec.*, MS., i. 44–6. June 3d, governor's order to comandantes, acknowledged by Sarría June 22d. *Arch. Arzob.*, MS., iv. pt ii. 140. The padres seem to have made no immediate reply. There is some reason to suppose that the above date should be June 3, 1826.

[32] April 2d, Duran notifies the governor of his assumption of the office. *Dept Rec.*, MS., i. 117; *Arch. Arzob.*, MS., iv. pt ii. 140. June 3d, comandante of S. F. has proclaimed Duran as vicario foráneo. *St. Pap. Sac.*, MS., xiv. 36. Oct. 15, 1824, bishop grants to president all the powers conferred by the former bishop. *Arch. Sta B.*, MS., xii. 320.

imposes."[33] Meanwhile the news of Sarría's refusal
had been sent to Mexico, and in June an order of
President Victoria was despatched to California that
the royalist prefect should be arrested and sent to
Mexico by the first vessel.[34] This order was carried
into effect in October, as appears indirectly from
Echeandía's order to Padre Duran to come to San
Diego and take the oath of allegiance in order that
he might assume the duties of prelate during Sarría's
arrest.[35] The arrest was, I suppose, nominal, merely
a suspension from his authority as prelate, involving
little or no interference with his personal liberty; and,
as we shall see later, he was not sent away at all. It
seems that Padre Martin of San Diego had based his
refusal to participate in religious services on his prelate's prohibition. The government called for a declaration as to the nature of that prohibition; and also
desired Padre Esténega to be informed of its great
satisfaction at his patriotic conduct in pronouncing a
stirring discourse at the taking of the oath.[36]

[33] Oct. 12th, Duran to Herrera, in *Arch. Arzob.*, MS., iv. pt. ii. 148.
[34] June 29th, Esteva to comandante general of Cal. *Sup. Govt St. Pap.*,
MS., iii. 4–5. P. Sarría was, however, to be treated with respect.
[35] Oct. 31st, E. to D. *Dept Rec.*, MS., ii. 6. In D.'s letter of Oct. 12th,
Arch. Arzob., MS., iv. pt ii. 148, he said that he could not act as prefect
until certain that Sarría was out of the province. This shows that Sarría's
arrest was probably effected by Argüello before Echeandía's arrival, or perhaps by order of the latter issued while en route.
[36] Sept. 2d, Minister Llave to governor. *Sup. Govt St. Pap.*, MS., iii. 1.
The general fact of the padres' opposition to the republic is mentioned by
nearly all who have written on California annals, and it is not necessary to
give specific references. Alvarado, *Hist. Cal.*, MS., ii. 20–5, and Vallejo, *Hist.
Cal.*, MS., i. 341–2, dwell on the fact that the padres never lost their feeling
of dissatisfaction and anger; that as a body they took subsequently but slight
interest in the progress of Cal.; and that through their influence the Indians
were disaffected and the difficulties of local government greatly increased.
Alvarado is much the more radical of the two. It was the policy, he says, of
emperor and clergy to make of the people their *burros de carga*. This, as
they well knew, could not be done with republicans. True, they might win
over many influential republicans; but there were so many factions that all
could not be controlled. Sooner or later the 'ass was sure to kick.' Therefore,
when they could not prevent the establishment of a republic, they wished to
leave the country; were not allowed to go and take with them the wealth of
the territory; were angry; preached against the existing government; and in
short, made all the trouble they could.
Among other classes besides the padres, there was no special manifestation
of feeling for or against the republic at this time. The masses now and later
were indifferent; the older officers and soldiers looked with deep regret on the

The old question of mission supplies still remained open as a ground of controversy. The reasons which had impelled the padres to give with a spirit of cheerfulness, real or feigned, had largely ceased to exist. Now most gave grudgingly, because they could not help it; or in a spirit of apathetic indifference to what might become of the mission property; or in a few cases refused in the interest of their neophytes. Padre Duran on one occasion told Martinez of San Francisco that he could send no more supplies, and it would be best to discharge the soldiers if there was a lack of rations. Martinez in turn asked the governor for permission to take the supplies by force. Padre Viader wrote that Santa Clara had to buy wheat for its neophytes, while the pueblo had plenty of grain to sell the presidios. "The moment the keys are taken from us by force," he wrote, "we will not take them back, nor attend to the temporal administration." The destitution was very great at San Diego, but the comandante in his letters implies that the padres gave all they could. The commandant of Santa Bárbara had a sharp correspondence with Padre Ibarra of San Fernando, trying to prove that the furnishing of supplies was by no means a special favor to the troops, but an ordinary duty of the missions until the expected memorias should come from Mexico, together with a new band of missionaries. The padre, however, was incredulous about the anticipated aid. "If you do not eat till then," he said, "you will need elastic bellies; and as to the coming missionaries, I will believe it when I see them, not before." He would, however,

change of government; and some of the younger Californians with the Mexican element were more or less enthusiastic republicans. The Indians had of course no choice, but their condition was in no respect improved by the change. Osio, *Hist. Cal.*, MS., 105-7, has something to say on the advantages of the Spanish rule. He notes that as late as 1842 an inválido hesitated to make a declaration before an alcalde, fearing that it was wrong for an old soldier of the king to do so. Alvarado, *Hist. Cal.*, MS., ii. 40-4, mentions a kind of secret politico-historical society formed by the youth of Monterey, with José Joaquin de la Torre as president, by which various schemes of independence from Mexico as well as Spain were discussed, and where even annexation to the U. S. was proposed, or a French or English protectorate.

not be surprised if Mexico were to send to California
for supplies. From San Luis Padre Luis Martinez
complained of everything in general, and in particular
of some 'missionaries' of a new sect, including one of
the Picos, who were travelling with a barrel instead
of a cross, and were making many converts to drunkenness, while the soldiers of the escolta did nothing
but destroy.[37] In Mexico the guardian made a detailed representation to Minister Alaman on the critical condition of affairs in California, owing to the fact
that the Indians were naturally disgusted at having
to support by their labor themselves, the padres, the
government, and the troops. He declared the amount
of unpaid drafts to be $259,151, and that of unpaid
stipends $153,712, begging most earnestly for at least
a partial payment to save the missions from ruin.[33]

The junta de fomento took up the question of
mission policy, which was regarded as one of the most
important matters submitted to that board. In its
dictámen on Echeandía's instructions,[39] the junta,
while regarding the necessity of reform as a matter
of course, called attention chiefly to the importance
of proceeding with great caution until a satisfactory
method could be devised for introducing a radical
change in the old system. Finally in April the mission plan was presented. In prefatory remarks the
history of the system was briefly traced, with a view
to show the growth of the monastico-military government in the Californias. "The junta is not ignorant
that from the Spanish system of discoveries and
spiritual conquests has resulted all the progress made

[37] Corresp. of Duran, Viader, and Lieut. Martinez in *St. Pap., Sac.*, MS.,
xiv. 22–4, 35–40. Destitution at S. Diego. *Dept St. Pap.*, MS., i. 110;
Guerra, Doc., MS., v. 201–2; Com. of Sta Bárbara vs. P. Ibarra. *Doc. Hist.
Cal.*, MS., iv. 731–2; *Guerra, Doc.*, MS., vii. 68–9. P. Martinez to Argüello,
Arch. Arzob., MS., iv. pt ii. 135. June 1st, 8th, Argüello on his efforts to obtain supplies from the missions. *Dept Rec.*, MS., ii. 35; *Guerra, Doc.*, MS.,
iv. 158.

[38] July 5th, Guardian Lopez to Alaman. *Arch. Arzob.*, MS., iv. pt ii.
143–8.

[39] For an account of the various reports and plans of the junta, see note 2,
this chapter.

in the Jesuit missions of old California, and in those
founded later in new California by the Fernandinos.
It knows the consideration and the praise which these
establishments have merited, not only from Spaniards,
but from enlightened foreigners; and it has given due
weight to all the reasons ordinarily urged in defence
of the system to show it to be not only just and convenient, but absolutely necessary. Still the junta has
not been able to reconcile the principles of such a
system with those of our independence and political
constitution, nor with the true spirit of the gospel.
Religion under that system could not advance beyond
domination. It could be promoted only under the
protection of escoltas and presidios. The gentiles
must renounce all the rights of their natural independence to be catechumens from the moment of
baptism; they must be subjected to laws almost monastic, while their apostles deemed themselves freed
from the laws which forbade their engaging in temporal business; and the neophytes must continue thus
without hope of ever possessing fully the civil rights
of society. The junta has not been able to persuade
itself that this system is the only one fitted to arouse
among the gentiles a desire for civil and social life,
or to teach its first rudiments, much less to carry it
to perfection. It believes rather that it is positively
contrary to the political aims in accordance with
which it should have been arranged, and still more to
the true spiritual aim which should be kept in view."
"The present condition of the missions does not correspond to the great progress which they made in the
beginning. This decadence is very noticeable in Lower California, and would suffice to prove that the system needs change and reform," especially in respect
of the temporal management by the friars. The
plan by which the junta proposed to effect the needed
reforms I append substantially in a note.[40] It shows,

[40] 'La Junta en suma reduce su dictámen para el arreglo de las misiones
de Californias á las proposiciones siguientes:' 1. Conversions among gentiles

like the prefatory remarks which I have quoted, the feeling on the subject in Mexico under the republican régime; and while as a whole it never became a law, it doubtless had an effect on subsequent legislation respecting secularization. In the colonization plan proposed by the junta a little later, the expense of bringing settlers from Mexico and an allowance for their support during a term of years were to be taken from the mission capital, which was supposed to have accumulated during the friars' administration; but the amount was to be 'equitably divided' between the sums due the missions for supplies and the funds actually on hand! Echeandía took some time to investigate the condition of mission affairs, and therefore did little or nothing this year which could indicate his policy.

Of the forty-seven vessels more or less clearly recorded as having been on the coast in 1825, seventeen were whalers; three were men-of-war; one was the national transport; respecting eleven or twelve we have only a mere mention, in some cases erroneous, of name and presence, with no information about their business; while of the remaining fourteen the objects, mainly com-

must be effected by *visitas* and *entradas* of friars and priests, who must obtain the permission of the government, and will receive their stipends as a *limosna* from the pious fund. 2. The supreme government should administer the pious fund, act upon the petitions of those who wish to convert gentiles, and assign to them their stipends and *viáticos*, but the territorial government may report on places for new conversions, and propose the priests, already in Cal., deemed qualified for the new ministry. 3. The right to *evangelizar* should not be restricted to members of any particular order. 4. The friars now in charge of the missions should remain in charge as curates. 5. To avoid burdensome taxes, etc., these friars as curates may receive their stipends as before from the pious fund. 6–7. There should be two friars in each mission, besides those temporarily residing or resting there while engaged in converting gentiles. 8. The missions to continue in this condition until formally made parishes and delivered to the bishop. 9. The government should reassume the administration of mission temporalities, forming the necessary regulations to prevent loss of property or damage to neophytes, and should distribute lands to the latter as soon as they are able to govern themselves. 10. The government should take measures to abolish the mission escoltas, but at the same time to afford full protection to persons and property. 11. The necessary changes in municipal laws, to correspond with this plan, to be referred to congress.

mercial, are well known. Nationally the fleet included twenty American craft, eight English, three Spanish, two Russian, two Mexican, one Californian, one French, and eight of unknown nationality.[41] Captain Cooper in the *Rover* started probably in February for a new voyage to China, not returning until the next year. The *Sachem* and *Spy* came from Boston for Bryant, Sturgis & Co., presumably under Gale's superintendence. McCulloch, Hartnell & Co.'s vessels were probably the *Pizarro* and *Junius*, and perhaps others, for the records are far from clear.

Of all the vessels of the year those which created the greatest sensation were three Spanish men-of-war which made their appearance in April and May. The 27th of April a large line-of-battle ship flying the stars and stripes of the United States was seen approaching Monterey. The people thought of 1818, "el año de los insurgentes," and made hasty preparations for a flight to the interior, while the governor prepared his garrison for defence.[42] Late in the afternoon the strange vessel anchored just beyond the range of the battery's guns, fired a salute, and sent an officer ashore, who shouted, "Viva la libertad!" and asked to see the governor. The commander soon landed, and proved to be José Martinez, an old acquaintance of the Argüellos. A short interview served to remove all fears,[43] and the motives of the strangers were soon explained.

[41] The vessels of 1825—see also list for 1825–30 at end of chap. v.—were: The *Apollo, Aquiles, Arab, Asia, Bengal* (?), *Cárlos Huat* (?), *Constante, Courier* (?), *Don, Eagle, Elena, Eliza, Factor, Inca* (?), *Juan Battey* (?), *Junius, Kiahkta, María Ester, Merope, Morelos, Nile, Pizarro, Plowboy, Recovery, Rover, Sachem, Santa Magdalena* (?), *Sta Rosa* (?), *Snow* (?), *Spy, Tartar, Tiemechmach* (?), *Tomasa, Warren, Washington, Whaleman, Young Tartar,* and nine American whalers not named.

[42] J. J. Vallejo, *Reminiscencias*, MS., 84–6, and Dorotea Valdés, *Reminis.*, MS., 2–5, have more to say of the fright of the people than others, though all mention it. Osio, *Hist. Cal.*, MS., 91–112, narrates the whole affair at some length. He says that Argüello was importuned to retreat, and that the artillery commander, Lieut. Ramirez, was especially desirous of securing his life, as he had just married a pretty wife with $8,000, but the governor refused to abandon the presidio.

[43] P. Altimira, however, still feared some hostile intention; May 12th he sent from S. Francisco a warning to Argüello, declaring that the men were bad, and should be looked upon with horror. He also recommended the sending

The ship was the *Asia*, or *San Gerónimo*, of seventy-four guns and six hundred men; and three days later her consort, the brigantine *Constante*, with sixty men, anchored in the harbor. These vessels had formed a part of the royal Spanish squadron operating against the rebels on the coast of South America. Together with the *Aquiles* and the transport *Garinton*, they had sailed from that coast for Manila in January 1824, after the fall of Callao, under Roque Guruceta. On the way the men revolted in March 1825, at Guahan, one of the Mariana Islands. They landed all the officers and passengers who would not join in their scheme, burned the *Garinton*, put José Martinez, formerly of the *Constante*, in command, and returned eastward with a view of surrendering the vessels to some of the American enemies of Spain. The *Aquiles* started first and was not seen again, and the others directed their course to California, as the most practicable route, and with a view of obtaining supplies. This was the account given by Martinez with more details on his later arrival at Acapulco.[44]

An agreement was signed on May 1st, by which Martinez formally surrendered the *Asia* and *Constante* to Argüello as an officer of the Mexican republic, under certain conditions intended to secure the safety of the men and the payment of their wages.[45] Thereupon

of the news to Mexico, and stated that the American schooner *Tartar* at San Francisco would carry a despatch for $1,500. Perhaps the padre had an understanding with Capt. Morrell, and was to have a share of the profits. *St. Pap. Sac.*, MS., x. 10–11. Morrell, *Narrative*, 209, mentions the man-of-war at Monterey, giving some details.

[44] '*Asia' y 'Constante,' Expediente de la Capitulacion, 1825,* in *Gaceta de Mex.*, Extra, June 15, 1825, which is devoted wholly to this affair, contains all the documents, and is the best authority. Jules Verne, the novelist, in *The Mutineers*, a story founded on this mutiny, gives many names and other particulars, which do not seem to be altogether inaccurate. The *Asia* had carried Viceroy O'Donojú to Vera Cruz in 1821, and Conde de Venadito to Habana. *Alaman, Hist. Mex.*, v. 329, 818–19. See also *Zamacois, Hist. Méj.*, xi. 611–13. The affair is also described in *Campaigns and Cruises in Venezuela*, i. 404–7.

[45] '*Asia' y 'Constante,' Tratado de Capitulacion de los Navíos en Monterey, 1825,* MS.; also in *Gac. Mex.*, Extra, June 15, 1825; signed by José Estrada (appointed by Argüello as comisionado), José Ramirez, José Cárdenas, and Antonio Ventura Roteta. Mention in *Dept St. Pap., Ben. Mil.*, MS., lvi. 8. May 3d, Argüello approves the contract in a communication to Martinez, and reappoints the old officers temporarily. Martinez was comman-

the officers and men came ashore, swore allegiance to independence and the federal constitution, pitched their tents on the beach, and for over twenty days made things lively at Monterey. First, however, they had a religious duty to perform. The holy virgin had been induced at a time of great peril by prayers and vows so to strengthen a weak sail that it bore the violence of the gale better than those thought to need no prayers; and now all the men walked barefoot with the sail to church, and rendered their thanksgiving with much ceremony.[46] Finally, when the merry-making was over, health restored, and some necessary refitting completed, the strangers embarked for Acapulco May 23d, under the charge of Captain Juan Malarin as chief navigator and bearer of despatches to the city of Mexico, by Argüello's appointment. The Mexican government approved the action of the Californian authorities, and assumed the obligation to pay the wages of the men to the amount of over $90,000. Whether the debt was ever paid is another matter. The new vessels thus unexpectedly added to the federal navy were sent round to Vera Cruz, and the *Asia* was subsequently known as *El Congreso*.[47] Several

der of the two vessels; Cárdenas and Antonio Ferrer were next in rank on the *Asia;* while Antonio Roteta and Manuel Galindo were the officers of the *Constante. Dept Rec.*, MS., i. 54.

[46] Torre, *Reminis.*, MS., 39–46, describes this church ceremony, and also that of swearing allegiance, at some length. Osio also gives some details. Vallejo, *Hist. Cal.*, MS., ii. 3–18, who gives considerable space to this affair of the *Asia*, tells us that in a quarrel about a girl, the *gachupin* Arnoldo Pierola killed Juan B. Lopez, and took refuge on the ship, where Lieut. Valle and the writer were sent to arrest him, but the crew refused to give him up. By careful precautions, further disturbances were prevented. The ladies presented two Mexican flags to the vessels, though, as appears from another document, they had to use blue stuff instead of green. Vallejo speaks of a grand ball on the *Asia*. All the old residents agree that money and sugar had not been so plentiful at Monterey for a long time. Sra Ávila, *Cosas de Cal.*, MS., 22–3, speaks of the ludicrous attempts of the sailors and marines to ride on horseback, and says further that their blasphemies shocked the Californians. Alvarado, *Hist. Cal.*, MS., ii. 93–101, notes that green corn was in season; also that the Indian maidens reaped a rich harvest of money, handkerchiefs, and beads from the strangers.

[47] June 11, 1825, Manuel Victoria, com. at Acapulco, to sec. war, announcing arrival of the vessels. May 21st, Argüello to com. at Acapulco on the surrender and Malarin's mission. June 11th, Martinez to com. Acapulco, announcing arrival and enclosing his narrative of same date. May 1st, the treaty as

men from the two vessels remained in California, but none of this number ever acquired any prominence in the territory.[48]

The third vessel of the fleet, the *Aquiles*, did not join the others at Monterey, but made her appearance at Santa Bárbara early in May; neither did her commander, Pedro Angulo, deem it best to surrender to the Mexican authorities. During their stay of a few days the crew and passengers contracted as many debts as possible, we are told, and otherwise behaved badly. Finally on their departure, having left behind the pilot with seven or eight men, they fired two cannon with ball cartridges against the presidio as a parting salute, and disappeared in the south-west.[49]

already cited, certified copy of Monterey, May 22d; and finally announcement of approval by Mex. govt on date of the gaceta, June 15th. All making up the *Asia y Constante, Expediente*. Sailing of the vessels on May 23d, *Guerra, Doc.*, MS., iv. 158. May 23d, Argüello to commandante at Acapulco, explaining the whole affair, and sending copies of contract. *Dept Rec.*, MS., i. 56. May 2d, Argüello to comandantes, giving an account of the surrender and plans. *Id.*, i. 117. Mention of the affair in *Niles' Reg.*, xxix. 74; *Gaceta de Mex.*, i. 1-4. Contract religiously carried out. *Mexico, Mem. Marina*, 1826, p. 3. The $90,000 paid. *Id.*, 1830, p. 1. Echeandía, on hearing of Argüello's action, had some fears that he had been tricked, and ordered more strict precautions. *St. Pap. Sac.*, MS., x. 32-3; *Dept St. Pap.*, MS., i. 68. Osio, not friendly to Echeandía, says that the latter was severely snubbed by the minister of war for his intermeddling, and that consequently he later took every occasion to annoy Argüello, killing him with *disgustos* in 5 years!

[48] In July 1828, 4 of the number remained in the Monterey district. *St. Pap., Ben.*, MS., i. 75-6. Manuel Fogó and Francisco Gutierrez named. *Dept Rec.*, MS., v. 17; vi. 45. David Spence, *Hist. Notes*, MS., 1-3, who gives a very clear narrative of the whole affair, says that 12 of the *Asia's* crew remained and became good citizens. I have also a letter of Spence to Hartnell of May 2d, announcing the arrival with some details. *Vallejo, Doc.*, MS., xxviii. 451. May 2, 1829, decree of president about the *Asia's* crew. *Disposiciones Varias*, ii. 60.

[49] May 6th, Guerra to Argüello, in *Dept St. Pap.*, MS., i. 113; *Id., Ben. Mil.*, liv. 7; *Dept Rec.*, MS., i. 227. June 25th, Esteva from Mexico to comandante of Monterey. If the *Aquiles* arrives give her no food; induce her to surrender like the *Asia;* take two officers as hostages; seize her sails; and report quickly. *Sup. Govt St. Pap.*, MS., iii. 8. Mrs Ord, *Ocurrencias*, MS., 18-19, says that when the commander of the vessel landed and called at Capt. Guerra's house, he found there a great crowd celebrating the wedding of her sister and Hartnell. With his companions he was invited to join in the festivities, and was induced by Hartnell to drink a good deal of wine with a view the better to learn his business, though without much success. Osio, *Hist. Cal.*, MS., 99-102, also speaks of the wedding, and tells us that Angulo, an ignorant Chileno, at first thought to hide his bad Spanish from so cultured a company by pretending to be a Frenchman; but Hartnell soon discovered he could not speak French. Learning that the *Asia* was at Monterey, Angulo hurried on board without waiting for anything, and sailed for Valparaiso, after sending a cannon ball into town.

One other visit to California this year requires special attention, from the fact that the voyager published his experiences in a book. I allude to that of Benjamin Morrell Jr., in the American schooner *Tartar*. Having sailed from New York in July 1824, he arrived at San Diego from the south in April 1825, perhaps bringing a cargo for Hartnell from Chili, but chiefly bent on catching seals. His description of San Diego, where he remained twelve days,[50] and his still more absurd description of his adventures on a hunting tour in the interior—where with seven Spanish companions he defeated fifty native mounted warriors in a desperate hand-to-hand battle, killing seventeen of their number, and himself receiving numerous wounds—leave no room to doubt that the valiant captain was a liar. He touched at Monterey and San Francisco, whence, finding that there was no prospect of success in the seal-fishery, he sailed in May for the Hawaiian Islands, going up to Cape Blanco and down to Socorro Island on the way. Many of Morrell's geographical and other details are tolerably accurate. His book was not published until 1832. He ventured on a prophecy "that long before another century rolls round the principal avenue of trade between the United States and the different seaports on the Pacific Ocean will be the river Colorado, as connected with the gulf of California. The China and India trade will of course ultimately flow through the same channel." Not a cargo has yet been known to be sent down the great cañon—but the century has not yet rolled round.[51]

[50] 'Its form is nearly circular, and it is surrounded by a wall about 20 feet in height, which forms the back sides of the houses. There are about 250 houses erected in this manner, from one to two stories high, built of freestone and neatly finished. There is also a large church, one nunnery, and a very neat little court-house. This town contains about 1,500 inhabitants, principally natives of the coast.' His way of saying that the women rode astride— as they did not—is very good, however: viz., 'They usually honor each side of the horse with a beautiful little foot and ankle.' A whale-boat was built during the stay.

[51] *Morrell, A Narrative of Four Voyages to the South Sea, etc., 1822–31.* N. Y. 1832. 8vo. 492 p. The matter on California is on p. 197-213. This was the

The customs revenue for the year was from $8,000 to $11,000, so far as may be determined from the records.[52] Vessels seem to have paid duties in accordance with the plan of 1824 and the subsequent action of the diputacion abolishing the duty on exported produce after January 1st, though the governor, owing to a 'forgetfulness which was natural,' neglected to publish the decree until March.[53] Echeandía's only action on commercial matters was a decree by which all trade was forbidden except at the four presidial ports, to the great inconvenience of the missionary traders. A little later, however, San Pedro was excepted, to accommodate the citizens of Los Angeles.[54]

Several of the foreign residents married hijas del país this year, but none did much else that calls for notice. Of new arrivals only about twenty names are known, of which number most are but visitors, chiefly masters of vessels; and only six have any claim to be considered as pioneer residents. John Burton, Robert Livermore, and Alpheus B. Thompson are the prominent names; but in the case of each there is a degree of uncertainty respecting the exact year of arrival, as fully explained elsewhere.[55]

The winter of 1824–5 was marked by an unprece-

second of the four voyages. Notices of Morrell's visit in the archives. *St. Pap. Sac.*, MS., x. 11, 14; xiv. 37; *Dept St. Pap.*, MS., i. 64–5. Blundering notice of the voyage in *Taylor's L. Cal.*, 43.

[52] The amount is given as $8,014 and elsewhere as $11,036, in *Dept St. Pap. Ben. Cust. H.*, MS., i. 101–2, 212. Duties at Sta Bárbara, $1,220. *Prov. St. Pap. Ben. Mil.*, MS., lvi. 1. Amount at S. Francisco, $1,061; at S. Diego, $471. Probably $11,000 was the total, and $8,000 the amount at Monterey.

[53] *Dept Rec.*, MS., i. 115.

[54] E.'s decree of Dec. 15th, in *S. Antonio, Doc. Sueltos*, MS., 101–3; *S. José, Arch.*, MS., vi. 23; *Vallejo, Doc.*, MS., xxviii. 82; *Dept St. Pap.*, MS., i. 94. Dec. 20th, S. Pedro excepted. *Vallejo, Doc.*, MS., xxviii. 83. Complaint that S. Diego did not get its share of the revenue. *Guerra, Doc.*, MS., v. 201–2.

[55] See Pioneer Register at the end of these volumes, ii.–v., for the names of all, including visitors. The pioneers proper of 1825, besides Burton, Livermore, and Thompson, are Fisher the negro, William Gralbatch, and James Grant. Of old residents, W. E. P. Hartnell and Wm. A. Richardson were married; Daniel Hill was baptized; and Capt. Henry Gyzelaar is said by Phelps—*Fore and Aft*, 242–3—to have been drowned in Russian River, though it may have been a year or two later.

dented fall of rain, from which damages more or less
extensive were reported throughout the length of the
territory.   At Sonoma many of the new adobe buildings were destroyed.   The voyager Kotzebue notes
the violence of the storms at San Francisco.   At Santa
Cruz the river overflowed the gardens and undermined
the buildings.   Considerable grain was spoiled in the
fields at different missions.   The southern rivers were
so swollen as to prevent the diputados from coming to
Monterey to ratify the federal constitution, and considerable changes in the course of the southern streams
and general drainage of the country are reported, notably at Los Angeles and San Diego.   More particulars will be found in local anuals.[56]   The rains were
on the whole beneficial to the crops in spite of the
local losses, for the harvest was 68,500 fanegas, the
largest of the decade except that of 1821.

[56] General mention not likely to occur in local anuals. *Leg. Rec.*, MS., i.
42; *Dept Rec.*, MS., i. 300–1.   A newspaper item, accredited to Salvio Pacheco and widely copied, states that from 1824 to 1826 hardly any rain fell.
Mention of the floods in *Alta Cal.*, Dec. 30, 1852; *Yuba Co. Hist.*, 67.

CHAPTER II.

ECHEANDÍA'S RULE—POLITICAL AFFAIRS.

1826–1830.

National Measures, 1826—Junta de Fomento—Echeandía at San Diego—Guerra for Congress, 1827–8—Colonization Regulations of 1828—Territorial Diputacion, 1827—Proposed Change of Name—Echeandía in the North—Diputacion, 1828–30—Election—Maitorena Sent to Congress, 1829–30—Acts of the Supreme Government—Padrés as Ayudante Inspector—Gomez as Asesor—California as a Penal Colony—Arrival of 130 Convicts—Carrillo Elected to Congress for 1831–2—Expulsion of Spaniards, 1827–30—List of Spanish Residents—Echeandía's Appeals for Aid—His Resignation—Appointment of Antonio García—The Californias Separated—Manuel Victoria Appointed Governor.

For the last half of the decade under consideration, the course of events adapts itself more conveniently to a grouping in topics than to strict chronological treatment, since the epoch, with the exception of the Solis revolt, was not one of radical changes and startling events, but rather of gradual progress toward the Mexican ideal of republicanism and the secularization of the missions. There was chronic and ever-increasing destitution among the troops, resulting in open mutiny, constant scheming to make both ends meet, with no little rascality on the part of the territorial financiers, and growing commercial industry under the auspices mainly of foreigners. Of the topics to be separately treated, usage, as well as convenience in this instance, gives the first place to politics, and to matters more or less closely connected with territorial and national government.

Politically, then, 1826 was wellnigh a blank. The national authorities attached some importance to California as affording by her rich missions a possible stronghold for Spanish reactionary sentiment, and they had a vague idea that there was a problem to be solved there; but having sent a political chief to study the state of affairs, a small military reënforcement, an administrator of finances, and a small amount of money and goods for him to administer, they felt that they had done a good deal, and were content to let California work out her own salvation for a time. Yet it seems that the junta de fomento was still engaged upon a general plan of government for the province, and for the report of this body, of whose acts we have unfortunately no record, all were waiting.[1]

Cheering news was also sent north that with the surrender of San Juan de Ulúa the Spaniards had lost their last foothold in Mexico, and also that the pope had recognized the Mexican independence. These events were celebrated at different points in the territory, by the governor's order, in April and May.[2]

Echeandía, sent to establish the republican régime, remained at San Diego engaged in studying the country's needs. He was not in robust health, was naturally inclined to be easy-going and dilatory, and was certainly in no haste to adopt any radical policy. Some items of business connected with the arrival of vessels claimed his attention; he slightly agitated the matter of secularization, trying one or two experiments with a view to test the feelings of the friars and the

---

[1] *Mexico, Mem. Relaciones*, 1827, p. 36–7. The minister says that in California very marked vestiges of the old monastico-military government still remain, presenting serious obstacles; but the governor is instructed to gather information, and the junta is at work on a plan.

[2] Corresp. of 1825–6, with notice of celebration at Sta Bárbara, Monterey, S. Buenaventura, and S. Fernando. Echeandía's order was dated April 15, 1826. *Dept Rec.*, MS., iii. 16; iv. 31; *Dept St. Pap., Ben. Mil.*, MS., lxxxvii.; *Id., Ben. Com. and Treas.*, MS., i. 11; *St. Pap., Ben.*, MS., i. 69–70; *Sup. Govt St. Pap.*, MS., xix. 26. Double pay for three days was ordered for soldiers; and some silver coins seem to have been distributed. At S. Fernando the padre refused to officiate, and the neophytes said some *pater-nosters* and *ave marias* on their own account.

capabilities of the Indians; and he was engaged together with José María Herrera in laying the foundations of what became later a very bitter quarrel. But
of these topics I shall speak elsewhere. Montereyans
were forming a prejudice against the new governor
because he chose to live in the south. The padres
disliked him because of the republic he represented
and his expected opposition to their interests; but the
governor attended to his routine duties in a manner
that afforded little or no ground of complaint.

The diputacion had no existence since its suspension by Argüello; but at the end of 1826 Echeandía
seems to have ordered a new election, and on the 18th
of February five electors *de partido* met at San Diego
to choose, not only diputados to reorganize the territorial diputacion, but also a diputado to the national
congress.[3] Pablo de Sola was on the first vote chosen
as representative in congress; but in view of the doubt
whether Sola could be deemed a resident of California
and of the urgent necessity that the territory should
be represented, the vote was reconsidered, and Captain
José de la Guerra y Noriega was unanimously elected,
with Gervasio Argüello as substitute. The term of
office was for 1827-8. Guerra did not start for Mexico until January 1828. His friends urged him not
to go, fearing that as a Spaniard he would not be well
received. Their fears were well founded, since he was
not admitted to congress, and even had to hurry back

[3] Dec. 5, 1826, Gov. orders that electors are not to start until further
notice. Dec. 31st, he orders them to start. *Dept Rec.*, MS., iv. 19-26.
The order for an election is not extant, but it appears from another document
to have been dated Nov. 14th. The five electores de partido, one for each presidio and one for Los Angeles, were Francisco de Haro, S. F.; Estévan Munras, Monterey; Cárlos A. Carrillo, Sta B.; Vicente Sanchez, Los Angeles;
and Agustin Zamorano, S. Diego. *Actas de Elecciones*, MS., 1-4; *Dept St.
Pap., Angeles*, MS., x. 1; *Guerra, Doc.*, MS., vii. 155-8, in which documents
is found the record of the action of the meeting. The only partido election
of which we have a record was that at S. F. on Jan. 1, 4, 7, 8, 1827, where
Haro was chosen over Joaquin Estudillo. Details given. *Vallejo, Doc.*, MS., i.
99-102; and the only primary elections recorded were that at S. F., *Id.*, and
that at San Antonio on Nov. 26th, where Eugenio Nactre was chosen to go to
Monterey and vote for the elector de partido. *Dept St. Pap., Ben. Mil.*, MS.,
lix. 17-19.

to California to avoid serious troubles, although he had left Spain at a very tender age.[4] Gervasio Argüello, the *suplente*, took the seat, but failed to distinguish himself or to be of much use to his constituents. The famous junta concluded its labors in behalf of California at the end of 1827; and in 1828 congress made an appropriation to give the territory a district judge.[5]

Among the acts of the supreme government, the decree of November 21, 1828, containing general regulations for the colonization of Mexican territory, deserves prominent notice. This was a supplementary decree, designed to give effect to the law of August 18, 1824,[6] by establishing rules for the guidance of the territorial authorities in making grants of land, as also of petitioners who might desire to take advantage of the law's provisions. With some slight modifications, these regulations were in force down to the end of Mexican power in California, and in this decade a few grants seem to have been made in accordance with them. I reproduce the substance of the rules in a note.[7]

[4] *Guerra, Doc.*, MS., vi. 99–100, 123, and passim. He sailed on the *María Ester*, carrying high recommendations from Echeandía. That he had not been admitted was known at home on Dec. 6th, *Dept Rec.*, MS., vi. 46–7; and his passport to return was signed by President Victoria on Dec. 16th, and viséd at S. Blas on May 16, 1829. Oct. 20, 1829, he speaks of his late *penoso viaje* in dunning Bandini for a debt. *Hayes' Mission Book*, i. 216. $1,000 of $5,000 due Guerra for mileage and salary was later collected in 1831. *Guerra, Doc.*, MS., iv. 209–10. June 18th, Argüello from Guadalajara thanks the junta electoral. *Dept St. Pap.*, MS., ii. 23. Vallejo, *Hist. Cal.*, MS., iii. 98, accuses Argüello of having intrigued, or at least used his influence, to keep Guerra from his seat. A pamphlet of 1828, giving sketches of the congressmen of 1827–8, speaks of him of California as *nada*, or 'nothing.' *Semblanzas de los Miembros.*

[5] The secretary of the interior mentions the completion of the junta's work in his report of Jan. 30, 1828, stating that a copy in print was distributed to members. *Mexico, Mem. Relaciones*, 1828, p. 22. Bustamante, *Cuadro Hist.*, v. 64, speaks of the junta. The *Aguila* newspaper mentioned a set of the records of the junta for sale. *Guerra, Doc.*, MS., iv. 175. It is remarkable that I have found none of these records in the archives.

[6] See chap. xxiii., vol. ii. this work. In forming these regulations of 1828, the plans proposed by the junta de fomento in 1825 were doubtless taken into consideration and adopted to a certain extent. See chap. i. of this volume.

[7] *Mexico, Reglamento para la colonizacion de los territorios de la república. 21 de Noviembre de 1828*, MS. Translation in *Halleck's Report*, App. No. 5; *Dwinelle's Colon. Hist. S. Francisco*, Add. 25–6; *Wheeler's Land Titles*, 8–9; i. *Rockwell*, 453.

1. Governors of territories may grant vacant lands to such persons, Mexi-

On May 12, 1827, the junta de fomento presented an *iniciativa de ley*, or general system of laws for the federal district, with the recommendation that the same be adopted by the government, as a kind of constitution for California and the other territories. There is no evidence that it was so adopted; and indeed, I find nothing to show that any general system of organic law was ever adopted as a whole; but it would seem that the different branches of territorial government were provided for by separate laws as needed from time to time.[8]

can or foreign, as will inhabit and cultivate them. 2. A person desiring lands shall, in a petition to the governor, express his name, country, etc., and shall describe the land by means of a map. 3. The governor shall at once ascertain if the conditions, as regards land and claimant, are those required by the law of 1824, and may consult the respective municipal authority. 4. This done, the governor may accede or not to the petition, according to the laws. 5. Grants to families or private persons shall not be valid without the previous consent of the diputacion, to which body the expediente shall be forwarded. 6. Not obtaining the approval of the diputacion, the governor shall report to the supreme government, with the necessary documents for its decision. 7. Grants to contractors for many families will not be valid until approved by the supreme government, to which must be sent the necessary documents, including the approval of the diputacion. 8. The governor shall sign a document to serve as a title to the party interested. 9. A record shall be made, in a book kept for the purpose, of all petitions and grants, including maps; and a quarterly report must be made to the supreme government. 10. No contract for a new settlement will be admitted, unless the contractor binds himself to introduce as settlers at least twelve families. 11. Non-compliance with the terms within a proper designated period shall invalidate the grant; but the governor may revalidate it in proportion to the part fulfilled. 12. The colonist will prove compliance with his contract before the municipal authority, in order, on the necessary record being made, to secure his right of ownership, with power to dispose of it. 13. New settlements shall be built with all possible regularity, and shall follow the rules of existing laws for other settlements. 14. The minimum of irrigable land to one person shall be 200 varas square; of agricultural lands, 800 varas square; and of grazing lands, 1,200 varas square. 15. Land for a house-lot shall be 100 varas. 16. Spaces between colonized lands may be given to adjoining proprietors who have cultivated their lands with most application, and have not received the full amount allowed by the law; or to their children, who may desire to combine the possessions of their families. 17. In those territories where there are missions, the lands occupied by them cannot be colonized at present.

In *Halleck's Report*, 121–2, a law of April 6, 1830, is cited, which authorized the reservation or taking of lands for forts, etc.; and also repealed art. 7 of the law of 1824 by prohibiting frontier colonization by adjacent foreigners. At least twice in these years, Oct. 7, 1827, and July 15, 1830, general orders were issued in California for owners of lands to appear and give information about them and the titles. *Olvera, Doc.*, MS., 1; *Dept St. Pap., Ben. Mil.*, MS., lxxi. 3.

[8] For an account of the acts of the junta de fomento, see chap. i., this volume. Of this *iniciativa de ley*, I shall not attempt to present more than a brief résumé or framework, as follows: 1. Attributes of the president as gov-

The junta of electors at San Diego, on February 19, 1827, also chose seven *vocales,* or members, and three *suplentes,* or substitutes, for the territorial diputacion, which was ordered by Echeandía to convene at Monterey a little later. It does not appear that he made any effort to have the sessions held in the south. The body assembled at the capital on June 14th, but several changes were necessary in its personnel to keep a quorum in attendance.[9] The governor now came north for the first time to preside at the meetings, and doubtless directed in great measure the legislative policy. The town was illuminated on

ernor of the federal district, who delegates his powers to a governor for each territory, reserving, however, the power of this and other appointments, with other faculties. 9 articles. 2. Attributes of the governor of the Californias. Appointed for 4 years, but removable at any time by the president, 35 articles. 3. Lieut.-governors, one for Upper and one for Lower California, appointed by the president for 4 years. 8 articles. 4. Council of government, 4 persons for Alta California, elected by the people for 4 years. 10 articles. 5. Ayuntamientos of alcalde, 3 regidores, and síndico for a population of 500 in Alta California. Elected, alcaldes yearly. 26 articles. 6. Administration of justice. Civil, 8 articles; criminal, 22 articles. 7. Judges learned in law; 5 in Alta California. 8 articles. 8. Superior tribunal of justice, consisting of a president and 2 ministers; no salary; 15 articles. 9. Ecclesiastical government under bishop of Sonora; 9 articles. 10. Military government under governor as comandante militar; 15 articles; with recommendations of strengthened defences, a comisario de guerra, and a military academy. 11. Navy, recommendation of a maritime force at S. Francisco and Monterey; and transfer of the navy-yard of S. Blas to Monterey. 7 articles and 3 notes. 12. Treasury and revenue, 4, 9 articles. 13. Commerce, 8 articles. 14. Subdivision of Alta California into 4 districts (practically agreeing with that which I have always followed); adopted by the junta on June 26, 1826. There is attached to the *iniciativa* also the *voto final* of the junta, dated May 13, 1827, and containing general conclusions on the prospects of the Californias and the labors of the board.

[9] The members elected on Feb. 19th were, in the order of their seniority: 1st, Mariano Estrada, 2d, Tiburcio Tapia, 3d, Ignacio Martinez, 4th, Antonio Mª Ortega, 5th, Juan Bandini, 6th, Anastasio Carrillo, 7th, Antonio Buelna, 1st, Supl., Nicolás Alviso, 2d, Joaquin Estudillo, 3d, Romualdo Pacheco. *Actas de Elecciones,* MS., 4–5; *Dept St. Pap., Ang.,* MS., x. 1. All seem to have been present at the first session or within a few days, but they were called away by private or military business until, on Sept. 1st, the two remaining vocales, apparently Estrada and Buelna, had to call in the ayuntamiento of Monterey, and with the aid of that body elect 5 provisional members, who lived in or near the capital and could be depended on. They were Francisco Pacheco, Estévan Munras, Juan José Rocha, Mariano G. Vallejo, José Castro. Sworn in on Sept. 19th. How the whole body now stood as respects seniority does not appear. Lieut. Martinez at first served as secretary, but on June 26th, Juan B. Alvarado was duly chosen, and awarded a salary of $25 per month. *Leg. Rec.,* MS., i. 47–89; *Dept Rec.,* MS., v. 67, 73, 75, 82, 87; *Vallejo, Doc.,* MS., ii. 170; *Dept St. Pap. S. José,* MS., iv. 47; *Id. Monterey,* vi. 3–4. Alvarado's salary was to be paid from the municipal funds of Monterey.

the night of the 13th, and sessions were held at short
intervals until the 20th of September. The subjects
considered were mainly those connected with commerce and finance, and especially with Herrera's administration of the revenues. Reserving those topics
for other chapters, I append in a note an abstract of
the legislative proceedings.[10]

[10] June 14th, oath of office taken by diputados before Echeandía, and Martinez chosen temporarily as secretary. June 16th, Comisario Herrera took the
oath. A reglamento for the dip. was begun and completed at the next session of June 19th. Details of routine rules for business need not be given;
suffice it to say that these rules were somewhat carefully prepared. There
were to be two regular sessions of 3 hours each week, each including a secret
meeting. The members were to be divided by the president into 3 sections
or committees: 1st, on missions and finance, 3 persons; 2d, on police regulations, 2 persons; 3d, on education, agriculture, industry, and govt of the
dip., 2 persons. The committees named were: 1st, Ortega, Bandini, and
Martinez; 2d, Estrada and Tapia; 3d, Carrillo and Buelna. June 23d, Estrada's
prop. that vessels be allowed provisionally to touch at the minor landing-
places with the governor's consent, approved and referred to committee.
Bandini introduced a *manifiesto* urging certain changes and reductions in
duties; that the supreme government be asked for teachers for a college or
academy; and that Los Angeles be declared provisionally the capital of the
territory, with the title of city. June 26th, tax on wine and brandy regulated
according to report of committee on finance. In afternoon Alvarado elected
secretary, Martinez resigning. June 28th, sec. sworn in. Additional regulations of the liquor traffic. June 30th, July 2d, liquor traffic continued. Martinez allowed to join his company in S. Francisco. July 7th, liquor regulations
concluded. Bandini's proposition to make Los Angeles the capital taken up,
but no action. Gov. proposed a change in the name of the territory. See text.
July 13th, Echeandía's proposition discussed and approved, subject to decision
of supreme government. Ortega not allowed to retire until Bandini should come.
Contador appointed. July 16th, petition from padres that vessels be allowed to
touch at the landings of Sta Inéz and Purísima. No power to act. July 17th,
18th, 20th, Sept. 19th–20th, action on revenue matters, involving the investi-
ation of charges against Herrera, and resulting measures directed against him.
See chap. iii. Pacheco as vocal suplente sworn in on July 20th. July 24th,
long discussion on Bandini's commercial propositions, in which Comisario
Herrera took part. See chap. iii. Contador Gonzalez takes oath of office.
Bandini and Tapia granted leave of absence; Suplentes Estudillo and Alviso
summoned. July 31st, Aug. 4th, 9th, 11th, 17th, Sept. 12th, regulations respecting live-stock and branches of commerce and police therewith connected.
Alviso sworn in Aug. 4th. Aug. 17th, Echeandía reports having ordered the prefect to establish a school in each mission. Sept. 1st, ayuntamiento called in and 5
new members elected provisionally. See note 9. Sept. 11th, report received
of removal of a local officer at Los Angeles. The next session regularly
recorded, after Sept. 20th, was on July 10, 1830. *Leg. Rec.*, MS., i. 47–
104. Incidental mention, *Arch. Arzob.*, MS., v. pt. i. 34; *St. Pap.*, *Sac.*,
MS., xix. 39; *Dept Rec.*, MS., v. 50, 126. June 22d, Echeandía to minister
of relations asks if the sub-comisario should attend as intendente, and if he
and the writer should have a vote. Alvarado, *Hist. Cal.*, MS., ii. 118–21,
represents Echeandía as having opened the sessions with a long discourse, in
which he explained the situation of the territory, the policy of Mexico, and
all that he had done since his arrival. This writer states that all the acts of
the diputacion in 1827–9 were really the work of Echeandía. Duhaut-Cilly,

One act of this diputacion merits further notice, which may as well be presented in the words of the original record: "The committee presented the proposition made by his excellency the president at the session of the 7th—this being July 13th—namely, that there be proposed to the supreme government a change in the name of the territory, and also in that of the Pueblo de Los Angeles, in order to distinguish the latter from the city of Puebla de Los Angeles, capital of the state of Puebla, which after close examination the committee reported for discussion, with the suggestions that the territory be named Moctezuma, and that to the pueblo be given the name of Villa Victoria de la Reina de Los Angeles; also that there should be proposed to the supreme government as a coat of arms for the territory 'an Indian with plume, bow, and quiver, in the act of crossing a strait, all within an oval having on the outside an olive and an oak,' in memory of the first peopling of these Amercas, which according to the most common opinion was by the strait of Anian; all of which, after sufficient discussion, was approved." So far as the records show, no attention was paid to this proposition in Mexico, and fortunately California escaped the burden of a new and inappropriate name, founded on one of the least reliable traditions of American antiquity.[11]

Echeandía did not extend his tour northward to San Francisco, perhaps not beyond Monterey; and I have not been able to find the general report on the

Viaggio, i. 282, who attended some of the meetings, tells us the diputados were mere puppets in the governor's hands. Echeandía would make a proposition supported by specious pretences and prosy arguments; sometimes by previous agreement one or two trusted ones would offer some weak objection for the president to overthrow; if any other dared to oppose, he was interrupted with a reprimand; did any one wince at the last moment, a look controlled his vote. This, of course, though amusing, is grossly exaggerated.

[11] _Leg. Rec._, MS., i. 62–3. On Nov. 3d, Echeandía forwarded this act to the secretary of relations, _Dept St. Pap._, MS., ii. 44, and he included with it the proposition to make Los Angeles the capital as well as a villa, though the legislative record does not show the diputacion to have approved Bandini's motion to that effect. Taylor mentioned this proposed change of name in a newspaper article, and from him apparently it was taken by Tuthill. _Hist. Cal._, 123.

condition of the country which he probably made as a result of his inspection.[12] For reasons with which the reader is familiar, Echeandía had a somewhat cool reception at Monterey; but by his policy at the capital he did much to remove the current prejudice, and to gain the good will of that class of Californians which constituted the progressive republican element. His course in the Herrera quarrel pleased Estrada and his large circle of friends, and he disavowed certain unpopular sentiments which his foes had attributed to him, such as approval of making California a penal colony.

Another affair which helped to give Echeandía a better standing at Monterey was his method of dealing with Captain Miguel Gonzalez. This Mexican officer had by virtue of his rank held the place of comandante de armas since 1826, greatly to the disgust of lieutenants Estudillo and Estrada, and of all the Californian officers and soldiers. Gonzalez is said—by his enemies, it must be remembered—to have been an ignorant, brutal, and despotic man, popularly known as El Macaco, the 'ugly ape.' The regular cavalry company, officers and men, accused him of arbitrary acts, and of partiality to the Mexican troops of his own artillery detachment and the others; while he complained of insubordination on the part of the Californians. It is not very important, even if it were possible, to investigate the details and merits of this quarrel. Mexican and Californian officers were inclined to look down, each upon the other, from a height of superiority; but the revolution gave commissions to many ruffians, and there is no special reason to doubt that Gonzalez was one of them. In February 1827 he wrote long and somewhat incoherent complaints to Echeandía, asking to be relieved of his

[12] Alvarado, *Hist. Cal.*, MS., ii. 127–35, says he was received enthusiastically at Sta Bárbara, contrary to his expectations, founded on the influence of the friars there; yet it was at this very time that two padres at Sta B. fled from Cal., as we shall see elsewhere. Vallejo, *Hist. Cal.*, MS., ii. 266–71, notes a grand reception at San José, and a rather cool one at Sta Clara.

command, but refusing to be subordinate in any way
to Estrada or Argüello. Usurping Estrada's authority over the presidial district outside of Monterey, he
put that officer under arrest; but Echeandía affirmed
Estrada's powers and ordered his release.[13] When the
governor came to Monterey in May, he soon took
sides against Gonzalez, administering frequent reprimands, and finally in November ordered him to prepare for a march to Santa Bárbara, in order that
peace might be restored by his absence. How far
Echeandía was influenced by the fact that Gonzalez
was the friend and father-in-law of Herrera,[14] we have
no means of knowing.[15] It would appear that Gonzalez did not accompany Echeandía to the south in
December, or that he returned immediately; for in
February 1828 he was suspended from his command
and put under arrest at Monterey by Estrada, at the
governor's order, after some investigations had been
conducted by Lieutenant Pacheco. At the end of
the year he was ordered to leave the country on the
María Ester, in accordance with instructions of May
31st from Mexico; but he was at San Diego as late as
April 1830.[16]

[13] Feb. 22, 24, 1827, Gonzalez to gov. *Dept St. Pap.*, MS., ii. 2–7, 10–11.
March 6th, Apr. 10th, gov. to Gonzalez. *Dept Rec.*, MS., v. 32, 36–7.
[14] Of Doña Alfonsa, the beautiful wife of J. M. Herrera and daughter of
Capt. Gonzalez, we shall hear more in later years.
[15] June 13th, Gonzalez to gov., protesting against firing a salute on corpus
cristi day. *Dept St. Pap.*, MS., ii. 25. July 14th, 27th, Sept. 27th, Nov. 16th,
19th, 20th, 21st, gov. to Gonzalez, with repremands for misconduct and disrespect—including the shooting at an alcalde, and allowing his wife to meddle
in official business. The order to prepare to march for Sta Bárbara was on
Nov. 16th. Nov. 21st, gov. to alcaldes, stating his orders for Gonzalez' departure and forbidding any insulting or sarcastic remarks about that officer or his
men or his family. *Dept Rec.*, MS., v. 64, 69–70, 92–3, 108–11.
[16] Dec. 15, 1827, Pacheco ordered to continue investigations. *Dept Rec.*,
MS., v. 117. Feb. 14, 1828, Echeandía to Gonzalez, ordering his suspension
and arrest for intrigue among the troops to keep himself in power; for disturbances at various places; for ignorance, disobedience, and inciting of insubordination. *Id.*, vi. 183–4. Feb. 22d, Estrada has arrested Gonzalez. *St.
Pap.*, MS., xii. 13. Feb. 29th (?), Echeandía's order to Estrada. *Dept St.
Pap.*, ii. 73. Nov. 9th, gov. orders Gonzalez to leave on the *María Ester.
Dept Rec.*, MS., vi. 131. Dec. 22d, to same effect. *Id.*, vi. 161. Dec. 9th,
however, he was ordered across the frontier by land en route to Loreto. *Id.*,
vii. 260. Apr. 23, 1829, testimony of Gonzalez at S. Diego about a statement
in a Mexican newspaper that he had destroyed a Spanish flag. *Dept St.
Pap., Ben. Mil.*, MS., lxxx.–vii. 72. Feb. 5, 1830, order from secretary of

Back at San Diego in April 1828,[17] Echeandía summoned his diputados to assemble, presumably at San Diego;[18] but there is no record of any action of the body this year, and little or no evidence that it met at all, except perhaps, as Alvarado says, to protest against the holding of meetings out of the capital, to listen to Echeandía's views on the subject, and to adjourn.[19] Later in the year, however, at an electoral junta held at San Diego on October 6th, the diputacion was reorganized by the choice of four new members.[20] All

war for Gonzalez to proceed to Mexico. *Sup. Govt St. Pap.*, MS., vi. 1. Inocente García, *Hechos*, MS., 40, 44, says that one of the offences for which Gonzalez was sent away was the arbitrary infliction on him, García, of 100 *palos* without trial, and he not being a soldier. Beechey, *Voyage*, ii. 57, 85, speaks of Gonzalez as having risen from the ranks by his own merit.

[17] En résumé, E., as shown by his corresp., had left S. Diego late in March 1827; was at Sta Bárbara during a large part of April; arrived at Monterey about the middle of May, and left there late in Nov.; was at Sta B. from Dec. until March; and returned to S. Diego early in April.

[18] April 10, 1828, Echeandía's summons to Estudillo, Alviso, Buelna, Ortega, Bandini, and Tapia to meet as agreed upon at the close of the last sessions, but not naming the place. *Dept Rec.*, MS., vi. 198. Buelna and Anastasio Carrillo mentioned as members in Sept. *Id.*, vi. 92. Aug. 9th, E. orders Habilitado Domingo Carrillo (of S. Diego) to pay out of the municipal funds Alvarado's salary of $25 per month as secretary. *Id.*, vi. 81. Other indications of Alvarado's presence as secretary at S. Diego as late as Dec. *Dept St. Pap.*, *Ben. Mil.*, MS., lxvi. 90–1. Alvarado's own version is confused in respect to dates, representing a first visit to S. Diego as having been in 1826, before E.'s visit to the north.

[19] Alvarado, *Hist. Cal.*, MS., ii. 139–40; iii. 14–22, tells us that when the diputados arrived at S. Diego they sent him as secretary to inform the governor of their presence and that they awaited his message. The first act on assembling in the large hall of the *comandancia* was to protest on motion of Buelna against meeting away from the capital. Echeandía received the protest courteously, and a few days later explained his theory that as comandante general he had the right to live where he could do most for the interests of the country, that is in his opinion at S. Diego. The diputacion replied that if he had that right, it as a body had it not, but was required by law to meet at the capital under the presidency of the senior vocal in the absence of the gefe político. Echeandía replied: 'I do not object. Let the diputados return to Monterey if they like.' The governor, however, had some resentment against Alvarado, in whose handwriting was the protest. Soon, on account of a quarrel with P. Menendez, chaplain of the troops—a Dominican whose wine he had been drinking and whose sermons he had been writing—Alvarado was summoned before the gefe político, and reprimanded for disrespect to a friar. A stormy scene followed, in which the young secretary—so he says—crowded Echeandía into a corner, pretended to have a dagger, and finally induced him to become calm, talk the matter over, and listen to reason. They parted friends, and E. went so far as to explain his real reason for choosing to live at S. Diego, viz., his fear of Herrera and his confederates, who had plotted to seize him and send him to Mexico!

[20] These were Cárlos A. Carrillo, Pio Pico, Vicente Sanchez, and José Tiburcio Castro, as 4th, 5th, 6th, and 7th respectively. *Actas de Elecciones*, MS., 8; *Leg. Rec.*, MS., i. 127; *Dept St. Pap.*, *S. José*, MS., ii. 12; *Dept Rec.*,

were summoned to assemble at San Diego on January 1, 1829; and they seem to have done so, part of them, at least, only to prove unmanageable, and to be dismissed by the gefe político. Immediately after the suspension of the southern session, a summons was issued for the diputados to convene at Monterey June 1st, and proceed to public business under the presidency of the senior vocal; but I find no evidence that any such meeting was held; in fact, Echeandía himself had no confidence that his summons would be heeded. Thus it may be said that in 1828–9 the legislature was not in session.[21]

In December 1829 Echeandía started northward again, and on the way summoned the diputacion to meet, this time at Santa Bárbara by reason of the troubles at Monterey. Possibly the body did assemble there, but only to adjourn;[22] for the troubles, to

MS., vi. 108. At the same time Manuel Dominguez, Salvio Pacheco, and Cárlos Castro were chosen as 1st, 2d, and 3d suplentes. The first three places were held respectively by Bandini, Anastasio Carrillo, and Buelna, who held over from the old board. *St. Pap., Sac.*, MS., xix. 42-3.

[21] Dec. 1828, summons to Pico, Sanchez, and Dominguez to meet at S. Diego on Jan. 1st. *Dept Rec.*, MS., vi. 159. Feb. 19, 1829, gov. permits Dominguez to retire because it is impossible to have any session, 3 of 5 members having refused to attend. *Id.*, vii. 88. May 22d, gov. says that the diputados summoned to S. Diego had not wished to come on account of the illegality of meeting except at the capital; therefore he asks them to go on at Monterey without his presence. *Id.*, vii. 164. April 10th, gov. tells the minister of relations that he suspended the junta on account of its 'desorganization,' attributable largely to the influence of Vicente Sanchez, prompted as he believes by Herrera. He proceeds to give a description of each of the 10 members in respect of character, ability, education, and property—in no case a flattering picture. Doubts that the diputados can be induced to leave their private affairs to meet even in Monterey. *Id.*, vii. 4-6. It does not seem likely, however, that Sanchez, a Los Angeles man, should have plotted in favor of Monterey. Don Pio Pico, *Hist. Cal.*, MS., 17-19, says that at S. Diego there was just a quorum, and that he prevented the session by insisting on its being held at Angeles, and withdrawing when his wish was not followed. He also went to Monterey, and met José T. Castro, the only other proprietary member present. April 9th, summons to convene at Monterey June 1st. *Dept Rec.*, MS., vii. 128. May 10th, Wm. A. Gale, in a letter to Cooper from S. Pedro, mentions the meeting ordered for June 1st. *Vallejo, Doc.*, MS., xxix. 354. It seems that Sanchez was suspended from his position as diputado in the course of this affair. *Dept Rec.*, MS., vii. 260.

[22] Dec. 8, 1829, E. from S. Gabriel to Sanchez, Pico, and Bandini, revoking the suspension of the first, and urging all to hasten as patriots to Sta Bárbara, in view of the critical condition. *Dept Rec.*, MS., vii. 260. Jan. 18, 1830, similar summons to the Carrillos. *Id.*, viii. 10. Feb. 5th, E. to comandante at Monterey, states that the diputacion did meet to devise means for the restoration of tranquillity. *Dept St. Pap.*, MS., ii. 128.

be described in the next chapter, having passed, the governor went at the end of March to the capital, where he succeeded with some difficulty in getting together four of the vocales,[23] and regular sessions were held from July 10th to October 7th, save that for one month during this period the members were allowed leave of absence to attend to their harvests. I append in a note an abstract of legislative action, much of which is noticed more fully elsewhere in connection with the special topics treated.[24]

The electoral junta which met at San Diego and

[23] *Dept Rec.*, MS., viii. 25, 53, 61; *Dept St. Pap.*, *Ben. Mil.*, MS., ii. 4; *Leg. Rec.*, MS., i. 130. The four were Buelna and José T. Castro, with Salvio Pacheco and Cárlos Castro as suplentes. Other members came in later.

[24] July 10th, the four members sworn in. Alvarado was still secretary. Castro and Buelna were named for 1st committee; Pacheco for the 2d; and Cárlos Castro for the 3d. July 14th, a proposition was presented by the committee on education, that schools be established at such missions as had none. July 16th, Juan B. Alvarado was appointed contador de propios y arbitrios (municipal treasurer), in accordance with a decree of the córtes in 1813. Salary, $15 per month. July 16th, secret session. Regulations on the proposed mission schools. July 20th, the matter of instructions to the newly appointed contador was referred to a com. The reglamento adopted in 1827 was modified in some respects, the changes including provision for 3 sessions a week, on Tuesday, Thursday, and Saturday. The president then submitted to the diputacion his plan for changing all the missions into pueblos. See chap. iv. July 23d, voted $30 dollars a month to P. Menendez as chaplain. The president made a speech on the necessity of making a beginning of establishing an ayuntamiento at Monterey and Sta Bárbara, according to the bando of Dec. 15, 1820, and decree of June 23, 1813, and consequently of assigning bounds to pueblo lands. A salary of $20 per month was voted for the teacher of S. Diego. July 24th, boundaries of the *egidos* of Monterey were fixed. See local annals. July 28th, boundaries of the jurisdiction of Monterey, continued. July 29th, same subject, continued. Also the secularization project taken up, and the first articles approved. See chap. iv. July 31st, Aug. 3d, approval of Echeandía's secularization plan concluded. Aug. 6th, the subject of convict settlers discussed, the dip. strongly disapproving the sending of any more of them to Cal., expressing a desire to get rid of those now here as soon as possible, but approving Echeandía's plan of a public workshop for such as had trades. It was voted to ask the sup. govt that only good and useful families be sent in the future. Aug. 10th, a reglamento in 6 articles for the contador de propios y arbitrios discussed and approved. Details of keeping the books of the office, etc. Aug. 13th, establishment of two convents approved as a supplement to the secularization project. Aug. 17th, a tariff of duties on timber established. See chap. v. Aug. 21st, 24th, certain members ask and receive leave of absence for 15 days. Others were to be summoned, but it seems this was not a success, since there were no more meetings for more than a month. Sept. 29th, at Bandini's request the difficulties of getting a quorum in attendance were put on record. Sept. 30th, approval of land grants to Ignacio Vallejo and Dolores Pico, in accordance with the colonization law of Nov. 24, 1828. Oct. 7th, sessions closed because several members wished to go home to attend to private business. *Leg. Rec.*, MS., i. 130-72.

chose the diputacion whose acts I have just recorded
assembled in obedience to a proclamation issued by
Echeandía on July 30, 1828, which not only ordered
an election, but prescribed in detail the methods to be
followed.[25]   The primary object was to elect a mem-

[25] *Echeandía, Bando sobre Elecciones, 1828*, MS. This document was in
substance as follows: 1–2. Elections to be primary, or municipal; secondary,
or of the partido; and tertiary, or territorial. Must be accompanied by public prayers. 3–6. Primary juntas shall include all citizens over 18 years of
age resident in the partidos. Sentenced criminals, men morally or physically
incapable, vagabonds, and domestic servants were not voters. 7–9. Primary
elections to be held on 3d Sunday in Aug. in plaza of the 4 presidios and 2
pueblos, presided by comandantes and alcaldes, in the morning after mass, a
secretary and 2 inspectors being chosen. 10–12. Challenging voters, etc. 13.
Municipal electors to be chosen as follows: 8 for S. Francisco; 5 for S. José;
9 for Monterey; 7 for Sta Bárbara; 7 for Los Angeles; and 13 (?) for S. Diego. 14–15. Method of voting. The voter to repeat the names of his candidates, to be written down by the sec. He may have the names on a list,
which the secretary must read aloud. 16–17. The president to announce the
result. A tie to be decided by lot. Each elector chosen to receive a copy of
the *acta*. 18–22. A candidate must be a citizen, etc.; 25 years old, or 21 if
married; able to read and write; holding no office, civil, military, or ecclesiastical. Cannot excuse himself. No weapons at the election. No other business to be done by the junta. 23–5. Secondary juntas, or partido elections,
to be held on 1st Sunday in Sept., at same places as the primary; under same
presiding officer; composed of the municipal electors before chosen. 26–8.
Three days before the election the electors meet and choose a secretary and 2
inspectors. Next day, credentials presented. Next day, report on credentials. 29–32. Election by secret ballot. If no one has a majority, there
must be a 2d ballot from the 2 highest candidates, a tie being decided by lot.
Three votes at least required for election. 33–5. An elector de partido must
have 5 years' residence in the partido in addition to the other qualifications.
(See 18–22.) Credentials, a certified copy of the *acta*, given to the successful
candidate, and also sent to the president of the territorial junta. 36–8. Tertiary or territorial junta to consist of the 6 electores de partido, and to meet
at S. Diego on 1st Sunday in Oct. being presided by the highest political
authority present. 39–41. Preliminary meetings for 3 days, as in secondary
elections. 42–6. Election first of a diputado, and then of a suplente.
Method as before, except that the meeting must be with open doors, the
voting *viva voce*, and 5 electors at least must take part. 47–52. Qualifications for a diputado to congress: 25 years of age, and two years of citizenship in the state if not born in it; 8 years of citizenship, and an estate of
$8,000 or income of $1,000, if not born in Mexican territory. Property qual-
ification not required of those born in Spanish America who have not joined
another nation. Certain high officials debarred. 53–6. Method and form of
credentials. 57. The day after this election of a congressman, the junta is
to renew the territorial dip. by electing the new members required, in the
same manner as before. 58. After the election, all officers, electors, and elect
shall pass to the church, where shall be sung a solemn te deum of thanksgiving.
On pp. 125–30, in continuation of the preceding bando, there are partial
records of the primary and secondary elections at the different places except
S. Francisco. The electors who met at S. Diego were Miguel Gonzalez de
Alava, for S. José; José Tiburcio Castro, for Monterey; Francisco Atanasio
Cota, for Sta Bárbara; Manuel Dominguez, for Los Angeles; and Agustin V.
Zamorano, for S. Diego. *Leg. Rec.*, MS., i. 126; *Dept Rec.*, MS., vi. 107;
Actas de Elecciones, MS., 6–7. In the last-named authority, the election of

ber of congress to take the place of Gervasio Argüello for the term of 1829–30; and on Sunday, October 5th, Lieutenant José Joaquin Maitorena of Santa Bárbara was chosen for the place, with Santiago Argüello as substitute. This was a most extraordinary choice; for Maitorena, though honest enough and good-natured, was unreservedly given up to drunkenness, and had retained his place in the Santa Bárbara company only because he had when sober some skill as an accountant. There were times, generally following illness and confinement in the *calabozo*, when, like Rip van Winkle, he 'swore off'; perhaps it was in one of these sober intervals that he was elected to congress. But the honor was too much for the poor fellow. He was very drunk at Tepic, where he was the object of much ridicule; he seems not to have been in a condition to take his seat as diputado, and he died in Mexico about the time his term of office expired.[26]

Maitorena by 3 votes and Argüello by 4 is recorded, as also in *St. Pap., Sac.*, MS., xix. 48; *Dept. St. Pap., S. José*, MS., iv. 74; and *Leg. Rec.*, MS., i. 130. Echeandía's bando is also found in *Dept. St. Pap., S. José*, MS., iv. 55–71. Aug. 1st, E. orders comandantes and alcaldes to publish the bando. *Dept. Rec.*, MS., vi. 74. Nov. 1828, Jan. 1829, E. orders Maitorena to start for Mexico. *Id.*, vii. 70; vi. 128. June 25, 1829, Echeandía explains to minister of justice the arrangement of election districts, S. Gabriel and S. Fernando being joined to Los Angeles, and Sta Clara and Sta Cruz to S. José. *Id.*, vii. 23.

[26] José Joaquin Maitorena entered the military service as a soldado distinguido, his father having been an officer in 1800; came to Cal. in 1801 as cadet in the Sta Bárbara company; was made alférez in 1806; and after several recommendations from governor and comandante he was finally promoted to be lieutenant of the company in 1827. *Prov. St. Pap.*, MS., xxi. 58; *Dept. Rec.*, MS., v. 39, 121–2; *Doc. Hist. Cal.*, MS., iv. 655–6. 1816–21, corresp. of Sola and Guerra, with frequent mention of Maitorena's drunkenness, and the resulting troubles to his family as well as to the public service. *Guerra, Doc.*, MS., iii. 95–6, 101, 113; iv. 4, 16–19, and passim; *Prov. St. Pap.*, MS., xx. 110. From 1822 to 1827 little is said on the subject, and it is probable that Don Joaquin behaved himself better than before. His actions at Tepic, where he stayed two months on his way to Mexico, are described in a letter of Manuel Varela, dated Tepic, Aug. 1, 1829. *Guerra, Doc.*, MS., vi. 135–7. He was constantly intoxicated; attracted the attention of everybody by his foolish actions and remarks; was initiated into a mock lodge of masons; and had a ludicrous quarrel with the treasurer to whom he applied for money on account of his *viáticos*. Cárlos Carrillo, in a letter from Tepic of April 2, 1831, gives the remaining details of Maitorena's life as learned from Navarro, the member from Lower Cal. In Mexico he was rarely in his right mind, and was not deemed in a fit condition to take his seat, though his credentials were admitted, and part of his salary was paid. He died probably late in 1830 of apoplexy caused by his dissipation. *Guerra, Doc.*, MS., iv. 199–200. The vagaries of this congressman are

·Thus California was not represented in the congress of 1829–30, for there is no evidence that Santiago Argüello went to the national capital at all; yet the territory received some slight notice from the Mexican authorities. The minister of the treasury department included in his report some information respecting Californian finances,[27] which, so far as it is intelligible, will be utilized elsewhere. The military establishment was also honored with brief mention, and an ayudante inspector, an officer unknown in California since the time of Captain Soler, was sent to aid General Echeandía, in the person of Lieutenant-colonel José María Padrés, who came up from Loreto in the summer of 1830.[28] To supply another urgent need of the territory, where there were as yet no lawyers, the licenciado Rafael Gomez was sent to California as asesor, or legal adviser. He arrived about the same time as Padrés, and took the oath of office at San Diego on August 18, 1830.[29] The political struggles, revolu-

also noticed in *Alvarado, Hist. Cal.*, MS., ii. 122–6; *Fernandez, Cosas de Cal.*, MS., 35–7; *Vallejo, Hist. Cal.*, MS., ii. 18–24. Alvarado attributes to him many good qualities, although admitting his faults. Maitorena left some kind of a quarrel with Capt. Miguel Gonzalez, which both Gov. Victoria and Gov. Figueroa were ordered to investigate; but finally in 1834 Capt. Zamorano suggested that, Maitorena being dead, the matter might as well be dropped. *Dept. St. Pap., Ben. Mil.*, MS., lxxiv.

[27] *Mexico, Mem. Hacienda*, 1830, annexes 24, 33, 37, 41, 43, 44, 52, 56, 57, 64. Aug. 17, 1829, law imposing a forced loan on California with other territories, and discounting salaries. Sept. 15th, decrees creating a fund for the war against Spain; but exempting the troops of California from the discount on pay, on account of their position on an Indian frontier. *Arrillaga, Recopilacion de Leyes*, 1829, p. 214–23; 1831, 24–36, 48.

[28] In *Mexico, Mem. Guerra*, 1830, annex. 1–3, the force in the Californias is given as 422 cavalry, supported at a cost of $131,440. Feb. 11, 1830, order to merge the S. Blas company into the regular presidial companies. *Sup. Govt St. Pap.*, MS., vi. 2. Arrival of Padrés at S. Diego on the *Leonor* on July 1, 1830. *Sup. Govt St. Pap.*, MS., vi. 9; *Carrillo (J.), Doc.*, MS., 27–8; *Dept. St. Pap., Ben. Mil.*, MS., lxxii. 21.

[29] Gomez's taking possession of the office. *Dept. St. Pap., S. José*, MS., iv. 91; *Id., Mont.*, vi. 6; *Id., Ben. Mil.*, lxxii. 21, 42; *Dept. Rec.*, MS., viii. 92. He had a salary of $3,000. The law creating the office seems to have been dated July or Aug. 29, 1829. In his report of Jan. 1831 the sec. of justice recommended that the asesor be made judge as well, with appeal to the nearest circuit court instead of Mexico, on account of the great distance. *Mexico, Mem. Justicia*, 1831, p. 7, annex 4. *Mexico, Mem. Hacienda* 1832, annex N. Oct. 12, 1829, *Virmond* from Mexico announces the appointment of the following officers for California: Rafael Gonzalez, administrator of customs at Monterey; Manuel Jimeno Casarin, contador of custom-house; Francisco Perez

tions, and counter-revolutions for the presidency, between Gomez Pedraza, Guerrero, and Bustamante, in the years 1828–30, made no impression, in fact were hardly known, in California.[30] Other national measures, with a single exception, require no special attention.[31]

The exception was in the matter of utilizing California as a penal colony for Mexican criminals. A small number of convicts had arrived, as we have seen, in 1825, and now orders were issued to send them from all parts of the republic.[32] These instructions, which the Mexican authorities had the assurance to regard as a means for improving the morals of the convicts and for colonizing California, were much more promptly obeyed, it is safe to say, than if they had been calculated to benefit the territory; and within a year more than a hundred criminals had been sentenced to presidio work in this northern Botany Bay.[33] Echeandía protested rather feebly, as soon as the news

Pacheco, comandante of the resguardo; and Lieut. Zamorano, promoted to captain. *Guerra, Doc.*, MS., vi. 145.

[30] Sept. 9, 1829, news of Pres. Guerrero's accession received. *Dept. Rec.*, MS., vii. 222. Feb. 19, 1829, gov. forbids communication with Acapulco, and adhesion to the plan de Perote. *Id.*, vii. 87. March 14th, communication reopened. *Id.*, vii. 109.

[31] Jan. 21, 1828, orders from Mexico circulated to send in bids for repairs on the public roads. May 21st, no bids. Echeandía, however, recommends the opening of a road to Sonora, and one from Sta Bárbara to S. Diego. *Dept. Rec.*, MS., vi. 173; vii. 17. Jan. 30, 1829, minister of justice wants a list of ayuntamientos, jurisdictions, prisoners, etc. *Sup. Govt St. Pap.*, MS., v. 1. Congress urged to give the Californias a form of government suited to their interests, since now the old Spanish laws prevail. *Mexico, Mem. Relaciones,* 1829, p. 21.

[32] April 29, 1829, secretary of justice issues a circular urging judges to sentence criminals to California presidios instead of Vera Cruz. Order transmitted by secretary of war. May 9th, further orders to governors of different states about forwarding convicts. *Arrillaga, Recop.*, 1829, p. 67–9. Oct. 21st, sec. of war to comandante of Acapulco. The govt will send to Cal. the families of such convicts as may desire it. *Id.*, p. 269–70. March 22d, the govt expects improvement in the morals of the convicts, is preparing a regulation for their management, and to give them the means of earning an honest living, forwarding their families, etc. *Mexico, Mem. Justicia,* 1830, p. 13, 19–20.

[33] I have before me the records of sentence of very many of these criminals, with name, place, date, and crime, in *Vallejo, Doc.*, MS., xxix. 408–80; *St. Pap., Ben.*, MS., i. 82–9; *Dept. St. Pap., Ben. Mil.*, MS., lxxx. 12–13; *Id., Ben. Cust.-H.*, MS., iv. 484–5. List of 80 convicts brought to Cal. on the *María Ester,* with full particulars, in *St. Pap., Ben.*, MS., i. 86–9; *Dept. St. Pap., Ben. Mil.*, MS., lxxii. 19. List of 60 convicts sentenced to California before Dec. 1829. *Vallejo, Doc.*, MS., xxxi. 85; *St. Pap., Sac.*, MS., xi. 10–12.

came, in September 1829, against the sending of any
but 'useful' convicts, since California had no jails, and
the local government could be responsible neither for
the safety of the criminals nor for the morals of the
community thus exposed to contamination.[34]   Of
course this had no effect; and in February 1830 the
María Ester brought up about eighty of the unwel-
come colonists from Acapulco to San Diego. Captain Holmes was not allowed to land them in the
governor's absence, and went on to Santa Bárbara in
March.   A sergeant and twelve soldiers were in
charge of the convicts.[35]

How to dispose of the new-comers was a question
of much perplexity. Nobody wanted anything to do
with them; and a month passed before any decision
was reached, perhaps before they were landed at all;
and then, late in April, thirty of the worst of them,
and probably many more, were sent over to Santa
Cruz Island with a supply of cattle and fish-hooks to
get a living as best as they could; while the rest were
set to work for private employers in the region of
Santa Bárbara and Los Angeles.[36]   Protests were re-

[34] Sept. 18, 1829, E. to sup. govt.   *Dept. Rec.*, MS., vii. 38–40. In *Doc.
Hist. Cal.*, MS., iv. 897, I find an unsigned document dated Mexico, April
25, 1830, purporting to be addressed by the diputado of Cal. to the sup. govt,
in which the writer protests against the sending of convicts. If there is no
error, this would indicate that Maitorena did make at least one honest effort to
serve his constituents.

[35] The *María Ester* left Acapulco Dec. 19th, touched at S. Blas and S. Lúcas,
and lost one convict on the voyage. The exact number varies from 77 to 83
in different documents. The *Enriqueta* was reported to be coming with more
convicts. *Dept. St. Pap.*, MS., ii. 133; *Id., Cust.-H.*, i. 32–3; *Id., Ben.
Cust.-H.*, iii. 55–6; *Dept. Rec.*, MS., viii. 25, 28, 50.

[36] Com. Carrillo's letters to the governor about landing the convicts on Sta
Rosa Island in March–Apr. 1830. *Dept. St. Pap., Ben. Mil.*, MS., lxxxviii.
1–3.   April 23d, the *María Ester* sailed for Sta Cruz Island with 31 of the
number, the missions furnishing some tools, cattle, hooks, and a little grain.
Carrillo (J.), Doc., MS., 22.   March 18th, Echeandía to comandante of Monterey from S. Luis Obispo, explaining his plan to send—apparently all—the
convicts to the islands. *Dept. Rec.*, MS., viii. 29–32.   Mrs. Ord, *Ocurrencias*,
MS., 25–7, says the convicts were in a naked and very filthy condition on
their arrival. Capt. Guerra furnished them with clothing, made a speech
encouraging them to good conduct, and personally employed 8 or 10. At the
islands a fire soon destroyed all they had, and after a time, getting no relief,
they built rafts, and all came over to the main, landing at Carpintería. The
narrator says that as a rule they became very good people. Nov. 2d, 13 of
those sent to the island had returned and presented themselves to the comandante. *Dept. Rec.*, MS., viii. 122.

ceived from all directions; and at Monterey a meeting
was held in May to pass formal resolutions and appoint
a committee to wait on the gefe político, and urge
the importance of sending the convicts back on the
same ship that brought them.[37] The diputacion passed
resolutions of similar purport in August, as has been
noted in the legislative records; but meanwhile, in
July, there had arrived the *Leonor*, Captain Fitch,
with fifty more convicts, about whom we have less
information than in the case of the first company.[38]
With few exceptions, no attempt was made to confine the criminals; but they were distributed through
the territory to earn their living under a surveillance
of the local authorities, more nominal than real. A
few escaped across the frontier; and of those who
served out their time, a large part remained permanently in California, where some were the founders of
respectable families.[39]

The sending of the convicts and the resulting discussions doubtless had an effect to embitter the feeling
that was beginning to exist between Californians and
Mexicans, particularly at Monterey, where the quarrel between Gonzalez and Estrada had originated a
sentiment of hostility which outlasted the Mexican
power in California. At the celebration of the independence on September 16, 1830, a free fight is said to

[37] May 1, 1830, resolutions signed by Juan Malarin, Mariano Soberanes,
José Castro, Antonio Osio, Juan B. Alvarado, Abel Stearns, Juan Cooper,
David Spence, and Wm Hartnell. 10 articles subsequently approved by
Echeandía. *Dept. St. Pap., S. José*, MS., v. 34–5. May 30th, alcalde (?) of
Monterey to governor, speaks of the excitement caused by the arrival, the
greater because of the part taken by convicts in the Solis revolt; and begs in
the name of the citizens that they be not permitted to land. *St. Pap., Sac.*,
MS., x. 89–90.

[38] July 21, 1830, arrival of the *Leonor* at S. Diego, where 23 of the convicts
remained. *Dept. St. Pap., Ben. Cust.-H.*, MS., iii. 54; *Dept. Rec.*, MS., viii.
83. In the *Atleta*, Apr. 1, 1830, it is stated that Gen. Berdejo levied a tax
of $3 on such presidiarios as wished for freedom, and many destined for
California were set at liberty.

[39] According to Vallejo, *Hist. Cal.*, MS., ii. 69–73, Echeandía excused the
Mex. govt for sending convicts, on the ground of ignorance. 'El Gobierno
ignoraba que existiesen familias decentes y de educacion en la peninsula,' he
said to Lieut. Sanchez. A squad of soldiers came as a guard of this last as of
the first convict band. These soldiers seem to have been sent back to the south
soon. Alf. Antonio Nieto commanded the last squad.

have taken place in the governor's house between the native-born youth of the capital and 'los de la otra banda,' Juan B. Alvarado and Rodrigo del Pliego playing the leading roles, and the occasion being an insulting toast by Pliego. Later in the year, as the records show, José Castro was arrested on a charge of posting pasquinades and of publicly expressing his patriotic contempt for the Mexicans.[40]

On October 3, 1830, five partido electors, chosen by the process already described, met at Monterey in accordance with Echeandía's proclamation of August 1st, and elected Cárlos A. Carrillo as diputado to congress for 1831–2, with Juan Bandini as substitute, José Antonio Carrillo and Agustin Zamorano being the defeated candidates. Next day, the 4th, they chose three new members, as required by law, to complete the territorial diputacion, with the same number of suplentes. The services of the officers thus chosen belong to the annals of another decade.[41]

[40] *Carrillo (J.), Doc.*, MS., 30–1; *Alvarado, Hist. Cal.*, MS., ii. 116; iii. 8–11; *Vallejo, Hist. Cal.*, MS., ii. 113–15. Incomplete record of proceedings in the Castro case. *Dept. St. Pap., Ben. Mil.*, MS., lxxi. 60–6. On another occasion, according to Alvarado, José Castro slapped Pliego's face in return for insulting remarks on the lack of education among the Californians.

[41] July 12, 1830, *Mexico, Reglas para las elecciones de Diputados y de Ayuntamientos, del distrito y territorios de la República, 1830.* Printed copy from department of the interior in *Vallejo, Doc.*, MS., xxx. 99; also in *Arrillaga, Recop.*, 1830, p. 253–63. Much of this law relates more particularly to the city of Mexico, its blocks, wards, etc.; but in so far as it applies to California, it does not differ materially from the regulations given in Echeandía's bando of 1828. Oct. 3, 1830, certificate of the election of Carrillo and Bandini, signed by Echeandía and by the electors, who were: Domingo Carrillo, of Sta Bárbara; Juan María Osuna, of S. Diego; José Antonio Carrillo, of Los Angeles; José Peña, of S. Francisco; and Juan Malarin, of Monterey. The document was also signed by the alcalde of Monterey, and by Francisco Pacheco and Antonio Buelna as witnesses. *Doc. Hist. Cal.*, MS., i. 57. Names of electors also in *Actas de Elecciones*, MS., 9–10; Luis Peralta, from S. José, was rejected for want of proper credentials. Notice of Carrillo's election in *Carrillo (J.), Doc.*, MS., 31; *Dept. Rec.*, MS., viii. 104. Record of municipal or primary elections at S. Francisco Aug. 15th; 9 electors chosen. *Vallejo, Doc.*, MS., i. 6; at Los Angeles, same date, *Los Angeles, Ayunt. Rec.*, MS., 6; at S. Diego, Aug. 22d, 13 electors chosen. It is difficult to account for the large number in comparison with other places. *S. Diego, Arch.*, MS., 16–17. The three vocales of the dip. chosen Oct. 4th to take the place of retiring members were Mariano G. Vallejo, 5th; Joaquin Ortega, 6th; Antonio María Osio, 7th. Suplentes: Francisco de Haro, 1st; Tomás Yorba, 2d; and Santiago Argüello, 3d. *Actas de Elecciones*, MS., 11; *Dept. Rec.*, MS., viii. 104. Oct. 7th, gov. notifies Vallejo of his election. *Vallejo, Doc.*, MS., i. 7.

From 1827 to 1829 the national government issued a long and somewhat complicated series of laws and regulations on the expulsion of all Spaniards from Mexican territory, the principal laws being those of December 20, 1827, and March 20, 1829.[42] By the terms of the former, the classes exempt from expulsion were quite numerous, including those Spaniards physically disabled, those over sixty years old, such as were married to Mexican wives or had children not Spaniards, professors of useful arts and sciences, and all who had rendered special services to the cause of independence, or who had manifested great affection for that cause. Such by taking the oath of allegiance might remain. The chief application of this law in California was of course to the friars, of whom I shall speak separately; but there were also other Spaniards in the territory. Echeandía seems to have interpreted the law, or instructions that may have been sent with it, to mean simply that resident Spaniards were to be reported and required to take the oath. Corresponding orders were issued and lists were sent to Mexico in 1828.[43]

[42] *Arrillaga, Recop.*, 1828–31, passim. Law of 1827 in *Id.*, 1828, p. 100–7; Law of 1829 in *Id.*, 1831, p. 224–6. See also *Sup. Govt St. Pap.*, MS., v. 2–5; xix. 44–54; *Dept. St. Pap.*, MS., v. 23; *Vallejo, Doc.*, MS., xxxi. 5; *Dispos. Varias*, ii. 55.

[43] *Españoles, Relacion de los Militares Españoles, que han prestado juramento, con expresion de sus clases, edades, servicios, etc., 1828*, MS. This list was forwarded by Echeandía to the minister of war on Dec. 6th, and contains the following names: Capt. José María Estudillo; Capt. José Bandini; Padre Antonio Menendez; Lieut. Narciso Fabregat; Capt. José de la Guerra y Noriega; Manuel Gutierrez, ranchero and capitalist, 82 years old, 40 years in Cal.; Vicente Cané, one of the *Asia's* men; Juan Mariner, retired artilleryman with rank of lieut.—over 60—33 years in Cal.; Manuel Gutierrez, 45 years, 7 in Cal.; Francisco Cáceres, 36 years, 11 in Cal.; José Amesti, 33 years, 7 in Cal.; Estévan Munras, 39 years, 8 in Cal.; Antonio Suñol, 35 years, 12 in Cal.; Ramon Espindola, artilleryman, 60 years; Antonio Peña, artilleryman, 50 years; Francisco García, invalido, 60 years; Joaquin de la Torre, 44 years, 25 in Cal.; Francisco Cayuelas, 80 years; Jaime Monyú, one of the *Asia's* men; as were also Manuel Fogó and Salvador García; José Fernandez, 25 years, 11 in Cal.; Luis Castro, deserter from the *Aquiles;* as were also José Nadal, Francisco Fernandez, Francisco Filibert, Ramon Obes, sergt., Pablo Sobradelas, José M[a] Iglesias, trader, Miguel Culebras, trader; Rafael Romero, 30 years, suspected thief; Juan Ign. Mancisidor, 40 years, supercargo; Antonio José Cot, already embarked; Francisco Martinez, has passport; P. Luis Martinez, has passport. Contrary to the indication in the title, many of those named had not taken the oath, but had been ordered to

The law of 1829 was more stringent than that of 1827, which it annulled, ordering the immediate expulsion of all Spaniards except those physically incapable of departure and those who were sons of American-born parents. I find nothing in the law indicative of any favor to such as had sworn allegiance; but so it was evidently understood in California, where it was promulgated in July. Nine men, nearly all deserters from the *Aquiles*, were selected for exile, two of whom, however, were allowed after all to remain; while all the rest on different pretexts, chiefly of infirmity and addiction to the republican cause, were deemed exempt.[44] Another branch of this national proscription was the decree of May 10, 1827, debarring Spaniards from holding any office or public employment until Spain should recognize the independence of Mexico. Some soldiers were discharged, and the officers Guerra, Es-

do so. There are several documents relating to different individuals of those named above in *Dept. Rec.*, MS., vi. 72, 95, 125–6, 153; vii. 204, 209; *Dept. St. Pap.*, MS., xix. 6–8, 19, 22, 45; *St. Pap., Ben.*, MS., i. 73–5. Nov. 22d, 1828, Echeandía orders investigation of an insult offered to the national flag on Sept. 16th; also outrages to old Spaniards. *Dept. Rec.*, MS., vi. 136. Dec. 1828, Valencia arrested for saying that neither he nor Maitorena nor the vecinos of Sta Bárbara had sworn to the independence. *Dept. St. Pap., Ben. Pref. y Jusg.*, MS., iii. 60. Dec. 14, 1827, R. C. Wyllie writes from Mazatlan to Hartnell that all the states are expelling Spaniards. *Vallejo, Doc.*, MS. xxix. 182. May 9, 1829, Echeandía orders arrest of a Spanish deserter who had forfeited his right to remain by serving two years under a foreign flag. *Dept. Rec.*, MS., vii. 156. May 30, 1829, J. M. Padrés wrote to the sup. govt, attributing the evils in Cal. to Spanish ideas, and complaining that the law on expulsion had not been executed. Oct. 6, 1830, Minister Alaman writes to the gov. for an explanation. *Sup. Govt St. Pap.*, MS., vi. 10–11.

[44] July 6, 1830, Echeandía proclaims the law of March 20, 1829. *Dept. Rec.*, MS., viii. 190-1. July 24th, E. orders passports for the 6: Culebras, Obes, Sobradelas, Francisco Fernandez, Iglesias, and Nadal. *Id.*, MS., vii. 208. Mancisidor was added to the list. The two exempted were Luis Castro, 60 years old; and Francisco Galindo, having a family (not in Echeandía's list). Aug. 11th, governor's report to minister of relations. *St. Pap., Sac.*, MS., x. 42–6. List of the nine at first deemed liable to expulsion. *Dept. St. Pap., Ben. Mil.*, MS., lxix. 29–30. List of nine Spaniards who ask to remain, mostly on the ground of infirmity. Munras, however, simply wants an extension of time. *Dept. St. Pap.*, MS., xix. 11–14. Aug., 2 Spaniards at S. Francisco; 2 at Los Angeles; and 16 at S. Diego. *Id.*, xix. 1–2, 19. Nov. 3d, list sent by gov. to Mexico of 12 who have claimed exemption. They were: Gutierrez (2), Fabregat, García (2), Suñol, Torre, Amesti, Munras, Fogó (or Fógué), José Fernandez, and Luis Castro. *St. Pap., Sac.*, MS., x. 49–52. Culebras asked for a passport to Ross, but was refused. *Dept. Rec.*, MS., vii. 235.

tudillo, and Fabregat were suspended for a time, though by decree of the president they received half-pay—quite as good as full pay in those days.[45] Yet another phase of the feeling against Spain was the patriotic alarm and enthusiasm caused by the report that a Spanish 'pirate' was cruising on the coast. "The time has come to show once more to the universe that before submitting to Spanish rule we will repose in the sepulchre," was the way the governor put it.[46]

Returning finally to Echeandía, and to matters more closely connected with the governorship, we note that from the beginning of 1827 he had insisted more and more earnestly in his communications to the supreme government on certain reforms and on further assistance to himself and the territory. He demanded a subordinate gefe político for Lower California; an ayudante inspector, who might assume the command in case of his illness or death; additional clerical aid, or the funds with which to procure such aid; more military officers and troops, priests, war-vessels, judges, and above all, money and improved financial management. And if such aid could not be afforded, he repeatedly asked to be relieved from his command.[47] Some of his requests were granted. José María

[45] Decree of May 10, 1827. *Dept. St. Pap., Ang.*, MS., ix. 3. Half-pay order, Oct. 1829. *Id., Ben. Com. and Treas.*, MS., ii. 7; *Dept. St. Pap., Ben. Mil.*, MS., lxxix. 13. Guerra and others suspended. *St. Pap., Sac.*, MS., x. 67; *Ord, Ocurrencias*, MS., 18. Sept. 3, 1829, discharge of soldiers ordered by Echeandía. *Dept. Rec.*, MS., vii. 220. July 15th, a soldier at Sta Bárbara discharged. *Dept. St. Pap., Ben. Mil.*, MS., lxx. 16. Cásares, or Cáceres, one of the Spaniards sent away, was a regidor of Monterey. *Dept. Rec.*, MS., vi. 171.

[46] *Dept. Rec.*, MS., vi. 94, 197, 264–6; vii. 83, 254. The pirate was reported to be the *Griego*, Capt. Juan de Mata; and the alarm lasted more or less from 1828 to 1830. The orders in 1828 were, however, that Spanish captains, supercargoes, pilots, etc., of vessels belonging to neutral nations were to be allowed to transact their regular business at the ports, but must be watched and not admitted to the interior. *Dept. St. Pap., Ben. Com. and Treas.*, MS., i. 105.

[47] Jan. 9, May 25, Oct. 17, 19, Nov. 7, 1827; Oct. 20, 1828; Aug. 11, 1829, E. to different national departments, complaining of difficulties, asking relief, and, particularly on Nov. 7, 1827, offering his resignation. *Dept. St. Pap.*, MS., ii. 44; *Dept. Rec.*, MS., v. 125–6, 131, 133; *St. Pap., Sac.*, MS., x. 40–1, 44–5.

Padrés and Rafael Gomez were sent to California as
ayudante inspector and asesor, respectively.[48]   The
military command of Lower California was detached
in the middle of 1829 and joined to the comandancia
general of Sonora;[49] and about the same time Colonel
Antonio García was appointed to succeed Echeandía
in the governorship.[50]   For reasons that I suppose to
have been connected with Bustamante's accession to
the presidency in January 1830, García did not come
to take possession of his office; and on March 8th
Lieut.-colonel Manuel Victoria was made gefe
político of Alta California, the *gefatura política* of the
peninsula being now detached as the *mando militar*
had been before, ·so that now the two territories were
again distinct.[51]   Victoria had been previously for a
time comandante principal of Lower California; he
came up from Loreto by land, arriving at San Diego
perhaps in December 1830; but he did not take possession of his office until the next year.   Meanwhile
in these last years Echeandía was busied chiefly with
mission affairs and commercial matters.   He had been

---

[48] Padrés had been comandante at Loreto and sub-gefe político of Lower
California.   I find no record showing the date of his appointment as ayudante
inspector; but in Feb. 1829 he seems to have been made sec. of the comandante
general.   *Sup. Govt St. Pap.*, MS., v. 1; and in July 1828 was ordered to
assume the command in Echeandía's place.   *Id.*, vi. 9.   Apr. 3, 1829, Rafael
Velez was approved as secretary of the comandancia, instead of Padrés, but he
never came. *Id.*, v, 3.
[49] June 1, 1829, gov. announces this change.   The two territories were
still subject in civil matters to the same gefe político. *Dept. St. Pap.*, *Ben.
Mil.*, MS., lxix. 2.
[50] Feb. 17, 1829, Moctezuma to Echeandía.   Orders him to deliver the
command to García.   *Sup. Govt St. Pap.*, MS., vi. 2.   May 1st, Gervasio
Argüello writes from Guadalajara that García has been appointed comandante
general.   *Guerra, Doc.*, MS., v. 227.   June 8th, Moctezuma to García.   Vessels are ready to take him to California, and the president desires him to sail
at once.   *Sup. Govt St. Pap.*, MS., v. 11.   July 17, 1828, Echeandía had
been ordered to give up the command to Padrés and proceed to Mexico.   *Id.*,
vi. 9.   Doubtless the political changes in Mexico had much to do with these
successive and confusing orders.   The records of this period are moreover
very incomplete.
[51] March 8, 1830, Victoria's appointment.   March 11th, Minister Facio to
Echeandía, ordering him to surrender the *gefatura* of California to Victoria,
and of Lower California to Monterde.   *Sup. Govt St. Pap.*, MS., vi. 6-7.
March 6, 1830, Capts. Juan Zamora, Juan Aguayo, Gerónimo Hernandez,
and Luciano Muñoz; Lieut. Leonardo Diez Barroso, and Alf. Mariano Crecero
have been destined to California. *Id.*, vi. 5-6.

more cordially received in the north in 1830 than at
the time of his former visit; and except among the
padres and their adherents, he had gained considerably
in popularity.[52]

[52] Gonzalez, *Experiencias*, MS., 26–7, describes his formal reception at Sta
Bárbara by the ayuntamiento.　Alvarado, *Hist. Cal.*, MS., ii. 156–7, says his
reception at the capital was enthusiastic, Lieut Estrada making for all the
citizens a speech of reconciliation, and the governor joining most heartily in
the ensuing festivities.

CHAPTER III.

IT is not my purpose to present financial statistics
in this chapter. Only fragments survive to be presented anywhere, and these will receive such slight
attention as they require, in connection with local presidio annals, commercial topics, and general remarks
on the subject of ways and means for the whole
decade. Here I have to speak of the management,
or mismanagement, of the territorial revenues, of the
insufficiency of those revenues, as administered, to
pay the soldiers or other employees of the government, and of the resulting destitution, discontent, and
finally revolt.

There is little or nothing that is new to the reader
to be said of the prevalent destitution in these years,
a destitution which oppressed only the troops.[1]   The

---

[1] Complaints are not very numerous in the archives, since the uselessness
of writing on the subject had been learned by long experience. The following minor items on this topic are perhaps worth preservation: 1826, Echeandía's complaints about the suspension of officers' pay. Only those officers who

rancheros and pobladores were at least as well off as in earlier Spanish times, the improved market for their produce afforded by the trading fleet counterbalancing the heavy duties that were now exacted. Few if any of these classes seem to have made an effort to do more than support themselves and families; and this, save to the incorrigibly lazy, was an easy task. The lands produced food both for the owners and for the Indian laborers who did most of the work; while the natural increase of their herds furnished hides and tallow more than enough to be bartered with the agents of Hartnell or Gale for groceries, implements, and clothing. So far as the records show, they did not even deem it worth their while to complain of excessive duties and consequent high prices.

For the support of the military establishment and to defray other expenses, the only resources were the duties collected on imports and exports—or the taxes on production, which practically took the place of the latter—the chief source of revenue, but one liable to considerable variation; contributions exacted from the missions as gifts, loans, sales on credit, or special taxes, given by the padres more and more grudgingly as the years passed by; and finally the supplies furnished di-

came with him to Cal. are paid, and there is much discontent among the others. *St. Pap., Sac.*, MS., xix. 32–4. Complaints heard by Beechey of non-payment of dues, and of excessive duties which greatly increased prices. *Beechey's Voy.*, ii. 10. March 30, 1826, petition of soldiers, alleging that they were getting *la racion, nada mas*, as in years past, notwithstanding the promises of the govt. Repeated June 7th. *Dept. St. Pap., Ben. Mil.*, MS., lvii. 13. April 30th, no funds to furnish $400 for the celebration of a great national event. *Id.*, lvii. 14. Hartnell lent the comisaría 264 cattle, which in 1839 had not been repaid. *Dept. St. Pap., Ben. Com. and Treas.*, MS., iv. 59. 1827, Feb. 1st, comisario has no funds to supply blankets; great want of money and food; impossible to get a loan. *Id.*, i. 79. Feb. 5th, gov. lends $600 in view of the urgent needs of the soldiers. *Dept. Rec.*, MS., v. 21. July 5th, complaint that S. Blas company do not get their share of supplies. *Id.*, v. 58. Nov. 21st, decree of national govt on a loan, part of which is to go to the relief of California. *Sup. Govt St. Pap.*, MS., xx. 8. 1828, March 3d, troops naked and in great want. Could get no part of their dues. *Dept. St. Pap., Ben. Mil.*, MS., lxvi. 68. Same date, gov. tells com. gen. that no supplies have been sent from Mexico for a considerable time! *Dept. Rec.*, vi. 7. March 10th, eight soldiers at Monterey granted leave of absence to go and earn their living for 3 months, for want of funds at Monterey. *Dept. St. Pap., Ben. Mil.*, MS., lxvi. 24–5.

rectly or indirectly by Mexico—that is, the $22,000 sent in 1825, possibly one or two small amounts sent later, and a few drafts on the national treasury which in one way or another foreign or resident traders were induced to accept as security for loans or in payment for goods supplied.[2] Theoretically, the national treasury should have paid the territorial expenses and received the net product of the territorial revenue; but practically, the territory was left to pay its own expenses, nominally about $130,000 a year, always excepting the small amounts furnished as before specified, and a considerable supply of very bad tobacco. To estimate the actual revenue with any approach to accuracy would probably have been wellnigh impossible at the time,[3] and is entirely so now. Fully collected and honestly administered, the total revenue could hardly have amounted to one half the nominal expenditure; and indications are not wanting that a considerable portion was lost to the troops through smuggling operations and the rascality of officials. Moreover, there were charges of partiality and injustice in the final distribution of the net product, cer-

[2] On the $22,000, see chap. i., this vol. At the same time $12,000 was ordered paid in favor of California through the comisario general at Arizpe; but I find no evidence that any part of the sum was ever paid. July 1826, record that $3,000 was sent to Cal. by the *Sirena* from the sup. govt. *Sup. Govt St. Pap.*, MS., iii. 6. In Jan. 1829, Enrique Virmond seems to have accepted drafts from the presidial comandantes to the amount of about $5,000 for goods supplied from the *María Ester;* and again in Dec. he supplied the same amount in goods and silver coin. *Dept. Rec.*, MS., vi. 1, 153, 168, 176. Virmond had exceptional facilities for getting his claims allowed by Mexican officials, and he probably lost nothing. Nov. 11, 1828, M. G. Vallejo authorized to borrow $500 payable on sight, or 15 days after sight of draft! *Vallejo, Doc.*, MS., i. 160. According to *Mexico, Mem. Hacienda*, 1830, annex. 33, the govt of Cal. had borrowed $7,262, of which sum $1,564 had been repaid down to June 29th. Hartnell also lent the govt $7,100 in 1827; the draft signed by Herrera was not accepted in Mexico, on account of some alleged irregularity; and on Nov. 20, 1830, Hartnell petitions the gov. on the subject. *Vallejo, Doc.*, MS., xxx. 154.

[3] Feb. 19, 1830, gov. informs the comisario general that commerce, carried on by a peculiar system, 'authorized by force of circumstances' in Cal., yielded barely two fifths of the expenses; while mission contributions, by dint of constant requisitions and annoyances, yielded not more than one fifth of the deficit. *Dept. Rec.*, MS., viii. 72. The revenue obtained from vessels is insufficient for garrison expenses; therefore, the missions advance grain and cattle, and the nation assumes the debt. Bandini's letter of 1828 in *Bandini, Doc.*, MS., 8.

tain presidios, and certain classes of troops, being favored or slighted.

During the Spanish rule, and the interregnum that followed, the provincial finances had been managed—for the most part honestly, if not always with great skill, so far as accounts were concerned—by the habilitados of the respective companies, one of whom in the later days had been named administrator, with very little authority over the others. On the establishment of the republic, Herrera had been sent, as we have seen, in 1825, as comisario to take charge of the territorial finances as a subordinate of the comisario general of the western states Sonora and Sinaloa. The instructions to Herrera are not extant; but it is evident from subsequent communications of himself and his superiors that he had exclusive control of the treasury department, and was independent of the gefe politíco, except that like any other citizen he was within the civil and criminal jurisdiction of that officer. The habilitados, the only persons in the territory qualified for the task, served as Herrera's subordinates for the collection of revenue at the presidios, so that locally there was no change. Whether the comisario appointed them voluntarily or in obedience to his instructions does not appear; but their duty was simply to collect the revenues and pay them over to Herrera, their duty as company paymasters in disbursing funds subsequently re-obtained from the comisaría being a distinct matter.

Naturally the habilitados were jealous from the first of the authority exercised by their new master, and were displeased at every innovation on the old method under Estrada's administration. Moreover, Herrera was a stranger, and worse yet a Mexican, being therefore liable to distrust as not properly appreciative of Californian ways. He was also a friend and relative of Captain Gonzalez, and involved to some extent in the quarrel between that officer and Estrada, which circumstance contributed not a little to his unpopularity. A quarrel resulted, the details of which it is neither desirable nor possible to follow closely. What were the relations between Herrera and Echeandía before they left Mexico, I do not know; but after their arrival in California there could hardly fail to be jealousy, especially on Echeandía's part; and at any rate, the latter soon became leader in the opposition to the comisario. I append some items from the correspondence of the times.[4]

Herrera was an intelligent and able man; his acts were approved by his superior officer; and I find in contemporary documents no proof of irregularities or unfaithfulness in his official conduct; though it would perhaps be presumptuous to found on the imperfect record an opinion that he acted wisely or

[4] March 3, 1826, com. gen. to Herrera. Reproves him for not sending accounts so that the great necessity of the troops might be known and relieved. *Dept. St. Pap., Ben. Com. and Treas.*, MS., i. 22. March 25th, Id. to Id., announces that all claims of Cal. may be presented at the comisaría. *Id.*, ii. 17. April 7th, H. to Echeandía. Charges that Lieut. Estudillo for a just reprimand becomes abusive. *Id.*, i. 41-2. May 11th, E. orders that all amounts due the treasury be paid at the comisario's office. *Dept. Rec.*, MS., iv. 37. June 27th, H. to E. Wishes to know why he is not recognized as gefe de hacienda; measures have been ordered without his consent or knowledge. He wishes E. to define his own position, so that he, H., may be freed from his burdens and report to the supreme government. *Dept. St. Pap.*, MS., i. 136. July 11th, H. to E. Defence of the practice of allowing vessels to touch at way points. *Dept. St. Pap., Ben. Mil.*, MS., i. 42-7. Sept. 11th, com. gen. to E. Asks him to order habilitados to send in their accounts to Herrera in two months, or he will appeal to Mexico. Reprimands him for exceeding his powers, using funds without Herrera's permission, treating H. as a subordinate and not as the gefe of all treasury branches, and not obeying the laws. Threatens to withdraw the comisario altogether if E. does not mend his ways. Accuses him of preventing the execution of Herrera's decree on the payment of duties, without authority to do so. H. was under no obligation to submit his orders or those of his superior to the gefe político. 'Watch also over those friars with their Spanish ideas.' The comisario must be supported, not opposed. In the appointment of a sub-comisario at Loreto, E. had also usurped authority. 'I can not permit you thus to interfere. The power of appointment rests exclusively with H. as my subordinate.' H. was not to be blamed for reporting these things, since he had positive orders to do so. *Id.*, i. 23-34. Oct. 16th, H. to E. on the details of business, explaining his efforts to get along with an insufficient revenue. Complains of habilitados for not rendering accounts, and for drawing drafts on him when they knew he had no money. Protests against paying one company more than another; and claims that in case of urgent need the soldiers should be preferred to officials. *Id.*, i. 56-60. Dec. 1st, H. complains that his orders are disregarded, and that Estrada refuses to render accounts. Repeats the complaint a little later, with threats to report to Mexico. Dec. 27th, 30th, orders from Mexico requiring half the revenues to be remitted to the national treasury! and that regular accounts be sent for publication in the *Gazeta* of Guadalajara. *Id.*, i. 72-3, 89-91, 14.

honestly throughout the quarrel, especially in opposition to the statements of several Californians who remember the controversy.[5] It is my opinion, however, that the class of Californians represented by Alvarado, Osio, and Vallejo look at Herrera's acts through the colored glasses of political prejudice; and that among other classes the comisario was by no means unpopular.

In April 1827 Echeandía ordered a secret investigation of Herrera's administration, to be conducted by Zamorano. The proceedings were begun at San Diego the 30th of April, and afterwards continued at Monterey and Los Angeles in May and June. The main charge was that the comisario had, on his way to California, invested a portion of the $22,000 of territorial funds intrusted to his care in effects to be sold for his own account and profit, though it was not claimed apparently that there was any deficit in his accounts, or that the money thus improperly used had not been refunded.[6] Zamorano as fiscal reported the

[5] No one has anything to say in Herrera's favor. Alvarado, *Hist. Cal.*, MS., ii. 111-17, 132-46, is especially bitter in his criticism, charging H. with dishonesty, embezzlement, conspiracy, usurpation, insolence, and pretty much everything that was bad. Osio, *Hist. Cal.*, MS., 122-3, is hardly less severe. Vallejo, *Hist. Cal.*, MS., ii. 62-3, tells us that H. 'did nothing but conspire and make trouble.' J. J. Vallejo, *Reminis.*, MS., 91-2, represents H. as intriguing with the support of the padres to unseat Echeandía and put himself in power. Duhaut-Cilly, *Viaggio*, i. 282-6, describes the quarrel without attaching much blame to Herrera; and it is to be noted that Mrs. Ord, one of the clearest-headed Californian writers, personally friendly to Echeandía, expresses no opinion on the merits of the parties to this quarrel. *Ocurrencias*, MS., 20-1.

[6] Herrera, *Causa contra el Comisario Sub-Principal de Californias, José María Herrera, 1827*, MS.; also an abridged record in the archives. Capt. Guerra testified that of the $22,000 the Sta B. Co. had got only $3,600; knew not what had become of the rest; had heard that the money was landed at S. Blas, and only a part reshipped with goods supposed to have been purchased with that money. Maitorena had heard of the investment of public funds, and had seen in the possession of Luis Bringas certain bales of goods, which he judged to be the ones bought by H. In a letter of later date, Maitorena attempts to show some irregularities in the collection of duties from the *Nile*, in 1825. Juan Bandini reserved his formal testimony until the matter should come before the diputacion; but declared it to be a matter of public notoriety that H. had misapplied the public funds. Alf. Romualdo Pacheco noticed at S. Blas that only $6,500 of the $22,000 was reshipped, and was told by J. M. Padrés that H. had invested the balance in goods, having admitted as much to him, Padrés. It was a notorious fact that Bringas had sold the goods at the presidios, towns, and missions of Cal. Alf. Juan José Rocha confirmed

charge well founded; and it must be admitted that the testimony against the comisario, though for the most part weak, furnished some grounds for suspicion —and nothing stronger under the circumstances—that certain packages of goods had been purchased with public money.   When we consider that these proceedings were conducted in secret, mainly by Herrera's enemies, that they were never carried further in public, that Herrera was never called upon for a defence upon any criminal charge, and that Echeandía was smarting under the rebukes of the comisario general, it seems wisest at the least to attach little importance to the accusations.

The matter was discussed by the diputacion in the sessions of July, Bandini and the president making all the speeches.   Bandini's deferred revelations proved to be the reading of a treasury report on the sums of

the statement as to what was seen in S. Blas.   Lieut. Estrada testified that the *Morelos* brought some 20 packages, including cigars and brandy, more than were on the manifest; and these goods were opened at Herrera's house, where and elsewhere they were sold by Bringas.   Deponent believed the goods belonged to H.   Luis Mariano Bringas, after much difficulty, was found and induced to testify at Angeles before the alcalde and Capt. Portilla. His testimony was clear enough, and to the effect that of the $4,500 in goods which he had brought to California and sold, $3,000 belonged to his friend Tejada, a trader of Saltillo, and $1,500 had been committed to him by H. as belonging to his (H.'s) cousin.   Full particulars were given of his dealings. But by the testimony of Ignacio M. Alvarado it was shown that Bringas, while refusing to testify on various pretences, had sent a messenger post-haste to Monterey and had received a message from H.   Capt. Portilla's opinion was, therefore, that Bringas had testified falsely under instructions from H., whose accomplice he was.   One of the documents exhibited by Bringas, in support of his testimony, was a draft bearing the name of Wm. A. Gale, written Galle, and pronounced a forgery by Gale himself, who denied that he had ever had any transaction with Bringas.   Moreover, Rodrigo del Pliego testified that H. had openly boasted of furnishing Bringas with papers that would serve his purpose, implying that the signatures were forged by him.   Zamorano's final opinion, rendered to Echeandía at the end of July, was that H. had invested a part of the public funds for his own account at Tepic, since of the $22,000 only about $8,500 in coin could be proved to have arrived in Cal.; and it was very likely that the bales of goods referred to represented the balance; though it was hard to prove, because H. had had plenty of time to replace the deficit in coin.   June 16th, Echeandía in a circular orders the apprehension of Bringas, who is to be compelled to testify. *Dept. Rec.*, MS., v. 53.   April 26th, E. to com. gen., says that H. has not acted properly, and that proceedings have been instituted to prove his misbehavior. *Id.*, v. 136. July 10th, H. to gov., with renewed complaints on the disregard of his orders by Martinez, Estrada, and Argüello. *Dept. St. Pap., Ben. Com. and Treas.*, MS., i. 76-9.

money intrusted to Herrera, and his own statement that he was positive of Herrera's misuse of the funds. The record of the previous secret investigations seems also to have been read. *Ternas*, or trios, of candidates for contador and treasurer were proposed in due form. Bandini then advocated the suspension of Herrera; but Echeandía opposed so radical a measure, arguing that the comisario would be so closely watched by the new officials that he could do no harm, and meanwhile the charges against him could be investigated by the supreme government. It is not easy to determine whether the governor's opposition was a mere pretence, or whether, while wishing to humble his rival, he doubted the expediency of suspending him on so slight evidence. On the first vote, four members were for suspension, one against it, and one besides the president did not vote. Subsequently another member was called in, the arguments were repeated, and Bandini obtained a secret vote in favor of suspension. It is not unlikely that this result had been prearranged, and that the arguments of Bandini and Echeandía were made merely for effect.[7]

Herrera was not suspended, because the candidates for treasurer declined to serve, and no suitable person for the place could be found; but Pablo Gonzalez was installed as contador from July 23d, and matters went on much as before, save that Herrera, offended at the charges of interfering with other officials, now declined to perform some duties thought to belong to him.[8] He neglected certain details of gathering sup-

[7] *Leg. Rec.*, MS., i. 91–101. For contador the *terna* was, 1. Pablo Gonzalez, 2. Joaquin Estudillo, 3. Manuel Dominguez. For treasurer, 1. José Antonio Carrillo, 2. José Antonio Estudillo, 3. Antonio María Osio. In the first vote Ortega, Bandini, Carrillo, and Buelna voted for suspension; Estrada against, and Tapia reserved his vote. Romualdo Pacheco was the suplente called in, but the final vote was secret, no names being given.

[8] Appointment of Gonzalez, who spoke English, as contador, July 23d. *Leg. Rec.*, MS., i. 64, 91; *Dept. Rec.*, MS., v. 71. Aug. 7th, Echeandía to com. gen. Says he has forwarded to the secretary of the treasury the secret investigations against H., whom the diputacion does not suspend for want of a suitable man to take his place. *Id.*, v. 138. Sept. 19th, H. to com. gen. complaining that the ministro de hacienda fails to answer his important questions. *Dept. St. Pap., Ben. Com. and Treas.*, MS., i. 91.

plies and serving out rations to prisoners, was summoned before the diputacion on September 19th, denied the right of that body to question him, but indulged in a wordy warfare with Echeandía in the legislative hall. Next day the governor evolved from his inner consciousness, and caused to be approved by the diputacion, the theory that the duty of a comisario subprincipal de hacienda was confined to 'systematizing the financial administration,' by reporting on needed reforms, and keeping accounts of net products of revenue.[9] Accordingly he notified Herrera of the result of his legal studies prompted by the comisario's misdeeds, and ordered him to restore to the habilitados all their former powers, and to confine his own authority to the narrow limits indicated above. Herrera thereupon, in obedience as he said to previous instructions from his superior, resigned his position, leaving the financial administration wholly in the hands of the gefe político, and asking for a passport to go to Mazatlan, which Echeandía refused. Thus the matter stood during the rest of 1827.[10]

[9] *Leg. Rec.*, MS., i. 86–90, 101–4. Sessions of Sept. 19th–20th. Echeandía supported his new theory with an elaborate argument. A new terna for treasurer was proposed, consisting of Santiago Argüello, Maitorena, and Ignacio Martinez; but military duties prevented their acceptance.

[10] Sept. 25, 1827, gov. to H. *Dept. Rec.*, MS., v. 91–2, repeated Sept. 27th. Sept. 26th, H. to Estrada, announcing his resignation. *Vallejo, Doc.*, MS., i. 110. Sept. 26th, gov. to Estrada, announcing and explaining the change. The complaint was in the matter of furnishing supplies and rations, and the theory was that Gov. Argüello had given up to H. at first powers to which he was not entitled. *Id.*, i. 109. Same date, Echeandía notifies Prefect Sarría of the change. *Arch. Arzob.*, MS., v. pt i. 38–9. Echeandía's argument quoted in *Vallejo, Hist. Cal.*, MS., ii. 172–4. E. says in 1829 that H. 'se suspendió y tenazmento se negó en el ejercicio de todas sus funciones desde el dia 26 de Septiembre de 1827, dejandolas al cargo de este gobierno.' *Dept. St. Pap., Ben. Mil.*, MS., lxx. 19. Sept. 29th, E. to H. Chides him for his refusal to perform duties belonging to his office, and refuses a passport. *Dept. Rec.*, MS., v. 93. October, E. asks minister of the treasury that the trial or investigation of himself and H. may take place in Cal. *Id.*, v. 130–1. Oct. 1st, E. to comandantes and prefect on his orders to H. *Id.*, v. 93–4; *Dept. St. Pap.*, MS., ii.41. Oct. 3d, E. to H. Never told him not to manage the funds entering his office; and if he persists in resigning the place, the treasury will be injured even more than it was by his assumption of the habilitados' duties and rights. *Dept. Rec.*, v. 95. Oct. 11th, H. to E., protesting against the orders which detain him in Cal. If the treasury interests were injured, it was because he was not allowed to go to report to his superior in order that the latter might put another man in his place; and the governor, to whom he was in no way responsible, was the only one to blame. If charged with criminal acts, he was ready for trial; if

Nor did 1828 bring any notable change in the situation. The habilitados attended to the revenues as of old, Estrada and afterward Vallejo of Monterey exercising a kind of supervision, until in November Manuel Jimeno Casarin, a young man brought to California by his brothers, the friars Jimeno, was appointed by Echeandía as acting comisario, or administrator of the revenues, his position being similar to that held by Estrada before the coming of Herrera;[11] and Juan Bandini was appointed at about the same time as subordinate comisario at San Diego. Meanwhile Herrera continued his protests against being kept in California; could obtain neither a trial nor a passport; but made some efforts to obtain material for a later prosecution of his adversary. Echeandía was greatly blamed by both the comisario general and the minister of the treasury for his course towards his foe; but he defended himself as well as he could in writing, and insisted on keeping Herrera in the territory and holding him responsible for all financial ills, present and prospective.[12]

not, there was no right to detain him. He wished to enjoy the wise laws of his country where they were respected and obeyed, and not remain where they were shamefully transgressed, as he was ready to prove. He also claimed his arrears of salary, he having received only $126 in a year, and having to sell his furniture to keep alive. *Dept. St. Pap.*, MS., ii. 51. Oct. 16th, E. to comandantes, alcaldes, etc., announcing his action towards H., urging habilitados to attend carefully to their duties, and explaining why H. was not allowed to depart—that is because at a distance it would be hard to prove H.'s frauds or justify his own action or that of the diputacion. *Dept. Rec.*, MS., 101, 103; *Dept. St. Pap.*, *S. José*, MS., iv. 49–50; *Dept. St. Pap.*, *Ang.*, MS., xi. 1. Oct. 28th, E. to com. gen. Thinks the administration of the revenue by the habilitados is injurious. With an administrator, vista, and guard at each port, the revenue might amount to $30,000 or $40,000 annually. *Dept. Rec.*, MS., v. 139. Nov. 27th, E. tells the comandante that the company officers had never been free from responsibility in the matter of finances. *Id.*, v. 105.

[11] *Dept. Rec.*, MS., vi. 13, 133; *Leg. Rec.*, MS., i. 286. Oct. 6th, P. Antonio Jimeno writes to P. Peyri about getting for his brother the position of collector of customs. Peyri replies that he should obtain a certificate of fitness, and security for $4,000. Perhaps Jimeno did not take possession until Jan. 1, 1829. *Vallejo, Doc.*, MS., xxx. 308.

[12] Jan. 11, 1828, gov. to min. of war. Defends himself against charges of usurpation by the min. of the treasury. Some of the charges had apparently been printed, for which satisfaction is demanded. *Dept. Rec.*, MS., vi. 18–19. Feb. 22d, H. asks for a passport to go and render his accounts at Mazatlan. *St. Pap.*, *Sac.*, MS., x. 101. March 1st and April 26th, com. gen. to E., blaming him and the diputacion for exceeding their powers, even on the supposition that H. was guilty as charged, in which case a report should have

A kind of revolt occurred in the north in October 1828, with which Herrera's name is connected as instigator by Alvarado, Osio, and Vallejo, without the slightest foundation so far as can be known. There is indeed very little information extant respecting the movement, although I have the statements of several old Californians on the subject, including two of the leaders, José de Jesus Pico and Pablo Véjar. It appears that on the 8th of October, a large part of the cavalry soldiers at Monterey, joined by those of the escoltas who left their missions, refused to serve longer unless they were paid, thereupon marching out of the presidio with their weapons. Touching subsequent events, there is no agreement among the narrators, beyond the fact that Lieutenant Romualdo Pacheco persuaded the rebels to return to their duties, several of the number being put in prison to await the decision of the supreme government on their fate.[13] All agree that want of clothing and food was

been sent to his superior officer. H. is also reprimanded on the same date for failing to report properly on E.'s misdeeds and other matters. *Dept. St. Pap., Ben. Com. and Treas.*, MS., i. 96–103. June 13th, H. to E. Protests against what is virtually his arrest, since he is not allowed to leave Monterey for Sta Bárbara and S. Diego to attend to business. *Dept. St. Pap.*, MS., ii. 58. July 1st, H. required by the pres. of Mexico to form a regular accusation against E.; nothing to be kept back. *Id., Ben. Com. and Treas.*, i. 92–3. Aug. 7th, E. says he did not intend to prevent H. from travelling by land within the territory. *Dept. Rec.*, MS., vi. 79. Sept. 15th, E. to com. gen. Says H.'s charge that he and the diputacion deprived him of his office is false. *Id.*, vi. 12–13. Nov. 7th, E. orders that H.'s salary be paid punctually. *Id.*, vi. 131. Same date, will not allow him to leave the territory till ordered to do so by the sup. govt. *Id.*, vi. 129. Dec. 4th, 9th, 17th, further correspondence, showing that H. went to S. Diego, apparently to make secret investigations against his foe, which caused additional complications not very clearly recorded. *Id.*, vi. 148, 150, 154–6, 158.

[13] Oct. 1828, escoltas from S. Luis Obispo to S. Juan Bautista have abandoned their posts. *Dept. St. Pap., Ben. Pref. y Juzg.*, MS., i. 6, 8–9. Oct. 18th, Echeandía orders comandante of Monterey to bring the rebels to trial by court-martial; but if he cannot master them, to offer a pardon. *Dept. Rec.*, MS., vi. 113. Oct. 20th, E. to min. of war. Says the escoltas left their posts, and with the other troops came with arms in their hands to demand their pay. Hopes by the aid of the artillery lately arrived to prevent such disorder; but needs officers. *St. Pap., Sac.*, MS., x. 36–8. Oct. 31st, Id. to Id. Mentions the revolt, and asks that the guilty ones be pardoned. *Dept. Rec.*, MS., vi. 36. Nov. 7th, comandante of Monterey has made known to the troops the governor's pleasure at their loyalty in rejecting the proposals by some degenerate *militares*. *Vallejo, Doc.*, MS., i. 159. Jan. 1829, fiscal's opinion in case of Francisco Soto for the revolt of Oct. 8th, and other insubordination, then in prison. Thinks the death penalty

the cause of the rising; and there is no reason to suppose that it had any politically personal significance. There is also a vague allusion to insubordination at San Francisco about the same time, but we have no particulars.[14]

In 1829 there was a practical cessation of the financial controversy in its old phases, the situation remaining unchanged, save that Antonio María Osio acted as comisario during part of the year in the place of Jimeno, and an opportunity was afforded Echeandía to rid himself of Herrera by sending him away as a prisoner for trial, on charges somewhat less unfounded than that of mismanaging the revenues. Discontent among the soldiers continued, resulting in a revolt more extensive and complicated than that of 1828, though not much more serious in its results. Destitution, resulting from non-receipt of pay and rations, and attributed naturally by the troops to some fault of the governor, was the leading motive of the soldiers; the participants in the last revolt, yet under

should not be inflicted. *Dept. St. Pap., Ben. Mil.*, MS., lxix. 24. Osio, *Hist. Cal.*, MS., 123–5, says 40 soldiers, not including the older sergeants and corporals, marched 12 leagues to Codornices Mt., and were induced to come back by Pacheco and the padres, the former offering to intercede for their pardon. Vallejo, *Hist. Cal.*, ii. 83–5, tells us the cavalry company went to Sauzal, could not agree among themselves, and when Pacheco put himself at their head, they instinctively obeyed his order to march back to their quarters, where they were under arrest for many months. Pico, *Acontecimientos*, MS., 10, says that 80 men wandered about for a month, when half went back and were pardoned. The rest, the leaders being Felipe Arceo, Raimundo and Gabriel de la Torre, Pablo Véjar, José de Jesús Pico, and Francisco Soto, remained away longer, but at last returned at the request of their friends and families, and were put in prison. Véjar, *Recuerdos*, MS., 8–9, says he and another man were sent to Estrada to say that they would serve no longer without pay; and that before they returned to duty Estrada promised pardon and some relief. Torre, *Reminiscencias*, MS., 8–9, says that Arces was leader, and that the rebels went as far as Sta Cruz, S. Juan, and S. José. Ávila, *Cosas de Cal.*, MS., 25–7, saw the rebels form in line near her husband's house to return with Pacheco. She says Véjar was the leader, and that while in prison all were terrified at threats of being put to death. Amador, *Memorias*, MS., 86, tells us it was a long time before all returned to duty. He and José de Jesus Vallejo, *Reminis.*, MS., 15–16, represent the soldiers as having been in a pitiable state of destitution when they were driven to insubordination. Mention of the affair in *Lugo, Vida*, MS., 13; *Larios, Convulsiones*, MS., 8; Ord, *Ocurrencias*, MS., 24.

[14] Oct. 20th, gov. to min. of war. *St. Pap., Sac.*, MS., x. 38–9.

arrest, were rendered reckless by current rumors that they were to be shot;[15] Herrera and some of the friars, from motives of personal hostility, were willing to encourage any movement directed against Echeandía; and finally the records, without clearly implicating any prominent individual, leave room for a suspicion that most of the officers at Monterey and San Francisco were at the least not very earnest in their opposition to the rebels, though lacking confidence in their success and courage to take risks.

In June two soldiers revealed to Alférez José Fernandez del Campo a plot of the troops to rise against the governor and all those *de la otra banda*, with a view to put all the offices in the hands of Californians. The outbreak at Monterey was to take place June 22d, but the plan was revealed on the 18th. The leader was Joaquin Solis, a convict ranchero, living not far from the presidio. Solis was a companion of Vicente Gomez, El Capador. Like him, he had rendered service in the war of independence, and like him, had been sentenced to California for brutal crimes, which, but for his past services, would have been more severely punished. This revelation strangely seems to have caused no special sensation. There was a formal examination of several witnesses, with some official correspondence. Difficulty was experienced in inducing any officer to act as fiscal, or prosecutor, and finally the matter was dropped for reasons not apparent. Stranger still, this affair was ignored in all the proceedings arising from later troubles.[16]

[15] June 9, 1829, order from Mexico that the soldiers under arrest for mutiny be set at liberty, after admonishment as to their duties. *Sup. Govt St. Pap.*, MS., v. 12. It does not appear that this order reached Monterey before the rising. The fact that the prisoners began the movement is stated by Pico, *Acont.*, MS., 10-13; Larios, *Convulsiones*, MS., 8-10; Ávila, *Cosas de Cal.*, MS., 25-8.

[16] June 23, 1829, com. of Monterey to Echeandía. Says a conspiracy of the Californians against the Mexicans had been detected, and his men had been under arms for 3 days, though the conspirators had not dared to break out. *Dept. Rec.*, MS., vi. 16. June 25th, Alf. Fernandez reported to the com. the revelations of Mariano Peguero, corporal of artillery, and of private Pedro Guerrero. Gabriel Espinosa and Raimundo de la Torre were named as concerned in the plot. The cavalryman, Juan Elizalde, confirmed the statements of Peguero

During the night of November 12th–13th, the soldiers at Monterey rose and took possession of the presidio. By a previous understanding, doubtless, though little or nothing was ever brought to light on the subject, there was no opposition in any of the barracks; but some of the men, especially of the infantry, seem to have been permitted to remain neutral by giving up their weapons. The ringleaders were Mariano Peguero, Andrés Leon, Pablo Véjar, and the two brothers Raimundo and Gabriel de la Torre, though even of these none would subsequently admit that he entered altogether willingly into the plot, or that he contemplated anything more serious than the sending of a 'representation' to the governor. Small parties, each including two or more of the men named, proceeded to the houses of Vallejo, the acting commandant of the company, Juan José Rocha of the artillery, Sergeant Andrés Cervantes, and of the acting comisario Manuel Jimeno Casarin, all of whom were roused from their slumbers on one pretext or another, and were locked up in the calabozo before dawn. Juan B. Alvarado and José Castro seem also to have been arrested. No resistance beyond verbal protest was attempted, except that the doors of Vallejo and Rocha had to be kicked down by Estévan Espinosa.[17]

and Guerrero. Follows a record of preliminary legal proceedings, leading to no intelligible result. *Dept. St. Pap., Ben. Mil.*, MS., lxix. 15–19. July 1st, gov. to com. of Monterey. Orders arrest of Solis, Espinosa, and Torre, and examination of Elizalde, Guerrero, and Fernando Curiel. *Dept. St. Pap.*, MS., ii. 96–7; *Dept. Rec.*, MS., vi. 187. July 8th, gov. orders artillery comandante to redouble his efforts to prevent the threatened revolt. *Id.*, vii. 193. Sept. 22d, José T. Castro, alcalde, assures Echeandía of the fealty of S. José. *St. Pap., Miss. and Colon.*, MS., ii. 7. Sept. 28th, Fernandez del Campo to alcalde. Must watch that no one carries forbidden arms. *Vallejo, Doc.*, MS., xxix. 419.

[17] The details of the arrests are given at considerable length in testimony to be referred to later. R. Torre, Véjar, Leon, Dolores García, Espinosa, and a few artillerymen composed the party that took Vallejo. He was called on pretext of an important message just arrived, but suspecting something, would not come out; therefore the door was kicked in after consultation. Peguero, Véjar, and Espinosa arrested Jimeno. Several witnesses testified that Alvarado and Castro were inprisoned. Ávila, *Cosas de Cal.*, MS., 25–8, was told by Véjar at the time that the object was to make the officers eat *morizqueta* and learn how the soldiers had to live. Spence, *Hist. Notes*, MS., 3–7, says Solis

The rebels thus secured Monterey without opposition, and similar easy success at all other points was anticipated.   There was the usual indulgence in prospective death or liberty as a figure of speech, but clearly none of the conspirators expected serious obstacles.   A leader was needed, none of the conspirators ranking higher than corporal, or feeling competent to take the command.   Raimundo de la Torre was accordingly despatched with a summons to Joaquin Solis, who came in from his rancho on the 14th and assumed the position of comandante general of the Californian troops.[18]   I suppose that all this had been prearranged, although Solis and the rest insisted on their trial, that the convict general now heard of the rising for the first time, and he even had the assurance to claim that he accepted the command to prevent the disorders that would naturally arise from leaving the rabble uncontrolled!

Now that there was a general, a plan or pronunciamiento was an absolute necessity.   Solis applied for such a plan—or, as he afterward tried to make it appear, for a petition or 'representation' to Echeandía on existing evils—to José María Herrera.   The ex-

took the officers of the presidio by stratagem.   Alvarado, *Hist. Cal.*, MS., ii. 148-59, says he and Castro were sleeping in the same room with Vallejo, when 10 soldiers came and marched all three to jail, where they spent the night on the bare ground, half-dressed.   Vallejo got a chance to make a speech, but to no avail.   The prisoners feared at first serious results from the reckless character of the conspirators.   Vallejo, *Hist. Cal.*, MS., ii. 86-96, 110-11; iii. 245, gives a similar narrative to that of Alvarado.   Says it was 2 A. M. when the soldiers came on pretence of giving him the mail-bag.   They were shut up with the lowest criminals, who were however soon released.   He was much relieved to hear from Jimeno, the last prisoner brought to jail, that the plot was to overthrow Echeandía, and not, as he had feared, to plunder the town and flee on one of the vessels in port.   Torre, *Reminis.*, MS., 10-21, says his brothers Raimundo and Gabriel were in command of the escoltas of S. Miguel and S. Luis respectively, and came with their men and those of S. Antonio and Soledad, arriving on the night of the revolt.   Osio, *Hist. Cal.*, MS., 125-51, tells us that Rocha, Vallejo, and Fernandez del Campo had repeatedly warned Echeandía of the danger, without his having paid the slightest heed. Véjar, *Recuerdos*, MS., 9-35, says Echeandía would certainly have been shot had he been in Monterey at the time, as the soldiers considered him responsible for all their troubles.

[18] Nov. 13, 1829, summons to Solis to take the command, in *Dept. St. Pap., Ben. Mil.*, MS., lxxii. 45, signed by Peguero, Leon, Gabriel de la Torre, and Petronilo Rios.   See also *Id.*, p. 40, 43, 53, 55.

comisario was in sympathy with any movement against the governor. We are told by Osio, Vallejo, Alvarado, and others that he was the prime mover in the revolt, Solis being merely a tool in his hands. I think this view of the case an exaggeration, and that Herrera, like several others perhaps who were never directly implicated, was willing to wait, and even aid so far as he could in safety. However this may have been, the troops counted on him to a certain extent,[19] and he at the least dictated the plan, which was written at his house by Petronilo Rios, and completed in the evening of November 15th. It was read aloud to a group of foreigners, including Hartnell, Spence, Cooper, Stearns, Anderson, McCulloch, and others who happened to be present, and who more or less approved the document, 'from motives of courtesy,' as David Spence afterward testified. It was read to the soldiers and approved by them the same night. Many claimed later not to have been pleased with the paper, since it was a plan of revolution, and not a petition for redress of grievances; but this was an afterthought in most cases.

The plan was made to embody the grievances of Herrera, as well as of the troops, and was directed against Echeandía as the author of all territorial evils.[20] The avowed object was to put the territory

[19] There are several vague allusions in the testimony to two *brazos fuertes*, on whom dependence was placed. One was supposed to be Herrera, and the other perhaps Capt. Gonzalez, or Lieut. Lobato, or Francisco Pacheco. Solis claimed to have acted in many things on H.'s advice after he had taken the command. H. in his testimony said he first knew of the trouble when in the night of the 12th he heard a noise in Jimeno's room next to his own, and rushed out sword in hand to defend him. Next day he was offered the comisaría, but declined, and advised the rebels to await the arrival of Osio, who already had the appointment from Echeandía. He again declined the office when offered by Solis. He was asked for advice, and gave it in the interest of good order. He subsequently agreed to dictate the plan on condition that the officers should be set at liberty, and with a view to secure respect for the authorities, to prevent outrages on persons and property; in fact, to control for the good of the territory so far as possible a revolution which he was powerless to prevent. *Dept. St. Pap.*, MS., lxxii. 71–4. It is fair to state that this defence was at least plausible, and that there is really no evidence of any weight against its accuracy, except the statements of persons liable to be influenced by prejudice.

[20] Solis, *Manifiesto al Público, ó sea Plan de Revolucion, 1829*, MS. It was signed by Solis, Peguero, Leon, Rios, and Gabriel de la Torre. In substance,

in the hands of a temporary governor appointed by the diputacion. There was no need of a such a revolution, or at least no reason to expect relief from such measures; the charges against Echeandía were grossly exaggerated, since he was merely a weak man placed in circumstances where a strong man could have done but little; but the prevalent destitution among the troops was real, and was perhaps a sufficient motive

the document was as follows: The sup. govt, which is ever anxious for our good, and to which we are ever obedient, sent a governor who has failed to comply with his instructions; has scandalously abused his authority; has devoted himself to his own interests and comforts and those of a few men about him; and has paid no attention to the complaints of hungry and naked soldiers. The laws call for a diputacion chosen by the people; but the gefe fails to either convoke that body or to explain his reasons for not doing so, and consequently agriculture, commerce, education, and other vital interests are grossly neglected. Two years ago the gov. suspended the comisario of the revenues for reasons not known, which has resulted in the most scandalous mismanagement of the public funds. The administration of justice and military discipline are in a state of detestable abandonment; immorality and crime are rampant; and all results directly from the ruler's neglect and lack of energy. Therefore, having endured all of misery and neglect that is humanly possible, having resorted in vain to every other expedient, the troops have resolved to use force, and to support the following plan: 1. The diputacion shall meet in due form with all its members. 2. When it has assembled Echeandía shall resign all his powers to the dip., which shall appoint a person worthy of confidence to serve until the arrival of a new gefe sent by the sup. govt, who will be immediately recognized. 3. Both this ayuntamiento (of Monterey) and those of other places will name proper persons to manage the revenues provisionally in accordance with the laws. 4. The troops will remain under their old officers, if the latter agree to this plan; otherwise they will choose a sergeant or corporal as comandante, who shall acknowledge the authority of the gefe appointed by the diputacion. 5. Commandants of troops will apply for pay and supplies to the respective administrators of revenue appointed as above, and never to missions or private persons. 6. Only alcaldes may apply to missions for supplies, giving proper receipts, and delivering the product to the administrators. 7. In very urgent cases the ayuntamiento and administrator may require a moderate loan from private persons, the amount being proportioned to their means. 8. Persons and property to be fully protected, especially in the case of foreigners belonging to a friendly nation. (Herrera added to this article a note in his own handwriting which extended the assurance of protection to the Spaniards already living in the territory—that is, leaving all further action against them for the sup. govt and the new governor to dispose of.) 9. An eloquent peroration, in which the pronunciados declare that they will never lay down their arms until their object is accomplished; that no violence will be used beyond what is necessary in defence of their rights; that there will be no persecution of opponents; that anxiety may be banished from the minds of all, citizens or foreigners; that the object was to reëstablish and not to overthrow the government; that 'the military apparatus which has caused alarm is only the effort of free men against tyranny, and the use of this last resource made everywhere to overthrow tyranny by soldiers overwhelmed by misery, weakened by hunger, and fully awakened by the painful spectacle daily presented to their eyes of a dear wife and tender children, naked, and on the point of becoming victims to indigence.'

for mutiny. It was natural enough that all existing evils should be popularly attributed to the ruler, and could the soldiers have induced some popular and intelligent officer to take the command, the movement would have been successful so far as the overthrow of Echeandía was concerned.

Soon after his arrival at Monterey, Solis transferred the imprisoned officers from the calabozo to the warehouse. Meanwhile Raimundo de la Torre was sent to San Juan, where he lay in wait for and captured Fernandez del Campo, an officer who at the time of the revolt was absent on an Indian expedition. His men joined the rebels, and the leader was brought to the presidio under arrest. Whether he also was locked up with the rest does not appear; but in a few weeks all the prisoners were released at the intercession of foreigners, and on the advice of Herrera, much against the wishes of some of the soldiers. Vallejo and Rocha were however sent south in the *Brookline*. Stephen Anderson carried copies of the plan to Santa Bárbara by water, and Meliton Soto, a citizen, was sent south with letters calculated to advance the rebel cause, while Raimundo de la Torre read the plan to the soldiers of every escolta from Soledad to San Luis Obispo. The ayuntamiento of Monterey, headed by Tiburcio Castro, the alcalde, accepted the plan, proclaimed it to the assembled citizens, and urged its acceptance by other towns.[21] Castro turned over the municipal funds, and replenished the rebel treasury by imposing a tax or loan of a few thousand dollars on the traders, chiefly foreigners. In accordance with the plan, an administrator of revenues was chosen, the position being given to Antonio María Osio, who accepted it.[22] When all had been arranged at the capital, General

[21] Nov. 16, 1829, Alcalde Castro to Solis, in *Dept. St. Pap., Ben.*, MS., v. 359-60.

[22] Nov. 16th, Tiburcio Castro's statement. *Dept. St. Pap., Ben.*, MS., v. 358. In his *Historia de California*, MS., 145, Don Antonio María naturally calls attention to the fact that he had been previously appointed by Echeandía.

Solis turned his attention to the north, leaving Francisco Pacheco in command at Monterey.[23]

Of the march northward and return we have few details; but there had been a previous understanding with the garrison, and neither at San Francisco nor at any point on the way did Solis encounter opposition. The northern tour consumed about a month, to December 20th. The ayuntamiento of San José accepted the plan as the best means of securing peace and order; or at least so I interpret a letter of Alcalde Archuleta, which that dignitary perhaps intended to be vague and unintelligible. At San Juan and Santa Clara Solis received supplies and money to the amount of a few hundred dollars; but Padre Duran at Mission San José, not in the comandante's route, declined to contribute, on the ground that he had no official knowl-

---

[23] Nov. 21st, Pacheco to Solis. Says he is not capable of undertaking the command, having neither talent nor disposition for it; but he was willing to serve his country in any possible way. The following items are from the various statements made from memory: Pablo Véjar, *Recuerdos*, MS., 9–17, says he had for a week the key of the comisaría, where there was a large box of silver coin, which fact he did not reveal, fearing the men would seize the money and give color to a charge that they had rebelled for plunder. He claims to have been a leader with Torre at first. Osio, *Hist. Cal.*, MS., 143–6, tells us that Castro was forced to lend $1,000 of the municipal funds, and that he, Osio, distributed over $3,000 in effects to the troops. He arrived the same day as Solis, and helped to secure the release of the prisoners. Estévan de la Torre, *Reminis.*, MS., 12–14, gives some details of the capture by his brother of Fernandez del Campo at S. Juan. Vallejo, *Hist. Cal.*, MS., ii. 86–90, attributes his release to the efforts of the foreigners headed by David Spence. He says Sergt Cervantes was also sent south in the *Brookline*. José de Jesus Pico, *Acont.*, MS., 10–13, says he was sent to intercept the mail at Soledad and to bring away the guard, succeeding in both undertakings. Gonzalez, *Revoluciones*, MS., 1–3, gives a brief account of the whole affair. Robinson, *Life in Cal.*, 69–70, says that Solis seized about $3,000 in the comisaría, and levied a contribution on the inhabitants. James O. Pattie's version of the Solis revolt is perhaps worth presenting apart. That part relating to this first phase of the affair at Monterey is as follows: In January 1830 (the date is wrong) my acquaintances informed me on landing 'that there was a revolution in the country, a part of the inhabitants having revolted against the constituted authorities. The revolted party seemed at present likely to gain the ascendency. They had promised the English and Americans the same privileges and liberty in regard to trade on the coast that belonged to the native citizens, upon the condition that these people aided them in their attempt to gain their freedom by imparting advice and funds. I readily appropriated a part of my little store to their use, and I would fain have accompanied them in hopes to have one shot at the general with my rifle. But my countrymen said it was enough to give counsel and funds at first, and it would be best to see how they managed their own affairs before we committed ourselves by taking an active part in them.' *Pattie's Nar.*, 222.

edge of any change in the government. He was perhaps the only man in the north who ventured to question the authority of Solis.[24] At San Francisco Solis and his army were received with an artillery salute; the whole garrison promptly joined the rebel cause; José Sanchez was made comandante instead of Martinez; and that is practically all that is known on the subject.[25]

At San Francisco Solis tried to induce Luis Argüello to take the chief command of the rebel forces. There is no documentary evidence of this fact, but it is stated by many of the Californians. The effort was natural; and José Fernandez says that the offer was made in his presence, Solis urging Argüello's acceptance, and promising to retire himself, so that Don Luis might not have to associate with a convict. But

[24] Nov. 22d, Solis announces that he is near S. Juan, and his men need clothing. *Dept. St. Pap., Ben.,* MS., v. 369. Nov. 25th, Alcalde Archuleta seems to accept the plan. *Id.,* v. 357–8. Amounts of money obtained, $140 at S. Juan; $100 at Sta Clara; and $200 at S. José. *Dept. St. Pap., Ben. Mil.,* MS., lxxii. 46. Nov. 26th, Solis, at Sta Clara, to ayunt. of S. José. Must have $100 from municipal fund or nearest mission in order to resume his march. *S. José, Arch.,* MS., vi. 14. Nov. 30th, *Id.* to *Id.* from S. F., again demands money to supply the troops. *Id.,* vi. 15. Dec. 1st, P. Duran declines to give $200 for a comandante general interino of whose authority he knows nothing. *Id.,* vi. 17. Dec. 4th, 6th, Solis, at S. Francisco, to the ayunt., arguing the case as against P. Duran. The beauties of the plan and the duties of all, including friars, under it are earnestly set forth. *Id.,* vi. 12, 11. Dec. 6th, Solis, back at Sta Clara, gives receipt for $100 of the tithes of S. José, and $200 of Sta Clara. *Id.,* ii. 49. Dec. 11th, Solis, at La Laguna, with complaint against the alcalde of S. José for nothing in particular. *Id.,* i. 35.

[25] Feb. 19, 1830, Martinez writes to Echeandía, that on Nov. 15, 1829, Solis was about to attack S. Francisco and he prepared to resist him, but found the troops so demoralized and so disposed to join Solis that he was obliged, not to accept the plan, but to remain neutral and await results. Nov. 30th, he was ordered to deliver the military command to José Sanchez and the habilitacion to Francisco Sanchez, and also to remain in his house as a prisoner. *Dept. St. Pap.,* MS., ii. 129. It would seem that on the final approach of Solis, Martinez had some idea of resistance, for Nov. 19th he wrote to S. José, asking for a reënforcement of 10 vecinos. *S. José, Arch.,* MS., i. 33. In Feb. and March 1830 Corporal Joaquin Piña, who had been in command of the artillery in the past Nov., was accused of insolence to Martinez on Nov. 28th, when he came by order of Solis, then at the mission, to demand ammunition for a salute. Piña denied the insolence, but in turn accused Martinez of having approved the plan when it was first read, Nov. 21st or 22d, and of having sent to Solis a written surrender of the presidio, much to the disgust of Piña, but with the approval of Francisco de Haro. *Dept. St. Pap., Ben. Mil.,* MS., lxxi. 21–8. All of the Californian writers mention the expedition to S. Francisco, but none give details. Osio, however, says that Solis met with no opposition from Martinez.

Argüello, while admitting that he would rejoice at the overthrow of Echeandía, had no disposition to head a revolution, and persisted in his refusal. A part of the San Francisco garrison was incorporated in the army of Solis, but most of the men deserted at San José on the march to Monterey.

On his return Solis received despatches warning him to make haste or Santa Bárbara would be lost to the cause. Accordingly after a short stay at the capital, he began his march southward with over one hundred men, Gabriel de la Torre commanding the cavalry and Lázaro Piña the artillery. Beyond the facts that the army was at San Miguel December 28th, got plenty of supplies at each mission, and was in such good spirits at Santa Inés that the men refused to accept the governor's *indulto* which met them at that point, we have practically no details respecting the march. Thus far all went well; but the leader had no ability, nor control over his men; the army had no elements of coherence, and would fall apart of its own weight at the slightest obstacle; yet if success should take the form of a hole, the fragments might fall into it.[26]

Let us now turn to the south. Echeandía heard of the Solis revolt November 25th, or a day or two earlier. On that date he revealed it to the officers and people in a circular, stating that he had convoked a council of seven officers, who were asked for a frank opinion whether his rule was satisfactory, and what changes if any could be advantageously made in the administration. The response was unanimous that he was a good governor, though Juan Malarin was named as the best man for the revenue department.

[26] The march south, organization of the army, trifling details. *Dept. St. Pap., Ben. Mil.*, MS., lxxii. 41, 45–6, 76–7, and scattering. Jan. 15, 1830, Alcalde Soberanes writes from Monterey that he has notice of Solis passing Purísima on Jan. 10th, and that Pacheco is awaiting him at La Cieneguita with 200 men. *S. José, Arch.*, MS., i. 37. Osio, *Hist. Cal.*, MS., 147, mentions that at Monterey Solis showed an inclination to give up the command; that his old companion Antonio Ávila threatened to oppose him if he continued to be the tool of Herrera; and that a sergeant of artillery went south in his army with the express purpose of betraying him (Lázaro Piña?), as he did.

Consequently he declares that the adherents of Solis, if they do not lay down their arms and leave the authorities free, shall be deemed traitors and accomplices of the Spanish invaders at Vera Cruz.[27] Two days later Echeandía reported the matter to the minister of war, announcing that he would start north in a few days to retake the capital. He declared his belief that Herrera was at the bottom of the revolt, hoping to gratify personal hatred, to avoid the rendering of accounts and exposure of his frauds, and either to escape by some vessel, or more likely to declare for Spain or North American adventurers. Echeandía does not fail to make the affair a text for discourse on the difficulties of his position, and the urgent need of aid from Mexico.[23] He left San Diego on December 1st and reached Santa Bárbara the 15th, after having made arrangements on the way for reenforcements to come from Los Angeles, and for a meeting of the diputacion, as elsewhere related.

At San Diego the rebellion obtained no foothold;[29] but at Santa Bárbara in the early days of December, before Echeandía's arrival, the garrison rose much as at Monterey, and held the presidio for nearly two days. The outbreak seems to have taken place just after the arrival of Meliton Soto with despatches from the north on the 2d. The coming of such a messenger had been expected, and a rising had been planned since the beginning of November. It was now settled

[27] Nov. 25, 1829, Echeandía's circular. *Dept. Rec.*, MS., vii. 257.

[28] Nov. 27, 1829, E. to min. of war. *St. Pap., Sac.*, MS., x. 53–5. He is hard pressed by numerous duties, the difficulty of maintaining harmony with disaffected Spanish friars, the fear of a neophyte uprising, the total want of funds, the difficulties of communication, etc. He wants officers, troops, priests, money, and above all, just now 50 men from Sonora to establish communication by land.

[29] Nov. 26, 1829, Echeandía orders the comandante to summon the militia in case of need to serve against Solis. *Dept. Rec.*, MS., vii. 258. Dec. 30th, Argüello assures E. that all at San Diego are opposed to the plan and determined to support the govt. *Dept. St. Pap.*, MS., ii. 92. Sergt José María Medrano was accused by P. Menendez of saying that he had expected the outbreak since July, and that had he been at Monterey he would have favored the plan; but after investigation the padre's testimony was doubted, and Medrano acquitted as a faithful soldier.

that the discharge of a musket at midnight of the 3d, eve of Santa Bárbara, should be the signal; but an accidental discharge brought on the outbreak prematurely at 11 A. M. Romualdo Pacheco, acting comandante, and Rodrigo del Pliego were seized and placed under arrest in Pacheco's house, guarded by a corporal and eight soldiers. Sergeant Dámaso Rodriguez was perhaps the leader of the rebels, or perhaps, as he afterward claimed, only pretended to be so to preserve order. No violence was done to persons or property. A distribution of warehouse effects was proposed, but was postponed until the soldiers of the mission guards should come to claim their share. The quelling of this revolt was a simple matter. The officers were released by Rodriguez and a few others, on the 4th, against the wishes of many. Pacheco easily won over a few soldiers, marched to the barracks next day, and advised the troops to return to their allegiance and duty. They were given until 9 P. M. to think of the matter, and they deemed it best to surrender, after six of the number, presumably the leaders, whom only Pacheco had threatened with arrest, had been given time to run away with Meliton Soto for the north.[30]

Echeandía put Santa Bárbara in the best possible state for defence. He obtained reënforcements of men,

[30] The best account is given in the testimony of the artilleryman Máximo Guerra. *Dept. St. Pap., Ben. Mil.*, MS., lxxii. 65–7. He names as implicated in the revolt and in the previous plans: Dámaso Rodriguez, Antonio Guevara, Vicente Rico, Joaquin Cota, Martinez, and himself, who were the 6 who ran away; also José María Perez, Luciano Félix, and Ex-alcalde Fernando Ticó, who spoke of Anastasio Carrillo as the prospective comandante. Soto in his testimony, *Id.*, 62–3, claimed to have had nothing further to do with the plot than, having business in the south, to carry letters for Solis, receiving $50 for the service. He was back at Monterey before Solis started for Sta Bárbara. Gonzalez, *Experiencias*, MS., 26–9, who was alcalde of Sta Bárbara at the time, gives a version agreeing with that of Guerra, so far as it goes. Dec. 8th, Echeandía at S. Gabriel wrote about the revolt, stating that Rodriguez was said to have only pretended to accept the command, that Pacheco had regained control by the aid of citizens, and that he was in pursuit of wounded (?) mutineers. *Dept. Rec.*, MS., vii. 259. Slight mention in *St. Pap., Sac.*, MS., x. 56. Mrs Ord, *Ocurrencias*, MS., 28–32, tells us that all the artillery revolted except Corporal Basualdo, who took refuge in the comandante's house.

animals, and supplies from the pueblo and missions,[31] stationed Pacheco with about ninety soldiers at Cieneguita, two or three miles from the mission, and awaited the approach of the rebel forces. The 7th of January, 1830, he issued a proclamation, in which he called upon the Monterey insurgents to surrender on condition of full pardon and liberty, except to the leaders, who would be simply imprisoned until their pardon could be obtained from Mexico. He believed the revolt to be due to the selfish aims and the crimes of Herrera, who had deceived the troops; and he warned them that in opposing him they were really in rebellion against the republic, a state of things that could lead only to blood and ruin.[32] Next day he received a communication from Solis, dated at Santa Inés or El Refugio the 7th, in which he was called upon to give up the command in accordance with the plan. He answered it the same day with a refusal. He ordered the rebels to present themselves unarmed for surrender, and renewed the argument against Herrera, claiming that the troops had received two thirds of their pay, and that there had been no complaint to him.[33]

None of the Solis men accepted the first offer of pardon received at or near Santa Inés. No obstacles had yet been encountered, and this revolt was so planned as to overcome everything else. It was yet hoped that the Santa Bárbara garrison might join the movement, and the rebel army marched bravely on to Dos Pueblos, even coming in sight of the foe on the 13th. Pacheco and his men immediately executed a

[31] Thirty-one citizens went from Angeles. *Dept. St. Pap., Ben. Mil.*, MS., lxxiii. 60–1. Dec. 20th, Echeandía directs padres of Sta Inés and Purísima to send to Sta Bárbara all people capable of bearing arms; also all spare animals and supplies to keep them from the hands of the rebels. *Dept. Rec.*, MS., vii. 266. Jan. 5, 1830, E. orders alcalde of Angeles to send armed and mounted citizens. *Id.*, viii. 2. Pacheco's advance guard consisted of 30 of the Mazatlan company, 8 artillerymen, 30 of the regular presidial company under Alf. Pliego, 20 of the S. Diego company under Alf. Ramirez, and about 100 neophytes with bows and arrows. *St. Pap., Sac.*, MS., x. 56.

[32] Jan. 7, 1830, proclamation. *Dept. Rec.*, MS., viii. 4.

[33] *Id.*, viii. 4–7.

change of base to prevent being cut off—that is, they retreated from Cieneguita as fast as their legs would carry them, and took refuge in the presidio.[34] Solis seems to have come somewhat nearer Santa Bárbara, but we know little in detail respecting what occurred for three days. Echeandía wrote to the minister of war: "On the 13th the rebels came in sight of the *divisioncita* of government troops, and from that time by their movements and frivolous correspondence endeavored to gain a victory; but knowing the uselessness of their resources and the danger of being cut off on their retreat, they fled precipitately at dusk on the 15th in different directions, spiking their cannon; and losing twenty-six men who have accepted the *indulto.*"[35] The last act of Solis before running away was to announce that his men were ready for a fight, and would never surrender until they got their pay.[36] The rebel chieftain described the events at Santa Bárbara thus: "Having taken a position between the presidio and mission, I found it impossible to enter either one or the other, the first because it was fortified, the second because of the walls pierced with loop-holes for musket-fire, and of all the people within, so that I knew we were going to lose, and this was the motive for not exposing the troops by entering. —— wrote me that the general had ordered Portilla to march with 150 men to surprise us, and seeing myself without means of defence for want of munitions, I determined to spike the cannon, and retire with my army to fortify myself in Monterey—*lo que verifiqué al mo-*

---

[34] The retreat is definitely stated only by Ord, *Ocurrencias*, MS., 29–39; Gonzalez, *Experiencias*, MS., 27–9; and Pico, *Acont.*, MS., 10–13; but all are good authorities.

[35] Jan. 26, 1830, Echeandía to min. of war. *St. Pap., Sac.*, MS., x. 58. He says the pursuit of the fugitives had to be suspended temporarily at Purísima. A list of 28 soldiers, who at this time surrendered themselves, is given in *Dept. St. Pap., Ben. Mil.*, MS., lxxvi. 23. Jan. 16th, E. announces the surrender of the 26th and his hopes of final success. Some additional correspondence of minor importance, from Jan. 8th to 18th. *Dept. Rec.*, MS., viii. 10. Jan. 13th, Pacheco tells E. that he has gained an advantage over the foe. *Id.*, viii. 85.

[36] Jan. 15th, Solis from 'Campo Nacional' to E. *Dept. St. Pap., Ben.*, MS., ii. 4. He was willing, however, to have a conference.

mento."[37] Dr Anderson wrote to Captain Cooper:
"You would have laughed had you been here when the
gentlemen from your quarter made their appearance.
All the people moved into the presidio, except thirty
women, who went bag and baggage on board the
Funchal. The two parties were in sight of each other
for nearly two days, and exchanged shots, but at such
a distance that there was no chance of my assistance
being needed. About thirty have passed over to this
side. The general appears to be perplexed what to do
with them. He seems as much frightened as ever."[33]
All my original witnesses state that cannon were fired,
but give no particulars save the important one that
nobody was hurt. Several represent the army of
Solis to have fled at the first discharge of Pacheco's
guns. At any rate, the rebel force fled, pursued at
not very close quarters, scattering as they advanced
northward, and wholly disbanded before they reached
the capital, where singly and in groups they soon
took advantage of the renewed offers of pardon. The
campaign of the south, and the battles of Santa Bárbara, Cieneguita, and Dos Pueblos—the first in which
Californians were pitted against Californians—were
over.

On the 18th Echeandía summoned the soldiers of
the north, that is, those who had surrendered, before
himself, Carrillo, and Zamorano. Each one was interrogated about the charges made in the plan. Each
declared that there were no grounds whatever for

---

[37] Jan. 20th, Solis, at S. Miguel, to José Sanchez. *Dept. St. Pap.*, MS., ii.
118. Solis at this time claimed to have over 100 men left, and to be confident
of success. He had only 40 men when he reached Soledad. *Id., Ben. Mil.*,
lxxii. 46. Jan. 15th, 16th, 18th, 28th, E. to Pacheco. Instructions about
the pursuit of the rebels, and the retaking of Monterey. *Dept. Rec.*, MS., viii.
85-90.

[38] Jan. 24th, Dr Anderson to Cooper. *Vallejo, Doc.*, MS., xxx. 7. The affair as reported at Monterey and reported by Pattie, *Narr.*, 225, was as follows: 'A continual firing had been kept up on both sides during the three
days, at the expiration of which Gen. Solis, having expended his ammunition
and consumed his provisions, was compelled to withdraw, having sustained
no loss, except that of one horse, from a sustained action of three days!
The cannon-balls discharged from the fort upon the enemy had so little force
that persons arrested them in their course without injury.'

complaint; whereupon the governor showed documents to prove that in 1829, one month with another,
the soldiers had received two thirds of their full pay.[39]
On the 24th the *Brookline* arrived at San Diego with
Vallejo and Rocha, the Monterey prisoners, and the
same day or the next there came the news that the
capital had been retaken. Pacheco was already on
his way north to assume the command at Monterey.[40]
On the 26th, Echeandía reported all he had done to
the supreme government, and did not fail to utilize
the occasion by expatiating on California's great dangers and needs.[41]

The recapture of Monterey was effected January
20th, largely by the aid of the foreign residents. It
was feared that Solis and his men, defeated at Santa
Bárbara, would devote their efforts to plunder, and
it was deemed prudent to act before their return.
There was no more difficulty in bringing about this
movement in favor of Echeandía than in effecting the
original revolt against him; yet David Spence indulged in a little Mexicanism when he wrote of the
affair that "with the firm resolution of death or victory, like bold British tars, we stood it out for twelve
days and nights."[42] Malarin, Munrás, Alvarado, and
José de Jesus Vallejo were most prominent among
those who aided the foreigners; and the citizens of
San José seem to have sent a party to assist in the
reëstablishment of the regular government.[43]   Fran-

[39] *Dept. St. Pap.*, MS., ii. 120–1.
[40] Arrival of Vallejo and Rocha. *Dept. St. Pap., Ben. Cust.-H.*, MS., iii.
58.   It is erroneously stated by some that these prisoners first carried the
news of the revolt to the south. Jan. 26th, Echeandía to Francisco Pacheco,
in reply to the latter's announcement that order has been restored at Monterey. *Dept. Rec.*, MS., viii. 12.
[41] Jan. 26th, E. to min. of war. *St. Pap., Sac.*, MS., x. 56–8.
[42] Feb. 4, 1830, Spence to Hartnell. *Vallejo, Doc.*, MS., xxx. 19.
[43] Meliton Soto in his testimony stated that Cooper's house was the headquarters, whence he went with Alvarado, Santiago Moreno, Alcalde Soberanes, and several citizens and foreigners to take possession of the artillery
barracks at 7 or 8 P. M. *Dept. St. Pap., Ben. Mil.*, MS., lxxii. 64. Galindo,
Apuntes, MS., 8–13, tells us that the alcalde of S. José sent 45 men, who
arrived at midnight and surprised the garrison. Pattie's account of events
at Monterey, from the time that Solis marched for the south—absurdly inaccurate in many respects—is as follows in substance: Solis marched on

cisco Pacheco was apparently still left in command, and Solis' men as they came straggling in were pardoned and incorporated in the garrison. Eight or ten of the ringleaders failed to present themselves, and patrol parties were sent out to find them. Solis himself, concealed near his rancho, was taken by a company of thirty men under Antonio Ávila. This man was a convict companion of Solis and Gomez, and he undertook the capture on a promise from Spence and Malarin to obtain from him a passport for Mexico. Neither Echeandía nor his successors could grant the pass, and Ávila had to stay in California.[44] Just after the capture of Solis, early in February, Romualdo Pacheco arrived with a force

March 28th with 200 men. Echeandía had no knowledge of the revolt. The insurgents were so elated at their victory at S. F. that they were sure of success, and decided to expel all Americans and Englishmen. Capt. Cooper's father-in-law, Ignacio Vallejo, reported this to the foreigners, and at a consultation it was decided to send to Echeandía notice of the impending attack on him at Sta Bárbara, which was done successfully by means of a letter forwarded by a trusty runner. April 12th news came of the battle and retreat. 'The name and fame of Gen. Solis was exalted to the skies.' 'The climax of his excellence was his having retreated without the loss of a man.' Capt. Cooper rolled out a barrel of rum, and when the admirers of Solis were sufficiently drunk, they were locked up, 50 in number, and the rest of the inhabitants took sides against Solis. 'Huzza for Gen. Echedio and the Americans! was the prevailing cry.' There were 39 foreigners who signed the rolls, and Capt. Cooper was chosen commander. They spiked the cannon of the castle, except 4 which they carried to the presidio; broke open the magazine for powder and ball; and stationed sentinels for miles along the road. The Spanish people were all locked up at night to prevent possible communication with the approaching general. In a few days Solis drew near; the Americans waited at their guns with lighted matches until the army was at the very gates, and then ordered a surrender. The soldiers obeyed, but Solis with 6 officers fled. Six Americans, of whom Pattie was orderly sergeant and commander, armed with rifles, were at once sent in pursuit to bring back the fugitives dead or alive. Minute details are given. Several shots were exchanged; one American was wounded, and a Mexican killed, with 4 bullets through his body; but the rest surrendered and were brought back to Monterey, where the American flag floated until Echeandía arrived! Pattie's Narr., 225-9.

[44] Spence, Osio, Vallejo (M. G. and J. J.), Alvarado, and others mention the promise to Ávila; but most of them state that the promise was kept, Echeandía granting the pass and $500 in money. Fernandez even speaks of Ávila as subsequently becoming a brigadier in Mexico. I have before me Ávila's petition to Gov. Figueroa in 1833, narrating the Solis capture. Dept. St. Pap., Ben. Mil., MS., lxxv. 13. Botello, Anales, MS., 53, mentions Ávila as being at S. Buenaventura in 1838. For some reason unknown to me, the Californians are disposed to regard Ávila very favorably, representing him as sent to Cal. for political offences merely; but in the records he stands as 'a vicious man of very bad conduct, who took part in various murders and assaults on travellers.' He was sentenced on Aug. 24, 1824, and

from the south, and took the command. Herrera was now put under arrest in his own house.

Now followed the formal investigation and trial of the imprisoned leaders. It was carried on at Monterey and Santa Bárbara, by Zamorano, Pacheco, Lobato, and Pliego, under instructions from Echeandía, and extended from January to June. The testimony [45] I have utilized in the preceding narrative, and it requires no further notice except in a single point. The evidence respecting the revolt was clear enough; but nearly all the troops were implicated; few men of any class had shown real opposition to the movement in the north; a rising of soldiers with the object of getting their pay was not a very serious offence from a military point of view; and pretty nearly everybody had been included in the various indultos offered. In fact, the criminal case was hardly strong enough to suit Echeandía's purposes respecting Herrera, the only one of the accused for whose fate he cared particularly. A more serious charge was needed, and grounds for it were easily found. After their defeat at Santa Bárbara, Solis and one or two of his men, wishing to gain the support of the padres, like drowning men clutching at straws, talked about raising the Spanish flag. It was easy to prove these ravings of the soldiers, and the foolish remarks of Padre Luis Martinez at San Luis Obispo. Particular attention was given to this phase of the matter in the investigation. [46] A revolt in favor of Spain would sound very differently in Mexico from a rising of hungry soldiers against

came on the *Morelos* in July 1825. *Prov. St. Pap., Ben. Mil.*, MS., li. 2; *Dept. St. Pap., Ben. Mil.*, MS., lvii. 3.

[45] *Solis, Proceso instruido contra Joaquin Solis y otros Revolucionarios de 1829*, MS. These documents do not contain the final sentence under which the prisoners were sent away.

[46] Pp. 78–105 of the *Proceso* noticed in the last note are entitled '*Autos que aclaran que el objeto de la faccion de Solis era de pronunciarse en favor del Gobierno Español.*' Meliton Soto, Raimundo de la Torre, and Máximo Guerra were said to have spoken in favor of a *grito* for Spain; and a letter of Solis, dated Jan. 17th, to P. Arroyo de la Cuesta, was produced, in which he announced his purpose to raise the Spanish flag, asked for a neophyte force to aid him, and said that the southern padres had agreed to the plan. p. 88.

their local chief, and Echeandía hoped he might now safely send Herrera out of the territory. Respecting the banishment of Padre Martinez, I shall speak in the following chapter.[47]

On May 9, 1830, the American bark *Volunteer*, John Coffin Jones, Jr., master, sailed from Monterey with fifteen prisoners on board to be delivered at San Blas. Herrera was confined to a room constructed for the purpose on deck; Solis and the rest were in irons.[48] We have no particulars about the reception of the prisoners by the Mexican authorities, but it is certain that they were discharged from custody without punishment.[49] Three at least of the soldiers, Torre, Véjar, and one of the Altamiranos, found their way back to California in later years; while Herrera, in spite of all Echeandía's accusations and precautions, was soon sent back, as we shall see, to take his old position as comisario de hacienda. California's first revolution was over, and little harm had been done.[50]

[47] Feb. 23d, Echeandía reported to min. of war the pacification of the territory, begged most earnestly for aid, and announced the fact that the revolution had really been in the interests of Spain. *St. Pap., Sac.*, MS., x. 61–3. April 7th, order from Mexico that Solis and his seven companions be tried for treason. Also thanks to E. for having suffocated the revolt. *Sup. Gov't St. Pap.*, MS., vi. 8. Miscellaneous communications respecting the trial in addition to those contained in the *Proceso*, in *Dept. St. Pap.*, MS., ii. 127–130; *Dept. Rec.*, MS., viii. 13, 22, 32, 36, 78.

[48] May 7, 1830, receipt of Jones for the 15 prisoners, as follows: José María Herrera, Joaquin Solis, Meliton Soto, Serapio Escamilla, Raimundo de la Torre, Pablo Véjar, Victoriano Altamirano, Gonzalo Altamirano, Leonardo Arceo, Mariano Peguero, Andrés Leon, Máximo Guerra, Antonio Guevara, Gracia Larios, Inés Polanco. *Dept. St. Pap., Ben. Mil.*, MS., lxxii. 17–18. Sailing of the *Volunteer* on May 9th. *Id.*, lxii. 28. Pattie, *Narr.*, 238–9, also sailed on the *Volunteer*, and names Capt. Wm. H. Hinckley as having been on board and leaving the vessel at S. Blas. The prisoners reached Tepic May 22d. *Guerra, Doc.*, MS., vi. 129. Those belonging to the Monterey cavalry company were dropped from the company rolls in 1836. *Dept. St. Pap., Ben. Mil.*, MS., lxxxii. 65. Six other men had been sent away from Sta Bárbara in February in the *Emily Marsham*, 3 of them, Joaquin García, José M. Arenas, and Antonio Peña, for complicity in the Solis affair. *Dept. Rec.*, MS., viii. 74.

[49] Torre, *Reminis.*, MS., 19–21, says that his brother Raimundo was tried by court-martial and acquitted; whereupon the rest were discharged without trial.

[50] The Solis revolt is described more or less fully in the following narratives, in addition to such as have been cited in the preceding pages: *Ávila, Cosas*, MS., 25–8; *Bandini, Hist. Cal.*, MS., 71–2; *Amador, Mem.*, MS., 86–90; *Fernandez, Cosas de Cal.*, MS., 59–64; *Pico, Hist. Cal.*, MS., 20; *Castro, Rel.*, MS., 19–23; *Pinto, Apunt.*, MS., 2; *Valdés, Mem.*, MS., 18–20. It is men-

Respecting the management of the revenues in 1829–30 there is little or nothing to be said beyond noting the fact that Osio, Jimeno, and Bandini are mentioned as comisarios during 1830, without much regard to chronology. It would seem that after the revolt Jimeno was restored to his old position; and that Bandini was appointed before the end of the year, though there is inextricable confusion, not only in dates, but in the offices of comisario, administrador, and contador.[51]

tioned in print by Mofras, *Explor.*, i. 293–4; Petit-Thouars, *Voy.*, ii. 90–1; Lafond, *Voy.*, 209; Pickett, in *Shuck's Rep. Men*, 227; Wilkes, *Narr.*, v. 173–4; Capron, *Hist. Cal.*, 37–8; Tuthill, *Hist. Cal.*, 130–1; Robinson, *Life in Cal.*, 69–70; and Flint, *Pattie's Narr.*, 222–30.

[51] See *Dept. St. Pap.*, MS., ii. 155–6; iii. 209–10; *Id.*, *Ben. Mil.*, lxii. 22; lxxiii. 53; lxxiv. 6; *Dept. Rec.*, MS., vii. 246–8; *Leg. Rec.*, MS., i. 269, 281–90.   Apr. 25, 1830, the Californian diputado in congress urged the uselessness of sending special officers to manage the revenues. *Doc. Hist. Cal.*, MS., iv. 898.   Jimeno was appointed contador on Sept. 30, 1829, by the min. de hacienda, but declined the place in Nov. 1830.   Oct. 21, 1830, Echeandía, Bandini, and Jimeno met at Monterey, and decided on the following customhouse organization at Monterey: administrador, with duties of comisario, at $1,000 per year; contador, with duties of vista, at $800; commandant of the guard, with duties of alcalde, at $800; guarda and clerk at $400; servant at $144; patron and two sailors at $144 and $96. *Dept. St. Pap.*, MS., ii. 155–6.

CHAPTER IV.

ECHEANDÍA AND THE PADRES—MISSION AND INDIAN AFFAIRS.

1826–1830.

MISSION PREFECT AND PRESIDENTS—THE QUESTION OF SUPPLIES—THE
OATH OF ALLEGIANCE—SARRÍA'S ARREST—FRIARS STILL MASTERS OF
THE SITUATION—COUNCIL AT SAN DIEGO—SOUTHERN PADRES WILL-
ING—NORTHERN PADRES REFUSE—FLIGHT OF RIPOLL AND ALTIMIRA—
THE FRIARS AS SPANIARDS—ECHEANDÍA'S CONCILIATORY POLICY—PE-.
TITIONS OF THE PEOPLE—EXILE OF MARTINEZ—PROGRESS TOWARDS
SECULARIZATION—MEXICAN POLICY—DIFFICULTIES—JUNTA OF APRIL
1826—DECREE OF JULY—EXPERIMENTAL FREEDOM—MISSION SCHOOLS
AND LANDS—PLAN OF 1829–30—APPROVAL OF THE DIPUTACION—AC-
TION IN MEXICO—INDIAN AFFAIRS—SANCHEZ'S EXPEDITION—VALLEJO'S
CAMPAIGN AGAINST ESTANISLAO—NORTHERN FORT—SEASONS.

VICENTE FRANCISCO DE SARRÍA retained the position
of comisario prefecto of the missions, and was not disturbed in the performance of his official duties from
1826 to 1830, though nominally in a state of arrest as
a recalcitrant Spaniard. Narciso Duran retained the
presidency until September 1827 when he was succeeded by José Bernardo Sanchez. The latter retained possession of the office until 1831, though
Duran was re-elected in May 1830.[1]

The old controversy between government and friars
respecting supplies for the troops continued of course
during these five years, but with no novel aspects.
In addition to commercial imposts, a secular tithe of

[1] *Arch. Sta B.*, MS., xi. 350, 358–60, 400; xii. 369. The guardian sent
Sanchez his patent June 9, 1827; and Duran notified him Sept. 30th. Sanchez was at first unwilling to accept. Duran was elected the second time May
26, 1830, Peyri and Antonio Jimeno being named as second and third suplentes.
Both Duran and Sanchez held the title of vicar under the bishop.

all mission products was exacted, citizens having presumably to pay this also in addition to their ecclesiastical tithes.[2] The method of collection was to exact from each mission the largest possible amount of supplies for escoltas and presidial garrisons, and at the end of each year to give credit on account for the excess of amounts thus furnished over the taxes. I find no evidence that any part of the balance was paid in any instance.[3] The padres gave less willingly than in former years, when there had been yet a hope of Spanish supremacy, but the quarrels in local and individual cases were much less frequent than might naturally be expected, or at least such controversies have left little trace in the records.[4]

[2] According to the plan de gobierno of Jan. 8, 1824, citizens paid 10 per cent in kind on all produce, while the missions were to pay a fixed rate per head of cattle or fanega of grain. By decree of Jan. 1, 1826, Echeandía, with the consent of Prefect Sarría, ordered that the tax be equalized between citizens and missions, the latter apparently to pay in kind. Decree of Jan. 1, 1826. *S. José, Arch.*, MS., iv. 13; *Sta Cruz, Arch.*, MS., 47–8; *Dept. St. Pap.*, MS., i. 123; *Vallejo, Doc.*, MS., xxviii. 81, 84, 86, including orders for circulation of the decree and some directions for the keeping of accounts. Aug. 25, 1827, Echeandía to Sarría, urging the importance and justice of this tax, which here and elsewhere in official accounts is spoken of as a 'loan.' *Dept. Rec.*, MS., v. 80; *Arch. Arzob.*, MS., v. pt i. 37; *Vallejo, Doc.*, MS., xix. 138. April 22, 1826, Echeandía to min. of war. Argues that the missions should also pay tithes. He is informed that some of them have $70,000 or $100,000 in their coffers. *St. Pap., Sac.*, MS., xix. 30–1. Oct. 31st, Herrera to Estrada on mission accounts. *Vallejo, Doc.*, MS., i. 98.

[3] June 23, 1826, circular from president received at S. Rafael to effect that the Mex. govt was going to pay all drafts presented within six months from Jan. 1st, and those not so presented would be outlawed. This news reached Cal. just after the expiration of the time! *Vallejo, Doc.*, MS., xxviii. 94. July 28, 1827, Echeandía notifies the prefect and comandantes that all creditors of the national treasury must present their claims to the comisario. *Dept. Rec.*, MS., v. 71.

[4] June 10, 1826, P. Duran to Herrera. Protests against furnishing the *diezmo* of cattle branded for the national rancho, when there has already been delivered during the year a much larger amount than that of the tithe. *Arch. Arzob.*, MS., v. pt i. 13–16. Nov. 30th, P. Viader, upbraiding Lieut Martinez for not sending money to pay for blankets, says, 'My friend, we have now arrived at a point of *date et dabitur vobis.*' *Vallejo, Doc.*, MS., xxix. 94. Dec. 18th, Duran says he likes to see the soldiers fill their bellies with meat, and not feel hungry. *Id.*, 95. April 19, 1827, draft by Habilitado Maitorena on habilitado general in favor of Sta Bárbara mission for $8,725, the amount of supplies furnished apparently before 1825. *Arch. Misiones*, MS., ii. 177–8. Feb. 27, 1827, gov. orders Lieut Ibarra, since all conciliatory and courteous means have failed, to go with a force to S. Diego mission, and bring away all the grain the mules can carry. Resistance will be regarded as an overt act against the nation. *Dept. Rec.*, MS., v. 27. Many certificates to effect that a padre has delivered provisions 'en calidad de préstamo para que se le reintegre por cuenta del

Meanwhile the missions got nothing from the pious fund through the Mexican treasury, in addition to the stipends of 1819–22, the payment of which has already been noted. It is not certain even that any of the latter amount, about $24,000, ever came to California, but probably some cargoes of mission goods were paid for by the síndico at Tepic out of that sum. Only fragments of the mission accounts have been preserved for these years.[5]

We have seen that the padres as a rule refused to take the oath of obedience to the constitution of 1824, or to solemnize by religious exercises any act of the republican government; and that Prefect Sarría had been put under arrest, though it had not been deemed wise to carry into effect the orders requiring the reverend prisoner to be sent by the first ship to Mexico. In fact, the friars were yet, in a great measure, masters of the situation, because they could keep the neophytes in subjection, and above all make them work. The great fear was that the missionaries

supremo gobierno.' *Arch. Arzob.*, MS., vii. passim. A large number of drafts of comandantes in favor of missions, 1825–30, in *Id.*, v. pt 2. June 7, 1828, Echeandía proposes that the expense of maintaining friendly relations with the Indians be deducted from the sums due the nearest missions. *Dept. Rec.*, MS., vi. 27. Oct. 7th, E. instructs Capt. Argüello to borrow $800 of the mission of S. José. *Id.*, vi. 109–10. Oct. 22d, E. orders Lieut José Fernandez and 30 artillerymen just landed to be quartered at S. Diego mission. *Id.*, vi. 115. Jan. 8, 1829, E. to Duran, urging him to 'lend' supplies, or sell them for a draft on the comisario of Sonora, which he doubts not will be paid promptly. *Id.*, vii. 53. May 4th, Vallejo complains of destitution at Monterey, and no aid from the missions. *St. Pap., Sac.*, MS., x. 80. Nov. 24th, similar complaints from Castro. *Dept. St. Pap., Ben.*, MS., v. 369–70. Dec. 6th, P. Duran says he has paid $200 on menace of force being used. *S. José Arch.*, MS., ii. 48. Jan. 15, 1830, P. Viader refuses to aid directly or indirectly in matters pertaining to war. *Id.*, i. 37. April 25th, congressman urges the injustice of imposing such heavy burdens on the missions. *Doc. Hist. Cal.*, MS., iv. 897–8. July 17th, com. of Sta Bárbara complains that the padre will neither give nor sell supplies. *Dept. Rec.*, MS., viii. 55.

[5] May 31, 1827, guardian to president, stipends of 1819–21 and most of 1822 paid. Certificates should be sent in for those of 1825–6. *Arch. Sta B.*, MS., xii. 400. June 27th, news received at S. Rafael; amount, $24,000. *Vallejo, Doc.*, MS., xviii. 97. The brig *Bravo* with mission goods was wrecked at Acapulco late in 1827, but the cargo was saved. *S. Luis Obispo, Lib. Mision*, MS., 7. Aug. 25, 1828, $6,861 in goods sent from Tepic to S. Blas for shipment, consisting of woollen and cotton stuffs, rice, sugar, rebozos, metates, and 25 pounds of cinnamon, shipped by the *María Ester*. *Id.*, 8–9; *Doc. Hist. Cal.*, MS., iv. 827–8.

would leave the territory en masse if too hard pressed. Had the situation of affairs, from a financial and military point of view, been more reassuring, the territorial authorities would not have been averse to assuming entire and immediate charge of all the missions; while the people, for the most part, would have rejoiced at the prospect of getting new lands and new laborers. But as matters stood, the rulers and leading citizens understood that any radical and sudden change, effected without the aid of the friars, would ruin the territory by cutting off its chief resources, and exposing its people to the raids of hostile Indians. Thus a conciliatory policy was necessary, not only to the government, but to the friars themselves. The latter, though they knew their power and often threatened to go, were old men, attached to their mission homes, with but a cheerless prospect for life in Spain, fully determined to spend the rest of their days in California if possible.

Sarría's condition of nominal suspension and arrest continued for five years or more. Once, in 1826, his passport was made out, and he went so far as to call upon his associates for prayers to sustain him on his voyage. There was no countermanding of the orders, but a repetition of them in November 1827, yet the padre remained. He seems to have been included with the rest in the proceedings against the friars as Spaniards, and the special orders in his case were allowed to be forgotten,[6] though as late as the middle

---

[6] May 1826, one of the padres claimed to have refused to perform mass, etc., by Sarría's order, and he signed a certificate to that effect. *Dept. Rec.*, MS., iv. 39. Oct. 31st, Echeandía notifies S. that he must leave Mexican territory. Nov. 13th, Sarría says he is ready. *Arch. Arzob.*, MS., v. pt i. 24. Beechey, in 1826, speaks of S. as waiting at Monterey to embark. *Voyage*, ii. 12. Vallejo, *Hist. Cal.*, MS., ii. 56–8, speaks of a personal interview between the gov. and prefect at Sta Bárbara. Oct. 31st, E. notifies S. that a successor will be named and a passport issued. *Dept. Rec.*, MS., iv. 11. Nov. 30th, sends the passport from S. Diego to Capt. Gonzalez at Monterey. *Id.*, iv. 17. Dec. 11th, S. to the padres. Has received his passport from the pres. of Mex. Is resigned, but asks for prayers. *Vallejo, Doc.*, MS., xxviii. 89. 1827, Duhaut-Cilly, *Viaggio*, i. 254–5, found S. kept as a kind of prisoner, and was asked to take him away, but declined, much to the gratification of the padres. Nov. 21, 1827, order from Mex. that S. be made to obey the

of 1828 the governor still pretended to be waiting for
a vessel on which to send him away.

On the 28th of April, 1826, Echeandía with Zamorano as secretary and the alcalde of Los Angeles met
padres Sanchez, Zalvidea, Peyri, and Martin at San
Diego to take counsel respecting the taking of the
constitutional oath by the friars. The representatives
of the latter said there was no objection to the oath
except that it compelled them to take up arms, or use
their influence in favor of taking up arms, for differences of political opinion. They would take the oath
with the supplement "So far as may be compatible
with our religion and profession;" but Echeandía
would not agree to any change in the formula, and
directed that a circular be sent out requiring each
padre to explain his views on the subject.[7] June 3d
the circular was issued through the comandantes to
the friars; but it was not so much a call for views
and arguments as for a formal decision in writing
whether each would take the oath or not.[8] The answers of the five padres of the San Diego district
were sent in on the 14th. Padre Peyri was willing
to take the oath, and was enthusiastic in his devotion
to the national cause. Martin had already sworn,
and did not approve of taking two oaths on the same
subject. The rest were ready to take the oath in the
manner indicated at the junta of April 28th; that is,
to be republicans so far as was compatible with their
profession and so long as they might remain in California. Replies from the Monterey jurisdiction, sent

orders of July 9, 1825, and Nov. 15, 1826, to depart. *Supt. Govt St. Pap.*,
MS., xix. 43. June 30, 1828, E. to min. of justice. S. will be sent away as soon
as there is a vessel for Europe or the U. S. *Dept. Rec.*, MS., vi. 30.

[7] *Dept. St. Pap.*, MS., i. 128-9. The old trouble was still active in 1826,
for on May 1st Capt. Argüello reported that yesterday having called on P.
Abella to take part in the celebration of the pope's recognition of national
independence, the padre refused. *Dept. St. Pap., Ben. Mil.*, MS., lvii. 13-14.
Next day it was complained that P. Esténega declined to perform religious
services in connection with the publication of certain bandos. *Arch. Arzob.*,
MS., v. pt i. 4. April 28th, record of the council referred to in the text.
Dept. St. Pap., MS., i. 128-9.

[8] June 3, 1826, E. to com. of Monterey. *Dept. St. Pap.*, MS., i. 134.

in on July 7th, were to the effect that the friars could not take the oath, and were ready to endure the penalty, though some of them promised fidelity and respect to the constituted authorities. The response from San Francisco and Santa Bárbara is not so far as I know extant.[9]

There was no further agitation of this matter during the year, though a warning was received from the comisario general against the disaffected friars, and especially against the president, who, as the writer had heard, talked of nothing but his religion and his king, protesting his willingness to die for either. "If this be true, it would be well to grant him a passport to go and kiss his king's hand, but to go with only bag and staff, as required by the rules of his order." I am not certain whether this referred to Duran or Sarría.[10]

During 1827 politico-missionary matters remained nearly in statu quo. No disposition was shown to disturb the padres further on account of their opposition to the republic, though there were rumors afloat that some of them were preparing to run away. Martinez, Ripoll, and Juan Cabot were those named in June as having such intentions, and Vicente Cané

[9] The position taken by the other padres will, however, be learned from a subsequent document. Answers of the S. Diego and Monterey friars in *Arch. Arzob.*, MS., v. pt i. 5–9, 17–20. Among the latter Sarría was not included, not being regarded as the minister of any particular mission. Abella 'came to this country for God, and for God will go away, if they expel him;' Fortuni 'no se anima á hacer tal juramento, pero sí guardar fidelidad;' Arroyo de la Cuesta 'was born in the Peninsula, and is a Spaniard; swore to the independence only in good faith to the king of Spain; has meditated upon the oath demanded, and swears not;' Uría 'finds it not in his conscience to take the oath;' Pedro Cabot 'has sworn allegiance to Fernando VII.;' Sancho, the same, and 'cannot go back on his word;' Juan Cabot 'cannot accommodate his conscience to such a pledge;' and Luis Martinez says 'his spirit is not strong enough to bear any additional burden.' Aug. 7th, Sarría addresses to the padres a circular argument on the subject, similar to that addressed in former years to Gov. Argüello, and called out by an argument of P. Ripoll, who it seems had wished to accommodate his conscience to the oath by bringing up anew the allegiance sworn to independence and Iturbide. *Id.*, v. pt i. 10–13.

[10] Aug. 16, 1826, com. gen. to Echeandía. *Dept. St. Pap., Ben. Com. and Treas.*, MS., i. 36–8. Beechey, *Voyage*, ii. 12, speaks of the dissatisfaction caused by the exacting of the oath, and says many padres prepared to depart rather than violate their allegiance to Spain.

gave evidence on the mysterious shipment of $6,000 in gold on the *Santa Apolonia* by Padre Martinez, an act supposed to have some connection with the plans for flight. Captain Gonzalez took a prominent part in the charges, and this was perhaps a reason why Echeandía and others paid very little attention to the subject.[11]

The rumors had some foundation, for at the end of December, or perhaps in January 1828, padres Ripoll and Altimira went on board the American brig *Harbinger*, Captain Steele, at Santa Bárbara, and left California never to return. They went on board the vessel on pretence of examining certain goods, and such effects as they wished to carry with them were embarked by stealth. Echeandía was there at the time, and David Spence tells us he was for some mysterious purpose invited to take breakfast on the brig before she sailed, but was prevented by other affairs from accepting.[12] Orders were at once issued to seize the *Harbinger* should she dare to enter any other port; but Steele chose to run no risks. The fugitives left letters in which they gave as their reason for a clandestine departure the fear that their going might be prevented otherwise, prompt action being necessary for reasons not stated. They were among the youngest of the Franciscan band, and in several respects less identified than most others with the missionary work in California, the reader being already familiar with certain eccentricities on the part of each. Their destination was Spain, which they seem to have reached in safety. A suspicion was natural that the two padres carried away with them something more than the 'sack and staff' of their order, that they took enough of the mission treasure to insure a comfortable voyage,

[11] Statement of Cané to E. about the $6,000 shipped in August 1826. *St. Pap., Sac.*, MS., xiv. 14–15. June 4, 1827, Gonzalez to E. *Id.*, xiv. 26–30. G. was very violent in his charges against the padres.
[12] Spence, in *Taylor's Discov. and Founders*, ii. no. 24. Alvarado, *Hist. Cal.*, MS., ii. 131–2, claims that while Ripoll and Altimira were making their escape with the mission wealth, Echeandía was being feasted by the other padres to avert suspicion. Vallejo, *Hist. Cal.*, MS., ii. 59–60, gives the same version.

and perhaps future comforts across the sea.   The truth
can never be known.   An investigation brought to
light nothing more suspicious than the transfer of certain barrels and boxes of wine, soap, and olives, with
perhaps other packages of unknown contents, from San
Buenaventura to Santa Bárbara.[13]   In their own letters, the padres said they had left the mission property
intact.   Duhaut-Cilly, however, had lately sold Ripoll
an English draft for 7,000 francs,[14] which he said
came to him legitimately from his stipend.   Though
Alvarado and Vallejo accuse the padres of having
stolen large sums, and their method of flight favored
the suspicion, I suppose that a few thousand dollars
was probably all they took, and that they had but little difficulty in justifying the act to their own satisfaction, in view of their past stipends either unpaid or
invested in supplies for the Indians.[15]

In reporting the flight of Ripoll and Altimira,
Echeandía suggested the expediency of granting
passports to those who had asked for them, with a
view to avoid such scandals; and he did send a pass
to Padre Martinez in September to prevent the disgrace of his intended flight.[16]   There was also a
scandal respecting the actions of President Sanchez,
whose letters and some goods being conveyed by John
Lawlor from San Gabriel to the sea-shore were stopped

[13] *Dept. St. Pap., Ben. Mil.*, MS., lxvii. 5–9, containing the testimony of
several men and the letters of Altimira to Geo. Coleman, the *llavero* of S.
Buenaventura, dated Jan. 23d from on board the vessel.   They contain kind
wishes for all in Cal., instructions about mission affairs, and good spiritual
counsels for Coleman.   The padre, according to Coleman's testimony, took a
small box of cigars and some books.
[14] *Duhaut-Cilly, Viaggio*, ii. 184–5.
[15] Mrs Ord., *Ocurrencias*, MS., 22–4, says they took no money at all.
Ripoll wept as he took leave of some of his Indians who went on board in
Steele's boat.   Jan. 25, 1828, Echeandía announces the flight, and orders the
Harbinger to be seized. *Dept. Rec.*, MS., vi. 174.   Jan. 28th, Alf. Pliego ordered secretly to investigate the robbery said to have been committed by Altimira. *Id.*, vi. 175.   Feb. 5th, Luis Argüello alludes to the flight. *St. Pap.,
Sac.*, MS., x. 102–3.   Mar. 26th, the authorities at S. Fernando college disa-
vowed having authorized or even known the flight. *Arch. Sta. B.*, MS., ix.
90–1.   Mar. 20, 1829, the Zacatecas college will replace Ripoll and Altimira.
Sup. Govt St. Pap., MS., iv. 2–3.
[16] Jan. 29, 1828, E. to min. of rel. *Dept. Rec.*, MS., vi. 22.   Sept. 23d,
E. to Martinez. *Dept. St. Pap.*, MS., xix. 6–7.

and searched by Alcalde Carrillo of Los Angeles, on suspicion of complicity in smuggling. Sanchez was indignant at what he deemed an insult, and demanded his passport; but Echeandía, by declaring the suspicions unfounded, and by conciliatory methods, succeeded in calming the worthy president's wrath.[17]

The law of 1827 on the expulsion of Spaniards from Mexican territory,[13] reaching California in 1828, had no other effect on the status of the missionaries than to give them another safe opportunity to demand their passports, as many of them did, some perhaps really desiring to depart. There was no disposition to enforce the decree, for reasons known to the reader.[19] Meanwhile the Spanish friars had been actually expelled from Mexico, and a most disheartening report came respecting the state of affairs at the college of San Fernando.[20]

There would seem to have been some complaint against Echeandía for not having enforced the law of 1827, for in June 1829, apparently before the arrival of the law of March 20th, he sent to Mexico a list of

[17] June 3, 1828, Lawlor to Sanchez. *Arch. Arzob.*, MS., v. pt i. 63-4. June 8th, Sanchez to E. *Id.*, 65-6. Aug. 21st, 29th, E. to S. and to the alcalde. *Dept. Rec.*, MS., vi. 84-5, 90.

[18] See chap. ii. of this volume.

[19] Oct. 20, 1828, Echeandía to min. of war. The padres are violent at the law for their expulsion, and are clamoring for passports and complaining of detention by force. *St. Pap., Sac.*, MS., x. 39-40. Dec. 6th, E. says that most of the 27 padres have agreed long before the date of the law to take the oath as was reported to Mexico on Dec. 6, 1826. (This report is not extant, but it is certainly not true that most had made such a promise.) If passports were issued as several have asked, the missions would be left without government and the territory without spiritual care. *Dept. Rec.*, MS., vi. 50. Duhaut-Cilly says he offered to carry the padres over to Manila; but he got a letter from Sarría, in which he said he was resolved not to abandon the flock intrusted to him by heaven until forced to do so, and he advised his companions to the same effect. The same writer notes the arrival of 3 Franciscans—they could not have been from California—at the Sandwich Islands on the French ship *Comète. Viaggio*, ii. 200-1, 219-20.

[20] March 26, 1828, P. Arreguin to Sarría. It had been at first proposed to dissolve the college; but finally the guardian and discretorio had decided to choose a vicario de casa, and had chosen the writer. He asks for Sarría's views about the policy of keeping up the college, where there were now Arreguin and 3 other priests, 2 sick Spaniards unable to depart, and 6 or 10 servants of different grades. *Arch. Sta B.*, MS., ix. 90-4.

the padres, with notes on the circumstances of each,[21] and a defence of his action, or failure to act, on the ground that all the padres except three were Spaniards, and it would have been absurdly impossible to expel them with nobody to take their place. He also urged that many of them be allowed to remain permanently in the territory. Only a few days later there came the law of March 20th, much more strict than the other, and it was circulated on the 6th of July. The announcement was that to all padres who had refused to take the oath passports would be given forthwith, while all the rest must show within a month the physical impediments preventing their departure as required by the law.[22] As before, no friar was expelled, and Echeandía had no idea of granting passports, though several, including Peyri, Sanchez, and Boscana, now demanded them, and though the governor really desired to get rid of certain unmanageable ones as soon as he could obtain others to take their places.[23] Not only did he send to Mexico a defence of his policy of inaction, showing the impossibility of the expulsion so far as California was concerned; but

[21] *Dept. Rec.*, MS., vii. 26–33. The following friars had taken the oath: Fernando Martin, 60 years old; Antonio Peyri, 70 years; Francisco Suñer, 71 years; and Márcos Antonio de Vitoria, 69 years, who however had subsequently retracted, though faithful and obedient to the government, of blameless life, and probably influenced by his excessive respect for his prelate. The following had taken the oath with some conditions: Gonzalez de Ibarra, Antonio Jaime, and Arroyo de la Cuesta; Boscana was ready to take the oath, and Barona, Zalvidea, and José Sanchez also with the conditions. This left 14 who would not take the oath, of whom Catalá, Viader, and Abella were over 60 years old; several were in bad health, and several were highly recommendable for their faithfulness. Should new padres come, E. proposed to grant passports to Arroyo, Ordaz, P. Cabot, Sancho, J. Cabot, Ibarra, Oliva, Duran, Esténega, Abella, and Uría, in that order. There were recommended to remain, Amorós, Catalá, Vitoria, Viader, Fortuni, Martin, Boscana, Sanchez, Zalvidea, and especially Peyri, Jaime, Barona, and Suñer. Martinez was the only one who had asked for a passport on the ground of not wishing to conform. Duhaut-Cilly, *Viaggio*, ii. 187–8, mentions the coming of the Dominicans President Luna and P. Caballero to S. Gabriel in June, to consult about the expulsion.

[22] July 6, 1829, E. to various officials. *Dept. St. Pap.*, MS., ii. 92–3, 97; *Id.*, *S. José*, ii. 16–17; *Dept. Rec.*, MS., vii. 190–1.

[23] July–September, applications of the padres for passports. *Arch. Arzob.*, MS., v. pt i. 54–7. Aug. 11th, Echeandía to min. of rel. *St. Pap.*, *Sac.*, MS., x. 43–6. In this document the gov. gives a very clear and complete statement of the whole matter.

the ayuntamientos of San José, Monterey, and perhaps other places, sent strong petitions on the evils
that must result from such expulsion, expressing for
the missionaries the deepest love and veneration, and
pleading eloquently that the people might not be deprived of their spiritual guardians.[24] I find no responses to these petitions, nor are there any definite
orders of later date on the subject, which, except in
certain particulars to be noted in the next paragraph,
seems to have been now allowed to rest. One of the
Spanish friars, however, received before the end of
1829 a passport to a land where it is to be hoped his
political troubles were at an end. This was the aged
and infirm Padre Jaime, who died at Santa Bárbara.

I have said that Echeandía deemed it desirable to
get rid of certain padres. Personal feeling was his
motive in part; moreover, it was important to remove
certain obstacles likely to interfere with his policy of
secularization, of which more hereafter. Prejudice
against all that was Spanish was the strongest feeling
in Mexico, and there was no better way for the governor to keep himself in good standing with the power
that appointed him than to go with the current. It
also favored Echeandía's plans respecting his enemy
Herrera, while increasing the importance of his own
services, to show the existence of a strong revolutionary spirit in favor of Spain. There was, however, but
a slight foundation on which to build. The padres
were Spaniards, and as a rule disapproved the new
form of government; but it is not likely that any of
them had a definite hope of overthrowing the republic, or of restoring California to the old system, and
the most serious charge that could be justly brought
against them was an occasional injudicious use of the

[24] Aug. 25th, *S. José, Peticion del Ayuntamiento en favor de los Frailes Españoles, 1829*, MS.; *Monterey, Peticion al Presidente y Congreso en favor de los
Frailes Españoles, 1829*, MS.   Oct. 22d, gov. approves the petitions. *Dept.
Rec.*, MS., vii. 239.   Oct. 12th, Virmond writes from Mexico that the president had not the slightest idea of expelling the friars. *Guerra, Doc.*, MS., vi.
145–8.

tongue.   Generally the prevalent rumors of treason
could be traced to nothing reliable.[25]

Of all the padres, Martinez of San Luis Obispo was
the most outspoken and independent in political matters, besides being well known for his smuggling pro-
pensities.   Echeandía deemed his absence desirable
for the quiet of the territory, and had issued a passport which had not been used.   It was thought best
on general principles to make an example; it was particularly desirable to give a political significance to
the Solis revolt, and Padre Martinez was banished on
a charge of complicity in that revolt in the interest
of Spain.   The evidence against him was not very
strong;[26] but there was little risk, since as a Spaniard
the accused might at any time be legally exiled.   He
was arrested early in February 1830, and confined in
a room of the comandancia at Santa Bárbara.   In
his testimony he denied all the allegations against
him, except that of giving food to the soldiers, as
others had also done and as it was customary for the
missionaries to do, whoever their guests might be.
He claimed to have tried to dissuade Solis from his
foolish scheme of raising the Spanish flag.   In a long
and eloquent communication addressed to Echeandía,

[25] Sept. 9, 1829, gov. to comandantes.   Has heard that some padre burns
daily two tapers before a portrait of Fernando VII.; and that another pre-
dicts from his pulpit the coming of the Spanish king.   Find out secretly who
do these things, and forward the result.   *St. Pap., Sac.*, MS., x. 25, 48; *Dept.
Rec.*, MS., vii. 44.   The guilty parties were not found.

[26] The evidence, some of the items resting on the statement of a single
soldier, was, so far as it is on record, as follows: That he had freely supplied
the rebels with food, had been very intimate with Solis and his leaders at San
Luis, had shown anger at certain soldiers when they said 'viva la república,'
had spoken mysteriously of his 'amo Francisquito,' in Spain or Mexico, had
shown a paper with 'viva Fernando VII.' written on it, had derided independence and liberty, and had lodged Alf. Fernandez del Campo in a room
which bore the inscription ' V. F. 7 ' on the ceiling.   *Solis, Proceso, etc.*, MS.;
Fernandez to Echeandía in *St. Pap., Sac.*, MS., x. 26–7.   Vallejo, *Hist. Cal.*,
MS., ii. 93–105, tells us that there were documents proving conclusively that
Martinez was plotting against the republic and carrying on a secret correspondence with the rebels in Mexico; but nothing of this kind was shown in
the recorded evidence, and the same may be said of a letter of encouragement
from Martinez found on the person of Solis at his capture, mentioned by Alvarado.   *Hist. Cal.*, MS., ii. 155.

protesting against the manner of his treatment, Martinez, while not attempting to deny his well known political sentiments, claimed that he was not such a fool as to suppose that Spain could be benefited by petty revolts in California, that he desired the welfare of the territory, and that in his opinion it could not be advantageously separated from Mexico. The two padres Cabot testified to having seen letters in which Martinez declined to take part in the political schemes of Solis, declaring that if the king wished to *conquistar* any part of America, he might do it himself, in his own way. Prefect Sarría also presented an argument to prove Martinez innocent.[27]

The 9th of March a junta de guerra, composed of six officers, besides the governor, met at Santa Bárbara to decide on the friar's fate. Echeandía explained, at considerable length, the difficulties in the way of administering a suitable penalty, and he seems to have counselled leniency, fearing or pretending to fear the action of the other padres; but after full discussion, it was decided by a vote of five to one to send him out of Mexican territory by the first available vessel.[28] Stephen Anderson, owner of the English brig *Thomas Nowlan*, was called in immediately, and gave bonds to carry the prisoner to Callao, and put him on board a vessel bound for Europe. Padre Martinez, on the same day, promised *in verbo sacerdotis* not to land at Manila or the Sandwich Islands, and on March 20th the *Nowlan* sailed.[29] The friar

[27] Martinez admitted to Lieut Romualdo Pacheco that he had received letters from Solis, urging him to arm his neophytes in defence of the Spanish flag soon to be raised. *St. Pap., Miss. and Col.*, MS., ii. 30–1. Testimony of Martinez and the PP. Cabot in *Solis, Proceso*, MS., 100–1, 98–9. March 4th, *Martinez, Defensa dirigida al Comandante General, 1830*, MS., in *Id.*, 93–8. Feb. 9th, *Sarría, Defensa del Padre Luis Martinez, 1830*, MS. Mrs Ord, *Ocurrencias*, MS., 31–6, gives some details of the padre's confinement in her father's house, and the efforts of members of the family to relieve the prisoner's wants in spite of the severity of Lieut Lobato. This writer and many other Californians think there was no foundation for the special charges against Martinez at this time.

[28] Record of the junta of March 9th, in *Solis, Proceso*, MS., 102–5. The officers were J. J. Rocha, M. G. Vallejo, Domingo Carrillo, M. G. Lobato, J. M. Ibarra, and A. V. Zamorano. A previous junta of Feb. 26th is alluded to.

[29] *Carrillo (José), Doc.*, MS., 21. The Spaniards A. J. Cot and family,

reached Callao in June, and subsequently arrived
safely in Madrid, whence he wrote to his friends in
California.   There were those who believed that he
carried away a large amount of money, an exploit
which, if actually accomplished, considering the circumstances of his departure, surpassed in brilliancy
all his previous deeds as a contrabandista.[30]   Even if,
as I suppose, he carried little or no gold at his departure, it is not probable that so shrewd a man of business had neglected in past years to make some
provision for future comfort.

The most important problem affecting the missions
was that of secularization; but it hardly assumed a
controversial aspect during this period. The missions,
as the reader is well aware, had never been intended
as permanent institutions, but only as temporary
schools to fit savage gentiles for Christian citizenship.
The missionaries themselves never denied this in theory,
but practically nullified the principle, and claimed perpetuity for their establishments by always affirming, no
matter whether the spiritual conquest dated back five
or fifty years, that the Indians were not yet fitted to
become citizens.   This was, moreover, always true,
even if it was a virtual confession that the mission
system was a failure, and it presented serious difficulties in the way of secularization.   The córtes of Spain
had decreed, however, in 1813, that all missions ten
years after foundation must be changed into pueblos,
subject to secular authority both in civil and religious
affairs,[31] and the success of independence made the

and J. I. Mancisidor sailed in the same vessel. Feb. 6th, Echeandía's order
to arrest Martinez. *Dept. Rec.*, MS., viii. 16.   March 9th, E. announces the
sentence to Prefect Sarría. *Id.*, viii. 27.

[30] Vallejo, *Hist. Cal.*, MS., ii. 96–100, says that he was the officer who
took Martinez on board. He walked very slowly, but as he was old and
corpulent, was not hurried. When they were alone in the cabin the padre
said: 'Perhaps you thought me drunk. Not so, my son, but see here'—proceeding to show that his clothing was heavily lined with gold! The young
alférez was glad to know that the friar had made provision for a rainy day,
and promised to keep his secret.

[31] See chap. xviii., vol. ii., for the decree of Sept. 13, 1813, and subsequent
developments in Cal.

change inevitable. The spirit of Mexican republicanism was not favorable to the longer existence of the
old missions under a system of land monopoly strongly
tinged with some phases of human slavery. If the
Indians were not fit for citizenship, neither were they
being fitted therefor.

Echeandía and the administration that appointed
him desired to secularize the missions, but understood
that it was a problem requiring careful study. Neither
party was disposed to act hastily in the matter: the
Mexican authorities largely perhaps because of indifference to the interests of a territory so far away;
and the governor by reason not only of his natural
tendency to inaction, but of the difficulties with which
on arrival he found himself surrounded. These difficulties, as the reader has learned, were insurmountable.
Had the territorial finances been in a sound condition,
had the military force been thoroughly organized and
promptly paid, had there been fifty curates at hand to
take charge of new parishes, had the territory been
to some extent independent of the missions—even with
these favorable conditions, none of which existed, secularization would have been a difficult task if not a
risky experiment, requiring for success at least the
hearty coöperation of the friars. Under existing
circumstances, however, which need not be recapitulated here, against the will of the padres, who, with
their influence over the neophytes and their threats
to retire en masse, were largely masters of the situation, any radical change in the mission status would
bring ruin to the territory.

The governor recognized the impossibility of immediate action; but in accordance with the policy of his
government,[32] with his own republican theories, with

[32] Jan. 31, 1825, min. of war to gov. A statement of grievances suffered
by the Indians of Cal. States that it is the president's desire to do away
with so vicious a system, but suggests that the reform should perhaps be one
of policy rather than of authority. It is not expedient to break up openly
the system of the padres, who if offended might by their influence cause great
evils. Still it was essential to check the arbitrary measures that oppressed
the Indians, and afford the latter the advantages of the liberal system—but

the spirit rapidly evolved from controversies with the
friars on other points, and with the urgings of some
prominent Californians who already had their eyes on
the mission lands, he had to keep the matter alive by
certain experiments intended to test the feelings and
capabilities of the neophytes.[33]   On April 28, 1826,
Echeandía and his secretary, Zamorano, held a consultation with padres Sanchez, Zalvidea, Peyri, and
Martin at San Diego, at which after the padres had
expressed their willingness to surrender the temporal
management, the governor made a speech on the importance of providing for the Indians of San Diego
and Santa Bárbara who desired to leave the *neofía*
and manage for themselves.   After discussion, it was
agreed that those of good conduct and long service
might be released, to form a pueblo at San Fernando
or San Luis, under regulations to be fixed by the governor.[34]

After later consultations not definitely recorded, at
which the plan was considerably modified, Echeandía
issued, July 25th, a decree, or proclamation, of partial
emancipation in favor of the neophytes.   By its terms
those desiring to leave the missions might do so, provided they had been Christians from childhood, or for
fifteen years, were married, or at least not minors,
and had some means of gaining a livelihood.   The
Indians must apply to the presidial comandante, who
after obtaining a report from the padre was to issue
through the latter a written permit entitling the
neophyte and his family to go wherever they pleased,

guardedly and slowly to avoid the license that might result from unwise
measures.   All is intrusted to E.'s experience and good judgment. *St. Pap.,
Miss. and Colon.*, MS., ii. 42, quoted by E. in 1833 in a letter to Figueroa.
    [33] According to *Alvarado, Hist. Cal.*, MS., ii. 109–10; *Vallejo, Hist. Cal.*,
MS., ii. 51–3; *Vallejo, Reminis.*, MS., 89–90, Echeandía, immediately after
taking his office, sent Lieut Pacheco to make a tour of inspection in the
southern missions.   The padres were not pleased; but Pacheco having some
trouble with P. Boscana at S. Juan Capistrano, went so far as to assemble the
neophytes and to make a political speech, in which he told the Indians of a
new chief who had come to the country to be their friend, and give them equal
rights with Spaniards.
    [34] *Dept. St. Pap.*, MS., i. 129–30.

like other Mexican citizens, their names being erased
from the mission registers. The cases of absentees
were to be investigated by the comandantes at once,
and those not entitled to the license were to be restored to their respective missions. At the same time
the padres were to be restricted in the matter of punishments to the 'mere correction' allowed to natural
fathers in the case of their children; unmarried males
of minor age only could be flogged, with a limit of
fifteen blows per week; and faults requiring more
severe penalties must be referred to the military
authorities.[35] The provisions of this order applied
only to the districts of San Diego, Santa Bárbara, and
Monterey; though in 1828 it was extended to that of
San Francisco, excepting the frontier missions of San
Rafael and San Francisco Solano.[36]

This order of 1826 was the only secularization
measure which Echeandía attempted to put in actual
operation before the end of 1830. It does not appear
that the missionaries made any special opposition, and
the reasons of their concurrence are obvious. First,
very few neophytes could comply with the conditions,
especially that requiring visible means of support.
Second, the decree required fugitives not entitled to
license to be returned to their missions by the military, a duty that of late years had been much
neglected. And third, and chiefly, experimental or
partial secularization was deemed by the friars to be
in their own interest, since they had no fears that the
neophytes would prove themselves capable of self-

[35] July 25, 1826, *Echeandía, Decreto de Emancipacion á favor de Neófitos, 1826*, MS. Received at S. Rafael Aug. 23d. *Arch. Misiones*, MS., i. 297. Forwarded by Lieut Estudillo to padre of S. Antonio. *Arch. Arzob.*, MS., v. pt ii. 114–17. Sergt Anastasio Carrillo sent by Capt. Guerra to proclaim the new order in the missions of the Sta Bárbara district, as he did at S. Fernando on Sept. 26th and at S. Buenaventura on Sept. 29th. *Doc. Hist. Cal.*, MS., iv. 789–92. Here the Indian was authorized, should the cabo de escolta and padre refuse to act in presenting his application for license, to leave the mission without permission and apply in person to the comandante. Vallejo, *Hist. Cal.*, MS., iv. 22, quotes the order of July 25th.

[36] June 20, 1828, gov. to comandantes and prefect. *Dept. Rec.*, MS., vi. 57.

government.   Respecting the result, we have no satisfactory information.   I find no record of the number
of neophytes who under the order obtained their freedom, nor of the manner in which they used their liberty.   Beechey, the English navigator, tells us that
the governor was induced by the padres to modify
his plans, and to try experiments with a few neophytes, who, as might have been expected, fell soon into
excesses, gambled away all their property, and were
compelled to beg or steal.[37]

While the governor doubtless used his influence to
imbue the neophytes with ideas of independence and
civil liberty, not conducive to contentment with mission
life,[33] no definite progress was made, except in the
preparation of plans, in the years 1827–9.   In July 1827
the prefect was ordered to see to it that a primary
school was supported at each mission, and compliance
was promised.[39]   In October of the same year, Echeandía called for a detailed report on the lands held
by each mission to be rendered before the end of the
year.   I find no such report in the records, though
the local reports for the next year did, in several
instances, contain a list of the mission ranchos.[40]

[37] *Beechey's Voyage*, ii. 12–13, 320.   A few doc. bearing on individual cases
of application for license. *Dept. St. Pap., Ben. Mil.*, MS., lvii. 23–4; *Dept.
Rec.*, MS., v. 65; viii. 34.   April 27, 1827, gov. says to com. of S. Diego that
as the Indians of S. Juan neglect their work and make a wrong application
of their privileges, they are to be admonished seriously that those who behave
themselves properly will obtain their full freedom when his plans are perfected, while others will be punished. *Dept. Rec.*, MS., v. 44.   May 20, 1827,
Martinez is to inform the Indians that in a few days E. will issue an order for
them to be treated the same as gente de razon. *Id.*, v. 46.   Dec. 6, 1826, E.
to sup. govt.   Speaks of the monopoly by the friars of all the land, labor,
and products of the territory; of their hatred for the present system of government; and of the desirability of making at least a partial distribution of
mission property among the best of the neophytes. *Id.*, v. 132–3.   Oct. 20,
1828, E. to min. of war, says the Ind. at most missions are clamoring to be
formed into pueblos. *St. Pap., Sac.*, MS., x. 39–40.

[38] Mrs Ord, *Ocurrencias*, MS., 52–4, says that the ideas instilled into the
minds of the neophytes by the gefe político made a great change in them.
They were not as contented nor as obedient as before. Osio, *Hist. Cal.*, MS.,
119–20, takes the same view of the matter.

[39] *Arch. Arzob.*, MS., v. pt i. 35; *Dept. Rec.*, MS., v. 54; *Leg. Rec.*, MS., i.
79–80.

[40] Oct. 7th. Echeandía's bando in *Olvera, Doc.*, MS., 1.   Names of mission
ranchos in the south. *Prov. St. Pap., Presid.*, MS., i. 97–8.   Bandini, in a

The order brought out, however, from the padres
of San Juan Capistrano, a defence of the Indian title
to the lands in California running back to the time
when, according to Ezra the prophet, the Jews wandered across Bering Strait to people America.[41]

In a communication of 1833 Echeandía, after alluding to his instructions, by which, as we have seen,
much was left to his own judgment, explained his acts
in these years as follows: "Intrusted with the task
of arranging the system of both Californias, supplying
as best I could in indispensable cases the lack of administration of justice, busied in regulating the treasury branches since the comisario abused his trust,
lacking the necessary supplies for the troops, at the
end of my resources for other expenses, struggling to
put in good order the necessarily tolerated traffic with
foreign vessels, anxious to establish regular and secure
communication with Sonora *via* the Colorado, combat-
ing the general addiction to the Spanish government
and the despotic system, encountering the abuses introduced in all branches by the revolution and enor-
mously propagated by the total neglect of the viceregal
government during the war of independence—occupied,
I say, with so many cares, without aid in the civil or
military administration, and finally having no Mexican
priests to take the place of the malecontent Spaniards
in divine worship, if they should abandon it as happened at Santa Bárbara and San Buenaventura, or
should be expelled as insufferable royalists, as some of
them are, and as was he of San Luis Obispo, who
favored the Solis revolt for Spain—which, though I
had the good fortune to suppress it, interfered with
the progress of good government—some of the missionaries mismanaging the property of their subjects,
and others refusing to remain under the federal gov-

letter to Barron, 1828, says the missions have seized upon nearly all the land
in the territory, so as to exclude private persons. *Bandini, Doc.*, MS., 8.
    [41] *Zalvidea and Barona, Peticion al Gefe Político á favor de los Indios, 1827,*
MS.

cial protest against the plan of secularization that was being prepared. This was partly because they believed that protests and arguments addressed to the territorial authorities would be without effect, partly because they still thought that secularization could not be effected for want of curates; but largely also, I suppose, because they had hopes of benefits to be derived from the struggle going on in Mexico. Bustamante's revolution against Guerrero was understood to be in the interest of a more conservative church and mission policy. There is no proof that the California padres were at the beginning in direct understanding with the promoters of the movement, but such is not unlikely to have been the case;[48] and there certainly was such an understanding directly after Bustamante's accession. At any rate, their hopes of aid from the new executive proved to be well founded, as we shall see. Meanwhile the national authorities were even more dilatory and inactive than those of the territory. Nothing whatever was done in the matter. The famous junta de fomento seems to have made some kind of a report on secularization before it ceased to exist. Congress took it up in 1830, but decided to leave the missions alone at least until the

---

[48] In the famous Fitch trial, *Fitch, Causa Criminal*, MS., etc., 339–40, President Sanchez, urged to arrest Echeandía for trial before an ecclesiastical court, declined to do so on account of the tumult it would cause, the prospect of an early change of governors, and the recommendations of Bustamante in his 'most esteemed private letter of April 11th,' which is quoted as follows: 'Your zeal should not rest a moment in a matter of so great interest; you will understand at once the rectitude of my intentions. Therefore I promise myself that you will not only aid by your influence and by every means in your power the success of my plans, but also take the greatest pains to reëstablish public tranquillity, which to my great sorrow is disturbed, and to bring about perfect peace and harmony among the people. This is my business, which I recommend very particularly to the prudence of your paternity, on whose aid I count for the accomplishment of my desires.' The president also uses, respecting the new governor, the following play upon words: 'Habiendo logrado ya esta desgraciada provincia su Victoria, seguramente se debe esperar que esta jurisdiccion eclesiástica usurpada, y oprimida, tambien conseguirá su *victoria*.' Vallejo, *Hist. Cal.*, MS., ii. 109–10, says that the padres learned of Bustamante's pronunciamiento just after the action of the diputacion, and that they immediately signed a petition to the govt against Echeandía, though pretending to the latter at the same time to be anxious to give up the mission temporalities.

arrival of the deputy from California; and finally the minister of relations approved Echeandía's plan and recommended it with the report of the junta to congress at the beginning of 1831.[49]

There are a few items of Indian affairs in the annals of these years that may as well be recorded here as elsewhere, none of them requiring more than a brief notice. In April 1826 Alférez Ibarra had apparently two fights at or near Santa Isabel, in the San Diego district, perhaps with Indians who came from the Colorado region. In one case eighteen, and in the other twenty, pairs of ears taken from the slain—a new kind of trophy for California warfare— were sent to the comandante general. Three soldiers of the Mazatlan squadron had been murdered just before, which deed was probably the provocation for the slaughter, but the records are unsatisfactory.[50]

Another event of the same year was an expedition under Alférez Sanchez, in November, against the Cosemenes, or Cosumnes, across the San Joaquin Valley. These Indians had either attacked or been attacked by a party of neophytes from Mission San José, who were making a holiday trip with their alcalde, and twenty or thirty of whom were killed, or at least never returned. Sanchez was absent a week, and though he had to retreat and leave the gentiles masters of the field, he had destroyed a ranchería, killed about forty Indians, and brought in as many captives.[51]

[49] Mexico, Mem. Relaciones, 1831, p. 33. Cárlos Carrillo, writing from Tepic, April 2, 1831, referred to information obtained from Navarro, the member from Lower California, that most of the congressmen had opposed any change in the status of the missions. Guerra, Doc., MS., iv. 200. Vallejo, Hist. Cal., MS., ii. 259, says a report was presented to congress on April 6, 1825, by J. J. Espinosa de los Rios, C. M. Bustamante, P. V. Sola, Tomás Suría, Tomás Salgado, Mariano Dominguez, J. M. Almanza, Manuel Gonzalez de Ibarra, J. J. Ormachea, and F. de P. Tamariz (the report of the junta alluded to by the minister?), in favor of including the mission lands in the colonization law of 1824. Jan. 15, 1831, Alaman to governor. The plan of founding two convents has been referred to the minister of justice. Sup. Govt St. Pap., MS., vii. 1.

[50] Dept. St. Pap. MS., i. 136-7; Id. Ben., Pref. y Juzg., iii. 81-3; S. Diego, Lib. Mision, MS., 96.

[51] Sanchez, Journal of the enterprise against the Cosemenes, 1826. 'Written

A new expedition was prepared, for which the troops of San Francisco under Sanchez were joined to those of Monterey under Alférez Mariano G. Vallejo, who was also, by virtue of his superior rank, commander in chief of the army, now numbering one hundred and seven armed men. Vallejo had not yet had much experience as an Indian-fighter, but he had just returned from a campaign in the Tulares, in which with thirty-five men he had slain forty-eight Indians and suffered no casualties.[55] Having crossed the San Joaquin River by means of rafts on May 29th, the army arrived next day at the scene of the former battle, where it was met as before by a cloud of arrows. The wood was found to be absolutely impenetrable, and Vallejo at once caused it to be set on fire, stationing his troops and his three-pounder on the opposite bank of the river. The fire brought the Indians to the edge of the thicket, where some of them were killed. At 5 P. M. Sanchez was sent with twenty-five men to attack the foe, and fought over two hours in the burning wood, retiring at dusk with three men wounded.

Next morning at 9 o'clock Vallejo with thirty-seven men again entered the wood. He found a series of pits and ditches arranged with considerable skill, and protected by barricades of trees and brush. Evidently the Indians could never have been dislodged from such a stronghold except by the agency that had been employed. Traces of blood were found everywhere, and there were also discovered the bodies of the two soldiers killed in the previous battle. The enemy, how-

MS., vii. 20. Osio, *Hist. Cal.*, MS., 129–30, gives some particulars about the loss of the two men, and says that Soto died of his wounds a little later at S. José. Alvarado, *Hist. Cal.*, MS., ii. 57–60, gives an absurdly exaggerated account of the battle and of the enemy's fortifications. Galindo, *Apuntes*, MS., 22–4, has a quite accurate narrative from memory, recalling even the name of the Rio Laquisimes, which may have been that now called the Stanislaus, though it is not certain.

[55] *Dept. Rec.*, MS., vii. 20. According to a document in *Vallejo, Doc.*, MS., xx. 280, Vallejo had been in two *acciones de guerra* as commander, one in the Sierra Nevada from S. Miguel, and the other in the Tulares, where he had one man killed and 15 wounded. May 16, 1829, Martinez orders Vallejo to march with Sanchez to chastise the rebels of Sta Clara and S. José assembled at Los Rios. *Vallejo, Doc.*, MS., i. 174.

ever, had taken advantage of the darkness of night and had fled. Vallejo started in pursuit. He encamped that night on the Rio Laquisimes, and next morning surrounded a part of the fugitives in another thicket near their ranchería on the Arroyo Seco. Here there were some negotiations, but the Indians declared they would die rather than surrender, and late in the afternoon the attack was begun. A road was cut through the chaparral with axes, along which the field-piece and muskets were pressed forward and continually discharged. The foe retired slowly to their ditches and embankments in the centre, wounding eight of the advancing soldiers. When the cannon was close to the trenches the ammunition gave out, which fact, and the heat of the burning thicket, forced the men to retreat. During the night the besieged Indians tried to escape one by one, some succeeding, but many being killed. Next morning nothing was found but dead bodies and three living women. That day, June 1st, at noon, provisions being exhausted, Vallejo started for San José, where he arrived on the fourth.[56]

[56] *Vallejo, Campaña contra Estanislao y sus Indios sublevados, 1829*, MS. This is the commander's official report dated at S. José June 4th. *Piña, Diario de la Expedicion al Valle de San José, 1829*. This is a diary kept by Corp. Lázaro Piña of the artillery, who accompanied the expedition. It extends from May 19th, the date of departure from Monterey, to June 13th, when they returned to Monterey. The details, beyond the limits of the actual campaign as given in my text, are unimportant. The original MS. was given me by Gen. Vallejo. June 5th, Martinez congratulates Vallejo on his defeat of the rebels at Los Rios. Regrets that he could not follow up the advantage gained. Orders him to S. Francisco to plan further operations. *Vallejo, Doc.*, MS., i. 175. Dec. 31st, Martinez states in the *hojas de servicios* of Vallejo and Sanchez that no decisive results were obtained, though 4 men were killed (?) and 11 wounded. *Id.*, i. 204; xx. 142. Oct. 7th, Echeandía pardons neophytes who had been in rebellion. *Dept. Rec.*, MS., vii. 230. Alvarado's narrative of this campaign, *Hist. Cal.*, MS., ii. 57–68, drawn evidently from his imagination, is so wonderfully inaccurate that no condensation can do it justice, and I have no space to reproduce it in full. Osio, *Hist. Cal.*, MS., 133–8, gives an account considerably more accurate than that of Alvarado, which is not saying much in its favor. He speaks of but one battle, in which the barricades of timber were broken down by the artillery, the order of 'no quarter' was given by Vallejo, the infuriated auxiliaries wrought a terrible carnage among the foe, and the pits dug for defences were utilized as graves. Galindo, *Apuntes*, MS., 22–6, names two soldiers, Espinosa and Soto, as fatally wounded, and says that Estanislao was captured. Bojorges, *Recuerdos*, MS., 14–22, who confounds the three expeditions, names Peña.

One phase of this campaign demands further notice.
One of the contemporary narratives, the diary of Piña,
represents that at least six of the captives, including
three or four women found alive in the second thicket,
were put to death, most of them by the order or with
the consent of the commander. Osio in his history
tells us that some captured leaders were shot or
hanged to trees, and Padre Duran made a complaint,
to which no attention was paid. Vallejo in his official
report says nothing respecting the death of the captives. At the time, however, Vallejo was accused by
Padre Duran, but claimed to be innocent.[57] Echeandía ordered an investigation of the charge that three
men and three women, not taken in battle, had been
shot and then hanged;[58] and the investigation was
made. From the testimony the fiscal decided that
only one man and one woman had been killed, the
latter unjustifiably by the soldier Joaquin Alvarado,
whose punishment was recommended.[59] There is no
doubt that in those, as in later times, to the Spaniards,
as to other so-called civilized races, the life of an Indian
was a slight affair, and in nearly all the expeditions
outrages were committed; but it would require stronger evidence than exists in this case to justify any special blame to a particular officer.[60]

In June 1827 orders were sent to Echeandía from
Mexico to found a fort on the northern frontier in the
region of San Rafael or San Francisco Solano. The

and Pacheco as the two killed under Sanchez, and says that Antonio Soto
died of his wounds at S. José.
   [57] *Arch. Sta B.*, MS., xii. 178.
   [58] Aug. 7, 1829. *Dept. Rec.*, MS., vii. 213.
   [59] *Dept. St. Pap., Ben. Mil.*, MS., lxx. 13. Lieut Martinez was the fiscal
to whom the case was intrusted.
   [60] A few items of Indian affairs for 1830: April, sergeants Salazar and
Rico sent with a force to prevent trouble at Sta Inés. Quiet restored in 3 days.
Dept. St. Pap., Ben. Mil., MS., lxxxviii. 1, 4. July–Sept., a grand *paseo
marítimo* proposed by P. Duran, in which the vecinos of S. José were invited
to join. The object was to visit the rivers and Tulares, and inspire respect
among the gentiles by peaceable methods. The mission would pay the expense.
S. José, *Arch.*, MS., i. 38-9. Dec., Arrival of suspicious Indians at S. Fernando. *Dept. St. Pap., Angeles*, MS., i. 95.

object was not only to protect those establishments
against gentile tribes, but also and perhaps chiefly to
prevent a further extension of Russian power. The
missions were to be called upon to furnish the required
aid in laborers, implements, and food, the corresponding instructions being also sent through the guardian
to the president. Echeandía's reply was to the effect
that there were no means to build a fort, but he would
try to construct quarters near San Rafael for a military
guard, and he did in March 1828 order Romualdo
Pacheco to go to the north and select a suitable site,
which is the last I hear of the matter.[61]

Respecting the seasons from 1826 to 1830, I find
nothing or next to nothing in the records; but I suppose that the winter of 1827–8 was a wet one, and
the next of 1828–9 one of unprecedented drought.
The flood is mentioned in various newspaper items, on
the authority of Vallejo and other old Californians,
and of trappers said to have been in the Sacramento
Valley; it is confirmed by one letter of the time, January 1828, which speaks of the flood at Monterey as
something like that of 1824–5.[62] The drought of 1829
is shown by the failure of the crops, the total harvest
being 24,000 fanegas, the smallest from 1796 to 1834,
and less than half the average for this decade; though
strangely I find no correspondence on the subject save
two slight items, one from San Rafael and the other
from San Diego.[63]

[61] June 6, 1827, min. of war to Echeandía. *St. Pap.*, *Miss. and Col.*,
MS., ii. 310; June 13th, guardian to president. *Arch. Sta B.*, MS., xii. 176–
7; Jan. 8th, 1828, E.'s reply. *Dept. Rec.*, MS., vi. 23; Mar. 25th, E. to Pacheco, ordering him to Nopalillos. *Dept. Rec.*, MS., vi. 196.
[62] *Vallejo*, *Doc.*, MS., xxix. 190.
[63] *Dept. Rec.*, MS., vii. 364; *Arch. Sta B.*, MS., xii. 181.

CHAPTER V.

ECHEANDÍA'S RULE—MARITIME AND COMMERCIAL AFFAIRS.

1826-30.

VESSELS OF 1826—REVENUE RULES—HARTNELL'S BUSINESS—HAWAIIAN
FLAG—COOPER AND THE 'ROVER'—LAWSUIT WITH ARGÜELLO—BEE-
CHEY'S VISIT IN THE 'BLOSSOM'—BOOKS RESULTING—TRADING FLEET
OF 1827—REGLAMENTOS ON LIQUORS AND LIVE-STOCK—EMBARRASSMENT
OF McCULLOCH, HARTNELL & Co.—CUNNINGHAM AT SANTA CATALINA—
VISIT OF DUHAUT-CILLY AND BOTTA—MARITIME AFFAIRS OF 1828—
RESTRICTIONS—SMUGGLING—AFFAIR OF THE 'FRANKLIN'—CANNON-
BALLS—AFFAIR OF THE 'KARIMOKO'—VESSELS OF 1829—CUSTOM-
HOUSE—ARRIVAL OF THE 'BROOKLINE'—GALE'S CORRESPONDENCE—
RAISING THE STARS AND STRIPES—LANG AT SAN DIEGO—THE 'SANTA
BÁRBARA' BUILT IN CALIFORNIA—SHIPS AND TRADE OF 1830—LIST OF
VESSELS, 1825-30.

THE vessels of 1826 were forty-four in number, including a few doubtfully recorded. There were twenty-
two American, eight English, five Mexican, four
Russian, three of the Hawaiian Islands, and one Californian, though the latter carried the American flag.
Eleven were whalers seeking supplies; one was on a
scientific and exploring expedition; and the rest, so far
as the records show, were engaged more or less exclusively in trade. Ten or twelve were included in the
list of the preceding year, having either remained over
from December to January or repeating their trip.[1]

---

[1] The vessels of the year, for more particulars about which see list at end
of this chapter, were the *Adam, Alliance, Argosy, Baikal, Blossom, Charles,
Courier, Cyrus, Elena, Eliza, Franklin, General Bravo, Harbinger, Inca, Inore,
Jóven Angustias, Kiahkta, María Ester, María Teresa, Mercury* (2), *Mero,
Moor, Olive Branch, Paragon, Peruvian, Pizarro, Rover, Sachem, Santa
Apolonia, Sirena, Solitude, Speedy, Spy, Thomas Nowlan, Timorelan, Triton,
Washington* (3), *Waverly, Whaleman, Young Tartar, Zamora.*

Vessels were not allowed to trade at way-ports, such as Santa Cruz, San Luis, Refugio, and San Juan Capistrano, without permission from the governor, which was easily obtained unless there was especial cause for suspicion. In June, Herrera, following instructions from his superior in Sonora, ordered that no vessel be allowed to load or unload in any other port than Monterey. He admitted that such a rule was ruinous to the territorial commerce, and said he had protested against it, but could not disobey orders. Echeandía, however, countermanded the rule provisionally, and it did not go into effect; but at the same time an *internacion* duty of fifteen per cent and an *avería* duty of two and a half per cent were added to the former import duty of twenty-five per cent, making a total of 42½ per cent, besides an anchorage tax of $10 for each vessel and a tonnage rate of $2.50 per ton.[2] Naturally these exactions displeased both the traders and the consumers of foreign goods; but they sought relief, not in written petitions, but in various smuggling expedients, in which they were rarely detected, and which therefore for this year at least find no place in the records.

For Monterey, the chief port of entry, I have no revenue statistics for the year. At Santa Bárbara, where accounts are complete, the revenue from customs was $7,446.[3] At San Francisco the recorded amount

[2] June 28th, Herrera to habilitados of S. Francisco, Sta Bárbara, and S. Diego, closing those ports. *Dept. St. Pap., Ben. Com. and Treas.*, MS., i. 16. July 5th, Id., insisting on internacion duty according to decree of Aug. 6, 1824. *St. Pap., Ben.*, MS., i. 67-8. July 11th, Id. to gov., insisting on the reformation of abuses, though said abuses were necessary. *Dept. St. Pap., Ben. Com. and Treas.*, MS., i. 42-7. July 22d, Id. to habilitados. Countermands order of June 28th until govt decides, but not that of July 5th. *Id.*, i. 51-2. Beechey, *Voyage*, ii. 10, 69, refers to the excessive duties. Jan. 24th, revised tariff of prices for products. *St. Pap., Sac.*, MS., x. 90-1. May 10th, decree of Mex. govt. All exports free of duty. *Sup. Govt St. Pap.*, MS., xix. 38. Sept. 26th, import duties as given in the text. *Dept. St. Pap., Ben. Mil.*, MS., lx. 2. July 17th, habilitado of Sta Bárbara understands that by the decree of Feb. 12, 1825, internacion duty is payable only on goods taken from the custom-house for other ports, foreign vessels having to pay only the 25 per cent and Mexican the 15 per cent of import duties. *Dept. St. Pap., Ben. Com. and Treas.*, MS., i. 48.

[3] *Dept. St. Pap., Ben. Com. and Treas.*, MS., i. 65. Partial statistics for each vessel are given in the list at the end of this chapter.

was $4,360;[4] and at San Diego, $1,666.   If the total
of $13,500 were doubled, it is evident that the
amount would be but a small part of the percentage
due on imports.   Only a few years later there were
complaints that no accounts had been rendered by
Herrera and his successors,[5] so that it is not strange
I have been unable to find complete figures.

All seems to have been *couleur de rose* in Hartnell's
business this year.   Echeandía granted a general
license for his vessels to touch at all the ports.   Mc-
Cullough from Callao, and the Brothertons from
Liverpool, wrote most enthusiastically of the prospects
for high prices, urging extraordinary efforts to buy
more hides and tallow, and expressing fears only of
rivalry from other firms, while four brigs, the *Inca*,
Speedy, *Eliza*, and *Pizarro*, were successfully loaded
with Californian produce.[6]   Gale's *Sachem* and the
other Boston ships must have interfered seriously
with Hartnell's purchases, but we have no information
beyond their names and presence on the coast.   Juan
Ignacio Mancisidor also did a large business, selling
the cargoes of the *Nowlan* and *Olive Branch*, and
taking away large quantities of mission produce,
though for him, as a Spaniard, trouble was in store.
The *Waverly* and her two consorts introduced the
Hawaiian flag to Californian waters, opened a new
branch of territorial trade, and brought to the country
William G. Dana, with others afterward prominent
among resident traders.

[4] Habilitados' accounts in *Vallejo, Doc.*, MS., i. passim; *Dept. St. Pap.,
Ben. Mil.*, MS., lx. 1–4.

[5] Figueroa to Mex. govt in 1834. *Dept. St. Pap.*, MS., iii. 209–10.

[6] Echeandía's permit of June 18 and Aug. 26, 1826, to Hartnell's vessels.
Dept. Rec., MS., iv. 48; *Vallejo, Doc.*, MS., xxix. 57.   Letters of McCulloch,
Begg & Co., Brothertons, for the year, in *Id.*, MS., xxix. nos. 4, 6, 12–15,
21, 40, 43, 52, 65.   Some beef was acceptable where hides and tallow were
not forthcoming.   The *Eliza* appears to have cleared at Callao for Costa Rica
to deceive rivals.   The *Esther*, sent to England with hides, had not been
heard of.   The tallow from each mission must be marked 'so that the peculiar
tricks of each padre may be found out.'   Cash is sent and more promised.
Anderson's competition in Peru was especially feared.   War between Buenos
Aires and Brazil made prospects better.   Yet P. Uria, from Soledad, protests
on June 11th against being obliged to sell exclusively to Hartnell, and will in
future accept the best offers.

Captain Cooper, in the *Rover*, came back from China in April 1826. The voyage had been made under a contract of 1824 with the government,[7] which had entitled the schooner to $10,000 for freight out and back, and the privilege of introducing $10,000 in goods free of duties. Besides some trading done by Cooper on his own account, he sold at Canton 375 otter skins for $7,000, investing the proceeds in effects for the Californian troops. Most of these effects were delivered after some delay to the habili-tado of San Diego. The delay, and much subsequent trouble, was caused by dissatisfaction on the part of the governor at the prices received and paid in China, and by personal difficulties in settling their accounts between Cooper and Luis Argüello, as master and owner of the vessel.[8] This last phase of the quarrel lasted until 1829, involving a lawsuit and various refer-ences to arbitrators. Argüello's side of the quarrel is not represented in the records; Cooper's letters are nu-merous, containing a great variety of uncomplimentary epithets for Don Luis. Arbitrators seem to have decided the case in Cooper's favor in the amount of $5,000, "which," writes the captain, "the damned rascal Argüello will never pay while California remains in its present condition."[9] To return to the *Rover:* the only incident of her voyage that is known was the throwing away of all Spanish papers on board, including invoices and the bill of sale to Argüello, and even of the Mexican flag, on account of revelations by a drunken sailor to the effect that the schooner was not American as pretended, but Mexican. This occurred at the Phil-

[7] See vol. ii. p. 520.

[8] Arrival of the *Rover*, and trouble about the landing of the cargo. *Dept. St. Pap., Ben. Mil.*, MS., lxxxvii. 68; *Id., Ben. Cust.-H.*, i. 18–20, 30; *St. Pap., Ben.*, MS., i. 71; *St. Pap., Sac.*, MS., xi. 1.

[9] Cooper's letters of 1826-9, in *Vallejo, Doc.*, MS., xxix., nos. 54, 113, 108, 117, 128, 200, 210, 234, 235, 292, 334, 387, with many more in the same volume, relating to details of C.'s business in those years, being of no special importance. It appears that Kierolf & Co., in China, had sent some goods by C. to Cal. on sale, and that by reason of his troubles with Argüello, he was unable to settle with that firm for several years. J. P. Sturgis was Cooper's correspondent at Canton.

ippine Islands.[10] On December 17, 1826, she sailed
for San Diego, in quest of documents by which she
might raise the Mexican flag. José Cárdenas was to
be master.[11] Nothing more is known of the *San
Rafael*, as it was proposed to call her, from contemporary documents; but two Californians tell us that
she was sent with a cargo to San Blas, and not allowed
to return by the Mexican authorities, who did not
like the idea of California having a vessel of her own.[12]

The visit of Captain Frederick William Beechey,
R. N., in H. M. S. *Blossom*, deserves notice as a prominent event, by reason of the books to the publication
of which it gave rise, and the information they contained about California.[13] Beechey had sailed from England in May 1825, despatched to Bering Strait, there
to await the arrival of Franklin and Parry of the arctic expeditions.[14] Sailing by Cape Horn, Valparaiso,

[10] Cooper's deposition of Dec. 23th, in *Dept. St. Pap., Ben. Mil.*, MS., lxiii.
9. The loss of the papers complicated the quarrel with Argüello. July 27th,
gov. ordered the sale of the vessel to Argüello, and the manner of her nation-
alization to be investigated. *St. Pap., Sac.*, MS., xii. 14.

[11] *Dept. St. Pap., Ben. Cust.-H.*, MS., i. 25.

[12] *Fernandez, Cosas de Cal.*, MS., 37–9; *Alvarado, Hist. Cal.*, MS., ii. 84–6.

[13] *Beechey, Narrative of a Voyage to the Pacific and Beering's Strait, to Co-
operate with the Polar Expeditions, performed in His Majesty's Ship Blossom,
under the command of Captain F. W. Beechey, R. N., F. R. S., etc., in the years
1825, 26, 27, 28. Published by authority of the Lords Commissioners of the Ad-
miralty. A new Edition.* London, 1831. 8vo, 2 volumes, maps and plates.
This edition is not mentioned by Sabin, being published by Colburn and Bent-
ley. The original in 4to form, 2 vols., had the same title, date, and publishers. There were published in 1832, according to Sabin, an American edition and a German translation. In the edition used by me the California
matter is found in vol. i. p. 471–2; vol. ii. p. 1–88, 319–21, 403; with descriptions of S. Francisco and Monterey harbors on p. 422–9; and observations of
latitude and longitude on p. 443. Only one plate relates to California, that
of 'Californian throwing the lasso.' In *Huish, A Narrative of the Voyages and
Travels of Capt. Beechey, etc.*, London, 1836, the California matter is given on
p. 415–60, somewhat condensed, and a portrait of Beechey forms the frontispiece. *Hooker* and *Arnott, The Botany of Captain Beechey's Voyage; comprising an account of the plants collected by Messrs. Lay and Collie, etc.* London,
1841. 4to, plates. The matter is arranged geographically in order of the countries visited; and California occupies p. 134–65, with one plate so far as Beechey's voyage is concerned; but on p. 315–409 is given a more important *California Supplement*, made up chiefly of a description of specimens collected by
Douglas later, with 23 plates. *Richardson* and others, *The Zoölogy of Captain
Beechey's Voyage; compiled from the collections and notes made by Captain Beechey, the officers and naturalist, etc.* London, 1839. 4to. The matter on California is scattered through the volume. The plates are splendidly colored.
From p. 160 there is a chapter on geology, which contains a 'geological plan'
and description of the port of S. Francisco, which I copy elsewhere.

[14] The *Blossom* mounted 16 guns. The chief officers under Beechey were:

and the Hawaiian Islands, he arrived in Kotzebue
Sound in July 1826, remaining in the far north until
October, when he was obliged by the closing-in of
winter and by want of supplies to sail for the south.
He anchored at San Francisco November 6th,[15] and
was hospitably received by Comandante Martinez and
Padre Tomás Esténega. Supplies were, however, less
plentiful than had been expected, and a party consisting of Collie, Marsh, and Evans was sent overland to
Monterey. This party was absent from the 9th to
the 17th,[16] during which time and subsequently Beechey and his men were occupied in making a survey
of San Francisco Bay and scientific observations about
its shores. No obstacles were thrown in his way, the
authorities asking only for a copy of the resulting
chart, which was given.[17] The Englishmen amused
themselves chiefly by excursions on horseback over
the peninsula, and especially from the presidio to the
mission, the inhabitants gaining an extraordinary revenue from the hire and sale of horses. The navigators
also visited Mission San José late in November. One
man was drowned and buried at San Francisco.

"By Christmas day we had all remained sufficiently
long in the harbor to contemplate our departure without regret; the eye had become familiar to the pic-
turesque scenery of the bay, the pleasure of the chase

lieutenants Geo. Peard, Edward Belcher, and John Wainwright; master,
Thomas Elson; surgeon and assistant, Alex. Collie and Thomas Neilson; purser,
Geo. Marsh; mates, Wm. Smyth and Jas. Wolfe; midshipmen, John Kendall
and Richard B. Beechey; clerks, John Evans and Chas. H. Osmer. The
whole force was 100 men.

[15] Announcement of arrival dated Nov. 7th, in *Dept. St. Pap., Ben. Cust.-
II.*, MS., i. 24.

[16] Collie's party, with an escort of Californian soldiers, travelled by way of
Sierra de S. Bruno, Rio de S. Bruno, Burri Burri, over the plain of Las Salinas, with Estrecho de S. José on the left, and Sierra del Sur on right, S. Mateo, Las Pulgas, Santa Clara, S. José, Ojo del Coche (?), plain of Las Llagas,
Rancho de Las Animas, Rio de Pájaro, plain of S. Juan, S. Juan Bautista,
Llano del Rey, Rancho Las Salinas, Monterey, and returned by the same
route. They were kindly treated by Capt. Gonzalez and Mr Hartnell. The
diary of this trip furnished Beechey a large part of the information published
about California.

[17] Jan. 25, 1827, gov. to Martinez. Presumes that Beechey laid before
him the necessary permit of the sup. govt to make a plan of the harbor. Orders him to forward the plan to S. Diego. *Dept. Rec.*, MS., v. 13.

had lost its fascination, and the roads to the mission and presidio were grown tedious and insipid. There was no society to enliven the hours, no incidents to vary one day from the other, and, to use the expression of Donna Gonzalez, California appeared to be as much out of the world as Kamchatka." The Englishmen sailed on December 28th for Monterey. Here they remained five days, cutting spars, and obtaining supplies from missions and from vessels in port, largely by the aid of Hartnell.[18] The supplies obtainable in California were, however, inadequate to the needs of the expedition; and on the 5th of January the *Blossom* sailed for the Sandwich Islands. After another trip to the Arctic, unsuccessful like the first, so far as meeting the ill-fated Franklin was concerned, Beechey returned to Monterey October 29, 1827,[19] remaining until December 17th, when he went again to San Francisco for water, finally sailing on January 3d for San Blas, and thence home via Cape Horn and Brazil, reaching England in October 1828.

It is thus seen that Beechey's visit was in itself an event of slight importance; but the observations published in the voyager's narrative were perhaps more evenly accurate and satisfactory than those of any preceding navigator. Beechey and his companions confined their remarks closely to actual observations. They were less ambitious than some of their predecessors to talk of things they did not understand, and thus avoided ridiculous blunders. It is not, however, necessary to notice their remarks at length here, for the following reasons: A large part is naturally devoted to local and personal matters, or to other topics treated in other chapters; notes of the scientific corps

[18] Jan. 4, 1827, Beechey writes from Monterey to the British consul in Mexico, recommending the appointment of Hartnell as vice-consul in Cal., in consequence of the increasing importance of English trade on the Pacific coast. *Vallejo, Doc.*, MS., xxix. 102.

[19] Notice of presence of the *Blossom* and 3 whalers on the coast in November. *Vallejo, Doc.*, MS., xxix. 168. Called the *Blondes*, at Monterey Nov. 8th. *Dept. St. Pap.*, MS., ii. 47. Mention of visit in *Soulé's Annals of S. F.*, 163–4.

on botany, zoölogy, and other branches, though of
great value, can of course receive in a work like this
no further attention than mere mention;[20] and what
remains of general description, respecting the country
and its institutions, on account of its very accuracy,
would be but vain repetition here. Had the visitor
been less careful and made more blunders, he would
receive more attention from me. Such is fame, and
the reward of painstaking.

The missions and the Indians claimed a large share
of Beechey's attention, as in the case of earlier visitors, and he was not blind to either the faults or ex-
cellences of the system or of the friars who had it in
charge.[21] Respecting the result of Echeandía's experiment at partial emancipation of neophytes, this
author happens to be wellnigh the only authority;
and he also translates an interesting diary of an expedition against the gentiles under Alférez Sanchez,
as noted in the preceding chapter. He gives consid-

[20] See note 13 of this chapter.
[21] 'Though the system they pursue is not calculated to raise the colony to
any great prosperity, yet the neglect of the missions would not long precede
the ruin of the presidios and of the whole of the district.' Vol. ii. p. 15.
' As to the various methods employed for the purpose of bringing proselytes
to the missions, there are several reports, of which some were not very cred-
itable to the institution; nevertheless, on the whole, I am of opinion that the
priests are innocent, from a conviction that they are ignorant of the means
employed by those who are under them. Whatever may be the system,...
the change according to our ideas of happiness would seem advantageous to
them, as they lead a far better life in the missions than in their forests.' p. 17.
' The produce of the land and of the labor of the Indians is appropriated
to the support of the mission, and the overplus to amass a fund which is
entirely at the disposal of the padres. In some of the establishments this
must be very large, although the padres will not admit it, and always plead
poverty. The government has lately demanded a part of this profit, but the
priests, who, it is said, think the Indians are more entitled to it than the
government, make small donations to them, and thus evade the tax by taking care there shall be no overplus.' p. 19–20.   'Though there may be occasional acts of tyranny, yet the general character of the padres is kind and
benevolent, and in some missions the converts are so much attached to them
that I have heard them declare they would go with them if they were
obliged to quit the country. It is greatly to be regretted that, with the
influence these men have over their pupils, and the regard those pupils seem
to have for their masters, the priests do not interest themselves a little more
in the education of their converts.' 'The Indians are, in general, well clothed
and fed.' p. 21–2.   'Nothing could exceed the kindness and consideration of
these excellent men to their guests and to travellers;' but they 'were very
bigoted men, and invariably introduced the subject of religion.' p. 33–4.

erable attention to commerce, presenting a clear statement on this subject.[22]   Like others, the English
navigator was enthusiastic in praise of California's climate and other natural advantages; but like others,
he wondered at and deplored the prevalent lack of
enterprise on the part of Mexican government and
Californian people, predicting an inevitable change of
owners should no change of policy occur.[23]   His geo-

[22] I may quote at some length on this topic, as being the subject proper of
this chapter. 'The trade consists in the exportation of hides, tallow, man-
teca, horses to the Sandwich Islands, grain for the Russian establishments,
and in the disposal of provisions to whale-ships,...and perhaps a few furs
and dollars are sent to China.   The importations are dry goods, furniture,
wearing apparel, agricultural implements, deal boards, and salt; and silks
and fireworks from China for the decoration of churches and celebration of
saints' days.   In 1827 almost all these articles bore high prices: the former in consequence of the increased demand; and the latter partly from the
necessity of meeting the expenses of the purchase of a return cargo, and
partly on account of the navigation.'   Great complaint of high prices, 'not
considering that the fault was in great measure their own, and that they were
purchasing some articles brought several thousand miles, when they might
have procured them in their own country with moderate labor only,' for example, salt and deal boards and carts.   'With similar disregard for their
interests, they were purchasing sea-otter skins at $20 apiece, whilst the
animals were swimming about unmolested in their own harbors; and this
from the Russians, who are intruders on their coast, and are depriving them
of a lucrative trade.   With this want of commercial enterprise, they are not
much entitled to commiseration.   With more justice might they have complained of the navigation laws, which, though no doubt beneficial to inhabitants on the eastern coast of Mexico, where there are vessels to conduct the
coasting trade, are extremely disadvantageous to the Californians, who having no vessels are often obliged to pay the duties on goods introduced in foreign bottoms.'   17% higher than on Mexican vessels.   Not only this, 'but
as a foreign vessel cannot break stowage without landing the whole of her
cargo, they must in addition incur the expenses attending that which will
in general fall upon a few goods only.   The imprudent nature of these laws
as regards California appears to have been considered by the authorities, as
they overlook the introduction of goods into the towns by indirect channels,
except in cases of a gross and palpable nature.   In this manner several
American vessels have contrived to dispose of their cargoes, and the inhabitants have been supplied with goods of which they were much in need.' p.
68–70.

[23] 'Possessing all these advantages, an industrious population alone seems
requisite to withdraw it from the obscurity in which it has so long slept
under the indolence of the people and the jealous policy of the Spanish government.   Indeed, it struck us as lamentable to see such an extent of habit-
able country lying almost desolate and useless to mankind, whilst other nations are groaning under the burden of their population.   It is evident from
the natural course of events, and from the rapidity with which observation
has recently been extended to the hitherto most obscure parts of the globe,
that this indifference cannot continue; for either it must disappear under the
present authorities, or the country will fall into other hands, as from its situation with regard to other powers upon the new continent, and to the commerce of the Pacific, it is of too much importance to be permitted to remain
longer in its present neglected state.   Already have the Russians encroached

graphical information is usually accurate and valuable; but a curious item is the idea, drawn from the Californians, that the great rivers running into San Francisco bay were three in number—the Jesus María, passing at the back of Bodega in a southerly course from beyond Cape Mendocino; the Sacramento, trending to the south-west, and said to rise in the Rocky Mountains near the source of the Columbia; and the San Joachin, stretching from the southward through the country of the Bolbones.

The vessels of 1827 numbered thirty-three, of which two or three arrivals depend on doubtful records. Fourteen were the same that had visited California the preceding year, some having wintered on the coast. Only four were whalers. The trading fleet proper was of about twenty craft. Of the whole number twelve were American, ten English, three Mexican, three Russian, two each French and Hawaiian, and one perhaps German.[24] Revenue receipts from fragmentary records, which are virtually no records at all, foot up about $14,000 for the year.[25] As the reader will remember, it was in this year that Herrera resigned, and the revenue branches were, if possible, in worse confusion than ever.

An attempt was made to remove some of the restrictions on the importation of foreign goods, deemed disadvantageous to Californian interests. The reforms desired were the free entry of foreign vessels into all the ports and embarcaderos, the subdivision

upon the territory by possessing themselves of the Farallones and some islands of Santa Bárbara; and their new settlement at Rossi is so near upon the boundary (no Englishman could admit it to be within California—author) as to be the cause of much jealous feeling—not without reason, it would appear.' p. 66-7.

[24] See list at end of this chapter. Vessels of 1827: *Andes* (?), *Baikal*, *Blossom*, *Cadboro*, *Carimacer* (?), *Comète*, *Courier*, *Favorite*, *Franklin*, *Fulham*, *Golovnin*, *Harbinger*, *Héros*, *Huascar*, *Isabella*, *Magdalena*, *María Ester*, *Massachusetts*, *Oliphant* (?), *Olive Branch*, *Okhotsk*, *Orion*, *Paraiso*, *Sachem*, *Solitude*, *Spy*, *Tamaahmaah*, *Tenieya*, *Thomas Nowlan*, *Tomasa*, *Washington*, *Waverly*, *Young Tartar*.

[25] Net revenue at S. F., $3,304. *Dept. St. Pap.*, *Ben. Mil.*, lxii. 8-11. See also figures in the list of vessels at end of this chapter.

of cargoes for convenience of sale and transportation,
and the reduction of duties to at most the original
twenty-five per cent by the removal of the internacion
and avería taxes, and even the tonnage dues. The
two first had already been accomplished practically,
since the authorities admitted that they had rarely
refused permission to engage in coast trade; and as
to the third, both governor and comisario were opposed to the high rates, and had been as careless as
they dared, and their subordinates even less careful.
The diputacion considered the matter in June and
July, and by the decision of that body and the resulting decrees, coast trade was legalized, subject to
the decision of the supreme government. The removal of the duties was recommended, the internacion
tax was restricted to goods carried inland more than
four leagues, while the missions were allowed to give
bonds for the tax pending the result in Mexico.[26]

[26] Jan. 22, and Aug. 6, 1827, Herrera regulates the details of trade between
private persons and foreign vessels, to prevent abuses of the illegal privileges
allowed of coast trade and division of cargoes. *Dept. St. Pap., Ben. Com. and
Treas.*, MS., i. 82–6. June 23d, July 24th, sessions of the diputacion. Bandini took a leading part in urging the reforms. *Leg. Rec.*, MS., i. 52–4, 64–
72. July 20th, gov. announces that foreign vessels may touch at Sta Cruz,
S. Luis, Purísima, Refugio, and S. Juan, by applying to the nearest comandante with a statement from the missionary that such visit is necessary. *Dept.
Rec.*, MS., v. 68; *Dept. St. Pap.*, MS., i. 144. Aug. 10th, com. of Sta Bárbara on same subject. *Dept. St. Pap., Ben. Mil.*, MS., lvii. 12–13. Aug. 7th,
Herrera announces the change respecting the internacion duty. *Dept. St. Pap.,
Ben. Com. and Treas.*, MS., i. 86–7. Aug. 22d, gov. to sup. govt, announcing the act of the dip.; also asking for one or two gunboats and
for a naval station at S. Francisco. *Dept. Rec.*, MS., v. 128–9. June 1st,
min. of war to E., announcing the president's permission for foreign vessels
to touch at the way-ports already named in this note and in the text. *Dept.
Rec.*, MS., vi. 176. Vallejo, *Esposicion*, 6, cites in 1837 a law of Nov. 16, 1827,
forbidding *comercio de escala* by foreign vessels. The tariff law of Nov. 16th,
Mexico, Arancel Gen., 1827, p. 5, allowed foreign goods to be introduced into
Cal. for three fifths the duties required elsewhere except in Yucatan; but if
reëxported, the other two fifths must be paid. Miscellaneous items on commerce for 1827: Rates of duties—import, 25% on value; avería, 2½% on do.;
internacion, 15% on do.; tonnage, $2.50 per ton (Mexican measurement); an-
chorage, $10 per vessel; collectors' compensation, 3%. *Dept. St. Pap., Ben.
Mil.*, MS., lxii. 5–10. Jan., national products free from export duty, except gold and silver. *Dept. St. Pap., Ben. Com. and Treas.*, MS., i. 71.
Jan. 31st, gov. says Sandwich-Island traders may touch at ports; but not
war-vessels, until it be proved that they sail under a proper flag and due
authority. *Dept. Rec.*, MS., v. 19. July 20th, Capt. Guerra says the
Mexicans in Cal. will probably abandon trade to the foreigners, who speculate in everything, and with whom they cannot compete. *Doc. Hist. Cal.*,

Meanwhile there came an order from Mexico, dated before the action of the diputacion, and permitting foreign vessels to touch at Santa Cruz, San Luis Obispo, Purísima, Refugio, and San Juan Capistrano. In its deliberations on revenue matters, the diputacion gave special attention to the duties on liquors, perfecting an elaborate reglamento, which was duly published by the governor. The proceeds of the liquor trade were devoted to the public schools.[27] Another prominent commercial topic, since hides and tallow were the chief articles of export, was that of live-stock regulations, to which the diputacion also directed its wisdom. The result was a series of twenty articles, in which the branding and slaughter of cattle, with other kindred points, were somewhat minutely regulated.[28]

The prosperity of 1826 in the business of Hartnell & Co. was followed by trouble and financial embarrassment in 1827–9. The exact nature of the reverses it is difficult to learn from the fragmentary correspondence; but I judge that John Begg & Co. failed, involving McCulloch, Hartnell & Co. to such an extent that the firm was obliged to delay its payments and to close the copartnership. Hartnell, however, paid all debts in California, and continued his business both for himself, with the aid of Captain Guerra, and as agent for foreign houses who sent vessels to the

MS., iv. 84. Grain raised only for home consumption, also wool; horse-hair somewhat sought by the French; padres unwilling to take money; exports amount to what 4 vessels of 300 tons can carry; 47% profit may be counted on; the export of tallow averages 1 arroba for each hide. *Duhaut-Cilly, Viaggio*, i. 232–3, 253; ii. 145–7, 150.

[27] *Reglamento de Contribuciones sobre Licores, 1827*, MS., approved at sessions of June 26th, 28th, 30th, July 2d, 7th. Gov.'s decree of July 12th, in *Dept. St. Pap., S. José*, MS., iv. 40–7. The tax was $5 per barrel of 160 quarts for brandy and $2.50 for wine in Monterey and S. Francisco jurisdictions; in the south $10 and $5 respectively, payable by all buyers and by the producer who might retail the liquor. This for native liquors. Foreign brandy and wine paid $20 and $10 per barrel. The regulations for the collection of this tax are somewhat complicated, and need not be given. Aug. 6th, Herrera announces that by superior orders a duty of 80% on foreign liquors and 70% on wines is to be exacted, besides the 15% of internacion. *Dept. St. Pap., Ben. Com. and Treas.*, MS., i. 87–8.

[28] *Reglamento sobre Ganados, aprobado por la Diputacion, 1827*, MS.

coast. The correspondence would indicate that he
went on loading vessels and trading with the padres
much as before. David Spence also went into business for himself. In connection with the financial
troubles, Hartnell made a trip to Lima, sailing at the
end of 1827, probably in the *Huascar*, and returning
in that vessel in July of the following year.[29]

Captain Cunningham of the *Courier*, in conjunction
probably with the masters of other American vessels,
thought to improve the facilities for coast trade by
erecting certain buildings and establishing a kind of
trading station on Santa Catalina Island. Cunningham was ordered by Echeandía to remove the buildings and promised to do so.[30]

Auguste Duhaut-Cilly, commanding the French
ship *Le Héros*, 362 tons, 32 men, and 12 guns, sailed
from Havre in April 1826, sent out by Lafitte & Co.
on a trading voyage round the world. He was accompanied by Dr Paolo Emilio Botta, afterward famous
as an archæologist and writer. This young scientist's
notes on the inhabitants of the Sandwich Islands and

[29] Mrs Hartnell, *Narrativa*, MS., 2–3, says that the rivalry of Cooper,
favored by the government, and of Spence soon obliged the firm of McC., H.
& Co. to liquidate. Alvarado, *Hist. Cal.*, MS., iv. 145, says that H. paid all the
debts of Begg & Co. in Cal. April, McCulloch advises H. to propose to Begg
& Co. a reform in the Cal. establishment, including a small vessel on the
coast under Mexican flag. Salting hides won't pay, nor will soap and candles.
Vallejo, Doc., MS., xxix. 125. July 1st, P. Viader to H. Speaks of Begg's failure, which he has expected for some time. *Id.*, 135. Fears for success of hide
business. *Id.*, 141. Aug. 6th, Begg & Co. say the prospect is bad. Mendoza (?) tallow better and cheaper than that of Cal. *Id.*, 148. Nov. 6th, P.
Sarría speaks of H.'s voyage, and sends letters of recommendation to friends
in Lima. *Id.*, 167. Jan. 5, 1828, Spence at Monterey to H. at Lima. *Id.*, 190.
May 1st, circular of Begg, Macala, and Hartnell to the padres of California,
announcing the dissolution of the firm of McC., H. & Co., and that H. will settle
all accounts and continue the business for himself. Warm thanks are rendered
for past courtesies, and H. is strongly recommended by the former associates.
Id., 224. July 14th, H. arrived by the *Huascar*. *Dept. Rec.*, MS., vi. 80.
July 16th, Cunningham speaks of a protested bill. *Vallejo, Doc.*, MS., xix. 257.
McCulloch continues his letters to H. Aug. 1st, gov. regrets Begg's want of
confidence in Mexican commerce. *Id.*, 265. Aug. 28th, balance sheet of $5,097
between Begg & Co. and H. *Id.*, 272. More accounts in October. *Id.*, 282.
Oct. 18th, certificate that H. furnished $14,397 in tallow, as he agreed in Lima.
Id., 283. The correspondence of 1829 is unimportant, but shows that H. still
owed considerable money in Lima, and that his creditors were pressing. *Id.*,
passim.

[30] *Dept. Rec.*, MS., v. 19; *Dept. St. Pap.*, MS., ii. 22.

California were added to an Italian translation of the voyager's narrative, made by his father, Carlo Botta, also famous as a poet and historian. Lieutenant Edmond Le Netrel also wrote a journal, a large part of which has been published.[31]

On January 27, 1827, the *Héros*, coming from Mazatlan, anchored at Yerba Buena. It yet lacked several months of the proper time for obtaining hides and tallow, but the time could be employed in arranging bargains with the padres; and while the captain remained at the port his supercargo, 'il Signor R——,' visited the missions of the district with samples of goods to be sold. After a month's stay, marked by adventures with grizzly bears and an earthquake, the traders sailed south March 7th, carrying three Indian prisoners condemned to confinement at San Diego. Touching at Santa Cruz, Monterey, Santa Bárbara, and San Pedro, they reached San Diego April 18th. Here the supercargo was left, while Duhaut-Cilly made a trip to Mazatlan and back before June 11th. 'Il Signor R——' proceeded northward to San Francisco by land, while the captain, having experienced an earthquake, and made a tour to San Luis Rey, anchored at Santa Bárbara on the 29th, and at San Francisco on July 17th. During this visit the Frenchman made excursions to Santa Clara, San José, and San Francisco Solano. In August they

[31] *Duhaut-Cilly, Voyage autour du monde, principalement á la Californie et aux Isles Sandwich pendant les années 1826, 1827, 1828, et 1829. Par A. Duhaut-Cilly.* Paris, 1835. 8vo. 428 p. plate. Of this original French edition I have only a fragment in my collection, and my references are therefore to the following: *Duhaut-Cilly, Viaggio intorno al Globo, principalmente alla California ed alle isole Sandwich, negli anni 1826, 1827, 1828, e 1829, di A. Duhaut-Cilly, capitano di lungo corso, cav. della Legion d'Onore, ecc. Con l'aggiunta delle osservazioni sugli abitanti di quei paesi di Paolo Emilio Botta. Traduzione dal francese nell' italiano de Carlo Botta.* Turin, 1841. 8vo. 2 vol. xvi. 296 p. 1 l.; 392 p. plates. The portion added to this translation, *Botta, Osservazioni sugli abitanti delle isole Sandwich e della California de Paolo Emilio Botta. Fatte nel suo viaggio intorno al globo col Capitano Duhaut-Cilly,* occupies p. 339–92 of vol. ii.; that part relating to Cal. is found on p. 367–78. These notes had originally appeared as *Botta, Observations sur les habitans de la Californie,* in *Nouv. Annales des Voyages,* lii. 156–66. *Le Netrel, Voyage autour du Monde,* etc. *Extrait du journal de M. Edmond Le Netrel, Lieutenant à bord de ce vaisseau* (*Le Héros*), in *Nouvelles Annales des Voyages,* xlv. 129–82.

sailed for Santa Cruz and Monterey. Here Duhaut-
Cilly found the French ship *Comète*, which had come
over from the Islands, as he claims, at the instigation
of the mysterious and treacherous Signor R——, and
to spoil the trade of the *Héros*, which venture was a
failure, as the author is delighted to observe. In
September they were at Santa Bárbara, having
anchored on the way at El Cojo to receive tallow
from Purísima. From San Pedro, about the 22d,
the captain, with Botta and a guide, visited Los
Angeles and San Gabriel, to feel another earthquake.
October 20th, after having broken his collar-bone by
a fall from a California *bronco*, Duhaut-Cilly sailed
again for Callao, again leaving il Signor R—— to continue his operations on board the *Waverly*. He came
back to Monterey May 3, 1828, made a visit to Bodega and Ross in June, was at Santa Bárbara and
San Pedro before the end of that month, revisited Los
Angeles and San Gabriel, and reached San Diego on
the 3d of July. Finally the *Héros* sailed August 27th
for the Islands. The Signor R—— had in the mean
time run away to Mexico.

From the preceding outline of the French trader's
movements, it is seen that his opportunities for observation were more extensive than those of any foreign visitor who had preceded him. No other navigator had visited so many of the Californian establishments. His narrative fills about three hundred
pages devoted to California, and is one of the most
interesting ever written on the subject. Duhaut-Cilly
was an educated man, a close observer, and a good
writer. Few things respecting the country or its
people or its institutions escaped his notice. His
relations with the Californians, and especially the
friars, were always friendly, and he has nothing but
kind words for all. The treachery of his supercargo
caused his commercial venture to be less profitable
than the prospects had seemed to warrant.[32]   I have

[32] Morineau, *Notice sur la Californie*, 151–2, says that both the *Héros* and

had, and shall have, occasion to cite this author frequently on local and other topics, and it is with regret that I leave the book here without long quotations.[33]

I find notice of thirty-six vessels on the coast in the year 1828, sixteen of which were included in the fleet of the preceding year, and several others had visited California before. Six were whalers.[34] A few meagre items of revenue amount to less than $6,000 at San Francisco and $34,000 at San Diego. In January Echeandía issued an order closing the way-ports, or embarcaderos, except San Pedro, to foreign vessels.[35] This was in accordance with orders from Mexico, and was enforced so far as possible. In July San Pedro was also closed by an order which declared that all coasting trade must be done in Mexican bottoms, that Monterey and Loreto were the only ports open to foreign trade, but that in cases of necessity trade might be permitted at the other presidial ports.[36] In September San Francisco and Santa Bárbara were closed provisionally; though ves-

the *Comète* brought cargoes, which, besides being too large, were ill-assorted and did not sell well.

[33] Mention of the *Héros* in *Dept. Rec.*, MS., vi. 32; *Dept. St. Pap.*, *Ben. Mil.*, MS., lxiii. 2; *Id.*, *Ben. Pref. y Juzg.*, MS., i. 2. Taylor, in *Brown's L. Cal.*, 43, mentions this voyage.

[34] See list at end of this chapter. Vessels of 1828: the *Andes*, *Arab* (under a Russian name), *Baikal*, *Becket* (?), *Brillante* (?), *Clio*, *Courier*, *Emily*, *Fenix*, *Franklin*, *Fulham*, *Funchal*, *General Sucre*, *Griffon*, *Guibale* (?), *Harbinger*, *Héros*, *Huascar*, *Karimoko*, *Kiahkta*, *Laperin* (?), *Magdalena*, *María Ester*, *Minerva*, *Okhotsk*, *Pocahontas*, *Rascow*, *Solitude*, *Telemachus*, *Thomas Nowlan*, *Times*, *Verale* (?), *Vulture*, *Washington*, *Waverly*, *Wilmantic*. I have fragments of the *Waverly's* original log for 1828-9. The author describes, p. 10, a celebration of St Nicholas day on the Russian vessels at Monterey Dec. 17th; also a fandango on shore. Peirce's *Rough Sketch*, MS., and *Memorandum*, MS., describe the *Griffon's* voyage as remembered by the author, who was on the vessel. Six vessels at S. F. in January are not named, but described by Morineau as a Russian frigate; a Russian brig of 200 tons loaded with grain for Sitka; an English schooner from New Albion; an American brig of 150 tons from Manila; a Hawaiian brig of 140 tons manned by kanakas; and a Mexican schooner of 100 tons from Sandwich Islands. *El Brillante* was at S. Diego from S. Blas, according to this author.

[35] Jan. 29, 1828, *St. Pap.*, *Sac.*, MS., x. 104. March 3d, Echeandía to com. gen. Has been obliged to keep open the four presidial ports and S. Pedro. *Dept. Rec.*, MS., vi. 7.

[36] July 8, 1828, gov.'s order. *Dept. Rec.*, MS., vi. 63, 77; *Dept. St. Pap.*, *S. José*, MS., iv. 53-4.

sels after discharging their cargoes at Monterey or
San Diego might visit the other ports to take away
produce, except money and breeding cattle, returning
to settle accounts.[37] I find no evidence, however, that
this order was obeyed this year. In the correspondence on revenue the only item worth notice was the
reduction of the internacion tax to ten per cent, presumably in response to the petition of 1827.[33] The
Russians were permitted to take otter on a small scale
for joint account of the company and the government. American vessels sought hides chiefly; those
from Mexico and Peru gave more attention to tallow,
while the Hawaiian buyers took away by preference
skins and horses.[39]

The traders were not pleased at the restrictions
which the Californian authorities could not well help
enforcing to a certain extent; and they redoubled
their efforts at smuggling. In most cases they were
successful, not much to the displeasure of any one in
California, and without leaving any trace of their
movements in the records; but occasionally by their
insolent disregard of appearances even, they came into
conflict with Echeandía. Two such instances in particular are recorded, that of the *Franklin* and that of

[37] Sept. 30, 1828, gov.'s order in *Dept. Rec.*, MS., vi. 103–3; *Dept. St. Pap.*,
S. José, MS., iv. 72–3. Nov. 26th, gov. permits foreign vessels, after dis-
charging their inward cargoes, to carry lumber from Monterey to Sta Bárbara.
Dept. Rec., MS., vi. 145. Nov. 30th, E. to min. of war, asking that S. Diego
be opened formally and fully to foreign commerce. *Id.*, vi. 52; *Dept. St. Pap.*,
MS., iii. 208.

[33] March 29, 1828, com. gen. sends decree of congress reducing the duty to
8% (on the goods for which bonds had been given?) if paid within 15 days
after publication of this order. *Dept. St. Pap., Ben. Com. and Treas.*, MS., i.
95. But in August Echeandía says the tax is 10%. *Dept. Rec.*, MS., vi. 86.
Feb. 1st, woollen and silk of Mexican manufacture free of duties. *Dept. St.
Pap., Mont.*, MS., i. 20. Goods still received as duties. *Vallejo, Doc.*, MS.,
xvii. 9, et passim. Consignees must declare tonnage of vessels on presenting
manifest of cargo. *Dept. St. Pap., Ben. Com. and Treas.*, MS., i. 93. June
20th, revenue from maritime duties belongs to the nation; taxes on retail
trade to the municipality. *Dept. Rec.*, MS., vi. 58. Sept. 30th, tonnage
$2.12½ per ton. *Id.*, vi. 103. Avería duties from July 1828 to June 1829,
$256. *Mexico, Mem. Hacienda*, 1829, doc. 29. Duties were computed by
Martinez at S. Francisco, by taking three fifths of the value, and the tonnage
was reckoned at $2.12½ per ton, less two fifths, a deduction for which he was
blamed by the governor. *Vallejo, Doc.*, MS., i. 157, 162.

[39] *Spence's Hist. Notes*, MS., 13.

the *Karimoko*. Captain John Bradshaw of the former
had been granted all possible privileges, his supercargo,
Rufus Perkins, being permitted to travel by land
from mission to mission;[40] but finally in July, at San
Diego, he was ordered to deposit his cargo in the
warehouse as security for duties, and pending the investigation of charges. He was accused of notorious
smuggling on the Lower Californian coast;[41] of having
illegally transferred the cargo of another vessel to his
own; of having touched at Santa Catalina in defiance
of special orders; of having refused to show his invoices or make a declaration; and of insolence to the
governor. Bradshaw and Perkins, being on shore,
promised obedience to the order; but asked permission
to go on board to make the necessary preparations,
and when there refused to leave the vessel, laughed
in the face of the Californians sent to convey and
enforce—so far as possible by threats—Echeandía's
order, and on July 11th changed anchorage to a point
near the entrance of the harbor. The governor circulated a warning to the padres and others to deliver no
goods to the *Franklin* should she escape,[42] as seemed
likely to happen, though Bradshaw still promised submission to legal proceedings. Meanwhile Echeandía
prepared to put a guard on the vessel, and applied to
Duhaut-Cilly for a boat. The French captain could
not refuse, but warned Bradshaw and interposed delays. On the morning of the 16th the *Franklin* cut
her cable and ran out of the port, the officers and
crew shouting their derision of the Mexican flag as
they passed the fort. Forty cannon-balls were sent
after the flying craft, with no apparent effect; but

[40] May 7, 1828. *Dept. Rec.*, MS., vi. 200.
[41] A warning had come from Loreto in May. *Dept. Rec.*, MS., vi. 203. Duhaut-Cilly, *Viaggio*, ii. 194–200, who was at S. Diego at this time, denounces
one Wm Simpson, a man whom Bradshaw had befriended, for having treacherously exposed the Yankee captain's crimes. He says there was some trouble
about a deposit of cargo to secure duties, but that it would have been amica-
bly arranged but for Simpson's act.
[42] July 12, 1828, gov. to comandantes, alcaldes, and padres. The *Franklin* is to be detained, if possible, should she dare to enter any port. *Dept. St.
Pap.*, MS., ii. 59–60.

Duhaut-Cilly met her a little later at the Islands, and
learned that two balls had entered the hull, two had
damaged the rigging, and that Bradshaw had been
wounded.[43]

The affair of the Hawaiian brig *Karimoko* occurred
also at San Diego late in the autumn.   John Lawlor, or Lawless, as it is often written, was master
of the vessel.   He it was who, after having employed
Domingo Carrillo to teach him Spanish, presented
himself to Echeandía to ask for a passport in the
following terms: "Buenos dias, Señor General; mi
quiero to voy to the missions y comprar cueros y
grease con goods; please mi dar permission.   Si quieres,
quieres; y si no, dejalo.   Adios, Señor General."[44]

[43] June 14th, 18th, July 9th, 11th, 12th, 13th, 14th, 16th, 23d, gov.'s communications on the subject. *Dept. Rec.*, MS., vi. 28, 32, 56, 61, 63–8, 72–3. *Duhaut-Cilly, Viaggio*, ii. 194–200. Further records dated in December respecting
the credits, etc., left behind by Bradshaw. *Dept. Rec.*, MS., vi. 53, 150–1, 162.
In 1841 a claim for damages was pending before the mixed commission in Washington. *Vallejo, Doc.*, MS., x. 131. On this affair of the *Franklin*, as in several
other matters, the testimony of James O. Pattie, who was at S. Diego at the time,
has to be noticed separately, since his statements are of such a peculiar character that they can neither be omitted nor used with other evidence in building up my narrative. (See next chapter for notice of Pattie's book.) Bradshaw
and Perkins were at S. Diego in March and April, and tried to aid Pattie,
partly as a countryman, and partly in the hope to get some furs which the
trappers had left on the Colorado. Bradshaw employed Pattie as a translator,
securing his occasional release for that purpose. In April or May he made a
trip in his vessel to Monterey. June 27th, his vessel was seized for smuggling. In the following examination of officers and crew Pattie served as interpreter ('Dice el Americano James Ohio Pettis, que sirvió de intérprete
á dicho capitan, dice que supo tenia este el propósito de largarse furtivamente
y de hacer fuego sobre la guarnicion si impedia su salida.' *Dept. Rec.*, MS.,
vi. 73), and was requested by Capt. B. 'to make the testimonies of his crew
as nearly correspond and substantiate each other as possible; for some of them
were angry with him, and would strive to give testimony calculated to condemn him. I assured him I would do anything to serve him that I could in
honor'! The taking of depositions was completed July 28th (Bradshaw had
really sailed on July 16th). Capt. B. told Pattie of his intention to run out
if the vessel were condemned, and offered him a passage on the *Franklin*. In
September Bradshaw was ordered to land his cargo, but refused. Pattie was
again employed as interpreter; and warned the captain and supercargo on
Sept. 11th of a plan he had overheard to arrest them, thus enabling them to
escape on board. A few days later he slipped anchor and ran out of the port
under a heavy shower of cannon-balls from the fort. 'When he came opposite it he hove to and gave them a broadside in return, which frightened the
poor engineers away from their guns. His escape was made without suffering
any serious injury. Their (three?) shots entered the hull of the vessel, and the
sails were considerably cut up by the grape.' *Pattie's Narr.*, 179, 185, 189–
201.

[44] *Vallejo, Hist. Cal.*, MS., ii. 60–1. It is said to have been Lawlor's
practice to hide about seven eighths of his cargo at some out-of-the-way spot on

On this occasion he had anchored at San Pedro and departed without paying $1,000 of duties. He had, in spite of repeated warnings, touched at Santa Catalina Island, and had even deposited goods there, besides breeding animals, the exportation of which was *contra bando.* The sails of the *Karimoko* were seized, and then Lawlor was ordered to go with part of his crew to bring over the island goods and live-stock, which were to secure the payment of the duties in arrears. He made all manner of excuses and pleas, including the suggestion that he could not make the trip without sails, and that his men on the island would starve if not relieved soon. The *María Ester* was employed to carry Santiago Argüello as investigating officer to Santa Catalina, and perhaps to bring over the effects; at any rate, Lawlor got a document in December certifying that all his duties had been paid; but in January of the next year he was again warned to quit the island of Santa Catalina within twenty-four hours.[45]

There were twenty-three vessels on the Californian coast in 1829, besides four doubtful English craft in Spence's list, eleven belonging to the fleet of 1828, only six appearing for the first time in these waters, and one being built in California.[46] Records of revenue

the coast or islands, and come to port with one eighth to get permission to trade.

[45] Oct. 28, Nov. 5, 1828, gov. to Argüello. *Dept. Rec.*, MS., vi. 121–2, 124. Nov. 6th. Id. to Virmond, to charter the *María Ester. Id.*, 129. Dec. 1st, Id. to Lawlor. *Id.*, 147. Dec. 13th (3d ?), Id. to Id., ordering him to pay duties and break up the island establishment. *Id.*, xix. 157. Dec. 5th, Id. to Id., arguing the case, with substance of Lawlor's communication. It seems that Lawlor pretended not to have been captain at the time of the S. Pedro transaction. *Id.*, vi. 149. Dec. 9th, receipt in full for duties. *Id.*, 154. Jan. 8th, 1829, gov. warns Lawlor to quit the coast. *Id.*, vii. 54.

[46] See list at end of this chapter. The vessels of 1829 were the *Alvins* (?), *American* (?), *Andes, Ann* (?), *Baikal, Brookline, Dhaulle, Franklin, Funchal, Indian* (?), *James Coleman* (?), *Jóven Angustias, Kiahkta, María Ester, Okhotsk, Planet, Rosalía, Sta Bárbara, Susana* (?), *Tamaahmaah, Thomas Nowlan, Trident, Volunteer, Vulture, Warren, Washington, Waverly, Wilmington;* also a Hawaiian schooner not named, Wm Aralon master, at S. Pedro in September. According to the *Honolulu Friend*, ii. 49–50, 4 vessels had arrived from Cal. in 1827, 5 in 1828, but none in 1829; 2 in 1830.

receipts are still more meagre than for preceding years.[47]   There was little or no change in commercial regulations; but the governor showed a disposition to enforce the orders of 1828 making Monterey and— provisionally—San Diego the only ports free to foreign vessels; and allowing such vessels to trade at the other ports only by special license and under strict precautions; that is, in a few instances a trader might carry goods duly examined and listed at Monterey or San Diego to other ports for sale by paying the expense of a guard to remain on board and watch each transaction.[48]   Something very like a custom-house was therefore maintained at Monterey and San Diego, each under a comisario subalterno, Osio and later Jimeno Casarin at the capital, and Juan Bandini in the south.[49]   A treaty between Mexico and England, by which English and Mexican vessels were put upon terms of equality in respect of duties, was forwarded from San Blas in July; but I find no evidence that the document had any effect in California.[50]

[47] Custom-house records seem to make the total receipts at S. Diego $117,267 for the year. *Dept. St. Pap., Ben. Cust.-H.*, MS., i. passim.   Total revenue at S. Francisco to May 31st, $1,177; at San Diego, $2,000.   In December for S. F., $1,264; for S. Diego in August, $826. *Dept. St. Pap., Ben. Mil.*, lxix. 27-9.   Gale states in a letter to Cooper, of May 10th, that the duties on the *Brookline's* cargo were $31,000, of which $26,000 have been paid. *Vallejo, Doc.*, xxix. 354.

[48] Gov.'s instructions of various dates. *Dept. Rec.*, MS., vii. 14, 81, 100-1, 116; *Dept. St. Pap.*, MS., ii. 94-5.   July 29th, min. of hacienda on the details of clearing national vessels for the coasting trade. *Vallejo, Doc. Hist. Cal.*, MS., i. 180.

[49] *St. Pap., Sac.*, MS., xix. 46-7.   Rather strangely, Gen. Vallejo, not only in his *Hist. Cal.*, but as early as 1837, *Exposicion*, MS., 5-6; *Doc. Hist. Cal.*, MS., iv. 299, represents the regular custom-house as having been established at S. Diego, and not at Monterey; but there is abundant evidence to the contrary in contemporary documents.   April 4, 1829, sup. govt allows state authorities to appoint customs visitadores at $4.50 per day on federal account. *Arrillaga, Recop.*, 1829, 56-7.   July 29th, Mex. custom-house regulations. *Id.*, 1833, 562-6.   Sept. 29th, regulations on ships' manifests, etc. *Id.*, 1829, 245-9.   Sept. 30th, decree ordering the establishment of a maritime custom-house in Alta California, under a visitador, subject to the com. gen. de Occidente.   The president has appointed Rafael Gonzalez administrator; Jimeno Casarin as contador; Francisco Pacheco, comandante of the guard; and Mauricio Gonzalez, guarda, at salaries of $1,000, $800, and $450. *Id.*, 1829, 249-51; *Doblan* and *Lozano, Leg. Mex.*, ii. 175-6; *Mexico, Mem. Hac.*, 1831, annex 9, p. 48.

[50] July 17, 1829, José María Lista, S. Blas, to captain of the port of Monterey. *Dept. St. Pap.*, MS., ii. 94.

Most notable among the vessels of the year was the *Brookline*, the successor of the *Sachem*, brought out by Wm A. Gale for Bryant, Sturgis, & Co., of Boston, and bringing probably the largest and best-assorted cargo of miscellaneous goods that had ever been offered to the Californians. Sailing from Boston in July 1828, she arrived at Monterey in February 1829. Alfred Robinson, who published a narrative of his voyage and life in California, in 1885 a resident of San Francisco, and probably the oldest American pioneer of California at this date living, came in the *Brookline* as supercargo's clerk. Gale was disappointed at the restrictions that had been imposed on foreign commerce since he left the coast, and which bade fair to interfere with the success of his trip; but his wares, and his prospective duties of $30,000, were a tempting bait; and without much difficulty he concluded an arrangement with Echeandía, by which he acquired practically all the privileges of old, was allowed to visit all the ports, and to pay his duties in goods.[51] José Estudillo was put on board with two or three soldiers, at Gale's expense, to watch proceedings, and prevent irregularities at Santa Bárbara, San Pedro, and San Francisco. It would perhaps be uncharitable to suggest, in the absence of proof, that these employees may have served Gale more faithfully than they did the revenue officers.[52] Gale was not satisfied with the manner in which he was treated, forming an unfavorable opinion of Echeandía's abilities and honesty, and suspecting favoritism toward his business

[51] *Robinson's Statement*, MS., 2-6, in which the writer gives many interesting items about the methods of trade in those days. *Robinson's Life in California*, 7-14, where the author speaks of the affair of the *Franklin* as having complicated matters by exasperating the authorities. Mention of arrival and movements of the *Brookline*, permission to trade, etc., in *Dept. Rec.*, MS., vii. 100, 116, 158, 191; *Vallejo, Doc.*, MS., i. 176; xxix. 316; *Dept. St. Pap., Ben. Pref. y Juzg.*, MS., i. 22; *Waverly, Voy.*, MS.

[52] April 28, 1829, Echeandía's instructions to Estudillo and the guard. All trading was to be done on board. *Estudillo, Doc.*, MS., i. 240; *Dept. Rec.*, vii. 138-9. July 13th, E. to com. of Monterey, on the privileges granted to Gale and the precautions taken. *Dept. St. Pap.*, MS., ii. 95-6. Sept. 12th, Gale allowed to cut wood. *Vallejo, Doc.*, MS., xxix. 412. Mar. 28th, Gale announces the plan to Cooper. *Id.*, 336.

rival, Hartnell; yet he seems to have done this year
and the next a larger business than any other trader.[53]

An interesting circumstance connected with the
Brookline's visit was the raising of an American flag
at San Diego, noticed in the newspapers on the authority of Captain James P. Arther.[54] He had visited
California before in the *Harbinger*, was mate of the
Brookline, and, like George W. Greene, one of his
companions, was still living in Massachusetts in 1872.
"Arthur and his little party were sent ashore at San
Diego to cure hides. They had a barn-like structure
of wood, provided by the ship's carpenter, which answered the purposes of storehouse, curing-shop, and
residence. The life was lonesome enough. Upon
the wide expanse of the Pacific they occasionally dis-
cerned a distant ship. Sometimes a vessel sailed
near the lower offing. It was thus that the idea of
preparing and raising a flag, for the purpose of attracting attention, occurred to them. The flag was
manufactured from some shirts, and Captain Arthur
writes, with the just accuracy of a historian, that Mr
Greene's calico shirt furnished the blue, while he furnished the red and white. 'It was completed and

[53] Gale's letters, chiefly to Cooper, in *Vallejo, Doc.*, MS., xxix. 325, 331,
336, 353, 354, 383, 400, 412, 434, 444. Feb. 22d, will begin to kill bullocks
to-morrow. Wishes Cooper to see Holmes and learn the particulars of the
Franklin affair. March 15th, comisario entrapped him into paying $800 ton-
nage. The governor's license to trade is 'opening the door just enough to
catch my fingers and jamb them.' March 28th, wishes his intention to
remain trading on the coast to be made public. May 8th, speaks of Hartnell's
protested bills. May 10th, is doing a good business. The whalers by smuggling injure legitimate trade. S. Diego is the 'centre of hell for strangers;'
suspects underhand work in his duties. Will bring no more American cottons
to Cal. Is not allowed to touch at Sta Catalina, and is drinking Monterey
water. Complains of Echeandía. July 19th, hopes Cooper will not lose his
head in the revolution. Sept. 12th, trade dull. Oct. 6th, will despatch the
Brookline sooner than he anticipated. Will pay $25 for large otter skins.
Oct. 31st, can undersell Hartnell, even if he can pay duties in his own way.
The *Franklin* business will do harm. Speaks of H.'s protested bills. Does
not believe H. honorable enough to pay, or that justice can be got under the
present imbecile government. His suspicions of underhand work in appraise-
ment are confirmed. Has raised the anchor left by the *Franklin*, but had to
give it up to prevent trouble. Hopes a new gov. will come soon.

[54] Capt. Arther in a note dated South Braintree, Mass., Sept. 24, 1872, in
which he regrets his inability to write his recollections of the affair, encloses
a clipping from the *Boston Advertiser* of Jan. 8th. See also mention in *S. F.
Call*, July 8, 1877.

raised on a Sunday, on the occasion of the arrival of the schooner *Washington*, Captain Thompson, of the Sandwich Islands, but sailing under the American flag.' So writes honest Captain Arthur. He further states that the same flag was afterwards frequently raised at Santa Bárbara, whenever in fact there was a vessel coming into port. These men raised our national ensign, not in bravado, nor for war and conquest, but as honest men, to show that they were American citizens and wanted company. And while the act cannot be regarded as in the light of a claim to sovereignty, it is still interesting as a fact, and as an unconscious indication of manifest destiny." [55]

Charles Lang, an American, with two sailors and two kanakas, was found in a boat near Todos Santos and arrested. He said he had come from the Sandwich Islands in the *Alabama*, with the intention of settling somewhere in California. The captives were brought to San Diego; and as Lang's effects, including a barrel-organ and two trunks of dry goods, seemed better adapted to smuggling than to colonization, they were confiscated,[56] and sold in June. The case went to Mexico, and afterward to the district judge at Guaymas, with results that are not apparent.

Among the vessels named as making up the fleet of 1829, there was one built at Santa Bárbara, and named the *Santa Bárbara*. This was a schooner of

[55] *Boston Advertiser.* It is well enough to regard this as the first raising of the stars and stripes, in the absence of definite evidence to the contrary; though such an event is by no means unlikely to have occurred before.

[56] Feb. 1829, investigation by Licut. Ibarra at Echeandía's order. *Dept. St. Pap., Ben. Mil.*, MS., lxix. 10–13, 25; liii. 90. The min. of war sent the case back on June 13th to be referred to the Guaymas judge. June 1st, Bandini ordered to sell the goods. Gov. says: 'After deducting the duties and 10 % due me as judge, you will allow me one half as *descubridor* and *promovedor*, and one half of the rest as *aprehensor;* the remainder you will take for having assisted at the taking'! *Dept. Rec.*, MS., vii. 169. Lang seems to have gone to Mazatlan on the *Washington. Vallejo, Doc.*, MS., xxix. 332. Lang was at S. Diego secretly on Dec. 24, 1828, where he met Pattie the trapper, and told him of his smuggling and otter-hunting purposes. He said he had a boat down the coast, and his brig had gone to the Galipagos for tortoise-shell. Pattie concluded to join Lang, but on going down to Todos Santos a few days later, found that he had been arrested. *Pattie's Narr.*, 208–10.

thirty-three tons, built for Cárlos Carrillo and William G. Dana for the coasting trade and for otter-catching. After certain delays and formalities, Echeandía granted the desired license for trade in August. José Carrillo was to be the captain, and the crew six men, more than half of whom must be Mexicans. Little is known respecting the career of this early—probably earliest—product of Californian ship-yards.[57]

Here I may introduce the romantic episode of Henry Fitch's marriage to a 'daughter of California,' a lady still living in 1880. The young American sailor had first arrived in 1826, and had soon surrendered to the charms of Doña Josefa, daughter of Joaquin Carrillo of San Diego, who in turn was won, as she states in a narrative written fifty years later,[58] by the handsome person and dashing manners of the captain. In 1827 he gave her a written promise of marriage. There were legal impediments on account of the fact that Fitch was a foreigner; but the young lady's parents approved the match, and a Dominican friar consented to perform the ceremony. It was hoped there would be no interference by either civil or ecclesiastical authorities, yet a degree of secrecy was observed.

[57] May 8, 1829, Echeandía orders the construction stopped until a proper permit is obtained. *Dept. Rec.*, MS., vii. 166. May 29th, gives the permit. Register must be obtained through the com. of Sta Bárbara. *Id.*, vii. 166. Aug. 12th, grants license for trading for one year. *Id.*, vii. 215–16. May 13th, E. had written to Mex. on the subject. *Id.*, vii. 10. Michael White, *California*, MS., p. 14–15, says that he built the schooner, with the aid of his cousin Henry Paine, for Capt. Guerra in 1830, out of materials saved from the wreck of the *Danube;* and that Thomas Robbins commanded her. After finishing this vessel, they built another of 99 tons for S. Gabriel, named the *Guadalupe*. A note in *Robbins' Diary*, MS., mentions the building of the *Santa Bárbara* in 1830, for Carrillo and Dana at La Goleta, or Hill's Rancho. The *Danube* appears not to have been wrecked until the spring of 1830, but this is not quite certain. In *Carrillo (J.), Doc.*, MS., 25, 27, 32, it is stated that 'José el Americano' (Chapman) was at work on a schooner for P. Sanchez of S. Gabriel in Sept. 1830; and that Guerra resolved to build another from the wreck of the *Danube*, but gave up the idea at the end of the year.

[58] *Fitch, Narracion de la Sra viuda del Capitan Enrique D. Fitch*, MS., dictated in 1875 by the lady at Healdsburg for my use. Some original papers relating to the marriage are annexed, including an authenticated copy of the marriage certificate.

As an essential preliminary, Padre Menendez baptized
the American, April 14, 1829, at the presidial chapel
of San Diego.[59] The friar promised to marry the
couple the next day; preparations were made, and a
few friends assembled late in the evening at the house
of the Carrillos.[60] At the last moment, however,
Domingo Carrillo, uncle of the bride, refused to serve
as witness; the friar's courage failed him, and the
ceremony could not proceed.[61] Neither the arguments and angry ravings of the Yankee *novio* nor the
tears and entreaties of the *novia* could overcome the
padre's fears and scruples; but he reminded Fitch that
there were other countries where the laws were less
stringent, and even offered to go in person and marry
him anywhere beyond the limits of California. "Why
don't you carry me off, Don Enrique?" naively suggested Doña Josefa. Captain Barry approved the
scheme, and so did Pio Pico, cousin of the lady.
The parents were not consulted. Fitch, though somewhat cautious on account of his business relations and
prospects on the coast, was not a man to require urging. Next night Pio Pico, mounted on his best steed,
took his cousin Josefa up on the saddle and carried
her swiftly to a spot on the bay-shore where a boat
was waiting; the lovers were soon re-united on board
the *Vulture*;[62] and before morning were far out on

[59] *Arch. Sta B.*, MS., xii. 345. Enrique Domingo Fitch, Domingo being
substituted for Delano at baptism, was a son of Beriah and Sarah Fitch of
New Bedford. Alf. Domingo Carrillo was godfather.

[60] Besides the immediate family, there were present Domingo Carrillo,
Capt. Richard Barry, Pio Pico, and Máximo Beristain. *Fitch, Causa Criminal*, MS., 345.

[61] This is the version given by Fitch and his wife in their testimony of the
next year. There is another version authorized by the lady herself, *Fitch,
Narracion*, MS., 4, and given by Vallejo, *Hist. Cal.*, MS., ii. 117–22; Vallejo
(J. J.), *Reminiscencias*, MS., 103–7; and Pico, *Hist. Cal.*, MS., 21–4, to the
effect that when all was ready and the padre had begun the service, Alf.
Domingo Carrillo, aid to the governor, appeared and forbade the marriage in
Echeandía's name. It is also more than hinted that Echeandía's motive was
jealousy, since the fair Josefa had not shown due appreciation of his own
attentions.

[62] Both the *Vulture* and the *María Ester*, the latter under command of
Fitch, were on the coast at the time and apparently at S. Diego, for it was
the *piloto* of the *María Ester* who took the lady in his boat. Why Fitch did
not sail in his own vessel does not appear; but Mrs Fitch says they went in

the Pacific. They were married on the evening of
July 3d at Valparaiso, by the curate Orrego, Capt.
Barry being one of the witnesses. Subsequently
they returned to Callao and Lima.

The elopement of Señorita Carrillo was naturally
much talked of in California; rumors were current
that she had been forcibly abducted from her home,
and the ecclesiastical authorities were greatly scan-
dalized. Next year, however, Fitch made his appearance in command of the *Leonor*, having on board also
his wife and infant son. He touched at San Diego in
July 1830, and thence came up to San Pedro. Here
he received a summons from Padre Sanchez at San
Gabriel, vicar and ecclesiastical judge of the territory,
to present himself for trial on most serious charges; but
he merely sent his marriage certificate by Virmond for
the vicar's inspection, and sailed up the coast for Santa
Bárbara and Monterey. Sanchez at once sent an order
to Monterey that Fitch be arrested and sent to San
Gabriel for trial, Doña Josefa being 'deposited' in some
respectable house at the capital. This order was executed by Echeandía at the end of August on the arrival of the *Leonor*.[63] The lady was sent to Captain
Cooper's house, and the husband was placed under
arrest. He claimed, however, to be unable to travel
by land. He protested against imprisonment as ruinous to his business, complained that the trial had
not been begun at San Diego, and asked that at least
he might be allowed to travel by sea. José Palomares, to whom as fiscal Padre Sanchez submitted this
request, gave a radical report against Fitch September 17th, declaring him entitled to no concessions, his
offences being most heinous, and his intention being
evidently to run away again. Yet Sanchez concluded
to permit the trip by sea, on Virmond becoming

the *Vulture*, and the part taken by Capt. Richard Barry in the matter confirms her statement.

[63] Aug. 29, 1830, E.'s order to Alf. Nieto to arrest Fitch. *Dept. Rec.*, MS.,
viii. 98.

bondsman for the culprit's presentment in due time; and on December 8th Fitch arrived at San Gabriel, and was made a prisoner in one of the mission rooms.

Meanwhile Mrs Fitch petitioned Echeandía at the end of October for release, and permission to go south by sea. The governor consented, and Doña Josefa sailed on the *Ayacucho* for Santa Bárbara, whence she proceeded on the *Pocahontas* to San Pedro, arriving at San Gabriel on November 24th, where she was committed to the care of Eulalia Perez of later centenarian fame. When her husband came, the house of Doña Eulalia was deemed too near his prison, and Josefa was transferred to the care of Mrs William A. Richardson. The fiscal pronounced Echeandía's act a gross infringement on ecclesiastical authority, declared him a culprit before God's tribunal, and urged that he be arrested and brought to trial. But Vicar Sanchez, though taking a similar view of Echeandía's conduct, thought it best, in view of the critical condition of affairs and the nearness of the time when Victoria was to take command, not to attempt the governor's arrest.

In December, Fitch and his wife were repeatedly interrogated before the ecclesiastical court, and Fiscal Palomares for a third time ventilated his legal learning. He now admitted his belief that the motives of the accused had been honest and pure, also that the affair might be settled without referring it to the bishop, but still maintaining the nullity of the marriage.[64] Fitch presented in his own behalf an elaborate argument against the views of the fiscal, complaining of his business losses, and of the threatened illegitimacy of his son, but for which he would be glad to have the marriage declared null and to marry over again.

[64] The objections to the marriage certificate—of which I have the authenticated copy made at this trial—were that it was slightly torn and blotted; that it included no statement of the city or church where the ceremony was performed; that the paper was neither legalized before 3 *escribanos*, nor viséd by the Chilian minister of foreign affairs. Moreover, P. Orrego, not being the curate of the parties, could not marry them without a dispensation from the bishop.

Many witnesses were examined, both at San Gabriel and San Diego. On the 28th of December the vicar rendered his decision, *Christi nomine invocato*, that the fiscal had not substantiated his accusations; that the marriage at Valparaiso, though not legitimate, was not null, but valid; that the parties be set at liberty, the wife being given up to the husband; and that they be *velados* the next Sunday, receiving the sacraments that ought to have preceded the marriage ceremony. "Yet, considering the great scandal which Don Enrique has caused in this province, I condemn him to give as a penance and reparation a bell of at least fifty pounds in weight for the church at Los Angeles, which barely has a borrowed one." Moreover, the couple must present themselves in church with lighted candles in their hands to hear high mass for three *dias festivos*, and recite together for thirty days one third of the rosary of the holy virgin. Let us hope that these acts of penance were devoutly performed. The vicar did not fail to order an investigation of the charges against Padre Menendez, who had acted irregularly in advising the parties to leave the country; but nothing is recorded of the result.[65]

Only seventeen vessels are named in the records of 1830, besides four that rest on doubtful authority; so that commercial industry would seem to show diminished prosperity; yet the records of this final year of the decade are less complete than before.[66] A Mexican report makes the revenue receipts at San Diego for

---

[65] *Fitch, Causa Criminal seguida, en el Juzgado Eclesiástico y Vicaría Foránea de la Alta California, contra Don Enrique Domingo Fitch, Anglo-Americano, por el matrimonio nulo contraido con Doña Josefa Carrillo, natural de San Diego. Año de 1830*, MS. This most interesting collection of over 30 documents, of which I have given a brief résumé, is the original authority on the whole matter. Jan. 9, 1831, Fitch writes from San Gabriel to Capt. Cooper, denying the rumors current at Sta Bárbara that he was doing penance; says P. Sanchez treated him very well, and seemed anxious to let him off as easy as possible. He has had trouble with the parents of Doña Josefa, who abused her, and he will not leave his wife with them. *Vallejo, Doc.*, MS., xxx. 171.

[66] See list at end of this chapter. The vessels of 1830 were the *Ayacucho, Brookline, Catalina* (?), *Chalcedony* (?), *Convoy, Cyrus, Danube, Dryad, Emily,*

the year $22,432, while the custom-house records
seem to make the amount $36,875.[67]   No vessel of the
year seems to require special notice, neither were
there any important modifications in trade or revenue
regulations.   Commercial and maritime annals of 1830
are thus wellnigh a blank.[68]   I append an alphabetical list of all the vessels, about 100 in number, besides doubtful records, touching on the coast in 1825–
30, with such items about each as are accessible
and apparently worth preserving.   I might add the
dates at which all the vessels, or most of them,
touched at the different ports on their successive
trips; but the information would be of great bulk
and little real value.[69]

Funchal, Globe, Jura, Leonor, María Ester, Planet, Pocahontas, Seringapa-
tan (?), *Thomas Nowlan, Volunteer, Washington* (?), *Whaleman.*   •

[67] *Unsueta, Informe, 1829,* doc. 9. *Dept. St. Pap., Ben. Cust.-H.,* MS., i.
passim.

[68] A few miscellaneous notes of minor importance are as follows: Feb. 19,
1830, one sixth of duties deducted, in case of national vessels from foreign
ports. *Dept. Rec.,* MS., viii. 22., April 23d, agreement between J. C. Jones,
Jr., and Cooper, by which the former is to furnish a vessel under Mexican
flag, for coasting trade, collecting furs, otter-hunting, etc., to be carrried on
by the two in partnership. *Vallejo, Doc.,* MS., i. xxx. 45.   Nov. 24th, gov.
says the vice-president complains that many vessels becoming nationalized do
not comply with the laws requiring officers and one third of the crew to be
Mexicans—a necessary formality to reduce the duties. *Dept. Rec.,* MS., viii.
125.   Aug. 17th, action of the dip. regulating the duties on timber exported—
the proceeds belonging to the *propios y arbitrios* fund. *Leg. Rec.,* MS., i. 166–7.
Mar. 31st, Mex. law on seizure of contraband goods.   *Arrillaga, Recop.,* 1831,
227–33.   Aug. 24, law on consumption duty on foreign goods. *Id.,* 1831, p. 233–
6.   Mexicans engaged in taking otter have no duties to pay to national treasury.   Two citizens of Sta Bárbara were engaged in the business at the islands.
Dept. St. Pap., Ben. Mil., MS., lxxxviii. 4.   June 30th, J. B. Lopez allowed
to take otter, paying from $1 to $3 per skin to the territorial treasury. *Dept.
Rec.,* viii. 52, 130.   In June Mancisidor writes to Guerra very discouragingly
respecting the prospects of the trade in Cal. hides and tallow.   This state
of things was largely due to the inferior quality of the Cal. products, resulting
from the carelessness of excessive speculation.   All dealers suffer, and some
will be ruined.   Cal. hides bring less than those of Buenos Aires, being too
dry and too much stretched. *Guerra, Doc., Hist. Cal.,* MS., vi. 140–1.

[69] List of vessels in Californian ports, 1825–30:
Adam, Amer. ship, 296 tons; Daniel Fallon, master; at S. Francisco in
Oct. 1826.
Alliance, Amer. ship; doubtfully recorded as having arrived at Monterey
in Oct. 1826.
Alvins, doubtful whaler of 1829.
America, doubtful whaler of 1829.
Andes, Amer. brig, 122 or 172 tons; Seth Rogers, master; on coast from
spring of 1828 (perhaps autumn of 1827) to spring of 1829; paid $430 at

Mont., and was in some trouble about duties at S. Diego, where she loaded salt meat.

Ann, Engl. ship; Burnie, master; in Spence's list for 1829.

Apollo, whaler; at Sta Cruz, 1825.

Aquiles, Span. man-of-war; Pedro Angulo, com.; at Sta B. in May 1825. (See text.)

Arab, Amer. brig. My fragment of her original log ends Jan. 5, 1825, at Pt Pinos. She re-appeared under a Russian name in 1828, having been sold to the Russ. Co.

Argosy, Russ. brig, 140 tons; Inestrumo, master; at Monterey and Bodega in 1826, from Sitka.

Asia, Span. ship of war, 70 guns, 400 men; José Martinez, com.; surrendered at Mont., 1825; also called *San Gerónimo*. (See text.)

Ayacucho, Engl. brig, 232 tons; Joseph Snook, master; arr. Mont. from Honolulu in Oct. 1830. (See later lists.)

Baikal, Russ. brig, 202 tons; up and down the coast from Ross to S. Diego each year from 1826 to 1830; Beuseman master, and Khlébnikof supercargo, in 1826; paid $1,216 at S. Diego; Etholin, master in 1828; brought vaccine matter in 1829.

Becket, Hamburg brig; doubtfully recorded as having trouble about smuggling at S. Diego in 1828.

Bengal, Engl. ship; in Spence's list for 1825.

Blossom, Engl. explor. ship; Beechey, com.; at S. Fran. and Mont. in autumn of 1826 and 1827. (See text.)

Brillante, perhaps at S. Diego from S. Blas in Jan. 1828.

Brookline, Amer. ship, 376 or 417 tons, from Boston; Jas O. Locke, master; Wm A. Gale, sup.; Alf. Robinson, clerk; Arther, mate; Bryant & Sturgis, owners; arr. Mont. Feb. 1829; paid $31,000 at S. Diego; wintered on the coast until 1830. (See text.)

Cadboro, Engl. schr, 71 tons; Simpson, master; at S. Fran. from Columbia Riv. Dec. 1827.

Catalina, Mex. brig; C. Cristen, master; Eulogio Célis, sup.; doubtful record in Hayes' list, 1830.

Chalcedony, bark; Jos Steel, master; doubtful record of 1830.

Charles, Amer. whaler, 301 tons, 21 men; S. Fran. 1826.

Clio, Amer. brig, 179 tons; Aaron W. Williams, master; came in 1828 to load with tallow for Chili.

Comète, French ship, 500 tons, 43 men; Antoine Placiat, master; came in 1827 as a rival to the *Héros;* tonnage at Mazatlan; duties, $1,048 at Sta B.

Constante, Span. man-of-war; surrendered with the *Asia* at Mont. in 1825.

Convoy, brig; at S. Fran. in Oct. 1830, paying $321.

Courier, Amer. ship, 200 or 293 tons; Wm Cunningham, master; Thos Shaw, sup.; Geo. W. Vincent on board; on the coast from 1826 (possibly 1825) to 1828, paying $937, $1,586, and $186 in duties on different occasions.

Cyrus, Amer. whaler, 320 tons, 22 men; Dav. Harriens, master; at S. F. in 1826; also at Sta B. Dec. 1830, with 1,500 bbls oil, to be coopered at S. Diego.

Danube, Amer. ship from N. Y.; Sam. Cook, master; arr. early in 1830, and was soon wrecked at S. Pedro; hull sold for $1,761 and cargo for $3,316 in Feb. to Dana and Guerra.

Dhaulle (or *Dolly?*), Amer. brig; Wm Warden, master; at Mont. July 1829, from Honolulu; carried 47 horses to the Islands.

Don, whaler; at Sta B. 1825.

Dryad, Engl. brig, from Columbia River; arr. Mont. Dec. 22, 1830.

Eagle, Amer. schr; at Sta B. Jan. 1825 (re-named *Sta Apolonia*, q. v.)

Elena, Russ. brig; Moraviof, master; 16 guns, 49 men, 10 officers; Karl von Schmidt and Nicolai Molvisto, passengers; wintered at S. Fran. 1825-6.

Eliza, Engl. brig; J. Morphew (or Murphy), master; 1825-6; $9,500 of cloth to McC., H. & Co.; paid $1,112 duties at Sta B.

Emily Marsham; at Sta B. Sept. 1828, from Sandw. Isl.; took prisoners from Sta B. in Feb. 1830; perhaps had returned in autumn of 1829.

Factor, Amer. whaler; John Alexy, master; at S. Fran. 1825.

Favorite, Engl. whaler, 377 tons, 35 men; John Fort (Ford?), master; at Sta B., from London, Oct. 1827.

Fenix, whaler, 300 tons; Wm Ratiguende (?), master, 1828.

Franklin, Amer. whaler, 294 tons; Wm Coffin, master; at S. Fran. 1826.

Franklin, Amer. ship, 333 tons; John Bradshaw, master; Rufus Perkins, and later J. A. C. Holmes, sup.; on the coast from 1827 to 1829. (See text for her troubles at S. Diego in 1828.)

Fulham, Engl. brig; Virmond, owner; came for hides and tallow, and wintered 1827-8.

Funchal, Engl. brig, 190 tons; Stephen Anderson, master, owner, and sup.; on the coast from autumn of 1828 to Feb. 1830, sailing from S. Pedro with 16,400 hides.

General Bravo, Mex. brig, 100 or 180 tons; Melendez, master; at Mont. Oct.-Dec. 1826, with tobacco.

General Sucre, Amer. brig; Cárlos Pitnak, or Pitnes (?), master; left a deserter S. Diego, 1828.

Globe, Amer. brig, 190 tons; Moore, master; at Monterey 1830, for Guaymas.

Golovnin, Russ. brig; at Mont. Dec. 1827.

Griffon, Amer. brig, from Honolulu; Peirce, master, 1828.

Guibale (or *Gaibale?*), Amer. schr, 121 tons; Thos Robbins, master; at Sta B. April 1828.

Harbinger, Amer. brig, 180 tons; Jos Steel, master and consignee; Thos B. Park, sup.; two trips from the Islands in 1826-8; paid $450, $576, $1,250; carried away two fugitive friars in Jan. 1828.

Helvetius, doubtful whaler of 1829. (See later lists.)

Héros, French ship, 250 tons; Auguste Duhaut-Cilly, master; trading on the coast 1827-8. (See text.)

Huascar, Engl. brig under Peruvian flag, 249 tons; Scott, Alex. Skee, or J. M. Oyagüe, master; Hartnell, passenger; cons. to McC., H., & Co., 1827-8; paid $610 at S. Fran.

Inca, Engl. brig, 170 tons, 11 guns; Wm Prouse (or Prause), master; from Callao to McC., H., & Co. in 1826 (possibly arr. in 1825); then to Liverpool in 128 days.

Indian, Engl. ship; in Spence's list of 1829.

Inore, Hawaiian brig, 155 tons, 1826.

Isabella (or *Sarah and Elizabeth*), Engl. whaler, 250 tons, 28 men; Edward David, master; Mrs Hartnell, passenger; at Sta B., from Mont. Oct. 1827.

James Coleman, Engl.; Hennet, master; in Spence's list for 1829.

Jóven Angustias, Mex. schr; at Sta B. Sept. 1829; also doubtful record of 1826.

Juan Battey, doubtful name of 1825; John Burton, master.

Junius, Engl. brig; Carter, master; at Mont. in 1825, paying $3,663 duties.

Jura, Engl. brig; at Sta B., from Mazatlan, May 1830.

Karimoko (or *Carimacu*), Hawaiian brig, 128 tons; John Lawlor, master; Wm Watts (?), sup.; on the coast 1827-8, paying $14 and $314. (See text for smuggling adventures.)

Kiakhta, Russ. brig, built in Cal., running between Ross and S. Fran.; wintered at S. Fran. 1825-6 and 1828-9; paid $95 and $1,548.

Laperin (or *Lapwing?*), Russ. brig; doubtful record of Nov. 1828.

Leonor, Mex. ship, 207 tons; 23 men; Henry D. Fitch, master; brought convicts in 1830. (See text for Fitch's runaway marriage.)

Magdalena (or *Victoria*), Mex. schr, 90 tons; Ramon Sanchez, master; on coast winter of 1827-8.

María Ester, Mex. brig, 170 or 93 tons; owned by Henry Virmond, who was on board in 1828; came from Lima or Mex. ports every year from 1825 to 1830; Davis, master in 1825; to McC., H., & Co.; paid $308; Fitch, master 1826-9; brought artillery in 1828; John A. C. Holmes, master in 1830; brought convicts. Possibly 2 vessels of same name.

Maria Theresa, Amer. whaler, 291 tons; Wm Guilcost, master; at S. Fran. 1826.

Massachusetts, Amer. whaler, 343 tons, 21 men; Seth Calheart (?), master; at S. Fran. Oct. 1827.

Mercury, Amer. whaler, 340 tons; Wm Austin, master; at Sta B. Nov. 1826.

Mero, Amer. ship, 300 tons; Barcelo Juain (?), master; doubtful record at Sta B. Nov. 1826.

Merope, Engl. ship from Calcutta and China; Espeleta, sup.; at S. Fran. Sept. 1825.

Minerva, Amer. whaler, 160 tons; D. Cornelio, master; at Sta B. Oct. 1828.

Moor, whaler of 1826.

Morelos (formerly *S. Cárlos*), Mex. transport; Flaminio Agazini, com.; at Mont. and S. Fran. 1825.

Nile, Amer. brig; Robert Forbes, master; trouble about $600 duties in 1825.

Okhotsk, Russ. brig, 150 tons; Dionisio Zarembo, master; on the coast 1827–8–9; paid $55 and $179; in trouble for having transferred cargo to *Kiakhta*.

Oliphant, brig; doubtful record as having loaded at Callao for Cal. in 1827.

Olive Branch, Engl. brig, 204 tons, 13 men; Wm Henderson, master; Jas Scott, sup.; cons. to Mancisidor from Callao for hides and tallow; wintered 1826–7, paying $510.

Orion, Amer. whaler, 350 tons, 22 men; Alfon Alfe (?), master; at Sta B. Oct., 1827, from Sandw. Isl.

Paragon, Amer. whaler, 309 tons, 23 men; Dav. Edwards, master; at S. Fran. 1826.

Paraiso (or *Paradise*), Hamburg schr, 123 tons, 11 men; Henry Adams, master; cons. to Mancisidor in 1827; paid $3,907 and $631.

Peruvian, Amer. whaler, 331 tons, 22 men; Alex. Macy, master; at S. Fran. 1826.

Pizarro, Engl. brig, 1825–6; cons. probably to McC., H., & Co.; paid $4,712, and $523.

Planet (or *Plant*), Amer. ship, 208 tons, 20 men; Jos Steel and John Rutter, masters, 1829–30.

Plowboy, Amer. whaler, Chadwick, master; at S. Fran. 1825.

Pocahontas, whaler, 309 tons, in 1828.

Pocahontas, Amer. ship, 21 men; John Bradshaw, master; Thos Shaw, sup.; autumn of 1830.

Rascow, whaler, 362 tons; Geo. Reed, master, 1828.

Recovery, Engl. whaler; Wm Fisher, master; at S. Fran. 1825.

Rosalía, Amer. ship, 323 tons; Bruno Colespedriguez (?), master; at S. Pedro, Oct. 1829.

Rover, Cal. schooner, 83 tons; Cooper, master; Argüello, owner; made a trip to China and back 1825–6, and then sailed for Mex. ports; paid $812; left $5,250 in goods at S. Diego. (See text.)

Sachem, Amer. ship, Bryant & Sturgis, owners; Wm A. Gale, sup.; on the coast from 1825 to Jan. 1827, when she sailed for Boston; duties as recorded $489, $2,063, $232.

Santa Apolonia (formerly *Eagle*), Mex. schr; Manuel Bates, master; Ramon Sanchez, sup.; Urbano Sanchez, owner; loaded with tallow at S. Luis Obispo in Aug. 1826.

Santa Bárbara, schr. built in Cal. 1829 for otter-hunting and coast trade.

Sta Rosa, doubtful name of 1825.

Seringapatan, East Ind. ship, grounded on Blossom Rock in 1830 (perhaps an error in date).

Sirena, vaguely mentioned as having brought money to Cal. in 1826.

Snow, doubtful record of 1825.

Solitude, Amer. ship, or Engl. brig; Jas or Chas Anderson, master, 1826–8.

Speedy, Engl. brig, to McC., H. & Co., 1826; carried $26,997 of tallow to Callao.

Spy, Amer. schr, 75 tons, accompanying the *Sachem* and offered for sale; Geo. Smith, master; on the coast 1825-7; also called in some records the *Spray*.

Susana, Engl. ship; Swain, master; in Spence's list for 1829.

Tamaahmaah, Hawaiian brig, 180 tons; Robt J. Elwell, master or sup. in 1827; John Meek in 1829.

Tartar, Amer. schr; Benj. Morrell, master; on the coast 1825. (See text for captain's adventures and book.)

Telemachus, Amer. brig; Jas Gillespie, master; from the Isl. in 1828 for trade and repairs; accused of smuggling.

Tenieya, Amer. brig; paid $232 at Sta B. 1827.

Thomas Nowlan, Engl. ship, 201 or 301 tons; Wm Clark, master, 1826-7; cons. to Mancisidor; paid $2,185 and $2,199; John Wilson, master, 1828-30; paid $858.

Tiemechmach (?), Amer. brig from N. Y.; John Michi (Meek ?), master, 1825.

Times, Engl. whaler, 407 tons; Wm Ross, master; at Sta B. Oct. 1828.

Timorelan, Haw. brig, 160 tons, seal-hunter; at Sta B. Sept. 1826.

Tomasa, at Sta B. 1827, paying $1,570; also doubtful record of 1825.

Trident, Amer. ship, 450 tons; Felix Estirten (?), master; at S. Pedro Oct. 1829.

Triton, whaler, 300 tons, 1825-6; Jean Opham, or Ibre Albet (?), masters. Perhaps two vessels.

Verale, Amer. schr, 140 tons; Wm Deny, master, 1828.

Volunteer, Amer. bark, 126 or 226 tons; Wm S. Hinkley, master; John C. Jones, owner; from Sandw. Isl. 1829-30; carried Solis and other prisoners to S. Blas in 1830; paid $4,054 at S. Fran.

Vulture (or *Buitre*), Engl. brig, 101 tons; Rich. Barry, master; Virmond, owner; from Callao 1828-9; paid $1,130.

Warren, Amer. whaler; Wm Rice, master, 1826; also Amer. ship, perhaps the same, at Mont. Dec. 1829.

Washington, Amer. schr, 52 or 140 tons; Robt Elwell, master from 1828; A. B. Thompson, sup.; from Sandw. Isl. 1825-6-7-8-9 and perhaps 1830; paid $49, $232, $93; carried horses to Honolulu.

Washington, whaler, 317 tons; Wm Kelley, master, 1826.

Waverly, Haw. brig, 142 tons, 9 men, 40 kanaka hunters; Wm G. Dana, master, 1826; carried away 1,428 guilders, 2,000 Span. dollars, 4 bars silver, 138 otter skins, 212 seal skins; Robbins, master, 1827-8; John Temple, passenger, 1827, from Islands; in 1829 carried horses to Honolulu.

Whaleman, schr; at S. Fran. winter of 1825-6; perhaps a whaler. Written also *Guelman*.

Whaleman, brig, 316 tons; Jos. Paddock, master; from Society Isl. 1830.

Wilmantic, Amer. whaler, 384 tons; Juan Bois, master, 1828.

Wilmington, Amer. ship, 364 tons; John Bon, master; at S. Pedro Oct. 1829. (Probably same as preceding.)

Young Tartar (or *Jóven Tartar*), Engl. schr, 95 tons; John Brown (?), master, 1826-7 (possibly 1825); paid $580; cargo insured in London 1827 for £4,000.

Zamora, Wm Sumner, master.

My authorities for the items of this list are more than 1,000 in number, chiefly in manuscript records. As each vessel would require a mention of from 1 to 20 titles, it is not practicable to give the references separately; and in a group for all maritime affairs they would be of little practical value; therefore I omit them, though I have the prepared list before me. The most important have been named in the notes of this chapter.

CHAPTER VI.

OVERLAND—SMITH AND PATTIE—FOREIGNERS

1826–1830.

The Eastern Frontier—The Trappers—First Visitors by the Over-
land Route—Jedediah Smith, 1826–8—Errors Corrected—Original
Documents—The Sierra Nevada Crossed and Re-crossed—First
Entry of the Hudson's Bay Company—McLeod and Ogden—Pat-
tie's Visit and Imprisonment, 1828–30—Flint's Narrative—Truth
and Fiction—A Tour of Vaccination—'Peg-leg' Smith—Trapping
License of Exter and Wilson—Vaca from New Mexico—Ewing
Young and his Hunters from New Mexico—Foreign Residents—
Annual Lists of New-comers—Regulations on Passports and Nat-
uralization.

For forty years California had been visited with
increasing frequency by foreigners, that is, by men
whose blood was neither Indian nor Spanish. England, the United States, Russia, and France were
the nations chiefly represented among the visitors,
some of whom came to stay, and to all of whom in
the order of their coming I have devoted some attention in the annals of the respective years. All had
come from the south, or west, or north by the broad
highway of the Pacific Ocean bounding the territory
on the west and leading to within a few miles of the
most inland Spanish establishments. The inland boundary—an arc whose extremities touch the coast at San
Diego and at 42°, an arc for the most part of *sierras
nevadas* so far as could be seen, with a zone of desert
beyond as yet unknown—had never yet been crossed
by man of foreign race, nor trod, if we except the

southern segment cut by a line from San Gabriel to Mojave, by other than aboriginal feet.[1]

Meanwhile a grand advance movement from the Atlantic westward to the Mississippi, to the plains, to the Rocky Mountains, and into the Great Basin had been gradually made by the fur-hunting pioneers of the broad interior—struggling onward from year to year against obstacles incomparably greater than those presented by the gales and scurvy of the Pacific. If I were writing the history of California alone, it would be appropriate and probably necessary to present here, en résumé at least, the general movement to which I have alluded, embodying the annals of the various fur companies. But the centre of the fur trade was much farther north, and its annals cannot be profitably separated from the history of the North-west. For this reason—bearing in mind also those portions of my work relating locally to Idaho, Montana, Nevada, Utah, New Mexico, and Arizona —I feel justified in referring the reader for the general exploration westward to other chapters of other volumes, and in confining my record here to such expeditions as directly affect Californian territory.

These began in 1826, when the inland barrier of mountain and desert was first passed, and from that date the influx of foreigners by overland routes becomes a topic of ever growing importance. It is well, however, to understand at the outset, that respecting the movements of the trappers no record of even tolerable completeness exists, or could be expected to exist. After 1826 an army of hunters, increasing from hundreds to thousands, frequented the fur-producing

---

[1] A few English and American deserters, leaving their vessels at Todos Santos or thereabouts, had on two or three occasions been sent across the frontier to S. Diego, forming an exception of little importance to my general statement. Another exception of somewhat greater weight rests in the possibility that trappers may have crossed the northern frontier before 1826. It is not improbable that Hudson's Bay Company men may have done so from the Willamette Valley on one or more occasions, though there is no more definite record than the rumor of 1820-1, that foreign hunters were present in the north, and the newspaper report of McKay's presence in Siskiyou in 1825.

streams of the interior, and even the valleys of California, flitting hither and thither, individuals and parties large or small according to the disposition of the natives, wandering without other motive than the hope of more abundant game, well acquainted with the country, as is the wont of trappers, but making no maps and keeping no diaries. Occasionally they came in contact with civilization east or west, and left a trace in the archives; sometimes a famous trapper and Indian-fighter was lucky enough to fall in with a writer to put his fame and life in print; some of them lived later among the border settlers, and their tales of wild adventure, passing not without modification through many hands, found their way into newspaper print. Some of them still live to relate their memories to me and others, sometimes truly and accurately, sometimes confusedly, and sometimes falsely, as is the custom of trappers like other men. I make no claim of ability to weave continuity from fragments, bring order from chaos, distinguish in every instance truth from falsehood, or build up a narrative without data; nevertheless, I proceed with confidence to write in this chapter and others of the men who came to California overland from the east.

Jedediah S. Smith was the first man who made the trip. From a post of the fur company established at or near Great Salt Lake a year or two earlier,[2] Smith started in August 1826 for the south-west with fifteen men, intent rather on explorations for future work than on present trapping.[3] Crossing Utah Lake,

---

[2] Smith was associated with Jackson and Sublette, and the post had been established by W. H. Ashley.

[3] *Smith, Excursion à l'ouest des Monts Rocky. Extrait d'une lettre de M. Jedidiah Smith, employé de la Compagnie des Pelleteries*, in *Nouv. Ann. des Voy.*, xxxvii. 208–12. Taken from an American paper. The news—perhaps the paper, but certainly not Smith's letter as might seem from the translation—was dated St. Louis Oct. 11, 1827. This brief letter, in which very likely wild work is made with names in the printing and translation, is in connection with the correspondence preserved in the archives, the best authority on the subject. The general accounts extant are full of errors, though each purports to correct errors previously made. Warner, *Reminiscences*, MS.,

he seems to have passed in a general south-westerly
course to the junction of the Virgin River and Colo-

21–9, errs chiefly in dates and order of events. He makes Smith start in
1824 and lead a party of hunters through the Green River country, south of
Salt Lake, over the Sierra Nevada near Walker Pass, into the Tulare Valley. In June 1825, leaving his men on the American Fork—whence the
name—he re-crossed the sierra with two men. Starting back for California
in the autumn of 1825 by a more southern route, he was attacked by the Mojaves while crossing the Colorado, and lost all his men but 2 or 3, with whom
he reached S. Gabriel late in 1826. The author of *Cronise's Natural Wealth
of Cal.*, after being at much trouble to unravel the various stories, 'gathered
the following particulars from those who knew Smith personally, and from
documents in the state archives:' 'In the spring of 1825, Smith, with a party
of 40 trappers and Indians, left their rendezvous on Green River near the
South Pass, and pushed their way westward, crossing the Sierra Nevada into
the Tulare Valley, which they reached in July 1825. The party trapped
from the Tulare to the American fork of the Sacramento, where there was already a camp of American trappers (?). Smith camped near the site of the
present town of Folsom, about 22 miles north-east of the other party. From
this camp Smith sent out parties, which were so successful that in October,
leaving all the others in California, in company with 2 of the party, he returned
to his rendezvous on Green River with several bales of skins. In May 1826
Smith was sent back with a reënforcement. On this trip he led his party
farther south than on the former one, which brought them into the Mojaves'
settlements on the Colorado, where all the party except Smith, Galbraith, and
Turner were killed by the Indians. These three made their way to S. Gabriel on Dec. 26, 1826, where they were arrested,' etc. Cronise also publishes
a translation of 2 documents from the archives, of which more later.

Thomas Sprague, in a letter of Sept. 18, 1860, to Edmund Randolph, published in *Hutchings' Mag.*, v. 351–2, and also in the *S. F. Bulletin*, states that
Smith, starting from Green River in 1825, reached and went down the Humboldt River, which he named Mary River from his Indian wife, crossed the
mountains probably near the head of the Truckee, and passed on down the
valley to S. José and S. Diego. Recruiting his men and buying many horses,
he re-crossed the mountains near Walker Pass, skirted the eastern base to
near Mono Lake, and on a straight north-east course for Salt Lake found
placer gold in large quantities. He was ordered to return and prospect the
gold fields on his way back from California, but near the gold mines he was
killed with most of his party.

Robert Lyon furnished to Angel, author of the *Nevada Hist.*, 20 et seq.,
a version somewhat similar to that of Sprague, including the discovery of
coarse placer gold near Mono Lake. His account seems to rest on the testimony, in 1860, of Rocky Mountain Jack and Bill Reed, who claimed to have
been companions of Smith.

An 'associate of the daring pioneer' corrected prevailing errors as follows
in the *S. F. Times*, June 14, 1867: 'He came into California in 1827, with
a trapping party from the rendezvous of the Rocky Mountain Fur Company,
on the Yellowstone River. He left his party on the American fork of the
Sacramento in the summer of that year, and with two men returned to the
rendezvous, where he fitted out a new party and returned in 1828 to the
American, where the two parties were combined, and moving northwardly,
he reached the Umpqua River,' etc.

It will be noticed that all these versions have the double trip and some
other points in common, and that the confusion is largely removed by the
original authorities, on which I found my text. Randolph, *Oration*, 313–14,
translating Smith's letter to P. Duran, and Tuthill, *Hist. Cal.*, 124–5, as well
as Frignet, *La Californie*, 58–60, mention Smith's arrival in 1826 in so general a manner as to avoid serious error. The same may be said of Douglas,

rado, down to the Mojave villages, and westward across the desert to San Gabriel.[4]

The Amajabes on the Colorado treated the party well, furnishing fresh provisions, and horses stolen from the Spaniards, and two wandering neophytes guided the sixteen Americans over the desert to the mission, where they arrived in December. The trappers gave up their arms, and the leader was taken to San Diego, where he explained his object, and submitted to Governor Echeandía his papers, including passports from the U. S. government, and a diary. The coming of the strangers naturally excited suspicion at first; but this was removed by Smith's plea that he had been compelled to enter the territory for want of provisions and water, it being impossible to return by the same route; and his cause was still further strengthened by a certificate of Dana, Cunningham, and other Americans, that the trapper's papers were all *en règle*, and his motives doubtless pacific and honorable.[5] He was therefore permitted to purchase supplies, and undertake his eastward march by a new route; but not, as

Private Papers, MS., 2d series, p. 1, Victor, *River of the West*, 34, and Hines, *Voyage*, 110, though these writers speak with reference to later events in Oregon, and derived their information from distinct sources. The *Yolo Co. Hist.*, *S. Joaq. Co. Hist.*, and other like works describe Smith's adventures, in some cases as accurately as was possibly from accessible data, still with various combinations of the errors already noted.

[4] The details of the route are worth preservation briefly, though not clear in all respects. Started Aug. 22d from Salt Lake, crossed the little Utá Lake, went up the Ashley, which flows into that lake through the country of the Sumpatch Indians, crossed a range of mountains extending s. e. to n. w., crossed a river which he named Adams for the president, and which flowed s. w. Ten days' march to the Adams again, which had turned s. e. (This is not clear; the text says, 'à dix journées de marche l'Adams River tourne au s. e., il y a là une caverne,' etc. Query—Did Smith pass from the Sevier to the Virgin, and suppose them to be one stream?) Two days down the Adams to its junction with the Seeds-Keeder, a river with many shallows and rapids, and having a sterile country on the south; farther to a fertile wooded valley inhabited by the Ammucheebès (Amajabes, or Mojaves), where he remained 15 days. This was 80 miles above where the Seeds-Keeder, under the name of Rio Colorado, flowed into the gulf of California. Re-crossing the Seeds-Keeder, he went 15 days west into a desert country, and across a salt plain 8 by 20 miles. Here the details cease abruptly, and he next speaks of his arrival in Upper California.

[5] Dated at S. Diego Dec. 20, 1826, and signed by Wm G. Dana, Wm H. Cunningham, Wm Henderson, Diego Scott, Thomas M. Robbins, and Thomas Shaw, in *Dept. St. Pap.*, MS., ii. 19–20. An English translation has been published in several works.

he wished, to follow the coast up to the Columbia via Bodega.[6]

The Californians supposed for a month that they were rid of their overland guests; but at the beginning of February 1827 some of them were seen at different places, particularly near San Bernardino, where Smith appeared on the 2d of February. There he left a sick man, and thence he seems to have sent a letter to Padre Sanchez by one of his men. The letter, as translated at the time, stated as the reason for return that the trappers in crossing a stream had been attacked by Indians, who killed eight of their number and stripped them of everything but their clothes—a statement that would seem to be false, though Smith bore the reputation of truthfulness.[7] At any rate, the trappers had tried without success to cross the Sierra, and were reported to be in a destitute condition. The two men to whom I have referred were, I suppose, Isaac Galbraith and Joaquin Bowman, who were detained at the time for examination, and who remained in the territory. Orders were issued to detain the whole party, but Smith had left San Bernardino before the orders could be executed.[8]

[6] Dec. 30, 1826. Echeandía reports Smith's arrival with 14 companions, 40 beaver skins, and many traps; also his visit to S. Diego and his apparent good faith. *St. Pap., Sac.*, MS., xix. 37–8. He enclosed Smith's diary to the minister of war, and it may come to light some day. Smith himself, *Excursion*, 210, says: ' Mon arrivée dans la Haute-Californie excita les soupçons du gouverneur, qui demeurait à San Diego. Il me fit conduire devant lui; mais plusieurs citoyens des Etats-Unis, notamment M. Cunningham, capitaine du *Courrier* de Boston, ayant répondu de moi, j'obtins la permission de retourner avec ma suite, et d'acheter des provisions; mais le gouverneur refusa de me laisser côtoyer la mer en allant vers la Bodega.'

[7] The letter is not extant, and its purport only is given in one of Argüello's letters to the governor. It is possible that there is an error somewhere, and that Smith in the original letter spoke of a fight in which he killed 8 Indians, especially as 2 women are also said to have been killed. Smith himself, *Excursion*, p. 211, gives no details nor even mention of having come in contact with the Spaniards at this time. He says, in continuation of quotation of note 6, 'I marched therefore E. and then N. E. (from S. Gabriel or S. Diego), keeping at a distance of 150 to 200 miles from the coast. I went nearly 300 miles in that direction,' through some fertile regions peopled by many naked Indians, and 'having reached a river which I named Kimmel-ché from the tribe living on its banks. I found beavers, etc. Here I remained some days; I intended to return to Salt Lake by crossing Mount Joseph; but the snow was so deep on the heights that my horses, 5 of which had died of hunger, could not advance. I was therefore obliged to re-descend into the valley.'

[8] Letters of Santiago Argüello to comandante of S. Diego and to gov., with

When next heard of in May, Smith had moved
northward and was encamped in the country of the
Moquelumnes and Cosumnes. Padre Duran, of
Mission San José, accused the Americans of having
enticed his neophytes to desert, but Comandante
Martinez pronounced the charge groundless.[9] New
communications and orders to investigate passed between the authorities; and a letter came to Padre
Duran from Smith himself, bearing date of May 19th.
It was a frank statement of his identity and situation,
of his failures to cross the mountains, and of the necessity of waiting for the snow to melt. He was far
from home, destitute of clothing and all the neces-
saries of life, save only game for food. He was particularly in need of horses; in fact, he was very
disagreeably situated, but yet, "though a foreigner
unknown to you, Reverend Father, your true friend
and Christian brother, J. S. Smith."[10]

The next day after writing this letter Smith started

references to replies and other communications, in *Dept. St. Pap.*, MS., ii.
33–7. Mention of Galbraith (Gil Brest) and the 'sick man' in *Dept. Rec.*,
MS., v. 89, 115, also of Galbraith in *Dept. St. Pap.*, MS., xix. 16–17. Bowman is mentioned as one of Smith's men in *Los Angeles, Hist.*, 19, by Mr
Warner, and there may be some mistake. The sick man may possibly have
been John Wilson, who was in custody in May as one of Smith's men. *Dept.
Rec.*, MS., v. 45; *Arch. Arzob.*, MS., v. pt i. 29, 33. Cronise calls Galbraith's companion Turner.

[9] May 16, 1827, Duran to com. of S. Francisco. 400 neophytes have been induced to run away. *Arch. Arzob.*, MS., v. pt i. 27. May 18th, gov. orders Martinez not to rely wholly on reports of the Indians, but to send out scouts to learn
who are the strangers and what their business; also to demand their passports
and detain them until further orders. *Dept. Rec.*, MS., v. 45. On same date
Rocha is ordered to institute proceedings against John Wilson, and take deposition of Daniel Ferguson, with a view to find out the aims of the strangers.
Id. May 21st, Martinez from S. José to gov. The Americans had nothing
to do with the flight of the neophytes. Sergt Soto has been ordered to investigate, find out what *gente* it is, not allow them to approach the missions, treat
them courteously, etc. A letter has been received from Smith to Duran,
which the latter would not receive, but which Martinez had had translated
and sent to Monterey for Hartnell to retranslate. The Indians say that there
are 12 of the strangers, the same who were at S. Gabriel, and they had killed
5 Moquelumnes in a fight. John Wilson, a prisoner at Monterey, has apparently not been missed, and he says something of the party having come from
Boston in 18 months to make surveys and buy lands of the natives (?). *Arch.
Arzob.*, MS., v. pt i. 28–33.

[10] May 19, 1827, Spanish translation of Smith's letter, in *Dept. St. Pap.*,
MS., ii. 18–19. English version, in *Randolph's Oration*, 313–14; and other
works. French version, in *Frignet, La Cal.*, 58–60.

homeward with but two companions. This was the first crossing of the Sierra Nevada, and the traveller's narrative, though brief and meagre, must be presented in his own words. "On May 20, 1827," he writes, "with two men, seven horses, and two mules laden with hay and food, I started from the valley. In eight days we crossed Mount Joseph, losing on this passage two horses and one mule. At the summit of the mountain the snow was from four to eight feet deep, and so hard that the horses sank only a few inches. After a march of twenty days eastward from Mount Joseph, I reached the south-west corner of the Great Salt Lake. The country separating it from the mountains is arid and without game. Often we had no water for two days at a time; we saw but a plain without the slightest trace of vegetation. Farther on I found rocky hills with springs, then hordes of Indians, who seemed to us the most miserable beings imaginable. When we reached the Great Salt Lake we had left only one horse and one mule, so exhausted that they could hardly carry our slight luggage. We had been forced to eat the horses that had succumbed."[11] There are no means of knowing anything about his route; but I think he is as likely to have crossed the mountains near the present railroad line as elsewhere.[12]

Smith returned from Salt Lake to California with eight men, arriving probably in October 1827, but

[11] Smith, *Excursion*, 211–12. With the quotation given, the letter ends abruptly.

[12] Still it is not impossible or unlikely that in this trip or on the return Smith went through Walker Pass, as Warner and others say, or followed the Humboldt or Mary, as Sprague tells us; but the gold discovery on the way as related by Sprague merits no consideration, in the absence of other evidence and the presence of evident absurdities. It is to be noticed that Warner describes this crossing of the sierra by Smith and two men accurately enough, except in date; and I think it probable that he has reversed the order of the two entries to California, the first being by Mojave in 1826, and the second by Walker Pass in 1827. On Wilkes' map of 1841, reproduced in vol. iv. of this work, Smith's route is indicated, on what authority is not stated, by a line extending s. w. from Salt Lake, and approaching the sierra on the 39th parallel, with a lake on the line in long. 119°, and three streams running N. between the lake and mountains. A peak in the sierra just N. of 39° is called Mt Smith; and Mt Joseph is at the northern end of the range in lat. 41°. This may all rest on accurate reports.

about the route followed or incidents of the trip nothing is known. The Californians apparently knew nothing of the leader's separation from his company, though the record of what occurred during his absence is meagre. On May 23d Echeandía issued instructions, by virtue of which the fur-hunter was to be informed that his actions had become suspicious, and that he must either start homeward at once, come to San José to enjoy the hospitality of California under surveillance until the supreme government could decide, or sail on the first vessel that could carry him beyond latitude 42°.[13] According to fragmentary records in the archives, it was supposed early in August that the strangers had gone. In September it was known that they were still present, and in October several orders were issued that they be brought to San José. It is not clear that any were thus brought in,[14] but it would seem that on Smith's return from the east late in October, he soon came, voluntarily or otherwise, to San José and Monterey with seventeen or eighteen companions.[15]

The 12th of November Captain Cooper at Monterey signed a bond in favor of his countryman. As the agent of Steel, Park, and others, and in the name of the United States, Cooper became responsible with his person and property for the good behavior of Jed-

[13] May 23, 1827, Echeandía to Martinez. *Dept. Rec.*, MS., v. 48.

[14] Gov.'s orders of Aug. 3d, Sept. 14th, Oct. 1st, 16th, in *Dept. Rec.*, MS., v. 73, 88, 94, 102. Bojorges, *Recuerdos*, MS., 12–14, the only one of my Californian writers who mentions this affair at all, says that Soto was sent out with 40 men to the Rio Estanislao, and brought in all the trappers to S. Francisco. As such orders had been issued, this is likely enough to be true, though perhaps it took place after Smith's return. Oct. 8th, Isaac Galbraith asks for an interview with Echeandía, wishing a license either to remain in the country or to rejoin his leader. He also corrects an impression that Smith is a captain of troops, stating that he is but a hunter of the company of Smith, Jackson, and Sublette. *Dept. St. Pap.*, MS., ii. 36–7.

[15] The Spanish records make the number 17, which is probably accurate, though records of a later event in Oregon speak of 18. Morineau, *Notice*, MS., 153–4, says that in October 1827 a caravan of 17 voyageurs arrived at S. Francisco from New Orleans. They sold some furs to a Russian vessel, bought horses, and returned by the same way they came. Carrillo, *Exposicion*, MS., 9, says that in 1827 one of the hunters passed through the country with 60 men, reached the house of the comandante general, made plans, etc., and went away unmolested!

ediah Smith in all that concerned his return to Salt Lake. In the document it was set forth that Smith and his men, as honorable citizens of the United States, were to be treated as friends, and furnished at fair prices with the aid in arms, horses, and provisions necessary for the return march by way of Mission San José, Strait of Carquines, and Bodega; but there was to be no unnecessary delay en route, and in future they must not visit the coast south of latitude 42°, nor extend their inland operations farther than specifically allowed by the latest treaties. To this bond Echeandía attached his written permission for Smith and his company to return, with one hundred mules, one hundred and fifty horses, a gun for each man, and divers bales of provisions and other effects which are named.[16]

Echeandía issued orders for a guard of ten men to escort the trappers to a point a little beyond San Francisco Solano, starting from San José;[17] but a slight change must have been made in the plan, for on the 18th the whole company arrived at San Francisco on the *Franklin* from Monterey.[18] This is really the last that is known of Smith in California, where four and perhaps five men of his party remained, besides Turner who came back later. I have accredited these men to the year 1826, though some of them probably came in the second party of 1827. The party doubtless left San Francisco at the end of the year or early in 1828, and proceeded somewhat leisurely northward, probably by a coast route as intended,[19] and not without some new misconduct, or what was vaguely alluded to as such by the authori-

[16] I have, in *Vallejo, Doc.*, MS., xxix. 171, the orginal of this interesting document kept by Cooper. Three copies were made, one sent to Mexico, one kept in the archives, and one given to Smith. It is written on paper provisionally 'habilitated' by the autographs of Herrera and Echeandía, bears a certificate of José Estrada, is signed John Bª R. Cooper. Then follows the autograph of the hunter. 'I acknowledge this bond, Jedediah S. Smith,' and closes with Echeandía's pass.

[17] Nov. 15th, E. to com. of S. Francisco. *Dept. Rec.*, MS. v. 107. Louis Pombert, a French Canadian, left Smith's party about this time and remained in the country. *Dept. St. Pap.*, MS., xix. 25–8.

[18] Argüello to gov. *Dept. St. Pap.*, MS., ii. 45.

[19] Bojorges, *Recuerdos*, MS., 14, says he left S. Francisco by water on an

ties.[20]   While attempting to ford the Umpqua River
he was attacked by Indians, who killed fifteen of the
company and took all their property. Smith, Turner, and two others[21] escaped to Fort Vancouver.
McLoughlin of the Hudson's Bay Company sent back
a party with one of the survivors to recover the lost
effects, in which they are said to have been successful. Jedediah Smith returned eastward by a northern route in 1829, and two years later he was killed
by the Indians in New Mexico. I append part of a
map of 1826 purporting to show 'all the recent geographical discoveries' to that date.

An important topic, perhaps connected indirectly
with Jedediah Smith's visit, is the first operations of
the Hudson's Bay Company's trappers in California.
Respecting these operations before 1830, I have no
original and definite information, except that contained in the statement of J. J. Warner, himself an old
trapper, still living in 1884, and an excellent authority
on all connected with the earliest American pioneers,
although he did not himself reach California until
the beginning of the next decade.[22]   Warner states

American vessel. It is possible, but not I think probable, that such was the
case, one of the vessels being chartered to take him up the coast to or beyond
Bodega. Warner says Smith started up the interior valley, but on account of difficulties in the way, turned to the coast 200 miles above Ross.
The men who remained, besides Galbraith and Bowman, were Bolbeda, Pombert, and probably Wilson.

[20] Feb. 1, 1828, gov. to Martinez. Alludes to the abuses committed by
Smith. *Dept. Rec.*, MS., vi. 178. Probably he had stopped on the way to
hunt and trap. June 26th, Cooper was thanked by J. Lennox Kennedy, U.
S. consul at Mazatlan, for his services in Smith's behalf; will send documents
to U. S. min. at Mexico. *Vallejo, Doc.*, MS., xxix. 250. But May 6, 1829, he
was ordered as bondsman by gov. to pay $176 due from Smith. *Dept. Rec.*,
MS., vii. 148. June 25, 1829, E. reports to the min. of rel. a rumor that the
Americans intend to take S. Francisco, a plan which he ascribes to the advent
of Smith. *Id.*, vii. 25.

[21] There is a discrepancy of one man in totals, but there is also a com-
pensating uncertainty about one of the men who remained in Cal. Cronise,
Nat. Wealth of Cal., 42, erroneously names two of the three survivors
Laughlin and Prior. Victor, *River of the West*, 35–6, names Turner and Black.
The particulars of the Umpqua fight belong to other parts of this series.
See *Hist. Or.* and *Hist. Northwest Coast.* The map given herewith is copied
from one in *Warren's Mem.* In *Pac. R. R. Repts*, xi. pl. iii., being a reduction
from A. Finley's map of N. America published at Philadelphia in 1826.

[22] *Warner's Reminiscences of Early California*, MS., 27–33. The author

that the party sent back from Fort Vancouver to avenge Smith's disasters was under the command of McLeod, and after recovering the stolen furs, traps, and horses, was guided by Turner down into the Sacramento Valley in 1828, where he made a successful hunt. Returning northward, however, he was overtaken by a snow-storm in the Pit River country, which he was the first to traverse.[23] He lost his animals, and was compelled to leave his furs, which were spoiled by melting snow before they could be moved.

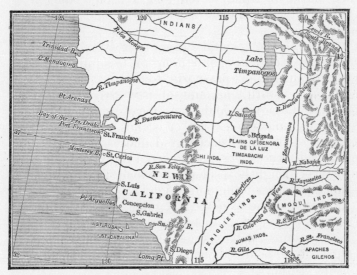

MAP OF 1826.

McLeod was discharged for his imprudence or for his bad luck. Meanwhile the company had hastened to despatch Ogden with another party of hunters up the Columbia and Snake, to proceed thence southward to Smith's trail,[24] by which he was to enter Califor-

[23] represents the manager of the company as having driven a shrewd bargain with Smith, and derived much profit from his disaster.

[23] The McLeod River, generally written McCloud, was named by or in honor of this hunter.

[24] That is one of Smith's trails, probably the most northerly, though Warner makes it the earliest.

nia, and thus get the start of any American trappers that might be sent as a result of Smith's reports. Ogden was successful in this movement, and entered the great valley about the same time that McLeod left it.[25] He also obtained a rich harvest of skins during his stay of eight months, and carried his furs to the north by McLeod's trail. These were the only visits of Hudson Bay trappers before 1832.[26]

The visit of the Patties to California in 1828–30 is the topic next demanding attention. Sylvester Pattie, a Kentuckian, lieutenant of rangers against the Indians in 1812–13, and later a lumberman in Missouri, joined a trapping and trading expedition to New Mexico in 1824, with his son James Ohio Pattie. The father was about forty years of age, and the son a school-boy of perhaps fifteen. With their adventures in New Mexico and Arizona for the next three years I am not concerned here. More than once they visited the Gila, and in September 1827 the elder Pattie was made captain of a company of thirty trappers, organized at Santa Fé to operate on the Colorado.[27] They reached the Colorado and Gila junction December 1st, or at least the Patties and six men did so, the rest having left the Gila, striking northward some two weeks earlier. The eight of Pattie's party were in a desperate strait. They understood from the Yumas that there were Christians down the river, and started to find them, floating on canoe rafts, trapping successfully as they went, and

[25] It seems rather unlikely that this could have been accomplished so soon as the autumn of 1828. Either it was in 1829, or Smith had reached Fort Vancouver early in 1828, instead of in the autumn as has been supposed.

[26] Similar versions of McLeod's and Ogden's expeditions, originating probably indirectly from Warner, but perhaps also from the recollections of other old trappers, are given in the county histories, newspaper articles, and other recent publications. See also *Hist. N. W. Coast*, i., this series. Cronise, *Nat. Wealth*, 41, says that French Camp, near Stockton, was located by a party of these trappers who encamped here from 1829 to 1838. In *Humphreys' Letter to Gwin, 1858*, p. 5, it is stated that Richard Campbell of Sta Fé came with pack-mules from N. Orleans to S. Diego in 1827. I find nothing more on the subject.

[27] Pattie, *Narr.*, 133, translates the passport given them.

reaching tide-water the 18th of January, 1828. They soon started back up the river, making little progress, and February 16th, having buried their furs and traps, they started westward across the desert. After terrible suffering they reached Santa Catalina Mission in Lower California the 12th of March. Ten days later, by Echeandía's order,[28] they started under a guard for San Diego, where they arrived the 27th. The company included, besides the Patties, Nathaniel Pryor, Richard Laughlin, William Pope, Isaac Slover, Jesse Ferguson, and James Puter,[29] most of whom sooner or later became permanent residents of California.

The narrative of James O. Pattie was subsequently printed; from it I have drawn the preceding résumé, and I have now to present in substance that part of it relating to California, introducing occasional notes from other sources, and reserving comment until the end.[30] On arrival at San Diego the strangers were

[28] March 22, 1828, E. to com. of S. Diego. Eight armed men have appeared at a frontier post with a *guia* of the N. Mex. custom-house as a passport. Arrest them and seize their arms. *Dept. Rec.*, MS., vi. 194; *Pattie's Narr.*, 170.

[29] All the names appear in the archives, in one place or another, though Ferguson is not clearly stated to have belonged to this company. Joseph Yorgens is named, perhaps a corruption of Ferguson's name, since Warner speaks of Ferguson, whom he must have known. Puter is mentioned only once, and there may be some error about his name. Pattie himself strangely names only Slover in his narrative, speaking also of a Dutchman; and on the other hand, Pattie's own name appears only once in the archives.

[30] *Pattie, The Personal Narrative of James O. Pattie, of Kentucky, during an expedition from St Louis through the vast regions between that place and the Pacific Ocean, and thence back through the city of Mexico to Vera Cruz, during journeyings of six years; in which he and his father, who accompanied him, suffered unheard-of hardships and dangers, had various conflicts with the Indians, and were made captives, in which captivity his father died; together with a description of the country, and the various nations through which they passed. Edited by Timothy Flint.* Cincinnati, 1833. 8vo. 300 pp. The editor, a somewhat voluminous writer of works largely fictitious, claims not to have drawn on his imagination, but to have changed the author's statement—apparently written—only in orthography and by an occasional abridgment.

The Hunters of Kentucky; or the trials and toils of traders and trappers, during an expedition to the Rocky Mountains, New Mexico, and California, by B. Bilson, New York, 1847, 8vo, 100 pp., is called by T. W. Field, see *Sabin's Dictionary*, viii. 569-70, 'a reproduction of Pattie's narrative, which the penury of the thieving writer's imagination has not empowered him to clothe with new language, or interleave with new incidents;' yet this reprint is much less rare than the original, and has been much more widely read. From it at the time of publication many people formed their ideas about the

brought before Echeandía and questioned, the younger
Pattie, who had learned a little Spanish in New
Mexico, serving as spokesman, and expressing his ideas
with great freedom on this as on every other occasion when he came into contact with the Spaniards.
The governor believed nothing of their story, accused
them of being spies for Spain—worse than thieves and
murderers—tore up their passport as a forgery, cut
short their explanations, and remanded them to prison.
On the way they resolved to redress their wrongs by
force or die in the attempt; but their arms had been
removed,[31] and they were locked up in separate cells.
The father was cruelly torn from the son, and died a
month later without being permitted again to see him.
The cells were eight or ten feet square, with iron
doors, and walls and floor of stone.   Young Pattie's
experience alone is recorded, as no communication
was allowed.   Nauseating food and continued insults
and taunts were added to the horrors of solitary confinement.   From his grated door Pattie could see
Echeandía at his house opposite.   "Ah! that I had
had but my trusty rifle well charged to my face!
Could I but have had the pleasure of that single shot,

Spanish Californians. In *Harper's Magazine*, xxi. 80–94, J. T. Headley
tells the story of Pattie's sufferings, taken from one of the preceding works,
and erroneously called the first overland expedition to California. Cronise,
Nat. Wealth of Cal., 45, says, 'the particulars of Pattie's journey were published with President Jackson's message to congress in 1836.'   The subject is
vaguely and incorrectly mentioned in *Greenhow's Hist. Ogn*, 366; and *Capron's
Hist. Cal.*, 37.   Warner, who knew personally most of Pattie's companions,
gives a valuable account in his *Reminiscences*, MS., 33–7.   The archive records are much less satisfactory than in the case of Jedediah Smith; but I
shall have occasion to refer to them on special points.

[31] Dr Marsh, *Letter to Com. Jones*, MS., 1842, p. 3, says they came to S.
Diego on a friendly visit, 'were well received at first, and shown into comfortable lodgings, where they deposited their arms and baggage.   They were
shortly after invited into another apartment to partake of some refreshment,
and when they returned found that their arms had been removed, and that
they were prisoners.   I mention this incident, trivial as it is, because I consider it as a characteristic trait of the whole Mexican people.   Gen. Echeandía in his own capital, with all his troops, could not take five American hunters without resorting to an artifice which would have been disdained by the
most barbarous tribe of Indians on the whole continent.   These poor men
were kept in close confinement a long time...Two or three of the number are
still in the country.'   Where Marsh got this version, which leaves even Pattie
in the shade, does not appear.

I think I would have been willing to have purchased
it with my life," writes the captive, and this before
his father died alone.   No attention was paid to pleas
for justice or pity.   Yet a sergeant showed much
kindness, and his beautiful sister came often to the
cell with sympathy and food, and even enabled the
prisoner to get a glimpse of his father's coffin as it
was hastily covered with earth.[32]

Captain Bradshaw of the *Franklin* soon got Pattie
out of jail for a day by the 'innocent stratagem' of
pretending to need his services as an interpreter; and
with an eye to business, he made an effort to get permission for the hunters to go to the Colorado and
bring the buried furs, but in vain.   In the proceedings against Bradshaw for smuggling, Pattie served
as interpreter; and later, by reporting certain orders
which he had overheard, he claims to have prevented
Bradshaw's arrest, and thus to have contributed to
the escape of the *Franklin*.[33]   Seth Rogers, A. W.
Williams, and W. H. Cunningham are named as
other American masters of vessels who befriended the
young prisoner, and gave him money.

Echeandía himself also employed Pattie as an interpreter, and at times assumed a friendly tone.   The
captive took advantage of this to plead his cause anew,
to discuss questions of international law, and to suggest that there was money to be made by sending
after the buried furs.   At the first he had known that
every word of kindness pronounced by Echeandía
"was a vile and deceitful lie," and after repeated interviews he perceived "that, like most arbitrary and
cruel men, he was fickle and infirm of purpose," and

[32] He calls the young lady Miss Peaks, and the couple may have been
Sergt Pico and his sister.   A certain *capitan de armas* is also mentioned as
of a friendly disposition, though he did not dare to brave the tyrant's rage.
The reference may be to Portilla or Ruiz.   It is remarkable that Pattie came
so often into contact with the governor, and not at all with the comandante.

[33] See preceding chapter for affair of the *Franklin*.   Pattie's statements
that Bradshaw's trial was concluded July 28th, that the *Franklin* ran out of
the harbor in Sept., and that she fired a broadside at the fort, are so positive,
so erroneous, and yet so closely connected with details of his own affairs, as
to leave a doubt as to the accuracy of those details.

thereupon proceeded to "tease him with importunities;" but under this treatment the general became surly. "How earnestly I wished that he and I had been together in the wild woods, and I armed with my rifle!" writes Pattie. This could not be, but he refused to translate any more letters, and the governor, striking him on the head with the flat of his sword, had him dragged again to prison to lie and rot.

The suggestion of profit from the furs had, however, taken root; and early in September the prisoners were released, allowed once more to see each other, and promised permission to go to the Colorado, greatly to their delight. "I was convinced that Mexico could not array force enough to bring us back alive. I foresaw that the general would send no more than ten or twelve soldiers with us. I knew that it would be no more than an amusement to rise upon them, take their horses for our own riding, flea some of them of their skins to show that we knew how to inflict torture, and send the rest back to the general on foot." Pattie was allowed to go to the mission to hire horses for the trip; but at the last moment Echeandía remarked that he could spare no soldiers to go with them. It did not matter, they said, though it spoiled their plan of vengeance. But the governor added that one must remain as a hostage for the return of the rest, and Pattie was the man selected. "At this horrible sentence, breaking upon us in the sanguine rapture of confidence, we all gazed at each other in the consternation of despair;" but Pattie urged them to go and follow their inclinations about coming back. They came back at the end of September. The furs had all been spoiled by the overflow of the river, and the traps were sold to pay the mule-hire. Two of the six, however, failed to return, having left their companions on the Colorado and started for New Mexico.[34]

[34] These two were probably Slover and Pope, since these are the only ones not recorded as being in California in 1829. Warner says Slover and Pope (with Geo. C. Yount, whom nobody else connects with this expedition at all) started

In the absence of his companions, Pattie, by advice of Bradshaw and Perkins,[35] had written a letter to Jones, consul of the United States at the Sandwich Islands, imploring intervention in his own behalf, and then he lay in his cell, harassed by continual threats of being shot at as a target, hanged, or burned alive. Soon came news from the north that the small-pox was raging in the missions. Fortunately Pattie had a small quantity of vaccine matter, and he resolved to make the best possible use of his advantage. Negotiations followed, which gave the young trapper many opportunities to show what could be done by the tongue of a free American citizen. In return for the liberty of himself and companions, he offered to vaccinate everybody in the territory; refusing his own liberty, refusing to vaccinate the governor himself, though trembling in fear of death, refusing even to operate on the arm of his beautiful guardian angel, the Señorita Pico, unless his proposition were accepted. There were many stormy scenes, and Pattie was often remanded to prison with a curse from Echeandía, who told him he might die for his obstinacy. But at last the governor had to yield. Certain old black papers in possession of the trappers, as interpreted by Pattie, were accepted as certificates of American citizenship, and in December all were freed for a week as an experiment.[36]

from New Mexico with the company, but returned from the Colorado without coming to Cal. There must be an error in Pattie's version of the departure of these two men; for I find that on Nov. 11, 1828, Echeandía informed the com. at Altar that he has issued passports to Pope and Slover, who started from N. Mexico for Sonora, but lost their way and entered Cal. *Dept. Rec.*, MS., vi. 13. Pope came back some years later, and has left his name to Pope Valley, Napa county, where he lived and died. May 1, 1828, E. had written to the com. of Altar about the 8 Americans detained at S. Diego, whom he thought it expedient to send back to the Colorado under a guard, that they might go to Sonora according to their custom-house permit. *Dept. Rec.*, MS., vi. 9. July 5th, the gov. of Sonora writes to the alcalde of Altar on the subject, and presumes that the com. gen. has already issued the proper instructions. The captives are alluded to as suspicious characters. *Pinart, Col. Doc., Son.*, MS., 43.

[35] Bradshaw had really been gone over a month at the time when these interviews are said to have taken place.

[36] It is implied by the writer that vaccination was a great mystery to the Californians, and even to the Russians, which is absurdly inaccurate, and

It was deemed best to take no risks. By a false promise to their friend, the capitan de armas, they got their rifles and pistols on pretence of cleaning them, and refused to return the weapons, which were concealed in the thicket. Charles Lang, the smuggler, now made his appearance secretly,[37] and the trappers determined to join him. Pattie with one companion left San Diego Christmas night, and went down to Todos Santos; but learning that Lang had been arrested, they returned. Their comrades were still at liberty; no trouble was made by Echeandía about their absence or the recovery of their arms; and in January and February 1829, Pattie vaccinated everybody at the presidio and mission. On February 28th a paper was issued to each, granting liberty for a year on parole;[38] and Pattie obtained also a letter to the padres, who were instructed to furnish supplies and horses for the journey, and "indemnify me for my services as far as they thought proper."

Pattie started immediately on his trip northward, called at mission, presidio, and pueblo, and arrived at San Francisco the 20th of June. He had vaccinated

forms a weak point in the narrative. It is not certain, however, that they had any vaccine matter in their possession in 1828, nor is it evident that Pattie could have kept that which he had from being taken. I suppose that all is exaggerated for effect, but that Pattie may have been really employed to vaccinate. Early in 1829 a Russian vessel brought vaccine matter, and W. A. Richardson was employed that year to vaccinate at the missions; and in 1821 the Russians had vaccinated 54 persons at Monterey.

[37] See p. 139, this volume, for Lang's adventures.

[38] Pattie's *carta de seguridad* of Feb. 28th is preserved in *Dept. Rec.*, MS., vii. 89. It is as follows: 'Whereas, Santiago Ohio Pattie, who came into this territory hunting beaver in company with other foreigners, without any license whatever, in March of the past year, appears to be a North American according to a custom-house permit given in New Mexico; and whereas, the comandante of this place reports him not to be vicious but of regular conduct, in the petition presented by Pattie on the 27th of this month for permission to travel and remain in the country, there being no consul nor mercantile agent of his nation, nor any Mexican bondsman, therefore I have determined to grant him provisionally this letter of security, that he may remain and travel in this territory for one year,' in accordance, so far as possible, with the laws of May 1 and Mar. 12, 1828.

I have not found the papers of the other men under this date, but in a list of Feb. 14th, *Dept. St. Pap.*, MS., xix. 44, Pryor, Puter, and Yorgens are named, Pryor being already at S. Luis Rey. He received a *carta de seguridad* April 52th. *Id.*, xix. 18–19. It is doubtful if any of them were kept in prison after their return from the Colorado.

in all 22,000 persons,[39] receiving from the padres certificates by which the value of his services was to be
finally estimated by a 'high dignitary' in the north.
After a week's visit to Ross, where everything pleased
the American, and where he received $100 for his
medical services,[40] he returned and presented his certificates to the padre at San Francisco. On July
8th John Cabortes, presumably Padre Juan Cabot,
presented the amateur physician a paper, by which
he gave him 500 cattle and 500 mules, with land on
which to pasture the same—to be delivered when he
had become a Catholic and a Mexican citizen. "When
I had read this," says Pattie, "I was struck dumb.
My anger choked me." But he soon recovered his
speech sufficiently to give the padre his opinion in
the matter, to say that he came from a country where
the laws compelled a man to pay another what he
justly owed him without condition of submission to
"any of his whimsical desires;" that as a protestant
he would not change his opinions for all the money
the mission was worth, and that as an American,
"rather than consent to be adopted into the society and
companionship of such a band of murderers and robbers," he would suffer death. For this "honest and
plain utterance" of his feelings, he was ordered to
leave the house; and, keeping his rifle ready for any
one the priest might send after him, he bought a
horse for three dollars, and started for Monte El Rey!

At the capital Pattie shipped on an American vessel, and for several months ploughed the Pacific,
touching at various ports. He does not name the
vessel, and he gives no particulars of his voyage, save

[39] Strangely enough there is no record in the archives respecting the ravages
of small-pox or Pattie's professional tour; yet his statement is confirmed by
the fact that the statistical tables show an extraordinary number of deaths
this year among the Indians of all the northern missions. (See note 36.) Sta
Cruz, S. José, and Sta Clara do not appear to have been visited at all. Here
in the extreme north only the few who had not had the small-pox were vaccinated.

[40] He had seen Don Sereldo, as he calls the Russian manager, at S. Diego,
and had been implored to come to Bodega and administer his remedy.

of the first week's terrible sea-sickness.   Back at Monterey,[41] he took a more or less active part, on both sides, in the Solis revolt, to which event considerable space is devoted in his narrative.[42]   At first the trapper had contributed in a small way to the rebellion fund, and had with difficulty been dissuaded from joining the army of Solis in the hope of getting a shot at Echeandía; but in the end he had become an ally of his old foe, who on his coming to Monterey received Pattie affably, and even listened with some patience to a repetition of his long-winded arguments and complaints.   Yet notwithstanding the portentous aspect of a document which Pattie had prepared by the advice of the Hawaiian consul, Jones,[43] for presentation to the American minister at Mexico, Echeandía ventured to doubt that his wrongs would be redressed, though he granted a passport that he might go to Mexico and try.   Spending three days *de fiesta* at San Cárlos in company with Captain William Hinckley, hunting otter profitably for ten days on the coast, presenting his rifle to Captain Cooper, and writing a letter of farewell to his former companions in the south, Pattie sailed on the *Volunteer* May 9th, in company with Solis and his fellow-prisoners, for San Blas.   At Mexico in June, at the office of Butler, American chargé d'affaires, he saw a communication of President Andrew Jackson in his behalf.   He was honored by an interview with President Guerrero, and had the pleasure of learning that Echeandía had been recalled.   I have his original letter of June 14, 1830, to friends in California, naming Lothlin (Laugh-

[41] He says it was Jan. 6, 1830; but if there is any foundation of truth in that part of the narrative which follows, it must have been about 2 months earlier.

[42] See chapter iii., this volume, on the Solis revolt, and especially Pattie's version of that affair.   His dates are all wrong; there are many absurd inaccuracies built on a substratum of truth; and there is apparently deliberate falsehood respecting his personal exploits in the capture of Solis.

[43] Pattie says that this consul, John W. Jones, to whom he had written from S. Diego, arrived at Monterey April 29th in his own brig from the Islands.   The reference is to John C. Jones, Jr., owner of the *Volunteer*, which arrived at about this time.

lin), Pryor, and Cooper, in which he explains that 'Kernal' Butler had been able to give no satisfaction, but had advised him to seek redress from the President of the United States. The adventurer reached New Orleans in August, and proceeding up the Mississippi, was soon introduced to Rev. Timothy Flint, who was to make his name and fame more or less immortal.[44]

I have thus presented, with fairness I think, the substance and spirit of Pattie's narrative, though obliged to omit many details, making no pretension to point out minor errors, and perhaps failing to give a full idea of the writer's bitter feelings toward his oppressors. The subject is entitled to the space I have given it, on account of the extraordinary nature of the adventures recounted, the early date of the visit to California, the extent of the author's travels in the territory, the fame of his book, and the accuracy of many of his statements. Yet from the spirit of the narrative, from the numerous erroneous statements, and from my knowledge of Echeandía's character, I have no hesitation in pronouncing Pattie's complaints of ill treatment grossly exaggerated. This opinion is confirmed by those of the company who remained in the country. Entering the territory without passports, the hunters were, according to the unwise policy of Mexican laws, liable to arrest. Presidio fare, and especially prison fare, in California at that time, was even less congenial to American hunters than was the narrow spirit of Spanish policy. Naturally they were disappointed at their reception, and disgusted with their situation, but they were not probably made the victims of any special oppression. James O. Pattie was, however, a self-conceited and quick-tempered boy, with a freedom of

[44] Letter in *Vallejo, Doc.*, xxx. 85. In 1883 a man whose name I cannot recall, apparently trustworthy, while visiting my Library, stated that his wife was a niece of Pattie, and that the latter had spent some time at her residence in San Diego in late years, or at least since 1850. The man promised to obtain from his wife a more definite statement on the subject, but I have not received it.

speech often amounting to insolence, and unlimited ability to make himself disagreeable. How far these peculiarities, and the young man's connection with the smuggling operations of Bradshaw and Lang, may have provoked Echeandía to the infliction of special penalties, I cannot say.

Thomas L. Smith, commonly called 'Peg-leg' Smith —a well known character in many parts of California, but chiefly in later times, who died in a San Francisco hospital in 1866—was one of the famous trappers and Indian-fighters of this early epoch. He was at times a companion of Jedediah Smith, and was the hero of many wild adventures in various parts of the great interior; but very few of his early exploits have ever been recorded with even approximate accuracy of time or place. He owes his position on this page to a report that he came to California in 1829, a report that I have not been able to trace to any reliable source.[45] Engaged in trapping in the Utah regions, he came to California to dispose of his furs. He was ordered out of the country, and departed, he and his companion taking with them, however, a band of three or four hundred horses, in spite of efforts of the Californians to prevent the act. Some accounts say that he visited the country repeatedly in those early years, and we shall find archive evidence of his presence a little later, acting with the horse-thieves of the Tulares, and known as 'El Cojo Smit.'[46]

In the spring of 1828 the Mexican government granted to Richard Exter and Julian Wilson[47] a pro-

[45] The story is told in many newspaper biographical sketches published at the time of Smith's death. I have before me the *S. F. Bulletin*, Oct. 26, 1866; *Nevada Daily Gazette*, Oct. 25, 1866; and others in *Hayes' Scraps, Cal. Notes*, ii. 309–12.

[46] As an item which I am unable to connect with any of the expeditions particularly accredited to this period, I may notice a record of Nov. 6, 1829, that five deserters from Upper California were captured on the frontier of the peninsula, one of whom, an Englishman, stabbed a neophyte, and was shot by another. *St. Pap., Sac.*, MS., xiv. 10–11.

[47] Exter, of Exter, Graves, & Co., Mexico, was connected with the General

visional license to hunt and trap in New Mexico and California, as well as on the coasts for sea-otter. They had asked for an exclusive privilege, which proposition was reserved for consideration by congress. The object in view was to derive a revenue from the territorial wealth of furs, and by a contract with these foreigners to prevent the constantly increasing clandestine operations of other foreigners, whom no revenue laws could control. The idea was a good one. Such a contract with a responsible and powerful company was perhaps the only means by which Mexico could partially protect her interests in this direction; but there may be some doubt whether Exter and Wilson possessed the requisite qualifications, since little is known about them. It does not appear that the exclusive privilege was ever conceded,[48] and nothing was ever done under the provisional permit. Vallejo and Alvarado say that there was a strong feeling in California against the scheme, and that when the two men came to the country in 1829, strutting up and down as if they owned it, Echeandía refused to recognize their authority, and they went away in disgust.[49]

In January 1830 a small party—of Mexicans apparently—came from New Mexico to Los Angeles under the leadership of José Antonio Vaca; but of their purposes and adventures we know nothing from the fragmentary records.[50] A somewhat better known

Pearl and Coral Fishing Association of London, and there are several letters from him to Hartnell, dated 1827, and not referring to the fur business, in *Vallejo, Doc.*, MS., xxix. 153–4, 163.

[48] April 28, 1828, provisional license granted. Hunting parties must be made up of at least two thirds Mexican citizens. *Mexico, Mem. Rel.*, 1829, p. 22. Aug. 7th, the comisario communicates the concession to Herrera. Exact accounts must be kept of number, size, and quality of skins. *Dept. St. Pap., Ben. Com. and Treas.*, MS., i. 106. Dec. 23, 1828, gov. announces the license in Cal., and says that the parties will be allowed to catch otter. *Dept. Rec.*, MS., vi. 162.

[49] *Vallejo, Hist. Cal.*, MS., ii. 124–5; *Alvarado, Hist. Cal.*, MS., ii. 128–9. Fernandez, *Cosas de Cal.*, MS., 58–9, mentions their failure to get an exclusive privilege, but says nothing of their having come to Cal.

[50] *Dept. Rec.*, MS., viii. 14, 18, 69; *Dept. St. Pap., Ben. Pref. y Juzg.*, MS., i. 31.

expedition is that of Ewing Young, the Tennesseean, or Joaquin Jóven as he was often called, who entered the territory later in the same year from New Mexico with a company of beaver-hunters of various nationalities. Warner says this party came by Jedediah Smith's old trail, and found Ogden's Hudson Bay trappers on the Sacramento.[51] After trapping for a short time in the Tulares, Young moved north and met the Indian alcalde of San José mission out on a hunt for runaway neophytes by order of the padre. The fugitives allied with the gentiles showed fight, but eleven of the trappers aided the alcalde to defeat the foe. Taking advantage of this service rendered, Young, with three of his men, came to the mission July 11th, showed his passports, explained his need of horses, and departed after promising to return in a week with furs to sell or to exchange for supplies.[52]

There is no record that the hunters returned to San José, though they may have done so; but at the end of July three Frenchmen came to Monterey, announcing their intention to return to New Mexico, having left the company.[53] In October the hunters were in the vicinity of Los Angeles, where the leader had great difficulty in controlling them, and where one man was killed.[54] It had been the intention to return from the Colorado in December to sell furs and buy

[51] *Warner's Reminis.*, MS., 37–9. In *Dept. St. Pap.*, ii. 84, 113, is Young's passport of 1829 signed by Henry Clay.

[52] July 15, 1830, report of José Berreyesa. *Dept. St. Pap.*, MS., ii. 135–9. One of Young's passports was viséd at Washington, March 20, 1828, by the Mex. minister. It permitted the bearer to go into the interior.

[53] These men were François Turcote, Jean Vaillant, and Anastase Curier. *Dept. St. Pap., Ben. Cust.-H.*, MS., ii. 4–5. In a letter to Capt. Cooper of Oct. 10th, Young says that the Frenchmen, who owed him money, had mutinied, and determined to stay in the country; but they had been forced to return with the party. He also speaks of the fight with Indians, but indicates that it was to recover stolen horses rather than to aid the neophytes. *Vallejo, Doc.*, MS., xxx. 135. Dec. 23d, Echeandía to alcalde of S. José. Speaks of 4 Americans who had come to the rancho of S. Pablo and must depart at once. There may be an error in this date. *Dept. Rec.*, MS., viii. 134.

[54] Warner says that James Higgins killed an Irishman known as Big Jim. José Antonio Pico reports the killing on Oct. 7th. He had orders to detain Young, but his force was too small. *Dept. St. Pap., Ben. Pref. y Juzg.*, MS., i. 97. Juan Higgins, probably the same, remained in Cal. for 5 or 6 years at least. *Dept. St. Pap.*, MS., iv. 156, 159.

mules; but Young had lost confidence in his men, and thought he would be fortunate to get safely home with his company by the aid of the Americans. He intended, however, to come back the following year.[55] There are several men named as being in California from New Mexico this year, some of whom may have belonged to this party; but Young and Higgins are the only ones known here later, unless Kit Carson may have made his first visit at this time.

Of the foreign residents who came to California before 1826, about fifty are mentioned in the records of 1826–30, a dozen or more having died or left the country. Some of the more prominent, like Hartnell, Spence, Cooper, and Gale, have been noticed in connection with commercial and maritime topics in the preceding chapter. All, including new-comers, were in this period as a class law-abiding citizens of considerable influence in their new home. Many were baptized, married, and naturalized. Space does not permit the introduction of personal experiences and achievements here, but the reader is referred to the biographic sketches presented elsewhere in this work.[56] In respect of general policy toward foreigners,[57] there was little or no tendency in California to exclusiveness or oppression in 1826, as has been seen from the commercial record, and especially from the privileges allowed to Captain Beechey, in contrast with the treatment of Vancouver at an earlier date and under another régime. Yet the Mexican laws were strict in requiring foreigners to show passports, and submit to surveillance; hence the precautions taken in the case of Jedediah Smith and his company; hence certain orders for the arrest of deserting sailors.

---

[55] Young to Cooper. *Vallejo, Doc.*, MS., xxx. 135.

[56] See alphabetical register of pioneers at end of vol. ii.–v. Also a list of pioneers who came before 1830, at the end of vol. ii. of this work.

[57] Aug., Dec. 1826, orders of sup. govt against admission of foreigners without passports circulated by gov. and comandantes. *S. José, Arch.*, MS., vi. 25; *Dept. Rec.*, MS., iv. 25.

Of new-comers for 1826, about sixty are named. It is not easy to decide exactly which of these are entitled to the name of pioneers, nor is it necessary, because I shall mention them all elsewhere. Here I name only such as remained in the country several years at least, traders who came often during a series of years and became well known to the people, men who though visitors now became permanent residents later, and men who died in California. Such for this year number twenty-five.[58] The most prominent names are those of Dana, Fitch, and Wilson; but ten or twelve lived long in the country and were well known.

In 1827 the general orders from Mexico promulgated by Echeandía, and more or less fully enforced, were to insist on passports, to keep a strict watch, render a monthly account of new arrivals, grant no lands to foreigners, and by no means to allow them to form settlements on coast or islands.[59] On the intercession of the English chargé d'affaires in Mexico, the local authorities were empowered to extend the passports of English residents for one year, while the papers of other foreigners might be extended so as to allow them time to make a regular application for renewal.[60] My list of newly arrived pioneers for the year contains twelve names, the total number, including visitors, being about thirty.[61] John Temple and

---

[58] For complete lists see Pioneer Register at end of these volumes. The pioneers of 1826 were the following: Louis Bolbeda, Joaquin Bowman, Michael Charles, Wm H. Cunningham, Wm G. Dana, Henry D. Fitch, Guy F. Fling, Benj. Foxen, Isaac Galbraith, Cornelius A. Johnson, John Littleton, Wm Logan, Thomas B. Park, Joaquin Pereira, Louis Pombert, John Read (?), Geo. J. Rice, James Scott, Joseph Steele, Wm Trevethan, John S. Turner, Geo. W. Vincent, John Wilson, John Wilson (trapper), and John H. Wilson the negro.

[59] Sup. Govt St. Pap., MS., iv. 1; Dept. Rec., MS., v. 19, 53, 95; Dept. St. Pap., S. José, MS., v. 12.

[60] St. Pap., Sac., MS., xvi. 1–3; Dept. Rec., MS., vi. 175. Barron and Forbes at Tepic were at this time pumping Bandini and Hartnell for information about California, and projecting a visit. Oct. 17, 1827, Eustacio Barron to Bandini. Bandini, Doc., MS., 7.

[61] See Pioneer Register at end of these volumes. Pioneers of 1827: Miguel Allen (born in Cal.), John Bradshaw, Geo. Coleman, Nicolas Dodero, Robt J. Elwell, John A. C. Holmes, Giovanni Glande, Joseph Jackson, John B. Leandry, Jean B. Mutrel, William Smith, and John Temple.

Robert J. Elwell became most prominent in California; though Bradshaw, Holmes, and Leandry were also well known men. It was during this year that the Californians were excited at the presence and actions of Jedediah Smith's trappers, their first American visitors by the overland route. As Smith arrived in December 1826, the names of his companions who settled in the country have been included in the list of that year, though they left the company of hunters, and some of them arrived, in 1827.

Orders of the Californian officials in 1828 respecting foreigners were of the same tenor as before; applications for naturalization were frequent; many strangers wished to marry Californian wives. Bands of trappers on the frontiers round about excited some apprehensions. A few immigrants of Mexican blood seem to have come in from Sonora, and all was faithfully reported to the minister of relations in Mexico.[62] In accordance with the decree of March 12, 1828, which declared that no foreigner could remain in Mexican territory without a passport, and regulated the holding of property by naturalized citizens,[63] a reglamento was issued by the president on May 1st prescribing in detail the methods to be observed in obtaining, granting, and using passports of various kinds. This document was doubtless forwarded to California later in the year.[64] I find about sixty new

[62] *Dept. Rec.*, MS., vi. 21, 27, 177, 192, 194; vii. 25; *St. Pap., Sac.*, MS., x. 98; *Vallejo, Doc.*, MS., xxix. passim. The Americans celebrated July 4th by burning much powder on the vessels at S. Diego.

[63] *Mexico, Decreto sobre Pasaportes y modo de adquirir propiedades los Estrangeros, 12 de Marzo de 1828.* 12 articles. In *Schmidt's Civil Law of Spain and Mexico*, 346-51, in Spanish and English; *Hayes' Mex. Laws*, 81-2.

[64] *Mexico, Reglamento para el ramo de Pasaportes—decretado por el Presidente en 1 de Mayo 1828.* Printed copy in *Pinto, Doc.*, i. 3. 25 articles, numbered as 22. Also in *Dept. St. Pap., Angeles*, MS., ix. 30-6; and part of it in *Vallejo, Doc.*, MS. Omitting minor details, this regulation was in substance as follows: The master of a ship, on arrival, must furnish a report of his foreign passengers, and each passenger a report of his name, business, etc., to the customs officer, who will grant a *boleto de disembarco* to such as are not Spaniards, and have a passport from the general government, or from duly accredited Mexican agents abroad, or a bond from the consul or agent of their nation at the port of landing, or of a Mexican citizen. The *boleto*, without which no foreigner could leave the vessel, must be presented within

names of foreigners in this year's records, several belonging to men whose presence is noted in consequence of the regulations just mentioned, but about whom no more is known than that they were here in 1828–9. Pioneers proper number eighteen, as per appended list.[65]   Several of these became in later times locally prominent; and one of the number, Henry A. Peirce, is still living in 1884, being in a sense the oldest living pioneer within my knowledge, though he has by no means resided continuously in California.   Two or three detected attempts at smuggling, together with the presence of Pattie and his trappers from New Mexico, were the leading topics of interest for 1828, as far as foreigners were concerned.

In 1829 Echeandía continued to circulate the passport regulations for the benefit of foreigners and of local officials.   He still received numerous applications for permits to remain, to travel, to marry, or to become naturalized, and called for full reports of resident foreigners.[66]   It is from these reports, and the various certificates connected with the applications above referred to, that I have obtained much of the information presented elsewhere respecting individuals; still the lists are incomplete, and have to be perfected from numerous scattered documents.[67]   Eche-

[24] hours to the civil authority of the port, who will visé the passport. To travel in the interior a *carta de seguridad* for a year must be obtained. Whatever passports a foreigner might have, he must present himself to the civil authorities of any place where he intended to remain over 8 days, and on each change of residence.   Due provision was made for renewal of licenses, penalties for failure to comply with the law, and for full reports to be sent to the government.

[65] Pioneers of 1828: Stephen Anderson, Louis Bouchet, John Brown (?), John Davis, Jesse Ferguson, Richard Laughlin, Timothy Murphy, Sylvester Pattie, Henry A. Peirce, Wm Pope, Nathaniel Pryor, Isaac Slover, Wm Taylor, James Thompson, Wm Warren (?) the negro, Edward Watson, Wm Willis, and Julian Wilson.   For biographical sketches, see Pioneer Register at the end of vol. ii.–v., this work.

[66] *Dept. Rec.*, MS., vii. 59, 86, 105, 176; *Dept. St. Pap.*, MS., xix. 20–2; *St. Pap., Sac.*, MS., xi. 4; *Vallejo, Doc.*, MS., xxix. 310.

[67] Naturalization records in *Dept. St. Pap.*, MS., xix. passim. List of 48 names dated Feb. 14th, in *Id.*, xix. 44.   List of 44 names in Monterey district Feb. 16th, in *Id.*, ii. 115.   List of 7 names in S. José, Feb. 5th. *Id.*, xix. 3.   List of 7 at Los Angeles Feb. 14th, in *Monterey, Arch.*, MS., vii. 24–5.   Apparently 2 foreigners at S. F. *Dept. St. Pap.*, MS., ii. 97–8.   There are no lists for Sta Bárbara or S. Diego.

andía heard this year and forwarded to the supreme government a rumor that the Americans were plotting to seize the port of San Francisco; while on the other side of the continent we find a rumor from Mexico, by way of England, that California with Texas was to be made over to the United States for a term of years, as security for a large sum of money to be spent in resisting Spanish invasion.[68] The new arrivals of the year, as named in an appended list, were seventeen,[69] or about thirty-five including visitors, or men about whom nothing more is known than their mention in lists of the year. Prominent names are those of Captain Hinckley, Alfred Robinson, and Abel Stearns. Robinson still lives in 1884, with none to dispute his title as the oldest pioneer, unless it be Peirce of 1828, as already mentioned, or Michael White, perhaps still alive, but about whose arrival in 1829 there is some doubt. The great excitement of the year was the Solis revolt, in which, as we have seen, the foreigners, though at first somewhat inclined to sympathize with the movement as promising them certain commercial advantages, later took a decided stand in favor of the regular authorities, and contributed largely to the restoration of the capital.

In February 1830 the Mexican government, in reply to reports respecting Abel Stearns and others in California who were seeking lands, directed Echeandía to distribute the public lands in accordance with the laws to such foreigners as could comply with all the requirements, taking care, however, that the Russians and

[68] June 25th, E. to min. of rel., in *Dept. Rec.*, MS., vii. 25. *Niles' Reg.*, xxxvii. 87. The *John Bull* says: 'The proposition of America must not be quietly listened to or tamely permitted; while we are earnest in our endeavors to put a stop to the power of Russia, we must not forget the necessity of checking the aggrandizement of America.'

[69] Pioneers of 1829—the '(?)' indicates uncertainty about the exact date of arrival: James D. Arther, Jas Breck, Walter Duckworth (?), James Flemming, Wm S. Hinckley (?), Geo. Kinlock (?), Lawrence (born in Cal.), John Meek, Manuel D. Olivera, Jordan Pacheco, John Rainsford, Alfred Robinson, Thos L. (Peg-leg) Smith (?), Abel Stearns, Chas A. Swain (?), Michael White (?), and Geo. Williams. See biog. sketches of them and also of the years' visitors in Pioneer Register at the end of these volumes.

Americans should be the least numerous, and be located in the central parts.[70]   A little later, however, foreigners of adjacent countries were prohibited from colonization on the frontier.[71]   It is not certain that any resident foreigner had yet obtained his final and complete papers of naturalization; though a few may have done so, and many had made application and complied with all the preliminary requirements, receiving certificates which served all practical purposes.[72]   Newcomers of this final year of the decade were fifty, of whom twenty-four named in a note may be regarded as pioneers proper.[73]   The arrival of Kit Carson this year is doubtful.   Bee, Jones, Nye, Snook, and Young were the names best known in the annals of later years. Some details about all the men named in this chapter and many visitors not here named may be found in the Pioneer Register appended to these volumes.   That register will also serve as an index through which may be found all that is recorded of any early Californian in this work.

[70] Feb. 2, 1830, Alaman to E. *Sup. Govt St. Pap.*, MS., vi. 4.

[71] Law of April 6, 1830, in *Halleck's Report*, 121–2.   Article 7 of the law of Aug. 18, 1824, was thereby repealed.

[72] The naturalization regulations, probably of 1828, are given in *Schmidt's Civil Law of Spain and Mexico*, 353–9, in Spanish and English.   The general purport had been circulated by Echeandía on June 4, 1829. *Dept. St. Pap.*, MS., xix. 20–1.   These rules prescribed in substance that any foreigner of two years' residence might, one year after having announced his intention, obtain a *carta de naturaleza* from the gov. by renouncing all allegiance to any foreign power, swearing to support the constitution and laws of Mexico, and presenting proof in due form of Catholic faith, means of support, and good conduct.   See also the Mex. passport regulations of Oct. 12, 1830, in *Arrillaga, Recop.*, 1830, p. 474–99.

[73] Pioneers of 1830; Henry J. Bee, John Burns, Kit Carson (?), James Cook, Phil. H. Devoll, Juan Domingo, *William Duckworth, John Ebbetts, James Harris, John Higgins, John C. Jones, *Geo. D. Kinlock, Laure, Allen Lewis, Gorham H. Nye, *Juan Pombert, Sam. Prentice, John Rice, John Roach, Ed Robinson (?), Jos F. Snook, Sam. Thompson, *Francis Watson, and Ewing Young.   Those whose names are marked with a * were born in Cal., their fathers being foreigners.

CHAPTER VII.

RULE AND OVERTHROW OF VICTORIA.

1831.

LIEUTENANT-COLONEL MANUEL VICTORIA was appointed
March 8, 1830, to succeed José María Echeandía as
gefe político of Alta California, and three days later
official notice was sent to the incumbent.[1] Victoria
was then at Loreto, where for several years he had
been comandante principal of Lower California; but
nothing is known of his career on the peninsula, nor
of his previous life beyond the current and probably
accurate belief in California that he was a native of
Acapulco, and commandant there in 1825, who had
won his rank by personal bravery in the war of independence.[2] Antonio García had previously been

[1] *Supt. Govt St. Pap.*, MS., vi. 6–7. Victoria's appointment and Minister Facio's communication of Mar. 11th to Echeandía.

[2] Com. at Acapulco 1825. *Gac. Mex.*, June 15, 1825. In June 1825, when
Victoria was about to leave Acapulco for Loreto, Enrique Virmond pro-

named to succeed Echeandía, and the substitution of
Victoria is believed to have been due to the success
of Bustamante in Mexico, and to Franciscan influence on the new administration. While there is no
positive proof of the Californian friars' intrigues in
the matter, yet Bustamante's revolution was widely
regarded as a reactionary movement in favor of the old
Spanish institutions. The padres were very bitterly
opposed to the mission policy of Echeandía, or of the
administration that he represented, and they openly
rejoiced at the new appointment as a glorious 'victory'
for their cause.[3]

Having notified Echeandía of his coming, and
named a day for the transfer of office at San Diego,
Victoria started northward from Loreto by land in
the autumn of 1830, arriving at San Diego in December, or possibly in November. He was disappointed
at not finding either the governor or any message
from him; but a despatch sent post-haste to the north
elicited from Echeandía a reply, to the effect that the
command would be turned over at Monterey, the
capital. A later despatch, however, named Santa
Bárbara as the place, and thither Victoria went,
arriving the 31st of December. Here he remained
about three weeks, engaging in a sharp correspondence with Echeandía, some of whose orders he countermanded, though not yet legally invested with
authority; but at last he came to Monterey, and on
January 31, 1831, assumed the formal command, taking the oath in presence of the ayuntamiento, assembled for the purpose.[4]

nounced him, in a letter to Guerra, 'un sujeto de las mejores prendas.'
Guerra, Doc., MS. Osio, *Hist. Cal.*, MS., 160–2, says he failed to gain the
confidence and esteem of the people in L. Cal.; but not much importance is
to be attached to this statement.

[3] See p. 108 this vol., with quotations from the statements of President
Sanchez on this subject.

[4] Robinson, *Life in Cal.*, 97, says V. arrived at Sta B. on Jan. 10th. The
rather meagre official correspondence on V.'s arrival and assumption of the
command is as follows: Jan. 14, 1831, V. to E., complaining of the delay in
turning over the office, and of the secularization decree. *St. Pap., Miss. and
Colon.*, MS., ii. 35–6; Jan. 19th, V. to min. of rel., narrating all that had

In explanation of the situation at the time of Victoria's arrival, of Echeandía's strange conduct in delaying the transfer of command, and of the bitter controversy that now began between the Californians and their new ruler, I must here refer briefly to a subject which will require full treatment in a subsequent chapter, that of mission secularization. The reader is familiar [5] with the Mexican policy on that matter, with Echeandía's investigation, experiments, and difficulties in attempting to carry out his instructions, and with the action of the diputacion in the summer of 1830 respecting a plan of secularization which was submitted to the national government for approval. Thus far proceedings had been strictly

occurred since his departure from Loreto, including the matter of secularization. *Sup. Govt St. Pap.*, MS., viii. 8–10; Jan. 19th, E. to V., in reply to letter of 14th, reserving full explanations for a personal interview, but conplaining of V.'s conduct in opposing his acts without legal authority, and announcing his intention to await his arrival at Mont. instead of marching to Sta B. as he had been ready to do. *St. Pap., Sac.*, MS., x. 76–8. Jan. 29th–31st, summons to ayuntamiento, and E.'s announcements of having given up the command. *Id.*, xiv. 25; *Dept. Rec.*, MS., ix. 89; *Dept. St. Pap.*, MS., iii. 5–6; *Id., S. José*, MS., iv. 94.

On the same topic a few extra-official statements may also be noted. Bandini, *Hist. Cal.*, MS., 72–3, tells us that V. on his arrival impressed the people of S. Diego as a simple, unostentatious man with benevolent ideas—but they were soon undeceived. Vallejo, *Hist. Cal.*, MS., ii. 137–8; Osio, *Hist. Cal.*, MS., 160–2; Vallejo, *Reminis.*, MS., 111; and Alvarado, *Hist. Cal.*, MS., ii. 168, state that on his way V. called on P. Peyri, at San Luis Rey, by whom he was most hospitably entertained, from whom he borrowed $6,000 more or less, to whom he promised all that the friars desired, and who at once wrote to his associates 'ya lo tenemos en el manguillo.' No doubt relations were most friendly between the two, but the authors named are bitterly prejudiced against V. and all his acts. Vallejo and Alvarado say he got large sums also at S. Juan and S. Gabriel—in fact, that avarice was one of his weak points, and that the padres were willing to buy him. In his diary of *Ocurrencias Curiosas, 1830–1*, MS., Guerra notes the presence of V. at Sta B. on Jan. 7th; declines to make predictions about his prospective rule; but says he seems a great friend of Pacheco, has very judicious views on the subject of missions; and in stature and flesh bears some resemblance to Echeandía. *Carrillo (J.), Doc.*, MS., 33. Mrs Ord remembers that V., instead of lodging as was customary at the comandante's house, went straight to the mission. Here Guerra went to call on the new governor, showing him every attention, and presenting his daughter, the writer. *Ord, Ocurrencias*, MS., 38–41. Osio, *Hist. Cal.*, MS., 162–4, says that V. arrived unexpectedly at Monterey, dismounting before the gov.'s house, and demanding, in an abrupt and offensive manner, an immediate surrender of the office. Echeandía promised the transfer for 9 A. M. next morning, and V. went to S. Cárlos to sleep.

[5] See chap. iv., this volume.

legal, and marked by no imprudent or hasty steps. The friars, however strongly opposed to seculariza- tion on general principles, had no just cause for com- plaint against Echeandía. There was now, however, a popular feeling in favor of the proposed changes far in advance of Echeandía's personal views, and largely due to the influence of José María Padrés, the newly arrived ayudante inspector. Padrés was a man of considerable ability. personally magnetic, and more- over a most radical republican. He soon became a leading spirit among the young Californians just be- coming prominent in public life, intensified their nas- cent republicanism, taught them to theorize eloquently on the rights of man, the wrongs of the neophytes, and the tyranny of the missionaries; and if he also held up before the eyes of the Carrillos, Osios, Vallejos, Picos, Alvarados, Bandinis, and others bright visions of rich estates to be administered by them or their friends, their young enthusiasm should by no means be termed hypocrisy or a desire for plunder.

But events in Mexico seemed to favor the friars, and were not encouraging to the views of Padrés and his disciples. It is not apparent whether or not the success of Bustamante or its bearing on Californian matters was known in July and August 1830, the date of the diputacion's acts; but when the day of Victoria's arrival drew near, and no approval of the plan came from Mexico, Echeandía was persuaded, probably without much difficulty, to essay a *golpe de estado*. Accordingly he issued, January 6, 1831, a decree of secularization, which he took immediate steps to carry into execution before turning over the com- mand to his successor. Victoria was known to be more a soldier than a politician, and it was hoped with the aid of the diputacion in some way to sustain the decree and reach a result favorable to the anti-mission party. Echeandía's act was wholly illegal, uncalled for, and unwise. It was simply a trick, and an absurd one. The opponents of Victoria were thus in the wrong at the beginning of the quarrel.[6]

While at Santa Bárbara Victoria heard of the decree of January 6th and prevented its publication in the south; while he reported the matter to the national authorities, denouncing Padrés, whom of course he had known well in Baja California, as the real author of the trick and as a man who was very dangerous to the best interests of the territory.[7] In the north, where the decree had been already published, the new ruler took immediate steps to prevent its execution. Nothing more need be said here of secularization,[8] but the wrath of the ayudante inspector and his party may well be imagined by the reader, and will be constantly apparent in the subsequent record.

Having assumed the command, Victoria issued the 1st of February an address to the people, a brief document, in which the author made known to his 'beloved fellow-citizens' his purpose to reform the evils that most afflicted the country, and his hope for cordial support from the inhabitants. "The laws must be executed, the government obeyed, and our institutions respected," he writes; "I have to favor honesty and to punish perversity, the first being in accord with my character, the second demanded by my honor and conscience."[9] All of this officer's communications, or at least all that have been preserved, were brief and to the point, showing the writer to be more of a soldier than politician, and lacking something of the usual Mexican bombast. Of his personal

[6] In a letter to the padres dated Nov. 18, 1832, E. says that V. factiously removed him from the command, and that he gave it up to save the country from disturbances (!), little thinking V. would 'audaciously prevaricate and break his oath.' *St. Pap., Miss. and Colon.*, MS., ii. 61. To Figueroa, on Mar. 19, 1833, he says that V. treated him with the greatest contempt in matters of government. *Id.*, ii. 55. The only defence of E. and his friends is the justice of their general views on the mission question and the Indians' rights, which of course has no real bearing on the matter at issue.

[7] *Sup. Govt St. Pap.*, MS., viii. 8-10.

[8] The subject is fully treated for the years 1831-5 in chap. xi.-xii., this volume, q. v.

[9] *Victoria, Manifestacion del Gefe Político de la Alta California á sus habitantes, 1831,* MS.

movements during the nine months of his stay in the north, we know but little, except what can be gathered from the dates of successive official documents to be noticed incidentally in the record about to be presented. He is said to have gone to San Francisco soon after taking the command, and subsequently to have spent some time on different occasions at Santa Clara.[10] In addition to his few letters on special topics, the governor made in June a general report on the industrial condition of California, a document which presents no matter for comment.[11] Echeandía retired to San Diego a few days after turning over the office, but did not yet leave the territory, as we shall see.

The annals of 1831, and of Victoria's rule, are confined to the revolutionary movement by which that rule was brought to an end, there being nothing else worthy of notice in the records of the year, so far at least as general history is concerned. The development of the revolution may best be explained by presenting as successive topics the several charges against the governor, which may be regarded as in a certain sense the causes of the popular feeling on the subject, though it is well to bear always in mind the chief cause, underlying all others as already shown. I begin with what was in reality the most serious and best founded accusation.

[10] Vallejo, *Hist. Cal.*, MS., ii. 137–40, speaks of a party given in V.'s honor at the house of Lieut Martinez, at which politics was more or less discussed. Amador, *Mem.*, MS., 122, mentions a tour of inspection before settling at the capital. Apr. 7th, José J. Gomez writes to Juan Bandini that V. had arrived at Monterey (from the north?) the day before, and was talking of going south soon. *S. Diego, Arch.*, MS., 18. Alvarado, *Hist. Cal.*, MS., iii. 7–8, tells a story to the effect that V. attempted to prosecute himself and José Castro for the part they had taken in publishing the secularization decree, authorizing Pliego, their enemy, to commence criminal proceedings. But when summoned—so says A.—they rode up before Pliego's office on horseback, refused to hear the documents read, and dashed off to Sta Clara. V. subsequently treated them very well, however, giving them a profitable license to take otter at S. Francisco.

[11] *Victoria, Informe General sobre California, 1830,* MS., dated June 7th. A general report on government with recommendations of reform may also be mentioned under date of Sept. 21st. *Dept. Rec.*, MS., ix. 146–9.

Victoria neglected to convene the diputacion, and even when urged to do so, flatly refused, greatly to the disgust of the members and their friends, the most influential element of the population. His conduct in this respect was doubtless illegal as well as impolitic, and gave the Californians just cause for complaint. He knew, however, that the vocales were for the most part the followers of Padrés and the promoters of Echeandía's *golpe de estado*, regarding their desire to assemble as merely a continuation of the trick, and supposing with much reason that the sessions would be largely devoted to schemes of interference with his own policy and measures. On January 29th, the day of Victoria's arrival at Monterey, Echeandía had summoned the vocales to assemble in the interests of public tranquillity.[12] I have no doubt the plan was in some manner to insist, with the aid of the diputacion, on the carrying-out of the secularization scheme. Efforts to convene that body were continued all the spring and summer. At first the ayuntamiento of Monterey, aided to some extent by that of San José, was the medium of appeal, though the governor in February assembled that body to explain how inopportune had been the petitions of Alcalde Buelna, and warned the municipal authorities not to meddle with matters that did not concern them.[13] The 30th of July diputados Vallejo, Osio, Ortega, and Castro petitioned the governor directly to convoke the assembly, and apparently some of the southern members either signed this petition or sent in another similar one; but Victoria showed no signs of yielding.[14]

[12] Jan. 29, 1831, E. at the request of the ayunt. of Monterey in extra session, to José Ortega, Tiburcio Castro, M. G. Vallejo, and suplente Francisco Haro in place of A. M. Osio. *Dept. Rec.*, MS., ix. 88; *Vallejo, Doc.*, MS., i. 216; *Monterey, Actos del Ayunt.*, MS., 30-1. Probably a similar summons was sent to other members.

[13] *Monterey, Actos del Ayunt.*, MS., 31-4, 38-40. Sessions Jan. 29th; Feb. 5th, 18th; Aug. 3d, 4th. Also vague allusions in the proceedings against Duarte, the alcalde of S. José. *Dept. St. Pap., Ben. Mil.*, MS., 14-51. Of the Duarte case I shall speak a little later.

[14] The petition is alluded to in *Leg. Rec.*, MS., i. 305-9, 332, but no details are given. On Aug. 24th V. writes to Alcalde Sanchez of Los Angeles·

The northern members repeated their petition September 11th, urging that the regular time for meeting was March 1st, claiming that urgent business required attention, and even threatening rather mysteriously, in case their request were denied, " to proceed according to law."[15]   This brought out from Victoria on the 21st an address, or manifiesto, to the public. In this document he defined in a very straightforward manner his position, alluding to the criminal motives and seditious plans of the opposing faction, "personal interests disguised in the habiliments of philanthropy," declaring his intention to thwart the schemes of his predecessor, and reminding good citizens that the way to prosperity and happiness lay in the direction of submission to law, and not of sedition. He stated that a majority of the diputados had been illegally elected, that he had reported everything to the national authorities, without whose orders he would not convoke the assembly, and that he counted on resources unknown to his enemies.[16]   In a report bearing the same date Victoria announced his suspension of the diputacion, and earnestly recommended the abolishment of all elective ayuntamientos and the restoration of military rule, except that certain judges might be appointed for Los Angeles and San José.[17] This radical overturning of all civil authority seemed a simple and effective measure to this honest soldier, who felt that he could preserve order more easily if

'As you are probably on good terms with Pico, persuade him to withdraw his petition for convoking the dip...It is my privilege to convene the assembly when I find it necessary; and up to the present time it has not been so; for I have just reasons which require me to await the decision of the sup. govt on my inquiries.' *Id.*, i. 329–30. Sept. 7th, V. writes a very curt and plain letter to Juan Bandini in reply to his of Aug. 7th. The subject is ostensibly financial matters, but it is apparent that Bandini was reckoned among the enemies of the new gov. on general principles. *Dept. Rec.*, ix. 43–5.

[15] Petition dated S. Francisco, in *Leg. Rec.*, MS., i. 330–2.

[16] *Victoria, Manifiesto á los Habitantes de California. 21 de Setiembre, 1831*, MS.; *Vallejo, Doc.*, MS., i. 245; *Pico, Hist. Cal.*, MS., 3; *Bandini, Doc.*, MS., 16. V. expressed like sentiments in a letter of Oct. 24th to the alcalde of Los Angeles, copied in *Leg. Rec.*, MS., i. 335–6.

[17] Sept. 21, 1831, V. to min. of justice, in *Dept. Rec.*, MS., ix. 146–9. The writer claimed that there were few if any persons fit for alcaldes, and that the offices were sought mainly for purposes of personal gain or revenge.

the territory were made a mere military comandancia. Small wonder, however, that the Californian republicans were unprepared for such a change! The four diputados, Vallejo, Ortega, Osio, and Castro, sent, September 18th, a representation to Mexico, complaining of the refusal to convoke the diputacion, of his evident hostility to the federal system, and of several arbitrary acts to be noted later. The 7th of November they sent another memorial in reply to Victoria's manifiesto, in which they called upon the supreme government to protect the people against the governor's oppressive usurpations.[18] Juan Bandini, substitute congressman from California, also wrote a reply to Victoria's proclamation, dated at San Diego October 10th, in which he refuted the charge of illegality in the elections, and argued very eloquently against the governor's right to deprive the country of the services of its diputacion on account of mere suspicions respecting the members. Pio Pico, senior vocal of the diputacion, issued a similar protest.[19]

The administration of justice was a subject which early claimed the new ruler's attention. It had been much neglected by the easy-going Echeandía, and crime had gone unpunished. Criminal proceedings had been often instituted, as we have seen in the local presidial annals of the last six years, but penalties had been rarely inflicted with fitting severity. Victoria had strict ideas of discipline, and no doubt of his ability to enforce the laws. He is said to have boasted soon after his arrival at Monterey that before long he would make it safe for any man to leave his handkerchief or his watch lying in the plaza until he might

---

[18] Copies of these documents in *Vallejo, Doc.*, MS., i. 215, 238, 241.

[19] *Bandini, Contestacion á la Alocucion del Gefe Politico D. Manuel Victoria, 1831*, MS.; *Pico, Protesta al Manifiesto de Don Manuel Victoria, 1831*, MS., dated Oct. 15th. Oct. 17th, J. M. Padrés in a private letter congratulates Vallejo and the other deputies on their efforts to throw off the ugly epithet of 'seditious' applied by the gefe político. He thinks the southern deputies have failed to do their whole duty. *Vallejo, Doc.*, MS., i. 239.

choose to come for it. How he carried out his ideas in this direction will be apparent from a few *causas célebres* of the year.

The case of Atanasio was pending when Victoria came. Atanasio was an Indian boy less than eighteen years of age, a servant in sub-comisario Jimeno's office, who had in 1830 stolen from the warehouse property to the extent of something over $200. The prosecution was conducted by Fernandez del Campo, Padrés, and Ibarra as fiscales; and the last-named demanded, in consideration of the youth and ignorance of the culprit, as well as on account of the carelessness with which the goods had been exposed, a sentence of only two years in the public works. The asesor, Rafael Gomez, after having sent the case back to the fiscal for the correction of certain irregularities, rendered an opinion April 18th, in favor of the death penalty; and by order of the comandante general Atanasio was shot at 11 A. M. on the 26th.[20] Gomez was an able lawyer, and I suppose was technically correct in his advice, though the penalty seems a severe one. Naturally the Californians were shocked; and though an example of severity was doubtless needed, Victoria was not fortunate in his selection. The circumstance that led to the culprit's detection seems to have been his using some military buttons for gambling with his comrades; and the popular version of the whole affair has been that an Indian boy was shot by Victoria for stealing a few buttons.[21]

In May 1831 the warehouse at San Cárlos was robbed on three different occasions, perhaps entered three times the same night, by Simon Aguilar, a Mex-

[20] *Atanasio, Causa Criminal contra el Indio Atanasio y ejecucion del reo, 1831,* MS.

[21] Estévan de la Torre, José M. Amador, Jesus Pico, Inocencia Pico de Ávila, José J. Vallejo, Juan B. Alvarado, and others give substantially this version. I have no space for minor variations, most of which are absurdly inaccurate. Osio, *Hist. Cal.,* MS., 165-6, says that Gomez sent a despatch to stay the execution an hour after the boy had been shot; and Vallejo, *Hist. Cal.,* MS., ii. 143, that Atanasio was a servant of Pliego, caused to be condemned by his master without the proper legal forms, and without any specification of the crime.

ican convict in the service of Gomez, and Eduardo Sagarra, a native of Lima. A neophyte boy, Andrés, furnished the keys, which he had managed to steal from Padre Abella, the complainant in the case. There was no doubt about the guilt of the accused, and the fiscal, Rodrigo del Pliego, demanded for the two men the death penalty, and for the boy, in consideration of his being only thirteen years old, two hundred blows. Gomez, the asesor, also decided that Aguilar and Sagarra should be shot, and that Andrés, after witnessing the execution, should receive one hundred blows, and be sent to the mission to work for six months, wearing a *corma*. The sentences were approved by Victoria, and executed May 28th at the presidio of Monterey.[22]

The famous Rubio case dates back to 1828. On the night of August 15th of that year, Ignacio Olivas and his wife, on returning from a fandango at San Francisco, found their little daughter aged five years, and son of one year, dead in their beds, the former having been outraged and both brutally treated. The soldier, Francisco Rubio, a vicious man who had been convicted of serious crimes while serving in the mission escoltas of Santa Inés and Solano, was suspected and arrested. The case was prosecuted in August and September by Lieutenant Martinez, and the testimony has been preserved. It was in evidence that Rubio had learned by inquiry that the parents were to attend the fandango without the children; that he knew how to open the doors; that tracks about the house agreed with his boot; that his clothing bore

[22] Records of the case in *Dept. St. Pap., Ben. Mil.*, MS., lxxiii. 8–11. Notice of the execution in *Dept. Rec.*, MS., ix. 25; *Guerra, Doc.*, MS., v. 102. Notices by P. Sarría of spiritual consolations and burial in the presidial cemetery of these two men, and also of Atanasio. Nos. 2784, 2892–3, in the register of burials at Monterey, copied in *Torre, Remin.*, MS., 25–6. Larios, *Convulsiones*, MS., 11, witnessed the execution and the flogging administered to the boy. So did Rafael Pinto, *Apunt.*, MS., 6–8, who was a boy at the time, and who received a terrible flogging from his brother-in-law, in order that he might never forget the day nor the solemn lesson taught by the event! Amador, *Mem.*, MS., 122–6, tells us that one of the padres interceded most earnestly with Victoria for a pardon.

blood-stains at the time of his arrest; that he had
tried to sell his shirt during the night; and that many
of his actions had seemed strange and suspicious to
his companions. Beyond his own statements and
protestations of innocence, there was no evidence in
his favor, or against any other person. Though circumstantial, the proofs were strong; sufficiently so, I
think, to justify the severest penalty. The case, however, dragged its slow length along, with no percepti-
ble progress, as was usual in California, through 1829
and 1830. Rubio was nominally imprisoned, but
during much of the time seems to have worked as a
servant about the presidio, with abundant opportunities for escape. When Victoria came he intrusted
the prosecution to José María Padrés, who began
active operations in May 1831. Alférez Vallejo,
who had declined to serve as fiscal, now made some
efforts in behalf of Rubio; but his testimony and
that of others called in to substantiate it tended
merely to show irregularity in one of the former proceedings, and that another man, having been charged
with similar crimes at San Francisco, might be guilty
in this instance. No new evidence was adduced in
Rubio's favor. He was defended by Pliego, a friend
of Victoria, who on account of technical irregularities, and because no one had seen his client commit the
crime, asked only that some other penalty than death
should be imposed. Padrés, an enemy of Victoria
and friend of Vallejo, expressed no doubt of Rubio's
guilt, but he also urged that imprisonment be substituted for death. Rafael Gomez reviewed the
testimony at some length, pronounced the accused to
be guilty, and recommended that he be shot behind
the house of Olivas. The sentence was finally approved by Victoria and executed August 1st, at 11.30
A. M.[23]

The case of Rubio, as just related from the original

---

[23] *Rubio, Causa Criminal por Asesinatos y Estupro, 1828–31*, MS.

records, would seem to be a very clear one, respecting which no blame could be imputed to Victoria; yet so bitter was the feeling against that official, that the execution has been almost uniformly regarded by Californians as a judicial murder, stamping Victoria as a blood-thirsty monster. The only reason for this strange belief, in addition to the popular feeling fostered by Vallejo and his friends, was the generally credited rumor that after Rubio's death an Indian confessed that he had committed the crime for which the innocent soldier had suffered. I am unable to say positively that this rumor, so confidently presented as truth by dozens of witnesses, was unfounded; but it may be noted that most persons speak indefinitely of the guilty Indian; that the few who venture on details of name, place, and date differ widely in such particulars; and finally that the later confession, if perfectly authentic, has no possible bearing on Victoria's action.[24]

Abel Stearns, an American but a naturalized citizen of Mexico, who had been in California since

[24] Besides being a partisan of Padrés in the general controversy, Vallejo had a personal grievance, arising from the fact that Victoria had condemned him to 8 days' arrest for insubordination in refusing to serve as fiscal in another case. *Dept. Rec.*, MS., ix. 18–19. Vallejo, *Hist. Cal.*, MS., ii. 140–7, says that he as prosecuting attorney informed Victoria that the signatures of the witnesses against Rubio were forgeries; that he and Padrés offered to aid Rubio to escape, but he refused; that the execution was an outrage; and that the real culprit confessed the crime in 1833. Alvarado, *Hist. Cal.*, MS., ii. 171, 183, iv. 81, regards the prosecution as a conspiracy against Rubio; and both he and Vallejo state that great reverses of fortune overtook Lieut Martinez at the time of Rubio's death, and were commonly regarded as divine punishments. Osio, *Hist. Cal.*, MS., 165–72, gives some particulars, more pathetic than probable, of the execution, and tells us that 6 or 7 years later Vallejo at Sonoma learned that Roman, a neophyte of S. Rafael, had committed the crime, and sent Sergt Piña to shoot him. Gabriel Castro in 1876 gave one of my agents a narrative in which I put no confidence, with minute details of the arrest and confession of Roman at S. Francisco, where he died in prison of syphilis. Ignacio Cibrian also gave a somewhat different version. In the evidence it appeared that a little brother of the victims said that a fierce coyote had come and killed the children; and Amador, *Mem.*, MS., 122–6, implies that Rubio's nickname of 'Coyote' was the main ground of his accusation. J. J. Vallejo, *Remin.*, MS., 112, tells us that Victoria was moved by the counsels of the padres and by his hatred of Padrés, who protected Rubio. The versions of Pinto, Pico, Weeks, Torre, and Galindo need no special notice. None doubt that Rubio was the victim of Victoria's oppression.

1829, was apparently a sympathizer with the party of
Padrés and Vallejo; or at least he was so regarded by
Victoria.   He had a land grant in the San Joaquin
Valley which required confirmation by the diputacion,
and he was therefore anxious for a meeting of that
body.   This was his only offence, so far as I can ascertain; but for it Victoria ordered him to leave the
country, refused to give or listen to any explanations,
and merely bade him present his claims and complaints to the supreme government.   The correspondence began in February.   In July, Stearns was refused permission to visit San Francisco to attend to
his business affairs, and on September 23d his passport was issued.   He soon sailed from Monterey,
but did not go farther than San Diego, or the frontier of Baja California.[25]   Nothing can be said in
defence of Victoria's arbitrary course in thus exiling
a Mexican citizen without trial or specification of
offence; but the provocation was I have no doubt
much stronger than it appears in the written record,
since Stearns was not a man disposed to submit quietly when his interests were threatened.

Another of Victoria's arbitrary proceedings was
that against Mariano Duarte, alcalde of San José, in
August and September.   Duarte had, after consultation with Alcalde Buelna of Monterey, tried to induce the ayuntamiento to petition for the convoking
of the diputacion.   This was his chief offence, "one
which has a very strong bearing upon the present
political state of the territory," in Victoria's eyes; but
there were others, brought forward by the other
municipal officers who disliked the alcalde, and included in the investigation.   Duarte had somewhat

---

[25] Correspondence between V. and Stearns in *Leg. Rec.*, MS., i. 321–9; *Dept.
Rec.*, MS., ix. 102, 106–7.   S. had, however, since Oct. 1830, a quarrel on
hand with Ex-alcalde Soberanes, for disrespect to whom he had been imprisoned, and justly as the asesor decided. *Monterey Arch.*, MS., i. 26–7.   Sept.
14, 1831, V. to min. of rel., accuses S. of pernicious conduct, of plotting with
Padrés to have the dip. meet, of trying to go to S. Francisco to join the
other plotters, and of being a vagabond dependent on Capt. Cooper. *Dept.
Rec.*, MS., ix. 145.

irregularly appointed certain regidores to fill vacancies, and had taken from the municipal funds compensation for teaching the pueblo school, whereas it had been the understanding that he was to teach for nothing—the estimated value of his services. Worse yet, Duarte allowed himself to be inveigled into a trap by his foes. A woman with more patriotism than modesty was induced to send the alcalde an amorous invitation, and he was surprised at her house by the watchful regidores. Rodrigo del Pliego was sent to San José to prosecute the case; and a little later Duarte was brought in irons to Monterey to be tried by a military court. There was no trouble in proving the truth of the only charge to which Victoria attached much importance, that of laboring to secure a meeting of the diputacion, and all went well for the governor until the opinion of the asesor was rendered September 30th. This opinion was to the effect that the charges against Duarte had been substantiated, but that in urging the ayuntamiento to coöperate with others in demanding a convocation of the assembly he had done no criminal act, and that as to the other offences a military court had no jurisdiction, and they must be sent to the supreme court in Mexico. Victoria seems to have made no effort to continue the prosecution in defiance of law.[26]

There was trouble likewise at Los Angeles, though the alcalde of that town, Vicente Sanchez, was a partisan and protégé of Victoria, being a man moreover who always had a quarrel on hand with somebody. In January Echeandía, acting on the legal advice of Gomez, had declared Sanchez as a diputado not competent to hold the place of alcalde, ordering that the first regidor take the place provisionally and a

---

[26] *Duarte, Causa Criminal seguida contra el Alcalde de S. José, Mariano Duarte, 1831*, MS. Lieut Ibarra was Duarte's defender, but his argument was devoted to showing his client to be an ignoramus. There is nothing in the narratives of Californians on this affair that deserves notice, though many mention it in their charges against Victoria. The decision of Gomez on the legality of the case was subsequently affirmed in Mexico.

new alcalde be chosen.[27] There is no record of immediate
action on this order; but on April 18th the ayuntamiento deposed Sanchez, putting Regidor Juan Alvarado in his place. At first Victoria did not object to
the change, but a few days later, probably learning
that it had been in some way in the interest of Echeandía's party, he discovered that the movement had
been a revolutionary and illegal one. So he wrote a
severe reprimand to Alvarado, ordered him to restore
Sanchez to office, and announced that he would soon
come down to Los Angeles to make an investigation.
The order was obeyed and Sanchez was reinstated.[28]
In June, for reasons that do not appear, Victoria saw
fit to revive the matter by sending Lieutenant Argüello to make investigations and administer rebukes.
The 21st of July he sent back the *sumario* that had
been formed by Argüello, and ordered that the regidores Alvarado and Perez, with six other citizens of
Los Angeles, should be put in prison. They were
never released by Victoria's order.[29]

One of Alcalde Sanchez's quarrels was with José
Antonio Carrillo. The exact nature of the trouble is
not explained; but in March Carrillo was taken into
custody as a defrauder. He escaped, but gave himself
up to the comandante of Santa Bárbara on March 21st,
and was kept in confinement there for some fifty days.
At the end of that time he was sent down to San
Diego, and immediately banished to San Vicente on
the frontier by Victoria's order. How Carrillo had
offended the governor is not recorded, but it is to be

[27] *Dept. Rec.*, MS., ix. 84–5.
[28] April 21st, 23d, V. to Alvarado. *Dept. Rec.*, MS., ix. 99–102. The com. of
Sta B. reports having felt some alarm when he first heard of Sanchez's removal,
but soon learned that no harm was intended. *Dept. St. Pap.*, MS., iii. 9–10.
April 25th, Alvarado to V., saying that Sanchez had been reinstated. April
26th, Sanchez to V., complaining of his wrongs at the hands of foes. Regidor José Perez was arrested, but let out on bail. *Dept. St. Pap., Ben. Pref.
y Juzg.*, MS., iii. 54–5.
[29] *Leg. Rec.*, MS., i. 307–8, 349–50; *Dept. Rec.*, MS., ix. 108–10. The six
citizens were Tomás Talamantes, Francisco Sepúlveda, José María Ávila,
Máximo Alanis, Demesio Dominguez, and José María Aguilar. Capt. Barroso took Argüello's place in August.

presumed that he had taken a prominent part in sending memorials from the south in the interest of the diputacion. He protested earnestly against his exile in June and July, demanding an opportunity to return, under bonds, to vindicate his honor; but all he could obtain was permission to move about from place to place on the frontier without returning to California while his case was pending. Nevertheless he did return, as we shall see.[30]

Finally José María Padrés, whom Victoria justly regarded as the leading spirit in the opposition to his measures, was summarily sent out of the territory without form of trial. In all his communications the governor had named Padrés as the cause of the country's ills.[31] Early in the summer he had been sent to San Francisco, where it was thought he could do less harm than at the capital; but he continued his plottings—so believed Victoria—in connection with Vallejo and several young Californians who were living there ostensibly engaged in hunting otter. In October the order for his banishment was issued, and early in November he was sent by sea to San Blas.[32] Of course Victoria had no authority for such an act.

I have thus catalogued the acts of Victoria's admin-

[30] Correspondence on Carrillo's case from March to August, in *Valle, Doc. Hist. Cal.*, MS., 17; *Leg. Rec.*, MS., i. 302–3, 313–20; *Dept. Rec.*, MS., ix. 32; *Dept. St. Pap.*, MS., iii. 14–16, 18; *Órd, Ocurrencias*, MS., 43–4. Alvarado, *Hist. Cal.*, MS., ii. 169–70, erroneously says Bandini was banished with Carrillo, and the two wrote a manifiesto, which was sent north. Some one put a copy under Victoria's pillow, and a reward was offered for his detection.

[31] Particularly in his report to the min. of rel. of Sept. 21st, in *Dept. Rec.*, MS., ix. 149–52.

[32] July 24th, Padrés at S. Francisco writes to Stearns, advising him to go to Mex. with his complaints against V. *Vallejo, Doc.*, MS., i. 234. Sept. 14th, V. to min. of war. Says that P. was sent to Bodega to make an inspection: but that he talked very freely to the Russians against the Mex. and Cal. govt. *Dept. Rec.*, MS., ix. 144. Oct. 17th, P. congratulates Vallejo on his opposition to V. *Vallejo, Doc.*, MS., i. 239. Oct. 19th, P. is to sail on the *Catalina*. Nov. 8th, he is to sail on the schooner *Margarita. Id.*, i. 242; *Dept. Rec.*, MS., ix. 53, 61. Figueroa, *Manifiesto*, 3–4, speaks of P.'s influence in favor of revolt. Alvarado, *Hist. Cal.*, MS., ii. 174–5, says P. left Monterey Dec. 8th, and that V. before exiling him had tried to buy him off. Both this author and Vallejo, *Hist. Cal.*, MS., ii. 142–7, say that P. left Cal. vowing to oust V., and in possession of news from Mex. that made him think it would not be very difficult.

istration, and they leave no doubt as to what manner
of man he was.   Personally brave, honest, energetic,
straightforward, and devoted to what he deemed the
best interests of the territory, he was yet more a comandante general than a gefe político.   His idea of
his duty was to preserve order and administer justice
by military methods, removing without regard to constitutional technicalities such obstacles as might stand
in the way of success in carrying out his good intentions.
All the Californians in their narratives credit him with
personal courage, but with no other good quality, save
that a few admit he paid better attention to the comfort as well as the discipline of his soldiers than had
his predecessors.   Nearly all, after mentioning more
or less accurately some of the acts which I have chron-
icled, express the opinion that Victoria was a cruel,
blood-thirsty monster, at whose hands the lives of all
honest citizens were in danger, some adding that he
was dishonest and avaricious as well, and others asserting that he was a full-blooded negro.   So strong is
popular prejudice, fostered by a few influential men.[33]
There is a notable lack of missionary correspondence
in the records of 1831, and I find only one contemporary expression of the padres' opinion respecting Victoria's acts, except that of course they approved his
abrogation of the secularization decree.   Padre Duran,
in the epilogue of his comments upon that measure,

[33] I shall give later references to all the Californian writers who have treated
of Victoria's rule.   Their sentiments are so uniform, that it is not necessary
to cite individual opinions.   In the memorial of the diputados to the Mex.
govt of Sept. 18th, *Vallejo, Doc.*, MS., i. 215, 238, the charges against V. are
his exile of Carrillo and Stearns, his arrest of Duarte, his refusal to convoke
the diputacion, his general opposition to the federal system, and his insults
to diputados and inhabitants.   A very complete résumé of V.'s acts and troubles, made up from his despatches and those of Echeandía and others, is found
in *Alaman, Sucesos de California en el año de 1831*, MS., the same being an
appendix to the minister's instructions to Gov. Figueroa in 1832.   The whole
subject is also fully treated in *Vallejo and Argüello, Expediente sobre las Ar-
bitrariedudes de Victoria*, MS., presented to the dip. on Feb. 17, 1832.   To
the usual charges Bandini, *Apuntes Políticos, 1832*, MS., adds the sending of
some Angelinos far among the savages toward Sonora to drive stock for a
favorite padre of the governor's, tampering with the mails at Monterey, and
abrogating the faculties of hacienda employees to the prejudice of the administration.

after affirming that the leading Californians aimed
solely at securing mission plunder and rejoicing at
Victoria's opportune arrival and suspension of the law,
wrote: "Interested parties, including some vocales of
the diputacion, sure of their prey, were disappointed,
and disappointment turned into hatred for the equitable Victoria. Never had they pardoned this just
chief for having rescued the booty already within
their grasp. They began to intrigue and hold secret
meetings, and for ten months of 1831 symptoms of
sedition have not ceased to keep the illustrious chief
in constant trouble. They sought to force him to
convene the diputacion, in order that with a semblance
of legality they might accomplish their desires,. . .un-
grateful for the sacrifices of the poor Indians; but Victoria never consented; and in November they proclaimed a plan of attack." The foreign residents are
equally silent,[34] but I suspect that their views were
more favorable to the governor than they cared to
admit generally to the strong element opposing him.
The Californians have weakened their cause by their
unfounded and exaggerated attacks on Victoria's personal character, for politically the cause was a strong
one. Victoria went far beyond the authority of his
office, in refusing to convoke the assembly, in trying
an alcalde by court-martial, and in banishing Mexican
citizens without forms of trial. He was not in sympathy with constitutional government; and his acts
were not to be defended by reason of the reactionary
character of the administration that appointed him,
the trick that was attempted by Padrés and Echeandía,
the formidable opposition which forced him to a more
arbitrary policy than he would otherwise have shown,
or the promptness and frankness with which he submitted all to the national authorities. Perhaps his
proceedings might even have justified revolt after a

---

[34] *Duran, Notas y Com.*, MS., epilogue. Spence, *Hist. Notes*, MS., 15,
merely says that V. was energetic and made every one respect order and law,
which did not please a certain class.

failure to obtain relief from Mexico. Under other circumstances, Victoria might have been an excellent ruler for California.

Thus far San Francisco in the extreme north had been the centre of opposition to Victoria, but the final revolt broke out in the extreme south at San Diego.[35] Some prominent men of the north are of opinion that the abajeños should not have all the glory, but I fear there is hardly enough of it to bear division. José Antonio Carrillo, supposed to be in exile on the frontier, but who came secretly to the vicinity of San Diego in November, was the real instigator of the revolt, seconded by Abel Stearns, another exile; but the active and ostensible leaders were Juan Bandini, diputado suplente to congress and sub-comisario of hacienda, and Pio Pico, senior vocal of the diputacion. Bandini in his history gives but a general account of the affair, but Pico enters into some detail, both of the actual revolt and of preliminary movements.[36] After ten or twelve days of preparatory plotting, Pico, Bandini, and Carrillo, on November 29th, drew up and signed a formal pronunciamiento, and that evening

[35] Vallejo, *Hist. Cal.*, MS., ii. 142-7, and Alvarado, *Hist. Cal.*, MS., ii. 172-3, state that the former, a member of the diputacion, was urged in letters from leading men in the south to take the initiative in a revolution to overthrow the tyrant. Vallejo went to Monterey to consult with the other northern vocales, but found them timid about resorting to rebellion. On his way back to S. F. he met V. at Sta Clara, and was offered by him all kinds of official favors if he would abandon the party of Padrés. This was just before the exile of the latter, and V. had received alarming news of growing uneasiness in the south.

[36] *Bandini, Hist. Cal.*, MS., 73-5; *Pico, Hist. Cal.*, MS., 24-34. Pico says that in the middle of Nov. his brother-in-law, José J. Ortega, came down from Monterey with news that V. was preparing to come south, and that he intended to hang Pico and Bandini for their efforts in behalf of the diputacion. He at once sent for J. A. Carrillo—also his brother-in-law—who came to his rancho of Jamul; both came to S. Diego in the night and had an interview with Bandini, and the three resolved on a pronunciamiento as the only means of thwarting V.'s plans. It took about two weeks to perfect their plans and to learn what men could be relied on. During this time Pico and Juan Lopez made visits to Los Angeles to enlist the Angelinos in the cause. They found that Alcalde Sanchez had about 70 (some others say 30 or 40) of the citizens in jail; but Ávila and other leaders disapproved of any rising until V. should have passed Angeles, when they would attack him in the rear, and the Dieguinos in front. Finally they heard from Stearns a confirmation of V.'s schemes as before reported.

with about a dozen companions started out to take possession of the presidio and garrison. Doubtless by a previous understanding with the soldiers, no resistance was made, though the forms of a surprise were gone through, the arms and barracks secured, and the officers placed under arrest.[37]

Next day the soldiers gave in their adhesion to the plan readily enough, but the officers, especially captains Portilla and Argüello, showed considerable reluctance. They shared the feelings of the rebels against Victoria—so they said, Portilla perhaps not quite truthfully—but they felt that for military men in their position to engage in open rebellion against their comandante general was a serious matter. At first they declined to do more than remain neutral under arrest; but finally they were induced to promise active coöperation on condition that Echeandía would accept the command. What part Echeandía had taken, if any, in the previous plottings cannot be known; but after much hesitation, real or pretended,[38] he consented to head the movement. The plan, slightly amended, was now made to embrace substantially the following points: the suspension of Victoria, the vesting by the diputacion of the political and military command in separate persons, and the provisional resumption by Echeandía of both commands until such act of the diputacion or the decision of the national government. This pronunciamiento was

[37] Bandini says there were 14 men in the first revolutionary party. Pico names, besides the 3 signers, Ignacio, Juan, and José Lopez; Abel Stearns; Juan María Marron; Andrés and Antonio Ibarra; Dámaso and Gervasio Alipas; Juan Osuna; Silverio Rios; another citizen, and a cholo to carry ammunition. Pico says he was deputed to arrest Capt. Argüello, whom he found at his house playing *tresillo* with his wife and Alf. Valle. He begged pardon for the intrusion, presented his pistols, and marched the two officers away to join Capt. Portilla, who had been arrested by Bandini. Valle, *Lo Pasado*, MS., 3–5, like most of the California writers, mentions the arrest of himself and the rest, but gives no particulars.

[38] E. was a timid man, not inclined to revolutionary acts, and moreover not in good health; therefore his reluctance to assume the responsibility of such a movement; yet I hardly credit the statement of the Vallejos and others that he refused the command until forced by Carrillo's threats to accept it.

finally signed December 1st by Echeandía, the three
original signers, and all the officials, whose names I
give with a translation of the document.[39] The reader

[39] *Pronunciamiento de San Diego contra el Gefe Político y Comandante General de California, Don Manuel Victoria, en 29 de Noviembre y 1 de Diciembre de 1831*, MS. Translation: 'Mexican citizens residing in the upper territory of the Californias. If the enterprise we undertake were intended to violate the provisions of the laws, if our acts in venturing to oppose the scandalous acts of the actual governor, D. Manuel Victoria, were guided by aims unworthy of patriotic sentiments, then should we not only fear but know the fatal results to which we must be condemned. Such, however, not being the case, we, guided in the path of justice, animated by love of our soil, duly respecting the laws dictated by our supreme legislature, and enthusiastic for their support, find ourselves obliged, on account of the criminal abuse noted in the said chief, to adopt the measures here made known. We know that we proceed, not against the sup. govt or its magistrates, but, as we are deeply convinced, against an individual who violates the fundamental bases of our system, or in truth against a tyrant who has hypocritically deceived the supreme powers so as to reach the rank to which, without deserving it, he has been raised. The supreme being, master of our hearts, knows the pure sentiments with which we set out: love to country, respect for the laws, to obey them and make them obeyed, to banish the abuses which with accelerated steps the actual ruler is committing against the liberal system. Such are the objects which we call pure sentiments and in accordance with public right. We will maintain this before the national sovereignty, and time will bear witness against what the breaker of laws chooses to call sedition. From the sentiments indicated may be clearly deduced the patriotic spirit which directs us to the proceeding this day begun; and at the thought that such sentiments are entertained by the people of Alta California, there is generated within us a complete conviction that our indispensable action will be supported and therefore sustained by all who live in this unfortunate country. As for the military officers in actual service, opposition is naturally to be expected from them to our plan, and we must allow them at first this unfavorable opinion demanded by their profession; but not so later, when they shall have fully learned the wise and beneficent intentions with which we act; for they also, as Mexican citizens, are in duty bound to maintain inviolate the code to which we have all sworn. We believe that your minds are ever decided in favor of the preservation of society, and your arms to be ready in the service of whoever may assure happiness, and in support of the laws which promulgate its representation. You are assured of the contrary spirit shown by the chief authority of this California, and we begin, in manifesting his criminal acts, with the infraction committed against the territorial representation, which has been suppressed on pretexts which confirm his absolutism, though you voted for the members to be the *arcas* of your confidence; the total suppression of the ayuntamiento of Sta Bárbara; the shooting of several persons by his order at Monterey and S. Francisco, without the necessary precedent formalities prescribed by the laws; the expatriation suffered by the citizens José Antonio Carrillo and Abel Stearns, without notification of the reasons demanding it; the scorn with which he has treated the most just demand which with legal proofs was presented by the very honorable pueblo of Los Angeles, leaving unpunished the public crimes of the present alcalde; and, not to weary you with further reflections of this nature, please consider the attributes which he has assumed in the department of revenues, making himself its chief, with grave injury to the public funds. We trust that after you know our aims you will regard the removal of all these evils as the duty of every citizen. We believe also that the public sentiment of the territory will never attempt to violate our rights, or still less provoke us to

who may have the patience to examine this state paper, California's first pronunciamiento, if we except that of the convict Solis in 1829, will find in it a good

make a defence foreign to our views (!). The said ruler has not only shown himself shameless in the violation of law, but has at the same time imperilled our security and interests by reason of his despotism and incapacity. You yourselves are experiencing the misfortunes that have happened during the short time of his management. For all these reasons, and with all obedience and subjection to the laws, we have proposed: 1st, To suspend the exercise of D. Manuel Victoria in all that relates to the command which he at present holds in this territory as comandante general and gefe político, for infraction and conspiracy against our sacred institutions, as we shall show by legal proofs. 2d, That when at a fitting time the excelentísima diputacion territorial shall have met, the military and political command shall fall to distinct persons as the laws of both jurisdictions provide, until the supreme resolution. These two objects, so just for the reasons given, are those which demand attention from the true patriot. Then let the rights of the citizen be born anew; let liberty spring up from the ashes of oppression, and perish the despotism that has suffocated our security. Yes, citizens; love to country and observance of the laws prescribed and approved by our supreme powers are the fundamental basis on which we travel. Property is respected; likewise the duty of each citizen. Our diputacion territorial will work, and will take all the steps conducive to the good of society; but we beg that body that it make no innovation whatever in the matter of the missions, respecting their communities and property, since our object is confined solely to the two articles as stated. To the sup. govt belongs exclusively the power to dictate what it may deem proper on this subject, and it promises to the padres to observe respect, decorum, and security of the property intrusted to their care. Thus we sign it, and we hope for indulgence in consideration of our rights and justice. Presidio of San Diego, Nov. 29, 1831. Pio Pico, Juan Bandini, José Antonio Carrillo.

'We, Capt. Pablo de la Portilla, etc. [see names at end], acquainted with the preceding plan signed by [names as before, with titles], according to which the people of this place surprised the small garrison of this plaza on the night of Nov. 29th, consider it founded on our natural right, since it is known to us in all evidence that the gefe político and comandante general of the territory, Don Manuel Victoria, has infringed our federal constitution and laws in that part relating to individual security and popular representation; and we find ourselves not in a position to be heard with the promptness our rights demand by the supreme powers of the nation, which might order the suspension which is effected in the plan if they could see and prove the accusations which give rise to so many complaints. But at the same time, in order to secure in the enterprise the best order, and a path which may not lead us away from the only object proposed, we choose and proclaim lieut.-col. of engineers, citizen José María de Echeandía, to re-assume the command, political and military, of the territory, which this very year he gave up to the said Sr Victoria—this until the supreme government may resolve after the proper correspondence, or until, the diputacion being assembled, distinct persons may in legal form take charge of the two commands. And the said chief having appeared at our invitation, and being informed on the subject, he decided to serve in both capacities as stated, protesting, however, that he does it solely in support of public liberty according to the system which he has sworn, coöperation for the best order, and submission to the supreme powers of the nation. Thus, all being said publicly, and the proclamation in favor of Sr Echeandía being general, he began immediately to discharge the duties of the command. And in token thereof we sign together with said chief—both the promoters of the plan who signed it and we who have seconded it—to-

many words. It was apparently the production of
Juan Bandini.

In a day or two the pronunciados, with about fifty
men under Portilla, set out northward, Argüello being left behind in command of San Diego. The little army arrived at Los Angeles December 4th, learning now, or perhaps the day before, that Victoria was
approaching from the north and was not far distant.
Of occurrences at the pueblo since the imprisonment
of eight citizens by Alcalde Sanchez at Victoria's order, as already related, we know very little; but it
would seem that there had been further trouble,
and that more citizens, perhaps many more, had been
added to the eight in jail, Andrés Pico being one
of the new victims. The captives were at once set
free by the San Diegans, and the obnoxious alcalde, Vicente Sanchez, was in turn put in irons.
The Angelinos accepted the plan with great enthusiasm, and next morning the rebel army, probably numbering about one hundred and fifty, marched out to
meet Victoria, who at the same time started with
about thirty men from San Fernando.

The date of Victoria's departure from Monterey is
unknown, as are his motives, and most details respecting his southward march. He must have started before the proceedings of November 29th could have
been known at the capital; but he probably was
warned of prospective troubles by letters from southern friends.[40] Full of confidence as usual in his abil-

day between 11 and 12 o'clock, on Dec. 1, 1831. José María Echeandía, Pio
Pico, Juan Bandini, José Antonio Carrillo, Pablo de la Portilla, Santiago Argüello, José María Ramirez, Ignacio del Valle, Juan José Rocha, and as comandante of the artillery detachment, Sergt Andrés Cervantes.'

[40] David Spence, *Hist. Notes*, MS., Robinson, *Life in Cal.*, 118-21, and
Tuthill, *Hist. Cal.*, 131-4, state that Portilla was the man who warned Victoria,
urging him to come south, and promising the support of his company, but
treacherously joining the rebels and leading them against the man he had
agreed to defend. I think there was some truth in this charge. That is,
Portilla was a Mexican officer in command of a Mexican company, and naturally a partisan of Victoria rather than of the Californians. He had a perfect right to warn the comandante, and very likely did so, intending to support him; but it would have required much more strength than he ever
possessed to withstand the movement of Nov. 29th; and the indications are

ity to restore order, the governor set out with Alférez
Pliego and ten or twenty men, leaving Zamorano, his
secretary, in command at Monterey. Even on arriving
at Santa Bárbara he seems to have got no definite information of the San Diego movement; but he was with
some difficulty persuaded by Guerra to increase his
little force before going to Los Ángeles, and was accordingly joined by Captain Romualdo Pacheco and
about a dozen soldiers.[41] His entire force was now
not over thirty men, nearly all I suppose of the
San Blas and Mazatlan companies. He expected no
fight; but in case trouble should arise, he doubtless
counted on the aid of Portilla and his Mazatecos.
Before he reached San Fernando, however, messengers overtook him from Santa Bárbara with definite
news of the open revolt at San Diego, in letters from
the rebel leaders to the Carrillo brothers, which by
advice of Guerra they had forwarded to put him on
his guard.[42] At San Fernando on December 4th,
Padre Ibarra had not heard of the revolt at San
Diego, and a messenger sent in haste to the pueblo
brought back word from Alcalde Sanchez that at
sunset there were no signs of revolution. Later in
the evening, however, when the revolutionists arrived
from the south, releasing the prisoners and locking up
Sanchez, a brother of the latter is said to have escaped with the news to San Fernando. And thus next
morning the hostile armies marched out from the

that the captain was put in command on the march to Los Angeles mainly
that he might be watched. Several Californians state that it was only by the
vigilance and threats of José Antonio Carrillo that Portilla was kept from
going over to the foe at the last. A contemptible weakness, rather than deliberate treachery, was Portilla's fault; besides, as we shall see, the valiant
commander and his men did no fighting when the hour of battle arrived.

[41] The widow Ávila, Cosas de Cal., MS., 29–30, states that provisions were
prepared at her house for Victoria's march, and that he left Monterey at dawn
with about 15 men. Gonzalez, Experiencias, MS., 29–30, and Ord, Ocurrencias, MS., 48–9, speak from memory of Victoria's arrival at Sta Bárbara.
The latter says Guerra warned Pacheco to be careful. 'Cuidado! que
aquellos son tercos; allí está José Antonio Carrillo.' Spence says Victoria
took 10 men from Monterey; Robinson, that he reached Sta Bárbara with 20.

[42] Pico, Hist. Cal., MS., 35–40. Pico's narrative of the whole affair is
remarkably accurate in every case where its accuracy can be tested, and is
therefore worthy of some credit where no such test is possible.

pueblo and mission respectively, the smaller force starting earlier or moving more rapidly than the other, since they met only a few miles from Los Angeles in the direction of Cahuenga.

Exactly what occurred at this unnamed battle-field on the forenoon of the 5th, so far as details are concerned, will never be known. The salient results were that two men, Captain Pacheco on the one side and José María Ávila on the other, were killed. Victoria was severely wounded. Portilla's force retreated to Los Angeles and to Los Nietos, and the governor was carried by his men to San Gabriel. After a careful study of all the testimony extant, I venture to present some additional particulars as worthy of credence. Portilla with his 150 men had halted on high ground to await Victoria's approach. Carrillo of the leading rebels was with the army; but Echeandía, Pico, and Bandini had remained behind. Victoria, approaching with his thirty soldiers, was urged by Pacheco not to risk an attack without reënforcements and additional preparations; but he promptly, perhaps insultingly, disregarded the captain's counsels.[43] He was brave and hot-headed, he did not believe Portilla's Mazatecos would fight against their comrades, and he attached little importance to the citizen rebels. Riding up within speaking distance, the governor was commanded by Portilla to halt, and in reply peremptorily ordered Portilla to come over with his soldiers to support his commander and the legitimate authorities. Noting a disposition to parley rather than to obey his order, Victoria ordered his men to fire; and some shots were fired, perhaps over the heads of the foe, since nobody was hurt. Portilla and his men now ran away, perhaps after one discharge of their muskets, and the Angelinos followed them; but two or three of the

[43] Pio Pico, Osio, Mrs Ord, and others state that some sharp words passed between the two officers, Victoria implying that Pacheco was moved by fear, and the latter indignantly repelling the taunt.

latter who had been in the pueblo jail, had personal grievance against Victoria, and were ashamed of their companions' cowardice—made a dash against the foe before retreating. José María Ávila was at the head of this party, and he first met Pacheco, whom he shot in the back with a pistol as the two horses were carried past each other by their impetus, after mutually parried thrusts of sword and lance by the respective riders. Pacheco fell dead with a bullet in his heart.[44] Ávila now rushed upon Victoria; Tomás Talamantes was close behind him, and on the other side at least two soldiers defended the governor. Of the ensuing struggle, which probably did not last three minutes, it is not strange that there are many popular versions; but Victoria received several lance-wounds. A soldier was shot in the foot. Avila after a desperate resistance was unhorsed and killed, shot perhaps by one of the soldiers,[45] and Talamantes, the only one of the pronunciados except Ávila who came into contact with the foe, escaped unhurt. Victoria's men attempted no pursuit, but bore the wounded governor to San Gabriel. Had it not been for his wounds, Victoria would have re-

[44] For a biographical sketch of Romualdo Pacheco, see local annals of Sta Bárbara later in this volume.

[45] José María Ávila was a native of Sinaloa, who came when a boy with his parents, Cornelio Ávila and Isabel Urquides, to Los Angeles. He was a wild and reckless fellow in his youth, but dashing and popular, noted for his skill in horsemanship. He amassed considerable property, and in 1825 was elected alcalde of Los Angeles, though suspended for a despotic exercise of power. On one occasion a citizen complained to Gov. Argüello that he had been arbitrarily imprisoned by the alcalde, who was called upon to explain, as he did in the following language: 'My motive for putting this person in jail was that I thought proper to do so; and because, besides that motive, I had other grounds, in the stating of which a good deal of time would be consumed; and since the man's complaint is only intended to take up your worship's time and mine, I close by stating that this is all I have to say, repeating myself obedient to your superior orders.' *Carrillo (J.), Doc.*, MS., 17–20. Ávila's late imprisonment by Sanchez at Victoria's order was the cause of his special wrath against the latter. Doña Inocencia Pico de Ávila, *Cosas de Cal.*, MS., 28–30, says that José María had a fight with one Nieto, and was condemned in consequence to a long imprisonment. He came to Monterey, staying at narrator's house, to induce Victoria to change the penalty to a fine; but the gov. refused, and Ávila went back very angry, vowing vengeance. As there is in the archives some reference to the troubles of Ávila and Nieto, this story may be accurate, though it is not clear how the former could have left the jail to visit Monterey on such business.

taken Los Angeles without difficulty; and it is by
no means unlikely that he would have crushed the
rebellion altogether.   Ávila and Talamantes had deposed the governor of California; and others had contributed nothing more potent than words.[46]

[46] It would serve no good purpose to present variations of testimony on
each point of this affair, which would be pretty much equivalent to giving
seven eighths of the narratives in full; but I append some items from various
sources, interesting for one reason or another.   The narrative of Juan Ávila,
nephew of José María, is worthy of especial notice as the testimony of an eye-
witness who is also a well known and respected man.   He watched the conflict from a little distance, having been advised by his uncle to take no active
part.   He, like one or two others, thinks that V. had advanced to Cahuenga
the night before.   He designates the battle-ground as the Lomitas de la
Cañada de Breita.   His version of the fight agrees in general with that in my
text, except that he says nothing of Talamantes, and states that Portilla's
men fired first.   His details after Pacheco's fall are as follows: Ávila rushed
among the soldiers in search of V., whom he gave a lance-thrust in the side,
unhorsing him, but when about to repeat the blow was shot in the spine by
the Mazateco Leandro Morales, and was himself unhorsed.   Pedro Guerrero
rushed up to kill him, but Á. shot him in the knee with his remaining pistol.
V. was so near that A., struggling on the ground, was able to grasp his foot
and throw him; but he rose again and killed A. with his sword.   *Ávila,
Notas*, MS., 11–15.   Osio, *Hist. Cal.*, MS., 178–89, gives a very full narrative.
His presentment of Portilla's grief at seeing the brave Mazatecos drawn up in
battle array against each other, of his fear that all V.'s men must inevitably be
killed in a bad cause, his orders to fire the first shot in the air, and the inter-
position of providence in the interest of an *economía de sangre*, is—though
given in sober earnest—amusingly absurd.   Osio's account of the fight agrees for
the most part with the preceding, but he says that V. got one of his wounds
from Talamantes.   He also mentions the absurd actions of a drunken man,
Francisco Sepúlveda, who came up at the last moment.   This writer gives the
impression that firing had continued, that the personal conflicts had taken
place in a shower of bullets, and that the rebels retreated only after the fall
of Ávila.   He is very severe in his remarks on their cowardice.   Pio Pico,
Hist. Cal., MS., 35–40, states that José Antonio Carrillo warded off Pacheco's
sword-thrust with his musket, and mentions Talamantes' services.   Bandini,
Hist. Cal., MS., 75–6, gives no particulars, but states that V. opened the fire
without consenting to give or receive explanations.   In a letter written a few
days later, Echeandía says: On Dec. 5th the citizens of Los Angeles 'pronounced with their ayuntamiento for the said plan, promising gladly to
sacrifice their lives and interests in its support.   This promise they kept and
are keeping, for that same day Victoria, whom we supposed in Monterey, presented himself in the vicinity of the pueblo, and, without accepting any
arrangement or even discussion, opened fire, thinking to subject them; but in
vain, because, anxious for their liberty, they gave themselves up to death, and
succeeded in putting Victoria on the brink of death, since seriously wounded
he retired his force to this mission.'   *Vallejo, Doc.*, MS., i. 245, xxx. 276.
Valle, *Lo Pasado*, MS., 3–5, says it was Guerrero who killed Ávila.   Mrs
Ord, *Ocurrencias*, MS., 49–50, says the report brought to Sta Bárbara was that
Ávila was wounded by Pacheco, wounded Victoria, and was killed by Isidoro
Ibarra.   Machado, *Tiempos Pasados*, MS., 27–8, calls the place of the fight
Arroyo Seco.   Amador, *Mem.*, MS., 135–6, had heard from Francisco Alviso, an
eye-witness, that it was Victoria who shot Ávila.   Manuel Castro, *Rel.*, MS.,
25–9, tells us that Ávila went out by permission of the rebel leaders to fight
single-handed with Pacheco and Victoria!   Steven C. Foster, *S. José Pioneer*,

There is little more to be said of the revolution or other events of 1831. Some citizens who took no part in the fight carried the bodies of Pacheco and Ávila to the pueblo, where funeral services were performed next day. The fugitive residents had recovered from their fright and returned to their homes, while Echeandía with a part of Portilla's veterans had also come to town from the camp at Los Nietos. The wounded governor lay at San Gabriel, in danger of death, as was thought, tended by Joseph Chapman as amateur surgeon, and by Eulalia Perez as nurse, if we may credit the old lady's statement.[47] His men, with two or three exceptions, had adhered to the plan or did so very soon; there was no possibility of further resistance; and this very day, December 6th, it is probable that he entered into negotiations through messengers with Echeandía, and made a formal surrender.[48] On the 9th he had an interview with Echeandía at the mission, at which he asked to be sent to Mexico, promising to interfere no more in the affairs of California. The general consented; and on the same day wrote and despatched to the north several letters, all of similar purport, in which he narrated all that had occurred, explained his own connection with the revolution, and summoned the diputacion to assemble immediately at Los Angeles to decide according to the plan on the persons to be intrusted with the political and military command.[49]

July 28, 1877, states that when the bodies were found, 'Ávila still grasped the lance-staff with a death-grip, while the point had been driven through Pacheco's body,' giving other inaccurate particulars. Many of the Californians in their narratives simply state that there was a battle and Victoria was wounded, and others say there was only a personal combat between Ávila, Pacheco, and Victoria.

[47] *Perez, Recuerdos*, MS., 22. She says the most serious wound was in the head, under the eye. Osio says that Charles Anderson was summoned with medicines from S. Pedro. From later letters of V. himself it appears that by the end of Dec. a troublesome discharge of blood from nose and mouth had ceased, and all his wounds had healed except one in the chest, which caused him much trouble ever after his arrival in Mexico. He had also many contusions which were painful. *Guerra, Doc.*, MS., iv. 180–3.

[48] Bandini and Pico say there was a surrender on that day.

[49] E. from S. Gabriel Dec. 9th to Vallejo, and to the ayunt. of S. José and Monterey, in *Vallejo, Doc.*, MS., i. 245; xxx. 276; *Dept. St. Pap.*, MS., iii.

About December 20th, Victoria left San Gabriel.[50] On his way south he spent some days at San Luis Rey with Padre Antonio Peyri, who decided to leave California with the fallen governor.   Meanwhile Juan Bandini at San Diego made a contract with John Bradshaw and Supercargo Thomas Shaw of the American ship *Pocahontas* to carry Victoria to Mazatlan for $1,600 in silver, to be paid before setting sail;[51] and the exile, arriving on the 27th, went immediately on board the ship, which did not sail, however, for twenty days.   I have before me an autograph letter addressed by Victoria to Captain Guerra on the 31st from on board the *Pocahontas* still in port,[52] in which he expresses confidence that his own acts will meet the approval of the national government, and that relief for the ills that afflict California will not be long delayed.   His wounds were rapidly healing, and but for grief at the fate of his compadre Pacheco and the bereavement of the widow, he would be a happy man. He urged Guerra to keep his friends the Carrillos if possible from accepting the new plan.   The vessel sailed on January 17, 1832, with Victoria and two servants, Padre Peyri and several neophyte boys, and Alférez Rodrigo del Pliego.[53]   On February 5th, hav-

20–1; *St. Pap.*, *Sac.*, MS., xii. 9.   He seems to propose also that the different comandantes should select a comandante general to act temporarily.

[50] Dec. 21st, Echeandía from Los Angeles announces that V. has already started for S. Diego to embark. *Dept. St. Pap.*, *S. José*, MS., iv. 94; *Vallejo*, *Doc.*, MS., i. 251.

[51] I have the original contract approved by E. on Dec. 27th, with the correspondence of E., Bandini, and Stearns on the subject, in *Bandini*, *Doc.*, MS., 18–24, 27–30.   See also *Leg. Rec.*, MS., i. 194, 211, 297–8.   The money—reduced to $1,500 by the fact that Pliego paid $100 for his own passage—was borrowed from foreigners and other private individuals, except a small sum obtained from the Los Angeles municipal funds.   Stearns acted as agent to obtain the money, and E. and Bandini became responsible for its re-payment. It was paid over to Bradshaw on Jan. 11th.   In February the dip. assumed the debt, but asked for time, greatly to Bandini's annoyance.   Of the final settlement I know only that in Sept. 1834, Bandini acknowledged the receipt of $300 from the ayunt. of Angeles on this account. *Dept. St. Pap.*, *Angeles*, MS., i. 148.

[52] *Doc. Hist. Cal.*, MS., iv. 925–7.

[53] References to embarkation of the passengers and sailing of the *Pocahontas* in *Bandini*, *Doc. Hist. Cal.*, MS., 18–30; *Id.*, *Hist. Cal.*, MS., 76–7; *S. José Arch.*, MS., v. 40; *Vallejo*, *Doc.*, MS., i. 254; xxx. 286, 290; *Guerra*, *Doc.*, MS., iv. 180–1; *Dept. St. Pap.*, MS., iii. 21–2.   There was a report

ing reached San Blas, Victoria wrote a letter to the Mexican authorities, in which, having told over again the events of the past year, he proceeded to explain the plans of Echeandía and the plotting diputacion. The result must inevitably be the utter ruin, not only of the missions, but of all the interests of California, and there was great danger of an attempt to separate the territory from Mexico.[54] July 10, 1832, he wrote again from Mexico to Guerra, stating that the government had at first intended to send him back to California, but had changed that plan. The wound in his chest still made his life miserable. He spoke of his strict obedience, of his patriotism, and his sacrifices; and predicted that "the wicked are not to prevail forever;" but he admitted having "committed the fault of not knowing how to satisfy political passions or to act in accordance with party spirit."[55]

At the time of writing the letter just referred to, Victoria was about to start for Acapulco, where he was on March 9, 1833; and that is the last I know of him. I append no biographical sketch, because all

current in Mexico that V. had been shipped on the schooner *Sta Bárbara*, in the hope that she would be wrecked. *Alaman, Sucesos de Cal. en 1831,* MS. For a biographical sketch of Padre Antonio Peyri, see the local annals of S. Luis Rey in a later chapter of this volume. Rodrigo del Pliego came to Cal. in 1825, his commission as alférez bearing date of Dec. 21, 1824. He had previously served in the Tulancingo dragoons, being retired as alférez of urbanos in Dec. 1821. He was attached to the Monterey company from the time of his arrival until August 1827; and then transferred to the Sta Bárbara company. He commanded a squad of the San Blas infantry company in 1826–7; made two minor expeditions against the Indians while at Sta Bárbara in 1828; and commanded 18 men of the S. Diego company in 1830 at the time of the Solis revolt. He returned to Monterey with Victoria in Jan. 1831, or a few months earlier; and served as prosecutor or defender in some of the celebrated cases under V.'s rule. Hoja de servicios, in *Dept. St. Pap., Ben. Mil.,* MS., lxxi. 18–20. In 1834 he seems to have been promoted in Mexico to the command of the Sta Bárbara company, but never returned to Cal. *Id.,* lxxix. 83. In 1828 he had been declared incompetent and ordered by the min. of war to return to Mex. *Dept. Rec.,* MS., vi. 12. Pliego was detested by the Californians, apparently without exception, as a cowardly sycophant. No one credits him with any good quality; the official records throw no light on his personal character; and the only thing to be said in his favor is that the Californians, being bitterly prejudiced against him and his friends, may have exaggerated his faults.

[54] *Alaman, Sucesos,* MS.

[55] *Guerra, Doc.,* MS., iv. 183–4. Tuthill, *Hist. Cal.,* 131–2, tells us that Victoria retired to a cloister. Robinson implies the same. Alex. S. Taylor somewhere says he died in 1868 or 1869.

that is known of him is contained in this chapter.
The Californians as a rule have nothing to say in his
favor; but the reader knows how far the popular prejudice was founded in justice. I have already expressed the opinion that under ordinary circumstances
Victoria would have been one of California's best
rulers.[56]

Of political events in the south in 1831, after Victoria's abdication, there is nothing to be recorded,
except that Echeandía held the command, both political and military, and all were waiting for the diputacion to assemble early in January. In the north the
news of the revolutionary success arrived about the
middle of December. San Francisco on the 19th, San
José on the 22d, and Monterey on the 26th, went
through the forms of adhesion to the San Diego plan.[57]

[56] The narratives furnished me by Californians, touching more or less fully
on V.'s rule, overthrow, and character—most of which I have already cited
on special points—are as follows: *Osio, Hist. Cal.*, MS., 160–89; *Pico, Hist.
Cal.*, MS., 24–40; *Vallejo, Hist. Cal.*, MS., ii. 136–59; *Alvarado, Hist. Cal.*,
MS., ii. 161–83; iii. 7–8, 48–50; iv. 81; *Bandini, Hist. Cal.*, MS.,72–7; *Amador,
Mem.*, MS., 122–8, 135–6; *Avila, Cosas de Cal.*, MS., 28–31; *Id., Notas*, 11–
15; *Bee, Recoll.*, MS., 2–3; *Boronda, Notas*, MS., 16–17; *Castro, Rel.*, MS.,
23–9; *Fernandez, Cosas*, MS., 64–6; *Gonzalez, Exper.*, MS., 29–30; *Galindo,
Apuntes*, MS., 16–21; *Larios, Convulsiones*, MS., 11–13; *Lugo, Vida*, MS.,
14–16; *Machado, Tiempos*, MS., 26–8; *Ord, Ocurrencias*, MS., 38–50; *Perez,
Recuerdos*, MS., 22; *Pico, Acont.*, MS., 18–23; *Pinto, Apunt.*, MS., 6–9;
Rodriguez, Statement, MS., 7; *Sanchez, Notas*, MS., 7–8; *Torre, Reminis.*,
MS., 22–30; *Valdés, Mem.*, MS., 21; *Valle, Lo Pasado*, MS., 3–5; *Vallejo,
Reminis.*, MS., 109–14; *Weeks' Reminis.*, MS., 73–4.

General accounts narrating briefly the events of V.'s rule, in *Marsh's Letter to Com. Jones*, MS., 4–5; *Robinson's Life in Cal.*, 118–21; *Petit-Thouars,
Voy.*, ii. 91; *Wilkes' Narr., U. S. Explor. Ex.*, v. 174; *Mofras, Exploration*,
i. 294; *Tuthill's Hist. Cal.*, 131–4, and *Los Angeles, Hist.*, 13. Mr Warner in
the last work makes the revolution a local event of Los Angeles annals.
These different writers speak favorably or unfavorably of V. according to the
sources of their information, or to their bias for or against the padres and
José de la Guerra on one side and the Bandini-Pico-Vallejo faction on the
other. Tuthill seems to have taken the versions of Spence and Stearns in
about equal parts. Mofras speaks very highly of Victoria, because of his dislike for the Vallejo party. The version of Robinson, a son-in-law of Guerra,
has been most widely followed.

[57] *Leg. Rec.*, MS., i. 348–9; *Monterey, Actos del Ayunt.*, MS.,42–3. Vallejo,
Sanchez, and Peña signed at S. F.; Leandro Flores for S. José; and Buelna
and Castro for the Monterey ayunt. Juan Higuera and Antonio Castro, of
the ayunt., declined on Dec. 25th to approve the plan; but Castro changed his
mind next day, Higuera still needing more time to think it over. At Sta
Bárbara the plan was signed on Jan. 1, 1832, by Rafael Gonzalez, Miguel
Valencia, and José María García; and it was approved by the ayunt. of Los

At least certain officials, civil and military, are made to appear in the legislative records of the next year as having signed the plan, with remarks of approbation on the dates mentioned. Rafael Gomez, the asesor, apprehensive of personal danger to himself as a partisan of Victoria, went on board the Russian bark *Urup* and tried to induce the captain to carry him to Sitka; but as he had no passport, his request was denied and he was set on shore at San Francisco.[58] The northern members, Vallejo and others, with Secretary Alvarado, started late in December for the south in response to Echeandía's summons to be present at the meeting of the diputacion.

Minor local events, with general remarks on such institutions and topics as are not very closely connected with or necessary to a full understanding of general annals, I propose to present once for all for the whole period of 1831–40, at the end of this volume. Another class of general topics, more purely historical in their nature, and more readily adapting themselves to chronological treatment, such as mission affairs, commerce, foreign relations, and Indian affairs, I shall group as before in chapters covering each a period of five years,[59] deeming this arrangement a much more satisfactory and convenient one for the reader than would be a more minute chronological subdivision. I shall of course refer to these topics as often and as fully as may be necessary to illustrate the annals of any particular year; but for 1831 I find no need for such reference, beyond what I have already said of

Angeles on Jan. 7th. Id. The pronunciamiento of S. F., Dec. 19th, is given in *Vallejo, Doc.*, MS., i. 248. Next day the artillery company recognized Echeandía. *Id.*, i. 250. Vallejo, *Hist. Cal.*, MS., ii. 152–3, claims to have started for the south with a small force in response to a letter from J. A. Carrillo, before he heard of Victoria's downfall.

[58] Certificate dated Dec. 22d, and signed by Zarembo, Khlébnikof, and Shélikof, in *Vallejo, Doc.*, MS., i. 310; Alvarado, *Hist. Cal.*, MS., ii. 181, implies that there were others besides Gomez who attempted to escape.

[59] For the period from 1831–5, see chapters xi.-xiv., this vol.; and for 1836–40, see vol. iv.

secularization to show the cause of the popular feeling against Victoria.

In addition, however, to what I have written about the occurrences of 1831 in California, there remains something to be said of what was being done in Mexico for California, that is, of the labors of Cárlos Carrillo, who had been elected in October 1830 to represent the territory in congress.[60] Don Cárlos reached Mexico in April 1831, after a flattering reception at San Blas and at other points on the way, and he was somewhat active in behalf of his constituents, in comparison at least with his predecessors, so far as we may judge from his own letters.[61] He may be regarded as the representative rather of Captain José de la Guerra than of the Californians, acting largely on that gentleman's advice; but it would have been difficult to choose a wiser counsellor. Carrillo complained to the national government of the arbitrary and unwise acts of the rulers sent to California, resulting to a great extent from the distance of the territory from Mexico. His proposed remedy was the separation of the political and military power, which should be vested in two persons, and his views on this subject met with some encouragement from the president and ministers, who even broached to Don Cárlos the expediency of accepting for himself the civil command. California's urgent need for an organic law was presented, as also the necessity of establishing courts of justice, and regulating the administration of finance. It was complained, moreover, that a great injustice had been done in the promotion of Mexican officers like Zamorano and Pacheco to captaincies over the heads of Californians who had grown gray in the service. Carrillo requested the territorial diputacion to petition congress for the reforms for

[60] See p. 50, this vol., for his election.
[61] *Carrillo, Cartas del Diputado de la Alta California, 1831-2*, MS. There are 14 letters in this interesting collection, besides several of other years, all to his brother-in-law, Guerra.

which he was working, including the appointment, or rather paying, of two competent teachers.[62]

Carrillo was a stanch partisan of the missionaries in these days, reflecting in that respect as others the sentiments of his brother-in-law, and therefore a large part of his correspondence was devoted to topics elsewhere treated. To the missions also was devoted, or to a closely allied matter, his exposition on the pious fund;[63] but this document merits at least a mention here, not only as containing a somewhat fair presentment of the country's general condition and needs, but as the first production of a Californian writer which was ever printed in form of book or pamphlet. Don Cárlos was an enthusiastic admirer of his native province, with great ideas of its destiny under proper management. He thought he was rapidly communicating his enthusiasm to the Mexican authorities, and on the point of success with his proposed reforms. Perhaps he was disposed to exaggerate his success; for the only evidences I find of Mexican attention to California at this time are a few slight mentions of statistical or financial matters in the regular reports of the departments.[64]

[62] *Dept. St. Pap.*, MS., iii. 169.

[63] *Carrillo, Exposicion dirigida á la Cámara de Diputados del Congreso de la Union por El Sr D. Cárlos Antonio Carrillo, Diputado por la Alta California. Sobre Arreglo y Administracion del Fondo Piadoso.* Mexico, 1831. 8vo. 16 p. Dated Sept. 15, 1831. This copy of a very rare pamphlet, the only copy I have ever seen, was presented to me in 1878 by Doña Dolores Dominguez, widow of José Carrillo, a son of the author. It has some slight corrections in ink, probably by the author or by Guerra.

[64] *Mexico, Mem. Relaciones*, 1832, p. 25, and annex. i. p. 11; *Id., Hacienda* 1832, annex. M.

CHAPTER VIII.

AN INTERREGNUM—ECHEANDÍA AND ZAMORANO.

1832.

The diputacion met at Los Angeles January 10, 1832.[1] Two subjects demanded and obtained almost exclusively the attention of this body, the vocales present being Pico, Vallejo, Osio, Ortega, and Argüello, with Yorba later and Alvarado as secretary. The first duty was a proper presentment of charges against Ex-governor Victoria, as a defence of the late revolutionary movement; and the second was to name a gefe político ad interim in accordance with the plan indorsed by the leaders of that movement. I append an abstract of proceedings at the meetings held in January and February.[2] So far as the action against

[1] Echeandía had on Jan. 5th sent out copies of the pronunciamiento of S. Diego, with remarks in defence of that document, concluding by asking the comandantes' opinion on the provisional command. *Vallejo, Doc.*, MS., i. 284.

[2] Session of Jan. 10th, dip. met in the casa consistorial; the oath was administered by Alcalde Dominguez; and Pio Pico, assuming the presidency

Victoria is concerned, I need add nothing to the abstract, because the whole matter has been exhausted in the preceding chapter.

In the matter of choosing a political chief trouble arose unexpectedly. The action of the diputacion in this respect had been very clearly marked out in the

as senior vocal, made a brief and modest address, congratulating the members on their meeting to act for the country's interests after having been for a year prevented from exercising their rights by the tyranny of Victoria. He made the customary admission of his own unworthiness, etc., and asked the aid of his associates in behalf of Cal. Pico's views having been approved, committees were appointed, credentials examined, etc. In the afternoon, Echeandía's summons to the members, dated Dec. 9th, was read. (p. 173-8.) Jan. 11th, after long discussion, in which the various charges were specified, it was unanimously voted to confirm, or approve, the suspension of Victoria; and Vallejo and Argüello were named as a committee to prepare a formal *expediente* on the subject for the sup. govt. Then on motion of Vallejo the diputacion proceeded in accordance with E.'s summons to choose a temporary gefe político, and it was decided according to the law of May 6, 1822, that Pico as senior vocal was entitled to the office. This action was to be sent to E. for circulation. Voted, that according to the Mex. law, the subcomisario, Juan Bandini, was entitled to a seat. Voted to continue the sessions at Angeles and not at S. Diego; but E. was to be invited to be present. Voted, as to the military command, that E. should notify the different officers to choose a temporary comandante general. (p. 178-83.) Jan. 12th, 13th, 14th, 17th, 18th, routine progress by the committee on charges against Victoria; Suplente Yorba takes the oath and his seat; Ortega and Osio named as a committee to prepare a *manifestacion* to the public; Vallejo granted leave of absence for ten days to visit S. Diego. (p. 183-5.) Los Angeles municipal accounts also considered in extra sessions of Jan. 14th, 17th, 23d, 27th. (p. 352-4.) Yorba's oath also in *Los Angeles, Arch.*, MS.. iv. 46-7. Jan. 17th, Ortega and Osio to Echeandía. *Dept. St. Pap.*, MS., iii. 26. Jan. 23d, three letters received from the gefe político provisional, Echeandía, in which he announced Victoria's departure; asked for records of the earlier sessions; and declared it impossible to leave his troops and come to Los Angeles. Jan. 26th-27th, on the 26th, Vallejo proposed that the oath be administered at once to Pico according to the law of Sept. 30, 1823; and as all approved, 'without waiting for a discourse offered by Echeandía' (?), the oath was administered by Vallejo, and Pico was formally declared gefe político interino, the corresponding report being sent to E. and all territorial authorities. Argüello thereupon made a speech, congratulating all on the arrival of the happy day when Cal. was ruled by one of her native sons; and Pico replied in fitting terms. (p. 186-9.) Pico, *Hist. Cal.*, MS., 41-2, states that when the oath was administered the necessary church utensils were lacking, and the padre refused the keys of the church, whereupon J. B. Alvarado entered the church by a skylight for the missing articles, and the oath was administered at the church door. Jan. 31st and Feb. 1st, E. writes to Pico acknowledging receipt of *actas* of Jan. 10th and 26th-27th, giving some advice respecting the policy of the new gefe, and expressing some dissatisfaction with Pico's appointment. *Dept. St. Pap.*, MS., iii. 27-38. Feb. 3d, a letter was received from Bandini, and the matter of his taking a seat it was decided to refer to the sup. govt. Letters from Echeandía were introduced (those referred to above), in which, with some suggestions on policy, powers, etc., he complains of having been 'violently,' or hastily, deprived of the office of gefe político. Osio and Yorba were named as a committee to report on the suggestions, relating among other things to pay of a secretary,

plan of San Diego and in Echeandía's summons to the members, and accordingly on January 11th Pio Pico, the senior vocal, was chosen to fill the position. Echeandía was duly notified, and at first expressed no dissatisfaction, though he seems to have wished the diputacion to adjourn to meet in the south, while that

etc.; and as to the complaints, it was decided that action had not been at all hasty or irregular, nor had it been necessary to wait for the presence of E. before swearing in Pico. Ortega was named to report on efforts to obtain from Mexico a constitution or organic law for California. Communications were also received from Bandini about the cost of Victoria's passage to S. Blas. This debt of $1,500 was assumed in the session of Feb. 4th. (p. 189–95.) In extra or secret sessions of Jan. 24th, 30th, Feb. 3d, 6th, the date and place of annual meetings were discussed without any definite conclusion. There was also some slight clashing between Pico and the rest, P. declaring that it was his place to direct the junta and not to be directed by it. (p. 352–5.) Feb. 10th, on motion of Ortega, Echeandía was again requested to proclaim, as soon as possible, the accession of Pico to the office of gefe, and to cease exercising political power himself; it was also ordered that the new gefe should have jurisdiction at once in those places where the civil authority was established, except at S. Francisco, Sta Bárbara, and S. Diego, which places were to be within the jurisdiction of the comandante general, until such time as the civil authority might be regularly organized and the necessity for military rule removed. (p. 196–7.) It seems that on Feb. 3d E. had objected to P.'s appointment in a communication, either to the dip. or to the ayuntamiento, to which latter body he writes on Feb. 6th. *Dept. St. Pap.*, MS., iii. 41. Feb. 11th, E. to P., in reply to note of 10th, asks by what right he has taken the oath, the law of Sept. 30, 1823, being anulled by art. 163 of the constitution. *Id.*, iii. 39. Feb. 12th, the ayunt. and citizens of Los Angeles held a meeting and formally declared that they would obey no other gefe político than Echeandía. This action was confirmed on Feb. 19th, J. A. Carrillo and José Perez dissenting. *Los Angeles, Arch.*, MS., iv. 50–3, 56–8; *Dept. St. Pap.*, MS., iii. 39–40. Feb. 13th, the action of the ayunt. against P. was received through E. P. made rather a bitter speech, and proposed that E. himself be invited to go before the ayunt. to explain why P. had been appointed according to the laws and to the plan of S. Diego; and also how insulting had been the action of the municipal body to the dip. and the laws. All but Yorba favored this, and the sending of a committee to reason with the ayunt. (p. 197–202.) Feb. 16th, a letter from E. was read, refusing to comply with the request of the dip. E. now declared the appointment illegal, because the military and political command could not be separated; there had not been 7 vocales present; some of them were related to Pico; and finally, P. was incompetent to perform the duties of the office. Still, rather than use force, he will give up the political command and hold the dip. responsible. P. in a very able speech refuted E.'s arguments, and claimed that, whatever his lack of talent, the people had chosen him as a vocal; but he refused to attend any more meetings or accept the office of gefe político until the dip. should vindicate its honor and freedom, and refuse to recognize E., who had evidently intrigued with the ayunt. against the territorial government. Vallejo followed with an argument against E.'s position, which he regarded as virtually a new pronunciamiento made with a view to keep for himself the political power. The speaker was, however, in favor of offering no resistance, but of suspending the sessions and leaving the responsibility of the new revolution with E. and his friends. All except Yorba approved this view, and it was decided to adjourn next day, reporting this action and the reasons to E. and to the national govt. (p. 202–9.) E.'s protest against P.'s appoint-

body desired him to come to Los Angeles. Each declined to yield, and the controversy may have been more bitter than is indicated in the records. At last, after waiting fifteen days, it was decided that the presence of the gefe provisional could be dispensed with, and on the 27th the oath of office was taken by Pico. Echeandía made no open opposition, but neglected to proclaim the change; and later, when the ayuntamiento of Los Angeles, doubtless at his instigation, refused on February 12th to recognize any gefe but Echeandía, the latter openly declared Pico incompetent, his election illegal, and the action of the diputacion a wrong to himself. Rather than resort to force, however, he proposed on the 16th to surrender the gefatura, holding the diputacion responsible for all disorders that might ensue. Echeandía's course can hardly be regarded otherwise than as contemptible and treacherous. Led by motives of personal ambition and personal resentment, he made use of his military power against the cause he had pretended to support. He may have been technically right in declaring the action of the diputacion illegal; for it is doubtful if in a frontier territory like California the civil and military power could be even temporarily separated by the people, but he knew this perfectly when he signed the plan, which was the only law under which the revolutionists could pretend to act.

Pico and his associates acted in a moderate and dignified manner at this juncture. The former de-

ment, also in *Dept. St. Pap.*, MS., iii. 42-3. Feb. 17th, Vallejo and Argüello presented their expediente against Victoria, a long presentment of all the charges, with copies of many documents on the subject, all of which has been utilized in the preceding chapter. Some slight routine business was transacted, and then the dip. adjourned for the reasons stated in the session of Feb. 16th. (p. 209 11, 298-350.) On this subject I may note here that on Feb. 6th, E. had sent to Mexico a full statement of the charges against Victoria and the causes of the revolt. *Alaman, Sucesos de Cal. en 1831*, MS., p. 23-9. Feb. 24th, at S. Diego the members of the dip., in forwarding to Mexico the expediente above alluded to, prefaced that document with a long statement of their late sessions at Los Angeles, of their efforts in behalf of their country, and of Echeandía's unexpected opposition and ambitious schemes to retain his political power. Their case as presented was a very strong one. (p. 253-68.) *Leg. Rec.*, MS., i. 173-355.

clined to retain the office in opposition to the will of
the general and the people of Los Angeles, and the
deputies, defenceless and averse to further civil dissensions, deemed it best to regard Echeandía's movement as a successful contra-pronunciamiento, which
relieved them of all further responsibility. They accordingly suspended their sessions on the 17th, rendering to the national government a full report of all
that had occurred, and holding themselves in readiness to meet again when the interests of the country
should demand it.   Pico made no further claims to the
office of gefe político, nor were any such claims made
for him. By the five members of the diputacion he
had been recognized from January 27th to February
16th, twenty days, and under the plan of revolt he
was entitled to the office.   Such is the substance of
Don Pio's title to be regarded as governor of California in 1832–3.[3]

While Echeandía was thus occupied with a revolutionary movement against his own friends in the
south, another Mexican officer was engaged in devel-
oping revolutionary schemes, equally selfish and ambitious, but far less treacherous, in the north. Captain
Agustin V. Zamorano and others pronounced at
Monterey against the plan of San Diego, and all who
had favored that movement. Zamorano had been
Victoria's secretary and friend, but so far as can be
known had taken no part in the troubles of 1831, had
made no effort to defend his unpopular master in his
time of need, but had perhaps promised neutrality.
Now that Victoria was out of the country, aware that
the popular feeling in favor of Echeandía was by no
means so strong as had been that against Victoria,
knowing that current disputes must be settled event-

[3] On the trouble between Pico and Echeandía, see, in addition to the records
already cited, *Pico, Hist. Cal.*, MS., 41–4; *Osio, Hist. Cal.*, MS., 189–92;
Vallejo, Hist. Cal., MS., ii. 159–64; *Alvarado, Hist. Cal.*, MS., ii. 184–90;
Ord, Ocurrencias, MS., 50–1; *Machado, Tiempos Pasados*, MS., 28–9. There
are no variations of statement requiring notice. P. says that E. subsequently
recognized him; but such does not appear to have been the fact.

ually in Mexico rather than in California, and being moreover free from all charges of complicity in the late revolt, the ambitious captain shrewdly saw his opportunity to gain favor with the national authorities, as well as temporary prominence in territorial affairs, and he acted accordingly.

Zamorano's first step was to secure the coöperation of the foreign residents of Monterey. These foreigners, though taking no decided stand, had been inclined to favor Victoria because of his strict preservation of order and administration of justice, caring very little for his sins against the spirit of Mexican institutions. As a rule, they disliked Echeandía, had no confidence in Pio Pico, were opposed to all revolutions not directly in the line of their own interests, and deemed their business prospects threatened by the rumored dissensions in the south. Therefore they were willing to act in defence of good order at the capital. They were convened by Zamorano on January 24th, and proceeded to organize a *compañia extranjera* for the defence of Monterey, during the continuance of 'existing circumstances,' against attack from the interior or from any other quarter. Nearly fifty joined the company, and elected Hartnell as their leader.[4]

[4] *Compañia Extrangera de Monterey, su organizacion en 1832*, MS. The company was not to be required to leave the town under any circumstances. Juan B. Bonifacio was 2d officer, or lieutenant, with Luis Vignes as a substitute in case of his disability. Such men as had to leave their work for military service were to receive 50 cents per day. The following men attended the meeting and signed the rolls of the company:

Agustin V. Zamorano,	Juan B. Bonifacio,	J. L. Vignes,
Wm E. Hartnell,	Timothy Murphy,	D. Douglas,
Thos Coulter,	Wm Taylor,	Nathan Spear,
Juan B. Leandry,	James Watson,	Santiago McKinley,
Geo. Kinlock,	John Rainsford,	Estévan Munras,
J. B. R. Cooper,	John Gorman,	José Iglesias,
José Amesti,	Chas Roe,	Walter Duckworth,
Luis Pombert,	Henry Bee,	Thos Raymore,
Samuel Mead,	R. S. Barker,	John Roach,
Wm McCarty,	Edward Watson,	Thos Doak,
John Thompson,	John Miles,	David Littlejohn,
Jas Cook,	Joseph Dixon,	Wm Garner,
Wm Johnson,	John Roper,	Pierre J. Chevrette,
Wm Gralbatch,	Guy F. Fling,	Chas R. Smith,
Juan D. Bravo,	John Burns,	Wm Webb.
Daniel Ferguson,		

I have in my possession the original 'orderly book' of the company, kept

Having thus enlisted the services of the foreign residents, the leaders of whom doubtless understood his plans, Zamorano summoned Asesor Gomez, Lieutenant Ibarra, Hartnell, and half a dozen other men of some prominence to a meeting February 1st; and to this junta, after having stated that northern California from Santa Bárbara to San Francisco did not accept the plan of San Diego, he submitted in substance the following questions: Are the acts of the diputacion at Los Angeles legal or illegal? In the latter case, in what person should be vested the civil and military command, Victoria having left the territory? Should a force be sent south for the defence of Santa Bárbara, as had been requested? Ought the sub-comisario of revenues at Monterey to obey the orders of Juan Bandini, his superior officer, but a leader in the revolution? After a thorough discussion, that is, after the members had approved Zamorano's views as previously agreed upon, the junta decided: First, that the acts of the diputacion must be considered illegal and null, since that body had been convened by an authority unknown to the laws and existing only by reason of revolution. Consequently no obedience or respect was due to rulers chosen by that body. Second, no gefe político should be chosen until the supreme government should appoint one, but the comandancia general should be filled ad interim, according to the military regulations, by the officer of highest rank and seniority who had taken no part in the rebellion, that is, by Zamorano, the two ranking captains Portilla and Argüello having for-

by its captain, from Feb. 8th, when active garrison duty was begun, to April 12th, when the captain resigned. *Hartnell, Cuaderno de Órdenes de la Compañia Extrangera de Monterey, 1832*, MS. On Feb. 23d, Edward Watson was dismissed for disrespect. March 25th, Hartnell, having to be absent, left Bonifacio in command. April 12th, the alcalde having requested the comandante of the post to dispense with Bonifacio's services, Hartnell took it as an insult to the company, and resigned. This was very likely the end of the organization. On Feb. 18, 1833, Hartnell informed the members that Gov. Figueroa, in his communication to Zamorano on Feb. 15th, had thanked the foreigners for their services, which he promised to make known to the sup. govt. *Vallejo, Doc.*, MS., ii. 12.

feited their rights.   Third, to remove anxiety, uphold
lawful authority, and prevent catastrophe at Santa
Bárbara, as large a force as can be spared should be
sent there at once, but not to attempt operations
against the rebels unless they should attack that place.
In case of such attack, the comandante may not only
repel the foe, but if circumstances permit, may advance
to San Diego and capture the rebel leaders.   He
must communicate the proceedings of this meeting to
the officer in command of the rebels, summoning them
all to give up their arms, and suspending all from
office.   Should they refuse, they are to be warned
not to advance beyond the points they now occupy.
Fourth, the comisario subalterno, Gomez, will not obey
Bandini, but communicate directly with the comisario
general in Sonora.   Fifth, the garrison at San Francisco having pronounced in favor of the legitimate
authority, and arrested their comandante, Sanchez,
who had approved the San Diego plan, the retired
lieutenant, Ignacio Martinez, shall be placed in command there.   Sixth, the acting comandante general
must report these proceedings to the supreme government, with mention of the services rendered by foreigners, and lists of soldiers and civilians who have
remained loyal.[5]

[5] *Pronunciamiento de Monterey contra el Plan de San Diego, ó sea Acta de la
Junta de 1º de Febrero 1832 en favor de la legítima autoridad y contra D. José
María Echeandía*, MS.   Copy certified by Zamorano on Feb. 2d, and several
other certified copies.   The signers were Capt. Agustin V. Zamorano, comandante of Monterey; Lic. Rafael Gomez, asesor of the territory; José Joaquin Gomez, comisario subalterno of Monterey; Salvador Espinosa, alcalde;
W. E. Hartnell and Juan B. Bonifacio, commanders of the foreign military
company; Juan María Ibarra, lieut of the Mazatlan company; Juan Malarin,
honorary 2d lieut of national navy; Francisco Pacheco, brevet lieut; and
José María Madrazo, sergt of artillery detachment.   Feb. 1st, Zamarano
reports the action of the junta to the alcalde of S. José. *S. José, Arch.*,
MS., iii. 9.   Feb. 2d, sends copies to S. F., S. José, and Branciforte. *Vallejo, Doc.*, MS., i. 289.   Feb. 6th, Z. announces to comandantes and alcaldes that the garrison and citizens of Sta Bárbara had 'pronounced' in
favor of legitimate authority, deposing the comandante, Alf. Domingo Carrillo, who had adhered to the S. Diego plan.   All accomplished in a most
happy manner. *Id.*, i. 290.   Feb. 12th, Z. to Echeandía, sends copy of the
proceedings of Feb. 1st, and the summons required by that document to
surrender, promising the clemency of the govt to him and his followers if
he accepts. *Id.*, i. 296.   April 2d, Alf. Sanchez, having repented, is restored

There are no records of a formal adhesion to Zamorano's plan at San Francisco, San José, Branciforte, and Santa Bárbara, though there are allusions to such adhesion at some of those places, and there can be no doubt that it took place at all during the month of February. Ibarra started with a military force for Santa Bárbara about February 9th; and in April, the defence of Monterey having been intrusted to the compañia extrangera and to another company of citizens organized for the purpose, Zamorano himself marched south with all the force he could raise, having learned that the so-called rebels were assuming a hostile attitude, and were not disposed to pay much attention to the *autoridad legítima*.

So far as the south is concerned, we know more of what was said than of what was done. The authors of my original narratives content themselves with the general statement that Zamorano having refused to recognize Echeandía, the latter consented to rule in the south, while his rival held sway over the north.[6] The earliest notice we have that a knowledge of the contra-pronunciamiento had reached the south is when on March 5th Echeandía reported to Pico the news of disturbances at Santa Bárbara, and proposed a meeting of the diputacion for consultation, offering to attend;[7] and next day were communicated more complete details respecting the proceedings at Monterey. There were informal meetings of officials for consultation at

to the command of S. F. *Id.*, i. 305. March 30th, Z. to alcalde of S. José. Has heard that the rebels of S. Diego have assumed a hostile attitude and are about to occupy Los Angeles, which at the beginning of the month had come out in favor of the legitimate authority. This makes it necessary for him to go to Sta Bárbara and perhaps farther; and he calls on the alcalde for 20 or 25 men, mounted and patriotic, to be sent at once, since by a rapid movement he hopes to secure the tranquillity of the country. *S. José, Arch.*, MS., ii. 60. Feb. 29th, Anastasio Carrillo in a private letter speaks of the force which Lieut Ibarra has at Sta Bárbara, with which he will force S. Diego to yield to the proposal of Feb. 28th (?). *Valle, Doc. Hist. Cal.*, MS., 25. April 8th, Z. was at S. Antonio on his way to Sta Bárbara. *Guerra, Doc.*, MS., vi. 152. Gonzalez, *Experiencias*, MS., 30-1, alcalde at the time, gives a few vague particulars about the action at Sta Bárbara.

[6] The names of authors and narratives are for the most part those given in note 56 of chap. vii.

[7] *Dept. St. Pap.*, MS., iii. 44.

San Diego on March 7th, 8th, and 13th; and it was probably at these meetings that Juan Bandini opened the batteries of his wrathful eloquence on the leaders of the northern movement, uttering some truths, but trusting largely to personal abuse to maintain his position.[8]

The 14th of March Echeandía made a formal reply from San Luis Rey to Zamorano's communication of February 12th. He accused the latter of having violated his personal pledges of neutrality, at the instigation of Rafael Gomez and his own personal ambition. He alluded to the facts that Victoria had recognized him as his successor in command, and that the officials at San Diego in recent meetings had utterly refused to recognize Zamorano as comandante general. Still Echeandía proposed a truce under conditions, which being observed, he would not use force to maintain his rights. Evidently nobody in California was thirsting for blood. The conditions were that Zamorano should leave commercial and other communication free between different parts of the territory, withdraw his forces from Santa Bárbara, leave the diputacion and ayuntamientos free to act as they might deem best in civil affairs, and leave also the comisario and the former comandantes of Santa Bárbara and San Francisco free in the exercise of their duties. On these conditions, by taking the oath prescribed in the constitution, he might regard himself as comandante general of the north until the decision from Mexico; but as Ibarra was intriguing with Los Angeles, Zamorano must decide very promptly, or he would begin hostile operations and make real the

[8] *Bandini, Apuntes Políticos de 1832*, MS., and another undated document in *Id., Doc.*, 26–31. Zamorano is accused of bad faith in keeping quiet for 42 days after Victoria's defeat to pronounce for him after his departure; Rafael Gomez was an intimate of Victoria, a prevaricator, an associate of unworthy persons, and a rum-seller; José J. Gomez was anxious for disorders in order to hide irregularities in his revenue accounts; Hartnell was a monarchist; Bonifacio, an ignorant foreigner, not naturalized; Espinosa had no authority outside of his municipality; and the other signers were for the most part incapable of understanding the pronunciamiento. There were only one captain and one lieutenant, as against 11 officers in favor of the plan of S. Diego.

streams of blood talked of, holding his opponents responsible before God and the world.[9]

The diputacion, willing to forget for the time its own wrongs at the hands of Echeandía, assembled at his call at San Diego to consider measures for checking the disorders that must result from the new pronunciamiento, "this duty devolving on the assembly for want of a gefe político." The members were unanimous in their condemnation of Zamorano's junta, especially of its attempt to suspend the diputacion, a body with whose acts even the national government had declared itself powerless to interfere, said Argüello, except after reference to congress. At a second meeting, March 22d, Pico expressed sentiments very similar to those of Bandini already cited; and it was resolved to issue a circular to the ayuntamientos, inviting them to preserve order, to recognize the diputacion, and to proceed with their ordinary municipal duties without paying the slightest attention to the junta which was tempting them into danger. After this rather mild action the assembly adjourned, apparently with the intention of meeting again at Los Angeles.[10]

But the legitimistas succeeded in their intrigues with the fickle ayuntamiento of Los Angeles, which body, on March 22d, laid before the people a communication from Zamorano, explaining the beauties of his system. To this system the assembled citizens "manifested themselves addicted;"[11] and Ibarra came immediately from Santa Bárbara with a part of his force and encamped in the pueblo of the Angels. At San Luis Rey the members of the diputacion en route for

---

[9] March 15, 1832, Echeandía to Pico, transcribing his communication of the 14th to Zamorano. *Vallejo, Doc.*, MS., i. 303.

[10] *Leg. Rec.*, MS., i. 211–20. March 18th, Pico to Vallejo, inviting him to attend the meeting of next day. *Vallejo, Doc. Hist. Cal.*, MS., i. 306. March 20th, Echeandía to Pico, reporting resolutions of the council of war at S. Diego March 7th, 8th, 13th, against Zamorano. Argüello and Vallejo had been present. *Dept. St. Pap.*, MS., iii. 44–5. The circular to the ayuntamientos was probably issued but intercepted by Zamorano's officials in the north.

[11] *Los Angeles, Arch.*, MS., iv. 59–60.

Los Angeles heard of the defection of that town, and also that Echeandía was engaged in active preparations for war. The most alarming symptom of approaching trouble was the attitude of the neophytes, who, as devoted partisans of Echeandía, were coming into camp from all directions and were being armed and drilled for offensive operations. The deputies now held a meeting at San Luis and devoted all their energies to the preservation of tranquillity and the prevention of bloodshed. It was voted to send a despatch to Ibarra, holding him responsible for any misfortunes that might result from an outbreak of hostilities, warning him of the inquietude of the Indians, and urging some arrangement to avoid a rupture. Similar notes were to be sent to both Echeandía and Zamorano.[12]

Echeandía expressed his willingness to make an arrangement for peace, but as no replies were received from Ibarra and Zamorano, he went on with his preparations, and an advance force of soldiers and Indians under Captain Barroso encamped at Paso de Bartolo on the San Gabriel River.[13] Ibarra deemed it best to retire to Santa Bárbara, perhaps by the order of his chief, who was now—early in April— hastening south from Monterey with reënforcements. Los Angeles was in turn occupied by Barroso and Echeandía, who in a day or two removed their forces to San Gabriel.[14]

[12] *Leg. Rec.*, MS., i. 220–2. It may be remarked that Ibarra's occupation of Los Angeles was in a sense a violation of Zamorano's plan of Feb. 1st, according to which his forces were not to advance beyond Sta Bárbara unless that place should be attacked.

[13] Alf. Ignacio del Valle, *Lo Pasado de Cal.*, MS., 6–7, relates that he was with Barroso at the Paso while his father, Lieut Antonio del Valle, was with Ibarra at Los Angeles.

[14] Many Californians state that Echeandía had over 1,000 Indians at the camp on the river; and Osio, *Hist. Cal.*, MS., 196–9, says that he entered Los Angeles at the head of 1,000 mounted Indians, whom, however, he dismissed with presents after retiring to S. Gabriel. Tuthill, *Hist. Cal.*, 134, following *Robinson's Life in Cal.*, 122, tells us that Echeandía gathered many Indians at S. Juan Capistrano, and inaugurated a series of robberies and murders. A state of anarchy and confusion ensued. There is no foundation for such a statement. Vallejo, *Hist. Cal.*, MS., ii. 161–77, narrates the particulars of a personal quarrel that occurred about this time between Echeandía and San-

Zamorano, on arrival at Santa Bárbara, was some-what less warlike than at Monterey, and was induced to consider the propositions for a truce, to which he had previously paid no attention. After some pre-liminary correspondence, not extant, between the two comandantes and the diputacion, an arrangement was concluded on the 8th or 9th of May; but Zamorano seems to have had very much his own way in dictat-ing the conditions[15] by which the military command was divided between Echeandía in the south and Zamorano in the north, while the diputacion was left with no authority at all, except such as the southern

tiago Argüello. The matter is also alluded to in *Leg. Rec.*, MS., i. 229–30. Vallejo also gives some details of the stay of the forces at S. Gabriel, where $20,000 were 'borrowed' and supplies were exacted, not much to the satisfac-tion of the padres, who were warm adherents of the other party.

[15] *Zamorano, Proclama que contiene los Artículos de las Condiciones con-venidas entre él y el Sr Echeandía en Mayo de 1832*, MS. This original procla-mation is dated May 9th. I have never seen the original agreement with signatures of the parties, or any copy of it; and I suppose that no such docu-ment was ever signed. The articles were in substance as follows: 1. Until the arrival of a ruler or of express orders from Mexico, California shall remain divided into two parts—one from S. Gabriel south, under command of Lieut-col. Echeandía, and the other from S. Fernando north, under Capt. Zamo-rano. The former could not advance any military force north of San Juan Capistrano; nor the latter south of S. Buenaventura—this, however, not to affect the ordinary mission escoltas of 5 or 7 men. 2, 4. Neither the dip. nor any gefe político named by that body shall issue any orders to the northern ayuntamientos; nor shall the dip. make any innovations in the southern mis-sions. 3, 5. Trade and travel must not be interrupted; and in case of convul-sions either party must afford prompt advice and aid. 6. Neither party can have with Los Angeles any other relations than the military ones heretofore existing between that town and the presidial comandantes. 7. Any armed advance contrary to art. 1 to be repelled without incurring responsibility; other faults to be promptly settled by official correspondence. 8. Mails to leave Monterey on the 7th, and S. Diego on the 22d of each month. 9. In opening official despatches from Mexico great delicacy to be used, and the responsibility to rest on the southern comandante. 10. Civilians who have taken no part in the contention may live where they please; others where they are (?). 11. Neophytes and gentiles are to be sent back unarmed to their respective homes. 12. For the sake of peace, these articles will remain in force until the chief named by the sup. govt shall have been recognized. Copy of this document also in *S. José, Arch.*, MS., ii. 90. Alvarado, *Hist. Cal.*, MS., ii. 188–9, claims to have been largely instrumental, by his personal intimacy with both leaders, in securing the formation of this treaty. Eche-andía did not admit that he had agreed to these articles except to Nos. 1, 5, and 8. This appears from his letter to Pico of May 22d. *Dept. St. Pap.*, MS., iii. 47–8, and from Zamorano's proclamation of July 7th. *Vallejo, Doc. Hist. Cal.*, MS., i. 314. His claim was that the others were suggestions not definitely decided on, or perhaps in some cases not accurately stated in Zamorano's proclamation. The diputacion, however, seems to have agreed with Z.'s version of the articles relating to that body. *Leg. Rec.*, MS., i. 250–2.

comandante might choose to give it in his district on matters not involving innovations in the missions.

The military forces were promptly withdrawn to the north and south by the respective generals, and the members of the diputacion retired to San Diego, where on May 15th they held a meeting, and addressed to the president of the republic a full report of what they had done for the good of California since February 24th, the date of their last representation. They declared that Zamorano's action had been wholly uncalled for, and that many of the statements in his pronunciamiento were false. They added to their report an argument in which they presented at some length their views on the causes of the evils afflicting California—evils due largely to the detestable and anti-republican mission system, and to the presence and intrigues of the friars, who sought a restoration of Spanish institutions. They more than hinted that Zamorano's movement had been in the interests of Spain, and they reiterated their opinion that the civil and military command should be vested in two distinct persons.[16] Again at the end of December did the diputacion meet, this time at Los Angeles, to take some final steps for vindicating the record of past acts and to adjourn, since the term of several members now expired, and the comandante of the north had refused to take any steps for a new election.[17]

One more episode of the Zamorano-Echeandía controversy demands brief notice, namely, the exploits

---

[16] Session of May 15, 1832. *Leg. Rec.*, MS., i. 231–52.

[17] *Leg. Rec.*, MS., i. 222–30. Dec. 30th–31st, it was voted to send a communication to the new chief in order to hasten his arrival; to send a protest to Zamorano, holding him responsible for violating the law by preventing an election and abrogating the faculties of the gefe político; to notify ayuntamientos of the dissolution of the dip., and call for acknowledgments of various exhortations to peace and good order sent to the municipal bodies; and finally to prepare a manifiesto to the people. The adjournment on Dec. 31st is recorded in *Los Angeles, Arch.*, MS., iv. 76. Aug. 2d, Echeandía had sent a communication to Pico on the subject of holding elections, in which he gives directions, proposes to preside, and speaks throughout as if he deemed himself still the gefe político. *Dept. St. Pap.*, MS., iii. 70–1.

of Antonio Ávila, a convict whom the reader will remember in connection with the Solis revolt of 1829, and some of his companion *presidiarios*. It seems that Vicente Sanchez came north as soon as released from the Los Angeles jail, and in his patriotic zeal enlisted Ávila and fifteen or twenty convicts to march south and aid in restoring the 'legitimate government,' promising them, in addition to other emoluments, their liberty. In the south they abandoned Sanchez, distrusting his promises and learning that he intended to use them for private rather than public service, and wandered about for a time in different parts of the country. The people naturally were alarmed when they knew that such a band of desperadoes were at large with arms in their hands, though it does not appear that they really committed any outrages. A charge of a design to overthrow Zamorano's and not Echeandía's power was trumped up against Ávila and his men, and after several unsuccessful efforts they were captured at Pacheco's rancho, disarmed, and subjected to trial at Monterey in June. No proof of revolutionary designs was adduced, but the convicts were kept under arrest until the new governor arrived, and were by him included in a general pardon to all combatants. Ávila in 1833 recovered his arms, but failed to obtain permission to go to Mexico until his term should have expired, notwithstanding his disposition to serve his country shown on at least two occasions.[18]

From June to December 1832 all was quiet politically, both in the north and south, and California under its dual military rule was by no means a badly

[18] *Ávila, Papeles Tocantes á la Sedicion de Antonio Ávila y otros Presidiarios en 1832*, MS. Vicente Sanchez declined to testify, on the plea that he was a diputado. June 13th, Zamorano to alcalde of S. José. Says Ávila's party are near Monterey, ready to present themselves on his (Z.'s) order; but as it is impossible for him to have any official relations with such people, it has been determined to capture them by force. He wants 9 or 10 men, who were later sent back because there were no muskets for them. *S. José, Arch.*, MS., ii. 57. June 19th, 23d, Z. to com. of S. F., on the same subject. *Vallejo, Doc.*, MS., i. 311–12.

governed territory, since we hear of neither disorders on the part of the people nor of oppressive acts by the rulers. Both parties, in fact, waiting for a new governor and a supreme decision on their past acts, were on their good behavior, and disposed to coöperate in the preservation of order. It may be a matter of some interest to decide who was the governor, or gefe político, of California this year. It has been customary to put Pio Pico's name in the list between those of Victoria and Figueroa; but as I have already shown, he has no claim to the honor. For some twenty days he claimed the place, which he ought to have had under the plan of San Diego, and was recognized by the four or five members of the body that elected him; but after February 16th he made no claims and performed no acts. Nor did the diputacion make any claims in his behalf. He refused on the date named to accept the office, and was never asked again to do so. There was no Mexican law making him gefe político without regard to his own acts, or those of his associate vocales, by virtue of his position as senior vocal. Zamorano, on the other hand, never made pretensions to be gefe político; in fact, one of the articles of his plan expressly declared that no such officer existed.

Either there was a vacancy or Echeandía was the governor. Echeandía was declared gefe político provisional in the plan of November 29th and December 1st, until he should give up the office to a person named by the diputacion. That plan was successful, and on December 6th Victoria surrendered the office to him. The diputacion recognized his title, and nobody formally denied it till the 1st of February. Then Zamorano's junta declared the office to be vacant; but the plan of February 1st was never entirely successful, being accepted only in the north. After January 27th he ought, according to his own pledges, to have surrendered the office, but he did not do so. On February 12th the Los Angeles ayuntamiento, the only civil organization in the south, recognized him, and declared it would not recognize any other, and it never did recognize any other; though by approving Zamorano's plan it virtually assented to the doctrine of a vacancy. The 16th of February Echeandía offered to surrender the office to avoid the use of force; but his offer was not accepted. The compact of May 8th–9th contained not a word against his claims to the office, even according to Zamorano's version of that compact; and Echeandía did not relinquish his claims, but on the contrary asserted them, and performed some few and slight acts, in the matter of elections and secularization, in his capacity of gefe político.[19] There was never any decision of the question by the Mexican authorities, nor in fact any necessity for such decision. If I give a chronological list of rulers elsewhere in this work, I must either use Echeandía's name for 1832 or leave the place blank. Meanwhile the reader may decide for himself.

Now Californian affairs in Mexico demand attention. Cárlos Carrillo, the congressman, was bitterly disappointed when he heard of the revolution against Victoria. The news seemed to weaken his eloquent eulogies of the Californians as a law-abiding people. He had flattered himself on having reached the brink of success in obtaining several advantageous measures for his constituents. Probably he had made less progress than he supposed, but the late events afforded the president and ministers a convenient excuse for refusing to carry out certain partial promises. All hope for a separation of the military and civil commands, for an organic law, for courts, for a proper

---

[19] July 19th, Z. in a proclamation to the people refers to E.'s rejection of certain articles of the compact and to his claim to be gefe político as subjects respecting which discussion had been voluntarily discontinued on account of the expected arrival of a new gefe at an early date. *Vallejo, Doc.,* MS., i. 314. Castillo Negrete in 1835 alludes to Echeandía as 'el intruso gefe político.' *Dept. St. Pap., Ben. Mil.,* MS., lxxviii. 53.

distribution of lands—and he might have added, "for my appointment as gefe político"—"has gone to the devil," he complains to Guerra, "and I am placed in a most awkward position after having sung the praises of the Californians in congress."[20] If we may credit Carrillo's own statements—and I find no other evidence on the subject—the Mexican authorities were disposed to be severe in their treatment of the revolting Californians; and it was only by the most untiring efforts that he saved the leaders, first from death, then from banishment, and finally had them included in an amnesty granted to the rebels of Vera Cruz.

The choice of a ruler to succeed Victoria now occupied, as far as the interests of so distant a territory ever did, the attention of Bustamante and his advisers. Circumstances seemed to require the appointment of a strong military man. The idea of separating the commands, if it had ever been entertained, was abandoned when the revolt was known, and at the same time Carrillo's chances disappeared, if he ever had any. Victoria says the first idea of the government was to send him back with a strong supporting force.[21] Then there was a thought of appointing Zamorano, as the ranking officer in California not involved in the revolt. This was recommended by Virmond, and very likely by Victoria and Padre Peyri, but Carrillo

[20] *Carrillo, Cartas del Diputado*, MS., 231–52. Jan. 20th, Carrillo called on the vice-president, receiving from him the news of disturbances in Cal. Bustamante threatened to send an armed force to bring that rebellious territory to order. C. told him it would be better to take away the Mazatlan company than to send more troops, who without pay would be sure to revolt. March 15th, Virmond has arrived and given an ugly account of home affairs. Victoria and Peyri are expected; and Pliego will say no good of the Californians. It is said that all officers who took part in the revolt will be dismissed the service. (Such an order seems to have been issued on Mar. 20th, so far as artillery officers were concerned. *Dept. St. Pap.*, MS., iii. 45.) April 14th, tired of official life, of struggles against obstinate diputados, of official promises never kept. Does not desire re-election, which Victoria tells him is talked of. Only by the most strenuous efforts, aided by four other deputies, he has saved the Californian revolutionists from the death penalty, but not from that of banishment for 4 years from the republic. Letters of April 21st and May 11th on Figueroa's appointment. C. in later years (p. 254–7) claimed that it was by his efforts that the Californian rebels were included in the amnesty granted to those of Vera Cruz.

[21] *Guerra, Doc.*, MS., iv. 183–4.

opposed it with all his might.[22]   The choice finally
fell on Brevet Brigadier-general José Figueroa, an
able and prominent man in Mexican affairs since 1820,
comandante general of Sonora and Sinaloa for five or
six years, and by reason of that position, more or less
acquainted with Californian affairs.   Politically he
was not in sympathy with Bustamante's administration, having been a supporter and intimate personal
friend of Guerrero; and it is believed that his appointment was a measure dictated less by a consideration
of his interests or those of California than by a desire
to get rid of a troublesome foe.[23]

[22] *Carrillo, Cartas*, MS., 235–6.   He says that Mexico was swarming with
claimants for command in the distant territories, impecunious nobodies at the
national capital, but ready to put on the airs of viceroys in Cal. *Id.*, p. 241–5.

[23] The first mention I find of Figueroa in contemporary records is in a private letter of Iturbide to Guerrero, dated Jan. 10, 1821, in which he urges the
patriot chieftain to put himself on the side of Spain, and asks him to send a
man of his entire confidence to treat with him on the subject, naming Figueroa
among several other 'individuos mas adictos á Vd.' *Mexico, Cartas de Iturbide
y Guerrero*, p. 2.   Antonio Ruiz de la Mota, one of Guerrero's men in the war
of independence, a man to whom F. rendered many favors in Cal., said that
F. as Guerrero's secretary took a prominent part in the negotiations by which
the two leaders were united and success insured; though at one time Guerrero
suspected his friend of treachery and proposed to have him shot. *Torre, Remin.*,
MS., 51–3.   In 1824 F. was appointed comandante general of Sonora, and
specially commissioned to organize an expedition at Arizpe to explore and secure the regions obstructed by savages; to inspect the mines, especially the
famous 'planchas de plata;' and to facilitate communication by land with
Cal.   In pursuance of these instructions, he marched in person to the junction
of the Colorado and Gila in 1825; but had to go back in haste to put down
the great Yaqui revolt, which lasted several years. *Retes, Portentosas Rique-
zas Minerales.*   His efforts to open communication between Son. and Cal. are
mentioned in the account I have given of Romero's expedition of 1823–6 in
chap. xxii. vol. ii.; and several of his letters are included in *Romero,
Documentos*, MS.   Elsewhere in my work in connection with the annals of
Sonora I have said something respecting this part of Figueroa's career; for
particular allusions to him, see *Pinart, Col. Doc. Son.*, MS., nos. 48, 52–3;
print, nos. 107, 110, 180–2; *Sonora, Actas del Primer Congreso Constitucional*
i. 74–5; *Figueroa, Observaciones de un Ciudadano*, MS., 1–7; *Opinion Pública
de Occidente*, July 30, 1829.   On Sept. 5, 1828, the name of Altar was officially
changed to Villa de Figueroa, and the general was formally declared a citizen
of Sonora.   Though of unquestioned bravery, he earned the cognomen of 'El
Pacífico y Calmoso;' always used his influence against local revolutions; and
was sometimes blamed for his indulgence to conquered Indian foes.   He left
Sonora in 1829, starting for the eastern coast to aid in repelling Spanish invasion, but not arriving apparently in time for that service.   On Dec. 20,
1829, he issued at Durango a proclamation calling upon the people to follow
him in support of Guerrero and the federal government against the rebels of
Campeche and Jalapa. *Atleta*, Jan. 7, 1830, p. 75.   In March 1830 he was arrested with several others by orders of Gen. Bachiller in Mexico on charge of
conspiracy, *Id.*, Mar. 25, Apr. 2, 25, 1830, p. 385, 416, 507; but as he was too
popular a man to be shot and too dangerous to be allowed to remain in Mex-

Figueroa received his appointment as comandante general and inspector at a salary of $4,000 April 17, 1832, and that of gefe superior político on May 9th, with instructions from the different ministries the 17th. His general instructions took the form of supplementary articles to those formerly given to Echeandía, not literally extant, as we have seen. Figueroa was to work for the perfect restoration of tranquillity, and to inspire confidence in the national government by explaining the causes which had led to certain changes in the system of republican administration. He was to supply complete statistics about California and all its institutions and industries. He was to give much attention to the neophytes, with a view to improve their condition and fit them for a change in the mission system. To give an impulse to trade, he must favor the exportation of surplus products and induce the missions to build small vessels. Colonization and the distribution of lands both to citizens and foreigners were to be encouraged in accordance with the laws, several special grants being recommended, as were active efforts to extend settlement toward 42° in the north. Indian policy toward the gentiles, movements and aims of the Russians and Americans, illegal operations of hunters and trappers, and abuses in connection with the rearing of cattle were among the matters to which the new ruler's attention was directed.[24] Special instructions were given on the subject of secularizing

ico, he was soon released to be exiled to California as governor. He held the honorary position of vice-governor of the state of Mexico until Dec. 7, 1833. *St. Pap., Miss. and Colon.*, MS., ii. 285, 293-4. He left Sonora in debt to the fondo de temporalidades to the amount of $3,000, which sum was ordered to be collected in 1834. *Dept. St. Pap., Ben. Mil.*, MS., lxxvii. 11. Cárlos Carrillo, when the appointment was first made, was told by a deputy from Sonora that Figueroa was a despotic fortune-hunter, and Virmond also spoke against him; but Minister Alaman spoke in the highest terms of the new appointee, and Carrillo himself after an interview formed a favorable opinion of him, freely expressed in his letters to Guerra, whom he advised to conciliate Figueroa's friendship by presenting him with a span of mules. On his appointment, see *Dept. St. Pap., Ben. Cust.-H.*, MS., ii. 18; *Id., Angeles*, xi. 2; *Id., Monterey*, ii. 21.

[24] *Figueroa, Instrucciones Generales para el Gobierno de California dadas ál Gen. Don José Figueroa, 1832*, MS. Dated May 7, 1832, and signed by the minister Ortiz Monasterio.

the missions, which in substance required the whole matter to be put back where it was before Echeandía's act of January 1831; but at the same time called for a continuance of investigation and reports with a view to an early change in the system.[25] With reference to the late revolutionary troubles, Figueroa was furnished with full reports from Victoria, Echeandía, and the diputacion, of the quarrel as viewed from different standpoints, and was instructed, after a secret and impartial investigation, to render a comprehensive report.[26]

The governor was provided not only with instructions on his duties, but with a force of some seventy-five officers and men who were to aid him in performing those duties. The soldiers, however, were cholos of a not very desirable class, from the region of Acapulco, but lately released from prison and pardoned for revolutionary attempts. Figueroa went to Acapulco in June to superintend the outfit of his company, and all sailed from that port July 17th in the brig *Catalina*.[27] The first landing was at Cape San

[25] May 17, 1832, Alaman to F. in *St. Pap., Miss. and Colon*, MS., ii. 33–5; *Arch. Arzob.*, MS., v. pt i. 102–6.

[26] *Alaman, Sucesos de California en 1831*, MS. Alaman also directs F. to obtain instructions from Victoria. *Sup. Govt St. Pap.*, MS., viii. 8. Victoria's influence is also apparent in Alaman's instruction of same date, May 17th, that Vallejo is not entitled to a seat in the dip. *Id.*, v. 9. As for Echeandía, a pardon was sent with orders to report at Mexico. *Id.*, xiii. 40. The complaints of the dip. against Victoria were also furnished; and F. was instructed to see that the dip. was renewed according to the laws, and to communicate this resolution to the complainants, as he did on July 7th. *Vallejo, Doc.*, MS., i. 316.

[27] July 1, 1832, F. at Acapulco appoints Lieut-col. Manuel Martinez temporary chief of the infantry embarked on the *Morelos* for California (?). *Dept. St. Pap.*, MS., iii. 54. July 5th, he announces to his soldiers their pardon, states that their imprisonment has not stained their honor, and explains that great reliance is placed in them to protect Cal. from Spaniards, Russians, and Americans. *Id.*, iii. 67–9. July 7th, to sec. of rel. Will attend to formation of a compañía de fronteras, and the sending of mails via the Colorado on arrival in Cal. *Id.*, iii. 52–3. July 14th, arms and munitions shipped on the *Catalina*, including 100 muskets and bayonets, 20,000 cartridges, and 2,000 flints, one 6-pounder with 200 charges. *Dept. St. Pap., Ben. Mil.*, MS., lxxxviii. 7. July 17th, force that sailed on the *Catalina* with F.: Lieut-col. Manuel Martinez and Lieut José Portu (who did not reach Cal.), Capt. Nicolás Gutierrez, Capt. Francisco Figueroa (brother of the general), Surgeon Manuel de Alva, 41 cavalrymen with 8 musicians under Sergt Estrada, 5 artillerymen under Sergt Buitron, and 9 infantrymen under

Lúcas on the 30th. Remaining here with his troops, Figueroa sent the vessel to San Blas and Mazatlan for money, additional troops, and a band of friars, all intended for California.[28] The *Catalina*, after taking on board ten Zacatecan friars—of whose coming to California I shall have more to say in another chapter—with Lieutenant Rafael Gonzalez and family, besides other officers and men not specified, sailed from San Blas on August 13th, and in five days reached Mazatlan.[29] Here, or at Rosario near by, Gutierrez received from the comisario general $20,000, and perhaps the rest of the $34,000 which had been promised;[30] and sailing on August 24th, the vessel touched on the 28th at Cape San Lúcas to take on board the general and his company.

That same day, the Acapulco cholos under Sergeant Nuñez revolted, and with the aid of the sailors seized the *Catalina* with everything on board, including the arms and money intended for California. Though thirty-eight men besides the friars were not involved in the mutiny, they were unarmed at the moment of the outbreak and made no resistance. The mutineers, after firing some shots at the party left on shore, sailed at midnight and went to San Blas to join in the revolutionary movement of Santa Anna against Bustamante. The reënforcement of men, munitions, and money was very acceptable; and it is not likely that any troublesome questions were asked about the manner in which they had been obtained.[31]

Sergt Nuñez—76 persons in all, including 4 women. *Id.*, lxxxviii. 6. The price paid the vessel for transportation was $8,416. *Id.*, lxxxviii. 7–8. May 10th, order from Mexico to com. at Acapulco to place volunteers at F.'s disposal. They were to have the preference in the distribution of lands. *Dept. St. Pap.*, MS., iii. 47–50. Only 9 volunteers seem to have been secured.

[28] Aug. 4, 1832, F. to com. of La Paz. *Dept. St. Pap.*, MS., iii. 56.

[29] Lieut Gonzalez had come from Mexico, starting July 26th, to take charge of the sub-comisaría at Monterey. He kept a brief journal of his journey from day to day. *Gonzalez, Diario de Mexico á California, 1832–3*, MS., which, either original or a copy in the author's handwriting, was given me by his son Mauricio. *Gonzalez, Memorias*, MS., 55.

[30] Aug. 11th, receipt of Gutierrez for $20,000. *Dept. St. Pap.*, MS., lxxiv. 46. By this date it would appear that the *Catalina* had touched at Mazatlan also on the way to S. Blas.

[31] Yet there was a report, or at least so F. stated to his men, that the

Figueroa and his men were now in a sad plight, with neither vessel, funds, arms, nor luggage. They went by land up to La Paz, where the last of the company arrived about the middle of October. The general reported his dilemma to the administrator of customs at Guaymas, who was urged to raise $10,000 and to furnish twenty-five muskets, with other supplies of absolute necessity.[32] The officials at Guaymas and Mazatlan seem to have exerted themselves in this emergency with some success; for on November 12th the *Catalina* had returned to La Paz and was ready to carry the party northward to their destination. On that date Figueroa delivered an address of encouragement to his men, reminding them of the evils that had overtaken or would overtake their rebellious companions, and of the good things awaiting them in California, "the land where the Aztecs lived before they came to Mexico."[33] They finally sailed from La Paz on December 13th, according to Gonzalez's diary, touched at Mazatlan from the 14th to the 17th, and arrived at Monterey on the 14th or 15th of January, 1833.

The news of Figueroa's appointment had arrived as early as July at least, and Echeandía on the 28th, in an address to the Californians, spoke of his joy at the approach of a new ruler, urging the people to render implicit obedience, but to be ready with the proofs of their loyalty and the reasons for having deposed Vic-

mutineers had been overpowered at S. Blas, part of the money recovered, and Rafael Nuñez sent to Guadalajara to be shot. *Dept. St. Pap.*, MS., iii. 58–61. Forbes, *Hist. Cal.*, 139–42, says that the party was well received by the revolutionists at S. Blas, and that $3,000 of the funds had been sent back to the friars. Gonzalez in his diary mentions no firing, and I doubt that any occurred. Mention of the affair at San Lúcas in *Alvarado, Hist. Cal.*, MS., ii. 194–5; *Castro, Relacion*, MS., 30; *Vallejo, Hist. Cal.*, MS., ii. 198–9; *Robinson's Life in Cal.*, 138–9; *Ryan's Judges and Criminals*, 39.

[32] Sept. 24th, F. at La Paz to administrator at Guaymas. *Dept. St. Pap., Ben. Cust.-H.*, MS., i. 33–5. Oct. 17th, Luis Valle, com. at Guaymas, to F. Will send the aid required.

[33] Nov. 12, 1832, F.'s address to his troops. *Dept. St. Pap.*, MS., iii. 58–61. I suspect that the date should be Dec. 12th. There had been some previous negotiations with the captain of the *Facio* to transport the troops. *Id.*, iii. 62.

toria. The 17th of October he wrote directly to Figueroa as his 'respected chief,' to express his submission to the national authority, and to explain that love of his country alone had prompted him to take part in the late pronunciamiento.[34] The people generally, many of whom knew something of Figueroa by reputation, were pleased at the prospect of seeing a regular government established again in the territory. The diputacion, as we have seen, voted at the final session of the year to send to the new gefe político an address of welcome and submission which should also be a defence of its own patriotic policy during the past two years. Such a document, if actually prepared, is not extant. Zamorano was doubtless less pleased personally than the other parties at the news of Figueroa's approach, on account of the well known political affinities of the comandante general; but having been involved in no revolutionary acts, he was even more confident of approval than the others. To Captain Antonio Muñoz, who came to relieve Fernandez del Campo in command of the artillery, and who arrived before Figueroa, Zamorano offered to resign his position of 'comandante general accidental of the north;' but Muñoz declined.[35] Evidently, though California was technically in a 'state of anarchy,' the new ruler was to encounter no opposition there.

[34] *Dept. St. Pap.*, MS., iii. 63–5, 73–4. E. takes advantage of the opportunity also to prepare for the defence of his late mission policy by dwelling on the powerful and baneful influence of the missionaries, all of whom with two exceptions are denounced as *apologistas* of Spain and all that is Spanish.

[35] *Dept. St. Pap.*, MS., iii. 79–82.

CHAPTER IX.

FIGUEROA'S RULE—HÍJAR AND PADRÉS COLONY.

1833-1834.

THE new ruler arrived at Monterey by the *Catalina* January 14, 1833, landing and taking possession
of his command the next day.[1]   With him came Captain Francisco Figueroa, his brother, Captain Nicolás
Gutierrez, lieutenants Bernardo Navarrete and Rafael
Gonzalez—the latter to take charge of the custom-
house—Surgeon Manuel Alva, about thirty soldiers,
and ten friars from the college of Zacatecas, who came
to reënforce the Fernandinos.

On the day of arrival, and apparently before landing, Figueroa addressed communications to the various local authorities, announcing his appointment,
and intention to devote all his energies to the welfare

---

[1] Figueroa's letter written in March. *Dept. St. Pap.*, MS., iii. 103.   Rather
strangely, there is in the archives no more definite record of his formal assumption of the command on Jan. 15th than this and the announcement mentioned
in my next note.

of the territory. He was naturally not quite sure what would be his reception from the different factions. Before leaving Mexico he had caused to be printed a proclamation, which he now circulated, together with a brief notice of his arrival, also printed, and as it seems at Monterey. This was the first use of type in California.[2] I suppose that he brought a small quantity of type with some kind of a hand-press, or stamp, for printing cards and brief notices, more as a curiosity perhaps than for actual use.

[2] The notice is as follows: 'El Supremo Gobierno Federal se ha servido confiar á mi insuficiencia el mando Político y Militar del Territorio, de cuyos destinos he tomado posecion el dia de ayer que desembarqué felizmente en este Puerto; y al tener el honor de comunicarlo á V. desfruto el de ofrecerme á su disposicion, protestandole la mejor voluntad para servirlo y complacerlo, y suplicandole acepte las seguridades de mi mas distinguido aprecio y consideracion. Monterrey, 16 de Enero de 1833. José Figueroa.' The name has the governor's rúbrica on the copy before me—the only one I have seen—*Earliest Printing in Cal.*—the one sent to M. G. Vallejo at S. Diego. The impression is bad, as if done by hand with imperfect apparatus. The 'à' (with grave accent) shows that the type was not the same used by Zamorano in later years.

The proclamation printed in Mexico was as follows: 'The comandante general, inspector, and gefe político superior of Alta California, to the inhabitants of the territory. Compatriots; at my arrival on your coasts I consider myself under obligation to address you to announce peace, order, and liberty. Boons so precious being assured, you will enjoy the abundant advantages with which nature enriched you. The contrary produces nothing but countless evils, misfortunes, and desolation. If a fatal moment of excitement has disturbed your repose, let peace return to occupy her seat in this delicious country, and with intrepid patriotism let us cast discord to barbarians who have no country or rights to respect. Peace is the true happiness of mortals; and I restore to you a gift so precious in the name of the supreme federal government, which has seen fit to confide to me the arduous task. A perpetual forgetfulness will efface the memory of the political errors which gave rise to the startling occurrences of year before last. In the law of April 25th last [printed May, but April substituted in ink], you will find guaranties and security. To me it belongs to carry them into effect, and I promise it shall be done. Fear nothing, fellow-citizens; the government works for your happiness. I, who come to execute its just desires, am resolved to overthrow whatever obstacles may impede the development of your prosperity. It remains for you, united and faithful, to present to the world a testimony of concord, of respect for authority, and of obedience to law. The laws will be my guide, and never shall an arbitrary policy or disorder deprive you of the just and moderate liberty secured in the compact of our institutions. Fulfill, therefore, your social obligations, and doubt not that your rights will be respected by your fellow-citizen and friend, José Figueroa.' In *Bandini, Doc.*, MS., 25; *Vallejo, Doc.*, MS., i. 288; *Dept. St. Pap., Angeles*, MS., x. 2-3. Written communications of similar purport issued, Jan. 14th-20th, to ayunt. of Monterey, with invitations to a thanksgiving mass at F.'s house Jan. 19th. *Dept. St. Pap., Mont.*, MS., vi. 20; *Dept. St. Pap.*, MS., iii. 84-5. To ayunt. of S. José. *Dept. St. Pap., S. José*, MS., iv. 113. To ayunt. of Branciforte. *Sta. Cruz, Arch.*, MS., 43. To military comandantes, through Zamorano. *Vallejo, Doc.*, MS., ii. 1.

In all Figueroa's communications, from his arrival to his death, there are evidences of his belief that by unremitting effort and the exercise of diplomatic talent he had overcome the difficulties in his way, and had succeeded in rescuing California from anarchy. This view of the matter was partly real and honest, so natural is it to magnify the importance of one's own achievements, and partly a pretence designed for effect in Mexico. The difficulties in this case were for the most part imaginary. There were no disorders; the factions vied with each other in their readiness to submit, and nowhere was there the faintest ripple of opposition. Figueroa is entitled simply to the credit of having been a sensible, industrious, and above all a popular man, who committed no acts of folly to create troubles where none existed. This at the first; for later he overcame certain obstacles of a somewhat more serious nature. Bandini is the only Californian who does not overestimate the importance of Figueroa's services in saving the country for Mexico, and Don Juan, it must be confessed, had a grievance against the governor, the nature of which will shortly appear.[3]

A Mexican decree granting an amnesty to all concerned in the irregularities of 1831-2, on the sole condition of future loyalty, was circulated by Figueroa, together with the announcement of his arrival.[4] Zamorano and his adherents affected a freedom from all need of amnesty, since their conspirings had been

---

[3] Bandini, *Hist. Cal.*, MS., 78, thinks any other man would have succeeded as well, as there was no opposition. Jan. 26th, the ayunt. of Los Angeles formally recognized Figueroa. *Los Angeles, Arch.*, MS., iv. 88. Feb. 2d, Alcalde J. A. Carrillo congratulates him. *Dept. St. Pap., Ang.*, MS., i. 104. Feb. 10th, Carrillo will harangue the Indians and tranquillize them. *Arch. Arzob.*, MS., v. pt i. 76. J. A. Menendez at S. Gabriel tells F. that at the missions his coming is regarded as the 'iris de paz que viene á disipar la espesa nube de las diferencias que tienen agitado el territorio.' *Id.*, v. pt i. 71.

[4] *S. José, Arch.*, MS., i. 48; *Sta Cruz, Arch.*, MS., 87. Jan. 19th, F. asks the padres to publish the amnesty and aid in promoting tranquillity. *Dept. St. Pap.*, MS., iii. 85. Notwithstanding the amnesty of April 25, 1832, I find an order to the comisario general dated Aug. 1833, that officers in Sonora and Cal. are to receive no pay until they prove they have had nothing to do with revolutionary plans. *Dept. St. Pap., Ben. Com. and Treas.*, MS., ii. 56.

in support of the government.   Figueroa humored
this somewhat plausible whim, thanked the legitimists
for their loyal services, made Zamorano his secretary,
and sent to Mexico a report altogether favorable to
the northern faction, according especial praise to the
compañia extrangera of Monterey, and also mentioning Ibarra and Carrillo in terms of approval.   If his
condemnation of the 'usurpation' of Echeandía's
party was more severe, and his praise for the 'loyalty' of Zamorano's party more flattering than was
called for by exact regard for the truth, the reason
must be sought in the policy of the administration
which this report was intended to please.[5]

Echeandía was not less cheerful and prompt in
his submission to Figueroa, with whom his relations
both personal and political had been most friendly in
Mexico, than was Zamorano; but he ridiculed his
rival's pretensions to be, more than himself, beyond
the need of amnesty, and in all his communications
he defended his past acts.   What he desired was not
pardon, but justification, and recognition of the positions he had assumed,[6] and he was annoyed at the
tone Figueroa felt himself obliged to adopt on the
subject.   On the day of his arrival Figueroa sent
Echeandía both an official and a private letter, and a
friendly correspondence followed.[7]   Echeandía rendered valuable aid to the governor in his preliminary
investigations on the subject of missions from February to April.   Orders brought by Figueroa required
him to report at Mexico, and he accordingly left Cal-

[5] *Figueroa, Informe al Ministro de Guerra sobre los Acontecimientos de 1831-2,
y Parte que tuvo en ellos el Capitan Agustin Zamorano, 1833*, MS.   Dated March
23d, and accompanied by copies (not given) of 38 documents furnished by
Zamorano in support of his policy.

[6] The govt in Oct. 1833 ordered an investigation of his services, etc., in
order to decide whether he should receive pay as governor or as lieut-colonel
of engineers. *Sup. Govt St. Pap.*, MS., xxi. 8.   I do not know what decision
was reached.

[7] Correspondence from Jan. 14th to Feb. 14th, with references to other
letters not extant. *Dept. St. Pap.*, MS., iii. 23-6, 76-8, 83-7, 96-100; *Arch.
Arzob.*, MS., v. pt i. 73.   Other communications on missions will be noticed
in another chapter, the latest from E. being dated March 19th.

ifornia never to return, sailing from San Diego May
14th, on the *Catalina*.   There is no record that he
subsequently appeared in public life; but in 1856 he
was practising his profession as engineer in Mexico,
and is reported to have died before 1871.   With this
officer's record during his residence of eight years and
more in California, the reader of the preceding chapters is acquainted, and it is not necessary to indulge
largely in repetitions; nevertheless, I append a biographical résumé.[8]   Echeandía we have found to be

[8] Of José María Echeandía before he came to California nothing is known
beyond the fact that he held the rank of lieut-colonel of engineers, and was
probably connected with a college of engineers in Mexico. He fairly represented Mexican republicans of the better class. His appointment was in
Jan. 1825. He sailed from S. Blas in June, remained at Loreto until Oct.,
arrived at S. Diego in Oct., and in Nov. received the command from Luis
Argüello. See chap. i., this vol., on his arrival; chap. ii. on his political acts
in 1826–30, including his visits to the north, his quarrel with Gonzalez, and
his complaints and offers of resignation; chap. iii. on his quarrels with
Herrera; chap. iv. on his mission policy and controversies with the padres;
and chap. vii.–viii. on his acts after giving up the command to Victoria on
Jan. 31, 1831. Also chap. xi. for additional particulars of his secularization
policy. Echeandía was probably under 40 years of age in 1825. In person
he was tall, slight, and well formed, with fair complexion, hair not quite
black, scanty beard—some say his hair and eyes were light, among them
Ignacio del Valle—and a pleasing face and expression. His health was very
delicate. In his speech he affected the Castilian pronunciation, noticeably
in giving the 'll,' 'c,' and 'z' their proper sounds. The following items from
various sources show something of his character. Gonzalez, *Experiencias*,
MS., 27, notes his affability to private soldiers. Valle, *Lo Pasado de Cal.*,
MS., 7–8, says he was so absent-minded as sometimes to ask his secretary
what his own name was before signing a document. J. J. Vallejo, *Reminiscencias*, 103–108, calls him a capricious despot, who would carry out a whim
without regard to results. David Spence, *Hist. Notes*, MS., 15, asserts that
he had no energy. Torre, *Reminiscencias*, MS., 22, speaks of him as popular
but over-indulgent and careless. Vallejo, *Hist. Cal.*, MS., ii. 46–7, 51, 110–
13, 116–17, and Alvarado, *Hist. Cal.*, MS., ii. 111, 140, 146–7, 166, are inclined to praise Echeandía in extravagant terms, mainly on account of his
somewhat radical republicanism. Pio Pico, *Hist. Cal.*, MS., 21, pronounces
him affable but apathetic. Shea, *Cath. Missions*, 109, quotes Alfred Robinson
as calling him 'the scourge of California, and instigator of vice, who sowed
seeds of dishonor not to be extirpated while a mission remains to be robbed.'
Tuthill, *Hist. Cal.*, 130, says 'he was contracted in his views, despotic in the
exercise of his powers, and selfish in his relations with foreigners.' Lieut
Romualdo Pacheco alludes to him as his worst enemy, but incapable of injur-
ing any one. Gale, writing to Cooper, *Vallejo, Doc.*, MS., xxix. 104, calls
him a man of undecided character, trying to please everybody.

June 6, 1832, orders for E. to report at Mexico. *Sup. Govt St. Pap.*, MS.,
viii. 40. Oct. 30, 1833, orders to investigate his services in order to reach a
decision about his pay. *Id.*, xxi. 8. In April 1828 he wrote to Guerra in
Mexico to pay his mother $100 without letting his wife know anything of
it. March 13, 1833, the comisario general alludes to an allowance of $100 to
María Salcedo, Echeandía's wife. *Dept. St. Pap., Ben. Com. and Treas.*, MS.,
ii. 65. Sailed from S. Diego, May 14, 1833. *Dept. St. Pap., Ben. Mil.*, MS.,

a man of considerable talent and good education,
affable and kind-hearted, but weak, irresolute, and
lacking energy. He was disposed to be upright and
faithful, but lacked strength of principle for emergen-
cies. In the administration of justice and the enforcement of military discipline he was notably inef-
fective. He has been abused extensively by partisans
of the friars, but no man could have escaped such
abuse without a complete surrender to the mission
monopoly and a reckless disobedience to his instructions. He favored secularization, and his views were
sound, but he was not hasty or radical in effecting
the change, but rather the contrary. True, at the
very end of his rule he was induced by Padrés to do
an illegal and unwise act, but that act did not go into
effect, and the padres had no good cause of offence.
No man in Echeandía's place, and faithfully representing the spirit of Mexican republicanism, could
have treated the friars better. His faults lay in another direction, as already indicated.

Figueroa's early relations with the diputacion, the
last of the powers he had to conciliate, are not clearly
recorded, but were doubtless altogether friendly.[9]
Before Figueroa's arrival some steps were taken by
the ayuntamientos for holding primary elections, and

lxxix. 23. Taylor, *Odds and Ends*, no. 14, says, with his usual inaccuracy,
that E. died in 1852. Mrs Ord, who knew him well in California, saw him
frequently in Mexico in 1855–6. He said that the allowance of half his pay
as director of the college of military engineers, which he left for his wife, had
not been paid while he was in Cal., and that he never succeeded in getting
it. He had some oil-mills and other property on which he with difficulty
supported himself until in 1835 providence sent an earthquake which so
damaged certain convents and dwellings of rich men as to render his profession of engineer very lucrative. In 1855 he was arrested for some opposition
to Santa Anna, but soon released. In 1871 Mrs Ord made inquiries for him,
and learned that he was dead, as were two step-daughters who had taken
care of him in his old age. *Ord, Ocurrencias*, MS., 42–3.

[9] Pico, *Hist. Cal.*, MS., 46, says that F. sent a special communication to
each of the members, announcing the amnesty. Pico replied with a defence
of his acts. Vallejo, *Hist. Cal.*, MS., ii. 200–3, relates that Osio, Alvarado,
and himself came at once to Monterey to offer their aid in maintaining order.
A long conference took place, and a dinner followed, and cordial relations
never ceased between the parties. Osio, *Hist. Cal.*, MS., 223, tells us that F.
issued orders for an election and hastened the meeting of the diputacion.

on March 24th the electors met at Monterey and chose four new members for the assembly, also electing Juan Bandini as deputy to congress, with José Antonio Carrillo as substitute.[10] There is no evidence that the body as now constituted ever held any session, or that any session was held in 1833 at all. It would seem that the election of March must have been declared illegal, for October 15th Figueroa ordered a new election to be held according to the Mexican plan of Zavaleta. This election was held the 1st and 2d of December, at Monterey, on the first of which days Bandini was again elected to congress, and on the second the diputacion was renewed by the election of all seven members.[11] They did not meet until May of the following year.

We have seen that a few years earlier orders had come from Mexico to establish a strong garrison in the region north of San Francisco Bay, with a view to protect that frontier from encroachments of foreigners; but nothing had really been effected beyond a slight correspondence and investigation by Echeandía.[12] Figueroa's instructions required him to pay particular attention to the same subject, it being

[10] Jan. 3, 1833, ayunt. of Los Angeles resolves to invite others to hold primary elections so that the new gefe may find everything ready. *Los Angeles, Arch.*, MS., iv. 77–8.   March 21st, 24th, meetings of the partido electors at Monterey.   The vocales elected were: 4th, J. A. Carrillo, 5th, Manuel Crespo, 6th, José Águila, 7th, Tiburcio Tapia; Suplentes, José Perez, F. J. Alvarado, and J. J. Vallejo. *Actas de Elecciones*, MS., 12–16; *Dept. St. Pap., Ang.*, MS., xi. 4–5.   March 23d, J. J. de la Guerra writes to his father that 'the enlightened'—that is, the electors—are living so scandalously—except his uncle Anastasio Carrillo—that 'even the English' are shocked. *Doc. Hist. Cal.*, MS., iv. 961.   This election left Vallejo, Ortega, and Osio as hold-over vocales in the 1st, 2d, and 3d places; but there was a decision from Mexico—Victoria's work?—dated May 17, 1832, that Vallejo as a military officer was not entitled to his seat. *Sup. Govt St. Pap.*, MS., v. 9.

[11] *Actas de Elecciones*, MS., 16–19; *Leg. Rec.*, MS., ii. 226–7.   The 7 vocales chosen were: 1. Cárlos Carrillo, 2. Pio Pico, 3. Francisco de Haro, 4. Joaquin Ortega, 5. J. A. Carrillo, 6. J. A. Estudillo, 7. José Castro.   Oct. 15th, F.'s order for an election. *Dept. St. Pap., Ang.*, MS., i. 134–6; x. 7–8.   Dec. 6th, F. orders surplus municipal funds to be sent in for the dip. *Vallejo, Doc. Hist. Cal.*, MS., ii. 193.   Bandini had left S. Diego for Mexico on the *Catalina* with Echeandía. *Dept. St. Pap., Ben. Mil.*, MS., lxxix. 23, 25.

[12] Chap. iv. of this volume.

deemed of the utmost importance that the northern
frontier up to latitude 42° be occupied by Mexicans,
either as settlers, soldiers, or missionaries, as soon
as possible. Accordingly in April the governor
announced his purpose to found a presidio. He
ordered Alférez Vallejo to make an exploration, select
a site, and offer lands to settlers, appealed to the missions for aid, called in the convict laborers from private ranchos to work on the proposed fortifications,
and reported his purposes to the government. The
prefect of the northern missions, however, while fully
approving the project, declared that no aid could be
depended on, and so far as I can learn, nothing was
accomplished before the end of the year.[13]

In March the governor had deemed the country
pacified, and good order restored, and so reported;
but his health was so impaired by rheumatic and
apoplectic attacks that he asked to be relieved of his
command.[14] His health improved, however, and from
July to September he made a tour of the south, occupied largely in studying the condition of the missions;
but while at San Diego on July 24th he addressed to
the minister of relations a confidential letter of warning against a "clique of conceited and ignorant men"
who were plotting to separate California from Mexico, and as a means to that end would do all in their
power through their representative, Bandini, to secure a separation of the military and civil commands,
and give the office of gefe político to a Californian.
He declared himself strongly opposed to any such
change, which would be "the germ of eternal discord,"
as there was not a single Californian even tolerably
qualified for the office. His warning has every appearance of being prompted by personal ambition,
though he disavowed any desire to retain the office

---

[13] Apr. 10th, 12th, F.'s letters to García Diego, and Apr. 15th, reply of
the latter. *St. Pap., Miss. and Colon.*, MS., ii. 299-308, Apr. 25th. P. Gutierrez to F. from Solano. *Dept. St. Pap.*, MS., iii. 116.
[14] March 25th, F. to min. of war. *Dept. St. Pap.*, MS., iii. 103.

himself.   He knew that the charge of a plan to secede
from Mexico was false, and his language was severe
and uncomplimentary, in marked contrast with that
he was wont to use in California; but there was in
Figueroa's character an observable element of policy
closely verging on hypocrisy.[15]

Having returned to the capital, the governor had
his attention engaged to some extent in October by a
minor revolt at San Francisco, where a few soldiers,
including the escolta at Santa Clara, attempted by
irregular and unmilitary methods—though no force
seems to have been used—to get rid of their comandante, Vallejo, whom they accused of ill treatment,
chiefly in the matter of furnishing food and clothing.
Vallejo was angry, and demanded the infliction of severe penalties; but a court-martial merely ordered a
transfer of eight men to other presidios.[16]

In addition to what has been presented in this chapter, beyond the routine of official correspondence,
much of which relating to missions, commerce, finance,
and other general subjects will receive some attention
elsewhere, there is nothing more to be said of events
in California during 1833; but I deem it best to go
on with the annals of the following year, before calling
the attention of readers to certain important developments in Mexico.

The diputacion, whose acts form a prominent element in the annals of 1834, assembled at the governor's house[17] in Monterey May 1st, with Figueroa
in the chair as president, and all the seven vocales in

---

[15] July 24, 1833, F. to min. of rel. in *Dept. St. Pap., Ben. Mil.*, MS.,
lxxxviii. 11–12. We shall see later that Bandini at this very time was working in congress for a separation of the commands. On Sept. 21st F. was at Los
Angeles. *Currillo (D.), Doc.*, MS., 79.

[16]*St. Pap., Sac.*, MS., xi. 49–54 ; *Vallejo, Doc.*, MS., ii. 119, 178, 195.

[17] Jan. 2, 1834, Figueroa to Sec. Alvarado about furnishing a room for the
meetings. Carpets, curtains, wall-paper, seats, etc., all deemed indispensable
for the dignity of the body, but the most necessary articles are to be obtained
first. An appropriation will be asked for to cover the expense. *Dept. St. Pap.,
Ben. Mil.*, lxxxviii. 19.   Alvarado gives a list of needed furniture to the value
of $299; only $10 in the box. *Id.*, 10.

attendance except Pio Pico. I append a résumé of proceedings at the successive sessions, as compact as it can be intelligibly made.[18] The president opened

[18] Sessions of the diputacion territorial of Cal. in 1834. Recorded in *Legislative Records*, MS., ii. May 1st, the oath was administered by the president; the members took their seats; and Figueroa delivered an address. Committees appointed: ways and means, J. A. Carrillo, Haro, and Estudillo; government and police, C. A. Carrillo, Pico, and Ortega; public works, Haro, J. A. Carrillo, and Castro; public instruction, C. A. Carrillo, J. A. Carrillo, and Estudillo; industry and agriculture, Ortega, Pico, and Castro; statistics, J. A. Carrillo, Haro, and Pico; colonization, Ortega, Castro, and Estudillo; vacant lands, C. A. Carrillo, Pico, and Ortega; municipal regulations, J. A. Carrillo, C. A. Carrillo, and Haro; roads and highways, Ortega, Castro, and Estudillo. Adjourned to 10 A. M. of next day. Alvarado, sec. Secret session. Information from Mex. that the European cabinets had agreed to make the Infante D. Francisco de Paula emperor of Mexico, with recommendations of zeal and vigilance. Passed to committee on govt. (p. 34–50.) May 2d, 6 despatches from the gov., of this and the past year, some enclosing orders from Mex. on secularization, duty on otter-skins, municipal regulations of Monterey, and furnishing of a hall for meetings, referred to com. On motion of Figueroa, the formation of regulations for proceedings of the dip. was made a subject of preference, and meanwhile Tuesday, Thursday, and Saturday were to be the days of meeting. J. A. Carrillo moved to fully organize the ayuntamiento of Sta Bárbara, and was told by the president to put his proposition in due form and let it take its course. (p. 51–4.) May 3d, 25 expedientes on land grants submitted for approval and referred to com. A letter of C. A. Carrillo, dated in Mex. 1831, was read asking the dip. to petition the govt for schools, and organic law, and the separation of the commands. Carrillo spoke on what he had accomplished in Mex., and the 1st and 2d points were referred. Communication from the ayunt. on expense of a road. Resignation of secretary offered on account of illness. Proposed that sessions begin at 10 A. M. and last 3 hours. Prop. that the comandante of Sta B. be deprived of judicial powers, and that 2 regidores be added to the ayunt., the place having 940 inhabitants—to be read three times. May 6th, petition of S. Diego for an ayuntamiento. Public buildings for Monterey. Prop. to have the mission lands surveyed, and to require inventories of mission property. May 10th, minor municipal matters of Monterey and Branciforte. Prop. to fix bounds of S. F. mission. Hours of meeting not settled. The Monterey road must be 'paralyzed' for the present for want of funds; *casas consistoriales* and jails should have the preference—so reports the com. Report in favor of accepting Alvarado's resignation. Also in favor of asking Mex. for $2,500 per year for schools, and for an organic law. Many land grants approved by the com. 2d reading of various propositions. (p. 55–68.) May 13th, foreign lumbermen. Artillery militia. Days fixed for discussion of certain matters. Haro's proposition to survey mission lands discussed and defeated. May 15th, Mex. secularization law of Aug. 17, 1833, referred to com. on missions(?). Regulation of weights and measures, also of brands, considered. Funds of Branciforte. Many minor measures postponed as belonging to general subjects to be treated as a whole. Further discussion on the Monterey *calzada*. Ortega complained of the imperfections of municipal govt and proposed the early formation of *ordenanzas* for the ayunt. Carrillo and Castro appointed to visit prisons. (p. 68–79.) May 17th, many land grants submitted, and approved. Sec. Alvarado agrees to serve a month longer. May 20th, petition for fixing mission boundaries sent back to await the arrival of Híjar, who was coming with a special commission to regulate secularization. (p. 80–6.) May 22d, duties of foreigners as citizens. Land grants. More discussion on mission bounds. Report on the Monterey *calzada*. Mission inventories. Proposition to assign lands and to stop the slaughter of mission

the sessions with an address, in which he reviewed the
condition of the country, and the character of the
legislation needed. In high-flown language the speaker
predicted great prosperity, now that Spanish tyranny
was a thing of the past, and the diputacion was at

cattle. (p. 86–93.) Figueroa absent on account of illness. May 24th, report of com. on missions on law of secularization. The national govt to be
asked for instructions. May 26th, secret session called to consider the reports of a conspiracy formed by P. Duran and Capt. Guerra. José María
Maldonado, sec. (p. 2–10.) May 27th, ayunt. of Sta B. Dip. declines to
call in suplente Estrada to take Pico's place. (p. 93–6.) May 30th, unimportant. Figueroa very busy in preparing correspondence for Mex. by the
Dorotea. June 3d, further discussion on secularization as per prop. of
May 24 (p 97 103.) June 12th, convicts. Pico's absence excused, as he was
ill. Minor communications answered. Petitions of individuals asking privileges or redress of grievances. Land grants. Mission lands again, and slaughter
of cattle. (p. 104–12.) June 16th, municipal funds. Land grants. Resignation
of Alvarado again postponed. June 17th, foreign citizens. Wild stock. First
reading of report on municipal and legislative regulations. June 19th, land
grants. First reading of several reports on topics already mentioned. (p.
113–21.) June 21st, Branciforte affairs. Land grants. Discussion on live-
stock regulations. Discussion on reglamento postponed until the absent members should arrive. (p. 121–9.) June 26th, much unfinished business. Sec.
Alvarado again, it not being quite clear what he wanted, but he was 'exonerated' from his place. His accounts and his position as contador were in
some way involved. Long discussion on some articles of a reglamento for
legislative proceedings. (p. 129–37.) June 28th, land grants. Discussion
of various matters relating to municipal govt. (p. 138–41.) July 1st, Maldonado elected sec. in Alvarado's place, and sworn in. Land grants. Munic.
govt continued. July 3d, land grants. Munic. govt. Com. on ways
and means instructed to hurry, as the dip. lacks funds. (p. 142–6.) July
5th, 8th, land grants. A moderate slaughter of mission cattle allowed. (p.
146–8.) Secret session of July 8th to consider charges of *malversacion* of mission property against P. Anzar. (p. 10–11.) July 10th, slaughter of mission
cattle at S. Luis Rey. Land grants. Minor reports read and days set for
discussion. Long discussion of reports on munic. revenues. (p. 149–63.) July
12th–15th, 19th, 22d, some land grants and unimportant matters. (p.
161–5.) On July 19th there was a secret (?) session, at which a prop. relating
to administrators of missions was considered; and on July 22d, when the
same subject was continued. (p. 11–13.) July 24th, munic. regul. and revenues. (p. 165–7.) July 26th, discussion on lands (not given). July 29th,
articles 8–53, titles 3–6, of a reglamento for the dip. discussed and approved.
(p. 168–80.) July 30th, land grants. Liquor tax. Completion of the reglamento. Tit. 8–14, art. 54–74. (p. 181–8.) July 31st, unimportant. Extra
sessions on administrators of missions, July 29th; on provisional regulation
for secularization, July 30th, 31st. 23 articles approved. (p. 13–28.) Aug.
1st, 2d, land grants and prop. to form an ayunt. for S. Diego and one for
Sta B., increasing that of Los Angeles. (p. 189, 28.) Oct. 17th–18th, extra
session to consider Híjar's claims as gefe politico and director of colonization.
(p. 190–6.) Pico sworn in. Oct. 22d, secret session on the same subject.
Report of com. 13 articles approved. (p. 29–34.) Oct. 23d, 25th, 28th,
30th, 31st, minor local matters. Few details. (p. 196–9.) Nov. 3d, discussion and approval on first reading on account of approaching end of the sessions, of several prop. relating to the colony and to secularization. Extra
session in evening, action on preservation of timber. Members authorized to
retire to their homes. (p. 199–212.) The sessions of May 1st–20th are also
recorded in *Dept. St. Pap., Ben.*, MS., ii. 45–96.

liberty to resume its deliberations. There was much to be done. All was yet in embryo; but the speaker had faith that by patient effort California, if she could not aspire to absolute perfection, might one day figure at the side of Jalisco and Zacatecas! One great obstacle had been the tendency of his predecessors to assume too many powers and duties for the political rule, as if representing an absolute government. A proper division of power according to the constitution should be effected, and the people must learn not to trouble the gefe político with every petty affair. Municipal government was in a sad state of disorganization; local officers incompetent, and the people lacking in respect for the authorities. Schools were neglected; and there were no jails nor other public buildings worthy of the national honor. Municipal revenues were far from sufficient for necessary expenses; he had been obliged to borrow money to fit up a room for this meeting. Agricultural and stock-raising regulations and restrictions had been oppressive. He reviewed the evils of the monastic despotism, and the measures taken and required to raise the neophytes from degradation, noted the necessity of certain public works at Monterey, and the importance of a fort on the northern frontier. His discourse was warmly approved by the vocales, and he took a very prominent part in subsequent proceedings.[19]

The labors of the diputacion were very largely devoted to the consideration of matters connected with the secularization of the missions, and in this respect will be more fully noticed in another chapter.[20] Another prominent matter was that of finance and revenue, of which I shall also have something to say separately.[21] Grants of public lands made by the

[19] Besides the copies of the speech in *Leg. Rec.*, MS., ii. 34–49; *Dept. St. Pap., Ben.*, MS., ii. 45–50, I have also, *Figueroa, Discurso de Apertura de la Diputacion Territorial en 1° de Mayo, 1834*, MS., the author's original blotter copy.

[20] See chap. xi. of this volume.

[21] The reports of the com. of ways and means on July 10th, 12th, 24th, 26th, 30th, on revenue and taxation, are given in *St. Pap., Miss. and Colon.*,

new governor in accordance with the laws were presented for investigation and approval at nearly every
session.   To these grants attention will be given in
the proper place.   The Híjar and Padrés colony, to
be treated fully later in this chapter and in the next,
furnished the assembly matter for discussion in the
later sessions of the year.   Action on municipal government, and many minor items of legislation, will
naturally come up more or less fully in connection
with local annals; here it need only be stated, that
not only were the older pueblo governments perfected,
but ayuntamientos, or town councils, were organized
at San Diego and San Francisco, where they had
never existed before.[22]   With the abstract of proceedings already given, the references of this paragraph,
and the mention of a grand ball given on November
1st, at the capital, in honor of this body,[23] I dismiss the legislative doings of 1834; but append at
some length the reglamento of the diputacion en
résumé, not only as a document of some interest and
importance, but as the first book ever printed in California.[24]

MS., ii. 238–53, much more fully than in the *Leg. Rec.* proper; and the
results were printed in the edict of Aug. 6th.   *Plan. de Propios y Arbitrios
para fondos Municipales, 1834,* in *Earliest Printing in Cal.*   I shall speak of
financial topics for 1831–5 in chap. xiii.

[22] *Leg. Rec.*, MS., ii. 188–9, 244–5. Figueroa's edict of Aug. 6th. *Dept. St.
Pap., Mont.*, MS., vi. 33.   F.'s orders on boundaries. *St. Pap., Miss. and
Colon.*, MS., ii. 217–20; *Vallejo, Doc.*, MS., ii. 316; xxxi. 133, 137, 140. *S.
Diego, Arch.*, MS., 30, 36, 56, 63.   There is some dispute respecting S. F.,
but of that more elsewhere.

[23] Printed invitation to this ball in *Earliest Printing in Cal.*

[24] *Reglamento Provisional para el Gobierno interior de la Ecma Diputacion
Territorial de la Alta California, aprobada por la misma Corporacion en
sesion de 31 de Julio del presente año.   Monterrey, 1834.   Imprenta de A. V.
Zamorano y Ca.* 16mo. 16 p.   I have never seen any other copy of this rare
little work than that in my possession.   It was presented to me by Cárlos
Olvera, son of Agustin Olvera.

Tit. i.—*Installation.*—Art. 1. Regular sessions will open May 1st, new
members taking the oath before the president.   2. Sessions to close on Aug.
31st; but the dip. will meet in extra sessions whenever convoked by the gefe
político.   3. Form of oath.   4. Then the pres. shall say aloud: 'The dip., etc.,
is declared legitimately constituted.'   5. One more than half the members must
be present for an ordinary session.

Tit. ii.—*Presidency.*—Art. 6. Duties of the pres.: (1) to open and close
the sessions; (2) to see that all observe 'órden, compostura, y silencio;' (3)
to present all communications; (4) to determine what subjects shall be discussed,

There yet remain to be noticed in the annals of 1834 a few detached topics before I take up the most prominent of all, the colony. The negotiations of

giving preference to those of common utility except by agreement on motion of some vocal; (5) to give the floor alternately to the members for and against; (6) to call members to order; (7) to sign the records as soon as approved, and correspondence to the govt and to ayuntamientos; (8) to convoke extra sessions for serious motives. 7. If his ruling is objected to, one shall speak for and one against, and the majority shall decide. 8. In performing his regular duties, he may remain seated; but in discussion, he must ask for the floor and be subject to the same rules as others.

Tit. iii.—*Secretary.*—Art. 9. Sec. appointed by the dip. according to law of June 23, 1813, receiving for the present $50 per month. 10. Duties: (1) to keep a record of proceedings 'laconic and clear,' without criticising speeches or reports; (2) to write and sign communications from the dip.; (3) to insert in the *acta* of 1st day of each month a list of *expedientes* in various stages of advancement; (4) to lay before the dip. different subjects in the following order: 1st, the *acta* of preceding session; 2d, official communications; 3d, private communications; 4th, propositions of members; 5th, reports fixed for discussion; 6th, reports for 1st reading.

Tit. iv.—*Sessions.*—Art. 11. Sessions public, lasting 3 hours from 10 A. M., and longer at the request of any member. 12. Sessions on Tuesday, Thursday, and Saturday, except holidays religious and secular. 13. Secret session following the public one whenever the subject may demand reserve. 14. Any member may ask for a secret session, and the pres. will call it. 15. In a secret session will be presented: (1) confidential communications to the dip.; (2) ecclesiastical and religious matters; (3) other subjects which the pres. may deem to demand reserve. 16. Secret sessions to begin by a discussion whether the subject requires such a session, and to close by asking if the proceedings are to be kept strictly secret. 17. Members must be present from beginning to end, decently dressed; be seated without preference; and observe the silence, decorum, and deportment corresponding to their position. 18. A member unable to attend for serious cause must notify the pres.; but a recorded permission of the dip. is necessary for more than 3 days' absence. 19. Such licenses cannot be granted to more than 2 members.

Tit. v.—*Motions.*—Art. 20. Motions must be presented in writing, signed by the author, to the sec., worded like the resolution which is desired. 21. Every motion to be discussed as soon as made; the author will explain his motives, and 2 members may speak for and against; then it goes to the proper committee. 22. No prop. can be approved without first passing to the com., except by express consent of the dip.

Tit. vi.—*Committees.*—Art. 23. To facilitate business, committees, both permanent and special, will be appointed to examine matters and put them in shape for final action. 24. The permanent committees will be on ways and means, colonization, vacant lands, missions, government and police, municipal regulations, public works, industry, public instruction, and statistics. The number may be increased or diminished by the dip. 25. The dip. will also classify special com. according to nature of business. 26. The pres. must name permanent committees on the day of installation after administering the oath. 27. A com. will consist of 2 or 3 members, but may be increased by consent of the dip. 28. No member shall refuse a place assigned him on a com. 29. On granting leave of absence, the dip. will name members to replace the absentees on com. 30. The same must be done when members of a com. have a personal interest in the matter considered; neither can such interested parties vote. 31. The gefe politico, or the senior vocal when acting as pres., cannot serve on com. 32. Com. must render their reports in writing, and conclude them with simple propositions to be voted

1833 respecting the fortification and settlement of the northern frontier have been mentioned. I may add that in the spring of that year, Vallejo had made a

on. 33. A com. report must be signed by a majority; the dissenting member to give his opinion in writing. 34. Com. may, call for any doc. or instructions from territorial archives or offices, except where secrecy is required. 35. A receipt must be given for such doc., and they must be promptly returned. 36. A com. may suspend action on a subject by reporting the reasons, and it will be considered in secret session. 37. A com. keeping an expediente in hand over 15 days must report to the pres. 38. Any member may be present and speak in com. meetings, but without a vote. 39. The chairman of a com., the one first named, will be responsible for all expedientes delivered to him.

Tit. vii.—*Discussions.*—Art. 40. Every report will have a 1st and 2d reading in different sessions, and discussion will immediately follow the 2d reading. 41. At the hour of discussion there must be read the original motion, the communication that gave rise to it, the com. report, and dissenting vote, if any. 42. The pres. will give the floor to members who ask it *en pro ó en contra*. 43. A com. report must first be discussed as a whole, and later each article separately. 44. Members to speak alternately for and against in order of asking the floor. 45. Members of the com. and the author of the prop. may speak three times, others only twice. 46. No one can be called to order except through the pres.: (1) when an article of this reg. is infringed; (2) when some person or corporation is insulted. 47. Speaking of faults committed by subordinate functionaries of the dip. is not cause for calling to order; but in case of calumny, the injured party retains his right to do so. 48. No discussion to be suspended except (1) for adjournment; (2) when the dip. may agree to give the preference to another more important subject; (3) for some suspensive motion approved by the dip. 49. Any member may call for the reading of any law or doc. to illustrate the matter under discussion, but not otherwise. 50. After the speeches according to this regl., the pres. will direct the sec. to ask if the question has been sufficiently discussed; if so a vote will be taken; if not, after one member has spoken on each side, the question will be repeated. 51. Discussion being declared sufficient, it shall be asked if the report shall be voted on as a whole; if yes, being approved in general, a discussion of the articles separately will follow; but if it be not approved as a whole, the question shall be to return it to the com. for amendment or not; and if the decision be in the negative, the proposition is to be considered defeated. 52. The discussion on any article being closed, it will be approved by vote, or returned to the com. 53. A report being rejected as a whole or in any of its articles, the dissenting report, if any, is to be discussed. 54. A measure having been approved may be amended by any member in writing before it is entered in the minutes; and the amendment being admitted shall be passed to the com.; otherwise it is to be considered as defeated.

Tit. viii.—*Voting.*—Art. 55. Voting to be done in one of two ways: (1) by the rising of those who approve, while opponents remain seated; (2) by calling of names. 56. All voting to be decided by an absolute plurality of votes. 57. In case of a tie, a new vote is to be taken after discussion; if there be still a tie, the matter is to be postponed until the next session; and if there be still no decision, it is to be settled by lot. 58. No member can be excused from voting on matters subject to his deliberation.

Tit. ix.—*Resolutions.*—Art. 59. The resolutions of the dip. shall be officially communicated to the gefe político when absent.

Tit. x.—*Ceremonial.*—Art. 60. Neither pres. nor members may wear arms at the sess. 61. Members presenting themselves to take the oath after the sess. are opened must be received at the inner door of the hall by two members named by the pres. 62. The dip. when in sess. will attend as a body at religious and political ceremonies.

tour of inspection to Bodega and Ross;[25] and that in the autumn the same officer had endeavored to begin in a small way settlements at Petaluma and Santa Rosa. Ten heads of families, fifty persons in all, agreed to settle at the former place, hitherto unoccupied; but the padre at San Francisco Solano, hearing of the project, sent a few men to build a hut and place a band of horses at that point in order to establish a claim to the land as mission property. Two or three of the settlers remained and put in crops at Petaluma, Vallejo himself having ten bushels of wheat sown on his own account. The padre's representatives also remained, and the respective claims were left to be settled in the future. Much the same thing seems to have occurred at Santa Rosa, where a few settlers went, and to which point the padre sent two neophytes with some hogs as the nucleus of a mission claim. All this before January 8, 1834.[26] In his speech of

Tit. xi.—*Guard.*—Art. 63. The dip. will have a military guard whenever it may be deemed necessary. 64. The guard will be subject only to the orders of the pres., who shall demand it from the proper authorities. 65. The pres. is to arrange the number of sentinels and report to the dip. 66. The guard shall form in line at the entrance and exit of the pres.; and the sentinel must shoulder arms at the arrival or departure of a member.

Tit. xii.—*Treasury.*—Art. 67. The surplus of municipal funds, and revenue from branches which the dip. and govt may designate, will constitute a fund for general expenses of the territory and the ordinary expenses of the dip. 68. To administer the fund, a person outside of the corporation shall be chosen, who, besides being of 'notorious integrity,' shall give bonds. Salary to be fixed by the dip. 69. The distribution of funds shall be made by the treasurer as he may be ordered; and he must render a monthly cash account.

Tit. xiii.—*Audience.*—Art. 70. Spectators must wear no arms, show respect and silence, and take no part in discussions by any demonstrations. 71. Any person disturbing order will be ordered sent out by the pres.; or if the offense be grave, arrested and delivered within 24 hours to the proper judge. 72. When such means do not suffice to prevent disorders, the pres. will adjourn the public session and continue a secret one. 73. The same course to be adopted when prudent measures fail to restore order when disturbed by members.

Tit. xiv.—*Observance of the Reglamento.*—Art. 74. This regl. is to be observed by the dip. provisionally. 75. Its observance will be absolute when it shall have been approved by the federal congress. 76. The dip. may resolve doubts respecting the articles, in accordance with art. 74–5, and may add to or amend them, reporting to congress.

[25] Vallejo's report was dated May 5, 1833. *Vallejo, Doc.*, MS., ii. 140. All that remains to be said of the Russians in California, from 1831 to 1846, will be found in chap. vi., vol. iv., *Hist. Cal.*

[26] All that is known of this earliest occupation is contained in three letters of Vallejo to Figueroa, the first dated Oct. 3, 1833, in *St. Pap. Miss. and*

May 1st to the diputacion, Figueroa mentioned the plan for northern settlement, but said nothing to indicate that any actual progress had been made.[27] The 14th of May, however, he sentenced a criminal to serve out his term of punishment "at the new establishment about to be founded at Santa Rosa."[28] In June the rancho of Petaluma was granted by the governor to Vallejo, and the grant approved by the diputacion, this being virtually an end of the mission claim.[29] Respecting subsequent developments of 1834–5 in the Santa Rosa Valley, the records are not satisfactory; but Figueroa, hearing of the approach of a colony from Mexico, resolved to make some preparations for its reception, and naturally thought of the northern establishment, which he resolved to visit in person. All that we know positively of the trip is that he started late in August, extended his tour to Ross, examined the country, selected a site, and having left a small force on the frontier, returned to Monterey the 12th of September.[30] To these facts there

Colon., MS., ii. 316–17; the second, of Jan. 8, 1834, in Vallejo, Doc., MS., ii. 211; and the third, merely stating that the padre had consented to the settlers' remaining temporarily, of Jan. 13th, in Id., ii. 218. It is in the latter letter that I find the name Sta Rosa applied to the region for the first time, though the valley had been certainly once and probably several times traversed by the Spaniards. There is a newspaper story to the effect that in 1829 Friar Aniaras (Amorós?) with a single companion wandering northward from S. Rafael, went up the Chocolami stream to Lúcas Point, where they baptized an Indian girl on the day of Sta Rosa, being driven away immediately after the ceremony by hostile gentiles. Gilroy Leader, March 19, 1875, and other papers. Fernandez, Cosas de Cal., MS., 87–8, also speaks vaguely of attempts in 1829 to found an establishment at Sta Rosa. It is very probable that the padres from S. Rafael or Solano reached this region on several occasions, and that the name Sta Rosa was applied from the day, during one of these visits, when some particular locality was explored or some notable event occurred; but I have found no original record of these occurrences.

[27] Leg. Rec., MS., ii. 48. He alludes, however, rather to the foundation of a fort than to settlement.

[28] Dept. St. Pap., Ben. Mil., MS., lxxviii. 23.

[29] Leg. Rec., MS., ii. 118–22. Vallejo's claim to Petaluma as finally confirmed by the U. S. authorities rested on a later grant by Gov. Micheltorena.

[30] This is Figueroa's own statement in his Manifiesto, p. 7, except the time of starting, about which I know only that F. was still at Monterey on Aug. 21st. Dept. St. Pap., MS., iii. 172. I find not a single document in any archive bearing on the subject. Vallejo, Hist. Cal., MS., iii. 22–7; Alvarado, Hist. Cal., MS., iii. 33–4; and Fernandez, Cosas de Cal., MS., 91–5, give long and circumstantial narratives, the last taken, as is claimed, from F.'s report to the min. of war, of F.'s expedition to the north, which they represent as

may be added, as probably accurate, the statements of several Californians, to the effect that the site selected was where Vallejo's settlers and the Solano neophytes had already erected some rude buildings, that the new place was named Santa Anna y Farías, in honor of the president and vice-president of Mexico, and that the settlement was abandoned next year, because the colonists refused to venture into a country of hostile Indians.[31]

An amusing episode of this year's history was a charge of conspiracy against "those irreconcilable foes of our country, Captain Don José de la Guerra y Noriega, Fr. Narciso Duran, Fr. Tomás Esténega, and Sergeant José Antonio Pico." The revelation reached the capital May 26th by a special messenger, who brought letters from Angel Ramirez, Antonio M. Lugo, and Padre Blas Ordaz, to the effect that Duran and Guerra had ridiculed often the federal system, that mysterious papers had been signed, that money had been transferred from San Gabriel to Santa Bárbara, and that the soldier Romero had been made to sign a paper by Pico without knowing its purport. Figueroa hastened to convene the diputacion in secret session to consider the momentous news. All the members were

---

an Indian campaign. Vallejo at the new settlement had some trouble with the Satiyomes under Sucarra, and a series of bloody battles ensued. The Indians were defeated, losing hundreds in killed and captives; but many soldiers were also killed; and finally Vallejo sent to F. for aid, and he came in person with a large force. The Indians were frightened and made a treaty. This is but a bare skeleton of the story, because, in the absence of any original evidence, I deem it either wholly unfounded or a gross exaggeration of some very trifling hostilities. If the expedition be considered a distinct and subsequent one from that mentioned by Figueroa, the improbabilities of the statements are increased rather than diminished. Richardson, *Hist. Vallejo*, MS., and in the *New Age*, and *Napa Reporter*, Oct. 17, 1874, tells a similar tale.

[31] In a letter of June 24, 1835, Figueroa alludes to a town which had been outlined and begun—but apparently abandoned—at Sta Rosa; but no name is mentioned. *St. Pap., Miss. and Colon.*, MS., ii. 406. Vallejo, *Hist. Cal.*, MS., iii. 10-11, says Zamorano surveyed the site, and F. struck the first blow. Juarez, *Narracion*, MS., 1-2, says the site of Santa Anna y Farías was on Mark West Creek. An article in the *S. José Pioneer*, July 20, 1878, affirms that it was on the land of the late Henry Mizer, just where Mark West Creek debouches into the Sta Rosa plain, near a large redwood tree! Several Californians state that F. was at the new town in the spring of 1835, but this was hardly possible.

in favor of decisive measures; José Antonio and Cárlos Carrillo, believing their personal influence would
check any outbreak that might result from "ignorance
and blind confidence in the Spanish friars," were instructed to proceed to the south at once; and a committee favored the arrest of the accused, and granted
the governor all needed powers to act. That same
day numerous orders were despatched southward to
military officers. Troops were ordered from place to
place; the general prepared to maintain at any cost
the republican integrity of California, and Captain
Gutierrez was intructed to arrest the conspirators and
bring them to an immediate trial. In five days José
Antonio Carrillo reported the charges unfounded. In
August Gutierrez reported to the same effect; and
Figueroa decided accordingly that the good fame of
the parties involved was unimpaired. Alfred Robinson gives probably the key of the mystery, when he
states that Guerra was negotiating for the purchase
of a rancho, an operation requiring a search of the
archives at San Gabriel, long conferences, and the signatures of several witnesses. It was the remark of
one of the latter, an ignorant fellow, distorted by the
personal enmity of certain persons, which created such
commotion at the territorial capital.[32]

I may note in passing that the junta of partido
electors met at Monterey October 16th–19th, and chose
José Antonio Carrillo as deputy to congress for 1835–
6, to succeed Bandini, who, as we shall see a little later,
had already returned to California. Mariano G. Vallejo was elected as substitute.[33] I may further allude
to the fact that Figueroa sent to the supreme government a comprehensive report on revenues and their
administration,[34] and the kindred fact that complaints

    [32] Leg. Rec., MS., ii. 2–10.   Communications of May 26th, 27th, 31st, Aug.
2d, 6th, in Dept. St. Pap., MS., iii. 149–56; 170–1; Dept. St. Pap., Ben. Mil.,
MS., lxxviii. 23–39.   Robinson's Life in Cal., 157–9.
    [33] Actas de Elecciones, MS., 19–21; Guerra, Doc., MS., vii. 159–63; Vallejo,
Doc., MS., ii. 313, 340.
    [34] Figueroa, Cosas Financieras de Cal., 1834, MS.   Dated Nov. 28th.   The
document will be noticed later.

of destitution among the troops came in frequently, especially from the south. Figueroa, even, could not feed and clothe troops to their satisfaction with fine words and loyal purposes. As of old, the missions were often called upon for supplies.

Let us turn backward to 1833, and southward to the capital of the republic, where Californian affairs were attracting more attention perhaps than ever before. This was largely due to the influence of José María Padrés, whose schemes of a few years before are fresh in the mind of the reader, and were by no means abandoned when their author was sent out of the country by Victoria in 1831. He left behind a party of ardent supporters in the far north, and went away vowing to return with full powers to carry out his proposed reforms. Of his influence and actions during 1832, and of his relations with Congressman Carrillo, nothing is known; but, not being politically in sympathy with the administration, he probably kept somewhat quiet in public and awaited his time. Privately, however, he was loud and enthusiastic in his praises of California, and labored earnestly to interest his friends in that country as a field for colonization. Many were led to regard his plans with favor, the most prominent of the number being José María Híjar, a gentleman of property, influence, and reputation. By the spring of 1833, the two had devised a project of taking a colony to California, and had made some progress toward its realization.

Now fortune began to smile on the *empresarios* most remarkably. In April Valentin Gomez Farías, a warm personal and political friend of Padrés, and perhaps already interested in his scheme, was elected vice-president, and became acting president on the retirement of Santa Anna. Soon, perhaps in June, there came the news that Figueroa was ill and desired to be relieved of office, which would throw the military command into the hands of Padrés himself, he

as ayudante inspector being already second in rank.[35]
Better still, he succeeded through his influence with
the president in obtaining for his associate Híjar on
July 15th the appointment of gefe político.[36] Next
day the same man was appointed director of colonization, or of the colony in process of organization, and of
the new establishments to be founded in California.
He was to receive a salary of $1,000, in addition to
that of $3,000 for his services as political chief, and he
might name a secretary to receive $1,500.[37] Padrés
himself, by the minister of relations, at what date does
not appear, was made sub-director.   About this time
there appeared on the scene to represent California
in congress a new deputy to take the place of Carrillo—none other than Juan Bandini, who as luck
would have it was one of Padrés' northern disciples,
and who lost no time in identifying himself with the
new schemes.[38] Largely by influence of the com-
bination, the law of August 17, 1833, was passed,

[35] July 12, 1833, Padrés ordered to assume the command if his chief should
continue disabled on his arrival. *St. Pap., Miss. and Colon.*, MS., ii. 288; *Figueroa, Manifiesto,* 4.   Sept. 12th, Com. gen. announces that P. is ordered to
Cal. to take command if F.'s illness continues. *Dept. St. Pap., Ben. Com. and
Treas.*, MS., ii. 57.   The order was answered by F. on July 18, 1834, by a
statement that his health was restored.

[36] July 15, 1832, García to Figueroa, who was at his own request relieved
with thanks for his faithful services. *St. Pap., Miss. and Colon.*, MS., ii.
206–7; *Figueroa, Manifiesto,* 5–6. This was received in February, and answered
on May 18, 1834, of course with a promise to deliver the office to Híjar on his
arrival.

[37] July 16, 1833, García to Híjar. *St. Pap., Miss. and Colon.*, MS., ii.
207–9.   Sept. 17th, Com. gen. Mendoza at Arizpe to Sub-com. Herrera, announcing Híjar's appointments and salary.

[38] Bandini. it will be remembered, had been elected in March. May 7th, administrator of customs at Monterey could give B. only $100 of $400 due him as
dietas. Dept. St. Pap., Ben. Cust.-H., MS., ii. 13.   He had sailed from S. Diego
in May 1833.   July 29th, a bill by Bandini in 10 articles on the favorite subject of dividing the commands and granting an organic law received its first
reading in congress. *St. Pap., Sac.*, MS., xviii. 51–3.   It will be remembered
that this same month, at S. Diego, Figueroa wrote an argument against the
measure and a warning against B.'s revolutionary schemes. Aug. 6th, Bandini
announces to the Californians that he has assumed his functions and will do
all in his power for their interests, the national authorities being well disposed. *Dept. St. Pap., Ang.*, MS., x. 5.   The announcement took the form
of a printed address to his constituents, preserved also in the Pioneer Soc.
Library, S. Francisco.   Of Carrillo I hear nothing in 1833, except that on Jan.
27th, perhaps as he was starting homeward, the comisario was ordered to pay
him $3,000 for viáticos. *Dept. St. Pap., Ben. Com. and Treas.*, MS., ii. 64;
and in 1834, $500 was paid him on the account. *Id., Ben. Mil.*, MS., lxxxi. 4.

requiring immediate secularization of the missions;
and a supplementary decree of November 26th authorized the adoption of such measures as might be
necessary to assure colonization and carry secullariza-
tion into effect, using "in the most convenient manner the revenues of the pious fund to furnish resources
for the commission and the families now in this capital bound for that territory."[39] I may add that besides the vice-president, the diputado from California,
the territorial gefe político, and the prospective comandante general, Padrés numbered among the adherents of his plan our old friends José María Herrera, now re-appointed sub-comisario of revenues, and
Angel Ramirez, who was sent to take charge of the
Monterey custom-house. Truly, the ayudante inspect-
or's star was in the ascendant, all obstacles to the
success of his schemes, whatever those schemes were,
being apparently removed.

Respecting the organization of the colony itself,
we have but little of original record. The terms offered were $10 to each family at the start, transporta-
tion by land to San Blas, three reals per day to each
person for rations during the march, free passage by sea
from San Blas to California, a farm from the public
lands for each man, rations to the amount of four reals
per day to each adult and two reals to each child for a
year, and a certain amount of live-stock and tools—all
the aid received after arrival, apparently in the nature
of an advance, to be repaid by the colonists later. The
system did not differ materially from that under
which earlier colonists had come to California.[40] The

[39] Copies of the secularization decrees of Aug. 17th and Nov. 26th will
be given in chap. xi. Figueroa's regulations of Aug. 9, 1834, were in accordance with the former.

[40] The $10 advance, 37.5 cents for travelling, and free passage by sea, are
mentioned in Híjar's original appointment. *St. Pap., Miss. and Colon.*, MS.,
ii. 207–8. Most of the colonists in their statements say that the allowance
for food, etc., on the march was 50 and 25 cents. Accounts rendered in Nov.
1834 show the ration in Cal. to have been 50 cents, and 25 cents to children
under 4 years; and the advance of live-stock to have been 4 cows, 2 yoke of
oxen, 10 horses, and 4 sheep to each man. Implements included 2 ploughs and
a variety of shovels, axes, hoes, crow-bars, etc. *Id.*, ii. 274–80. See also
Híjar's instructions, to be mentioned later.

result was, that more than 250 persons were enlisted, of whom 204—99 men, 55 women, and 50 children— were entitled to rations and other aid after their arrival in the promised land.

Híjar and Padrés, like other colonization agents in all times and countries, painted the attractions of the country in bright colors. Then, as in much later times, California was represented, in respect of climate and other natural advantages, as an earthly paradise. There is little evidence, however, that these men made false promises, or went far beyond the limits of honest enthusiasm. Some of the Californians speak of promises to distribute the mission wealth, including the neophytes as servants; of promised opportunities to gain an easy fortune by employing native otter-hunters and pearl-seekers, or to live luxuriously in idleness; and of other inducements equally absurd and false; but the testimony of respectable citizens who were members of the colony does not confirm these theories. Again, it has been the fashion to ridicule the material of which the colony was composed,[41] as having been altogether unfit for colonists. The truth is, that the men were of a class far superior to any that had before been sent as settlers to California. Many were educated, some had property, and all had a trade or profession. There was a notable absence of the low and criminal classes of Mexicans; and the subsequent record of those who remained in the country was favorable. True, they came mostly from the city, and the number of artisans was somewhat too predominant over that of agriculturists; yet such farm laborers as could have been obtained from

[41] The colony contained 19 farmers, 11 painters, 12 seamstresses, 8 carpenters, 8 tailors, 5 shoemakers, 5 tinners, 5 silversmiths, 2 hatters, 2 physicians, 2 barbers, 2 saddlers, 2 blacksmiths, 2 printers, 2 goldsmiths, and also a mathematician, gardener, surgeon, machinist, ribbon-maker, rebozo-maker, midwife, distiller, candy-maker, vermicelli-maker, navigator, founder, porkman, musician, vintager, apothecary, boatman, and carriage-maker, *St. Pap., Miss and Colon.*, MS., ii. 275-6, besides 6 teachers and the officers. Forbes, *Hist. Cal.*, 142-3, says they were of every class except that which would have been useful—artisans and idlers, but not a single farmer—'goldsmiths proceeding to a country where no gold or silver existed,' etc.

the Mexican provinces would not have done so well by far, either for themselves or for California.[42]

In connection with the colonization project, a commercial company was formed, with the colony leaders and other prominent men as partners, about which little is known, except that it was called the Compañía Cosmopolitana, and that its object was to purchase a vessel and engage in the exportation of Californian products. Of course it was only by some such commercial scheme that the empresarios could legitimately hope for profit beyond the salaries of a few officials; and it is very certain that a patriotic desire to develop the resources of California was not their sole motive. General Anaya is said to have been president, and Juan Bandini vice-president, of the company. Agents were sent to Acapulco to purchase a vessel, securing the brig *Natalia,* to be paid for in tallow.[43] A considerable sum was to be received from the government for transportation; effects to a certain amount could be smuggled on the first trip;

[42] Among those who came with the colony and have been more or less well known and prominent as citizens may be mentioned Ignacio Coronel and family, Agustin Olvera, José Ábrego, Victor Prudon, Francisco Guerrero, Jesus Noé, Mariano Bonilla, Zenon Fernandez, Auguste Janssens, Florencio Serrano, José Mª Covarrubias, José de la Rosa, Gumesindo Flores, Francisco Castillo Negrete, Fran. Ocampo, Nicanor Estrada, Juan N. Ayala, Simon O'Donojú, and Chas. Baric.

[43] The brig *Natalia* was sold on June 21, 1834, by Miguel Palacios at Acapulco, to Bandini and other agents of the company for 7,200 arrobas of tallow payable in Cal.; and José Noriega was sent in her as supercargo to represent Palacios and receive the purchase value. He was to receive from the co. $50 per month and his expenses until his return to Acapulco. The vessel, as we shall see, was wrecked at Monterey; and as late as 1841 Noriega, who lived and afterwards died in Cal., had received neither his salary nor any part of the promised tallow, though there had been some legal proceedings in the matter. Letters of Noriega to Guerra, in *Doc. Hist. Cal.,* MS., iv. 1003–4, 1107–9. Bandini, *Hist. Cal.,* MS., 64–6, says Anaya, afterwards president of Mexico, was president and himself vice-president; and he states that besides Híjar and Padrés, Judge Castillo Negrete and Sub-comisario Herrera were partners, as were several respectable Mexican merchants. He says the vessel 'was paid for, and that without any mission tallow' (?). Ministers Lombardo and García, Vice-president Farías, and other prominent officials are named as partners by some Californians, perhaps without any authority. According to José Ábrego—letters in *Vallejo, Doc.,* MS., xxxi. 132; and in *García, Apunte,* MS., (appendix)—shares in the co. were $100 each; himself with Bandini and Oliver (Olvera?) were sent to Acapulco to receive the *Natalia;* and the price was to be $14,000. Bandini says that the doings of the company were published in the daily *Fenix* early in 1834.

it was not doubted that the *Natalia* could be made to pay for herself; and it was hoped that such a monopoly of a growing California trade might be secured as to justify the purchase of other vessels and enrich the partners. So far as is apparent, the paid-up capital of the Compañía Cosmopolitana was nothing.

It has been supposed that there were also connected with the colony certain mysterious schemes of a political nature, by which Gomez Farías hoped, in case his administration should be overthrown, to find in California a refuge for himself and his political friends, a stronghold from which as a centre to work for a restoration of his power in Mexico, or at the last, a rich province where he and his partisans might live in affluence and security There is some slight evidence, as we shall see, that suspicions of this kind were entertained in Mexico; but I deem them for the most part unfounded; though the vice-president may very likely have deemed it desirable to put even so distant a territory as California under the control of his political friends.[44]

Vallejo, Osio, Alvarado, and other Californians who more or less fully reflect their views, denounce the whole colonization plan of Híjar and Padrés as a deliberately concocted plot to plunder the missions under the protection of the highest political and military authorities, who were themselves to share the spoils. This is to go much further than is justified by the evidence. The enterprise of Híjar and Padrés was on its face a legitimate one. Colonization had long been regarded by intelligent men as a measure of absolute necessity for California's welfare, and the impolicy and impossibility of attempting to continue the old monastico-missionary régime was equally apparent. The objects ostensibly were praiseworthy; the

[44] Antonio Coronel, *Cosas de Cal.*, MS., 13, says he has never been able to trace the rumors of political plots to any reliable source; though Florencio Serrano, *Apuntes*, MS., 24–5, thinks there were circumstances that indicated an intention to declare Cal. independent of Mexico in certain contingencies.

methods lawful, and the good fortune of Padrés in securing the aid of the government was not in itself an evidence of corruption. As a matter of course, the empresarios intended to make money; it was certainly not wise to intrust to them such unlimited powers, and it is quite likely that such powers would have been abused by them had they been able to carry out their plans. It is perhaps well for their reputation that they were not submitted to the temptation; but they are entitled to the benefit of the doubt; and in view of subsequent developments charges of contemplated robbery do not altogether become the party which largely controlled the final disposition of the mission estates.[45]

The rendezvous of the colonists at the capital was at the abandoned convent of San Camilo, where a grand ball was given just before the departure, in April 1834. Among the lower classes of the Mexican population—the *léperos*—there seems to have prevailed an idea that California was a land inhabited exclusively by savage Indians and Mexican convicts, and that families from the capital were being in some way deceived or exiled to that dangerous country against their will. Janssens, Coronel, Abrego, Híjar, and others agree that hostile demonstrations were made by the mob, which attempted to prevent the departure of the colonists. I think this action was one not likely to have originated with the léperos, but that it must have been prompted by persons, possibly the friars,

[45] Alvarado, *Hist. Cal.*, MS., ii. 223–30, is particularly violent in his denunciation and ridicule, giving full credence to every rumored accusation against Híjar and Padrés of deception towards the colonists, of schemes of plunder, and of political plots. Osio, *Hist. Cal.*, MS., 224–30; and Vallejo, *Hist. Cal.*, MS., ii. 309–10, 349–50, take substantially the same view. The animus of these writers on the subject will be more apparent later. By writers generally who have mentioned the colony the scheme has been more or less emphatically condemned, by most on account of the supposed worthless character of the colonists, by some on account of its connection with secularization, and by others because of the personal and political aims of the promoters. Naturally Juan Bandini, *Hist. Cal.*, MS., 59–66, is an earnest defender of the project. Valle, *Lo Pasado de Cal.*, MS., 40–1; and Machado, *Tiempos Pasados*, MS., 31, state that Bandini was commonly regarded in southern California as the author of the scheme.

who were interested in opposing the enterprise. A company of mounted policemen was furnished by the government to restrain the hostile element, and the emigrants started in April 1834 on their long journey—the men on horseback and the women and children in large covered carts drawn by mules—and proceeded the first day to Tecpantla.[46]

The march to the sea, as remembered by members of the expedition, was attended by no special hardships or incidents requiring mention, the travellers being hospitably received everywhere along the route, at some towns even with public demonstrations of welcome and good-will. There was a delay of some weeks at Guadalajara, and a still longer stay at Tepic. It is said that on account of difficulties in obtaining prompt payment of government funds, Híjar was compelled to raise money by mortgaging his estates in Jalisco;[47] but there is a notable lack in the archives of all information respecting the finances of the colony. On July 20th the company left Tepic for San Blas, where two or three days later a part went on board the *Natalia*, to avoid the mosquitoes, as Janssens says. Nine days later the *Morelos* arrived and the rest of the colonists embarked. There had been some desertions, as well as a few enlistments, en route, and at their first sight of the ocean still others lost heart and turned back; but some 250 proceeded on the voyage.

On the 1st of August, probably, the two vessels set sail. The Cosmopolitan Company's brig *Natalia* had on board Híjar, Bandini, and the naval officer Buenaventura Araujo, and her commander was Juan Gomez.

[46] Bustamante, *Voz de la Patria*, MS., ix. 4–6, says they started, 400 in number, April 14th, after committing many excesses. Híjar's instructions, to be noticed later, were dated April 23d, which was probably very nearly the date of departure.

[47] The salaries of Híjar and Padrés had been paid in Mexico down to the time of departure. *Dept. St. Pap., Ben. Mil.*, MS., lxxix. 64, 77. July 20, 1833 (4?), an estimate of expenses for surveying instruments and travelling expenses for two commissioners and six teachers, with their families, to amount of $6,985, was approved and sent to sub-comisario of California. *Dept. St. Pap., Ben. Com. and Treas.*, ii. 47–50.

On the national corvette-of-war *Morelos*, Captain Lúcas Manso, were Padrés, Judge Castillo Negrete, the new asesor, Cosme Peña, and Sub-comisario Herrera. A day or two out of port the vessels were separated. The *Natalia*, the faster sailer of the two, was struck by a squall off Cape San Lúcas and had a somewhat narrow escape. There was also much sickness, resulting in several deaths.[48] The brig was bound for Monterey, but in view of the sickness on board the commander was induced by Bandini, and by Híjar who was himself very sea-sick, to put in at San Diego, where she anchored the 1st of September.[49] The new-comers were hospitably received at San Diego, the officers and prominent individuals being the guests of Bandini and his friends, while the rest were distributed at various private houses or lodged in tents and warehouses. In a few days a vessel in port took about half the number up to San Pedro, whence they went inland to San Gabriel. Most of the rest soon went up to San Luis Rey. At these two missions they remained for a month and more, and then—except those who established themselves permanently in different parts of the south—started toward the northern frontier, passing in small detachments from mission to mission, and receiving nothing but kind treatment from padres, administrators, settlers, and neophytes.[50] The *Natalia*, after having perhaps been

[48] Híjar, nephew of José María, *California en 1836*, MS., p. 110–12, speaks of troubles between Gomez and Araujo on the voyage, in connection with which the latter at one time forcibly assumed the command. Janssens gives some details of the gale.

[49] *Dept. St. Pap.*, MS., iii. 172–3; iv. 72–5. One record makes the number of passengers 129 and another 140. Martin Cabello came on the *Natalia*, to be receptor of customs at S. Diego. Híjar speaks of a banquet at the house of Bandini. Serrano says that for two days the families were sheltered in the hide-houses on the beach and fed by the foreign owners of those houses. Machado thinks that they were detained in quarantine for fear of the measles, at a spot called Huisache, for a time. Several died and were buried at the mission. Janssens notes the kindness of the San Diegans, who would take no pay from the colonists for entertainment.

[50] Janssens is the only one who mentions the sea-trip to S. Pedro. Híjar notes a long stay at Sta Bárbara; a division at S. Luis Obispo, one party being bound for Monterey and the other to Sonoma, and the fact that many remained at the different missions, including himself and seven companions at

aground for a time at San Diego, sailed north with the effects of the colony. Lying at anchor in Monterey, she broke her cables in a gale on the afternoon of December 21st, and was driven on the beach about two miles above the town, where she soon went to pieces. Three men lost their lives.[51]

There is a popular tradition that the *Natalia* was the same vessel on which Napoleon had escaped from Elba, in 1815. This statement is repeated by almost every writer who has mentioned the colony. No one presents any evidence in its support, but I am not able to prove its inaccuracy.[52]

The *Morelos*, with Padrés and the rest of the colonists, 120 in number, also had a narrow escape from shipwreck in a gale off Point Concepcion, according to the statement of Antonio Coronel; but she arrived safely at Monterey on September 25th, and the newcomers were as warmly welcomed at the capital as

S. Juan Bautista. Serrano says some of the colonists endured great hardships on the way north, and that he and others determined to quit the colony and look out for themselves. Híjar also tells us that the colonists made firm friends of the neophytes as they passed along, by kind treatment and by sympathy for their sufferings under missionary tyranny. Moreover, Araujo, in a letter of Sept. 18th to Híjar, the director, says: 'I have already predisposed them [the neophytes] in our favor, explaining to them as well as I could how philosophically we are armed,' etc. *Guerra, Doc.*, MS., vi. 154. Pico, *Acontecimientos*, MS., 25, recalls the arrival at Purísima, whence he helped convey them to S. Luis. Oct. 20th, Lieut-col. Gutierrez informs Figueroa that some of the colonists had done good service in quelling Indian disturbances. They were thanked in the name of the govt. *St. Pap., Miss. and Colon.*, MS., ii. 281.

[51] Record of day, hour, and place in *Dept. St. Pap., Ben. Mil.*, MS., lxxix. 73–4. Janssens, *Vida*, MS., 41–4, gives a vivid description of the disaster and the efforts of the Montereyans to rescue the officers and crew. In these efforts a negro servant of Joaquin Gomez particularly distinguished himself, saving several lives by his own exertions. A part of the cargo was washed ashore, and much of it was stolen despite the efforts of a guard. The cook and two sailors were drowned, and the mate Cuevas was badly hurt. Híjar, *Cal. en 1836*, MS., 123–8, also gives some details. Many newspaper writers, perhaps following Taylor in *Pacific Monthly*, xi. 648–9, have stated since 1860 that parts of the wreck were still visible, having furnished building-material for over 30 years to the people of Monterey. One piece of newspaper eloquence, in 1878, when the timbers were still visible, merits quotation. 'The company, like the brig *Natalia* which brought them here, was wrecked, and the ribs of its records, like those of the old brig, can only be seen in the ebb of the tide of the present back to the beginning of the history of Sonoma County.' *Sac. Record-Union*, June 25, 1878.

[52] Híjar says that a French captain who visited the coast in 1846 declared the identity, and I think it likely that the tradition has no better foundation.

their companions had been at San Diego.[53] They also started northward before the end of the year, their destination being San Francisco Solano, though we have but little information respecting their exact movements at this time. Of the reception accorded to the directors, of the obstacles encountered by Híjar and Padrés, and of some rather interesting political complications, I shall speak in the following chapter.[54]

[53] The date of arrival is given in *Figueroa, Manifiesto*, 8. Sept. 26th, Padrés announced his arrival with 120 colonists, who intended to settle north of S. Francisco Bay. *Dept. St. Pap., Ben. Com. and Treas.*, MS., iii. 43–4. On Sept. 12th, a demand for grain had been sent to Sta Cruz in expectation that the vessels would arrive in a few days. *Sta Cruz Rec.*, MS., 22. Coronel, *Cosas*, MS., 9–10, says that the inhabitants vied with each other in their kindness and hospitality to the strangers. *Alvarado, Hist. Cal.*, MS., ii. 230–2, tells us that Padrés, 'factotum, monopolizador general, y consejero supremo,' was at first warmly welcomed by his old friends and partisans, of whom the writer was one. He tells also an absurd story of a mortifying incident that occurred. Two ladies came off in the boat with Padrés, expecting to see nobody in Cal. except soldiers, friars, convicts closely guarded, and Indians ready to become their servants. As they drew near the shore, they beheld two beautiful and well-clad ladies of Monterey in the crowd awaiting them, and said, 'Sr Padrés, how is it possible that these girls can be our servants? We look as much like servants as they.' Padrés bit his lip, and the ladies insisted on returning to the ship to 'dress up' before landing. Nov. 1st, a ball was given, partly in honor of the colonists, and partly of the diputacion. *Earliest Printing in Cal.* Dec. 13th the *Morelos* was still in port. Manso in command; Lieutenants Valle, Anaya, and Azcona; 2 'aspirantes,' 3 mates, 2 mechanics, 7 gunners, and 7 boys. *Dept. St. Pap., Ben. Mil.*, MS., lxxix. 85.

[54] My statements of Californians on the Híjar and Padrés colony, in addition to documentary authorities, are the following, the same being cited on particular phases of the subject only for special reasons: *Janssens, Vida*, MS., 7–59; *Coronel, Cosas*, MS., 1–17; *Híjar, Cal. en 1836*, MS., 2–11, 59–62, 108–12; *Serrano, Apuntes*, MS., 1–12, 24–7; *Abrego*, in *Vallejo, Doc.*, MS., xxxi. 132, and in *García, Apunte*, append., MS.; *Vega, Vida*, MS., 8–17; *Bandini, Hist.*, MS., 59–66, 76. The preceding were all written by men who came with the colony; the following by men who with a few exceptions had personal knowledge of the subject: *Osio, Hist. Cal.*, MS., 225–40; *Alvarado, Hist. Cal.*, MS., ii. 223–45; iii. 1–5, 27–33; *Vallejo, Hist. Cal.*, MS., ii. 222–3, 272–4, 306, 309–10, 349–51; *Vallejo, Reminis.*, MS., 43–56; *Fernandez, Cosas*, MS., 71–86; *Pinto, Apunt.*, MS., 3–6; *Pico, Acont.*, MS., 25–6; *Machado, Tiempos Pasados*, MS., 30–1; *Galindo, Apuntes*, MS., 28–31; *Botello, Anales*, MS., 15–17, 176; *Ord, Ocurrencias*, MS., 63–8; *Gomez, Lo que Sabe*, MS., 375–9; *Larios, Convulsiones*, MS., 13–14; *Ávila, Notas*, MS., 10–11; *Pico, Hist. Cal.*, MS., 49–55; *Espinosa, Apuntes*, MS., 1–2; *Torre, Remin.*, MS., 48; *Amador, Mem.*, MS., 138–42; *Gonzalez, Revol.*, MS., 4–6; *Valle, Lo Pasado*, MS., 11–14; *Castro, Rel.*, MS., 31–5; *Arce, Mem.*, MS., 3–5: *Marsh's Letter*, MS., 5–6; *Brown's Statement*, MS., 9–10; *Green's Life and Adven.*, MS., 29. The printed mentions of the subject are found in *Figueroa, Manifiesto; Forbes, Hist.*, 142–5; *Wilkes' Narr.*, v. 174; *Petit-Thouars, Voy.*, ii. 89; *Mofras, Explor.*, i. 295–6; *San Miguel, La Repub. Mex., Parte Ecles.*, 18–21; *Rosa, Ensayo*, 30–1; *Randolph's Oration; Payno* in *Revista Científica*, i. 83; *Robinson's Life in Cal.*, 161–7; *Tuthill's Hist. Cal.*, 136–9; *Ferry, Californie*, 18–19; *Mora, Otras Sueltas*, i. cclviii.–ix.

CHAPTER X.

FIGUEROA, CASTRO, AND GUTIERREZ—THE COLONY.

1834-1835.

Santa Anna Orders Figueroa not to Give up the Command to Híjar—
Quick Time from Mexico—Híjar Demands the Mission Property—
His Instructions—Action of the Diputacion—Lost Prestige of
Padrés—Bando—Controversy—Bribery—Submission of the Direct-
ors—Aid to the Colonists—At Solano—New Quarrel—Rumored
Plots—Revolt of Apalátegui and Torres—Pronunciamiento of the
Sonorans—Surrender—Legal Proceedings—Figueroa's Orders—
Seizure of Arms at Sonoma—Arrest of Verduzco and Lara—Exile
of Híjar and Padrés—Figueroa's Manifiesto—Sessions of the
Diputacion—Carrillo in Congress—Los Angeles Made Capital—
Foundation of Sonoma—Death of Figueroa—Life and Character—
Castro Gefe Político—Gutierrez Comandante General—Estu-
dillo's Claims.

Thus far all had gone well with the empresarios,
but obstacles were now encountered that were destined
to prove insurmountable. The first and most serious
had its origin in Mexico. On the 25th of July, 1834,
some six days before the colony sailed, President
Santa Anna, having taken the reins of government
into his own hands in place of Vice-president Gomez
Farías, issued an order to Figueroa not to give up the
office of gefe político to Híjar on his arrival in California, as he had been ordered, and had promised to
do.[1] We have no official information respecting the
motive that prompted this countermand; but there
can be no doubt that Santa Anna regarded as excess-

[1] *Figueroa, Manifiesto*, 7-8. Order transcribed to com. of S. Francisco on
Oct. 21st. *Vallejo, Doc.*, MS., ii. 314. The order is: In answer to yours of
May 18th, 'ha dispuesto S. E. conteste á V. S. que no entregue el citado mando
y continue desempeñando la Gefatura.' Lombardo.

ive the powers conceded to the empresarios, and that
he was actuated by a suspicion, not so well founded
but perhaps even more potent than the former motive,
that political and revolutionary plans in the interest
of Gomez Farías were involved in the scheme. There
was no lack of persons in Mexico whose policy it was
to foment this suspicion, without regard to its accuracy. Abrego and Osio affirm that the directors sailed
from San Blas in defiance of orders from Mexico to
delay the departure of the colony; but I believe this
to be an error.[2]

The countermand of July 25th was sent to California in all haste overland by a special courier, who
placed it in Figueroa's hands near Monterey the 11th
of September, and with it another despatch from
Híjar at San Diego, announcing his arrival at that
port on the 1st. The trip was much the quickest on
record between the national and territorial capitals,
and the fame of that courier who braved the terrors
of Indians, deserts, and starvation, coming alone by
way of the Colorado, has never ceased to be talked of
in Californian families.[3] Governor Figueroa had re-

[2] *Osio, Hist. Cal.*, MS., 229–30; *Ábrego, Cartas*, MS. Bandini, *Hist. Cal.*,
MS., 61–4, denounces it as a strange and arbitrary act to annul the appointment without giving reasons, and thus to create confusion in the important
matter of colonization. Vallejo (J. J.), *Remin.*, MS., 46–8, understands that
Santa Anna's order was prompted by the friars. After the order was issued, on
Sept. 30th, the com. gen. of Jalisco sent to Mexico the statement of the surveyor Lobato left at Tepic, that Padrés had repeatedly threatened in case of
any change in Mexico to make Cal. independent or annex it to the U. S.
Sup. Govt St. Pap., MS., x. 4–5.

[3] Figueroa, *Manifiesto*, 7–8, mentions the receipt of the despatches on Sept.
11th. Most state that the time made was 40 instead of 48 days. Osio says
the man was detained by the Indians at the Colorado, who threatened to kill
him, but at last built him a balsa to cross the river in exchange for his horse,
equipments, and most of his clothing. He nearly perished on the way to
S. Luis Rey, being 3 days without water. His reward was $3,000. Serrano
relates that Lieut Araujo by an ambush captured the courier near S. Gabriel,
and took him to Híjar, who was urged to hurry to Monterey and secure his
office; but he refused to resort to such expedients, and released the captive.
Amador says the man was Rafael Amador, his cousin. Torre states that the
courier arrived about 11 P. M. at Monterey, and was welcomed by the firing
of cannon. Espinosa was one of the escort furnished by Lieut Valle to guard
the man northward from Monterey to meet Figueroa. He describes his
dress, notes the feasts given in his honor, and says Figueroa gave him 4 mules
on his departure. Valle also mentions having furnished the escort for the
trip towards Sta Rosa. Vega was told the man had at first mistaken his des-

ceived no official notice respecting the colonists, but he
had deemed it best to make preparations for their arrival, and with that object in view had visited the Santa
Rosa Valley, as already related, and there selected a
site for the new town. It was on his return, one
day's journey before reaching the capital, that he
received the countermand from Mexico. He sent to
Santa Cruz and other places for such supplies as could
be furnished, and awaited the arrival of the colonists.
It may be here stated that secularization had been
already begun in accordance with the law of 1833 and
regulations of 1834; and several of the missions were
in charge of administrators.

The *Morelos* entered the harbor on September 25th,
and the immigrants, as we have seen, were made as
comfortable as possible Padrós at first claimed the
position of comandante general, but of course in vain,
since his claim was conditional on Figueroa's illness;[4]
then he presented his appointment as sub-director of
colonization and officially demanded aid for his colonists. The situation was embarrassing. In the absence of instructions to the contrary from the war
department, Padrés as ayudante inspector was Figueroa's subordinate officer, notwithstanding his appointment of sub-director from the minister of relations;
and there was no legal authority for expending public
funds for the support of the colony. So confident had
been the directors in the success of their plan in
every detail, that they had made no provision for the
slightest contretemps. There was, however, as yet no
controversy.

The 14th of October Híjar arrived by land from
San Diego, and after the customary courtesies of re-

tination and gone to Monterey in N. Leon. Gonzalez recalls the meeting of
the courier and Figueroa at the writer's rancho of Leñadero. Galindo thinks
the man was to receive $1 per hour, if successful. Híjar affirms that the man
was sick and had to stop at S. Juan Bautista, where the writer was, another
man being sent on in his place. J. J. Vallejo calls him Hidalgo. I may perhaps safely suggest that some of the items cited are not quite accurate.

[4] *St. Pap., Miss. and Colon.*, MS., ii. 285-6, 290-1. An order of Dec. 7th
(1833 ?) is alluded to as countermanding that of July 12th.

ception, was shown by Figueroa the order forbidding
a transfer of the civil authority. Though bitterly
disappointed, Híjar could make no objection, and fell
back on his commission as director of colonization,
which Figueroa consented to recognize. At an interview on the 15th Híjar presented the instructions
addressed to him in his double capacity as gefe político
and director, instructions to which Figueroa assented,
and which I append in a note.[5] Next morning the
latter received a demand from the director to be put in
possession of the mission property according to article
1 of the instructions, the governor being asked to issue
the necessary orders to administrators and comandantes. Figueroa, rather strangely as it would seem,
promised compliance, but proposed to consult the
diputacion. The reply on the 17th was simply a plea
for haste on account of disorders at the missions, the
approach of planting-time, the neglect of the friars,
the sufferings of the neophytes, and the needs of the
colony. The comandante general was to be held responsible for damages caused by delay. Accordingly
the diputacion was convened the same day, and before
that body was laid a full statement. Figueroa had,
he said, no desire to retain the gefatura. He would

[5] *Híjar, Instrucciones á que Deberá Arreglar su Conducta D. José María
Híjar, Gefe Político de la alta California y Director de Colonizacion de esta y de la
baja,* in *Figueroa, Manifiesto,* 11–14; *St. Pap., Miss. and Colon.,* MS., ii. 270–3;
Jones' Report, no. 12. Art. 1. He will begin by occupying all the property
belonging to the missions; the military comandante to furnish all necessary
aid required. 2. For a year from arrival each colonist is to receive 50 cents
per day, or 25 cents if under 4 years of age. 3. Travelling expenses to be
paid by govt, and the colonists to receive the *monturas* bought for their transportation. 4. Selection of favorable sites for settlements. 5. The frontiers
to be settled as soon as possible. 6. Plan of the new towns. 7. Native settlers to be mixed with the Mexicans, but no town to be inhabited exclusively
by Indians. 8. House lots. 9–10. Farming lands to be granted in full ownership. 11. The movable property of the missions having been distributed
(according to law of secularization?) one half of what is left is to be sold to
the best advantage. 12. Not over 200 head of stock of the same kind to be
sold to one family. 13. The remaining half of movable property to be kept
on govt account and to be devoted to expenses of worship, support of missionaries, education, and purchase of implements for the colonists. 14. The
gefe pol. and director to report in detail at first and annually on the disposition and condition of the property after the distribution as above. 15. He is
also to report at least once a year on the condition and needs of the colonists.
Dated April 23, 1834, and signed Lombardo.

gladly give it up to the senior vocal, or to any person who might legally receive it.   He had no desire to oppose the colonization project, but had some doubt whether it was as director or as gefe político that Híjar was to receive the mission property, and he desired advice as to the proper course for him to pursue.   Of course this humble tone was all assumed, yet it was rather neatly done.[6]

Thus the tide of fortune for Padrés and his associate had begun to ebb.   Instead of finding themselves invested with the civil and military authority, they were simply directors of colonization, and their powers even in that capacity were left to the tender mercies of the diputacion.   The members of that body, it is true, had been a few years earlier admirers and partisans of Padrés, or at least were largely under the influence of those partisans, such as Bandini, Vallejo, and Osio; but though we may be sure the ayudante inspector exerted all his eloquence and influence to retain the favor of his old friends, his power over them seems to have been lost.   Vallejo and Alvarado admit candidly that the chief reason for this defection was the fact that Padrés had brought with him twenty-one Mexicans to become administrators of the missions; whereas, under the old plans, the Californians were to have those places.   I have no doubt this was, to a certain extent, the true state of the case, though I do not suppose that all the places had been promised to Mexicans.   Figueroa's mission policy was substantially identical with that of Echeandía and Padrés in the past, to which the Californians had committed themselves.   He had actually made a beginning of secularization; all was going well, and the Californians were filling the desirable places.   Why should they favor a change in favor of strangers?

Whatever their motives—and they were not altogether selfish—the vocales had the soundest of legal

[6] *Figueroa, Manifiesto*, 14–22; *St. Pap., Miss. and Colon.*, MS., ii. 209–10.

reasons for refusing to accede to Híjar's demands. To suppose that the government in depriving him of the office of gefe político had intended to leave intact all the powers given to him in his double capacity was an absurdity; nor was it credible that the whole matter of secularization and disposition of mission property was to be intrusted to a mere director of colonization, deemed unfit for the civil rule. Doubtless the administration in its haste had been led into carelessness in not specifying what powers if any were to be left to Director Híjar. The diputacion met on the 17th of October, and listened to a speech from Figueroa, receiving documents illustrating the subject-matter. The matter was referred to the committee on government. It was decided to reserve discussion for secret sessions, and next day Híjar was called upon to show his instructions. At the secret session of the 21st the committee, consisting of José Antonio Carrillo, Pio Pico, and Joaquin Ortega, rendered its report, which was discussed and approved article by article without opposition. On the same day it was published by Figueroa in a ponderous bando.[7]

In a preamble to their report, Carrillo and his associates made an able and even eloquent presentment of the case. Considerable attention was paid to national aspects, for it seems that an effort had been made to show that Santa Anna's revocation of Híjar's commission was in some way a threat to federal institutions, and a warning was uttered against the folly of taking part in the strife that was agitating the republic, so long as the rights of California were not attacked, and especially so long as the territory was under the guidance of so wise and popular a ruler as Figueroa.

[7] *Legis. Rec.*, MS., ii. 190–6, 29–34; *Figueroa, Manifiesto*, 22–33. Of the document as finally published I have an original—*Figueroa, Bando en que publica la Resolucion de la Diputacion Territorial contra las Pretensiones de Don José María Híjar, Director de Colonizacion, 21 de Oct. de 1834*, MS., sheet 12x50 inches. Oct. 19th, Figueroa demands from H. his instructions for the dip. They were sent the same day. *St. Pap., Colon. and Miss.*, MS., ii. 211. Oct. 21st–22d, F. sends to the alcalde of Los Angeles his address to the dip., and the action of that body. *Dept. St. Pap., Ang.*, MS., xi. 23–6.

Orders of the government were for the most part clear, and should be obeyed. The innocent colonists were, however, in no way to blame for the failure of the directors to provide for their welfare, nor for the carelessness of the government in issuing indefinite orders; and for them the territorial authorities should provide in every possible way. The Indians, moreover, ought not to be despoiled of their property— their only reward for a century of slavery—as would be the case if Híjar's original instructions were carried out; and on this point the government should be fully informed. The decision of the committee, approved by the diputacion, and published in the governor's bando, was in substance as in the appended note.[8] Figueroa was to remain gefe político; Híjar was to be recognized as director of the colony, but must not interfere with the missions, and all possible aid was to be afforded to the colonists. The course decided upon was an eminently just and proper one.

Híjar addressed to Figueroa, October 23d, a communication, in which he attempted to refute successively all the positions assumed by the diputacion. This letter, with Figueroa's arguments against each point interpolated between its disjointed paragraphs, fills fifty-four pages of print.[9] Both disputants dis-

---

[8] 1. The order of July 25th must be obeyed, and Figueroa will continue to act as gefe político. 2. Hijar may fulfil his special commission of director of colonization, subject to the territorial government and the regulations which may be adopted by the diputacion. 3. H. is to have nothing to do with secularization, and is not to receive the mission property. 4. Until the sup. govt may decide, the secularization regulations of the dip. will be carried out, and the Indians will be put in possession of their property. 5. (a) The gov. will cause to be given to the colonists on arrival the tools and other aid called for in the instructions, the same to be taken *pro rata* from the different missions; (b) he will also furnish necessary food on account of the allowance to each person; (c) the director will be subject to the gefe, and will report to him, giving estimates of expenses, etc.; (d) the mission lands belong to the Indians, and no colony shall be established on them. 6. The gefe will retain H.'s instructions, giving him a certified copy if desired. 7. (a) This document is to be reported to the sup. govt, which (b) is to be asked to revoke the instructions so far as they despoil the Indians of their property; to approve the regl. of the dip.; and (c) to separate the political and military command. 8. This action of the dip. shall be circulated for the information of the public.

[9] *Figueroa, Manifiesto*, 35–89.

played ability in their written arguments, besides using some severe language; but they went, much further than was necessary or than I have space to follow them, beyond the real question at issue into the rights of the Indians, the equities of secularization, and the constitutional powers of national and territorial authorities. A private conference of leading men was held the 25th, at which Híjar's letter was read, and arguments in support of Figueroa's position were made by the lawyers Luis del Castillo Negrete and Rafael Gomez. Another conference was to be held the next day; but meanwhile Híjar invited Figueroa to breakfast, and tried to bribe him—so says the governor—to deliver the mission property, offering to enrich him, not only with that very property, but with credit and influence in Mexico and $20,000 or more from Jalisco.[10] Figueroa does not appear to have deemed that his honor required anything more than a refusal of the offer; and after a long argument, offered not to oppose, if the diputacion would consent, the delivery of the mission property, on condition that no part of it should be disposed of until a decision could be obtained from Mexico. This proposition was not accepted at the conference that followed, at which Híjar and Padrés are said to have finally given up the contest, admitted the justice of all that the diputacion had done, and announced their purpose to take the colony to Baja California. All protested against this project as ruinous to the colonists, and begged the directors to remain, which they finally consented to do, some slight modifications in the resolutions of the 21st being agreed upon, which modifications, with Híjar's letter of the 23d, were submitted by Figueroa to the diputacion on the 29th.

The diputacion on November 3d, while administering to Híjar a severe reprimand for his "jumble of erroneous ideas, unfounded imputations, and gratuitous

[10] *Figueroa, Manifiesto,* 92.

criminations," agreed to the changes proposed, and required of the director a written acquiescence; which action was communicated to him on the 4th by Figueroa.[11] Híjar replied two days later with a protest and more arguments instead of the desired agreement; but he announced his purpose, for the welfare of the colonists and the good name of Mexico, to disregard for the present his own wrongs of outraged honor, and remain with the colony wherever it might be sent, earning his living with a spade if necessary. Accordingly preparations were made for the settlement of the colonists on the northern frontier. Padrés was call upon to decide whether he would assume the duties of ayudante inspector or of sub-director; and he replied by resigning the former position.[12] Figueroa addressed to the minister of relations on the 9th two communications in defence of the policy that had been pursued with the directors. On the 20th, and again on December 8th, he wrote to the secretary of war, explaining his course with Padrés, who it seems after resigning his military position once had tried unsuccessfully to obtain command of the northern frontier. He declared that Padrés was already plotting mischief, and that the territory would never be safe until that officer should be removed. He also offered his own resignation of the comandancia general.[13]

I have already noticed the arrival of the colony in two divisions at San Diego and Monterey in September 1834, the stay of the southern division for a month

[11] *Figueroa, Manifiesto*, 93–106; *Leg. Rec.*, MS., ii. 205–7. The changes were as follows: (1) In art. 2, the words 'laws and regulations on the subject' were to be substituted for 'regulations which may be adopted by the dip.' (2) Híjar was to have his original instructions returned. (3) If Híjar would agree in writing to the resolutions as amended, he was to receive his full salary of $4,000. (4) The gefe político was authorized to settle any further questions of detail without reference to the dip. Nov. 4th, F. informs the min. of rel. that H. is to remain as director, subject to the civil government, and to receive $4,000; but after the colonists are once located under municipal govt, it is thought no director will be needed, and the salary may be saved. *St. Pap., Miss. and Colon.*, MS., ii. 213. H.'s reply of Nov. 6th is also in *Id.*, ii. 213–17.

[12] Nov. 8th, 9th, *St. Pap., Miss. and Colon.*, MS., ii. 270, 279, 287–8.

[13] *St. Pap., Miss. and Colon.*, MS., ii. 283–92; *Figueroa, Manifiesto*, 48–55.

or more at San Luis Rey and San Gabriel, and their gradual progress northward. Immediately after the agreement with Híjar, particularly on November 12th, orders were issued for a *pro rata* furnishing by the missions of necessary supplies. There are also some fragmentary items of record respecting transportation in November and December;[14] but all that can be definitely learned is that during the winter a majority of the whole company, the rest being scattered throughout the territory, were gradually brought together at San Francisco Solano, which mission was already in charge of Mariano G. Vallejo as comisionado for secularization. Padrés was with them, and Híjar made some visits to Solano. The intention was to found a settlement on the northern frontier, perhaps at Santa Rosa, though it does not clearly appear that any of the colony actually went there, or indeed that any had lands assigned them at San Francisco Solano. Early in March 1835 a new correspondence took place between Híjar and Figueroa. Supplies had come in slowly, barely in quantities sufficient to keep the colonists alive. Híjar now desired to make a beginning of the new town, and called on the governor to state definitely whether he could furnish the required aid. Figueroa admitted that he could not furnish all that was required by the instructions, though he would do, as he had done, all that was in his power.

[14] Nov. 5, 1834, Ramirez notifies receptor at S. Francisco that the brig *Trammare* will bring the colonists' luggage north and may land it on Angel Island. *Pinto, Doc.*, MS., i. 125–6. Nov. 8th–9th, Híjar's estimates of livestock, tools, supplies, etc., for the colony, amounting to $45,000 for a year. *St. Pap., Miss. and Colon.*, MS., ii. 274–8, 280. Nov. 12th, miscellaneous orders to missions with some details of supplies to be furnished. *Dept. St. Pap.*, MS., iii. 188; *St. Pap., Miss. and Colon.*, MS., ii. 279–82; *Valljo, Doc.*, MS., 325–8. Dec. 19th, the gov. says to the comisionado of S. F. that if the colonists have not yet gone to the other side, they are to be detained until the rains are over. *St. Pap., Miss.*, MS., ix. 61. Coronel speaks of the journey in oxcarts or on horseback, of crossing the strait of Carquines in boats managed by S. José neophytes, and of being lodged in such of the mission buildings as were not occupied by Vallejo and his troops. *Cosas de Cal.*, MS., 12. Most Californian writers give no information beyond the bare fact that most of the colonists went to Sonoma. Some state that there was now considerable ill feeling between them and the native inhabitants, arising largely from the troubles of the leaders.

He advised, however, that on account of scanty means and the general unfitness of the men for frontier settlers, the idea of a new town be abandoned, and the colonists be allowed to select, each for himself, their own residence and employment. Híjar protested against this plan, as opposed to the views of the Mexican government; but Figueroa insisted, and issued the corresponding orders. The colony was thus disorganized, but there are records of aid furnished to families at different points throughout 1835. There is no more to be said of the colonists as a body. Most of them remained in the country to constitute a very respectable element of the population.[15]

In a defence of his own course, written later, Figueroa, presenting the documents in the case chronologically, interspersed among them his own comments. From his remarks it would appear that almost from the day of arrival, in September 1834, to the outbreak in March 1835, soon to be noticed, certain members of the colony under the leadership of Padrés were engaged in plots to secure the territorial government by force, Híjar being meanwhile an indifferent spectator, if not an active participant in these intrigues.[16] I suspect that Figueroa's fears at the time were to a considerable extent unfounded, and that his subsequent presentment of them was much exaggerated in detail to suit his own purposes. The colonists

[15] Correspondence of Híjar and Figueroa, March 1–4, 1835, in *Figueroa, Manifiesto*, 117–28; *Dept. St. Pap.*, MS., iv. 8–9. Orders and correspondence of March 5th to April, on transfer of the families from Solano to the homes they might select, and on supplies furnished. *Vallejo, Doc.*, MS., iii. 14–16; xxiii. 5; *St. Pap., Miss.*, MS., vii. 72–4; *Dept. St. Pap., Ben.*, MS., v. 377–9. Account by Padrés April 12th of amounts paid to colonists, aggregating $2,604. *Dept. St. Pap., Ben.*, MS., v. 371–2; *Id., Cust.-H.*, MS., vii. 662–4. Fragmentary records of supplies furnished to families, June to August. *Dept. St. Pap., Ben. Mil.*, MS., lxxx. 11; lxxxi. 46; *Id., Ben.*, v. 372–5; *Id., Ben. Com. and Treas.*, iv. 9; *St. Pap., Miss.*, MS., vi. 15; *Vallejo, Doc.*, MS., xxiii. 12.

[16] *Figueroa, Manifiesto*, passim. In Oct., before the action of the dip., they are said to have worked hard to alarm the public with charges of centralism and oppression. p. 22–3. After that action of Oct. 21st, some in their anger talked loudly and recklessly of their original plans. p. 33–5. About

were of course bitterly disappointed at the failure of
the directors to keep their promises, and many of them
were disposed to throw the blame on Figueroa and
the Californians.   It is the nature of disappointed
Mexicans to conspire; there were some reckless fellows like Araujo who were perfectly willing to make
trouble; and it is not likely that Padrés, or even Híjar perhaps, would have regretted or opposed any
revolutionary movement offering chances of success.
But such chances, against a popular ruler, the leading
Californians, and the friars, were known to be but
slight.   Therefore I doubt that Híjar and Padrés
made any definite plans to overthrow the territorial
government, and especially that Figueroa, as he claims,
was acquainted from the first with the details of such
plots.

There was, however, an attempted revolt at Los
Angeles March 7, 1835. The night before, about
fifty Sonorans, who had lately come to California, and

the time of settlement with Híjar, or in Nov., Araujo instigated two attacks
of the Cahuilla Indians on the S. Bernardino rancho.   Verduzco at the same
time tried to induce the neophytes of S. Luis Rey to revolt against the escolta;
but his plot was discovered and frustrated.   Lara on his way north tried to
enlist the neophytes of different missions in support of his plots, as was proven
by his diary, which fell into Figueroa's hands. p. 106–7.   Padrés concealed
the 200 rifles and ammunition he had brought, advised the colonists to have
nothing to do with Figueroa, and daily harangued them at Sonoma on their
wrongs at the gefe's hands. p. 108–114 (also F.'s reports to Mex. on Padrés
already cited).   In February two persons from S. Antonio reported a plot;
and several members of the colony revealed the revolutionary plans.   Híjar
meanwhile was intimate with the conspirators, and must have known their
schemes. p. 110–11.   The desire in March to unite the colony was for the
purpose of revolution; and to defeat this movement was F.'s chief reason for
allowing it to be scattered. p. 116–17.   When the news came of trouble in the
south, F. was investigating the matter at Sta Clara and S. Juan. p. 128–9.
Oct. 15, 1834, Capt. Portilla from S. Luis Rey. Has discovered that Verduzco
sought to surprise the guard and seize the arms. *Dept. St. Pap.*, MS., iii.
174–5.   Oct. 21st–22d, F. to Gutierrez and to 8 comisionados to investigate the
disturbances, arrest the leaders, and assure the Ind. that the charges of the
revolutionists were false. *Id.*, iii. 175–6. Araujo, on Sept. 18th, says, 'I have
already predisposed the neophytes in our favor,' this being perhaps the purport of the 'diary' referred to by F. *Guerra, Doc.*, MS., vi. 154.   Oct. 22d,
F. warns alcalde of Angeles to look out for revolutionary movements. *Dept.
St. Pap.*, MS., iii. 177; *Id., Ang.*, xi. 28.   Oct. 28th, Carrillo at Sta Bárbara has taken steps to prevent Araujo from seducing the neophytes. *St. Pap.,
Miss.*, MS., ix. 29.   Jan. 27, 1835, president has heard of Araujo's plots and
orders him to be sent out of the country. *Sup. Govt St. Pap.*, MS., xi. 1.

who were living in the town or the adjoining ranchos,
assembled at Los Nietos, and at daybreak entered Los
Angeles armed with lances and muskets, under the
leadership of Juan Gallardo, a cobbler, and Felipe
Castillo, a cigar-maker. They seem to have seized
certain weapons at the houses of foreign residents as
they came in. Marching to the town hall, and using
force to obtain the keys, they took a cannon and a
quantity of ammunition stored there temporarily, or
in a private house near by, in anticipation of an Indian
campaign. Without committing further acts of violence, the Sonorans stationed themselves near the
entrance of the hall, while the leaders took steps to
summon the alcalde. That official, Francisco J. Alvarado, at once convened the members of the ayuntamiento by tap of the drum, and the citizens generally
left their beds to attend the meeting. Gallardo then
submitted, with a respectful letter for the approval of
the illustrious corporation, a plan which explained the
presence of himself and followers, and by which it was
proposed to restore California to the splendid prosperity of former times by simply removing Figueroa
from the command.[17]

[17] *Pronunciamiento de Apalátegui en Los Angeles, contra Don José Figueroa,
7 de Marzo de 1835*, in *Figueroa, Manifiesto*, 131–3; *Los Angeles, Arch.*, MS.,
iv. 155–9; *Bandini, Doc. Hist. Cal.*, MS., 39. 'A multitude of citizens having assembled to devise means to save California from the evils which she
has suffered and is suffering under the administration of Gen. D. José Figueroa,
and considering—1. That this chief has not complied with divers orders given
him by the sup. govt of the Union to improve the condition of the inhabitants of this country; that, abusing their docility, he has exceeded the powers
granted him by the laws, by unduly assuming the political and military commands against the federal system and against express laws which forbid this
union of the commands; that with the law of secularization he has made a
scandalous monopoly, reducing the mission products to an exclusive commerce,
and treacherously inducing the dip. to regulate a general law according to his
whim; that, in infringement of the treasury regulations, he disposes of the
soldiers' pay at his own will without the knowledge of the chief of revenue,
and without the formalities prescribed by law; 2. That the dip. has no
power to regulate or make additions to a general law, as it has done in the
case of that on the secularization; 3. That as the missions are advancing
with giant strides to total ruin, through the measures dictated for the shut-
ting-out of the natives and the distribution of their property; and, 4. That
some commissioners, either by gross ignorance in the management of this class
of business or by their own malicious conduct, have proposed to advance
their private wealth by ruining that of the missions, with notable injury to
the natives who have acquired that property by their personal toil—have re-

The ayuntamiento in session with the citizens discussed the propositions of the plan, referred them to a committee, and finally decided by a plurality of votes that it had no authority to act in such a matter, and that Gallardo must apply elsewhere for support—in fact, according to one record the ayuntamiento went so far as to disapprove the plan, though having no army with which to enforce its disapproval. A committee consisting of Guirado, Osio, and Ossa was sent to communicate the decision and to request the pronunciados to remove their force across the river. This they declined to do, but promised to preserve the peace, and held their position until about four o'clock in the afternoon. Pio Pico and Antonio M. Osio, both of whom were in town on this eventful day, assert that the rebels were waiting for money that had been promised but was not forthcoming.[18] However this may have been, at about the hour mentioned Gallardo and Castillo respectfully informed the ayuntamiento that as

solved as follows: Art. 1. Gen. José Figueroa is declared unworthy of public confidence; and therefore the first alcalde of the capital will take charge provisionally of the political power; and Capt. Pablo de la Portilla of the military command as the ranking officer in accordance with army regulations. Art. 2. The resolutions of the dip. on regulations for the administration of missions are declared null and void. Art. 3. The very rev. missionary fathers will take exclusive charge of the temporalities of their respective missions as they have done until now, and the comisionados will deliver the documents relating to their administration to the friars, who will make the proper observations. Art. 4. By the preceding article the powers of the director of colonization to act according to his instructions from the sup. govt are not interfered with. Art. 5. This plan is in every respect subject to the approval of the gen. govt. Art. 6. The forces that have pronounced will not lay down their arms until they see the preceding articles realized, and they constitute themselves protectors of an upright administration of justice and of the respective authorities.' It nowhere appears who were the signers of the plan, if any, in addition to Gallardo and Castillo. All the copies close with the note 'here the signatures.' Figueroa devotes p. 134-46 of his *Manifiesto* to a series of arguments in reply to the successive articles of the plan, exhibiting very much more of skill and satire and anger than the subject deserved.

[18] *Osio, Hist. Cal.*, MS., 236-8; *Pico, Hist. Cal.*, MS., 50-5. Robinson, *Life in Cal.*, 164-7, gives a full narrative with a translation of the pronunciamiento. Other accounts in *Alvarado, Hist. Cal.*, MS., iii. 1-5; *Fernandez, Cosas de Cal.*, MS., 80-2; *Vallejo, Remin.*, MS., 55-6; *Botello, Anales*, MS., 15-16; *Ávila, Notas*, MS., 10-11; *Ord, Ocurrencias*, MS., 66; *Galindo, Apuntes*, MS., 30; *Tuthill's Hist. Cal.*, 138-9. Nearly all represent this as a revolt in the interests of the colony or its directors. In *Los Angeles, Hist.*, 14, it is spoken of as a revolt of Torres and Apalatey to place Ijar at the head of affairs.

the plan had not been approved by that body, after the exercise of what was doubtless better judgment than they themselves had brought to bear on it, they had decided to give up the instigators of the movement, and to throw themselves, if any wrong had been unwittingly done, on the indulgence of the legal authorities. Accordingly they gave up two men, and disbanded their force.

The two men given up, locked in jail, and sent next day to Lieutenant-colonel Gutierrez at San Gabriel for safe keeping, were Antonio Apalátegui, a Spanish *escribiente*, or clerk, and Francisco Torres, a Mexican doctor, or apothecary, who had come with the colony, and who lately had left Monterey with despatches from Híjar to the authorities in Mexico. All the Sonorans agreed that these men had instigated the revolt, Apalátegui being the active agent. The ayuntamiento on the evening of the 7th issued an address to the people, in which the events of the day were narrated, and a similar report respecting the doings of 'una reunion acéfala de Sonorenses' was forwarded the same night to Figueroa. Unconditional pardon was granted to the Sonorans, and some twenty of the number started immediately for Sonora, where many of them were arrested and submitted to a close examination respecting their deeds in California. The taking of evidence and other routine formalities of the case against Apalátegui and Torres occupied two months, and in May they were sent off to Mexico as disturbers of the public peace and conspirators against the legitimate authority.

The testimony and correspondence respecting the Apalátegui revolt as preserved in the archives form a very voluminous record, of which I offer a partial résumé in the accompanying note.[19] From the whole

[19] March 3d, Lieut.-col. Gutierrez to Figueroa, that he suspected Torres and is watching him. *Dept. St. Pap.*, MS., iv. 7–8. March 7th, record of events at Angeles—including ayunt. session; two letters of Gallardo to the ayunt.; Gutierrez to the ayunt. and to F.; and ayunt. to F. and to the people, in *Los Angeles Arch.*, MS., i. 36–8, 41–3; iv. 152–64; *Dept. St. Pap., Ben.*, MS., ii. 17–25; v. 185–96; *Dept. St. Pap., Angeles*, MS., i. 174–5; *Figueroa, Manifiesto*, 130–1, 146–7. March 8th, 10th, 11th, 14th, corresp. on subsequent

it appears that the Sonorans had no special grievance
to redress, but were easily induced to join what they
were led to regard as a general and popular movement, which they abandoned as soon as they learned
its unpopularity; that the immediate motives of the
leaders Gallardo and Castillo are not known; that

alarms and rumors. One or two arrests were made, and the Sonorans feared
punishment and sent a committee, including Wm A. Richardson, to plead for
them with Gutierrez. On March 19th, F. sent a full pardon and permission to
return to Sonora. *Dept. St. Pap., Ben.*, MS., ii. 25-7; v. 191-6; *Dept. St.
Pap.*, MS., iv. 23. March 11th to May 6th. *Apalátegui* and *Torres, Causa
seguida contra ellos por Conspiradores, 1835*, MS., 100 p. Testimony and legal
proceedings, with some additional papers, in *Dept. St. Pap.*, MS., iv. 21-3;
Dept. St. Pap., Angeles, MS., ii. 12-13. Fragmentary testimony of Hidalgo
and others at Monterey in *Dept. St. Pap., Ben. Mil.*, MS., liii. 77-86. Gallardo and Castillo testified that A. and T. had seduced the Sonorans, assuring them that the happiness of Cal. depended on the movement, and that all
the settlers and the ayunt. were in favor of it, and had given the pronunciados $2 each. T. they said had furnished $60 to buy lead, etc. A. deposed
that T. and Gallardo had led him into the affair; but admitted that he himself had written the plan and lent $200 for distribution. He said that Ga-
llardo was the leader, and had secured the re-payment of the $200 by pledging
his horses. He thought that many citizens of Los Angeles and some foreigners of Sta Bárbara knew of the plot in advance. T. swore that he had made
many objections to the plan shown him by A. and Gallardo after they had
'pronounced;' that he had loaned a little money without knowing for what it
was to be used; and that he had never favored nor instigated the movement.
Miguel Hidalgo testified at Monterey that T. at Los Angeles had tried to induce him and others to join a plot, though speaking very guardedly. All efforts to prove by this witness an understanding with Hijar or others failed
completely. Several foreigners, including Dr Wm Reid, Hugo Reid, and
Santiago Johnson, testified that they knew nothing of the revolt except by
rumors; but they said some arms had been taken from them or other foreigners.
There was some evidence respecting the manufacture of lances and the payment of various sums of money, implicating none but Gallardo. A.'s defender
was Julian Padilla, Osio declining; and T. was defended by Regina de la
Mora. The fiscal was Manuel Requena. There is nothing in the legal routine that requires notice. The defence was confined mainly to protests, complaints of irregularities in the proceedings, and declarations of the ease with
which the innocence of the accused was to be shown before the sup. court in
Mexico. On June 13th, the asesor, Cosme Peña, reviewed the case; and June
30th the alcalde rectified certain errors. April 10 to May 6, 1835, *Apalátegui* and *Torres, Averiguacion en Sonora del Tumulto hecho en Los Angeles por
varios Sonorenses á Instigacion de los dichos Gefes*, MS., 50 p. About a dozen men
were examined in this Sonora investigation, and the general purport of their
testimony was that the Sonorans had joined what they were led by Apalátegui to regard as a general movement of Los Angeles, the prominent citizens
of the south, and the foreign residents, made with a view to restore the missions to the padres, and that they had abandoned the scheme as soon as its
true nature was known. The record is a fragment, and the result not known.
March 13th, Figueroa at S. Juan Bautista to ayunt. of Angeles on the events
of March 7th. Original in *Coronel, Doc. Hist. Cal.*, MS., 23-34; *Figueroa,
Manifiesto*, 147-51. Same to alcalde of Monterey. Original in *Vallejo, Doc.*,
MS., xxxi. 175. Same to alcalde of S. Diego. *Hayes, Miss. Book*, i. 228.
Same to Gutierrez in *Dept. St. Pap.*, MS., iv. 9-10. Replies of Argüello and
Portilla. March 21st, all right at S. Diego and S. Luis Rey. *Id.*, iv. 13-14.

Antonio Apalátegui, who may have had a personal grievance against Figueroa, was the active instigator, though hardly more prominent than Gallardo; that Torres probably encouraged the plot, though acting with much caution and secrecy; and finally that there is no evidence to connect either the colony or its directors with the movement in any way. There is room, however, for a plausible conjecture that Torres, in behalf of himself and his associates, was disposed to test by experiment the strength of Figueroa's popularity in the south.

Figueroa was at San Juan Bautista on March 13th when he heard of the affair at Los Angeles. His theory was that that revolt was part of a deliberate plan on the part of Padrés and Híjar to overthrow him and seize the mission property. That same day, in addition to the despatches which he sent south, as already noticed, he sent to Híjar an order suspending him and Padrés from their positions as directors, directing them to give up all arms and munitions to Vallejo, and to start at once for Mexico to answer before the supreme government for their conduct in California.[20] At the same time he ordered Vallejo at Solano to receive the surrender of Híjar and Padrés, to seize all the arms and ammunition in possession of the colonists, to arrest Francisco Verduzco and Romualdo Lara, and to embark all on board the *Rosa*, a Sardinian bark then in the port of San Francisco, to the captain of which vessel the corresponding instructions, or request rather, were forwarded at the same

March 19th, ayunt. of Angeles receives written thanks from F. *Los Angeles, Arch.*, MS., iv. 165. March 30th, thanks expressed by F. verbally. *Id.*, iv. 166. In April Mariano Bonilla, a teacher of the colony, was removed from his school at Monterey and ordered to be sent away for complicity in this affair; but he did not leave Cal. *St. Pap., Miss.*, MS., ix. 28. May 7th, A. and T. taken to S. Pedro. *Dept. St. Pap., Angeles*, MS., ii. 13. The date of sailing on the *Loriot* is not known.

[20] *Figueroa, Manifiesto*, 157–8; *Dept. St. Pap., Ben.*, MS., ii. 27–9. F. claims to have been fully aware of the plots that were being formed, and of the purposes with which Torres had been sent to Los Angeles, but had calmly awaited the outbreak before taking any definite action. It is true that on Mar. 4th he had warned Vallejo to look out for any attempt at revolt. *Vallejo, Doc.*, MS., iii. 13.

date.[21] Vallejo received the order on the 14th,
"watched the colonists until their preparations called
for prompt action, and then suddenly fell upon them
on the 16th at 4 P. M., arresting Verduzco, Lara, and
others," who the next day were taken on board the
Rosa at San Francisco.[22] On the 15th, several sessions of the Monterey ayuntamiento were held to
approve all the governor had done and proposed to
do; though the latter seems not to have made known
his orders to Vallejo, and the ayuntamiento declined
to name the persons who ought to be sent away.
Next day Figueroa issued a printed address to the
people, announcing that "the genius of evil has
appeared among you, scattering the deadly poison of
discord," declaiming in the most bitter terms against
Híjar and Padrés, congratulating all that he has been
able to save his beloved country, and promising a
more complete vindication of his policy later.[23] On the
17th, Híjar, still at Solano, replied to Figueroa's order
of the 13th with a protest against the insult offered
him, a declaration of his belief that the revolt was
purely imaginary, a denial of the governor's right
to suspend him, an expression of his determination
to drag his prosecutor before competent tribunals,
a complaint of unnecessary outrage at the hands
of Vallejo, but at the same time an announcement of
his disposition to yield to force and obey the order to

[21] March 13, 1835, F. to Vallejo in *Dept. St. Pap.*, MS., iv. 11–12; *Id.*,
Ben., ii. 29–31. Private note of same tenor and date, in *Vallejo, Doc.*, MS.,
iii. 18. Ignacio Coronel, Rafael Padrés, and other suspected persons were
also to be sent on board the *Rosa*. Request to capt. of the *Rosa*, who was
desired to take the prisoners to S. Blas if possible—the same being also communicated to the captain of the port at Monterey, in *Dept. St. Pap., Ben.
Mil.*, MS., lxxxvii. 69. F. to Alf. Valle. *Valle, Doc.*, MS., 40.

[22] *Vallejo, Doc.*, MS., iii. 25. 37 rifles were seized besides other munitions. *Id.*, xxiii. 4. Mar. 19th, Verduzco to Padrés from the *Rosa. Id.*, iii.
21. March 20th, Vallejo certifies that before the rifles were taken 2 parties of
the colonists had departed to other parts of the territory. Also that no
resistance was made. *Id.*, iii. 22. Vallejo went back on the 18th to Solano
after putting his prisoners on the bark.

[23] *Monterey, Actos del Ayunt.*, MS., 73–80. *Figueroa, el Comandante Gen.
y Gefe Político de la Alta Cal. á los Habitantes del territorio.* Monterrey, 1835,
1 sheet, in *Earliest Printing in Cal.; Castro, Doc.*, MS., i. 22; *Figueroa, Manifiesto*, 151–4.

depart.[24] Neither Híjar nor Padrés was arrested
at Solano, but at San Francisco on March 26th they
went on board the *Rosa* in obedience to Figueroa's
orders as exhibited by Vallejo, and the vessel sailed
for Monterey.[25]

The *Rosa*, after lying at anchor in the port of Monterey for a week or more, carried the prisoners down
to Santa Bárbara, where—numbering with their families twenty-four persons—they arrived on April 16th,
and three days later were transferred to the American
brig *Loriot*, with the supercargo of which vessel Figueroa had made a contract for transporting them with
Torres and Apalátegui to San Blas.[26] On May 8th–
9th the *Loriot* was at San Pedro, but the exact date
of sailing for San Blas does not appear in the record.
Before his departure, Padrés addressed to Figueroa
a formal and indignant protest against the summary
and illegal treatment which he had received, accusing
the governor of having been influenced from the first
by hostility to the colony.[27] With the exiles were

[24] *Figueroa, Manifiesto*, 158–62; *Guerra, Doc. Hist. Cal.*, MS., v. 106–9.

[25] March 26th–27th, Vallejo to Figueroa, Id. to Híjar, H. to V. in *Vallejo,
Doc.*, MS., iii. 24, 26; vi. 349.   Coronel had not been arrested.   H. and P.
had started for Monterey by land when ordered to return and embark on the
Rosa.   March 30th, some fears of trouble at Monterey reported to F. in the
south, who orders watchfulness, and arrests if disorder occurs but not otherwise. *Dept. St. Pap.*, MS., iv. 15–16.   March 31st, F. at Angeles to Vallejo,
ordering him to form a representation on the acts of H., P., and the rest, their
revolutionary projects, seduction of Indians, etc. *Id.*, iv. 17.   April 4th, F. to
V.   Has heard of the sailing of the prisoners; V. must keep the effects seized
for the present, and try to discover where the rest of the rifles were that had
been brought by Padrés. *Id.*, iv. 19–20.   Passage money, etc., to capt. of the
Rosa. Id., iv. 17–19; *Dept. St. Pap., Ben. Mil.*, MS., lxxxi. 6.

[26] Figueroa had tried to engage the Mexican brig *Catalina*, Capt. Frederico
Becher, for the service. *Dept. St. Pap.*, MS., iv. 20–1.   Contract with A. B.
Thompson of the *Loriot*, dated Apr. 11th, to sail after Apr. 30th; to carry to
S. Blas and maintain on the voyage Híjar and Padrés with their families,
Torres, Apalátegui, Verduzco, Lara, Bonilla, Araujo, and some others, with
families and luggage; and to receive on return of the vessel $4,000. *Id.*, iv.
24–6.   Duties due from Thompson and Robinson were to be deducted from
the amount.   Apr. 17th, Padrés to F.; is ready to continue his voyage as ordered.   Apr. 30th, F. instructs captain not to touch at any other port than
S. Blas. *Id.*, iv. 27–9.   Same date, H. to Guerra, asserting his innocence,
though it cannot be proven 'in this unhappy country, where the laws are
trampled on.' *Guerra, Doc.*, MS., v. 109–10.   24 persons landed on Apr. 19th.
Dept. St. Pap., Ben. Mil., MS., lxxxi. 6–7.

[27] May 8th, *Padrés, Protesta que Dirige D. José María Padrés al Gefe Político,
1835*, MS.   May 9th, Gutierrez is at S. Pedro guarding the prisoners and
forming a *sumario. Dept. St. Pap.*, MS., iv. 38.

sent reports of the gefe político explaining his action in the matter, together with the indictments more or less legally substantiated in each case. The documentary process against Apalátegui and Torres was quite elaborate and has been sufficiently noticed; that against the parties arrested in the north is not extant, if it ever existed in any more definite form than the somewhat vague accusations of Figueroa and Vallejo.[23]

On the sailing of the *Loriot* from San Pedro, in May 1835, the famous colonization scheme of Híjar and Padrés, with its attendant controversies, may be regarded as having come to an end, though over two hundred of the colonists remained to swell the population of California. Figueroa devoted the remaining few months of his life to the preparation of an elabo-

---

[28] Mar. 31st, F. to sec. of the interior, reporting the plots of H. and P. and his own policy, without mention of the arrests in the north—also some accompanying correspondence. *Vallejo, Doc.*, MS., xxxi. 182–3, 185, 198.   May 5th, F. to sec. of state.   Reports his later proceedings.   H. and P. go to Mex. to answer to the sup. govt, whose employees they are; Torres and Apalátegui go as prisoners at the disposal of the sup. court; Verduzco, Lara, and Rafael Padrés are also implicated in the revolt, and are to await the result of their trial (that is, probably the *sumario* in a complete form was not sent with them); and Lieut Araujo goes because he is of no use in Cal., is sick, and has asked to be removed, besides being being an adherent of Híjar. *Dept. St. Pap.*, MS., iv. 29–31.   April 15th, Vallejo at Solano sends to F. the proceedings or investigations against the colonists.   The documents are not given; but in his letter V. states that the coming of Híjar, Verduzco, and Lara caused great excitement; that they openly talked of surprising the garrison; that he overheard them plan to capture him, first occupying the church; that he was on the watch for 9 days until the order came from F.; that he seized and disarmed them on the 16th, as they were cleaning their weapons; and that the wife of Padrés exclaimed on that occasion, 'I am glad they have been headed off for being so slow.' *Vallejo, Doc.*, MS., iii. 28.   May 21st, F. sends V. 27 pages of proceedings against Padrés and associates, instructing him to continue them as fiscal.   Other allusions to these papers. *Id.*, iii. 23, 50, 52.   Vallejo, *Hist. Cal.*, MS., iii. 39–42, says that the colonists at Solano instead of going to work spent their time in plotting and gaining the good will of the Indians, Lara and Verduzco spending in presents for the Indians the $2,000 that F. had paid for the support of the colony.   They told him he was lucky in making the arrest just when he did, for half an hour later they would have seized him.   They accused Pepe de la Rosa of having betrayed their plots, but unjustly, since Rosa's interviews with Vallejo were as a printer and not as a politician.   Brown, *Statement*, MS., 9–10, who was at Solano at the time of the arrests, thinks Rosa did give the information.   Alf. Ignacio del Valle took a prominent part in protecting the country from imaginary plots, as is shown by the records and by his own statement. *Valle, Lo Pasado de Cal.*, MS., 13–14.   Coronel, *Cosas de Cal.*, MS., 12–14, is sure there were no thoughts of revolt at Sonoma.   Janssens, *Vida y Aven.*, MS., 51–7, also regards the charges as having been invented by F. and V. to get rid of H. and P.

rate defence of his own policy, which was a very complete history of the whole affair, and has been fully utilized with other documents in the preceding pages. It was besides one of the earliest specimens of California printing—in fact, the second book printed in the territory.[29] As a defence, the production is somewhat too elaborate and earnest. The governor's action at the beginning in refusing to give up the command and the mission property, as later in banishing Apalátegui and Torres, were so manifestly just and proper as to require no justification. His acts in other phases of the controversy, not perhaps without a certain foundation of justice and policy, would show to better advantage without the declamatory arguments in their support with which the volume is largely filled. The author's very earnestness and violence at times betray the weakness of his cause. The charge of bribery against Híjar should have been made sooner or not at all. I have elsewhere expressed my belief that the revolutionary plots of Híjar and Padrés were largely imaginary.

Of the men exiled from California at this time, Híjar will re-appear in the history of a later period; but of the rest I know nothing. I have found no record bearing upon their reception and treatment in Mexico, nor any evidence that the directors ever published a reply to Figueroa's manifiesto, or took any other steps to vindicate their conduct in California. For them the colony and the Compañía Cosmopolitana were disastrous failures. Of Padrés I would gladly append a biographical sketch, as I have done of other promi-

---

[29] *Figueroa, Manifiesto á la República Mejicana que hace el General de Brigada José Figueroa, Comandante General y Gefe Político de la Alta California, sobre su conducta y la de los Señores D. José María de Híjar, y D. José María Padrés, como Directores de Colonizacion en 1834 y 1835.* Monterrey, 1835. Imprenta del C. Agustin V. Zamorano, 12mo. 184 p. This book was being printed when the author died, and contains some obituary matter to be noticed later. An English translation was printed in S. Francisco in 1855. *Figueroa, The Manifiesto which the General of Brigade, etc.*, S. F. 1855, 8vo, 104 p., the title on the cover being *Missions of California.* As has been seen, the originals of most documents published in the *Manifiesto* are extant, either in my collection or in some of the archives.

nent men; but beyond his first coming in 1830 as ayudante inspector, his influence with Echeandía and the Californians in behalf of radical republicanism and secularization, his exile by Victoria in 1831, his connection with the colony as just related, and something of his character which the reader has learned in these chapters, I have no information to offer.

At the election of October 1834, four or five men were chosen to replace the outgoing vocales of the diputacion;[30] but that corporation did not assemble, chiefly because three of the members were ill, until August 25, 1835, the sessions continuing, according to the records, until October 12th. I append a brief résumé of the business transacted.[31] President Figueroa's opening address was short, being a congratulation on the escape of the country from dangers that had

[30] The election record, *Actas de Elecciones*, MS., 19–21, does not show who were elected. The hold-over members were J. A. Carrillo, Estudillo, and Castro; and the new diputacion seems to have been composed as follows: 1st vocal, José Antonio Carrillo, absent as congressman; 2d, José María Estudillo, excused on account of sickness. *Dept. St. Pap., Ben.*, MS., ii. 17; 3d, José Castro; 4th, Juan B. Alvarado (though it is not clear whether he was 4th or 5th or 6th, and in one record, *Dept. St. Pap.*, MS., iv. 42–3, Figueroa summons him as a suplente); 5th, Manuel Jimeno Casarin; 6th, Antonio Buelna; 7th, absent and unknown (perhaps J. A. de la Guerra); suplente, present, Salvio Pacheco; secretary, José María Maldonado. *Leg. Rec.*, MS., ii. 212–15.

[31] Aug. 25, 1835, examination of credentials; appointment of committees; and address by the pres. Buelna granted leave of absence on account of illness. (p. 212–16.) Aug. 27th, Sec. Maldonado offered his resignation, and asked to be paid $120 due him. Aug. 29th, land grants submitted for approval. Sept. 1st, ditto; Maldonado submitted an index of documents in the archives, and retired, his place being taken by Alvarado. Sept. 3d, land grants; and wild cattle. (p. 217–18.) Sept. 5th, commun. from Los Angeles on cutting timber; from the alcalde of Monterey on boundaries of the capital. Sept. 10th, petition of inhabitants of S. Francisco to be attached to the jurisdiction of S. José for convenience of all concerned. Sept. 12th, 15th, 21st, land grants. (p. 219–21.) Sept. 26th, commun. from J. M. J. Gonzalez on appointment as police commissioner at Sta Inés. Oct. 10th, teacher at Sta Clara resigns; and Ignacio Coronel wants an appointment as teacher at S. Buenaventura. Oct. 12th, land grants. Prop. to place the portrait of the late Gen. Figueroa in the hall of sessions. (p. 221–2.) Oct. 14th, land grants. Oct. 15th, claim of Estudillo to be *gefe politico ad interim*, backed by the ayunt. of S. Diego, referred to com., but no action. Acting gefe pol. Castro authorized to collect his salary. Munic. fund of Monterey. Land grants. Oct. 16th, Salvio Pacheco granted leave of absence for sickness. No formal adjournment. *Leg. Rec.*, MS., ii. 212–26. On p. 262–9 are found also many communications of no available importance connected with the acts of the dip.

lately threatened; and the routine of business at successive sessions was for the most part unimportant, though I shall have occasion to notice elsewhere a few of the topics treated. The president was occupied with other matters, and the chief aim of the legislators was apparently to devise acceptable excuses for obtaining leave of absence. It is remarkable that Figueroa did not bring before the diputacion his policy and acts toward Híjar and Padrés with a view to strengthen his record with the approval of that body; but for some reason this was not deemed necessary.

At the election of October 1834, José Antonio Carrillo had been chosen diputado to congress, with Mariano G. Vallejo as substitute.[32] Carrillo seems to have been at his post early in 1835, and his influence is apparent in an order of President Barragan dated May 23d, publishing the following decree of congress: "The pueblo of Los Angeles in Alta California is erected into a city, and it will be in future the capital of that territory." So well pleased was Don José Antonio with this achievement in behalf of his town, that he secured an impression from the type on white satin, which, tastefully bordered in blue, perhaps by Señora Carrillo, is in my collection.[33] The order was not officially published in California until December; but the news came that such a change was contemplated, and the effect at Monterey may be imagined.

[32] See chap. ix. of this volume.
[33] *Pico, Doc.*, MS., i. 1. The satin copy is mentioned by several Californians. Decree also given in *Dept. St. Pap., S. José*, MS., ii. 135; *Id., Mont.*, iii. 47; *Arrillaga, Recop.*, 1835, 189–90, where it is said to have been published on June 10th; *Dublan* and *Lozano, Leg. Mex.*, iii. 51. Decrees of congress dated March 21 and October 26, 1835, that diputados from Cal. are to have voice and vote in forming laws and decrees. *Id.*, iii. 91; *Dept. St. Pap., Mont.*, MS., iii. 56; *Sup. Govt St. Pap.*, MS., xi. 1–2. June 13th, order concerning payment of *dietas* and *viáticos*. *Arrillaga, Recop.*, 1835, 223–6. Oct. 15th, min. of war to gov., diputados ordered to proceed to Mex. without excuse. *St. Pap., Sac.*, MS., xvi. 14. Dana, *Two Years before the Mast*, 196, says inaccurately that the form of sending representatives to congress was gone through; but there was little communication with the national capital, so a member usually stayed permanently, knowing there would be revolutions at home, and if another member should be sent, he had only to challenge him and thus decide the contested election.

A meeting of the ayuntamiento was called October 12th, before which body reasons most unanswerable and convincing—to the people of Monterey—were adduced why the proposed change of capital would be a measure outrageously detrimental if not fatal to all the best interests of the territory.[34] A report of Hartnell and Pacheco as a committee was approved, sustaining objections to the change, and recommending a protest. This action was passed immediately to the diputacion, which body on the 14th confirmed it, resolved that the reports of the territorial congressmen were based on selfish interests, decided to remain with the gefe político "at this capital" until further action; and sent the whole expediente to Mexico by the *Catalina* on the 15th.[35]

Figueroa still bore in mind the importance to Mexican interests of founding a frontier settlement and garrison north of San Francisco Bay. In fact, he had temporarily suspended the enterprise only from fear of what he chose to regard as the revolutionary plans

[34] Of these reasons I note the following: Monterey has been the capital for more than 70 years; both Californians and foreigners have learned to regard it as the capital; interests have been developed which should not be ignored; and a change would engender dangerous rivalries. The capital of a maritime country should be a port, and not an inland place. Monterey is a secure, well known, and frequented port, well provided with wood, water, and provisions; where a navy-yard and dock may be constructed. Monterey has a larger population than Los Angeles; the people are more moral and cultured (!); and the prospects for advancement are superior. Monterey has decent buildings for govt uses, to build which at Los Angeles will cost $30,-000; and besides, some documents may be lost in moving the archives. Monterey has central position, mild climate, fertile soil, developed agriculture; here women, plants, and useful animals are very productive! Monterey is nearer the northern frontier, and therefore better fitted for defence. It would be unjust to compel the majority to go so far on government business. It would be impossible to assemble a quorum of the dip. at Los Angeles. The sensible people, even of the south, acknowledge the advantages of Monterey. Monterey had done no wrong to be deprived of its honor, though unrepresented in congress; while the last three deputies have had personal and selfish interests in favor of the south.

[35] *Monterey, Acuerdo del Ayuntamiento y de la Diputacion contra el propuesto Cambio de Capital en favor de Los Angeles, 1835*, MS. In *Monterey, Actos de Ayunt.*, MS., 118–20, the matter was first brought up on the 10th and the report approved on the 13th. Carrillo's letter with the decree was received Dec. 31st. *Id.*, 146. This action of the diputacion, as we have seen, is not given in the legislative records.

of Híjar and Padrés.   As soon as these *bêtes noirs*
were fairly out of the country, therefore, he instructed
Vallejo to establish at once garrison, town, and colony.
His letters accompanying the instructions to Vallejo
were dated June 24, 1835, and the site was to be in
Sonoma Valley, instead of that formerly chosen at
Santa Rosa.   The chief motive announced was a desire to check the possible advance of Russian settlement from Bodega and Ross.   Vallejo was authorized
to issue grants of lands, which would be confirmed,
and the only precaution urged was that the Mexican
population should always be in excess of the foreign;
that is, that the granting of lands should be made
an obstacle rather than an aid to foreign encroachment.   The young alférez was praised and flattered
without stint, and urged to strive for "that reward
to which all men aspire, posthumous fame," even if he
should be called upon to make personally some advances of necessary supplies for the colony.   The
truth is, that Figueroa was not quite easy respecting
the view that would be taken in Mexico of that part
of his policy toward Híjar and Padrés which had
caused the abandonment of the northern settlement;
but with such a settlement actually established he
would have no fears; hence his zeal.[36]   The instructions that accompanied these letters are not extant,
nor have we any official record respecting the founding
of the town.   We know only that at the ex-mission
of San Francisco Solano, where he had spent much of
the time for nearly a year as comisionado of secularization, Vallejo established himself with a small force
in the summer of 1835, and laid out a pueblo to which
was given the original name of the locality, Sonoma,
Valley of the Moon, a name that for ten years and
more had been familiar to the Californians.   Vallejo

[36] June 24, 1835, confidential letters of Figueroa to Vallejo—or what
purport to be and probably are copies of such letters—furnished by Vallejo
to Gen. Kearny in 1847, in *St. Pap., Miss. and Colon.*, MS., ii. 406–8; also
printed with English translation in *Californian*, Apr. 13, 1847; *Calif. Star*,
March 13, 1847; *Jones' Report*, no. 24.

soon gained, by the aid of his military force, and especially by alliance with Solano, the Suisun chief, a control over the more distant tribes which had never been equalled by the missionary and his escolta, a functionary who, however, still remained as curate. Quite a number of families, both Californians and members of the famous colony, settled at Sonoma.[37]

José Figueroa died at Monterey September 29th, at 5.30 P. M., from the effects of an apoplectic attack, after about a month's illness. The funeral ceremonies, with firing of guns and other military honors, took place at the capital October 2d, being attended by all the people of the vicinity, and by prominent men from all parts of the territory. The body was embalmed rudely and taken to Santa Bárbara by the *Avon*, which sailed the 17th, to be deposited in a vault of the mission church on the 29th. There the remains were to lie, according to Figueroa's request, until the Mexican government should send for them to render fitting honors to the memory of a warrior who had distinguished himself in the struggle for independence. Mexico never did anything of the kind, and the Californians were not much more zealous in perpetuating his memory. The diputacion, on motion of Juan B. Alvarado, passed some very eulogistic resolutions in the sessions of October 10th–14th, providing for the hanging of Figueroa's portrait in

[37] Details given by Vallejo, *Hist. Cal.* MS., iii. 11–22, and less fully by Alvarado, *Hist. Cal.* MS., ii. 199–202, the same having been reproduced in different combinations by several newspaper writers are so manifestly inaccurate in so far as they can be tested as to be of no value. The general idea conveyed is that of an expedition into a new frontier country, including battles, maritime adventures, and treaties with thousands of hitherto hostile Indians; the past 10 years of peaceful occupation and Vallejo's own past residence at Sonoma being substantially ignored. The foundation of the town is also made to precede the expulsion of Híjar and Padrés. Vallejo mentions the following names on his way to Sonoma: Pt Novato; Embarcadero of P. Ventura, or Lakeville; Pt Tolai, on Midshipman's Creek; and Pulpula, or Pope's Landing. Vallejo also states that W. A. Richardson assisted him in making the survey. In 1861 Santiago Argüello assured Judge Hayes, *Emig. Notes*, 454, that he was the founder of Sonoma, having made the map, etc. 500 soldiers is a favorite newspaper statement of Vallejo's force. 25 would perhaps be a more accurate estimate.

the legislative hall, with the inscription "Benefactor of the Territory of Alta California;" for a suitable monument to be erected at Monterey; and for the printing of the resolutions in the manifiesto about to be published. The monument was intrusted to the ayuntamiento, which body before the end of 1835 had gone so far as to devise an appropriate inscription in Latin and Spanish, and to ask officially how the cost was to be paid. Here the matter ended for all time.[38]

A biographical sketch of Figueroa, as in the case of his predecessor Victoria, is not required here, because all that is known of his life has been told in this and the two preceding chapters. In person, he was a little below medium height, thick set, with a swarthy complexion, black and abundant hair, scanty

[38] Sept. 29th, Zamorano to comandantes, and private letters to Vallejo and Valle announcing the death. *Vallejo, Doc.*, MS., iii. 74–5. Record of the death also in *S. Diego, Arch.*, MS., 59; *Dept. St. Pap.*, MS., iv. 56. On Sept. 26th the American médico Stokes had joined the council of doctors to consider the governor's case. *Dept. St. Pap., Pref. y Juzg.*, MS., v. 53. Sept. 3d, F. had been at S. Rafael. *Id., Ben. Mil.*, lxxviii. 8. Military honors ordered, including a gun each half hour for about a week, besides special artillery evolutions on the day of funeral. *Id., Ben. Mil.*, lxxx. 20–1. Valle, *Lo Pasado de Cal.*, MS., 15, speaks of having been at Sta Cruz where he heard the first guns without knowing the occasion. Figueroa had ordered a grand celebration of the national fiesta on Sept. 16th. *Id.*, 19–20. Transfer of the remains to the south on the *Avon*, and ceremonies at Sta Bárbara. *Dept. St. Pap.*, MS., iv. 58–9; *Id., Ben. Mil.*, lxxx. 23. The mission books of Sta B. contain no record on the subject, probably because the deposit in the vault was not intended as a permanent one. Accounts of the embalming of the body by Drs Alva, Stokes, Cooper, and others, in *Gonzalez, Memorias*, MS., 17–18; *Dye's Recol.*, MS., 3; *Gomez, Lo que Sabe*, MS., 178–9; *Pinto, Apunt.*, MS., 12–13. It is stated by Gonzalez and Gomez that the remains were removed from the vault in 1845, at which time the coffin was opened and found to contain nothing of the body but dust; and it was thought this effect was due to the arsenic used in the embalming process. From Mexico there came in time an order dated Feb. 8, 1836, that the remains should be placed where Figueroa had desired. *Sup. Govt St. Pap.*, MS., xii. 1. Action of the dip. and ayunt., in *Figueroa, Manifiesto*, 177–84; *Leg. Rec.*, MS., ii. 222, 268–9; *Monterey, Actos de Ayunt.*, MS., 122, 134–5; *Robinson's Life in Cal.*, 168–72; *Vallejo, Hist. Cal.*, iii. 60–7. The inscription to be put on the monument was as follows in substance: 'To the Eternal Memory | of General José Figueroa | Political and Military Chief | of Alta California | Father of the Country | dedicate this monument | the Provincial Diputacion | and the Ayuntamiento of Monterrey | at public expense | as a mark of gratitude. | Died in this capital | Sept. 29, 1835 | at the age of 43.' General mentions of F.'s death, with more or less eulogy, in nearly every case, in *Pico, Acont.*, MS., 26–7; *Ord, Ocurrencias*, MS., 68–9; *Galindo, Apuntes*, MS., 31; *Castro, Rel.*, MS. 35–6; *Amador, Mem.*, MS., 142; *Fernandez, Cosas*, MS., 70–2, 84–5; *Vallejo, Reminis.*, MS., 116; *Alvarado, Hist. Cal.*, MS., ii. 238–9; iii. 37–40; *Vallejo, Hist. Cal.*, MS., iii. 55–9; *Tuthill's Hist. Cal.*, 139–40.

beard, piercing eyes, protruding lip, and large prominent teeth. He is believed to have had a large admixture of Indian blood. In manner, he was extremely affable and fascinating, especially in his intercourse with inferiors. His favorite vice was gambling; and though there is some evidence that he had a family in Mexico, he kept a mistress, and left a natural daughter in California. He brought to the country a military reputation, considerable experience, good administrative abilities, and great skill in the arts by which personal popularity is acquired. His term of office in California was brief, and the circumstances of his rule were favorable. His enemies were for the most part men of straw; his partisans were then and later the controlling element of the population. Even the padres were forced by circumstances into a partial and negative support of his policy. Moreover, he did some really good work in organizing territorial and local government, and he made no serious errors. He was liberal in the matter of land grants and in his policy toward foreigners. He antagonized no class, but flattered all. Hence an enviable reputation, for the Californians have nothing but praise for the character and acts of Figueroa. He has been fortunate in his fame. Eulogy has been exaggerated; I think the man's acts and correspondence show traits of character that under less favorable circumstances would have given him a much less favorable record. Nevertheless, he is probably entitled to his position in history as the best Mexican governor ever sent to rule California.[39] In several following chapters I

[39] Some miscellaneous items about Figueroa: Bandini is the only prominent Californian who did not share the enthusiasm for F., and even he in his *History* and correspondence did not deem it expedient to speak very decidedly against the popular sentiment. Osio, *Hist. Cal.*, MS., 240–8, narrates that F. was silent partner with Angel Ramirez in a monte game at the capital, which was broke up by the alcalde, tells of his giving a banquet in honor of a newly married Indian couple, and himself leading the dance with the bride, and states that his sympathy for the natives made him too lenient in punishing their crimes. F.'s physical appearance is spoken of particularly in *Pico, Hist. Cal.*, MS., 56–7; *Botello, Anales*, MS., 13–17; *Avila, Notas*, MS., 16; *Valdés, Mem.*, MS., 23; *Vega, Vida Cal.*, MS., 13; *Serrano*,

shall have occasion to speak frequently of Figueroa, though in this I leave him in his tomb.

In May 1835 the gefe político had notified the supreme government that he should be obliged to surrender the office temporarily to the senior vocal of the diputacion and seek relief for his illness away from the capital. He then intended to make the change in June, but did not do so until after the diputacion had assembled. On August 29th he issued an order to José Castro as senior vocal to assume the office as acting gefe político during his necessary absence. Corresponding circular orders were sent the same day to the different alcaldes.[40] It is not known what part of the time in September Figueroa was absent from Monterey, nor what duties if any José Castro performed as acting gefe in that month. He doubtless presided at several sessions of the diputacion at any rate. Just before his death, however, in accordance with the national law of May 6, 1822, and with the strong popular feeling in favor of a separation of the commands, Figueroa disposed that Castro should succeed him as gefe político ad interim, while Lieutenant-colonel Nicolás Gutierrez, as the ranking officer in California, was to assume the position of comandante general. Gutierrez had been summoned to the capital by letter of September 22d, and arrived a few days after Figueroa's death. After urging various excuses—ill health, want of ability, aversion from stepping into

Apuntes, MS., 28–30; *Torre, Reminis.*, MS., 32, 36–7, 51–2. All speak in praise of his character, as in *Arce, Memorias*, MS., 5–6; *Pico, Acont.*, MS., 24, 27; *Pinto, Apunt.*, MS., 12–14; *Marsh's Letter*, MS., 5–7; *Spence's Notes*, MS., 16–17; *Ord, Ocurrencias*, MS., 54, 61, 68. Alvarado and Vallejo, *Hist. Cal.*, MS., passim, are very enthusiastic in their praise of the man and all his acts. Requena, in *Hayes' Miscellany*, 29, says that F. bought the Alamitos rancho in 1835 for $500. Mention of a family in Mexico and heirs to the California estate. This in 1854 in connection with a suit of Stearns about Alamitos. *Doc. Hist. Cal.*, MS., i. 518. The idea expressed by Tuthill and others that F. was harassed to death by his enemies, or worn out by his labors in behalf of Cal., has little foundation in fact.

[40] Aug. 29, 1835, F. to C. to alcaldes, and to prefect of missions. *Dept. St. Pap.*, MS., iv. 48; *Id., Ang.*, xi. 37–9; *S. Diego, Arch.*, MS., 50. *Arch. Arzob.*, MS., v. pt ii. 11–12. In *Monterey, Actos Ayunt.*, MS., 125–7, the date is Aug. 27th, when F. announced the change to dip. and ayunt.

the place of a deceased friend, and his Spanish birth—
for declining the command, he at last yielded to the
decision of a council of war and accepted the office on
the 8th of October.[41]

Castro was in reality third vocal in rank of seniority, though the oldest who had been present in the
sessions of this year. José Antonio Carrillo was in
Mexico, but José Antonio Estudillo was at San Diego,
being excused on account of illness. To him doubtless the gefatura belonged, unless so ill as to be unable to perform the duties. The ayuntamiento of San
Diego took this view of the matter at the session of
September 21st, held on receipt of the circular of
August 29th, and sent a corresponding protest. This
would seem an excellent foundation for a quarrel; but
the records are vague respecting subsequent developments. Estudillo's claims were never allowed, apparently never even considered at the capital, and
were abandoned soon by himself and friends. Possibly he was really too ill to take the office; and it is
also possible that, as Bandini states, Castro turned
over the office to the comandante general without
much objection early the next year to avoid turning
it over to Estudillo.[42] Castro at any rate assumed the

[41] Oct. 8, 1835, Gutierrez to Castro, to comandantes, and to ayuntamientos.
Dept. St. Pap., MS., iv. 56-8; *Id.*, *Ben. Com. and Treas.*, iii. 70-81;
Id., *S. José*, v. 1-2; *S. Diego, Arch.*, MS., 56-8; *Hayes' Doc. Hist. Cal.*,
MS., 31. Oct. 9th, order in the garrison order-book for Gutierrez to be recog-
nized, signed by Capt. Muñoz. *Dept. St. Pap., Ben. Mil.*, MS., lxxx. 22.

[42] Sept. 21, 1831, action of ayuntamiento in favor of Estudillo. *S. Diego,
Arch.*, MS., 56-7; *Hayes' Doc.*, MS., 29; *Dept. St. Pap., Pref. y Juzg.*, MS.,
iii. 34; Oct. 10th, Castro to alcalde of S. Diego, complaining that no answer
had been received to the circular of Aug. 29th, which had conveyed the information of his appointment 'on account of the absence and sickness of the vocal
to whom it belonged.' (There had been nothing of the kind in the circular.)
He had heard that there was some difficulty at S. Diego about recognizing
him (he must naturally have seen the protest of Sept. 21st, sent to Figueroa),
and asks for information without delay. *S. Diego, Arch.*, MS., 61. In *S.
Diego, Index*, MS., 15, allusion is made to a reply of the ayunt. sustaining
E.'s claims. Oct. 15th, communications from E. and from the ayunt. were
received by the dip. and referred to a committee; but there is no record of
discussion or of results. *Leg. Rec.*, MS., ii. 222-4. In *Savage, Doc.*, MS.,
42-4, is an undated record or argument on the subject, apparently emanating
from Bandini, in which Castro's arguments are referred to, thus implying that
there had been a correspondence and refusal by Castro. At the same session
the payment of Castro's salary was authorized at $3,000 per year. Jan. 22,

office, was supported by the diputacion, and recognized by all the local authorities of the territory, meeting no opposition except that alluded to in San Diego.   He ruled until January 1836; but during his term there was nothing in connection with political annals which calls for notice here.   Castro carried out as nearly as possible his predecessor's plans, performed faithfully the few routine duties required of him, and if he had no opportunity to make himself famous, he at the least committed no serious or disgraceful errors.[43]

1836, Capt. Portilla to Gutierrez.   Says that Pio Pico did not recognize Castro's right to be gefe político. *Dept. St. Pap., Ben. Mil.*, MS., lxxxi. 31.   In a complaint of the alcalde to the gefe político in April 1836, the síndico is charged with having presented in the name of the people a paper inviting other ayuntamientos not to recognize Castro.   He also went about inciting the Indians to a campaign against Monterey, affirming that Capt. Portilla would take command of the movement. All this in Dec. 1835. *S. Diego, Arch.*, MS., 98.   Whether this 'plan' had anything in common with that accredited to Bandini and investigated by Gov. Chico's orders the next year, I am not quite certain. *Id.*, 104, 116.   Bandini's statement is in his *Hist. Cal.*, MS., 79–80, but he gives no particulars.   José María Estudillo, *Datos*, MS., 7, says that his father was invited by Figueroa to take the gefatura, but declined.   Botello, *Anales*, MS., 17–18, gives the same version.

[43] General mention of Castro's succession and rule, including in most cases the transfer to Gutierrez in Jan. 1836: *Alvarado, Hist. Cal.*, MS., iii. 41–5, stating that Zamorano worked hard to induce Figueroa to give both commands to Gutierrez at the first; *Larios, Convulsiones*, MS., 15–16; *Pinto, Apunt.*, MS., 14–15; *Pico, Acont.*, MS., 27–8, saying C. expected opposition from G., and gathered some of his friends and relatives about him; *Valle, Lo Pasado*, MS.; *Vallejo, Hist. Cal.*, MS., iii. 69–74, mentioning some troubles with P. Mercado; *Galindo, Apuntes*, MS., 31–2, characterizing the hesitation of G. to accept the command as mere pretence; *Serrano, Apuntes*, MS., 30; *Vallejo (J. J.), Reminis.*, MS., 117, complimenting C. for having kept the country free from the strife of factions; *Juarez, Narr.*, MS., 7, offsetting C.'s good record at this time against his bad one of later years; *Botello, Anales*, MS., 18–19; *Tuthill's Hist. Cal.*, 141; *Ord. Ocurrencias*, MS., 84–5; *Mofras, Explor.*, i. 298; *Marsh's Letter*, MS., 7.   The last two omit all mention of C.'s rule, and make G. succeed Figueroa.

CHAPTER XI.

MISSIONS AND SECULARIZATION.

1831-1833.

ECHEANDÍA'S PLAN OF 1830—DECREE OF 1831—THE COMISIONADOS—VIEWS OF THE PADRES—CARRILLO'S EFFORTS IN MEXICO—THE PIOUS FUND—EVENTS OF 1832—DIPUTACION AND FRIARS—ECHEANDÍA'S REGLAMENTO—NOTES OF PADRE SANCHEZ—BACHELOT AND SHORT—EXILES FROM THE HAWAIIAN ISLANDS—NEW MISSIONARIES IN 1833—THE ZACATECANOS—DIVISION OF THE MISSIONS—TROUBLES IN THE NORTH—FLOGGING NEOPHYTES—SUPPLIES FOR SAN FRANCISCO—MISCONDUCT OF PADRE MERCADO AT SAN RAFAEL—MASSACRE OF GENTILES—FIGUEROA'S INSTRUCTIONS ON SECULARIZATION—ECHEANDÍA'S REGULATIONS—FIGUEROA'S POLICY—EXPERIMENTS IN THE SOUTH—PROVISIONAL RULES—EMANCIPATION IN PRACTICE—PROJECTS OF PRESIDENT DURAN—FIGUEROA'S REPORT AGAINST SECULARIZATION—MEXICAN DECREES OF 1833—PRESIDENT AND PREFECT.

MOST important of general matters for the half-decade, after or even before political events and annals of the colony, is the affairs of the missions, especially in the phase of secularization. So closely is this subject connected with the general history of the territory, that I have been obliged frequently to give it more than mere passing mention in the last four chapters; yet it is absolutely necessary, at the cost of some slight repetition, to treat the matter separately and fully. As a fitting introduction, I refer the reader to what I have written on secularization for the preceding period of 1826–30, including Echeandía's instructions, policy, and efforts.[1] I also append in a note the substance of Echeandía's plan, as ap-

[1] See chap. iv., this volume.

to support on home resources; being in constant trouble on account of the soldiers of the escoltas, often favorites and servants of the padres and corrupters of the neophytes; knowing well that to insure the integrity of the nation and tranquillity and prosperity at home, it was best to abolish once for all the oppression of the neophytes by establishing a secular government, since once converted from slaves to proprietors they would become enthusiastic supporters of the federal system, a means of defence against foreign schemes, and of support to the territorial government and troops; desiring to release the missionaries for the founding of new missions; therefore I proposed to consolidate the security and good order of the territory by converting into free men and proprietors the 18,000 *forzados, indigentes reducidos* in the old missions, in order to advance rapidly to the civilization of the multitude of gentiles who also with their lands belong to our nation, thus avoiding the necessity of foreign colonization. Therefore I repeat, at the beginning of 1831, all being ready for the regeneration intrusted to me, and for which I had striven so hard, mindful of the laws and of the benefits to result, taking advantage of the most fitting occasion to develop the power of right by which was to be restrained the colossal arbitrary power of the missionaries—I took steps to put the neophytes under the civil authorities, deeming this the fullest possible compliance with the laws and superior orders."[4]

The special pleading quoted, or condensed from the author's original verbosity, was of course all beside the true question at issue. The territorial government, as Echeandía well knew, had no power to secularize the missions. Nevertheless, a decree of secularization was issued January 6, 1831. It was an illegal and even revolutionary measure, devised by

---

[4] *Echeandía, Carta que dirige á Don José Figueroa, 1833*, MS., p. 44–50. Though put in quotation-marks, what I have given is but a brief résumé of the author's endless and complicated words and phrases.

José María Padrés in supposed furtherance of his own interests or radical theories, and those of a few friends. I have already had something to say of this *golpe de estado.*[5] Had it been accomplished some months earlier, there might have been a plausible hope on the part of Padrés and his party for success; but now when Victoria was already in California, it was a most absurd and aimless scheme, unless indeed it was intended to have the effect it did have; that is, to drive Victoria to the commission of arbitrary acts and thus lay the foundation for a revolution. The results politically have been related.

The decree of January 6, 1831, was for the most part in accordance with the plan of 1830. From the original in my possession I form the appended résumé.[6] San Cárlos and San Gabriel were to be organ-

[5] See chap. vii., this vol. The views of Padrés in this connection, already well known to the reader, are given at some length in *Osio, Hist. Cal.*, MS., 155–64; *Vallejo, Hist. Cal.*, MS., ii. 254–62; *Alvarado, Hist. Cal.*, MS., ii. 160–1; *Guerra*, in *Carrillo (J.), Doc.*, MS., 31–2; *Robinson's Life in Cal.*, 97; *Figueroa, Manifiesto*, 2–3.

[6] *Echeandía, Decreto de Secularizacion de Misiones, 6 de Enero, 1831*, MS. Also in *Dept. Rec.*, MS., ix. 65–77; *Arch. Sta B.*, MS., ix. 435–70. The document is signed at Monterey on Jan. 6th, by E. and, in the secretary's absence, by José María Padrés.

Preamble.—Whereas, 1. All Mexicans enjoy the rights granted by the organic law except the mission Indians; 2. The law of Sept. 13, 1813, expressly provides that the missions be formed into towns; 3. Grave evils will result from the continued granting of licenses as heretofore; 4. The dip.—being convinced that the neophytes live in a state of discontent, that most of the friars have declared themselves opposed to independence and the national govt, and that the decay of the missions must follow—decreed in August last in accord with my propositions the manner of distributing lands and property; therefore I have deemed it proper to decree for the present as follows: 1. S. Gabriel and S. Cárlos are to be organized as towns, the latter retaining the name of Carmelo. 2. At S. Gabriel 4 comisarios to be elected, dependent on the ayunt. of Los Angeles until the population be determined, and to be elected under the direction of a trustworthy person selected by that ayunt. 3. Same at S. Cárlos, dependent on ayunt. of Monterey. Elections to take place on 3d and 4th Sundays of Jan.; officers to enter upon the discharge of their duties on Feb. 1st. 4. The ranchos of each mission to continue subject to it, and to have a sub-comisario if the number of inhabitants be considerable. 5, 6. Identical with art. 5, 6, of the plan of 1830. 7. All inhab. of the two missions 25 years old, or 18 years if married, are entitled to grants of land in fee simple; but the lands cannot be subjected to entail or mortmain. 8, 9, 10. Correspond with 8, 7, 12, of the plan. 11. Unmarried neophytes of 25 years or more to have only half the house lot granted by art. 6; and to have a smaller share of live-stock, tools, etc., than the others. 12–17. Correspond in substance to art. 10, 14, 11–13, 16, 17, 18, of the plan. 18. An administrator is to be appointed for each town; and for this purpose

HIST. CAL., VOL. III.   20

ized at once into towns, the surplus property after
distribution to neophytes passing under the control of
secular administrators. A similar change was to be
effected at most of the other missions as rapidly as
the comisionados appointed to superintend the distribution could attend to their duties. Suitable provision was made for the support of the ministers,
and for the education of Indian children.

Governor Victoria had arrived at Santa Bárbara
on his way to assume the command, the transfer of
which Echeandía purposely delayed for the advancement of the secularization scheme, and he took steps
to prevent the official publication of the bando of January 6th in the south.[7] His exact instructions from

heads of families are to choose three men to be named to the ayunt., which
body will forward the names to the gov. with a report on qualifications.   19.
The administrator to have charge of all property remaining after the distribution, the same to be delivered to him by inventory.   20. The citizens interested will appoint the necessary majordomos, who will be under the
administrator's direction.   21. They will also propose to the comisario the
proper salaries of administrator and majordomos, to be laid before the
ayunt. and gov.   22. Corresponds to art. 17–18 of plan.   23. The minister
will be allowed $1,000 at S. Gabriel and $600 at Carmelo, including the
sínodo of $400.   24. At S. F., S. José, Sta Clara, S. Juan Bautista, Soledad,
S. Antonio, S. Miguel, Sta Inés, S. Buenaventura, S. Fernando, S. Juan
Capistrano, and S. Diego, comisarios, administrators, and majordomos will
be chosen as provided in art. 2–4, 18, 20; but in other respects they will continue under the community system until the comisionados for the distribution of lands, etc., shall have concluded their labors at S. Gabriel and S.
Cárlos, when they will attend to these.   25. The ministers of these missions
will be furnished by the administrators with support and servants in addition
to their sínodos until a proper allowance for their spiritual services is determined on.   26. At Sta Cruz, S. Luis Obispo, Purísima, Sta Bárbara, and S.
Luis Rey only comisarios and majordomos are to be chosen, the administra-
tion remaining for the present in the hands of the padres.   27. In the future,
for the purposes indicated, S. F. will belong to the port of the same name; S.
José and Sta Clara to the ayunt. of S. José; Sta Cruz, S. Juan, Soledad, S.
Antonio, S. Miguel, and S. Luis Obispo to that of Monterey; Purísima, Sta
Inés, Sta Bárbara, and S. Buenaventura to the comandancia of Sta Bárbara;
S. Fernando and S. Juan Capistrano to the ayunt. of Los Angeles; and S.
Luis Rey and S. Diego to the comandancia of S. Diego.   28. With all pos-
sible haste a school is to be establised at S. Gabriel and at Carmelo, in which
reading, writing, and arithmetic will be taught as well as the best morals
and politics.   29. Each of the southern missions up to Sta Inés will send 4
clear-headed pupils over 18 years of age to the school at Monterey.   30.
Each of the northern missions will send 4 Indian pupils to Carmelo.   31.
The pupils to be chosen by the comisarios and administrators.   32. Teachers
to have $40 or $50 according to skill; and to have also $15 for each proficient
pupil produced in 6 months, or $5 for each at the end of a year.   33. Per-
sons deeming themselves competent to teach will make application to local
authorities.

    [7] Jan. 7, 1831, Guerra says the new *mandarin* expresses very sensible

Mexico are not known, but the spirit of the administration which he represented was favorable to the friars; and he understood perfectly not only the illegality of Echeandía's act, but its motive and the influence of Padrés in the matter. In the north the bando was more or less fully published in January. The document with the proper instructions and requests was sent not only to local officials, but to the padre prefect and bishop, who were urged to instruct and prepare the friars for the change.[8] The ayuntamiento of Monterey on the 8th chose a comisionado for each of the seven missions of the district.[9] José Castro and Juan B. Alvarado were sent to San Miguel and San Luis Obispo respectively, where they read the decree and made speeches to the assembled neophytes. At San Luis, and probably at all the missions of the district, the comisarios were elected; but at San Miguel, after listening to the orators, the neophytes expressed a very decided preference for the padre and

views in regard to the missions—that is, of course his views were favorable to the padres. *Carrillo (J.), Doc.*, MS., 33. Jan. 14th, V. to E. Has just seen 'by a lucky accident' the edict, which contains provisions entirely contrary to superior instructions and orders. He has taken steps to counteract the evil results, but holds E. responsible if any occur. *St. Pap., Miss. and Colon.*, MS., ii. 35–6. Jan. 19th, V. to sup. govt, denouncing the decree as a scheme for plundering the missions, instigated by Padrés. It was published at Monterey and probably at S. Francisco; but elsewhere it was deemed too risky. *Sup. Govt St. Pap.*, MS., viii. 8–10. Yet the decree was known in the south; for on Jan. 21st, Com. Argüello at S. Diego directs to the com. gen. an argument against making the proposed change at S. Gabriel, chiefly because the troops could not get along without the supplies furnished by that mission. *Dept. St. Pap.*, MS., iii. 1–3. Echeandía in 1832 stated that the devil had prompted Victoria to prevent the publication in the south and afterwards to nullify the decree in the north, giving no reasons for such shameful conduct! *St. Pap., Miss. and Colon.*, MS., ii. 61. On the general fact of V.'s nullification of the decree, see *Tuthill's Hist. Cal.*, 131; *Halleck's Report*, 125; *Ord, Ocurrencias*, MS., 38–9; *Amador, Memorias*, MS., 126–8.

[8] Jan. 6, 1831, E. to bishop of Sonora. *Dept. St. Pap., Ben. Mil.*, MS., lxxiii. 52. Same to prefect. *Id.*, lxxi. 6–7; *Dept. Rec.*, MS., ix. 77. Same to comandantes and ayuntaminentos. *Id.*, viii. 136. Jan. 12th, same to Zamorano, recommendations on distribution of land at S. Gabriel. Zamorano may have been appointed comisionado for that mission. *Id.*, ix. 78. Jan. 12th, same to com. of Escoltas, who are to aid Alcalde Buelna in publishing the decree, and to obey not the padres' orders but those of the comisarios, after such have been chosen. *Id.*, ix. 79.

[9] *Monterey, Actas del Ayuntamiento, 1831–5*, MS., 25. The comisionados were Juan B. Alvarado for S. Luis Obispo, José Castro for S. Miguel, Antonio Castro for S. Antonio, Tiburcio Castro for Soledad, Juan Higuera for S. Juan Bautista, Sebastian Rodriguez for Sta Cruz, and Manuel Crespo for S. Cárlos.

the old system.[10] On account of Victoria's arrival the matter went no further than the election of
comisarios; nor is there any record that it went so
far in the districts of San José and San Francisco.

For the rest of 1831, during the exciting epoch of
the revolt against Victoria, there is little to be said of
mission history, and the project of secularization was
at a stand-still. There is a notable absence in the
archives of missionary correspondence for the year;
and the padres have thus evaded—whether to any
extent voluntarily or through accidental loss of papers I am not quite sure—a definite record of their
attitude in the quarrel that distracted the territory;
though there can be no doubt that their sympathies
were strongly in Victoria's favor. The bishop replied
in March, by stating briefly that he had no curates at
his disposal, and by requesting information upon all
that concerned the welfare of California.[11] It would
seem that even Victoria had some instructions not altogether opposed to secularization, for in August
President Duran issued a circular, in which he asked
of the padres, apparently by the governor's order,
their opinions of a scheme for emancipating the neophytes and distributing the estates on a basis including the maintenance of religious service, the support of
the padres, and the retention of community property

[10] *Dept. St. Pap.*, MS., iii. 3–5; *Dept. Rec.*, MS., ix. 85. The Indians
said they respected the government and the decree, but by reason of their
poverty and ignorance they desired no change. Alvarado, *Hist. Cal.*, MS.,
iii. 6–7, narrates his efforts at S. Miguel, where from a cart in the mission
courtyard he vividly pictured the advantages of freedom to the Indians; then
requested those who wished to remain under the padre to stand on the left
and those preferring freedom on the right. Nearly all went to the left at
first, where they were soon joined by the small minority who had not the
courage of their convictions. Alvarado says the Indians of S. Luis and
S. Antonio expressed the same views. Jan. 21st, E. to alcalde of Monterey.
The election of comisarios at S. Cárlos was illegal and void; and a new one
must be held. *Dept. Rec.*, MS., ix. 84. Jan. 25th, alcalde of Monterey to
Sebastian Rodriguez. Will introduce the new system (at Sta Cruz) after Feb.
1st. *Monterey, Arch.*, MS., xvi. 9.

[11] March 22, 1831, bishop at Fuerte to gov. *St. Pap., Miss. and Colon.*,
MS., ii. 58. Echeandía interpreted this as an acceptance of the change, but
says that later, when he heard of Victoria's acts, the bishop began to throw
obstacles in the way. *Id.*, ii. 53.

to a certain amount with which to found new missions. There are extant the replies of only three friars, two of whom opposed and one approved the proposition.[12]

At the end of December Duran prepared—probably for use in Mexico, with a view to prevent a renewal of Echeandía's original scheme, now that Victoria had fallen—a series of commentaries on the decree of January. It was one of the ablest documents that was ever written by a friar in California, but one which cannot be presented en résumé, and much too long for literal reproduction. On the decree, article by article, Padre Narciso expends the full force of his talent and learning, with not infrequent volleys of wit, sarcasm, ridicule, and bitter denunciation. Not a weak spot, and there were many, is overlooked, and not a weapon is neglected. In the paper there is much of sound argument, shrewd special pleading, evasion of real issues, and Franciscan prejudice, but little misrepresentation of facts. The standard position of all missionaries, that the Indians were absolute owners of the soil and all the mission property, but that they were still children requiring parental control, and that the friars alone were qualified to exercise that control, was presented over and over in a great variety of ingenious forms. Echeandía's lack of authority to make the changes was insisted on, as were many legal discrep-

---

[12] The circular was dated Aug. 13th, and is not extant, its contents being known only from the three replies. P. Juan Cabot writes from S. Miguel Aug. 24th, that while he would be glad to be freed from his cares, he can see no way of distributing the estates without producing ruin. The Indians of his mission would have to be scattered at long distances in order to get a living, and he could not be responsible for their spiritual care. P. José Sanchez deemed the execution of the project probably inevitable, but sure to result, as it was intended to, in total destruction to the missions. Taking into consideration what had happened in Baja California and Sonora, he could see no possibility of good results here. 'So far as it concerns me personally,' he writes, 'would that it might be to-morrow, that I might retire between the four walls of a cell to weep over the time I have wasted in behalf of these miserables!' P. José Joaquin Jimenez of Sta Cruz wrote in October that in view of the reasons urged by the government, and of the fact that the burden was becoming insupportable to the friars, it would be wisest to free the Indians and distribute the property on the basis proposed; but also that the Indians should be obliged to keep their share and to work. *Arch. Sta B.,* MS., viii. 13–19.

ancies between the decree and the law of 1813 on which it purported to rest, and strong points were made by ridiculing the pretended desire to civilize and educate the Indians in view of what the gente de razon had accomplished in that direction for themselves. In a note I give some brief quotations from Padre Duran's *epílogo*.[13]

There was no trouble about the furnishing of supplies in 1831. Naturally the padres were disposed to do their best, and the only records in the matter are one or two orders from Victoria to comandantes, intended to prevent excessive demands on the missionaries.[14] At the beginning of the year, and probably in consequence of the secularization movement, a passport for Habana was tendered to Duran as soon as a successor at San José could be procured. He apparently had asked license to retire.[15] Three missionaries died at their posts, padres Boscana, Barona, and Suñer, while no Franciscans came to fill up the de-

[13] *Duran, Notas y Comentarios al Bando de Echeandía sobre las Misiones, 1831*, MS. Dated Dec. 31, 1831. 'It would be better, with less bluster about the Indians, to begin with the gente de razon. Let the latter begin to work, to found establishments and schools, and to practise arts and industries; then will be time to lead the Indians to follow a good example. Are they, but yesterday savages, to go ahead and teach the way to civilized men? To form such projects of giving freedom to Indians after having taken a million dollars of their hard earnings for the troops, and to leave in their endemic sloth the others, who as a rule know nothing but to ride on horseback? Truly, I know not from what spirit can proceed such a policy, or rather I know too well. Why not write what all say? Why say *á medias palabras* what all say *á voca llena?* What all believe is that, under the specious pretext of this plan, there was a secret plan for a general sack of the mission property, the leaders in the plot intending to convert as much as possible of the booty into money, to be enjoyed in foreign lands. But God willed that Victoria should arrive,' etc. 'The interested parties, including certain members of the diputacion, who counted on the spoils, were disappointed, and their disappointment changed into hatred for Victoria, whom they have never pardoned for having rescued the prey which they deemed already within their clutches.' Then follows an account of the revolution down to Victoria's overthrow. I suppose a copy of this document may have been carried to Mexico by P. Peyri, who accompanied Victoria.

[14] *Dept. Rec.*, MS., ix. 5; *Dept. St. Pap.*, MS., iii. 6–7.

[15] *Dept. Rec.*, MS., ix. 86. Mofras, *Explor.*, i. 272–3, tells us that in 1831, P. Sanchez having died of grief at the invasions of the civil powers, most of the other friars being subjected to indignities, determined to retire; and thus these venerable men, who had devoted 30 or 40 years of their life to civilizing Indians, were driven from a country 'qu'ils avaient arrosée de leurs sueurs et fécondée par la parole apostolique,' taking nothing with them but a coarse woollen robe—all of which is very pathetic and inaccurate.

pleted ranks. Padres Jesus María Martinez and Francisco Cuculla, Dominicans from Baja California, seem however to have spent a considerable portion of the year in the territory.

Meanwhile in the Mexican congress Cárlos Carrillo was exerting all his influence and eloquence in opposition to any change. He was a partisan of the friars, and foresaw nothing but ruin in secularization. He expressed his views at considerable length in letters to Captain Guerra, which may be taken as copies for the most part of his private and public arguments at the capital.[16] A branch of the same subject, and one of more urgent importance at the time than secularization proper, was the disposition to be made of the pious fund, a topic under discussion in congress. The estates of the fund had been for twenty years neglected, and for the most part unproductive; the question was how to make them again productive, and how to apply the revenues. Hitherto the estates had been administered in one way or another by the government; the revenues over and above the expenses of administration had been constantly dwindling; and for a long time no aid had been given to the missions. Now it was proposed to dispose of the property, in perpetuity or for a long period, by emphyteutic sale, which of course would involve a great sacrifice of actual value, and would yield a very slight revenue, but which would put into the hands of the government a large amount of ready money. The friends of the missions favored a renting of the estates on the most advantageous terms possible for short periods, and were assisted by many who cared nothing for the missions, but were opposed to a wanton sacrifice of property.

Don Cárlos prepared an elaborate argument against the proposed sale, and intrusted it to a fellow-mem-

[16] *Carrillo, Cartas del Diputado*, MS., passim. Especially letter of April 25, 1831. p. 200–9. Oct. 19, 1831, the min. of justice and eccl. aff. replies to the síndico of Cal. missions that the mission property cannot be regarded as belonging to the public treasury. *S. Luis Ob., Arch.*, MS., 11.

ber to be delivered in the hall of congress; but the
'gran pícaro,' when he got the floor, made a speech
on the other side.[17]   Fortunately, others took up the
defence of Carillo's views and gained a victory, temporarily, over his opponents.   Moreover, his argument, a strong presentment of the subject, under
date of September 15th, was made public in print.[18]
The author said but little about religion, or justice to
Indians or friars.   He admitted that the missions
were not accomplishing much for civilization, but he
considered the whole matter from the standpoint of
Mexican interests.   He extolled California as a most
valuable possession, the occupation and retention of
which were due solely to the missionaries.   Faulty as
the system might be, it had subdued Indians and
gained northern territory for Spain and Mexico.
During the troubles of the past twenty years, the
missions had not only been self-supporting, but had
contributed over half a million dollars to the support of the troops, besides offering the only encouragement to a growing and profitable commerce.   In
other words, California had been supported and saved
for Mexico by the earnings of the Indians, under the
mission system.   But for the missions the territory
to-day would be in possession of savages or of a foreign power.   Only by maintaining the missions, and
especially by founding new ones in the north, could
the country be saved from foreign aggression in the
near future.   Moreover, this method involved no expense to the national treasury.   A rich property existed which could be legitimately applied in this way
to national defence.   The duty and policy of Mexico
were clearly to make that property as productive as
possible, and to apply the revenues solely to the support and extension of the California missions.[19]   Don

[17] *Carrillo, Cartas del Diputado, 1831*, MS., p. 214–15.
[18] *Carrillo, Exposicion dirigida á la Cámara...sobre Arreglo y Administracion
del Fondo Piadoso.*   Mexico, 1831.
[19] If there was any weakness in Carrillo's argument, it was in his exaggeration of the unanimity of sentiment in Cal. in favor of the friars and his own

Cárlos won the victory, for his propositions, attached in thirteen articles to the *exposicion*, were almost literally adopted in the law of May 25, 1832,[20] by which the estates were to be rented for terms not exceeding seven years, and the product was to be devoted exclusively to the missions. True, the victory was a barren one, for the missions derived little or no benefit from it; but neither had they profited by the fund in the past since the revolution against Spain began. Nor could they under any system have got their dues while the Mexican revolutionary troubles continued.[21]

Naturally little was done or even attempted in the matter of secularization during the political and military interregnum of 1832, yet some theorizing was indulged in, which it is well to notice. The diputacion, in addition to defending its past acts toward Victoria, or rather as a part of that task, spoke very bitterly against the friars in their reports of February and May. By means of their wealth, it was charged, and through the fanaticism of the people, the padres had influence, and used it unscrupulously to disseminate Spanish ideas, and plot against the federal system, breaking the laws, corrupting officials, and making themselves abhorred by intelligent citizens—that is, by the writers and their friends. Some had fled to Spain with gold and silver belonging to the missions. Their commercial frauds were well known. Why should they be allowed to profane our institutions, and propagate among the young and ignorant their sentiments in favor of Fernando VII.? Why had not the laws against them been enforced in California as

views, and in his fears of a revolution if this public sentiment should be disregarded.

[20] *Arrillaga, Recopilacion*, 1832, p. 114–16; *Fondo, Piadoso de Californias, Ley y Reglamento*. Mex., 1833. 12mo. 20 p. Gleeson, *Hist. Cath. Church*, ii. 136, says that the fathers were by this act deprived of $50,000 per year.

[21] The padres entered into an agreement with Enrique Virmond to furnish goods or money and take drafts on the govt to the amount of their stipends; and this was approved by the govt May 9th, 12th. Espinosa to guardian and to gov. *Arch. St. B.*, MS., x. 271–2; *Sup. Govt St. Pap.*, MS., viii. 12.

elsewhere? By them the neophytes were cruelly
beaten, forced to work, treated as slaves, without
having obtained the slightest benefit from sixty years
of mission training. Truly Pico, Vallejo, and Osio
were becoming very radical republicans and ardent
patriots, according to the Mexican ideal.[22] However,
they were angry at the time, and were declaiming for
effect in Mexico, as was Carrillo in a more temperate
way at the capital.

Acting as comandante general in the south, according to the terms of the treaty with Zamorano, Echeandía had the assurance to meditate the enforcement
of his decree by preparing on November 18th a supplementary reglamento, as if the events of the past
months had been but a mere temporary interruption
of his plans. The document, appended in a note,[23]

[22] Reports of Feb. 24 and May 15, 1832, in *Leg. Rec.*, MS., i. 244–9, 265–6.
Alférez José Sanchez about this time, as prosecuting officer in a criminal case,
made use of some very violent and sweeping denunciations of the friars
for their cruelty to the Indians. *Dept. St. Pap., Ben. Mil.*, MS., lxxiii. 6–7.
In his circular of Nov. 18th, Echeandía represented the Indians as complaining bitterly of their oppression by the padres. *St. Pap., Miss. and Colon.*,
MS., ii. 63–4.

[23] *Echeandía, Reglamento de Secularizacion, 18 de Nov. 1832*, MS. The
doc. was sent on Nov. 18th to Padre Sanchez, to each of the southern
missions, probably to local authorities in the south, and to Pres. Duran in
the north. On Jan. 13, 1833, it was sent to the min. of rel. in Mexico; and
on Feb. 7th, to Figueroa. The copy sent to F. is in my possession, and to it
are joined several responses from the friars. Reglamento.—Art. 1. Pursuant
to edict of Jan. 6th, after a record of population and property is made, the
property for pobladores is to be distributed to neophytes of ten years' standing, if married or widowers with minor children—except those who may wish
to continue in community, those incapacitated for work, and those who
neglect their families. 2. The distribution to be made at the mission or ranchos not far distant, and having a settled population, to such as reside there,
or were born there, and have the preceding qualifications. 3. The assignment of *egidos* and distribution of community property, etc., that cannot be
effected at once will await the first opportunity. 4. All thus detaching
themselves from the community shall pay from their private property parish
dues according to their circumstances, and in due time tithes. 5. The heads
of families will choose from their own number the necessary alcaldes and police officers; and this govt will appoint a comisionado to direct and correct
them, and to do all that is conducive to the best Christian and civil order.
6. Other neophytes will continue to work in community; but this govt will
regulate all relating to their food, raiment, wages, labor, and punishments.
7. The community service will terminate as the neophytes may fulfil the conditions prescribed for detachment, or as it is seen that the detached maintain
good order and progress in their town. 8. Out of the community property will
be paid tithes and parish dues, support of aged and sick, expenses of divine
worship, schools, jails, and others conducive to public welfare; and it is un-

was intended to apply only to the four southernmost missions. It did not go so far in some respects as was provided by the decree of January, and introduced some new features not authorized by that decree. It was not apparently published in regular form as a bando, but was rather submitted for approval to the friars. It was prefaced with an argument on the necessity of secularization under superior, laws and instructions, a statement of the enthusiasm with which the Indians had welcomed the author's efforts, a presentment of their complaints of injustice and a general discontent under the padres' management which threatened serious consequences, a mention of good results at San Juan Capistrano, where the padres were said to have voluntarily given up the temporalities, and a plea to the missionaries to accept their duties as parish priests.

Padre Sanchez replied in a long series of critical notes on both preface and reglamento.[24] This criticism is one to which it is impossible to do justice

derstood that at the proper time a part will be used for the foundation of new missions among neighboring gentiles. In order to a beginning of regular administration, the branch of vineyards will be separated at once so that all labor in them may be done for wages, deducting expenses from the product. 9. The missionaries now in charge will be treated as parish priests and as depositaries of the community property, signing the account to be rendered annually by the chief steward, who on recommendation of heads of families will be appointed from their number by this govt. The curate is to have all parochial dues besides his *sinodo* until the sup. authority may decide.

[24] *Sanchez, Notas al Reglamento de Secularizacion, 1832,* MS. The document has no date. The concluding note is as follows: 'It seems to me that I have given some convincing proofs, not perhaps of absurdities—I do not venture to say that—but of *inconvenientes* as they appear to me at first reading. I do not wish to engage in a prolonged dispute with Echeandía; let him do what may seem best. I have expressed my views, not so much for him, as for an instruction to the padres that they are by no means to lend themselves to any such coöperation as is demanded by that gentleman; since to do so would be to subscribe to the ruin of their missions, and to the ignominy of all the insults, suspicions, and distrust expressed in the plan, which were by no means necessary if only the welfare of the Indians were sought. Let Sr Echeandía then do what he pleases about the missions, but let him not count on the coöperation of the padres, which he himself must know to be absurd. The missionaries will serve as such and in no other capacity, until the curia eclesiástica, in accord with the sup. govt communicating with us through our prelate, may see fit to order a competent change—and so long as they are given the necessary food to support life, which failing they have the natural and divine right to shake off the dust of their shoes and go to other labors wherever they may be found.'

here, and to which may be applied much of what I
have said about Duran's notes on the original decree.
Sanchez, giving his attention chiefly to the preamble,
begins by suggesting that precepts on obedience to
law would come with better grace from one who had
given a better example than Echeandía.   His pretensions to teach the padres their obligations and rights,
or to change their status, are met with protest and
ridicule.   If the laws and his instructions required
him to secularize the missions, why had he waited
six years, until the arrival of his successor, before
acting?   If the Indians of the south, as was certainly
true, were assuming a threatening attitude, it was due
to the license they had enjoyed under Echeandía, and
to his unwise act in having put arms in their hands
against Zamorano, being thus a reason for a return to
the old restraint rather than for additional license.
As to the enthusiasm of the Indians for Echeandía,
the padre has little to say beyond reminding him that
there are several ways of winning popularity among
school-boys, one of the most successful being to let
them do as they please.   Of course he dwells on the
theory that the Indians were children and 'savages
of yesterday;' and of course he fails to recognize the
fact that this theory in itself was a condemnation of
the mission system in all but missionary eyes.   In the
reglamento itself the padre easily found no end of
faults and inconsistencies; yet in one of his notes he
expressed a degree of favor for an experimental emancipation and distribution of property at a few of the
oldest missions.   President Duran also issued at his
mission of San José a series of notes so similar in argument and expression to those of Sanchez as to require
no further notice.[25]   The answers from the padres of
San Diego, San Luis, and San Juan, that from San
Gabriel not being extant, were to the effect that they
left the matter entirely with the prelate.   Martin

[25] *Duran, Notas á una Circular ó Bando intimado por El Sr D. José María
Echeandía á las cuatro Misiones, 1832*, MS.   20 p.   Original.

said that since May 20th the neophytes at San Diego
had managed temporal affairs for themselves—except
the wine-cellars.   Ánzar said he was a Mexican, and
would cheerfully coöperate with the governor if permitted.   Zalvidea would be glad personally to be relieved of the burden.   He had toiled over twenty years
and had not saved a *medio real*.[26]   There is no record
that Echeandía took any further steps before the end
of 1832.

Padre Antonio Peyri left California at the beginning of the year with Victoria; and Padre Antonio
Menendez, a Dominican who for some six years had
served as chaplain at different places, died in August.
There may be noted here also as an interesting item,
the arrival of two priests who remained about five
years in the country.   They were Jean Alexis Auguste Bachelot, apostolic prefect of the Sandwich
Islands, and Patrick Short.   The two, with a companion, had arrived at the Islands in July 1827 from
France, to establish Catholic missions; but prejudice
was aroused against their teachings, largely, it is believed, through the intrigues of protestant missionaries, and in December 1831 they were banished,
"because their doings are different from ours, and because we cannot agree," as King Kaahuamanu stated
it.   They sailed on the *Waverly*, Sumner, master,
which landed them at San Pedro on January 21, 1832,
whence they were taken to San Gabriel and kindly
treated.   There is not much to be said of their stay
in California.   Bachelot remained at San Gabriel as
assistant minister, his name appearing often in the
mission registers.   Short soon came north, and he
was engaged with Hartnell in an educational enterprise at Monterey in 1834.   An order came from
Mexico to expel them as Jesuits and as having no
papers; but the governor did not enforce it.   In 1837,
however, although the ayuntamiento of Los Angeles

---

[26] *Vallejo, Doc.*, MS., xxxi. 25, copies of the letters attached to the reglamento.

made an effort to retain him as curate, Bachelot, accompanied by Short, sailed on the *Clementina,* and landed at the Islands in April. Persecutions were renewed, from which they were relieved by the French and English navigators Petit-Thouars and Belcher. Short sailed in October for Valparaiso, and Bachelot soon departed for the South Sea Islands, dying on the voyage in 1838.[27]

With Governor Figueroa, at the beginning of 1833, there came to California a missionary reënforcement of ten friars. They were Franciscans, all Mexicans by birth, and belonged to the college of Nuestra Señora de Guadalupe de Zacatecas, being called Guadalupanos, or more commonly, Zacatecanos, as the earlier friars had been known as Fernandinos from the name of their college. Immediately after their arrival, that is in February, they were put in charge of the seven missions from San Cárlos northward, their prefect, Francisco García Diego, going to reside at Santa Clara. The Fernandinos of these missions retired to the southern establishments.[28]

[27] See full and interesting accounts in *Petit-Thouars, Voy.*, ii. 325–48; *Hon. Polynesian*, ii. 31, 81, from *N. Amer. Review*, Oct. 1840. I have obtained much information from an obituary of Bachelot and a collection of documents published by Capt. Sumner in his own defence against the charge of cruelty to the priests en voyage, in *Honolulu, S. Isl. Gazette*, Oct. 6, Nov. 29, 1838. Autograph letter of P. Short, Mar. 19, 1834. *S. Antonio, Doc. Sueltos*, MS., 118. Corresp. on the order of expulsion from California. *Dept. St. Pap., Ang.*, MS., xi. 16, 34. *Los Angeles, Arch.*, MS., iv. 269. Bachelot's services desired as curate. *Id.*, iv. 289. Short at Purísima March 1837. *Vallejo, Doc.*, MS., xxxii. 77. Proposition to found a school at Monterey—mentioned also by several Californians. *Dept. St. Pap.*, MS., iii. 131–2; *Vallejo, Doc.*, MS., xxxi. 9. Short at S. Gabriel on April 16, 1832. Bachelot on various dates from 1832–7. *S. Gabriel, Lib. Mision*, MS., 16, 39, 59. Short at S. Juan Oct. 1832, and called a member of the 'Sacred Congregation of the Perpetual Worship of the Most Holy Sacrament.' *S. Juan B., Lib. Mision*, MS., 15. Arrival at Honolulu Apr. 17th; and departure of Short Oct. 30th. *Hon., S. I. Gazette*, Apr. 22, 1837; *Peirce's Rough Sk.*, MS., 2. Robinson, *Life in Cal.*, 122, and Mofras, *Explor.*, i. 294–5, mention the arrival of the French priests. Alvarado, *Hist. Cal.*, MS., ii. 191–3, tells us that Pres. Duran made their arrival an excuse to call for contributions for the cause of propaganda fide in China and Japan, and that $2,000 were collected.

[28] The new-comers were Francisco García Diego, prefect, who went to Sta Clara, succeeding Viader, who left Cal.; José María de Jesus Gonzalez Rubio, S. José, succeeding Duran who went to Sta Bárbara; José María de Jesus Gutierrez, Solano, in place of Fortuni, who went to S. Luis Rey; Rafael de

Considering the importance of the subject, there is a remarkable absence of original records respecting the coming of the Zacatecanos and the division of the missions; though it cannot be doubted that much was written at the time which is no longer extant, as is the case respecting many important topics of mission history during these last years. It will be remembered that in 1817 the southern missions were ceded by the college of San Fernando to that of Orizaba; but on account of troubles in Mexico and of the dissatisfaction of Californian friars—who were, however, willing to give up the northern, deemed the poorest establishments—the change was not consummated.[29] The necessity for a reënforcement continued more and more urgent, and San Fernando was in a state of disorganization so complete that it could do nothing of itself; but of the negotiations of that college with others I know nothing until letters of 1832 announced from Tepic that the Zacatecanos were coming.[30] The cession of the northern missions was evidently agreed upon in Mexico; but there is nothing to show to

Jesus Moreno, with García Diego at Sta Clara; José Lorenzo de la Concepcion Quijas, S. Francisco, succeeding Esténega, who went to S. Gabriel, but soon Q. was transferred to Solano; Antonio Suarez del Real, who succeeded Jimeno at Sta Cruz, the latter going to Sta Inés; José María del Refugio Sagrado Suarez del Real, brother of Antonio, at S. Cárlos, freeing Abella for the ministry of S. Luis Obispo; Jesus María Vasquez del Mercado, S. Rafael, in place of Amorós, who had died the year before; José Bernardino Perez, who served for a time as secretary to Prefect García Diego; and finally, Francisco de Jesus Sanchez, of whom we know nothing in Cal. for 8 or 9 years, and who possibly was left in Baja California to arrive later. The preceding is derived from the registers of the different missions, showing merely the presence of a padre at a mission on a given date; for there is no record of the assignments and transfers, with a single exception, that of Gonzalez to S. José on Feb. 13th. *Corresp. de Misiones*, MS., 39–41.

[29] See vol. ii. p. 407, of this work.

[30] Jan. 24, 1831, Martiarena at Tepic says to Capt. Guerra, in announcing his appointment as síndico, that Fr. Bernardino Pacheco is going to Cal. as a friar of S. Fernando college, which 'according to the agreement is to furnish 10 friars and the college of Zacatecas 11; the latter will be able to comply, but not the former, which has not more than 7 friars.' *Guerra, Doc.*, MS., vi. 130. April 21, 1832, Cárlos Carrillo, in Mex., says 10 friars from Zacatecas are going, as he is told by the min. of eccl. aff. and by the guardian, who have had great difficulty in obtaining so many. At S. Fernando there are only 4. *Id.*, iv. 242–3. July 18th, Martiarena says the 10 friars are at Tepic and are to sail on the *Catalina*, to take charge of the ceded northern missions. *Id.*, vi. 129.

what extent the Fernandinos in California knew or
approved what was being done. Beyond the presence
of the ten in Baja California, at the time Figueroa's
soldiers revolted,[31] there is no account of their journey,
no official record of their arrival, and no list of their
names. President Duran in a circular to the padres,
January 23d, devoted to several general matters, but
especially to the urgent calls of the college for aid,
alluded to the cession as a matter in which he should
lose no time, having already permitted the Zacatecan
prelate to station his friars so as to learn the routine
and prepare for a formal delivery of the missions.
He hoped the change would enable some of their
number to go to the relief of the mother college, and
declared that no one might hope for a license from him
to retire to any other destination.[32] In assigning his
padres to their different stations on and about February 13th, Prefect García Diego used the following formula: "Inasmuch as the supreme government of the Mexican republic has intrusted to our
college some of the missions of Alta California,
which hitherto the worthy sons of the college of San
Fernando have administered with such honor; and it
having been agreed between the venerable discretories
of both colleges that there should be delivered to us
the missions of the north as appears from orders
which I have shown to the Very Rev. Padre President Fr. Narciso Duran; therefore," etc.[33] Soon
a *concordat funeral* was concluded between the two
bands of missionaries, by which each agreed to say
twenty masses for the soul of any member of the
other band who might die; and thus the new order of
things was permanently established.[34]

[31] *Dept. St. Pap., Ben. Cust.-H.*, MS., i. 35.
[32] *Duran, Cordillera á los Padres en Enero de 1833*, MS.
[33] This in the appointment of Gonzalez to S. José. *Corresp. de Misiones*,
MS., 39–41. García assumed formal charge of Sta Clara on March 6th. *Sta
Clara, Paroquia*, MS., 19.
[34] *S. José, Patentes*, MS., 190–1; *Coronel, Doc.*, MS., 11–12; *Arch. Obispado*, MS., 52. General mention of the transfer in *Mofras, Explor.*, i. 274,
who states that the division was made in Cal. to avoid disputes, the old

The Zacatecanos were as a class by no means equal morally or intellectually to their predecessors, as will be apparent from their actions in later years; and besides this inferiority, there were naturally many difficulties to be encountered by them at the first, arising from their inexperience and a certain degree of prejudice felt against them by neophytes and others. It did not take them long to learn that their lines had not fallen to them in places altogether pleasant; and in September we find their prefect begging for a certificate of the miserably sad condition in which he and his associates found themselves, for exhibition to the government on returning to his college; for "we cannot subsist here longer, because the climate is destroying our health."[35]

Their troubles in 1833, to say nothing of the climate, were of a threefold nature, arising from the unmanageable character of the neophytes, from the difficulty of furnishing supplies to the presidio, and from Padre Mercado's conduct at San Rafael. The Indians did not behave in a manner at all satisfactory to their new masters, who resorted freely to the use of the lash. Vallejo, comandante of the San Francisco district, made complaint to Figueroa on the subject, and the latter to Prefect García Diego, with a notification that flogging was forbidden by the laws. The prefect seems to have made an earnest effort to remedy the evil; and though some of the padres were disposed to be obstinate, no special complaint is recorded after the issuance of a pastoral letter on the subject on the 4th of July.[36]

Spanish friars not being able to tolerate the lax morals of the Mexicans. Alvarado, *Hist. Cal.*, MS., ii. 205, 209–10, says the Zacatecanos wanted all the missions; but the Fernandinos refused, and finally succeeded in convincing the stupid Mexicans that, as there were 21 missions and only 10 friars, a division was necessary! Wilkes, *Narrative*, v. 173, states that the new friars were in every way inferior to the old ones, and totally unfit for missionaries. *Vallejo, Hist. Cal.*, MS., ii. 197–8; *Robinson's Statement*, MS., 8; *Ord, Ocurrencias*, MS., 55–6.

[35] Sept. 5, 1833, García Diego to Figueroa. *Arch. Azob.*, MS., v. pt i. 41.
[36] May 5th, 31st, Vallejo to Figueroa. *Vallejo, Doc.*, MS., ii. 41, 52. The complaint is of flogging at the 4 missions, nothing being said of S. José.

Throughout the year at frequent intervals Vallejo complained that the soldiers of his company at San Francisco were in great destitution, and that the missions did not furnish sufficient food for the garrison, or even for the escoltas. He gave many details of the privations endured and of his personal efforts to obtain relief, and he expressed rather freely the belief that the Fernandinos would not have permitted the soldiers to suffer so.[37] The complaints were forwarded by Figueroa to the prefect, who professed the best possible intentions, but pleaded poverty, and could not understand "why Don Guadalupe was making so much trouble about the matter." Figueroa issued an order December 1st, fixing the yearly amount of supplies to be furnished by the missions of Monterey and San Francisco jurisdictions, including live-stock with which to replenish the national ranchos.[33]

Vallejo was also prominently concerned as complain-

Vallejo had an interview with the minister of S. Francisco, who said 'it would not be expedient at any time to discontinue flogging the Indians; for his part he would perpetuate this paternal correctional mode of punishment so fitting for that class of people. If he were forced to act otherwise, he knew the road by which he had come,' that is, he would leave the country. On being shown the law he replied, 'Lashes, lashes, and more lashes for these people so devoid of honor!' Vallejo admitted that at Sta Clara, García Diego had good intentions, yet he allowed the majordomo, Alviso, to flog. May 13th, June 14th, F. to García Diego. Id., ii. 142, 153; Arch. Arzob., MS., v. pt i. 80. June 16th, P. Gutierrez to F., claiming that the Indians, having no shame or honor, could be controlled only by fear; and that the law was intended for more advanced people in Mexico. Dept. St. Pap., Ben., MS., ii. 12–14. June 30th, García Diego to F. Id., ii. 15; Arch. Arzob., MS., v. pt i. 80–1. He declares his intention to abolish flogging. 'Mi genio, mis ideas, mi sensibilidad, todo junto se opone á esta costumbre que jamas aprobaré.' Yet he has to work slowly. July 4th, García Diego, Carta Pastoral á los padres Zacatecanos contra la costumbre de azotar á los indios, 1833, MS.

[37] Letters of V. and F. Vallejo, Doc., MS., ii. 15, 45, 47, 99–101, 107, 116, 128, 148, 152, 179. Feb. 21st, F. to G. D. Dept. St. Pap., Ben. Mil., MS., lxxix. 4. Apr. 15th, G. D. to F., explaining his difficulties, the poverty of the missions, his efforts, and hopes of better success. St. Pap., Miss. and Colon., MS., ii. 308–9. May 25th, June 15th, same to same. Arch. Arzob., MS., v. pt i. 77–8.

[38] Dept. St. Pap., Ben. Mil., MS., lxxiv. 47–8; Id., Ben. Cust.-H., MS., ii. 78–81. The requisition was for 1,458 fanegas of wheat, 318 fan. beans, 936 arrobas of lard, 50 cargas of flour, $1,632 worth of soap, 834 pairs of shoes, 139 blankets, 80 shields, 80 cueras, 80 cananas, 80 musket-cases, 8 saddles, 200 broken horses, 34 pack-mules, 1,690 cows and heifers, 810 steers and bulls, 200 mares and foals, 20 oxen, 20 ploughshares, 12 axes, shovels, hoes, pickaxes, crowbars, 4 adzes, chisels, saws. To be contributed pro rata. The cattle for the ranchos were to be a loan to be repaid in 6 years.

ant in the troubles with Padre Mercado at San Rafael. In May a controversy arose on the subject of mission discipline, the padre demanding the surrender of an offender arrested by the corporal of the escolta, who refused, by Vallejo's order, as he claimed. Mercado in an arrogant and threatening manner defended his authority to punish the neophytes as he pleased, while the comandante, though ordering the neophyte in this case given up, denied the padre's right to interfere in any but minor offences.[39] In August, Corporal Ignacio Pacheco of the escolta, asking for meat for his men, was told by Mercado that "he did not furnish meat to feed wolves," whereupon Pacheco caused a sheep of the mission flock to be killed, and the padre was furious. In the resulting correspondence Mercado used very intemperate and insulting language both to Vallejo and to the soldiers, whom he repeatedly designated as a pack of thieves. In turn he was charged by Vallejo with falsehood.[40] Finally on November 16th a body of gentiles belonging to the rancherías of Pulia approached San Rafael, as they had been encouraged to do by Figueroa through Vallejo, with a view to encourage friendly relations. Fifteen Indians of the party came under Toribio to speak with the padre, who put off the interview until next day. During the night a robbery was committed, which was attributed by Mercado to the guests, and they were therefore seized and sent as prisoners to San Francisco. On the morning of the 20th, the warlike missionary, fearing as he claimed that the gentiles would attack the mission to liberate their companions, sent out his majordomo Molina with thirty-seven armed neophytes, who surprised the strangers, killed twenty-one, wounded many more, and captured twenty men,

[39] Letter of Vallejo May 9th, and of Mercado May 9th, 17th, in *Vallejo, Doc.*, MS., ii. 43, 141, 149.

[40] Letters of Pacheco and Mercado Aug. 22d, and of Vallejo Aug. 23d, Oct. 18th, in *Vallejo, Doc.*, MS., ii. 84, 110, 167-8. Vallejo advises Pacheco to act very carefully, to avoid all disputes, and to take no supplies without politely asking the missionary first.

women, and children, having on their side five wounded, one of the number mortally. This achievement was coolly reported by Mercado to Figueroa in a letter of the 25th, with a request for reënforcements to aid in pacifying the rancherías. The governor was naturally indignant that his promises to the Indians had been thus shamefully violated, and with the advice of Asesor Gomez, sent the case to Prefect García Diego, the competent ecclesiastical judge. The prefect suspended Mercado from his ministry, summoned him to Santa Clara, and announced his intention to send him to his college for trial. Meanwhile Vallejo, by Figueroa's orders, liberated Toribio and his companions at San Francisco; went to San Rafael with a military force and freed the captives there; and then made a tour through the rancherías to Solano, pacifying the excited Indians, and explaining to them Figueroa's kind intentions and the wickedness of Padre Mercado, dilating on the latter topic very reluctantly—perhaps. In the middle of the next year, Mercado was freed from arrest and restored to San Rafael, two friars having been sent to make an investigation, and having learned from fourteen witnesses that the padre had nothing to do with the outrage![41]

Returning to the topic of secularization, or to progress in that direction during 1833, I have first to notice Figueroa's instructions on this point from the Mexican government — instructions that emanated from the same administration which had appointed Victoria, and similar in spirit probably to those given that officer, and certainly to those under which Écheandía

---

[41] *Mercado, Expediente de papeles tocantes á la matanza de Indios hecha por órden del P. Ministro de S. Rafael, 1833,* MS., in *Monterey, Arch.,* i. 32-7; *Vallejo, Doc.,* MS., ii. 200; xxxi. 58; *Arch. Arzob.,* MS., v. pt ii. 3; *Dept. St. Pap.,* MS., iii. 137-8; *Id., Ben.,* ii. 9-10; being communications of Mercado, Figueroa, Vallejo, Gomez, Sanchez, and García Diego, some of them duplicated in the different archives referred to. The affair is also briefly mentioned in *Vallejo, Hist. Cal.,* MS., iii. 74-5; *Alvarado, Hist. Cal.,* MS., ii. 211.

had acted.   The necessity for a change was recognized,
and the duty of the new ruler, as of his predecessors,
was to ascertain and report the best practical methods.
Minister Alaman disapproved in the vice-president's
name Echeandía's decree of 1831: both because he
had gone far beyond his authority in issuing such a
decree, and because some of its provisions were not
in accord, as pointed out, with the law of 1813, on
which it purported to be founded; and he ordered
Figueroa, if Echeandía's order had to any extent been
obeyed, to restore the missions to the position they
held before its publication.   Yet he was to study the
question closely, to ascertain what missions were in a
condition to be secularized according to the law of
1813, and to report such a plan as he might deem
most expedient.[42]

Figueroa's general instructions from Minister Ortiz
Monasterio, also bearing the date of May 17th, authorized him to go practically much further toward
secularization than did the document just mentioned.
Article 4 was as follows: "It being a matter of the
greatest necessity that the neophytes rise from the
state of abasement to which they find themselves reduced, you will cause to be distributed to such as are
fitted for it such fields of the mission lands as they
may be capable of cultivating, in order that they may
thus become fond of labor and may go on acquiring
property; but there must be kept undistributed the
lands necessary for the support of divine worship,
schools, and other objects of common utility.   By
this means, for the mission system may be gradually

[42] May 17, 1832, Alaman to F., in *St. Pap., Miss. and Colon.*, MS., ii. 33–
5; *Arch. Arzob.*, MS., v. pt i. 102–6. Cárlos Carrillo wrote from Mex. in 1832
that no change would at present be made in the mission system. *Carrillo,
Cartas*, MS., 231.   As an evidence of F.'s feeling on the mission system, I
cite a recommendation in favor of a neophyte of S. Juan Capistrano, directed
to Echeandía in 1826, from Sonora, in which he doubts not that E. 'will
protect those unfortunates who from necessity have to bear all the rigor of
those friars.' *Dept. St. Pap., Ben. Mil.*, MS., lvii. 21.   F., in his *Manifiesto*,
2–3, notes his instructions, or their general purport.   July 7, 1832, from Acapulco he promises the min. of rel. to obey his instructions on arrival. *St. Pap.,
Miss. and Colon.*, MS., ii. 36–7.

substituted another more adapted to the interests of the territory, the influence of the missionaries may be lessened until they retain only the spiritual administration, and thus in fact the missions may be secularized. Yet for all this, it is necessary to act with prudence and tact, so as to cause no discontent among the missionaries, with whom care is to be taken to preserve the greatest harmony; and to that end are enclosed private letters written by the vice-president to some of the most influential friars." [43]

Before Figueroa's arrival in the middle of January 1833, I find no record that Echeandía had taken any steps to carry into effect his regulations beyond the appointment of comisionados; [44] but on January 29th, possibly before he knew of Figueroa's arrival, he issued a new regulation for officers of justice and police in the missions of San Diego district. The order dealt chiefly with the penalties for various minor offences and the routine duties of the local officers who were to inflict them. It was probably never enforced, and requires only a mention, with the remark that it was intended to relieve the Indians from arbitrary and excessive punishments. [45] Echeandía informed Figueroa that he had been about to commence the distribution of lands at San Diego, but had suspended operations on hearing of the new governor's arrival. In the same communication he denounced the policy and acts of the friars, and urged Figueroa to adopt

---

[43] *Figueroa, Instrucciones Generales*, MS., p. 33–4.   In art. 5, Indian youths are required to be selected and sent to Mexico for education, with a view to make ministers of them later.

[44] These were Capt. Portilla at S. Luis Rey, Alf. Ramirez at S. Diego, Alf. Rocha at S. Juan Capistrano, and Alf. Valle at S. Gabriel. *Dept. St. Pap.*, MS., iii. 87, 89.   Feb. 10th, the comandante of S. Luis calls for reënforcements to check disorders among the Indians arising from the distribution of lands. *Id., Ben. Pref. y Juzg.*, v. 76.

[45] *Echeandía, Reglamento para los encargados de justicia y policía en las misiones del departamento de S. Diego, 1833*, MS.   An annexed note says: 'This regulation was ordered to be observed to restrain the arbitrary way in which missionaries, majordomos, and corporals of escolta caused the neophytes to be flogged, imprisoned, and outraged in other ways for any fault in the community labors or in other precepts which they were tyranically forced to observe. Echeandía.'

strict measures in favor of the Indians.[46] Finally,
on March 19th, Echeandía directed to Figueroa the
long letter, already often cited, in which he fully
reported and defended his past policy. In this communication, besides the arguments already noticed, he
attempted, in a manner satisfactory to himself, to
overthrow the reasoning of Minister Alaman against
his famous decree, and he also proposed a scheme of
converting gentiles on the frontiers, through the
agency of old neophytes and military guards.[47]

Meanwhile Figueroa prepared to make the investigations required by his instructions. His views were
for the most part identical with those of Echeandía,
but he had of course to encounter the same obstacles
which had prevented that officer during the earlier
years of his rule from carrying out his instructions.
He announced February 18th to Echeandía his policy
and his general approval of the latter's views, stating
that he hoped to begin the distribution of lands at
San Diego in April. This was to be made known to
the Indians, who were to be informed of the governor's purpose to protect their liberties but at the
same time to allow no license.[48] After some delay on
account of illness, Figueroa went south at the end of

[46] Feb. 7, 1833, E. to F., in *Vallejo, Doc.*, MS., xxxi. 25, enclosing documents to prove the abuses committed by the friars of the south, and the
malicious exaggeration of all they say against the proposed reforms. Each
padre does as he pleases, on the excuse that to do otherwise he must have his
prelate's orders, which are not given. The prelate is Duran, a Spaniard and
pronounced royalist, only saved from expulsion by his intimate friendship
with Victoria. The *gente de razon* pay no parochial tax, are entertained
gratis by the friars, and receive loans and gifts from the missions; therefore
the magistrate who attempts to protect the Indians is a shining mark for
popular attack. Still he has been regaining little by little the civil authority
usurped by the friars, and urges Figueroa to continue the same policy. On
the same date were sent the complaints of a S. Diego Indian, Tomás Tajachi,
against Argüello particularly, whom Echeandía thought it best to replace with
some officer less obnoxious to the Indians. *Arch. Arzob.*, MS., v. pt i. 74–6,
107–9.

[47] *Echeandía, Carta que dirige á D. José Figueroa, 1833*, MS., p. 38–41,
56–7.

[48] Feb. 18, 1833, F. to E., and also to Santiago Argüello. *Vallejo, Doc.*,
MS., xxxi. 26–7. F. evidently feared a revolt of the Indians. Feb. 10th,
J. A. Carrillo writes that he has complied with orders as to sustaining the
gov.'s authority; and will go to S. Gabriel with the síndico of the ayunt. to
harangue the Ind. and tranquillize them. *Arch. Arzob.*, MS., v. pt i. 76.

June. The result of his investigations was to convince
him that any general measure of secularization would
be ruinous, and that a change of system, though
necessary, must be very gradually effected. So he
reported to the Mexican government, and to President Duran and Prefect García Diego in July.[49] To
the secretary of the interior he described the character and circumstances of the neophytes, representing
them as totally unfit by nature and training for sudden emancipation. To the prelates he stated that
the partition of lands at San Diego would be only
partial and provisional, though insisting that all qualified neophytes must be freed from missionary control,
and calling for their views on the general subject.
He also issued a series of regulations on gradual
emancipation, to go into effect provisionally until approved by the diputacion and by the supreme government.[50]

[49] July 15, 1833, F. to Duran; July 20th, to sec. of int.; July 27th, to
García Diego. *Vallejo, Doc.*, MS., xxxi. 27, 33, 29. F. describes the neophytes as children, with a natural predilection for the customs of their ances-
tors, and for a savage life without work. During their reduction they had
learned, perforce, only to cultivate the soil imperfectly, to practise some
rude industries, and to manage horses, besides receiving a slight and superficial religious instruction. They had been kept intentionally in the most
abject ignorance, the padres having always opposed their education. If freed
at once from their degrading servitude, they would soon from proprietors
become beggars, having bartered their possessions for liquor and gewgaws.
They would return to the wilderness and join the wild Indians in stealing
cattle and horses for sale to New Mexicans and foreigners.

[50] *Figueroa, Prevenciones provisionales para la emancipacion de Indios reducidos, 15 de Julio, 1833,* MS.
1. The gefe político will determine the number to be emancipated in each
mission and the time at which it is to be done, appointing the comisionados
deemed necessary to carry out these *prevenciones*. 2. Those emancipated will
be those who have been more than 12 years Christians, married or widowers
with children, knowing how to cultivate the soil or having some trade, and
having 'application to work.' The selection is to be made by the comisionados in conjunction with the ministers of each mission. 3. The emancipated
are to remain subordinate to the respective authorities, and to the padres of
the mission who will exercise over them the functions of parish priest in all
that concerns the spiritual administration. 4. The emancipated will receive
seed for their first sowing, and for a year the customary mission rations; but
during that time they must assist the mission during planting and harvest,
and at other times as they may be summoned—not all at a time—by the minister and the alcalde acting in concert and so arranging the tasks that neither
the mission work nor that of private individuals shall suffer. 5. The comisionados in accord with the ministers will select a fitting spot as near the
coast as possible, and between the missions on the high road, where the

Shortly before the *prevenciones de emancipacion* were issued, President Duran had written to Figueroa a strong letter on the subject, basing his opposition to emancipation on the state of things which he had found to exist at Los Angeles, and by which he claimed to have been undeceived and surprised. The

emancipated may form a pueblo if there be a sufficient number of families. There they will be given lots of a size corresponding to the amount of land at the place, where they may build their houses so as to form streets and plaza symmetrically as provided by ancient and modern laws. Lands will likewise be assigned for *egidos* of the pueblo. 6. The newly founded pueblos—according to decree of May 23, 1812—will remain for the present attached to the nearest municipality or military command, which, in accordance with laws and regulations in force and with these *prevenciones*, will care for the police, embellishment, order, and other objects of economical government in the pueblos intrusted to their care. 7. As the emancipated cease to be minors and enter upon the enjoyment of citizens' rights, the authorities will see that they are considered on terms of equality with others in elections and hold municipal offices according to fitness and good conduct. Still in order that they may be accustomed and taught to govern according to the federal system, there are to be appointed annually from their number an alcalde, 2 regidores, and a síndico procurador, to be intrusted with the economical government of their pueblo, but to remain subject in the administration of justice, civil and criminal, to the judges of first instance and other superior tribunals. 8. They must immediately build houses in regular order on their lots, which they must enclose with fruit trees or other useful trees. 9. The minister and comisionado will assign the best land nearest the pueblo, where there will be given to each family a field, and to the pueblo grazing lands and 2 *caballerías* of land for *propios*, all in the name of the Mexican nation. 10. Fields to be 200 varas square, and common grazing lands in proportion to the amount of live-stock up to 2 *sitios* or a little more. 11. Products of land and property of the *propios* to be applied to expense of worship, church, public buildings, schools, etc. Such property to be administered by a majordomo, elected for 4 years from the emancipated and watched by the alcalde and priest, who may remove him for cause, and who are to use the product of the property for the purposes specified, with the approval of the gefe político. Routine of annual reports and accounts. 12. The comisionado and priest to render full report with lists, etc., of the new foundations. 13. The gefe político to give titles to lands, and license to use a mark for cattle. 14, 15. Each family to receive from the mission property 2 mares, 2 cows, 2 ewes, with implements, etc., but all subject to variation according to the circumstances of the mission and judgment of comisionado and priest. 16. 100 cattle and 25 horses to be given for the *propios* if the mission has sufficient to do so; otherwise, what it can give. 17. Each individual will mark his animals; but for two years they are to be tended in common by persons appointed alternately by the alcalde for the purpose. For one year no animal can be killed or sold; nor afterwards all the stock of any individual. Penalty, a return to mission life. 18. They will enjoy in common the use of water, grass, wood, etc., on the lands assigned for *egidos* and pasturage. 19. The land to be the property of the individual to whom it is assigned, and of his heirs; but it cannot be divided nor transferred. 20. No mortgage, lien, or mortmain title can be imposed on the land, under penalty of confiscation. 21. The emancipated must aid in the common work of the pueblo on ditches, dams, corrals, rodeos, constructing church and other public buildings. They must mark the boundaries of their fields with useful trees. 22. Land left vacant by the death of the owner without heirs reverts to the nation. 23. The emancipated

two or three hundred Indian vecinos of that town
were beyond all comparison more unfortunate and
oppressed than any in the missions. Not one had a
garden, a yoke of oxen, a horse, or a house fit for a
rational being. Instead of the equality so much
talked about, the Indians swept the streets and did
all the menial work. For offences scarcely noticed
in others, they were bound naked over a cannon to
receive 100 blows. They were in reality slaves, being bound for a whole year by an advance of some
trifle, since no Indian ever looked beyond the present.
They had no ambition for liberty except for savage
liberty and vicious license, which they would purchase
at the cost of a thousand oppressions. Duran was
convinced by experience and from conversation with
practical men that emancipation would result in slavery
or savagism to the Indians and in destruction to all
their property; and he begged the governor to consider well the results before deciding a subject "worthy
the wisdom of a whole congress."[51] Yet on receipt
of the regulations Duran offered no general opposition to the plan, limiting his criticism to the recommendation of here and there a minor change in some
of the articles, calling for no special attention. His
closing suggestion was as follows: "If after three or
four years it shall be noted that the *emancipados*
depend on wild fruits for subsistence, that they
allow their live-stock to decrease, that they neglect
their planting and other labors in a spirit of vagabondage, or that they manifest no zeal or liking for a
rational and civilized life, and if, being several times
warned, they do not mend, then they shall be returned

who may neglect their work and stock, or dissipate them, or abandon their
homes to give themselves up to vagabondage, idleness, and vice, will be submitted anew to the mission by decision of the alcalde and priest, who must,
however, give two previous warnings, with time to reform.   24. The authorities will attend to the exact enforcement of these regulations, and will be
responsible for infractions if known and not prevented.
    [51] July 3, 1833, D. to F., in *Arch. Arzob.*, MS., v. pt i. 88–91. On June
17th, D. had written on the unsatisfactory condition of the Indians at S.
Diego and S. Luis, made worse by the pernicious example of Portilla's soldiers. *Id.*, v. pt i. 78–9. Also to same effect on July 19th. *Id.*, 101.

to their missions," the author having of course little doubt that they would eventually be thus returned.[52]

While Figueroa's plan was not so radical as to greatly excite the opposition even of friars, yet when he attempted its execution he encountered obstacles and found no popular enthusiasm in its favor. It was tolerated by the padres as an experiment not seriously interfering with the mission system, nor very destructive to their interest in the mission property, but sure to result in proving the utter incapacity of the Indians for self-government. But, for the same reasons largely, it was only passively approved by the gente de razon, who saw in it no direct avenue to the mission lands and herds and servants, while the neophytes themselves were ambitious only to have the property to dispose of as they pleased, and could see little that was attractive in pueblo life under authority, in a living that was to be earned, in having fields that must be tilled, and cattle that could not be bartered. The governor, however, made an earnest effort to give the Indians the civil liberty so little prized by them, but so valuable in the eyes of Mexican theorists. He visited the southern missions in person, exhorting the assembled neophytes and explaining to them the advantages of the proffered freedom. Of one hundred and sixty families at San Diego and San Luis, qualified according to the standard established, only ten could be induced to accept emancipation before Figueroa started on his return to the north.[53] He persevered in his efforts nevertheless, appointing captains Argüello and Portilla as comisionados. The results cannot be exactly known. Some families were emancipated at San Diego and San Luis, but not enough apparently to form a new pueblo; though they received lands, managed their own property, and became citizens.

[52] *Duran, Crítica sobre las Prevenciones de Emancipacion, 1833*, MS. Dated at S. Diego July 16th.
[53] Oct. 5th, F. at Sta B. *St. Pap., Miss. and Colon.*, MS., ii. 72.

At San Juan Capistrano the experiment was tried
on a larger scale. All seem to have been emancipated, and lands were assigned at the mission, which
thus became virtually a pueblo in October, under the
prevenciones of July, and certain special supplementary rules issued at this time. I find no evidence
that any neophytes at all were emancipated this year
north of San Juan.[54]

In addition to his efforts in the direction of experimental and partial emancipation, Figueroa also kept
in view his obligation to report on a plan for formal
secularization. In August he called upon the diputacion, and on the prelates of the two missionary

[54] July 19, 1883, F. appoints Argüello comisionado for S. Diego, notifying
also Duran. *Vallejo, Doc.*, MS., xxxi. 31–2. Sept. 21st, Portilla to F. On
the 23d he will begin the distribution to the neophytes of San Juan Capistrano of their lands at S. Mateo, the best site on the mission tract. The
Ind. of S. Luis will build their houses at once (where it is not stated), while
the women harvest the melons. In another letter of the same date P. says
the Ind. of S. Juan are not willing to go to S. Mateo, not understanding why
their lands should not be assigned at the mission, where they have already
well watered lots on which they are supporting themselves without aid from
the mission. F. at first ordered a temporary suspension of the distribution at
S. Mateo, and on Oct. 13th granted the petition of the Ind., ordered lands
to be assigned at the mission under the rules, and issued some supplementary
rules for their guidance. *Id.*, xxxi. 38. On Oct. 5th, he had announced his
intention in a report to Mexico to emancipate all the neophytes of S. Juan,
who seemed more civilized than others. *St. Pap., Miss. and Colon.*, MS., ii.
72. It may therefore be supposed that these regulations were put in force.
Sept. 27th, Argüello to F. Reports progress, or lack of it, at S. Diego and
S. Luis. He says that of 59 heads of families at S. Diego only two wished
for emancipation, unless they could have their property to do what they
pleased with it; but there were 14 families of 33 persons from S. Dieguito
who wished to join the two and form a pueblo, and he had granted their
petition and was going to assign their lands. (It is not stated where, nor is
there any evidence that he did so.) At S. Luis Rey he was even less successful; for out of 108 families none desired emancipation, though 4 married
men were somewhat non-committal on the subject. *Id.*, xxxi. 36–7. Oct.
3d, M. G. Vallejo to F. Thanks God that the true owners of the missions
begin to enjoy their rights. 'I have rejoiced from the bottom of my heart
at the liberation of these poor people from the clutches of the missionaries.
The great supply of men and dollars the padres have hitherto had will now,
though rather late, come to an end!' *St. Pap., Miss. and Colon.*, MS., ii. 318.
Oct. 15th, in a decree on elections F. declares that the neophytes are not
citizens, but the *emancipados* can vote. *Dept. St. Pap., Ang.*, MS., xi. 12;
Id., S. José, MS., iv. 131. Nov. 26th, F. directs Portilla to warn the 'townsmen' of S. Juan that they must do nothing but what is allowed in the reglamento, and must obey orders sent to Portilla. The ayunt. of Los Angeles
has nothing to do with the management of their property—only having
jurisdiction in civil and criminal matters. P. is to instruct them in their
rights and duties, and bid them pay no heed to idle rumors. *Dept. St. Pap.,
Ben. Mil.*, MS., lxxix. 12.

bands, to state what missions were in a condition to
be secularized under the law of 1813; what objections
to secularization existed; and what would be the best
means to be employed.[55] The diputacion held no
session this year, or at least has left no record of its
reply; but both Duran and García Diego gave their
views on the subject, the former in several communications, the latter in a single one dated September
24th. There was nothing in the argument of the
Zacatecan prefect that demands extended notice.
He admitted that all the missions under his charge—
except Solano, which lacked some weeks of the required ten years—were subject to secularization according to the law of 1813; but he believed that law
could not be applied to California without inevitable
ruin to the missions and to the neophytes.[56]

President Duran of course opposed the change, and
used to some extent the old arguments, with which,
coming from him and others, the reader is familiar;
but he also seems to have put himself as fully as possible in the governor's place, and admitting for the
time that a change was inevitable, to have given in
good faith his views respecting the best means to be
employed. He noted two great obstacles to be overcome: first, the natural apathy, indolence, and in-
competency of the neophytes, acknowledged by every
intelligent man who had any experience in the matter;
and second, the burdens imposed on the missions by
circumstances, chiefly that of supporting the troops

---

[55] Aug. 2, 1833. *St. Pap., Miss. and Colon.*, MS., ii. 96; *Arch. Arzob.*,
MS., v. pt i. 106.

[56] *García Diego, Parecer del Padre Prefecto sobre Proyecto de Secularizacion,
1833*, MS. The law, he claims, was made 2,000 leagues away by men who had
no knowledge of the character and needs of Californian Indians. Emancipated,
the Ind. would return to nakedness and savagism. Good men would not be
chosen for alcaldes. The govt had never secularized the missions of Tarahu-
mara and Sonora, though older than those of Cal. The padres would content
themselves with saying mass and confessing applicants. It is only by force
that Ind. can be made to attend to religious duties. The bishop has no
curates, and the friars would not serve as such, etc. It would seem that F.
also addressed his inquiries to others; for Oct. 19th, Alf. José Sanchez reports S. F., S. José, and Solano as in a condition to be secularized, the Indians being altogether competent. *St. Pap., Miss. and Colon.*, MS., ii. 96.

as they had done for over twenty years. Of course the Indians would do nothing for the support of the troops after secularization, and if any of their property were taken by force, they would find means to do away with the rest and escape to the wilderness and savagism. Therefore, before effecting any radical change, the government must be sure respecting resources for the future. The padre disclaimed any opposition by himself or his associates from motives of interest to their college or to themselves. The law of 1813 was altogether inadequate, having been framed by men who knew nothing of the subject in its Californian phases. The ten-year rule should be ignored, and some other adopted, if the results of half a century's work were to be saved.

Three plans were suggested by Duran. The first was to establish a new line of missions and presidios east of the old line, secularize the old establishments into Indian pueblos, and give the neophytes their choice between remaining in the pueblos or being attached to the new missions. This would effectually prevent them from escaping from civilization, and would also free the territory from the danger of attack and outrage at the hands of renegade neophytes, hostile gentiles, and ambitious foreigners. This plan, though the best, was probably impracticable, because the national government could not be induced to bear the expense. The second plan, though not so expeditious, was sure, and would lead to the same result. It was to have a bishop appointed for California, a live man, not bent on leading a life of ease, and to give him the exclusive control of all tithes under the protection but not direction of the governor. With the means placed at his disposal, the bishop could in a few years have in operation a seminary of ecclesiastical education, a college of missionaries, a cathedral, and all the necessary agencies for converting gentiles and furnishing curates. Then the missions might be secularized without risk. The third expedient, less desirable than the others, was a partial and experimental secularization of certain old missions, eight of which are named, where there have been no new conversions for many years. A portion of the property might be distributed, and the rest kept as a community fund, administered by stewards of their own choice, free from tithes, and devoted to the support of the spiritual administration. The missionary should have for a time a fatherly control, and the alcaldes and majordomos should be responsible for losses and evils resulting from a failure to follow his advice. The neophytes should be made to understand that if they neglect their privileges they will be again put under the padres. With these precautions, if also the government will see that the gente de razon are obliged to set a better example, the evils of secularization may be reduced to a minimum.[57]

Figueroa had now become convinced that any general measure of secularization would be productive of great injury to the interests of California. In his report of July 20th, he had advocated a gradual emancipation, in which he thought the friars might be induced to coöperate.[53] Now, having heard that a bill for secularization had been introduced in congress, he made haste to lay before the government, in his report of October 5th, the results of his own experience and the views of Duran and García Diego, with whom he agreed to the extent of opposing any sudden and radical change in the mission system, as involving total destruction of all the property with possible danger to the security of the territory. He was inclined to favor Duran's plan of a partial and experimental change at the oldest missions.[59] It

[57] *Duran, Proyectos de Secularizacion de Misiones, 1833*, MS. On Oct. 10th Duran asks earnestly that Gov. F. use his influence to have the padres relieved of the mission temporalities, promising to serve *en lo espiritual* until ministers can be sent to replace them. No reason is given except that the padres are old and worn out.

[58] *Vallejo, Doc. Hist. Cal.*, MS., xxxi. 33.

[59] *Figueroa, Informe en que se opone al Proyecto de Secularizacion, 1833*, MS. The 8 missions mentioned by Duran were: S. Juan Capistrano, S. Buenaventura, Sta Bárbara, Purísima, S. Antonio, S. Cárlos, Sta Cruz, and S. Francisco.

must be noticed that Figueroa had reported in favor
of expelling Padres Duran and Sarría from the territory. Their conduct in private and religious matters
was praiseworthy; but politically they were opposed
to the national interests, and they had not scrupled
to use their official position, influence, and wealth to
spread their opinions, opposing the distribution of
lands, freedom of the press, and popular sovereignty,
and desiring the reëstablishment of the inquisition.[60]
Figueroa's advice, whatever might otherwise have
been its effect, came too late. The national congress,
without waiting for the governor's report, and largely
through the influence of the Híjar and Padrés party,
as we have seen, had not only discussed a bill for
secularization, but had passed it on the 17th of August.[61] This law simply provided that the missions

---

[60] Aug. 17, 1833, F. to sup. govt, in answer to an order referring to him
Echeandía's complaints against the friars and Victoria's defense of their conduct. *Dept. St. Pap.*, MS., iii. 139–40.

[61] *Decreto del Congreso Mejicano secularizando las Misiones, 17 de Agosto de
1833.* In *Arrillaga, Recopilacion*, 1833, p. 19–21; *Dublan* and *Lozano, Leg.
Mex.*, ii. 548, iii. 96; *Vallejo, Doc.*, MS., ii. 165; *Halleck's Report*, 125, 148–9;
Dwinelle's Colon. Hist., add., 26–7; *Jones' Report*, 59; *I. Rockwell*, 455;
Wheeler's Land Titles, 9–10; *Bandini, Doc.*, MS., 36; *Hayes' Mission Book*, i.
218; *Lassepas, Baja Cal.*, 206–7; *Muhlenpfordt, Mejico*, ii. 450. Art. 1. The
govt will proceed to secularize the missions of Upper and Lower California.
2. In each mission shall be established a parish under a priest of the secular
clergy, with a salary of from $2,000 to $2,500, as the govt may determine.
3. These curates can collect no fee for marriages, baptisms, burials, or any
other service. As to fees of pomp, they may receive such as may be expressly
allowed in the tariff to be formed with the least possible delay for that purpose by the bishop of the diocese and approved by the sup. govt. 4. To the
parishes are given the churches of each mission, with the sacred vessels, vestments, and other appurtenances now possessed by each; and also such rooms
adjoining the church as in the judgment of the govt may be deemed necessary for the most fitting service of the parish. 5. For each parish the govt
will provide a burial-ground outside the settlement. 6. $500 per year are
assigned as an endowment for public worship and for servitors in each parish.
7. Of the buildings belonging to each mission, there shall be assigned the
most appropriate as a dwelling for the curate, with land not exceeding 200
varas square; and the other buildings shall be used as an ayuntamiento-
house, primary schools, public establishments, and work-shops. 8. In order
to provide promptly and effectually for the spiritual needs of the Californias,
there is to be established a vicar-generalship at the capital of Alta Cal., with
jurisdiction over both territories; and the diocesan will confer the corresponding powers, as complete as possible. 9. As an endowment of this vicarship
$3,000 are assigned, from which all expenses of the office must be paid, no fees
being allowed on any pretext. 10. If for any reason the curate of the capital or of any other parish shall hold the vicarship, he will receive $1,500 in
addition to his allowance as curate. 11. No custom can be introduced oblig-

should be converted into parishes, under the management of the ordinary ecclesiastical authorities, and regulated some details of that management. Respecting the real difficulties of secularization, the disposition to be made of mission property, and the obstacles existing in California, it was silent. Supplementary regulations were apparently contemplated, though not mentioned; and such regulations, or what may in a certain sense be construed as such, will be noticed a little later in the instructions to José María Híjar. By the law of August 17th, the expense of putting curates and a vicar in charge of the missions, and also as it appears of supporting them in their new positions—that is, all the expense arising from the execution of the law—was to be paid from the pious fund. By a later decree of November 26th, the government was authorized "to adopt all measures to insure the colonization, and make effective the secularization of the missions, of Alta and Baja California, using for that purpose in the most convenient manner the estates of the pious fund of those territories, in order to furnish resources to the commission and families now in this capital and intending to go there."[62]

We have seen that ten new padres had come to California in 1833 to reënforce the missionary band; but two of the Fernandinos died this year, José Bernardo Sanchez, ex-president, and Luis Gil y Taboada;

ing the inhabitants of Cal. to make oblations, however pious they may be or necessary they may be declared; and neither time nor consent of the citizens can give them any force or virtue. 12. The govt will see to it that the diocesan do his part in carrying out the objects of this law. 13. When the new curates have been named, the govt will gratuitously furnish a passage for them and their families by sea; and besides may give to each for the journey by land from $400 to $800, according to the distance and number of family. 14. The govt will pay the passage of returning missionaries; and in order that they may return comfortably by land to their college or convent, may give to each from $200 to $300, and at discretion whatever may be necessary in order that those who have not sworn the independence may leave the republic. 15. The sup. govt will meet the expenses authorized by this law from the product of the estates, capital, and revenues at present recognized as the pious fund of Cal. missions.

[62] Decree of Nov. 26, 1833, circulated by the secretary on the same date, and published in a bando of Dec. 2d. *Arrillaga, Recop.*, 1833, p. 311–12; *Sup. Govt St. Pap.*, MS., ix. 1; *Hayes' Mission Book*, i. 218.

and one, José Viader, left the country.   If we add to
these losses the five padres who had died, and one
who had left California in 1831–2, we have a gain of
only one during the three years covered by this chapter, notwithstanding the coming of the Zacatecanos.

Narciso Duran succeeded Sanchez as president of
the missions in June 1831, being also prelate, vicar,
ecclesiastical judge, and apparently vice-prefecto,[63]
there being no change in 1834–5 or the period included in the following chapter.   Duran's authority
was confined to the missions south of San Antonio
after the coming of the Zacatecanos in March 1833.
Padre Sarría, as already noted, had held the office of
comisario prefecto down to 1830; but while there is
no record of his ceasing to hold that office or that a
successor was appointed, neither is there any evidence
that he or any other friar performed any duties of
the position after 1830, and he is spoken of in 1833
as ex-prefect.[64]   Therefore we must conclude that the
office of prefect was abolished during these years so
far as the Fernandinos were concerned.   It is to be
noted that Padre Sanchez issued several papers after
he left the presidency in 1831, which by their tone
would indicate that he still held some authority over
the friars, but there is no other evidence that such was
the case.   In the north, García Diego was comisario
prefecto of the Zacatecanos during the period covered
by this chapter and the next, Rafael Moreno being
president and vice-prefect from the beginning of 1834.[65]

[63] *Arch. Arzob.*, MS., v. pt i. 43; *S. Gabriel.*, *Lib. Mision*, MS., 41; *Arch.
Sta B.*, MS., vii. 7; *Arch.*, *Obispado*, MS., 23.   He is in a few documents addressed as prefect, but this was probably an error.

[64] *Arch.*, *Misiones*, MS., ii. 678.   In *Id.*, 702, Duran is addressed by
Figueroa as presidente prefecto.

[65] *S. José*, *Patentes*, MS., 190-213.   Both were re-elected in 1835.   P.
Gonzalez was made prefect provisionally in 1835.

CHAPTER XII.

MISSION AND INDIAN AFFAIRS.

1834-1835.

Emancipation—Indian Pueblos—The Diputacion—Figureoa's Policy—
Mexican Law of April 1834—Provisional Regulations of August
9th—Híjar's Instructions—Their Meaning—The Reglamento in
Practice—Local Results—Ten Missions Secularized—Views of the
Padres—Supplementary Regulations of Nov. 4th—Destruction of
Mission Property by the Friars—Slaughter of Cattle—Stipends
in 1835—Mission Supplies—Mission Ranchos—García Diego's Suggestions—Local Items of 1835—Six Missions Secularized—The Fernandinos Content—Mexican Decree of Nov. 9th—Mission Statistics, 1831-5—Seasons—Pestilence—Indian Affairs, 1831-5.

There is no positive record that Figueroa's eman-
cipatory experiments had led to the foundation of any
other Indian pueblo than that at San Juan Capistrano
before the end of 1833. It is possible, however, that
two others were founded before that date, San Dieguito
by the ex-neophytes of San Diego, and Las Flores by
those of San Luis Rey. At any rate, Figueroa in
his opening address before the diputacion, May 1,
1834, stated that the three pueblos had not only been
established, but were flourishing, the difference between the condition of the townsmen and of the neophytes being already noticeable.[1] And this is all
that is known of secularization in the first quarter of
the year.

In his discourse the governor recapitulated his past
efforts, and announced that the results of his plan of
gradual emancipation, though impeded by his other

[1] *Figueroa, Discurso de Apertura, 1834,* MS.

onerous duties and by lack of competent subordinates, had been most encouraging until interrupted by the arrival of the secularization law of August 17th, which compelled him to await further instructions. The law was submitted to the diputacion with a request for advice as to its enforcement. The deliberations of that body on mission management in May and June were extensive, but barren of results. Various propositions, relating to the measurement or assignment of mission lands, to the prevention of unnecessary slaughter of mission cattle, to the enforced rendering of inventories by the padres pending secularization, were introduced, referred to committees, reported back, and discussed; but practically nothing was accomplished. In view of the Mexican law of August 1833, and of the knowledge that Híjar had been appointed commissioner of colonization, Figueroa felt doubtful about his powers to take any action, and the vocales were easily induced to adopt his views. It was resolved June 3d that the gefe político had no authority to execute the law, though some steps might be taken should circumstances require it; that the diputacion should recommend the assignment of certain property to the municipal funds of the new pueblos, and that the government should also be urged not to delay secularization even in the absence of regular curates, since the friars could act as such temporarily.[2]

Though still doubtful, or at least affecting doubt, as to his powers in the matter, Figueroa was induced to change his mind so far as to admit that the 'cir-

[2] *Leg. Rec.*, MS., ii. 44–6, 51, 60–1, 67–8, 70–2, 83–6, 88–9, 92–5, 98–103, 108–11. The mission property recommended for the *fondo de propios* included 1,000 head of cattle and horses, the gardens and vineyards, land for tillage and for the stock, and the surplus buildings after secularization was provided for. May 2d, the governor's old inquiry of Aug. 2, 1833, as to what missions were in a condition to be secularized under the law of 1813, was received, which is another proof that there had been no session in 1833. By the action of May 22d and June 15th the unnecessary slaughter of mission cattle was prohibited. But more on this elsewhere. It was ordered that vacant mission lands should be granted according to the colonization law. This was published in a bando. *Arch. Obispado*, MS., 90; *Sta Cruz, Arch.*, MS., 11.

cumstances' required action as provided for in the previous resolutions, without awaiting special instructions from the government or the arrival of its commissioner. The reason alleged was that in the long interval between the passage and enforcement of the secularization law, the mission property was in danger of being wasted by maleadministration—a reason not wholly without force. In reality, however, the position of Figueroa in 1834 did not differ much from that of Echeandía in 1831. Each desired to advance the scheme of secularization, each had instructions to that effect, each founded his action on a national law—of Spain in one case and of Mexico in the other—each expected the early arrival of a successor, each preferred from motives of personal pride and for the personal interests of friends and supporters that the change should be inaugurated by himself rather than by his successor, and each had the support of the diputacion. Both knew perfectly well that they had strictly no legal right to act in the matter, and that the motives alleged, though of some weight, were not urgent for immediate action; yet both chose to assume the responsibility of such action. Figueroa's act, if somewhat less arbitrary and uncalled for than that of Echeandía, was none the less a trick. Unlike Echeandía's, but largely from accidental causes, it proved to a certain extent successful. It is by no means impossible that more was known in California of the instructions to Híjar and the plans of Padrés than was admitted in public discussions and correspondence.[3]

[3] April 16, 1834, congress passed a decree, published by bando on April 19th, as follows: '1. All the missions of the republic shall be secularized. 2. The missions shall be converted into curacies, the limits of which shall be designated by the governors of the states where said missions exist. 3. This decree is to go into full effect within four months from the date of its publication.' *Arrillaga, Recop.*, 1834, p. 134–5; *Dept. St. Pap., Mont.*, MS., vii. 6; *Sup. Govt St. Pap.*, MS., x. 1; *Hayes' Mission Book*, i. 220; *Id., Legal Hist. S. Diego*, i. 57; *Jones' Report*, no. 13. This law seems never to have been mentioned in Californian discussions, and was probably not understood to apply to Cal., as very likely—from the use of the terms 'governors' and 'states,' and the existence of a special law—it was not intended to apply; yet had F. known of this decree, he might have used it somewhat plausibly in defence of his course. In *Figueroa, Manifiesto*, passim, there is much argument for

Provisional regulations for the secularization and administration of the missions were proposed to the diputacion July 19th by the Carrillos. Don Cárlos was for some reason, doubtless satisfactory to himself, less radically opposed to secularization than he had been a few years earlier. After full discussion, Figueroa still maintaining a slight pretence of opposition, they were approved article by article in the secret sessions of July 30th and 31st, re-read and finally approved August 2d, and officially promulgated in a printed bando by the governor August 9th.[4]

and against his action.   In *Mexico, Mem. Justicia,* 1834, p. 30, it is stated that the execution of the laws of Aug. 1833 and April 1834 has been prevented by lack of priests, largely due to the ravages of cholera.

[4] *Figueroa, Reglamento Provisional para la secularizacion de las Misiones de la Alta California, 9 de Agosto, 1834.*   Printed document in *Earliest Printing in Cal.*   Also in *St. Pap., Miss. and Colon.,* MS., ii. 253–62; *Bandini, Doc.,* MS., 37; *Arch. Sta B.,* MS., viii. 264–75; x. 254–65; *Dept. St. Pap., Mont.,* MS., iii. 30–42; and with something of the discussions in *Leg. Rec.,* MS., ii. 12–28.   English translations in *Halleck's Report,* 147–53; *Jones' Report,* 65; *Dwinelle's Colon. Hist. S. F'co,* append., 31; *I. Rockwell,* 456; *Hayes' Mission Book,* i. 220.   1. The gefe politico, according to the spirit of the law of Aug. 17, 1833, and to his instr. from the sup. govt, acting in accord with the prelates of the friars, will partially convert into pueblos the missions of this territory; beginning in Aug. (erroneously printed 'next August,' it having been discussed in July) with 10 missions and continuing with the others successively.   (In the original proposition the last clause was 'so far as his duties may allow,' the definite date and the specification of missions being substituted after much debate.)   2. The friars will be relieved from the administration of temporalities, and will exercise only the functions of their ministry in spiritual matters until the formal division of parishes be made and curates provided by the govt and bishop.   3. The ter. govt will reassume the admin. of temporalities, directively, on the following plan.   4. The approval of this regl. will be solicited from the sup. govt by the quickest route.

Distribution of property and lands.—5. To each head of a family, and to all over 20 years old, will be given from the mission lands a lot not over 400 nor less than 100 varas square.   In common, will be given them enough land to pasture their stock.   *Egidos* shall be assigned for each pueblo, and at the proper time *propios* also.   6. Among the same individuals there shall be distributed pro rata, according to the judgment of the gefe pol., one half of the live-stock, taking as a basis the latest inventories rendered by the missionaries.   7. There will also be distributed to them, proportionally, half or less of existing chattels, tools, and seed indispensable for the cultivation of the ground.   8. All the remaining lands and property of every kind will remain under the charge and responsibility of the majordomo or employee named by the gefe pol., at the disposal of the sup. govt.   9. From the common mass of this property provision shall be made for the subsistence of the padres, pay of majordomo and other servants, expenses of worship, schools, and other objects of public order and improvement.   10. The gefe pol., intrusted with the direction of temporalities, will determine and regulate after proper investigation, the expenses which it may be necessary to incur, both for the execution of this plan and for the preservation and increase of the property.   11. The

These regulations, which I give nearly in full, were certainly, whatever may have been the legality of their issue, much more wisely and carefully prepared than any that had preceded them, resembling in many points the prevenciones on gradual emancipation, leaving much to the judgment of the friars, and

missionary will choose that one of the mission buildings which suits him best for his dwelling and that of his attendants; and he will be provided with the necessary furniture and utensils. 12. The library, sacred vessels, church furniture, etc., shall be in charge of the padre, under the responsibility of a sacristan chosen by him and paid a fair salary. 13. General inventories shall be made of all mission property duly classified, account books, documents of every class, debts, and credits—all to be reported to the sup. govt.

Political government of the pueblos.—14. The political govt shall be organized in conformity with existing laws; and the gefe pol. will give the proper rules for the establishment of ayuntamientos and holding of elections. 15. The economical management of the pueblos shall belong to the ayunt.; but in the admin. of justice they will be subject to the judges of 1st instance constitutionally established in the nearest places. 16. The emancipated will be obliged to aid in the common work which in the judgment of the gefe pol. may be deemed necessary for the cultivation of the vineyards, gardens, and fields remaining for the present undistributed. 17. They will render to the padre the necessary personal service.

Restrictions.—18. They may not sell, burden, nor convey the lands given them; nor may they sell their stock. Contracts made against these orders shall be void; the govt will reclaim the property and the buyers will lose their money. 19. Lands, the owners of which die without heirs, shall revert to the nation.

General rules.—20. The gefe pol. will appoint the comisionados whom he may deem necessary for the execution of this plan. 21. The gefe pol. is authorized to settle whatever doubt or matter may arise in connection with the execution of this regulation. 22. Until this regul. is put in force the missionaries are prohibited from slaughtering cattle in considerable quantities, except the usual slaughter for the subsistence of neophytes, without waste. 23. The debts of the missions shall be paid in preference out of the common property, on such terms as the gefe may determine. And for exact compliance there shall be observed the following rules: 1. The comisionados as soon as appointed will go to their respective missions to carry into effect the plan, presenting their credentials to the friar, with whom they are to preserve harmony, politeness, and due respect. 2. At first the com. will receive all accounts and documents relating to property; then the general inventories will be formed in the order given, an estimate of two intelligent persons sufficing for the live-stock. As entered in the inventory, all passes from the control of the friar to that of the com.; but no innovation is to be made in the system of work, etc., until experience proves it to be necessary. 3. The com. and majordomo are to see that all superfluous expenses cease. 4. Before making an inventory of field property the com. must explain to the Indians this regulation and the change it is to effect in their condition. Their lots are to be immediately distributed. The com., padre, and majordomo will select the place, give to each what he can cultivate within the fixed limits, and allow each to mark his land in the most convenient way. 5. The com. must pay no debts of the mission without an express order from the govt, to which a report must be made in order that the number of cattle to be distributed may be determined. 6. Implements will be distributed for individual or common use as the com. and padre may decide; but grain is to remain undistributed, and the neophytes will receive the usual rations. 7. What is known as the

evidently intended to conciliate as far as possible the
good-will of the missionaries and to use all possible
precautions against the evils to be feared from a sudden and radical change.

In the middle of October, after some progress had
been made in carrying into effect the law under Figueroa's regulations, Híjar appeared on the scene with
instructions dated April 23d which contained certain
articles regulating the law of August 1833, or at least
were the only regulations on the subject that the
Mexican government had deigned to issue. I append
those articles in a note.[5] Their exact meaning is
not quite clear, since, literally interpreted, they contain not a word to authorize the distribution of any
portion of the mission property to neophytes. This
fact enabled Figueroa and his friends to denounce
with much plausibility the whole scheme as one of deliberate plunder. I suppose, however, that the failure
of the government to define specifically the Indians'
rights was but a part of the general carelessness observable in all official transactions relating to the col-

'nunnery' is to be abolished at once. The girls and boys are to be given to
their parents, to whom their parental duties are to be explained. 8. The
com., after investigation, will propose as soon as possible one or more persons
deemed fit for majordomos, with the salary that should be paid them. 9.
Rancherías at a distance having 25 families may form a separate pueblo if
they wish to do so, otherwise they will form a *barrio* or ward of the main
pueblo. 10. The com. will report the population, in order to prepare for elections, which so far as possible are to conform to the law of June 12, 1830.
11. The com. will take all necessary executive steps demanded by the state
of business, reporting to the govt and consulting it in serious or doubtful
cases. 12. In all else the com., padre, majordomo, and Indians will act as
prescribed in the reglamento.—Monterey, Aug. 9, 1834. José Figueroa;
Agustin V. Zamorano, secretary.
    [5] *Híjar, Instrucciones.* Art. 1. He will begin by taking possession of all
the property belonging to the missions of both Californias. Art. 7. Special
care shall be taken to attach the Indians to the settlements, mixing them
with the other inhabitants, but not permitting any settlement composed of
them only. Art. 9. Each family of colonists to receive certain land, live-
stock, and implements (of course from the mission property). Art. 11. The
distribution of movable property belonging to the missions having been made
(was this merely the distribution to the colonists as per art. 9? or did it include also a distribution to neophytes as a part of secularization?), one half
of what is left shall be sold in the most advantageous manner. Art. 13. The
remaining half is to be kept on account of the govt, to pay expenses of worship, education, etc. Art. 14. An annual report on the mission property required from the director of colonization.

ony. Secularization included as an essential element, by the whole spirit of Spanish laws, the distribution of mission lands and property to the Indians. Híjar and Padrés always claimed to be advocates and defenders of aboriginal rights; and while their strongest motives, as in the case of all men in a like situation, were personal rather than humanitarian, I deem it unlikely that there was any intention of perpetrating so gross an outrage as was implied in a literal interpretation of the instructions considered independently of other laws. I suppose rather that the plan was to put the neophytes, at least in theory, on equal terms with the colonists in the distribution of property. It can serve no useful purpose to speculate upon what might have been the results if Híjar's instructions had been carried out. The revocation of his commission as gefe político enabled Figueroa very justly to annul those instructions; else he would have found himself with his reglamento very much in the position of Echeandía with his decree of January 1831. The controversy has been fully treated elsewhere; and the arguments of the two rivals on their respective systems and authority for regulating secularization, though lengthy and interesting, do not call for further notice.[6] The Híjar and Padrés colony as planned seemed destined to exert a radical and controlling influence on the fate of the California missions; but in reality it had no effect beyond the imposition of a heavy tax for a year or two to support the families, and a diminution of the opposition which Figueroa might otherwise have expected from the friars.[7]

The records of what was actually accomplished this year under Figueroa's provisional regulations are meagre, as we shall find the annals of secularization

[6] See *Figueroa, Manifiesto*, 44–80.
[7] Janssens, Híjar, and other members of the colony are inclined to insist that the opposition to the directors arose largely from their efforts in behalf of the Indians, whose property the other party wished to control.

in all years. There are in the archives vague local items indicating the presence of a comisionado and the introduction of the new system in nine missions. Such fragmentary information as can be derived from these items, I give in a note.[8] The tenth mission was perhaps San Cárlos, which would naturally have been one of the first, though there is no evidence on the subject. Most of the items bear date of November, and in but few missions was much progress made before December.

The padres have not left themselves on the record on either side of the contest between Figueroa and Híjar; nor do they appear to have made any attempt to interfere seriously with the enforcement of the provisional regulations. Before their publication, President Duran had written a letter of general discontent to the governor, complaining of the uncertain prospects in the matter of secularization, of the scarcity and illness of friars, of the refusal of the Zacatecanos to take charge of more than eight missions, of the

[8] There is nothing in relation to S. Diego. At S. Luis Rey, Capt. Portilla was comisionado in Nov., and the accounts turned over by P. Fortuni showed assets of $46,613 and liabilities of $14,429. In Dec. the Ind. refused to work, and ran away, taking most of the horses and killing many cattle; but in Jan. they began to come back and behave better. *St. Pap., Miss.*, MS., xi. 49–53; *Hayes' Mission Book*, i. 223, 227. No record for S. Juan Capistrano, except that Juan José Rocha, probably the comisionado, acknowledges on Nov. 22d receipt of resolution to secularize the mission. *Dept. St. Pap., Ben. Mil.*, MS., lxxxviii. 18. At S. Gabriel an inventory was made in Nov. 1834. *St. Pap., Miss.*, MS., vi. 12–14; and Lieut-col. Gutierrez was doubtless the com., being in charge early the next year. Lieut Antonio del Valle was the com. at S. Fernando, and was engaged in Oct. in making inventories. *Guerra, Doc.*, MS., vi. 150; *Vallejo, Doc.*, MS., xxxi. 134. At Sta Bárbara Alf. Anastasio Carrillo was com. from Sept., with José María García as majordomo from Oct. *St. Pap., Miss.*, MS., ix. 24–31; xi. 1. Domingo Carrillo was com. of Purísima in Nov. *Id.*, xi. 23. There is no record for S. Luis, S. Miguel, S. Antonio, S. Cárlos, S. Juan, or Soledad. Santa Cruz was delivered to Alf. Ignacio del Valle as com. on Aug. 24th; and Juan Gonzalez was majordomo from Oct. This establishment was now known as Pueblo de Figueroa; and the Ind. were reported to behave admirably under the new system; though there was a little trouble with the padre about the rooms to be occupied by him. *St. Pap., Miss.*, MS., ix. 66–71; x. 6; *Sta Cruz, Arch.*, MS., 12, 23; *Valle, Lo Pasado*, MS., 9–10. There is no record of secularization this year at Sta Clara or S. José. At S. F. de Asis, Joaquin Estudillo took charge as com. in Sept. *St. Pap., Miss.*, MS., ix. 62. At S. Rafael an inventory was taken in Sept.; the pueblo was marked out in Oct. by Ignacio Martinez, who was probably the com.; and stock was distributed in Dec. *Id.*, v. 58–9; x. 11. S. F. Solano was perhaps not fully secularized until next year.

action of some troops who had sustained the Indians rather than the padres, and of new troubles, not explained, which had come upon himself. "The Indians should not be entirely subjected nor entirely free," yet he saw no practicable middle course, and begged Figueroa to take counsel of unprejudiced persons such as foreigners.[9] Prefect García Diego received in May from the guardian of his college a copy of the secularization law, with orders to obey its provisions and instructions on the methods of surrender to curates. He congratulated the Zacatecanos on the adoption of a measure which would enable them to retire. About the same time he received and circulated an order forbidding the padres to take any part in politics, or to criticise the policy of the government.[10]

Duran seems to have made a report on the plan embodied in the provisional reglamento, which is not extant, but which, on being presented to the diputacion, was referred to a committee, and resulted in a series of supplementary regulations adopted in the extra session of November 3d and issued in a bando by Figueroa on the 4th. No radical changes were introduced by this document, which seems to indicate that Duran and the other friars were inclined to look somewhat favorably on the new system as administered by the governor, or at least, that it was more favorable to their interests than any substitute likely to be obtained.[11]

[9] July 22, 1834, D. to F. *Arch. Arzob.*, MS., v. pt ii. 4–5.
[10] May 22, 1834, F. to Casarin. *Dept. St. Pap.*, *Mont.*, MS., vi. 30. June 20th, García Diego to padres. *Arch. Obispado*, MS., 90. May 23d, same to same. *S. José, Patentes*, MS., 203–8. Alvarado, *Hist. Cal.*, MS., ii. 217–23, tells us that the Zacatecans were in a fury. They prepared a protest to the pres. against the plundering policy, calling for F.'s trial and removal. Backed by Zamorano and Sanchez, they sent the protest south for the signatures of the Fernandinos, not one of whom would sign the document, and some of whom talked very warmly in favor of the regl., mainly to annoy the Zacatecanos, whom they despised as intruders. I believe, however, there is no reason to credit Alvarado's statements on this and like subjects.
[11] *Reglamento de Misiones secularizadas, aprobado por la Diputacion en 3 de Nov. 1834*, MS., in *Vallejo, Doc.*, xxxi. 131; *Leg. Rec.*, MS., ii. 199–205; translation in *Halleck's Report*, 153–4; *Jones' Report*, 60; *Dwinelle's Colon. Hist.*, S. F'co, add., 34; *Hayes' Legal Hist. S. Diego*, i. 57. Art. 1. Conformably to the law of Aug. 17, 1833, salaries of $1,500 are assigned to curates.

A special matter that may best be noticed here is the slaughter of mission cattle by the friars in 1834 and the following years, together with a wanton neglect and destruction of other property. Many of the missionaries regarded secularization as an outrage upon themselves, their college, and their neophytes; and when they became convinced that the disaster could not be averted, at different times, but chiefly in 1834, they ceased to care for the buildings, vineyards, and gardens as in former times, and attempted to realize in ready money as large an amount as possible, which of course could best be done by a slaughter of cattle for their hides and tallow. Accordingly such a slaughter was effected, to some extent in all the missions, but notably at San Luis Rey, San Ga-

of first-class parishes, and $1,000 to those of the second class. 2. Parishes of the first class shall be, S. Diego and S. Dieguito; S. Luis Rey, Las Flores, and annexed settlements; S. Gabriel and Los Angeles; Sta Bárbara mission and presidio; S. Cárlos and Monterey; Sta Clara and José de S. Guadalupe; and S. José, S. Francisco Solano, S. Rafael, and the colony (7 in all, incorrectly grouped in Halleck's and other translations). Parishes of the second class, S. Juan Capistrano, S. Fernando, S. Buenaventura, Sta Inés and Purísima, S. Luis Obispo, S. Miguel, S. Antonio and Soledad, S. Juan Bautista and Sta Cruz, S. Francisco mission and presidio. In parishes of more than one place, the curate will reside at that first named. 3. The comisario prefecto García Diego will reside at this capital. The gefe pol. will ask from the bishop in his behalf the faculties of vicario foraneo. His salary shall be $3,000. 4. In all other respects the vicar and curates are to conform to the law of Aug. 17th. 5. Until the govt shall provide regular curates, the prelates will do so (from the friars) provisionally, by consent of the gefe pol. 6. $500 per annum shall be paid in each parish for church expenses and servants. 7. All these salaries and expenses of worship shall be paid from the common property of the extinguished missions, in money if there be any, or in produce at current rates—the gefe pol. to give the necessary orders. 8. Art. 17 of the regl., requiring the Ind. to render personal service to the friars, is abrogated. 9. The gefe will cause to be assigned buildings for the residence of curates, ayuntamientos, schools, etc., according to art. 7 of the law. 10. Other points of Duran's recommendations may be attended to by the gefe pol. under art. 17 of the regl. 11. All to be communicated to the prelates and by them to their subordinates.

My original is the one sent by Figueroa to Comisionado Valle at S. Fernando, whom he directs to assign the curate's dwelling at once. Salaries are to commence on Dec. 1st, after which date it will not be necessary to supply the padre with subsistence or service, except on salary account. On Oct. 30th F. had issued a resolution of the dip. that although the Ind. towns still bore the name of missions, they were not lawfully so, since they ought to have been secularized ere this, and should therefore be considered as towns of the republic, subject to the same laws as other towns, being under the civil authorities of the head towns of the respective districts. *St. Pap., Miss. and Colon.*, MS., ii. 263-4.

briel, and Purísima, by outsiders who contracted to kill the cattle and deliver half the hides to the padres. Such is the charge, and though exaggerated in detail, I have no doubt it is well founded; indeed, so far as I know, the padres have left in the records no denial of its truth. Naturally the documentary evidence on this subject is slight; but we have seen that in June the diputacion forbade the slaughter of cattle except in the usual quantities, and by members of the community; and a similar prohibition was deemed necessary in the reglamento of August. I append a few notes from the archives and something of what has been said on the subject.[12]

[12] July 16, 1834, F. to alcaldes, publishing the act of the dip. of the 12th. It is stated that the slaughter was then going on at Purísima, S. Luis, and S. Gabriel. *Pico, Doc. Hist. Cal.*, MS., i. 9–10; *Dept. St. Pap., Ang.*, MS., xi. 21–2; *Sta Cruz, Arch.*, MS., 10–11; *Vallejo, Doc.*, MS., xxxi. 95–6. June 20th, Prefect García Diego circulates the order to the Zacatecanos. *Arch. Obispado*, MS., 90. July 8th, 10th, 12th, permission asked by S. Cárlos and S. Luis to slaughter cattle for payment of debts. *Leg. Rec.*, MS., ii. 148–51, 163. From May to July 5,700 cattle were killed, leaving 2,850 hides for the mission, the rest belonging to the 'porcioneros.' *St. Pap., Miss.*, MS., x. 4.

Osio, *Hist. Cal.*, MS., 203–6, attributes the slaughter largely to the feeling of the Fernandinos against the Zacatecanos. The padre of S. Luis Obispo was ordered by his prelate to convert the mission wealth as rapidly as possible; and he bought $20,000 worth of cotton, woollen, and silk goods which he distributed among the neophytes. Over 5,000 hides from S. Gabriel were shipped at S. Pedro. When P. Esténega came to that mission he found all the cattle destroyed, so that he had to appeal to the Yorba rancho for meat, fat, and milk. Gov. Chico in 1836 said the friars 'annihilated the best part of the funds to allay the covetousness that they deemed to be the primary cause of secularization,' executing 'matanzas espantosas de ganado,' and abandoning 'toda clase de arbitrios de su progreso.' *Earliest Printing in Cal.* Bandini, *Hist. Cal.*, MS., 51–3, tells us that 2,000 cattle were killed in a single day at one mission, the meat and fat being left in the fields. F.'s government only pretended to interfere, to save a portion of the stock for a particular purpose indicated in a letter to friends in Mexico, which the author saw, but which he takes good care not to quote or explain. J. J. Vallejo, *Reminis.*, MS., 54–5, though a friend of the padres, admits the destruction, and thinks it was justified by circumstances. Pio Pico, *Hist. Cal.*, MS., 157, says he had a contract at S. Gabriel, employing 10 vaqueros and 30 Indians, and killing over 5,000 cattle. Pico, *Acont.*, MS., 24, speaks of a very extensive slaughter at Purísima under Domingo Carrillo, the administrator. Estudillo, *Datos*, MS., 33–4, tells us that after a time nothing but the hides was saved. Some 20,000 head were killed at the S. Jacinto ranch of S. Luis Rey. Robinson, *Life in Cal.*, 159–61, says the ruin was more preceptible at S. Gabriel than elsewhere. The contractors really took two hides for every one they gave the padres. Hayes, *Emig. Notes*, 486, thinks the slaughter began in 1832. Mrs Ord, *Ocurrencias*, MS., 70–3, is inclined to doubt that any wanton slaughter was effected at most missions; but she understood that 30,000 cattle were killed at S. Gabriel, and remembers that there were fears of a pestilence from the rotting carcasses. Truman, in the *Castroville Argus*,

The venerable ex-prefect Padre Francisco Vicente Sarría, of the Fernandinos, died in 1835; and his associate, Francisco Javier Uría, had died the year before. These are the only changes to be noted in the missionary personnel, except that Padre Perez of the Zacatecanos disappears from the records after 1835. I do not know what became of him.

By submitting to heavy discounts, certain friars seem to have succeeded in collecting a portion of the sums due them on account of sínodos this year. This was accomplished through the agency of Virmond, who for approved missionary drafts on the pious fund obtained others on the national treasury which were paid in custom-house orders negotiable at 25 or 30 per cent discount for cash. As usual, the accounts are incomplete, and it is impossible to state exactly what sums were obtained; but at one time $7,200 were paid to the padres of six missions; and the college of San Fernando seems to have got a bill accepted for the sínodos of nine friars from the beginning of 1830 down to the respective dates of their decease. Meanwhile the pious-fund estates remained, not yet rented according to the law, in the hands of a directive junta. Of the revenue from June 1832 to March 1834, amounting to $56,250, the sum of $25,691 had been expended on the colony; $23,567 had been taken as a loan by the government; $4,713 paid out in miscellaneous expenses; and $1,523 paid over in missionary stipends.[13]

Sept. 23, 1871, gives a very exaggerated account of the destruction and shipment to Spain of all the property at S. Juan Capistrano by P. Zalvidea; and Taylor, *Cal. Farmer*, Feb. 1, 1861, tells us that the padre of S. Gabriel unroofed the buildings, used the timbers for firewood, had the cattle killed on halves, and distributed the utensils to the neophytes, who were ordered to cut down the vineyards, but refused.

[13] *Mexico, Mem. Relaciones*, 1835, p. 36–7, no. 10. May 2, 1835, F. to the govt says that Deppe, Virmond's agent, had paid $7,200 to padres of S. Antonio, Sta Inés, Purisima, S. Miguel, S. Juan Capistrano, and S. Francisco, for 1831-2-3. He advises a suspension of such allowances, or of such payments, on the ground that the padres manage the missions in their own way and have plenty of resources. In cases of actual necessity, the sínodos could be paid from the mission products, and the whole considered as a loan to the govt. (In view of the secularization laws already enforced or to be enforced

Demands for supplies from the missions were often refused in 1835, both by the padres and by the comisionados, but always on the plea of absolute want of means. The changes of the last few years had left many of the establishments in such a condition that they could barely feed and clothe the Indians, who were not disposed to look at all favorably on any sharing of their earnings with the troops. To what extent, if any, the community cattle and other property were sacrificed in aid of the troops or for the furtherance of private interests I have no means of knowing; but I suppose that the swindling operations charged upon the government and the administrators, with much probability of truth, did not commence until later, and that in 1834–5 the authorities contented themselves for the most part with the legitimate taxes on mission products.

In respect to general regulations and progress of secularization, there is little to be noted in the annals of 1835. No approval of the reglamento came from Mexico, nor disapproval for that matter, and in California little or nothing was changed in the current system. Figueroa devised a plan for establishing separate ranchos at each mission for the support of the padre and of public worship; and even made a beginning at San Cárlos and Santa Cruz. García Diego approved the measure warmly in May, perhaps had

immediately, the meaning and force of F.'s argument are not apparent.) June 17th, F. certifies the drafts of 6 padres, 4 of them for stipends of 1834 and 2 for 1831–4, aggregating $4,800. *St. Pap., Miss. and Colon.*, MS., ii. 294–8. Oct. 7th, Virmond to Guerra. On the discounts necessary to obtain money. Calls for a full power of attorney, and will do his best. *Guerra, Doc.*, MS., vi. 147–8. Dec. 23d, same. Speaks of the draft in favor of the college in favor of PP. Catalá, Suñer, Boscana, Barona, Amorós, Sanchez, Gil, Uría, and Sarría; and calls for doc. to prove their claims. *Id.*, vi. 146–7. Dec. 16th, there is no way to recover the losses of two or more of the missions by the death of the insolvent Síndico Martiarena at Tepic. *Id.*, vi. 130. A list of padres showing sums due to each from 1811 to Dec. 1, 1834. The total sum is $248,000; and the amount received from 1811 to 1830 by the padres still living in 1834 was $19,200 out of $85,600 that should have been paid. *Fondo Piadoso de Cal., Demostracion de los Sínodos que adeuda á los Religiosos del Colegio de S. Fernando, 1811–34*, MS. Oct. 14th, directors of pious fund to pres. of missions, calling for certified accounts of sums due. *Doc. Hist. Cal.*, MS., iv. 994–5.

suggested it first himself, but in August, after reflection, changed his opinion, basing his opposition
on the governor's lack of authority to make such an
innovation on the Mexican laws against the foundation
of any *obras piadosas* whatever, on the animosity that
would be felt against the padres so long as they administered any property, on the insufficiency of the
means proposed, and on the injustice of freeing the
gente de razon from all responsibility for the support
of religion.[14]   On account of this opposition or of Figueroa's early death, the scheme was carried no further.
From the Fernandinos we hear nothing; and their silence may indicate that in the south secularization was
proving more or less satisfactory.   In the north, however there were complaints of demoralization among
the Indians, and of other difficulties, which prompted
Prefect García Diego to suggest certain modifications
of the rules, not adopted so far as can be known.[15]

[14] May 29, Aug. 3, 1835, G. D. to F. *St. Pap., Miss. and Colon.*, MS., ii.
333, 336–9.   June 15th, guardian of the col. at Zacatecas wrote to prefect that
the missions must not be considered nor called parishes, nor the missionaries
curates, since no legal and formal transfer had been effected.   And the transfer could be made lawfully to only priests able to show all their papers in due
form. *Corresp. de Misiones*, MS., 45–7.   Aug. 15th, G. D. to the padres.   The
guardian requires statistical information about the missions. *S. José, Patentes*,
MS., 211–12.

[15] *García Diego, Reglas que propone el P. Prefecto para gobierno interior de
las ex-misiones, 1835*, MS.   His suggestions were: 1. Total separation of the
quarters chosen by the padre for himself and servants and those of the comisionado and majordomo.   2. That the Ind. be compelled to render personal
service to the padre, whose servants should not only be supported by him, but
controlled and corrected in a parental way, independently of all interference
from the com.   3. That in view of disorders that have resulted among the
single women since they were set free, they should be returned to the padre's
exclusive control, aided by an alcalde of his own choice.   4. That the allowance of $500 per year for expenses of religious worship should be paid to the
padre at the beginning of the year, he to keep a book of accounts which was
to be inspected by his prelate.   5. That the padres should be authorized to
enforce attendance on religious duties by the same means used in the case of
children.   6. That com. be instructed to aid the prelate with animals and
vaqueros when travelling, or the friars travelling by order of their prelate.   7.
The com. and majordomos also to furnish carriers of correspondence between
the prelate and friars.

Dana, *Two Years before the Mast*, 199, speaks of the prevalent immorality
among the Indian women in 1835–6.   May 21st, F. orders com. not to make
loans of mission effects which may prejudice the establishment. *St. Pap., Miss.*,
MS., ix. 27.   Oct. 12th, Vallejo to F., expressing the opinion that not all the
neophytes are fit to be intrusted with the management of their own property;
and advising that a part be made to live in community, the property being

Locally we have a series of items in continuation of those presented for 1834. These show that six additional missions were secularized this year, San Diego, San Luis Obispo, San Antonio, Soledad, San Juan Bautista, and San Francisco Solano. No change had yet been made so far as the records show at San Buenaventura, Santa Inés, San Miguel, Santa Clara, and San José. Thus in sixteen missions the friars had been deprived of the temporal management; comisionados had at first taken charge, and at several of the establishments had completed their labors; inventories of all mission property had been made; a portion of the lands and other property had been distributed to the neophytes; the padres had become temporarily curates; and majordomos, often unofficially called administrators, had succeeded the comisionados, or were managing the estates under their supervision. Figueroa's provisional reglamento was practically in force, though the author was dead, and, so far as can be determined from meagre records, the result at many missions was not unsatisfactory.[16] It is unfortunate that we may know

managed by majordomos. *Vallejo, Doc.*, MS., iii. 43. Dec. 27th, F. says that the sum of $500 for church expenses is excessive; and orders that payment be made only for what is actually needed. *St. Pap., Miss.*, MS., ix. 10.

[16] At S. Diego Joaquin Ortega became majordomo in April. *St. Pap., Miss.*, vi. 38–9. There is no record of any com. having served since 1833. In Nov. the Ind. pueblo of San Pascual was in existence with 34 families. Document in *Hayes' Mission Book*, i. 230; *Id., Emig. Notes*, 497. No record of S. Dieguito. At S. Luis Rey Portilla as com. had troubles of a not important nature with Ortega of S. Diego, and with the padre, who was not pleased with the rooms assigned him. *Dept. St. Pap.*, MS., iii. 3–7; *St. Pap., Miss. and Colon.*, MS., ii. 340–1. Early in the summer he transferred the charge of the property to Pio Pico, as majordomo, against whom in Nov. the Ind. made loud complaints. *Hayes' Mission Book*, i. 229; *Julio-César, Cosas de Indios*, MS., 4–5. Inventory of August, assets, $203,737; debts, $9,300. *St. Pap., Miss.*, MS., vi. 10–11. An inventory of S. Juan Capistrano makes the assets $54,456; debts $1,420. *Id.*, v. 48–9. At S. Gabriel there is no record of the appointment of a majordomo, Gutierrez being still in charge in Jan. *Dept. St. Pap., Ang.*, MS., ii. 3. Antonio del Valle became majordomo of S. Fernando on June 1st; and to him the Ind. complained of P. Ibarra's removal of money and goods. *St. Pap., Miss.*, MS., ix. 8; xi. 3. In *Id.*, xi. 3–4, is a record that Cárlos Carrillo was sent to secularize S. Fernando, but the Ind. refused to recognize him. This is unintelligible, unless the name should be S. Buenaventura. For Sta Bárbara there are several inventories for the year; and in May José María García took charge as maj. *Id.*, ix. 24–5. At Purí-

so little about the practical working and immediate results of the new system; and especially that the padres' views are not extant. Here and there a friar had a personal quarrel with the new administration about the assignment of rooms . or servants, or presented a complaint that the ex-neophytes were ill treated, but for the most part they were silent. They seem, more particularly the Fernandinos in the

sima Joaquin Carrillo as maj. was put in charge in Aug. by his brother Domingo. Assets were $29,981. *Id.*, vi. 16.

Manuel Jimeno was ordered by the gov. in Oct. to secularize S. Luis Obispo; and Santiago Moreno was made maj. the same month. *Id.*, ix. 14–15, No record for S. Miguel. Manuel Crespo was the com. to secularize S. Antonio; and Mariano Soberanes was maj. until Sept. 10th, when he was succeeded by José Ramirez. The inventory at the transfer showed assets of only $7,883. *Id.*, vi. 16; xi. 30. P. Mercado made very bitter complaints in Dec. of the treatment of the Indians by Ramirez, and of the deplorable results, the regulations being flagrantly disregarded, and the prosperity of the mission ruined. *Leg. Rec.*, MS., iii. 3–6; *S. Antonio, Doc. Sueltos*, MS., 120–1. At S. Cárlos, Torre, *Reminiscencias*, MS., 37–9, tells us that Joaquin Gomez was the com. (probably in 1834), and José Antonio Romero the first majordomo. Figueroa, as I have said elsewhere, issued some orders for the formation of a rancho for the support of the church. *St. Pap., Miss. and Colon.*, MS., ii. 334–5. For Sta Cruz there are full inventories in 1835. Total, $84,334. *Sta Cruz, Lib. Mision*, MS., 1–3; *St. Pap., Miss.*, MS., v. 54. Secularization was deemed complete on Dec. 1st, at which time $10,576 had been distributed in effects to the Ind. *Id.*, ix. 66–7. Ignacio del Valle was to receive a gratuity of $300 for his services as com. *Id.*, ix. 69; *Sta Cruz, Parroquia*, MS., 20. Juan Gonzalez was the maj. of this Pueblo de Figueroa. *Savage, Doc.*, MS., i. 20. Nicolás Alviso was the first maj. in charge of Soledad, where he had perhaps been com. as well. *Dept. St. Pap., Ben. Mil.*, MS., lxxx. 10. The inventory of Aug. showed a total of $47,297. *St. Pap., Miss.*, MS., v. 57. At S. Juan Bautista the aggregate value was put down as $138,973, after $8,439 had been distrib. to the Ind.; and the debt was only $250. *Id.*, vi. 17–18. Tiburcio Castro was the maj. and apparently the com., there being some trouble both with the Ind. and the padre. *Id.*, x. 15–16; *St. Pap., Miss. and Colon.*, MS., ii. 342–3.

No secularization was yet attempted at Sta Clara, though many neophytes were given licenses of emancipation. *Arch. Arzob.*, MS., v. pt ii. 14; *Vallejo, Doc.*, MS., iii. 17. Neither is there any record of secularization at S. José. In the inventories of July the San Francisco property was valued at $67,227, the buildings being $33,969; and there was $7,222 of debt. *St. Pap., Miss.*, MS., vi. 19–20; *Vallejo, Doc.*, MS., xxxi. 220. The inventory is very complete in detail. Com. Estudillo, having trouble with P. Gutierrez, was replaced for a while by Ignacio del Valle; and Gumecindo Flores took charge in July as maj. *Sta Cruz, Arch.*, MS., 74; *St. Pap., Miss.*, MS., ix. 63; vi. 19; *Valle, Lo Pasado*, MS., 10. There is nothing about S. Rafael in 1835 except a grant of lands at Nicasio to ex-neophytes. *Vallejo, Doc.*, MS., iii. 29. M. G. Vallejo was the com. who secularized S. F. Solano, and appointed Antonio Ortega as maj. There was a quarrel with P. Quijas, who went in his wrath to live at S. Rafael; and the Ind. were also somewhat troublesome on account of their desire to live in their old rancherías. Vallejo resigned in Dec. *Vallejo, Doc.*, MS., iii. 11–12, 40, 45, 47, 57; *St. Pap., Miss. and Colon.*, MS., ii. 345; *Pinto, Doc.*, MS., i. 51. The foundation of Sonoma, really a part of the secularization of this mission, is noticed elsewhere.

south, to have accepted the new system as the least unfavorable that could be hoped for; and to have devoted themselves in good faith to the performance of their new duties. Their cause was lost; but they had made a long fight, and were personally glad to be relieved of onerous duties; and their prospects were not unfavorable for passing their last years in comfort. It was unfortunate for the country that the system was to be disturbed, and the old controversies were to be to some extent revived.

The disturbance was to come from Mexico, where radical changes in the form of government were effected in 1835, centralism as interpreted by the ambitious dictator, Santa Anna, gaining a victory over federalism. This change, requiring but mere mention for my present purpose, was in its general aspects favorable to the church and to the friars; and one of its immediate results was the passage by the congreso constituyente on November 7th, of the following decree: "Until the curates mentioned in article 2 of the law of August 17, 1833, shall have taken possession, the government will suspend the execution of the other articles, and will maintain things in the state in which they were before the said law was made."[17] This decree, practically repealing the secularization law, and sure if enforced to create greater confusion in the management of the missions than had ever existed before, was not known in California until after the end of 1835, and therefore a presentation of its effects belongs to the next half-decade of mission annals.

Regular mission statistics cease almost entirely with the secularization in 1834, even for the establishments that were not secularized until some years later. Nothing but occasional, special, and fragmentary reports are extant for the period from 1835 to 1846, all ob-

[17] Decree of Nov. 7, 1835, in *Arrillaga, Recop.* 1835, p. 583-4; *Halleck's Report*, 154; *Jones' Report*, 63; *Hayes' Mission Book*, i. 222-3.

tainable data from which reports I shall give from
time to time as occasion may require.   Therefore I
deem it best to present here for the period of four
years a statistical statement like that which I have
before appended to the annals of each decade.   It is
not, however, likely that the reports were as carefully
made during the last few years as for earlier periods.
Most of the padres were careless in the matter, and a
few probably misrepresented the condition of their
missions in respect of agriculture and live-stock.

In 1830 there had been 26 missionaries in charge
of the 21 missions.   In 1835 there were still 26, since
10 Zacatecanos had come to take the place of the 8
Fernandinos who died and the two who left the country.   Only one, Padre Abella, was left of those who
came before 1800.

The neophyte population decreased from 18,000 to
15,000, only one mission, San Luis Rey, showing a
gain.   San Luis had still the largest population, and
as to the smallest there was close rivalry between
San Cárlos and San Francisco.   San Rafael showed
the largest percentage of loss, but the figures in this
case are not reliable, Santa Clara and Santa Cruz
coming next.   Baptisms numbered 3,500, an average
of 875 against 1,300 for the past decade.   Solano had
the largest number, 555, followed by San José with
414 and San Luis Rey with 385; while Santa Cruz
had only 23, and San Francisco perhaps less.   Deaths
numbered 4,250, an average of 1,062 against 1,445
for the past decade, San José having the largest number, 659, and San Francisco the smallest, 36.

In cattle there was a loss of 16,000 head, from 156,-
000 to 140,000; though 10 missions showed a gain,
chiefly in the north.   Horses decreased from 16,600
to 12,000; though 8 missions gained.   Sheep decreased from 150,000 to 130,000, there being a gain
in 8 missions.   San Luis Rey still led in cattle and
sheep, closely followed by San José and Santa Clara.
The average yield of grain crops decreased from 57,-

500 fanegas to 32,700 fanegas per year, or more than
40 per cent. Solano and San José were the only
missions that gained in their average; while the largest loss was 73 per cent at San Juan Capistrano.
The best total crop was 40,000 fanegas in 1831, and
the worst was 25,000 fanegas in 1833.

For this period of four years I may say, as I have
said of the last decade, that the losses in the different
branches represented in the statistics obtainable are
much less than would be expected from what is known
of the current mission history; but, as I have already
warned the reader, these statistics are much less reliable than those of former years.

I find no evidence that there occurred in the years
1831–5 any noticeable season of flood or drought;
though both have been rather vaguely ascribed to
that period by newspaper writers, who founded their
statements ostensibly on the recollections of old residents. As there is no agreement on the subject, the
statements are not worth particular reference, one of
the most widely circulated being that of a flood in
1832—though a terrible drought is also ascribed to
the same year—in support of the theory of decennially
occurring inundations. Memoranda of Thomas O. Larkin at Monterey show light rains in the autumn of
1833, heavy rains in February and April 1834, a dry
spring, with three days' rain after the middle of May,
and no heavy rains until the last half of December in
1835.[18] A terrible pestilence, an intermittent fever
often prevalent in that region, is reported as having
almost depopulated the whole valleys of the Sacramento and San Joaquin in 1833. Warner, with Ewing Young and a party of trappers, passed up the valleys in the autumn of 1832, noting a dense Indian
population; but in the following summer when the
party returned the country was strewn with the remains of the dead wherever a village had stood, and

[18] Larkin in *S. F. Chronicle*, March 25, 1856, in *Vallejo, Doc.*, xxxvi. 214.

from the head waters of the Sacramento to Kings River only five living Indians were seen. The trappers themselves were attacked by the fever, and some of their servants died. There may be something of exaggeration in this narrative; but there is no reason to question the general accuracy of Warner's statement; especially as Vallejo wrote in May of the same year that a pestilence, which he supposed to be the smallpox, was causing fearful ravages on the northern frontiers; and as Edwards in 1837 found on every hand abundant and revolting signs of the pestilence, which was described to him by Ewing Young from personal observation. Young said he saw hundreds lying dead in a single rancheria.[19]

The topic of Indian affairs, as distinguished from mission annals, or relating mainly to the hostile acts of the native gentiles or refugees, assumes no special importance in 1831–5, and may be noticed as appropriately here as anywhere. Local alarms of minor importance and generally unfounded need not be mentioned at all in this connection, nor the constant but petty depredations of prowling thieves on live-stock from one end of the territory to the other. In 1833, from February to June, there was an excitement in the San Diego district consequent upon the reported plan of the neophytes to unite with the gentiles and seize the mission property. There was some evidence that invitations had been sent to the different missions; and that El Cajon was the rendezvous from which the attack was to be made the 20th of June. It was also rumored that the movement had a political significance, being intended to support Echeandía's views respect-

[19] Warner in *Los Angeles Star*, 1874; *Hayes' Legal Hist. S. Diego*, i. 34–7; *Yuba Co., Hist.*, 24. Day in *Hesperian*, ii. 2; May 18th, Vallejo to comandantes, etc., in *Vallcjo, Doc.*, MS., iii. 32; *Edwards' Diary*, MS., 27. Vallejo says the contagion came first from the northern English settlements and later from Ross. He recommends vaccination and other precautions. The traveller from whom the account in the *Hesperian* was taken may have been Warner or another of his party.

ing the distribution of mission lands. After much correspondence between the governor and local authorities, including calls upon the comandantes and alcaldes for aid, a small force was sent to El Cajon under corporal Gonzalez to seize Tajochi and other ringleaders. No resistance was made, the Yuma allies, if there had been any such, having run away. Tajochi was sentenced after trial to two years of public work, and three of his associates received shorter terms of punishment. The political element was perhaps imaginary; and it is not impossible that the plot for a general revolt was equally so.[20] Palomares and Bojorges, old Indian-fighters, mention rather vaguely some expeditions from San José out into the valleys the same year, in one of which the name Calaveras was applied to a battle-field on which thirty unburied bodies of the foe were left. This is partially confirmed by a report in the archives of an expedition by Regidor Peralta from San José, in which he killed twenty-two Moquelumnes in November.[21]

Complaints were frequent of depredations committed near each of the southern missions in 1834, and especially at San Gabriel. The Indians went so far as to steal the holy vessels used at the rancho of San Bernardino, and to hold Padre Esténega as prisoner for a while when he went there to protest. Lieutenant Araujo and others connected with the Híjar colony were supposed to be in some way implicated in the troubles here, referred to in current correspondence as a 'revolt,' in which four or five Indians seem to have been killed.[22] This was in October, and at the end of December San Bernardino was attacked

[20] *Dept. St. Pap.*, MS., iii. 89, 117–23; *Id., Ben. Mil.*, lxxv. 5–8; lxxix. 13–14; *Id., Ben. Pref. y Juzg.*, v. 39; *Id., Ang.*, i. 99–100; xi. 3, 9.
[21] *Palomares, Mem.*, MS., 32–8; *Bojorges, Recuerdos*, MS., 9–11; *Dept. St. Pap., Ben. Pref. y Juzg.*, MS., i. 15, v. 45; *S. José, Arch.*, MS., v. 27. Peralta met Joaquin Jóven (Ewing Young) and his cattle-thieves, also a party of Frenchmen.
[22] *Dept. St. Pap.*, MS., iii. 175–205; *Id., Ben. Mil.*, lxxxviii. 14–17. An expedition against the Navajos by citizens of Los Angeles is mentioned in January. *Id., Ang.*, i. 139, 141.

again, the buildings were sacked and burned, and several persons killed, wounded, or captured, the survivors taking refuge at San Gabriel or the other ranchos. The excitement was great in January and February; but the records afford but slight information about details or results.[23] The campaigns of Vallejo and Figueroa in the north, and their bloody battles with the fierce Satiyomes near Santa Rosa, which must have occurred in 1834 if at all, I have noticed elsewhere, expressing my opinion that, if not purely imaginary, these events as related by several writers were grossly exaggerated.[24] I may also allude to the hostilities said to have accompanied the founding of Sonoma with like incredulity.

In 1835 Vallejo seems to have marched northward from Sonoma to aid the chief, Solano, in reducing the rebellious Yolos.[25] He had in view also an expedition to the Tulares in July; but it was given up.[26] Robbers from the Tulares gave great trouble at San José and the adjoining region; and it appears that the citizens became somewhat too fond of making raids in that direction, and were apt to make no distinction between horse-thieves and inoffensive women and children. Figueroa was obliged to issue strict orders to prevent outrages.[27] The native inhabitants of San Nicolás Island in the Santa Bárbara Channel are said

[23] *Dept. St. Pap.*, MS., iv. 1–3; *St. Pap.*, *Sac.*, MS., xii. 6–8, being reports to Figueroa with calls for aid. This and other similar events will be noticed somewhat more fully in local annals.

[24] See chap. ix. of this vol. The writers who narrate this affair are there named. I may be in error; but I do not believe that such an event, especially as it involved the death of a dozen soldiers, could have occurred without leaving some slight trace in the archives. The killing of even a single soldier in an Indian fight of those days was a very startling event.

[25] *Vallejo, Report on County Names, 1850*, p. 532, in *Cal., Journal of Senate,* 1850. Charles Brown claims to have accompanied an expedition apparently identical with this. He says the force consisted of 60 Californians, 22 foreigners, and 200 Indians, lasting nearly three weeks in the rainy season. 100 captives were taken, and some acts of fiendish barbarity were committed by Solano and his men. Narrator was wounded.

[26] *Vallejo, Doc.*, MS., iii. 55, 59. Letter of Vallejo and Figueroa.

[27] *Dept. St. Pap.*, *S. José*, MS., iv. 164–5. Osio, *Hist. Cal.*, MS., 244–6, is disposed to blame Figueroa for his leniency toward Indians, which to some extent accounted for their depredations.

to have been removed in 1835 to the main, with the exception of one woman, who was found and brought over eighteen years later.[28] At San Luis Rey a plot was revealed to capture no less a personage than the governor when he should arrive from the north. An examination of arrested plotters in April indicated, however, nothing more serious than a design to protest against the granting of Temécula rancho, which the Indians claimed as their own property.[29]

While Indian hostilities were thus for the most part trifling as recorded, yet in one phase of the subject they were much more serious than could be made to appear from a series of petty local items, even if all those items were extant, which is far from being the case. The constant depredations of renegade neophytes, in alliance with gentile bands, and instigated by New Mexican vagabond traders and foreign hunters, kept the country in a state of chronic disquietude in these and later years, being the most serious obstacle to progress and prosperity. Murders of gente de razon were of comparatively rare occurrence, but in other respects the scourge was similar to that of the Apache ravages in Sonora and Chihuahua. Over a large extent of country the Indians lived mainly on the flesh of stolen horses, and cattle were killed for their hides when money to buy liquor could not be less laboriously obtained by the sale of other stolen articles. The presence of the neophytes and their intimate relations with other inhabitants doubtless tended to prevent general attacks and bloody massacres, as any plot was sure to be revealed by somebody; but they also rendered it wellnigh impossible to break up the complicated and destructive system of robbery. Far be it from me to blame the Indians for their conduct; for there was little in their

[28] *Nidever's Life and Adventures*, MS., 68–72. Sparks and Williams were among the men who removed the Indians in 1835, as they stated to Nidever, who himself found the woman in 1853.

[29] *Dept. St. Pap., Ben. Mil.*, MS., lxxx. 13–19.

past training or present treatment by white men to encourage honest industry.[30]

[30] Davis, *Glimpses of the Past*, MS., 282-9, relates at some length the exploits of Estanislao and Yoscolo, two ex-neophyte chiefs. Yoscolo made a revolt at Sta Clara, seized 200 Indian girls from the nunnery, took large numbers of cattle, and went to the Mariposa region to join Estanislao, who had run away before. Vallejo made an expedition against them, but was outgeneralled by the Indians. Later Yoscolo made another successful raid on the missions, and retired with his force to the Sta Cruz mountains, where he was soon defeated after a hard battle, and his head exhibited on a pole at Sta Clara. There is much confusion evidently in the events thus outlined; but there is probably some foundation of fact besides what is recorded in a previous chapter about Estanislao and Vallejo's campaign.

CHAPTER XIII.

MARITIME, COMMERCIAL, AND FINANCIAL AFFAIRS.

1831-1835.

NINETEEN vessels were on the coast in 1831, including one launched this year from a California port,
most of them laden with goods from different lands,
chiefly from Boston, to be exchanged in the regular
way for hides and tallow.[1] Respecting the fleet of
this year, as to a great extent of most others at this
period, we have to content ourselves with the vessels'
names, those of their officers in most cases, and various
items of destination, nationality, tonnage, cargo, and
dates, collected from many sources and embodied as

---

[1] See list for 1831-5 in this chapter. Vessels of 1831: *Ayacucho, Baikal,
California, Catalina, Convoy, Dryad, Eliza, Fanny, Fibian, Globe* (?), *Guadalupe, Harriet, Leonor, Louisa, Marcus, Margarita, Pocahontas, Urup, Volunteer, Whalehound* (?), and *Wm Little*. The *Guadalupe* was a schooner of 6
tons, framed by Joseph Chapman at S. Gabriel, hauled in carts to S. Pedro,
where she was put together and launched. Robinson, *Life in Cal.*, 100, was
present at the launching, and describes her as the second vessel built in Cal.
Warner, *Remin.*, MS., 63-7, says she was built in 1831-2 for Wolfskill,
Yount, and other otter-hunters. He calls her the *Refugio*.

Customs revenue at S. Francisco for 8 months in 1831, $2,419. *Unzueta,
Informe*, doc. 9. Revenue at S. Diego, June 1830 to June 1831, $389.
Mexico, Mem. Hacienda, 1832, doc. 3; *Prieto, Rentas*, 204, doc. 2.

before in a list note.   What adventures the traders had, if any; what obstacles they encountered; what goods they smuggled; what duties they paid; what profits they gained—must be left to the imagination. There is nothing to indicate that they had any especial difficulty in obtaining cargoes on account of the current political disturbances, or that controversies on commercial topics arose with Victoria.

The fleet of 1832 numbered twenty-four vessels, of which four were old acquaintances, seven were whalers, and five doubtful names from the lists of Spence and Hayes.[2] In several respects available items about these vessels are even less complete than before; but a few of these items, in the absence of maritime topics more exciting, may be noticed as follows: The *Pocahontas* carried away the exiled governor, Victoria, with some companions in misfortune, including Padre Peyri.   The *Waverly* brought padres Bachelot and Short, who had been exiled by protestant influence from the Hawaiian Islands, and who spent several years in California as already related.   Captain Sumner on touching at Santa Bárbara for water was arrested with his officers, and his vessel put under a guard; but investigation revealing no cause of suspicion, he was permitted to sail after a few days.   The *Newcastle* brought Thomas O. Larkin as a passenger, and from this year a resident.   The whaler *Wm Thompson*, after obtaining fresh supplies at San Francisco, came back into port a few days after sailing with a part of her crew in a state of mutiny.   By order of General Zamorano, aid was rendered to restore obedience; the mutineers were put in irons; and four deserters from another vessel were added to the crew; but the territorial treasury could not bear the expense

---

[2] Vessels of 1832: *American, Anchorite, Ayacucho, Balance, Bolívar, California, Chalcedony, Crusader, Don Quixote* (?), *Friend, Josephine* (?), *Jóven Victoriano, Newcastle, Plant, Phœbe* (?), *Pocahontas, Roxana, Singapartan, Spy* (?), *Tranquilina, Urup, Victoria* (?), *Waverly,* and *Wm Thompson.*
  Customs revenue at S. Francisco for the year ending June 30, 1832, $30 (?). *Prieto Rentas,* 204, doc. 2.

of sending the criminals to San Blas, as was desired
by the captain.   Finally the *Bolívar*, under a permit
to purchase horses for coin at San Francisco by paying tonnage dues, managed to smuggle goods to the
amount of $10,000, Padre Viader of Santa Clara be-
ing the purchaser, if we may credit the charges of
Alférez Vallejo.

There were thirty-one vessels in the fleet of 1833,
including six whalers and five doubtful names.[3]   The
Catalina, a Mexican brig, brought from Cape San Lúcas in January Figueroa, the new governor, and the
ten padres Zacatecanos, carrying away in May Ex-
governor Echeandía, Congressman Juan Bandini, and
Captain Barroso.   The *Facio* brought Don Juan Forster on his first visit to California, and also brought
the news that Gomez Pedraza had occupied the pres-
idential chair.   The *Volunteer* on approaching San
Francisco defeated in a race the *Ayacucho*, thought
to be the fastest sailer on the coast.   So states Davis,
who was on the *Volunteer;* and the same writer records the festivities attending the marriage of Thomas
O. Larkin on board the same vessel at Santa Bárbara.
This bark also brought reports of a privateer on the
coast with hostile intent, but nothing came of it.
The only other vessel requiring special mention was
the *Loriot*, which, by reason of alleged otter-catching
and other smuggling operations, was seized at San
Francisco in September by Alférez Sanchez.   The
sails were put on shore to prevent flight, but the rud-
der could not be removed.   The cargo was transferred
by water from the Yerba Buena anchorage to the
presidio landing, and thence, as rapidly as one small
cart could carry it, to Vallejo's house, where Supercargo Thompson was at first confined.   Soon he was
released on bail, with John Reed on the bond, and in

[3] Vessels of 1833: *Alert* (?), *Ayacucho, Baikal, Barnstable* (?), *Bolívar* (?),
*California, Catalina, Chalcedony, Charles Eyes, Crusader, Don Quixote, Dryad,
Enriqueta* (?), *Facio, Fakeja, Friends, General Jackson, Harriet Blanchard,
Helvetius, Isabel, Kitty, Lagoda, Leonidas* (?), *Leonor, Loriot, Margarita,
North America, Polifemo, Roxana, Sta Bárbara, Volunteer.*

November, after Judge José Antonio Carrillo at Los Angeles had considered the case, both captain and vessel were permitted to depart, John C. Jones having given bonds for submission to the results of a subsequent trial. Of final results nothing is known. Jones, owner of several of the vessels trading at this time from Honolulu, was United States consul for the Hawaiian Islands.

Thirty-two vessels are named as being in California ports in 1834,[4] a year in which the hide-and-tallow trade was more brisk than usual, in consequence perhaps of the unwonted slaughter of mission cattle. Items of revenue as given in my note are somewhat less incomplete than in previous years;[5] and for many of the vessels there are records of the number of hides and the *botas* of tallow taken away from different ports, indicating that there was but little difficulty in obtaining cargoes this year. The coming of the colony on the *Natalia* and *Morelos* has been noted elsewhere; as have the wreck of the former vessel at Monterey, and the tradition of her identity with the craft that took Napoleon from Elba; and I find no circumstances connected with the presence of other vessels of the year that call for special notice.

The fleet of 1835 consisted of twenty-three vessels, besides nine doubtfully recorded, most of them in David Spence's list.[6] Custom-house records are com-

---

[4] Vessels of 1834: *Avon, Ayacucho, Bonanza* (?), *By Chance, California, Clarita* (?), *Crusader, Don Quixote, Europe* (?), *Facio* (?), *Feighton* (?), *Jóven Dorotea, Lagoda, Leonor, Llama, Loriot, Magruder, Margarita, Martha, Morelos, Natalia, Pacífico, Peor es Nada, Polifemia, Pulga* (?), *Refugio, Rosa, South Carolina, Steriton, Tansuero* (?), *Urup, Wm Sye.*

[5] Miscellaneous items of revenue not belonging to particular vessels: Receipts at the Monterey custom-house, July–Dec. 1834, $28,531; expenses, $2,270; balance paid to comisaría. *Dept. St. Pap., Ben. Cust.-H.*, MS., vii. [399–67]. Receipts June 30, 1833, to June 30, 1834, $50,109. *Prieto, Rentas*, p. 204, doc. 2–3. About 1834 the exports from S. Pedro were over 100,000 hides and 2,500 quintals of tallow. *Mofras, Explor.*, i. 362.

[6] Vessels of 1835—see list of 1831–5 at end of this chapter: *Alert, Avon, Ayacucho, Bolívar, California, Catalina, Clementina, Clementine, Diana, Facio, Framen* (?), *Gange, Garrafilia, Iolani, Juan José* (?), *Lagoda, Leon* (?), *Leonor, Liverpool Packet, Loriot, Margarita, Mariquita, María Teresa* (?), *Matador* (?), *Peor es Nada, Pilgrim, Polifemia, Primavera* (?), *Rosa, Sitka, Trinidad* (?), *Wilmington.* Revenue statistics for 1835: Receipts at Monterey custom-

paratively complete, showing the total revenue from duties to have been about $50,000 for the year. Of the vessels, the *Rosa* and the *Loriot* were employed by the territorial government for the exile of the colony revolutionists; while the *Pilgrim* and *Alert* were the Boston ships on which Richard H. Dana had his experience of 'Two Years before the Mast,' resulting in one of the most fascinating and widely read books ever written about California. I refer the reader to a list at the end of this chapter for more particulars about the vessels of 1831–5.

I have now to notice commercial regulations and other general phases of the subject—briefly, for modifications were neither frequent nor radical. Governor Victoria issued an order a few days after assuming his office, by which he required a strict enforcement of the Mexican revenue laws. Declaring Monterey the only legal port, at which exclusively foreign vessels must discharge their cargoes and pay duties, he forbade the introduction of prohibited goods, the continuance of retail trade by the vessels, and the payment of duties in kind. Bandini, then in charge of the comisaría, not only denied Victoria's right to interfere at all in matters of revenue, but defended the abuses complained of, on the ground that they had arisen chiefly from the peculiar circumstances and necessities of California, and that they had the tacit sanction of the government.[7] It does not appear that Victoria's

house for the year, $48,125, though there is a variation of a few thousand dollars in different accounts; salaries and other expenses, $6,991; balance paid into the comisaría.

[7] Feb. 9, 1831, V. to B. and Gomez. *Sup. Govt St. Pap.*, MS., vii. 1; *Leg. Rec.*, MS., i. 268–9. Mar. 7th, B.'s reply. *Id.*, i. 269–73. April 13th, V. proposed the imposition of tonnage dues on whalers and the abatement of the duties exacted from Russian vessels. *Dept. Rec.*, MS., ix. 123. Echeandía represented that trade with foreign vessels had been well regulated at the beginning of 1831. *St. Pap., Miss. and Colon.*, MS., ii. 43, 45. June 27th, Mexican regulations. *Arrillaga, Recop.*, 1831, p. 324–46. May 17, 1832, instructions to Figueroa. Commerce to be fostered and exports of surplus products, to which end the missions should be induced to build small vessels for the coasting trade; Californians should be encouraged to engage in commercial pursuits, especially in otter-hunting, with a view to drive out foreigners; and

order had any real effect, though for the next four years the law requiring each vessel to come first to Monterey for a settlement of duties was more strictly enforced than before. After an understanding had been reached with the customs officers by means of state-ments, exhibition of papers, inspection and appraisal of cargo, the vessel became at once a movable sales-room, opened successively at each port up and down the coast until the cargo had been disposed of and the hides received in payment had been stored at San Diego—a process generally requiring two years of time and several visits to each port. The aim of the traders was to make the agreement at Monterey as favorable as possible; and so entirely dependent on customs receipts was the government, that the super-cargoes could often dictate terms. By the connivance or carelessness of officials, the way was often left open for a transfer of cargo at sea or at the islands, so that several cargoes could be sold under one permit. This method of smuggling was more common among the Sandwich-Island than the Boston ships; and many cargoes were thus transferred without the vessel that brought them ever entering California ports. Whalers in quest of fresh supplies smuggled large quantities of goods, and the Russians engaged to less extent in similar operations, both these classes being favored on account of the fact that their coming afforded the inhab-itants a market for vegetables and grain. So far as the records indicate, there was very little smuggling car-ried on by vessels that touched on the coast without a permit of some sort.

Under Figueroa's political administration during 1833–5, no evidence appears that changes were effected in the commercial system,[8] though there were frequent

complete reports on commercial topics should be rendered. *Sup. Govt St. Pap.*, MS., viii. 13, 35, 38–9. Oct. 26th, Zamorano approved of exempting whalers from all charges, as the sale of supplies to them was a direct benefit to the inhabitants; but he required them, like other vessels, to come first to Monterey. *Vallejo, Doc.*, MS., i. 327.

[8] Jan.–Feb. 1833, Pavon, director general de rentas, to officers in Cal. about the taking of govt drafts for past loans in payment of duties. The last

suggestions of needed reforms. In October 1833 Bandini introduced in congress a proposition to open San Diego and San Francisco to foreign trade, making Monterey, Santa Bárbara, and San Pedro minor ports for coasting trade in national vessels; but he was unable to carry the point, and Monterey still re-

order was that they might be taken to the extent of 40 per cent if the balance was in money. *Dept. St. Pap., Mont.*, MS., vii. 1-2. Feb. 5th, heavy tonnage dues have driven away the whalers to the Sandwich Islands, greatly to the injury of Cal. The rate should be reduced to 1 real per ton. *Id., Ben. Cust.-H.*, ii. 8. Feb. 16th, allow no discharge of cargo without a certificate from Monterey. Let no ships enter mission harbors. *Id.*, ii. 17. March 4th, foreign vessels mock the laws. Having paid a small duty, they manage to make several trips. *Id.*, ii. 9. May 7th, S. Francisco and Sta Bárbara are the hot-beds of smuggling. Additional guards required. *Id.*, ii. 13-14. May 31st, introduction of prohibited goods still continued. Any attempts of the revenue officers to enforce the laws meet with a storm of popular discontent and threats. National vessels afford no relief, selling at high prices and avoiding payment of duties on the claim of having paid in Mexico. *Id.*, ii. 14-15. June 5th, gov. not in favor of export duties. *Id.*, ii. 23-4. July 27th, sub-comisario favors granting permit to a Russian vessel to get salt and to salt meat without paying tonnage. *Id.*, ii. 19-20. Sept. 19th, a full list of vessels with details must be sent to Mex. by each mail. *Id., Mont.*, vii. 2-3. Oct. 15th, Bandini's proposition in congress. *St. Pap., Sac.*, MS., xviii. 54. Oct. 22d, seizure of $3,711 in gold-dust at S. Diego, from Guaymas. *Dept. St. Pap., Ben. Mil.*, MS., lxxix. 38-9. Oct. 24th, decree of congress. Foreign goods brought in Mex. vessels will enjoy a discount of 20 per cent in duties. *Id., Mont.*, vii. 3-4. Nov. 2d, order respecting manifests. *Arrillaga, Recop.*, 1833, p. 134-9; *Pinto, Doc.*, MS., i. 61-2; *Dept. St. Pap., Mont.*, MS., vii. 4-5. Nov. 18th, all trade with gentiles forbidden; and all traders in such cases to be treated as smugglers. *Id.*, ii. 28; *Id., Ben. Mil.*, lxxix. 16; *Sta Cruz, Arch.*, MS., 96. Nov. 18th, order from Mex. that whalers pay $10.50 each for the building of piers. *Dept. St. Pap., Ben. Cust.-H.*, MS., ii. 28. Dec. 27th, gov't orders to be received in part payment of duties. *Id., Com. and Treas.*, iii. 20. Aug. 21, 1834, administrator of customs to the receptor at S. F. He must go on board of any foreign vessel arriving and demand a certificate that duties have been paid at Monterey. If she has no certificate, no part of her cargo can be landed and no trade allowed; but she must proceed to Monterey. A Mexican vessel with national goods may discharge all her cargo and trade on paying duties or giving bonds for such payment; but if from a foreign port or laden with foreign goods she must proceed to Monterey like a foreign vessel. Lighters and boats from Ross or Bodega need not be sent to Monterey; but may trade by submitting to inspection and appraisal and paying duties. Any attempt to abuse this privilege to be punished with confiscation. *Pinto, Doc. Hist. Cal.*, MS., i. 115-19; *Dept. St. Pap., Ben. Cust.-H.*, MS., ii. 1-3. Foreigners seem to have paid $5 per month for use of shanties and salting-places at S. Diego. *Id., Pref. y Juzg.*, vi. 69. Aug. 6th, Figueroa's decree on duties imposed for municipal revenues. *Dwinelle's Colon. Hist. S. F'co*, add., 29-30; *S. Diego, Arch.*, MS., 54. March 15, 1835, 2 per cent 'derecho de circulacion' paid on money sent from Cal. to S. Blas. *S. Diego, Arch.*, MS., 3. July, Aug., no sailor from a Mex. vessel shall be allowed to land in Cal. without special cause. *Dept. St. Pap.*, MS., iv. 47-8; *St. Pap., Miss.*, MS., xiv. 43. Sept. 5th, Mex. custom-house regulations. *Arrillaga, Recop.*, 1835, p. 452-5. Bandini's report on the administration of revenues in 1824-35, dated May 1835. *Bandini, Informacion del Visitador de Aduanas*, 1835, MS.

mained the *puerto habilitado* of California in the eyes
of everybody but Don Juan and his San Diego friends.

Bandini's troubles, and especially his controversy
with Angel Ramirez, constitute a prominent feature
of commercial history at this period, even if they were
not, as Don Juan was disposed to believe, the grand
turning-point of Californian destinies. Bandini was,
as we have seen, a leading spirit in the grand scheme
of Híjar and Padrés, and in the Compañía Cosmopolitana. Though not able to close the port of Monterey in favor of San Diego as he wished, he did obtain
an appointment as visitador, or inspector of the California custom-houses. He started for home with the
colony in 1834, filled with the most enthusiastic hopes.
Member of a great commercial company without in-
investing a cent of capital, in a sense the representative of the company in California, having at his disposal a stanch vessel, Híjar and Padrés in full possession of the political and military power, the mission
wealth virtually under the control of his associates,
and last, but far from least, himself provided with a
commission by virtue of which he could remove such
obstacles to his interests as might arise in the revenue
department, the road to a princely fortune seemed
broad and open before the ambitious ex-congressman.
The failure of the general scheme, in its political,
military, and even commercial aspects, has been sufficiently noticed, and it is only of Bandini's experience
as visitador that I have now to speak. He was not
more successful than Híjar in securing recognition of
his authority. In the autumn of 1834, soon after his
arrival, he presented his credentials to Ramirez, the
administrator, and announced his purpose to begin by
inspecting the Monterey custom-house. Ramirez, of
whom I shall have something to say later, was a man
always disposed to look out for his own interests; and
though supposed to be a partisan of the colony clique,
he foresaw the triumph of Figueroa, and deemed it

wiser to save something from the general wreck for himself than for Bandini. He accordingly declined to permit any interference in his office until orders to that effect should come from his superior officer, the director de rentas in Mexico. In vain did Don Juan entreat and argue and protest; Don Angel had the advantage, being doubtless supported by Figueroa. He declined to yield or to enter into any controversy, and reported the state of affairs to his superior. He also ordered subordinate officials at other ports not to submit to Bandini's interference, though the latter had things very much his own way for a time at San Diego, which he persisted in regarding as the open port of California.[9]

Whether Ramirez ever received any order from the director does not appear. Bandini afterward declared that such an order was received and disregarded. However this may have been, Don Angel soon found a more effective weapon against his opponent, in an accusation of smuggling. Bandini had brought from Acapulco on the *Natalia*, of which he was the supercargo, various effects, exceeding $2,000 in value, for his own use and for sale on his own account. These goods were landed at San Diego free of duties, on the assurance of the visitador that all was *en régle*, except a small quantity lost in the wreck at Monterey.

---

[9] Sept. 13, 1834, Figueroa congratulates Bandini on his appointment. *Bandini, Doc.*, MS., 38. Dec. 7, 1834, B. to Ramirez, with his appointment of March 17th. B.'s salary was to be $3,000, and he had received $1,000 in advance. Reply of R. same date. *Dept. St. Pap., Ben. Cust.-H.*, MS., vii. 1-4; additional correspondence between the two at Monterey, Dec. 9th-11th. *Id.* vii. 4-5, 7-8; *S. Diego, Arch.*, MS., 25-6. Dec. 12th, R. to dir. gen., enclosing correspondence with B. *Dept. St. Pap., Ben. Com. and Treas.*, MS., iii. 6-8. Dec. 13th, B. to the sup. govt. *S. Diego, Arch.*, MS., 27. March 16 -17, May 6, 1835. R. to receptores of S. Diego, S. Pedro, and S. F., with orders that no interference by B. be permitted. *Pinto, Doc.*, MS., i. 141-2, 147; *Dept. St. Pap., Ben. Cust.-H.*, MS., vii. 14-15. April 5th, R. to dir. gen., accusing B. of a well understood plan to use his appointment as visitador for the making of a fortune at the expense of the treasury; he explains the steps he has taken, his determination not to recognize B.'s authority without special orders, and also alludes to complaints of smuggling to be investigated. *Id., Ben. Com. and Treas.*, iii. 8-10. May 5th, B. to min. of hacienda, a full report on administration of customs in past and present. *Bandini, Informacion*, MS.

An investigation was made by Judge Castillo Negrete. The facts were clear enough. Bandini himself confessed the introduction of the goods, with no explanation so far as can be known. Indeed, in his later ravings he never deigned to deny the charge, nor to explain his action, but simply affected to regard it as an absurdity that he could have been engaged in contraband trade. The judge accordingly suspended him from office, declaring the goods confiscated, together with the sum of $700 due the accused from the territorial treasury.[10]

Bandini's disappointment and indignation at this disastrous ending of all his brilliant hopes for wealth and power may be more adequately imagined than described.[11] He lost no opportunity during the next few years of reporting in writing upon his wrongs,

[10] Investig. of the charge of smuggling, comprising a dozen documents, in *S. Diego, Arch.*, MS., 44–6; *Dept. St. Pap.*, MS., iv. 71–87; *Id.*, *Ben. Pref. y Juzg.*, ii. 154–5; *Id.*, *Ben. Cust.-H.*, vii. 12; *Pinto, Doc.*, MS., i. 145–6. The temporary suspension was dated May 7, 1835, and the permanent suspension May 14, 1836. The goods smuggled in by B. included 6 bales of sugar, 25 cases of table oil, 1 barrel of tobacco, some wine, ribbons, and jewelry, and 6 or 8 bales of unknown effects. Santiago Argüello was reprimanded for negligence in the matter. Lawsuits begun respectively by Ramirez and Bandini were left unaffected by the decision; but we hear no more of them.

[11] Richard H. Dana, *Two Years before the Mast*, 276–7, speaks of B. as follows: 'Among our passengers [from Monterey to Sta Bárbara on the *Alert*, Jan. 1836] was a young man who was a good representation of a decayed gentleman. He reminded me much of some of the characters in Gil Blas. He was of the aristocracy of the country, his family being of pure Spanish blood, and once of considerable importance in Mexico. His father had been governor of the province [all these items are erroneous], and having amassed a large property, settled at San Diego, where he built a large house with a court-yard in front, kept a retinue of Indians, and set up for the grandee of that part of the country. His son was sent to Mexico, where he received an education, and went into the first society of the capital. Misfortune, extravagance, and the want of any manner of getting interest on money soon ate the estate up, and Don Juan Bandini returned from Mexico accomplished, poor, and proud, and without any office or occupation, to lead the life of most young men of the better families—dissipated and extravagant when the means are at hand; ambitious at heart, and impotent in act; often pinched for bread; keeping up an appearance of style, when their poverty is known to each half-naked Indian boy in the street, and standing in dread of every small trader and shopkeeper in the place. He had a slight and elegant figure, moved gracefully, danced and waltzed beautifully, spoke good Castilian, with a pleasant and refined voice and accent, and had throughout the bearing of a man of birth and figure. Yet here he was, with his passage given him, for he had no means of paying for it, and living on the charity of our agent. He was polite to every one, spoke to the sailors, and gave four reals—I dare say the last he had in his pocket—to the steward who waited upon him'!

and even tried to collect his salary; but he received no attention whatever from the Mexican authorities, and was exasperated the more on that account. His treatment at the hands of Ramirez and Figueroa— for he blamed the governor hardly less than the administrator—was in his view not only the greatest outrage of modern times, but the cause from which sprung all of California's subsequent evils. His writings on the subject are but wordy and declamatory protestations of his own patriotism and the baseness of his foes, always in general terms, for he avoided specification both in defence and attack. Once, however, he determined after much hesitation to produce evidence that could but prove Ramirez's revenue frauds and triumphantly justify his own acts. The evidence turned out to be a statement of José Antonio Carrillo that Don Angel was an 'apostate friar'![12] The truth is, that while Angel Ramirez was a scoundrel in comparison with Juan Bandini, the latter allowed his disappointment to run away with his judgment in this quarrel, and did not leave a dignified or flattering record. Subsequently he retrieved his fortunes to some extent, and regained his temper. He also had the pleasure of knowing that his foe had died in disgrace and poverty.

In 1834 Figueroa made a report to the Mexican government on the condition and past history of commercial industries, including something also of financial management. He explained his own efforts to introduce order and compliance with the national laws; but admitted that in some respect such compliance was impracticable under the circumstances. His concluding suggestions were that Monterey should be opened to foreign trade, and the other ports to the coasting trade; that foreign vessels be allowed to engage for five years more in the coasting trade; and

---

[12] *Bandini, Acusaciones contra Angel Ramirez, 1834–7*, MS. Directed to the min. of hac., pres. of Mex., director de rentas, and Gov. Chico.

that a regular custom-house be established at Monterey.

The fur trade is a branch of Californian commerce respecting which we have but little information for the period covered by this chapter. Foreigners secured most of the otter skins by contraband methods; the Indians killed a few animals as in former years; and in several instances Californians were regularly licensed by the territorial authorities to engage in otter-hunting on the coast. Hardly a vessel sailed without carrying away more or less skins, which all traders were eager to obtain. The authorities, both of nation and territory, understood the importance of this export, and made some weak and unsuccessful efforts to develop it, or at least to secure the legal revenue which even as carried on at the time it should yield.[13]

A slight controversy about the obtaining of salt from the *salinas* near Los Angeles in 1834 brought the general subject before the authorities. The pueblo claimed the *salinas* and refused the request of San Fernando and San Gabriel to use them. The decision locally is not known, but from communications between Ramirez, Herrera, and Figueroa, it appears that the *estanco* on salt had not been very strictly en-

[13]*Figueroa, Cosas Financieras, 1834,* MS. March, 1831, Victoria permits otter-hunting on condition that two thirds of the crews be Californians; that S. Francisco be the northern limit of hunting; and that duties be paid on the skins taken by the Aleuts for their share. *Dept. Rec.,* MS., ix. 94; April, the Kadiaks offered to give instruction in the art of taking otter. *Vallejo, Doc.,* MS., xxx. 200. April, Pacheco at Sta Bárbara denies having permitted otter-hunting. *Dept. St. Pap., Ben.,* MS., ii. 5. Aug., hunting free to Californians, so long as there is no intercourse with foreigners or abuse of gentiles. *Dept. Rec.,* MS., ix. 41. In 1832 Estrada, Castro, Ortega, and Alvarado were licensed to take otter in S. Francisco Bay; hired Aleuts and bidarkas from the Russians; obtained the services of mission Indians from S. José; and did quite a prosperous business for a time. *Alvarado, Hist. Cal.,* MS., ii. 39–40; iii. 8; *Vallejo, Notas,* MS., 36–8. Sept. 8th, Zamorano to com. of S. Francisco. *Vallejo, Doc.,* MS., i. 323. Subject mentioned in the instructions to Figueroa. *St. Pap., Miss. and Colon.,* MS., ii. 221–2. Feb. 16, 1833, Figueroa permits Teodoro Gonzalez to hunt otters from Monterey to Sta Bárbara. *Dept. St. Pap.,* MS., iii. 92–5. May 2, 1834, proposition to impose a tax on skins exported considered in the dip. *Leg. Rec.,* MS., ii. 51. Robinson, *Statement,* MS., 19, says he collected about 3,000 otter skins in one year, which he sent to China. The best were worth $60.

forced, and that even foreign vessels had taken away loads without paying duties.[14]

In 1835 Abel Stearns was suspected of carrying on extensive contraband operations at San Pedro. He had a warehouse near the shore never inspected by any revenue officers, and used, as was believed, for the storing of hides purchased of settlers who paid no slaughter tax, and goods illegally landed from vessels. The pueblo was so far away that on the arrival of a ship there was plenty of time for smuggling goods ashore at San Pedro or Sta Catalina before Receptor Osio could arrive on the spot. In March the citizens of Los Angeles complained to the governor, and asked that Stearns' establishment be suppressed. An investigation was ordered, but all we know of the result is that a committee reported in September against the spoliation of Stearns' property and the blotting-out of San Pedro as a prospective settlement. It was recommended rather that guards be established to prevent smuggling, and that the complainants present some proof of Don Abel's guilt if they had such proof.[15]

Financial topics are not very distinct from those of commerce, and the personnel of treasury and revenue officials may be taken as a connecting link. Their names may be presented with a greater approximation to accuracy than their exact titles and powers, to say nothing of their accounts. Juan Bandini had received in 1830 the appointment of comisario principal ad interim, virtually the same position that Herrera had held; but he in reality exercised no authority, and, as he himself confessed, was prevented "by many circumstances" from carrying out superior orders or organizing his department. Victoria refused to recognize Bandini's authority except locally at San Diego,

[14] *Dept. St. Pap.*, MS., iv. 88–97.
[15] *Stearns, Expediente de Contrabando, S. Pedro, 1835*, MS., in *Los Angeles, Arch.*, MS., i. 44–59; *Dept. St. Pap., Ben. Cust.-H.*, MS., vii. 11–12; *Id., Angeles*, ii. 12. Being communications of Gov. Figueroa, Administrator Ramirez, Receptor Osio, and the complaint of citizens.

and refused to be moved by his arguments and protests. Don Juan succeeded in having his resignation accepted before the end of 1832. Victoria at the beginning of 1831 seems to have found Joaquin Gomez, administrator of customs, in charge at Monterey, Antonio María Osio, contador and perhaps sub-comisario under Bandini, being temporarily in charge at San Francisco. No change was made, except that Gomez was regarded as sub-comisario and Osio was not allowed to return, though ordered to do so by Bandini. At the same time José María Padrés held the office of visitador of customs by Echeandía's appointment dated January 15th.[16]

The nominal control of Bandini ceased at an unknown date in 1832. In October, José Mariano Estrada, by Zamorano's appointment, succeeded Joaquin Gomez as sub-comisario at Monterey, the latter having resigned after many complaints of irregularities on his part; and Figueroa, who re-appointed him in February, states that on his arrival in January 1833 Estrada was the only treasury official in California.[17] With Figueroa came Rafael Gonzalez with an appointment as administrator of customs, assuming

[16] *Bandini, Manifiesto á la Diputacion sobre Ramos de Hacienda Territorial, 1832*, MS. Correspondence of Bandini and Victoria in *Id.*, i. 273–80; *Dept. Rec.*, MS., ix. 112–13. Sept. 18, 1831, V. to min. of war on treasury and revenue abuses. He alludes to Bandini as a 'mercenary employee,' with whom traders make illegal arrangements, and who believes himself dependent only on the com. gen. *Dept. Rec.*, MS., ix. 143–4. May 21st, law governing the offices of comisarios and subalterns. *Vallejo, Doc.*, MS., xxx. 215. It is possible that Gomez was put in office at Monterey by Victoria and not before his arrival, though Figueroa says he took charge in January. *Dept. St. Pap.*, MS., iii. 210; and he is spoken of as comisario on Jan. 14th. *S. José, Arch.*, MS., v. 39. April 7th, Gomez writes to Bandini that his place—'so good a thing' in most countries—is full of hardships in this; and he is anxious to get out of it to eat his frijoles in peace. *S. Diego, Arch.*, MS., 18. Appointment of Padrés. *Dept. Rec.*, MS., ix. 80. It seems that Francisco Pacheco was acting as *guarda* without pay. *Id.*, ix. 63. Osio at S. Francisco. *Dept. St. Pap., Ben. Mil.*, MS., lxxiii. 54; *Vallejo, Doc.*, MS., xxi. 14.

[17] Dec. 6, 1834, F. in *Dept. St. Pap.*, MS., iii. 210. Estrada succeeds Gomez Oct. 18th. *S. José, Arch.*, MS., v. 23; *Vallejo, Doc.*, MS., i. 326. Reports of the matter by Zamorano and Estrada; also the appointment by F. Feb. 16th. *Dept. St. Pap., Ben. Cust.-H.*, MS., viii. 307–8, 312, 316–22. There is in *Dept. St. Pap., Ben. Com. and Treas.*, MS., ii. 94, what seems to be a resignation of the comisaría by Bandini on March 20, 1833; though in his *Informacion* he says his resignation was accepted in 1832.

the office in January; and in May, Estrada resigning, Gonzalez became also sub-comisario ad interim. He held the former position until succeeded by Angel Ramirez in July 1834, and the latter until October of that year, when our old friend José María Herrera returned from Mexico with the colony to resume his former position.[18] Bandini came back as visitador de aduanas in 1834; but his troubles in that connection have been already noticed.

From 1833 a few subordinate revenue officers were appointed, not only for Monterey, but for the other ports. Pedro del Castillo was made receptor at San Francisco. Santiago E. Argüello held the same position at San Diego until October 1834, when he was succeeded by Martin S. Cabello, who came with an appointment from Mexico. José María Maldonado had charge of the customs at Santa Bárbara until July 1835, and later Benito Diaz. Antonio María Osio was receptor at Los Angeles, having jurisdiction over San Pedro, and having also to watch over the inland trade with Sonora. At the capital four sub-

[18] Gonzalez appointed Aug. 6, 1832. Salary, $1,000. *Dept. St. Pap., Ben. Com. and Treas.*, MS., ii. 24. Took possession Jan. 14 (?). *Id., Cust.-H.*, ii. 5–6; *S. José, Arch.*, MS., ii. 53. Becomes comisario May 14, 1833. *Dept. St. Pap., Ben. Cust.-H.*, MS., ii. 16–17. Osio, *Hist. Cal.*, MS., 357–9, ridicules Gonzalez, alias 'Pintito,' as a very stupid fellow, appointed by favor of Director-gen. Pavon. He once pompously objected to the large quantity of *idem* imported according to the invoices. Also noted by Robinson, *Life in Cal.*, 140. Angel Raminez appointed admin. Sept. 12, 1833. *Dept. St. Pap., Ben. Com. and Treas.*, MS., ii. 58. Took possession July 1, 1834. *Dept. St. Pap.*, MS., iii. 211; *Id., Ben. Cust.-H.*, ii. 1. Furnishes bonds in $2,000 (or $4,000) June 23, 1835. *Id.*, iii. 89, 86; but is also said to have been in possession in May. *Dept. St. Pap.*, MS., iii. 152; *Id., Ben. Mil.*, lxxviii. 24; *Leg. Rec.*, MS., ii. 2–3. Herrera's appointment Jan. 12, 1833, or Dec. 24, 1832. *Dept. St. Pap., Ben. Com. and Treas.*, MS., ii. 66; *Id., Ben. Mil.*, lxxix. 51, 81. Receives the office from Gonzalez Oct. 7th or 11th. *Id.*, iii. 46; *Id., Ben. Mil.*, lxxviii.; *St. Pap., Sac.*, MS., xii. 14; or as Figueroa says on Oct. 1st. *Dept. St. Pap., Sac.*, MS., iii. 211. Feb. 1, 1833, Admin. Gonzalez complains of lack of a suitable pier and buildings, boats, furniture, scales, etc., for want of which two thirds of the revenue is lost; also of calumnies against himself as against all who came from Mexico. He recommends 9 employees at Monterey, and a receptor at each of the other ports. *Dept. St. Pap., Ben. Cust.-H.*, MS., ii. 6–7, 12. July 1, 1834, Admin. Raminez to dir. gen., explaining difficulties and recommending additional officers. *Id., Com. and Treas.*, iii. 2–4. Dec. 6, 1834, Figueroa to the sec. de estado on the past succession of officials and their failure to leave any records. *Dept. St. Pap.*, MS., iii. 209–11.

ordinate officials were appointed in July 1834, by the recommendation of Ramirez: Francisco Figueroa as contador, Juan B. Alvarado as vista, Francisco P. Pacheco as comandante of the guard, and Eugenio Montenegro as corporal of the guard. The two former had a salary of $600, and the latter of $400. Lieutenant Araujo, who came and departed with Híjar and Padrés, was a naval officer who was sent, with perhaps a few subordinates, to command the California marine service.[19]

There was no lack of official correspondence respecting the theory and practice of financial management in this as in other periods; but much of what was written related to petty routine details, none of it had any apparent effect in the way of reform, and part was clearly not intended to have any other effect than the throwing of responsibility for existing evils upon other shoulders than those of the writers. The receipts at the custom-house were far from sufficient to meet the expenditures of the civil and military budgets; and the complaints from all quarters of hard times were constant, as were also contentions respecting the division of revenues, each official and class of officials fearing with much reason that some other would gain an advantage. In the absence of complete statistical data, we may only conjecture that mutual jealousy and precautions secured a comparatively just distribution among military, political, and treasury employees.[20]

[19] Authorities on local revenue officers. *Dept. St. Pap.*, MS., iii. 109; *Id.*, *Angeles*, xi. 8; *Id.*, *Mont.*, vii. 5; *Id.*, *S. José*, v. 122; *Id.*, *Ben. Cust.-H.*, ii. 1, 10, 16–17, 23, 25; iv. 5; vii. 8–14; viii. 14; *Id.*, *Com. and Treas.*, ii. 58; iii. 4–5, 59, 67–8; *Id.*, *Pref. y Juzg.*, ii. 156; *Id.*, *Mil.*, lxxv. 1–3; lxxvi. 30; lxxvii. 14–20; lxxviii. 1; lxxx. 3; *Monterey*, *Arch.*, MS., vii. 61; *St. Pap.*, *Sac.*, MS., xvi. 13–14; *S. Diego*, *Arch.*, MS., 33, 44; *S. José*, *Arch.*, MS., ii. 50; *Pinto*, *Doc.*, MS., i. 25–6; *Vallejo*, *Doc.*, MS., ii. 72; xxiii. 1.

[20] July 20, 1831, a general reglamento for treasury officers in all parts of the republic. *Mexico*, *Regl. Tesorería Gen.*, p. 14, 28. June 5, 1832, Gervasio Argüello is ordered to conclude his duties as habilitado general at Guadalajara and return to California. *Sup. Govt St. Pap.*, MS., viii. 41. Argüello had for a long time performed no duties; whether he had succeeded in drawing any part of his pay as lieutenant of the S. Diego company does not

The Californians were not much troubled by taxation in these days, having in 1831–3 to pay only a tax on the sale of liquors, which was rather a duty than a tax, to provide for municipal expenses. A high official having in 1832 refused to pay the duty on divers barrels of brandy, the merchants also declined payment until he should be forced to comply with the law; and in consequence the public schools had to be closed for a time. A timber and wood impost was also collected at Monterey. Expenses of the diputacion had to be paid from the surplus of local funds, a surplus usually not existing, as Figueroa learned by repeated applications for money with which to fit up a legislative hall. No tax was ever collected in California for national purposes, though there were occasional vague refer-

appear. He did not return. April 1833, complaints of habilitados' hardships by Vallejo. *Vallejo, Doc.*, MS., ii. 31. A visitador to go to Cal. from Mexico to restore order in the treasury departments and put the presidial companies on their old footing. *Mexico, Mem. Guerra*, 1833, p. 5; *Id.*, *Mem. Hac.*, 1831, p. 28; *Arrillaga, Recop.*, 1832-3, p. 110. Of course nothing of the kind was done. Dec. 1833, for many years retired officers and men have not been paid. *Dept. St. Pap., Ben. Cust.-H.*, MS., ii. 46. Jan. 1834, Figueroa had to borrow $300 to fit up a room for the dip. *Id., Ben. Mil.*, lxxxviii. Feb., etc., confusion as to whether Cal. belonged to the comisaría of Sinaloa or Sonora, orders coming from both with complaints. The com. gen. of Sonora had the real command. *Id., Ben. Com. and Treas.*, iii. 20-7, 57-66. Officers may have certificates so as to negotiate for their pay. *Sup. Govt St. Pap.*, MS., xxi. 10. April, Figueroa appeals to missions for relief. *Arch. Arzob.*, MS., v. pt ii. 2. Sept., troops to be paid in preference to others. *Sup. Govt St. Pap.*, MS., x. 3; xi. 1. Regulations of Sept. 21, 1834, for comisarios, etc., in *Arrillaga, Recop.*, 1833, p. 386-536. Dec. 8th, gov. to min. of war on his financial troubles and the urgent necessity for aid from Mexico. *St. Pap., Miss. and Colon.*, MS., ii. 289. Nov. 1835, Com. Gen. Gutierrez to Gov. Castro, complaining that the troops are not getting half rations. *Dept. St. Pap., Ben. Mil.*, MS. lxxxviii. Complaints that the civil employees do not get their proper share of the revenues. *Dept. St. Pap.*, MS., iv. 69. Items of fin. statistics 1831-5. 1831, receipts for Jan., $2,132, including $500 in goods on hand Jan. 1st, and $201 in supplies from missions; expenditures, $1297. *Vallejo, Doc.* MS., xxi. 1, 15. Revenue of the year, $32,000; expenses, $131,000. *Soulé's An. S. Fran.*, 80. 1832, Aug, 11th, Capt. Gutierrez received from com. gen. of Sinaloa $20,000 at Rosario to bring to Cal. *Dept. St. Pap., Ben. Mil.*, MS., lxxiv. 46. 1833, estimates for the 6 presidial companies of the Californias, $128,440. *Mexico, Mem. Hacienda*, 1832, doc. 0. Payments from sub-comisaría July to Dec., $22,954. *Dept. St. Pap., Ben. Com. and Treas.*, MS., ii. 39. Net proceeds, July 1833 to June 1834, $47,768, expenses being $2,842. 1834, total payments from sub-comisaría, $76,587. Loans from missions are among the receipts. *Dept. St. Pap., Ben. Com. and Treas.*, MS., iii. 39-48. Due to officers and men June 30th, as per adjustments, dating chiefly from 1833, but 7 from earlier dates, $53,835. *Id., Ben. Mil.*, lxxvii. 15-16. 1835, total payments from sub-comisaría, $46,394. *Id., Com. and Treas.*, iii. 75, 83-5; iv. 1-2.

ences to the matter in communications from Mexico; and no tax was ever assessed upon property according to its value, all exactions being in the nature of duties on articles changing owners, or of licenses. By a law of October 1833 all citizens were relieved from the civil obligation to pay tithes, and most citizens took advantage of the privilege, some officers settling with their conscience by offering in payment claims of the government for back pay. What tithes may have been collected before the law was published in California in May 1834, there are no means of knowing. Deliberations on ways and means for municipal funds were frequent in meetings of ayuntamiento and diputacion from November 1833, and the result was a law or plan published by the governor on August 6, 1834, and appended substantially in a note.[21]

I append also an alphabetical list of all the vessels that touched at Californian ports in 1831–5. The names number ninety-nine, but more than twenty

[21] *Plan de Propios y Arbitrios para fondos municipales de los Ayuntamientos del territorio de la Alta California, 1834.* Printed bando signed by Figueroa and Zamorano, in *Earliest Printing*; also in *Dept. St. Pap., Mont.*, iii. 25–30; *Los Angeles, Arch.*, MS., i. 23–30; *Dwinelle's Colon. Hist.*, add., 29–30. The substance is also given several times over in proceedings of dip. and ayunt., with reports of committees, discussion, articles not finally embodied in the plan, etc., in *St. Pap., Miss. and Colon.*, MS., ii. 222–53; *Leg. Rec.*, MS., ii. 154–67, 181–2. Art. 1. Ayunt. to apply for assignment of *egidos* and *propios* lands. Art. 2. The *propios* in small tracts may be leased at auction; and present holders will pay as required by the ayunt. Art. 3. Grantees of town lots for building, of 100 varas square, will pay $6.25, and 25 cents per front vara for a smaller lot or for the excess in a larger one. Art. 4, 5. For the grant and registration of a brand for cattle, $1.50. Art. 6. For killing cattle or sheep for market, 6.25 cents per head; hogs, 25 cents. Art. 7. Shops for sale of dry goods are to pay $1 per month; grocery and other shops, and bar-rooms, 50 cents. Art. 8. Each weight and measure, sealed by the *fiel ejecutor*, 12.5 cents. Art. 9. Circuses and other shows, $2 for each performance. Art. 10. Billiard-rooms, $1 per month. Art. 11. At the 5 ports, including S. Pedro, 12.5 cents for each parcel landed from foreign vessels, and 6.25 cents from national vessels. Art. 12. The 25 cents per ton on foreign vessels to be asked for in behalf of the treasuary of the dip. Art. 13. Hunters are to pay 50 cents each on large otter and beaver skins. Art. 14. Fines for minor offences, imposed by alcalde or gefe, to go into the munic. fund. Art. 15, 16. Liquor taxes are reduced as follows: National brandy to $3, Angélica, $2, and wine $1.50, per barrel; foreign brandy to $1, gin $1, wine and beer 50 cents, per gallon. Art. 17. A voluntary contribution be requested from each vessel anchoring at Monterey, for the building of a wharf. Art. 18. Tax of $3 on each auction sale. Art. 19–21. Provisions for execution of the law.

rest on doubtful records. Eleven had visited the coast in the preceding half-decade. Twenty-two were whalers in quest of supplies. Of the rest, twenty-three were under United States colors; thirteen carried the Mexican flag, seven the English, four the Russian, three the Hawaiian, and one the Italian. One was a government vessel; two came from the Columbia River for supplies; and the rest came to trade for Californian products—seventeen from Honolulu, fourteen from South American and Mexican ports, and nine from Boston.[22]

[22] Alphabetical list of vessels in Californian ports in the years 1831-5:

Alert, Amer. ship, 342 tons; Faucon, master, transferring command on arrival to Thompson; Bryant & Sturgis, owners; Alf. Robinson, resident supercargo; arrived from Boston in June 1835. Davis thinks she was also on the coast in 1833 under Penhallow.

American, whaler; at S. Fran. in Nov. 1832.

Anchorite, whaler; at S. Fran. in Nov. 1832.

Avon, Amer. hermaph. brig, 88 tons, 16 men; Wm S. Hinckley, master; John C. Jones, owner; two or three trips from Honolulu in 1834-5; duties, $2,101, $1,719, and $2,374. According to Dana, she also engaged in smuggling. Jones was on board in 1835. She carried Gov. Figueroa's remains to Sta B. from Monterey.

Ayacucho, Engl. brig, 204 or 160 tons, 13-25 men; John Wilson, master; Stephen Anderson, and later Jas Scott, supercargo; on the coast from Callao each year 1831-5 for hides and tallow; duties, $4,721 in 1832; $4,416 in 1834; $4,020 in 1835. She was regarded as the fastest sailer on the coast.

Baikal, Russ. brig, 202 tons; Livovich Iliasovich (?), master; at S. Fran. spring of 1831 and autumn of 1833.

Balance, whaler; Ed Daggett, master; at S. Fran. Nov. 1832; 21 men, most of them ill with scurvy.

Barnstable, Jas B. Hatch, master; Henry Mellus, sup. Probably erroneous record in Hayes' list for 1833.

Bolivar, Amer. brig, 212 tons; from Honolulu to buy horses 1832; $400 tonnage; accused of smuggling; perhaps in 1833; Nye, master; also at end of 1835; Dominis, master.

Bonanza, Engl. schr, doubtful record of 1834.

By Chance, Amer. schr; 84 tons; Hiram Covell, master; at Mont. 1834, from Panamá; duties, $1,907.

California, Amer. ship, 379 tons; Bryant & Sturgis, owners; arr. from Boston in 1831, and left in April 1833; 'C——,' master; Wm A. Gale, sup., who remained at her departure; came back in 1834, remaining until 1835; Jas Arther, master.

Catalina, Mex. brig, 160 or 138 tons, 13 men; brought govt stores in 1831; John C. Holmes, master. Brought Gov. Figueroa in Jan. 1833, and made another trip to Mazatlan and back in 1833. Jos Snook (called Esnuco), master. Also on the coast in 1834-5; Fred. Becher, sup. (R. Marshall, master; and E. Celis, sup., according to Spence). Under U. S. flag, according to Dana. Cargo, $12,555; duties, $1,550.

Chalcedony, Amer. brig; Jos Steel, master; on the coast in 1832-3.

Charles Eyes, Engl. bark, 255 or 219 tons, 14 men; Thos Chapman, master; on the coast 1833 from Callao.

Clarita, doubtful record of 1834.

Clementina, Mex. schr; doubtful record of 1835.

Clementine, Engl. brig; Jas Hanly, master; from Honolulu 1835, consigned to Nathan Spear; duties, $3,261; carried away horses and hides in Dec.

Convoy, Amer. brig, 137 tons, 13 men; Pickens, master; from Honolulu in 1831.

Crusader, Amer. brig. (later perhaps Mexican), 160 or 110 tons; from Sandw. Isl. 1832–3; Thos Hinckley or Thos Sturgis, master or sup.; duties, $2,273; from Callao in 1834; Wm A. Richardson, master.

Diana, Amer. brig, 170 tons; from Honolulu via Sitka in 1835; duties, $363.

Don Quixote, Amer. bark; John Meek, master; Wm S. Hinckley, sup., from Honolulu 1833–4; duties, $475.   Complaint of unlawful privileges granted her.   Spence puts her in his list for 1832, also with Smith as master.

Dryad, Engl. brig; from Columbia River; paid duties, $1,416, in Jan. 1831, but had arrived in Dec. 1830.   Touched at S. Fran. again in Nov. 1833, for Honolulu, with David Douglas, the scientist, and Chief Factor Finlayson on board.   Douglas had also come to Cal. on the first trip, remaining some time in the country.

Eliza, at Sta Bárbara Oct. 1831.

Enriqueta, Amer. schr., 62 tons; Lewis (or Levi) Young, master; on the coast 1833.   Perhaps same as the *Harriet*, q. v.

Europe, 1834.   See *Urup*.

Facio, Mex. brig, 11 men; Santiago Johnson, master; Johnson & Aguirre, owners; from Guaymas in 1833.   John Forster took her back.   Perhaps on the coast in 1834.   In 1835 she was grounded at S. Pedro, and was rescued by the *Pilgrim*.

Fakeja (*Fakir ?*), whaler, 339 tons; R. Smith, master; at Mont. in Dec. 1833.

Fanny, whaler; at S. Fran. Oct. 1831.

Fibian (*Phœbe Ann ?*), on the coast to trade in 1831.

Framen, doubtful name of 1835.

Friend, Amer. whaler, 404 tons; L. B. Blindenburg, master, 1832–3.   Also 2 whalers not named at S. Fran. Oct. 1832.

Gange, French whaler; H. Chaudiere, master; Mont. Sept. 1835.

Garrafilia, Amer. brig, 170 tons; at Mont. 1835; duties, $361.

General Jackson, Amer. whaler; at Mont. Nov. 1833.

Globe, mentioned on doubtful authority 1831.

Guadalupe, Cal. schr, 60 tons; built by Jos Chapman, and launched at S. Pedro in 1831.   *Robinson's Life in Cal.*, 100.

Harriet, whaler, 417 tons, 34 men; at S. Fran. Oct. 1831.

Harriet Blanchard, Amer. schr, 62 or 66 tons; Carter, master; Shaw, sup.; Jones, owner; took 30 horses for Honolulu in 1833.

Helvetius, Amer. whaler; at S. Fran. Oct.–Nov. 1833.   Possibly on the coast before; as Chas Brown always claimed to have come on her in 1829.

Iolani, Hawaiian schr, 48 tons, 6 men; Jas Rogers, master; Nic. García, consignee; at Mont. in spring of 1835; duties, $776.

Isabel, Amer. whaler, 242 tons; J. C. Albert, master; S. Fran. and Mont. 1833.

Josephine, schr under Wm A. Richardson, lost at Sta Catalina Isl. in 1832, acc. to Hayes' list.

Jóven Dorotea, Mex. schr; Benito Machado, master; at Mont. May 1834.

Jóven Victoriano, brig; at S. Fran. Sept. 1832.

Juan José, Mex. brig; consigned to Pedrorena in 1835, acc. to Spence's list.

Kitty, whaler; at S. Fran. in Nov. 1833.

Lagoda, Amer. ship, 292 tons; John Bradshaw, master; Bryant & Sturgis, owners; Robinson, owner's agent; on the coast from autumn of 1833 to spring of 1835.

Leon, French ship; Bonnet, master.   Mentioned on uncertain authority as having come to the coast in 1835 for cattle and hay for French troops in the Pacific; probably later.

Leonidas, Mex. brig; formerly the U. S. *Dolphin*; Malarin, master; named by Davis for 1833.

Leonor, Mex. ship, 207 tons; Henry D. Fitch, master; on the coast from S. Blas in 1831; came back in 1833-4, and also in 1835, under Chas Wolter; Fred. Becher, sup.; duties, $1,419.

Liverpool Packet (?), whaler of 1835.

Llama, Engl. brig, 140 tons; Wm M. Neill, master; from Columbia River in 1834 for supplies; duties, $874.

Loriot, Amer. schr, 70 tons; Gorham H. Nye and A. B. Thompson, master and sup.; on the coast 1833-4. See text for her seizure at S. Fran. Back again in 1835 and carried Híjar and Padrés to S. Blas in May, returning in Aug.; duties, $4,024. More smuggling.

Louisa, Amer. bark, 174 tons, 16 men; Geo. Wood, master; J. C. Jones, owner and sup.; from Honolulu via Sitka in 1831; took hides and horses. Wm H. Davis, since well known in Cal., was on board as a boy 9 years of age.

Magruder, Amer. schr, 15 tons, 4 men; Wm Taylor, or Faiton, master; from Honolulu in 1834 for sale.

Marcus, whaler, 286 tons, 23 men; N. S. Bassett, master; at S. Fran. Oct. 1831.

Margarita, Mex. schr.; carried J. M. Padrés from Mont. 1831; back on the coast 1834-5; duties, $547, $479.

María Teresa, Mex. brig; Spence's list 1835.

Mariquita, Mex. sloop; Agustín Poncabaré, master (or J. Chaseagre); from S. Blas 1833, and again 1835; duties, $171.

Martha, whaler, 359 tons, 31 men; Tim. W. Riddell, master; at Mont. Oct.- Nov. 1834.

Matador, Mex. brig; cons. to J. Parrott in 1835, acc. to Spence's list.

Morelos, Mex. sloop of war; Lieut L. F. Manso, com.; Luis Valle, master. Brought part of the colony and several officers to Cal. in Sept. 1834.

Natalia, Mex. brig, 185 tons, 13 men; Juan Gomez, master; Comp. Cosmop., owner; Juan Bandini, sup. Brought part of the colony to Cal., and was wrecked at Mont. in Dec. 1834.

Newcastle, Amer. brig; Stephen Hersey, master; from Boston via Honolulu in 1832.

North America, Amer. whaler, 388 tons; Nathaniel Richards, master; at Mont. Nov. 1833.

Pacífico, Mex. brig; from Guaymas, cons. to Aguirre, in 1834; duties, $280. Some trouble about 1,156 marks of silver bullion.

Peor es Nada, Mex. schr, 20 tons; built at Mont. by Joaquin Gomez and launched Aug. 30, 1834; sailed for south in Oct. under Chas Hubbard, under charter to Isaac V. Sparks and others for otter-hunting; returned Mar. 1835 under John Coffin, making a second trip to south in the autumn.

Phœbe (?), whaler of 1832.

Pilgrim, Amer. brig, 155 tons, 14 men; Frank A. Thompson, master, succeeded by Ed H. Faucon; Bryant & Sturgis, owners; Robinson, agent; on the coast from Jan. 1835, having perhaps arrived in 1834; cargo, $12,000.

Plant, Amer. brig; B. & S., owners; sailed from Boston with the *California,* but had to put in at Rio de Janeiro for repairs; arr. in 1832 and soon sailed for home via Honolulu.

Pocahontas, Amer. ship, 300 tons; Bradshaw, master; Shaw, sup.; remained on the coast from 1830 to Jan. 1832, carrying away Gov. Victoria and Padre Peyri.

Polifemia, Russ. brig, 180 tons; N. Rosenberg, master; on the coast in 1833-4-5; duties, $383; accused of smuggling.

Primavera; Mex. brig; C. Bane, master; in Spence's list for 1835.

Pulga, at Mont. Sept. 1834; doubtful.

Refugio, Mex. schr; at S. Fran. 1834; duties on salt, $15. Said by Warner to have been built at S. Pedro in 1831-2. Perhaps same as the Guadalupe, or confounded with that vessel.

Rosa, Sardinian ship, 425 tons, 24 men; Nic. Bianchi, master; A. A. Cot, consignee. 'A large, clumsy ship, with her top-masts stayed forward and high poop-deck, looking like an old woman with a crippled back,' says Dana. Arr. in 1834, and in 1835 carried the colony conspirators from S. Fran. to Sta B.

Roxana, Amer. brig; Frank Thompson, master; B. & S., owners; on the coast in 1832-3; Gale & Robinson, agents. The *Riojana*, Cal. schr; Wm Ayala, master; probably the same craft.

S. Feighton, whaler, 351 tons, 25 men; Benj. H. Lawton, master; at Mont. Oct. 1834.

Santa Bárbara, Mex. schr, 40 tons, 5 men; Thos Robbins, master; at Sta B. June 1833 from Mazatlan with 6 passengers; built in Cal. See list 1829.

Singapartan (*Seringapatan* of 1830?), Engl. whaler; at S. Fran. 1832.

Sitka, Russ. bark, 202 tons; Basilio Waccodzy (?), master; at S. Fran. and Mont. 1835.

South Carolina, Amer. ship; Jos Steel, master; at Mont. Aug. 1834; duties, $10,631.

Spy, doubtful mention, 1832.

Steriton, whaler; at Mont. Sept. 1834.

Tansuero (or *Traumare*), Engl. brig, 215 tons; L. Amist, master; from Sandw. Isl. in 1834.

Tranquilina, whaler, 309 tons, 22 men; Geo. Prince, master; at S. Fran. Nov. 1832.

Trinidad, Mex. brig of Spence's list for 1835.

Urup, Russ. brig; Dionisio Zarembo, master; wintered 1831-2; duties, $1,107; also 1834; Basilio Idirbe (?), master; duties, $1,953.

Volunteer, Amer. bark, 226 or 150 tons, 11 men; Jos O. Carter, master; John Ebbetts, sup.; on the coast 1829-31; also in 1833; Shaw, master; Jones, owner and sup.; Sherman Peck, asst sup. Carter took her back, Jones and Shaw returning on the *H. Blanchard* to Honolulu.

Victoria, Brewer, master; in Spence's list for 1832.

Waverly, Hawaiian brig; Wm Sumner, master; arr. S. Pedro Jan. 1832, bringing the exiled priests Bachelot and Short from Honolulu. Remained but a few days.

Whalehound, doubtfully recorded whaler 1831.

William Little (*Guillermo Chiquito*), sloop, 36 tons, 7 men; Little or Henry Carter, master; from Honolulu for produce and horses in 1831.

William Lye (or *Syne*), whaler, 389 tons, 30 men; D. A. Riddell (or Reyder), master; at Mont. Oct. 1834.

William Thompson, whaler; Stephen Potter, master; at S. Fran. Nov. 1832; crew mutinous.

Wilmington, whaler; at Sta B. Nov. 1835; 1,900 bbls oil.

CHAPTER XIV.

PIONEERS AND FOREIGN RELATIONS.

1831-1835.

OVERLAND IMMIGRATION—NEW MEXICAN ROUTE—WOLFSKILL'S PARTY—
YOUNT AND BURTON—JACKSON'S COMPANY—WARNER—EWING YOUNG'S
SECOND VISIT—CARSON, WILLIAMS, SPARKS, AND DYE—GRAHAM AND
LEESE—ACROSS THE SIERRA—CAPTAIN JOE WALKER—NIDEVER—BON-
NEVILLE'S NARRATIVE—HUDSON'S BAY COMPANY TRAPPERS—OTTER-
HUNTING IN CALIFORNIA—NEW MEXICAN HORSE-THIEVES—CHINO PANDO
—FOREIGN POLICY—FEARS—OFFER OF PURCHASE BY U. S.—SPANIARDS
—PIONEER NAMES—THOSE WHO CAME BEFORE 1830—NEW-COMERS OF
EACH YEAR—ALPHABETICAL LISTS—DOUGLAS THE BOTANIST—THOMAS
COULTER'S VISIT—MORINEAU'S MEMOIR—VISIT OF HALL J. KELLEY—
JOHN COULTER'S LIES—DANA'S 'TWO YEARS BEFORE THE MAST.'

OVERLAND immigration of trappers and traders into
California continued to some extent during 1831–5.
Several parties came in by the Gila routes from New
Mexico, and at least one crossed the mountains farther
north, as the companies of James O. Pattie and Ewing Young and Jedediah Smith had done at an earlier date.[1] The subject retains all its fascination and
importance of the preceding period, and also, unfortunately, its meagreness of record. Warner and Nidever furnished me in their personal recollections
most interesting and valuable information, as have
other immigrants of that epoch in greater or less degree. Bonneville and Joe Meek have had their recollections recorded by the pens of Irving and Victor.
Statements of Joe Walker and other path-finding
pioneers have found their way more or less fully and

[1] See chap. vi. of this vol. on overland expeditions of 1826–30.

accurately into newspaper print; and the archives indicate from time to time the presence of trapper bands at the coast settlements or in the interior valleys. With all this, the record is neither complete nor satisfactory in all respects, and there is little likelihood that it can ever be much improved.

In the autumn of 1830, William Wolfskill fitted out a company in New Mexico to trap in the great valleys of California. He was a Kentuckian by birth, thirty-two years of age, with some eight years' experience of trapping and trading in the broad territories surrounding Santa Fé from the north to the south-west. He had been a partner of Ewing Young, then absent in California, and he was assisted pecuniarily in this enterprise by Hook, a Santa Fé trader. There is extant neither list of the company nor diary of the trip; but the expedition took a route considerably north of that usually followed, left Taos in September, crossed the Colorado into the great basin, and pressed on north-westwardly across the Grande, Green, and Sevier rivers, then southward to the Rio Vírgen, trapping as they went. It seems to have been the intention to cross the mountains between latitudes 36° and 37°; but cold weather, with symptoms of disorganization in the company, compelled the leader to turn southward to Mojave. Thence he crossed the desert westward, and arrived at Los Angeles early in February 1831. Here the party was broken up, some of its members returning to New Mexico a few months after their arrival, and others remaining in California. Of the latter those subsequently best known as residents were, besides Wolfskill, George C. Yount and Lewis Burton. Of the individuals of this and other companies I shall have more to say later.[2]

[2] The authorities on Wolfskill's company are *Warner's Remin.*, MS., 39-41, 63-7; and the *Story of an Old Pioneer* written by ' B.' for the *Wilmington Journal*, 1866; also in substance in the *S. F. Bulletin* of Dec. 17, 1858. Other newspaper sketches are either taken from these, or are inaccurate. Other members of the party, remaining for a time or permanently in Califor-

The next expedition to be noticed came also from Santa Fé under the command of David E. Jackson, formerly a partner of Sublette, but now associated with Young and Waldo. He left Santa Fé in September 1831, with nine hired men and a negro slave. His purpose was to purchase mules in California for the Louisiana market, and he brought, besides letters from Young and Hook to Cooper, a large amount of silver for that purpose. Coming by way of Santa Rita, Tucson, and the Gila, he reached San Diego in November, starting on his return in February 1832. I have several of his letters to Captain Cooper. The only member of Jackson's party who is known to have remained in California was J. J. Warner.[3] It should be noted that some members of all these early parties, after returning to New Mexico, came back to live in California in later years; and these men are accustomed to date their pioneership from the year of their first visit, as I would gladly do if it were possible to ascertain the names and dates.

Ewing Young started on his second trip to California from Taos in September 1831, but as he trapped the Gila and other streams on the way, he did not reach Los Angeles until April 1832. He had with him thirty men, most of whom, with Jackson's party, were soon sent back to New Mexico in charge of the mules and horses purchased, not so many as the partners had hoped to obtain, and part of which were lost in fording the Colorado. Owing to defective traps, Young's beaver catch had not been large, and he resolved to retrieve his fortunes by a hunt in California,

nia, were Samuel Shields, Francis Z. Branch, John Rhea, Zacarias Ham, François le Fourri, Baptiste St Germain, Bautista Guerra, and Juan Lobar. Eight of the 11 are mentioned under date of April 1831, in *Dept. Rec.*, MS., ix. 95. A Mr Cooper is named in the *Story, etc.*, as one of the company. Which of the Coopers is not apparent.

[3] *Vallejo, Doc.*, MS., xxx. 237, 241, 280; xxxi. 4; *Warner's Remin.*, MS., 11–15, 42–3. There are 2 or 3 men in the arrivals of 1831, not otherwise accounted for, who may have come with Jackson or Wolfskill. Such are Braun, Gibson, Cebet, Romero, and Pardo. There are many newspaper items in which Warner's arrival this year is mentioned, with no details. Dye, *Recollections*, MS., also relates from memory the fitting-out of Jackson's party.

where he spent several years before going to Oregon.
Eight or ten of his men also remained, prominent
among whom were Moses Carson, Isaac Williams,
Isaac Sparks, and Job F. Dye.[4]

In the winter of 1832–3 another party arrived from
New Mexico, under circumstances nowhere recorded,
so far as I have been able to learn. This party, the
exact date of whose arrival is not known, included
Joseph Paulding, Samuel Carpenter, William Chard,
and Daniel Sill.[5] There are half a dozen other men
of some prominence whose arrival is accredited to this
period, and some of whom may have come with this
company. Such were Cyrus Alexander of 1832;
Lawrence Carmichael, Isaac Graham, and Jacob P.
Leese of 1833; and Joseph L. Majors of 1834.[6] Most
of these men were well known in California a little
later; but of their coming there is nothing more to
be said. The way from the south-east, notwithstanding the natural perils of the desert and the ever im-
minent danger of Apache hostilities, was in a certain
sense an open one, and was often traversed by parties
of two or three persons. It may be noted in this

[4] Dye, in his *Recollections of Cal.*, a MS. written for me, and *Recollections
of a Pioneer*, published in the *Sta Cruz Sentinel*, May 1, June 19, 1869, gives
a complete narrative of this expedition, with many interesting details of personal adventure. Other authorities are *Warner's Remin.*, MS., 11–21, 43–51;
Los Angeles Hist., 19; *Nidever's Life and Adven.*, MS., 36–7. Warner names
as those who remained in Cal., Carson, Williams, Sparks, Ambrose Tomlinson,
Joseph Dougherty, Wm Emerson, and Denton. Dye names as members of
the company, Moses Carson, Sparks, Williams, Dye, Wm Day, Benj. Day,
Sidney Cooper, Jos Gale, Jos Dofit, John Higgins, James Green, Cambridge
Green, James Anderson, Thomas Low, Julian Vargas, José Teforia, and John
Price. He also names as members of his original company from Arkansas,
whom Nidever represents as having left that company and joined Young,
Pleasant Austin, Powell Weaver, James Bacey, and James Wilkinson. Hace
is added by Nidever. Some of these names are doubtless erroneous. Most
of the men returned to N. Mexico, and some came back again. The two Days
and Price at any rate were in Cal. a few years later, and may possibly have
remained on this trip. Both Dye and Nidever mention the murder of Anderson by Cambridge Green in Arizona, for which Green was delivered to the
authorities at Los Angeles. He escaped from prison some time later.

[5] *Los Angeles Hist.*, 19, Warner being the authority.

[6] *Warner's Remin.*, MS., 58–61; and miscellaneous records of individual
arrivals. Wm Ware and James Craig should perhaps be named in this connection.

connection that John Forster came up from Guaymas to Los Angeles by land in 1833, guided by a native [7]

Still one more detachment from the army of trappers in the great basin came into California before 1835, and this time by a northern route over the Sierra. The general operations of this army in the broad interior, and the summer rendezvous of 1832–3 in the Green River Valley, have been described by Irving in his narrative of Bonneville's adventures. The same author records the formation of a company sent by Captain Bonneville under Joseph Walker to make explorations west of Great Salt Lake, and devotes a chapter to the adventures of that company.[8] The aim, as given by this authority, was to explore the region surrounding the lake, the extent of which body of water was greatly exaggerated by Bonneville. The company consisted of about forty men, some fifteen of whom were free trappers.[9] The start from Green River was in July 1833, and after hunting a few days on Bear River, they went on to the region just north of the lake. Whatever may have been Walker's original intentions or instructions, his men could not live in the desert, and they went westward in search of water, which was found in the head streams of the Mary or Ogden river, since called the Humboldt. I suppose their destination from the first had been California, though Bonneville may perhaps have had different views; at any rate Walker's men

[7] *Forster's Pioneer Data*, MS., 10.

[8] *Irving's Adventures of Bonneville*, 184–8, 324–42; also given in substance in *Warren's Memoir*, in *Pac. R. R. Repts.*, xi. pt i. p. 31–4. The first published narrative of this expedition was in the *Jonesborough, Tenn., Sentinel*, of March 8, 1837, a brief account from the statement of Stephen Meek, who had returned to Tennessee, and reprinted in *Niles' Register*, of March 25th, vol. lii. p. 50.

[9] Geo. Nidever, *Life and Adven.*, MS., was one of these. The original company of about 40 under Robert Bean had left Ft Smith in May 1830. It included Graham, Naile, Williams, Price, Leese, and Dye. It was divided in N. Mex. in the spring of 1831. Both Nidever and Dye give many details down to this division, and N. later. He says nothing of any instruction to explore the lake, but states that Walker when joined by the writer was bound for Cal.

followed the Humboldt down to its sink. There was trouble with the Indians along the way, respecting which the exact truth can hardly be known, except that the trappers' conduct was dastardly, though their outrages were exaggerated by Bonneville and others.[10]

From the Humboldt sink Walker's men crossed the desert and the Sierra into California by a route about which there is much uncertainty. Said Bonneville to Irving: "They struck directly westward, across the great chain of Californian mountains. For three and twenty days they were entangled among these mountains, the peaks and ridges of which are in many places covered with perpetual snow. For a part of the time they were nearly starved; at length they made their way through them, and came down upon the plains of New California. They now turned toward the south, and arrived at the Spanish village and post of Monterey." Stephen Meek tells us "they travelled now four days across the salt plains, when they struck the Californian mountains, crossing which took fifteen days, and in fourteen days more they reached the two Laries"— Tulares—"killed a horse, and subsisting on the same eleven days, came to the Spanish settlements." Joseph Meek is represented as giving the route somewhat definitely westward to Pyramid Lake, up the Truckee River, and across the mountains—by the present railroad line very nearly—into the Sacramento Valley, and thence southward. This authority also states that they met a company of soldiers out hunting for cattle-thieves in the San José Valley, and were taken as prisoners to Monterey.[11] Finally a newspaper version, founded on Walker's own statements, and corroborated to some extent by that of Nidever, gives what I suppose to have been the correct route from the sink, south-westward by what are now Carson

---

[10] For some details, see *Hist. Utah*, chap. ii., this series.

[11] *Victor's Riv. West.* And Sebastian Peralta with a party of vecinos from S. José did meet early in Nov. a company of so-called French trappers bound to Monterey. *S. José, Arch. MS.*, v. 27.

Lake and Walker lake and river, over the Sierra near the head waters of the Merced, and down into the San Joaquin Valley.[12]

Whatever the route, they reached Monterey in November 1833; and all authorities agree that with fandangos and aguardiente they passed a gay winter at the capital; though somewhat strangely their presence there has left but slight traces in the archives.[13] George Nidever and John Price are the only members of the company known to have remained in California, though Frazer and Moz were probably of this party. Several other men known to have arrived in 1833 may have belonged to it.[14] In the spring Walker with most of his men started to return, skirting the Sierra southward and discovering Walker Pass. Thence they kept to the north-east, and by a route not exactly known, rejoined Bonneville on Bear River in June 1834.[15] That officer was altogether disgusted with

[12] Biographical sketches of Capt. Jos R. Walker in *Sonoma Democrat*, Nov. 25, 1876; and in *S. José Pioneer*, Sept. 1, 1877. Thompson of the *Democrat* was well acquainted with Walker; and the article in the *Pioneer* was founded on an interview. One account says he saw Mono Lake, and the other that he discovered Yosemite. On Walker's tombstone is an inscription: 'Camped at Yosemite Nov. 13, 1833.' According to the *Pioneer*, 'his first attempt to descend to the west was near the head waters of the Tuolumne, which he found impossible; but working a little to the south-west he struck the waters of the Merced.' Nidever states that they came down between the Merced and Tuolumne, and soon arrived at Gilroy's rancho.

[13] The only allusions to Walker's party that I have found are, 1st, a letter of Wm L. Saunders to Walker of June (Jan.?) 1, 1834, in relation to a bill against S. left with Capt. Cooper for collection. *Vallejo, Doc.*, MS., xxxi. 91; and, 2d, John Price's petition for a permit to remain, in which he is said to have come with Walker late in 1834. *Dept. St. Pap., Ben. Cust.-H.*, MS., vii. [201].

[14] A writer in the *Sta Cruz Sentinel*, June 14, 1873, names John Nidever. John Hoarde, Thos Bond, Daily, Capt. Merritt, Wm Ware, and François Lajeunesse as having come with Walker.

[15] Irving says 'they passed round their southern extremity [of the mountains], and crossing a range of low hills, found themselves in the sandy plains south of Ogden's River; in traversing which they again suffered grievously for want of water.' Two Mexicans had joined the trappers on their return, and gladly aided in their atrocities. Stephen Meek says they 'left on April 1st, and in 10 days struck the snow bank on the south side of the Salt or California mountain. Before reaching the plains on the north side of the mountain, they had to leave 30 horses, 9 mules, and 25 cattle in the snow. In the fore part of May, reached St. Mary's River,' and July 4th the Bear River. Warren says the return route was nearly that of Frémont in 1842, known as the Sta Fé trail to California. Finally Joseph Meek carries his party to the Colorado, down to the Gila, back to Bill Williams Fork, across to the Colo-

such details of "this most disgraceful expedition" as
he had patience to hear. "Had he exerted a little of
the lynch law of the wilderness," says Irving, "and
hanged these dexterous horsemen in their own lazos,
it would but have been a well merited and salutary act
of retributive justice. The failure of this expedition
was a blow to his pride, and a still greater blow to his
purse. The Great Salt Lake still remained unex-
plored; at the same time the means furnished so lib-
erally to fit out this favorite expedition had all been
squandered at Monterey"—so infinitely more important was it to explore the desert lake than to cross the
continent!

I have thus mentioned all the parties of trappers
known to have entered California in this period, except those of the Hudson's Bay Company from the
north, respecting whose presence I find only a few
vague allusions. Warner tells us that Young, in the
autumn of 1832, found the San Joaquin already
hunted, and on American Fork met Michel with a
large force of Hudson's Bay Company trappers. In
March 1833 John Work applied to Figueroa for a
permit to get supplies for his trappers, and in April
Padre Gutierrez at Solano complained of the presence
of forty men at Suisun calling themselves hunters,
but willing to buy stolen cattle, and otherwise disposed to corrupt the neophytes.[16] Kelley on his way
to Oregon in the autumn of 1834 was overtaken by
Laframboise and party coming from the south. In
June 1835 it was reported that the trappers had
their headquarters upon an island formed by the
Sacramento and Jesus María rivers; and in Novem-

rado Chiquito and Moqui towns, and thence north to the starting-point, accom-
panied most of the way by a large party of hunters under Frapp and Jervais!
[16] March 18, 1833, Work to Figueroa. March 20th, 6 beaver-hunters at
Solano desiring leave to visit S. F. *Dept. St. Pap.*, MS., iii. 101–2. Apr. 7th,
P. Gutierrez to F. *Id.*, iii. 111. Warner, *Remin.*, MS., 47, says that be-
tween 1832 and 1840 Frapp, Breager, and Fitzpatrick of the Rocky Mountain
Fur Co. each came to Cal. with a party of trappers. See *Hist. Northwest
Coast*, this series.

ber, Laframboise, the leader of the beaver-hunters, was warned by Comandante Vallejo at Sonoma to suspend his operations.[17]

Over thirty hunters had been added to the population of California by the expeditions that have been mentioned, and most of them resorted to hunting and trapping as a means of living, for some years at least. This they did with and without license, with their own license or with that of another, separately or in bands of foreign comrades or in partnership with Californians and Mexicans, and paying taxes when they could not avoid it.[18] Wolfskill on his arrival associated himself, as did Yount, with the earlier comers, Prentice, Pryor, and Laughlin. He built a schooner at San Pedro, and in her hunted otter up and down the coast in 1832. Being a Mexican citizen, with a passport from the governor of New Mexico, he was able to get a license, but he soon abandoned the business to become a settler. Ewing Young, with Warner and others, also engaged in otter-hunting for a time in 1832, building two canoes at San Pedro with the aid of a ship-carpenter; and with these

[17] *Vallejo, Doc.*, MS., iii. 55, 81. The Columbia-river trappers and traders usually retired in summer northward, to return in Sept. Vallejo speaks of orders of the govt made known to Laframboise the year before against taking beaver; but in a spirit of hospitality he offered to permit a temporary encampment at Sonoma, otherwise the Frenchman must retire within 24 hours or be treated as a smuggler.

[18] In his report to the min. of rel. on June 7, 1831, Victoria complains that he is unable to prevent foreigners from reaping all the profits of the fur trade. For want of a vessel he could not prevent fraudulent hunting at the islands, and the interior was overrun by foreigners who cared nothing for law. *Dept. Rec.*, MS., ix. 135–6. A. B. Thompson's arrest and the seizure of his vessel at S. F. have been already noticed. Pryor, Prentice, Lewis, and White were accused of complicity with Thompson, and the confiscation of their boat and goods was ordered in Sept. 1833. *Monterey, Arch.*, MS., i. 29–30; *Dept. St. Pap., Ben. Pref. y Juzg.*, MS., iii. 24–5. In July 1833 Figueroa says that vessels have taken otter in notorious violation of law of nations, and such craft must be seized. *S. Diego, Arch.*, MS., 2. 1834, a legal argument citing authorities on eminent domain in the matter of taking otter. *Doc. Hist. Cal.*, MS., i. 184, 134. April 10, 1834, the Russian colonial gov. reported that sea-otter and beaver would soon be exterminated by Americans, with the aid of Indians, in violation of Mexican laws. *Zavalishin, Delo o Koloniy Ross*, 9. Alfred Robinson, *Statement*, MS., 18–20, gives some details about otter-hunting during this period. So does Wm H. Davis, *Glimpses*, MS., passim.

canoes, a yawl, and two kanakas, they visited Point
Concepcion and the channel islands. Soon, however, they started inland with a larger party to
trap on Kings River in October. In 1833 Young
trapped up to Klamath Lake and back, then made a
short trip to the Gila and Colorado, and went to
Oregon with horses in 1834. He lived and died in
Oregon, making several visits to California to buy
live-stock in later years. The presence of 'Joaquin
Jóven' and his hunters is noted in the archives.[19]
George Nidever with Yount at first hunted on the
north side of San Francisco Bay and at the mouth
of the San Joaquin, and later with Sill and others
on the southern coast and Santa Bárbara islands
under Captain Dana's license.[20] This hunting under
another's license was a common method of evading the
spirit of the laws, and avoiding inconvenient delays;
and it was profitable to the holder of the document,
who exacted a large percentage of the skins taken,
having it in his power to effect a confiscation of all in
case of non-compliance with his demands. Job Dye
represents himself as having lost five months' time
and all the skins he had taken, by venturing to
question Don Roberto Pardo's system of dividing the
spoils.[21] He later hunted in partnership with the
padre of San Luis Obispo, and then made a trip

[19] Elsewhere in this chapter I notice Young's departure for Oregon, with
Hall J. Kelley. Oct.–Nov. 1833, a party of S. José vecinos out in search of
stolen horses met Jóven's party in the valley, and recovered 27 animals,
though there were many more which he would not give up. Young also
visited S. José with 4 of his men. The S. José party, under Sebastian Peralta,
killed 22 Moquelumnes on this expedition. *S. José, Arch.*, v. 27; *Dept. St.
Pap., Ben. Pref. y Juzg.*, MS., v. 45–6. In June 1835 Vallejo writes that 7
foreign fugitives from Monterey had passed on toward the Columbia with
stolen horses. One named Oliver was found sick at Suisun, and said his companions had gone on to join Joaquin Jóven. *Vallejo, Doc.*, MS., iii. 55.

[20] Brown, *Narrative*, MS., 27–8, mentions the operations of Yount and
Nidever in S. F. Bay. Capt. Cooper and other foreigners got licenses to
hunt in 1833–4, on condition that not over one third of their crews should be
foreigners; but on one occasion Castro and Estrada were authorized to complete their crews with foreign sailors. *Dept. St. Pap.*, MS., iii. 76, 144–5,
157–8, 167, 187–9; *Vallejo, Doc.*, MS., xxxi. 3, 18.

[21] In 1831 Victoria revoked Ortega's license because he allowed foreigners
to hunt under it. *Dept. Rec.*, MS., ix. 1, 42, 80–1.

down the coast with McIntosh. Meanwhile Burton, Sparks, and others made a not very successful trip to the peninsular coasts in the *Peor es Nada*.

Another phase of overland communication demands passing notice. New Mexicans of Spanish blood came like the foreigners by the Colorado routes to California, where as a rule they had a bad reputation. They came ostensibly for purposes of trade, bartering sarapes and blankets for mules and horses;[22] but they were suspected with much reason of driving away stolen as well as purchased animals, of inciting the neophytes to steal, and even of being in league with gentile bands of the Tulares. Complaints were frequent during 1831–5, but it was in 1833 that the greatest excitement was felt, as indicated by contemporary correspondence. Early in January, the ayuntamiento of Los Angeles passed strong resolutions on the subject, and forbade the purchase of any animal without the intervention of some local juez;[23] and an attempt was made to enforce the rule and punish offenders, with Figueroa's authority and support. Parties of armed vecinos, under various jueces del campo,

[22] There were of course legitimate traders, and a few New Mexicans became permanent and respectable citizens of California. On the overland trade I quote from the *Los Ángeles, Hist.*, 18: 'With Mr Wolfskill's party there were a number of New Mexicans, some of whom had taken sarapes and frazadas with them for the purpose of trading them to the Indians in exchange for beaver skins. On their arrival in Cal. they advantageously disposed of their blankets to the rancheros in exchange for mules. The appearance of these mules in New Mexico, owing to their large size compared with those at that time used in the Missouri and Sta Fé trade, and their very fine form, as well as the price at which they had been bought in barter for blankets, caused quite a sensation, out of which sprung up a trade carried on by means of caravans or pack-animals, which flourished for some 10 or 12 years. These caravans reached Cal. yearly. They brought the woollen fabrics of New Mexico, and carried back mules, silk, and other Chinese goods. Los Angeles was the central point in Cal. of this trade. Coming by the northern, or Green and Vírgen river routes, the caravans came through the Cajon Pass and reached Los Angeles. From thence they scattered themselves over the country from S. Diego to S. José and across the bay to Sonoma and S. Rafael. Having bartered and disposed of the goods brought, and procured such as they wished to carry back and what mules they could drive, they concentrated at Los Angeles for their yearly return.'
[23] *Los Angeles, Arch.*, MS., iv. 86–7.

scoured the country to seize all animals for which no proper bills of sale could be shown, at the same time arresting offenders; and though the main success was in covering much paper with ink, yet Antonio Ávila succeeded in restoring a large band of mules stolen from San Luis Obispo mission, and in arresting one or two parties of New Mexicans, including Juan de Jesus Villapando, or 'Chino Pando,' the leading culprit, who soon broke jail and escaped to New Mexico. Other parties were pursued unsuccessfully, but all had the effect to open the eyes of the authorities to the extensive thieving operations going on. An appeal was sent to the governor of New Mexico, who was informed by Figueroa that, so general had become the outrages committed, "every man coming from that territory is believed to be an adventurer and a thief." Legal proceedings were instituted against Villapando at Santa Fé, and against the parties arrested in California, most of whom escaped from the jail, and a grand military expedition was sent out under Alférez Dámaso Rodriguez against the robbers. The exact result is not known, for little appears on the subject after 1833. It is probable that the archive record is incomplete, but also that this New Mexican branch of industry was subsequently conducted on a smaller scale and with more caution.[24]

[24] March 10, 1831, gov. to com. of Sta Bárbara on the complaints he has received. *Dept. Rec.*, MS., ix. 5–6. April, arrival at Angeles of a caravan of 30 under Antonio San Estévan. *Dept. St. Pap.*, *Ben. Pref. y Juzg.*, MS., iii. 52. Avila and Lugo sent out after thieves. *Id.*, *Angeles*, i. 102–4, 112–13; *Ávila, Notas*, MS., 9–10. Affairs of Jan.–March 1833, including complaints of padres and vecinos, official correspondence, results of expeditions, and legal proceedings. *Nuevo Mexico, Expediente de Abigeato, 1833*, MS. Similar papers in *Los Angeles, Arch.*, iv. 73; *Dept. St. Pap., Angeles*, MS., i. 109; xi. 3–4. Jan. 21, 1834, a party arrives from N. Mexico with 1,645 sarapes, 341 blankets, 171 coverlets, and 4 *tirutas*—claiming exemption from taxes under a decree of 1830. *Dept. St. Pap., Ben.*, MS., ii. 16. Feb. 4th, Elwell writes Hartnell that 125 New Mexicans have come to buy mules; and will probably steal what they can not buy. *Vallejo, Doc.*, MS., xxxi. 64. Feb. 21st. gov. of N. Mexico is proceeding against Villapando. *Dept. St. Pap., Angeles*, MS., xi. 15. April 3d, part of José Antonio Aveita's company bound for the Tulares and must be arrested. *Id., Ben. Mil.*, lxxxviii. 17–18. July 30th, P. Abella complains of the N. Mexicans staying at his mission and selling liquor to the Indians. *Arch. Arzob.*, MS., v. pt ii. 6.

Overland immigration being thus disposed of, I have to notice briefly several general topics of foreign relations. Californians were as a rule favorably disposed toward foreigners in these years, there being doubtless less prejudice against them in the minds of citizens than against the Mexicans. The benefits they had conferred in past years, and were still conferring commercially, were appreciated both by citizens and authorities, while the harm they were doing and likely to do troubled the latter much more than the former, and not even them very seriously. Notwithstanding the irregularities committed by the trappers and deserters, foreigners were not discouraged by illiberal regulations and restrictions from settling in the country; while citizenship, wives, and lands were easily obtained by those whose conduct was regular. Newcomers had to comply with certain formalities, and they were occasionally reminded that they were under surveillance, but no cases of oppression are recorded.[25]

[25] April 9, 1831, gov. to alcalde of Angeles. The 8 persons just arrived must make the declarations required by law of May 1, 1828, and give bonds for good conduct, after which *cartas de seguridad* will be granted. *Dept. Rec.*, MS., ix. 95-6. In *Forster's Pioneer Data*, MS., appen., is a *carta de seguridad* issued to Juan Forster by the vice-president to travel for one year in the republic. It is a printed blank filled out with name, dated April 4, 1832, and numbered 1031. Sept. 23, 1831, form of oath required from a Portuguese for naturalization. *Dept. Rec.*, MS., ix. 114. Nov. 8, 1832, six foreigners from whale-ships are on their way to S. José. They must be arrested and sent to Monterey. *S. José, Arch.*, MS., ii. 59. Jan. 1833, art. 9 of Monterey municipal laws. Foreigners on entering or leaving town must show their passports. *Dept. St. Pap.*, MS., iii. 160. April 1833, Figueroa is requested to remove from Solano to Monterey 3 turbulent and anti-catholic foreigners. *Id.*, iii. 116. Nov. 18, 1833, F. issues strict orders prohibiting foreigners from hunting. Patrols must be sent out monthly, and all offenders arrested and treated as smugglers. Hunters who are Mex. citizens must have a license. *Sta Cruz, Arch.*, MS., 95; *Dept. St. Pap., Mont.*, MS., ii. 82; *Id., Ben. Mil.*, lxxix. 16-17. May 17, 1834, F. submits to asesor García Diego's question if foreigners wishing to marry Cal. girls must have the gefe's permission, as required by Victoria. *Id.*, iii. 148. June 21st, dip. considers the question if married and land-owning foreigners must aid in community work of the pueblos. *Leg. Rec.*, MS., ii. 127-8. July 25th, none of the foreigners at Sta B. have *cartas* or certificates. *Dept. St. Pap.*, MS., xix. 33. Nov. 9th, all foreigners on ranchos must appear before alcalde. Foreigners without passes and fugitive sailors to be arrested. *Id., Ben. Pref. y Juzg.*, iv. 33-4; *Id., Cust.-H.*, iii. 14. Nov. 22d, Americans at Los Angeles protest against being obliged to do military service, except in case of an emergency, being protected by treaty between U. S. and Mexico. *Id., Los Angeles*, MS., i. 154-6. July 12, 1835, F. instructs the alcalde of S. Diego about the steps to be taken by Thos Ridington or any

The danger of territorial encroachment by foreigners was not in these years regarded as very threatening in California. True, it was sometimes alluded to by governor and congressmen, but less often and less earnestly than might be accounted for by the fact that it was the strongest argument that could be urged in pleas for attention, aid, and protection from the supreme government. Thus Cárlos Carrillo, in his argument for mission occupation of the north in 1831,[26] urged that the natural wealth of California was becoming well known to the world; and there were powers that recognized no right of domain not founded on actual possession—a threatening circumstance for that part of California north of San Francisco Bay. Victoria in the same year announced a doubtful rumor that the Americans were trying to found an establishment in the Tulares, informing the minister of war that he would prevent the entry of these foreigners without compromising the national dignity.[27] Figueroa's instructions of 1832 required that no obstacles be put in the way of foreigners desiring to settle in accordance with the colonization laws, and especially that a projected colonization scheme of Henry Virmond at Sonoma—about which nothing more is known —be aided; yet the government also recommended especial care that not more than one third of the inhabitants of any settlement should be foreigners, and attached great importance to the foundation of frontier posts, and the strict maintenance of Mexican supremacy up to latitude 42°, the limit fixed by treaty with the United States.[28] Figueroa's efforts in this direction have already been noted; but in his report of

other foreigner desiring naturalization. 1. He must prove that he came legally to Cal. 2. Apply to the ayunt., his original application being retained in the archives and he receiving a certified copy. 3. He must appear before the district judge and prove that he is a catholic, a good citizen, and has a trade by which to gain a living. 4. An expediente of all these steps and documents must be presented to the gefe pol. S. Diego, Arch., MS., 49, 56; Hayes, Doc., MS., 22.
[26] Carrillo, Exposicion, 8.
[27] May 6, 1831, V. to min. of war. Dept. Rec., MS., ix. 129-30.
[28] Figueroa, Instrucciones, MS., p. 35-6.

April 1833 he made some very serious charges against foreign residents. Not only did these adventurers hunt and trap in defiance of the laws, but they took advantage of their hunting expeditions as a pretext to explore the whole country and conciliate the gentiles, giving at the same time bad advice to citizens, and all with the intention, or under the guidance of men who had the intention, of eventually seizing this part of the republic.[29] The Russians and Americans were chiefly feared; and the former were somewhat more alarmed about the ambitious views of the Yankees than were the Californians themselves, being in fact the parties most directly interested; though, as we have seen, Californian ambition on the part of Russia was confined to a very few individuals. Zavalishin states that repeated warnings were given in Russian reports.[30]

Voyagers to California had frequently spoken and written of its natural advantages and its great prospective value as a national possession, and they had also pointed out clearly the ease with which it might be wrested from Spain or Mexico. But while individual foreigners probably—Americans and Russians certainly—thought and spoke of the time when California might belong to their respective countrymen,[31] I doubt if any scheme of encroachment had yet taken definite form in the councils of any nation. There was, however, a proposition for the purchase of northern

[29] April 12, 1833, F. to min of war. *St. Pap., Miss. and Colon.*, MS., ii. 303–4. In March P. Gutierrez of Solano had complained of dangers to be apprehended from foreign settlers on lands in that region, but this was with a view to local mission interests rather than those of the nation. *Dept. St. Pap.*, MS., iii. 101–2. June 5, 1834, F. sends to Mex. an account of the foreigners in Cal.—document not extant—but believes the number to be really much greater than appears, since many are not registered. *Id.*, iii. 139.

[30] *Zavalishin, Delo o Koloniy Ross*, 13–14. The Russian American governor in April 1834 mentioned the coming of 163 armed Americans with their families to settle, and Baron Wrangell, in a report of his mission to Mexico, stated that the U. S. minister had openly said, 'Oh, this part of California we will not lose sight of. We have parties there who gather and forward all possible information; and the time is not far off when northern California will come into our confederation.'

[31] Morrell, in his *Narrative*, published in 1832, draws in print a glowing picture of Cal. as it would be under the rule of the U. S.

California by the United States during the administration of General Jackson.   August 6, 1835, Forsyth,
secretary of state, wrote to Butler, chargé d'affaires
in Mexico, "it having been represented to the president
that the port of St Francisco, on the western coast of
the United Mexican States, would be a most desirable
place of resort for our numerous vessels engaged in
the whaling business in the Pacific, far preferable to
any to which they now have access, he has directed
that an addition should be made to your instructions
relative to the negotiations for Texas.   The main object is to secure within our limits the whole bay of St
Francisco.   If you can induce the Mexican government
to agree to any line which will effect this, you are authorized to offer a sum of —— in addition to the sum you
were directed to offer, etc.   You are to endeavor first
to obtain the following boundary, which is considered
the most eligible: Beginning at the gulf of Mexico,
proceed along the eastern bank of the Rio Bravo del
Norte to the 37th parallel of latitude, and thence along
that parallel to the Pacific.   This line may probably
be supposed to approach too near, if not to include, the
Mexican settlement of Monterey.   If this objection
should be urged, you can obviate it by explaining that
we have no desire to interfere with the actual settlements of Mexico on that coast, and you may agree to
any provision effecting the great object of securing the
bay of St Francisco, and excluding Monterey and the
territory in its immediate neighborhood."[32]   The sum
offered is given by some authorities as $5,000,000.   The
reply of the Mexican government has eluded my search,
but Dwinelle tells us that the proposition was favorably received, and would have been accepted had it
not been for the efforts of British diplomates.[33]

---

[32] *U. S. Govt. Doc.*, 25th cong., 1st sess., H. Ex. Doc. No. 42; *Congres-
sional Debates*, xiv., append., p. 131; *South. Quart. Rev.*, xv. 93–4.
[33] *Dwinelle's Address before Pioneers*, p. 19. In the *South. Quart. Rev.*, viii.
197, it is stated that Forsyth offered $5,000,000 'for the whole country of
California.' In *Niles' Register*, lxviii. 211 (1845), is quoted from the *London
Times* the statement that $5,000,000 was offered 'for the port of San Francisco,

Forbes has a chapter on 'Upper California considered as a field for foreign colonization,' written as early as 1835, though published later. He is enthusiastic in praise of the natural advantages of the country; but while he deprecates the Mexican restrictive policy and lack of energy, and indulges in brilliant dreams of what California would be under the rule of such a power as England, he evidently believes that there was no immediate danger of encroachment by any foreign power. He believes, however, that Russian policy on the Pacific coast should receive some attention from the American and European powers.[34]

Spaniards were still regarded as foreigners; but the attempts to enforce Mexican restrictions on the subject in California were so few and slight as hardly to merit mention. Victoria brought instructions to expel the Spaniards not legally entitled to remain, and he issued a circular on the subject in October 1831, a document not intended to apply to the padres, and not enforced at all, except that Cáceres, the only Spaniard in the San Francisco district, was ordered by Vallejo to leave the republic. Moreover, a citizen granted a license to take otter was forbidden to employ a Spaniard in his crew. That Victoria had failed to carry out his orders in this respect was one of the charges presented against him by the diputacion in 1832; but Figueroa adopted no more radical policy, though for political reasons he recommended the expulsion of padres Sarría and Duran, and his orders from Mexico seem not to have required any greater precautions in the case of Spaniards than other foreigners.[35]

one of the finest naval positions of the world,' and the editor thinks the *Times* mistaken about the date, and that the proposition was made earlier by President Adams, the price including Texas. He says: 'At that time Mexico was revelling in an unlimited credit with English capitalists, and for the sake of a few millions would not entertain a project for dismembering her empire.'

[34] *Forbes' Hist. Cal.*, 146–9, 309–25.

[35] *Dept. Rec.*, MS., ix. 60, 113; *Vallejo, Doc.*, MS., i. 278; *Leg. Rec.*, MS., i. 250; *Dept. St. Pap.*, MS., vi. 24.

Exclusive of transient visitors and of men about whom the records show only their presence in California at one date, the number of foreign residents, properly called pioneers, who came to the country before 1830 was 180, as per lists that have been already given.[36] Of this number 140 are known to have been in the country after 1835. Meanwhile in 1831–5, as named in the annual lists given later in this chapter, there came 170 more of the same class, of whom 160 left records of their presence after 1835. Therefore we may take 300 as a near approximation to the foreign male population in 1835, including sons but not daughters of pioneers by native wives. The number includes visitors who did not become residents until later; but there were doubtless a few whose presence after the year mentioned has left no trace in the records. It was the new-comers who a little later were to cause the authorities so much trouble rather than the older foreign residents. The latter were for the most part well-behaving citizens, many with Californian families, and all with Californian habits of life more or less deeply rooted. Now, as before and later, the trade of the country was largely in their hands, and as yet they meddled but slightly in territorial or local politics. They were as a rule well liked by the Californians; and though 'taking life easy,' they still exhibited a degree of energy that excited admiration, if not imitation. There are no startling adventures or great achievements to be noted in connection with any name in the list; neither did any fall into especial disgrace or misfortune. Some were married, and others baptized; a few obtained naturalization papers, and many got passports; several received land grants, the foundation of future fortunes; of many we have nothing at this time be-

[36] See list at end of vol. ii., this work; also annual lists for 1825–30 in chap. i., vi. of this volume. See also, for brief biographic notices of foreign residents and visitors, the Pioneer Register at end of vol. ii.–v., this work, which will serve also as index, including references to all that is written of any early Californian in any part of the work.

yond the bare record of their presence; and some are not mentioned at all, though known to have been in the country earlier and later.

Under date of 1831 may be noticed the visit of David Douglas, the famous Scotch botanist. He had spent five or six years in the north in an earnest and adventurous search for botanical specimens, as elsewhere related,[37] and he came down from the Columbia on the *Dryad* to investigate the flora of California, arriving at Monterey in December 1830. He brought letters from Captain Beechey to Hartnell, with whose family he became very intimate, and by whose aid he easily obtained in April a *carta de seguridad* to prosecute his researches for six months.[38] He remained in the country twenty months. His name appears on the rolls of the compañía extrangera in January 1832; and in a table of latitudes and longitudes promised to Governor Victoria and subsequently furnished to Figueroa, the variation of the compass at Monterey is dated August 1832.[39] Parry quotes a letter to Hooker, written at Monterey November 23, 1831, in which is given a slight description of the country and of the writer's botanical discoveries, but nothing of his personal adventures. He hoped to secure a passage to the Columbia River direct, but was obliged to wait until August 1832, and sail on an American schooner for Honolulu, and thence to Vancouver in October. There was a current rumor in later years that he had

[37] See *Hist. Northwest Coast*. Douglas' journal was published by Hooker in the *Companion to the Botanical Magazine*, ii. 79, etc., which I have not seen. An account of his adventures was published by Somerville in the *Overland Monthly*, vii. 105–13; and more briefly by Stillman in *Id.*, ii. 262. Whether the journal was seen by those writers I do not know; if so, it can have contained but very meagre details of Douglas' experience in California. A more complete account, quoting some of Douglas' letters to Hooker and referring to others, taken I suppose from the *Bot. Mag.* as above, is found in *Parry's Early Botanical Explorers of the Pac. Coast*, in the *Overland*, 2d ser., i. 409–14.

[38] *Dryad* at Monterey in Jan. *Vallejo, Doc.*, MS., xxi. 15. *Carta*, dated April 20, 1831, in *Dept. Rec.*, MS., ix. 97. Sept. 1, 1829, Beechey to Hartnell, in *Vallejo, Doc.*, MS., xxix. 407. He writes from London, and speaks of having met Guerra at Tepic.

[39] Nov. 25, 1833, Douglas to Figueroa, in *Vallejo, Doc.*, xxxi. 52, with the table of geographical positions on the same sheet, as follows:

found on the roots of his California plants gold enough to make a watch-seal![40] In November 1833 a vessel en route from the Columbia to Honolulu with Douglas and Chief Factor Finlayson on board touched at San Francisco in distress; and the botanist from his 'tent on the hill at Yerba Buena' wrote to Hartnell, recounting some of his later hair-breadth escapes in the far north, sending warm regards for friends at Monterey, and expressing his hope of meeting them again—"though not, God willing, before I see the 'land o' cakes.'"[41] He never saw either Scotland or California again; for in July 1834, during one of his solitary excursions at the Islands, he fell into a pit

	Latitude.	Longitude.
Sta Bárbara (landing)	34° 23′ 41″	119° 14′ 0″
Sta Bárbara (Noriega's house)	34° 25′ 0″	119° 14′ 30″
Sta Inés	34° 36′ 4″	119° 52′ 57″
Purísima	34° 40′ 14″	120° 8′ 54″
S. Luis Obispo	35° 16′ 20″	120° 22′ 21″
S. Luis Obispo (anchorage)	35° 10′ 56″	120° 19′ 0″
S. Miguel	35° 45′ 5″	120° 29′ 47″
S. Antonio	36° 0′ 18″	121° 5′ 1″
Sta Lucía (summit)	36° 11′ 49″	121° 10′ 14″
Soledad	36° 24′ 19″	121° 11′ 30″
Monterey (anchorage)	36° 36′ 0″	121° 44′ 0″
Monterey (Hartnell's house)	36° 35′ 43″	121° 44′ 21″
Monterey (Pt Pinos)	36° 38′ 30″	121° 46′ 37″
Monterey (Pt Carmelo)	36° 31′ 40″	121° 48′ 42″
Monterey (North Pt Carmelo)	36° 33′ 23″	121° 45′ 42″
Monterey (Cipres Pt)	36° 34′ 47″	121° 46′ 9″
Monterey (S. Cárlos)	36° 32′ 19″	121° 45′ 33″
Cerro de Buenaventura (top.)	36° 31′ 32″	121° 25′ 39″
Sta Cruz	36° 58′ 14″	121° 40′ 2″
Sta Cruz (mouth of river)	36° 57′ 33″	121° 40′ 0″
Sta Cruz (Pt Año Nuevo)	37° 0′ 52″	121° 41′ 21″
S. Juan	36° 50′ 55″	121° 18′ 4″
Cerro del Gavilan (top.)	36° 31′ 32″	121° 20′ 0″
Sta Clara	37° 21′ 4″	121° 45′ 53″
S. José	37° 31′ 47″	121° 48′ 2″
S. Francisco (Yerba Buena)	37° 48′ 15″	122° 20′ 27″
S. Rafael	37° 58′ 26″	122° 38′ 27″
S. Francisco Solano	38° 17′ 9″	122° 18′ 26″

[40] *Roberts' Recollections*, MS., p. 10, the writer being personally acquainted with Douglas, but not claiming to have heard the story from him. A similar rumor seems to have reached England, where it was reported after the gold discovery that flakes of gold were found on the roots of pines sent home by Douglas and others, who were blamed for not having found the gold or announced the discovery. *Quart. Review*, 1850, no. 87, p. 416.

[41] *Douglas's Letter to Hartnell, 1833*, in *Vallejo, Doc.*, MS., xxxi. 49. The letter was dated Nov. 11th, and on Nov. 25th, as we have seen, another was sent to Figueroa. Parry notes also from his letters that he anchored in Drake Bay, and landed at Whalers Bay, or Sauzalito.

and was trampled to death by a wild bull that had
fallen in before him. The botanical results of his trip
in California, that is, descriptions of the specimens
sent to England, were published by Sir William
Hooker in 1841.[42]

New-comers in 1831, as named in various records,
number fifty-four, and half of them, or twenty-seven,
as named in the appended list, are entitled to be considered pioneer residents.[43] Many spent the rest of
their years in California, and were locally well known,
but the most prominent names in later annals were
those of Burton, Davis, Forbes, Vignes, Warner,
Wolfskill, and Yount. Three of the whole number,
Davis, Warner, and Weeks, were living in 1884, all
of whom contributed their reminiscences for my use.
In that part of this chapter devoted to the overland
immigration from New Mexico, and of a former
chapter to the maritime annals of the year, all has
been said that is known respecting the actions of foreigners in 1831. As a class, they took no part in
the political disturbances of that year, though Abel
Stearns was one victim of Victoria's wrath who conspired for his overthrow; and Captain Bradshaw of
the *Pocahontas* was employed to carry away the fallen
governor.

In the spring of 1832 the foreign residents of Monterey were induced to take part in politics, so far as

[42] *Hooker and Arnott's Botany of Capt. Beechey's Voyage, California Supplement*, p. 316–409. Robinson, *Life in Cal.*, 107, who met Douglas at Monterey, says: 'I was told he would frequently go off, attended by his little dog,
and with rifle in hand search the wildest thicket in hope of meeting a bear;
yet the sight of a bullock grazing in an open field was more dreadful than all
the terrors of the forest. He once told me that this was his only fear, little
thinking what a fate was in reserve for him.'

[43] Pioneers of 1831: Wm Bale, Francis Z. Branch, Lewis T. Burton, Jos
O. Carter, Cooper (died), Wm H. Davis, Geo. A. Ferguson, James A. Forbes,
Thos Fuller, Jos Gibson, John Gorman, Wm L. Hill, Henry Kelley, James
Kennedy, Wm McMichael (?), John Matthews, Wm Matthews, John Rhea,
Pierre Romero, Sam. Shields, Smith (died), Wm Stenner, Louis Vignes, John
J. Warner, James W. Weeks, Wm Wolfskill, and Geo. C. Yount. For some
particulars about these men and others who visited Cal., see the Pioneer
Register at end of vol. ii.-v., this work.

to band themselves as the Compañía Extranjéra, under command of Hartnell, in support of Zamorano's movement against Echeandía and the diputacion, so far as the defence of the capital was concerned. Enough has been said elsewhere of this matter;[44] and its only interest in this connection lies in the fact that the rolls of the company furnish the names of forty-one foreigners, about half of them new-comers.

The second name on the list was that of Thomas Coulter. He was an English scientist, who after extensive travels in Mexico had arrived in California in November 1831, by what route or conveyance I have been unable to learn, but probably by sea.[45] Of Dr Coulter's travels in California, not extending north of San Francisco Bay nor east of the Tule lakes, we know only what may be learned from a paper communicated to the London Geographical Society in 1835, which is, that from March to July of 1832 he made a trip from Monterey via San Gabriel to the Rio Colorado and back.[46] His notes are for the most part geographical in their nature, and are sufficiently indicated on his map, which I here reproduce. One

[44] See chap. viii. of this vol.
[45] Stillman, in *Overland Monthly*, ii. 262, quotes a letter written at Monterey in 1831, in which Douglas speaks of having met Coulter. He had been in Sonora in the winter of 1829–30. Parry, *Early Bot. Expl.*, 413, also quotes the letter, and says C. returned to England in 1833.
[46] *Coulter's Notes on Upper California. Communicated by Dr Thomas Coulter. Read 9th March 1835*, in *Lond. Geog. Soc. Jour.*, v. 59–70, with a map. Also extract in *Nouv. An. Voy.*, lxxv. 30–52. The author corrects the 'great popular error' respecting the Tule lakes which has 'raised these comparatively insignificant ponds to the rank of a great inland sea.' He was unable to explore the eastern regions, but questioned the hunters about them. Some geographical positions are given by the use of the chronometer, based on Beechey's longitude of Monterey. The remains of one of the two Colorado missions were found 'on a point of rock projecting a little into the river, and constituting the extreme southern point of the Rocky Mountains.' The region from S. Pedro to S. Bernardino is described as 'the only point of either Californias, south of S. Francisco, capable of sustaining a large population.' 'Any efforts for the purpose of colonizing Upper California should be directed towards the portion north and east of S. Francisco and east of the Tule lakes, which is fertile, well wooded and watered, and of sufficient extent to make its colonization worth while as a speculation.' The white population is estimated at 6,000; while the author notes the rapid decrease and approaching annihilation of the Indians. The neighborhood of S. F. Bay is declared to be the 'only part of the country likely ever to become of much interest to Europeans.'

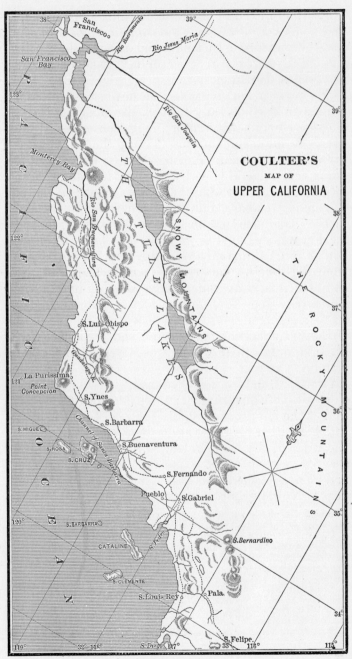

COULTER'S MAP.

other item in the bibliographical annals of California, and not a very important one from any point of view, may be accredited to this year, namely, the publication of *Morrell's Narrative* of a visit made in 1825, as described in an earlier chapter.

My pioneer list for 1832 contains forty-five names, a number that would be increased to eighty by the addition of transient visitors.[47]   Seven or eight, however, are doubtful names so far as the exact date of arrival is concerned.   Among the best known Californians who came this year, were Alexander, Carson, Black, Chard, Dye, Larkin, Sparks, Spear, West, and Williams.   Carson and Dye were the only survivors in 1880, and the former still lived, I think, in 1884. Larkin was destined to be most prominent of all, and with him on the *Newcastle* came Mrs Rachel Holmes from Boston, whom Larkin married the next year, the first American woman who came to live in California.

Foreign residents had a good friend in Figueroa, who came in January 1833, and was liberal in his policy. Thanks were rendered for the services of the Compañía Extrangera, and the so-called loyalty of its members to the legitimate government; and this is all that is to be said of the foreigners in politics or as a class.   A bibliographical item for the year may perhaps be supplied by the work of the Frenchman, M. P. de Morineau, who seems to have spent some time in California about 1833, and who published a memoir on the results the next year.[48] Nothing more is known of his visit; nor does the

[47] Pioneers of 1832: Cyrus Alexander, Allen (?), Alexis Bachelot, Robt S. Barker, James Black, Wm Blake (?), C. T. Briggs (?), Lemuel Carpenter, Moses Carson, Wm G. Chard, James Craig (?), Benj. Day, Wm Day, Denton, Ferd. Deppe, Wm Dickey, Joseph Dixon, Sant. Duckworth (born in Cal.), Job F. Dye, Hazel Fuller, José Garner (born in Cal.), Geo. Gay, Thos Grant, Chas Hall, Arch. Johnson (?), Michel Laframboise (?), Thos O. Larkin, J. O. E. Macondray, John D. Meyer, Joseph Paulding, Dan. Rice, Wm B. Richardson, Patrick Short, Dan. Sill, Phil. O. Slade, Isaac J. Sparks, Nathan Spear, John Thompson, Ambrose Tomlinson, Phil. J. Walter, John Ward (?), Wm Ware (?), Mark West, Geo. Williams, and Isaac Williams.   See Pioneer Register at end of these volumes.

[48] *Morineau, Notice sur la Nouvelle Californie*, in *Nouv. Ann. des Voy.*, lxi.

resulting memoir require special attention here. It was a brief but tolerably accurate presentation en résumé of Californian history, statistics, people, institutions, manners and customs, closing with a recommendation of the country as a field for French commerce. I have occasion to cite it elsewhere on several points.

I append the names of forty-seven pioneers who came in 1833, though in a few cases the year of arrival is not quite certain.[49] There were some thirty-five more who came, but did not stay or return. The leading names according to subsequent prominence as citizens are Forster, Graham, Johnson, Leese, and Walker. Four of all the list, Forster, Leese, Nidever, and Meek, were living in 1880; Meek and Leese I think also in 1884.

An interesting incident of 1834 is the visit of Hall J. Kelley. He was a Yankee school-master, an intelligent and energetic young man, an enthusiast on the subject of Pacific-coast settlement, whose eccentricities finally developed into insanity, and whose projects and writings are noticed fully in my *History of Oregon*. Kelley crossed the continent from Vera Cruz to San Blas in 1833. On his way he had interviews with prominent Mexicans, and wrote a letter to president Santa Anna on his project of settling California after he should have effected his purpose in Oregon. From San Blas he took passage by water

137–57; also in *Soc. Geog., Bulletin*, xvi. In the *United Service Journal, 1834*, pt i. p. 94, it is stated that Morineau wrote his memoir for Humboldt. He probably made his visit earlier than 1833, and perhaps with Duhaut-Cilly in 1827–8.

[49] Pioneers of 1833: José Allen (born in Cal.), Arch. Banks, Wm Brander, Chas Brown, Sam. Campbell (?), Lawrence Carmichael, Thos Cole, John B. Cooper, Cecilio Doak (born in Cal.), James G. Dove, Chas Fippard, Jos Florin (?), John Forbes, John Forster, Foster (? died), Wm J. Foxen (born in Cal.), Eph. Frawell, Geo. Frazer, Isaac Graham, Wm Gulnac, Elias Hayes, Harry Hicks, Jos Hicks, Fran. Higares, Wm M. Hooper, James Johnson, Wm Keith, Jacob P. Leese, Thos Lewis, Louis Mathurin, Steph. H. L. Meek, Geo. Nidever, Sherman Peck, Thos Pepper (?), Wm Place, John Price, Thos Ridington, Francis L. Ripley (?), James Scott, Pierre J. Sicard, John F. Smith, Peter Storm (?), Wm Thompson (?), Jos R. Walker, James Whitmarsh, Chas Wolter, and Henry Wood. See Pioneer Register at end of vol. ii.-v., this work.

to La Paz, and thence with much toil and hardship
found his way by land to San Diego, where he arrived
April 14, 1834. Thomas Shaw of the *Lagoda* gave
him a passage to San Pedro, and after a visit to Los
Angeles he arrived at Monterey in June, also visiting
San Francisco. Here he broached to Governor Figueroa his scheme for surveying, mapping, and eventually settling the interior valleys, receiving in reply a
letter of June 26th, in which Figueroa approved his
plans without being able to authorize or pay for their
execution until he could consult his superiors. At
Los Angeles Kelley had met Ewing Young and his
trappers, whose presence and operations have been
noted in this chapter, and had urged them to make a
trip to Oregon. Near Monterey he met Young again,
and succeeded in enlisting him with seven companions
for the journey. They started by way of San José in
July with about a hundred horses and mules; and were
soon joined by seven more hunters—a rough party
of 'marauders,' as Kelley calls them, including two
of Walker's men—with some sixty more animals.
Marching up the great valley, suffering from fever,
threatened by the Indians on account of outrages committed by the 'marauders,' and overtaken on the way
by Laframboise and his Hudson's Bay Company trappers, the party arrived at Vancouver in October. A
charge from Figueroa of having stolen horses caused
Young much trouble, and imbittered all his life in
Oregon. He claimed to have purchased all his horses,
and that if any had been stolen they were those
of the 'marauders;' and I have no proof that such
was not the case, though obviously the Californians
had no means of drawing fine distinctions between the
different parties roving through the valleys. Kelley
made a map of the Sacramento Valley, and he wrote a
memoir in 1839, containing an excellent description
of California, which was published by congress. He
continued to write for some forty years, at first to
overcome obstacles and carry out his projects of settle-

ment in the far west; and later to make known his early efforts, to seek a reward, and particularly to complain of the gross wrongs of which he had been the victim. He honestly believed himself to have been the first and most efficient promoter of American colonization on the Pacific coast, and that he had been robbed of the honor and profit that should have resulted from his services.[50]

Another visit of the year was probably apocryphal. Dr John Coulter, in a narrative of adventures in the Pacific published in London, devoted seven chapters to his experience in California, covering a larger part of the year 1834, so far as can be judged from the single date given in the book.[51] The author's knowledge of Californian geography was perhaps derived from earlier books, with a general idea of institutions; but all the rest was evidently evolved from his imagination, since, if he ever saw the country at all, his narrative shows no trace of that fact. It is for the most part an account of absurdly impossible personal adventures, with allusions to magnificent ruins and relics of antiquity: Indians clad in doeskin, decked with gay feathers and paint and silk scarfs and silver bracelets and coronets, and armed with tomahawk and rifle; canoes floating on stream and lake; robbers with their deadly lassos infesting every trail; with lofty pines, shady magnolias, cochineal-feeding prickly pears, and broad ranges of hazel-nut!

[50] *Kelley's Memoir; Id., History; Id., Narrative*, etc., passim. I have formed my narrative from disconnected statements in these and other writings of the author. There is no reason to question its accuracy. Kelley claimed that Sutter's occupation of the Sacramento Valley was suggested by his reports.

[51] *Coulter, Adventures on the Western Coast of South America, and the interior of California...By John Coulter, M. D., author of 'Adventures in the Pacific.'* London, 1847. 12mo. 2 vol. The matter on California is found in vol. i. p. 127–88. Dr Stillman, in *Overland Monthly*, ii. p. 263, has justly characterized the book as a tissue of lies. Coulter claims to have been left at S. F. sick with rheumatism from the whaler *Stratford*, Capt. Lock, and to have sailed later in the *Hound*, Capt. Trainer, to rejoin his vessel at Tahiti. His time after his malady had been cured by the temescal was spent in visits to all the northern missions, and with hunters and trappers in the broad interior.

Besides the ordinary sources of information, we have for 1834 two formal lists of foreigners in the Monterey district, and a similar list for the Angeles district, so that probably few names have been missed. Of the ninety foreigners who appear in the records, however, many besides those known to be visitors do not reappear after 1834–5; and the pioneers proper as named in my list are thirty-six.[52] Prudon, Reid, and Stokes were perhaps those best known in California; and so far as I know, Janssens was the only survivor in 1884. The coming of the Mexican colony added several to the number of foreign residents, as had the New Mexican caravans of 1831–2 and Walker's overland expedition of 1833.

In 1835 also California had its visit, resulting in a book, both of a very different class from Coulter's of the preceding year, being Richard H. Dana's *Two Years before the Mast*, a work that requires but brief notice at this date, as no other about California has had more readers. The author, since a prominent lawyer and lecturer as well as writer of well known books, was then a boy in Harvard College, who shipped as a common sailor on the *Pilgrim*, with a view to cure a weakness of the eyes that interfered with his studies. He arrived at Santa Bárbara in January 1835, and left San Diego to return in May 1836 on the *Alert*, having visited repeatedly every port on the coast, and spent four months at the hide-houses of San Diego. His book was a connected narrative of his experience and observations during the two years' absence from Boston, and was first published in 1840.[53] Notwithstanding its truth,

---

[52] Pioneers of 1834: Wm J. Bailey, Chas Baric, Thos G. Bowen, John Colbert, Dav. Cooper, Luther Cooper, J. M. Covarrubias, Nathan Daly, Wm Daly, Wm Garue, Horatio N. Hartnell, Henry Herd, Jos H. Hill, Gerard Hope, Chas Hubbard, Aug. Janssens, Chas Johnstone, Robert King, Wm Lumsden, John C. McLeod (?), Jos L. Majors, Misteril, Albert F. Morris, Pierre Olivier, Matt. Pelham, Dav. Philips, Victor Prudon, Hugo Reid, James Rogers, Thos Russell, Matias Sabici, John Smith, James Stokes, Wm Taylor, Andrew Watson, Ezekiel Whitton.
[53] [*Dana*] *Two Years before the Mast. A Personal Narrative of Life at*

Dana's narrative had all the fascination of Cooper's and Marryatt's sea-stories, and it was doubtless this charm mainly that caused its immense popularity; yet it was instructive no less than fascinating, as it contained the most realistic picture extant of sailors' life and treatment in American trading vessels, with intelligent observations on the countries visited. Of the Californian hide trade, in all its details, Dana presented a view which has never been surpassed. His opportunities were small for studying the history and institutions of the country; but his remarks on the places and men and customs that came under his personal observation were not only interesting, but with some exceptions accurate. The current popular idea of California from 1841 to 1848 was founded largely on this book, with those of Forbes and Robinson. The author's appreciation of the western land is summed up in the remark, 'In the hands of an enterprising people, what a country this might be!' but he adds, "Yet how long would a people remain so, in such a country? If the 'California fever,' laziness, spares the first generation, it is likely to attack the second." An addition to the late editions, "Twenty-four Years After," is second in fascination to no part of the original.

I have but sixteen names to record in my list of pioneers for 1835, and six of these are doubtful in respect of date. Including visitors, the total number of new-comers is but thirty-six. None acquired any special prominence, unless it may be Henry Mellus; and none but Watson, I think, survived in 1884.[54]

Sea. N. Y., 1840, 16mo, 483 p.; *Id.*, 1847; *Id.*, 1857; ed. of London, 1841, 8vo, 124 p.; Dutch translation: *'Twee jaren voor den mast.' Deventer, 1842,* 8vo, 2 vol.; 'New edition, with subsequent matter by the author,' Boston, 1869, 12mo, 470 p.; *Id.*, 1873. In the original edition the author's name did not appear on the title-page. The additional matter in the author's edition is a narrative of a second visit to California in 1859.

[54] Pioneers of 1835: Fred. Becher (?), James Bridger (?), Martin Cooper, John Coppinger (?), Wm H. Crowell (?), Wm Daylor, Wm Forbes, Manuel King, Allen Light (?), Henry Mellus, Henry Plummer, John O'Brien, L. V. Prudon (?), Robt Robinson, Stephen Simmonds, Thos Watson (born in Cal.) See for biographical sketches of pioneers, natives, and visitors, the Pioneer Register at end of vol. ii.–v., this work.

CHAPTER XV.

RULE OF GUTIERREZ AND CHICO.

1836.

I take up again the thread of political annals dropped at the end of 1835.[1] In accordance with a prevalent desire of the Californians, Figueroa at his death had separated the political and military com-mands, intrusting the latter, according to army regu-lations, to the ranking officer Lieutenant-colonel Nicolás Gutierrez, and the former, according to a Mexican law of somewhat doubtful application to a territory, to José Castro, as senior vocal of the dipu-tacion. The only objection had come from the south in behalf of José Antonio Estudillo of San Diego, who was really the senior vocal, but was absent from the capital on account of illness. Estudillo was doubtless entitled to the position of gefe político ad interim, and the prospective honor may have done

---

[1] See chap. x. of this volume.

much to restore his health; but for some reason that the records fail to make apparent, the efforts in his favor were ineffectual.

On January 2, 1836, Castro transferred the gefatura to Gutierrez, as both announced to local authorities in letters of that date.[2] The alleged motive of the transfer was an order of the supreme government, dated January 21, 1835, that for the national good the civil and military commands should be vested in one person. This order was probably in reply to some of Figueroa's past suggestions and the efforts of Californians in congress; but it is strange that it did not arrive sooner. The lawyers, Cosme Peña and Castillo Negrete, the diputacion, and the ayuntamiento of Monterey approved the union of the two commands, which Gutierrez himself affected to oppose at first.[3] It is remarkable that the change should have been so quietly effected, and given rise to so little correspondence, that Castro and his Californian friends should have surrendered the power to a Mexican without at least a war of words. True, the rule of Gutierrez was accidental, prospectively brief, and hardly worth a contest; true also, that the current correspondence may possibly have disappeared in great part from the archives; yet enough of mystery remains to indicate an understanding between Castro and Gutierrez, and to give some plausibility to Juan Bandini's theory that the former surrendered the command to the latter in order to keep it from Estudillo—that personal and local prejudices were more potent than the popular feeling against Mexican rulers.[4]

[2] Jan. 2, 1836, C. and G. to ayunt. of Los Angeles, S. Diego, and Monterey. *Dept. St. Pap., Angeles*, MS., xi. 43; *Id., Mont.*, iv. 80; *S. Diego, Arch.*, MS., 69, 71. Bando of G., same date. *Dept. St. Pap., S. José*, MS., v. 9. G. to com. of Sonoma. *Vallejo, Doc.*, MS., iii. 144. All these communications are nearly in the same words, some of them in print. March 7th, he signs his name and rank as 'Nicolás Gutierrez, Teniente Coronel de Caballería Permanente, Comandante General, Inspector, y Gefe Político de California.' *Doc. Hist. Cal.*, MS., i. 252.

[3] Dec. 15–19, 1835. *Monterey, Actas del ayunt.*, MS., 141, 143–4; *Dept. St. Pap., Ben. Pref. y Juzg.*, MS., iii. 46.

[4] *Bandini, Hist. Cal.*, MS., 79–80. *Vallejo, Hist. Cal.*, MS., iii. 75–8, asserts that there was much discontent, and even vague talk of revolt, at the

The rule of Gutierrez lasted four months, and I find no indication of opposition, discontent, or controversy during that period. Like his predecessor, he confined his efforts to the performance of routine duties, giving little or no offence to either people or politicians, though there must have been a constantly growing feeling against Mexican rulers, fomented to a certain extent by those who chose to style themselves federalists. The establishment of centralism in Mexico was not yet officially proclaimed in this far north, but the tendency was known and discussed. A communication from the minister of relations, dated June 5, 1835, and circulated by the governor on January 10th, called attention to the possibility of future changes in the form of government, and to various petitions on the subject already made public in the newspapers, at the same time urging upon territorial authorities the necessity of the strictest precautions against such disorders as might arise from popular feeling founded on vague rumors and utilized by revolutionary leaders.[5] National affairs received no further public attention during this brief rule; but two or three topics of a local nature merit brief notice here, both on account of their importance and of their results.

By a national decree of May 23, 1835, Los Angeles was made a city and capital of California. I have noticed this fact elsewhere, and also the burst of indignation with which the news was received at Monterey.[6] Two days after his accession, Gutierrez gave

north in Castro's favor, and in the south for Estudillo; but in March there came an earthquake that led people to forget politics in favor of prayer. Several Californians, as Pinto, *Apunt.*, MS., 14-15; Estudillo, *Datos*, MS., 7-8; and Castro, *Relacion*, MS., 36-7, imply that while there was dissatisfaction, Castro yielded to Gutierrez's demand to prevent disorders and promote peace. Robinson, *Life in Cal.*, 173, followed by Tuthill, *Hist. Cal.*, 141, states that Gutierrez succeeded in accordance with the will of Figueroa, implying that Castro's temporary rule was simply in consequence of Gutierrez's absence in the south; but this is an error.

[5] Jan. 10, 1836, Gutierrez to alcaldes, forwarding communication of June 5, 1835. *S. Diego, Arch.*, MS., 72.

[6] See chap. x. of this volume.

official publication to the decree, thus honoring the
city of the Angels, and in February some efforts were
made to secure proper buildings for temporary public
use in the new capital; but the Angelinos were so
lacking in public spirit that no citizen would furnish a
building rent free, as the governor required, and the
matter dropped out of sight for more than a year.[7]
All the same, Los Angeles soon distinguished itself
by producing the first Californian vigilance committee.
Domingo Félix, who lived on the rancho bearing his
name, near the town, was married to María del Rosario Villa, who had abandoned her husband to become
the mistress of a Sonoran vaquero, named Gervasio
Alipas. After two years of frequent efforts to reclaim
the erring woman, met with insults from her paramour whom he once wounded in a personal encounter,
Félix invoked the aid of the authorities, and the wife
was arrested at San Gabriel, and brought to town on
March 24, 1836. Through the efforts of the alcalde
and of friends, it was hoped that a reconciliation had
been effected, though Alipas and his brother threatened vengeance. Two days later the couple started,
both on one horse, for their rancho; but on the way
the husband was stabbed by the paramour, and his
body was dragged by the man and woman with a reata
to a ravine, where it was partly covered with earth
and leaves.

By March 29th the body had been found and both
murderers arrested. There was great excitement in
the city, and on April 1st the ayuntamiento, summoned in extra session to take precautions, resolved
to organize a force of citizens in aid of the authorities
to preserve the peace.[8] The danger was real, but no

[7] Jan. 4, 1836, gov. to alcaldes. *Dept. St. Pap., Angeles*, MS., xi. 40; *S.
Diego, Arch.*, MS., 70–1. Jan. 21st, receipt of the decree by ayunt. of Los
Angeles. *Los Angeles, Arch.*, MS., iv. 183. Feb. 6th, demand for buildings.
Vignes would rent a hall for $400 and contribute $75 of that sum. Stearns
and Sanchez had also halls to rent, but none for free use until a suitable edi-
fice could be erected. *Id.*, i. 70–3.

[8] *Los Angeles, Arch.*, MS., iv. 189–92. A. M. Osio was invited to be pres-

good citizens could be induced to aid the officers of the
law, for they had resolved on a summary infliction of
the penalties which justice demanded, but which, as
they well knew, were not to be expected from the
ordinary course of law in California, where there was
no tribunal authorized to inflict the death penalty on
a civilian. At dawn on April 7th about fifty of the
most prominent citizens met at the house of John
Temple and organized a 'junta defensora de la seguridad pública,' of which Victor Prudon was chosen
president, making an eloquent address, the original
draft of which is in my possession. Manuel Arzaga
was made secretary, and Francisco Araujo was put in
command of the armed force. During the forenoon,
while the organization was being perfected, two messengers were sent in succession to Padre Cabot at San
Fernando, whose presence was required on the pretext that a dying Indian needed his spiritual care;
but the weather was bad and the padre refused to
come.

About two o'clock P. M. a copy of the popular *acta*,
with a demand for the prisoners to be delivered up
for execution within an hour, was sent to the alcalde,
Manuel Requena.[9]   Half an hour later the junta

ent and take part in the deliberations, and did so, but he says nothing of the
affair in his *Hist. Cal.*   See *Popular Tribunals*, this series.

[9] This document is preserved in *Los Angeles, Arch.*, MS., i. 81–91, with
other records bearing on the same affair. I quote as follows: '*Salus populi
suprema lex est.* The subscribing citizens, at the invitation of the rest,
justly indignant at the horrible crime committed against Domingo Félix,
bearing in mind the frequency of similar crimes in this city, and deeming
the principal cause thereof to be the delay in criminal cases through having
to await the confirmation of sentences from Mexico, fearing for this unhappy
country a state of anarchy where the right of the strongest shall be the only
law, and finally believing that immorality has reached such an extreme that
public security is menaced and will be lost if the dike of a solemn example is
not opposed to the torrent of atrocious perfidy—demand the execution or the
delivery to us for immediate execution of the assassin Gervasio Alipas and
the faithless María del R. Villa, that abominable monster who cruelly immo-
lated her importunate husband in order to give herself up without fear to her
frantic passions, and to pluck by homicide from the slime of turpitude the
filthy laurel of her execrable treason (!)...Let the infernal couple perish.
Such is the vow of the people, and we protest in the face of heaven that we
will not lay down the arms with which we support the justice of our demand
until the assassins have expiated their foul crimes...Public vengeance demands a prompt example, and it must be given. Still reeks the blood of the

marched out to the parsonage near the court and jail, and at three P. M. the alcalde was notified that the hour had expired. The ayuntamiento in session had received and considered the demand, which it was decided to refuse after two committees had been sent out to reason with the crowd.[10] Narciso Botello, the secretary, having refused to give up the keys, they were taken, the guard was arrested, and the criminals were taken from the jail to be shot—the man at 4:30 P. M. and the woman half an hour later. It was discovered that Alipas had his shackles nearly filed off. The bodies were exposed at the jail door for two hours, and then placed at the disposal of the authorities. The alcalde fearing further disturbances, the junta volunteered to serve for a few days as a guard to aid the authorities in preserving order,[11] and was then disbanded.[12] About the results of this affair, I shall have to say something a little later.

About the time of these events at Los Angeles, there were current rumors of prospective revolutionary troubles of a nature not clearly defined at San Diego. The only foundation for such rumors perhaps was a memorial presented by Bandini and others, in which they deplored the ravages of Indian raiders,

Álvarez, of the Potiñon, of the Jenkins, and of other unhappy victims of the fury and passions of their impious murderers...The world shall know that if in the city of Los Angeles judges tolerate assassination, there are virtuous citizens who know how to sacrifice their lives in order to save that of their compatriots...Death to the homicide!' There follow 55 signatures, including 14 foreigners. Four other communications are given respecting the giving-up of the keys and return of the bodies.

[10] Los Angeles, Arch., MS., iv. 186–8.

[11] April 10th, a bando was published by the ayunt., providing for the volunteer organization for defence, and threatening prompt and severe punishment to all disturbers of the peace. Dept. St. Pap., Ang., MS., ii. 69–70. It does not appear what danger was apprehended.

[12] Prudon, Vigilantes de Los Angeles, 1836, MS., is an original narrative written at the time by the president of the junta, and is the most complete extant. To it is prefixed Prudon's address on accepting the presidency. I have cited several archive records; and may refer also to a report made on May 4th by the ayunt. of Los Angeles to that of S. Diego, narrating events in some detail. S. Diego, Arch., MS., 103. Full accounts are given by Botello, Anales del Sur, MS., 20–5; Sanchez, Notas, MS., 9–11; and Alvarado, Hist. Cal., MS., iii. 60–9. The affair is also mentioned by Day in Hesperian, ii. 150–1; in Los Angeles, Hist., 14, and Hittell's Hist. S. F'co, 79–80.

the decadence of the missions under the reglamento
of secularization, the decline of agriculture and
trade, and the lack of tribunals of justice, proposing
as a remedy the calling for a general assembly of
military, civil, and missionary representatives, which
body should proceed to reorganize the military, industrial, financial, and judicial system of California without awaiting approval from Mexico. On April 14th
an extra session of the ayuntamiento was held, at
which the news from Los Angeles was received and
considered, together with the current rumors of
trouble nearer home. It was decided to send the
governor a record of the meeting, with an assurance
of San Diego's loyalty, the rumors being groundless.
They also forwarded the citizens' memorial.[13] April
23d, Gutierrez replied, accepting in good faith and
with gratitude the assurance of San Diegan patriotism, but declaring that the formation of the proposed
assembly could not be carried out consistently with
fidelity to the national government.[14] There is no
evidence that the occurrences at either Los Angeles
or San Diego had any political or revolutionary meaning whatever, or that Gutierrez regarded them as
having any such meaning.

But a new ruler was en route for California, sent
to rule that country in accordance with the *bases* of
October 1835, which overthrew the federal constitution and system of 1824, but which provided for no
very radical immediate changes in the territory. The
president's choice fell upon Colonel Mariano Chico, a
member of congress at the time from Guanajuato, who

---

[13] *S. Diego, Arch.*, MS., 96–7. March 21st, Bandini to Vallejo. Be-
wails the sufferings of Cal. caused by the misdeeds of some of her sons and
of others; but hopes for better days. Regrets that differences of political
opinion should have produced a seeming coolness between the two. *Vallejo,
Doc.*, MS., iii. 182. On Jan. 11th, a meeting of citizens had been called to
consult on steps to preserve order. *S. Diego, Arch.*, MS., 71.

[14] *Dept. St. Pap., Angeles*, MS., xi. 47–50; *Hayes, Doc.*, MS., 49. On
April 22d, Gutierrez had written to Vallejo that attempts at revolt in S.
Diego and Los Angeles would prevent him from sending an officer to the
north as was desired. *Vallejo, Doc.*, MS., iii. 197.

was appointed December 16, 1835, to succeed Figueroa, apparently before that officer's death was known, and arrived at Santa Bárbara on the *Leonor*, as I suppose, after the middle of April 1836, the exact date being unknown.[15] Beyond the facts that Chico was a diputado, and that members of his family in Guanajuato had taken a somewhat prominent part in the revolutionary struggle, I know nothing of the man before his arrival in California. As we know, the people had a strong feeling against Mexican officials as a class, and were opposed to centralism so far as they had any political opinions; it is also stated that letters and newspapers from Mexico had given Chico an unfavorable reputation in respect of both political and private character;[16] yet I do not think there was any prejudice against him or his politics that would have proved a serious obstacle to a man skilled in the art of gaining popularity.

Having spent a few days at Santa Bárbara at the house of Cárlos Carrillo, whom he had known in Mexico,[17] Don Mariano started north by land, escorted by about eighteen soldiers, and accompanied by Jacob P. Leese, the company also including, I presume, Doña Cruz, a woman introduced by the governor as his niece, of whom more anon. He arrived at the capital May

---

[15] Aug. 1, 1835, J. A. Carrillo wrote to his brother Cárlos from Mex. that Figueroa's course was disapproved, and a successor—name not given—would sail on the *Leonor*. *Vallejo, Doc.*, MS., iii. 185. The date of appointment may have been Dec. 15th, as an order of minister Tornel to deliver the command to him seems to bear that date. *Sup. Govt St. Pap.*, MS., xi. 2–3. The date is given as Dec. 16th in *Dept. St. Pap., S. José*, MS., iv. 109; and *Id.*, *Ben. Mil.*, lxxxi. 16. The permission of congress had to be asked for his appointment on account of his being a congressman. Dec. 24th, $400 had been advanced 'for account of secret expenditures,' and $2,000 on account of his salary. *Id.*, xxxi. 11–12, 16. I have no date for the arrival of the *Leonor*, except that she anchored at S. F. on May 19th. *Pinto, Doc.*, MS., i. 30–1. Several writers mention the fact that Chico landed at Sta Bárbara.

[16] *Osio, Hist. Cal.*, MS., 249–51; *Alvarado, Hist. Cal.*, MS., iii. 47; *Vallejo, Hist. Cal.*, MS., iii. 78–80.

[17] Mrs Ord, *Ocurrencias*, MS., 90, says that she—then Mrs Jimeno—was ill of a fever when Chico called at the house of her father, Capt. Guerra. He insisted on seeing the sick woman, and she was told later that in her delirium she had made some rather queer remarks to the governor. Hittell, *Hist. S. F.*, 81, on the authority of Leese, mentions Chico's stay at Carrillo's house and his consultations with Guerra.

1st, and was received by Gutierrez and the citizens
with the usual ceremonial welcome.[18] On the 2d and
3d the offices of comandante general and gefe político
were formally turned over by Gutierrez to Chico, which
event—celebrated at night by a grand fiesta and ball
—was duly communicated to local authorities the
same days,[19] when he also issued a printed address announcing his appointment, arrival, and patriotic intentions, together with the death of President Barragan,
learned while en route.[20]

He issued another proclamation on the 20th, lauding
centralism extravagantly, denouncing federalism, and
congratulating the Californians with flattering words
on their glorious future under the new régime. "The
constitution of 1824," wrote Don Mariano, "child of
inexperience and haste, was an abortion of blunders
fruitful in disorders, which you endured for eleven
years; it was your idol while worthy; but the oracle
once proven false, and your forbearance wearied, you
decided with your brethren of the interior to melt
that false idol, though respecting still its relics until
the substitution of the new image which is being prepared to serve you as a deity." "The olive of peace

[18] Alvarado, *Hist. Cal.*, MS., iii. 50–2, and Vallejo, *Hist. Cal.*, MS., iii.
80–3, tell us that officers and citizens marched out to meet the gov., all except the presidio officers wearing federal badges expressive of their political
sentiments; and that when Chico made the remark that he was glad to meet
so many good people, Alvarado replied that they had not come out to welcome him, but Domingo Carrillo, whom he had arrested at Sta Bárbara for
his political opinions and had brought along as a prisoner. I have no reason
to believe that Carrillo had been arrested at all, that any such badges were
worn, or that any such insult was offered by Alvarado to the new governor.
The exact date of Chico's arrival is given in *Gomez, Diario de Cosas Notables
en Monterey, 1836,* MS. A brief but important original narrative by D. Rafael
Gomez.

[19] The *comandancia* was transferred on May 2d, a day before the *gefatura*,
as appears from a communication of Chico to the com. at Sonoma. *Vallejo, Doc.*,
MS., iii. 199; and *Gomez, Diario*, MS. May 3, 1836, Chico and Gutierrez to
different ayunt. *Dept. St. Pap.*, MS., iv. 108; *Id., Mont.*, vi. 37; *Id., S. José*, v.
8; *Id., Angeles*, xi. 53; *S. Diego, Arch.*, MS., 102; *Id., Index*, 25. Chico
recognized at Los Angeles May 10th. *Los Angeles, Arch.*, MS., iv. 193–4. At
S. Diego May 12th, being congratulated on the 14th by Alcalde Argüello.
S. Diego, Arch., MS., 99. May 28th, congratulated by J. M. Estudillo at S.
Francisco. *Arch. Arzob.*, MS., v. pt ii. 15.

[20] The only copy of this original print that I know of is preserved in the
Mercantile Library of S. F., in *Taylor's Specimens of the Press*, no. 5.

sprouts in this far north; let our fraternity fertilize its root, let our concord water it until it rises in majesty to touch the heavens." "California was ever the centre of discretion, an example of docility, a model of subordination and obedience to supreme authority. She has preserved intact her customs, healthful and free from the poison of revolution, and is ready to climb the hill of fortune as a state; she may be the nursery to produce for the country citizens best fitted to advance its greatness."[21] Something more of declamation than of argument is to be noted in this paper, the contents of which were delivered as an address on the day of taking the oath of adherence to the bases of the new constitution. The governor took immediate steps to have the oath taken in all parts of the territory, as was done at some places—probably at all—before the end of July, without opposition apparently.[22]

Chico had sent an order to Comandante Vallejo the 4th of May, at Sonoma, to come to Monterey for consultation on important matters, and to bring with him such forces as could be spared from the northern frontier, an order which was repeated on the 17th.[23] On the 6th he had sent a similar order through the alcalde of San Diego for Juan Bandini to come at

[21] Printed original in *Earliest Printing. Dept. St. Pap., Angeles*, MS., x. 19. Literally copied by Vallejo, *Hist. Cal.*, MS., iii. 105–8, who quotes as follows from a letter of Pablo de la Guerra on the subject. 'The "bear," to deceive the Californians and prevent their detection of his falsehood, has spoken in mystic language; I would rather undertake to decipher the responses of the Delphic oracle.'

[22] May 29, 1836, swearing of the bases at S. Diego with great rejoicings, firing of guns, shouts, and ringing of bells, 'un acto tan grato como lisonjero á todo Mexicano,' as described by Capt. Portilla in a communication to his com. gen. *Dept. St. Pap., Ben. Mil.*, MS., lxxxi. 36; *S. Diego, Arch.*, MS., 110, 115. June 1st, swearing of the bases by the military of the south at S. Gabriel, as reported by Gutierrez. *Dept. St. Pap.*, MS., iv. 109–11; *Id., Ben. Mil.*, xxxi. 18. On or about June 11th, the oath was taken at Sta Bárbara, P. Duran refusing to say mass. *St. Pap., Miss. and Colon.*, MS., ii. 373–4. June 19th, the oath administered at Los Angeles by Chico himself, who made a speech on the beauties of centralism. 'This people heard the discussion with pleasure.' *Los Angeles, Arch.*, MS., iv. 195–6. July 11th, Chico finds it strange that Vallejo has not reported the swearing of the bases by his troops. *Vallejo, Doc.*, MS., iii. 219.

[23] *Vallejo, Doc.*, MS., iii. 200, 201, 205–6.

once to the capital for a conference.[24]   On the 11th Chico had issued another printed proclamation, or bando, this time on commercial topics, prohibiting the retail trade on board of foreign vessels which had so long been practised on this coast, requiring a landing of all cargoes at Monterey, and imposing other restrictions more in accordance with Mexican laws than with Californian usages.[25]   On the 16th he had issued an order that Abel Stearns must come to Monterey or leave the country;[26] and finally he delivered on the 27th an address at the opening of the sessions of the diputacion—a document also circulated in print.

In his discourse Chico spoke first of the general difficulties that had beset his path, and which he had hitherto been obliged to meet alone without the wise counsels of the vocales now fortunately assembled. Next he referred at considerable length to the troubles at Los Angeles, but his views on this topic will be noticed later.   Thirdly he noticed the measure of May 11th on the regulation of commerce, expressing his belief that if not perfect it could not fail to prevent many existing abuses.   The constant ravages of thieves among the herds of horses and cattle were alluded to as one of California's greatest evils, which, however, he had taken steps to check by the aid of the newly arrived law of December 29th, which brought such malefactors within the ordinary military jurisdiction. Fifthly and chiefly, the subject of missions received attention; and in this respect the situation seemed to the governor most critical.   He declared himself at a loss, and in his perplexity "awaited the counsel of your excellency to lead the government like Ariadne's thread from so strange a labyrinth."   What with an imperfect system of secularization partially carried

[24] *San Diego, Arch.*, MS., 104.   The order reached Bandini June 8th or 10th.

[25] May 11, 1836, Chico to the people. *Earliest Printing.*   Also May 11th, he issued an order for the formation of local cuerpos de seguridad y policía. *S. Diego, Arch.*, MS., 106.

[26] *Dept. St. Pap., Angeles*, MS., xi. 52.

out by incompetent men, the destruction of property by the padres, the insubordination of the neophytes, and the new complications introduced by the national decree of November 7th, he saw no way of advance or retreat by which to save the missions from total ruin, but would do his best, and would thankfully receive suggestions. Finally he asked indulgence for his errors, in consideration of his zeal for the country's wellbeing. This discourse, if it displays no extraordinary wisdom on the part of the speaker, shows nothing of weakness, petulance, arrogance, or strong political prejudice, nor does it contain anything specially apt to displease the Californians [27]

According to the new bases, the republic was to be divided into departments, each ruled by a governor and a junta departamental; and though additional legislation was required to create the departments, and though in reality no change had as yet been legally made in the old names so far as California was concerned, yet the old diputacion was now called a junta departamental, and Chico, in his discourse, even spoke of California as a department. At an election held at Monterey on the 25th—for what reason or by what authority I do not know—four new members were chosen to complete the junta, and one of them tried to avoid serving on the plea that according to a Mexican law the body should have but five members; but Chico decided that there was no new law affecting the number or attributes of the vocales in a territory, and that only the name could properly be considered as changed. The sessions opened, as I have stated, on May 28th with a speech from Chico. He made another speech on June 1st, in advocacy of his proposition to send an agent to represent the interests of California in Mexico, in addition to the diputado in congress.[28] The plan was favorably con-

[27] Chico, Discurso pronunciado por el Sr Gefe Político de la Alta California ...al abrir sus sesiones la Ecsma Junta Departamental el 27 de Mayo de 1836, in Earliest Printing; also in Bandini, Doc., MS., 40.
[28] Chico, Alocucion á la Junta Departamental 1 de Junio, 1836, MS.

sidered, and a trio of candidates was proposed for the
position; but nothing came of it. There is nothing
else in the proceedings of the junta at this session
demanding further notice than is given in the appended
record.[29]

Early in June Chico started for the south, and was
absent from the capital a month. This brings me to
the troubles encountered by this ruler, which were
destined to overwhelm him. It is not easy to fathom
these troubles entirely, or to determine with exacti-
tude what manner of man Don Mariano was. The
Californians in their recollections of olden times are

[29] *Leg. Rec.*, MS., iii. 1–3, 13–31. May 25th, election of 4 members, J.
Gomez, Spence, R. Gomez, and Crespo. May 28th, opening of the session.
Rafael Gomez desired to be excused, on the grounds that he had not been 7
years a resident and that the junta should legally have but 5 members—both
overruled later. The vocales in order of seniority seem to have been as follows: 1st, José Castro; 2d, J. B. Alvarado; 3d, José Ant. de la Guerra; 4th,
Rafael Gomez; 5th, David Spence; 6th, Manuel Crespo; 7th, Joaquin Gomez.
Alvarado presided—though it is not apparent why he rather than Castro took
that position—and J. M. Maldonado was secretary. The committees were,
proprios y arbitrios, J. Gomez and Spence; colonization and vacant lands,
J. Gomez and Guerra; missions, Spence and R. Gomez; government and
police, Crespo and Castro; reglamento and municipal orders, Alvarado and
Castro; public works and industries, Spence and Guerra; instruction and statistics, Alvarado and Castro.
May 31st, June 2d, representation of P. Mercado against José Ramirez.
No details. June 1st, Chico's prop. to send an agent to Mex. Chico reported
that he had forbidden the appointment of an alcalde by the ayunt. of S. Francisco for the region north of the bay. June 4th, Chico's recommendation on
supervision of mission accounts, disapproved on Sept. 5th. June 16th,
meetings to be on two days of the week, as determined by the president, instead of on Tuesday, Thursday, and Saturday. June 21st, prop. for an agent
in Mex. approved. Trio named: Alvarado, F. J. Castillo Negrete, and Rafael Gomez. Com. appointed to form instructions. June 23d, sec. and his
salary. June 30th, secularization of Sta Inés and S. Buenaventura. Inventories of Sta Clara, S. José, and S. Miguel. July 1st–4th, various minor matters; and more about the agency for Mex. July 6th, Joaquin Gomez refused
leave of absence. July 7th, Gomez proposed to revoke the license granted by
Figueroa to Kostromitinof to build a warehouse at S. Fran., and to have the
building destroyed after the next shipment; no such permission to be given
in future. Chico's order forbidding the appointment of an alcalde for the
northern frontier approved. July 19th, Chico says it is customary for the
oldest vocal to preside in the absence of the gefe. July 18th–26th, land grants,
petition of Jas Burke, etc. July 29th, more about instructions to the agent.
Complaints of Alvarado against Chico (addressed to minister of relations and
not really a part of the legislative record). Aug. 30th, approved that no permission be given foreigners to erect warehouses at the ports; but it was said
that Kostromitinof had not yet built any. The records are brief, vague,
confused, and probably very incomplete for the whole session.

unanimous in denouncing him as a tyrant, a rascal, and a fool. He was the object not only of hatred as Victoria had been, but of ridicule.[30] As in Victoria's case, the popular feeling was, to some extent at least, unfounded; and it has doubtless been exaggerated in the telling, largely through the influence in later years of men who had political reasons for magnifying the governor's faults. His public acts, as recorded in contemporary documents, could not have been specially offensive to any class of Californians, and many of the acts imputed to him by later narratives are so absurdly improbable as to cast serious doubt on the accuracy of the rest. It is clear enough that Chico was neither despot, villain, nor insane, but

[30] Choleric, respecting nothing when suffering from bile; revengeful; came to Cal. in the hope of bettering his fortunes. *Osio, Hist. Cal.*, MS., 249–88. 'Militarate de mala ley, stubborn as a school-boy, destitute of all good breeding, with no idea of the advantages to be gained by a conciliatory policy, pompously ostentatious, believing himself a general, a statesman, and an apothecary, insolent as Nero, religious and profane at the same time, cowardly, mad, and a corrupter of public minds.' *Alvarado, Hist. Cal.*, MS., iii. 45–140. This writer tells many stories of Chico, some of them too absurd for notice. 'Scandalously avaricious.' *Bandini, Hist. Cal.*, MS., 80–3. Mrs Ord, *Ocurrencias*, MS., 82 98, says he was very unpopular; and relates that the Indian Juan Cristóbal at Sta Bárbara pronounced him a rascal at first sight, running away in great fear, especially on account of his goggles; and when the padre explained that he was a good man, etc., the Indian still insisted— 'wait a little and thou wilt see how he acts, and then tell me if he is good or bad; let us see who wins, thou or I.' Chico nicknamed 'Oso Chico' because of his crazy and lewd disposition; 'loco y impúdico.' *Hartnell, Narr.*, MS., 11. Had all the vices and no virtues—all the attributes necessary to make a man worthy of hatred. *Vallejo, Hist. Cal.*, MS., iii. 82–153. Haughty and domineering. *Fernandez, Cosas de Cal.*, MS., 97–9. A man fitted to strengthen the provincial prejudice, of disagreeable manners, one with whom no one could be on friendly terms. *Botello, Anales*, MS., 19–22. Despotic and arbitrary, the very opposite of Figueroa. *Castro, Rel.*, MS., 37–8. Ill-tempered and quarrelsome; insolent and immoral. *Pinto, Apunt.*, MS., 16–19. Violent, despotic, and hated by all. *Pico, Acont.*, MS., 18–19, 28–31. No common sense; spent his time in inventing remedies and studying flowers. *Vallejo (J. J.), Remin.*, MS., 118–21. Impetuous and lacking in tact. *Coronel, Cosas*, MS., 18. Irascible, imprudent, and capricious. *Serrano, Apuntes*, MS., 31–6. Devoid of sense, quarrelling with everybody. *Arce, Mem.*, MS., 7–8. Peevish and perhaps mad. *Torre, Remin.*, MS., 57–61. Insolent and slovenly. *Galindo, Apuntes*, MS., 33–4. Treated with deserved contempt. *Larios, Convulsiones*, MS., 16. The worst ruler that could have been sent to Cal. *Valdés, Mem.*, MS., 23–5. As 'quijote' as a Spaniard. *Amador, Mem.*, MS., 144. Soon lost every friend he chanced to make. *Ávila, Notas*, MS., 18–19; and more to similar effect, in *Janssens, Vida*, MS., 63–72; *Gonzalez, Exper.*, MS., 32; *Gonzalez, Revoluciones*, MS., 9–10; *Sanchez, Notas*, MS., 11–12. The above references are made to include all that the writers say of Chico's rule, and many of them will not require further mention.

being unpopular, he might as well have been all three, so far as results are concerned.

On his arrival in California he had to encounter the ordinary inherent difficulties of his position, which were by no means trifling, as had been discovered by all his predecessors. As a Mexican he had to meet a strong prejudice, and as a centralist a still stronger opposition, there being a party of young men in the country who claimed to be ardent federalists, and for whom revolution, as a word, had no terrors. Chico succeeded Figueroa, a man distinguished for his arts of flattery and conciliation; having himself none of those arts, and no extraordinary ability with which to overcome difficulties. He was perhaps personally petulant and disagreeable; at any rate, he made enemies and no friends, and the current was started against him. His pretty 'niece,' Doña Cruz, turned out to be his mistress; and the respectability of Monterey was easily persuaded to consider itself shocked by such immorality in high places.[31] The restrictive bando of May 11th on commerce may have displeased a powerful element among the foreigners, and his persecution of Abel Stearns, of which and its motives little is really known, tended in the same direction, though there is very little in support of the charge that he was specially hostile to foreigners.[32]

[31] Stories are told going to show that Doña Cruz was not altogether faithful to her lover, and gave the governor no end of trouble by her freaks of inconstancy.

[32] Chico's orders against Stearns are dated May 16th, June 26th, and July 30th. *Dept. St. Pap.*, MS., iv. 120; *Id.*, *Ben. Pref. y Juzg.*, vi. 5–6; *Id.*, *Angeles*, xi. 52. No motive is given; but by Stearns and others it is implied that the cause was his connection with the movement against Victoria. From the haste of both Victoria and Chico to proceed against Stearns on their arrival, it is not unlikely that each had some secret instructions on the subject from Mexico. Stearns came to Monterey, and was allowed to go back, under bonds, to settle his business in a month and leave the country. July 8th, Stearns writes to Chico complaining of the injury done him, and threatening to hold the govt responsible. *Dept. St. Pap., Ben. Pref. y Juzg.*, MS., vi. 2–3. Eulogio Célis, a Spaniard, who seems to have been supercargo of the vessel on which Chico came, was also forbidden to re-enter Cal. *S. Diego, Arch.*, MS., 114, 120.

Osio, *Hist. Cal.*, MS., 254–6, narrates that Stearns, hurrying to obey the order, came to Monterey and was at first politely received with others, not

It should be remembered, however, that on account of Texan complications in 1835–6, the Mexican government and its representatives had no reason for friendly feelings toward Anglo-American foreigners at least. I find no contemporary evidence of controversy before Chico's departure for the south; but it is not unlikely that the storm was raging in certain circles not represented, naturally, in public records. Alvarado and Vallejo state that at this time, or possibly during Chico's absence, they with Castro and Gabriel de la Torre planned a revolution at the house of Captain Cooper; but that Chico, by subsequently revolting against himself, rendered the carrying-out of their plans unnecessary.[33]

being known to the gov.; but on hearing his name, Chico sprung up, and pointing his finger at him, cried out, 'Are you the rascal Abel Stearns whom I sent for to punish as his criminal acts deserve? Are you the American scoundrel who rose against Gen. Victoria, and whom I shall hang to-morrow at the flagstaff? Are you the audacious foreigner, without honor, who has dared to enter this room among honorable men? Be off, and await to-morrow the result of your rascality!' Alvarado, *Hist. Cal.*, MS., iii. 71–6, asserts that at a secret meeting to consider Chico's opposition to foreigners he (A.) was sent to interview the gov., whom he warned that if he persisted in his measures all foreign capital and vessels would be withdrawn, greatly to the injury of Cal. Chico said the foreigners would not be allowed to withdraw their capital; and when A. said there was no law to prevent it, burst out laughing, and remarked that his visitor had evidently not acquainted himself with the modern Mexican system of politics and forced loans. A. explained that the Californians would side with the foreigners if any such outrage were attempted; and Chico, after storming a while, became more reasonable, said he would postpone violent measures for a time, and finally asked the young diputado to take a cup of chocolate with himself and Doña Cruz. He was, however, sadly disappointed when he learned that A. could tell him nothing about the medical properties of California plants.

Of the foreigners who have given their opinions about Chico, Spence, *Hist. Notes*, MS., speaks of 'the despot general who was a fitter subject for the lunatic asylum than for governor. He respected neither law nor justice, but acted solely according to his own caprice and whims.' Dr Marsh, *Letter*, MS., p. 7, says 'he was the friend of Victoria, pursued the same outrageous course of conduct, and shared the same fate. He arrived fully determined to take vengeance on those who had been instrumental in expelling Victoria.' Alfred Robinson, *Life in California*, 173: 'Prejudiced against many Californians, and violently incensed at the foreign residents, Chico commenced a tyranny that soon brought him into disgrace; and finally ended in his expulsion from the territory.' Petit-Thouars, *Voyage*, ii. 92, and Wilkes, *Narrative*, v. 174–5, attribute his downfall to his arbitrary conduct and a quarrel with the judge of the district. Tuthill, *Hist. Cal.*, 141, follows Robinson's version.

[33] *Alvarado, Hist. Cal.*, MS., iii. 126, 140, 48–9; *Vallejo, Hist. Cal.*, MS., iii. 82–92, 100. Vallejo relates that on receipt, May 13th, of Chico's order of May 4th (*Vallejo, Doc.*, MS., iii. 200–1), he started for Monterey. At S. José he met Célis and Becher, who warned him against the 'cold-blooded,

The doings of the junta defensora, or vigilance committee, at Los Angeles in April, were the current topic of public attention when Chico landed at Santa Bárbara. These "scandalous events—a tumultuous meeting of citizens who allowed themselves to be seduced by four malicious and wayward men, putting themselves above authority and law in despite of sound morals"—seemed to the new ruler matters of the greatest moment and fraught with terrible peril to California. He saw a political significance in the movement, believing that the alleged cause was not the real one, but that "a resolution meditated by occult anarchical spirits to overthrow the government inspired in the incautious Angelinos the fatal idea of revolt under a pretext apparently sound, in order that

fierce, brutal, hypocritical, insolent, centralist governor,' who had arrested Carrillo at Sta Bárbara and many of the leading men at Monterey. Vallejo went back to Sonoma and started again with a force of 22 soldiers, 10 citizen volunteers, and 14 Indians. At S. José Juan Alvires was told to be ready for action if needed. One day was spent at Pájaro at the rancho of J. J. Vallejo, who was ready to render aid against the centralist. At 11 A. M. on May 26th, having been admitted to the presidio by the corporal of the guard, Don Guadalupe formed his men in a line before the governor's house and knocked at the door. It was opened by an old man in a morning gown, green cap, and slippers, who said, 'I am the man you have come to see; are you not Alférez Vallejo, who commands on the Sonoma frontier?' 'Yes, and I want to see Comandante General Chico,' was the reply, whereupon he went and put on his uniform, and returned, saying, 'Señor Alférez, here is the general of California.' A long interview ensued, minutely described. Chico complained of Vallejo's delay in coming, but after a long discussion, the latter, by the aid of a map drawn on the spot, succeeded in convincing Chico that the trip from Sonoma could not have been made quicker! Then Chico questioned his visitor closely about the northern frontier and his Indian policy. The Indians were also called in and questioned. Finally the governor expressed great satisfaction and praised the young officer's conduct; asked him to take a glass of wine brought by Doña Cruz, whose bright eyes almost caused the alférez to forget the charms of his own young wife; and accompanied him to the door, telling him to stay at Monterey as long as he liked. Vallejo then went out to meet his friends, who had gathered to defend him in case of need, and were much surprised to know that 'Guadalupe had tamed the bear.' It was their opinion and the narrator's that Chico had intended to arrest Vallejo, but had been frightened by his resolute acts and by his military escort. (The interview, according to Vallejo's own version, would indicate rather that Chico was a quiet, gentlemanly officer, who had no hostility against the alférez, and was pleased by his independence and bluff manners.) It was then that the plan of revolution was formed, to be carried out if Chico should continue his arbitrary conduct, and a written agreement was made, of which each of the conspirators kept a copy. Alcalde Estrada so far assented to the plan as to agree not to endure from Chico any direct infringement of the written laws.

later they might be induced to serve the sinister aims into which more than once the avowed and secret directors of this mutiny have been initiated, causing bitter days for this department." So urgent did the danger seem, that he wished to go in person to Los Angeles, but was dissuaded by friends, who told him that as the command had not yet been transferred, his authority would probably not be recognized at the pueblo. Therefore he hastened to Monterey, and soon sent Gutierrez south with a force to restore order. All this, with something of results, and the fact that the expedition had burdened the treasury with a loan of $2,000, was communicated at length to the junta and to the people in the governor's discourse of May 27th.[34] It was doubtless in connection with this expedition that the order to Vallejo had been issued as already related.

On April 26th, in accordance with orders from Monterey, Alcalde Requena had commenced proceedings against members of the so-called mob of April 7th; but as all declared there were no leaders, and that over fifty culprits must be punished if any, the alcalde could only report to the governor enclosing a list of the names.[35] It was on May 4th that Chico issued orders for Gutierrez to march south to quell the disorders at Los Angeles; but we know very little of the expedition, save that it cost $2,000, met no resistance, and according to Chico's discourse was successful in

[34] *Chico, Discurso, etc.* Jacob P. Leese, as already stated, came north with Chico; and according to the statement of Hittell, *Hist. S. Francisco*, 81, based presumably on Leese's own account, 'on the way Chico asked him for an account of the affair at Los Angeles, of which Noriega at Sta Bárbara had given him a very unfavorable opinion. Leese told the circumstances, and produced the copy of the record, which entirely satisfied the governor, who promised that he should not be troubled about it. A desire to learn the particulars of the execution at Los Angeles was probably one of Chico's motives for requesting Leese's company; and the conviction in his mind that the people acted properly may have had some influence in inducing him to give a letter that assisted Leese in obtaining the order for laying out the town of Yerba Buena.' Evidently there is a mistake about Chico's conviction, whatever may have been his course towards Leese personally.

[35] Record of May 4th. *S. Diego, Arch.*, MS., 103. Chico also mentions in his *Discurso* the means adopted by the mob to shield the leaders.

overawing the Angelinos to such an extent that they
"pointed out their deceivers, that justice might pursue them." Some arrests were made and arms were
seized in the city and adjoining ranchos before and
after Chico's arrival.[36]

Why Chico went to the south at all is not clear;
neither is it possible to give any connected narrative
of what he did there, except to make himself very unpopular. He reached Los Angeles about the middle
of June, having a few days before presided at the
swearing of the bases at Santa Bárbara, as he did at
the city on the 19th. He granted some kind of an
amnesty to those concerned in the tumult of April,
excepting four men from the amnesty, by an order of
June 20th; and next day he issued a bando requiring the delivery of all arms that were yet in private
possession, under severe penalties.[37] Osio says that
after storming for a while, and terrifying the timid
Angelinos with his threats of hanging and shooting,
Chico calmed down and astonished the prisoners by
dismissing them with pardon, after a mild reprimand.
This writer says, however, that he subsequently lost
his temper again, and caused several arrests; but the
prisoners were released after he left the country.
Several Californians tell us that Prudon and Araujo
were banished, and that the latter never returned;
but I think that no one received any greater punishment than a brief arrest.

The governor, being called to Monterey by 'important affairs,' left San Gabriel for the north on

---

[36] May 4, 1836, Chico's order to Gutierrez, and to alcalde to give him aid.
Dept. St. Pap., MS., iv. 108. May 18th, Prudon and Arzaga arrested. Sepúlveda and Juan Ávila not yet. *Guerra, Doc.*, MS., vi. 155. May 28th, arms
seized from 24 persons, 13 of whom were foreigners. *Los Angeles, Arch.*, MS.,
i. 98–101. June 3d, Gutierrez to Chico. Is gathering in all the arms, and will
go to S. Diego, leaving Ibarra in command. *Dept. St. Pap., Ben. Mil.*, MS.,
lxxxi. 37. June 8th–18th, collection of arms by alcaldes at the ranchos. *Id.*,
Angeles, ii. 50–2. Nov. 20th, arms collected at S. Gabriel, perhaps in connection with some other matter. *Id.*, ii. 65–6.

[37] The 4 men not included in the amnesty were José Perez, Vicente
Sanchez, José Sepúlveda, and Juan Ramirez, said to have headed a second
meeting of citizens. *Dept. St. Pap., Ben. Pref. y Juzg.*, MS., vi. 7. They
may have been the 4 'díscolos maliciosos' of Chico's *Discurso.*

June 28th, and reached Monterey the 8th of July. Before his departure, he gave to Gutierrez full authority to act in all matters pertaining to the civil or military command in the south. This officer was at San Diego, making investigations respecting the 'plan' of Bandini and others, to which I have already referred. The result was forwarded on July 13th for consideration at the capital; but its nature is not revealed.[38] There can be no doubt that Chico acted most unwisely in assuming the position that he did respecting the tumults in the south. There was probably no political significance in them at all. Such popular uprisings for speedy justice, when supported by the best citizens, are nearly always for the best, whatever may be the theoretical majesty of the law. Chico was technically right in his adherence to law and order, but he should have seen that he could accomplish nothing against a whole town, as he did see after going south, and have congratulated himself that the trouble did not occur in his term of office. All he effected was to make himself cordially hated by the citizens of Los Angeles and San Diego.

In yet another affair, Chico while in the south laid the foundations of a controversy that was destined to alienate from him whatever share he had in the patriotic good-will of even the staid and conservative Santa Bárbara. On his way southward he came to Santa Inés the 10th of June, and the padres Jimeno not only refused him animals and other aid for his journey, but failed to award him the ceremonial reception due to his rank, or even the courtesies always shown to travellers at the missions. Such was Chico's own version of the affair; that of the padres, confirmed by Señora Jimeno, their sister-in-law, who was present at Santa Inés, was that as much courtesy was shown

[38]July 1st, 13th, Gutierrez from S. Luis and S. Diego to Chico, who on June 25th had announced his departure for the 26th. *S. Diego, Arch.*, MS., 116; *Dept. St. Pap., Ben. Mil.*, MS., lxxxi. 25, 28. June 27th, Chico at San Gabriel, ready to start next day. *Vallejo, Doc.*, MS., iii. 216. At Monterey July 8th. *Gomez, Diario*, MS.

to the governor as was possible on short notice, his coming not being known in advance at the mission.[39] Arriving at Santa Bárbara the same day, Chico presented a complaint on the subject to Prefect Duran, who did not attempt to deny or justify the alleged discourtesy of the friars, paying very little attention to the charges,[40] but offering a long argument to the effect that unsecularized missions were under no obligation to furnish aid to the government. This argument, and the resulting secularization of Santa Inés and San Buenaventura, will receive attention in another chapter. Duran also flatly refused to celebrate mass at the swearing of the bases, on the ground of his allegiance to Spain.

It does not appear that there was any controversy during Chico's presence at Santa Bárbara. If there was any exhibition of ill temper in the governor's in-

[39] June 23d, Chico to junta, including the substance of his letter of June 11th to P. Duran. *St. Pap., Miss. and Colon.*, MS., ii. 368–73. C. says that his coming had been announced formally by a vaquero sent from Buenavista, that Manuel Jimeno told him at Oso Flaco that he was expected that very day, and that all the people of the mission were on the *qui vive* for his arrival. Therefore he was surprised when P. José Jimeno came out to meet him, with the remark that no facilities could be afforded since his coming had not been known, and moreover that he and his brother were 'mere pilgrims in that Jerusalem.' P. Victoria was courteous, but the Jimeno brothers showed such marked disrespect and contempt for his office that he was compelled to decline even to take a seat proffered him on a bench in the ante-kitchen. At the foot of the hill he was overtaken by the majordomo, who begged permission to bring animals for his service, an offer which was accepted. Sra Jimeno, *Ord, Ocurrencias*, MS., 87–97, says she was at Sta Inés recovering from a serious illness, and P. Antonio Jimeno had come there to celebrate her birthday on June 11th. They were at dinner when an Indian announced the general's coming. Chico came in a carriage; the three friars went out to meet him; one opened the door of the carriage, another offered his hand, while P. José Jimeno expressed regret that ignorance of the time of his arrival prevented a more ceremonial reception, though the mission bells were now ringing. Chico was invited in to dinner, but declined, and reëntering his carriage, was driven to Huejote. To that place the padres and Sra Jimeno sent a fine repast, which Chico refused, saying, 'Vuelvale Vd. esa comida á esos frailes, pues no quiero nada de ellos.'

[40] June 15th, Duran to C., will not treat of the occurrences at Sta Inés, because he has already made verbal explanation, and will speak of them again. 'For, after all, those padres are my brethren, and I cannot but insist on acting as peacemaker until I succeed in obtaining from you a complete indulgence in favor of those poor friars, whose offence I believe could have been none other than surprise and inadvertence; and I trust that you will entertain the same opinion when you know them better.' *St. Pap., Miss. and Colon.*, MS., ii. 374–5.

tercourse with the padres, it has left no trace in his written communications, which are dignified in manner and matter. He reported the matter to the junta, and that body decided before his return to Monterey that the missions were under obligations to aid the government; and expressed much regret and surprise at the offensive conduct of the padres toward the chief magistrate of the territory, something that had never been witnessed in the country before, even in the case of a private traveller.[41] After Chico's return it was decided by him and approved by the junta that Duran should be ordered to Monterey and expelled from California, for having refused to celebrate mass at the swearing of the bases, and for publicly maintaining that the national independence was ·illegal, unjust, and anti-Catholic. This action was consistent enough with the past policy of the diputacion, and, as will be remembered, had been recommended by Figueroa; yet it is not unlikely that the chief motive of this support of Chico by the junta was to promote, through Duran's well known popularity at Santa Bárbara, the disaffection of that conservative people, hitherto unmanageable in the interest of political agitators. The order was sent to the alcalde July 25th; and all that we know of the result by contemporary records is that on August 4th, after Chico's departure, Padre Duran announced to the alcalde that he could not go to Monterey by land, but must await the *Leonidas*.[42] It is stated, however, by several persons who must have known the facts, that when an attempt was made to put the padre prefecto on board a vessel, the people of the town rose en masse, women in the front ranks, and prevented the

[41] Report of com. on missions, June 29th–30th. *St. Pap., Miss. and Colon.*, MS., ii. 385. July 4th, Alvarado to Vallejo. The padres Jimeno and P. Duran treated Chico with so much disrespect that he was obliged to take from them the temporal management of Sta Inés and S. Buenaventura. *Vallejo, Doc.*, MS., iii. 218.

[42] July 25, 1836, Chico to alcalde of Sta B. Aug. 4th, P. Duran to same. *Dept. St. Pap.*, MS., iv. 115–16, 122.

local authorities from executing Chico's orders.[43] The popular version ascribes Chico's 'persecution' of Duran to the latter's refusal to punish the padres Jimeno, and to his denunciation of the governor's vices; but the dates and tenor of the two original documents cited will suggest to the reader very many discrepancies in all that is said by Californians about this, like every other part of Chico's rule.

The governor's popularity at the capital had not increased during his absence, and he soon became involved in the final troubles of his Californian experience. These troubles are stated with great unanimity by those who write from memory to have grown out of a scandalous liaison between José María Castañares, a clerk in the custom-house, and Doña Ildefonsa, wife of the sub-comisario, José María Herrera. This *causa célebre* is fully recorded in the archives, many of the original papers being in my possession. The record is bulky, and most of the details,

---

[43] *Valdés, Mem.*, MS., 24; *Janssens, Vida*, MS., 65; *Gonzalez, Experiencias*, MS., 32; *Pinto, Apuntaciones*, MS., 17. Mrs Ord, *Ocurrencias*, MS., 93–7, says that two officers came to Sta B. from the north to arrest Duran, arriving in the night. Domingo Carrillo warned Capt. Guerra; and narrator with a little brother was sent to warn P. Duran, who replied: 'Tell the patriarch to have no fear; blessed are they that suffer persecution for justice, for theirs is the kingdom of heaven.' The agents of Chico gave Duran some days for preparation, and then he went to the beach in a carriage. All the women of the place crowded about the carriage, and declared that the padre should not go on board the vessel. When a climax of cries and tears and general excitement had been reached, the men, hitherto concealed in a *sauzalito* near by, came up to support the women; and Duran, against his own desire, real or pretended, was taken home. Sta Bárbara for the first time was in open revolt against the govt. Alvarado, *Hist. Cal.*, MS., iii. 79–86, tells us that Capt. Guerra, knowing that Duran was to be exiled, and not being at liberty to divulge the secret, called his young son, and gave him money to go and buy all the eggs he could get for P. Duran, who was to be sent away, but it was a great secret, and must be told to nobody. Of course the youngster told everybody, as was his custom with all secrets—and also so as to get the eggs for nothing and pocket the money—and when the soldiers went to make the arrest, they found Duran surrounded by a crowd of women, who declared they would defend him with their lives. The soldiers did not dare to make the attack, and Chico was notified that he must send Mexican soldiers to take the padre! Vallejo, *Hist. Cal.*, MS., iii. 120–4, states, as does Alvarado, that Duran's chief offence was having preached against the governor's immorality. Chico was furious, and prepared to send an armed force to make his authority respected at Sta B.; but was dissuaded, or prevented by his other troubles, from carrying out his plan.

for obvious reasons, cannot be printed; indeed, I have neither space nor plausible pretext for presenting more than the brief outline necessary for historical purposes.

The amours of Castañares and Ildefonsa, a daughter of Captain Miguel Gonzalez, were more or less notorious in Monterey for some time before the persons more directly interested chose to make trouble. Doña Ana, wife of Castañares and daughter of Rafael Gonzalez, administrator of customs, began to agitate the matter in February 1836, and was prosecuted by Herrera for slander.[44] Doña Ana wasted no sentimentality on such a subject as her husband's faults, and for a time had exerted herself to separate the guilty pair, and thus prevent scandal. She was more than a match for all the others combined in energy and shrewdness, and had provided herself with abundant proofs, including the lovers' letters. She had even piloted no less a personage than Governor Gutierrez to a point where with her he overheard Ildefonsa's confession of her guilt, together with the cheering admission that when she had resisted on account of her friendship for Doña Ana, Castañares had threatened to remove that obstacle to their felicity by the use of poison. The case lasted from April to June, and was then dismissed by Herrera, who in May had begun another prosecution against Castañares and Ildefonsa for adultery.[45] On May 28th, the guilty couple were arrested. Castañares was locked up in jail and Ildefonsa deposited, as was the custom, in the house of a respectable citizen. The 30th of July Herrera withdrew his suit and consented to the liberation of the prisoners, on condition that Castañares

<hr/>

[44] *Castañares, Causa seguida contra Ana Gonzalez (Castañares) por haber hablado del adulterio de Alfonsa Gonzalez (Herrera) y de J. M. Castañares, Abril–Junio, 1836*, MS. About 50 documents, of which the longest is Doña Aña's defence of April 11th, including her charges.

[45] *Castañares, Causa Criminal contra J. M. Castañares é Ildefonsa Gonzalez por adulterio, seguida á pedimento del esposo de esta, José María Herrera, Mayo–Julio, 1836*, MS. This is a rather brief record, but many of the documents bearing on this case were also introduced in the next. See note 46.

should leave the place, and not come within twelve leagues of the sub-comisaría so long as he remained in California. Meanwhile another bitter controversy had been raging between Doña Ana and Herrera, who hated each other much more heartily than they did their unfaithful spouses. Herrera had been so rash as to make in his previous slander suit some rather annoying charges against the lady's character; and now Doña Ana brought suit to obtain certain documents needed for her own justification, but which, as her opponent declared, she intended to use 'extrajudicially' to his own detriment by keeping the scandal alive. I have the original records of this suit, which was made to include pretty much all that pertained to the other two in the way of testimony, charges, letters, and pasquinades, many of the pieces being more amusing than instructive. The end seems to have been a reference to the supreme court on some technicality.[46]

One of Herrera's alleged reasons for suspending his prosecution of Castañares at the end of June was that "the public tranquillity had been disturbed by events growing out of the matter, and harmony lost between the authorities, so that very serious consequences were to be feared unless the cause of contention were removed." This is all I find in records of the time to connect the Monterey scandal with Chico's troubles;[47] but the Californians tell the story in substance as follows: While Castañares was in prison, and his paramour in enforced seclusion, a company of *maromeros*, or rope-dancers, gave a performance in one of the presidio buildings, at which, as usual on such rare occasions, everybody was present. The best place was reserved of course for the governor, who on entering

---

[46] *Castañares vs Herrera en Asuntos de Calumnia, 1836, Junio–Julio.* The original papers in *Doc. Hist. Cal.*, i. 257–380. Several hundred documents, bearing the autographs of nearly every prominent man in Monterey either as court officials or witnesses.

[47] Alvarado, however, in his charges of July 29th, accused Chico of having meddled with the case of Castañares, which belonged to the ordinary jurisdiction.

was accompanied, not only by his mistress Doña Cruz, but by her friend Doña Ildefonsa Herrera, who had been liberated for the occasion. There was much indignation and excitement at the appearance of this notorious pair in the place of honor, and some ladies left the room in disgust. Then Alcalde Ramon Estrada, who felt that his authority as a judge had been insulted by Ildefonsa's presence, was induced to release Castañares from the jail and give him a prominent seat at the show, from which he is said to have ostentatiously saluted his paramour at the governor's side. Chico was beside himself with rage, and perhaps had hot words with Estrada on the spot. At any rate, next day he marched with a military escort to the hall of the ayuntamiento, took away from Estrada his alcalde's *vara*, and subsequently placed him under arrest in his own house—some authorities speaking even of his being locked up in jail, of an attack on his house, and of insults to his aged father, Don Mariano.[48]

The exact date of the quarrel with Estrada is not known, though his arrest would seem to have been on June 27th; nor is it possible to determine the chronologic order of succeeding events. The popular excitement was great. Teodoro Gonzalez, the regidor, took the position of alcalde, and seems to have incited the citizens to resist Chico's encroachments on the rights of the municipal authorities. The military force at Monterey was small, and most of the soldiers were in sympathy with Chico's enemies. The governor feared that not only his authority but his life was in danger. The cannon at the castillo were kept loaded and manned; and Chico remained for the most part

[48] *Serrano, Apuntes*, MS., 31–5; *Gonzalez, Revoluciones*, MS., 7–10; *Osio, Hist. Cal.*, MS., 263–76; *Torre, Remin.*, MS., 58–61; *Alvarado, Hist. Cal.*, MS., iii. 92–5; *Vallejo, Hist. Cal.*, MS., iii. 128–40; *Pico, Acont.*, MS., 30–1; *Pinto, Apunt.*, MS., 18–19; *Janssens, Vida*, MS., 63–72; *Vallejo (J. J.), Remin.*, MS., 118; *Fernandez, Cosas de Cal.*, MS., 97–9. To go more closely into details than I have done would be to give the different versions pretty nearly in full, for it must be confessed there is but a slight resemblance between them.

in his own house under the protection of a guard. This critical state of affairs lasted several days, perhaps more than a week.[49] As early as July 15th, orders were sent to the southern troops to come to Monterey; on the 23d came the *Leonidas* with news of Santa Anna's defeat and capture in Texas, on which topic a flamingly patriotic proclamation was issued next day to the Californians; and on the 27th affairs had apparently approached a crisis, since on that day the governor suspended Cosme Peña, a prominent counsellor of his foes, from his office of asesor, and sent now and urgent orders for the troops to come by forced marches to the capital.[50]

No reënforcements made their appearance. Indian ravages on the Sonoma frontier and at San Diego served Vallejo and Portilla as convenient excuses for not promptly obeying the orders of their chief. The popular feeling at Monterey was more turbulent than ever, or at least was made to appear so to the governor, by advisers who desired to increase his fears. At last, on July 29th, he sent a communication to the diputacion, stating that as there was great popular excitement on account of his suspension of the alcalde and asesor, as bodies of men were in arms near the town, and as he had no physical or moral support, he had determined to go to Mexico at once.[51] The diputa-

[49] Janssens tells us that José Castro offered to raise a company of men to support Chico, but was induced by the people to change his plans; but I attach no importance to this statement.

[50] July 15, 1836, Chico to Gutierrez. Let Capt. Portilla march at once with the Mazatecos and artillery. *S. Diego, Arch.*, MS., 120; *Hayes, Doc.*, MS., 61. July 23d, arrival of news from Texas. *Gomez, Diario*, MS. July 27th, let the troops hasten by double marches. *S. Diego, Arch.*, MS., 119; *Id., Index*, 30. July 29th, G. to C. Portilla on one pretext or another will not start. *Id.*, 119, 122. July 31st, G. to C., in answer to letter of 27th. Portilla and Muñoz will start at once and march rapidly. No danger in the south; but fears serious troubles at Monterey, and warns him to be on his guard. Regrets the annoyances to C. from Peña's revolutionary promptings, etc. *Dept. St. Pap., Ben. Mil.*, MS., lxxxviii. 28–9. July 27th, Cosme Peña suspended. *Vallejo, Doc.*, MS., xxxii. 29. Vallejo, *Hist. Cal.*, MS., iii. 124–6, says Chico's order to him to march with his force was dated July 23d, and was accompanied by another very flattering letter of thanks for past services dated July 10th, but really written on the same day as the order. A translation of Chico's proclamation of July 24th is given in the *Honolulu, S. I., Gazette*, Nov. 12, 1836.

[51] The only original record of this consultation of the dip. is a report of the

cion, composed of men who had come to consider Chico as their enemy, and had been for some time plotting to drive him from the country, seems to have approved the governor's plan, after some efforts to impose conditions respecting the succession, glad to have him go voluntarily without the necessity of actual revolt, and not believing that he would succeed in returning with reënforcements, as he threatened to do.[52]

On the same day, July 29th, Chico had chartered a vessel for his voyage to Mazatlan, as he announced to Herrera.[53]   Also on that date, Alvarado, in behalf of the diputacion and of the people, wrote a series of charges against the governor, addressed to the minister of relations, and designed to prevent Chico's return with support from the supreme government.[54]   On the 30th, Chico officially informed local authorities that popular commotion, beyond his control from lack of troops, and by reason of disaffection in the ayuntamiento and diputacion, obliged him to go to Mexico

com. of govt and police, Crespo and Gomez, dated the same day, in *Vallejo, Doc.*, MS., xxxii. 30. The com. recommends that to avoid public disorder, Chico shall restore the suspended officials; deliver the political command to the presiding vocal (Alvarado), to be by him delivered to the 1st vocal, now absent (Castro); and deliver the military command to the ranking officer. On these conditions the dip. would take steps to protect his person until his departure! Alvarado and Vallejo narrate many particulars, more interesting than accurate, I think, of interviews at this time between Alvarado as president of the dip. and Chico, particulars designed to prove that the latter was insane. They also speak of an order given to Zamorano by Chico, in his wrath that he was not urged to stay, to attack the junta with a military force, the attack being repelled by the people under Gonzalez. Alvarado states that the junta was at first disposed to reject Chico's proposal to go for troops as an insult, but was persuaded by himself that he would get no troops and this was the easiest way to get rid of him.

[52] Rafael Gomez in his *Diario*, MS., written at the time, expresses the bebelief that Chico will not come back; and he also confirms the bad reputation given Chico by the Californians.

[53] July 29, 1836, Chico to Herrera. Offers to collect the $6,000 placed at disposal of Cal. by the Guaymas comisaría. *Dept. St. Pap.*, MS., iv. 118–20.

[54] *Leg. Rec.*, MS., iii. 28–9. California, the 'theatre of abomination, disorder, and desolation.' Chico, after disposing of Castañares, a criminal belonging to the ordinary jurisdiction, has suspended and ordered the arrest of the alcalde; searched scandalously the house of an old and honored citizen; disregarded the faculties of the ayunt. which tried to take steps for protecting the persons and property of this municipality; suspended the asesor, and insulted the members of the dip.; and finally, in a note to this body, promises to resign, although he has sent for troops from different points, to the great danger of the territory, that they might come and foment the disorder. He had also made dangerous concessions to the Russians.

in quest of aid by which to restore order. In his absence, Gutierrez would hold both commands from August 1st. Gutierrez was advised to adopt such a policy as to check the conspiracy against the government.[55] There is some evidence that Chico had promised at first to leave the *gefatura* in the hands of the diputacion; and he is also said to have left orders to institute suits against Estrada and Cosme Peña.[56]

Chico sailed from Monterey on the *Clementine* July 31st, and from San Pedro on August 10th.[57] Of his departure, as of his rule, many queer stories are told. He presented Alvarado with a 'universal recipe' for the cure of all maladies, and shouted to him as he stepped into the boat, "Bring up crows to peck your eyes out!" He embraced an old Indian woman on the beach, saying, "Of all the men in this country thou art the best." He raved at Muñoz and Portilla for not coming up with reënforcements; declared he would return with 5,000 men; and shouted, with one foot in the boat, "Me voy Chico, pero volveré Grande." He left his gold watch to be regulated in California, transferred the command in a sealed packet not to be opened until midnight, and thanked a man for having caught his hat when running in the street on the day of the mob. He was prevented by the people from landing at Santa Bárbara. At San Pedro he put on board his vessel large quantities of tallow, stolen by the aid of Gutierrez from San Gabriel and other missions, to be disposed of at Mazatlan in payment for

[55] July 30, 1836, Chico to comandantes, alcaldes, etc. *Dept. St. Pap.*, MS., iv. 121; *Hayes, Doc.*, MS., 65; *S. Diego, Index*, MS., 31; *Vallejo, Doc., Hist. Mex.*, MS., iii. 225; xxxii. 31. July 30th, Chico to Gutierrez. *Dept. St. Pap.*, MS., iv. 119–20. The rebels have tried to seduce Guadalupe Vallejo, but the result is not known.

[56] *Gomez, Diario de Cosas, Notables*, MS. This should be excellent authority, the diary having been written at the time, by Rafael Gomez, an able lawyer and a Mexican.

[57] *Gomez, Diario*, MS.; *Dept. St. Pap.*, MS., iv. 118–19; *Hayes, Doc.*, MS., 65; *S. Diego, Index*, MS., 31. The *Clementine* was chartered from Wm Hinckley. Her captain is said to have been Wm Hanley. She had come from Honolulu in March. According to *S. Diego, Arch.*, MS., 119, it appears that about July 22d Lieut Navarrete had been ordered to Mazatlan on business for Chico; but he did not go.

goods which he had bought for the California market on private speculation. These statements are made chiefly by Alvarado, Osio, Vallejo, and Bandini; if any of them have a remote foundation in fact, I have not discovered it.

Chico never came back, and of his efforts and reception in Mexico nothing is really known. There were rumors, probably unfounded, of his having raised 200 men at one time for a return, and others that he was disgusted with the country, as was Doña Cruz, making no effort to regain his office, and contenting himself with a few bitter speeches in congress, in which body he took his old seat as diputado. He left property in California to the amount of several thousand dollars, which was confiscated by Vallejo and Alvarado the next year for the benefit of their new government, and as an indemnity for the harm that Chico had done in the country.[58] A Don Mariano Chico, whom I suppose to have been he of Californian fame, was governor of *Aguas Calientes in 1844,[59] and in 1846 he was comandante general of Guanajuato, still a radical centralist. He resigned in consequence of troubles with the new governor, publishing a pamphlet in defence of his conduct and views.[60]

In exposing the exaggeration and absurdity of most of the charges made against Governor Chico, I have

[58] Aug. 20, 1836, Vallejo to Alvarado, private letter enumerating Chico's scandalous acts. He had plundered the treasury, not only taking all the money but obtaining a draft on Mazatlan from Herrera. His real object in chartering a vessel under pretence of sending for aid had been to run away with all the plunder he could get his hands on. *Vallejo, Doc.*, MS., iii. 228. Feb. 21st, 1837, Vallejo to Malarin, ordering him to furnish an account of the effects left in his charge by Chico. Tells Alvarado that the amount is about $4,000, which is to be placed in deposit until an investigation is made about the amount carried away which belonged to the presidial companies. *Id.*, iv. 71. Feb. 27th, the amount proved to be $2,031, all that was left of $6,000 which had originally been invested by Chico for mercantile transactions. It was to be paid over by Malarin to Hartnell. *Id.*, iv. 76; *Dept. St. Pap., Ben. Mil.*, MS., lxxxi. 79–80. March 14th, the money to go into the state treasury to meet expenses of the govt. *Vallejo, Doc.*, MS., iv. 82. Alvarado, *Hist. Cal.*, MS., iii. 173–4, says that the existence of the money was discovered through a letter from Chico to Gutierrez which fell into Vallejo's hands.

[59] His report on the industrial condition of the department of Sept. 30th is given in *Mexico, Mem. Agric.*, 1845, appen. 3–7.

[60] *Chico, Dos Palabras del General.* Guanajuato, 1847. 12mo, 15 p.

perhaps been led to say more in his defence than was justified by the facts. He was assuredly not the villain and fool that the Californians picture him, but he had no special fitness for his position, little executive ability, and no qualities perhaps much above the commonplace. He was an educated man, and his weaknesses were of the tongue rather than the pen. That he was hot-tempered and personally disagreeable can hardly be doubted, when no one has a word to say in his favor; but his annoyances were great; his foes have had most to do in fixing his reputation, and there were divers political and personal motives for reviling his memory during the next ten years. He seems to have been a man of about forty-five years, of medium height and slight form. His complexion was light, his black hair sprinkled with gray, and he generally wore spectacles. The troubles that resulted in his departure must be regarded as revolutionary, having been fomented by a clique who desired to get rid of him, and rejoiced that circumstances enabled them to effect their purpose without coming into open conflict with the national government, and thus to try their wings in easy flights.

CHAPTER XVI.

GUTIERREZ, CASTRO, AND ALVARADO—REVOLUTION.

1836.

GOVERNOR CHICO, frightened away from California
at the end of July, had left both civil and military
commands, in accordance with the laws though against
the wishes of the diputacion, to Nicolás Gutierrez,
who was at the time acting as military commandant of
the south, and who did not reach the capital for more
than a month. Meanwhile I suppose that Captain
Zamorano was acting as representative of the governor's authority at Monterey, being comandante of the
post, at least until August 8th, when Captain Muñoz
arrived from the south with the reënforcements ordered by Chico, and possibly assumed the command
by virtue of his seniority in rank. I have, however,
no record of any act of authority exercised by either of
those officers. Gutierrez arrived the 6th of September.[1]

[1] Dates of arrival of Muñoz and Gutierrez fixed by *Gomez, Diario*, MS. Aug.
14th, alcalde of S. Diego reports that all is tranquil. Aug. 17th, Gutierrez

The second rule of Gutierrez, like the first, was a most uneventful period, if we except the stirring events that ended it. From contemporary records we can learn but little of his acts or of his policy, respecting which we must form our idea mainly from what preceded and what followed, from acquaintance with attendant circumstances and men concerned, and from the testimony of certain Californians. This testimony might be accepted with somewhat more implicit faith had it proved more accurate in respect of Victoria and Chico.

In recording the governor's arrival, Rafael Gomez wrote in his journal: "It appears that his intention is to carry forward the arbitrary measures which his predecessor began and which were the cause of his departure. Would that this might prove not so, for such conduct brings disorder."[2] Padre Abella complained of his interference in mission affairs and of his apparent intention to cause the friars all possible annoyance.[3] This is all I can find of contemporary complaint, and that of the friar grew out of special local troubles. On the other hand, I have a letter of Gutierrez, who wrote on October 7th: "I have summoned Don Pablo de la Portilla to give up to him the political and military commands, because I observe it is not pleasing to some persons that I should retain them. I do it most gladly, since I have no other aspiration than to separate myself from public affairs and to live in peace and quiet. You and all sensible men

---

from S. Gabriel as 'comandante militar de la demarcacion del sur,' and not as comandante general or gefe político, acknowledges receipt. He was still at S. Gabriel on Aug. 20th. *S. Diego, Arch.*, MS., 123-4. Sept. 17th, Portilla to G., announcing that the soldiers at S. Gabriel had refused to serve longer without pay or clothing. *Dept. St. Pap., Ben. Mil.*, MS., lxxxi. 23-4. Sept. 23d, G. orders an election for first Sunday in Oct., secondary election the following Sunday, and final meeting of electors at Monterey on Nov. 6th to choose a dip. The primary and secondary elections took place at S. Diego on Oct. 9th, 16th. Andrés Pico was the elector de partido. *S. Diego, Arch.*, MS., 130-2, 134. I find no further records of this election in any part of Cal.

[2] *Gomez, Diario de Cosas Notables*, MS.

[3] *Carrillo (J.), Doc.*, MS., 35-8.

know the fatal consequences of political convulsions, and I will make any sacrifice to prevent them."[4]

The Californians are much less violent in their denunciations of Gutierrez than of Chico and Victoria, their charges against him being for the most part general and rather vague. There is, however, a general agreement that he was an immoral man, unduly addicted to wine and women; a few make special charges of minor importance; a few find no fault with his conduct, and many condemn him in general terms, as if such were their obligation, hardly knowing why.[5] Juan B. Alvarado and Mariano G. Vallejo, particu-

[4] Oct. 7, 1836, G. to J. A. Estudillo, in *Estudillo, Datos,* MS., 57-8, 20-1. The writer urges his friend to inform him of anything likely to disturb the public peace, and regrets to learn that the 'torch of discord has extended its deadly train to S. Luis Rey, attracting with its flame the administrator of that property,' Pio Pico, at least so he has heard but can hardly believe. Botello, *Anales,* MS., 46, mentions the proposition to give the command to Portilla; so also does Alvarado, *Hist. Cal.,* MS., iii. 142.

[5] The widow Ávila, *Cosas de Cal.,* MS., 7-11, relates at considerable length that her husband, Miguel Ávila, síndico of Monterey, on account of having caught the wife of Capt. Muñoz and two other ladies bathing in a pool of water which supplied the town, and remonstrated with them for filling the water with soap, was arbitrarily imprisoned by Gutierrez, who replied to his wife's entreaties with threats to shoot her husband. But he was finally so frightened by the threatening attitude of the ayunt. and people, that Ávila was released. The lady attributes the governor's troubles largely to this affair. Pinto, *Apuntaciones,* MS., 20-1, also mentions Ávila's arrest, and the popular indignation thereat. He says it was believed that Chico had left instructions to G. to treat harshly all who opposed him. According to Bandini, *Hist. Cal.,* MS., 83, he took the advice and followed in the footsteps of Chico. Osio, *Hist. Cal.,* MS., 277-301, says there was much satisfaction at the appointment of the popular G., the intimate friend of Figueroa; yet he showed a strange melancholy on taking the command, supposed to arise from the necessity of obeying Chico's orders. Pio Pico, *Hist. Cal.,* MS., 100-1, speaks of his fondness for Indian girls in the south. David Spence, *Hist. Notes,* MS., 17, says he attempted to harass those suspected of having taken an active part against Chico; also was disposed to manage the revenues. Botello, *Anales,* MS., 22, tells us that the people merely sought a pretence to revolt against Gutierrez. J. J. Vallejo, *Remin.,* MS., 117, 121-2, speaks of his concubines, and of his following the course marked out by Chico, whose return he expected. Of courteous manners, but much addicted to drink. *Arce, Mem.,* MS., 8-9. Quarrelled with everybody. Threatened to put narrator in jail because he asked to have his land grant confirmed. *Pico, Acont.,* MS., 31-2. Did nothing to deserve hostility. *Janssens, Vida,* MS., 70-2. Affable, but kept a harem. *Lugo, Vida, Cal.,* MS., 15. Vicious, corrupt, and gave a bad example; but this was not the cause of his overthrow. *Coronel, Cosas de Cal.,* MS., 19. Have seen him intoxicated. *Ávila, Notas,* MS., 18. Addicted to scandalous vices; not arbitrary or despotic; wasted public funds. *Serrano, Apuntes,* MS., 36. Not a bad man, but fond of women. Many scandals were current about him in this respect. *Galindo, Apuntes,* MS., 32. Unpopular. *Ord, Ocurrencias,* MS., 98.

larly the former, speak of the governor's immorality in establishing in his *palacio* a seraglio of Indian girls from San Gabriel; but their chief argument against him is based on his treatment of the diputacion. Not only, according to these gentlemen, did Gutierrez refuse to deliver the office of gefe político to the senior vocal, as was desired and expected, but he insulted that body through its president, sent to confer with him; said he "had no need of diputados of pen and voice while he had plenty of diputados of sword and gun;" and even gave orders to disperse the diputacion by force, so frightening the members that they did not dare to reassemble at Monterey.[6]

The truth is, that Gutierrez, a Spaniard by birth though serving on the insurgent side during the revolution, was an inoffensive, easy-going, unpretentious, and not unpopular man. He was a faithful officer, of moderate ability, and of not very strict morals. He was neither dishonest, arrogant, nor arbitrary in his conduct. As a Mexican officer he was loyal to his national allegiance; he had no right according to the laws and his predecessor's instructions to turn over the civil command to the diputacion; and as a Spaniard he had to be somewhat more cautious respecting his conduct than if he had been born in Mexico.[7]

[6] *Alvarado, Hist. Cal.*, MS., iii., 112-24. With many details of his own interviews with the gov., and also the efforts of Angel Ramirez, Alvarado's friend, and having much influence over G. and all the Mexicans. Vallejo, *Hist. Cal.*, MS., iii. 154, etc., agrees in the main with Alvarado's statements, he not having been at Monterey at the time.

[7] G. as remembered by the Californians was of medium height, rather stout, of light complexion, reddish hair, beard slightly sprinkled with gray, and with a cast in the right eye which caused him to be nicknamed 'El Tuerto.' He came to Mexico as a boy, and his first service was as a drummer. Torre, *Remin.*, MS., 68-70, saw him give an exhibition of his skill as a drummer at a serenade on Figueroa's birthday. Abrego, in *García, Apuntes*, MS., appen., says that G. was one of 300 Spanish prisoners taken by Gen. Bravo, and whom he offered to liberate to save his father's life. The father was shot, but Bravo freed the men, most of whom, including the young drummer, remained in the insurgent ranks. He had served with Figueroa, was his intimate friend, and came to Cal. with him in Jan. 1833, as captain. His commission as lieut-colonel was dated July 18, 1833. *Dept. St. Pap., Ben. Mil.*, MS., lxxix. 79. In 1834-5 he was comisionado for the secularization of S. Gabriel. All else of his life in Cal. is contained in this chapter and the preceding. I know nothing of him after he left the country.

Neither his character, acts, nor policy had much influence in exciting the opposition that resulted in his overthrow. Pretence for a quarrel with him was sought by certain persons, was of course not difficult to find, and would have been found had the difficulty been much greater.

For some twenty-five years, since the *memoria* ships ceased to come, there had been a feeling that California was neglected and wronged by the home government. The Mexican republic after the success of the revolution did nothing to remove that feeling. The people, though enthusiastic republicans in theory, waited in vain for the benefits to be gained from republicanism. The influence of the missionaries, men of education and devoted to Spain, tended strongly to foster the sentiment of aversion to all that was Mexican—an influence that increased rather than diminished as the padres lost their temporal prestige and became prone to refer bitterly if somewhat secretly to the olden times. The sending of convicts and *cholo* soldiers from Mexico went far to intensify provincial prejudice. The Californians came to regard themselves proudly as superior in blood and morals to those *de la otra banda*. Mexicans of little experience or ability were given commissions in the presidial companies and sent to command veterans who had grown gray in the service and believed themselves entitled to promotion. When commerce brought a degree of prosperity, it was in spite of Mexican revenue laws, and Mexican officers were sent to manage the revenues. Complications growing out of the colony scheme had an effect to widen the breach. Foreigners, with interested motives but sound arguments, labored to prove that California had received nothing but neglect and ill treatment from Mexico. Last but not least, there were various personal interests and ambitions thrown as weights on the same side of the scale.

The result was in 1836 a strong popular feeling amounting almost to hatred against the Mexicans "of

the interior," and a belief that Mexico should furnish
for California something more or something less than
rulers, and laws made with no reference to the country's needs. The popular feeling was not one of disloyalty to Mexico as a nation. The Californians were
far from entertaining as yet so radical an idea as that
of absolute independence; but they beleived that territorial interest should be consulted by the nation, and
that no more Mexican officers should be sent to rule
California. Alvarado, Carrillo, Castro, Pico, Vallejo,
and other young Californians of the same class, the
men who had for the most part supplied the diputacion with members, the politicians of the country, not
only shared the popular sentiment, but were disposed
to utilize it for their own as for their country's interests. They were willing to furnish from their own
number men to rule California and handle its scanty
revenues. Even they were not yet prepared to advocate entire separation from Mexico; but they were
men of some education, who had come much in contact with foreigners, and had imbibed to some extent
liberal views. Some of them had become more than
half convinced that Mexican ways of doing most
things were not the best ways. Yet they shrewdly
feared foreign influence, and were disposed to be cautious. Their present purpose was to gain control of
the country; later there would be time to determine
what to do with the prize. Their success against Victoria had given them self-confidence, and made the
word 'revolt' less terrible in their ears. Later success
in getting rid of Chico by other methods still further
flattered their self-esteem. The rise of centralism
gave to their schemes an aspect of national patriotism;
while rumors that centralism was on its last legs au-
gured comparative safety. Manifestly their time had
come. Hence the rising against Gutierrez, whose
character and acts, as I have said, were unimportant
factors in the problem.

Juan B. Alvarado, second vocal and president of

the diputacion, was the leading spirit in this movement. He was at this time twenty-seven years of age, and employed as *vista*, or inspector, in the custom-house. His public life had begun in 1827, when he was made secretary of the diputacion, holding the place until 1834. His father, Sergeant José Francisco Alvarado,[8] died in 1809, three months after the birth of his only son, and his mother, María Josefa, daughter of Sergeant Ignacio Vallejo, subsequently married Ramon Estrada. Juan Bautista learned from his mother and from the soldier-schoolmasters of Monterey to read, write, and to cipher more or less, besides his *doctrina* and the art of singing in the choir at mass. Governor Sola took an interest in the boy, and gave him a chance in his office to improve his penmanship and acquire some knowledge. He was observant and quick to learn. He and his companions, José Castro and Guadalupe Vallejo, were fond of reading, especially when they could get contraband books and elude the vigilance of the friars. He learned much by his association with foreigners, besides acquiring a smattering of English. He aided Padre Menendez, the chaplain, as secretary for a time, and was employed as clerk and collector by different foreign traders, who gave him a good reputation for intelligence and honesty.

In 1836 Alvarado was a young man of much practical ability, of good character, of tolerably steady habits, though rapidly acquiring too great a fondness for strong drink, and of great popularity and influence with all classes, though he had been one of the first to resent Mexican insults to his countrymen, and had consequently been involved in personal difficulties with Rodrigo del Pliego and others *de la otra banda*. He was perhaps better qualified than any other of the younger Californians to become a popular and successful leader. He was not so dignified nor so rich as Vallejo, and was perhaps not the superior of José

[8] See biographical sketches.

Antonio Carrillo in ability for intrigue. He had somewhat less education from books than some members of the Guerra and Estudillo families, but in practical efficiency, as in personal popularity, he was above them all. He was backed by the foreign residents and traders, who doubtless expected to control his policy for their own private and commercial interests, and some of whom very likely hoped in the end to gain political advantages for their respective nations. On the other hand, Alvarado was incited by a few Mexicans, notably by the lawyer Cosme Peña and the ex-friar Angel Ramirez, administrator of customs and the young vista's superior officer. Both were influenced by personal motives, and had no doubt of their ability to control the new administration. There is much reason to believe that Ramirez had special need of a governor who would look with friendly charity on the state of his official accounts.

I come now to the final outbreak against Gutierrez, respecting which no original documentary evidence exists.[9] The ordinary version in narratives that have

[9] The earliest account of the revolution extant is one sent by a resident, whose name is not given, and printed in the *Honolulu, S. I. Gazette* of Dec. 2, 1837. The author does not credit the report that the foreigners were largely instrumental in causing the movement. The Frenchmen, Petit-Thouars, *Voyaje*, ii. 92–100, Mofras, *Exploration*, i. 298–300, and Lafond, *Voyages*, i. 210, attribute the revolt mainly to the instigations and promises of the Americans; and Mofras thinks the presence of the U. S. man-of-war *Peacock* a few days before had an influence. Wilkes, *Narrative*, v. 175–9, tells us that Alvarado was acting under the direction of foreigners who intended to hoist a new flag, to banish all Mexicans, to declare Cal. an independent state, and to have themselves all declared citizens. These declarations were supposed to emanate from Ramirez and 'Penné,' who wished to make use of the foreigners for their own ends. Greenhow, *Hist. Or.*, 367, attributes the movement to strong popular opposition to centralism. Gleeson, *Hist. Cath. Church*, 144–9, says the conspirators acted ostensibly with a view of gaining their independence, but really for purposes of plunder. Some general printed accounts of the revolution of 1836, to most of which I shall have no occasion to refer again, being mostly brief and more or less unimportant: *Cal. Star*, Feb. 26, 1848; *Honolulu Polynesian*, i. 6; ii. 86; *Farnham's Life in Cal.*, 60–6, the same being printed in the *Sta Cruz Sentinel*, Feb. etc. 1869; *Tuthill's Hist. Cal.*, 143–4; *Randolph's Oration; Dwinelle's Address before Pioneers*, 20; *Niles' Register*, lii. 85; *Robinson's Cal. Gold Region*, 59–61; *Pickett*, in *Shuck's Rep. Men*, 227–8; *Holinski, La Californie*, 196–7; *Hartmann, Geog. Stat. Cal.*, i. 37; *Ferry, Californie*, 19–20; *Ryan's Judges and Crim.*, 42-3, 51; *Nouv. An. Voy.*, lxxxv. 251; *Yolo Co. Hist.*, 10–12, and other county histories; also many newspaper

been published, is to the effect that Gutierrez, in consequence of a quarrel with Ramirez and Alvarado about some details of revenue precautions, such as the stationing of guards on a newly arrived vessel, ordered the arrest of Alvarado, who escaped by flight, and at once proceeded to incite a revolution. This was the version sent at the time to the Sandwich Islands by a resident foreigner, confirmed by Alfred Robinson, from whose narrative it has been taken by Tuthill and other writers. It is also partially confirmed by several Californians, and has, I think, a slight foundation in fact. At any rate, Alvarado and José Castro left the capital in October, and making San Juan their headquarters, began active preparations for a rising of the settlers, native and foreign.[10]

accounts. Some of the preceding mentions and narratives are accurate so far as they go; and in others the errors are so petty and apparent as to merit no pointing-out. Castañares, *Col. Doc.*, 19, is the only Mexican who has done more than mention the affair. He says the revolt was instigated and supported by the Americans. Foreigners who mention the revolution more or less fully in unpublished statements are Marsh, *Letter*, MS., 7–8; Bee, *Recollections*, MS., 6–21; Janssens, *Vida*, MS., 71–9; Brown, *Statement*, MS., 10–11; Weeks, *Remin.*, MS., 99; Davis, *Glimpses*, MS., 120 et seq., and the U. S. consul at Honolulu in a despatch of March 12, 1837, to the secretary of state, in *Savage, Doc.*, ii. 174–6. Spence and Munras published a card in the *Honolulu Polynesian*, i. 163, denying the truth of an article attributed to them in the *S. Luis Potosí Gaceta*. Manuscript narratives by Californians are: *Osio, Hist. Cal.*, MS., 303–18; *Alvarado, Hist. Cal.*, MS., ii. 202–3; iii. 125–85; *Vallejo, Hist. Cal.*, MS , iii. 154–207; *Bandini, Hist. Cal.*, MS., 83–6; *Castro, Rel.*, MS., 39–42; *Torre, Remin.*, MS., 62–70; *Gomez, Lo que Sabe*, MS., 13–18, 44–5; *Vallejo (J. J.), Remin.*, MS., 122–3; *Serrano, Apuntes*, MS., 27–41; *Arce, Mem.*, MS., 8–10; *Ávila, Cosas de Cal.*, MS., 8–13; *Fernandez, Cosas de Cal.*, MS., 99–106; *Pinto, Apunt.*, MS., 21–31; *Valle, Lo Pasado*, MS., 17; *Ord, Ocurrencias*, MS., 99; *Pico, Acont.*, MS., 32–40; *García, Hechos*, MS., 50–7; *Coronel, Cosas de Cal.*, MS., 21; *Galindo, Apuntes*, 34–5—and following pages of each narrative for succeeding events in 1836–7.

[10] In the *Honolulu, S. I. Gazette*, Dec. 2, 1837, it is stated that Ramirez sent Alvarado to ask for a guard to prevent smuggling. Gutierrez assented, but suggested that the guard must be stationed on board the vessels, and not on shore. A. replied that R. simply wanted a guard, and could station it to suit himself. The gov. was angry and threatened to arrest A. as a revolutionist, and A. thought it best to leave town the same night. Robinson, *Life in Cal.*, 173–4, affirms that the quarrel was one of etiquette in the matter of placing guards. Tuthill, Mofras, Petit-Thouars, Wilkes, and Farnham give the same version in substance, though the latter adds some fanciful embellishments, as is his custom when no absolute lies suggest themselves. *Osio, Hist. Cal.*, MS., 304–6, says that Ramirez was negotiating future customs dues to raise money for gambling, balls, etc. Gutierrez interfered to prevent the abuse, Ramirez became insolent and talked of revolt, Alvarado joined in the quarrel, and both were threatened with arrest. G. changed his mind and wished to conciliate A., but could not find him. *Ávila, Cosas de Cal.*,

This version, while not altogether inaccurate, makes the revolt the result of a quarrel between the governor and a revenue officer, ignoring entirely the political aspects of the matter and the agency of the diputacion. Alvarado, on the other hand, ignores the revenue quarrel, and exaggerates perhaps the political element, choosing naturally to look upon himself as president of the diputacion, rather than as an officer of the custom-house. There can be no doubt that the diputacion was concerned in the movement, or that Alvarado, the leading spirit, acted in its name, the quarrel about revenues being but a minor element in a complicated whole. It is therefore proper to present the version given by Alvarado himself and supported by other Californians, though in the absence of contemporary documents I cannot vouch for its entire accuracy.

From one of his stormy interviews with Gutierrez, Alvarado returned to the hall to find it empty, the diputacion having adjourned in its fright to meet at San Juan, whither the president hastened to join his fellow-vocales.[11] A meeting was held at once, at which Estévan Munras and other prominent citizens took part. Vocal Antonio Buelna made a radical

---

MS., 8–9, and Gomez, *Lo que Sabe*, MS., 44–5, state that A. was believed by G. to have been the writer of a pasquinade against him posted at a street-corner. Janssens, *Vida*, MS., 71–2, says that meetings had been held beforehand, at which a pretext for the quarrel had been devised.

[11] There is a little mystery about this diputacion. A new election was to have been held on Nov. 6th, but now the body must have been constituted as in the sessions following the May election, recorded in the last chapter—that is, 1. Castro, 2. Alvarado, 3. Guerra, 4. R. Gomez, 5. Spence, 6. Crespo, 7. J. Gomez. Alvarado represents Crespo as having been a spy of the gov., excluded when a secret session was held; and Spence is said to have met with the body, though not a member; while nothing is said of the two Gomez. Buelna, who took a prominent part, may have been a suplente called upon to act in the absence of one of these. There is no record whatever of the October sessions. Estévan de la Torre, *Reminis.*, MS., 62–4, says that one day Gutierrez entered the hall of the dip. when drunk, and had hot words with Alvarado, whom he ordered under arrest after suspending the session. J. M. de la Torre, narrator's father, furnished horses and accompanied Alvarado to S. Juan that night. J. J. Vallejo, *Remin.*, MS., 122–3, has yet another version. He says that Gutierrez sent out spies to mingle with the people and learn who were prominent in fomenting discontent. Learning that Alvarado and Castro were the leaders, he ordered the arrest and exile of the former, who, being warned, was aided by Tia Boronda and Isaac Graham to escape.

speech against Gutierrez as a centralist who disregarded the rights of the people as represented by the diputacion, a body which he had repeatedly insulted and had even threatened to dissolve by force. He argued that Gutierrez had no right to hold both commands; and advocated a resort to force to rid the country of its oppressor. Spence and Munras, mindful of their commercial interests, opposed the use of force, but favored a petition to the supreme government, leaving matters in statu quo for the present. This policy was not acceptable to the majority, who, on motion of Castro, voted that if Gutierrez would not give up the civil command he must be exiled. This was signed by Castro, Buelna, Alvarado, and Guerra. Spence refused, but promised aid to the cause. Alvarado was appointed to solicit the coöperation of Vallejo at Sonoma, and Castro was ordered to take command of the citizens in arms. Meanwhile the governor learned what course affairs were taking, and sent Crespo to San Juan to negotiate, offering to make some concessions; but the agent was not received, and the answer sent back was to the effect that the diputacion, representing the people, had undertaken the preservation of federal institutions, and the governor must prepare to defend himself.

Alvarado went first to Monterey and had an interview with Angel Ramirez, who was somewhat alarmed at the plan of visiting Sonoma and making Vallejo prominent in the enterprise, fearing that Vallejo's friendship for Bandini might interfere in the success of his own plans. Alvarado stopped at the house of Tia Boronda, and there had a meeting with Isaac Graham, the hunter, upon whom he prevailed without much difficulty to arouse his countrymen and join the revolutionary cause. During this interview, glancing out of the window, Alvarado saw Captain Muñoz and eight soldiers rapidly approaching the house, whereupon he rushed out, mounted Graham's horse which

was standing at the door, and dashed off at full speed,
with the bullets whistling about his head!

Next Don Juan Bautista hastened to Sonoma,
receiving aid and encouragement along the way
from the rancheros and others at San José, San
Francisco, San Pablo, and San Rafael, at which latter
place the padre invited him to take the benefit of
church asylum.   At Sonoma he found his uncle
Vallejo more cautious and less enthusiastic in the
cause than he would have wished.   The comandante
was very strong and independent, monarch of all he
surveyed on the northern frontier, and correspondingly timid about running unnecessary risks.   While
patriotically approving the views of Alvarado and his
associates, and ready in theory to shed his blood in
defence of popular rights, he counselled deliberation,
remembered that the northern Indians were in a
threatening attitude, required time to put his men in
a proper condition to leave their families, and after a
ceremonious introduction to the chief Solano and
his Indian braves at Napa, sent his nephew in a boat
to San José, with instructions to rouse the people and
await further developments.[12]

At San José Alvarado found many citizens ready to
aid in the cause and eager for active operations.   His
associates overruled his desire to wait for Don Guadalupe, though it was thought best to inspire confidence
in the movement by using Vallejo's name as leader
of the pronunciados even without his consent.   Soon
after, Alvarado wrote to his uncle as follows: "When
I parted from you at Napa, my sentiments of patriotism and my personal situation both animated me all

[12] Both Alvarado and Vallejo, in their *Hist. Cal.*, MS., very naturally
try to conceal the latter's hesitation at this time, stating that 200 men
were promised and great enthusiasm was shown for the cause. Osio, however, tells us that Alvarado got but little satisfaction from Vallejo, and came
back very much discouraged, and Alvarado himself, in a letter written a few
days later and soon to be noticed, clearly implies that Vallejo had refused to
take a leading part in the movement.   Chico, it will be remembered, had not
been certain on his departure which side Vallejo would take.   Chas Brown,
Statement, MS., 10-11, remembers Alvarado's visit to Sonoma.   He says no
troops went south.

the more ardently to do a good deed for my country. I returned with regret at not having succeeded in obtaining your company in attaining an object of public beneficence; and I was in great trouble. At San José I met Castro, Buelna, and Noriega; and we agreed to make a *pronunciamiento.* We formed a plan, and with thirteen men started for Monterey. Immediately we recognized the enthusiasm of the inhabitants in defence of a just cause. On the way they aided us with arms and supplies.... We called the expedition the 'vanguard of the division of operations,' giving out that you were bringing up the rear with the rest of the forces, and that you were the chief of the army. It was necessary to employ this ruse, for in this belief many people joined us."[13]

Castro at San Juan and among the rancheros of the Salinas and Pájaro valleys had also been successful in organizing a little revolutionary army; and about seventy-five mounted Californians,[14] armed with lances and such old muskets—for the most part unfit for use—as could be found on the ranchos, assembled apparently at Jesus Vallejo's rancho on the Pájaro. They had a Mexican flag and plenty of fifes and drums obtained at the mission of San Juan. There are no narratives which throw any light on the details of these preparations.

The strongest part of the revolutionary force, from a military point of view, was Graham's company of riflemen. Graham was a Tennesseean hunter who had come from New Mexico three years before. He was a wild and reckless fellow, a crack-shot, a despiser

<hr/>

[13] *Alvarado, Carta confidencial á D. Guadulupe Vallejo, 7 de Nov. 1836,* MS. This is a document of the greatest historical importance, one of the very few original records extant upon this revolution. It establishes Vallejo's position in the matter; and it raises grave doubts about the accuracy of Alvarado's statements on the formal meeting of the diputacion at S. Juan before his visit to Sonoma.

[14] Jesus Pico, *Acont.*, MS., 32–8, claims to have captured all the govt horses and brought them in for the use of the army. Inocente García, *Hechos*, MS., 50–6, was the standard-bearer. The number of the men is given in different narratives all the way from 60 to 400.

of all Mexican 'varmint,' who had opened a distillery
not far from San Juan. His place was a favorite
loafing-place for foreigners; and having agreed to aid
Alvarado, he had no difficulty, by a free use of aguardiente and eloquence, in raising a company of twenty-
five or thirty men of various nationalities, most of them
sailors, with perhaps half a dozen American hunters.
Graham was aided in his work of recruiting by William R. Garner, and John Coppinger was made his
lieutenant, both Englishmen; while Louis Pombert,
a Frenchman, as a kind of sergeant was next in command. There is no list of names extant. A good
deal of admiration has been expressed by different
writers following in the lead of Farnham, for the brave
and noble Graham, cavalier of the wilderness, and his
gallant band of Kentuckian riflemen, taking up arms
for Californian independence, not without a hope of
bringing their adopted home under the stars and
stripes! Their motives and their services have been
greatly exaggerated; yet the presence of a few real
hunters, and the superiority of the guns carried by
the rest, made this company the most formidable part
of the revolutionary force. If the sailors were not
very expert marksmen, it was all the same to the
Mexicans, to whom all were *rifleros Americanos.*
Doubtless the leaders were promised recompense in
lands and privileges; and it is not unlikely that a few
of the foreigners looked at the whole enterprise from
a political point of view; yet we may be very sure that
the Californian leaders were inclined to use their allies
rather than be used by them.[15] It must be remem-

[15] Farnham's remarks on the services of the 50 foreigners who, with 25
Californians loitering in the rear, expelled the Mex. governor after insisting
on political conditions which were promised but were never fulfilled, are too
absurd to merit refutation. Other writers naturally exaggerate Graham's
services and are somewhat over-enthusiastic about the American element in
his company—the writers being Americans themselves, or foes of Alvarado
for various reasons, or, if French or English, writing before Cal. became a
part of the U. S. Dr Marsh, *Letter*, MS., 7–8, gives the composition of the
company substantially as in my text. The writer of the account in the *Honolulu, S. I. Gazette*, Dec. 2, 1837, says: 'It is true that many foreigners were
hired by the govt to serve in the ranks, but they no doubt did it for the pay,

bered, however, that there was a foreign influence in
the whole affair quite distinct from that exerted by
the members of Graham's company.

It was apparently on the evening of November 3d
that the revolutionary forces under José Castro approached the capital. I quote from Alvarado's letter,
as the best authority extant, the following account of
what happened during the next few days: "Finally
we arrived at Monterey with upwards of 100 men.
The place was fortified with over 50 men assembled
in the plaza. On the night of our arrival we passed
on with some strategy and took the castle, and the
height near the house of Linares, so that the plaza,"
that is, the presidio within the walls of which Gutierrez had his garrison, "was commanded. With aid
from the people of the town, from the merchants, and
from the vessels, except that of Don Federico Becher,
we armed ourselves sufficiently and sent a flag of truce,
with a demand that Gutierrez should surrender the
plaza at discretion. In it were all the officers, including Portilla who had lately arrived, and a multitude of
convicts whom Gutierrez had armed. The reply being
delayed, we fired a cannon-shot from the fort, and the
ball was so well directed that we put it into the *zaguan*
of the comandante's house, while the officers were con-
versing in the court. Such was their fright that they
were not to be seen for an hour. Then Gutierrez replied that he would not surrender. Such was the
anger of the division that every man dismounted, arms
in hand, to attack. We had also a company of 25
riflemen. When the movement was seen from the
plaza, they sent a messenger to stop it, and to suppli-

knowing well the character of the revolution, and that there would not be
much danger.' Vallejo, *Hist. Cal.*, MS., iii. 195, remarks that the Mexicans
exaggerated the foreign influence for effect in Mexico. Alvarado, *Hist. Cal.*,
MS iii. 141-2, admits that the foreign company was of the greatest use to
him, that the leaders did good service, and that he promised them lands.
Bee, *Recoll.*, MS., 6-11, who was a member of the company, gives a not very
clear account of its operations. He says Garner was chosen 1st lieutenant and
Coppinger 2d, though the former did not serve.

cate that we should not attack; and in a few minutes
Gutierrez sent a communication offering to surrender
on condition that we would give guaranties to the
men of his party, without preventing such of them as
desired to do so from following him. We accepted
the conditions, and presented ourselves in Monterey
in the most admirable order. The infantry marched
to the sound of Mr Hinckley's music, and the cavalry
with trumpets. The officers retired from the plaza,
except one who remained to deliver the post." [16]

The account just quoted, written at the time by
Alvarado, the leader of the movement, in a private
letter, intended to have no other effect than to inform
Vallejo of what had occurred, is doubtless a correct
one. Other records throw no doubt on its accuracy,
except perhaps in the statement that the surrender
was made in consequence of evident preparations for
a charge. In later narratives written from memory,
Alvarado, like other Californians, has introduced
some exaggerations and erroneous statements. It is
no part of my duty to reproduce the errors of such
statements, but only to utilize the testimony which I
have gathered so far as it may reveal the truth. I
append a few details, the accuracy of which there is no
special reason to question. [17]   There is a general agree-

---

[16] *Alvarado, Carta Confidencial*, MS.

[17] Alvarado, *Hist. Cal.*, MS., iii. 142–59, says that Spence was sent by
Gutierrez to make a tour of inspection on the night the army arrived. They
were surprised to find the fort not guarded. Their numbers were soon increased by the inhabitants, sailors, etc., to over 300. The fort might easily
have been defended. José Ábrego furnished the ball that was fired, and
Peña aimed the gun, being allowed 15 minutes to 'read up' artillery practice.
Two small cannon were landed from Hinckley's vessel. The foreigners were
anxious to attack the presidio. Late in the evening Castillero and Crespo
came out with torches and a flag of truce to propose surrender. Terms were
made verbally at 1 A. M., and in writing next morning after the dip. had
held a meeting. Villavicencio was sent to receive the arms, which Muñoz
gave up. Gutierrez went with his officers to the house of Joaquin Gomez.
Vallejo, *Hist. Cal.*, MS., iii. 154–80, gives the same version in substance as
Alvarado. He says half the force halted at the lagunita, while the rest went
to take the castillo. Spence in his report exaggerated to Gutierrez the number of the attacking force. The prisoners were sent on board the *Clementine*
the same day of the surrender, though she did not sail for some days. According to Garcia, *Hechos*, MS., 50–6, Buelna commanded the S. José division,
and García with his own party joined the rest at the leñadero. Graham
wished at the first to besiege Monterey and shoot every man that presented

ment that the revolutionists on approaching the town divided their forces, kindled fires, sounded their trumpets and drums, and did all in their power to make it appear that their force was large; that the fort was taken on the night of arrival without the slightest resistance; that Gutierrez made no effort to defend himself, and took no precautions to avert attack; that the cannon-ball which hit the presidio was the only one in the castillo which a gun could be found to fit, the gunners being Balbino Romero and Cosme Peña the lawyer; that J. A. de la Guerra was at one time admitted to the presidio blindfolded as a representative of Castro; that ammunition and other aid was obtained from the foreign vessels in port, Hinckley of the *Don Quixote* openly favoring the Californians, while Steele and French of the *Caroline* and *Europe* were but little more cautious in their support; and finally, that Castro's force had been much increased and that of the governor weakened by desertions from the presidio. The force at the disposal of Gutierrez has been greatly exaggerated. It could not have been over seventy-five men at the beginning of the siege, only fifty of the number being soldiers. Castro had at first about the same force, besides Graham's men.

himself! At dawn Ramirez and Cosme Peña came to the castillo with a paper, on which was written, 'Federacion ó muerte de California la suerte.' J. J. Pico, *Acontecimientos*, MS., 32–8, says that he was sent south with a party to intercept Portilla's 25 men who were approaching, which he accomplished (?). He and Pinto, *Apunt.*, MS., 21–7, think that two shots were fired, one of which struck the church. Harry Bee's whole narrative on this affair is notable only for its inaccuracy. *Recollections*, MS., 6–21. Osio, *Hist. Cal.*, MS., 308–15, gives the hour at which different events occurred, but they are obviously incorrect. Mofras, *Explor.*, i. 298–300, and Petit-Thouars, *Voyage*, ii. 92–9, state that Gutierrez and his officers had been promised permission to remain if they chose, and were sent away in violation of this promise. Mofras says Larkin and John C. Jones aided the revolutionists. Wilkes, *Narrative*, v. 175–9, tells us that the ball fired was an 18-pounder, and the firing at dawn. Robinson, *Life in Cal.*, 174–5, says the ball weighed 4 lbs. Janssens, *Vida*, MS., 72–6, by request of Escobar and Negrete, formed a patrol of citizens to preserve order during the siege. Gomez, *Lo que Sabe*, MS., 13–17, and others state that Francisco Soto did good service by getting into the presidio with divers bottles of brandy to promote desertion. Torre, *Remin.*, MS., 64–5, gives a very good account of the whole affair, but in it, as in the statements of Bandini, Ord, Coronel, Avila, and Jesus Vallejo, there is nothing not already noticed.

The castillo was taken, and the siege of Monterey began in the night of November 3d.[18] During the next day several communications, some of them in writing, passed between Castro and Gutierrez, but only one of them is extant. It was written by the governor to his foe after the cannon-shot was fired, the act being rather plausibly alluded to by the writer as an 'act of violence.' In this document Gutierrez points out the inconsistency of Castro's demand that the *gefatura* should be surrendered by the same person to whom he himself had delivered it, with pleasure as he said, earlier in the year in accordance with laws that had not been changed. Another inconsistency of the diputacion was in wishing to exercise in advance certain powers for which that body had petitioned the supreme government. He declares that he has personally no desire to retain the command, which he would gladly have given up to Portilla, but the hostile movements of Castro and his associates render it necessary that he should maintain his own military honor as well as the dignity of the Mexican republic. He has accordingly determined, after consultation with his officers and the ayuntamiento, to fight to the last in defence of the laws, as is clearly his duty. Yet if Castro and his supporters desire to prevent the shedding of blood, they are invited, in the name of the country, of law, and of justice, to a peaceful conference with representatives of the government in presence of the ayuntamiento, at a place to be named by that corporation. Hostilities are in the mean time to be suspended, and the governor promises to approve the decision of the conference if consistent with his own responsibilities and the national honor. The tone of the letter is dignified, and shows an earnest desire to avoid further troubles.[19]

[18] Petit-Thouars, Mofras, Wilkes, and others say it was on Nov. 2d, and there are no means of proving that it was not so; but one day and two nights are all I can find room for in the siege.

[19] *Gutierrez, Carta Oficial del Gefe Político á D. José Castro, proponiendo conferencias, 4 de Nov. 1836*, MS. Two letters had been received from Castro before this letter was written.

There is no evidence that Castro consented to the conference proposed; and at 9 P. M. a junta de guerra was held in the presidio to consider what was to be done. There were present Comandante General Gutierrez; captains Portilla, Muñoz, and Castillero; lieutenants Navarrete and Estrada; alféreces Ramirez and Valle; the surgeon Alva; Crespo, the phlebotomist; the district judge, Luis del Castillo Negrete; the governor's secretaries, Bonilla and Gonzalez; Romero, the teacher; and Zamorano, secretary of the comandancia. The officers were called on for reports. Muñoz stated that the foreigners were about to mount two guns at the houses of Pacheco and Ábrego, with which to destroy the presidio. Others reported the desertion of twenty soldiers and nine convicts. It was also made known that the artillery were disposed to surrender, and the infantry had left their post. Such being the situation, it was decided after discussion to make an offer of surrender on condition that life and property should be protected and no insults be offered to the capitulating force. The proposition was sent to Castro, who agreed to it verbally, requiring, however, a delivery of arms. This gave rise to a new debate. But it was found necessary to yield, as the garrison was now reduced to thirty-five men, worn out by fatigue and hunger, in an exposed position commanded by the artillery of the foe, while the enemy had a strong position, the support of the people and of the ships, and a force of two hundred men, "nearly all foreigners, and chiefly Americans." Castro was accordingly notified that the garrison would march out and stack their arms at the artillery barracks. These proceedings were signed by all members of the junta, each of whom retained a copy.[20]

We have no further record of the surrender; but know that early on the next day, the 5th, the revo-

---

[20] *Junta de Guerra y Rendicion de Monterey, 4 de Nov. 1836*, MS. This is one of the original copies made at the time, in the handwriting of Mariano Romero.

lutionist Californians took peaceful possession of the presidio. The Mexican officials, having given up their arms, went to the house of a citizen to remain until their fate should be decided. The day was devoted mainly, like several following days, to festivities of triumph, in which everybody—except the Mexican officials perhaps—participated. I quote in continuation from the concluding portion of Alvarado's letter: "All the officers except Valle and Zamorano we have embarked to-day on the *Clementine* for Cape San Lúcas, also Herrera, Luis Castillo, a few soldiers, and some of the worst convicts...There are no forces in the territory to resist us; on the contrary, they are waiting to join us. To-day Buelna and Villa start for Santa Bárbara to have sworn the bases of the new Californian government. The federalists will win in Mexico, and we shall remain, if fate be propitious, erected into a free and sovereign state. The officers and Gutierrez, ashamed of their aberrations and seeing liberty shine with honor, wept bitterly. Gutierrez sent a letter, confessing his faults, giving satisfaction, and expressing regret at leaving a country where he had intended to live forever. It is wonderful, uncle, with what order our expedition has been conducted. Everybody shouts *vivas*, for California is free!"[21]

The *Clementine* sailed from Monterey on November 11th for Cape San Lúcas with about seventy passengers—enforced and voluntary exiles, including among the latter many of the Híjar and Padrés colony who were not contented in their new home.[22] Gutierrez, Muñoz, Navarrete, and the two Estradas had been put on board the vessel four or five days before she sailed, and were the only officers who were really forced to leave the country. There was much feeling against Sub-comisario Herrera and Judge Castillo Negrete, but they would have been permitted to remain if they

---

[21] *Alvarado, Carta Confidencial*, MS. The date of surrender is also given in *Gomez, Diario*, MS.

[22] *Gomez, Diario de Cosas Notables*, MS.

would have submitted to the new order of things.
Castillo Negrete was very violent against the revolutionists. He vented in verse his spite against the men
whom he regarded as leaders, Peña, Ramirez, and
Hinckley, before leaving Monterey, and having sailed
on the *Leonidas*, stopped at San Diego to incite the
southerners to resistance. Don Luis never returned,
but was subsequently gefe político of Baja California.[23]
Portilla, Castillero, Valle, and Zamorano were permitted to remain in California, but the latter chose at
first to depart, though he soon returned to the San
Diego frontier, as we shall see, to promote southern
resistance to Alvarado. The *Clementine* after landing
her passengers at Cape San Lúcas returned to Monterey in December. The Californian leaders have been

[23] His verses were as follows:

> A California ha perdido
> La turbulenta anarquía
> De su gobierno escogido
> Por eso lo ha conducido
> A accion tan atroz y fea;
> Y para que al mundo vea
> El tal gobierno como anda
> Del triumvirato que manda
> Te voy á dar una idea.
>> El proto-libertador
>> Primer hombre del Estado
>> Es un fraile renegado
>> Gran perjuro y gran traidor
>> De oficio administrador.
>> Es de muy ancha conciencia
>> Derrochador sin clemencia
>> Sagaz revolucionario
>> Jugador y perdulario
>> Sin Dios, ni patria, ni ciencia.
> Ocupa el lugar segundo
> En el Californio Estado
> Un filósofo relajado
> Cibarrita é inmundo;
> Que quiere rejir el mundo
> Bebiendo mezcal sin taza
> Y con alma bien escasa;
> Pues de sabio es presumido
> Cuando el pobre no ha podido
> Saber gobernar su casa.
>> Del Estado es Almirante
>> Y privado consejero
>> Un navegante extrangero
>> Contrabandista intrigante
>> Estafador y bien pillo
>> Con el cual cumplo el trecillo
>> Que gobierna torpemente
>> Y que abusa impunemente
>> Del Californio sencillo!

Vallejo, Hist. Cal., MS., iii. 186–7; *Alvarado, Hist. Cal.,* MS., iii. 159–68.
The charges embodied in this rhyming tirade were for the most part well
founded, so far as the three victims were concerned; and the space devoted by
Alvarado and Vallejo to their refutation shows that Don Luis chose well his
weapon of annoyance.

accused of having acted in bad faith when they exiled
Gutierrez and his companions. The charge has no
foundation; there was no stipulation that they might
remain; and to have permitted it would have been
a very stupid proceeding. I add some brief notes respecting the men who went away at this time.[24]

[24] Of Nicolás Gutierrez, his life and character, all that is known has been
told in this and the preceding chapters, and in chap. x. of this volume. He
came to California as a captain with Figueroa in Jan. 1833. His terms of
office as ruler ad interim of the territory were as follows: Comandante general
from Sept. 29 (assumed office Oct. 8), 1835, to Jan. 2, 1836; gefe político
and comandante general, Jan. 2d to May 2d; and from Aug. 1 to Nov. 5,
1836. He took away with him some trunks containing effects belonging to
the late José Figueroa. Dept. St. Pap., Ben. Mil., MS., lxxxi. 34. Nothing
is known of him after he left California, except that on April 21, 1837, he
wrote from Mazatlan to Joaquin Gomez that he would probably see him back
again soon in command of an expedition that was being prepared. Vallejo,
Doc., MS., xxxii. 83.

Licenciado Don Luis del Castillo Negrete was a Spaniard, his father having been an attorney of the council of Indies. He was educated at Alcalá,
Toledo, and Granada in philosophy, mathematics, and law, leaving Spain
after 1820. These facts appear from diplomas and certificates shown in
Monterey. Vallejo, Hist. Cal., MS., iii. 180-9, with samples of some of his
literary productions, one of which I have already presented. He arrived at
Monterey Sept. 25, 1834, Sta Cruz, Arch., MS., 77, with his family, having
been appointed district judge of Cal., of which office he took possession on
Oct. 1st. He also acted as legal adviser to Gov. Gutierrez. After leaving
Cal. Don Luis was sub-gefe político of Baja California from May 1837 to
June 1842. See Hist. N. Mex. States, ii. In March 1839 he was trying to
collect back pay due for his services in Cal. Dept. St. Pap., Ben., MS., v.
344-5. He died Nov. 25, 1843. Moreno, Doc., MS., 21. He is represented
as having been a very able lawyer, and a brilliant, accomplished gentleman.
The Californians say he was unscrupulous; but this may have been because
he was inclined to ridicule rather than sympathize with their political projects. Alvarado and his associates would have liked to secure his coöperation, but this was not consistent with his official position and his plans for the
future; besides, he had a great dislike for Angel Ramirez and Cosme Peña, the
latter being not only a rival lawyer but a rival poet. Don Luis had a brother
who was a general in the Mexican army; and a Luis del Castillo Negrete, who
in 1871 was a diputado in Sinaloa, Ures, Estrella del Occidente, Jan. 5, 1872,
was perhaps his son or nephew.

Francisco Javier del Castillo Negrete was a brother of Luis, who came to
Cal. with the judge; served as Gov. Chico's secretary; perhaps sent by Chico,
just before his own departure, on a mission to Mexico. He was subsequently
comandante of the frontier in Baja California. In Aug. 1854 he was in San
Francisco in very destitute circumstances, as he wrote to Gen. Vallejo. Vallejo, Doc., MS., xiii. 379. Francisco is said to have had some of his brother's
brilliant qualities, being somewhat less reserved and more popular.

José María Herrera first came to Cal. in 1825 with Gov. Echeandía, as
comisario de hacienda for the territory. Of his early life, or any part of his
record outside of Cal., I know nothing. With his career here, his quarrel
with Echeandía dating from 1827, and his expulsion from the country in 1830
for complicity in the Solis revolt, the reader is already familiar. See chap.
iii. of this vol. Herrera came back in 1834, at the same time as Castillo
Negrete, to resume his old position and manage the territorial finances. During this second term he engaged in no controversies officially, and so far as

As commander-in-chief of the victorious revolutionary army, José Castro was comandante general of California from November 5th, the date of Gutierrez's surrender, to the 29th, when his successor assumed the office, and as president of the diputacion, he was governor for a still longer period, until December 7th. It has been customary to date Alvarado's rule from the fall of Gutierrez, and to ignore Castro altogether in the list of rulers for this period; but in reality, Alvarado at this time had no authority, whatever his influence may have been. Don José was a grandson of Sergeant Macario Castro,[25] and a son of Corporal José Tiburcio Castro, who had been alcalde of San José. His mother was an Álvarez. He was born

can be known, gave no cause for complaint. His name, however, became again disagreeably prominent in connection with the troubles growing out of the scandalous liaison between his wife, Doña Ildefonsa Gonzalez, daughter of Capt. Miguel Gonzalez, and José María Castañares, as fully narrated in chap. xv. Herrera is described as of medium height and inclined to corpulency, with fair complexion, black hair, and thick beard. He was affable in manner, of much business ability, skilful in argument, and well educated. Some leading Californians have given him a very bad character, under circumstances known to the reader. I do not undertake to decide just to what extent the charges rest on prejudice. A man of the same name was contador of the custom-house at Guaymas in 1839. *Pinart, Col. Doc. Son.*, MS., iii. 116.

Capt. Juan Antonio Muñoz was appointed in 1830 to proceed to Cal. and succeed Alf. Fernandez del Campo in command of the artillery. He arrived late in 1832 and was offered by Zamorano the *comandancia accidental*, but declined, remaining inactive until Figueroa came, *Dept. St. Pap.*, MS., iii. 79–82, and then took his proper command. There is nothing to be noticed in his Californian career of four years, except that he was very much disliked by the people; and I find no record respecting him before his arrival or after his departure in exile in 1836.

Lieut Bernardo Navarrete came with Figueroa in 1833. In Aug. 1834 he was commissioned captain of the Monterey company; but there is no record that he received the commission before his banishment in 1836. *Dept. St. Pap., Ben. Mil.*, MS., lxxix. 83. Chico proposed to send him on a commission to Mexico, but Francisco Castillo Negrete seems to have gone in his place. He commanded the cavalry during the final siege of Monterey. Like Muñoz, he was disliked by the Californians, for reasons which, except his being a Mexican, are unknown.

Alférez Patricio Estrada was also sufficiently under the ban of Californian displeasure to be sent away in 1836. He had come with Echeandía in 1825; commanding a detachment of the Piquete de Hidalgo.

Nicanor Estrada left the country in 1836, not in the *Clementine*, and perhaps voluntarily. He worked as a blacksmith. In Mexico he had been a captain of cavalry, and came with the colony as a kind of political exile. In Nov. 1835, notice was sent that his rank had been restored. *Dept. St. Pap., Ben. Mil.*, MS., lxxxi. 1.

[25] See biographical sketches.

about 1810, and his early educational advantages had been substantially the same as those of his companions Alvarado and Vallejo, though he had profited by them somewhat less than either of the others, being less observant and ambitious. He had no experience as a soldier or in clerical duties; but he had served several terms as vocal in the diputacion; had sometimes presided over that body, and had once, as its president, been gefe político ad interim, from September 1835 to January 1836.

The popular movement having proved successful, the Mexican ruler having been deposed, and these victories having been properly celebrated in fiestas at the capital, it became necessary to organize the government under a new régime. The plan of the pronunciamiento, drawn up on November 3d, but not extant, would seem to have been rather vaguely worded, so as not to make it quite certain what the revolution was to accomplish. The leaders have been accused of making it vague intentionally, or worse still, of having promised to declare California entirely independent of Mexico, in order to secure foreign support, subsequently breaking the promise. I have no reason to believe that any such pledge was made. At any rate, Alvarado knew well that popular feeling would not support such a step; and it is probable that from the first the intention had been merely to insist on Californian rulers, under the pretence of a revolt against centralism. Doubtless a pressure was brought to bear by Americans, after success had been achieved, in favor of absolute independence. Indeed, it is said, and I have heard Alvarado himself admit, that a lone-star flag had been prepared; and the project of raising it over the presidio was discussed. Possibly Alvarado was not personally much opposed to the plan, but he feared, while respecting, the influence of foreigners. His associates were yet more timid; opposition was feared from the south even to changes less radical; his Mexican supporters protested against disloyalty to the federal constitution; and David Spence and other foreigners deemed it wise to curb American ambition. The Californians hesitated, if at all, but for a moment; the Texan experiment was not to be tried in California, and the Mexican flag still waved over the capital.[26]

The day after the surrender of Gutierrez, November 6th, the diputacion met, that is, four of its members did so. I am unable to explain why Spence, Gomez, and Crespo took no part in this and subsequent meetings. Respecting the proceedings at this and other sessions, we have no other record than the printed addresses and decrees issued from time to time. The first of these, signed by Castro, Alvarado, Buelna, and Noriega, was an address of congratulation to the people.[27] The second production was a record of

[26] Bandini, *Hist. Cal.*, MS., 85–6, says the persons who favored independence were chiefly Mexicans. Mofras, *Explor.*, i. 300, tells us that the Americans had a lone-star flag all ready, which they wished to hoist, putting Cal. under the protection of the U. S., and promising the aid of the *Peacock* which would soon return; but the Mexicans Peña and Ramirez, Spence, Amesti, Munrás, and Deleissèques succeeded in preventing the movement. Petit-Thouars, *Voyage*, ii. 99, gives in substance the same version, and adds that the Americans then withdrew in disgust, except a few riflemen who got $2 a day for their services. Wilkes, *Narr.*, v. 178–9, says the courage of Alvarado and the diputacion failed them at the last moment, and they refused to keep their promise of raising the flag—adding some absurd details. Gleeson, *Hist. Cath. Church*, i. 148–9, follows Mofras. Serrano, *Apuntes*, MS., 27, 38–9, insists that the lone-star flag was actually raised, and that Castro trampled the Mexican flag under foot. Inocente García, the standard-bearer, claims to have prevented Capt. Hinckley and others from raising the new flag on one occasion, and to have insisted on hoisting the national banner. Robinson mentions the Texan flag which was said to have been prepared. Alvarado, *Hist. Cal.*, MS., iii. 199–204, admits that he thought favorably of putting Cal. under a European or American protectorate.

Robinson, *Life in Cal.*, 177, says that several Mexican vessels in the harbor were seized and afterward released. It is claimed by Alvarado, Vallejo, and others that they had some difficulty in preventing outrages on Mexicans, instigated largely by Graham and his men. It was partly to save them from injury and insult that Gutierrez and others were kept on board the vessel for some days before she sailed.

[27] 'The most excellent diputacion of Alta California, to its inhabitants: Californians: Heaven favors you; you are doubtless its chosen portion, and therefore it is leading you with propitious hand to happiness. Until now you have been the sad victim of servile factions, whose chiefs, content with a passing triumph, taxed to the utmost your long-suffering patience. As obedient sons of the mother country, and faithful defenders of your dear liberties, you swore solemnly before God and men to be free, and to die rather than be slaves. In this spirit, you adopted forever, as a social compact to direct you, the federal constitution of the year twenty-four; your government was

proceedings at the extra session of November 7th, signed by the same men and published as a circular. At this meeting the plan of the original pronunciamiento was submitted for revision and approval. This document in its original form is not given, and it is consequently impossible to state what changes were introduced. It had been somewhat vaguely worded, and perhaps intentionally so; but Alvarado explained that its informalities were due to the haste and confusion of the campaign, since the intention of the *pronunciados*, as was well known, was simply to resist the oppressions of the rulers sent from Mexico since the adoption of the new system; and he moved that the plan be drawn up as in the appended note.[27] This

organized at cost of immense sacrifices, which unnatural sons trampled on, ignoring them in order to found upon your ruins their own fortune and criminal advancement; and when it seemed that you were already the sure patrimony of the aristocratic tyrant, you boldly waved the banner of the free: "Federation or Death is the destiny of the Californian." Thus have you shouted, and a cry so sweet will be indelibly engraved upon your hearts, in whom (sic) the sacred fire of love for the country is seen to burn incessantly. You have tasted the sweet nectar of liberty; the bitter cup of oppression may not be tendered you with impunity. California is free, and will sever her relations with Mexico until she ceases to be oppressed by the present dominant faction called central government. To accomplish so interesting, so grand an object, it remains only that we, the inhabitants of this soil, united, form a single wish, a single opinion. Let us be united, Californians, and we shall be invincible, if we use all the resources on which we may count. Thus shall we make it clear to the universe that we are firm in our purpose, that we are free and federalists! José Castro, Juan B. Alvarado, Antonio Buelna, José Antonio Noriega. Monterrey, Nov. 6, 1836.' Government Press in charge of citizen Santiago Aguilar. 1 leaf.

Original print in *Earliest Printing*. Also in *Bandini, Doc.*, MS., 42; *Guerra, Doc.*, MS., i. 151-2; *Vallejo, Hist. Cal.*, MS., iii. 195-6; and translation, somewhat less literal than mine, in *Hopkins' Translations*, 3-4, printed also in the *S. Francisco Alta*. The Noriega who signs was José Antonio de la Guerra. It was a whim to sign his name Noriega, which he had no right to do. Alvarado, *Hist. Cal.*, MS., iii. 169-73, says that two copies of the address were sent to every place to be posted in regular form on the doors of *alcaldía* and church.

[28] *Plan de Independencia Californiana adoptada por la diputacion en 7 de Nov. 1836*. Original print, 1 leaf, with rubric of the four signers in *Earliest Printing*. Also in *Castro, Doc.*, MS., i. 33; *Vallejo, Doc.*, MS., xxxii. 41; *Bandini, Doc.*, MS., 41; *Los Angeles, Arch.*, MS., iv. 210-11; *Dept. St. Pap., Angeles*, MS., x. 17. Translation in *Hopkins' Translations*, 4-5, in which one unfortunate error is to be noted, where debida á las fatigas de la campaña is rendered 'the result of the labors of the company.'

1. Alta California is declared independent of Mexico until the federal system of 1824 shall be reëstablished. 2. The said California is erected into a free and sovereign state, establishing a congress which shall pass all the particular laws of the country, also the other necessary supreme powers, the pres-

plan was unanimously adopted by the diputacion, and
being submitted on motion of Castro to the leaders
of the pronunciados, was by them also approved, without much opposition, it may be supposed, since those
leaders were Castro and Alvarado. Next day President Castro issued the first of a series of decrees emanating from the diputacion in its new capacity, in which
the people are duly informed "that the said supreme
legislative body has decreed as follows: 'The constituent congress of the free and sovereign state of Alta California is hereby declared legitimately installed.'"[29] On
the 13th, as 'commander of the vanguard of the division of operations,' Castro issued a printed proclamation
to the people, congratulating them on their escape from
tyranny, exhorting them not to falter in the good work,
reminding them that death was preferable to servitude, and that federalism must become the system of
the nation. "Viva la federacion! Viva la libertad!
Viva el estado libre y soberano de Alta California!"[30]

The next record carries us forward to the time when
Vallejo, having arrived from Sonoma, assumed the
military command, tendered him, as we have seen, by
the diputacion on the 7th. Mariano Guadalupe Vallejo was a young man of about thirty years, who
had recently received a lieutenant's commission in the
Mexican army, and was comandante of the northern

ent most excellent diputacion declaring itself constituent. 3. The religion
will be the catholic apostolic Roman, without admitting the public worship of
any other; but the government will molest no one for his private religious
opinions. 4. A constitution shall regulate all branches of the administration provisionally, so far as possible in accordance with the said (federal?)
constitution. 5. While the provisions of the preceding articles are being
carried out Don Mariano Guadalupe Vallejo will be called to the comandancia
general. 6. The necessary communications will be made to the municipalities of the territory by the president of the excelentísima diputacion.
   [29] *Castro, Decretos de la Exma Diputacion erigida en Congreso Constituyente,
por su Presidente,* no. 1–10, 1836, in *Earliest Printing.* Nos 1–4 are signed
by Castro as diputado presidente, and by Juan B. Alvarado as diputado sec-
retario; nos 5–9 by Castro and by J. A. de la Guerra as sec.; and no. 10 by
Alvarado as gov. and Cosme Peña as sec. It is possible that this series was
continued, but I have found no later numbers. Nov. 10th, Castro to comis-
sario de policía at Branciforte, forwarding the bases adopted by the diputacion to be sworn at the villa. *Sta Cruz, Arch.,* MS., 74.
   [30] *Dept. St. Pap., Angeles,* MS., x. 14–16.

frontier, with headquarters at Sonoma. He was the
son of the 'sargento distinguido' Ignacio Vallejo and
of María Antonia Lugo, being, on the paternal side at
least, of pure Spanish blood, and being entitled by
the old rules to prefix the 'Don' to his name. In
childhood he had been the associate of Alvarado and
Castro at Monterey, and his educational advantages,
of which he made good use, were substantially the
same as theirs. Unlike his companions, he chose a
military career, entering the Monterey company in
1823 as cadet, and being promoted to be alférez of
the San Francisco company in 1827. He served as
habilitado and as comandante of both companies, and
took part, as has been recorded in preceding chapters,
in several campaigns against the Indians, besides acting as fiscal or defensor in various military trials. In
1830 he was elected to the diputacion, and took a
prominent part in the opposition of that body to Victoria. In 1832 he married Francisca Benicia, daughter of Joaquin Carrillo, and in 1834 was elected diputado suplente to congress. He was a favorite of
Figueroa, who gave him large tracts. of land north
of the bay, choosing him as comisionado to secularize San Francisco Solano, to found the town of Sonoma, and to command the frontera del norte. In his
new position Vallejo was doubtless the most independent man in California. His past record was a good
one, and both in ability and experience he was probably better fitted to take the position as comandante
general than any other Californian. He was not personally so popular as either Alvarado or Castro, because chiefly of his reserved, haughty, aristocratic, military manner; yet it is evident that his name and his
strength carried great weight with the people, since
the revolutionists were forced to represent him as their
leader, even without his consent. The reasons of his
conservatism were well enough known, and little doubt
was felt that he would accept the command offered him.
Accordingly Alvarado, in his letter of November 7th,

already cited, explained to his uncle the use that had
been made of his name, declared the movement a success, and urged the importance of his presence at the
capital. Don Guadalupe obeyed, and came from Sonoma with a small force.[31]

It was on November 29th that Vallejo took the
oath of allegiance to the new government, assumed
the position of comandante general, and issued a proclamation to the Californians—a document expressing
patriotic purposes in the usual grandiloquent language
of Spanish American officials.[32] It was feared that
some objection might be made in certain quarters to
a general who held no higher military rank than that
of lieutenant, and accordingly on the day the oath
was taken the constituent congress voted Vallejo a

[31] Vallejo, *Hist. Cal.*, MS., iii. 197–202, tells us that he started from Sonoma with a large force before he knew what had taken place, but sent back
all but 50 of his men when he heard at S. José that Gutierrez had fallen.
He only knew of his appointment by the shout of viva el comandante general! by which he was greeted at Monterey. Nov. 7, 1836, Castro to Vallejo. Official notice of his appointment. 'The people expect of your patriotism a compliance with their wishes.' *Vallejo, Doc.*, MS., iii. 264. Nov. 16th,
Vallejo from str. of Carquines to Castro. Will start at once for Sonoma, and
thence for Monterey; though it is inconvenient, as he expects 62 Indian chiefs
to make treaties. *Id.*, iv. 42.

[32] *Vallejo, Proclama del C. Mariano G. Vallejo en el acto de prestar el jura-
mento de las baces adoptadas por la Ecs^{ma} Diputacion de la Alta California.*
Monterrey, 29 de Nov. de 1836. Imprenta del Sup. Gob., etc., 1 leaf, in *Earliest
Printing; Vallejo, Doc.*, MS., iii. 269; *Bandini, Doc.*, MS., 43; *Dept. St. Pap.,
Angeles*, MS., x. 13; and with French translation in *Petit-Thouars, Voyages*,
MS., iv. 1–3. 'Fellow-citizens: the sovereign legislative assembly of the
free state of Alta California calls me to its aid, and I obey its supreme determination, putting myself at the head of the brave men who surround me, and
accepting the comandancia general for the public welfare, whose slave alone
I am. Yes, fellow-citizens, I swear to you before God I would promise to
secure your happiness, if, as my soul abounds in love for the country, my
knowledge were sufficient to second my good intentions and the purity of my
desires. Yet I will strive to that end, and I will succeed in showing that I
am a citizen who loves the liberty of a country so often outraged with impunity. If I succeed, my reward will be the well-being of the sovereign people
to which I have the honor to belong; but if it may not be so, my fitting recompense will be a cold stone, which, confounding me among insensible beings,
shall publish "Here lies a Californian who yielded to death rather than to
tyranny!"' etc. In translating this and other documents in my notes, I have
thought it best to give the author's words as literally as possible, taking
pains, however, never to exaggerate in English any vagueness, inelegancy, or
absurdity of the original Spanish. On Nov. 28th, Alvarado wrote to Valentin Cota at Sta Bárbara a friendly letter, declaring that prospects were very
bright, though the leeches might yet make trouble. *Cota, Doc.*, MS., 5–6.

colonel of cavalry, the commission being issued in December.[33]

On December 4th the legislators brought their minds to bear on revenue management. It was decided to suppress all the old offices connected with the custom-house, and to intrust all the business to a collector at a salary of $1,000 and a clerk at $360.[34] At the next session provision was made for the organization of a 'civic force to sustain the system of government adopted,' for which purpose the ayuntamiento was required to prepare at once lists of inhabitants between fifteen and fifty years of age. The staff of the squadron was to consist of a colonel, lieut-colonel, sergeant-major, and standard-bearer. The government was also authorized to organize an infantry company of riflemen. The leading commissions in the civic militia were subsequently given to Alvarado and Castro respectively, both commencing their military career with a rank that in Spanish times could have been reached only by long years of service in the lower grades.[35]

It was now deemed necessary to choose a chief executive of the new government in place of Castro, who had hitherto acted in that capacity as president of the diputacion. Accordingly, at the session of December 7th, Juan B. Alvarado was declared to be governor ad interim of the state, with a salary of

[33] Castro, Decretos de la Dip., no. 2, Nov. 29th. Commission Dec. 11th, in Vallejo, Doc., MS., i. 11; Petit-Thouars, Voyage, iv. 20.

[34] Castro, Decretos, no. 3. Ramirez seems, however, to have remained in charge of the custom-house until Dec. 21st at least; and Hartnell was the first recaudador.

[35] Castro, Decretos, no. 4, Dec. 5, 1836; also in Petit-Thouars, Voyage, iv. 3–6. Alvarado's commission as colonel was issued Dec. 11th, by Castro as president. Earliest Printing. As by decree no. 4 the colonel was to be appointed by the govt, and Alvarado had since become the chief executive, he was freed from the duty of appointing himself, and the president authorized to issue the commission on Dec. 7th, by no. 6 of Castro, Decretos. Of Castro's own commission as lieut-col. I have no record, save that from about this time that prefix was attached to his name. On Dec. 12th, Alvarado, as col. and governor, commissioned José Jesus Vallejo as captain of artillery in the civic militia, Earliest Printing; and also Valentin Cota of Sta Bárbara to be captain, Guerra, Doc., MS., v. 305; and Miguel Ávila to be alférez. Ávila, Doc. Hist. Cal., MS., 253.

$1,500, the *tratamiento* of 'excellency' and a secretary at $1,000,[36] to which position Cosme Peña was soon appointed. Of Alvarado's inauguration, of the speech that he may have made, and the proclamation he may have issued, there is no record.

Three important decrees were issued the 9th of December. By the first, each ayuntamiento was directed to choose at its next session a diputado to join the members of the congress and aid in the formation of a constitution. A second divided the state temporarily into two cantons, or districts, the first that of Monterey, including the municipalities of San Francisco and San José; the second that of Los Angeles, including Santa Bárbara and San Diego. Each canton was to have a gefe político, to be the governor in the first, and in the second a man subordinate to the governor and appointed by him from a trio to be elected at Los Angeles January 15th by comisionados named by the ayuntamientos. As no such election was ever held, and as the system never went into effect for reasons that will appear later, it seems unnecessary to go further into details. By the third decree some of the late restrictions on commerce were removed; duties were fixed at forty per cent on foreign

---

[36] *Castro, Decretos de la Dip.*, no. 5, Dec. 7, 1836; *Petit-Thouars, Voyage*, iv. 6–9. Art. 1. Alvarado to be gov. ad interim. Art. 2. To serve until the appointment of another to serve 'constitutionally.' Art. 3. His attributes are: 1. To appoint officials in accordance with the bases and laws. 2. To care for the security and tranquillity of the state. 3. To command the militia. 4. To enforce the bases and laws, and issue the necessary decrees to that end. 5. To see that justice be promptly and fully executed. 6. To appoint and remove administrators of missions, take accounts through comisionados, and report to congress on mission matters requiring attention. 7. To fine corporations, subordinate authorities, and private individuals to extent of $100 for disrespect to the govt, or $200 for failure to comply with duties; or to suspend officials, reporting at once to congress. Art. 4. To have the title of excellency. Art. 5. To have $1,500 per year. Art. 6. In case of disability, his duties to be performed by the pres. of the congress. Art. 7. To take the oath of office before the pres. Art. 8. To have a secretary and a clerk, or more than one if necessary, appointed by himself. Art. 9. The secretary's duty is to extend the minutes and sign all decrees and orders. Art. 10. Sec. to have a salary of $1,000, and clerk $375, without fees. Art. 11. The sec. to take the oath before the state govt. Art. 12. This decree to be published, etc. Signed by Castro and by Guerra. Alvarado, *Hist. Cal.*, MS., iii. 184–5, tells us that there was much discussion about the title of the new ruler, between gefe político, president, and governor.

goods, with tonnage dues at eight reals per ton, and coasting trade was permitted to foreign vessels under a permit from the government. This was in appreciation of the aid rendered by foreigners to the cause of freedom.[37]

Thus far the Californians had been successful in their armed protest against centralism. They had got rid of their Mexican ruler, and had made a start in the experiment of governing themselves. The machinery of government was working smoothly enough at the capital. The beginnings under the new régime had been marked by no hasty or unwise steps. The leaders were among the best and the ablest of the Californians, abounding in patriotism, if somewhat lacking in experience. It would be going too far, perhaps, to say that the new administration had before it an open road to permanent success, for the inherent difficulties of the situation were great. Possibly it is fortunate in a sense for Alvarado and his associates that they can point to the opposition of their countrymen as an insurmountable obstacle in their way, for it is certain that such opposition removed every hope of a notable success. Yet I have much reason to believe that Alvarado would have effected a marked improvement in the condition of California had he been allowed to do so, and that the internal quarrels, which needlessly monopolized his attention and energy, were from every point of view a misfortune to the country.

The bases of the new system were of course forwarded, with the various proclamations and decrees therewith connected, to every part of the state; and I suppose that they were approved with the usual forms and oath of allegiance everywhere in the northern districts, though strangely enough not a single record of such local proceeding has rewarded my search.

---

[37] *Castro, Decretos*, nos 7, 8, 9, Dec. 9, 1836; *Vallejo, Doc.*, MS., 51-3; *Petit-Thouars, Voyage*, iv. 12-20; *Dept. St. Pap., S. José*, MS., iii. 55-60.

In the south a strong opposition developed itself, to be treated fully in the following chapter. Alvarado determined to visit the south in person. He obtained from the congress a concession of extraordinary powers,[38] gave his civil authority as far as possible to General Vallejo, whom all local authorities were ordered to obey,[39] and started southward on Christmas, with some fifty soldiers and Graham's riflemen, a part of the force being sent by water on the *Clementine*, which had returned from Cape San Lúcas. Vallejo at about the same time was called away to Sonoma to settle some trouble with the Indians, and Lieut-colonel Castro was left in command. There is nothing more to be said of affairs at the north in 1836, except that Angel Ramirez, having been removed from the administration of the revenues, and having been unable to control Alvarado as he had hoped to do, was perhaps already engaged in plotting future mischief.[40] There is no indication that north of Santa Bárbara there was any disaffection among Californians, though some of the more timid looked forward with anxiety to the result of the governor's campaign in the south, and still more anxiously to the time when their revolt should be known in Mexico.

[38] *Castro, Decretos*, no. 10, Dec. 20, 1836; *Petit-Thouars, Voyage*, iv. 21. This, the final order of the series, is issued by 'The citizen Juan B. Alvarado, colonel of the civic militia, superior gefe político of the first canton, and governor of the free and sovereign state of Alta California.' Countersigned by Secretary Peña.

[39] Dec. 23, 1836, Alvarado to civil authorities and private persons. In *Vallejo, Doc.*, MS., iv. 45. Vallejo in return conceded his military authority to Alvarado so far as the south was concerned. His order to comandantes of the south is dated Dec. 17th. *Id.*, iv. 43.

[40] Alvarado, *Hist. Cal.*, MS., iii. 190–4, and Vallejo, *Hist. Cal.*, MS., iii. 241–3, tell us that the former on his way south found evidence that Ramirez and P. Mercado were plotting at S. Antonio, and sent a note of warning to Vallejo. Alvarado thought of arresting Ramirez, but had some hope that he would conspire with the south and thus drive Juan Bandini over to the governor's side.

CHAPTER XVII.

ALVARADO'S RULE—TROUBLES IN THE SOUTH.

1836–1837.

Causes of Southern Opposition—Sectional, Local, and Personal Prejudice—The News at Angeles—San Diego Aroused—Plan of November—Counter-plan of Santa Bárbara—New Ayuntamientos and
New Plan—Letters of Prominent Men—Castillo Negrete—Osio—
Bandini—Pio Pico—Cárlos Carrillo—Alvarado in the South—
The Barbareños Submit—Angelinos Obstinate—Dieguinos Patri-
otic but not Warlike—Defensive Measures—Campaign and Treaty
of San Fernando—Alvarado at Los Angeles—Castro's Arrival—
Another Plan—Speeches—Fears of Attack from Sonora—Castro
at San Diego—Diputacion Sustains Alvarado—Plan de Gobierno—
Intrigues of Osio and Pico—Los Angeles Submits—Governor's
Manifiesto of May—Return to Monterey—Events in the North,
January to May.

That the changes effected at Monterey were not approved in the south was due almost entirely to sectional, local, and personal causes. The provincial prejudice was as strong in one part of California as in
another. The arribeños were not more radical federalists than were the abajeños, nor were they more
unanimously opposed to Mexican rulers. The loyalty
of the sureños and their natural shrinking from revolutionary measures were not notably more pronounced
than the same sentiments among the norteños. It
was San Diego and Los Angeles, not Monterey and
San José, that had begun the revolt against Victoria
in 1831. It was the south that sustained Echeandía,
and the north that supported Zamorano's counter-
revolt in behalf of the supreme government. There
was not much opposition to Gutierrez personally in

either section. Alvarado was personally popular in
both sections. The padres Fernandinos in charge of
the southern missions were disposed rather to favor
than oppose the change. El sur, as fully as el norte,
had felt the effects of Mexican oppression and neglect,
real or imaginary. The benefits, if any, to be derived
from independence could be nowise sectional. Other
reasons for southern opposition must be sought.

A strong sectional feeling had been in process of development since 1825, when Echeandía, charmed with
southern climate and southern ladies, had seriously
wounded the pride of Monterey, by fixing his residence
at San Diego. Most representatives to congress had
been from the south, which was deemed a slight to
northern talent; but on the other hand, Argüello and
Castro had ruled as governors, while Pico and Estudillo had failed to secure recognition. Custom-house
quarrels had waxed hot between San Diego and Monterey, to the advantage of the latter; but the southern pueblo had gone far ahead of San José in population, even gaining the rank of city. In the struggle
for the capital, Los Angeles had gained the victory,
on paper, which caused a burst of indignation in the
north; but Monterey had thus far evaded a delivery
of the spoils, and the Angelinos were furious. A division of the missions between the friars of two colleges had a slight tendency to widen the breach.

The first feeling on hearing what had happened
was one of surprise and of timidity. Yet the people
were not more timid than the arribeños, but their
courage had not, like that of the others, been braced
up by the excitement of personal participation in stirring events or by the eloquence of popular leaders.
Soon, however, there was developed in the minds of
the southerners a still more potent sentiment, to the
effect that the revolution had been the work of northern men, and that they would not only monopolize the
glory and prestige arising from the achievement, putting on airs of superiority, but would probably claim

the lion's share of the offices and other benefits of the new system. Before the avowed policy of the new administration was fully known, the most absurd rumors were current, but Los Angeles had much reason to believe that the change was at the least not favorable to its own possession of the capital, and this was ample cause for the opposition of that city. San Diego entertained similar hopes and fears, though in less marked degree, respecting the custom-house. But the opposition in the extreme south was due mainly to another cause, the influence of Juan Bandini. This gentleman saw in the movement at Monterey but one figure, that of his hated foe, Angel Ramirez.

Judge Castillo Negrete on his way to Mexico spent a few weeks in the south, where he attacked with argument, invective, and ridicule the revolutionary leaders, devoting all his energies to fanning the flame of popular discontent already kindled by local prejudice. The result was, that the most exaggerated ideas of Alvarado's policy were instilled into the public mind, so far as the people at large could be induced to think of the subject at all. The conditional element of the plan of independence was ignored altogether; Mexico had been defied, and California, defenceless, was exposed to the rapacity of foreign nations, if not indeed already virtually delivered to agents of the United States. All Mexicans had been or were to be banished, and their property confiscated, perhaps their very lives endangered. The south was to have no voice in the new administration. Even the catholic faith was dishonored, and protestant heresy was to be encouraged. Such were the fears which certain individuals deemed it for their interest to inculcate, and it is wonderful what unswerving loyalty and patriotism, what respect for the power of Mexico, what devotion to the true faith, and what ardent zeal to put themselves right on the record and avert the terrible consequences of Mexican wrath were all at once developed in the southern mind and heart, as represented by the ayuntamientos of Los Angeles and San Diego. I proceed with the chronological narrative.

In his letter of November 7th, before cited, Alvarado stated that commissioners would start next day to submit the new plan for approval in the south.[1] There are indications that such agents were despatched about that time, but we have no record of their negotiations, and they do not appear to have gone beyond Santa Bárbara. So far as I can learn, the first news of events at Monterey came on the *Leonidas,* which touched at Santa Bárbara about the 15th. The tidings spread to Los Angeles, where, on the 17th, Alcalde Requena called an extra session of the ayuntamiento. The rumor was that Gutierrez was prisoner, Mexican officials had been banished, and an armed force was en route for this city, to compel adhesion to a plan of unknown purport, but believed to involve a change in the existing order of things. The people were called in, and it was resolved not to recognize any authority not legally established, and to send a committee, headed by Síndico A. M. Osio, to meet the approaching force and learn the objects of its coming.[2] Next San Diego heard the news, from Rocha at San Gabriel, and assembled its ayuntamiento on the 22d. In the discussions great importance was attached to the part taken

[1] *Alvarado, Carta Confidencial,* MS. Buelna and Villavicenció are named. It would seem that the former at least could not have gone, yet some statements indicate that he did.

[2] *Los Angeles, Arch.,* MS., iv. 197-200. The arrival of the *Leonidas* with the district judge and Capt. Muñoz (?) on board was mentioned. Regidores Valdés and Herrera were the other members of the committee. Nov. 19th, an account of the meeting was sent to J. J. Rocha, administrator of San Gabriel, who acknowledged receipt on Nov. 20th. *Dept. St. Pap., Angeles,* MS., ii. 66. Osio, *Hist. Cal.,* MS., 318-20, mentions the prominent part taken by the síndico, not naming himself, now and later. Osio says the opposition of Los Angeles was, 1st, because it was ridiculous to form a state with only 9,000 inhabitants, 300 of them educated; 2d, because of foreign and American coöperation, savoring too much of annexation; 3d, because greater powers than those of the national congress had been assumed in granting religious tolerance. These and 'other reasons' caused Angeles to hesitate in recognizing a govt whose elevated principles might very likely prove top-heavy.

by foreigners in the northern outbreak. On the recommendation of Alcalde Argüello and Comandante Salazar, it was decided to send two comisionados to consult with the authorities of Los Angeles and Santa Bárbara on the course to be taken. "The national honor and integrity being at stake, not a moment should be lost." Juan Bandini and Santiago E. Argüello were appointed for this commission,[3] and reached Los Angeles in time to take part in the meetings of the ayuntamiento and people, November 25th–26th. At the first of these meetings a plan was adopted to save the country. By its terms the plan of Monterey was rejected as an act of violence; other ayuntamientos were invited to send each three persons to Los Angeles to elect a provisional gefe político; the law making Los Angeles the capital was to be strictly enforced; military officers not engaged in the Monterey movement were to be invited by Comandante Rocha to choose a temporary general; Los Angeles was to await the coöperation of San Diego and Santa Bárbara only, to carry out this plan; and these resolutions were to have effect until the national laws should be again in full force. This was approved by the people, and it was voted to place on file a list of adherents, to place under surveillance all who refused to sign it, and to arrest the emissaries said to be coming from the north. Next day, besides communications from Monterey, one was read from the alcalde of Santa Bárbara, who represented his municipality as declining to approve the plan of Monterey until a provisional congress should meet in a central locality, and

[3] Nov. 22, 1836, acta of the ayunt. Letter of Alcalde Argüello to Alcalde Requena, and instructions in 7 articles to the comisionados. *S. Diego, Arch.*, MS., 137–8. The agents were to have an interview with Gutierrez, if possible, to make known the perfect loyalty of S. Diego, and it was understood that one of their duties would be to aid in devising means for the selection of a legitimate temporary ruler. Nov. 22d, Alcalde Argüello orders mission administrators to furnish all needed aid to the comisionados on their journey, and he tells him of S. Diego mission, 'the national honor demands that you furnish me two horses'! *Id.*, 141.

guaranties be offered of protection to lives and property of Mexicans.[4]

Bandini and Argüello returned home, and their report of what had taken place at Angeles was presented at the ayuntamiento meeting of the 29th, a report which, like the speeches made, was full of loyalty and brave determination to avenge the insult to the Mexican nation, with expressions of surprise and regret that selfish interests had prompted certain unprincipled men to "abuse the candor of the Californians, and compromise them so shamefully." This was simply 'Bandini versus Ramirez.' San Diego of course approved the plan of Los Angeles, and the three electors named in accordance therewith were Bandini, S. E. Argüello, and J. M. Marron, Pio Pico being substituted for Bandini a few days later on account of the latter's illness. Meanwhile the troops at San Diego and San Luis became infected with a revolutionary spirit and refused to do duty—that is, they 'struck' for pay or supplies now that there might be urgent need of their services. This delayed the electors, and it is not quite certain that all of them reached Los Angeles at all.[5]

All seemed favorable now for the establishment of a separate provisional government in the south, which should either defeat the Monterey administration, or at least exact favorable terms of compromise; but obstacles began to present themselves. The action of the garrisons at San Diego and San Luis seemed to

[4] *Los Angeles, Arch.*, MS., iv. 200–12. Sessions of Nov. 25th–6th. Action of citizens of Sta B. on Nov. 20th, announced by Alcalde Dana on Nov. 23d, also in *Dept. St. Pap., Angeles*, MS., ii. 67–8. Art. 3 of these Sta Bárbara resolutions is unintelligible. The Los Angeles plan, as reported by a committee of the ayunt., is also given in *Los Angeles, Arch.*, MS., i. 106–8, with a preface condemnatory of the people of Monterey, who, 'hallucinated with the idea of ruling all California themselves, have been deceived by adventurers.'

[5] Nov. 28, 1836, report of the comisionados; Nov. 29th–30th, acta of ayunt. of S. Diego; Dec. 1st, notice sent to Angeles; Dec. 3d–4th, Pico's appointment; Dec. 2d, 9th, 11th, corresp. between Argüello, Salazar, and Pico about the revolt of troops; Dec. 16th, Alcalde Argüello complains that communication has ceased with the ayunt. of Los Angeles, and that all his patriotic efforts have been in vain. *S. Diego, Arch.*, MS., 139–43, 147; *Los Angeles, Arch.*, MS., i. 107–20.

indicate that the soldiers even of the south were not
so intensely patriotic as to serve without food. Castillo Negrete was invited to take up his residence at
Los Angeles, and give the loyal sureños the benefit
of his counsels; but he declined the honor and the
service.[6] And finally, at a session of the ayuntamiento December 10th, a communication was received
from Santa Bárbara, the ayuntamiento of which place
declined to indorse the Angeles plan, proposing one
of its own instead. The Barbareños refused to take
part in any sectional election held in the interest of
either Monterey or Los Angeles; but favored a general junta composed of four delegates from each presidio and three from each town, to meet at Santa Inés,
to work for the interests of the whole territory, and
to choose provisional rulers. The Angelinos were
now discouraged, seeing nothing desirable in the plan
of Santa Bárbara. They voted that nothing could
be done, thanked San Diego for its proffered coöperation, put on file with approval a protest of Castillo
Negrete against the northern iniquity, and adjourned.[7]

Such was the situation at the end of December
1836. At the beginning of 1837 new ayuntamientos
were installed; a fact which seems to have instilled
new life and courage into both Angelinos and Dieguinos. The result was a new plan of Los Angeles,
dated January 3d. Its purport was as follows: 1.
The plan of Monterey, so far as it relates to indepen-

---

[6] *Los Angeles, Arch.*, MS., iv. 213–14; *Dept. St. Pap., Angeles*, MS., ii.
58.

[7] *Los Angeles, Arch.*, MS., iv. 215–19. Several proclamations of Vallejo
and others in the north were also received and put on file. It was even allowed that these documents might be shown to such sound-minded and reliable men as had a curiosity to read them. The plan of Sta Bárbara, apparently dated Dec. 9th, was in 4 articles. The 1st approved the preceding
resolutions of Nov. 20th (see note 4); the 2d proposed the junta at Sta Inés;
3d, authorities to be provisional until approved by national govt; and, 4th,
refusal to take part in a sectional election, or counter-revolt. Dec. 29th, Alcalde Argüello sends a package of papers to the sup. govt by the *Leonidas*,
and desires Castillo Negrete to put in a clear light in Mexico the patriotic
desires and efforts of himself and of San Diego in this crisis. *S. Diego, Arch.*,
MS., 149.

dence from Mexico, is not recognized. 2. The electors at the proper time will come 'to this capital' and proceed to elect a diputacion according to law. 3, 4. Until the new diputacion meets, the ayuntamiento of this city will be the chief authority, but will turn over the command to the first vocal according to law. 5. All to be submitted for approval to the supreme government. San Diego was filled with joy at the receipt of this plan on the 7th, and gladly promised support, though article 1 was deemed by the ayuntamiento not strong enough, and article 3 was feared to be illegal. The election was to be on the 29th, before which date several things happened, as we shall see.[8]

I have before me several communications, private letters for the most part, written by prominent men in November and December 1836, which deserve notice here, as throwing much light on this southern complication. Three of these papers are from the pen of Castillo Negrete, who, as we have seen, tarried a little in the south on his way to Mexico. The first is a letter of advice, dated at Santa Bárbara November 18th to Lieutenant Domingo Carrillo, comandante of the post, respecting his duty in this emergency. After being duly instructed about the Monterey iniquity, Carrillo was counselled to give his men an unlimited leave of absence until recalled to service in the name of the nation. All arms should be secreted, that they might not fall into rebel hands. The troops might however legally venture to aid the municipal authorities in preserving order, always providing the

[8] S. Diego, Arch., MS., 151-3; Los Angeles, Arch., MS., i. 126-7. Gil Ibarra and José Sepúlveda were the new alcaldes of Los Angeles; José Antonio Estudillo held the office at S. Diego. On Jan. 2d the former ayunt. had received the 9 decrees of the congreso constituyente, and had even as a matter of courtesy acknowledged the receipt to Juan B. Alvarado. Los Angeles, Arch., MS., iv. 225-7. Andrés Pico was the elector of S. Diego. Osio, Hist. Cal., MS., 320-2, says that Alcalde Ibarra was a nobody, and that the whole opposition to Alvarado was managed by the ex-síndico, that is, by Osio himself, through the 2d alcalde Sepúlveda as an obedient agent. I shall have more to say of Osio's course.

said authorities were loyal! Finally the comandante ought to assemble his officers in a council of war to put on record their patriotic purposes. Thus might they hope to escape the terrible consequences of revolt against Mexico.[9]

The licenciado's letters had a semi-official character, as his communication to Carrillo had been written in his capacity of legal adviser of the comandancia, and the other two as district judge of California under the overthrown administration. From on board the *Leonidas* at San Diego, Don Luis in December directed to the ayuntamiento of Los Angeles a long exposition on the state of affairs. I regret that I have not space to reproduce it nearly in full, for a résumé does it no justice; but I present a few quotations in a note.[10]

[9] *Castillo Negrete, Consejos al Comandante de Sta Bárbara, Nov. 1836*, MS. Original document. Nov. 20th, the judge certifies that Carrillo has remained true to the legitimate authority. *Id.*, 9–11. Meanwhile Carrillo had perhaps followed the advice given by granting leave of absence to his men, to earn a living as they could. At any rate, I find such a discharge for one private dated Nov. 19th. *Vallejo, Doc.*, MS., iii. 266. Carrillo was later removed by Alvarado.

[10] *Castillo Negrete, Exposicion que dirige el Juez de Distrito al Ayuntamiento de Los Angeles sobre el Plan revolucionario de Monterey, Dec. 1836*, MS. The day is left blank, but was probably Dec. 5th or 6th. 'A power usurpatory of our rights, disturber of our repose, pretends to take from us at the same time order and liberty...California's first necessity is to reëstablish a legitimate government...Californian inexperience may be the victim of revolutionists, who, seducing some incautious ones and favored by foreign smugglers, have set up in Monterey the throne of anarchy, and fixed the focus of a faction which is moved by unnatural men, without God, law, or country, and headed by four hallucinated deputies without skill or foresight, as blind instruments of the former...American adventurers and corrupt citizens found their hopes on public calamity, on the ruin of the national treasury, on the protection of smuggling, and on the squandering of mission property...Four ill-advised diputados, abusing the name of diputacion, without powers, mission, or faculties, without having consulted public opinion, constitute themselves sovereigns and arrogate to themselves perpetually all legislative, executive, and judicial powers...It is not our duty to obey a diputacion not legally convoked.' (Yet there is no evidence that the dip. convoked by Chico had ever been permanently adjourned.)...'They are perjurers, breaking the oaths they took before God and men; traitors to the country, having forgotten the holy principle "against the country there is no right."'...The so-called congreso constituyente merely follows the inspirations of a frantic philosopher, an old revolutionist, and a vicious foreign smuggler...The universal and urgent interest of the territory is to preserve peace, prevent the shedding of blood, and protect life and property, being ruled by our respective ayunt. until the laws are again enforced...Let us check that faction which seeks to rule us without our consent, else the country will be covered with laws, the legislators will be loaded with salaries and privileges. With republican phrases they will sow discord, plunder the treasury, and attack private for-

The argument is an exhaustive, brilliant, and powerful one; though the author's denunciations of the
revolutionists and their policy are more bitter and
violent than there was any need to make them, their
animus being somewhat too clearly traceable to a personal dislike of two or three men. The remedy proposed was suggested at the end in a series of eight
resolutions, on which, with some exaggeration, even
of the author's estimate of metropolitan powers, was
founded the plan of January 3d already noticed. Don
Luis issued also another formal protest against the
Monterey movement, embodying more briefly his
views as expressed in the exposition, and intended to
explain the motives which obliged him to leave the
territory, for he did not feel at liberty to remain as
invited and help the Angelinos to carry into effect his
suggestions.[11]

Antonio M. Osio, síndico of Los Angeles, who in
later writings claims to have been the chief promoter

tunes, and respect neither God nor men...Have we not seen them break the
compact made on the field of Monterey, imprisoning some, expelling others,
and forcing capitulated soldiers into their service?' (This charge had little
if any foundation in fact.) He goes on to say that the electors sent to the
capital at the time fixed by law to renew the dip. were treated with scorn
and not permitted to act. It is true that there was a summons for Nov. 6th,
but there is no other evidence that the electors were not allowed, or even
attempted to perform their duties. Again, he speaks of 'the blind instruments of Ramirez, Peña, and Hinckley, who would make of Cal. another
Texas, and tear the national flag...Shall we be then like the Texans, victims
sacrificed to foreign ambition? God forbid!...There is no ayunt. of higher
rank than that of Los Angeles, since it is a city and by law the capital; therefore it should take the initiative.'
He then suggests the following plan: 1. The ayunt. of Los Angeles to
invite the others to form a 'common centre of union' to protect public welfare and avoid the disasters of an impending civil war. 2. The electors
already chosen to meet at Los Angeles and elect a new dip. 3. The dip. as
soon as formed to have the right to name a gefe político and com. gen. 4.
The appointment of those rulers to be, however, provisional and subject to
the decision of the sup. govt. 5. The authorities of Los Angeles to write to
the 4 diputados of Monterey, begging them in the name of the country to
desist from their fatal purpose and favor the new election 'at the capital.'
6. Angel Ramirez, Cosme Peña, and Wm Hinckley to be sent to Mexico for
trial. 7. The new dip. to preserve order, etc., and to declare null the oaths
taken in support of independence. 8. The ayunt. to consult the people of the
city before acting on this proposition.
[11] *Castillo Negrete, Protestacion del Juez de Distrito contra el Plan de Monterey 6 de Dic. 1836*, MS. This and the preceding communications were received at Los Angeles on Dec. 10th.

of the opposition to Alvarado, also wrote some letters which indicate that he had plans of his own, though they do not make quite clear the purport of his schemes. The 25th of November he sent to Antonio del Valle a copy of the Los Angeles plan of that date, with a letter, to be shown also to the Carrillos, in which he says: "Although the plan touches some points that we have not spoken of, I think they"—that is, the Carrillos and Osio's friends—"will agree to what I propose, according to our scheme, the difference being very slight. It is necessary to choose rulers, and we shall play very badly the instrument in our hands if we cannot make Vallejo comandante general. If the political command is separated—which is not expedient in such cases—we can give it to my uncle Don Cárlos [Carrillo], who is well known here and *en la otra banda*, not a bad choice perhaps, whether he wishes it or not. Our friend Don Juan Rocha agrees to meddle in nothing, but merely to keep order with his soldiers. I have told Don Juan Bandini he had better go home and keep quiet, since in this fandango only Californians will be allowed to dance. This did not please him, but it is best that he keep quiet, though a friend. I will do all in my power to fulfil my promises. I have already spoken with some friends, who are ready to follow me. The comisionados from Monterey will be sent by the alcalde out of this jurisdiction. Rocha will not admit them at San Gabriel, and if they go to San Diego the Apostle Andrés [Pico] will send them about their business." [12]

Next day Osio addressed Vallejo himself in a letter which throws but little light on the preceding. He had been stunned with surprise and sorrow, he wrote, at hearing what had happened at Monterey. He was sure Vallejo had nothing to do with the plan, but that Castro and Alvarado had used his name without per-

---

[12] *Osio, Carta sobre Combinaciones políticas, 25 de Nov. 1836*, MS. Osio in his history says nothing of these plans, which I do not pretend to understand fully.

mission. It could result in nothing but misfortune, and would make California the laughing-stock of the world. Mexico could reconquer the territory, without expending a dollar, by simply turning loose on its property a horde of Sonoran vagabonds. Vallejo must devise a speedy remedy; organize some kind of a temporary government satisfactory to the people if not strictly legal; and finally, go as a deputy to Mexico to explain matters. Independence is a foolish dream at present; and the writer quotes from Vallejo's old conversations with Echeandía, to the effect that California might one day be independent—but only when their great-grandchildren should reach an advanced age! So far as intelligible, Osio's plan would seem to have involved a surrender to Mexico and centralism on condition that Vallejo should be made governor and general.[13]

Juan Bandini, as a matter of course, had something to say on the subject. In a letter of December 3d to Vallejo he represents himself as delirious with sorrow at what has occurred. The picture has no bright side. He loves California better than the land of his birth, but all his efforts and those of others in behalf of the country are now rendered vain and of no effect just when the prospects seemed fairest. The result cannot fail to be disgrace and shame and vengeance. The Californians were mad to expose their plans without force to support them, to attempt to resuscitate the lost cause of federalism. "It is hard to contend against one's own opinions, but it is harder to see a friend mixed up in so terrible a predicament." Not a word of southern remedial plans.[14]

[13] Osio, Carta á Vallejo, 26 de Nov. 1836, MS. The writer implies that a very extensive revolt in the south, in which the Indians were to have taken part, had been prevented by prompt measures; and he declares that the 'Yanques' must be taught to let politics alone.

[14] Bandini, Carta a Vallejo, sobre revoluciones 3 de Dic. 1836, MS. Pio Pico adds a word of remembrance on the margin of Bandini's letter; and on the same date writes to Vallejo on the subject. He expresses no disapproval of the plan; but doubts that Vallejo is concerned in it, as Alvarado claims. Were it so, surely he, Pico, would have been given a share in the enterprise. Vallejo, Doc., iii. 275.

On the 7th Don Juan made a long report to the
minister of hacienda on his favorite topic, using the
revolution as a new weapon against his old foe, Angel Ramirez, who had caused the outbreak solely to
cover up his revenue frauds. The Californians had
been led into a trap, and the real intention was to
annex the territory to some foreign power. He sends
documents to show that the south has disapproved
such criminal plans, and that 'I have coöperated' in
this holy work.[15] Five days later he wrote again to
Vallejo, in reply to a defence of the revolution. He
reasoned earnestly and eloquently. He was still
sure that Mexico would wreak a terrible vengeance
on all concerned, and trembled for his friend, who
had been so unfortunately misled. The whole matter
had in his mind no other phase than the punishment
to be expected from Mexico and the agency of Angel Ramirez.[16]

Cárlos Antonio Carrillo took a more cheerful view
of the situation. On the 5th of December he expressed his approval of what Castro and Alvarado
had done, though he feared the article on independence could not be sustained for want of force. He
attached little importance to the federal phases of the
plan, for what had the federal government ever done
for California? He hoped much from the proposed
junta at Santa Inés, and would do his best to unite
the south. He favored giving the civil as well as
the military command to Vallejo, as Osio had also
urged. In two subsequent letters Don Cárlos declared himself to be fully converted by the arguments
advanced, and an enthusiastic supporter of the whole
scheme, independence and all. He even hoped to
induce the south to share his views. He had heard,
however, that Bandini, Rocha, and others had sent
to Sonora for aid, and wished Vallejo to come south

---

[15] *S. Diego, Arch.*, MS., 145. Bandini to min. of hac., Dec. 7, 1836.
[16] *Bandini, Carta Particular á Vallejo sobre Cosas Políticas, 12 de Dic.
1836*, MS.

with as large a force as possible.[17]   Several writers, treating the subject superficially, have confounded these events with those of later date, and represented Don Cárlos as Alvarado's chief opponent from the first.

Alvarado had left the capital on or about Christmas. His army consisted of some sixty Californians, and twenty-five foreigners under Graham and Coppinger. Part of the force went down the coast on the *Clementine*, landed at El Cojo, and joined the rest at Purísima.   Letters received before starting and on the way left little doubt of a kind reception at Santa Bárbara.   Messengers sent forward from Purísima brought back confirmation of favorable prospects, and the forces of the Estado Libre arrived at the mission January 3d, being cordially received by the Barbareños of all classes.[18]

Conservative Santa Bárbara, as we have seen, though favoring a general junta in central California and requiring pledges that Mexicans should not be persecuted, had virtually favored the Monterey plan from the first by refusing to accept the opposing plan of Los Angeles.   Cárlos Carrillo and his friends had expressed their approval.   Valentin Cota had been in communication with Alvarado and received from him a captain's commission.[19]   And, what was much more

[17] *Carrillo, Cartas de Don Cárlos al Gen. Vallejo, Dic. 1836*, MS.   The last letter was dated Dec. 23d.   The leaders of the opposition, besides Bandini and Rocha, were said to be Manuel Dominguez, Vicente Sanchez, Estudillo, Requena, and Arenas.   Félix Gallardo had been sent to Sonora by Rocha and paid $60 and two horses.

[18] J. J. Pico, *Acontecimientos*, MS., 38–9, claims to have commanded the party that went by sea; but Alvarado, *Hist. Cal.*, MS., 189–94, says the commander was Benito Diaz.   He tells us that Capt. Hinckley had volunteered to take a force in his vessel and conquer the south; but his offer was declined, a peaceful settlement being hoped for.   This writer and Vallejo, *Hist. Cal.*, MS., iii. 245, name Jacinto Rodriguez as the agent sent forward from Purísima.   Pinto—*Apunt.*, MS., 24–7—appointed alférez in Alvarado's force, gives some details of recruiting men for the expedition.   He went to Sta Cruz and obtained 35 men.   The total force was 200 men.   Janssens, *Vida*, MS., 87, says that Villa and Buelna, the comisionados, had visited Sta Bárbara before Alvarado's coming.

[19] *Cota, Doc.*, MS., 5–6; *Guerra, Doc.*, MS., v. 303–5.

important, José de la Guerra y Noriega and Padre
Narciso Duran had determined to support the new
government.   These gentlemen have not left on record any expression of their views at this time.   To
what extent, if at all, they were influenced by a spirit
of antagonism as Spaniards to everything Mexican,
or by the fact that a son of Guerra was one of the
four revolting diputados, it is impossible to determine;
but there is much reason to conclude that they looked
upon Alvarado's success, now that the movement had
gone so far, as more likely to bring about peace and
prosperity than would be the success of the southern
faction with its radical sectional policy and wavering
support.

At any rate, the support of Duran, Guerra, and
Carrillo made the way clear at Santa Bárbara.   President Duran went out to meet Alvarado, whom he received at the mission with all the honors paid in olden
times to the governor, walking by his side to the
church where the religious ceremonies *de estilo* were
performed.   This was on January 3d; a few days were
spent in interviews with leading men; and on the
6th the ayuntamiento and people with great enthusiasm and all possible ceremony and noise took the oath
of allegiance to the new system, the new governor,
and the congreso constituyente.   "The people here
are even more enthusiastic for the cause than those
of Monterey," wrote Alvarado to Castro and Vallejo.[20]

[20] Jan. 9, 1837, Alvarado to Castro.   Official and private letters in *Vallejo,
Doc.*, MS., iii. 152; iv. 8.   Jan. 12th, A. to V.   Private letter in *Vallejo,
Corresp.*, MS., 37–8.   In these letters Alvarado manifests much real interest
in the country's welfare; hopes for a peaceful settlement of all troubles; and
gives to Cárlos Carrillo the chief credit for the brilliant success at Sta. Bárbara.   The fact of Sta. Bárbara's adhesion at some date before Jan. 11th is
recorded in *Los Angeles, Arch.*, MS., iv. 234.   In his *Hist. Cal.*, MS., iii.
205–13, Alvarado narrates his experience at Sta. Bárbara.   He says that P.
Duran tried to impose some favorable conditions for the missions; but yielded
the point, when Alvarado declared that he was pledged to complete the work
of secularization.   So great was the enthusiasm that the gov. thought once
more of absolute independence for Cal., and consulted Duran about blessing
and raising a flag of that purport; but the friar declined to bless the flag,
and dissuaded him, so that the project was dropped.   *Vallejo, Hist. Cal.*,
MS., iii. 245–9.

The news was not, however, altogether cheering from the south. There was still a strong party at Los Angeles that would not be conciliated. In the letters cited, Alvarado explained the situation to his northern associates; expressed his opinion that it would be necessary to overcome the obstinacy of the Angelinos by a show of force; and ordered Castro to come immediately by sea to San Pedro with a reënforcement, and to meet him at Los Angeles, whither he would soon start.[21] Meanwhile he made preparations for his march, enlisting some recruits for his army, both native and foreign.[22] He also found time to address two communications to the recalcitrant ayuntamiento of Angeles, in which he tried to demonstrate the justice of his cause, the groundless character of the fears that had been entertained, and the falsehood of the charges that he would adopt a sectional policy or deliver his country to the hands of foreigners or disturb any Mexican who should abstain from plots against the new system. He declared that his resources were ample to sustain the conditional independence declared, and that federalism was already tottering throughout the nation. He hoped sincerely that Los Angeles would follow the example of Santa Bárbara, receive him in a spirit of conciliation, and unite with other towns in working for the welfare of the whole country. His military force, he said, was more than sufficient to enforce his views, but he hoped his countrymen would not oblige him to use it against them.[23] At last with a force of eighty men, besides the riflemen, the governor began his march by way of

[21] Jan. 9, 1837, A. to C., in *Vallejo, Corresp.*, MS., 44–5. It would seem that Vallejo also was urged to come to the south. *Id.*, 37–8. Sra Ávila, *Cosas de Cal.*, MS., 16–17, notes the rejoicings at Monterey, especially among the women, when the news of Sta Bárbara's adhesion came.

[22] Nidever, *Life and Adven.*, MS., 87–8, was one who joined Graham's riflemen at Sta Bárbara. The number was at last about 40. They were paid $2 a day, and promised the privilege of taking up lands later. They served about 20 days.

[23] *Alvarado, Comunicaciones al Ayuntamiento de Los Angeles, 7 y 16 de Enero, 1837*, MS. The second letter was written at S. Buenaventura.

San Buenaventura, at which mission he was on the 16th–17th.

Let us turn now to the southern ayuntamientos, which illustrious and patriotic bodies we left jubilant over the plan of January 3d, evolved mainly from the brain of Castillo Negrete, as a measure which was to save the country from northern tyranny. By the 8th Alvarado's complete success at Santa Bárbara was known at Angeles, and rumors were current that he intended to extend his march southward. Accordingly the people were called to arms. All persons sympathizing with the foe were ordered to leave the city, the mission funds at San Fernando to the amount of $2,000 were taken by the municipal authorities 'for safe keeping,' scouts were stationed on the Santa Bárbara routes, the southern missions were notified to be ready with supplies, and San Diego was requested to send at once an armed force of patriots to aid in repelling the invader.[24] San Diego had from the first been full of zeal for the cause, and had on one or two occasions reproached the Angelinos for their lukewarmness. The ayuntamiento had still an unlimited supply of patriotic and warlike phrases for its ally; but to be thus suddenly called upon for such aid as men and muskets and a cannon was really very startling. This was a radical measure, and required caution and deliberation. It was clear that if the rebels of Monterey were really threatening an invasion of the 'law and order' towns, something must be done. Therefore it was resolved to await more particulars of news from the north, and to inquire what it was proposed to do with the force asked for! And nearly a week later, when a reply had been

---

[24] Jan. 6th, 8th, sessions of ayunt., in *Los Angeles, Arch.*, MS., iv. 228–32; *Dept. St. Pap., Angeles*, MS., ii. 96–7; *S. Diego, Arch.*, MS., 154. On Jan. 11th the news was received officially that Sta Bárbara had adhered to the northern cause, and refused to send electors accordingly to the plan of Jan. 3d; also that S. Diego would accept that plan. On the same day Alvarado's first letter was received, and it was resolved that his authority could not be recognized. *Los Angeles, Arch.*, MS., iv. 233–4.

obtained from the alcalde of Los Angeles, San Diego went to work in earnest. On or about the 18th, twenty men under Pio Pico and Regidor Francisco M. Alvarado started northward, in time to arrive at Los Angeles after the war was over.[25]

The Angelinos, notwithstanding the lack of support from San Diego, pushed forward their preparations for defence. The mission money was partly expended in this work; the soldiers at San Gabriel were summoned to the city; one Charlefoux, with a band of thirty or forty Indian-hunters and 'traders' in horses, was induced to join the patriot army; citizens and rancheros were enlisted; and by the 16th a force of about 270 men was stationed at San Fernando, under Alférez Rocha as commander-in-chief, Alcalde Sepúlveda having been the leading spirit in directing the preparations, and issuing on the 17th an address in which the citizens were called upon to prove by their deeds that, however far others had followed the Monterey faction out of the path of duty, there were left men who were ready to defend the honor of their beloved country. It would seem also that Sepúlveda had sent to Alvarado a copy of his address, or certain propositions embodying the same sentiments, and that his commissioners may have brought back from San Buenaventura the governor's second communication already cited.[26]

[25] Jan. 10th, 12th, 16th, sessions of ayunt. Jan. 11th, corres. of Alf. Salazar, and his call for money and supplies. Jan. 14th, 16th, 18th, 23d, Alcalde Estudillo to Osuna, Cabello, Fitch, etc., about preparations for the march. *S. Diego, Arch.*, MS., 155–66; *Los Angeles, Arch.*, MS., i. 128–35. Jan. 17th, Pio Pico says he will start with 25 men next day, picking up recruits on the way. *Dept. St. Pap., Angeles*, MS., ii. 101. Alvarado, *Hist. Cal.*, MS., iii. 180–1, 217–18, 225, 232, tells us that Salazar was a friend of Castro, and purposely interposed obstacles; also that Capt. Fitch supplied only moistened powder. He is very bitter against the Dieguinos as braggarts, who would do nothing but talk, and to whom 'the Supreme Being had denied the gift of veracity.'

[26] Jan. 11th, 16th, sessions of ayunt. *Los Angeles, Arch.*, MS., iv. 234–7. Jan. 15th–17th, communications of Sepúlveda and Rocha. *Dept. St. Pap., Angeles*, MS., ii. 94–102. José Perez was accused by Sepúlveda of talking in favor of the Monterey faction. The Indian allies are called Chaguanosos by Janssens and others, and Shauanoos (Shawnees?) by Osio. The chief is called Shalifú. Osio, *Hist. Cal.*, MS., 321–40, gives many details of the prepara-

Alvarado's letter of the 16th was read at an ayuntamiento meeting of the 17th. The allusion in it to his large resources for war seemed to the Angelinos a very forcible point of his argument, and they were convinced by a careful study of the document that the policy of Don Juan Bautista was not so oppressive or unpatriotic perhaps as had been feared. Another letter from Antonio M. Osio was read, in which the writer solicited powers to form an arrangement with Alvarado on an equitable basis, providing that the ruler should be a Californian. After a long discussion, it was resolved to send Sepúlveda and Osio as comisionados, with authority to effect a settlement in accordance with the following resolutions: 1. The ayuntamiento is anxious to avoid bloodshed, even at the cost of some sacrifice not involving disrespect to laws and oaths. 2. The plan of independence from Mexico cannot be accepted, though there is no objection to a declaration in favor of the federal system. 3. The Roman catholic religion must be the only one permitted, and persons publicly holding other views must be prosecuted as hitherto. 4. No officer or citizen is to be molested for opinions respecting this revolution upheld by him prior to the ratification of this treaty. 5. The state of things decided upon is to be binding upon both parties until the supreme government shall decide, with the understanding that Los Angeles is not to be held responsible for the

tions for defence, in which he himself was the leading man and Sepúlveda's counsellor. He aroused great indignation against the Monterey plan by assuring the women that under it protestant priests were to be tolerated who would marry any girl that desired it to any foreigner, whatever his religion! The women were terrified, and exhorted their husbands and sons to fight for their daughters and sweethearts and the catholic faith. Their conduct is praised as heroic. Osio gives the force as over 300 in 4 companies. He says that Sepúlveda and Manuel Dominguez went to S. Buenaventura to have an interview with Alvarado, to persuade him to retire and be content with ruling the north until the sup. govt should decide, and above all to ascertain the military strength of the enemy. They were kindly received, but the succeeding particulars are not intelligibly expressed by Osio, though the spies learned that Alvarado's force was far inferior to their own. All expected blood to flow, and the privilege of shooting Alvarado had been awarded by common consent to Sepúlveda.

treaty, since it is made merely to prevent bloodshed in California.[27] Next day Sepúlveda wrote that every man capable of bearing arms should be sent to the front, as the people of Monterey were approaching and had replied to his messages that on the 19th they would be within gunshot on the plain of San Fernando.

Alvarado, with his army of 110 men and two pieces of artillery, had left San Buenaventura on the 17th, and after a day's march in the rain had halted for the night at Cayeguas rancho, whence he despatched the message cited above, and where he had a conference with Osio and others sent by Sepúlveda, a conference resulting in nothing beyond an agreement to hold another nearer San Fernando on the 19th.[23] Next day Alvarado advanced to the Calabazas rancho, where, or perhaps at Encino, he met Sepúlveda and Osio on the 19th. The comisionados had meanwhile reported at San Fernando the inferiority of Alvarado's force, thus arousing a somewhat warlike spirit, if we may credit Osio's statement; but they had also re-

[27] Jan. 17th, 18th, session of ayunt. *Los Angeles, Arch.*, MS., iv. 238–41; *Dept. St. Pap.*, MS., xi. 61–5. On Jan. 18th Pio Pico's letter was received, with news that he was coming with 25 men; and the news was forwarded to S. Fernando. *Id., Angeles*, ii. 83. The S. Diego force, 20 strong, arrived on Jan. 21st (too late to be sent to S. Fernando, as will be seen later). *Los Angeles, Arch.*, MS., 243–7. Ignacio Coronel was comandante at S. Gabriel after Rocha's departure. *Dept. St. Pap., Angeles*, MS., ii. 99–100. Jan. 18th, Sepúlveda to Alcalde Ibarra. *Id.*, ii. 100–1. Janssens, *Vida*, MS., 88–9, claims to have commanded the garrison at S. Gabriel.

[23] Osio, *Hist. Cal.*, MS., 291–7, still speaking of himself as 'the friend of Sepúlveda,' and not naming the other comisionados, gives some details of the negotiations at Cayeguas on the evening of Jan. 17th and morning of the 18th, though he gives no dates. He attributes the failure to the 'pertinaz arrogancia licurga' of Alvarado and Peña, who put on airs of importance, and insisted on seeing the comisionados' credentials, which of course was impossible, as they had none. Osio says also that Cárlos and Anastasio Carrillo were on the spot working to prevent a conflict. Alvarado, *Hist. Cal.*, MS., iii. 215–25, like Vallejo, *Hist. Cal.*, MS., iii. 249–59, says he refused to treat because the comisionados, whom he says were Osio, Valle, and Lugo, insisted on addressing him as 'chief of the northern forces,' instead of governor, some of them even carrying their familiarity so far as to call him Juanito. In a report written a few days later, Alvarado—*Carta en que relata la Campaña de San Fernando, 22 de Enero, 1837*, MS., being addressed to Gen. Vallejo, and also to the ayunt. of Monterey—says nothing of these preliminary negotiations. He says his force was 80 men, but I think this cannot have included Graham's men.

ceived the ayuntamiento's instructions of the 17th to form a treaty. Andrés Pico, who accompanied them, had brought from the south the news not only that reënforcements were coming, but that Pio Pico and two associates were on the way as comisionados for San Diego, and in order that those gentlemen might take part in the negotiations they were again postponed until the next day.[29]

On the morning of the 20th, as Pico had not arrived, Sepúlveda and Osio, probably accompanied by others, went again to Encino or Calabazas. Instead of proceeding to negotiate a treaty, however, they merely showed to Alvarado their instructions, which had been intended to be kept secret, and obtained his approval of them in writing on the margin, together with an additional promise, written in pencil, not to molest any one, Mexican or Californian, for having taken up arms under the alcalde's orders. The document, with which the reader is familiar, was regarded by the governor as not conflicting in any essential point with the plan of Monterey, and as one which he was amply authorized to sign by virtue of the 'extraordinary powers' which had been given him. The comisionados now set up the claim that, as a treaty had been signed, Alvarado should at once disband his forces and retire to the north. To this, of course, not being a man entirely out of his senses, Don Juan Bautista would not listen; and after long discussions, he brought the matter to a close on the 21st by sending a message to Sepúlveda that if San Fernando was not surrendered

[29] Mainly the version of Osio, *Hist. Cal.*, MS., 297–300, 341–2, but confirmed more or less fully by contemporary records. Osio represents the leaders and men at S. Fernando as much disgusted with the ayuntamiento's instructions, which were the work of Alcalde Ibarra and his adviser Requena. He also says that Andrés Pico had a secret conversation with Alvarado, which suggested to 'the friend of Sepúlveda' grave suspicions of some trick. Alvarado himself, in his *Hist. Cal.*, MS., affirms that the negotiations were broken off as before by the refusal of the comisionados to recognize him as governor, though one of them went so far as to call him 'excelencia;' whereupon he called them fools, and sent them off 'con cajas destempladas.' He also tells of an Indian, Mauricio, who was hired to return to S. Fernando with the tale that Castro had arrived with a large reënforcement.

on the messenger's return he would take it by force. The order was obeyed at once, Rocha's men retired toward the city, and Sepúlveda came out in person to tell the Monterey chief that the stronghold of the patriots was at his disposal. Alvarado accordingly occupied the mission with his army late in the afternoon of the 21st, and next day reported his success to his associates in the north.[30]

On January 21st, before the fall of San Fernando was known in the city, a meeting of the ayuntamiento was held, at which Pio Pico, Joaquin Ortega, and Martin S. Cabello, having presented their credentials as representatives of San Diego, were added to the comisionados appointed and instructed on the 17th, and the instructions were modified or enlarged so as

[30] Alvarado, Carta en que relata la Campaña de S. Fernando, MS. The writer does not state what the agreement was, but simply says it differed very slightly from the established plan. He says his men were anxious to fight, and were with difficulty restrained. The agreement is given in Los Angeles, Arch., MS., iv. 249–50; Dept. St. Pap., MS., xi. 64–5, and is literally as follows: 'The citizen Juan B. Alvarado, governor of the free and sovereign state of Alta California, declares his acceptance of the resolution passed by the illustrious ayuntamiento of the city of Los Angeles on the 17th inst, and by virtue of the extraordinary faculties with which he is invested, does hereby conform to all that is contained in the articles expressed in the aforesaid resolution. Field of San Fernando, Jan. 20, 1837. Juan B. Alvarado, Lic. Cosme Peña, secretary.' Osio, Hist. Cal., MS., 343–8, says that Alvarado was surprised and delighted at getting such favorable terms at such a critical moment, when the most he had hoped for was to be allowed to rule over the regions north of Sta Bárbara. The 'friend of Sepúlveda' was sad to think of the mothers of Los Angeles, and Alvarado, on learning the cause of his melancholy, promised that during his rule the decree of religious tolerance should not be enforced, and the girls should not be encouraged to marry protestants, Jews, and heretics. This author says nothing of the attempt to prevent Alvarado from remaining in the south. He says it was a hard task for Sepúlveda and his 'friend,' not only to curb their own wrath, but to calm the warlike leaders at S. Fernando, especially Rocha, who raved like a madman, declaring that in future he would take a barber with him in his campaigns to bleed him, since it was the only way ever to see blood in Californian wars. Jan. 23d, Cárlos Carrillo writes to Vallejo, expressing his joy at the triumph of 'our cause.' Vallejo, Doc., MS., iv. 14. On Jan. 31st the current news at S. Diego was that the northern leaders had surrendered! So writes Alcalde Estudillo to the comandante of fronteras, who had been ordered to send aid, but had not done so because he learned from 'unofficial sources' that it would be useless. S. Diego, Arch., MS., 165. May 26th, Comandante Martinez at S. Francisco has learned of the victory at S. Fernando over 270 men. Dept. St. Pap., MS., iv. 161–2. Mention of the S. Fernando campaign in Janssens, Vida, MS., 87–9; Avila, Notas, MS., 20; Botello, Anales, MS., 27; Nidever's Life, MS., 85–8.

to provide that their purport must not be divulged to the northerners, and no one of the latter must be permitted under the treaty that might be formed to enter Los Angeles.[31] Don Pio started for San Fernando with his twenty men, and met Rocha's army in full retreat. It was a good opportunity to make a show of his own valor by expressing disgust and rage at a state of things so disgraceful, but he gradually became calmer, and did not attempt to retake the mission with his brave but tardy Dieguinos.[32]

The ayuntamiento met again on the 22d, when the occupation of San Fernando must have been known, though it was not mentioned at the meeting, to listen to a report from the comisionados and a letter of thanks from Alvarado, who announced that on arrival in the city he would give a greater proof of his gratitude. But the Angelinos were in no mood for kindly greetings; and after due deliberation, they decided that their instructions as approved by Alvarado should be deemed in no sense to constitute a binding treaty, since no signatures of the comisionados were affixed to it, and because the latter had not in truth been free agents, having been forced, as it were, to show their instructions by the threatening attitude of the invader's troops. Therefore, all the arrangements were declared null and void. California was not a sovereign state, Alvarado was not its governor, and Los Angeles was again ready to defend the national integrity. Orders were accordingly issued to post guards and take other measures for active defence.[33]

[31] Los Angeles, Arch., MS., iv. 243-4, 246-7.
[32] Osio, Hist. Cal., MS., 348-9, who was of course in the rear guard of the retreating force, describes Pico's wrath. He tells us also that Cabello insulted Sepúlveda on account of his agency in making such a treaty. Firearms were drawn, but no blood spilt. Osio himself lost his temper and talked of cowards when Requena claimed that the instructions had been misunderstood. Pico himself, Hist. Cal., MS., 59-62, pretends to have gone on to S. Fernando, had a long interview with Alvarado, and obtained from him certain concessions which insured peace, and made it possible for the governor to enter Angeles.
[33] Session of Jan. 22d. Los Angeles, Arch., MS., iv. 248-52.

The result of all these reactionary and defensive measures was—and without any intermediate diplomacy, so far as the records show—that Alvarado entered the city without resistance, probably on the 23d, certainly within two or three days. He was accompanied by Graham's company and by the Monterey militia, leaving the Santa Bárbara volunteers at San Fernando. Castro, with thirty or forty men, arrived from Monterey on or about the same day.[34] Rocha's soldiers were at San Gabriel. The volunteers of the Angeles army had disbanded, but the twenty Dieguinos were still encamped in the city, and aided the northern troops in preserving order.

The ayuntamiento met once more on the 26th. The meeting was attended also by Alvarado, J. J. Pico, and Miguel Avila of Monterey, by Pio Pico, Ortega, Cabello, and Regidor Alvarado of San Diego, and by A. M. Osio of Los Angeles. No allusion was made to the resolutions adopted at the last session, but the object was to take into consideration the agreement made with Alvarado at San Fernando.[35] The governor addressed the meeting in defence of the new system, and proposed a plan in six articles on which he thought all might agree, thus avoiding future controversy. This plan was referred to a committee of three, Pio Pico, Cabello, and Osio, who reported it back with certain modifications, mainly intended, as it would seem, to obscure its exact meaning and provide for subsequent variations of interpretation.[36] The

[34] Jan. 9th, Alvarado orders Castro to come south with 20 men by sea. *Vallejo, Doc.*, MS., iv. 9. Jan. 14th, Castro to Vallejo. Will start in 3 days. *Id.*, iv. 11. Jan. 17th, C. says he will start at 4 P. M. with 50 men by land, as the *Clementine* is not ready. *Id.*, iv. 12. Alvarado, *Hist. Cal.*, MS., iii. 216, 226–30, says that to raise. funds Castro had to pledge his own property to Spence and Malarin. The debt was paid by Alvarado after 1841. The two officers lodged at the house of Abel Stearns. The city was carefully patrolled but no disturbance occurred.

[35] It is spoken of as the agreement made by the 2 alcaldes and the S. Diego comisionados with Alvarado, and would seem therefore to have been distinct from that of Jan. 20th; but there is no record to show its nature. It was perhaps the interview mentioned by Pico. See note 32.

[36] The plan was in substance as follows, the portions in parentheses being the committee's additions: 1. Alta California proclaims the federal system

gist of it was that a new diputacion should assemble at
Santa Bárbara on February 25th, to adopt or reject
what had been done at Monterey, always supporting
federalism, and insisting on a native ruler. It was
formally approved by all parties. Then followed
speeches of congratulation at the victory achieved over
difficulties that had threatened to set Californians at
enmity one with another. Pio Pico wished to be put
on record as saying that he would support a native
ruler to whatever section he might belong. Antonio
M. Osio declared that " sooner than submit to another
Mexican mandarin, he would retire to the forest and
be devoured by wild beasts;" while Alvarado, in a
closing speech, promised a faithful fulfilment of the
compact.[37]

of 1824 (since the new system of centralism has not been sworn by the dip.,
and the system now ruling in the nation is not known). 2. The dip., to be
chosen by electors according to Mexican law, will assemble and take into consideration what has been decreed in favor of the Monterey system. (The dip.
will meet and act in accordance with the laws in force.) 3. All that has
been done will remain in force until the dip. meets. 4. The present govt
will summon the electors or decree the election. (To meet at Sta. Bárbara
on Feb. 25th.) The two copies do not agree. 5. The decree dividing Cal.
into 2 cantons is null and void. 6. Until the federal system shall have been
restored, no ruler appointed by the Mexican govt shall be admitted. (As
soon as possible the sup. govt will be informed by competent authority that
order is restored, and asked to appoint an *hijo del pais* to govern Cal.) In the
discussions on art. 6, it was agreed on both sides that no Mexican ruler would
be likely to be admitted, but it was urged that Mexico should be allowed to
grant a native ruler in answer to a request, rather than be ordered to do so.

[37] Ayunt. session of Jan. 26th, in *Los Angeles, Arch.*, MS., iv. 254–62; *S.
Diego, Arch.*, MS., 156, 163–4; *Bandini, Doc.*, MS., 45. Osio, *Hist. Cal.*, MS.,
352–5, gives a different account, saying nothing of the plan adopted and of
course nothing about his own speech. He says that Alvarado on reaching
Angeles summoned the ayunt. to meet within an hour, caused himself to be
recognized as governor, and then thanked the members for their resolution of
the 22d, since it relieved him from all his agreements, made only because of
his inferior force, especially from his promise not to punish any one for past
acts—at which all turned pale! Alvarado, *Hist. Cal.*, MS., iii. 230–7, and Vallejo, *Hist. Cal.*, MS., iii. 249–59, narrate events at Angeles substantially in
accordance with the records. Botello, *Anales del Sur*, MS., 28–9, and Pico,
Acont., MS., 40–3, though both participants in these events, add nothing to
our knowledge of them.

Jan. 30th, Alvarado demanded and received what was left of the money
taken from S. Fernando, with which to support his men. *Los Angeles, Arch.*,
MS., iv. 267–9. J. J. Pico says he went with three men to get the money,
about $1,500. Osio says he delivered the money, $1,785, and that Alvarado
told him he was a fool not to have taken half the amount for his trouble!
Also on Jan. 30th Alvarado complained that several men were plotting mischief, and urged the ayunt. to adopt prompt measures. *Los Angeles, Arch.*,
MS., iv. 267. Vallejo says that 9 men, including Pio Pico, were arrested.

Having issued on the 1st of February a summons for the electors to meet on the 25th, Alvarado, in letters sent northward on the 2d and 3d, narrated briefly what had occurred at Angeles. Officially he stated that the modifications of the original plan, to which he had assented, were not essential, while it had been necessary to make concessions to conciliate public opinion in the south. In a private letter he explained that under the present plan he hoped to reach, though by a roundabout course, his original aim, by managing to secure a majority in the new diputacion. Otherwise it would have been necessary to maintain a military force permanently in the south, which would have been an intolerable burden to the treasury.[33] Leaving Castro with thirty men to garrison San Gabriel and preserve order,[30] Alvarado left San Fernando February 5th, and two days later arrived at Santa Bárbara, where he found the popular enthusiasm unabated, and where his first act was to send home the Monterey troops and Graham's riflemen.[40]

Thus far all had gone well with Alvarado in the south; but there followed during February and March

[33] *Alvarado, Carta en que relata los Sucesos de Los Angeles, 2 de Feb. 1837,* MS., the same letter being sent to different officials. Feb. 3d, Alvarado to Vallejo, private letter, in *Vallejo, Doc.,* MS., iii. 176. He says that Domingo Carrillo refused to take the oath, and was removed from the command at Sta Bárbara. Rocha may have to be removed also. At S. Diego under Salazar there is really no garrison.

[39] *Los Angeles, Arch.,* MS., iv. 273-4.

[40] Feb. 9, 1837, Alvarado to Vallejo, Estrada, and alcalde of S. José, in *Vallejo, Doc.,* MS., iv. 29; *Dept. St. Pap.,* MS., iv. 160-1; *Id., S. José,* v. 43. Nidever, *Life,* MS., 85-8, says the riflemen were paid off at Sta Bárbara. Alvarado tells us that he wished to retain Graham's men, but was advised by Castro that there was danger of not being able to pay them, and that it would be best to discharge them while no dissatisfaction existed. The foreigners were complimented in speeches and departed in good humor.

Some references to printed accounts of the troubles in the south, some of them extending over several years, and all very inaccurate and inextricably confused wherever they are more than a bare mention, are: *Mofras, Explor.,* i. 301-2; *Petit-Thouars, Voyage,* ii. 92-9; *Forbes' Hist. Cal.,* 150-1; *Wilkes' Narr.,* v. 175-9; *Robinson's Life in Cal.,* 173-7; *Gleeson's Hist. Cath. Church,* i. 144-9; *Ferry, Californie,* 20-1. Manuscript statements on the southern campaigns, adding nothing to what has been given, are: *Castro, Relacion,* MS., 41-4; *Marsh's Letter,* MS., 8; *Vallejo, Remin.,* MS., 123-5; *Lugo, Vida,* MS., 23-5; *Arce, Memoria,* MS., 12-13; *Robinson's Statement,* MS., 15, 26; *Galindo, Apuntes,* MS., 36-8.

a period of inaction which was unfavorable to his complete success, even if it did not develop any actual triumph for his opponents. Notwithstanding the concessions gained, and their pretended enthusiasm, many influential southerners still chose to regard themselves as vanquished or tricked foes, rather than conciliated friends of the plan as it stood. They withheld that hearty support which alone could have resulted in political harmony. Pio Pico's actions were mysterious, and he was suspected of exerting all his influence secretly against the government. Manuel Requena and other recalcitrant Angelinos were sent by Castro to the governor, expecting to be banished to Sonoma, but were released by Alvarado on signing an agreement not to meddle in politics.[41] Alvarado's letters to General Vallejo at this time show the anxiety which he felt, containing alternate expressions of confidence and discouragement. Early in March the report was circulated, with quieting effects, that Vallejo was intending to come south with a hundred men.[42]

[41] Feb. 11, 1837, Alvarado to Vallejo, in *Vallejo, Doc.*, MS., iv. 32. Requena's companions were Vicente Sanchez, Luis Arenas, Juan Gallardo, Antonio del Valle, J. M. Ramirez, Juan Salazar, Antonio Avila, and others. Rocha was in the number summoned, but ran away. Alvarado allowed him to return, but not to be comandante or administrator. Botello, *Anales*, MS., 69-70, says that Requena was sent into a kind of exile at Sta Inés, until in 1838 he retired to L. California. Janssens, *Vida*, MS., 89-92, describes the adventures of himself, Orozco, Rojas, and others, who fled from Los Angeles and also took refuge in the peninsula.

[42] Mar. 4th, ayunt., in answer to a request for quarters and supplies for Vallejo's men, refused to incur any expense; but resolves that there are plenty of supplies and probably buildings also to be had for money. *Los Angeles, Arch.*, MS., iv. 285-6. Feb. 27th, March 13th, 16th, announcement of Vallejo's coming at S. Diego. *Dept. St. Pap., Angeles*, MS., xi. 70-2; *S. Diego, Arch.*, MS., 173. March 6th, all quiet; but there may be trouble, as some don't wish Cal. to be a state. Governor's course approved by all good men. Robbers being strictly dealt with. Alvarado to Vallejo, in *Vallejo, Doc.*, MS., iv. 209. March 12th, Cárlos Carrillo says to Vallejo that the people of Los Angeles are very well disposed, even more addicted to the new system than the Barbareños. *Id.*, iv. 214. March 9th, the people well disposed. 'If freedom is not secured now, Californians will be slaves forever and forfeit the respect of men.' Civic force at Sta Bárbara, 150 men in good discipline. Arms bought of the *Bolivar*. Has gained favor by granting lands. The old folks are pleased with the title of 'governor,' as it reminds them of old times. The U. S. consul at Honolulu writes to Dana that 'there is nothing to fear from Mexico, which is not thinking of California. The present rulers of the state have more to fear from their own people, so many of them will want office. Chihuahua, Jalisco, and Zacatecas have pronounced against the central govt.' Alvarado

Besides disquieting rumors from the north, of which I shall speak later, there was an alarming report that a force of two hundred men—Sonorans, Indians, and Americans—under Lieut-colonel Juan José Tobar, were marching by the Rio Colorado on California, having failed in their revolutionary and mining schemes at Quitovaca. A brother of Captain Portilla, and other men who had left California were said to be engaged in this expedition. This was soon discovered to be a false alarm; but in consequence of it, Alvarado had made hasty preparations for defence; urged Vallejo to have his force ready to march at a moment's notice; gone in person to Los Angeles, apparently causing the re-arrest of some of the malecontents there; and had sent Castro and Capt. Villavicencio with a force to San Diego. Castro's orders were, in case the rumors should have any apparent foundation, to remove or spike all the guns, to leave not a single horse between San Diego and San Gabriel, and to distribute all supplies at the missions in such a manner as to prevent them falling into the hands of the enemy.[43] To what extent Castro found it necessary to carry out these measures in the south does not appear; neither is there anything in the local politics of San Diego at this time which demands notice, except that on March 18th the ayuntamiento, on receipt of certain communications from Alvarado, refused to recognize him as governor, or Vallejo as general.[44]

to Vallejo, in *Id.*, iv. 212. March 19th, the cause has yet many foes. Opinion in Angeles seems favorable; but no reliance can be placed on that town. 'It should be burned.' *Id.*, iv. 219.

[43] March 19, 1837, Alvarado to Vallejo. Official and private letter. *Vallejo, Doc.*, MS., iv. 215, 219. March 26th, Alvarado on coming to Angeles with 50 men found the rumor false. *Id.*, iv. 224. March 25th, the matter presented by Alvarado to the ayunt. *Los Angeles, Arch.*, MS., iv. 287-9.

[44] *S. Diego, Arch.*, MS., 172. The theory advanced was that Alvarado's authority as comandante of the northern forces had ended with the treaty of Jan. 26th. It is to be noted, however, that this *acta*, though in the secretary's handwriting, has no signatures. March 25th, Alvarado complains that his communications to the S. Diego ayunt. are not answered. That body should be mildly exhorted to rejoin the rest of the state. *Los Angeles, Arch.*, MS., iv. 289. Hayes, *Emig. Notes*, 480, states that the troops which went to Angeles in 1837 disbanded for want of pay, and never returned, the presidio going rapidly to decay. Alvarado, *Hist. Cal.*, MS., and Vallejo, *Hist.*

The election provided for in the plan of Los Angeles took place at Santa Bárbara either February 25th or at least before March 5th, on which date the deputies elected were summoned to meet, also at Santa Bárbara, March 25th.[45] The four new members elected seem to have been Pio Pico, Antonio M. Osio, Manuel Jimeno Casarin, and José R. Estrada, one of the last-named two being perhaps a suplente in place of José Castro.[46] The governor's summons, much to his disappointment, was not promptly obeyed, and the diputacion could not be organized in March. Pico and Osio refused to attend at all, a policy that may safely be termed disgraceful in view of their speeches in the Los Angeles meeting of January 26th. Six members assembled April 10th, however, at Santa Bárbara, Juan A. Alvarado, Guerra, Buelna, Jimeno, Estrada, and Francisco J. Alvarado of San Diego as a suplente for Pio Pico, with Victor Prudon as secretary.

On the first day of the session the governor presented a manifiesto on the condition and needs of the country. April 11th this document was submitted to a committee consisting of Jimeno, Buelna, and Estrada, all Monterey men it will be noted, who reported favorably on the views therein expressed, and submitted a series of eight propositions for the approval

Cal., MS., iii. 261-2, connect Castro's visit to S. Diego with a revolutionary movement at that place.

[45] There are no records of the election that I have been able to find. Feb. 19th, Francisco Sanchez at S. F. writes that he has been summoned to Sta B. as an elector. *Vallejo, Doc.*, MS., iv. 38. March 5th, the pres. and sec. of the electoral junta announced the result, which was communicated officially to Pio Pico on March 9th. Original summons in *Pico, Doc.*, MS., ii. 155. This doc. is also notable as bearing a seal of the 'Gobierno Supremo del Estado Libre y Soberano de la Alta California,' neatly and elaborately executed with a pen, the only sample existing, for it was never engraved.

[46] It will be remembered that there had been much mystery about the composition of the diputacion since May 1836, and it is not yet cleared up. It would seem that now the 4 who had acted in Nov. 1836 were regarded as holding over, Castro being prevented from acting by other duties, because Alvarado had said several times before the election that he had four votes secure when the new dip. should meet. March 25th, Alvarado informed the ayunt. of his inability to assemble the members elect, and his intention to summon the suplentes. *Los Angeles, Arch.*, MS., iv. 287-8.

of the meeting, propositions which confirmed in substance all that had been done by Alvarado's government, and empowered the diputacion under its new organization to continue as a constituent congress of the state.[47] The resolutions were unanimously approved, and thus a new plan was added to the long list. The diputacion acted the same day on certain land grants, but there are no definite records of any subsequent sessions. The result was communicated to the two southern ayuntamientos by Alvarado, who presented it as a faithful fulfilment of the agreement of January 26th, and hoped for a hearty support. He was bitter, however, in his complaints against Pico and Osio. He chided San Diego for its action of March 18th, and declared his purpose now to enforce the system adopted, being "weary of his own leniency," and disgusted at the conduct of those Californians who still "sighed for the tyrant's yoke." Los Angeles nevertheless on April 18th rejected the action of the congress, as not in accordance with the treaty, which, as the Angelinos chose to regard it, had simply provided that all should be put back in the old condition under a gefe político and territorial diputacion.

---

[47] *Plan de Gobierno adoptado por la Diputacion en Sta Bárbara, 11 de Abril, 1837*, MS.; mentioned in *Dept. St. Pap., Angeles*, MS., xi. 75. Art. 1. Cal. pronounces for the system that the majority of the nation has adopted (federalism of course is meant), and therefore the action of the dip. of Nov. 7, 1836, remains in force, except art. 3, which is included in the constitution of 1824. (The article on the catholic religion.) 2. The dip., including the deputies appointed by the ayunt. (?), is to continue as a congreso constituyente, to meet, after its adjournment at this place, as soon as convoked by the govt. 3. Decrees 8 and 9 of the congress (those on a division of the state and on foreign commerce) are repealed, not having served the purpose intended; and the Mex. laws on the points involved are restored. 4. The sup. govt will remain invested with the extraordinary powers conferred in order to consolidate the system in case of difficulty arising. 5. The national govt shall be petitioned, it being understood that Cal. is an integral part of the Mex. republic, to restore the federal system. 6. Mex. shall also be asked to allow, by means within her power, that Cal. may govern herself as a free and sovereign state. 7. Pending the supreme decision desired on these petitions, Cal. will remain under the form of govt expressed in the manifiesto and these propositions. 8. A certified copy of this acta shall be sent to the national govt.

April 13th, Alvarado issues the corresponding decree, repealing decrees 8 and 9 in accordance with art. 3. *Vallejo, Doc., Hist. Cal.*, MS., iv. 228, in MS., though ordered printed.

San Diego, on the other hand, expressed on April 27th cordial approval of the plan in general, though still preferring to remain non-committal, and postponing the act of swearing allegiance until some doubts could be cleared away respecting the system alluded to in article 1, fearing, perhaps, it might be centralism![48]

About the same time that Angeles repudiated the plan of April 11th, Pico and Osio made their tardy appearance at Santa Bárbara with a plan of their own, for which they sought approval from the congressmen, though it was really a rejection of all that had been done.[49] There was no action by the congress, but Alvarado simply sent the proposition to Castro to be presented to the ayuntamiento, to which body he also addressed a letter filled with indignation at the conduct of those " unworthy diputados who proposed a return to the tyrant's yoke and perpetual slavery— the very men who had so lately declared their purpose to be devoured by wild beasts rather than submit to a Mexican despot." The congress shared in his indignation, the governor said, and the ayuntamiento was expected to share it; yet if the latter body should per-

[48] April 16, 1837, Alvarado to ayunt. of Angeles and S. Diego. *Dept. St. Pap.*, MS., xi. 78–82; *Hayes' Doc.*, MS., 72. Apr. 22d, session of ayunt. *Los Angeles, Arch.*, MS., iv. 291–4. Apr. 27th, session of ayunt. *S. Diego, Arch.*, MS., 101. In the acta last alluded to, the signatures of the secretary and síndico of the S. Diego ayunt. did not appear, because those officers 'had been carried off by an armed force for some unknown cause.' This state of things had been announced on April 24th by Alcalde Estudillo, who asked that steps be taken for their restoration, addressing Alvarado as governor of the state, and announcing ' a decided enthusiasm in favor of *armor patrio*' on the part of the people. It appears that in consequence of the action of March 18th, Alvarado had sent Eugenio Montenegro to arrest the two officers, J. M. Teran and Domingo Amao, who escaped from custody while being taken to S. Gabriel. As late as September, Amao, who had fled to the frontera, had not returned to his post as secretary. *S. Diego, Arch.*, MS., 173, 175, 186.

[49] The plan of Pico and Osio was as follows: 1. The territory of Alta California reëstablishes the order of things existing before the pronunciamiento of Monterey. 2. The laws of Mexico shall be respected and obeyed, whatever may be the system she has adopted. 3. The treaty of Los Angeles between governor, ayunt., and comisionados shall be observed (?). 4. After the preceding articles shall have been carried out, the officers of the army shall be invited, by the person on whom the office of gefe político may legally devolve, to coöperate in restoring order. 5. The result of action on these propositions is to be communicated to the ayunt. *Los Angeles, Arch.*, MS., iv. 296–7.

sist in its folly, he would not use force, but would hold it responsible for results. "The fate of the Californians is in your hands, and it behooves you to reflect carefully on what you will do."[50]

At a meeting of the ayuntamiento, May 1st, the governor's letter and Osio's propositions were read, and a long discussion ensued. No one had anything to say in favor of the new propositions. Four members, Ibarra, Valdés, Herrera, and Alvarado, declared themselves in favor of the resolution of April 22d, involving, as they understood it, a full compliance with the convention of January 26th. The other four, Sepúlveda, Lugo, Pantoja, and Lopez, urged a recognition of the existing government, and full compliance with all its orders and decrees. Next day the discussion was resumed. Sepúlveda made an earnest appeal; Ibarra's party declared itself convinced, and a unanimous vote was secured in favor of the resolution that "the ayuntamiento of the city of Los Angeles recognizes the present system of government, and the orders and decrees emanating therefrom, without prejudice to the laws in force, decreed by the legislation of Mexico." José Castro was present at this meeting, and it is just possible that Alvarado's opponents regarded their votes as the best means for avoiding an involuntary sojourn at Sonoma.[51]

Alvarado now regarded the triumph of his cause as complete, and on May 10th issued a long and grandiloquent manifiesto of congratulation to the people of California. In this document he declared that, in accordance with his promise, he had been indefatigable and successful in making his countrymen free

---

[50] Alvarado to ayunt. of Los Angeles, April 28, 1837. *Dept. St. Pap.*, MS., xi. 75–8. The ayunt. on April 29th ratified its action of the 22d, though it was said there was danger of some members being carried north for their opposition to Alvarado. *Los Angeles, Arch.*, MS., iv. 295.

[51] Sessions of May 1st, 2d. *Los Angeles, Arch.*, MS., iv. 296–301. Alvarado writes also May 1st to clear up the doubts at S. Diego suggested in the action of April 27th, proving that the federal system was undoubtedly the one intended, and pleading, with much flattery, that though he had arrested their síndico and sec., their escape proved that they had not been very harshly treated. *S. Diego, Arch.*, MS., 176, with a seal in ink and pencil.

men; that despite the few backward steps he had
been obliged to take in order to 'economize blood,'
all had been regained by the action of the Santa Bárbara congress, as approved now throughout the south;
that there was now but one opinion in California, and
nothing to fear except from abroad—to meet which
latter danger the people were exhorted to stand firm
and united, worthy of their grand achievements and
destinies.[52] The governor now despatched a messenger
by land to Mexico to communicate to the government
the final action at Santa Bárbara, bearing also despatches in which Sonora was urged to join California
and make a stand for federalism.[53] Castro, perhaps
without Alvarado's orders, withdrew his force from
San Gabriel to Santa Bárbara. Flattery and some
more substantial rewards in the shape of office or
lands were distributed among southern friends of the
cause. For instance, Alcalde Sepúlveda was made a
captain of the civic militia. Thanks were publicly
rendered to Padre Duran, and the cattle of the presidial rancho of San Julian were distributed among
the soldiers, the rancho itself being given to José de
la Guerra.[54] Finally, Alvarado and Castro started for

[52] *Alvarado [Manifiesto del] Gobernador Interino del Estado Libre y Soberano de la Alta California, á sus habitantes. Monterrey, Mayo 10 de 1837. Imprenta del Supremo Gobierno á Cargo del C. Santiago Aguilar.* Folio, 2 leaves,
in *Earliest Printing; Estudillo, Doc.*, MS., i. 248; *Vallejo, Doc.*, MS., xxxii.
85; *Dept. St. Pap., Angeles*, MS., x. 19–20; and with French translation in
Petit-Thouars, Voyage, iv. 24–33. Despite the imprint, it was issued at Sta
Bárbara on May 10th, and printed at Monterey later. With all its vapid and
high-sounding Mexicanisms, the document contains also many eloquent expressions of patriotic good sense. A peculiar freak of the printer is to be
noted in the printing of the word *aristocrata* wrong side up—evidently not
an accident, since the same thing occurs in the proclamation of Nov. 6, 1836.
May 9th, Alvarado tells Vallejo that all troubles are at an end. The opponents from Angeles and S. Diego came to Sta Bárbara to promise solemnly
not to disturb the peace. *Vallejo, Doc.*, MS., iv. 237. May 10th, he thanks
and congratulates the ayunt. of Los Angeles. *Dept. St. Pap., Angeles*, MS.,
xi. 86.
[53] *Alvarado, Manifiesto.* He offers all California's resources to aid Sonora
in overthrowing the central system in the republic. Vallejo, *Hist. Cal.*, MS.,
iii. 209, thinks this was a somewhat rash offer under the circumstances.
[54] Jan. 4, 1837, order for distribution of the movable property. *Guerra,
Doc.*, MS., vi. 28. Vallejo, *Hist. Cal.*, MS., iii. 260–1, thinks the grant of
the rancho was an unwise and illegal act, being also an interference with his
own rights as general.

Monterey, where they arrived the 30th of May. Castro was called back in a hurry by the news of new troubles in the south, to be described later.[55]

Affairs in the north from January to May 1837 may be very briefly recorded. After Castro's departure on January 17th, Ramon Estrada was left in command at Monterey with about a dozen men. The capital was abandoned for the most part to women and foreigners, and the only excitement was in the receipt of news from Don Juan Bautista in the south. General Vallejo at Sonoma, besides watching over Indian tribes on the northern frontier, busied himself in enlisting and drilling recruits, with a view of restoring the presidial companies to something like their old strength, and of more thoroughly organizing the civic militia in preparation for possible emergency. Some success was achieved, especially at San José de Alvarado and San Juan de Castro, towns which, since the revolution of November, had been honored with additions to their original names. Some of the new recruits were sent to Sonoma to learn military discipline.[56] One other matter occupied the general's atten-

---

[55] June 1, 1837, Alvarado to Vallejo. *Vallejo, Doc. Hist. Cal.*, MS., iv. 242. Felipe García, in *Taylor's Discov. and Founders*, ii. no. 25, testifies that the people of Sta Bárbara used to express their sentiments respecting the 'big captains' of the north as follows:

Quien del país encendió el pasto—Castro.
Quien roba hasta hacer viejo—Vallejo.
Quien la aduana ha destrozado—Alvarado.
I para vivir sosegados
Deben de ser fusilados
Alvarado, Castro, y Vallejos.

[56] Jan. 6, 1837, Vallejo sends 50 cans of powder to Monterey. *Vallejo, Doc.*, MS., iv. 52. Jan. 7th, V. to com. of San Francisco, on recruiting young men for the presidial companies, in *Vallejo, Ordenes de la Comandancia Gen.*, a collection of printed orders of 1837-9, on paper of uniform size, bound in a volume, but not paged; one of the earliest books printed in California. Similar orders were sent to all comandantes. In his *Hist. Cal.*, MS., iii. 243-5, Vallejo says that about 60 young men came to Sonoma and were drilled by Lieut Sabas Fernandez, while Salvador Vallejo was sent to Ross for arms and clothing. Jan. 12th, V. to Alvarado. 3 companies of 80 men each organized at S. F. and Alvarado, and one of 30 at Sonoma. All enthusiastic in 'the cause.' *Vallejo, Doc.*, MS., iv. 55. Jan. 20th, same to same, on available forces under captains J. J. Vallejo at S. José, Francisco Sanchez at S. Francisco, and Salv. Vallejo at Sonoma. *Id.*, iv. 57. Jan. 24th, V. to alcalde of S. José, asking for 30 men, to recruit whom Alf. Prado Mesa is sent. *Vallejo, Ordenes.*

tion; namely, the conduct of Becher, supercargo of the Mexican vessels *Catalina* and *Leonor*, which was thought to be sufficiently suspicious to justify a seizure of his property and credits at San Francisco, to the amount of $11,000. It was believed that the government might justly use this property for its defence, should it prove that Becher had promoted hostile acts.[57]

At the end of January Vallejo put his brother Salvador in command at Sonoma, and early in February marched with fifty men to Monterey.[58] His avowed purpose was to watch the progress of affairs in the south, and to protect the government from certain persons whose conduct had given rise to suspicions of active infidelity, especially at San Juan. It was during this visit that he wrote to Alvarado to have quarters prepared for one hundred men whom he had ready to send down by sea. I do not suppose he had any real intention of going to the south, but it was thought the statement, supported by the known departure from Sonoma, would help Alvarado.[59] The nature of the plots at San Juan is not very clearly revealed; but before Vallejo's arrival a number of convicts had been disarmed by William R. Garner, Quintin Ortega, and Mariano Castro; and arms had also been seized at various ranchos. Vallejo caused the

[57] Jan. 12th, 20th, V. to Alvarado, in *Vallejo, Doc.*, MS., iv. 56-7. March 17th, A. to V. Fears much from Becher's hostility, since he has discovered our plans to buy two vessels with which to operate against the centralists. He pretends to clear for Callao, but it is feared he will touch at a Mexican port with bad reports. Castro will watch him at S. Diego. *Id.*, iv. 216. Oct. 27th, Richardson, Becher's agent, has received order to cancel attachment of $5,000. *Id.*, iv. 341.

[58] Jan. 30th, instr. to Capt. Salvador Vallejo. Should any Mex. force appear, he was to assure the foe that the northern Californians would maintain their rights if they had to destroy all the property they possessed. *Vallejo, Doc.*, MS., iv. 17. On Jan. 24th, the general had announced his purpose to go to Monterey. *Id.*, iv. 59.

[59] Feb. 21st, V. to A., in *Vallejo, Doc.*, MS., iv. 66; *S. Diego, Arch.*, MS., 170. Feb. 20th, the gen. had addressed the gov. on the importance of reorganizing the presidial companies. *Vallejo, Ordenes.* Glad to hear of success, but warns A. to beware of Los Angeles. *Vallejo, Doc.*, MS., iv. 65. Feb. 25th, urges the necessity of looking out for the northern towns as of much greater importance than those of the south. *Id.*, iv. 75.

arrest of Rafael Gonzalez, Francisco Pacheco, and Juan Quintero, the first of whom and eight convicts were sent to Sonoma.[60] At Monterey there were found some symptoms of approaching trouble, fomented by Angel Ramirez, Captain Figueroa, and other Mexicans, who circulated rumors of intended persecution and exile of their countrymen. A proclamation of the general seems to have quieted the popular excitement. "We do not confound the vices of governments with those of individuals," writes Vallejo. "We repel the aggressions of the one and punish the faults of the others. Virtue, honesty, and good behavior will be respected in all. Live in peace and union, and I will protect your lives and property."[61]

The general was back at Sonoma by the middle of March; but late in that month was roused to renewed activity by the report of an impending attack from Sonora. He issued orders for all troops to concentrate at Monterey; while with fifty men he hastened to Santa Clara. The report, as we have seen, proved without foundation.[62] Another affair which created some local excitement was the arrest of Lieutenant Antonio M. Pico, who had been sent by the governor to negotiate a loan at Ross, but who on the way was accused of attempting to incite revolt among the

[60] Feb. 14th, Garner to com. of Monterey. *Vallejo, Doc.*, MS., xxxii. 72. Feb. 16th, Vallejo to D. A. Rodriguez. *Id.*, iv. 64. Feb. 21st, same to Alvarado. *Id.*, iv. 66. Feb. 27th, Mota, one of the prisoners, offered to reveal the names of the leaders if set free. *Id.*, iv. 86.

[61] *Vallejo, Proclama del Comandante Gen., 24 de Feb. 1837.* Original print, 1 leaf, in *Earliest Printing; Vallejo, Doc.*, MS., iv. 40; xxxii. 75; and with French translation, in *Petit-Thouars, Voyage*, iv. 22-3. In his *Hist. Cal.*, MS., iii. 262-8, Vallejo claims, however, to have arrested Angel Ramirez, who tried to bribe his Indians to seize the general. He was released after 2 days. March 6th, Alvarado thanks the gen. for his activity. *Vallejo, Doc.*, MS., iv. 208. March 9th, A. says his govt owes only $5,000, of which half will be paid from the *Bolivar's* duties. *Id.*, iv. 212. March 14th, Santiago Estrada put in command of Monterey. *Id.*, iv. 81. March 18th, no person unless well known to enter S. Francisco without a passport from the gov. *Id.*, iv. 84.

[62] March 27, 1837, orders to different officers, Capts J. J. Vallejo, Francisco Sanchez, Salvio Pacheco, and J. M. Alviso. 'Good Californians must rush to the defence of their country, threatened with invasion.' Also letter to Alvarado. *Vallejo, Doc.*, MS., iv. 85-9. April 4th, 26th, false alarm, forces may retire. *Id.*, iv. 92-3, 234.

militia at San José and San Francisco, perhaps at the
instigation of the southern Picos. He was sent to
Sonoma, much to the displeasure of the alcalde of San
José, who deemed his authority interfered with.[63]   Finally, Alvarado arrived from the south at the capital
on October 30th, but was obliged to announce, in the
same letter that made known his arrival, the occurrence of new troubles at Los Angeles which had
caused Castro with sixty men to be sent back in haste,
and which necessitated an interview with the general
at the earliest moment.

[63] *Vallejo, Doc.*, MS., iv. 95, 221, 231; *Alvarado, Hist. Cal.*, MS., iv. 46–
7. A. says he escaped by breaking his parole. The arrest was on April 21st
or 22d. April 24th, Vallejo writes to deny some rumors that he is hostile to
the present govt. May 16th, complains that his letters are not answered. *Vallejo, Doc.*, MS., iv. 233, 98. A., writing from S. Antonio on his way north,
wrote very bitterly of the disgraceful acts of the citizens of San José, who
were said to have threatened to overthrow him because he was a relative of
Vallejo. 'Perhaps they don't know that I have just conquered hundreds of
brave citizens who opposed me.' He speaks also vaguely of some prisoners
coming by sea from the south, whom it would be necessary to shoot at Monterey. *Id.*, iv. 235.

CHAPTER XVIII.

SAN DIEGO PLAN—ALVARADO AND CARRILLO.

1837.

BANDINI'S MOVEMENTS—PLOTS ON THE FRONTIER—ZAMORANO, PORTILLA, AND ESTRADA—PLAN OF MAY—SEIZURE OF LOS ANGELES—DON JUAN AT SAN DIEGO—THE ARMY AT ANGELES AND SAN FERNANDO—CASTILLE-RO'S COMMISSION—OATH OF CENTRALISM IN THE SOUTH—ALVARADO AT MONTEREY AND SANTA CLARA—RUMORS FROM MEXICO—RAMIREZ RE-VOLT—MONTEREY TAKEN AND RETAKEN—ALVARADO RETURNS TO THE SOUTH—TREATY WITH CASTILLERO—ALVARADO SWEARS TO THE CON-STITUTIONAL LAWS—HIS MOTIVES—DIPUTACION AT SANTA BÁRBARA—CASTILLERO SENT TO MEXICO—THE 'CALIFORNIA'—VALLEJO REFUSES TO ACCEPT CENTRALISM—CÁRLOS CARRILLO'S APPOINTMENT—ALVARADO'S POSITION—CARRILLO ASSUMES OFFICE AT ANGELES—SAN DIEGO OBEDI-ENT—NOT SO STA BÁRBARA—LETTERS OF VALLEJO AND ALVARADO.

JUAN BANDINI had followed the advice of Osio to "go home and keep quiet," so far at least that the records are silent about him from December 1836 to May 1837. During this period he lived on his fron-tier rancho, and spent all the time which troublesome Indians left at his disposal in plotting against Alva-rado's government, or rather in devising schemes by virtue of which, when Mexican supremacy should be fully restored, his own agency in bringing about that result might be so apparent as to obtain proper recog-nition and reward. He had an understanding with Captain Portilla and other prominent men at San Diego; while across the line, in full sympathy with Don Juan, was Captain Zamorano, who after his vol-untary exile at the fall of Gutierrez, had found his way back to La Frontera. Zamorano, like Bandini

and Portilla, was very quiet and careful in his movements; but Captain Nicanor Estrada, who had been
exiled with Gutierrez but had also returned from Cape
San Lúcas, was more active in enlisting men, preparing arms, and arousing enthusiasm for the cause, being
assisted by a party of refugees from the north, who
had fled from Los Angeles at Alvarado's approach in
January. Not much is known in detail of the preparations; but fifty or seventy-five men were enlisted,
including, I suppose, remnants of the old compañía de
fronteras, and were armed as well as circumstances
would permit. Indian hostilities, to be mentioned
later, interfered somewhat with the progress of these
patriotic efforts.[1] Osio and Pico were secret supporters
of this movement, and their plan already noticed was
doubtless a part of it, those gentlemen having changed
their mind about the policy of being "devoured by
wild beasts" rather than obey a Mexican mandarin.
Strangely, in their narratives they say little or nothing of events in these months, though the former has
described so minutely the preceding occurrences.

It will be remembered that late in April, San Diego
had approved the new system as expressed in the
Santa Bárbara plan of April 11th, though postponing
on a frivolous pretext the formal swearing of allegiance.
If the ayuntamiento took any action later on receipt
of Alvarado's explanation, it is not recorded. On

---

[1] These preparations are briefly related, and subsequent events more fully,
in *Bandini, Hist. Cal.*, MS., 86–97. The author regards the treaty of Jan.
26th at Los Angeles as merely a trick of Alvarado to disarm the south, and
the action of the dip. at Sta Bárbara on April 11th as a flagrant violation of
that treaty. The subsequent 'persecution' of S. Diego by Alvarado in sending Castro to take away the cannon, and in arresting members of the ayunt.,
rendered the Dieguinos desperate. They went to the frontier, and in a few
days raised 70 men, but had to suspend operations for a time to fight Indians.
The same version in much more grandiloquent language is given in *Bandini,
Sucesos del Sur, Mayo y Agosto*, 1837, MS., a report to the minister of hacienda, dated Aug. 4th, in which, of course after a new tirade against Angel
Ramirez, Don Juan tells how 'S. Diego never faltered in her heroic devotion
to Mexico,' and how, 'resolved to sacrifice our existence in favor of the national government, we planned for victory or an honorable death.' He does
not name Zamorano. *Janssens, Vida*, MS., 90–121, was one of the refugees
from Angeles, and, if we may credit his story, which there is no one to con-
tradict, took a very prominent part in all this campaign.

May 21st, Bandini and his associates, with a part of
their armed force, came to San Diego and openly proclaimed their purposes. Zamorano, styling himself
comandante general and governor ad interim, addressed
the ayuntamiento, enclosing the plan which the soldiers and citizens had already approved, and asked that
body to coöperate for the 'national decorum,' which
of course it did at once. Bandini and S. E. Argüello
were named as comisionados to present the plan at
Angeles, carrying also a letter from Zamorano, similar
to that already mentioned.[2] The plan of this pro-
nouncement contained, as a matter of course, since
Bandini was concerned in its production, more words
and more articles than any that had preceded it. I
append some particulars in a note;[3] but the general

[2] May 21, 1837, Zamorano to ayunt. *S. Diego, Arch.*, MS., 178; *Dept. St.
Pap., Angeles*, MS., xi. 83-5. There is no formal record of the session at S.
Diego. Janssens says that he and J. M. Alvarado were also members of the
commission. Zamorano must have assumed the command by consent of Portilla, who was his senior.

[3] *Plan de San Diego que proclamaron Zamorano, Bandini, y otros en 21 de
Mayo 1837*, MS. Art. 1. Alta California is restored to order and obedience
to the sup. govt under the system adopted by decree of Oct. 23, 1835. 2. The
civil and military command is to be vested in the officer of senior rank as per
superior order of Jan. 21, 1835. 3. The dip. having taken an active part in
the revolution of the north, its authority is ignored until the campaign be
over, order restored, and new elections held. 4. All acts of the dip. since
Nov. 7, 1836, declared null and void. Such of its resolutions as have proved
beneficial may be sanctioned by the new dip. later. 5. The person alluded
to in art. 2 will take the oath before the ayunt. of Los Angeles, capital of
the territory. 6. Volunteer forces supporting the sup. govt are to be disbanded by the comandante when peace is restored. 7. The gefe will recommend to the sup. govt as highly meritorious the services of soldiers and volunteers who may aid in re-organizing the territory. 8. The leaders of the rebels of Nov. 7th, and officers commissioned by the sup. govt, who may present
themselves, acknowledging their error, and asking clemency, will be favorably
recommended to the sup. govt, to which authority those not doing so will be
given up for judgment. 9. Troops from sergeant down, on presenting themselves, will be re-admitted to the service, the act being credited to them as a
merit. 10. All the forces organized as civic militia by the northern rebels
are hereby dissolved. 11. Persons of the latter class, on presenting themselves, may retire to their homes, or serve as volunteers for the sup. govt.
12. Loans made in favor of the just cause will be reimbursed from the public treasury. 13. The new dip. is to make a respectful representation through
the gefe político to the sup. govt of the strong desire of the people of Cal. for
a separation of the civil and military commands. 14. Until the new dip. is
installed, there is to be a junta of 5 members appointed by the gefe as coun-
sellors in cases of difficulty. 15. This junta will be presided over by one of
its members, the pres. being changed each month. 16. The junta's duties:
to resolve doubts of the gefe; to have charge of the public funds; and to
appoint a treasurer. 17. The treasurer to be paid a salary fixed by the gefe.

purport, as in the plan of Osio and Pico, was to undo
all that had been done since November 5th of the past
year, to recognize the full authority of Mexico under
any system, to rule the country under southern and
'loyal' auspices until the national authority should be
fully restored, and to treat the rank and file of those
who had favored the Monterey rebellion as 'erring
brethren' worthy of pity and forgiveness. The comisionados on arrival at Los Angeles seem to have
acted secretly for a day or two, making known their
mission only to a few trusted partisans like Ibarra,
Requena, and Botello. It will be remembered that
half the ayuntamiento had ratified the Santa Bárbara
plan more from fear of arrest and exile to Sonoma
than from any other motive, and the fear was still entertained.[4] It was therefore deemed necessary to secure
the garrison and guns before appealing to the people.

It was probably on the evening of May 26th that
the seizure was effected by Bandini and his associates
without resistance, and by an understanding with the
comandante of the guard. The sentinel was surprised
and disarmed. A few soldiers of the civic militia
were disturbed in a game of cards to surrender the
post and arms, including the gun brought by Castro
from San Diego, while Captain Sepúlveda at his own
house was brought to terms without any suspension
of harmonious relations by his guest Pio Pico.[5] Next

18. All insults, etc., to the pronunciados of Nov. 7th are to be severely punished.   19. A copy of this plan to be sent to other ayunt. for adoption.   20.
This plan to be sent immediately by extra mail to the Mexican government.

[4] Janssens narrates at some length that, on account of this fear of arrest,
the comisionados arrested Capt. Andrés Pico at S. Luis Rey on the way north,
and compelled him to make the most solemn pledges to keep quiet and not interfere.

[5] Bandini says he executed this movement with 8 companions at 7 P. M.,
not giving the date. Janssens implies that it was done on the night of arrival
by the 4 comisionados, including himself, aided by 4 others, including Ibarra
and the Frenchman Baric. He gives many details, makes Bandini a great
strategist and hero, and implies that the inhabitants were made to believe for
a day that Bandini had a strong garrison in possession, with a large military
force approaching. Janssens was sent in a day or two to enlist Charlefoux
and his 25 riflemen in the cause, which he did successfully. Botello, *Anales*,
MS., 37-40, who was at the time sec. of the ayunt., thinks there had been
some discussion in that body before the capture, which was effected by 12 or

day the ayuntamiento met to listen to Bandini's eloquence and take his plan into consideration. Alcalde
Sepúlveda took part in the debate and mildly opposed
the San Diego plan, but the majority approved it;
and while no formal vote of approval appears on the
records, it was decided that the document should be
published next day, together with a second address
read by Bandini. Another session was held on the
30th to devise means to prevent conflict and bloodshed, and to this end three comisionados were appointed to treat with Alvarado.[6]

Bandini remained at Los Angeles only a few days,
"maintaining his position with great difficulty, but resolved to die rather than yield." Then in consequence
of alarming reports of Indian hostilities, the ayuntamiento in a secret session of May 31st voted at Bandini's request to suspend all politico-military movements and negotiations, in order to send a force to
the southern frontier in obedience to the call of the
'governor and general,' Zamorano. Botello, a prominent southerner who accompanied the force, says that
the movement was hastened by reports of Castro's
approach from the north, but this may be an error.
Bandini and his men carried with them the captured
guns and entered San Diego in triumph. It was a
proud day in the life of Don Juan when the Dieguinos came out in procession to welcome with shouts
the return of their conquering hero. Indian troubles

15 men, including himself, Capt. Santiago Johnson, Pablo and Emilio Véjar,
acting in collusion with Alf. Palomares, who commanded the guard. The
sentinel was a boy named Lara. There were later rumors of a plot by Sepúlveda to recapture the guns and barracks.

[6] May 27th, 30th, session of ayunt., in *Los Angeles, Arch.*, MS., iv. 302–14.
Of Don Juan's address I have only a fragment of the original blotter. *Bandini,
Discurso ante el ayunt. de Angeles el 27 de Mayo, 1837*, MS., in which I find
nothing worthy of notice, his views being already well known to the reader.
The comisionados named were Antonio M. Lugo, Andrés Pico, and Anastasio
Carrillo. The instructions given for their guidance—*Instrucciones á que debe
sujetarse la comision nombrada por este ayuntamiento de Los Angeles, 30 de Mayo,
1837*, MS.—required them in 10 articles to submit the plan to Alvarado,
and if it were rejected all hostilities must be suspended and all armed bodies
must remain where they were until an arrangement could be effected to last
until the Mexican troops should come, when the chief of the latter would
act according to his orders.

were of short duration. The enthusiasm was great, and volunteers freely offered their services. Charle-foux and his New Mexican hunters had been induced by Janssens to join the force, and in a few days the 'army of the supreme government,' perhaps one hundred and twenty-five strong, was ready for an advance,[7] and began its march northward the 10th of June.

Captain Portilla was in active command of the expedition, though the self-styled governor and general, Zamorano, with Nicanor Estrada, Bandini, and Argüello, seems to have accompanied the force. They entered Los Angeles June 16th, in time, as Bandini says, to witness "the shameful dispersion of Castro's force," and the flight of the leader in such haste as to leave behind some of his wearing apparel. Janssens goes still further, and states that the advance guard of the foe was met at the Santa Ana rancho, but threw down their arms and fled in disorder on seeing the southerners prepare for a charge, not stopping until they reached San Fernando.[8] Castro was certainly at Los Angeles on the 12th, when his presence, and the absence of the opposition members at an extra session, enabled the versatile ayuntamiento to turn another political somersault, "rectifying their vote in defense of the state government, and ignoring the acts of Ibarra and his followers, which had disturbed the public order."[9] He doubtless

[7] May 31st, ayunt. sess. at Angeles, and vote to send a force south. *Los Angeles, Arch.*, iv. 316–18. Bandini says the reports of Castro's coming did not arrive until he left Angeles; and this is confirmed by Janssens, who claims to have been left behind at Los Angeles as a spy, staying at the house of Ignacio Coronel. On the first news of Castro's approach he was sent south by Pio Pico in great haste to warn the S. Diego leaders. May 30th Zamorano writes to alcalde of S. Diego about the Indian wars. *S. Diego, Arch.*, MS., 177.

[8] Bandini says Castro had 80 or 90 men at Angeles, while the others numbered 90. Janssens calls the southern force 125, and Botello, 250. The latter speaks of Rocha coming to meet them at Paso de Bartolo with a few men, at first supposed to be foes. This was perhaps the foundation of Janssens's story. Botello tells us also that a few of Castro's stragglers were captured.

[9] June 12th. *Los Angeles, Arch.*, MS., iv. 315.

retired to San Fernando, and later to Santa Bárbara, but as to the manner of his departure it is best not to attach much importance to the unsupported statements of his enemies.

Meanwhile, Captain Andrés Castillero arrived at San Diego, bringing the constitutional laws of December 29, 1836, which replaced the federal constitution of 1824; and the oath of allegiance to the new system was taken with great enthusiasm by the assembled ayuntamiento and *vecindario* on June 12th. After the ceremony Castillero hastened away, and joined the army at San Luis Rey the same night, when he represented himself as a comisionado of the supreme government.[10] Having arrived with the army at Los Angeles, he proceeded by virtue of his commission to summon the ayuntamiento, which body, together with all officials, soldiers, and citizens, took the oath of allegiance to the constitutional laws on June 18th, with all due religious rites and social festivities.[11] On or about the 21st, Portilla's forces moved forward and occupied San Fernando, whence Castro had retired to Santa Bárbara.[12]

[10] June 12th, session of ayunt. *S. Diego, Arch.*, MS., 179. It is noticeable that Castillero's name is not mentioned, and Alcalde Estudillo speaks of the laws as having been received *extrajudicialmente*. It was only after some discussion that it was deemed proper to take the oath. This circumstance, not mentioned by Bandini and Botello, gives some plausibility to the charges of those writers that Castillero's commission was a mere pretence invented to serve his own ends between S. Diego and S. Luis. Bandini goes so far as to intimate that Castillero's instructions, which he saw, were a forgery, suspected by him to be such at the time. It is not very probable that Castillero would have gone so far in his deception as to forge papers, though under the circumstances he is likely enough to have resorted to much verbal deception and exaggeration. Alvarado, in a letter of Sept. 1st, stated that Castillero was not, as he claimed to be, a comisionado. *Vallejo, Doc.*, MS., iv. 306. The captain, it will be remembered, was one of the officers who surrendered at Monterey in Nov. 1836. Of his subsequent movements until he appeared at S. Diego in June 1837 nothing is known. He may have gone to Mexico with Gutierrez, and have been sent back as a commissioner, or he may have resumed his command as captain of the compañía de fronteras, his special commission to have the central system sworn to being sent to him from Mexico.

[11] *Los Angeles, Arch.*, MS., i. 138-9; iv. 319-21; *Id., Ayunt. Rec.*, 5. The *acta* was communicated to the min. of war.

[12] Bandini speaks of dissatisfaction with Portilla's acts, in consequence of which the command was offered to himself, but declined. Why Zamorano did not command is not very clear, but I think it possible that he did not

Alvarado on arriving at Monterey May 30th had immediately heard of the new troubles in the south, including Bandini's seizure of the Angeles garrison, and had despatched Castro back in haste with sixty men. This he announced to Vallejo in a letter of June 1st, and a few days later he sent more details about the plan of San Diego and the defensive preparations at Santa Bárbara, where three guns had been mounted at the Rincon Pass, and whither Castro was already hastening with aid. Still more alarming news, however—for Alvarado had no doubt of his ability to control the south—was that contained in the newspapers, to the effect that Mexico was organizing a force to be sent to California, a report that doubtless accounted for the actions of Bandini and his associates.[13] An interview between the governor and general was held at Santa Clara about the middle of

leave S. Diego at all. June 20th, ayunt. receives request from Portilla for arms, supplies, etc., to continue his march and enforce the new constitution. An appeal was accordingly made to the people. *Los Angeles, Arch.*, MS., iv. 322. Same date. Portilla addressed as com. gen. *Dept. St. Pap., Angeles*, MS., ii. 102. June 30th, Portilla at S. Fernando as comandante militar interino, asks Ignacio Coronel to take command at S. Gabriel, raise volunteers, and get supplies from the mission. *Coronel, Doc.*, MS., 187; *Dept. St. Pap., Angeles*, MS., ii. 103. Same date, Portilla complains that some of his men are returning home without leave. *Id.*, ii. 105–6.

[13] June 1st, Alvarado to Vallejo. *Vallejo, Doc.*, MS., iv. 242. June 6th, same to same, from Sta Clara, in *Id.*, iv. 243, says that Castro's men have very few arms; he must be aided; Salvador Vallejo wishes to go south with a company, and Villa will command another; the general urged to make haste. June 7th, V.'s reply, in *Id.*, iv. 102. Wishes Salvador to return, that he may come down, for the northern frontier must not be left unprotected. Prompt steps must be taken; Angeles could not have been taken without collusion; other towns will perhaps turn against their benefactors if there is any hope of aid from Mexico, but the coming of such a force is very doubtful. June 8th, V. orders Alf. Prado Mesa to put his men at Sta Clara at the governor's disposal, and Capt. Sanchez at S. F. to hold himself and force in readiness for action. *Id.*, iv. 246-7. June 12th, Alvarado, at Sta Clara, to Castro, in answer to letters of 5th and 8th. Is indignant at the falsehood of S. Diego and the cowardice of those who yielded at Angeles. Agrees with C. that vigorous measures are called for; the Californians must be made free whether they wish it or not. Capt. Sepúlveda must be court-martialled. All enemies of the system may be arrested and sent north, if it seems best. Arms and ammunition will soon arrive from Honolulu by the *Clementine*. Will come to Sta B. himself as soon as he can see Vallejo, who should come to-morrow. *Id.*, xxxii. 89. Vallejo, *Hist. Cal.*, MS., iii. 282–5, describes the interview at Sta Clara as having been on June 13th–18th; and says that he promised the gov. his hearty support, though he objected to some of his acts in the south, and deemed the north as the part of the country needing most attention.

June, and immediately after, the former sailed from Monterey for Santa Bárbara, where he arrived in time to send back on June 21st the news of what had occurred at Los Angeles, now in the power of the southern forces. Vallejo was, as usual on receipt of an appeal for aid, busied with some important expeditions against the Indians, but on the 25th he issued orders to different subordinates to mass their troops at Monterey in expectation of active service.[14]

Before returning to the south, it is as well to record an important political event which occurred early in July at Monterey, namely, a counter-revolt against Alvarado's authority by the very Mexicans who had aided to put him in power. Angel Ramirez and Cosme Peña were the leaders. They had expected to control the governor's policy in their own interests, and had failed. Ramirez had lost his position in the custom-house before the end of 1836. Peña had gone south with Alvarado as secretary, but had soon returned, being succeeded by Victor Prudon. We have seen that there had been some ill feeling on the part of the Californians toward the Mexican residents, fomented perhaps to some extent by foreigners, and that Vallejo had been obliged to make some arrests earlier in the year, issuing a proclamation which had promised protection and temporarily allayed discontent. Ramirez, however, continued his plottings; and the present time, in view of the news from the south and from Mexcio, was regarded as a favorable opportunity for active operations. Vallejo's orders to mass troops at the capital had not apparently been promptly obeyed, else the revolt would hardly have been practicable.

The active leaders at Monterey were Captain Francisco Figueroa, Juan N. Ayala, and Sergeant Santia-

[14] June 25th, V. to A., com. of Monterey, Capt. Sanchez, Alcalde Alvirez, and Capt. J. J. Vallejo, in *Vallejo, Doc.*, MS., iv. 251, 254-6; xxxii. 91; *Vallejo, Hist. Cal.*, MS., iii. 289-91. San José was evidently suspected of disaffection, and was to be watched.

go Aguilar, director of the printing-office. Ramirez
and Surgeon Alva were absent from the town, exerting their influence among the rancheros, and at San
José and San Juan. Cosme Peña was in town, but
worked secretly, afterwards pretending that he had
been forced into a passive compliance in the plot.
Captain Villavicencio had just started with most of
his men to join Castro in the south, and Jesus Pico,
left in command, was absent from his post, when at 5
P. M. on July 1st, the Mexicans, perhaps thirty or
forty in number, under Figueroa, seized the fort and
arms without resistance, holding possession until the
3d.[15] Villavicencio was hastily recalled; Pico raised
a few men in the interior; Graham volunteered with
a part of his riflemen; the Mexican garrison was in
its turn besieged, and a message was despatched to
Vallejo.[16] Figueroa's men, frightened by the warlike
preparations, and disappointed in not getting reënforcements from the country, offered to surrender if
Vallejo would come to protect them, claiming that their
revolt had been solely with a view to protect their
lives, which had been threatened by Pico and others.
Vallejo replied favorably, knowing that there was
really much bitter feeling against the Mexicans, and
promised protection to all, with punishment to but
few, if their statement should prove true; but before
this reply arrived, Figueroa surrendered, all his men

[15]Florencio Serrano, *Apuntes*, MS., 41–50, is the only participator in this
movement on the Mexican side who has told the story, and he fails to throw
much light on it. He says they found at the fort 4 or 5 men playing cards,
but at the presidio nobody at all, Pico having run away at the first alarm.
There were 50 Mexicans in all, and Alva returning from the country reported
a failure to get reënforcements. Spence, Estrada, and Munras had frequent
interviews with Figueroa and Peña. Mrs Ávila, *Cosas de Cal.*, MS., 14–16,
states that during the Mexican occupation, the Indian servants, at the instigation of the Mexicans, plundered the houses of their masters.

[16]July 3d, Villavicencio to Vallejo, in *Vallejo, Doc.*, MS., iv. 266, announcing both the capture and recapture; but there had been a previous despatch, for on the same day, July 3d, V. announced from Sonoma his own
departure for Mont., and later in the day he wrote from Petaluma on his way.
July 3d, V. to com. of S. Francisco and alcalde of Monterey. *Id.*, iv. 264–5.
V. was at S. Rafael on July 6th, when he heard that Mont. had been retaken.
Id., iv. 272.

were made prisoners, and the leaders were put in irons.[17]

Vallejo came down to Santa Clara, and caused the arrest of several men in that region, including Angel Ramirez. All except the leaders were released within a few days. Those leaders were at first delivered to Captain J. J. Vallejo for safe keeping at his rancho;[18] but were soon sent to Sonoma, both Vallejo and Alvarado agreeing that they must be very strictly guarded until all political troubles should be at an end.[19] Those sent to Sonoma, and held in captivity there as late as the end of August, were Ramirez, Alva, Figueroa, Peña, Ayala, Aguilar, Manuel Crespo, and José María Maldonado. I have no definite information about

[17] It would seem from V.'s letter from Petaluma, that the Mexicans had made their offer to surrender on July 1st, the same day they took the fort. In telling the story of the recapture, Serrano claims to have prevented a disaster by seizing Ayala's hand as he was about to apply the match to a loaded cannon. Osio, *Hist. Cal.*, MS., 316–17, 376–80, tells us that the lighted match was dashed from the man's fingers by a bullet from the rifle of one of Graham's men! Other Californian writers who speak more or less fully of this Monterey revolt are: *Torre, Remin.*, MS., 75–9; *Arce, Memorias*, MS., 11; *Pico, Acont.*, MS., 44–5; *Pinto, Apunt.*, MS., 27–9; *Botello, Anales*, MS., 24–5; *Alvarado, Hist. Cal.*, MS., iii. 174–5, 240–1; *Vallejo, Hist. Cal.*, MS., iii. 292–6; *Fernandez, Cosas de Cal.*, MS., 101; *Ord, Ocurrencias*, MS., 100–1; *Coronel, Cosas de Cal.*, MS., 22; *Galindo, Apuntes*, MS., 38-9; *García, Hechos*, MS., 68–70. Vallejo regards A. M. Pico's attempts, already noticed, as a part of this same plot. Harry J. Bee, *Recollections*, MS., 6–21, and in *S. José Pioneer*, Jan. 13, 1877, gives a narrative from memory of this affair, so absurdly inaccurate that it merits no further attention.

[18] July 4th, com. of Monterey to Capt. V. The prisoners may either be kept at the rancho or sent to Sonoma. *Vallejo, Doc.*, MS., iv. 268. Gonzalez, *Revoluciones*, MS., 10–11, says the prisoners were given up to him as alcalde on his demand.

[19] July 8th, Vallejo to Villavicencio. The Monterey prisoners and all suspected persons to be sent to Sonoma under a strong escort. *Vallejo, Doc.*, MS., iv. 273. July 9th, same to Alvarado. Fears that the lives of Mexicans are in danger. All would certainly be killed should any native chance to perish in future troubles with Mexico. The persons named in an enclosed list (not given) should be shipped out of the country. *Id.*, iv. 275. July 9th, Villavicencio to Vallejo, with orders from Alvarado of July 6th, that no leniency be shown to any man that took up arms to capture the fort. *Id.*, iv. 274. July 11th, Vallejo to Alvarado. Has arrested Ramirez. Has abundant proof of his plots to upset the govt. *Id.*, iv. 279. July 11th, Vallejo to ——. Leonardo Félix and Pedro Chabolla arrested; Mesa and Higuera detained for examination. *Id.*, iv., 278, 259. July 14th, Vallejo to J. J. Vallejo. Peña is in great terror. To save bother his irons may be removed and he may be treated a little better than the others; but must be kept secure and not allowed to speak to any one. *Id.*, xxxii. 99. Aug. 9th, Alvarado recommends great precautions with the captives. *Id.*, iv. 292. Aug. 31st, list of the captives at Sonoma. *Id.*, iv. 304, 307.

the date of their release, except that of Figueroa on August 31st; but several Californians state that after leaving Sonoma they were scattered at different missions for a time under surveillance before being restored to entire liberty.

Let us now turn to the south, where at the end of June Alvarado with Castro and the 'civic militia of the state' at Santa Bárbara was awaiting the approach of the 'army of the supreme government' encamped at San Fernando under Portilla and Juan Bandini. There is a notable and unfortunate lack of exact data respecting what was said and done in these days, there being no record at all on the side of the northerners, and only a very vague one from the standpoint of the abajeños.[20] It is clear, however, that Castillero as commissioner of the supreme government, but regarded by Bandini and his associates as fully in sympathy with their plan, went to Santa Bárbara in the early days of July and had an interview with Alvarado. We may only conjecture what was said at that interview, but the result was that Alvarado agreed to take the oath of allegiance to the constitutional laws, and thus restore California unconditionally to Mexico. So far as sectional issues were concerned, this was Alvarado's greatest victory and the most crushing defeat he had administered to the south in all this play at politics and war. The country being restored to its

[20] Osio, *Hist. Cal.*, MS., 361–73, who says that the 'amigo de Sepúlveda,' though the first man to whom Bandini applied for support, refused to promise more than not to use his influence against the Dieguinos, next speaks of the difficulty experienced in getting a little coin to distribute among the soldiers when the oath was taken; tells of Sepúlveda's arrest and temporary detention by the southerners in spite of his own efforts; notes some faults of Macedonio Gonzalez in matters having no bearing on the political situation; and finally, explains that Castillero was clever enough to manage the leaders on both sides for his own interests, favoring Alvarado finally as the one who could help him most. Bandini in his report of Aug. 4th—*Sucesos del Sur*, MS.—stated that his force marched on victoriously to within 30 leagues of Sta B., when the rebels demanded a truce, the result being that the so-called state govt was destroyed, and Cal. restored to Mexico. In his *Hist. Cal.*, MS., 96–7, Bandini says that 'Castillero deceived us vilely, sold his honor for a few dollars, and joined Alvarado and Castro against us, so that by his intrigues we fell into the power of our adversaries.'

national allegiance, the diputacion would naturally resume its powers, and Alvarado would become governor ad interim as senior vocal of that body. There was left no pretext for southern opposition. The army of the supreme government must be disbanded, the elaborate plan of San Diego had melted into thin air, and there were no temporary offices to be filled, not even that of treasurer. Centralism was triumphant, for which the abajeños cared nothing. Mexico was victorious, which gave them very little joy, but the arribeños still controlled California, and southern patriotic intrigues would go for naught in the final settlement. No wonder Bandini deemed his party 'vilely deceived' by its pretended friend Castillero; yet what more could the Mexican comisionado insist on than submission to the national authority?

On the other hand, Alvarado as an advocate of federalism and Californian independence suffered a defeat, somewhat humiliating in view of the recent proclamation of his purpose to make the Californians free in spite of themselves. He has written nothing, then or since, which throws much real light on his motives;[21] yet it is not difficult to conjecture with approximate accuracy the arguments by which Castillero induced him to triumph in defeat. Experience had now proven that the south could not be depended upon to support the governor in the position he had assumed, but would seize upon every pretext to revolt in order to gain sectional advantages or gratify personal prejudices. Even in the north there were signs of disaffection at San José, growing out of a local quarrel; while the Mexican residents had gone so far as to rise in arms and seize the capital. United effort, by which alone

[21] In a letter of July 12th to Vallejo he refers to a previous communication narrating all that had occurred since their last interview; but unfortunately that document is not extant. *Vallejo, Doc.*, MS., iv. 282. In a letter of Sept. 1st, however, A. says he was strong enough to defeat the conspirators of both north and south. The plan of S. Diego was simply to seize the offices. When the Dieguinos saw Alvarado's force they put themselves hypocritically under the constitution, abandoned their position, and acted disgracefully. *Id.*, iv. 307.

success was attainable, could not be secured, and there
was much ground for discouragement. Not only did
Castillero present these facts in a strong light, but he
also confirmed the report that a strong force was being fitted out in Mexico to reconquer California. It
was merely a question under what leaders the country
should be restored to its national allegiance, and he
made no secret of his preference for Alvarado. To
aid in the final triumph of the men who had dealt so
unfairly with him seemed no part of the governor's
duty, and his desire to remain in office was naturally
strong. Moreover Castillero assured him that by his
influence with the government, if sent to Mexico as a
commissioner, he could prevent the sending of the military force, which would of course be ruinous to the
country, and could probably secure a confirmation of
Alvarado's title as governor. Finally, there can be
but little doubt that Castillero brought the news that
by the decree of December 30, 1836, one day after the
adoption of the constitution, the Californias had been
formed into a department, and that thus one of the
main objects sought by Alvarado's party had been
secured.[22] It is not strange that under the circumstances Don Juan Bautista was converted to centralism.

It was on July 4th that Portilla announced the
agreement of the northern pronunciados to accept the
constitutional laws, and the consequent withdrawal of
his army to San Gabriel.[23] On July 9th Alvarado
issued a proclamation to the people, a very graceful
effusion, albeit not very explicit as an explanation of
his late change of front, bearing evident marks of hav-

---

[22] Mexico, Leyes Constitucionales, 29 de Dic. 1836, in Arrillaga, Recop. 1836,
(2) 317–78. Decree of Dec. 30th, making the Californias a department, in Id.,
379–80. It does not appear that Castillero brought official news of this decree, though Alvarado immediately called himself gov. of the dept of Alta
Cal.

[23] July 4th, Portilla to ayunt. of S. Diego. Hayes' Doc., MS., 73; Id., Mission
Book, i. 322; S. Diego, Index, MS., 42. The communication is headed 'Division of operations of the sup. govt.' July 8th, a similar document read
to ayunt. of Angeles, and congratulations expressed for so happy a result.
Los Angeles, Arch., MS., iv. 323.

ing emanated from the mind as well as pen of the versatile and eloquent Frenchman, Victor Prudon.[24] This proclamation was first delivered as a speech by the governor on the occasion of swearing allegiance to the Mexican constitution, an event celebrated at Santa Bárbara on the date named, July 9th, with all possible ceremony and enthusiasm. From this date, barring certain mysterious indications of irregularity in the composition of the diputacion, which, as they excited no comment either in Mexico or among Alvarado's enemies in California, need not greatly trouble either historian or reader, Alvarado may be regarded

[24] *Alvarado, [Proclama del] Gobernador Interino del Departamento de la Alta California á sus habitantes, 9 de Julio, 1837*, MS. Issued at Sta Bárbara. 'Compatriots! Liberty, peace, and union form the trinal intelligence that should rule our destinies. Our arms gave us the first; a wise congress assures to us the second; and upon ourselves depends the last, without which we have neither liberty nor peace. Let us then preserve inviolate that union, sacred ark which holds the custody of our political redemption. War against the tyrant only! Peace among ourselves! The solidity of an edifice consists in the union of its parts; a single stone torn out from an arch causes the columns to totter, bringing ruin to a structure that would mark the age of time did its component materials remain united. Not otherwise disunion brings ruin to the moral edifice of a society. The territory of Alta California is immense; its coasts are bathed by the Pacific Sea, which, placing us in contact with the nations, develops our industries and commerce, fountains of abundance.' (See newspapers of later years!) 'The benignity of our climate, the fertility of our soil, and—I say it in your behalf—the suavity of your customs and excellence of your character are so many privileges with which the Omnipotent has favored us in the distribution of his gifts. What country can count so many advantages as ours? Let us then strive to give it in history a place as distinguished as that which it occupies on the map. The constitutional laws of 1836 guarantee to us our rights, and even extend them beyond our moderate desires. The august chamber of national representatives is ready to consider a bill to be presented by us for our greater welfare and prosperity; our votes may be cast in favor of the citizen whom we deem worthy to occupy the supreme magistracy of the nation—and what more do you wish? The very laws assure us that we are not again to fall a prey to the despotism and ambition of a tyrant like D. Mariano Chico. The department of Alta California can henceforth be governed only by a native or a citizen. Yes, friends; the enthusiasm and pleasure which you feel on receiving such news is well founded. I share your pleasure, and I close in order that you may no longer have to restrain your joy. Give it free course, and shout with me—Viva la Nacion! Viva la Constitucion del año de '36! Viva el Congreso que la sancionó! Viva la Libertad! Viva la Union!'

Also in *Hayes, Doc.*, MS., 75; forwarded by Alvarado to ayunt., and received at S. Diego on July 31st. *S. Diego, Arch.*, MS., 183. July 24th, the proclamation had been read at Monterey, causing great enthusiasm. *Vallejo, Doc.*, MS., xxxii. 103. Sent to Sonoma to be sworn July 12th. *Id.*, iv. 280. And it would seem that the people of Sta Cruz went to Monterey on July 17th to take the new oath. *Sta Cruz, Arch.*, MS., 20. The fact that the oath was taken at Sta Bárbara on July 9th is mentioned by Alvarado in a letter of July 12th to Vallejo. *Vallejo, Doc.*, iv. 282.

as legally the governor ad interim of California, his revolutionary term ending with his new oath.

In his letters sent northward, though unfortunately the most important of them describing the negotiations with Castillero is missing, the governor described the state of affairs as on the whole satisfactory, his enemies being filled with confusion.[25] The southern friars, represented by Padre Duran, now consented to take the long-delayed oath of allegiance, on the ground that Spain had recognized the independence of Mexico, while the Zacatecanos of course made no objection, having already sworn to the bases.[26] The diputacion assembled as early as July 16th at Santa Bárbara; but we have no record of its acts, except that on the 21st it resolved, 1st, that in consequence of certain doubts arising in relation to the election laws, a commission of two persons should be sent to the national capital to treat with the supreme government; and 2d, that the senior vocal, on whom by law devolved the office of gefe político, should notify the ayuntamientos and other authorities that the diputacion was assembled in extra session. He was also authorized to carry out the first resolution.[27]

It is probable that the diputacion took no other action, and that the governor had no other use for its services at this time, after securing its indorsement of his title, with authority to send a commission to Mexico. It had been determined from the first by Alvarado and Castillero that the latter should go to

[25] July 9th, 12th, 17th, Alvarado to Vallejo, in *Vallejo, Doc.*, MS., iv. 269, 282–3. Pio Pico still disposed to favor the vagabonds at S. Gabriel, and Portilla for gefe político, being instigated by Zamorano. Bandini gone home, convinced that it is no use to struggle longer.

[26] July 8th, Duran to Alvarado, in *Vallejo, Doc.*, MS., xxxii. 96. July 12th, P. Moreno to A. *Arch. Arzob.*, MS., v. pt ii. 18.

[27] These resolutions were published at Sta Bárbara on Aug. 2d, and at Monterey on Aug. 13th. *Vallejo, Doc.*, MS., iv. 289; xxxii. 105, 107. Sent to Los Angeles July 29th. *Dept. St. Pap., Angeles*, MS., xi. 90–1. The first meeting of July 16th is mentioned by Alvarado on July 17th. *Vallejo, Doc.*, MS., iv. 283. There is also a short address of Alvarado to the dip. in *Id.*, xxxii. 121, undated, but probably delivered at this time. It contains congratulations on 'California Libre,' and states that only a few points require action at this time.

Mexico in the former's behalf, and the doubts on election laws were simply a pretext. Early in July the governor began to speak of the project in his letters, expressing his belief that Don Andrés, with the aid of his brother, could exert in Mexico a greater influence in favor of himself and Vallejo than any other man; meanwhile Castillero made a trip to the southern frontier to restore order among the men of his command.[28] He returned in August, and sailed after the middle of that month on the schooner *California,* reaching Acapulco the 15th of September. His mission was to prevent the sending of a Mexican force to California, to defend Alvarado's acts and policy before the government, and to obtain if possible a confirmation of his title as governor together with that of Vallejo as general. It is not very unlikely that he carried with him a moderate sum of money to be placed "where it would do most good"—else, knowing much of Mexican methods, he would hardly have been so confident of success.

The *California* was a schooner called originally the *Clarion,* and at the Sandwich Islands the *Kaniu;* brought this year from Honolulu by Henry Paty; and by him sold to Alvarado for the state government. She was paid for in mission produce, and was commanded during this year and the next by Thomas M. Robbins of Santa Bárbara. The governor had at first intended to purchase two vessels with mission funds; and had hoped to use them profitably, not only in commercial enterprises and to protect the revenues,

[28] Alvarado to Vallejo. *Vallejo, Doc.,* MS., iv. 282–3, 306. Osio, *Hist. Cal.,* MS., 373–5, tells us that A. first appointed on this commission Cárlos Carrillo and 'another' (Osio himself I suppose), who were summoned to Sta B. to receive their instructions. But it was suggested that one of them, the 'other' probably, had the defect of telling the truth on all points, which would be inconvenient; and therefore A. announced that to his great regret the scheme would have to be abandoned. Finally Castillero accepted the place (probably as a man of some wealth), from a desire to give himself importance by appearing in person before the president. The Cal. records name no companion of Castillero, though the commission was to consist of two; but Bustamante, *Gabinete, Mex.,* i. 36, mentions the arrival at Acapulco on Sept. 15th of Castillero and Nicolás Estrada as comisionados. I know of no such Californian, but it may have been Capt. Nicanor Estrada.

but also for purposes of defence against Mexico, and even as the nucleus of a west-coast navy with which to enforce federalism in the nation! Circumstances changed, however; funds were not too plentiful; and one vessel was deemed sufficient.[29]

Alvarado's position as governor was now temporarily secure. On September 4th he circulated for publication the Mexican decree of December 30, 1836—nine days after the news of Alvarado's revolt reached the capital—making California a department, authorizing the national government to designate provisionally the capital and the authorities to act until the regular elections could be held; and empowering the junta departamental to divide the department into districts and partidos. Not even yet, though published in the usual form, had this decree been received 'officially,' and for the present nothing was done in consequence of it. Alvarado in later times claimed that he had not before known of the fact that California had been made a department.[30] About the middle of September he returned once more to Monterey.

If Alvarado's position was for a time comparatively secure, that of Vallejo had no longer any foundation to stand upon. He had no claim to the military command, which now belonged to the ranking officer in the territory. The governor recognized this fact in his letters of July; stated that both Portilla and

[29] March 9th, Alvarado to Vallejo, about his projected purchase of 2 vessels. *Vallejo, Doc.*, MS., iv. 212. There is no record of the actual purchase, which is however spoken of by several Californians. The movements of the *Kaniu* at the islands, and her sailing for Cal. in May 1837, are recorded in the *Honolulu, S. I., Gazette*, 1836-7. The pay of the crew began Aug. 14th. There were 16 men and a boy, only 5 being of Spanish American blood. G. Robinson (William ?) was 1st pilot, and later W. Reed 2d pilot. *Dept. St. Pap., Ben. Cust.-H.*, MS., v. 13-14.

[30] Sept. 4th, A.'s order for publication of decree. Published at S. Diego before Dec. 16th. *S. Diego, Arch.*, MS., 183-4, 190. Alvarado, *Hist. Cal.*, MS., iv. 15, says he had heard rumors from Castillo Negrete through Zamorano, which were not believed. I have not much doubt that he knew all about it at the time of his arrangement with Castillero. The news of Alvarado's revolt was announced to congress by minister Tornel on Dec. 21st according to *Bustamante, Voz de la Patria*, MS., xi. 60-1.

Zamorano desired the position; but desired Vallejo to aid him in giving it to Captain José de la Guerra, on the ground that it was better that it should be held by a friend than a foe.[31] Vallejo replied in a printed letter of July 20th, the meaning of which is not quite clear, but in which he declared the separation of the civil and military commands to be impracticable, and thus apparently showed a desire to see Alvarado share in his own fall.[32] He, however, saw the necessity of resigning his position, and based his resignation on the alleged ground of his unwillingness to swear allegiance to the central constitution, "such oaths having become bywords in the whole country." At the same time all military officers were ordered to meet at Monterey to choose a comandante general.[33] The San Francisco company, on receipt of orders from Alvarado to take the oath, addressed a protest to Vallejo, in which they declared that they had once sworn to die in defence of federalism, and asked to be discharged from the service rather than change their political faith.[34] I suppose that Vallejo and other officers and soldiers in the north were subsequently induced to take the oath in support of centralism; but I find no definite record of the fact. The council of war for the election of a comandante had not been held as late as October, and probably was not held at all, the aim of Vallejo and Alvarado being perhaps to postpone definite action until the result of Castillero's efforts could be learned. Portilla insisted that the choice must fall on the senior officer, meaning himself. Some officers

[31] July 12th, 17th, A. to V., in *Vallejo, Doc.*, MS., iv. 282–3.
[32] *Vallejo, Carta impresa al Gobernador, 20 de Julio, 1837*, in *Earliest Printing*. There is a possibility of error, as the date was printed 1838 and changed in ink—apparently by Vallejo's direction—to 1837.
[33] No date, probably early in August, Vallejo to dip. and to Alvarado. *Vallejo, Doc.*, MS., iv. 202.
[34] Aug. 16th, Com. Sanchez to V., in *Vallejo, Doc.*, MS., iv. 294. Aug. 31st, protest of the company, *Id.*, iv. 305. This is probably what Alvarado, *Hist. Cal.*, MS., iii. 181–3, ridicules as Berreyesa's revolt at the instigation of southern agents.

in their letters expressed a preference for Vallejo.[35]
There seems to have been no final decision in the
matter. It does not appear that Vallejo's resignation was accepted by the diputacion, or that any
other officer attempted to exercise the command.
All waited for news from Mexico.

And this news came sooner than looked for, and in
an unexpected form. It was an announcement that
Cárlos Carrillo had been appointed provisional governor of the department of Californias. It reached
Monterey October 30th, and Los Angeles ten days
earlier, in letters from Luis del Castillo Negrete and
José Antonio Carrillo at La Paz, enclosing certified
copies of the appointment to Alvarado and the ayuntamiento, and the original probably to Don Cárlos himself at San Buenaventura. There is not much to be
said of the circumstances in Mexico which had led to
this appointment. I have no copy of the report which
Gutierrez rendered on his arrival in exile, though it
is not difficult to conjecture its purport. The Mexican government was too busy with troubles at home
to devote much attention to a distant territory, but
finally it did go so far as to make preparations for
sending 1,000 men under General Iniestra to restore
the wayward California to her allegiance.[36] Money
and arms, however, were scarce. The fitting-out of
the expedition progressed slowly, and before it was
completed the Californian congressman, José Antonio
Carrillo, devised a method of suspending it altogether,

[35] Sept. 1st, Alvarado expresses a high opinion of V.'s services, and hopes
the Mexicans will not succeed in breaking the friendship of the two. *Vallejo,
Doc.*, MS., iv. 306-7. Sept. 20th, Portilla to 'Lieut M. G. Vallejo,' saying
that ill health may prevent his attendance at the council. *Id.*, iv. 313. Oct.
1st, Alf. Salazar to Vallejo. Cannot come in time, but votes for V. *Id.*, iv.
315.

[36] I have no official record of these preparations, but there is no reason to
doubt the reports current in California at the time, founded on articles in the
newspapers and the statements of J. A. Carrillo, Castillero, and others. Osio
and several others name Gen. Iniestra. Greenhow, who names Gen. Urrea as
in charge of the movement, Mofras, Forbes, Marsh, and others tell us that on
hearing of the rebellion Mexico 'fulminated furious proclamations,' etc., but
I have seen no such papers.

at the same time advancing the interests of his own family and sparing his country the threatened infliction of cholo soldiers. He persuaded the government that California was not really disloyal or hostile to Mexico; but had been driven to her present rebellious attitude by the arbitrary acts of Mexican rulers. Instead of sending an army at great expense, it would be sufficient merely to appoint a native ruler—his brother Don Cárlos for example, well known in Mexico and popular at home—whom California would gladly recognize and thus return to her allegiance. The administration was glad to be persuaded, and willing to try the experiment. The appointment was issued in a hurry by the minister of state on June 6th; Don José Antonio left Mexico two days later, and from La Paz en route sent the papers ahead in August.[37]

Los Angeles of course was delighted with Carrillo's appointment. True, Don Cárlos was not in sympathy with the abajeños, and had been a partisan of the other side throughout the late controversies, but "anything to beat Alvarado and the pronunciados del norte" was the Angelinos' motto, and they made such haste that Carrillo to the letter announcing his appointment had to attach his thanks for their acknowledgment, their congratulations, and for a grand illu-

[37] June 6, 1837, Minister Peña y Peña to Cárlos Carrillo, announcing his appointment by the president, with power to fix the capital provisionally wherever circumstances might require. Copy from the original in the possession of the Carrillo family, in *Carrillo, Doc.*, MS., i. Also in *Dept. St. Pap., Angeles*, MS., xi. 92-3; and translation in *Hopkins' Translations*, 6. July 21st, Antonio M. Ercilla announces the news from Tepic, where J. A. Carrillo then was, to Guerra, *Guerra, Doc.*, MS., vi. 145; but it does not appear when this was received—possibly a little earlier than by the other route. Aug. 20th, J. A. Carrillo at La Paz to Alvarado, with certified copies. *Dept. St. Pap.*, MS., iv. 165-6. Oct. 20th, Castillo Negrete's despatch from Baja California with similar copies read before ayunt. of Los Angeles. Cárlos Carrillo's letter of Oct. 24th received on Nov. 4th. *Los Angeles, Arch.*, MS., iv. 326-30. Oct. 25th, Cárlos Carrillo to Alvarado, with news. *Dept. St. Pap.*, MS., iv. 169-70. Oct. 25th, same to Vallejo. *Vallejo, Doc.*, MS., iv. 337. Oct. 31st, Alvarado's proclamation of the news, which came 'by yesterday's mail.' *Dept. St. Pap., Angeles*, MS., x. 20-1; *S. José, Arch.*, MS., vi. 5; *Hopkins' Translations*, 6-7. Petit-Thouars, *Voyage*, ii. 100, who was at Monterey at the time, says the news came on Nov. 1st.

mination of the city in his honor. He also pledged his word to make Los Angeles the capital on assuming the government, a very impolitic promise to be made so early, but Don Cárlos, an easy-going, kind-hearted man, was all at sea in matters of political management.

Alvarado's submission to the national authorities and his acceptance of the constitutional laws were not known in Mexico at the time of Carrillo's appointment. José A. Carrillo, writing from La Paz to Alvarado, presented a strong argument in favor of such submission, showing the impracticability of resisting Mexican power, alluding to the difficulty he had had in preventing the sending of one thousand soldiers, and claiming that the most essential object of the revolutionists had been secured with a native ruler. He urged Alvarado to submit to the new governor, and promised in such case to go in person to Mexico, and obtain all necessary guaranties of pardon and protection for the revolutionary leaders, that is, to undertake the very mission in which Castillero was now employed. Don Cárlos announced his appointment to Alvarado and Vallejo in friendly modest letters, expressing much diffidence in respect to his own capabilities, but hoping to succeed by earnest effort with the aid of his good friends. He made no formal demand for a transfer of the office, but left Alvarado to take such action as might seem proper in consequence of his announcement.

Don Juan Bautista now found himself in a very peculiar situation. Of course he had hoped to retain the command, and was disappointed at the prospect of losing it, especially when any day might bring news from Castillero which would secure him in its possession. With this feeling, however, neither the writer nor reader of history is called upon to feel any special sympathy. His personal disappointment furnished no justification for refusing or delaying compliance with the orders of the government which he had sworn to obey. There were, however, other and more serious complications. Alvarado had placed himself at the head of a revolution, and while he had surrendered in a sense and acknowledged the supremacy of the national laws, yet the government had not accepted his surrender, Castillero having had no authority whatever in the matter. In the eyes of the government at the time of this last appointment he was simply a rebel chief, ordered virtually, not to transfer the governorship, but to obey the governor. Was he under obligation to come down from the vantage-ground of success and high position, to place himself without guaranties as a private citizen at the mercy of a power that might legally shoot him as a traitor? Could he disregard the fate of his associates whose position was like his own? Surely no successful rebel was ever known to give such excessive proofs of devotion to his country. Again, Alvarado looked upon himself at this time as the legitimate ruler of California. He was so considered by the people, even by Cárlos Carrillo, and there was not much reason to fear that President Bustamante would not so recognize him, knowing the circumstances, even if he should insist upon naming a successor. An order to the incumbent to deliver the office was, by custom if not by law, as necessary to a change of rulers as was the appointee's order to receive it, and the recognition implied in such an order was of vital importance to Don Juan. Thus a way seemed open to the delay so urgently demanded by the safety of the former rebels as well as by Alvarado's ambitious hopes.

In his proclamation of October 31st, the governor made known to the people the news which he had unofficially received, and of which he hoped to receive confirmation by the next mail, adding, "All the department may be sure that I shall deliver the command to the nominee on receiving the slightest intimation from the supreme government." Within a few days he notified the ayuntamientos in due form, speaking of "the nearness of the time when I shall deliver the command to Carrillo."[38] Don Cárlos unwisely yielded to the counsel of his advisers, and chose to regard Alvarado's position and his request in a private letter for a conference as insulting to himself and threatening to the peace of the country, speaking of 'frivolous pretexts' for delaying obedience, and hinting vaguely by a negative assertion at fears that "you aspire to the place I occupy."[39] Meanwhile the ayuntamiento of Los Angeles on receipt of the governor's communications refused to recognize any other authority than that of Carrillo, who was invited to come and establish his government in that city before replying to Alvarado.[40]

Could Alvarado have obtained an interview with Don Cárlos—his so-called 'uncle,' that is, cousin to the lady whom a real uncle had married—he would probably have succeeded in making him understand the full force of the reasons for delay, and of his right to insist at least on the guaranty implied in recognition of his title; and thus further disagreement might perhaps have been avoided. But Carrillo's new southern friends knew better than to trust their easily influenced protégé within the reach of Juan Bautista's eloquence; and if there was any uncertainty about results, it was removed by the arrival of José Antonio Carrillo at the beginning of December. This gentleman feared the influence of Castillero in Mexico, knowing how little the administration cared who was governor of California so long as there was no rebel-

[38] Nov. 3d, 7th, Alvarado to ayunt. *Dept. St. Pap., Angeles*, MS., xi. 98; *Sta Cruz, Arch.*, MS., 57–8; *Hopkins' Translations*, 7. A private letter of Alvarado to Carrillo of Nov. 4th is not extant, nor the official note of the 3d.

[39] Nov. 14th, Carrillo to Alvarado, in reply to letters of Nov. 3d, 4th, private letter in *Vallejo, Doc.*, MS., iv. 345; official note in *Dept. St. Pap.*, MS., iv. 167–8. On Nov. 18th, before receiving C.'s reply, A. wrote to Vallejo a private letter, expressing the same views as in his communications to C.—that is, his willingness to give up the rule on receipt of an order from Mexico. *Vallejo, Doc.*, MS., iv. 346.

[40] Nov. 18th, session. *Los Angeles, Arch.*, MS., iv. 329–30. Carrillo's letter of Nov. 14th to Alvarado had also been forwarded to this body. *Dept. St. Pap., Angeles*, MS., xi. 96–8.

lion to call for Mexican troops and money. He feared Castillero's arrival with an order that if no change had yet been made in the governorship none need be made. It was as much for his interest to avoid a delay in the transfer as for Alvarado's interest to secure it. His influence over his brother was of course great, and the latter followed his lead without hesitation.

On December 1st the Angelinos, as representatives of the supreme government, took possession of a house that had been rented as a temporary capitol.[41] Next day Juan Bandini seems to have delivered an oration before the ayuntamiento.[42] On the 4th the same illustrious body in an extra session received formal notice that Don Cárlos would take the oath of office, thus assuming the governorship, on the 6th, at 9 A. M. It was thereupon resolved to prepare the *sala capitular*, to open a subscription for funds wherewith duly to solemnize the act, to issue tickets of invitation to prominent citizens, to obtain a big cannon from San Gabriel for salvos, and to illuminate the city for three nights. At last the day arrived, and the ayuntamiento met in public session; José Antonio Carrillo made a speech; Cárlos Carrillo took the oath and delivered an address; mass and te deum followed at the church; and the enthusiastic Angelinos proceeded to their new governor's house to shout their vivas and overload him with congratulations.[43]

The address of Don Cárlos was circulated among the people.[44] It was of the congratulatory and grand-

[41] *Los Angeles, Ayuntamiento Records*, MS., 24. The house was that of the widow Josefa Alvarado, rented of John Temple for $360 per year, the negotiations having begun in September.

[42] There is some mystery about this speech, which is fragment of a blotter in Bandini's handwriting, headed 'Discourse pronounced by the Síndico J. B. in the session of Dec. 2d,' in *Bandini, Doc.*, MS., 46. Bandini was not a síndico at all in that year or the next. The speech, however, amounts to nothing, being apparently an argument in favor of a meeting of the asamblea departamental.

[43] Sessions of Dec. 4th, 6th. *Los Angeles, Arch.*, MS., iv. 331–5.

[44] *Carrillo, Discurso que pronunció al tomar el mando político en Los Angeles, el 6 de Dic.* 1837, MS.

iloquent type deemed suitable for such occasions. Its purport was: "The.end of all our troubles has come, the political sea is calm, nothing but happiness ahead. Your wishes are fulfilled now that a Californian rules California. It was my brother who brought us the gift of peace and my appointment; but for his intercessions, a thousand bayonets would now gleam on our shores. I·recognize my own unworthiness, but I trust in your coöperation. Let us be united, asking heaven's blessing." There was not the slightest intimation that any opposition was expected, and no attempt to explain the irregularity and haste with which the office was assumed. The action at Angeles was ratified at San Diego on December 9th.[45]

The support of Santa Bárbara was essential, and Don Cárlos sent his brother José Antonio as a comisionado to obtain it, instructing him to lay before the ayuntamiento the disasters which must result from the coming of the military expedition now ready to start from the Mexican coast.[46] Yet, notwithstanding the comisionado's eloquence and influence, his threats of bringing a force from Mexico, and the fact that Cárlos Carrillo was a Santa Bárbara man with many relatives and friends in that place, the Barbareños could not be induced to support the present plan and policy of Los Angeles. They had sworn allegiance to Alvarado, and regarded their oath as binding until the command should be in due form transferred to another. Moreover, they recognized their own need, as Alvarado's associates and supporters, of formal guaranties from Mexico, and they could but regard Carrillo's present actions as savoring of treachery.[47]

[45] Dec. 8th, Carrillo to ayunt., with his appointment, etc. Dec. 10th, Francisco Alvarado to C., with news of the ratification, enthusiasm, etc. *S. Diego, Arch.*, MS., 189–90. Dec. 10th, C. orders the ayunt. of Angeles to proclaim him gov. in its jurisdiction. *Dept. St. Pap., Angeles*, MS., xi. 99.

[46] Dec. 8, 1837, appointment and instructions of Cárlos to J. A. Carrillo in *Soberanes, Doc.*, MS., 70.

[47] In a letter of Dec. 20th, Alvarado informs Vallejo of the arrival of 2 men from Sta Bárbara, with news of Carrillo's efforts and threats at that place. They report a bitter feeling against D. Cárlos. *Vallejo, Doc.*, MS., iv. 361.

During the rest of the year nothing was accomplished on either side, save that the Zacatecan friars, through their prefect, expressed their recognition of Carrillo as governor,[48] and that Castro was sent down with an escort of ten men to take command at Santa Bárbara. Castro was instructed to forward communications from the north and south, aid the local authorities in preserving order, keep a close watch on fomenters of opposition to the government, but not to use force without orders, it being especially desirable to avoid a rupture.[49] Correspondence continued in December. The governor had been offended by Carrillo's letter of November 14th, and had not answered it, but now he wrote a reply, which was forwarded by Castro. It was a dignified and forcible presentment of the matters at issue, expressing deep regret at Carrillo's hasty assumption, without legal formalities, of a command which the writer was willing to turn over to him legally, and at his refusal to consult with the man whom he had recognized as a legitimate ruler respecting certain matters that could not be treated in writing. He closed by renewing his proposal for a conference, which might take place at San Miguel, and by which further sectional strife might be prevented.[50]

General Vallejo also wrote on December 26th letters to Alvarado and the two Carrillos. To the former he declared that his right to await orders and guaranties from the Mexican government could not be questioned; that the threat to bring a force from Mexico was but braggadocio to frighten cowards; and that were it not for the expected arrival of the *California* at an early date, he would not hesitate to march

---

[48] Dec. 14th, P. Moreno to the friars. *Arch. Obispado*, MS., 59.
[49] Dec. 25, 1837, Alvarado's instructions to Castro. *Soberanes, Doc.*, MS., 74–5, in 9 articles.
[50] Dec. 26, 1837, Alvarado to Cárlos Carrillo. *Soberanes, Doc.*, MS., 78–81; *Vallejo, Doc.*, MS., xxxii. 118. Same date, to Vallejo. Advises him to keep military men on good terms, so that they may be disposed to obey his orders. *Id.*, iv. 364.

with his soldiers to the south in Alvarado's support; yet under existing circumstances it would doubtless be best to avoid violent measures.[51] To José Antonio Carrillo he wrote that his boasting and threats at Santa Bárbara had aroused not fear, but indignation that a son of California could adopt such a course, rebuking him for his hasty action and advising prudence. Let them wait till the vessel should arrive with despatches, and then the command would be legally and gladly surrendered, although the legitimate ruler had been grievously insulted.[52] In writing to Don Cárlos, Vallejo adopted a milder tone, appealing to his good sense and patriotism, and begging him not to plunge the country needlessly into a sectional strife by ignoring the rights of a ruler whom he had himself aided to put in power. Alvarado could not yield, even if he wished to do so, and leave his friends unprotected, while Carrillo assuredly could not rule successfully without northern support. Why not then secure that support by showing a conciliatory spirit, and consenting to a slight delay, or at least to a conference?[53]

Answers to these letters, though not extant, were evidently not conciliatory. The sum total of all that can be said against the position of Alvarado and Vallejo at this time is that they perhaps hoped to receive by the *California,* not an order to surrender their power, but authority to keep it. This hope on their part, causing them to desire delay, was neither more nor less culpable than Carrillo's fears on the same subject prompting haste. Otherwise, Alvarado's ground was tenable legally and morally, besides tending to

[51] Dec. 26th, V. to A., in *Vallejo, Doc.,* MS., iv. 368. He hints that Carrillo may have heard in Mexico of some proposition to cede California to the U. S., which may account for his haste to get possession.

[52] Dec. 26th, V. to J. A. Carrillo, in *Vallejo, Doc.,* MS., iv. 367.

[53] Dec. 26th, V. to Cárlos Carrillo, in *Vallejo, Doc.,* MS., iv. 365. In a later letter to J. A. Carillo, not dated, Vallejo accuses him of having asked congress to expend $60,000 in sending an army to Cal.; and says that had his commission and the appointment of D. Cárlos been genuine, they should have gone like men to lay their papers before the governor, and to come to an understanding. It seems that Carrillo had replied to V.'s first letter, asserting that his threats were exaggerated. *Id.,* xiv. 13.

peace and harmony, while Carrillo's position was inconsistent, partisan, and sure to result in sectional strife. Don Cárlos, a strong supporter of Alvarado's government, on receipt of his appointment with power to select his capital, at once, without consulting his chiefs or associates, offered to make Los Angeles the capital. Then he simply notified Alvarado of his appointment, not recognizing the latter's title, even so far as to ask for a transfer of the office. He merely waited for Alvarado as a rebel chief to submit humbly to him as representative of the supreme government; and at the governor's suggestion of delay for at least a conference and the legal formalities of a transfer, he wrote insulting letters in reply, and by an irregular assumption of the governorship at Los Angeles became virtually leader of the faction that had so long struggled against Alvarado and himself. That Carrillo was a weak man, easily influenced by others, is far from sufficient excuse for this act of treachery. Don Cárlos deserved no sympathy, and he got none, even from his own town of Santa Bárbara, until long years had caused the facts to be forgotten. In time foreign residents and writers, and even many Californians, were taught to regard him as a leader of the sureños from the beginning, defrauded of the governorship by the plots of a northern faction.

Naturally Carrillo's partisan acts in favor of the south, his treatment of his former associates, and his brother's loud threats of bringing an army from Mexico excited much anger in the north, not only among the leaders, but among the people. The leaders' interests, depending on the *California's* expected arrival, were in favor of peace; therefore Alvarado, Vallejo, and Castro kept their temper tolerably well; but had the governor chosen to yield, it is almost certain there would have been a revolt in the north. That is, Carrillo's policy had brought about a renewal in a new form of the old sectional quarrel, the worst possible result for California.   It was Carrillo's fault, and not Alvarado's.   Here as elsewhere, such a quarrel once begun, there is very little room for sympathy or blame for either side.[54]

[54] Testimony about the events of this period, from printed matter and from statements of Californians, does not as a rule add anything to our knowledge derived from contemporary documents. Most Californians content themselves with stating that Alvarado refused to recognize Carrillo, approving or disapproving his policy according as they lived in the north or south. Alvarado, *Hist. Cal.*, MS., iv. 23–32, gives a much fairer and more accurate version of these than of some earlier events, agreeing for the most part with his letters written at the time. Vallejo's statements, *Hist. Cal.*, MS., iii. 277–320, are very much less complete and satisfactory than are his original letters. Osio, *Hist. Cal.*, MS., 382–5, does not indicate, either under his own name or anonymously, what part he took; nor does he give many details; but he seems to have some words of blame both for Alvarado and for J. A. Carrillo. Bandini, *Hist. Cal.*, MS., 97–9, states that Alvarado had no intention of giving up the office, but made a new revolution to avoid it. Carrillo was defeated through bad management on his side. J. J. Vallejo, *Reminis.*, MS., 123–5, seems to regard Carrillo's appointment as the result of southern intrigue, and represents him as having 'raised the standard of revolt'! Botello, *Anales*, MS., 43–8, tells us that Alvarado and his friends resisted Carrillo on one pretext or another, but really to prevent the abajeños from avenging their past wrongs and to keep them from moving the capital and custom-house. He admits that it was the intention of the sureños to clip the wings of the northern clique. In the brief account sent to the Islands, and published in the *Honolulu S. I. Gazette*, May 5, 1838, and *Honolulu Polynesian*, ii. 93, Nov. 20, 1841, Alvarado is said to have agreed to give up the command on being shown Carrillo's commission and receiving guaranties from him of protection for the life and property of himself and friends, which Carrillo refused. Mentions more or less accurate, but all incomplete and brief, of Alvarado vs Carrillo, some extending beyond the point to which I have brought my narrative, are as follows: *Marsh's Letter*, MS., 8; *Ord, Ocurrencias*, MS., 103–8; *Pico, Acont.*, MS., 47–8; *Serrano, Apuntes*, MS., 54–9; *Valle, Lo Pasado*, MS., 19–21; *Coronel, Cosas*, MS., 24; *Janssens, Vida*, MS., 122–8; *Castro, Rel.*, MS., 41–2; *Galindo, Apuntes*, MS., 39–40; *Gonzalez, Experiencias*, MS., 33; *Avila, Notas*, MS., 21. Also the following in print: *Belcher's Voyage*, i. 137; *Mofras, Explor.*, i. 301–2; *Robinson's Life in Cal.*, 178–9; *Laplace, Voyage*, vi. 190–1; *Greenhow's Hist. Or.*, 367; *Forbes' Hist. Cal.*, 150; *Farnham's Life and Trav.*, 290; *Tuthill's Hist. Cal.*, 144–5; *Los Angeles Hist.*, 14.

CHAPTER XIX.

DON JUAN BAUTISTA AND DON CÁRLOS.

1838.

Don Cárlos Closes Northern Ports—Sends for Mexican Troops—
Castro's Plan—A Spurious Appointment—Carrillo's Letters—
Military Preparations—Castañeda at San Buenaventura—Santa
Bárbara Threatened—News from Mexico—Battle of San Buena-
ventura—Los Angeles Taken—Alvarado at San Fernando—Don
Cárlos at San Diego—A New Plan—Tobar in Command—Cam-
paign of Las Flores—Treaty—Negotiations at San Fernando—
Escape of the Pretender—Vallejo Favors Don Cárlos—News by
the 'Catalina'—Arrival of Castillero—Recognition of Alvarado
and Vallejo—An Island for Carrillo—Abajeños Despondent—
Arribeños Triumphant—Re-arrest of Carrillos and Picos.

The state of affairs was not greatly changed in January 1838. On the 3d, however, in view of critical
circumstances arising from 'polyarchy,' Carrillo from
his capital at Angeles proceeded to close, so far as he
could do so by a decree, the ports of Monterey and
San Francisco, "until the north should submit to the
supreme government," and to establish the custom-
house at San Diego.[1] Such an act did not tend in any
marked degree to conciliate the people from Santa
Bárbara northward.

Next, through his brother, he sent to Mexico a request for 200 armed men to aid in making his authority
respected, after which Don José Antonio was sent on
the 6th to labor again with the obstinate Barbareños.
He was aided by the Valles, Don Antonio and his

[1] *S. Diego, Arch.*, MS., 193; *Hayes, Doc.*, MS., 79; *Id., Emig. Notes*, i.
363. Published at S. Diego and S. Luis Rey on Jan. 8th. *S. Diego, Arch.*,
MS., 210.

son Ignacio, and by the Picos, Don Pio and his brother Andrés. They offered to Castro and Villavicencio as their ultimatum that Don Cárlos on Alvarado's submission would countermand his request for 200 armed Mexicans, and would give guaranties for the lives of the rebels against Chico and Gutierrez. He would also consent to an interview at San Buenaventura. Castro promised to go as a comisionado to Monterey to make known the propositions to Alvarado, whom, with Vallejo perhaps, he would induce to return with him to Santa Bárbara, where negotiations might be continued. He started on the 11th, and both the Carrillos addressed letters to Alvarado, urging him to submit.[2]

Castro believed that there was really danger of a force coming from Mexico, and his object in coming north was to consult with Alvarado. He proposed and the governor approved a sudden attack on Los Angeles, to be followed by the sending of Don Cárlos and some twenty others to the north as prisoners. This plan was submitted to Vallejo,[3] who probably disapproved it or counselled delay, not putting much faith in Carrillo's threats. Of course there was no thought of accepting the latest propositions. In these days the theory became current that Carrillo's appointment was spurious, since neither Alvarado, nor

[2] Jan. 9, 1838, J. A. Carrillo to A. *Dept. St. Pap.*, MS., iv. 172-6. 'Juanito, you know my firmness; accept the invitation and confide in me. Do not adhere to a caprice which will injure you and your country.' Jan. 16th, Cárlos Carrillo to A. *Id.*, iv. 179–80. Drops all resentments, and is willing to comply with all that has been stipulated; that is, is willing that his rival should yield. Same date, C. C. thanks Castro for promising to use his influence with A. *Id.*, iv. 176–7. Jan. 19th, A. to Vallejo, private letter. Castro had arrived Jan. 18th. The Barbareños were reported very bitter against Carrillo; and one night they would have killed his agents if Castro had not prevented it. *Vallejo, Doc.*, MS., v. 22. On Jan. 15th A. had written to V. that J. A. Carrillo had said at Sta Bárbara that Don Cárlos had shown at Los Angeles his original appointment and guaranties for the late revolutionists. *Id.*, v. 20.

[3] Jan. 19, 1838, A. to V., in *Vallejo, Doc.*, MS., v. 22. He announces his intention to go south soon, says J. A. Carrillo is de facto governor in Los Angeles, abusing everybody; there are two parties at Angeles; Carrillo brought a Capt. Castañeda from Mexico, who has been offered the command at Sta Bárbara. He (Alvarado) has 40 men at Monterey, 10 at S. Juan, 20 at Sta Bárbara, all anxious to fight.

anybody else outside of Angeles at least, had as yet been favored with a glimpse of the original. Even the document of which an alleged copy had been shown, was not legal as was claimed, because it did not bear the president's signature. The latter theory had perhaps some force as a technicality; and to the former a degree of plausibility was given by Carrillo's mysterious actions. At any rate, they served their purpose, and strengthened Alvarado's cause somewhat at the north.

Throughout February also Alvarado waited, being content that affairs at the south should remain in statu quo, and believing that favorable news from Castillero was more likely to arrive than was Carrillo's reën-forcement.[4] Correspondence was continued, though it brought no progress toward a settlement. J. A. Carrillo had informed Vallejo of the request for Mexican troops, and the latter wrote to Don Cárlos in reply a very earnest letter of reproach for having paid no attention to his past communications, and for his hasty and unwise policy, which was sure to result in civil war. "If it be true," he said, "that troops have been sent for, you may be sure the command will not be given up, nor will those wrongfully termed rebels tamely submit." Yet he would like to see Carrillo legally in possession of the command, and as an 'affectionate cousin' hoped that all would result in tranquillity.[5] On February 15th both Carrillos answered Vallejo's communications of December 26th, which they claimed not to have received until the day before. Both said in substance: "Your arguments

---

[4] Vallejo, on Jan. 29th, had given the command at Sonoma to D. Salvador, and announced his purpose to march southward. *Vallejo, Doc.*, MS., v. 25. He had been at S. F. on Feb. 1st, and ordered a small force from that place to Sta Clara; but the ayunt. interposed obstacles and could find no men. *Soberanes, Doc.*, MS., 86–8.

[5] Feb. 10, 1838, V. to Cárlos Carrillo, in *Vallejo, Doc.*, MS., iv. 31. Feb. 14th, Capt. Villavicencio wrote to Alvarado from Sta Bárbara that Carrillo was making enemies, and it was rumored that he had summoned the Indians to his aid. Even Capt. Casteñeda was displeased, and had been heard to deny that Carrillo had any commission from the govt. Had A. decided to yield, the writer and others had formed a plan of revolt. *Id.*, v. 29.

have no force. We hold authority from the supreme
government. It is your duty simply to obey. You
have refused. We have sent for troops. If evil
comes of it, yours is the fault." Don Cárlos claimed
to have " exhausted every conciliatory means," and
declared that Alvarado's invitation to a conference
had involved an attempt to degrade his authority.
Don José Antonio denied having threatened to bring
one thousand armed men, but defended the request
for one fifth of that number; ridiculed the " Quixotic
enterprise of conquering Mexico;" and declared that
whatever orders the much-talked-of schooner might
bring, they would come addressed to the governor and
not to rebels.[6]

The position assumed in these communications and
others of the time entirely ignored all that had been
done by Alvarado since November 1836. It was the
old position of Los Angeles and San Diego striving
for the capital and custom-house. Considered as the
position of Bandini, Requena, Ibarra, Portilla, and
others who had never submitted to Alvarado except
when forced to do so, it possessed to a certain extent
the merit of consistency; but as that of Cárlos Carrillo it had no merit whatever. Meanwhile Don
Cárlos continued to act as governor in the south by
issuing the usual routine orders on minor matters
connected with the civil administration.[7] And late
in February he seems to have resolved on certain
military movements, for in obedience to his order
Alcalde Estudillo sent a force of citizens under Pio
Pico with a supply of ammunition from San Diego
to Los Angeles.[8]

Portilla was still acting as general in the south,
with headquarters at San Gabriel. Manuel Trujillo,

[6] Feb. 15, 1838, Carrillos to Vallejo, in *Vallejo, Doc.*, MS., v. 30-1.

[7] Four of these orders dated Feb. 10th, 16th, 19th, relating to land
grants, commerce, and Indians, are given in *Hopkins' Translations*, 7–8.
Also 8 others, on police matters, mails, passports, etc., dated Feb. 6–18th, in
S. Diego, Arch., MS., 194–5.

[8] Feb. 20, 1838, C. to Estudillo. Feb. 25th, E. to C. Several communications. *S. Diego, Arch.*, MS., 195, 197, 211.

a recent arrival, was Carrillo's secretary. Early in March San Diego was warned to be on the lookout for any force that the northerners might send down in Hinckley's ship, since it was said that Alvarado was coming south with an army;[9] and a few days later Captain Juan Castañeda, a Mexican officer who had come to the country with José Antonio Carrillo, was sent with a force to occupy San Buenaventura.[10] This occupation was effected probably on March 12th, without disaster, and soon Castañeda was instructed to advance and attack Santa Bárbara before it could be reënforced from the north. He was to form his own plan of attack, but was to lose no time. He must allow no conditions, but insist on immediate surrender at discretion, after which the leaders were to be kept in close confinement. "No more consideration must be shown for those faithless rebels."[11]

[9] March 3, 1838, C. to the encargado of S. Diego, *Hayes, Doc.*, MS., 81; *S. Diego, Arch.*, MS., 195. Estudillo promised on March 5th to observe all possible caution, and on March 7th sent the warning down to Todos Santos across the frontier. *Id.*, 211.

[10] March 10, 1838, Portilla's instructions to Castañeda. *Vallejo, Doc.*, MS., v. 38. He was to hold the mission and prevent the northern revolutionists from using its resources—it will be noticed that Cárlos Carrillo was the administrator of this mission—to cut off all communication with Sta Bárbara, and if attacked by the enemy in overwhelming numbers, to 'save the national honor' by retreating. Should he find the place already in possession of the foe, he might use his judgment as to the possibility of dislodging them. A letter of J. A. Carrillo to his brother on March 10th, *Dept. St. Pap.*, MS., iv. 182-3, seems to indicate a degree of displeasure that some of his ideas had not been adopted.

[11] March 16, 1838, Portilla to Castañeda. 3 despatches. Alf. J. A. Pico is to join him with a reënforcement. *Vallejo, Doc.*, MS., v. 42-4. March 12th, Carrillo warned Castañeda against Sergt Macedonio Gonzalez, who was to be closely watched. And on March 15th, he had recommended a Mexican named Badillo, who has a plan 'favorable to our views.' *Id.*, v. 40-1. March 16th, Manuel Requena also wrote to Castañeda that a reserve force was being organized to aid him. 'A Mexican officer accustomed to victory will not be defeated in California.' 'Laurels of victory await you!' *Id.*, v. 45. March 17th, Carrillo to 1st alcalde. Orders him to go with the sec. of the ayunt. to S. Buenaventura, escorted by 15 armed men, that the citizens of Los Angeles there may have a civil authority at their head. The sec. is to report all occurrences until the gov. can come in person. *Id.*, v. 46. March 18th, J. M. Covarrubias to Castañeda. Reënforcements will be sent. Fullest confidence felt by the writer and by others, who sign their names on the back of the same letter; viz., Pio Pico, Trujillo, Zamorano, Requena, A. and Joaquin Carrillo, Ignacio del Valle, and two others. *Id.*, v. 49. March 18th, Carrillo and Portilla to Castañeda. He must accelerate his movements and attack Sta Bárbara before Alvarado can arrive or the garrison escape. He must not however pursue the rebels, should they escape, farther than

Castañeda, in obedience to his orders from Portilla, left San Buenaventura probably March 17th, and took a position with his force in sight of Santa Bárbara, demanding the immediate surrender of the place. Comandante Villavicencio, though his force was small, had two or three small cannon so placed as to defend the approaches. He refused to surrender, and despatched a courier in all haste to the north for reën-forcements, while Captain Guerra and Padre Duran went out to parley with the besiegers. I have no means of knowing exactly what arguments these venerable diplomatists used, but such was their force that Castañeda did none of the brilliant things expected of him by the Angelinos. The captain most assuredly dis-obeyed in a disgraceful manner the orders of his chiefs Carrillo and Portilla, which with his force of over one hundred men he might easily have executed. Whether his course was inspired by fear of Villavi-cencio's guns, or was the result of deliberate treach-ery to Carrillo, as Botello intimates, or of an agree-ment with Guerra afterward broken by Castro, as Pio Pico seems to think, I do not know; but after remain-ing three or four days, perhaps at the Cerro del Vol-untario, he retired to San Buenaventura.[12]

Purísima. The gov. will leave Angeles on Monday so as to enter Sta Bár-bara on Wednesday. *Id.*, v. 50–2. It is noticeable that several letters of Carrillo, Portilla, and other prominent men at Angeles at this time bear the mysterious sign 'Fu....u,' which evidently had some hidden significance. On March 20th Carrillo acknowledges the receipt of $1,000 from Pio Pico as a loan to the treasury in aid of Castañeda's movement. On July 5, 1843, Gov. Micheltorena indorsed this by a marginal decree that it should be paid when convenient. Indorsed by Pio Pico to Andrés Pico, and by the latter to Pablo de la Guerra. *Guerra, Doc.*, MS., i. 232–3.

[12] Botello, *Anales del Sur*, MS., 50–2, who as sec. went with the alcalde of Angeles to Castañeda's camp, says that he pretended not to have men enough, though his officers urged an attack, and friends in Sta Bárbara sent word how easily it could be taken. Castañeda was said to have had some differences with Carrillo before starting. Pico, *Hist. Cal.*, MS., 63, says that the agree-ment was that Castañeda should retire to S. Buenventura and no troops on the other side should pass Carpintería, that is, until Alvarado and Carrillo could hold a conference. Lugo, *Vida*, MS., 18–19, tells us the comisionados persuaded them to retire, promising mediation with the northerners. Pinto, *Apuntaciones*, MS., 29–34, claims to have been present at the interview be-tween Villaviciencio and Andrés Pico, after the negotiations with Guerra and Duran, when an arrangement was made to stop hostilities until Alvarado should come. *Valle, Lo Pasado*, MS., 21, merely says that Castañeda re-

In the north, during the first half of March, they were content to wait as before, news from the south being unexciting, and the governor also suffering for a time from illness.[13] Then came the information that Don Cárlos had sent a force to San Buenaventura, thus assuming the offensive. The force was understood to be small, and Carrillo not apprehensive of any immediate attack. Alvarado resolved on prompt action, and sent Castro with fifteen men to Santa Bárbara to join the garrison of that place, attack the abajeños by surprise, and to send Don Cárlos and his leaders as prisoners to Monterey. It was the plan suggested by Castro earlier, the execution of which had been postponed. "It is time to put an end to these political discussions," wrote the governor.[14]

There were particular reasons, it seems, for prompt action on both sides at this time. Alvarado learned that a despatch from Castillero for him had been intercepted by Carrillo; and he, on the other hand, intercepted a letter from Don Cárlos to his wife. In that letter it was announced that the *California* had reached Acapulco; that some of Alvarado's official letters had been published in government journals of September

treated, pleading insufficiency of force. Mrs. Ord, *Ocurrencias*, MS., 108–10, says that Villavicencio's garrison of 20 or 25 men was increased to 100 men by the citizens. She says that Castañeda came only to Carpintería. Farnham, *Life in Cal.*, 290–4, gives a very amusing but of course inaccurate account of the Sta Bárbara campaign. Mention only in *Alvarado, Hist. Cal.*, MS., iv. 41–2; *Pico, Acont.*, MS., 48–9; *Estudillo, Datos*, MS., 22–3; *Gonzales, Experiencias*, MS., 33–5; *Janssens, Vida*, MS., 126; *Valdés, Mem.*, MS., 27.

[13]March 4, 1838, Alvarado to Vallejo. Thinks of going south in 8 days. *Vallejo, Doc.*, MS., v. 36. March 12th, friends in Los Angeles send encouragement. Same to same. *Id.*, v. 39. March 12th, V. to J. A. Carrillo. A rather severe answer to his last letter, suggesting that it is as well to drop protestations of friendship for a while until things are more settled. 'I am neither centralist, federalist, nor monarchist, but ranchero, caring little for systems while we have neither population nor capital.' *Dept. St. Pap.*, MS., iv. 183–5. There is also a letter of Alvarado to Cárlos Carrillo, in *Vallejo, Doc.*, MS., iv. 30, not dated, and probably written a little later. It is a repetition of the old views expressed somewhat independently.

[14]March 18, 1838, A. to V., in *Vallejo, Doc.*, MS., v. 48. He wants a few men sent from Sonoma and S. Francisco. March 13th, Villavicencio to A. from Sta Bárbara. Sends 4 documents to undeceive him about Carrillo's intentions, one being doubtless Portilla's order to Castañeda to occupy S. Buenaventura. *Dept. St. Pap.*, MS., iv. 185-6.

1837, and that Captain Robbins had been rewarded with some position in accordance with Alvarado's recommendations. It was implied also that the government was inclined to favor Alvarado as governor. The party in power when official despatches should arrive would manifestly have the advantage; therefore Castro had orders to win or lose in fifteen days.[15]

Santiago Estrada was the courier sent by Villavicencio to announce to the governor Castañeda's appearance in front of Santa Bárbara with one hundred and fifty men. Estrada met Castro on the way at San Luis Obispo, and hastened that officer's movements; at Buenavista rancho his strength gave out, and he forwarded a letter to Santa Clara.[16] All available force was at once placed at Alvarado's disposal by the general, Salvador Vallejo being sent by forced marches from Sonoma.[17] I have no details respecting the march southward of Alvarado and his reënforcements. April 5th he was at Santa Inés, and six days earlier at Buenavista had heard of Castro's success.

Castro, after joining his escort to Villavicencio's force and the Santa Bárbara volunteers, had probably about one hundred men, with whom, taking along also a few cannon, he hastened on to San Buenaventura. His approach to the mission seems to have been un-

[15] March 18, 1838, Alvarado to Vallejo from S. Juan, in *Vallejo, Doc.*, MS., v. 47. Bustamante, in his *Gabinete Mex.*, i. 90, MS. (not in the printed edition), also says it was on Sept. 22d that the return of California to allegiance was announced in congress. Bustamante had predicted this return in Dec. 1836, and that it would be effected through the friars.

[16] March 22, 1838, Estrada's original letter, forwarded by Alvarado to Vallejo the same day. *Vallejo, Doc.*, MS., v. 53–4. He says Castañeda's force was encamped at the 'Laguna de Sal this side of Montecito,' which corresponds to the Cerro del Voluntario mentioned in different statements.

[17] March 24, 1838, V. to Sanchez, Martinez, com. at Sta Clara, and to Capt. Vallejo, in *Vallejo, Doc.*, MS., v. 55–8. Same date, A. to V. from Sta Clara. Will march next day for S. Juan. Is determined to avenge himself and punish the southerners for their shabby treatment of him. Does not need a large force to do it. *Id.*, v. 60. March 28th, Lieut Martinez, rancho de la Merced. Was lame, having been thrown from a horse; could not get any *civicos* to go, but helped Salvador with horses, etc. *Id.*, v. 62. March 24th, V. to A. Mentions the orders he has issued. An accident to his leg prevents him from coming in person. Is glad the time has come to act with decision. *Dept. St. Pap.*, MS., iv. 187–8.

suspected until he had surrounded it, or at least cut off its communications with Los Angeles.[18] On the morning of March 27th, Castañeda was notified by Castro, from the campo militar of the 'northern division of operations,' to evacuate the place within one hour under assurance of protection to life and property, else force would be employed. He returned the summons, writing on the back that in case of an evacuation it must be with all the honors of war. In a second note Castro declined to make further concessions, and repeated his demand, and on the back of this note was returned Castañeda's refusal to surrender except as before offered. Yet a third summons was sent, with a threat of opening fire at once; and the reply was, "Do as you please."[19] Firing soon began.

The battle of San Buenaventura, though much powder was burned, was not a bloody one. Castro reports to the governor the 28th: "I have the pleasure to inform you that after two days of continuous firing, and with the loss of only one man killed on our side, the whole force of 110 men which defended this place has fled on foot under cover of night; and at this moment I have determined that a company of mounted infantry under Captain Villa, and another cavalry company of lancers under Captain Cota, shall start in their pursuit, myself remaining here with the rest of the division and the artillery to protect this place, which would be very advantageous for us in case the escaped rebels should join the force of Don Cárlos and return to save their honor."[20] Next day he announced his success

<hr />

[18] March 26, 1838, Castañeda to com. of Sta B., asking that 4 men who had been given leave of absence be sent back. *Vallejo, Doc.*, MS., v. 61. March 27th, Carrillo to encargado at S. Diego, asking for a gun, the wheels to be obtained from Fitch, also munitions. *S. Diego, Arch.*, MS., 195.

[19] In *Pico, Doc.*, MS., ii. 3-5, 7-8, I have the originals of Castro's first and second summons with the replies of Castañeda. The latter's 2d and 3d replies are in *Dept. St. Pap.*, MS., iv. 189.

[20] March 28, 1838, Castro to Alvarado, forwarded by the latter to the Monterey alcaldes on April 4th from Sta Inés. *Vallejo, Doc.*, MS., xxxii. 155; also in *Dept. St. Pap.*, MS., iv. 188-9. March 30th, Alvarado from Buenavista announces the victory, the news having just arrived by a courier from Sta B., to administrators of missions from S. Juan northward. He says the forces on each side were about 100 men; and he has 80 men who are to start south-

in having captured 70 of the fugitives, with 50 muskets and other arms.   The soldiers were to be set free
according to the laws of war; the officers were sent to
the governor as prisoners.[21]

Naturally accounts of this battle written from memory, though numerous, present many discrepancies.
There is a very general tendency to grossly exaggerate the forces engaged, really a little more than 100
men on each side, and to speak of assaults repelled,
and other purely imaginary details.   Castañeda's force
had, as it would seem, no artillery, but included a party
of New Mexicans armed with rifles.   Castro's approach was altogether unsuspected until at dawn he
made his presence known, having by that time seized
all the garrison's horses, cut off communication with
Angeles, and also probably cut off the water supply,
thus obliging the soldiers to quench their thirst mainly
with the mission wine.   Two guns were placed on
the shore-side in the direction of the chapel, and one
perhaps on the elevation back of the mission.   Early
in the fight a rifleman from the church tower killed
one of Castro's men.[22]   The guns were then directed
upon the church, which in 1874 still bore some slight
marks of the cannonade, and from the walls of which
in the course of certain repairs some time in the past
decade a cannon-ball is said to have been taken.   The
"continuous firing of two days" was perhaps continuous only with considerable intervals between the volleys, and it could not have continued into the second
day for a longer time than was necessary to make

---

ward at once. *Vallejo, Doc.*, MS., v. 64. The doc. is indorsed at Merced by
Martinez, at S. Pablo by J. Castro, and at S. Rafael by Murphy, between 8
A. M. and 7.30 P. M. of April 2d. In *Id.*, v. 63, is what purports to be a copy
of a similar note to Gen. Vallejo; but the copyist has intentionally changed
its figures so as to exaggerate grossly the forces engaged.

[21] March 29th, Castro to Alvarado. *Dept. St. Pap.*, MS., iv. 190–1. March
31st, Capt. Cota asks to have the prisoners Ignacio Alvarado, Teodoro Yorba,
and Enrique Sepúlveda left with him at Sta Bárbara, he being responsible
for them. *Id.* Castro's report forwarded from Sta Inés to Vallejo on Apr. 5th.
Vallejo, Doc., MS., v. 72–3; xxxii. 128. April 9th, great rejoicing at S. Francisco at the news. Sanchez to V. *Id.*, v. 76.

[22] The man is called by most Californians Cordero or Cornado. Alvarado
says he was Aquilino Ramirez; and Jesus Pico calls him Olivas.

known the flight of the garrison during the night. The fugitives, or such of them as kept together, were easily overtaken by the horsemen near Saticoy on March 28th. Castañeda and a few of his officers were sent under arrest to Santa Bárbara, and perhaps to Santa Inés. Nearly all the Californians state that after the occupation Castro found concealed in the mission church certain other men of some prominence, who were sent north with the other prisoners. There is a general agreement that Andrés Pico, Alcalde Luis Arenas, and Ignacio Palomares were of this number.[23] There are no contemporary records respecting any of the prominent prisoners, nor the circumstances and length of their captivity.[24]

Escaping fugitives, who seem to have met on the way Pio Pico at the head of a small reënforcement,

[23] Others named, most of them and perhaps all incorrectly, are J. A. Carrillo, Gil Ibarra, Manuel Requena, Manuel Alva, Ignacio del Valle, and José Ramirez. Yorba, Alvarado, and Sepúlveda (see note 21) were probably of the number found in the church. Arenas was at Sta Inés on April 6th, giving testimony on that day against Carrillo. *Dept. St. Pap.*, MS., xviii. 13–14.

[24] Botello, *Anales*, MS., 52–63, was one who ran away from the mission with the rest, and unlike the rest escaped to carry the news to Carrillo. José Carrillo, son of D. Cárlos, also escaped, but was re-arrested at Sta Ana. Botello notes some suspicious actions on the part of Castañeda, which seem unimportant. Alvarado, *Hist. Cal.*, MS., iv. 36–41, testifies that the New Mexicans had been promised all the mares at S. Fernando for their services, and were therefore known as Yegueros. Osio, *Hist. Cal.*, MS., 385–90, puts Tobar in command instead of Castañeda, states that the garrison did not succeed in escaping from the mission, and describes some of the abuse shown by Alvarado when drunk to the prisoners at Sta Inés. Salvador Vallejo, *Notas Históricas*, MS., 75–80, gives one of the most absurdly inaccurate narratives of the affair extant. García, *Hechos*, MS., 86–92, claims to have been sent to S. Luis Obispo with the prisoners, who he says were soon set at liberty. Pinto, *Apuntaciones*, MS., 34–7, aided in capturing Andrés Pico and the rest, who were hidden under the sacred vestments, etc., in the sacristy. He says Castro at first threatened to shoot Surgeon Alva. Gonzalez, *Experiencias*, MS., 35–6, says that only a few volleys were fired. Mrs Ord, *Ocurrencias*, MS., 110–11, heard the firing all day at Sta Bárbara. Pio Pico, *Hist. Cal.*, MS., 63, and Ávila, *Notas*, MS., 21–2, narrate that Pico with 20 men on his way to join Castañeda met some of the fugitives at Sta Clara River. Valle, *Lo Pasado*, MS., 22–3, as well as Botello, mentions José Carrillo's arrest. An account of these events, dated March 30th, was published in the *Honolulu S. I. Gazette*, May 5, 1838. In it Castro is said to have made several arrests on his first arrival at Sta Bárbara, including that of D. Pedro Carrillo. Farnham, *Life in Cal.*, 294–8, evidently used the version in the *Gazette*, and added to it in his usual 'opera bouffe' style of writing history. Brief narratives also in *Valdés, Mem.*, MS., 27–9; *Forster's Pioneer Data*, MS., 14–15; *Castro, Relacion*, MS., 44–5; *Arce, Mem.*, MS., 13–15.

soon carried to Los Angeles the tidings of the disaster at San Buenaventura. Cárlos Carrillo had time to collect his friends and the remnants of his demoralized army and retire to San Diego before Castro came and took possession of the city, probably on the 1st of April.[25] Very little can be learned about events of the next two weeks and more. Castro's only act at Angeles, so far as known, was to issue a recommendation, or credentials, to a committee of citizens who went to meet Alvarado with a view to secure a cessation of hostilities.[26] On April 8th he had retired to San Fernando, whence he modestly acknowledged the receipt of Alvarado's letter expressing satisfaction with his past achievements, and promised still more good service when his force should be joined by that of the governor.[27] Alvarado, having left Santa Inés as late as the 6th, and spent perhaps a few days at Santa Bárbara, joined Castro at San Fernando on or before April 16th. On this date he addressed another letter to Don Cárlos, deploring the latter's policy and the resulting hostilities, but reminding his 'dear uncle' that there was yet time to prevent serious calamities by submitting his credentials to the diputacion and consenting to a conference.[28]

Meanwhile Carrillo was at San Diego again preparing for war, at the instigation of Bandini, Zamo-

[25] March 31, 1838—after Carrillo had departed, but before Castro's arrival —the ayunt. sent a committee of 3, Lugo, Covarrubias, and José Carrillo, to urge Don Cárlos to come to the city, where the presence of his Excellency was deemed necessary for the protection of lives and property. *Los Angeles, Arch.*, MS., v. 2-3. Same date, showing that Don Cárlos had not yet reached S. Diego, alcalde of S. Diego announces the sending of the gun desired and 6 men, all that could be induced to go to Angeles. *S. Diego, Arch.*, MS., 197; *Hayes, Doc.*, MS., 83. April 1st, same to Carrillo. A bark in sight which may be the one of which the gov. had written, viz., Hinckley's vessel. *S. Diego, Arch.*, MS., 197.

[26] April 1st, Castro to Alvarado. *Dept. St. Pap.*, MS., iv. 192. There is not a word about events since the fall of S. Buenaventura.

[27] April 8, 1838, C. to A. *Dept. St. Pap.*, MS., iv. 197-8. Alvarado's letter had been dated the day before, probably at Sta Bárbara. He had 50 men with him, probably Salvador Vallejo's northern troops.

[28] April 14th, A. to Carrillo. *Dept. St. Pap.*, MS., iv. 201-2. He begs Don Cárlos to leave the 4 or 5 vagabonds who advise him, and to form an alliance with himself.

rano, and the rest. Here, as in the north, we have but few particulars of the preparations;[29] the chief support of the would-be governor's reviving hopes seems to have been the arrival from Sonora overland of Captain Juan José Tobar, said to have been somewhat distinguished as an Indian-fighter and guerrillero. Tobar arrived on April 4th and was at once made general in place of Portilla. It does not appear that he came in any official capacity, or accompanied by more than a small escort; but Don Cárlos, wishing to make the most of his new ally, announced that he had come to quell the disorders in California, implying of course that he brought a force with which to accomplish that object. Carrillo, however, desiring to treat the citizens fairly, had induced Tobar to suspend his operations until the result of communication with Castro could be known. So he informed the ayuntamiento of Los Angeles, to which body Tobar also wrote, expressing his desire to try gentle means first, and authorizing an announcement "in my name to the troops with the northern rebels that they shall be pardoned if they present themselves before me with their arms within fifteen days which expire on the 25th—otherwise I shall be inexorable in punishing them."[30]

From volunteers at San Diego, refugees from Los

---

[29] April 4, 1838, Ortega to Carrillo. Is at his orders, but excuses himself from going to meet him. April 11th, sends from S. José del Valle some rumors about the northern forces. *Dept. St. Pap.*, MS., iv. 196. April 4th, Encargado Estudillo orders all to come from the mission. 'The gov. is waiting for you to have a conference on various matters.' *S. Diego, Arch.*, MS., 198. Apr. 5th, 10th, P. Caballero, at Guadalupe. B. Cal. sends cattle and report of arms and ammunition to Carrillo. *Dept. St. Pap.*, MS., iv. 192, 198-9. Apr. 6th, justice of S. José del Valle tells Carrillo that both as legitimate gov. and as a cousin he may count on him. *Id.*, iv. 221. Apr. 14th, Osuna, S. Luis, to Carrillo, has been unable to secure the services of Linares. Castro said to be advancing. *Id.*, iv. 200. April 19th, 20th, Pio Pico, S. Luis, to Carrillo. Is ill and cannot meet him. Regrets Carrillo's illness. *Id.*, iv. 195.

[30] April 11, 1838, session of ayunt., when the letters of Carrillo and Tobar were read. It was resolved to send the former to Castro. The people after hearing the other letter at a public meeting 'dissolved without uttering a word.' *Los Angeles, Arch.*, MS., v. 4-7. April 9th, Tobar to the ayunt. *Dept. St. Pap., Angeles*, MS., xi. 102-3.

Angeles, recruits obtained across the frontier—for
Carrillo's jurisdiction, if he had any, extended over the
peninsula—and the remnants of Portilla's men, Don
Cárlos formed an army of 100 men or more for his new
general, who soon marched northward. At Las
Flores, after passing San Luis Rey, he heard that the
enemy had left Angeles for the south, and here Tobar's army made a stand, perhaps on the same day that
Castro's force came in sight, and probably on the 20th
or 21st of April. An adobe building of the rancho
served as barracks, and an adjoining corral as a fort.
Three cannon were mounted so as to command the
approaches, the gunners being protected, and weak
points strengthened, by a judicious arrangement of
hides, pack-saddles, and whatever else was at hand.
Juan Bandini and José Antonio Carrillo seem to have
been present as well as Don Cárlos. Requena, Ibarra,
and other prominent Angelinos were also within the
fortified corral.[31]

Meanwhile Castro and Alvarado had united their
forces, obtaining volunteers also from Santa Bárbara
and perhaps from Angeles, and had marched south
from that city with over 200 men, occupying the mission of San Juan Capistrano about the same time that
Carrillo reached Las Flores.[32] An advance guard of

[31]Botello, *Anales*, MS., 64–8, Janssens, *Vida*, MS., 129–39, and Coronel,
Cosas de Cal., MS., 25–8, give some meagre details. The last two were present, Janssens having charge of one of the guns. Botello, being disabled, remained at S. Luis with Pio Pico's family. Don Pio, *Hist. Cal.*, MS., 63–70,
accounts for his own absence by claiming to have discovered in advance that
Carrillo intended to capitulate, and he was busied with plans to surprise S.
Buenaventura, and thus counteract the cowardly policy of D. Cárlos!

[32]Ignacio Ezquer, *Mem.*, MS., 5–10, who was temporarily in charge of S.
Juan, the administrator having gone to join the southern army, tells us that
J. A. Carrillo with a small party from the south came one evening and in-
quired about Castro's men, of whom nothing had been heard. He intended
to sleep at the mission, but finally decided to go to the arroyo near by to spend
the night, taking along a supply of wine and aguardiente. At midnight, narrator was roused from sleep by the arrival of Castro's men. Later, much
liquor was consumed, and narrator was compelled to get drunk, not losing
consciousness, however, until the new-comers had fired a cannon toward the
port, thus scaring away the sleepers at the arroyo, who left some of their ac-
coutrements behind. Pinto, *Apunt.*, MS., 74–5, confirms the story that the
gun was fired on account of Alvarado's suspicions that there might be foes in
that direction, and that some horses were found tied there. Alvarado, *Hist.*

Tobar's force under J. A. Carrillo seems to have previously visited the mission and retired. It was on April 21st that the northern army appeared in battle array before the improvised fort which protected the southern foe.

The combat at Las Flores was for the most part one of tongue and pen, though a cannon was fired once or twice from the corral, doing no harm—so say several witnesses, confirmed by a letter written at the time. A flag of truce was sent—from which side first is not quite clear—with a demand, not for surrender, but for an interview. Don Juan Bautista had no motive for fighting if he could accomplish his purpose by other methods; the cannon had a threatening aspect, and Tobar might be a man who would not hesitate to use them; besides, he had not much doubt of his ability to control his uncle in an interview. On the other hand, there is some reason to believe that Tobar really intended to fight, trusting to his guns to make up for disparity of numbers. Many of his men were imbued to a certain degree with their leader's valor. Cárlos Carrillo, freely charged by his associates with cowardice, declined to assume the responsibility of shedding blood, forbade the discharge of a single gun, and went out to meet his nephew on the bloodless field of diplomacy. Tobar finally retired in disgust, with many companions, not pausing until he had crossed the frontier; and Don Cárlos was left to his peaceful methods of warfare. Zamorano, of whom very little is known since the failure of his aspirations to the governorship with Alvarado's submission to Mexico in July 1837, probably crossed the frontier about the same time as Tobar. He came back four years later, only to die; and as nothing is known of

Cal., MS., iv. 82-95, and Vallejo, *Hist. Cal.*, MS., iii. 369-72, represent that the southerners had occupied S. Juan, and retired at Castro's approach. They add that Salvador Vallejo being sent forward to occupy S. Juan by 'conciliatory' means, did so by sending a threat to hang all who did not instantly surrender; or, as one says, he charged bayonets and rushed madly through all the mission buildings from which the foe had retired!

his experience in the mean time, I append a biographical sketch. He was a man of much ability, honor, and energy; of exemplary conduct, though ambitious; and never warmly in sympathy with the Californians.[33]

[33] Coronel, Botello, and Janssens are those who complain most bitterly of Carrillo's cowardice. Osio, *Hist. Cal.*, MS., 390–4, describes Don Cárlos as 'fluctuating between fear and ignorance.' This writer also speaks of a gun planted by Alvarado on a hill, and of the enemy's water supply being cut off. Also of Carrillo's running to the beach and escaping in a boat. Alvarado, *Hist. Cal.*, MS., iv. 87–108, insists that Tobar, after he found out what kind of men he was fighting with, came to an understanding with Castro, who purposely left the way clear for his escape. Several persons, with no special advantages for knowing anything on the subject, speak of a previous understanding between Alvarado and Carrillo, which is absurd. Salvador Vallejo, *Notas Hist.*, MS., 64–7, talks of a conflict between 400 mounted Californians and 500 Sonorans and Ópatas, of a bayonet charge, a rout, horses killed, a hot pursuit, etc.! Pinto, *Apunt.*, MS., 07–8, says that some cannon shots were fired. Juan Forster, *Pioneer Data*, MS., 15–17, on whose land the battle took place, says he watched the operations without taking any part. Also brief accounts in *Valle, Lo Pasado*, MS., 23; *Sanchez, Notas*, MS., 3–5; *Meadows' Graham Affair*, MS., 1–3; *Pico, Acont.*, MS., 52–3; *Estudillo, Datos*, MS., 23; *Ord, Ocurrencias*, MS., 111–13; *Arce, Mem.*, MS., 15–17; *Lugo, Vida*, MS., 19–21; *Ávila, Notas*, MS., 21–4; *Castro, Relacion*, MS., 45–8.

I know nothing of Capt. Tobar's life after this visit to Cal., and little of his earlier record. In 1828 he was stationed at Altar under Gen. Figueroa's orders. In 1832 he revolted, seizing Pitic and Guaymas; and in 1835 issued a manifiesto at Arizpe in defence of his past acts. It was probably in the character of a political refugee that he came to Cal. He is described as a very tall man of fine appearance and great bravery, about 50 years of age. There were later rumors, probably unfounded, of his intention to return with a larger force. *Pinart, Col. de Sonora*, MS., no. 38, print, 362. April 24th, Tobar to Carrillo, bidding him farewell, with thanks for his kindness. Is at S. Diego, and is about to leave Cal. *Dept. St. Pap.*, MS., iv. 203.

Agustin Vicente Zamorano is said to have been a native of Florida, his parents being Spaniards. Of his early life, save that he received a good education, nothing is known until he entered the army on May 1, 1821, as cadet. In July he was attached to the 6th battalion, taking part in several battles on the insurgent side under generals Bustamante and Quintanar, and being made alférez in October. In Oct. 1824, he was transferred to the corps of engineers; and came to California with Gov. Echeandía in 1825. He served as Echeandía's secretary for 5 years; was married in Feb. 1827 to María Luisa, daughter of Santiago Argüello; was made lieutenant in 1828, still of the battalion and engineers; and early in 1831, on Echeandía's recommendation, was commissioned captain of the Monterey company. Record of military service in *Dept. St. Pap., Ben. Mil.*, MS., lxxvii. 2–3; *St. Pap., Sac.*, MS., x. 36, 68. Marriage, *Arch. Sta B.*, MS., xii. 342; *Dept. Rec.*, MS., vi. 30–1; vii. 108. In 1832 he refused to accept the results of the revolt against Victoria; made a counter-revolt against Echeandía: and sustained himself as comandante general of the north until the arrival of Figueroa in 1833, as related in chap. viii.–ix., of this volume. He served as Figueroa's secretary in 1833–5; and in addition to his duties as captain of the presidio, conducted a printing-office at Monterey, having succeeded in obtaining a press and type in 1834. All the products of this press down to his departure bore his name, and I have in *Earliest Printing* many specimens, together with Zamorano's circular and scale of prices. He was not a printer by trade. In June 1835 he was made captain of the S. Diego company. *Dept. St. Pap., Ben. Mil.*, MS., lxxix. 85.

Several interviews were held at Las Flores, midway between the two armies, by the rival governors and their representatives, before a satisfactory settlement could be effected. Alvarado, describing those negotiations from memory, mentions three interviews. The first was broken off by Carrillo's familiar way of addressing Don Juan Bautista as Juanito, or Johnny. The liberty was not displeasing to Alvarado, but his companions, Castro, Villa, and Salvador Vallejo, insisted on the use of his proper title, which Carrillo's friends, Requena and Tobar, would not permit. Next day, however, the two rivals withdrew out of hearing of the rest to have a conference untrammelled by official etiquette. Don Cárlos now showed his original appointment, and was much grieved that Don Juan did not at once yield to so convincing an argument, but before they parted some progress was made toward a temporary settlement which would remove the necessity for further warfare.[34]

On April 23d Alvarado sent a despatch to Vallejo and other officials in the north, stating that for three days with his 250 men he had besieged the foe, 100 strong with three cannon, at Las Flores, preventing their advance to attack the peaceful inhabitants of the north. Don Cárlos was among the besieged, but after several interviews had offered nothing satisfactory to the Californian people. Yet a complete victory by force of arms, the only way left, could not fail to follow within a few days.[35] That same day,

His efforts with the sureños against Alvarado, prompted by personal ambition and the hope of gaining favor in Mexico rather than by sympathy with, or opposition to, the south, have been recorded in the preceding chapter. The last definite record of his presence was on March 18, 1838, at Angeles, when he signed a letter to Castañeda. It is possible that he left the country immediately on the fall of Los Angeles; but he probably remained for a while to support Carrillo's claims. I know nothing of him during his absence. In 1842 he came back with Gov. Micheltorena as lieut-colonel and inspector; but died soon after landing at San Diego in August, leaving a widow who long survived him. One of his daughters married Gen. José María Flores, and another was the wife of Henry Dalton.

[34] Alvarado, Hist. Cal., MS., iv. 95–107. I omit further details, which are, I suspect, much more amusing than accurate.

[35] April 23, 1838, A. to V. Vallejo, Doc., MS., v. 77. Same to ayunt. of

however, a treaty was signed which I give in full.[36]
By its terms the opposing factions were to be for the
most part disbanded; Carrillo was to accompany Alvarado to San Fernando, where an arrangement was
to be made respecting the governorship; and until
such arrangement had been made, Vallejo was to be
recognized as general.

It was after the general terms had been agreed
upon, but before they were signed, that Tobar was
allowed to escape, either by intention or carelessness
on the part of Castro. The treaty was virtually a
surrender by Don Cárlos, who indeed, consistently
with his aversion to the use of cannon, could do
nothing but surrender. He may have had some
hopes of success in the consultation to be held at San
Fernando, but there was nothing in the treaty on
which to found such hopes. A few southerners rep-

S. José. *S. José, Arch.*, MS., vi. 6; circular in *Vallejo, Doc.*, MS., xxxii.
129.

[36] *Tratado de Las Flores entre Alvarado y Carrillo, 23 de Abril, 1838.* Original MS. Copy in *Bandini, Doc. Hist. Cal.*, MS., 77.

'In the space between the northern and southern forces of Alta California,
on the field of Las Flores, April 23, 1838, the subscribers have agreed upon the
following articles: Art. 1. The force of the south at Las Flores will be disbanded
absolutely, the citizens (volunteers) retiring to their homes with the arms
belonging to them. Soldiers in said force will march under their respective
chiefs to protect the points where they belong. Art. 2. The artillery and
munitions belonging to the said division will remain at the disposition of the
departmental government. Art. 3. The division of the north near the said
pueblo will disband its auxiliary citizen soldiery at the same time that the
disbanding mentioned in art. 1 takes place—there remaining as a guard for
Don Cárlos Antonio Carrillo and Don Juan Bautista Alvarado 75 men chosen
by their respective chiefs. Art. 4. Don C. A. Carrillo will proceed, accompanied by Don J. B. Alvarado, with the escort cited in the preceding article,
to the establishment of San Fernando for the purpose of arranging there
gubernatorial matters pertaining to Alta California, this not being done in
the city of Los Angeles, named by a law as capital of the department, for
lack of resources to do so in the present circumstances. Art. 5. Meeting in
the said establishment, both gentlemen named in the preceding article will
agree upon what is necessary for the tranquillity of the country. Art. 6.
Persons in the division of the south remain entirely at liberty to live, work, or
settle at any point of Alta California; assured that they will not be molested
for having manifested their opinion on this occasion, on condition that they
never use their arms to break this agreement, others concerned enjoying the
same guaranties on the same conditions. Art. 7. Gen. Tobar will be recognized
as an officer of the Mexican army, and will be shown all the consideration
due to his position. Art. 8. Pending the arrangement indicated in art. 5,
Lieut. M. G. Vallejo will be recognized as comandante general of Alta California. Cárlos Anto Carrillo. Juan B. Alvarado.'

resent Alvarado as having promised to give up the command and as having broken his pledge; but he made no such promise in writing, and there is no reason to believe that he did so verbally. If he failed to carry out the treaty of April 23d faithfully in any respect, it must have been in not promptly disbanding his forces, and there is no evidence against him on this point.[37]

The northern army now retraced its march by way of San Gabriel to San Fernando, taking along the captured cannon, which were soon sent to Monterey on Steele's vessel, and escorting the two rival governors, who were now on the best of terms. True, Don Cárlos suggested en route that his position seemed more like that of a prisoner under guard than of a ruler attended by an escort. Don Juan replied, "If you are a prisoner, so am I, as we are marching side by side." At San Fernando in the early days of May their respective claims to the governorship were discussed. Carrillo could only show his original appointment and urge his rival's duty to submit to the supreme government. Alvarado could no longer deny that the document was in a certain sense genuine; indeed, he had probably never had any real doubt on the subject, but he still insisted that the appointment should bear the president's signature, and he made the new point that he had no official knowledge of Peña y Peña's signature, or indeed of his appointment as minister of state.[38] He also, in addition to the old arguments with which the reader is familiar, attached much weight to the fact that Don Cárlos,

[37] May 14, 1838, Com. Sanchez to Vallejo, announcing his return from the southern campaign with the S. Francisco troops. *Vallejo, Doc.*, MS., v. 78. This indicates compliance with the treaty. Alvarado, *Campaña de Las Flores y Sucesos de Abril–Mayo, 1838*, MS., a letter to Vallejo from Sta Bárbara May 22d—a most important original document—stated that Carrillo, before signing the treaty, wished to be allowed to escape and to go to Lower California, where he thought he could make himself recognized as governor, but he persuaded him that this was an impracticable scheme.

[38] Carrillo's appointment was simply an announcement that the president had made him governor, dated from the *Ministerio de lo Interior*, and signed Peña y Peña. Copy from original in *Carrillo (P.), Doc.*, MS., 1.

during the year that had elapsed since his appointment, had not, as he admitted, received a single official communication from the government. Had the negotiations proceeded uninterruptedly, Don Cárlos remaining under Alvarado's influence, it is probable that they would have resulted in an agreement to await orders from Mexico to transfer the command. The two had already partially agreed on a convention of representatives from each pueblo; when José Antonio Carrillo, Juan Bandini, and Pio Pico made their appearance, and soon regained control of their weak-minded chieftain. With them Don Cárlos went away to Angeles, announcing his intention to remain in that city where he was still recognized, but promising to commit no further hostilities.[39]

Alvarado went to Sta Bárbara about May 10th. He had advised Carrillo not to go to Angeles, but had not otherwise attempted to detain him. It appears that he had well founded hopes of a reaction in his own favor among the Angelinos. On the 14th over sixty citizens, headed by Juan Gallardo, José M. Herrera, Vicente Moraga, Pedro Dominguez, and Antonio Aguilar, presented a petition to the ayuntamiento, in which they represented, with all due deference to the supreme government, that the appointment of Cárlos Carrillo as governor had not produced the beneficial results intended, since the appointee had shown himself to possess none of the qualities necessary in a ruler, but had on the contrary committed serious blunders, notably in exciting hostilities at San Buenaventura and Las Flores, where "only by divine dispensation had California been saved from mourning and sorrow." Therefore, the petitioners advised submission to the government of the north in accordance

---

[39] *Alvarado, Campaña de la Flores*, MS. May 2d, A. to J. J. Vallejo. Says that as the state is now entirely pacified, it has been determined to release all political prisoners. *Vallejo, Doc.*, MS., xxxii. 132. May 3d, A. to alcalde of S. José. Tranquillity restored; Tobar fled; artillery in my possession; Don Cárlos pardoned; shall soon come north, etc. *Hopkins' Translations*, 8-9.

with public opinion and for the country's good. No
action was taken, because the petition was not written
on stamped paper, but next day when that irregularity had been corrected, the people were summoned and
the subject discussed on its merits. Eight citizens
took part in the discussion, and of twenty-eight whose
names were not on the petition twenty-two voted
for what was asked in that document, while only one,
Sérbulo Varela, voted in favor of Carrillo. The
matter was finally referred to a committee, which reported that while the ayuntamiento had no right to
criticise the acts of Carrillo, yet a clearly defined
public opinion demanded the recognition of Alvarado
as governor pending the decision of the government.
This was approved by a plurality of votes, the result
being formally communicated to the people and to
Carrillo, who was still addressed as governor. Thus
did the versatile city of the Angels accomplish
another political somersault.[40]

Of course the two Carrillos and their supporters
were not disposed to accept the position in which the
ayuntamiento had placed them. Some of the number,
like Requena, Portilla, and Trujillo, had crossed the
frontier with Tobar; while others, as Pico, Bandini,
Ibarra, and Botello, were left to continue the agitation. Before they had time, however, to carry into
execution their new plan, whatever it may have been,
the leaders were arrested on or about May 20th.
Alvarado, promptly informed of the troubles that were
brewing in the city, had sent Villavicencio with twenty-five men from Santa Bárbara to nip the conspiracy

---

[40] Sessions of ayunt., May 14–15, 1838. *Los Angeles*, *Arch.*, MS., v. 8–23.
The citizens taking part in the discussion were Tiburcio Tapia, Vicente
Sanchez, Abel Stearns, Antonio Ign. Ávila, José Sepúlveda, Felipe Carrillo,
Ignacio Machado, and Francisco J. Alvarado. The committee was composed
of Vicente de la Osa, Sanchez, Castillo, Sepúlveda, Stearns, and Tapia. In
the lists of about 90 citizens, only one foreigner appears besides Stearns, and
that was Miguel Blanco, or Michael White. In *Dept. St. Pap.*, *Angeles*, MS.,
ii. 112, is an incomplete blotter-copy of the *acta* of the committee, of which
Stearns was made pres. and Castillo sec. According to the *Los Angeles
Ayunt. Rec.*, MS., 24, there would seem to have been also an earlier petition
on the subject signed by 28 citizens.

in the bud. The governor states, both in his letters
written at the time and in his later recollections, that
the arrests were made by the citizens of Los Angeles,
who delivered the prisoners to Villa on his arrival;
but other evidence is to the effect that the captain's
force made the arrests, searching the houses of prominent citizens for that purpose. At any rate, there
were seized and carried as captives to Santa Bárbara,
Cárlos Carrillo, José A. Carrillo, Pio Pico, Gil Ibarra,
Narciso Botello, Ignacio Palomares, and José M. Ramirez. Bandini escaped. It seems that the prisoners
taken at San Buenaventura had probably been released
before this time; but Andrés Pico was now re-arrested, together with Ignacio del Valle and Roberto Pardo
at Santa Bárbara.[41] Pio Pico was quite ill at the
time, and served out a short term of nominal imprisonment at the presidio.[42] Cárlos Carrillo was released
on parole after a few days, promising not to leave
Santa Bárbara and to let politics alone, a promise
which he kept religiously till opportunity offered to
escape.[43] The other captives, eight in number, were

[41] *Alvarado, Campaña de Las Flores*, MS.; *Id., Hist. Cal.*, MS., iv. 109–
11. Botello, *Anales*, MS., 71–88, says he was taken at Requena's house and
taken to Carrillo's, where Ibarra and Ramirez were soon brought in. Pio Pico
had been at Carrillo's house, but went to that of Doña V. Sotelo de Dominguez, where he was found by Villa's men hidden under the floor of a chamber.
At Sta Bárbara all were confined in one room under that occupied by Alvarado. Jesus Pico, *Acont.*, MS., 50–2, was with Villavicencio. He says J. A.
Carrillo was found under a pile of hides. Cárlos Carrillo was taken in charge
by Villavicencio, his godson, and treated very kindly. Mrs Ord, *Ocurrencias,*
MS., 113–17, remembers the arrival, when her mother—Carrillo's sister—addressing Villavicencio, said, 'Is it possible, José María, that thou hast brought
as a prisoner thy second father?' He replied, 'Godmother, I am ordered and
must obey, but I have cared for him on the way as if he were my own father.'
J. J. Warner, *Los Angeles, Hist.*, 14, says he had an arm broken in resisting
arrest for refusing to have his house searched by a party under Alf. Espinosa;
and on June 30th Warner made a complaint before the alcalde that Agustin
Martinez on May 14th had entered his house sword in hand, forced him into
the street, and dangerously wounded him. *Los Ang., Arch.*, MS., i. 156–7;
Id., Ayunt., MS., 18.
[42] Pico, *Hist. Cal.*, MS., 76–83, remarks that though at first subjected to
petty annoyances, he was finally allowed the freedom of the presidio, and was
even taken in P. Duran's coach to be *padrino* at a christening, Alvarado giving him $200 to be expended in gifts.
[43] Alvarado says he simply took Don Cárlos to his wife, saying, 'Here,
aunt, I bring uncle to you for safe-keeping. Try to make him understand
that he is too old now for school-boy pranks.'

started on May 22d for the north, being mounted on horses more famous for docility than speed, and protected by an escort of fifteen men well mounted and armed. Jesus Pico commanded the escort to Buenavista, Santiago Estrada to San Juan Bautista, Jesus Vallejo to San José, and Corporal Galindo beyond that point. They reached Sonoma the 3d of June, and were kept in confinement there by Vallejo until the end of September, or a little later.[44]

In his letter of May 22d Alvarado complimented his officers and men for their conduct during the campaign, announcing his intention of keeping up a force of about one hundred men for the present, and of going soon to Los Angeles in person.[45] General Vallejo in turn congratulated him on his triumphs, urging him to follow up his victory in such a manner as to secure permanent peace, and not allow the troublesome element in the south to recover from their de-

---

[44] May 22, 1838, Alvarado to J. J. Vallejo, ordering him to come with a guard to meet the prisoners. *Vallejo, Doc.*, MS., v. 86. May 30th, Gen. Vallejo to Sanchez at S. Francisco and Murphy at S. Rafael. Must furnish horses, boats, etc. *Id.*, v. 90–1. June 1st, J. J. Vallejo to Gen. V. His illness prevents him coming in person, but sends Corp. Galindo. *Id.*, v. 92. June 6th, Gen. V. to Alvarado. Prisoners arrived 3 days ago and are kept secured. Not allowed to communicate with the people. *Id.*, xiv. 24. June 9th, Vallejo to Lieut Ramirez. Cannot grant his request for release without orders from the gov. *Id.*, v. 94. June 20th, A. to V. May show some leniency to such of the prisoners as are grateful for the kindness with which they have been treated. *Id.*, v. 98. Aug. 9th, A. to ayunt. of Angeles. Grants request for liberation of political prisoners at Sonoma. *Dept. St. Pap., Angeles*, MS., xi. 108. Sept. 22d, A. to V. He is to free the prisoners as soon as they bind themselves to respect the governor's authority and not to disturb the peace of the country; but they are not to be allowed to come south until Don Cárlos and others have presented themselves as invited. *Vallejo, Doc.*, MS., v. 181. Botello says the prisoners, or the 4 Mexicans at least, were very cruelly treated at Sonoma, being shut up in a floorless room, without beds, and given insufficient food. *Osio, Hist. Cal.*, MS., 393–4, 398–9, tells us that Vallejo would not speak to them, gave them food that only excessive hunger enabled them to swallow, and would not permit them to receive food presented by the people. Ignacio del Valle, one of the prisoners and a Mexican, says they were treated well enough. *Lo Pasado*, MS., 25–9. Two of them, Ibarra and Palomares, had the small-pox while at Sonoma.

[45] *Alvarado, Campaña de Las Flores*, MS. He also asks Vallejo's advice about opening negotiations with Sonora. Salvador Vallejo, one of the officers complimented, in a letter to Gen. Vallejo says that Juan Bautista is no military man, and he has had to use his sword several times on the officers, by which they have been brought at last into tolerable discipline and respect for their superiors! *Vallejo, Doc.*, MS., v. 87.

feat.[46] To the ayuntamiento of Los Angeles the
governor, for some reason inexplicable to me, instead
of a letter of thanks for its action of May 15th, addressed a severe lecture on the evils of its past course,
with earnest advice for the future to attend strictly
to municipal affairs and let state politics alone.[47]

At the end of May, Alvarado was invited by the
ayuntamiento to visit Los Angeles, his presence being required there to preserve peace and restrain certain turbulent citizens. He accepted the invitation,
but seems not to have made the visit until late in
June; and the only incident to be noticed in connection with it, and even this may very likely refer to a
previous visit, was a plot to assassinate the governor,
which he claims to have discovered in time to prevent its success. The plot was revealed by a veiled
woman who did not make herself known. Alvarado
had reason to believe, however, and has always believed, that the lady to whom he owed his life was
none other than Doña Concepcion Argüello, the
heroine of the Rezánof romance.[48] Meanwhile San
Diego through its alcalde, Estudillo, had the impu-
dence to inform Alvarado, the 'gefe de la division del
norte,' that the people could not recognize any other
ruler than Carrillo. Reports came also that Zamorano, Portilla, and others were plotting mischief on
the frontier; but Alvarado promptly sent word to

[46] May 25th, V. to A. *Dept. St. Pap.*, MS., iv. 206–7; *Vallejo, Doc.*, MS.,
v. 88.   The general is very enthusiastic on the subject.   'The fate of California depends only on the conditions you make with the rebels.'

[47] May 27th, A. to ayunt. of Angeles. *S. Diego, Arch.*, MS., 207; *Dept. St.
Pap., Angeles*, MS., xi. 104–6.   The communication was also sent to S.
Diego.   June 6th, Vallejo suggests the propriety of chartering a vessel on
which to send away a party of vagabonds who do nothing but make trouble.
He also suggests a revision of mission administrators' accounts. *Dept. St.
Pap.*, MS., iv. 208–9.

[48] May 31, 1838, ayunt. to A., with invitation. *Los Angeles, Arch.*, MS.,
v. 26–7.   June 6th, 10th, A. accepts and orders a house for his use to be prepared. *Dept. St. Pap., Angeles*, MS., xi. 107.   June 9th, ayunt. receives his
letter. *Los Angeles, Arch.*, MS., v. 28.   June 20th, still at Sta Bárbara, but
going to Angeles to reorganize the town. *Vallejo, Doc.*, MS., v. 98.   Alvarado, *Hist. Cal.*, MS., iv. 65–71, tells the story of the plot, which was to be
carried out by certain convicts, and gives his reasons for believing Doña Concepcion to have been his benefactress.

those gentlemen that if he heard of their crossing the line as threatened with a Mexican force, he would first shoot ten prominent men of the south, and then march to defeat the invaders![49] On the other hand, cheering rumors came from Honolulu by the *Don Quixote*, brought by the *Clementine* from San Blas, that Captain Robbins of the *California* spoke of having favorable despatches for Alvarado, having been himself made a naval captain by Alvarado's recommendation.[50] Severe earthquakes were felt in the north late in June.

In July there were no new developments of a political nature.[51] August was a more eventful month. In its earliest days Cárlos Carrillo, the 'Pretender,' escaped from Santa Bárbara in company with his son Pedro and José María Covarrubias. They fled in a boat, probably with the connivance of Dana and other foreigners during the governor's absence; but Don Cárlos, whose management and luck were equally unfortunate on sea and land, was driven by stress of weather to land near Point Dumetz, whence he was aided by friends to join the 'Carlist' conspirators on the San Diego frontier. Carrillo's alleged motive for flight was the fear that he would be one of the ten men whom Alvarado had threatened to shoot on the approach of Mexican troops. Yet Don Cárlos forgave his persecutors, and promised to do all in his power to have them pardoned when the supreme government should have enforced his recognition! He even had the assurance to recommend his family to Alvarado's care.[52]

[49] June 26th, Estudillo to Alvarado. *San Diego, Arch.*, MS., 201. June 20th, A. to Vallejo. *Vallejo, Doc., Hist. Mex.*, MS., v. 98.

[50] June 20th, Alvarado to Vallejo. *Vallejo, Doc.*, MS., v. 98. Is organizing a permanent force of 100 men to be stationed at S. Fernando, where they will be drilled by the 'unfortunate but able' Castañeda, who was so poor that Alvarado had to give him a jacket to wear.

[51] The printed letter of July 20th from Vallejo to Alvarado bears date of 1838, but probably belongs to 1837. (See chap. xviii.) July 26th, V. to officials, circular in which he complains that communications addressed to him often come open. Angel Ramirez has tampered with the mails at San Luis Obispo. Vigilance is required. *Vallejo, Doc.*, MS., v. 119.

[52] July 30, 1838, C. to A., explaining the reasons of his flight, and bidding farewell. *Dept. St. Pap.*, MS., iv. 214–15. Aug. 16th, Alcalde Olivera to

If Alvarado was not very seriously alarmed at the flight of Don Cárlos, he was indeed troubled by letters from the north announcing the partial defection of no less a personage than General Vallejo. José Antonio Carrillo had utilized the time of his imprisonment at Sonoma by holding long interviews with the general, and had succeeded in convincing that dignitary of his good faith, and of the genuineness of his brother's appointment. So Vallejo stated in his letters of August 10th–11th, and in them advised the recognition of Don Cárlos, or at least the holding of a convention at Santa Clara with a view to such recognition. Of the real motives for delay in giving up the command, he said little or nothing. The point of his long and able argument addressed to Alvarado was to this effect: Carrillo's title being valid, it would be necessary to yield sooner or later; Alvarado and his associates had from the first in good faith disclaimed any purpose to retain the command; with all his triumphs he had been so fully occupied in quelling revolts, that he had had no time to introduce needed reforms; experience proved there was no hope for a cessation of sectional troubles; to yield voluntarily while in the full tide of success would not only be flattering to their own pride, make a good impression in Mexico, and check

A., excusing himself for not having prevented Carrillo's flight. He had watched the vessels, but never thonght of his attempting a boat voyage. *Id.*, iv. 223–4. Aug. 18th, A. tells Vallejo it seems to be his fate to act the part of papa to the families of his adversaries while they are absent on a campaign against him. For instance, Zamorano and others whom he won't mention. *Vallejo, Doc. Hist. Mex.*, MS., v. 145; *Alvarado, Hist. Cal.*, MS., iv. 74–82. Capt. John Paty of the *Plymouth* carried the news to the Islands, where it was published in the *Honolulu S. I. Gazette*, Nov. 17, 1838. Paty said that Carrillo escaped on the *Kamamalu's* launch in the night. Alvarado took no notice, except to fine Carrillo $100 for departing without a passport. Alvarado asserts that about the same time correspondence was seized bearing the mysterious sign 'Fu....u.' Carrillo's escape is mentioned in *Pico, Hist. Cal.*, MS., 70; *Ord, Ocurrencias*, MS., 114–15; *Pinto, Apunt.*, MS., 38–9. The Hawaiians were somewhat disposed to ridicule the course of events in California; witness the following in the account just cited: 'The task of recording great political events, of taking the profiles of revolutions, and sketching the contour of national changes, falls to the lot of our brethren of the quill in more enlightened realms; ours only is the duty of the historian of mighty deeds! It is for us to tell of the bloody revolutions of California, to portray the magnificent characters of her champions, and to chronicle the deeds of glory which cluster around the brows of her sons!'

dissensions at home, but—a still more practical advantage—would enable Alvarado and his party really to control public affairs for a time in their own way, since Don Cárlos would come north to establish his government, remaining in their power until the whole matter should be finally settled.[53]

All these things José Antonio Carrillo had promised in behalf of his brother. Furthermore, becoming acquainted with the general's particular hobby, he had agreed that in case of the change being effected the presidial companies should be at once reorganized. He had realized the importance of playing his best card, for he better than any other understood the nature of the despatches to be expected from Mexico. That he succeeded in winning over Vallejo to his views is not strange. Few men in California could resist his crafty eloquence; moreover, there was much force in his arguments, as reflected in the general's letters, if faith could be placed in his promises and in his statements respecting the feeling in Mexico. Alvarado lacked that faith, and with much reason. The plot lately discovered against his life at Angeles had not left him in a conciliatory mood. He had no doubt that his past successes would be avenged by the imprisonment or exile of himself and friends should the Carrillos gain control before the arrival of guaranties from Mexico, and the recent flight of Don Cárlos, in ignorance of his astute brother's plans, was by no means a propitious circumstance.

The governor's hesitation, if he hesitated at all, was

[53] *Vallejo, Tres Cartas Reservadas en que insta el reconocimiento de D. Cárlos Carrillo como Gobernador. Agosto, 1838*, MS. Addressed on Aug. 10th, 11th, to Alvarado, Castro, and Villavicencio. Other letters were doubtless written of similar purport, and Carrillo wrote still others to Don Cárlos and friends in the south, which latter seem not to have been delivered by Alvarado until later. Vallejo wished the matter kept secret; and the plan if approved was to emanate ostensibly from Alvarado himself. The letter to the governor was long and minute in detail; the others shorter. Alvarado, *Hist. Cal.*, MS., iv. 76-9, says he sent back a flat refusal, chiding Vallejo for his disaffection, which was doing much harm in the south. He deeply regretted the general's course.

not however of long duration; for in a day or two an
event occurred which put a new face on the whole subject. On August 13th, the *Catalina* arrived at Monterey with news from Mexico. Castillero wrote that he
had been successful in his mission, and that he would
soon arrive in California as a comisionado from the national government. Just how far he entered into details is not known, as his letter is not extant; but from
this and other private communications it was known
that Alvarado and his associates had nothing to fear,
even if they were not to be continued in power. There
came also official despatches about the war with
France, addressed to the governor and general respectively. One package of correspondence was sent
in haste to Sonoma, while Jesus Pico started at once
to deliver the other to Alvarado at Los Angeles.
Vallejo, on August 17th, circulated to military authorities the despatch respecting the French war
"addressed to him" by the Mexican government.
From San Fernando on the 18th Alvarado wrote a
long letter to the general, communicating the good
news, and next day issued a proclamation, in which,
besides alluding to the French war, he announced
also the 'happy results' of Castillero's mission to
Mexico, without specifying what those results were.[54]

There was of course no further thought of giving
up the governorship to Carrillo before Castillero's arrival, and Vallejo's plan of a convention at Santa Clara

[54] Aug. 13, 1838, J. J. Pico to Vallejo, announcing arrival of *Catalina*.
California expected in 10 or 12 days with money, arms, and clothing. *Vallejo,
Doc.*, MS., v. 137. Aug. 17th, V.'s circular. *Id.*, v. 144. Aug. 18th, Alvarado to V. from S. Fernando. *Id.*, v. 145. Aug. 19th, A. sends his proclamation to V. *Id.*, v. 147. Same date, the proclamation sent to Los Angeles
and San Diego. *Dept. St. Pap., Angeles*, MS., xi. 108; *S. Diego, Arch.*, MS.,
208. Sept. 3d, Estudillo to A., 'gefe de la division del norte.' His proclamation has been published. *Id.*, 201. Sept. 14th, 18th, the proclamation
sent to Carrillo at his request. *Id.*, 202. June 20th, a letter from Virmond
in Mexico to Vallejo, which may very likely have been received by the *Catalina*. *Vallejo, Doc.*, MS., v. 97. The writer announces Castillero's success,
and the favorable ideas of the president towards Cal., and particularly toward
Vallejo. Says he, Virmond, has often taken the part of the Californians.
Castillero is about to start. Money, arms, and clothing will be sent. Understands that the *California* is to carry the mails on the coast.

was kept a secret among the few who knew anything about it.[55] There was nothing to do but await the arrival of the *California*. Don Cárlos, after being landed by his boatmen, who carried his luggage back to Santa Bárbara, had wandered for many days on foot, harassed with fears of pursuit, until on arrival at San Luis Rey he had heard the news from Mexico, and had written to Alvarado a letter begging for amnesty. Meanwhile Vallejo, on September 1st, asked to be relieved of the command, that he might attend to his private interests and those of his colony at Sonoma;[56] but there is no evidence that any attention was paid to his request, and soon the general had to issue a proclamation to quiet certain popular rumors that he was in league with the enemies of Alvarado. These rumors he pronounced false, declaring that his views had not changed since 1836, and that he would resign sooner than be false in any way to his friends.[57] Meanwhile the prisoners had been liberated, and there are some vague indications that they tried to make trouble at San José and elsewhere, by representing that Vallejo was in sympathy with the Carrillos. No

[55] Sept. 19th, A. to V., in *Vallejo, Doc.*, MS., v. 177. This is the governor's only reply to V.'s plan of Aug. 10th, so far as the records show. He says that on account of the favorable news, he did not deliver the letters to southerners; that Castro, Villa, and S. Vallejo had declared that as military men their duty was to obey the gov., and that J. A. Carrillo's letter to himself was an insult, and would not be answered. He mentions rumors of a pronunciamiento against Carrillo on the frontier; and speaks of Don Cárlos' adventures and demand for pardon.

[56] *Vallejo, Oficio impresso en que quiere renunciar el mando militar, 1° de Set. 1838.* In *Earliest Printing; Vallejo, Ordenes*, 9-14; *Dept. St. Pap.*, MS., iv. 258. This communication, which is quite long, seems to have been addressed to Alvarado, but possibly to the min. of war. In it he urges the reorganization of the presidial companies as the only means of averting utter ruin at the hands of the Indians.

[57] No date, blotter of the proclamation, in *Vallejo, Doc.*, MS., iii. 287. Oct. 22d, J. J. Vallejo urges his brother not to give up his command. *Id.*, v. 213. Nov. 9th, Salvador Vallejo, from Sta Bárbara, to the gen. Speaks of rumors that he is in league with the southerners; and blames him for having opened his ears to J. A. Carrillo, who has 'made a bag of him.' Says Alvarado is drinking too much. *Id.*, v. 260. Nov. 10th, D. A. Rodriguez, S. Francisco, to Vallejo. Reports a conspiracy at S. José, prompted by J. A. Carrillo and Angel Ramirez—A. M. Pico and Pedro Chabolla being leaders, with accomplices at Sonoma. The outbreak to be on Nov. 15th. *Id.*, v. 229. Nov. 18th, J. J. Vallejo, Yerba Buena, to his brother. Urges him in 2 letters to quiet the people by a proclamation.

blame can be attached to General Vallejo for his course in this matter; but he was unfortunate in his choice of a time for proposing his plan, and was over-credulous in listening to the special pleading of Don José Antonio.

The *California* had been expected to follow the *Catalina* in a few weeks at most; troubles with France and other obstacles, however, caused Castillero's departure from Mexico to be delayed from July to September. On November 15th, the schooner anchored at Santa Bárbara, and Captain Castillero, now comisionado of the supreme government, landing in bad health, sent communications to Alvarado, who was absent, and to Vallejo at Sonoma. These communications informed the governor and general that by virtue of documents brought by the writer in his official capacity they would be able to retain their positions, that the *California* had also brought arms and other war-stores, and that a personal conference was necessary at the earliest opportunity.[58]

The most important of the documents brought from Mexico by Castillero were as follows, in the order of their respective dates: a decree of June 30th dividing the republic into twenty-four departments, one of them the Californias, with capitals as before;[59] a commission as captain of the presidial company of San Francisco for Lieutenant Guadalupe Vallejo;[60] an expression of thanks for the gift of the *California* from the departmental to the national government;[61]

[58] Nov. 17, 1838, Castillero to Vallejo, transcribed in a later letter of the latter. *Vallejo, Doc.*, MS., v. 251; xxxii. 168; *Earliest Printing.*

[59] Decree of June 30th, in *Arrillaga, Recop.*, 1838, 284–5; *Sup. Govt St. Pap.*, MS., xxi. 22; xii. 4; *Vallejo, Doc.*, MS., v. 225. This decree divided the departments into 2 sections, Californias being one of those which was to elect a diputado to congress for 2 years on Oct. 1st. It is likely, however, that this decree came also before on the *Catalina* in August.

[60] July 9, 1838, original appointment and commission, 2 documents, in *Valljo, Doc.*, MS., i. 12.

[61] July 10th, the goleta to be used as a *paquete mercante. Dept. St. Pap.*, MS., iv. 127; *Vallejo, Doc.*, MS., v. 110¾. There is no other evidence that such a gift had been thought of in Cal. July 20th, decree of amnesty. *Id.*

a decree of amnesty for all political acts and opinions
during the past troubles; an order addressed to Cárlos
Carrillo to the effect that the senior vocal of the territorial junta should act as governor temporarily, a
copy of the same being forwarded also to Alvarado;[62]
an order to the governor to grant lands on the coast
islands to Mexicans who might ask for them, giving
preference to Antonio and Cárlos Carrillo, who were
to have exclusive possession of one of the islands in
consideration of their patriotic services;[63] an appointment of Vallejo as comandante general in consideration
of his distinguished services;[64] and finally private
letters to both Alvarado and Vallejo from President
Bustamante, who expressed his high esteem for those
gentlemen, and confidence in their patriotism and
ability to direct the affairs of California in the future.[65]

Truly Don Andrés had served his masters most
faithfully, and all had resulted well for the revolutionists of 1836. Men of the southern faction have

[62] July 20th, min. of the interior to Carrillo. 'The president, learning
with satisfaction that Alta California has returned to constitutional order,
and as the law of amnesty draws a thick veil over all political occurrences,
directs that, in order to carry out the constitutional law, the 1st vocal of the
junta territorial of that department shall exercise the powers of governor;
steps being taken at once for the election of the junta departamental, and a
terna being sent to the sup. govt for the regular appointment, the pres. relinquishing for this time the powers given him by the constitution in the
frontier departments,' forwarded by Alvarado, as 1st vocal, to ayunt. of
Angeles on Dec. 10th. *Dept. St. Pap., Angeles*, MS., xi. 109–10; also transcribed by Alvarado, who received it from Castillero, to Vallejo on Dec. 10th.
Vallejo, Doc., MS., v. 268; also English translation, in *Hopkins' Translations*,
9. According to *Dept. St. Pap.*, MS., iv. 126, the order, or a similar one,
was dated June 2d.

[63] July 20th, min. of the int. to gov. *St. Pap., Miss. and Colon.*, MS., ii.
387; *Mont. Arch.*, MS., ii. 13; *Leg. Rec.*, MS., iii. 92; *Bandini, Doc.*, MS.,
48; *Halleck's Rept*, 180–2; *Jones' Report*, no. 28. The gov. was to act in accordance with the junta; and the avowed object was not only to settle the
islands, but to prevent foreigners from occupying them to the injury of commerce and fisheries. Sta Rosa Island was granted to the Carrillos in accordance with this order.

[64] July 23d, appointment as comandante militar of Alta California, signed
by Moran, min. of war. Original in *Vallejo, Doc.*, MS. i. 13. Aug. 21st,
Moran to com. gen. Orders that the auxiliary troops continue in service until
further orders. *Soberanes, Doc.*, MS., 96.

[65] Sept. 13th, original letters with autograph signatures, in *Vallejo, Doc.*,
MS., v. 166; xxxii. 158. The writer regrets the delay in Castillero's departure, which could not be avoided. He hopes Vallejo will look out for foreign
invaders: Castillero's commission seems to have been finally issued on Sept.
7th. *Dept. St. Pap.*, MS., iv. 127; *Sup. Govt St. Pap.* MS., xiv. 1.

been wont to deplore the base ingratitude of Mexico in thus rewarding rebels, while the loyal sureños for all their suffering and sacrifice got no thanks. The reader knows that southern loyalty to Mexico was but a very flimsy pretence. But for his own injudicious acts and utter incompetence as a ruler, Cárlos Carrillo would merit a degree of sympathy; as it was, his island grant was quite as much as he deserved. His appointment had been obtained by his brother on the representation that it would bring California back to her Mexican allegiance; but Alvarado had accomplished all that before Carrillo's appointment was known there, and all subsequent disorders had resulted from the refusal of Don Cárlos to await the decision of the supreme government. The president had been made to understand that Alvarado and his associates were the men who could control California, and whose good will was of some value to the national administration. Well would it be for the reputation of Mexico if her record were as clear on every matter of state policy. Alvarado has often been represented, by writers who have disposed of several years' annals in a paragraph, as having accepted centralism in gratitude for his recognition as governor; but he had really sworn to the constitution a year before he was so recognized. Another theory that has been current to some extent is that Castillero brought from Mexico two blank commissions to be filled up in favor of Alvarado or Carrillo as circumstances and his own judgment should dictate, having also duplicate papers by which to reward with an island estate the one who should not receive the governorship. The reader with the facts before him will perhaps agree with me that this version is improbable to the verge of absurdity.[66]

[66] This version of duplicate documents is mentioned as a rumor by several Californians in their memoirs; and it was given currency by Peachy in an argument in the New Almaden case, an item from which has been widely circulated in the newspapers. Osio, *Hist. Cal.*, MS., 394-6, describes the matter very unintelligibly. Bandini, *Hist. Cal.*, MS., 99, deemed the action

Alvarado and Vallejo proclaimed the tidings in print to the people, at the same time congratulating themselves and their friends in private letters; little else was accomplished before the end of the year.[67] There was, however, some further revolutionary trouble at San Diego, resulting in several arrests on Christmas night. The Carrillos were there, and naturally the objects of much popular sympathy. That there was any intention of resisting the orders from Mexico and continuing the struggle against the governor may perhaps be doubted; but reports of such plans, real or imaginary, reached Alvarado at Santa

of Mexico disgraceful. *Serrano, Apuntes*, MS., 56-8, says that the minor officials from Castro down for whom Castillero brought commissions were known as *oficiales de Catarrillo.* Alvarado notes the arrival of Castillero in his *Hist. Cal.*, MS., iv. 42-3, 111-13. A piece of doggerel, composed by one José Elisalde and sung by the S. Diego soldiers, gives their view of the whole matter, a game of cards being used as an illustration. *Romero, Mem.*; MS., 5; *Hayes' Emig. Notes*, 495.

"Bautista buscó barajas
Castro se les barajó.
Montenegro paso el monte
Y Don Pio lo tapó.
Luego vino Castillero
Y la carpeta se llevó."

[67] In demanding his salary later, Alvarado seems to have dated his taking possession of the office from Oct. 1, 1838; why, is not very clear. *Dept. Rec.*, MS., x. 6. Nov. 21st, *Alvarado [Proclama del], Gefe Politico Interino de la Alta California á sus Habitantes, 21 de Nov. 1838. Impreso en Sonoma; Imprenta del Gobierno*. In *Earliest Printing*. In this proclamation the governor congratulates the people on the happy ending of all dissensions; thanks Castillero; announces his own honest purpose to sacrifice everything for his country; and advises all to forget their resentments and get ready for the coming elections. Nov. 21st, Alvarado to Vallejo. Official and private letters. He says the appointment of Carrillo had been due to underhanded work, and the govt had been glad to cancel it. *Vallejo, Doc.*, MS., v. 245-6. Nov. 22d, Castillero to Vallejo, private letter. *Id.*, v. 248. Nov. 27th, *Vallejo, Circular impreso en que anuncia su Nombramiento de Comandante General, Nov. 21, 1838*, in *Earliest Printing; Vallejo, Doc.*, MS., v. 251; *Savage, Doc.*, MS., i. 20. This circular merely transcribes Castillero's letter of Nov. 17th. Nov. 30th, P. Gonzalez congratulates Vallejo, and tells him the news was celebrated at S. José with salutes, music, te deum, etc. *Vallejo, Doc.*, MS., v. 258. Dec. 3d, Vallejo congratulated in letters from José R. Gonzalez, Ignacio Peralta, and Simeon Castro. *Id.*, v. 263-5. Dec. 10th, Alvarado publishes in a bando, and includes in letters to Vallejo and others, the news of Castillero's arrival and the order of the sup. govt respecting the governorship. *Id.*, v. 268; *Dept. St. Pap., Angeles*, MS., x. 21-2; *Id., S. José*, v. 44-6. Dec. 15th, the news and orders published at Angeles. *Los Angeles, Arch.*, MS., v. 38-9; *Dept. St. Pap.*, MS., xviii. 8. Dec. 17th, P. Duran congratulates Alvarado. *Arch. Arzob.*, MS., v. pt ii. 20. Dec. 22d, a new proclamation by Alvarado, urging the people to be true to the govt and not listen to revolutionists. *Dept. St. Pap., Angeles*, MS., x. 23. Dec. 29th, Alcalde Arenas orders comisarios of ranchos to publish Alvarado's appointment. *Dept. St. Pap., Angeles*, MS., ii. 135-6.

Bárbara, and he sent Castro with twenty-five men in great haste southward. At any rate, it gave the officers and men a chance to display the new uniforms lately received by the *California*. The *pastorela* was being performed at Bandini's house, Don Juan himself not being present apparently, and all prominent Dieguinos were assisting in the festivities of Christmas, when Castro and his force surrounded the house after midnight. The two Carrillos and the two Picos, with Joaquin Ortega, were taken prisoners. Alcalde Estudillo was wanted also, but hid in a loft, and was declared by his wife and son to be absent from home. Next day Castro started northward with his captives. Ortega was soon set at liberty.[68]

[68] Dec. 22, 1838, Alvarado to Vallejo. Carrillo plotting to upset the govt, enlisting men on the frontier and in Sonora. A letter of (or to) Ignacio del Valle had been seen revealing the plots. *Vallejo, Doc.*, MS., v. 278. This is the only contemporary document on the subject; but there are later proofs of the prisoners being at Sta Bárbara. It seems that there was a project formed to rescue them at S. Luis Rey; and that Estudillo did go to that place or near it. J. M. Estudillo, *Datos*, MS., 24–6, says his father returned because the prisoners disagreed and decided that no attack should be made. Another version from the Estudillos, in *Hayes' Emig. Notes*, 343–4; *Id.*, *Miscellany*, 41, is that Castro and his men were to be made drunk at a banquet at San Luis and then attacked; but Estudillo turned back because his heart failed him at the thought of shedding blood. Pio Pico, *Hist. Cal.*, MS., 71–6, says the prisoners were armed and the majordomos were ready to help; but Estudillo, after coming within a mile, disappointed their hopes by going back. Rafael Pinto, *Apuntaciones*, MS., 39–43, who was with Castro, tells us the plan was arranged by Andrés Pico, who was allowed to go home for a while under Pinto's care before starting from S. Diego. The plan was for each of the captives to stab one of the captors to the heart at the supper-table at the moment of Estudillo's attack! Mention of the affair also in *Ord, Ocurrencias*, MS., 115–16; *Machado, Tiempos Pasados*, MS., 34–5; *Ezquer, Memorias*, MS., 13–14; *Janssens, Vida*, MS., 142; *Alvarado, Hist. Cal.*, MS., iv. 113–16.

CHAPTER XX.

ALVARADO'S RULE—POLITICAL EVENTS.

1839-1840.

Governor and General at Santa Bárbara—Carlist Prisoners—Don Cárlos Yields—End of the Conflict—Military Discipline—Presidial Companies—Diputacion as a Junta at Monterey—Division of California into Districts and Partidos—Prefects—Plots of Ramirez and Padre Mercado—Life of Angel Ramirez—Sedition at Branciforte—Flag Tumult at Los Angeles—Castillero Elected to Congress—Vocales Elected—War with France—Jimeno Acting Governor—Alvarado Married by Proxy—Arrival of the 'California'—Alvarado Appointed Governor—Cosme Peña—Castañeda Sent to Mexico—Annals of 1840—Sessions of the Junta Departamental—Tribunal de Justicia—Monterey the Capital—Conspiracy of Carrillo and Gonzalez.

There yet remained some traces, albeit not bloody ones, of the past two years' conflict to be obliterated before the rulers of the department, now invested with unquestionable authority, could proceed in the work of reorganization, and open for California the path to complete prosperity, hitherto closed by sectional dissensions and other obstacles now for the most part removed, if the proclamations of the time were to be credited. The reader may suspect that new difficulties, or the old ones in new forms, were likely to be encountered. In the first days of the new year General Vallejo arrived at Santa Bárbara from the frontera del norte to bear his share of the post-bellum burdens; the first public business in order was mutual congratulation by governor and comandante.[1]

[1] Jan. 1, 1839, Vallejo to Alvarado, transcribing his promotion of July 23d. *Vallejo, Doc.*, MS., v. 1. Jan. 2d, V. congratulates A. on his recogni-

At the same time arrived Lieutenant-colonel Castro with his four or five Carlist prisoners from San Diego. Cárlos Carrillo was allowed the freedom of the town under parole by Alvarado. The others were soon turned over to Vallejo, who sent them on board of vessels then lying at anchor in the roadstead, with orders to the captains that no communication was to be allowed with persons on shore. José Antonio Carrillo was confined alone on the *Leonidas;* the rest, the Picos, Covarrubias, and José Carrillo,[2] were committed to the care of Robbins on the schooner *California.* Vallejo relates that the penalty included a short trip out to sea in order that true repentance might be developed by the terrors of sea-sickness—not a bad idea, but perhaps an afterthought of later years.[3] The *California's* prisoners were kept on board four days, and released January 19th—from their floating dungeon at least.[4] Don José Antonio seems not to have recovered his freedom until somewhat later, having aroused Vallejo's wrath by stating that his solitary confinement had been from fear that he would implicate the general himself in his plots against the government.[5]

On the 19th Cárlos Carrillo, being released from his parole, probably at the same time the other pris-

tion as gov. *Id.,* v. 2; *St. Pap., Miss. and Colon.,* MS., ii. 389.   Jan. 2d, A. in turn congratulates V. *Vallejo, Doc.,* MS., vi. 160.

[2] It is not quite clear whether the last two had been arrested with the rest at S. Diego or subsequently.

[3] *Vallejo, Hist. Cal.,* MS., iii. 392–400; *Alvarado, Hist. Cal.,* MS., iv. 50–4, 117–19. Pico, *Hist. Cal.,* MS., 71–6, says they spent a few days on the vessels, and were then released. Feb. 5th, Don Pio wrote from S. Luis Rey that he had rejoined his family. He had been ill, but was urged homeward by a desire to make known his liberty and the end of all political differences. *Dept. St. Pap.,* MS., iv. 244.

[4] Jan. 15th, Vallejo's orders to captains of the two vessels to receive the prisoners on board. *Vallejo, Doc.,* MS., vi. 13–14. Jan. 19th, order to place the *California's* prisoners at Castro's disposal. *Id.,* vi. 15.

[5] Jan. 23d, V. to Capt. Castañeda. Orders an investigation of the charges against Carrillo. *Vallejo, Doc.,* MS., vi. 19–20. The result does not appear. It is possible that Don José Antonio was released on the 19th like the rest, or that all were kept under arrest for some days after leaving the vessels. Three men of bad character were sent out of the country at this time on the *Leonidas.* These were Pedro and Pablo Saenz and Máximo Guerra. Jan. 24th, V. to captain of the *Leonidas Id.,* vi. 22.

oners left the vessels, addressed to Alvarado a letter, in which he formally recognized his legitimate authority as governor, relinquishing his own claims, and promising to give up all official documents in his possession. This communication was circulated on the 23d by the governor, with an order that Don Cárlos be not molested for his past acts and opinions, quickly followed by a publication of the Mexican decrees authorizing a grant of coast islands, and forbidding all persecution for complicity in the past disturbances. Thus ended the long conflict between Alvarado and Carrillo, though the latter made some efforts subsequently to collect a salary for his term of office, and certain debts contracted by him at Los Angeles as governor were paid from the departmental treasury.[6] He did not obtain the island of Santa Rosa until some years later, not deeming it at the time, perhaps, a very desirable acquisition.[7]

General Vallejo found matters at Santa Bárbara in a condition which did not square at all with his ideas of military discipline. Don Guadalupe, proud and pompous in manner, had been a soldier from youth. He was a martinet by disposition and education, and at Sonoma, among Indians and soldiers paid from his own pocket, had been wont to put on the airs of a

[6] Jan. 19, 1839, Cárles Carrillo to Alvarado, offering his submission. Circulated to different officials on Jan. 23d. *S. Diego, Arch.*, MS., 215; *Sta Cruz, Arch.*, MS., 58; *Vallejo, Doc.*, MS., vi. 169. Jan. 24th, A. publishes decree of July 20, 1838, on grant of islands. *S. Diego, Arch.*, MS., 216. Jan. 25th, A. proclaims communication from the sec. of the int., condoning all political offences. Original in *Coronel, Doc.*, MS., 65; *S. Diego, Arch.*, MS., 217; *Sta Cruz, Arch.*, MS., 59. Jan. 27th, A. to sup. govt. Announces the complete restoration of tranquillity through the efforts of Castillero and himself. *Sup. Govt St. Pap.*, MS., xv. 9. Feb. 5th, S. Diego juez de paz, in name of the inhabitants, congratulates A. *S. Diego, Arch.*, MS., 221. Sept. 22d, Carrillo to Vallejo. Urges him to influence A. to give him an order on some vessel for his salary as gov. from Dec. 6, 1837, to Jan. 21, or 25, 1839. *Vallejo, Doc.*, MS., viii. 166. July 1, 1840, sub-comisario's account, approved by A., shows $1,141 to have been paid for 'extraordinary expenses,' that is, supplies furnished to D. Cárlos 'en el tiempo que fué gobernador.' *Id.*, xxvi. 97.

[7] Alvarado, *Hist. Cal.*, MS., iv. 121-2, says he at first told Don Cárlos that the president had ordered that he should be given an island and sent to live on it, sarcastically proposing to give him a servant who would say every morning, 'How has your Excellency slept?' The old man begged not to be condemned to such a fate.

petty sovereign.   Colonel Alvarado and Lieutenant-
colonel Castro, on the contrary, had never been soldiers at all.   They knew little of military discipline,
and had not cared to enforce the little they knew.
To their officers they were 'Juanito' and 'José,' and
the men were correspondingly familiar and careless.
Captain Vallejo proposed to change all that, and
Alvarado had no objections to the experiment, though
doubting the practicability of enforcing strict discipline in an army not regularly paid.   The new régime
was introduced at once.   In a few days the guard-
house was crowded with offending soldiers, while pretty
much every officer in the place was under arrest.   The
Carlist prisoners, as we have seen, were promptly sent
on shipboard, and no attention was paid to the importunities of weeping sisters, cousins, and aunts.   A
lieutenant and a citizen in conversation ventured to
criticise the comandante's acts.   The officer was reprimanded, legal proceedings were begun against the citizen for disrespect, and Castro was placed under arrest
for not having arrested the others.   Castillero was
snubbed.   Padre Duran, coming to plead for some
prisoners, was forced by a sentinel to await his turn
for an audience with the general, and on announcing
his errand, was informed that he might retire unless
he had something to say about church matters.   Captain Guerra y Noriega was ordered to take the command of Santa Bárbara, and declining on the ground
of ill health, was ordered under arrest at his own
house, and informed that it was his duty simply to
obey orders, though his petitions presented later in
proper form would receive due attention.   Some were
amused and others offended at these new methods.
Don Guadalupe soon found himself involved in such
a tempest of protest and entreaty that he was forced
to yield.   At a grand party at the house of Guerra y
Noriega, all shook hands, made peace, and received
the surrender of the general, who was forced to admit

that in an army of unpaid relatives, the old Spanish discipline must be somewhat modified.[8]

Vallejo not only turned his attention to the impracticable scheme of restoring discipline, but he also made earnest and oft-repeated efforts, unfortunately without success, to restore the old presidial companies on which he believed the country's permanent prosperity to depend. The companies had now no real existence except that of San Francisco, supported at Sonoma at Vallejo's own expense. Alvarado was less enthusiastic in the matter, but whatever his desires, he could barely find funds to support the few men already in arms. He however ordered the municipalities to furnish recruits to the number of seventy. Vallejo also addressed his representations in favor of military reorganization to the minister of war, asking for money, arms, and chaplains, but getting nothing beyond 'authority' to reorganize the companies. The government had authorized the retention of the civic militia in the service, but as there was no present need of that force and no money with which to support it, the members were allowed to retire to their homes. It was early in March that Vallejo returned to the north and reëstablished his headquarters at Sonoma.[9]

[8] *Vallejo, Hist. Cal.*, MS., iii. 392–418; *Alvarado, Hist. Cal.*, MS., iii. 59; iv. 116–19. Jan. 28th–30th, corresp. between V. and Guerra, in *Vallejo, Doc.*, MS., vi. 174–9.

[9] Some military items, Jan.–April, 1839. Jan. 3d, supplies brought by Castillero from Mexico: 598 coats, 477 pants, 297 shirts, 298 stocks, 289 shoes, 200 cloaks, 400 caps and casques, 400 *maletas*, 200 *chabrases*, 100 muskets, 200 carbines, 99 sabres, 49 lances, 4 trumpets, 3,000 flints, 15,580 cartridges. *Vallejo, Doc.*, MS., xxv. 15. Alf. Lázaro Piña with 9 men of the S. F. company at Sta B. as Vallejo's escort. *Id.*, xxv. 10. Jan 7th, 11th, 19th, Vallejo to Alvarado, urging organization of presidial companies, or of permanent militia. *Id.*, v. 3; vi. 165; *Dept. St. Pap.*, MS., iv. 242. Jan. 27th–29th, recruits called for. Quota of Angeles 40, S. Diego 10, Branciforte 15, Sta Bárbara 5. *S. Diego, Arch.*, MS., 219, 221; *Vallejo, Doc.*, MS., vi. 175. Jan. 31st, V. authorizes the auxiliary forces to disband temporarily. Names captains J. A. de la Guerra, Valentin Cota, and A. M. Ortega; lieutenants Manuel Cota, Juan P. Ayala, Felipe Lugo, and Octavio Gutierrez; alféreces Clemente Espinosa, Guillermo Navarro, Hilarion García, Isidoro Guillen, Tomás Romero, Antonio Olivera, Joaquin de la Torre, and Ignacio del Valle. *Id.*, vi. 33, 183. Feb. 6th, V.'s appeals to min. of war for repairs of fortifications, etc., describing present condition, explaining dangers of foreign encroachment, recommending officers for promotion, etc. *Id.*, vi. 217–24. Authorized from Mexico to incur the expense of repairing fortifications Aug. 5th. *Sup. Govt*

Alvarado had in the mean time convoked the diputacion to assemble at the capital. He issued an election proclamation for the formation in March of a new junta departamental, and returned to Monterey at the end of January, being accorded the enthusiastic ceremonies of a public reception, with the usual salutes, speeches, races, feasting, and dancing.[10]

The diputacion, its composition being unchanged since 1837, met at Monterey the 25th of February. Vocal Pico was absent during the sessions, and Osio served as secretary. After delivering a short address upon the recent measures adopted in Mexico for the benefit of California, Alvarado declared the body legally installed as a junta departamental. The sessions continued until March 7th, and action was taken upon three subjects. First, the approaching elections for members of the junta and a deputy to congress were declared legal, despite the non-attendance of electors from Baja California, if a majority of all the electors were present. Second, Alvarado's proposition to divide the department into districts, to be noticed presently, was approved. And finally a *terna* of three names was made out from which a permanent governor was to be selected by the supreme government. The names in order of preference were Juan B. Alvarado, José Castro, and Pio Pico.[11]

St. Pap., MS., xv. 8–9. Complaints of Sergt Petronilo Rios in command of artillery at Monterey about trouble in getting funds and supplies from the sub-comisario. *Vallejo, Doc.*, MS., vi. 269, 334–5, 465. March 13th, Prefect Castro orders from S. Juan the formation of a company of auxiliaries to protect the district from Indians. *Doc. Hist. Cal.*, MS., i. 392. March 14th, V. to min. of war. Appeal for chaplains. *Vallejo, Doc., Hist. Cal.*, MS., vi. 228. March 31st, J. A. Pico ordered to Sonoma from S. Diego, and wants 2 men for an escort. *Hayes' Miss. Book*, i. 328. No comandante, nor munitions, so far as known to Judge Osuna, at S. Diego. *S. Diego, Arch.*, MS., 221. April 25th, V. says the order to retain the auxiliary troops in service will entitle Alvarado to the military *fuero. Vallejo, Doc.*, MS., vi. 437. April 26th, Capt. Guerra wants $12,000 of back pay. *Id.*, vi. 487.
    [10] Jan. 17th, call for election. *S. Diego, Arch.*, MS., 214; *Vallejo, Doc.*, MS., xxxii. 174; *Estudillo, Doc.*, MS., i. 249. The order convoking the members of the old dip. is not extant. Jan. 29th, A. sails for Monterey. *Sta Bárbara, Lib. Mision*, MS., 47. Reception mentioned in *Alvarado, Hist. Cal.*, MS., iv. 124–5.
    [11] *Leg. Rec.*, MS., iii. 30–6, 47–8. The members present were Alvarado,

According to the laws of December 1836, the republic was to be divided by congress into departments, and each department by its junta into districts and partidos.[12] The corresponding decree of the junta was issued by Alvarado on February 27th, dividing the department of Californias into three districts, one of them belonging to the peninsula exclusively. Of the others, the first district extended from the Sonoma frontier to San Luis Obispo, with the capital or head town at San Juan de Castro; and the second from El Buchon to Santo Domingo on the peninsular frontier, with the head town at Los Angeles. The first district was divided at Llagas Creek into two partidos, of which the second had its *cabecera* at San Francisco mission, and the second district was divided at the space between San Fernando and Cahuenga, Santa Bárbara being the *cabecera* of the second partido.[13] By the laws of December 30, 1836, and March 20, 1837, each district was to have a prefect appointed by the governor and approved by the supreme government; each partido, except one in every district, was to have a sub-prefect appointed by the prefect and approved by the governor.[14] Accordingly the prefects were named on the same day that the division was made, or the next, José Castro being appointed in the first district, and Cosme Peña in the

Buelna, Guerra, Jimeno, Estrada, and Osio. The organization of temporary courts of 1st instance was discussed, without result so far as the record shows.
[12] *Leyes Constitucionales*. Ley vi. art. 1–3, in *Arrillaga, Recop.*, 1836, p. 367. Also decree of Dec. 30, 1836, ordering the division in Californias and the appointment of prefects, in *Id.*, p. 379. In the *Mexico, Providencia de la Suprema Corte de Justicia—que se proceda á la division del territorio de los departamentos* of Nov. 11, 1837, governors were directed to have the division made at once if not already done, *Id.*, 1838, p. 572; but this instruction had probably not reached Cal. In making the division, it does not appear that any restrictions were imposed as to number, extent, or population of districts.
[13] Feb. 27, 1839, decree of junta dividing Cal. into districts and partidos, in *Leg. Rec.*, MS., iii. 33–4; *S. Diego, Arch.*, MS., 220; *Vallejo, Doc.*, MS., vi. 274; *Dept. St. Pap., Angeles*, MS., x. 26, xi. 112; *Estudillo, Doc.*, MS., i. 254; *Dept. St. Pap.*, MS., iv. 246. The 3d district in Baja California was not divided into partidos at this time.
[14] *Mexico, Reglamento Provisional para el Gobierno interior de los Departamentos, 20 de Marzo, 1837*. Art. 61–121 on prefects and sub-prefects, in *Arrillaga, Recop.*, 1837, p. 202, 214–23. Translation in *Hall's Hist. S. José*, 489–517.

second, though the latter was not approved in Mexico.[15]
The prefects may be regarded as a kind of petty
governors, their functions being executive rather than
judicial; further explanation of the system is deferred,
and the somewhat complicated record of successive
changes in the incumbents of the prefectura will be
cleared up in local annals. The same law of March
20, 1837, which defined the powers of prefects, made
provisions also respecting ayuntamientos, which deprived California of those bodies except at the capital,
justices of the peace taking their place. This provision was put in force by the dissolution of the ayuntamientos at the end of 1839.[16] It may be noted here
that an attempt was made in the peninsula to oppose
the union with Alta California, there being a preference for union to Sinaloa—at least in the mind of Gefe
Político Castillo Negrete, who had no fondness for
the position of prefect under his old foe Alvarado.[17]

The attention of the people was occupied in March
to a slight extent with the elections, but in April and
May there were several more exciting topics of popular interest. Angel Ramirez was accused of new
plots to rouse the Indians, being supported by Padre
Mercado, and by certain persons who were dissatisfied
with the *terna* for governor. Ramirez had been arrested for complicity in the revolt of July 1837, and
for much of the time since that date had been compelled to live at certain missions under surveillance.
Whether he was yet entirely free does not appear;

[15] I have not found any regular appointments of prefects, but Alvarado
named Castro and Peña in his letter of Feb. 28th to Vallejo, *Vallejo, Doc.*,
MS., vi. 277, and it is evident from many documents that the appointments
were issued on that date or on the 27th. The approval of the division and of
Castro's appointment by the sup. gov. was on Aug. 7th. *Dept. St. Pap.*, MS.,
iv. 131, 280; *Sup. Govt St. Pap.*, MS., xv. 10, 12; *Estudillo, Doc.*, MS., i. 262.
Before the news reached Cal. in Sept., Peña had already resigned and had
been succeeded by Tiburcio Tapia.

[16] Nov. 7, 1839, gov. to prefect, ordering dissolution of ayunt. *Dept. St.
Pap., Angeles*, MS., xii. 19. Details in local annals.

[17] July 16, 1839, Luis Castillo Negrete to some clergyman. No attention
is to be paid to orders from Alta California till the change now pending in the
senate shall have been decided. *Castro, Doc.*, MS., i. 37.

nor is it possible to determine whether the charges made at this time were well founded. Both Ramirez and Mercado were detained for some time at San Antonio, it being Alvarado's intention to send them both out of the country.[18] Perhaps Don Angel escaped to the Tulares and spent some months in the rancherías of gentile tribes. He returned, however, to live again for a time at the missions, and died early in the next year at San Luis Obispo. He had suffered long from a terrible disease, and died at last without receiving the rites of the church. His had been a strange eventful career as friar, soldier, customs officer, and conspirator. He was known in California as an able and brilliant man, but without a redeeming trait in respect of honor and morality. There is nothing in the record to show that his most unenviable reputation was undeserved.[19]

[18] April 3, 1839, Cosme Peña at Sta Bárbara to Alvarado. Reports a plot brewing to rouse the Indians of S. Antonio and other missions. Also plots to prevent the attendance of southern members elected to the junta. *Vallejo, Doc.*, MS., vi. 359. April 11th, Alvarado to Vallejo. Sends Peña's communication. Ramirez is to remain at S. Antonio until he can be shipped away in the *California*. Has his eyes on the friars. Ex-gov. Carrillo has not yet sent the papers he promised. *Id.*, vi. 404. April 29th, A. to V. The padre (Mercado?) detained at S. Antonio, and will be sent away as the general desires. *Id.*, vi. 497. Pinto, *Apunt.*, MS., 75–80, says he was sent to arrest Ramirez at S. Luis Obispo, but he escaped, through a warning from Administrator Moreno, to the Tulares. Inocente García, *Hechos*, MS., 68–70, was administrator of S. Miguel. He says that Victor Arroyo was arrested by him and sent in irons to Monterey for complicity in this plot. Tiburcio Álvarez had also been concerned in it.

[19] All the Californians agree that Angel Ramirez had been a friar of the Merced order, and later a captain in the insurgent army. Ábrego, *Cartas*, MS., gives a few details learned from his uncle in Mexico. It seems that Ramirez had left his convent in 1820 and fought under Gen. Anaya. He allowed the escape of some royalist intrusted to his charge, and this saved his life later when himself captured by the Spanish forces. He was several times under arrest before coming to California. The government desired, says Osio, *Hist. Cal.*, MS., 302–3, 316–17, 380–1, to remove him as far as possible from Mexico, where his intrigues caused constant trouble. Janssens saw him serving in command of Vice-president Gomez Farías' body-guard. Vallejo, *Hist. Cal.*, MS., iii. 71–4, 187–8, 298–9, tells us he was a protégé of Gen. Ugarte y Loyola of New Galicia. 'Had he been president he would have conspired against himself.' Says Alvarado, *Hist. Cal.*, MS., ii. 224, 'El capitan fraile tenia mas mañas que un burro de aguador.' In 1833 he was made administrator of the Monterey custom-house, and arrived in the spring of 1834 overland, bringing a mistress with him. He was very free with his money and that of the government, giving many expensive dinners and balls, which, with his social qualities, gave him much popularity. He knew everybody, and was skilled in all the arts of a demagogue. He was

At Branciforte, certain evil-doers disobeyed and even ridiculed the alcalde's orders. Comandante Castro sent Lieutenant Soto with a force to aid the municipal authorities. Nine, all members of the Robles, Salazar, and Soria families, were arrested. On the march back to San Juan the prisoners refused to obey orders, and were fired upon, Avelino Robles being killed and Nicolás Robles badly wounded. Reports based on this affair and the plots of Ramirez, were circulated in the south, to the effect that the whole north was in revolt; but Prefect Peña issued a denial of such reports, presenting the death of Robles and the imprisonment of his companions as a salutary example for the benefit of the Angelinos, showing the energy of the government and the inevitable consequences of insubordination.[20]

Yet despite the warnings thus given by the prefect, a tumult occurred before the month was over in the city of Los Angeles, or 'Los Diablos' as it was

accused of embezzling the public funds, but no definite proofs exist. Juan Bandini's fruitless efforts to investigate his management of the revenues are well known to the reader, who also remembers the part taken by Don Angel in support of Alvarado's revolution of 1836. He thought he could control Alvarado more easily than Gutierrez, but learned his mistake when he made the attempt, being removed from his office in December 1836. Castillo Negrete described him in verse as 'El proto-libertador—Primer hombre de Estado—Es un fraile renegado—Gran perjuro y gran traidor—De oficio administrador—Es de muy ancha conciencia—Derrochador sin clemencia—Sagaz revolucionario—Jugador y pendulario—Sin Dios, ni patria, ni creencia.' Unable to control the governor, he engaged in plots against him; and was arrested in July, 1837. Later he lived at the missions, closely watched, and always suspected. Torre, *Remin.*, MS., 79, García, *Hechos*, MS., 71–2, and Serrano, *Apuntes*, MS., 53–4, describe not very clearly his mission life, stating that at the last he was treated with great indignity. He died at San Luis Obispo on Feb. 6, 1840, and was buried next day by P. Abella. After postponing confession from time to time, he at last promised to attend to his spiritual welfare after taking a short sleep, but from that sleep he never awoke, and thus died without the sacraments. *S. Luis Obispo, Lib. Mision*, MS., 55. His disease was syphilis contracted among the Indians. A writer in the *Californian*, Nov. 21, 1846, attributes his death to poison. On account of his promise to confess, his body was buried in the mission cemetery.

[20] April 19th, Castro to Vallejo, with marginal order of the latter that the prisoners be tried by military law. *Vallejo, Doc.*, MS., vi. 456. May 2d, Prefect Peña's circular, in *S. Diego, Arch.*, MS., 223; *Monterey, Arch.*, MS., ix. 7–8; *Dept. Rec.*, MS., x. 24–5. May 23d, Castro to Vallejo. No proceedings by military law because the gov. had banished the prisoners from Cal. or from the Monterey district. V. blames C. for having permitted an 'incompetent authority' to interfere. *Vallejo, Doc.*, MS., vii. 131.

re-christened by Don Cosme at this time. Peña was naturally not popular, especially among the class that had so bitterly opposed Alvarado in the past, and there were occasional manifestations of the feeling against him. One ground of displeasure was that he had established his office at the house of Abel Stearns, in front of which he had raised the flag of the prefec- · ture and planted a cannon. It was said that Stearns had used the flag-staff as a post to which cattle were tied for slaughter, thus insulting the dignity of the Angelinos. On Sunday, May 19th, while Peña was absent at San Pedro, some fifteen young men, armed and mounted, had assembled to pull down the flag, and perhaps to sacrifice a calf in burlesque before it. On his return the prefect caused the arrest of the ringleaders, Varela, Sepúlveda, and Yorba, to be tried for sedition, and obtained a guard of ten soldiers from Santa Bárbara. Next, the citizens sent protests to the ayuntamiento, which body asked Peña to remove the flag to the public buildings, where it would be respected. Peña in anger surrendered the prefecture to Alcalde Tapia, and both reported to the government at Monterey. The reply was to impose a fine of five dollars on each signer of the memorial, which had also been sent by twenty citizens to the governor, and one of ten dollars on each member of the ayuntamiento. Peña was, however, ordered to Monterey, and Tapia left in charge of the office. Quiet was restored by the middle of June.[21]

The primary elections had taken place in March, and on May 1st the seven partido electors met at

<hr />

[21] General accounts, Peña to Vallejo, on June 8th. *Vallejo, Doc.*, MS., vii. 191. Peña to Alcalde. *Dept. St. Pap., Ben.*, MS., iv. 39-47. May 22d-25th, action of ayunt. *Los Angeles, Arch.*, MS., v. 87-8; *Dept. St. Pap.*, MS., xviii. 15-16. May 25th, Tapia to Alvarado. *Dept. St. Pap., Ben. Pref. y Juzg.*, MS., v. 2-3. May 25th, com. of Sta Bárbara to Vallejo. Has sent a force under Lieut Pardo. *Vallejo, Doc.*, MS., vii. 142. June 1st, Tapia announces that all is quiet. *S. Diego, Arch.*, MS., 227. June 3d, gov. to Pref. Tapia, imposing fines. *Dept. St. Pap., Angeles*, MS., xi. 114-17. June 12th-17th, action at Angeles on the fines, which there was a willingness to pay, though Tapia was exempted in July. *Id.*, v. 22, 38, 43, 57; *Los Angeles, Arch.*, MS., v. 94-5.

Monterey as a junta electoral. The result of their labors was that on the 2d Andrés Castillero was elected as congressman, with Antonio M. Osio as substitute; and on the 3d seven members of the new junta departamental to meet on the 1st of August, were chosen as follows: Manuel Jimeno, Tiburcio Castro, Anastasio Carrillo, Rafael Gonzalez, Pio Pico, Santiago Argüello, and Manuel Requena.[22] May 13th and 14th the old junta, or four of its members, held meetings to ratify the late election, and to empower the new congressman to receive from the supreme government the product of the pious-fund estates for the payment of public expenses.[23] Two or three days later Don Andrés sailed on the *California* to occupy his new post. It is as well to state here that though the newly elected junta was convoked for August 1st, no meeting was held at that time nor in this year at all. The vocales would not present themselves, and the substitutes could not be summoned until the junta had approved the excuses of the regular members![24]

Vallejo in the mean time did not cease to urge military reorganization, especially with a view to secure the northern frontier from foreign aggression. On May 10th in one of several letters to the minister of

---

[22] Records of this election and of the local elections of March, in *Leg. Rec.*, MS., iii. 36–43. The partido electors were Osio and Santiago Estrada for Monterey, Felipe Lugo and Joaquin Ortega for Angeles, Covarrubias for Sta Bárbara, José Fernandez for S. José, and Francisco Guerrero for S. F. The substitute vocales chosen were José Castro, J. R. Estrada, Ignacio del Valle, Cárlos Castro, Ignacio Martinez, J. J. Vallejo, and A. M. Pico. Order for the election issued Jan. 17th. *S. Diego, Arch.*, MS., 214; *Vallejo, Doc.*, MS., xxxii. 174; *Estudillo, Doc.*, MS., i. 249. Further records of local elections. *Doc. Hist. Cal.*, MS., i. 397; *Dept. St. Pap.*, MS., iv. 250. May 5th, Alvarado proclaims the election of Castillero and Osio. *S. Diego, Arch.*, MS., 245.

[23] *Leg. Rec.*, MS., iii. 43–4. May 16th, Alvarado to sup. govt. *Sup. Govt St. Pap.*, MS., xv. 9. Aug. 7th, Castillero not successful in obtaining the pious fund. *Dept. St. Pap.*, MS., iv. 131; *Vallejo, Doc.*, MS., xxxii. 196, 282. Castillero expected to sail from Sta Bárbara May 13th. *Id.*, vii. 64. The vessel left S. Diego on June 7th.

[24] Aug. 1st, junta convoked for this date. *Pico, Doc.*, MS., ii. 163; *Dept. St. Pap.*, MS., iv. 276. Aug. 12th, Castro to alcaldes. No quorum obtained. *Sta Cruz, Arch.*, MS., 40; *Dept. St. Pap., Mont.*, MS., iv. 82–3. Aug. 14th, election approved in Mexico. *Dept. St. Pap., Angeles*, MS., x. 28.

war he described at some length his past efforts and
success in colonizing the region north of the bay. He
required not only approval of what he had done, but
aid to carry on the work, including certain commercial
concessions to the colonists; for he could not longer
support the military force from his own resources, and
at the same time meet the constantly increasing demands of the settlers for aid.[25]   A few recruits were
obtained for the regular companies, but they were of
a vagabond class which the municipal authorities were
glad to get rid of, and which the general did not desire for soldiers.[26]   There was trouble also because the
governor discharged militia officers without the comandante's consent, and otherwise interfered in military
matters.[27]   The chief difficulty, however, was a financial one.   There was of course a quarrel about the
distribution of revenues, the army not getting its share,
as was believed by military men, and each company
being defrauded, in the opinion of its officers.   The
chief complaint came from Santa Bárbara, as Sonoma
interests were protected by the presence of the general, Monterey with the custom-house had the first
handling of the funds, and San Diego had no company
to support.   Both in the south, and to some extent

[25] May 10, 1839, V. to min. of war on needs of the northern frontier. *Vallejo, Doc.*, MS., vii. 28.   Other communications on military needs, in May.
Id., vii. 26, 27, 29, 37.   June 10th, V. to Alvarado.   A printed appeal for
regular military companies and an escolta for each mission.   'Nothing but
the old system can save the country.' *Vallejo, Ordenes*, 15–21; *Id., Doc. Hist.
Cal.*, MS., xxxii. 206.   Same date, to min. of war. *Dept. St. Pap.*, MS., iv.
258.   Dec. 1st, V. begs Castillero to get aid for the troops. *Vallejo, Doc.*,
MS., viii. 334.

[26] May 10th, V. to Alvarado.   No criminals will be accepted. *Vallejo, Doc.*,
MS., vii. 43.   May 24th, Capt. Villavicencio got 12 recruits in the south,
unfit for soldiers, but turned over to Castro. *Id.*, vii. 138.   May 31st, V.
calls the recruits physically unfit or grossly immoral. *Id.*, vii. 156.   June 1st,
the wicked recruits to be sent back to Angeles. *Id.*, vii. 167.   Nov. 12th, V.
to A.   Sends a decree of Jan. 26th, requiring regular companies to be filled
by draft. *Id.*, viii. 274.   Nov. 26th, A. says the conscription will be carried
into effect when instructions arrive. *Id.*, viii. 318.

[27] May 19th, V. to A., complaining of the discharge as a dangerous precedent, and begging the gov. as colonel to revoke his order and put himself
under the general's orders. *Vallejo, Doc.*, MS., vii. 117.   June 7th, Capt. S.
Vallejo will obey the general's orders, notwithstanding his dismissal by the
gov. *Id.*, vii. 185.   July 5th, Alf. Andrés Pico refuses to take command at
S. Luis Rey as ordered by Vallejo. *Id.*, vii. 316.

in the extreme north, the 'clique at the capital' was
charged with spending the public moneys almost exclusively for the benefit of local interests and personal
friends.[28]

In June the war between Mexico and France took
a large share of attention from the authorities, both
military and civil.   As the war had ended three
months before, the real danger of an attack on Californian coasts was not great; however, as tidings of
peace had not yet reached the north, an opportunity
was afforded for a brilliant display of national patriotism in preparing to repel the possible attacks of
French corsairs.   The resulting complication of military orders, interwoven with complaints respecting
defective fortifications and other means of defence,
was very nearly a reduplication of similar alarms in
the old Spanish times.   The only result was that expenses were considerably increased during the month,
and that a little work was done on one or two
forts.   French residents were not molested, though
closely watched, if orders were obeyed; on the last
day of the month the news of peace was circulated.[29]

[28] May 25th, Vallejo to Guerra at Sta B. Explains the distribution of $10,000
received for the army as its share of the *California's* duties, $25,000; S. Fran-
cisco co., with 60 men, got $2,000; Monterey, 30 men, $1,500; Sta Bárbara,
15 men, $1,000; S. Diego, $500; staff and unattached officers, $1,000; war
material paid for, $1,300; chest of medicine, $250; Sta B. artillery, $200;
capt. of port and other officers at S. F., $350; Alf. Ignacio del Valle, $100;
the rest for relief of old inválidos in small sums. *Vallejo, Doc.*, MS., vii. 140.
July 5th, com. of Sta B. to V., complaining of neglect from the Monterey
authorities. *Id.*, vii. 310. Complaints from S. Luis Rey. *Id.*, vii. 313–14.
July 10th, V. to Alvarado. Complains that the comisario refuses to obey his
requisitions. *Id.*, vii. 70. Orders payment of $1,000 each to Sta B. and S.
Diego, and offers to lend $10,000 to the treasury. *Id.*, vi. 144, 146–7; vii. 358.
$1,400 in goods and $100 in money paid to Monterey co. from Feb. to July.
Id., vii. 388.   July 22d, Comisario Ábrego expects to pay one fourth of dues
for past month. *Id.*, vii. 406. Aug. 6th, only one soldier at S. Diego. *S. Diego,
Arch.*, MS., 234. Aug. 7th, not a cent's worth of anything received for the
artillery this year. *Vallejo, Doc.*, MS., viii. 22, 17. Sept. 3d, men at S. Luis
Rey—S. Diego co.—left the service against orders to earn a living by their
work. *Id.*, viii. 69–70. Sept. 8th, Capt. S. Vallejo complains that the S.
Francisco co. is neglected by the comisario. *Id.*, viii. 86. Sept. 11th, Vallejo
to Lieut J. M. Ramirez. Cannot relieve his wants, having no resources. *Id.*,
viii. 133, 137. Oct. 27th, Ábrego says Capt. Castañeda and the habilitado of
S. F. refused $4,000 proffered, because the amount included 1,000 hides at
$1.50. *Id.*, viii. 233.   Nov. 3d, northern troops to have $2,500 from the first
duties. *Id.*, viii. 252.
[29] Over 40 communications on this alarm. *S. Diego, Arch.*, MS., 221, 229–.

From July to September lampoons of an insulting
and threatening character, and directed against the
departmental rulers, were posted at different places,
and anonymous letters of similar purport were sent
to Alvarado. At the same time rumors were current, for the most part without foundation, of plots
in the south, and even of a hostile expedition approaching from Sonora. Vallejo evidently did not
share in the alarm felt or feigned at the capital, as he
refused to put certain troops asked for under the governor's orders till he should be informed respecting
the exact nature of the suspected plots.[30] In these
months Alvarado, as was often the case during his
rule, was unable to attend to his official duties on
account of illness, and his secretary, Jimeno Casarin,
acted much of the time as governor, especially in
July; however, Don Juan Bautista had sufficiently
recovered his health in August to marry Doña Martina, daughter of Francisco Castro. The marriage
took place at Santa Clara on August 24th, but Alvarado was not present, being represented by José
Antonio Estrada. Eight days later the bride came
to the capital, where the festivities lasted several
days.[31]

The national schooner *California* arrived September
15th at Santa Bárbara, on her return voyage from

---

[30] *Dept. Rec.*, MS., x. 13; *Dept. St. Pap.*, MS., iv. 256-7; *Id.*, *Angeles*,
xii. 6; *Vallejo, Doc.*, MS., vi. 119-36; vii. 67-9, 174, 176, 189, 206-20, 249,
404. Communications from Mex. Jan.-April. *Sup. Govt St. Pap.*, MS., xv.
2-4. June 25th, news of peace in a private letter of Guerra. *Vallejo, Doc.*,
MS., vii. 264. Officially published June 30th. *Id.*, vii. 275. Oct. 31st,
orders had been received from Mexico to strengthen coast defences. *Id.*, viii.
240.

[30] Lampoons and anonymous letters at Sta Bárbara and Monterey. *Va-
llejo, Doc.*, MS., vii. 310, 321; *Alvarado, Hist. Cal.*, MS., iv. 140-4; *Vallejo,
Hist. Cal.*, MS., iv. 7-14. Reports of the Sonora expedition brought to S.
Diego in August, contradicted in Sept. *Vallejo, Doc.*, MS., viii. 58, 67.
Plots in the south in Sept. *Id.*, viii. 76, 88.

[31] Copy of record from Sta Clara mission book, in *Vallejo, Doc.*, MS.,
xxxii. 293. P. Gonzalez performed the ceremony. *Alvarado, Hist. Cal.*,
MS., iv. 169-72, tells us it was the arrival of La Place that kept him from
going in person to Sta Clara, and he also says the rings used at the wedding
were of California gold.

HIST. CAL., VOL. III. 38

Acapulco.[32]   She brought Mexican despatches of August 6th and 7th, announcing Alvarado's appointment as governor, *en propiedad,* and promoting Vallejo to the rank of colonel.[33]   All that had been done by governor or junta was approved, except the appointment of Cosme Peña as prefect of the second district; but that gentleman had already given up his position to another, and he soon took his departure for Mexico, to be heard of no more in California.[34]

The despatches brought by the schooner were officially circulated a few days after their arrival by Acting-governor Jimeno, the prefects, and subordinate officials; and the news of Alvarado's appointment was duly celebrated in different parts of the department, especial enthusiasm being shown at Los Angeles, where on a Sunday the flag was hoisted, salvos were fired, a

[32] Sept. 15th, capt. of port reports arrival. *Vallejo, Doc.,* MS., viii. 149; *Cooper's Log-book of the 'California,'* MS., entry of same date.

[33] Aug. 7th, min. of int. sends Alvarado's appointment. *Dept. St. Pap., Angeles,* MS., xi. 12–13; *Id., Mont.,* iv. 16–17.   Aug. 6th, Pres. Bustamante to V., congratulating him and Alvarado, and thanking him for his services. *Vallejo Doc.,* MS., viii. 11.   Aug. 6th, V.'s appointment and commission as colonel of the defensores de la patria, sent by min. of war. *Id.,* i. 14–15.   Also Aug. 2d, 4th–6th, commun. from min. of war to Vallejo in reply to his letters of February, approving his measures, sending commissions for several officers, and promising additional aid. *Savage, Doc.,* iv. 308, 310, 312, 314–15.   Sept. 17th, 22d, V. was congratulated by Cárlos Carrillo and Cosme Peña on his appointment as comandante general *en propiedad. Id.,* viii. 157, 165.   But there was no such appointment, since that of July 1838 had been permanent and not temporary.

[34] The licenciado Cosme Peña was a Mexican lawyer who came to California with the Híjar and Padrés colony in 1834, as asesor to succeed Gomez. I know nothing of his previous career.   In the discharge of his official duties he showed himself to be a man of fair ability and education, but he was a hard drinker, and unfortunate in his domestic relations.   After being involved in many scandals, his wife left him in 1837 and started overland for Sonora. The party was attacked by Indians on the Colorado, and the lady is said by Ignacio Coronel to have become the wife of a chief.   Don Cosme had trouble with Gov. Chico, and was at one time suspended from his office.   In the autumn of 1836, he took a prominent part in Alvarado's revolution—though far less influential than he was represented by Castillo Negrete, his bitter enemy—and was made governor's secretary.   He subsequently joined in the counter-revolt of Angel Ramirez and other Mexicans, and was imprisoned for a time at Sonoma; but Alvarado still felt disposed to befriend him, and made him prefect of Los Angeles.   He held this place several months, but of his acts nothing is known beyond the events of the 'flag tumult' mentioned in this chapter.   Vallejo, who in his *Hist. Cal.,* MS., iii. 188–91, quotes from Peña's poem on the 'Fall of Man,' states that he went from California to Guaymas, where he served as a judge.   None of the Californians have much to say in Don Cosme's favor.   He left two daughters in the country.

man was wounded by the premature discharge of a cannon, and at night the city was illuminated. Alvarado was, however, ill again, and did not take the oath and formally assume the governorship till November 24th, the transfer being announced next day by himself and Jimeno.[35]

Now that the governor and comandante militar were secure in the possession of their respective positions, a serious misunderstanding had developed between the two, resulting in a quarrel which lasted as long as their control of public affairs, and in a suspension of that control a few years later. The causes were somewhat complicated. It will be remembered that in November 1836 Vallejo, though his opinions were substantially in accord with those of Alvarado and Castro, had declined to engage actively in the revolution against Gutierrez, but had, without his own knowledge or consent, been made military commander, a position he was very willing to accept after the first success had been achieved at Monterey. His coöperation was absolutely necessary to the revolutionists, and the position of general was a reward very flattering to the young lieutenant. His subsequent support of the cause was most cordial and effective, and was fully appreciated by his associates. Without his aid Alvarado's project must have failed, and this aid was none the less, but rather more, effective that Vallejo remained in the north instead of personally taking part in the southern campaigns. While disapprov-

[35] Sept. 20th, Jimeno to prefect and Vallejo with several doc. from Mexico. *Dept. St. Pap., Mont.*, MS., iv. 16–17; *Vallejo, Doc.*, MS., viii. 160–3. Sept. 21st, John Temple to Larkin, hopes the news of Alvarado's appointment will prove true. *Larkin's Doc.*, MS., i. 24. Sept. 22d–23d, further circulation of the appointment by Jimeno through prefects. *S. Diego, Arch.*, MS., 238, 241; *Vallejo, Doc.*, MS. viii. 167, 169; *Sta Cruz, Arch.*, MS., 56. Sept. 30th, congratulations of P. Duran. *Arch., Arzob.*, MS., v. pt ii. 25–6. Oct. 5th–9th, receipt of the news at Angeles. Dolores Sepúlveda was the man wounded. *Los Angeles, Arch.*, MS., v. 96–7; *Dept. St. Pap., Angeles*, MS., v. 87–9; *Id., Ben. Pref. y Juzg.*, v. 21. Nov. 12th, Vallejo has learned with pleasure the appointment and will give it due publicity. *Vallejo, Doc. Hist. Cal.*, MS., viii. 273. Nov. 24th, A. takes the oath and the office as announced on the 25th. *Id.*, viii. 313, 315; *Dept. St. Pap.*, MS., xii. 18; *Id., Mont.*, iv. 18.

ing some of the governor's acts, such as his disposition of the San Julian rancho, the general made few complaints, and threw no obstacles in the way of success. Later, at an unfortunate time, as already related, the comandante was induced by José Antonio Carrillo to advocate the recognition of Don Cárlos as governor. Though kept secret as far as possible, enough of this matter leaked out to cause the circulation of rumors not flattering to Vallejo; and while there is no evidence of serious ill feeling between the two principals at the time, yet it may be regarded as certain that both were left in a state of mind not unfavorable to future controversy, and that others had their cue for the provocation of such controversy.

The trouble began after the arrival of Castillero and the submission of the south to Alvarado's rule. The new rulers had now to organize the interior government of the country, and the military branch was to Vallejo all-important. To reörganize the presidial companies and put the army on a sound footing was the one thing to be done before thinking of other reforms. Vallejo's plans were perhaps, under the circumstances, impracticable; at any rate, his enthusiasm was not shared by Alvarado, who soon became indifferent, and was disposed to regard Vallejo's importunities as unwarrantable interference in the affairs of state. He even took the liberty of discharging certain officers, thereby greatly offending the general, whom he had not consulted in the matter.[36] Alvarado was much troubled in these days by the demands of office-seeking friends and other petty cares, being also nervous and ill from the effects of too much aguardiente, so that his duties were left largely in the hands of his secretary. Neither Jimeno nor Castro

[36] May 19, 1839, in reproving the gov. for his dismissal of the officers, a measure positively revoked by himself, V. says, 'Sr Governor, you flatter yourself with being in power, but you must not forget the force that sustains your power. No government has existed without the military.' *Dept. St. Pap.*, MS., iv. 255–6. Vallejo, *Hist. Cal.*, MS., iv. 25–8, represents A.'s mission policy as having had much to do with his opposition at this time.

was specially well disposed toward Vallejo. Ábrego, in charge of the revenues, naturally favored the governor and people of Monterey, rather than the comandante and absent officials. Trouble arose, as already stated, in connection with the distribution of military funds and supplies, and complaints came in from all directions that the 'Monterey clique' was spending the public money for the exclusive benefit of its friends. To what extent these charges were well founded, it is impossible to determine; Alvarado, while his difficulties were not fully appreciated out of the capital, and while his old foes were willing to make the most of the coolness between him and Vallejo, was certainly subjected to influences not favorable to an impartial distribution of the revenues, or to a wise administration of the public interests.

There is no reason to question Vallejo's honest desire for the welfare of his country. He spent his own money freely to advance his plans of military reform. He believed his former associates were neglecting their duties, and his pride was deeply wounded by their attitude, which seemed to say, "Our need of you ended with the cessation of armed opposition to our rule; attend to your northern frontier; put your force at our disposal when we call for it; and leave us to govern in our own way." When, therefore, the governor did ask to have the troops of Monterey and San Juan put under his orders to avert dangers in the south, Vallejo refused until the exact nature of the danger should have been explained, declaring that his troops would be always ready to support the law, but not its abuse.[37] He attempted, however, to bring about an interview, for some time unsuccessfully.

[37] Sept. 9th, V. to A., in answer to demand of Aug. 14th. *Dept. St. Pap.*, MS., iv. 278–80. Sept. 26th, Jimeno says the danger is past, and the force no longer needed! *Vallejo, Doc.*, MS., viii. 179. Aug. 10th, Castro would be glad to meet V., but wishes him to come south. V. had ordered him to come to Sonoma. *Id.*, viii. 33, 35. Sept. 4th, J. J. Vallejo, S. José, to the gen. Has not succeeded in having an interview with Alvarado and Castro to avert calamities. A. is controlled by Castro, and things have a suspicious air. *Id.*, viii. 77. Sept. 6th, Prado Mesa writes very bitterly against the 'clique.' It

About this time the chief, Solano, conceived the project of making a visit to Monterey with an escort of Indian braves. He had been invited by Alvarado in 1836 to pay him a visit, and had promised to do so; but his action at this time was doubtless prompted by Vallejo, who thought it well to frighten the potentates of ·the capital with a hint at his reserve power. He of course had no real intention of inflicting on the people of Monterey a large force of Indians; but he perhaps at first exaggerated the number to be sent.[33] In the middle of October, the general announced that Solano had asked and received permission to visit the capital with eighty Indians. I do not know if the visit was made; but if so, it was probably with a smaller number, who formed part of the general's escort, as he was at San Francisco October 22d and 23d, en route to Monterey.[39]

Having arrived at the capital, Vallejo asked for an interview with the acting-governor—it does not appear that he had any communication personally with Al-

is time to bring them to their senses. *Id.*, viii. 78.   Sept. 8th, V. to gov. Desires a conference at Sta Clara. *Id.*, viii. 84.   Sept. 24th, Jimeno, being about to turn over the office, cannot grant the interview; besides, a gov. has no right to leave the capital. *Id.*, viii. 171.   Oct. 9th, J. A. Carrillo to V. The political condition promises nothing but misfortune.   Thinks of selling his property and leaving the country.   He is always suspected, and even his private letters are not safe. *Id.*, viii. 199.

[33] Sept. 3d, Pablo de la Guerra, in the name of his own and other Sta Bárbara families, protests against V.'s proposed sending of Solano with 2,000 Indians.   He begs V. not to run such a risk for the sake of frightening Alvarado. *Vallejo, Doc.*, MS., viii. 73.   Oct. 2d, Salv. Vallejo to Guerra.   Has urged his brother in vain not to send Solano to Monterey.   Hopes to influence Solano, however, not to take more than 1,000 Indians. *Id.*, viii. 192. These letters purport to be copies of originals, and are in the handwriting of a man whom I have often detected in questionable practices.   Doubtless the numbers are pure inventions, and the dates are suspicious.   Possibly the whole is a forgery, but it is not unlikely that Vallejo may have made a threat and used large figures.

[39] Oct. 16th, V. to Alvarado, announcing Solano's departure. *Vallejo, Doc.*, MS., viii. 216.   *Ochenta* in the original is changed clumsily into *ochocientos* by the same genius mentioned in the last note.   Document also in *Dept. St. Pap.*, MS., iv. 282.   Proofs of V.'s trip and presence at S. Francisco on Oct. 22d-3d, and indications that he had 31 men in all. *Vallejo, Doc.*, MS., viii. 210, 223, 225.   Dorotea Valdés, *Reminis.*, MS., 7–8, claims to remember Solano's visit at Monterey.   Fernandez, *Cosas de Cal.*, MS., 96, 101–3, remembers his passing through S. José with hundreds (!) of Indians.   He says Solano kept his men in very good order, but both he and V. acted in a very proud, arrogant manner.

varado, who was perhaps absent—and such an interview was held on October 30th. Doubtless the comandante was independent and dictatorial in manner, and Jimeno stubborn rather than conciliatory. Next day the former wrote a letter, stating that the conference had ended without results; that he had been able to get no satisfaction for Alvarado's interference in military affairs; and that not the slightest attention had been paid to his pleas for reforms in financial and commercial management. He would therefore go home to attend to his duties as best he could without support, and to hope that the 'ruler of nations' might save California from the impending ruin.[40] He soon resolved, however, to go to the national capital to lay before the president in person California's needs a project he had had in mind for some months, but which, after ordering all officers to vote for a comandante to serve during his absence, he abandoned before December, and decided to send Captain Castañeda instead as his comisionado. The captain, after some trouble in raising funds for his journey, sailed from San Diego late in December. Later there came from Mexico a denial of Vallejo's request for leave of absence.[41]

[40] Oct. 29th, V. to Jimeno, asking for an interview. *Dept. St. Pap.*, MS., iv. 283. Oct. 30th, J. consents, naming the governor's house, at 4 P. M. *Vallejo, Doc.*, MS., viii. 236. Oct. 31st, V. to J., complaining, as in the text. *Id.*, viii. 241. Nov. 1st, J.'s answer. Is surprised that the conference should be deemed at an end, and evades the matters at issue. Thinks there is not much danger, and that V. should have confined the discussion to the military topic. *Id.*, viii. 247. Nov. 13th (17th), V.'s reply from Sonoma. Independent and sarcastic. Peace will not last long, and the country is on the road to ruin. Implies that he may have occasion to go to Mexico to explain the true situation and needs of his country. *Id.*, viii. 295; *Dept. St. Pap.*, MS., iv. 284-5. Nov. 25th, Alvarado to V., in reply to the last. Will sacrifice his life to preserve the peace that now exists, etc. *Id.*, viii. 316. Dec. 13th, V. to comandante of S. José. 'There seems to be a determination to lead the country to ruin and exasperate its best citizens.' *Id.*, viii. 373.

[41] Sept. 4th, 17th, mentions by J. J. Vallejo and Eulogio Célis of the general's plan of going to Mexico. *Vallejo, Doc.*, MS., viii. 77, 158. Nov. 18th, V. announces his intention. Says he has the right to name his successor, but prefers to leave the choice to the officers, who are to send in their votes. *Id.*, viii. 306. Dec. 1st, V. to Pres. Bustamante. Has decided to send Castañeda, but at the same time asks for leave of absence. *Id.*, viii. 333. Dec. 3d to Jan. 10th, ten letters with votes, mostly for Capt. Guerra. *Id.*, viii. 326, 344, 351, 378, 393, 396-7; ix. 12. Dec. 7th, trouble with the comisario

The annals of 1840 group themselves naturally about four general topics, Vallejo versus Alvarado, sessions and acts of the junta, alleged conspiracy of Carrillo and Gonzalez in the south, and the Graham affair. The last subject will be presented separately in the next volume; the others demand present attention.

The controversy between governor and comandante waxed hotter and hotter throughout the year. Each accused the other of interference in matters beyond his jurisdiction, and each was disposed to restrict the other's prerogatives to very narrow limits. Vallejo recalled the old Spanish times when the two commands were united in one person, and looked upon himself as invested with all the powers of the old comandante general, while to Alvarado he accorded the petty civil authority of the Spanish gobernador. Alvarado, on the contrary, held that in a republican government the military authority was subordinate to the civil, expecting Vallejo to use his troops as directed, to preserve order and protect the country. Both were independent and assumed superiority. Mutual 'friends' were ever ready to widen the breach; the old topics of disagreement still existed, and new ones were added. The respective merits of the parties, as usual when a quarrel has once begun, are not worth much consideration; the controversy, however, was as effective an obstacle to all real progress in California as had been the earlier one of Alvarado against Carrillo.

Alvarado had appointed Hartnell as visitador to carry into effect his regulations for the management

about funds, and Alvarado's passport for Castañeda to go on a military commission 'as far as S. Diego.' *Id.*, viii. 358-60. Dec. 20th, Casañeda at S. Diego, has got money from Célis. *Id.*, viii. 384. April 23, 1840, min. of war to V. The pres. would be glad to see him, but the leave of absence cannot be granted, as there is no officer to take his place on the frontier. *Id.*, ix. 116. March 10, 1840, Alvarado to min. of int. All quiet; pay no heed to Castañeda's loud talk and false reports. *Dept. Rec.*, MS., xi. 65-6. April 21st, 24th, letters from Castillero and the min. of war to V., announcing that Castañeda will soon return to Cal. with needed military supplies. *Id.*, ix. 115, 118.

of missions, as will be more fully explained elsewhere. Vallejo would not permit Hartnell to take possession of San Rafael in pursuance of his instructions, and even arrested the visitador, and carried him across the bay as a prisoner, for having ventured to interfere in matters concerning the northern frontier without his consent.[42] His position was, not only that by virtue of his military jurisdiction and office of director of colonization he had exclusive control of Indian affairs north of the bay, but that San Rafael was no longer a mission, the property having once been distributed and only restored partially under his solemn promise of redistribution—a promise for the fufilment of which the Indians were clamorous, and which he would fulfil at any cost.

The distribution of the public funds continued of course to be a subject of contention. Vallejo accused Ábrego of not dividing the revenues equally as the law required between civil and military employees. He called often for exact statements of the division; he denied the governor's right to interfere in military accounts, and gave his communications the form of positive orders. Ábrego, on the other hand, delighted in the governor's interference against the 'autocrat of Sonoma,' called upon Vallejo to show his commission as comandante general or be content with a captain's pay, and refused to pay the salary of Richardson and

[42] May 14, 1840, Hartnell to gov. The Indians objected to the change, and referred to Vallejo's promises. They could not be made to understand that the comandante had nothing to do with missions. The arrest was at S. F. after H.'s return, and he was taken back by V., but released probably next day, after agreeing that V.'s views in this particular case were correct. *St. Pap., Miss.*, MS., xi. 15–17. May 16th, H. left S. José for Monterey yesterday, and the gov. is now satisfied, writes the judge of S. José to Jimeno in answer to an order to investigate the arrest. *S. José, Arch.*, MS., iii. 38. Jimeno's inquiry about the arrest. *Dept. St. Pap., S. José*, MS., v. 69. The matter was agitated as early as Jan. 22d, when Alvarado complains of V.'s disposition to dictate to him about the distribution at S. Rafael. *Vallejo, Doc.*, MS., ix. 25. V.'s argument on the matter to H. and A. *Id.*, xiv. 17; ix. 106. April 4th, A. begs V. to let H. act according to the regulations. *Id.*, ix. 97. April 9th, V. repeats his arguments, but seems to promise compliance. *Dept. St. Pap.*, MS., v. 3–4. Alvarado, *Hist. Cal.*, MS., iv. 145–57, narrates the affair, except the arrest, and says that it displeased some of V.'s friends at Sta Bárbara. Mentioned by Vallejo, *Hist. Cal.*, MS., iv. 202–3.

Guerra appointed port-captains, as was claimed, illegally.[43] Vallejo's refusal to show his commission was mainly to snub the comisario doubtless; possibly he also wished to conceal the fact that his title in that document was comandante militar, and not general. Meanwhile routine military correspondence was unimportant, except promises from Mexico of supplies, some of which arrived before the end of the year.[44]

Alvarado now regarded Vallejo as an enemy, and would not even call on him when he came to Monterey.[45] On April 1st he convoked an extra session of the junta, and declared to that body that 'certain men' were plotting against the lawful authorities, and promoting insurrection. He implied clearly that Vallejo was in league with these men; indeed, Vallejo, Pico, and J. A. Carrillo were the only ones named, and it was against the first that his charges were most bitter. He accused the comandante of circulating predictions of impending disaster; of massing his troops at Sonoma, whence they could operate against the government; of refusing aid, both against the Indians at San José and to put down a revolt in the south; of refusing recruits and leaving the south defenceless; of sending

[43] Correspondence between Vallejo and Ábrego on financial topics, including some rather sharp sayings on both sides, with Ábrego's complaints to the director de rentas. *Dept. St. Pap., Ben.*, MS., iii. 140–1, 150–1, 166–7; *Id., Ben. Mil.*, lxxxviii. 31–4; *Id., Ben. Com. and Treas.*, iv. 15–16, 48–9; *Vallejo, Doc.*, MS., ix. 6, 14, 31, 144, 176, 202, 213. Alvarado, *Hist. Cal.*, MS., iv. 193–200, declares that he never authorized any unfair division of the money.

[44] Jan. 1st, 'fuero' of the defensores not under arms ceases. *Dept. St. Pap., Mont.*, MS., iv. 20. April 9th, military stores sent from Sonoma to Monterey. *Vallejo, Doc.*, MS., ix. 101, 104; xiv. 255. April 7th, recruiting, 15 men to be raised. *Dept. Rec.*, MS., xi. 11. Apr. 12th, com. of Sta B. complains. No pay, while the sub-prefect is paid regularly. *Vallejo, Doc., Hist. Cal.*, MS., ix. 112. July 12th, V. sympathizes and hopes for relief from Mexico, not from the departmental authorities. *Id.*, ix. 175. Aug. 20th, a *comandancia militar* authorized on the northern frontier. *Id.*, x. 223. Aug. 21st–22d, relief promised from Mexico. Letters from Castillero and Virmond. *Id.*, ix. 226, 229. The relief included 500 muskets. Nov. 26th, *Catalina* has brought part of the stores. *Id.*, ix. 327. 50 sabres detained at Mazatlan. *Savage, Doc.*, MS., iv. 324–5. Other routine commun. in *Id.*, iv. 321, 326, 328, including the order for a mil. command. at Sonoma.

[45] Jan. 22d, A. to V. Says he is glad to get advice from intelligent men, though he will not bind himself to follow it; he does not care for the opinion of fools and men who act for their own interests. *Vallejo, Doc.*, MS., ix. 25. March 16th, V. chides him for not calling, and thus making a public display of the dissensions between them. *Id.*, ix. 72.

Castañeda to work against the governor in Mexico, with a view of securing both commands for himself; and of being the prospective author of the outbreak he so confidently predicted. Alvarado's motive in calling the meeting was to obtain authority to spend money in supplying the prefects with arms for the protection of the country. The junta accordingly gave him the powers he desired, should Vallejo, who was 'merely comandante militar,' persist in neglecting his duties with sinister views.[46]

All that Alvarado appears to have done in consequence of this action was to order Castro to form a company of auxiliary troops for the public security, and to retain at Monterey some of the arms and munitions brought by the *Catalina*.[47] I find no reply of Vallejo to the action of the junta, which perhaps he did not hear of until later, as the session was a secret one. He continued his complaints and arguments, however, and no progress was made toward reconciliation.[48] Californian prospects had no bright side to the general in those days. His despondency and bitter opposition to the administration at Monterey were founded to a considerable extent on wounded pride, and disappointment at not being able to control affairs, yet his motives were honest, his positions were for the most part tenable, and Alvarado had no reason to suspect him of treacherous or revolutionary designs.

[46] Session of April 1, 1840. *Leg. Rec.*, MS., iii. 75–8. Pico was to be fined and Carrillo forced to attend to his duties. This was a committee report, and no final vote appears.

[47] *Dept. St. Pap., Ben. Com. and Treas.*, MS., iv. 54; *Vallejo, Doc.*, MS., ix. 351.

[48] April 15th, V. to his brother, in a very despondent tone; can never forgive those who have brought about the coming evils; desires to die, since his efforts have been fruitless; hopes the crisis will come soon to teach a lesson to those who believe a train of civil employees can save the country; will not abandon his post till his resignation is accepted; dwells on the continual slights to which he is subjected. *Vallejo, Doc.*, MS., xxxiii. 57. April 25th, to minister of war. Cannot make his authority respected, and should not be held responsible for results. *Id.*, ix. 124–5. He probably sent in his resignation about this time, as he states in his history. Sept. 1st, argument in a private letter to Alvarado, in answer to the latter's claim that he was trying to enforce the laws. *Id.*, ix. 241.

Indeed, it is probable that such a suspicion was but a pretence.

The junta, or four of its seven members, assembled at Monterey February 16th under the presidency of Alvarado, holding regular and extra sessions till the end of May. I append a résumé of the proceedings in a note.[49] The prominent matters presented

[49] Feb. 16, 1840, Jimeno, Castro, Argüello, and Gonzalez were present and took the oath. Requena and Carrillo absent on account of sickness. Pico not heard from. The gov. delivered an address on the state of public affairs. under the following heads: police and municipal regulations, agriculture, commerce, education, administration of justice, and ways and means. 'It is for you as a body to shower the most abundant benefits on the country you represent, reaping as the fruit of your tasks the eternal gratitude of its dearest sons.'

Feb. 18th–22d, a *Reglamento para el gobierno interior de la Junta Depaartmental, 1840* (variations from the former reglamento given in *Leg. Rec.*, MS., iii. 66–9), was formed by a committee and adopted. Regular sessions were to be held from Jan. 1st to June 30th of each year, on Tuesdays and Fridays. The junta was to have a sec. and two subordinates at $800, $300, and $200. The changes in detail from the reglamento of 1834 (p. 252 of this vol.) were for the most part unimportant. Feb. 18th, Argüello was made temporary sec., and Feb. 22d Pico appeared and took his seat. Feb. 25th, proposition on tribunals of justice. Committees formed: taxes and municipal administration, Pico; education, agriculture, and industries, Castro and Gonzalez; commerce and constitutional changes, Argüello. (Feb. 27th, various doc. from Mex. submitted, including Alvarado's appointment as gov. p. 94.) Feb. 29th, excuses of Carrillo and Requena. (Dr Den's certificate of Carrillo's illness. p. 66.) March 3d, 9th, 10th, 13th, tribunal of justice; land grants; excuses of Carrillo and Requena; suplentes to be summoned; Zenon Fernandez chosen as sec. March 18th, question of the capital. Fernandez sworn. March 21st, Gonzalez asks for leave of absence on account of illness, age, and incapacity. About salary of vocales, $1,500 per year. March 24th, capital. (March 26th, Gonzalez's excuses not accepted. 'Every public functionary is a mark for the shots of scandal.' p. 82.) March 27th, 29th, 31st, lands, capital. (Salaries to date, $725. p. 99.) (April 1st, secret session to consider acts of Vallejo, Pico, and Carrillo. Gov. authorized to arm the civil officers, as elsewhere related. p. 63–4, 69–78.) April 3d, land grants. April 4th, 9th, 23d, threatening attitude of foreigners. Graham affair. (April 8th, Jimeno's report on coast and mission lands. p. 90–2.) April 9th, Jimeno's report passed to com. April 28th, prop. to forbid distillation and importation of liquors from wheat, corn, and barley, as being injurious to Californian farmers. Castro allowed to go home to attend to matters left pending by his son who had gone to Mexico with the prisoners, (Jimeno's land report approved by com., also prohibition of distilled liquors on April 30th. Salaries for month, $500. p. 79, 83, 87, 92, 96.) May 1st, land bill approved. May 5th, liquor bill approved, except the article on importation. Census. May 8th, census. May 12th, eleven land grants referred to com. Census bill. Secretary's salary raised to $1,000. May 15th, census bill. May 19th, land grants. 27 referred and 11 others approved. May 22d, land grants, 14 referred and 27 approved. May 26th, 29th, 30th, 16 grants approved. (May 30th, Alvarado reported perfect tranquillity, obtained permission to leave the capital if necessary, and declared the sessions closed. p. 78.) *Leg. Rec.*, MS., iii. 49–65, with additional records of various dates not

for the consideration of the junta, and requiring further notice here, were the establishment of a supreme court and a settlement of disputes respecting the capital. The tribunal de justicia, in accordance with the law of May 23, 1837, was to consist of four ministros, or justices, a fiscal, or attorney, and a secretary. The places were filled in the session of March 10th by the appointment of Juan Malarin, J. A. Carrillo, J. A. Estudillo, and A. M. Osio, in that order, with Juan Bandini as fiscal and Mariano Bonilla as secretary. The last named was the only one who had any legal knowledge, and as a measure of conciliation the south was given a majority of the members.[50] The tribunal does not appear to have assumed its duties until May 1842, when Bandini, declining to serve as fiscal, was succeeded by J. M. Castañares, and Bonilla as secretary by Narciso Botello.

March 18th Jimeno introduced a resolution that the junta should propose Monterey as the capital, with the title of city, and that it be regarded so pending a decision. His reasons were the resolutions of the diputacion in 1836; the fact that the decree making Angeles the capital had not been officially received; and some evidence which appeared in the government journal to the effect that Monterey was regarded as the capital in Mexico. The matter was referred to

in order, but introduced by me under their dates in parentheses so far as they have any importance. *Id.*, p. 66–96. Hartnell was paid $30 per month for the building occupied by the govt. *Dept. Rec.*, MS., xi. 6. Items referring to these sessions of 1840, in *Dept. St. Pap., Angeles*, MS., xii. 43; *Id., Ben. Com. and Treas.*, iv. 46; *Dwinelle's Colon. Hist. S. Fran.*, add., 70–2. In Oct.–Nov., Jimeno was again acting as governor on account of Alvarado's illness. *Leg. Rec.*, MS., iii. 95; *Dept. Rec.*, MS., xi. 24, 69; *Arch. Arzob.*, MS., v. pt ii. 28.

[50] *Mexico, Arreglo Provisional de la Administracion de Justicia 23 de Mayo, 1837*, in *Arrillaga, Recop.*, 1837, p. 399. Chap. iii. on 'Tribunales Superiores de los Departamentos.' p. 408. Also decree of July 15, 1834, on the same subject, in *Id.*, 1839, p. 175, being the one cited in California at the time of the appointment, as per *Dept. Rec.*, MS., xi. 55; *S. Diego, Arch.*, MS., 252. Action of the junta Feb. 25th to March 10th, in *Leg. Rec.*, iii. 57–8; *Vallejo, Doc.*, MS., xxxiii. 38. May 19, 1841, members cited to instal the tribunal. Bandini sent excuses, which were accepted. Narciso Botello appointed secretary. *Dept. Rec.*, MS., xii. 44–6.

Argüello as a committee, and he, although a southern man, reported in favor of the resolution, declaring that Monterey from its position should be the capital, and that it had virtually been recognized as such by the supreme government.   Pico insisted on obedience to the law of May 1835 making Los Angeles the capital, but Argüello cited the later law of December 30, 1836, authorizing the government to designate the capital provisionally.   On March 27th the resolution was adopted, Pico protesting in violent language against this action as illegal and outrageous.   Don Pio went so far as to quit the hall in wrath, for which he was officially rebuked and fined by the junta; but the fine was remitted when he apologized and retracted his protests.[51]

Finally, the conspiracy of José Antonio Carrillo demands our notice. If estimated from the bulk of the record, it was an important matter indeed.   In August, Joaquin Pereira, a Portuguese, revealed to Judge Olivera of Santa Bárbara that Carrillo had proposed to him to join in an attempt to seize that place by surprise, he having one hundred and fifty men already enlisted for the enterprise.   Macedonio Gonzalez had gone to the southern frontier to raise troops, only the resolution of Cárlos Carrillo being awaited to begin operations.   Pereira ran away soon after making the revelation; and, so far as I can determine from the mass of papers before me, not a particle of evidence was found in corroboration of his statement.   Yet Carrillo was regarded in these times with much suspicion by the administration at Monterey, and Prefect Argüello, who seems to have become all at once an *arribeño*, attached some importance to the charges, or pretended to do so.   A complicated correspondence ensued; Carrillo was arrested

[51] *Leg. Rec.*, MS., iii. 58-9, 63-78, 81-2, 84-5. The knowledge of foreign plots (Graham affair), to oppose which he would sacrifice his life, had much to do with his apology; so he said.

and taken to Monterey to be released; Gonzalez was
brought as a prisoner to Angeles, and perhaps even
sent to Sonoma; and finally, in May of the next year,
the Carrillos were officially vindicated from all accusations, and restored to 'good reputation and fame.' It
seems unnecessary to notice in detail the documents
in the case, though they contain much that is amusing, if not very instructive.[52]

[52] Over 50 communications on the Carrillo-Gonzalez conspiracy. *Dept. St.
Pap.*, MS., v. 20–44; xviii. 62–3; *Id.*, *Angeles*, i. 21–6, 38; iii. 19–40, 53, 57;
xii. 30–7, 63; *Id.*, *Ben. Pref. y Juzg.*, i. 13; iv. 5; vi. 73–7; *Dept. Rec.*, MS.,
xi. 21–3; xiii. 33; *S. Diego, Arch.*, MS., 258, 285; *Vallejo, Doc.*, MS., ix. 223;
xxxiii. 139; *Doc. Hist. Cal.*, MS., iv. 1066; *Hayes, Doc.*, MS., 136. Carrillo's
trip to Monterey as a prisoner was made from Sept. 27th to Oct. 7th. Gonzalez was a sergeant of the frontier garrison of Lower Cal., and very influential with the Indians. He had left his post in 1837 for the north, *Vallejo,
Doc. Hist. Mex.*, MS., i. 74, being an order for his return, and had been engaged in the plots of Bandini and Zamorano. According to *Dept. St. Pap.,
Ang.*, MS., xi. 125, he was arrested and sent to Sonoma in Dec. 1840.

CHAPTER XXI.

LOCAL ANNALS OF SAN DIEGO DISTRICT.

1831–1840.

Military Commandants—Decrease and Disappearance of the Presidial Organization—Fort and Other Buildings—Population—Private Ranchos—Summary of Events—Politics and Indian Depredations—Treasure on the Colorado—Civil Government—Ayuntamiento—Criminal Record—San Diego Mission—Padre Martin—Statistics—Secularization—Ortega as Administrator—San Luis Rey—Padre Peyri—A Prosperous Mission—Slaughter of Cattle—Chronologic Happenings—Pio Pico in Charge—Hartnell's Investigation—Mission Ranchos—San Juan Capistrano—Statistical View—Annals of Emancipation—Administration of the Argüellos—The Ex-neophyte Pueblos of San Juan, San Dieguito, Las Flores, and San Pascual.

Santiago Argüello was captain of the San Diego presidial company until 1835, when he retired from the service, but he was often absent from his post. Agustin V. Zamorano was appointed captain in 1835, and held the position on the rolls during the rest of the decade; but he was here only in 1837–8, and never assumed command of the company. Captain Pablo de la Portilla was nominally commandant of the post by the seniority of his rank whenever present, until he left California in 1838. Rodrigo del Pliego, always absent, was on the rolls as lieutenant until about 1838, when José Antonio Pico was raised to that rank. The company alférez was Juan Salazar until he was ordered to the north in 1839, José A. Pico also holding that rank apparently from about 1834, when he was promoted from that of sergeant, and Andrés Pico becoming alférez in 1839. Salazar was habilitado, and more often than any other during the decade is named as acting commandant, though every other officer of the company held the command at times.[1]

The military organization was, however, but a shadow of its former strength. In 1830, as we have seen, the total force was about 120 men. During the first half of this decade the presidial cavalry company shows a muster-roll varying from 35 to 25. Six artillerymen and three Mazatecos are mentioned in 1833; nine and 17 of the same classes in 1836. In 1835, of the 27 soldiers 11 were on duty at the presidio, 13 at San Gabriel, and one at San Juan. In 1837 the troops were sent north in the sectional disputes, and never returned as a body. From that date the presidio was abandoned, though a force of one soldier is reported in 1839. The organization had, however, been kept up at San Luis, where in September 1839 the remaining eight soldiers quit the service to save themselves from starvation. Pay-rolls of the company show a theoretical expenditure of from $800 to $900 per month, never paid. It appears that a sum of $500 was sent down from the capital in 1833; the commandant was notified in 1839 that there was $1,000 in the treasury for his company; and presumably the men did not live without occasional rations. Military correspondence is devoted almost exclusively to complaints of destitution.[2]

[1] For presidio annals of S. Diego in 1821–30, see vol. ii. p. 539 et seq. The scattered archive references for the official list as given above I do not deem it worth while to present, they being more bulky and complicated than important. Many of them are included in note 2.

Santiago E. Argüello was receptor of customs in 1833–4; and was succeeded by Martin S. Cabello under a Mex. appointment of July 22, 1833. He was required to give bonds for $2,000. *Dept. St. Pap., Mont.*, MS., vii. 5; *Id., Ben. C. & T.*, iii. 21. He had trouble with the local authorities in 1836, and the place was held for a time by Andrés Pico. In 1837–8 Bandini, Pico, and Cabello are named confusedly as in charge of the revenues; and in 1839–40 nothing appears on the subject. *S. D. Arch.*, MS., 5, 41, 95, 107, 118; *Dept. St. Pap., Cust.-H.*, MS., iv. 1–4; *Hayes, Doc.*, MS., 8.

[2] May 17, 1832, want of resources prevents the organization of a frontier co., as the gov. thinks. Minister Alaman urges the necessity. *Sup. Govt St.*

Of the presidio buildings nothing is known except that they were abandoned in 1835 or a little earlier, and in ruins long before 1840. Probably much of the material was brought down to build the little town of 30 or 40 houses that had sprung up at the foot of the hill. After Castro's raid of Christmas 1838, earthworks were hastily thrown up on the ridge for the town's protection, and a cannon was brought over from the castillo. This castillo, or fort, at Point Guijarros, had no garrison or guard after 1835, if it had one before. An investigation in 1839 showed the existence of nine cannon, two of them service-able, with 50 canisters of grape and 300 balls. It was intended to put a guard in charge of this prop-erty, but the enterprise failed; and in January 1840, the remnants of the fort and *casa mata* were sold to Juan Machado for $40. A few of the guns were perhaps removed; one may still be seen at San Diego; and the rest, after being spiked by an American cap-tain in 1842, are said to have been thrown into the bay during the war of 1846–7.[3]

Pap., MS., v. 7–8.   June 1833, comisario sends $500 to S. D. *Dept. St. Pap.*, *Ben. C. & T.*, MS., ii. 86.   April 17, 1834, Alf. Salazar cannot go to Mont. for want of a shirt and jacket.   Has only a poor cloak to cover the f ightful condition of his trousers. *Id.*, *B. M.*, lxxix. 55.   Gov. has called on presi-dent and padres to furnish supplies. *Id.*   June 1835, S. D. must furnish its quota of artillery militia. *Leg. Rec.*, MS., ii. 263–5.   Oct. 1835, list of offi-cers and men of the co. and their whereabouts. *S. D. Arch.*, MS., 55.   Feb. 7th, decree reëstablishing the local militia. *Id.*, 82–3.   Aug. 1836, com. suc-ceeds in borrowing three guns for his troops. *Id.*, 122.   1839, plenty of corn and wheat at the mission, but nothing else. *Vallejo, Doc.*, MS., vii. 313–14. Four fire-arms and pikes borrowed. *Id.*, 243.   Final disbandment at S. Luis, and complaints of Pico. *Id.*, viii. 69–70.   Only one soldier at S. D.; therefore the juez de paz cannot execute the prefect's orders. *S. D. Arch.*, MS., 234. July, $1,000 ready for the co. *Dept. St. Pap.*, *Ben.*, MS., iii. 162.   For mus-ter-rolls, pay-rolls, names of company officers, etc., and complaints of des-titution, see *Dept. St. Pap.*, *B. M.*, MS., lxii. 30; lxxiv. 45; lxxv. 5, 10–12; lxxvii. 14, 20; lxxviii. 2, 4; lxxix. 23–4, 40, 54, 82; lxxx. 26; lxxxi. 3, 19, 29, 35; lxxii. 1, 28, 64; lxxiv. 4; *Dept. St. Pap.*, MS., iii. 1, 8–10; iv. 2, 4; *St. Pap., Sac.*, MS., iii. 35, 37, 117; x. 4; xii. 6; xiii. 16; xiv. 16–20, 43; *Dept. Rec.*, MS., ix. 47; *S. D. Arch.*, MS., 30, 82, 158, 180; *Id. Index*, 33; *Hayes, Doc.*, MS., 12, 13, 19, 28; *Vallejo, Doc.*, MS., i. 283; iii. 176; iv. 315; vi. 7, 24–5, 90–1, 264; vii. 103–5, 312; viii. 253.

[3] Not a building of the presidio left in 1839; all in ruins. *Vallejo, Doc.*, MS., vii. 8; viii. 23–4.   It was therefore necessary to buy a house in town for a proposed garrison.   The earthwork on Stockton Hill mentioned in *Hayes' Em. Notes*, 364; *Id. Miscel.*, 41; *S. D. Union*, June 20, 1876.   On what be-came of the guns, *Romero, Mem.*, MS., 3.   Photograph of one of the guns

The population of the district, not including neo-phyte and gentile natives, has been given as 520 in 1830.[4] There are absolutely no statistics for this decade. There was probably a small decrease in the first half, and subsequently a very large one, caused by the scattering of the military force and by the depredations of Indians at the ranchos. Bandini, without giving figures, states that the depopulation was very rapid after 1836.[5] As an estimate, I put the population in 1840 at 150, the smallest figure for more than half a century. The number of foreigners was nine in 1836, and ten in 1840, three of them having families.[6] The neophyte population of the three missions, 5,200 in 1830, had decreased to 5,000 in 1834. After the secularization there are no definite statistics, but there are indications that in 1840 the ex-neophytes whose whereabouts were known, at the missions, in the pueblos, and in private service, may have been 2,250. Of gentiles and fugitives, as in other periods, the number cannot be given. I append a note on the ranchos occupied by private citizens during this period.[7] Most of them had to be abandoned at

in the plaza at Old Town, with inscription, *El Jupiter. Violati fulmina regis. Carolus tertius, etc. Manila. Año de 1783,* in *Hayes' Em. Notes,* 550-2. Reports on the castillo and guns in 1839. *Vallejo, Doc.,* MS., vi. 269; viii. 21, 264; xxv. 204. April 1839, alcalde says he has never received any munitions or artillery, but will have a search made. *S. D. Arch.,* MS., 221. Sale of the castillo to Machado. *Hayes' Em. Notes,* 494; *Id. Doc.,* 115. Aug. 1835, mention of a contribution, plans, etc., for building a church and casa consistorial. *S. D. Arch.,* MS., 56. May 1837, Padre Duran authorizes the alcalde to select a building for a chapel and to fence in a campo santo. *Hayes' Miss. B.,* 411. Douglas, *Journal,* MS., 88, describes S. D. as a town of 50 houses in 1840; estimated exports, $10,000.

[4] See vol. ii., p. 544 of this work.

[5] *Bandini, Hist. Cal.,* MS., 8. In 1839 the number of votes cast for electors was 31. *S. D. Index,* MS., 53.

[6] *St. Pap., Sac.,* MS., xii. 15; *Dept. St. Pap., Ang.,* MS., iii. 39.

[7] San Diego ranchos in 1831-40, according to land commission and district court lists in *Hoffman's Reports,* list for 1836 in *S. D. Arch.,* MS., 110, and other authorities. Those marked with a * were finally rejected by the L. C. or U. S. courts. Agua Caliente, granted in 1840 to José A. Pico; claimant under a later grant, J. J. Warner. Cueros de Venado, owned by J. M. Marron in 1836; not presented to the L. C. under this name. Jamacha, granted in 1840 to Apolinaria Lorenzana, who had asked for it and obtained the necessary certificates from the padres in 1833-4. Cayetano Gaitan was in charge 1836. Lorenzana claimant before L. C. *Jamul, granted to Pio Pico in 1831. Andrés Pico in charge 1836. Pio Pico claimant before L. C. Jeus,

one time or another on account of Indian depredations. The inhabitants of the town still pastured
their cattle and raised crops, as they had done before,
on lands regarded as common. The cultivated fields
were chiefly in Soledad Valley, where the cultiva-
tors built *enramadas* for temporary residence. They
claimed no property in the land, but he who tilled a
field one year acquired a respected right to do so the
next. The town lots had been at first assigned by
the military commandant; and the first written title
from the alcalde is said to have been that given to
Tomasa Alvarado in 1838.

Events at San Diego during this decade, as in
most others, were neither numerous, important, nor

owned by M. I. Lopez in 1836. Not before the L. C. *Melyo, granted in
1833 to Santiago E. Argüello, who was the claimant before L. C. Nacion,
not yet granted to private ownership. J. A. Estudillo in charge 1836. Otay,
granted in 1829 to José A. Estudillo, whose heirs, Victoria Dominguez et al.,
were claimants before L. C. Sant. E. Argüello in charge 1836. Paguai,
granted Sept. 7, 1839, and confirmed May 22, 1840, to Rosario Aguilar, but
refused by the grantee. *Hayes' Em. Notes*, 488. Peñasquitos, granted in
1823 and again in 1834 to F. M. Ruiz and F. M. Alvarado, the latter being
owner and occupant in 1836 and later claimant before L. C. Rosario,
mentioned in 1828; in charge of Manuel Machado 1836; not before the L. C.
under this name. San Antonio Abad, mentioned in 1828; Sant. E. Argüello
in charge 1836; not before the L. C. San Dieguito, granted provisionally to
Silva family 1831. *Dept. Rec.*, MS., ix. 97. Granted in part, 1840 or 1841,
to Juan M. Osuna, who is named as owner in 1836, and whose heir was claimant before L. C. San Isidro, mentioned in 1828; owned and occupied by
José Lopez in 1836; not before the L. C. Secuan, Juan Lopez 'solicitante' in
1836; not before L. C.; probably in Lower Cal. *Soledad, regarded as a
part of the town commons and formally made such in 1839. Granted by
Gov. Carrillo in 1838 to Fran. M. Alvarado; claimant before L. C. Cave J.
Coutts. San José del Valle, granted in 1836 to Silvestre de la Portilla, who
was also the claimant before L. C. In charge of Francisco Villa 1836. *Temascal, occupied by Leandro Serrano in 1828 and owned by him in 1836.
Granted by Gov. Echeandía, no date given. Claimants, Josefa Montalva et
al. *Temécula, granted to J. A. Estudillo in 1835; claimants before L. C.,
V. D. Estudillo et al. Granted provisionally to Andrés and Pio Pico, June
2, 1840. *St. Pap. Miss.*, MS., x. 4. Tecate, owned and occupied by Juan
Bandini in 1836. Not before L. C. (Bandini was driven out by Indians, and
in 1838 obtained a grant of Jurupa farther north.) Tia Juana, on the frontier, granted to Santiago Argüello in 1829. Abandoned for a time on account of Ind. raids. Vallecitos, granted to José M. Alvarado in 1840; L.
Soto claimant before L. C.

Feb. 5, 1835, Com. Argüello turns over to alcalde papers relating to applications of soldiers for lands, as being no longer within his powers. *S. D.
Arch.*, MS., Jan. 12, 1835. Joaq. Carrillo petitions the alcalde for a grant
of the mission lands, since S. D. is no longer a presidio, but a pueblo. *Id.*, 32.
Information on the general subject of lands and town lots. *Hayes' Em. Notes*,
480.

exciting. A chronological summary is appended, consisting of references to items of political and military affairs as given in other chapters, interspersed with such other petty happenings as seem worthy of brief notice.[8] This little community was intensely patri-

[8] Chronological summary of S. Diego events, 1831. Revolt against Gov. Victoria, Nov.–Dec. See p. 200–4, 210, this vol. Arrival of Jackson's trading party from Sta Fé in Nov. *Id.*, 387.

1832. Meetings of officials and of the diputacion, March–May, and position of the Dieguinos in the struggle against Zamorano and the plan of Monterey. *Id.*, 225–9.

1833. Departure of Ex-gov. Echeandía in May, *Id.*, 244. Petition of the inhab. for an ayuntamiento. *Id.*, 249. Visit of Gov. Figueroa, July. *Id.*, 247. Fears of an attack from the Indians, neophytes, and gentiles combined, with rumors of political designs. Ringleaders arrested. *Id.*, 358–9. Bandini in congress tries to have the post of S. Diego opened to foreign trade. *Id.*, 369. March 26th, a soldier under arrest was forcibly released by a corporal and 7 privates, all belonging to the L. Cal. forces. *Dept. St. Pap., B. M.*, MS., lxxix. 9. Nov. 12th, a fall of meteors alarmed the people, and sent them in haste to the church. It also broke up an interesting game of monte. *Ezquer, Mem.*, MS., 3.

1834. Arrival of the *Natalia*, Sept., with part of the Híjar and Padrés colony. p. 267 of this vol. Bandini as inspector of customs, and his smuggling operations. *Id.*, p. 371. Nov., according to the reglamento, S. Diego and S. Dieguito formed a parish of the 1st class, salary $1,500. *Id.*, 347–8. Nov.–Dec., robberies by Indians of frequent occurrence. The com. gen. will 'take steps,' but meanwhile Capt. Portilla is to make a *salida* asking the alcalde for volunteers. *Hayes' Miss. Book*, 221, 224–5. Dec. 18th, 21st, election of an ayuntamiento for the next year, as recorded elsewhere in this chap.

1835. First ayunt. in session attending to municipal affairs. S. Diego in behalf of Estudillo opposes Castro as gefe político. This vol., 299–300. Visit of R. H. Dana. *Two Years before the Mast*. Feb. 11th, Gov. Figueroa writes to alcalde about a school, for which it seems the people had offered to pay. *Hayes' Doc.*, MS., 17. Feb. 4th, effort to organize an expedition against the Cahuillas who are threatening Sta Isabel. *Id.*, 37. Large force of gentiles said to be threatening S. Luis Rey. Arms to be collected and funds raised by contribution. *Los Ang. Arch.*, MS., iv. 150–1. April, examination of Ind. accused of having plotted to seize Gov. Figueroa at S. Luis. This vol., 361.

1836. Vague rumors of revolutionary troubles. Bandini's plan for a general assembly to save the country, and assurances of S. Diegan loyalty. This vol., 419–20. May 29th, oath of allegiance to the new Mex. constitution. *Id.*, 423. Oct. 9th, 16th, primary and secondary election. Andrés Pico sent to Monterey as partido elector. *Id.*, 446. S. Diego to be a part of the 2d or southern district, that of Los Angeles, according to Alvarado's plan. *Id.*, 475. News of Alvarado's revolution or the plan of Monterey; S. Diego loyal to Mexico; acts of the ayunt., the people, and of Bandini in Nov.–Dec. *Id.*, 481–5. The existence of hidden treasure at the ruined missions on the Colorado was reported by Indians; or at least their stories about certain coins in their possession gave rise to a belief in such treasure. The foreigners Thos Russell and Peter Weldon were leading spirits in the matter; the alcalde was an interested party; and Receptor Cabello made a formal demand for the treasure in behalf of the national treasury! A party actually went to make the search, finding nothing; and the matter was investigated by the ayuntamiento, Russell and Weldon being arrested. This matter furnished a subject for comment from Feb. to July. *S. D. Arch.*, MS., 95–6, 108, 114;

otic, fully imbued in these times with politico-military zeal under the leadership of her prominent citizens Bandini, Pico, and the rest. In 1831 she began the first revolution against Mexican authority, that expelled Governor Victoria, and should have made Pio Pico a San Diegan governor. But in 1836 she developed intense loyalty to Mexico, in opposition to Alvarado's revolutionary plan; and both then and

Id. Index, 24; *Alvarado, Hist. Cal.*, MS., iii. 55–6. Indian depredations, chiefly in Jan.–March, with reference to authorities for many but confused details. This vol., 67–8.

1837. Port open to coasting trade only by decree of Feb. 17th. Vol. iv., 84. Enthusiasm of S. Diego against Alvarado. Troops sent north too late. This vol., 485, 494–5, 505. Arrest of municipal officers by Alvarado's agents, and partial conversion of the ayunt. in April. *Id.*, 508. Plots of Bandini, Portilla, and Zamorano. S. Diegans march north and capture Los Angeles in May. *Id.*, 515–21. Oath to the central constitution June 12th. S. Diego supports Gov. Carrillo, Dec. *Id.*, 540. Depredations of Indians on the frontier. Ranchos destroyed and the town threatened. Expeditions by citizens and by the troops enlisted to oppose Alvarado. *Id.*, 68–9. The hostile bands included fugitive neophytes, rancho employés, and savages from the interior. Claudio was a leader. Leiva, Molina, Camacho, and another were killed at Jamul. Tia Juana, Tecate, and most of the frontier ranchos were plundered. There was an absurd tendency to connect, for political effect, the hostility of the Indians with the plan of Monterey; and there were some controversies between civil and military authorities as to the methods of conducting the defence. This year's ayunt. was the last elected.

1838. Jan., Gov. Carrillo's decree establishing the custom-house at S. D. This vol., 545. Feb., force of citizens under Pio Pico sent to Los Angeles. *Id.*, 548. April, Carrillo defeated, retires to S. D.; new preparations, Tobar's arrival, and campaign of Las Flores. *Id.*, 556 et seq. June, S. D. still refuses to recognize Alvarado. *Id.*, 568–9. Same in Sept.; but Carrillo at S. Luis submits. *Id.*, 572–3. More political trouble in Dec.; Castro's raid at Christmas and arrest of the Carrillos and Picos. *Id.*, 577–8. A heavy storm of rain and snow in Dec. was very destructive to sheep. *St. Pap. Miss.*, MS., ix. 36. No depredations by Indians this year; but in April and Sept. there was some correspondence on precautions and suspicious movements of the natives. *S. D. Arch.*, MS., 204; *St. Pap. Miss. and Colon.*, MS., ii. 388.

1839–40. The Indians of the frontier were still on the war-path, especially in 1839, and few if any of the ranchos escaped plunder, most of them being entirely abandoned at different times. So far as can be judged from the records, nothing effectual was done by either local or territorial authorities to punish the marauders, though there was no lack of complaints and promises and plans. See this vol., 69–70. Details are too bulky for separate reproduction, and when combined give no satisfactory result. In March 1839 an election was held under the new laws, Fitch presiding; and Andrés Pico and J. A. Estudillo were sent as electors to Los Angeles to vote for congressman and members of the junta. *S. D. Arch.*, MS., 222. In Oct., Belcher, the English explorer, visited the port and remained five days, but he gives very slight description of the place. *Belcher's Narr.*, i. 325 et seq. In 1840 several foreigners were arrested to be exiled with Graham to S. Blas, but little is known of particulars. This vol., 14–15, 24, 30–1. J. B. Leandry's visit to S. D. on this business with orders from the prefect. *S. D. Arch.*, MS., 254. Romero, *Mem.*, MS., 5, thinks it was in 1840 that the last channel between the river and False Bay was closed by a flood.

in the sectional strife of 1837–8 her favorite sons struggled valiantly by word of mouth and pen in support of Cárlos Carrillo and southern interests. Some Dieguino forces even took part in the bloodless campaigning; their town was more than once invaded by the northern foe; and prominent citizens were made captives. Next to political excitements, and often far surpassing them, were those arising from depredations of hostile Indians, especially in 1836–7 and 1839. Again and again the frontier ranchos were plundered until most of them had to be abandoned; and the town itself was often thought to be in danger, with neither soldiers, arms, nor supplies for effectual defence. A search for hidden treasure on the Colorado was a local topic of comment in 1836; popular elections of municipal rulers were held for three years; complaints of hard times and various pressing needs were always in order; petty controversies between local officials furnished occasional opportunity for consuming the small supply of paper and ink; and for the rest the people must content themselves with their social diversions, with waiting for news of northern complications, and the anchoring in their bay of the trading craft that came not infrequently to carry away their little store of hides and tallow.

Civil government in San Diego, as distinct from the military rule, began with the installation of the first ayuntamiento in 1835. This town council, consisting of alcalde, two regidores, and a síndico, was elected in December of each year to serve during the next year. I append the official list for the decade.[9]

[9] Ayuntamiento of S. Diego elected Dec. 21, 1834, to serve during the year 1835: alcalde, Juan María Osuna; regidores, Juan B. Alvarado and Juan María Marron; síndico, Henry D. Fitch; sec., appointed at $20 per month, soon reduced to $15, José M. Mier y Teran; jueces del campo, Bonifacio Lopez, appointed by ayunt., Jan., Matías Olivas in Aug. At the election 13 electors voted, and Pio Pico got two votes for alcalde. *S. D. Arch.*, MS., 28–9. The inhab. on Sept. 22d had petitioned the govt to give them an ayunt. in accordance with the laws. *Leg. Rec.*, MS., ii. 234–41. Fran. Basualdo was at first appointed sec., but not approved by the assembly, being a military man.

1836: alcalde, Santiago Argüello; regidores, Juan María Marron and Manuel Machado; síndico, Jesus Moreno; sec., Domingo Amao; jueces de

The alcalde had jurisdiction over the whole district, appointing the administrators of missions and owners of ranchos to serve as subordinates, or comisarios de policía. For three years only, 1835–7, the ayuntamientos were continued, and then the alcalde's place was filled by a juez de paz appointed by the governor each year in 1838–40. The change was made because the population was less than that required for a legal ayuntamiento; and from January 1838, San Diego was ordered to recognize Los Angeles as cabecera de partido. Details of municipal affairs, meagrely recorded, are more important as illustrating the system than as part of local annals; but I give a few items in a note.[10] From 1839 this district formed part of

campo, Andrés Ibarra and Ignacio Lopez; juez de policía, Juan B. Corona (?); comisarios de policía, José Corona, Esculano Olivas, Juan B. Alvarado, Henry D. Fitch, and as substitutes, Fran. Ruiz, Andrés Ibarra, Matías Olivas, Ramon Osuna, and the administrators of missions and proprietors or overseers of all ranchos in the district. At the election of ayunt. Andrés Pico got 5 votes and Argüello 6. *S. D. Arch.*, MS., 63; *Hayes, Doc.*, MS., 34. The secretary's salary was still a matter of contention, but was not raised from $15. Mier y Teran served in the early part of the year, but was removed for various faults, and in return made charges against the alcalde. *S. D. Arch.*, MS., 66. The 2d regidor was elected for two years, so that Marron held over. The alcalde found fault with the síndico as an unruly and dangerous man. *Id.*, 98.

1837: alcalde, José Antonio Estudillo; regidores, Francisco M. Alvarado and Francisco Ruiz; síndico, José M. Mier y Teran; sec., Domingo Amao. No other officials named. Election of Dec. 18, 1836, in *S. D. Arch.*, MS., 144. Machado should have held over as 1st regidor, but declined to serve on account of bad health.

1838: no ayuntamiento as per governor's order of Dec. 9, 1837. *Id.*, 190. Juez de paz, José A. Estudillo; sec., José F. Álvarez. No election. Estudillo held the office at first temporarily as 'encargardo,' and then permanently by the governor's appointment. Fitch acted at E.'s request in June. *Id.*, 300. Sec. Amao having run away, Governor Carrillo appointed Álvarez in March. *Id.*, 195–6.

1839: juez de paz, Juan M. Osuna; 2d juez, or suplente, Juan M. Marron. No sec. named. Osuna was elected by the people on Jan. 1st to succeed Estudillo at the latter's request.

1840: juez de paz, Juan M. Osuna; suplente, Juan M. Marron; treasurer (depositario de fondos propios), J. A. Estudillo to April, Francisco M. Alvarado from May. Fitch and J. M. Alvarado had been appointed justices of the peace by the prefect in Dec. 1839 for 1840; but in Jan. the gov. restored those of the preceding year. *Hayes, Doc.*, MS., 102–20. The prefect had made the appointment on the nomination of the justices, as there was no sub-prefect to propose candidates. Perhaps the governor's act was founded on this irregularity. Fitch took the oath of office and began to act. Alvarado declined to take the oath because he could not write. *S. D. Arch.*, MS., 249. The secretary's salary was now $10. *Dept. St. Pap., Ang. Pref. y Juzg.*, MS., iii. 48.

[10] Many communications received by the alcalde from the govt and by

the third prefecture and of the Los Angeles partido,
not having sufficient population for a sub-prefect.
The criminal record presents no *causas célebres,* and
but a meagre array of petty cases. Methods of court
procedure and principles involved in the administration of justice call for no general remark. The subject is best disposed of, like most others connected

him forwarded to the sub-alcaldes or comisarios at the ranchos. *S. D. Arch.,*
MS., passim. July 1835, Los Angeles alcalde claims jurisd. over criminal
matters at S. D., requiring a mule-thief to be sent to him. Jan., trouble
between S. D. alcalde and the com. at S. Luis Rey, the latter claiming the
right to its own alcalde and regidores. Feb. 10th, alcalde instructed by
gov. that his political authority does not extend beyond the presidio settlement; but in the administration of justice his jurisdiction extends to all the
settlements. Jan. 5th, animals must be kept out of town under penalty of
a fine. Vagabonds, drunken persons, etc., must be fined. Jan. 7th, papers
relating to a rancho turned over to alcalde by commandant. Jan. 8th, fines
for persons carrying prohibited weapons. Penalties for petty thefts. Juez de
campo to attend to hide trade. Merchants must submit their measures and
weights to the ayunt. Jan. 12th, schools considered. Feb. 19th, committee
to investigate qualifications of applicants for lands. Mar. 19th, work on the
casa consistorial must cease for want of supplies for the prisoners. People
called on for contributions. May 3d, a dispute on a private debt referred by
gov. to ayunt. May 19th, Joaquin Carrillo forbidden to sell his garden, at
his wife's petition and on order of the gov. Sept. 22d, alcalde wishes to know
if he may force traders to sell at less extravagant prices. Sept. 25th, complains that Argüello refuses to pay his *degüello* tax.
1836. Indian alcaldes paid 1 real per day. Man. Silvas employed on 'ne-
gocios subalternos' at $3 per month. May, trouble between alcalde and the
encargado at Temascal, the latter refusing to obey the former's summons.
1837. March, síndico makes a report of receipts and expenditures. Ayunt.
agrees that each regidor shall take his turn in aiding the alcalde. Dec. 9th,
gov.'s order that there is to be no election for ayunt. 1838. Jan. 17th, S.
Diego must recognize Los Angeles as cabecera, and electors must go there to
vote. 1839. June, prefect orders juez de paz of S. D. to select Indians for
auxiliaries. Colorado Ind. claim the right to elect their alcaldes. 1840.
Juez de paz Fitch needs an escolta de tropa to enforce the liquor laws; also
a secretary, as he cannot write Spanish. Prefect appoints the depositario de
fondos propios. No expenditure without prefect's orders. No pay for acting
as receptor or captain of the port. A tax was imposed on the hide-salting
establishments of foreigners, as had been done before in 1834. *Dept. Rec.,* MS.,
xi. 8; *Dept. St. Pap., Pref. y Juzg.,* MS., vi. 69. See also, for preceding items,
S. D. Arch., MS., 30–1, 42, 58, 99, 113, 172, 190, 214, 231, 246, 249, 264; *Id.
Index,* 19, 64–5, 130–4; *Hayes Doc.,* MS., 13–14, 24, 70, 112; *Id., Miss.
Book,* 226.
Items of revenue and finance. Customs revenue, year ending June 1831,
$389, all paid out to employés. *Mexico, Mem. Hac.,* 1832, doc. 3. Libro de
fianzas 1833–4, referred to in *Dept. St. Pap., Cust.-H.,* viii. 15. Alcabalas or
excise tax 1834 to April, $10,007. *Id., Ben. Mil.,* lxxvi. 4. Aug. 1839, Ramon
Osuna appointed collector of tithes. *S. D. Arch.,* MS., 235. Munic. receipts
1839, $76; expenditures, $77. Same May to July 1840, $29. Sept. to Nov.
$51 and $29. July 1840, some hides were declared to have been unlawfully
seized, but there was no money to pay for them. *Id.,* 266.

with local annals of the period, in a list of original
items as appended.[11]

[11] 1831. Charges of rape and incest by a girl against her father, a military officer. The evidence was not strong enough for conviction, but the
girl was removed from her father's control on account of his cruelty. *Dept.
St. Pap.*, *B. M.*, MS., lxxiv. 11–29. 1833. Much gambling among both Indians and gente de razon. *Ezquer*, *Mem.*, MS., 2–3. 1835–40. Municipal
police regulations, instructions to jueces de campo, etc., most relating to the
killing of cattle, carrying weapons, punishment for petty thefts. *S. D. Arch.*,
MS., 51, 162, 168; *Id. Index*, 106–9. 1835. For want of funds to support
prisoners, they were put to work for any citizen who would feed them. *S. D.
Arch.*, MS., 38. Domingo sentenced to 4 years of presidio for murder of
Cruz. *Hayes' Miss. B.*, 310; *Dept. St. Pap.*, *Ang. Pref. y Juzg.*, MS.,·ii. 21.
A prominent citizen granted by the alcalde a separation from his wife who
had lost $2,000 by gambling. *S. D. Arch.*, MS., 63. There are many petty
gambling cases before conciliadores in these years. 1836. F. M. Alvarado
fined $50 and $25 to the Ind. he had flogged, 'a scandalous proceeding.'
Fine reduced to $25 and 'satisfaction' to complainant. *Id.*, 67. A Mex. for
applying his brand to the cattle of others, and an Ind. for forging the síndico's name to a permit for a keg of aguardiente, sent by the alcalde to Lieut.
Gutierrez as no longer to be tolerated in the jurisdiction. *Id.*, 113–14. Penalties in the alcalde's court: stealing cattle or horses, one to three months of
public works; stealing brandy, 2d offence, 1 year with chain; not informing
against a thief, $3 and 3 days' arrest; Ind. for rape, 1 year with chain; Ind.
servant of Bandini for carrying off a woman, 6 months; running away and
stealing a horse, 20 days; coming from S. Miguel without a pass and robbery, 1 month; robbing a room, banishment for municipality. *Id.*, 67. Two
ex-convicts arrested as vagrants. *Id.*, 71. Thos Russell fined $10 and loss of
his pistol for sending a challenge to Lumsden. *Id.*, 67. Prisoners all at work
for private citizens, says the com., being blamed for the escape of a convict.
Dept. St. Pap., *B. M.*, MS., lxxxi. 19. Bandini supposes that an Ind. murderer
being a christian will come under jurisdiction of the alcalde, and not of the
mil. com. *Hayes' Miss. B.*, 302. Sept., an Ind. who 'tuvo inconsequencias'
with his wife after prayers went and hanged himself. J. J. Ortega and two
others went to look at the man and reported to the chief alcalde. Then the
1st regidor and sec. went to the spot, and looking upon the hanging man
asked three times in the name of God who had killed him. Getting no reply,
they proceeded to examine the body, and being satisfied he had hanged himself, ordered him to be taken down. *Id.*, 301. Dec., Russell banished for
escape from prison. *S. D. Arch.*, MS., 63. 1837. Ind. for killing a calf
fined $2 and 45 days on public works. Fine for gambling, $2.50 for each
party. The alcalde founds his decisions on the laws of 1827 and 1833. *Id.*,
191. Feb., there were 14 prisoners on public works, three of them allotted
to Fitch to repair the plaza road. *Id.*, 172. Síndico ordered to patrol the
town with a guard of citizens. *Id.*, 161. Five prisoners at work on a court-
house and jail deemed more important than a church. No place to keep the
prisoners at night unless some citizen would give up a room. Contributions
called for, and 8 fan. corn received. *Id.*, 166–7. 1839. Prefect calls for a
list of 'ociosos y mal entretenidos.' Alcalde replies that owing to his efforts
there are no idlers in town. *Id.*, 228. Prefect asked to decide about two ex-
neophytes who stole a cow. Alcalde understands that such are to be again
'reduced' to their mission. *Hayes' Miss. B.*, 334. Prefect says a thief must
be sent to the alcalde of Los Angeles, from mission to mission, with the papers
in the case. *S. D. Arch.*, MS., 237. 1840. There being no troops or jail,
Fitch needs an escolta to enforce laws against drunkenness, etc. *Hayes, Doc.*,
MS., 118. Feb., citizens, chiefly foreigners, subscribe $828 as a reward for
discovery of the murderer of Luis Juan. *S. D. Index*, MS., 65.

At the San Diego mission padres Martin and Oliva continued their ministry, the latter throughout the decade, the former until his death in 1838, after twenty-six years of continuous service.[12] Down to 1834, when statistics come to an end here as elsewhere, the padres had baptized 160 Indians, buried 312, married 127 couples, and had on their register 1,382 neophytes. At the end of the decade there were about 800 nominally under control of the ex-mission authorities, though there were only 50 at the mission proper.[13] Naturally secularization is the

[12] Fernando Martin was a native of Robledillo, Spain, born May 26, 1770. He became a Franciscan in 1787 at the convent of Ciudad Rodrigo, where after completing his studies he served as preacher until 1809, when he volunteered for the American missionary field, leaving Cádiz in March and arriving at the Mex. college of S. Fernando in June 1810. The next year he was appointed to Cal., and after vexatious days at Acapulco and elsewhere on account of a pestilence and of insurgent troubles, he reached L. Cal. in April 1811, and came up to S. Diego by land, arriving on July 6th. His missionary service began at once, and he never served at any other establishment. He was an exemplary friar, of whom little was heard beyond the limits of his mission, yet he was accredited by his superior in 1820 with more than average ability and zeal. He was one of the few friars who took the oath of republicanism. His death occurred on Oct. 19, 1838. *Autobiog. Autog. de los Frailes*, MS.; *Sarria, Informe de 1817*, MS.; *Arch. Sta B.*, MS., iii. 123; *Duhaut-Cilly, Viaggio*, ii. 19–21; *St. Pap. Miss.*, MS., ix. 36.

[13] Statistics of 1831–40: decrease of pop. 1,544 to 1,382; baptisms 160; deaths 312; marriages 127; decrease in large stock 8,822 to 3,417; horses and mules 1,192 to 307; sheep 16,661 to 8,616. Largest crop 6,849 bush. in 1831; smallest 1,710 in 1834; average 3,561, of which 2,395 wheat, yield 7.33; barley 903, yield 5.54; corn 202, yield 18.

Stat. of 1769–1834: bapt. 6,638, of which 3,351 Ind. adults; 2,685 Ind. child., 602 child. de razon. Marriages 1,879, of which 166 de razon. Deaths 4,428, of which 2,573 Ind. adults, 1,575 Ind. child., 146 adults de razon, 134 child. de razon; death rate 5.32 per cent of pop. Largest pop. 1,829 in 1824. Down to about 1806 females exceeded males slightly; but this was reversed later. The proportion of children under 8 years varied from $\frac{1}{3}$ in early years to ₅ in later. Largest no. of cattle 9,245 in 1822; horses 1,193 in 1831; mules 330 in 1824; asses 37 in 1801; sheep 19,450 in 1822; goats 805 in 1789; swine 120 in 1815; all kinds 30,325 in 1822. Total product of wheat 132,077 bush., yield 10 fold; barley 81,187 bush., yield 11 fold; corn 24,112 bush., yield 47 fold; frijoles 4,299 bush., yield 9 fold.

Miscell. stat. of 1834–40: July 1834, P. Martin loans the presidio $1,533. *Dept. St. Pap., Ben. C. & T.*, MS., iii. 39. 1835–8, distrib. to neophytes in 4 years, 439 shirts, 202 skirts, 673 blankets, 116 fan. maize, 2,110 wheat, 22 frijoles, 140 barley. *St. Pap. Miss.*, MS., vi. 38–9. See ground plan of the mission buildings perhaps of 1839. *Id.*, vii. 3. Value of church effects $4,802; due from inhab. $560. *Id.*, vii. 2. June 24, 1839, Hartnell's report; S. Diego has 2 vineyards of 8,600 cepas and 517 olive trees, fields for 1 fan. corn and 8 alm. frijoles; Sta Isabel 5,860 vines, fields for 30 fan. wheat, and 20 fan. barley; Sta Mónica 8,000 vines, fields for 2¼ fan. corn, 2 fan. frijoles. *Id.*, xi. 23–5. Feb. 1839, admin. says the mission with estates of Sta Isabel and Sta Mónica is in ruins, people all fled except 50. *Id.*, ix. 37. May, P. Oliva says Sta

leading topic of mission annals; but at San Diego only slight additions can be made to what has been given in the general narrative. After a certain amount of theorizing and agitation by Echeandía in 1829–33, followed by an experimental emancipation of chosen neophytes by Figueroa in 1833–4, Alférez Ramirez and Captain Argüello being successively comisionados, the mission was finally secularized in 1835, and was put in charge of José Joaquin Ortega, who kept the place of majordomo or administrator until replaced by Juan M. Osuna in 1840.[14] After secularization, affairs are said to have continued very much as before. The Indians had never been so closely confined to the mission routine here as farther

Isabel has 560 souls. *S. D. Index*, MS., 135. 1839 (?), Sta Isabel 344 inhab., Sta Mónica 116, mission 320, total 780, also 16 de razon. *St. Pap. Miss.*, MS., vii. 2. June, 1840, debts of the mission to J. A. Aguirre $446, W. E. Hartnell $350, Ant. Cot $69, Joaq. Ortega $1,748, Rosario Aguilar $54; total $2,668. *Vallejo, Doc.*, MS., xxxiii. 12; *Pico, Pap. Miss.*, MS., 47–51.
[14] On secularization in general, see chap. xi.–xii. this vol., and chap. ii. vol. iv. 1831, acc. to Echeandía's decree of Jan. 6th, comisarios, etc., were to be chosen, but no immediate change made. This vol., 306. Blas Aguilar was the majordomo this year. 1832, Echeandía's efforts in the south; views of P. Martin and others. *Id.*, 316. 1833, Echeandía's regl. of Jan., José M. Ramirez appointed comisionado. Figueroa's experimental plan. Sant. Argüello comisionado and his efforts in July–Sept. *Id.*, 326–32. 1834. Ind. pueblos. *Id.*, 339. No record of progress this year. *Id.*, 346. Nov. 22d, Juan José Rocha acknowl. receipt of the decree of secularization for S. D. *Dept. St. Pap., B. M.*, MS., lxxxviii. 18. 1835, actual secularization, Joaquin Ortega in charge from April as majordomo at $50 per mo.; no details. This vol., 353. June, the alcalde is informed by gov. that respecting punishment of Ind. he is to consult the asesor. *S. D. Arch.*, MS., 50. 1836, Jan., alcalde at the town summons the majordomo to appear before him to propose candidates for mission alcalde and regidores—though the mission ayunt. was to have control of petty local matters, not of admin. of justice. *Id.*, 71; *Mont. Arch.*, MS., ix. 2. Several doc. vaguely indicating a controversy between Alcalde Argüello and Ortega. *Hayes' Miss. B.*, 316–17. 1837, Ortega as majordomo, generally called administrator, at a salary of $600. The padre takes O.'s place during his absence. *Id.*, 318. Jan., mission ayunt. chosen. *S. D. Arch.*, MS., 167. Belcher, *Narr.*, i. 327, describes the mission Ind. as armed with bows and arrows. 1838, Rosario Aguilar named a majordomo under Ortega. *St. Pap. Miss.*, MS. v. 55. 1839, Feb., administrator has trouble in causing the gentile chiefs to respect his authority. *Id.*, xi. 35, May 7th, P. Oliva claims that Sta Isabel is not a 'sitio valdío' as claimed, but a mission with 580 Ind. *Hayes' Miss. B.*, 329. June, alcalde ordered by prefect to aid Inspector Hartnell in restoring fugitive ex-neophytes to the missions. *Hayes' Miss. B.*, 332. June 24th, Hartnell reports the mission Ind. in a very naked condition and clamorous for the removal of the administrator in favor of the padre. *St. Pap. Miss.*, MS., xi. 24–5. 1840, under Alvarado's regulations Ortega was removed, and Juan María Osuna was made majordomo in July by Hartnell. *Arch. Misiones*, MS., ii. 1077; *S. D. Index*, MS., 135–6. Ortega not permitted to go to Sta Isabel.

north, and the change was therefore somewhat less abrupt. Of the gradual decadence, not much more rapid than it had been before 1834, as of the minor troubles and controversies and complaints, we have but the most fragmentary record.

Padre Antonio Peyri at the end of 1831 left San Luis Rey, an establishment which he had founded and in 33 years of faithful service had brought to the front rank of California missions, and quit the country in company with the exiled Governor Victoria. He was one of the most prominent Fernandinos, though he chose to devote his energies mainly to his local task; and he was unwilling to remain and witness the overthrow of all his plans, being grievously disappointed at Victoria's failure to establish what he had foolishly hoped would prove a new régime for the missions.[15] After Peyri's departure

[15] Antonio Peyri was born Jan. 10, 1769, at Porrera, Catalonia, Spain; took the Franciscan robe in the convent at Reus Oct. 25, 1787; sailed from Cádiz May 8, 1795; and left his college in Mex. for Cal. March 1, 1796, arriving in July. He served two years at San Luis Obispo, and in 1798 was a founder of San Luis Rey, where, and at the branch establishment of S. Antonio de Pala, he served continuously thereafter. By his superiors he was accredited with distinguished merit as a manager, but not with fitness for high office. *Autobiog. Autog. de los Padres*, MS.; *Sarría, Informe sobre los Frailes 1817*, MS.; *Arch. Sta B.*, MS., iii. 123–4. He was less unfriendly than most Spanish friars to the republic, and took the required oath in 1826; but in the same year petitioned the president of Mex. to relieve him of his mission administration. *Arch. Arzob.*, MS., v. pt i. 23. In 1829 he demanded his passports, being as a Spaniard included in the law of March 20th, and though offered exemption by the governor, insisted in his demand, asserting that he was an old man no longer fit for service. *Id.*, 56–7. He obtained from the Mex. authorities permission to retire with full payment of past stipend. *Guerra, Doc.*, MS., vi. 145, 148. The padre sailed on the *Pocahontas* Jan. 17, 1832, from S. Diego for Mazatlan on his way to Mexico; see p. 210, this vol. The tradition is that he had to leave S. Luis secretly, and that his neophytes, 500 strong, hastened to S. Diego to prevent his departure, arriving only in time to receive his blessing from the receding ship. *Bidwell, Cal.*, MS., 185–7, learned from one of the Indians who aided his departure that he kneeled on the hill and prayed for the mission as his last act. Peyri took with him from the mission funds about $3,000, the amount of stipend due him, as he wrote to Capt. Guerra. He is accused by the republican foes of Victoria of having contributed large sums to support the latter's cause, and of having carried away secretly, hidden in barrels of grain and olives, other large amounts in gold and silver. Pio Pico, *Hist. Cal.*, MS., 159–60, learned from Juan Mariner, a Catalan trusted by Peyri, that the padre took 32 barrels of olives, each containing money. Vallejo, *Hist. Cal.*, MS., ii. 156–9, makes it 14 bbls of flour, and says the S. Blas customs offi-

Padre José Antonio Ánzar, a new-comer, served in 1832, being accused of some irregularities; Buenaventura Fortuni was the minister in 1833–6; in 1837–9 there is no record except of Oliva and Abella as visiting friars; and in 1840 Father Francisco Gonzalez de Ibarra took charge. San Luis was the only mission to show a gain in population for 1831–4, and at the end of that period, with a register of 2,844 neophytes, it stood at the head of the list, not only in respect of population but in the number of its live-stock. Additional statistics are appended.[16]   In 1840

cers refused to land the suspicious cargo. Leandro Serrano, sometime major-domo of S. Luis, talks of 10 kegs of silver dollars passed of as brandy. *Hayes' Em. Notes*, 205; *Id. Miscell.*, 92. I suppose all this to be unfounded. Forbes, *Cal.*, 22, saw Peyri on his way to Mex., publishes his portrait as a frontispiece of his book—said by old Californians to be a good likeness—and describes him as the beau ideal of the old-time fraile with his jolly figure, bald head, and white locks. Nearly all speak well of him. Fray Antonio left Mex. in Feb. 1834, and by way of New York and France reached Barcelona in June. Instead of the tranquillity he had expected for his old age, he found only turmoil and strife. It was not even safe to visit his native town. He bitterly regretted having left Cal., and confessed his great error; but the doctors told him that his age and infirmities made a return voyage dangerous, even if his funds had not been exhausted. He had brought from Cal. two young neophytes, Pablo and Agapito, whom he had placed in the Propaganda college at Rome, where they were contented and the objects of much interest. All this I learn from the friar's original letter written at an inn at Barcelona, and mailed at Marseilles in April 1836, to Stephen Anderson in Edinburgh. *Vallejo, Doc.*, MS., iii. 1. Taylor, *Discov. & Found.*, no. 35, p. 201, says he died at Rome in 1835, drawing on his imagination for the fact. The tradition in Cal. is that one of the neophytes completed his education as a priest, but nothing definite is known of his career. See also, on the life and character of Peyri, *Vischer's Missions of Cal.*, p. vii.–viii.; *Du-haut-Cilly, Viaggio*, ii. 36; *Hughes' Cal. of the Padres*, 32; *Hayes' Memorab.*, 73; *St. Pap. Miss.*, MS., v. 15; *Dept. St. Pap.*, MS., ii. 53–4; *Id.*, xix. 18; *Lancey's Cruise*, 168; *S. Diego Union*, June 19, 1873; *Perez, Recuerdos*, MS., 23–7; *Ord, Ocurrencias*, MS., 75; *Vallejo, Remin.*, MS., 31–2; *Mofras, Explor.*, i. 343.

[16] Statistics of San Luis Rey 1831–4: increase in pop. 2,776 to 2,844; baptisms 385; marriages 161; burials 324. Decrease in large stock 27,978 to 13,000; horses and mules 2,468 to 920; sheep, etc., 26,658 to 15,300. Largest crop 7,825 bush. in 1831; smallest 2,307 in 1834; average 4,684, of which 2,325 wheat, yield 5.74 fold; 1,030 barley, yield 5.5 fold; 1,202 corn, yield 53 fold; beans 102, yield 6.87 fold.

General statistics 1798–1834, the whole period of mission existence: total no. baptisms 5,591, of which 3,539 adult Ind., 1,862 Ind. children, 192 child. de razon; average per year 151. Total of marriages 1,425, of which 9 gente de razon. Deaths 2,859, of which 1,445 Ind. adults, 1,367 Ind. child., 12 and 35 ad. and child. de razon; average death rate 4.42 per cent of pop. Largest pop. 2,869 in 1826. Sexes about equal down to 1809; then the excess of males increased to about 10 per cent. The proportion of children under 8 yrs was about ⅓, rather more before and less after 1812. There were generally from 20 to 50 persons de razon living at the mission. Largest no. of cattle

there were about 1,000 of the ex-neophytes at mission, pueblos, and ranchos more or less under control of local authorities. Secularization began here as at San Diego with Figueroa's experimental emancipation in 1833, resulting in the forming of an ex-neophyte pueblo at Las Flores, with but a small population. The final secularization was accomplished in November 1834 by Captain Portilla as comisionado, and Pio Pico remained in charge as majordomo and administrator until succeeded by José A. Estudillo in August 1840.[17] After the securalization the decline in pop-

27,500 in 1832; horses 2,226 in 1828; mules 345 in 1828; asses 5 in 1827; sheep 28,913 in 1828; goats 1,300 in 1832; swine 372 in 1819; all kinds 58,767 in 1828. Total product of wheat 114,528 bush., yield 9 fold; barley 94,600 bush., yield 16 fold; corn 101,442 bush., yield 182 fold; beans 10,215 bush., yield 23 fold.

Miscell. statistics of 1831-40. Accounts of 1834 as rendered by P. Fortuni to Capt. Portilla: assets $46,613, debts $14,429. *St. Pap. Miss.*, MS., xi. 53. 1835: Inventory Aug. 22d; valuation $203,737; debts $93,000; the church 64x10 varas, of adobes, tile-roofed, floor of clay, board ceiling, 9 doors, 18 windows, 4 adjoining rooms, all valued at $30,000, included in the total, as also the 6 ranchos valued at $40,437, the most valuable being Pala, Sta Margarita, and S. Jacinto. *Id.*, vi. 10-11. Jan., May, nothing but cattle for the needy troops of S. Diego. *St. Pap., Sac.*, MS., x. 4; xiv. 44. 1839: Lists of debts amounting to $15,656 in May and $14,639 in Aug. The largest creditors were Juan Ebbetts, J. A. Menendez, Thos Shaw, P. Fortuni, Thos Park, John Temple, P. Ibarra, and Pio Pico. *Pico, Pap. Miss.*, MS., 47-51, 57; *Vallejo, Doc.*, MS., xxxiii. 12. Long list of debtors owing from $3 to $173, or 1 to 30 beasts, each. *Pico, Pap.*, 53-5; Bandini, *Hist. Cal.*, MS., 9-10; Osio, *Hist. Cal.*, MS., 218-20; and Julio César, *Cosas de Ind.*, MS., 1-2, give some particulars about the mission ranchos, without definite dates or figures, agreeing in substance with information given on p. 555 of vol. ii.

[17] Chron. summary of events at S. Luis Rey during the decade: Echeandía's preliminary agitations here as at S. Diego. For gen. account of secularization, see chap. xi., xii., this vol., and chap. ii., vol. iv. 1831: Gov. Victoria at S. Luis, departure of P. Peyri. This vol., p. 183, 210. Julio César, *Cosas de Ind.*, MS., 4, says that one of the neophyte boys carried away by Peyri came back to Cal. in later years. 1832: Echeandía at S. Luis, writings against Zamorano, Ind. ready to fight, meeting of the diputacion. This vol., p. 225-7. Capt. Pablo de la Portilla appointed comisionado by Echeandía. *Id.*, 326. 1833: Portilla continued in office. His efforts at emancipation under Figueroa's instructions. Small results. *Id.*, 330-2. Feb., Com. Portilla needs 15 or 20 men to prevent disorders among the Ind. on account of the division of lands. *Dept. St. Pap., Pref. y Juzg.*, MS., v. 76. Oct., Rosario Aguilar, majordomo at Pala, knocked down and left for dead by Simon, an Ind., who was arrested. *S. D. Arch.*, MS., 20.

1834: Great slaughter of mission cattle; 5,700 head killed on shares from May to July, the mission getting half the hides and tallow. This vol., p. 348-9. In July, after the slaughter was well advanced, permission was asked of the dip. *Leg. Rec.*, MS., ii. 148-51, 163. Estudillo, *Datos*, MS., 33-4, puts the number killed at about 20,000. In Sept., Oct., a part of the Hijar and Padrés colony were at S. Luis. This vol., 267-8. Some of them accused of inciting a revolt. *Id.*, 281. Actual secularization in Nov., Portilla receiving the property from P. Fortuni. *Id.*, 346. Besides trouble caused by

ulation was more rapid than that in wealth, the Indians succeeding in retaining partial control of the rich
mission ranchos of Santa Margarita, Pala, Santa Isa-

the Ind. running away in appreciation of their new liberty, Portilla seems to
have had some difficulty with the padre.   Dec. 30th, Figueroa advises him to
'contemporizar' with the friars, who have the right to select their own residence. *Arch. Arzob.*, MS., v. pt ii. 7.
    1835: Pio Pico in charge as majordomo, or administrator. This vol., p.
353.   Ind. plot, or rather protest against the loss of the mission rancho of
Temécula. *Id.*, 361.   Oct., the admin. is forbidden to disturb Portilla in the
possession of his rancho S. José del Valle. *S. D. Arch.*, MS., 62.   Nov., Ind.
go to S. Diego to complain before the alcalde that they are not given the
promised liberty, but are severely treated by Pico.   The alcalde reports to
gov. that the danger is serious. *Hayes' Miss. B.*, 229; *S. Diego Index*, MS.,
131.
    1836: Pico still majordomo and encargado de justicia.   His troubles with
the Ind. still continued.   In June he imprisoned Pablo Apis, a leader among
the neophyte petitioners, for redress of wrongs; but they forced him to release
the prisoner, and both parties went to S. Diego to make charges before the
alcalde.   The latter sent a small guard to S. Luis, retained Apis and 4 others
under arrest, urged Pico to use great care so as not to lose the crop, and reported to the gov.   The corresp. is complicated, but no definite results are
indicated.   Evidently Don Pio was not as popular a manager as had been P.
Peyri. *S. D. Arch.*, MS., 112; *Id. Index*, 133; *Dept. St. Pap., Pref. y Juzg.*,
MS., iii. 32-3; *Savage, Doc.*, MS., iii. 64-5; *Hayes' Miss. B.*, 297-9, 303-4,
293.   Sept., alcalde ordered to aid Pico in retaking fugitive neophytes from
the gentiles in the interests of religion. *Id.*, 308.   Soldiers 'strike' for pay
and rations. This vol., p. 483-4.   1837: Arrest of Andrés Pico.   Castillero
joins the southern army here in June. This vol., p. 518, 521.   1838: This
year, like the preceding, sectional strife so fully occupied the minds of all that
the records bear but slight trace of anything else.   Campaign of Las Flores
April. *Id.*, 558 et seq.   Ex-gov. Carrillo at S. Luis in Sept. *Id.*, 573.
    1839: March, the mission must support the fam. of soldiers absent on
service. *S. D. Index*, MS., 134.   May, an Ind. widow asks prefect to be released from the mission to support herself and daughters.   She is overworked
and gets no clothing. *Los Ang. Arch.*, MS., i. 160-1.   June 5th, Pico complains to Visitador Hartnell that the Ind. are constantly running away and
taking refuge at Los Angeles. *Vallejo, Doc.*, vii. 179.   June 14th, prefect
instructed by Hartnell to aid Pico in his efforts to recover all fugitives. *Dept.
St. Pap., Ang.*, MS., v. 26-7.   June 24th, H. says the vines are much injured by worms.   Mission debts and credits about $15,000.   Weaving in
progress. *St. Pap. Miss.*, MS., xi. 25.   July, in Pico's absence P. Ibarra was
put in charge of the mission. *Vallejo, Doc.*, MS., vii. 324; viii. 12.   P. claimed
that during an earlier absence much property had disappeared.   Andrés
Pico declines to take command. This vol., p. 591.   Oct.-Nov., trouble between Pico and admin. at S. Juan about some cattle at a rancho claimed by
both.   Hartnell after investigation decided that P. should have 4,000 and the
other 2,000.   Pico at once sent a man to kill his 4,000, and there were none
left! *Vallejo, Hist. Cal.*, MS., iii. 363-8.   Nov. 7th, com. of S. Luis to be
tried for the crime of freeing a known criminal, Morillo. *Dept. St. Pap., Ang.*,
MS., xii. 20.
    1840: Andrés Pico in temporary charge, Pio being absent in the early
months.   In July Hartnell appointed José A. Estudillo as majordomo under
Alvarado's new regulations.   Pio Pico made much trouble about transferring
the office; but it appears that the difficulty was chiefly on matters of etiquette.
Don Pio felt sore at the loss of his place, and deemed himself aggrieved by
some informality in the manner of demanding a transfer.   Moreover he had
become personally responsible for mission debts to the amount of $2,000, and

bel, Temécula, and San Jacinto throughout this decade, though not much longer.

Father Barona died in 1831, and Zalvidea continued in charge of spiritual affairs at San Juan Capistrano throughout the decade, having, however, but little to do with the management of temporalities even in the early years. The population in 1834 had decreased to 861, and in 1840 was probably less than 500 with less than 100 at the pueblo proper; while in its crops San Juan showed a larger deterioration than any other establishment.[18] Here secularization

he wished to get rid of this responsibility before turning over the property. Original correspondence in *Arch. Misiones*, MS., ii. 1069–70, 1083; *Hartnell, Diario*, etc., MS., 35, 38, 57–60; *Vallejo, Doc.*, MS., xxxii. 351; xxxiii. 91, 94; *St. Pap. Miss.*, MS., xi. 5–9. Finally Hartnell came to S. Luis on Aug. 4th, and from the 10th to 16th the transfer of property to Estudillo was formally made, it being discovered that the number of cattle at the mission ranchos was much less than the inventory of 1839 called for, but also that the said inventory had been grossly inaccurate by the fault of Cárlos Castro, who had not taken the trouble to count. *Hartnell, Diario*, MS., 18–20. Meanwhile there was some difficulty about Joaquin Ortega taking charge at Sta Isabel as ordered by the gov., the Indians protesting. *Id.*, 58; *Hayes' Miss. B.*, 344. Pico had long been trying in different ways to get possession of Temécula rancho against the wishes of the Ind. Feb. 13th, P. Ibarra to Duran, with particulars. *Arch. Misiones*, MS., ii. 1021–2. After surrendering the administratorship he contained his efforts, and seems to have obtained a temporary grant or permission to occupy. Nov. 5th, Capt. Juan and his band are resolved that the Picos shall not put their stock at Temécula, claiming that rancho as the best grain land of the mission; but P. resolved to succeed. *St. Pap., Miss.*, MS., x. 3; xi. 9–11. Nov. 22d, Majordomo Estudillo and 11 Ind. had come to Angeles to oppose the grant, resolved to quit the mission if it was confirmed. *Dept. St. Pap., Pref. y Juzg.*, v. 11. Dec. 15th, Gov. Jimeno to encargado of S. Luis. Assure the Ind. of Temécula that they shall not be disturbed. *Dept. Rec.*, MS., xi. 51–2. Pico himself, *Hist. Cal.*, MS., 98–100, says that the ex-mission was very prosperous under his honest and systematic management; but not so under his successor. John Forster, *Pioneer Data*, MS., 21–2, also declares that Pico's administration was exceptionally honest and efficient. Julio César, *Cosas de Ind.*, MS., 4–5, asserts that all the administrators were cruel despots, and Pico the worst of all.

[18] José Barona was born at Villa Nueva, Spain, March 22, 1764, became a Franciscan at Velorado, July 18, 1783, left the convent at Calahorra Sept. 2, 1794, arrived at the college of S. Fernando Aug. 24, 1795, and came to Cal. Jan.–May, 1798. He served at S. Diego in 1798–1811, and at S. Juan Capistrano in 1811–31. He was regarded by his superiors as a faithful worker of medium merit. *Autobiog. Autog. de los Padres*, MS.; *Arch. Sta B.*, MS., iii. 125; *Sarria, Inf. sobre Frailes 1817*, MS., 43–4. As early as 1817 he was in broken health, and desirous of retirement. In 1823 he was rudely treated by some soldiers at S. Juan; and after 1827 he spent most of his time at S. Luis as an invalid. But little appears about him in mission or secular records. He died at S. Juan Aug. 4th, and was buried on the 6th by P. Zalvidea. *Guerra, Doc.*, MS., i. 240. Statistics of San Juan Capistrano 1831–4: decrease in pop. 926 to 861; baptisms 149; deaths 200. Decrease in large stock

assumed a form slightly different from that at the
other missions, since all the neophytes were emancipated under Figueroa's experimental system of 1833,
the lands being apportioned to them by Captain Portilla as comisionado, and a regular Indian pueblo being organized in November.[19]   It is not quite certain

10,978 to 8,059; horses and mules 178 to 59; sheep, etc., 5,019 to 4,080.   (In
1838 there were 494 cattle, 448 horses, and 9 mules.)   Largest crop 1,625
bush. in 1831; smallest 300 (?) in 1834; average 790.

General stat. 1771–1834, the whole period of the mission's existence: total
of baptisms 4,404, of which 1,689 Ind. adults, 2,628 Ind. child., 4 and 83 de
razon; average per year 69; total of marriages 1,168, of which 24 de razon;
total of deaths 3,227, of which 1,255 Ind. adults, 1,898 Ind. child., 24 and 30
de razon; average per year 50; death rate 5.88 per cent of pop.   Largest
pop. 1,361 in 1812.   Females slightly in excess of males down to 1811.
Children decreased from ¼ to ⅛ of the pop.   Largest no. of cattle 14,000 in
1819; horses 1,355 in 1806; mules 183 in 1813; asses 4 in 1813; sheep 17,030
in 1800; goats 1,353 in 1784; swine 206 in 1818; all kinds 31,270 in 1819.
Total production of wheat 140,700 bush., yield 19 fold; barley 7,760 bush.,
yield 21 fold; corn 89,875 bush., yield 100 fold; beans 5,375 bush., yield 22
fold.

Sept. 12, 1832, P. Zalvidea sends a keg to S. Luis to be filled with conse-
crated wine, that at S. Juan having soured.   *Sta Cruz Arch.*, MS., 11.   1835:
Inventory of mission property, formed by the padre and four comisionados.
Total amount including buildings $54,456; debts $1,410 (credits $13,123;
buildings $7,298; furniture, tools, etc., $14,708; church $1,250; sacred uten-
sils $15,568, ranchos S. Joaquin and Mision Vieja $12,019, library $490).   *St.
Pap. Miss.*, MS., v. 48–9.   1838: Live-stock turned over by Sepúlveda to his
successor Argüello as mentioned above. *Id.*, vi. 33.   Income of the storehouse
$2,372, expenditure $1,717. *Id.*, vi. 37.   1839: S. Juan owes $1,600 besides
the padre's stipend.   Credits $5,000. *Id.*, xi. 26.   1840: List of debts amount-
ing to $1,556. *Vallejo, Doc.*, MS., xxxiii. 12; *Pico. Pap. Mis.*, MS., 47–51.

[19] Chronological summary for S. Juan Capistrano 1831–40: 1832: Padre
allowing the Ind. to manage their own affairs.   His views on Echeandía's
reglamento. This vol., p. 315–17; *St. Pap., Miss. & Colon.*, MS., ii. 63; *Vallejo, Doc.*, MS., xxxi. 25.

1833: Alf. Rocha was appointed comisionado by Echeandía, *Dept. St. Pap.*,
MS., iii. 87, but took no action.   Capt. Portilla was appointed by Figueroa
later, and in Oct. effected the emancipation of all the neophytes.   See a few
details in this vol., p. 332.

1834–7: No definite records.   Rocha mentioned as comisionado in 1834.
Id., 346.   S. Juan to be a parish of the 2d class according to the reglam. of
Nov. *Id.*, 348.   J. A. Pico is named by Ezquer, *Mem.*, MS., 3–4, as comisionado to secularize the mission in 1834, and he seems to have held that position in Feb. 1836. *Dept. St. Pap., Ang. Pref. y Juzg.*, MS., ii. 21.   Francisco Sepúlveda became administrator in 1836 or 1837, apparently.

1838: Sepúlveda succeeded by Santiago Argüello in Jan.   Occupation of
S. Juan by the army of Alvarado and Castro in April during the Las Flores
campaign. This vol., p. 558.   June, Argüello promises to exert himself to
prevent the spread of small-pox. *Vallejo, Doc.*, MS., v. 100.   A.'s salary
was $1,000. *St. Pap. Miss.*, MS., vi. 32.

1839: April, Delfin, a neophyte, in behalf of all the neophytes, charges
the administrator with wasting and misapplying the mission effects, so that
the Ind. are deserting, tired of working without results.   The admin. cul-
tivates fields for himself with Ind. labor; puts his own brand on the best
horses; and buys animals with mission brandy.   Only 60 Ind. at work.

that all the steps were completed, nor is anything known of pueblo annals for a year. It would appear, however, that whatever was accomplished had to be undone under the regulations of the next year, and that the mission was secularized like the rest in 1834. José Antonio Pico and Francisco Sepúlveda were successively in charge during 1834–7; and Santiago Argüello from January 1838. The Indians, having had a foretaste of liberty, became more and more discontented, and were clamorous for a return to pueblo life and self-government. Hartnell failed to satisfy them on his tour of 1839; and finally in 1840 they were left in charge of Padre Zalvidea, aided by

They ask for a just administrator, and one who has not so large a family. *St. Pap. Miss.*, MS., vi. 34–7. Gov. Alvarado instructed Hartnell to investigate, and he found the charges against Argüello unfounded, though the Ind. were discontented, and wished the padre to manage their affairs. *Id.*, xi. 26–8. Hartnell's visit was early in June, and he refused to make any immediate change, though he seems to favor a trial of their plan of saving the expense of an administrator. He found affairs in a bad state, only 80 Ind. at the mission, and some gente de razon disposed to make trouble. The prefect was instructed to aid in the restoration of fugitives. *Hartnell, Diario*, MS., 31, 42, 69–72. In Aug. Argüello says he cannot improve the condition of affairs on account of constant desertions, robberies, and the prefect's refusal to allow the arrest of runaways. *St. Pap. Miss.*, MS., xi. 43–6.

1840: Ramon Argüello was left in charge during his father's absence; but the Ind. were bitterly opposed to the whole family. Hartnell in June was authorized to set the Ind. free if he could make satisfactory arrangements. *Arch. Miss.*, MS., ii. 1111; *Hartnell, Diario*, MS., 86. On arriving in July to put in force the new reglamento, he first appointed Ramon Argüello as majordomo, but the Ind. would not submit, showing great excitement. Then a proposition of Andrés Pico to rent the mission, support the padre with the old and sick, and pay fair wages to all ex-neophytes who would work. Also one of J. A. Estudillo to take the mission as majordomo for 5 or 6 years for one third of the product of the estates instead of a salary, binding himself to care for the padre and Ind., to repair the buildings, and to add his own oxen and horses for working purposes to the mission stock. But the Ind. would listen to nothing of the kind, insisting on being formed into a pueblo. It was finally agreed that temporarily, until the govt could make arrangements about the pueblo, Padre Zalvidea should have charge of the property, the Ind. promising to work faithfully under his administration. *Hartnell, Diario*, MS., 5–6. Hartnell's reports to govt, and his correspondence with Pico and Estudillo. *Id.*, 60–4; *Arch. Miss.*, MS., ii. 1075. Sant. Argüello much offended at his son's removal. *St. Pap. Miss.*, MS., xi. 11. P. Zalvidea had refused absolutely to remain in permanent charge, or as curate at the proposed pueblo, unless families de razon should also be allowed to settle there, and some civil authority be established over the Ind. alcaldes. At the end of Dec. he appointed Agustin Janssens as acting majordomo; approved by govt in Feb. 1841. *Janssens, Doc.*, MS., 5-6. Correspondence with a neophyte who tilled land at Trabuco. *Id.*, 3–4. Janssens had been living for a time at Trabuco as representative of Capt. Argüello, who was soliciting a grant of the rancho.

Agustin Janssens, with the promise of complete emancipation as soon as arrangements could be made. In these last years a very large part of the Indians were absent at Los Angeles and at the ranchos.

There were three pueblos of ex-neophytes in the district besides San Juan Capistrano, namely, San Dieguito, Las Flores, and San Pascual, about all of which there is a most unfortunate lack of information. They were composed of Indians selected from the different missions for their intelligence, good behavior, industry, and fitness in all respects for earning their own living and managing their own affairs. They were feeble approximations to such towns of civilized and christianized natives as all the missions had been intended under the original system to become; but in every respect except the choice of the best Indians, the conditions were unfavorable to success. San Dieguito, Las Flores, and San Juan were perhaps organized in 1833, the two former from the ex-neophytes of San Diego and San Luis respectively;— and in May 1834 they were represented by the governor as in a flourishing condition. San Dieguito seems to have had about 15 families at the start; and at the time of Hartnell's visit in 1839 they were complaining that their best lands had been taken away. Las Flores had 196 inhabitants in 1836, and they were so far advanced in politics that they presented charges against their Indian alcaldes, who were replaced by others after investigation by Pio Pico. In 1839, Hartnell found 49 families of 143 souls, and in four years they had rid themselves of half their property; but the rest of the live-stock, valued at $867, was distributed with a warning that unless they did better they would be again reduced to mission life. San Pascual was organized in November 1835, with 34 families of 113 souls from San Diego. Nothing more is known of it during the decade.[20]

    [20] On the pueblos, see this vol., 339; *St. Pap. Miss.*, MS., xi. 25–6; vi. 52; *Dept. St. Pap., Ang.*, v. 78; *Hartnell, Diario*, MS., 42; *Hayes' Miss. B.*, 230, 305, 497; *Id., Doc.*, 66; *S. D. Arch.*, MS., 114.

CHAPTER XXII.

LOCAL ANNALS OF LOS ANGELES DISTRICT.

1831–1840.

A Centre of Political Agitation— Chronologic Summary and Index— Local Occurrences—Indian Hostilities—Day and Stearns—Vigilance Committee—Sectional Warfare—Carrillo's Capital—Tumult of the Flag—Arrest of Foreigners—Increase of Population —Private Ranchos—Ayuntamiento and Municipal Affairs—Criminal Record—A Race—The Prefecture—Peña, Tapia, and Argüello—Port of San Pedro—San Gabriel—Padres Boscana and Sanchez—Statistics—Secularization—Events—Bandini's Reforms —San Fernando Rey—Father Cabot—A Prosperous Mission— Antonio del Valle as Comisionado—Chronologic Record.

During this decade Los Angeles was a centre of political agitation and of military achievement. From the expulsion of Governor Victoria in 1831, after a battle fought not far from town, there was hardly a month in which the Angelinos did not feel themselves to be responsible in a peculiar manner for the salvation of California, either from the arbitrary encroachments of Mexican despots or from the mad folly of Monterey patriots, whose methods of resisting despotism did not merit the approval of abajeño office-seekers, and who were blind to the claims of the angelic city as capital of the province. Especially in the struggle against Alvarado and in favor of Cárlos Carrillo as governor did the zeal of Los Angeles manifest itself, though it was strongly reën-forced by eloquence from San Diego. But in this struggle the south was destined to defeat, for Santa Bárbara when not hostile was lukewarm, San Diego if eloquent was not warlike, and the arribeño leaders, instead of being annihilated by the patriotic plans and pronunciamientos of their opponents, showed an alarming tendency to use actual force in the play at war. All the complicated and ludicrous sequence of positions assumed—not to say somersaults accomplished—by the illustrious ayuntamiento and citizens of the southern metropolis has been fully presented in the political annals of the country, so that the appended summary [1] assumes largely the form of an index to

[1] Chronologic summary of Los Angeles events during the decade. 1831. Stearns banished by Victoria. This vol., p. 194. Also troubles of Alcalde Sanchez, imprisonment of regidores and citizens, and arrest of José A. Carrillo. *Id.*, 195–6. Dec., arrival of the revolutionary forces from S. Diego, fight near Cahuenga, defeat of Victoria. *Id.*, 204–10. Arrival of Wolfskill's party from Sta Fé in Feb. *Id.*, 386. On Oct. 5th, the chaplain's house was accidentally burned. *Dept. St. Pap., Ben. Pref. y Juzg.*, MS., iii. 18–19.

1832. Jan. 7th, ayunt. adheres to the S. Diego plan. This vol., p. 212. Jan.–Feb., the diputacion in session. Vain efforts to make Pio Pico gov. The ayunt. declares for Echeandía against Pico. *Id.*, 216–20, 231–2. Feb.–April. Ibarra's intrigues, the ayunt. turns from Echeandía to Zamorano, northern force retires, southern force under Barroso at Paso de Bartolo, Angeles, and S. Gabriel, a truce. *Id.*, 225–7. Dip. meets in Dec. *Id.*, 229. Arrival of Ewing Young's trappers in April. *Id.*, 387.

1833. Jan.–Feb. Angeles recognizes and congratulates Gov. Figueroa. *Id.*, 242. Padre Duran's views on the condition and treatment of Ind. in the town. *Id.*, 329–30. Excitement arising from acts of N. Mex. traders and horse-thieves. *Id.*, 395. Botello speaks of a school this year kept by Vicente Moraga at $15 per month.

1834. Controversy about the salt-fields. *Id.*, 374. Ind. troubles of Oct.–Dec., chiefly in S. Bernardino region. *Id.*, 359–60. More details as follows: Oct. 23d, report of Gen. Gutierrez to gov. On 19th the chief Marona reported the advance of 4 chiefs and 200 Ind. on S. Gabriel at the instigation of Hijar and Araujo. P. Esténega and Araujo went to meet them on the 20th. The padre was detained and plundered, but given up to Araujo at La Puente, and the chief testified that the Ind. had risen at A.'s instigation. Lieut J. M. Ramirez was sent against the Ind. on the 21st, and Araujo was ordered to Mont. *Dept. St. Pap.*, MS., iii. 179–83. Oct. 23d, Ramirez's report of his campaign. He attacked 60 Ind. on the 21st, killing 4; and later attacked 200, forcing them to retreat. *Id.*, 177–8. Figueroa's orders of Oct. 31st for precautions, etc. *Id.*, 183–7. Further corresp. It appears that the Ind. had stolen the sacred vessels and other property at S. Bernardino. *Id.*, 190–1. Dec. 16th, Serrano has been warned to leave Temascal by Ind., who say the Angeles district is to be attacked by Colorado River bands. *Id.*, 205. From Gutierrez's report of Feb. 6, 1835, it appears that in the last days of Dec. the rancho of S. Bernardino had been attacked, plundered, and burned. Ramirez with a force of 58 men marched on Jan. 5th. Meanwhile 6 or 8 wounded refugees came in, reporting that 13 persons had been killed, that several families had escaped to other ranchos, and others had been made captives. They said the leaders were ex-neophytes of S. Gabriel and that further hostilities were intended. *Id.*, iv. 1–3. Unfortunately nothing is known of the result of Ramirez's campaign, and nothing more of the massacre. I suppose the number killed may have been exaggerated, and that all were Indians. In *St. Pap., Sac.*, MS., xii. 6–8, is a report showing that in Jan.–Feb. 1835, rumors of impending attack were still current in the district, and that most ranche-

preceding chapters of this volume. There are interspersed, however, various other matters of considerable local interest, most of which, like the political de-

rías in the mountains were in arms to repel invasion by more distant tribes. Nov. 22d, American residents protest against being obliged to do military service except in case of invasion or other great emergency. One of their number has been put in jail for refusal to serve. *Dept. St. Pap. Ang.*, MS., i. 154-6.

1835. March, Apalátegui and Torres revolt against Figueroa in the supposed interest of Híjar and Padrés. This vol., p. 281-6. Charges against Abel Stearns as a smuggler. *Id.*, 375. Angeles made a city and capital by Mex. decree of May 23d, news not received till late in the year. *Id.*, 292, 416. In Sept. Wm Day bought a barrel of wine of Abel Stearns, and finding it sour wished the seller to take it back. Stearns refused, and a quarrel ensued, during which S. attacked D. with a stick, and was in turn stabbed in four places, one cut nearly severing his tongue. Day was arrested and kept in jail for a year, while complicated and intermittent legal proceedings were carried on against him. Day was not only put in jail but handcuffed, and certain Mexicans under Manuel Arzaga broke into the jail and removed his irons, for which they are said to have been banished. *Dept. St. Pap., Ben.*, MS., v. 67-74, 93-156, *Botello, Anales del Sur*, MS., 0-14.

1836. Jan. 4th, publication of the decree making Angeles the capital, lack of zeal in furnishing public buildings. This vol., p. 416-17. Jan. 28th, drunken Ind. to be arrested and put to work on the city water-works. *Los Ang. Ayunt. Rec.*, MS., 70. March-April, murder of Domingo Félix, and the resulting vigilance committee. This vol., p. 417-19. June, oath to the bases constitucionales. *Id.*, 423, 432. April-June, Gov. Chico's visit and troubles connected with his investigation of the vigilance committee. *Id.*, 430-2. Sept., troops at S. Gabriel decline to serve longer without clothing. *Dept. St. Pap., B. M.*, MS., lxxxi. 23-4. Nov.-Dec., news of Alvarado's revolution, meetings of ayunt. and citizens, patriotic plans against the plan of Monterey. This vol., p. 481-4. Dec., Angeles with S. Diego and Sta B. to form a district according to Alvarado's plan, not carried out. *Id.*, 475.

1837. Jan., new plan against revolution; correspondence of leading men; seizure of the mission funds; hostile preparations; campaign of S. Fernando; treaties and protests; Alvarado and Castro at Angeles; peace and congratulations. *Id.*, 484-503. Arrest of 9 or 10 Angelinos by Castro. *Id.*, 504. April-May, the city again asserts its opposition to the new govt, but finally deems it best to submit. *Id.*, 507-9. May-June, a new pronunciamiento; S. Diego plan; Bandini captures the town; Portilla advances in warlike array, but Castillo arrives with the new constitution, and Alvarado ends the war by submitting to Mexico. *Id.*, 518-21, 526 et seq. Oct.-Nov., news of Cárlos Carrillo's appointment as gov., and great joy of the Angelinos. *Id.*, 534-8. Dec., Don Cárlos sworn in before the ayuntamiento. *Id.*, 539-40.

1838. Jan.-Feb., Carrillo at Angeles as the capital. *Id.*, 545 et seq. March, a military force sent north only to be defeated; several prominent citizens made prisoners of war. *Id.*, 549 et seq. April, Castro again in possession of the town, but many citizens escape to the south. *Id.*, 556. May, Carrillo returns with Alvarado after the unsuccessful campaign of Las Flores; revolt of citizens in favor of Alvarado; ayunt. and citizens decide against Carrillo; but after further plots Carrillo and other prominent citizens are sent to the north as prisoners, all is peace again, and Alvarado is entertained by the Angelinos. *Id.*, 564-9. About this year, according to Botello, Janssens, and Mrs Ord, Ignacio Coronel, aided by his daughter and wife, opened a primary school in town.

1839. Jan., the quota of Los Angeles in the call for recruits for the army is 40 men. This vol., p. 583. May, tumult of the flag, or troubles of Pre-

velopments alluded to, have received elsewhere all the attention they merit. Such matters were the meetings of the diputacion in 1831–2; the depredations of New Mexican 'traders' in 1833; Indian hostilities involving the destruction of San Bernardino in 1834; the Apalátegui revolt, wounding of Abel Stearns, and the promotion of Angeles to be a city and capital in 1835; vigilance committee's operations in 1836; the prefect's troubles and flag tumult of 1839; arrest of foreigners, acts of the Chaguanosos, Stearns' contraband operations, and the Carrillo conspiracy in 1840.

Both town and district must be regarded as reasonably prosperous during the decade. The population in 1830 has been given as 1,160, or 770 for the town, and 390 at the ranchos and missions. The chief authorities for the following period are a padron of 1836 and a voting list of 1839, as given with a few other details in a note.[2] While the statistical basis is not entirely

fect Cosme Peña. *Id.*, 588–9. Sept., news of Alvarado's confirmation in Mexico as governor of Cal.; popular rejoicing at Los Angeles. *Id.*, 594–5. June 5th, precautions ordered against the small-pox. *Dept. St. Pap., Ang.*, MS., v. 21–2, 25. Aug. 16th, 21 citizens send a petition to the ayunt. on the state of the town cemetery, which has been used since 1822, and is totally inadequate to present needs, endangering the health of the community. They ask that a suitable site for a new burial place be selected, and that the ayunt. and priest consider the matter of removing all remains from the old campo santo. The ayunt. referred the matter to a committee, and approved its report in Oct. in favor of a new cemetery to be established at the cost of the petitioners with coöperation of other citizens. *Coronel, Doc.*, MS., 92–4. But nothing was accomplished for 5 years.

1840. April, arrest of some 14 foreign residents, who were sent to S. Blas with Graham and his companions. Vol. iv., p. 14. May–June, pursuit of the Chaguanosos and N. Mexican horse-thieves. *Id.*, 77. Oct., more of Stearns' smuggling operations. *Id.*, 95. Conspiracy of José Antonio Carrillo, who was carried to Monterey as a prisoner, an affair which caused much correspondence with but little foundation. This vol., p. 606–7.

[2] Population of Los Angeles: 1833, John Forster thinks there were about 200 families in the town. *Bancroft's Pers. Obs.*, MS., 90. 1834, 21 Americans sign a petition. *Dept. St. Pap., Ang.*, i. 156. 1836, padron of Angeles jurisdiction showing of gente de razon, 603 men, 421 women, and 651 children; total, 1,675; Indians, 553. *Los Ang., Ayunt. Rec.*, 13. List of 358 men available for the protection of the city, including 8 at S. José, 4 at Alamitos, 3 at Lugo's, 17 at Sta Ana, 5 at Las Bolsas, 5 at S. Antonio, 48 at Sta Gertrudis, 21 at S. Gabriel, and a few at other ranchos. *Id.*, 5. The census of 1836 is also mentioned as above in *Los Ang. Co. Hist.*, 33–4, and the names of foreigners, 40 in number, are given; also in *Los Ang. Arch.*, i. 121 –4. 1837, from the padron of the preceding year 274 (or 264) men were selected as fit for military service. *Id.*, i. 137; iv. 279. 1838, names of about 90 citizens in petitions, etc. *Id.*, v. 8–23. 1839, original list of voters, with

satisfactory, I think the population of gente de razon in 1840, including 40 or 50 foreigners, some of them with families, may be safely put at 1,800, or 1,100 in the city and suburbs with 700 at the ranchos and missions, a gain of 640 during the decade. The Indian population, exclusive of gentiles and refugees in distant rancherías, may be regarded as about 1,500. I append a list of some 30 ranchos,[3] more than half of

age, occupation, and residence. The whole number is 153, living in town 87, on the ranchos 53, at the missions 13. There were 99 laborers, 24 rancheros, 12 merchants, 15 men of different trades, besides a clerk, school-master, and an administrator; 54 could write. Abel Stearns is the only foreigner named. *Coronel, Doc.*, MS., 51–64.

[3] Ranchos of the Los Angeles district 1831–40. Those marked with a * were rejected by the Land Commission or U. S. courts. Alamitos, 6 leagues, confirmed in 1834 to Juan J. Nieto, heir of Manuel Nieto; Abel Stearns, claimant before L. C. Francisco Figueroa lived here in 1839, it having been bought by Gov. Figueroa for $500 in 1835. Azuza, 4 leagues, granted to Ignacio Palomares and Ricardo Véjar in 1837, 1840, and to Luis Arenas in 1841, including S. José; Henry Dalton cl. Ballona, 1 league, granted in 1839 to Agustin Machado, who was the claimant. The Talamantes and 5 voters in all lived here in 1839. Boca de Sta Mónica, 1½ leagues, granted in 1839 to Fran. Marquez et al., Isidor Reyes et al. claimants. Bolsas, 7 leagues, confirmed in 1834 to widow of Manuel Nieto, José J. Morillo claimant. The Ruiz, 3 voters, lived here in 1839; 5 men in 1836. For half of Las Bolsas, Ramon Yorba et al. were claimants. Brea, 1 league, granted in 1828 to Ant. J. Rocha, who was claimant; nothing in the records of 1831–40. Cahuenga still ungranted. In Feb. 1833, though occupied by the mission, it was claimed by the ayunt. as ejidos of the town. *Cajon de Muscupiabe, granted in 1839 to Juan Bandini, who was claimant. *Cañada de los Pinacates, ¼ league, granted in 1835 to José and J. M. Cruz; M. Antonio Cruz claimant. Cañada de Sta Ana, 3 leagues, granted in 1834 to Bernardo Yorba, who was claimant. 17 men in 1836; 12 voters in 1839. Cerritos, 5 leagues, granted in 1834 to Manuela Nieto, John Temple claimant. Said by Requena to have been sold for $4,000. Ciénega de las Ranas, see S. Joaquin. Ciénegas, 1 league, granted in 1823 to Fran. Ávila; no record in this decade; claimant, Januario Ávila. Coyotes, 10 leagues, confirmed in 1834 to J. J. Nieto; A. Pico et al. claimants. 4 voters lived here in 1839. In 1840 this rancho was decided to belong to J. B. Leandry, though Tomás Sanchez claimed it, having lived there 8 years as renter of a part. *Dept. St. Pap.*, MS., v. 15–16. Cuati (Huerta), granted in 1830 to Victoria Reid, who was claimant. Cucamonga, 3 l., granted in 1839 to Tiburcio Tapia; L. V. Prudhomme claimant. Habra, 1½ l., granted in 1839 to Mariano Roldan; A. Pico et al. claimants. Jurupa, 7 (or 14) l., granted in 1838 to Juan Bandini; claimants, Bandini and Louis Robidoux. Nogales, 1 l., granted in 1840 to José de la Cruz Linares; M. de Jesus García et al. claimants. Ojo de Agua, granted to Encarnacion Sepúlveda in 1840. Not before the L. C. Paso de Bartolo Viejo (sometimes called S. Rafael), 2 l., granted in 1835 to Juan Crispin Perez; Pio Pico et al. claimants. Rincon, 1 l., granted in 1839 to Juan Bandini; B. Yorba cl. *Rosa de Castillo, granted in 1831 to Juan Ballesteros; A. Lestrade cl. San Antonio, confirmed in 1838 to Ant. M. Lugo, who was claimant. 5 men here in 1836. San Francisco, granted in 1839 to Antonio del Valle, much against the wishes of the S. Fernando Ind.; Jacoba Félix cl. San Joaquin, 11 l., granted in 1837, 1842 to José Sepúlveda, who was the cl., including Ciénega de las Ranas. San José, granted in 1837, 1840 to R. Véjar and Ign. Palomares, who were cl. (see

the number newly granted, which were occupied by
private owners during the decade, information being
mainly drawn from the later records of the Land
Commission. Municipal affairs were managed by an
ayuntamiento elected each December for the following year, until late in 1839, when justices of the peace
took the place of alcaldes and regidores. Jueces de
campo for the environs of the town and auxiliary
alcaldes at the ranchos were subordinate to the ayuntamiento. A full official list is appended,[4] with such

Azuza). The Félix, 4 voters in all 1839; 8 men in 1836. S. José de Buenos
Aires, belonged to Alanis and Polanco in 1840. Near Sta Mónica. *Leg.
Rec.*, MS., iii. 59, 82–3. *San Pascual, 3 l., granted in 1840 to Enrique
Sepúlveda and José Perez; M. M. Lugo de Foster et al. cl. San Pedro, 10 l.,
granted in 1822 to Juan J. Dominguez; M. Dominguez et al. cl. 4 voters in
1839. San Rafael, 8 l., granted in 1784, 1798 to J. M. Verdugo, whose heirs
were cl. Two Verdugos and another voter in 1839. San Vicente, 4 l., granted in
1837 to Francisco Sepúlveda, who was cl. Included Sta Mónica. *Leg. Rec.*,
MS., iii. 59, 82–3; *Carrillo (D.), Doc.*, MS., 79–80. Santa Ana, see Cañada de
Sta A. and Santiago de Sta A., Santa Catalina Isl., solicited in 1840 by Louis
Vignes and J. M. Ramirez for sheep-raising, but not granted. *Dept. St. Pap.*,
Pref. y Juzg., MS., vi. 77; *Id., Ang.*, xii. 40–1, 97. Santa Gertrudis, 5 l.,
conf. in 1834 to widow of Manuel Nieto, S. Carpenter cl. 48 (?) men in
1836; 10 voters in 1839. Report on this rancho in 1833 in *Cota, Doc.*, MS.,
1. Santa Mónica, see Boca de Sta M. In 1840 it was decided that neither
Marquez nor Reyes had any title to the lands which had been held by Alvarado and Machado. *Leg. Rec.*, MS., iii. 59, 82–3. Santiago de Santa Ana,
11 l., granted in 1810 to Antonio Yorba, whose heirs were the cl. In 1836
three men; in 1839 three Lugos and another voter. Sauzal Redondo, 5 l.,
conf. in 1837 to Antonio Ign. Avila, who was the cl. *Topanga Malibu, 3
l., granted in 1804 to J. B. Tapia; L. V. Prudhomme cl. No record in 1831–
40. Tujunga, 1½ l., granted in 1840 to Pedro Lopez et al.; cl., D. W. Alexander et al. Virgenes, 2 l., granted in 1837 to J. M. Dominguez; cl., M.
Ant. Machado. Two voters in 1839. *Las Vírgenes, gr. in 1834 to Domingo
Carrillo, whose heirs were the cl. See record of cases in *Hoffman's Reports*,
also *Hayes' Miscell.*, 29–31; *Id., Doc.*, MS., 12. On pueblo lots, see cases nos
422, 477, 688 before the L. C. In 1836 the matter of titles to town lands
was agitated, and it appeared that no one had a written title, grants having
been made verbally at first by military comisionados and later by the ayuntamiento. Owners were ordered to petition for regular titles to stop boundary disputes. *Los. Ang. Arch.*, MS., i. 76–8; ii. 72; *Id., Ayunt. Rec.*, 4;
Leg. Rec., MS., iii. 3.

[4] Municipal government at Los Angeles, with list of officials. Chief
authorities: *Los Ang. Arch.*, MS., i., iv., v.; *Id., Ayunt. Rec.*, MS., *Dept.
St. Pap.*, MS., xviii.; *Id., Ang.*, i.–v., xi.; *Id., Ben. Pref. y Juzg.*, iii., v., vi.;
Id., Ben., iv.–v.; *Leg. Rec.*, MS., i., ii.; *Valle, Doc.*, MS., besides hundreds
of scattered references.

1831. Alcalde Vicente Sanchez; 1st regidor Juan B. Alvarado; síndico
Gil Ibarra. Sanchez was always in trouble. His election was declared void
because he was a member of the assembly, and the 1st regidor took his place.
He was suspended in April, but reinstated by Victoria, to be again suspended
and imprisoned by V.'s opponents in Dec. Tiburcio Tapia is named as alcalde in May. *Dept. St. Pap.*, *Ben. Pref. y Juzg.*, MS., iii. 56. The auxiliary

items as are extant respecting routine happenings in connection with pueblo government. As has been remarked, this versatile town council assumed an in-

alcaldes were Juan Perez at Sta Gertrudis, Manuel Gutierrez at S. Pedro, Julio Verdugo at S. Rafael, Rafael Pico at Simí, and Yorba at Sta Ana.

1832. Alcalde Manuel Dominguez; regidores Juan N. Alvarado, José Man. Cota, Felipe Lugo, Ignacio María Alvarado, Juan Ballesteros; sec. Vincente de la Ossa; alcalde aux. at Sta Ana Tomás A. Yorba. Jan. 27th, pay of sec. raised to $20. *Leg. Rec.*, MS., ii. 352. The election for the ayunt. of the next year in Dec. had to be postponed on account of an epidemic which prostrated all the officers and most of the people.

1833. Alcalde José Ant. Carrillo; regidores Felipe Lugo, Ignacio M. Alvarado, Antonio Machado, José Sepúlveda; síndico Tiburcio Tapia; sec. Ossa, and Vicente Moraga temporarily in Feb. and May; jueces de campo Antonio M. Lugo and Ricardo Véjar; aux. alcaldes Perez at Sta Gertrudis, Verdugo at S. Rafael, Bernardino Yorba at Sta Ana, and Man. Dominguez at S. Pedro; A. M. Osio receptor. Jan. 4th, the aux. alcaldes chosen. Jan. 5th, sessions of the ayunt. to be Tuesday and Wed. at 10 A. M. Jan. 9th, Machado's offer to repair the priest's house gratuitously accepted. Feb. 7th, sec. removed for neglect of duty, subject to action of dip. Feb. 28th, com. appointed for state election. April, ayunt. refuses to remit fine of T. A. Yorba, who in 1832 had failed to attend election on excuse of ill health. The dip. in 1834 approved the refusal. July, the election of a second alcalde recommended to gov. Aug. 29th, ayunt. refuses to obey gov.'s requisition for 20 men to fill the ranks of the S. Diego comp. Carrillo being chosen member of the dip., the 1st reg. was to take his place as alcalde, either permanently or temp., as the gov. should decide, and the decision was in favor of the former. Sept. 7th, the gov. wants more reasons, etc., respecting a 2d alcalde. Sept. 20th, complaints of Carrillo's absence, but ayunt. could not excuse him from attendance at Monterey. Munic. receipts. Jan.–Sept., $977, including $417 tax on wines and liquors, $448 fines, expend. $928.

1834. Alcalde José Perez, regidores José Sepúlveda, Vicente de la Ossa, Januario Ávila, síndico Vicente Moraga, sec. Moraga till May, Manuel Arzaga from June. Perhaps also Moraga ceased to be síndico in the middle of the year, for his resignation seems to have been accepted in July, though he seems to have acted in Nov. Botello, *Anales*, MS., 10, says M. was removed for carelessness and inability. Jueces de campo Lugo and Ignacio Palomares. Munic. receipts, $919, includ. liquors $321, fines $150, gambling licenses $214, dry goods shops $39, expend. $986, includ. ayunt., school, and constable $465, church $6, sec. $96. In Sept. $24.50 sent to dip. at Mont. for powder and flints. Dec., munic. treasurer to have 8 per cent. May 30th, síndico cannot act as secretary. There were complaints that Perez was a tool of J. A. Carrillo, through whom judicial decisions could be bought. It was charged that an assassin was let off for $200. Not too much credit should be given to these charges as they may have originated from personal and political controversies, the merits of which cannot be known.

1835. 1st alcalde Francisco Javier Alvarado, 2d alcalde Domingo Romero; regidores Januario Ávila, Vicente de la Ossa, Ignacio Palomares, Rafael Guirado, Juan N. Alvarado, Juan de Dios Bravo; síndico Narciso Botello, sec. Manuel Arzaga; jueces de campo Antonio I. Ávila, José Serrano, Ignacio M. Alvarado; aux. alcaldes Perez at Sta Gertrudis, Tomás Yorba at Sta Ana, Domingo Carrillo at Los Berros (?), encargado de indios Tib. Tapia. Munic. receipts $580, expend. $583. Botello, *Anales*, MS., 12, says Arzaga was removed about June and he, B., acted as sec. Jan., business hours at the alcalde's office fixed at 10 A. M. to noon, and 3 to 5 P. M. Feb., gov. orders alcalde to follow implicitly the orders of the district judge, his superior. March 30th, meeting presided by the gov. April, gov. urges the speedy installation of the

teresting variety of attitudes in the political controversies growing out of the struggle between north
and south, and as a consequence town officials had

tribunal de vagos acc. to law of March 3, 1828. Aug. 28th, com. gen. sends
alcalde 4 men to force the Sonorans and citizens to respect his authority.
    1836. 1st alcalde Manuel Requena, 2d alcalde Tiburcio Tapia; regidores
Rafael Guirado, Juan M. Alvarado (3d not named, but probably Bravo), Ba-
silio Valdés, Felipe Lugo, José María Herrera; síndico Abel Stearns to June,
Antonio M. Osio from July; sec. Narciso Botello; jueces de campo Ant. I.
Ávila, José M. Lugo, Juan Ramirez; encargados de justicia, or aux. alcaldes,
Perez at Sta Gertrudis, Julio Verdugo at S. Rafael, Manuel Dominguez at S.
Pedro, José Ant. Yorba at Sta Ana Abajo or S. José (Jesus Félix also at S.
José), Teodosio Yorba at Sta Ana, Bernardo Yorba at Cajon de Sta Ana, Mariano R. Roldan at Alamitos. Munic. receipts, $664, expend. $518. Botello
as collector and treasurer claimed 8 per cent, but was allowed only three per
cent for commission. Jan., ayunt. resolves that troops which had been asked
for and arrived, as there was no food for them, should go to S. Gabriel, and
the com. gen. should be requested to send troops to be supported on their
pay. Gov. orders a plan to be made of lands for fondo legal y ejidos. Also
cost of a govt building to be estimated. Feb. 4th, tribunal de vagos established consisting of Requena and the 1st and 2d regidores Guirado and Alvarado. March, the diputacion to occupy two rooms offered by Sanchez and
Stearns. May, gov. approves alcalde's proposal to permit certain persons to
carry arms. Dec. 13th, appeal of comandante at S. Gabriel, that he has no
means of supporting his troops, who wish leave to earn a living for themselves.
Ayunt. decides that the admin. of S. Fernando must be asked for aid.
    1837. 1st alcalde Gil Ibarra, 2d alcalde José Sepúlveda; regidores Val-
dés, Lugo, Herrera, Francisco Pantoja, Bernardino Lopez; síndico Ignacio M
Alvarado, sec. Narciso Botelo, aux. alcalde Manuel Duarte at Sta Gertrudis.
No record of the others. Munic. receipts $381, expend. $460. Feb., the two
permanent committees on police and on lands not yet chosen on account of
political convulsions. Sept. 21st, order of gov. received to suspend 1st alcalde, who is to report for trial to the Sta Bárbara alcalde. Ayunt. resolves
to petition gov. for a suspension of the order until the accusations against
Ibarra can be investigated. Dec. 22d, Gov. Carrillo gives order for election
of substitutes for those members of the ayunt. whose resignation has been accepted.
    1838. 1st alcalde Luis Arenas, 2d alcalde José Perez; regidores Ignacio
Palomares, Bernardino Lopez, Juan Ballesteros, Antonio Machado, Januario
Ávila, José del Cármen Lugo; síndico Vicente de la Ossa, sec. Narciso Botello;
jueces de campo José M. Lugo, Agustin Machado, Emigdio Véjar, Máximo
Valenzuela; comisarios de policía, or aux. alcaldes, Antonio M. Lugo, Tib.
Tapia, Raf. Guirado, Fran. M. Alvarado, id. suplentes Julian Chavez, Cristóbal Aguilar, Isidro Alvarado, Isidro Reyes. The services of the ayunt. were
more or less interrupted by the arrest and enforced absence of its members,
especially Alcalde Arenas and Sec. Botello. Munic. receipts $837, expend.
$834. Aug. Perez and Ballesteros appointed to revise the policía de los
campos.
    1839. 1st alcalde Tiburcio Tapia (until May), 2d alcalde Manuel Domin-
guez; regidores Antonio Machado (acting síndico and acting 1st alcalde after
May), Januario Ávila, José del C. Lugo, Fran. M. Alvarado, José Sepulveda,
Juan Crisóstomo Véjar; síndico Vicente Sanchez (elected but not sworn in),
sec. Botello, and later Ignacio Coronel. At the election of this ayunt. in
Dec. 1838, the law of July 12, 1830, was followed, the new law not having
been received. In Nov. the ayunt. was abolished, and the two alcaldes, Dominguez and Machado, were ordered to act as jueces de paz pending the regular appointment. It is notable that on the 1st alcalde becoming prefect it

some exciting adventures to relieve the monotony of their regular duties; but these experiences growing out of national and territorial patriotism were permitted to absorb the surplus of zeal that might otherwise have been devoted to local controversies; so that the record of town affairs is somewhat tame, even when supplemented by the criminal record and items connected with the administration of justice.[5] These

was not the 2d alcalde but the senior regidor that took his place. Munic. receipts $739. July 17th, proposition to rent the salt-fields and tax asphaltum for municipal revenues. Feb., Capt. Juan de Dios Padilla refuses to obey a summons from the alcalde. Also reprimanded for not removing his hat in the juzgado. May, prefect proposes 2 jueces de paz at the capital and one at each mission, also at S. Pedro and Sta Ana. Ayunt. expresses regret at prefect's illness. July, 2d regidor fined $10 for misdemeanor in the case of Temple. Nov. 7th, governor's order to dissolve the ayunt; order rec'd Nov. 21st. Dec., no síndico required under the new system, but a depositario must be appointed to dispose of funds only on prefect's order.

1840. Jueces de paz Felipe Lugo and Juan B. Leandry; jueces de campo Ramon Ibarra, Juan Ramirez, Enrique Véjar, Antonio Ignacio Ávila for the environs of the town; for the ranchos Ignacio Palomares at S. José, Mariano Roldan at Los Coyotes, Bernardo Yorba at Cajon de Sta Ana, Tomás Yorba at Sta Ana, José Yorba at Sta Ana Abajo, Francisco Figueroa at Alamitos, P. Dominguez at S. Pedro, Juan Sepúlveda at Palos Verdes, Felipe Talamantes at La Ballena, Julio Verdugo at Los Verdugos. Pio Pico collector of tithes appointed July 16th, to receive 5 per cent for commission. Ranchos established for less than 5 years were exempt. Tithes might be paid in cattle and horses. Munic. receipts $567, expend. $517. Proceeds of stamped paper 1st quarter $57, 3d quarter $12. Complaints in Feb. that accounts have not been rendered, and that neither schoolmaster nor sec. of ayunt. has been paid. Feb., Lugo and Leandry complain to prefect that certain men oppose them and criticise their conduct. They are willing to resign or to answer any charges. Sept., subaltern jueces are informed that they have but 3 days in which to return answers to their superiors.

[5] Administration of justice at Los Angeles. 1831. A man fined $5 for branding cattle out of season. *Dept. St. Pap.*, MS., iii. 8. 1833, Jan.-Feb., ordinances of ayunt. against carrying forbidden weapons, playing forbidden games, and selling liquor after 8 P. M. *Los Ang. Arch.*, MS., iv. 74, 84–5, 89–90; *Dept. St. Pap. Ang.*, MS., i. 99, 110. Also similar regulations in other months. Nov., owners of ranchos must be made to burn the carcasses of cattle slaughtered. *Los Ang. Arch.*, MS., iv. 75. 1834. By complaint of J. A. Carrillo alcalde Perez seized some silver on the *Pacífico*. J. A. Aguirre, the owner, succeeded in proving the seizure illegal, and that the whole affair was a plot of Carrillo and Perez, who were to share the profits, and who were accused of other conspiracies against the wealthy Spaniard. They were condemned to pay damages for the ship's detention, and the alcaldes were reprimanded for neglect of duty. *Dept. St. Pap. Ben.*, MS., v. 1–15, 64–7. 1835. April 8th, bando of Alcalde Alvarado containing municipal ordinances in 19 articles. *Id., Ang.*, i. 157–60. May, Yorba writes to Capt. Guerrera that thefts of horses and cattle at the ranchos are of frequent occurrence, and the alcaldes take no energetic steps to prevent such outrages *Guerra, Doc.*, MS., vi. 151. July, prisoners have to be transferred to S. Gabriel for want of guards and insecurity of prison in town. *Los Ang. Arch.*, MS., i. 60–1. Oct., a military court to sit at S. Gabriel to try men who

petty items as appended have a certain interest and value as an element in pueblo annals, even if in the absence of causas célebres they call for no special remarks in my text.

killed cattle at Los Nietos for their hides. *Id.*, iv. 283. Nov. no food furnished to prisoners; but for charity they would starve. *Dept. St. Pap. Ben.*, MS., v. 67. Dana, *Two Years before the Mast*, 196–7, tells how a Mexican entered a naturalized Yankee's house and stabbed him to the heart. Americans seized the murderer, and as the gov. and gen. declined to interfere, with the aid of 30 or 40 trappers they took possession of the town, appointed a judge and jury, and shot the man after his conviction in spite of a proclamation from a general 'with titles enough for an hidalgo.' This is a story of some interest, but I think it has no foundation in fact.

1836. See reference to murder of Félix and acts of vigilance committee elsewhere. Jan 2d, new series of munic. regulations. *Dept. St. Pap., Ang.*, MS., ii. 72. Jan. 14th, ayunt. complains of an 'epidemic of crows'! and calls for a contribution for the slaughter of the birds; else a bando will be issued. *Los Ang. Ayunt. Rec.*, MS., 64. Jan. 28th, danger of hydrophobia. No man must keep more than two dogs, and those securely tied. All the rest must be killed, and the 2d alcalde offered to furnish poison on credit as the treasury was empty. *Id.*, 68. Feb., inhab. willing to build a prison; meanwhile the curate's house to be used. *Dept. St. Pap., Ang.*, MS., x. 44, 54. March, 12 prisoners, 7 of them out on bail, 1 for murder, 1 assault with wounds, 6 for larceny, 2 for stealing cattle. *Id., B. M.*, lxxxii. 28. Six suspicious persons found sleeping in the fields at S. Francisco rancho, with 3 English muskets and a pistol. *Id., Ang.*, ii. 48. Aug., still 12 prisoners, including 2 assassins. *Id.*, vi. 9.

1837. Feb., the junta de guerra mentioned above (Oct. 1835) had condemned to death the men convicted of *cuereando*. The ayunt. asks for a commutation to exile or some milder punishment; but the culprits were to be marched through the streets with a crier proclaiming their crimes on the way to their destination. *Los Ang. Arch.*, MS., iv. 283–4. Jesus Pico, *Acontecimientos*, MS., 43, says he was charged with conducting the men, 8 in number, to Monterey, en route for Sonoma. He remembers the names of Romero, 2 Valdés, José García, and Antonio Valencia. Manuel Arzaga was living with the wife of a man absent at Guaymas. By advice of Padre Duran, the alcalde ordered the guilty couple to be parted, the woman to be delivered to P. Esténega at the mission, until her husband should come, and Arzaga to be sent to S. Diego and closely watched. The two managed to meet again, and at the padre's complaint new orders were issued in Nov. *S. Diego, Arch.*, MS., 188.

1838. German, *Sucesos*, MS., 2–3, says that Ritillo Valencia, for firing a pistol at Domingo Altamirano, was sent to Mont. in irons. July 7th, police regulations in 22 articles. *Los Ang. Arch.*, MS., v. 29–37. Oct., Antonio Valencia being tried for murder of Ant. Águila. *Dept. St. Pap.*, MS., xviii. 11. Nov., nine keepers of shops petition for the privilege of selling liquor on feast days after the 'toque de las ánimas,' as the only means of gaining a living, so dull was trade. Referred to the gov. *Los Ang. Ayunt. Rec.*, MS., 52.

1839. Jan., police regul. in 10 articles for the year. *Los Ang. Arch.*, MS., v. 48–51. Feb., Jose M. Cota, son of the owner of Los Cerritos, sent to the gov. as a cattle thief. *Dept. St. Pap.*, MS., xviii. 19–20. May, decree against vagrants, who must be made to work. *Dept. Rec.*, MS., x. 25; *Vallejo, Doc.*, MS., vii. 10; *Mont. Arch.*, MS., ix. 9. Criminal proceedings against Francisco Limon for outrage on a little Indian girl at S. Fernando, resulting in her death. Sentenced to 2 years in presidio. Sentence sent to Mex. for approval. *Dept. St Pap., Ben.*, MS., iv. 1–4. Decree against sale of liquors

In February 1839, in accordance with a Mexican law of 1836, Governor Alvarado divided Upper California into two districts and appointed Cosme Peña prefect of the second, or Los Angeles district, Santa Bárbara being a partido under a sub-prefect. The licenciado Cosme Peña was appointed prefect and took possession of the office on April 11th, promising great things in his installation speech; but he soon became involved in troubles with the people, not being either personally or politically popular, and after the flag tumult recorded elsewhere, on May 25th under the pretext of illness he turned over the office

on feast days. *Id., Ang.*, MS., v. 9, 65–6; *S. D. Arch.*, MS., 224. Aug., 5 prisoners escape from jail. Alcalde complains that citizens refuse to do guard duty. *Los Ang. Arch.*, MS., i. 167–8. A soldier at S. Luis claimed by alcalde for criminal trial. Com. J. A. Pico declines to give him up; but is ordered by Vallejo to do so if the crime was committed before enlistment. *Vallejo, Doc.*, MS., viii. 53. Nov., alcalde fined by prefect $20 for permitting card-playing in a tavern on Sunday. *Dept. St. Pap., Ang.*, MS., v. 102–3. Dec., Joaquin Ruiz on trial for being ringleader in an attempt to release Ant. Ávila from prison. The fiscal, in consideration of R.'s talent and poverty, and his father's large family, and intemperance, recommends a penalty of only 2 years presidio. *Id., Ben.*, v. 382–3.

1840. A horse-race between animals owned by Andrés Pico and Fernando Sepúlveda, a minor, led to a dispute and a suit against S. for the stakes, which Francisco Sepúlveda, Fernando's father, was forced to pay by alcalde Lugo. The matter was sent to the gov., who on the advice of the judge of the 1st district decided that Lugo must pay back the stakes, and be suspended until he should do so, but retaining the right to sue for a recovery from the parties to whom they had been paid. Lugo replied in a long and somewhat skilful defence, refusing to be suspended except by the junta after legal proceedings or to pay the stakes. He claimed that the gov. and Mont. judge had argued as partisan attorneys and not as judges; that they had made many blunders; that the affair was none of their business, but belonged to the superior tribunal, and if there was no such body it was their fault. He says that the elder Sepúlveda was present at the race, and had in other races paid his son's losses without objection. The final decision is not given. *S. Diego Arch.*, MS., 265. Very few public women at Angeles at this period. *Arnaz, Recuerdos*, MS., 14–15. Jan.–March, bandos with police regulations in 14 art. *Dept. St. Pap., Ang.*, MS., iv. 2, 43–6. March, many Angeles prisoners confined at Sta B., claim for $20 a month for their support. *Id.*, 50. May, three prisoners allowed to serve in an exped. against horse-thieves under bonds. *Id.*, 109. June, edict to prevent careless management of the salt works. *Id.*, 112–13. A woman exiled for pursuing an innocent Irishman, Jas Boxe, and keeping him from his wife. *Los Ang. Arch.*, MS., i. 191–5. July, 22 prisoners; 10 cattle-thieves, 3 homicides, 6 thieves, 2 assassins, 1 charged with rape. 4 were sent to Sta B., 4 kept in jail, and the rest released on bail for want of room and food. *Dept. St. Pap.*, MS., xviii. 24. Aug., prefect orders that Ant. Valenzuela must not molest Domingo Romero, accused of incest, which will be investigated by the prefectura. *Los Ang. Ayunt. Rec.*, MS., 44. Nov., a man sentenced to 3 months public works for drawing a knife to kill a citizen in the court-room. *S. Diego Arch.*, MS., 263.

to Alcalde Tapia, and went to Monterey. Tapia was acting prefect till August, though Machado took his place in June and July; and on the 10th of August he was formally appointed by the governor, Peña having resigned. In September came the news that the latter's appointment had not been approved in Mexico. It does not appear that any action was taken in Mexico on Tapia's appointment, and perhaps it was never intended to be permanent; at any rate in May 1840 he asked to be relieved on account of illness, and Santiago Argüello was appointed to the office. The prefect's salary was $2,000 and that of his secretary—Francisco Castillo, succeeded before the end of 1839 by Narciso Botello—was $700. The prefect as an executive officer exercised a general authority over the ayuntamiento and over all local officials in the district; but there is nothing in his routine acts of 1839–40 that demands special notice.[6]

[6] On the prefecture and tumult of the flag see this vol. p. 585–9. Peña's appointment announced March 7, 1839. *Dept. St. Pap. Ang.*, MS., x. 112–14. I omit miscellaneous references to authorities for this and the following points. April 11th, Peña installed, and makes a long speech. *Id.*, ii. 164; *Id., Pref. y Juzg.*, iv. 53; v. 79; though there are other documents indicating the 13th or 15th as the date. *Dept. St. Pap.*, MS., xviii. 17–18; *Id., Ben. C. & T.*, iv. 26. April 13th, P. to Vallejo on the good disposition of the people. *Vallejo, Doc.*, MS., vi. 410, 439. April 16th, J. M. Covarrubias named as sec., and he may have held the place for a time before Castillo's appointment. *Dept. St. Pap., Ben. C. & T.*, MS., iv. 28. April 22d, Prefect Peña directs alcalde not to allow administrators of missions to remove fugitive Ind. from town without consent of alcalde and prefect. *Id., Ang.*, ii. 165. May 25th, Peña directs Tapia to take charge ad int. *Savage, Doc.*, MS., iii. 48; *Hayes' Doc.*, MS., 92–3. Same date, notifies govt. and administrators to same effect. *Dept. St. Pap., Pref. y Juzg.*, MS., v. 5; *S. Diego, Arch.*, MS., 225. May 26th, Tapia assumes the office. *Dept. St. Pap. Ang.*, MS., v. 10. June 12th, prefect orders that Ind. shall be collected at the missions. *S. Diego Index.*, MS., 134. June 21–3. Machado takes the office ad int. *Dept. St. Pap., Pref. y Juzg.*, MS., v. 7; *Id., Ang.*, v. 20. Peña's resignation July 31st, accepted Aug. 10th, and Tapia appointed same day. *Id., Pref. y Juzg.*, v. 24, 29; *Id., Mont.*, iv. 12. Castillo reigns as sec. Aug. 21st, and Botello acts ad int. *Id., Pref. y Juzg.*, MS., v. 25; *Coronel, Doc.*, MS., 94. Nov. 5th, prefect fines alcalde $20. Nov. 29th, orders alcalde to convoke ayunt. for an extra session. Botello appointed sec. Oct. 5th–7th. *Los Ang. Arch.*, MS., v. 100; *Dept. St. Pap. Ang.*, MS., v. 86, 90. May 24th, Tapia asks to be relieved on account of illness. *Id., Pref. y Juzg.*, vi. 69. May 30th, Argüello appointed. *Id., Ang.*, iv. 111; xii. 31; *Dept. Rec.*, MS., xi. 15–16; *S. D. Arch.*, MS., 255. June 2d, Argüello accepts, June 17th, installed, making a speech. *Dept. St. Pap., Ben.*, MS., ii. 32–3; *Id., Pref. y Juzg.*, vi. 72; *Hayes' Em. Notes*, 511–14; *Id., Doc.*, 127. Sept. 9th, prefect has released the sub-prefect, whom he believes innocent. *Dept. St.*

The port of San Pedro, though a large quantity of country produce was shipped there, and few trading vessels failed to visit it, had as yet neither local authorities nor other residents. There was, however, a sub-alcalde at the Dominguez rancho a few miles inland. In 1831-2 there were some slight attempts at ship-building. From 1833 Antonio M. Osio as receptor at Los Angeles had charge of the port trade as well as of the inland commerce with New Mexico. A part of the colony landed here in 1834. Osio states that 5,000 hides from the mission cattle were shipped here in that year, while Mofras writes of an annual shipment about that time of 100,000 hides, 2,500 centals of tallow, and several cargoes of soap. Abel Stearns had a warehouse, and in 1835 and other years was accused of doing a profitable contraband trade. The fugitive governor, Chico, is said to have touched at San Pedro in his flight, in 1836, to take on board a quantity of stolen tallow. Dana's experience of several weeks in loading hides here is described in his famous narrative; and Belcher gives a slight description of the place as it appeared in 1839.[7]

At San Gabriel in 1831-2 the names of padres Jesus María Martinez, Francisco Gonzalez de Ibarra, Vicente Pascual Oliva, and the Dominicans Francisco Cucullu and Mariano Sosa appear occasionally on the mission registers; but the regular ministers were fathers Boscana and Sanchez, until their deaths which occurred respectively in July 1831 and January 1833.[8]

Pap., P. y J., MS., vi. 77. Expenses of office in Oct. $52; in Nov. $6. Id., iii. 52, 56.

[7] See this vol. pp. 267-9, 288, 349, 363, 366, 369, 375, 384, 393, 442; vol. iv. 80, 95, 146; Mofras, Explor., i. 362; Dana's Two Years, 107 et seq.; Belcher's Voy., i. 322; Douglas' Jour., MS., 87-8. And on Osio's appointment as receptor, Dept. St. Pap., MS., iii. 109; Id., Cust.-H., ii. 10-25; vii. 12-13; Id., Ang., xi. 8; Id., Pref. y Juzg., ii. 156.

[8] Gerónimo Boscana was born on May 23, 1776, at Llumayor, island of Mallorca, and took the Franciscan habit in the convent of Jesus extra muros at Palma on Aug. 4, 1792. After acting for nearly four years as professor of belles lettres, he started for America June 5, 1803; arrived at Mexico Oct. 24th; started for Cal. Feb. 17, 1806; and landed at Monterey June 6th. His missionary service was at Soledad in 1806; at Purísima in 1806-11, at San

Sanchez was succeeded by padre Tomás Eleuterio Esténega, who came down from the north on the

Luis Rey in 1812-13, at San Juan Capistrano in 1814-26, and at San Gabriel in 1826-31. Though accredited by his superiors in 1817 and 1820 with 'regular' merit and ability somewhat more than medium, yet some doubt was felt about his qualifications as a spiritual guide, and he was spoken of as one whom for reasons known to the guardian it would not be well to leave alone at a mission. *Autobiog. Autog. de los Padres,* MS.; *Sarría, Informe sobre Frailes, 1817,* p. 44; *Id., Informe de Mis. 1819,* p. 115. His chief ministry was at S. Juan Capistrano, where he devoted much study to the manners and customs of the natives, especially their religious traditions. His writings, on this subject, found among his papers and long in possession of Capt. Guerra y Noriega, were published by Robinson in 1846 under the title of *Chinigchinich.* He is described by Eulalia Perez, *Recuerdos,* MS., 26, and others as of less than medium stature, fair complexion, considerably bent in his old age; an inveterate snuff-taker; kind-hearted and well liked generally, but subject to occasional spells of apparent lunacy when he seemed to be angry with himself and every one about him. The portrait published with his book is said to look like him. His sudden removal from S. Juan in 1826 and the disparaging hints in reports of superiors as noted above give some weight to the charges of Vallejo and others that the padre was guilty of immoral relations with his neófitas. He tried unsuccessfully to get his passport and quit the country in 1829 under the law expelling Spaniards. *Arch. Arzob.,* MS., v. pt i. 55. His death occurred on July 5, 1831; and he was buried next day in the San Gabriel church on the San José side of the presbytery near the remains of Padre Nuez. *S. Gabriel, Lib. Mis.,* MS., 40; *Guerra, Doc.,* MS., i. 243-4.

José Bernardo Sanchez was born Sept. 7, 1778, at Robledillo, Spain, and became a Franciscan in the convent of N. Sra Sta María de Gracia at S. Miguel *supra Tagum,* Oct. 9, 1794. Leaving Spain in Feb. 1803, he reached his college in Mexico in Aug., and came to Cal. in 1804. He served at S. Diego in 1804-20, at Purísima in 1820-1, and at S. Gabriel in 1821-33, until his death on July 15th. In 1817-20 he was regarded by his superiors as of distinguished merit and ability far above the average, but was suffering, and in hopes of early retirement. *Autobiog. Autog. de los Padres,* MS.; *Sarría, Inf. sobre Frailes, 1817,* MS., 39-40; *Arch. Sta B.,* MS., iii. 130. In 1806 Sanchez accompanied Sergt Pico on an expedition against the Ind.; in 1818, he took an active part in preparations to resist Bouchard's insurgents; in 1821 he went with Payeras on an exploring and baptizing tour among gentile rancherías; in 1828 he was greatly aggrieved by a charge of smuggling, and asked for a pass to retire; in 1829, he again desired a passport as a Spaniard who had not taken the oath; and in 1831-2 he was active in opposing Gov. Echeandía's project of secularization. From 1827 to 1831 he held the high position of president, performing its difficult duties with great credit. He is described as fair and fat, of lively disposition, generous and hospitable, with a multitude of friends of all classes. He was an able manager of temporal affairs, and took great pride in the prosperity of his mission, being greatly disappointed and perhaps soured by the disastrous results of secularization, against which he had struggled in vain, even to the extent of slaughtering the mission cattle at the last as recorded in this chapter. Mofras, *Explor.,* i. 272-3, says that Father Sanchez died of grief; and Eulalia Perez, *Recuerdos,* MS., 14-15, adds that about a month before his death he was insulted, jostled, and struck by his neophytes, which had a deplorable effect both on his mind and body. It is possible that this story has some slight foundation in fact, though, if so, it is strange that no more definite record appears. His body was buried on Jan. 16, 1833, by Padre Oliva at the foot of the altar in the presbytery of the mission church. *Guerra, Doc.,* MS., 244; *S. Gabriel, Lib. Mis.,* MS., 40; cited also in *Los Ang. Express,* Sept. 16, 1874, by J. J. Warner. The remains were disturbed but not removed in Dec. 1850, at the burial of P. Ordaz.

arrival of the Zacatecanos and remained in charge of San Gabriel during the rest of the decade. Father Alexis Bachelot from the Sandwich Islands also lived here most of the time in 1832–6. The neophyte population decreased only about 30 down to 1834; but by the end of the decade nearly 1,000 had left the community, leaving about 400, though I suppose there were still about 1,000 ex-neophytes whose whereabouts was somewhat definitely known. A considerable increase in cattle down to 1834, but not probably making allowance for the slaughter of that year, is shown by the regular reports; but by 1840 the livestock had almost entirely disappeared.[9] The record of secularization at this establishment is very meagre even in comparison with the others. Colonel Gutierroz was the comisionado to effect the change in 1834,

[9] Statistics of 1831–4. Decrease in pop. 1352 to 1320. Baptisms, 175; largest no. 64 in 1832; smallest, 30 in 1831. Deaths, 144; largest no. 85 in 1832; smallest 8 in 1834. Increase in large stock 25,725 to 26,220; decrease in horses and mules 2,225 to 220; sheep, 14,650 to 6,660. Largest crop, 4,315 bush. in 1834; smallest, 407 in 1832; average crop, 2,440, of which wheat 1,755, yield 7.33 fold; barley 157, yield 9.8 fold; corn 432, yield 61 fold.

General statistics of 1771–1834, the whole period of the mission's existence. Total no. baptisms, 7,854, of which 4,355 Ind. adults, 2,459 Ind. children, 1 adult and 1,039 children of gente de razon; average per year, 123. Total of marriages, 1,955, of which 241 de razon. Deaths, 5,656, of which 2,916 Ind. adults, 2,363 Ind. children; 211 and 186 de razon; annual average, 88; average death rate, 7.61 per cent of pop. Largest pop., 1,701 in 1817. There was a slight excess of males down to 1803, and a greater excess later. The proportion of children varied from ⅓ at first to 1/10 at the last. Largest no. of cattle, 26,300 in 1828; horses, 2,400 in 1827; mules, 205 in 1814; asses, 6 in 1794; sheep, 15,000 in 1829; goats, 1,380 in 1785; swine, 300 in 1802, 1803, and 1822; all kinds, 40,360 animals in 1830. Total product of wheat, 225,942 bush., yield 16 fold; barley (for only 11 years), 1,250 bush., yield 10 fold; maize, 154,820 bush., yield 145 fold; beans, 14,467 bush., yield 28 fold.

Miscell. stat. of the decade. Feb. 1833. J. M. Marron borrows 200 cattle for 5 years from P. Esténega. *Marron, Pap.*, MS., 10. 1834. There were 4,443 head of cattle thus lent out. The mission debts were $8,271, and credits $11,153. There were 163,579 vines in 4 vineyards, and 2,333 fruit trees. Artillery, 4 small cannon, one of them lent to the ayunt., and 3 pedreros. *St. Pap., Mis.*, MS., vi. 12–14. Nov. 26th, amount of supplies to S. Diego presidio $49,665, to Sta Bárbara $6,895, no period specified, perhaps since the foundation. *Dept. St. Pap., B. M.*, MS., lxxix. 52–3. 1839. Hartnell's report of June 24th, 369 souls all contented. Debts $4,000 (or $6,000), credits $10,500; 1,100 cattle, 1,700 horses, 1,040 sheep. *St. Pap., Mis.*, MS., xi. 28–9; *Hartnell, Diario*, MS., 72–4. Dec. 31st, Bandini distributes $1,615 of clothing among 233 Ind. *Id.*, vi. 42–3. 1840. April. In the list of effects to be surrendered by the administrator were 72 cattle, 715 sheep, and 3 hogs. *St. Pap. Mis.*, MS., 41. Debt at the same date $3,230, of which $1,944 was due to P. Esténega. *Pico, Pap., Mis.*, MS., 47–51.

a year marked also by the wholesale slaughter of the
mission cattle by order of the padres, and by the destruction of the San Bernardino branch by hostile
savages.[10] Gutierrez turned over the control to Juan

[10] Chronologic summary of S. Gabriel events. 1831. Gov. Victoria
wounded, cared for at the mission in Dec. This vol., p. 206, 210. To be
secularized and a school established under Echeandía's plan. *Id.*, 305–6. A
schooner framed here to be launched at S. Pedro. *Id.*, 363. Death of P. Boscana, this chapter. 1832. Echeandía's forces encamped here in April. This
vol., 227. P. Bachelot begins his service as assistant minister. *Id.*, 317.
1833. Alf. Ignacio del Valle appointed as comisionado for secularization in
Jan., but nothing accomplished. *Id.*, 326. J. A. Carrillo goes in Feb. to
harangue and tranquillize the Ind. *Id.*, 327. Death of P. Sanchez and arrival
of P. Esténega. This chap. This year a controversy between the mission and
J. J. Nieto at Sta Gertrudis was settled by arbitration. N. had borrowed
8,000 (?) mission cattle on shares 8 or 9 years before. It was decided that
N. should have all the cattle at Los Cerritos and the mission ⅔ of all the rest;
and in Oct. that N. should give up 3,000 head. There was more trouble that
had not been settled 3 years later. *Dept. St. Pap., Ben..*, MS., v. 167–84.
    1834. Part of the Mex. colony here from Sept. This vol., 267. Beginning
of secularization, Col Nicolás Gutierrez made comisionado and an inventory
prepared in Nov. *Id.*, 346–8. Slaughter of the mission cattle, private individuals taking contracts from the padre to kill cattle on shares for their hides
and tallow. *Id.*, 348–9. Indian depredations at S. Bernardino Oct.–Dec. *Id.*,
359, and annals of Los Angeles in this chap. Controversy about right of the
mission to use the salinas. *Id.*, 374. Lugo, *Vida*, MS., 107, represents S.
Bernardino as a very prosperous establishment, and says that extensive
improvements in the buildings were in progress when the destruction occurred. This year a garrison was organized at S. Gabriel, to consist of a sergeant and 8 men from Portilla's Mazatlan company. *Dept. St. Pap., B. M.*,
MS., lxxxviii. 26.
    1835. Col Gutierrez still in charge, but no records of progress in secu-
larization. The insurgents Apalátegui and Torres imprisoned here in March.
This vol., 284. A painting of S. Gabriel is mentioned as having been made
by Ferdinand Deppe this year from a drawing made on the spot. Later in
possession of Daniel Hill at Sta Barbara, and photographed for Vischer's
work. *Taylor's Discov. and Found.*, ii. no. 42, p. 216; *Hayes' Scraps, Angeles*,
iv. 84.
    1836. No record of mission affairs except that Juan José Rocha was in
charge as majordomo, being appointed in Feb. June 1st, oath taken to the
new 'bases' or centralism. This vol., p. 423. Sept., soldiers refuse to serve
without pay. *Id.*, 446. The governor's alleged immoral conduct. *Id.*, 448.
1837. José Perez succeeded Rocha as majordomo early in this year. Nothing
known of events at the mission except occasional mention of the presence of
portions of the northern or southern forces during the sectional wars. This vol.,
pp. 495, 501, 503, 510, 528. Of 1838 still less is known, not even the administrator's name appearing. Coronel, *Cosas de Cal.*, MS., 219, represents the mission as still rich and in good order in 1838, but his view would seem to be
exaggerated.
    1839. Juan Bandini was administrator, having probably been appointed
the year before. In March he claims that he found the mission property in
a very bad condition, but has restored it to prosperity. But he offers his
resignation, and asks that the $500 due him for salary be paid in mares and
other mission effects, as there is plenty of everything but cattle. He informs the govt in a private letter that he has already taken 40 young bulls,
but will return them if the gov. thinks it best. The resignation seems to
have been accepted, but reconsidered, as B. continued to serve through the

José Rocha in 1836; the latter was succeeded in 1837 by José C. Perez; and he by Juan Bandini probably in 1838. Nothing is known in detail of the administration of these men, but in the middle of 1839 the mission had still 1,700 horses, 1,100 cattle, and 1,000 sheep. Local events in these years are swallowed up in the maelstrom of political doings at Los Angeles. In 1839–40 we have the visits of Visitador Hartnell, and the transfer of the estate from Bandini to Father Esténega. Live-stock now included 72 cattle and 700 sheep, yet Don Juan claimed to have done much for the welfare of the ex-mission.

At San Fernando Father Ibarra continued his ministry alone until the middle of 1835, when he retired temporarily to Mexico. His successor was Pedro Cabot from San Antonio, who served until his death in October, 1836.[11] From this time till August,

year. March 20–2. *St. Pap., Mis.*, MS., x. 1–2; *Vallejo, Doc.*, MS., xxxii. 185, In June Hartnell made his first visit, reporting Bandini's accounts all right, the property in good condition, and the Indians content. He authorized B. to kill 100 cattle and to buy $2,000 worth of clothing to be paid for in brandy and other produce of the next year. In July B. appointed Rafael Guirado as clerk at $15 per month. *Hartnell, Diario*, MS., i. 53–4, 72–4; *Arch. Miss.*, MS., ii. 887–9.

1840. In a letter of Feb. P. Duran quotes P. Esténega to the effect that the mission has to support 38 gente de razon, that there is not a candle, no tallow to make a candle, and no cattle fat enough to supply the tallow. 'What a scandal! and what a comment on secularization!' says Duran. *Arch. Misiones*, MS., ii. 1017. March, Bandini speaks of the orange orchard as the only one in Cal., and he has given it special care, having restored it with over 100 trees. *St. Pap. Mis.*, MS., vi. 42. At the end of April Bandini turned over the property by inventory to P. Esténega, *Id.*, 41, but did not leave the mission or entirely give up the management. In May three droves of mares were stolen by Indians. From July 25th to Aug. 1st. Visitador Hartnell was here on his second tour. Bandini was absent at first, but came on the 28th. The Ind. complained bitterly that B. had carried off mission property, chiefly horses and carts (probably as per letter to gov. in 1839, as above); also that he had opened a dram-shop, sold mission brandy to the Ind., and then punished them for getting drunk! Hartnell declined to comply with the prefect's request that the administrator be ordered to supply his house with grain, soap, lard, etc. On Aug. 1st José Crispin Perez was appointed as majordomo to manage affairs under the supervision of P. Esténega. *Hartnell, Diario*, MS., 21, 37, 64, 91–2, 99–100. H. was also at S. Gabriel on Aug. 18th–19th. Also in July and Aug. there were reports that the savages were on the point of renewing their hostilities at San Bernardino.

[11] Pedro Cabot, a brother of Padre Juan Cabot, was born at Buñola, Mallorca, on Sept. 9, 1777. He became a Franciscan at Palma, Dec. 22, 1796; came to Mexico, June–Sept. 1803; and to Cal. Feb.–Aug. 1804. His mis-

1838, I find no mention of any minister, but Ibarra may possibly have served. Then came Blas Ordaz, who remained during the rest of the decade. Down to 1834 the decrease in neophyte population was less than 100; in live-stock there was no falling-off whatever if the registers may be trusted; and the crops were still good. Thus this mission was exceptionally prosperous at this period; and at the end of the decade there were still about 400 Indians in the ex-mission community, statistics being more voluminous than at the missions further south.[12] Lieutenant Antonio del Valle was commissioned to secularize the establishment in 1834, and the next year became

sionary service was at S. Antonio in 1804–28, and again in 1829–34; at Sole-dad in 1828–9; and at San Fernando in 1835–6. He was rated by his superi-ors as of distinguished merit and scholarship, well qualified for any position in Cal., even the prelacy. *Autobiog. Autog. de los Padres*, MS.; *Serría, In-forme sobre Frailes, 1817*, MS., 59–60; Payeras in *Arch. Sta B.*, MS., iii. 133. Fray Pedro was known as a dignified, scholarly, courteous man, nicknamed El Caballero in contradistinction to his rougher brother Juan, nicknamed El Marinero, than whom, however, he was hardly less popular. Both were noted for their hospitality at S. Antonio and S. Miguel, their adjoining mis-sions, and were beloved by all classes, notwithstanding Pedro's polished manners, retiring disposition, and tendency to asceticism. He gave much attention to the language of his neophytes, and he was an uncompromising royalist, declining to take the oath to republicanism in 1825–9. In July 1836 he was determined to quit the country and to persevere in his demands for a passport; and declined most positively Duran's request to serve as pres-ident in case of his (D.'s) departure. In Aug. he was called to shrive the victims of the vigilantes at Angeles, but declined to come. His remains were interred in the mission cemetery on Oct. 12th, by Padre Ibarra. Copy of the burial register by Taylor in *S. F. Bulletin*, Apr. 25, 1864. Money due him is said to have been paid to a nephew who came from Spain.

[12] Statistics of S. Fernando 1831–4. Decrease in pop. 827 to 792. Bap-tisms 89; largest no. 36 in 1834; smallest 16 in 1832. Deaths 124; largest no. 45 in 1832; smallest 19 in 1834. Cattle remained at 6,000 while horses and mules decreased from 560 to 520 by the loss of 40 mules; sheep remain-ing at 3,000. Largest crop 2,370 bush. in 1834; smallest 830 in 1831; average 1,530 bush., of which 940 wheat, yield 12 fold; 470 corn, yield 80 fold; beans 45, yield 9 fold.

Stat. for 1797–1834. Total of baptisms 2,839, of which 1,415 adult Ind., 1,367 Ind. children, 57 child. de razon; average per year 74. Total of mar-riages 849, of which 15 gente de razon. Deaths 2,028, of which 1,036 Ind. adults, 965 Ind. children, 12 and 15 de razon. Annual average 54; death rate 6.61 per cent. of pop. Largest pop. 1,080 in 1819 (or 1,100 in 1805, which may be an error). Sexes nearly equal; children from ¼ to ⅓. Largest no. of cattle 12,800 in 1819; horses 1,320 in 1822; mules 340 in 1812; asses 1 to 3 every year till 1819; sheep 7,800 in 1819; goats 600 in 1816; swine 250 in 1814; all kinds 21,745 animals in 1819. Total product of wheat 119,000 bush., yield 19 fold; barley, only raised in 6 years, 3,070 bush., 14 fold; maize 27,750 bush., 83 fold; beans 3,624 bush., 14 fold.

Miscell. stat. of 1834–40. 1834, P. Ibarra delivered to comisionado $20,000

majordomo, retaining the position, apparently to the
satisfaction of all concerned, until 1837, when he was
succeeded by Anastasio Carrillo.   From the middle
of 1838, Captain José M. Villavicencio served as administrator, though often called away by supposed
military duties, and leaving the management of the
estate to Carrillo, Castillo, and Perez.[13]   Hartnell

in hides, tallow, etc., and $5,000 in coin. *Guerra, Doc.*, MS., vi. 150. Dec.,
mission furnishes $1,000 for Hijar's colony. *St. Pap., Mis.*, MS., vii. 77-8.
1835, July, inventory apparently incomplete, total value $41,714.   The
church is 40 x 6 varas, tile-roofed, board ceiling, brick floor, adobe walls, 3
doors, 7 windows with wooden bars; sacristy, 8 varas sq. with one door and
window, worth $1,650; credits $5,736; buildings, $15,511; 32,000 vines worth
$16,000; 1,600 fruit-trees, $2,400; library of 191 vol., $417. *Id.*, vi. 22-3.
1836, amounts paid, $2,226 to Ignacio del Valle, P. Cabot $1,003, P. Duran
$1,048, P. Ibarra $500. *Id.*, vii. 68-71. Supplies for troops, $2,159. *Id.*, vi.
74-8. 1837, March, inventory of $153,639. *Id.*, vii. 67. 1838, June, inven-
tory of $156,915; credits $14,293, buildings, $56,785, house utensils, $601,
goods in storehouse, $5,214, liquors, etc., $7,175, live-stock, $53,854; S.
Francisco rancho, $1,925, grain, $618, tannery, $544, carpenter shop, $127,
blacksmith, $789, soap works, $512, mills, $200, tools, $368, tallow works,
$2,540, church, $1,500, ornaments, etc., $4,348, library, 50 works, ————;
debts, $1,689. *Id.*, viii. 13-14. 1839, June 23, Hartnell's statement of prop-
erty on hand 'for distrib. among Ind. or trade'? 8,547 head of live-stock
(by another report of this date the live-stock on the different mission ranchos
was 3,590 cattle, 2,044 horses, 2,887 sheep, 25 asses, 57 mules, and 47 hogs),
280 hides, 50 arrobas wool, 314 arr. iron and steel, 13 bbls. liquor. *Id.*, vii.
8. Accounts; Sept. income $1,439, expend. $822; Nov., $2,687 and $1,789;
Dec. $11,282 and $4,899. Paid to P. Ordaz this year $661.   Hide and tallow
acct income $48, expend. $290.   Stock deliv. to Bandini Nov. 1st, $393.
Due the mission Nov. 1st, $271; Dec. 11th, $805; supplies to govt from June
1838 to Dec. 11, 1839, $6,775; supplies to Sta B. company, $516; to others,
$247.   Mission debts Nov. 30th, $4,344. *Id.*, vii. 8-15.   1840, inventory of
property June 19th, 4,130 cattle, 2,637 horses, 2,500 sheep, 60 mules, 33
asses, 30 hogs; Dec. 31st, 2,270 cattle, 60 hogs, all the rest about the same
as in June.   Grain in June, 236 fanegas; in Dec., 1,157 fanegas, worth $2,295.
Hides and leather in June, 124; in Dec., 59, worth $88. Wool, June, 140 arr.;
Dec., 15 arr., worth $22. Soap, June, $150; Dec., $190. Brandy and wine in
Dec. 58 bbls., $2,360. Tallow and lard, Dec., 81 arr., $119.   Oil, 9 bbls.,
$504.   Iron, 180 arr., $720.   Total value in Dec., not including live-stock,
land, or buildings, $6,300.   Receipts for 9 months of the year (June-Aug.
lacking), $9,874; expend., $11,069. *Id.*, 8-15, 13-14; ix. 19-21.
   [13] Chronologic summary of S. Fernando events. 1831. Gov. Victoria here
on his march south against the rebels; also the bearing of Echeandía's secularization plan, never put in operation, on this mission. This vol. p. 205,
306. 1832-3. Nothing in the records. 1834. Antonio del Valle as comisionado takes charge of the mission estates by inventory from P. Ibarra in Oct.
This vol. p. 346. S. Fernando to be a parish of 2d class with salary of $1,000
under the reglamento of Nov. *Id.*, 348. Slight controversy about the use of
the salt fields. *Id.*, 374. 1835. Valle was on May 25th appointed to be
majordomo, or administrator, at $800 salary from June 1st. In July, Ind.
complain that last year two boxes of money had been shipped away; there
was now a box of silver, and they demanded that strict accounts should be
required from P. Ibarra before his departure. *Id.*, 353; *St. Pap., Mis.*, MS.,
xi. 3. Recommendation that a guard be placed at S. Francisco rancho to

found all except the accounts in comparatively excellent condition on the occasion of his official visit in 1839; but matters were less satisfactory in the next year.

prevent cattle-stealing. *Id.*, 2. In July the admin. reports that horses are being constantly stolen, and that Ind. who have taken refuge at the mission are the thieves. *Dept. St. Pap., Ang.,* MS., i, 172.

1836. The death of Padre Cabot and the probable return of P. Ibarra are mentioned elsewhere in this chap. Valle remained in charge of the establishment. In *Dept. St. Pap., Ang.,* MS., ii. 23–9, is a records of the exploits of Rafael, or El Cuyuya, a locally famous robber, who was often arrested and as often escaped from the jail here and at Los Angeles and Sta Bárbara. All the power of the district seemed insufficient to keep him confined or to keep him separated from two of his favorite women, whom he always rescued from their imprisonment. 1837. In March Valle, who is highly praised by Duran and others, was succeeded by Anastasio Carrillo as majordomo. *St. Pap., Mis.,* MS., vii. 67–8. In Jan. strange Ind., said to be aided by gente de razon, made a raid on the mission horses, some of which were recovered after two fights, in which several Ind. were killed and wounded. *Dept. St. Pap., Ang.,* MS., ii. 97–8. Mission funds, $2,000, taken for ' safe keeping' by the Angeles authorities in their efforts to resist Alvarado in Jan. This vol. p. 404. Southern garrison under Rocha stationed here, but the mission is captured by the northerners. *Id.*, 495–501. In June Castro retires and Portilla for the south takes possession. *Id.*, 521. 1838. The administration is given up in June by Carrillo to Capt. José M. Villavicencio. *St. Pap., Miss.,* MS., viii. 13. Mission mares pledged to N. Mex. allies of the south for their aid. This vol., p. 555. Castro's force here in April. *Id.*, 556. Alvarado and Carlos Carrillo at S. Fernando after the campaign of Las Flores. *Id.*, 562–4. A permanent force to be stationed by Alvarado. *Id.*, 569.

1839. Villavicencio still administrator and military commandant; but Francisco del Castillo seems to have been in charge temporarily during a part of this year or the preceding. On the division into prefectures, etc., S. Fernando was attached to the Sta Bárbara partido, the boundary being between the mission and Cahuenga. *Id.*, 585. From June 16th to the 24th, Visitador Hartnell was at this mission, where he found 416 Ind., well contented except with the granting to Valle of the mission rancho of S. Francisco, which they claimed to need. The crops were good and there were no grasshoppers or rust. Valle had not yet moved his family to the rancho. The clerk, Madariaga, was discharged as unfit for the place. Villavicencio's and Castillo's accounts were found in a confused and unintelligible condition. *Hartnell, Diario,* MS., 1, 2, 13, 74–7; *St. Pap., Miss.,* MS., xi. 29–30. 1840. Villavicencio seems still to have held the office, but to have been absent much of the time, leaving affairs in charge of Juan Perez, and later Anastasio Carrillo. Hartnell made his visit Aug. 20th, but nothing is recorded of his acts and the results, except that it was the governor's interference with his orders removing Perez in favor of Carrillo that caused the visitador to resign his position on Sept. 7th at Sta Bárbara. *Hartnell, Diario,* MS., 15–16, 21, 65. Nothing known of mission affairs this year except the statistics given in the preceding note.

CHAPTER XXIII.

LOCAL ANNALS OF SANTA BÁRBARA DISTRICT.

1831–1840.

GAIN IN POPULATION—PRESIDIAL ORGANIZATION—MILITARY ITEMS—SUM-
MARY OF EVENTS—SANTA BÁRBARA IN THE POLITICAL CONTROVERSIES—
CHICO AND DURAN—MUNICIPAL AFFAIRS—OFFICIAL LIST—SUB-PREFEC-
TURE—GRANTS OF PRIVATE RANCHOS—SANTA BÁRBARA MISSION—
STATISTICAL VIEW—ANNALS OF SECULARIZATION—SAN BUENAVENTURA
—FATHERS SUÑER, URÍA, AND FORTUNI—POPULATION, AGRICULTURE,
AND LIVE-STOCK—MAJORDOMOS AND ADMINISTRATORS—SANTA INÉS—
FATHER ARROYO DE LA CUESTA—STATISTICS OF DECADENCE—A GAIN IN
CATTLE—MODERATE PROSPERITY—LOCAL HAPPENINGS—LA PURÍSIMA
CONCEPCION—SECULARIZATION—INVENTORIES.

THE population of Santa Bárbara district, not including San Fernando, which was legally within its
jurisdiction, increased from 630 in 1830 to about 900
in 1840, so far as the meagre and contradictory records
afford a basis for estimate.[1] During the same period
the ex-neophyte Indian population decreased from
4,400 to 1,550, the latter number including 750 in
town and on the ranchos, in addition to 800 still living in the ex-mission communities. Adding the totals
of population for the three districts of San Diego,
Los Angeles, and Santa Bárbara, we find that in

---

[1] July 1834, a pop. of over 1,000 is claimed for Sta Bárbara; and the April
padron is said to have shown 940, probably including Ind. except neophytes,
and perhaps exaggerated to secure an ayuntamiento. *Leg. Rec.*, MS., ii. 58,
241, 243. The padron referred to is in *St. Pap., Mis.*, MS., v. 45. Dec. 31,
1834, a padron which makes the pop. 792, including 414 adults, 378 children,
52 Ind., and 64 foreigners. *Dept. St. Pap., Ben. P. y J.*, MS., vi. 1. An
undated padron, possibly incomplete, shows a pop. of 614 souls in 'the port
and inmediaciones.' *Guerra, Doc.*, MS., i. 135. In June 1841 there were 262
men between the ages of 18 and 60 years. *Dept. St. Pap., Ben. P. y J.*, MS.,
iv. 13. In July 1834 there were 9 Amer. married to natives, but not naturalized. *Id., Ben. Mil.*, lxxix. 112–13.

Southern California the gente de razon had increased during the decade from 2,310 to 2,850; while the christianized Indians had decreased from 9,600 to 5,100, of which latter number only 2,250 were still living at the missions.

Here the military or presidial organization of early times was still kept up, and fragmentary records appear from time to time to remind us of the old Spanish forms, though never sufficiently complete to afford satisfactory information on any phase of the subject. I append the items such as they are.[2]   José

[2] Sta Bárbara military items. 1831. Lieut Romualdo Pacheco, commandant; Alférez Rod. del Pliego; but the former was killed and the latter left Cal. this year. Pay-roll for the year $9,029; 44 men, 22 inválidos, 8 artillery. $350 for relief of the troops from the *Ayacucho*, and loan from James Burke in Oct. and Dec. *Dept. Rec.*, MS., ix. 50; *Pinto, Doc.*, MS. i. 1832. Capt. José de la Guerra y Noriega, and also Lieut Juan M. Ibarra named as commandant. Dom. and Anast. Carrillo alféreces; 19 soldiers named; 3 officers, 35 men, 19 inválidos. Pay-roll for 5 months $4,999. 1833. Ibarra, comandante; capt., Guerra y Noriega; alférez, Domingo Carrillo; sub-comisario subalterno, Anastasio Carrillo. Pay-roll for the year $11,615; 3 officers, 32 men, 6 artill., 5 Mazatecos. In his account of Dec. 31st A. Carrillo charges himself $6,710; credits $6,725. Net yield of post-office $51; stamped paper $27. Mission supplies for the year $2,270. The comisario at Mont. ordered in Jan. to send $2,000 for Sta B. Complaints of destitution. Sales of livestock from rancho nacional $675. Some orders were issued by Gov. Figueroa at Guerra's request on the restocking of the rancho; tithe cattle to be used for this purpose. *Guerra, Doc.*, MS., v. 177; *Vallejo, Doc.*, MS., xxxi. 53; *Dept. St. Pap.*, MS., iii. 91-2; *Id.*, *B. M.*, lxxvi. 12.

1834. Ibarra comandante; Anast. Carrillo habilitado. 2 officers, 33 men, 18 inválidos, 5 artillery, 5 Mazatecos. Pay-roll for the year, $10,671. May, 36 coats, hats, etc., and 72 shirts—probably showing the company to number 36 men—ordered to be distributed. *Dept. St. Pap., Ben. C. & T.*, MS., iii. 32-3. April, com. calls on gov. for materials to repair soldiers' quarters, in a ruinous condition. *Id.*, *B. M.*, lxxix. 54. Efforts to obtain a loan of cattle from the missions for the rancho nacional. *Arch. Arzob.*, MS., v.'pt ii. 2. Morineau, *Notice*, 148, speaks of a field cultivated for the soldiers' support. 1835. Ibarra and Carrillo as before, the latter sometimes as acting comandante. 2 off., 31-4 men, 16 inval., sergeants Tomás Romero, Juan P. Ayala, and Isidoro Guillen. Pay-roll for 11 months $9,474. Deducted from pay for montepio and inválidos $348. Oct., aid asked for a capt. of artillery with a corporal and 4 men who go to Sta B. *Dept. St. Pap., Ben. C. & T.*, MS., iii. 92. Actual payments for year ending July 1st, $1,912, leaving due the comp. $7,373. *Id., Ben. M.*, lxxxi. 2. Supplies from pueblo de los Berros, $1,038. *Id., Ben. P. y J.*, vi. 17. 1836. Ibarra com. of post; Lieut Domingo Carrillo com. of the comp.; A. Carrillo habilitado. 3 off., 29-32 men, 16 inval., 6 artill., 9 Mazatecos, 2d alférez Pablo Pacheco. Pay-roll for 6 months $5,163; inválidos for the year, $1,560; deduction per month for montepio and inválidos, $29.

1837. José de la Guerra y Noriega, comandante. In *Guerra, Doc.*, MS., i. 131-4, is a list of 116 men, among whom the 625 head of live-stock at S. Julian rancho should be distributed; but the list contains many names of men no longer in the company or at Sta B. The rancho had been granted by Alva-

de la Guerra y Noriega was nominally captain of the presidial company, sometimes acting as comandante, and continuously after 1837. Lieut Juan M. Ibarra of the Mazatlan company acted as comandante in 1833–6. Domingo and Anastasio Carrillo were the company alféreces down to 1836, when the former became lieutenant, and Pablo Pacheco second alférez. Later Roberto Pardo and José Lugo held these places, and Ignacio del Valle appears as habilitado. Down to 1836 the cavalry company numbered from 40 to 30 rank and file, with 20 to 15 inválidos, the pay rolls varying from $1,000 to $600 per month, and there being generally half a dozen artillerymen and as many Mazatecos in the force. In later years the nominal force was about half as large, but in both periods more than half the men were not actually serving as soldiers; and rarely was there any need of their services. The district was quietly prosperous, but the appended résumé of events is hardly more than an index of what has been recorded in other

rado to Guerra y Noriega. Ingress for the year, $3,529; paid out to troops $3,238; effects in store May, $308. June 10th, José Ign. Lugo represents that he was retired from mil. service 30 years ago at $8 per month; but has never received a cent. Owes $350 and wants it paid on acct. Gov. replies that he must present his acct to the comisaría 'when established'! *Dept. St. Pap., Ben. Mil.*, lxxx. 81–2.

1838. Antonio de la Guerra named as comandante; also J. M. Villavicencio. List of officers and men in the company of civic militia. Capt. Valentin Cota, lieut Juan P. Ayala, and Roberto Pardo, Alf. José Ant. Olivera, rank and file 38 men. *Cota, Doc.*, MS., 13. 1839. Com. José de la Guerra y Noriega; also Alf. Roberto Pardo. Habilitado, Alf. Ignacio del Valle, also acting com. Sergt José Lugo was promoted to be 2d alférez. Anast. Carrillo named as comisario subalterno. In *Soberanes, Doc.*, MS., 146, is mentioned a cavalry comp. of capt., alférez, and 15 men, whose pay amounts to $462 per month. Other reports show 17–19 men and 11–12 inválidos. Pay-roll for the year, $7,630. Jan., Lieut. Octaviano Gutierrez reports the artillery to be 7 guns, 2 of them 6 pounders, the rest 4; 4 of them brass and 3 iron; 4 of the 7 dismounted or useless. *Vallejo, Doc.*, MS., xxv. 11. There was much discontent respecting the distribution of mil. funds by the Mont. authorities. In Aug. Guerra says the artill. comp. has received nothing since he was in command. *Id.*, viii. 22, 17, 170, 205. Five recruits called for from Sta B. *Dept. St. Pap.*, MS., xviii. 56–7. 1840. Guerra y Noriega com., Ignacio del Valle habilitado. 19 men (one report says 32–3, perhaps including inválidos). 2d alf. José Lugo. In Aug. G. complains that the comp. is reduced to 8 or 10 available men, and there are no supplies for more. Sub-lieut Pardo has been long away, and G. is incapacitated by age and infirmities. *Vallejo, Doc.*, MS., ix. 224. Complains of unjust discrimination, since the sub-prefect gets his salary regularly. *Id.*, 112. Pay-roll for the year $8,457.

chapters.[3]   Santa Bárbara was always conservative in politics, taking no part in the movement of· 1831 against Victoria, but supporting in the interest of

[3] Chronologic summary of Santa Bárbara events. 1831. Jan., Gov. Victoria here on his way north. This vol., p. 182. March, imprisonment of J. A. Carrillo from Los Angeles. *Id.*, 196. Victoria's last visit in Nov., joined by Capt. Pacheco. *Id.*, 205. A forest fire on the hills endangering the town, driving the people to the beach, covering the decks of vessels with cinders, but turned aside by the green vineyards of the mission, is described by Robinson, *Life in Cal.*, 98. 1832. Jan. 1st, adherence to the S. Diego revolutionary plan. This vol., p. 212. Feb.–May, action of Sta B. in support of Zamorano against Echeandía. Ibarra's forces in possession. *Id.*, 223–8. Arrival and arrest of Capt. Sumner of the *Waverly*. *Id.*, 364. 1833. Marriage of Thos. O. Larkin on a vessel in the port. *Id.*, 365, 408. Bandini's efforts in congress to make Sta B. a puerto menor. The port is described as a hot-bed of smuggling. *Id.*, 369. April, pacification of Mex. celebrated with great festivities. *Dept. St. Pap., B. M.*, MS., lxxix. 31. May, an Ind., attempting to climb the flagstaff to arrange the halyards, fell and was killed. *Id.*, 28. 1834. Nothing in the records. 1835. Career of the convict Badillo, released this year. This vol., p. 16. Foreigners said to have known of the Apalátegui revolt at Angeles in advance. *Id.*, 285. April, sailing of Híjar, Padrés, and the other prisoners. *Id.*, 288. Oct., remains of Gov. Figueroa deposited in the mission church. *Id.*, 295. Removal of the Ind. from S. Nicolás Isl. by Sparks, Williams, and others. *Nidever's Life and Adven.*, MS., 68–72; and many newspaper sketches in connection with accounts of the rescue of an Ind. woman 15 years later. R. H. Dana arrived here in Jan., and often visited the place during this year and the next, his adventures being described in his *Two Years before the Mast*, 63, and passim. He describes Sta B. as 'composed of one-story houses built of sun-baked clay, or adobe, some of them whitewashed, with red tiles on the roofs. I should judge that there were about a hundred of them; and in the midst of them stands the presidio, or fort, built of the same materials and apparently but little stronger.' See also *Robinson's Life in Cal.*, 40 et seq., for descriptions and views which may apply to Sta B. in this—or any other early decade. 1836. April, arrival of Gov. Chico from Mex. This vol., p, 421. June, oath to federalism. Gov. Chico's visit and troubles with P. Duran. *Id.*, 423, 432–6. Nov.–Dec., news of Alvarado's revolution. Sta B. declines to join Los Angeles against the north. *Id.*, 481–4, 491. 1837. Jan., Gov. Alvarado and his army received and supported by the Barbareños. *Id.*, 491–3. Garrison from Sta B. at S. Fernando. *Id.*, 501. Feb., Alvarado's return from the south. *Id.*, 503. April, session of the diputacion, approving Alvarado's movement. *Id.*, 506–7. Pico and Osio present themselves with a new plan. *Id.*, 508. Castro and his force come here from S. Gabriel. *Id.*, 510. June–July, return of the gov. from the north in consequence of new opposition at Angeles; he accepts centralism, which is approved by Sta B.; meeting of the diputacion. *Id.*, 522–3, 526–32. Dec., the Barbareños refuse to support Cárlos Carrillo; Castro in command; threatened attack from the south. *Id.*, 540–1, 549–50. 1838. Jan., new and vain attempts of Carrillo to obtain support. *Id.*, 545–6. March, approach of Castañeda and southern army; Castro and Alvarado come from the north; campaign of S. Buenaventura; southern prisoners at Sta. B. *Id.*, 551–5. May, a force is sent to Angeles, and Carrillo with others is brought back as a prisoner. *Id.*, 564–6. Carrillo escapes in Aug. *Id.*, 569. Nov., arrival of Castillero with news of Alvarado's confirmation in Mex. *Id.*, 574. Dec., S. Diego prisoners brought by Castro. *Id.*, 578. Murder of

tranquillity Zamorano's cause in 1832. Political and other annals of 1833–5 contain nothing notable; but in 1836 the policy of Governor Chico and his controversy with Padre Duran created an excitement among the Barbareños that had much effect on later events. During the sectional troubles of 1837–8 this town exercised a great and probably controlling influence. Through the efforts of Guerra y Noriega and Duran its support was given from the first to Alvarado; and though naturally loyal to Mexico and averse to revolution, the citizens refused to aid Los Angeles and San Diego in their factious opposition to the plan of Monterey. Nor did they waver in their support of Alvarado, even when Cárlos Carrillo, one of the most popular of their number, urged his claim as governor. When these troubles were at an end the course of local happenings again became monotonous in 1839–40. Captain Guerra y Noriega, like Vallejo in the north, had hoped for a restoration of the old presidial organizations, but the hope was a vain one, and the aged captain's efforts barely kept in existence the skeleton of his garrison.

The municipal records of Santa Bárbara have been for the most part lost, so that respecting the pueblo government, administration of justice, criminal cases, and even list of officers, only a slight record can be formed from miscellaneous scattered documents.[4]

Capt. Bancroft by Ind. at Sta Rosa Isl. Vol. iv., p. 90–1. Views of Sta B., in *Forbes' Cal.*

1839. Jan., Alvarado, Vallejo, and the southern prisoners; the general's attempts to enforce military discipline. *Id.*, 580–3. May, Lieut Prado and 10 men sent to maintain order at Angeles. *Id.*, 589. Election; Covarrubias elector for Sta B. *Id.*, 590. Complaints respecting the distribution of revenues. *Id.*, 591–2. June, sub-prefect can find no *pus vacuno* to vaccinate Ind. *Dept. St. Pap., Ang.*, MS., v. 23. Visit of a British explorer. *Belcher's Voy.*, i. 320–2.

1840. Revelation of the Carrillo conspiracy. This vol., p. 606. Arrest and imprisonment of foreigners in connection with the Graham affair. Vol. iv., p. 14–17, 28.

[4] Sta Bárbara municipal government and official list. 1831–2. Alcaldes Rafael Gonzalez, Miguel Valencia; regidor or síndico José María García. *Guerra, Doc.*, MS., ii. 197; *Leg. Rec.*, MS., i. 348; *Gonzalez, Experiencias*, MS. Gov. Victoria was accused of having suppressed the ayuntamiento. This vol. p. 202. In 1832 the diputacion left Sta B. under the jurisdiction of the com.

The successive alcaldes, or justices of the peace from 1839, were Rafael Gonzalez, José Antonio de la Guerra, José María García, José María Valenzuela,

gen. as a place where the civil govt was not fully organized—that is, was disposed to favor Zamorano. *Id.*, 218.   1833.   Alcalde, or judge of 1st instance, José Antonio de la Guerra. *Dept. St. Pap.*, MS., iii. 90; *Id.*, *Ben.*, *P. y J.*, iii. 77.   Valentin Cota juez auxiliar. *Carrillo, Doc.*, MS., 112.   In April, Gov. Figueroa states that Sta B. has no ayunt. or constitutional alcalde. The so-called alcalde, or his place, was created by the dip. without formalities of law, and he is merely a juez conciliador.   He asks the opinion of Asesor Gomez, who replies that to decide the appointment illegal under the Span. laws and to put the citizens under military rule would open political wounds not yet healed. *Dept. St. Pap.*, *B. M.*, MS., lxxvi. 6-9.   José M. Maldonado was receptor in charge of the revenues from this year. This vol. p. 377.

1834.   Alcalde José M. García (several references for different months). In Aug. the dip. voted to create an ayunt. with alcalde, 4 regidores, and síndico, after discussion and the receipt of petitions. *Leg. Rec.*, MS., ii. 188-9; this vol. p. 249-50.   In July the extent of the alcaldía was given as from S. Fernando to Purísima, 55 l. from east to west, and 25 l. north to south. *Dept. St. Pap.*, *B. M.*, MS., lxxix. 87.   1835.   Alcalde José María Valenzuela. Oct. 12th, election of Rafael Gonzalez declared null by José Castro. *Dept. St. Pap.*, *Ben.*, MS., ii. 31.   Cármen Dominguez juez de campo.   No trace of the ayunt. as provided by the dip.   Wm G. Dana was perhaps captain of the port in these years.   Benito Diaz succeeded Maldonado as receptor by appointment of July 3d, salary $400. *Id.*, *Ben.*, *Cust.-H.*, vii. 10, 14; viii. 14. 1836. Alcalde Wm. G. Dana.   James Burke in July wished to be excused from serving as regidor. *Leg. Rec.*, MS., iii. 27.   Diaz suspended in Dec. as receptor. *Dept. St. Pap.*, *Ben.*, *Cust.-H.*, MS., iv. 1.   1837.   Alcalde Diego Olivera; regidor Santiago Lugo.   José Ant. de la Guerra was capt. of the port; and Diaz, notwithstanding his suspension, still served as receptor.   1838.   Alcalde Diego Olivera; síndico Ramon Valdés.   Munic. receipts, taverns at 4 reals per month, stores, $1, billiards, otter-skins, $159, liquors, $64, fines, $4, lots and brands, $4, total, $232; expend., secretary's pay at $15 per month, $123, sacristan, $87, church and office expenses, $22, total, $232. *Dept. St. Pap.*, *Ben.*, *P. y J.*, MS., ii. 26-30.

1839.   Sta B. made cabecera of 2d partido of 2d district. This vol. p. 585. Sub-prefect, appointed in April, Raimundo Carrillo, salary, $365; Sec. Francisco Castillo, who resigned in Aug.   Alcalde Antonio Rodriguez, síndico Vicente Valencia.   These were elected for the year; but under the prefecture system from April there were appointed as jueces de paz, José María Rojo and Antonio Rodriguez, the latter becoming 1st juez on Rojo's removal in July.   Pedro Cordero was appointed, probably at the same time, as 2d juez, or suplente.   Manuel Lorenzana served as alguacil at $5 per month. José Ant. de la Guerra was still capt. of the port at $30 (or $50).   Diego Olivera was made tithe-collector in Dec.   Munic. receipts and expend., $330. *Dept. St. Pap.*, *Ben.*, MS., ii. 31-2.   May 31st, sub-prefect's decree with munic. regulations in 23 articles. *Id.*, *Ben.*, *P. y J.*, v. 9-10.   June, juez orders comandante to remove the slaughter-pen from the Arroyo de la Viña, as a nuisance. He may put it on the beach toward the castillo, or north of the town. *Sta B. Arch.*, MS., 5-7.   This order caused a controversy, and after reference to the govt, Capt. Guerra seems to have had his own way. *Dept. St. Pap.*, MS., iv. 258-71.   July, a 2d síndico appointed. *Dept. St. Pap.*, *Ang.*, MS., xi. 9. Judicial cases must be referred to Los Angeles. *Id.*, v. 93.   Business is stopped because the juez can find no competent secretary. *Sta B. Arch.*, MS., 11, 13.   In July there was a controversy between the civil and military authorities. José Andrade was arrested for debt, and brought before the juez de paz; but Capt. Guerra claimed that the man was his servant, and as such

William G. Dana, Diego Olivera, Antonio Rodriguez, José María Rojo, and José Antonio Olivera. In the early years of the decade there seems to have been much doubt respecting the legality of the civil government and the exact extent of military jurisdiction. In 1834, on petition of the citizens, the diputacion voted to give the town a regular ayuntamiento; but the only evidence that such a body existed in 1835–8 is the occasional mention of a regidor or síndico. In 1839 Santa Bárbara was made a partido of the second prefectura, and Raimundo Carrillo served as sub-prefect this year and the next. About twenty ranchos were granted to private ownership during tho decade,[5] but beyond the dates of concession and names

entitled to the military fuero, and finally took him by force from the civil custody. After much trouble at home the matter was referred to Monterey and Sonoma, where the final decision was rendered in favor of the captain, and Justice Rojo lost his place. The justice of the decision may be questioned, since Andrade seems to have been only nominally, and to a very slight extent a servant. *Vallejo, Doc.*, MS., vii. 301, 305–9, 409, 416; viii. 32; *Sta B. Arch.*, MS., 7–9; *Dept. St. Pap.*, MS., iv. 273–4; *Doc. Hist. Cal.*, MS., iv. 1029–31.

1840. Sub-prefect Raimundo Carrillo. Jueces de paz, Antonio Rodriguez and Pedro Cordero, resigning in Feb. *Dept. St. Pap., Ben. P. y J.*, MS., vi. 60; but Joaquin Carrillo is also named in Jan. *Id., Ang.*, iv. 17, 19. José Ant. Olivera and Ramon Valdés appointed in April or May. *Id.*, xii. 28, 31; *Id., Ben., P. y J.*, vi. 69; and served for rest of year. Síndico (?), treasurer, or depositario, Juan Camarillo, succeeded by Jacinto Lorenzana; sec., Fran. Castillo, and later Manuel Ponce de Leon. Munic. receipts for the year $662.75, expend. $666.50. *Id., Ang.*, iii. 63, with monthly accts in *Id.*, iv. passim. Jan., a woman for abandoning her husband was ordered put in irons or a *corona*, pending investigation, there being no secure place of confinement. *Sta B. Arch.*, MS., 13. Feb.–April, Narciso Fabregat and other traders ask that either the order closing shops on feast-days be enforced or repealed, since many open their shops on pretence of living there. *Dept. St. Pap.*, MS., v. 1, 54. June, sub-prefect ordered to exile a woman living in concubinage. *Id., Ang.*, i. 1. Oct., the Sonoran Jesus Valdés, or El Tuerto, killed by José M. Losaga. *Los Ang. Arch.*, MS., i. 221–2.

[5] Private ranchos of Sta Bárbara district (included with those of Los Angeles in earlier decades). See *Hoffman's Reports*. Those marked with a * were rejected by the land com. or U. S. courts. Álamos, granted in 1839 to José de la Guerra, who was the claimant. Calleguas, 1837, José Pedro Ruiz; G. Ruiz et al. cl. Casmalia, 21., 1840, Antonio Olivera, who was cl. Conejo, still in possession of Capt. Guerra y Noriega. Guadalasca, 1836, Isabel Yorba, who was cl. Jesus María, 1837, Lúcas Olvera et al.; L. T. Burton et al. cl. Lompoc, 38,000 acres, 1837, Joaquin and José A. Carrillo, who were cl. Nipomo, 15 l., 1837, Wm G. Dana, who was cl. Ojai, 1837, Fernando Ticó, who was cl. Pozas, 6 l., 1834, J. Carrillo; José de la Guerra y Noriega cl. Punta de Concepcion, 1837, A. Carrillo, who was cl. Refugio, 6 l., Ant. M. Ortega et al., who were cl. Rincon, 1 l., 1835, Teodoro Arellanes, who was cl. Saca, 1838, Antonio; Antonia de la Guerra de Lataillade cl. Rio de Sta Clara, 1837, Valentin Cota, who was cl. San Julian, 6 l., 1837, Geo. Rock, only a

of owners, we have no details of what the occupants were doing. It is noticeable that none of the titles were rejected in the litigation of later times. Sir James Douglas in 1840 wrote of Santa Bárbara as a larger town than Monterey, estimating the annual exports of hides and tallow at $25,000.

Santa Bárbara mission remained in charge of Padre Antonio Jimeno until late in 1840, with Padre Narciso Duran as associate from the end of 1833. Antonio Menendez, the Dominican chaplain of the presidio, was buried at the mission in April 1832. The neophyte population, 711 in 1830, decreased to 556 in 1834, the year of secularization. In 1836 it was 480; and in 1840 not more than 250.[6] In

'dummy' for Capt. Guerra y Noriega, who was cl.   San Pedro, 1 l., 1838, Joseph Chapman, whose heirs were cl.   Santa Ana, 1837, Crisogono Ayala, et al., who were cl.   Santa Clara, or El Norte, 1837, Juan Sanchez, who was cl.   Santa Cruz Isl., 1839, Andrés Castillero, who was cl.   Santa Rosa, 3½ l., 1839, Francisco Cota; M. J. Olivera de Cota cl.   Sespe, or San Cayetano, 61 l., Cárlos Ant. Carrillo, who was cl.   The original grant was for 2 l., which was fraudulently changed to 6 l.; but the courts finally cut it down.   See *S. F. Bulletin*, Oct. 10, 1878.   Simí, formerly occupied by the Picos.   In 1831, Romualdo Pacheco was granted the use of a portion.   *Guerra, Doc.*, MS., vi. 29–30.   Sisquoc, 1833, María Ant. Caballero; James B. Huie cl.   Tepusquet, 2 l., 1837.   Tomás Olivera; A. M. Cota et al. cl.   Tinaguaic, 2 l., 1837, Victor Linares; Wm D. Foxen cl.

[6] Sta Bárbara statistics of 1831–4.   Decrease in pop. 711 to 556.   Baptisms 80 children; largest no. 29 in 1831; smallest 16 in 1834.   Deaths 200.   Increase in large stock 3,259 to 3,819; decrease in horses and mules 759 to 419; sheep 3,480 to 2,700.   Largest crop 3,700 bush. in 1834; smallest 2,700 in 1832; average 2,400, of which 1,476 wheat, yield 7 fold, 435 barley 12 fold, 405 maize 47 fold, 57 beans 12 fold.

Statistics of 1834–40.   Inventory of March 1834, credits $14,953, buildings $22,936, furniture, tools, goods in storehouse, vineyards, orchards, corrals, and animals $19,590, church $16,000, sacristy $1,500, church ornaments, etc., $4,576, library $152, ranchos $30,961 (S. Antonio $9,421, Dos Pueblos $12,055, S. Márcos $6,111, Sta Cruz $1,650, S. José $1,050, Guyzapa $674), total $113,960, or less debt of $1,000, $112,960.   *St. Pap.*, *Miss.*, MS., vi. 49–50.   Monthly wages to mission employés, priest $125, teacher $83, 1st majordomo $40, 2d id. $17, expense of worship $41, 10 servants at $6, $60, total $367.   1835–6.   Pop. 506, 481, baptisms 9, 13, marriages 5, 3, deaths 50, 25.   March 1835.   Inventory of church, etc., agreeing with that cited above, except that 8 bells are valued at $3,290.   *Id.*, v. 46–7.   Of the effects of 1834 $2,484 had been distrib. among the Ind.   *Id.*   1838.   Live stock of all kinds 1,212 animals.   Detailed inventory of property as turned over by Carrillo to Cota.   Receipts Jan.–March $569, expend. $324.   Salaries, padres $1,500, surgeon Nicolás $100, admin. Cota $480, majordomo Valenzuela $240, clerk Ponce de Leon $120, corporal Vicente $144, sacristan Lino $72, blacksmith $120, total per year $3,276.   *Id.*, viii. 6–8.   1839.   Pop. 246 according to Hartnell's report.   *Diario*, MS.   555 by a report in *St. Pap.*, *Miss.*, viii. 1, which

cattle there was a slight gain down to 1834, and good crops were harvested to the last; even after the secularization a considerable degree of prosperity in livestock and agriculture is indicated by Hartnell's statistics of 1839. The buildings were also kept in better condition that at most other establishments. Alférez Anastasio Carrillo was the comisionado to secularize Santa Bárbara,[7] and the successive administrators

must include scattered Ind. Cattle 1,770, horses 609, sheep 2,250, mules 30, asses 4, goats 22, 70 hides and sides of leather, 40 parchments, 42 salted skins, 150 cheeses, 59 arr. tallow, 188 arr. iron, grain sown 33 fan. wheat, 6 fan. barley, 3 fan. maize. *Hartnell, Diario*, MS., 88. Feb. 27th, account of supplies to govt since 1837, total amount $4,360, on which is credited $740. *St. Pap., Miss.*, vi. 25. 1840. Due the mission from Scott, Thompson, Cot, and Park, $1,479. *Vallejo, Doc.*, MS., xxxiii. 12; *Pico, Pap. Mis.*, MS., 47–51.

General statistics of 1786–1834, the whole period of mission history. Total no. of baptisms 5,679, of which 2,490 Ind. adults, 2,168 Ind. children, 1,021 children de razon; average per year 116. Marriages 1,524, of which 200 gente de razon; average 31. Deaths 4,046, of which 2,446 adult Ind., 1,288 Ind. children, 160 and 152 gente de razon; average among neophytes 77; death rate 8.03 per cent of pop. Largest pop. 1,792 in 1803. Males in excess of females except in 1801–10. Children from $\frac{1}{4}$ to $\frac{1}{3}$ in earlier years, later $\frac{1}{8}$ to $\frac{1}{5}$. Largest no. of cattle 5,200 in 1809; horses 1,337 in 1816; mules 340 in 1823, asses 1 to 3 each year; sheep 11,066 in 1804; goats 200 in 1792 and 1820; swine 200 in 1823; all kinds 16,090 in 1809. Total product of wheat 152,797 bush., yield 14 fold; barley 24,733 bush., 17 fold; maize 19,084 bush., 72 fold; beans 2,458 bush., 11 fold.

[7] Summary of Sta B. mission annals. 1833. P. Duran favors the partial, or experimental secularization. This vol., 335. 1834. Anastasio Carrillo comisionado, with José M. García as majordomo, at $40 per month, and Leandro Gonzalez as maj. de campo at $16.50 from October. *Id.*, 346. In Nov. Carrillo complains that the funds are not sufficient to pay the expense of $367 per month, and says the padres will perform the teacher's duties for a small fee. *St. Pap., Miss.*, MS., ix. 32–3. In Nov. P. Uría of S. Buenaventura was buried here. *Sta B. Lib. Mis.*, MS., 37. 1835. García was left in charge from June 1st by the comisionado, at $50, Raimundo Carrillo being llavero and clerk at $30. *Id.*, 24–5, 27–8, 30–1. Mariano Bonilla had been appointed teacher at $1,000, but there were difficulties about his salary, and also about his supposed connection with the colony revolt. *Id.*, 26, 28, 32–3. 1836. Raimundo Carrillo succeeded García as administrator on June 20th. *Id.*, vii. 53. 1837. In Dec. Carrillo writes that he has broken up a place where Manuel Gonzalez sold liquor to the Ind. There are other offenders of the same stamp who hinder progress at the mission, and he desires the commandant to interfere. *Cota, Doc.*, MS., 9–12. 1838. Oct. 13th Carrillo turned over the estate to Manuel Cota, under whom Manuel Ponce de Leon served as clerk at $12, and José M. Valenzuela as majordomo. *St. Pap., Miss.*, MS., viii. 6–8; *Vallejo, Doc.*, MS., xxxii. 287. In March Carrillo complains that the troops are killing cattle, and is told by the comandante that Castro had authorized the officers to kill all the cattle needed without asking permission of the administrator. *St. Pap., Miss.*, MS., vi. 26. In July the Ind. demanded clothing and the yield of the fisheries, else they would not work. *Id.*, ix. 38. 1839. Cota still in charge though suspended temporarily in July; also Valenzuela; but Ponce de Leon was replaced by Antonio Garraleta in April. P. de L. writes to Hartnell to complain about his pay. *Vallejo, Doc.*, xxxii. 287.

were José M. García in 1835–6, Raimundo Carrillo in 1836–8, Manuel Cota in 1838–9, and Leandro Gonzalez from 1840. In 1837–8 the support of Alvarado's army was a heavy tax on the mission resources; yet as we have seen these resources were by no means exhausted. There was trouble in 1839 with Cota, who was opposed by the padres and Indians and was suspended by Visitador Hartnell, after which for a time at least the neophytes became more contented and industrious under Father Duran's supervision.

Father Suñer of San Buenaventura died at his post in 1831, and his associate Father Uría died in 1834; but Blas Ordas had come to this mission in May 1833, and his ministry continued till 1838; while Buenaventura Fortuni, coming in the middle of 1837, served until his death in 1840. Padre Antonio Jimeno served temporarily during Fortuni's illness, and seems to have become the regular minister at the end of 1840.[8]

Feb. 6th an ex-neophyte applies to com. gen. for a renewal of his certificate of emancipation obtained from Gov. Figueroa, but since lost. *Id.*, vi. 232. Feb. 18th, Cota urges the gov. to restore the live-stock taken during the late wars. *St. Pap., Miss.*, MS., ix. 38–9. July, visit of Hartnell 1st to 15th. He found the accounts in bad condition and the Ind. much dissatisfied with Cota's management; and he finally suspended the administrator, who was accused of cruelty to the Ind. and insolence to Duran, and was also disrespectful to H., who resisted Cota's respectful petition to be reinstated, advising the govt against it. Duran was authorized to expend $500 for clothing for the Ind. *Diario*, MS., 3–4, 11–12, 14, 41–2, 78–82, 88–9. July 8th, original letter from a neophyte complaining of the alcaldes. *St. Pap., Miss.*, MS., viii. 6. July 10th, Hartnell to Duran explaining that he has suspended Cota and put affairs in charge of the alcaldes under D.'s direction. D. replies that he will aid by advice and to protect the Ind., but will have nothing to do with the temporal administration. 'The old times have gone by never to return.' *Arch. Miss.*, MS., ii. 919. July 18th, govt approve H.'s conduct. *Id.*, 921. Oct. 25th, Duran to Hartnell on petty details of mission affairs. He seems to represent the Ind. as doing much better without the administrator. *Id.*, 951. Nov. 18th, Cota seems to write as admin. He says the mission has long depended on manufactures rather than stock-raising and agriculture. *St. Pap., Miss.*, MS., ix. 39. 1840. Feb. 15th, P. Duran urges the appointment of an administrator. *Arch. Miss.*, MS., ii. 1017; and Leandro Gonzalez is appointed at $1,000 from May 15th. *St. Pap., Miss.*, MS., viii. 6; *Dept. St. Pap., Ang.*, MS., xii. 33. Hartnell's second visit was from Aug. 27th to Sept. 7th, but there is nothing in the records respecting his acts or the condition of affairs. *Diario*, MS., 15–16. Dec. 18th, P. Fortuni of S. Buenaventura buried here. *Sta B. Lib. Mis.*, 38.

[8] Francisco Suñer was born in Jan. 1758, at Olot, Cataluña, taking the

The falling-off in neophyte population down to 1834, when there were 626 in the community, was much less marked than in the past decade; and in livestock there was an actual gain, agricultural operations being also moderately successful to the end. After

Franciscan habit at Barcelona on April 14, 1779. Here he served from 1800 as predicador conventual and as comisario visitador of the 3d order. Leaving Cádiz in April, 1804, he reached the Mexican college in July, and in 1808 came to Cal. His missionary service was at S. Cárlos in 1808-9, San Juan Capistrano in 1809-13, San Luis Rey in 1814-16, Sta Bárbara in 1816-23, and S. Buenaventura in 1823-31. He was rated by his superiors as of medium ability. *Autobiog. Autog. de los Padres*, MS.; *Payeras, Inf. de 1820*, MS., 128; *Sarría, Inf. sobre Frailes*, 1817, MS., 50-1. He was a preacher of more than ordinary eloquence, but his usefulness as a missionary was seriously impaired by his broken health, on account of which he made frequent efforts from 1814 to obtain a passport for retirement, and which probably had much to do with a brusque manner and irritable temperament that made him generally unpopular. From 1824 he was blind. He took the oath of republican allegiance in 1826. His death occurred on Jan. 17, 1831, and he was buried next day in the S. Buenaventura church. *S. Buen., Lib. Mis.*, MS., 25, 67.

Francisco Javier de la Concepcion Uría was born May 10, 1770, at 2 P. M. at Aizarna, villa de Sta Cruz de Cestona, province of Guipúzcoa, Spain. In *Doc. Hist. Cal.*, MS., iv. 1-3, I have his original certificate of baptism. He became a Franciscan Jan. 13, 1789, at S. Sebastian; left Cádiz May 8, 1795; and came to Cal. in 1797. After serving at S. Fernando in 1797-1805, he retired to his college, but came back at the end of 1807, serving at Sta Cruz in 1808, Sta Inés in 1808-24, Soledad in 1824-8, and S. Buenaventura in 1828-34. Accredited by his superiors with distinguished merit and ability. *Autobiog. Autog.*, MS.; *Sarría, Inf., 1817*, MS., 51-2; *Payeras, Inf.*, 1820, MS., 129; *Arch. Sta B.*, MS., x. 444. Padre Uría was stout in physique, jolly in manner, addicted to pleasantries and jokes, indulging sometimes in coarse language, kind-hearted and well liked though at times very quick-tempered. He was an excellent manager of temporal affairs, and was noted for his generosity, especially to the Indians. Some of his letters are found in *Guerra, Doc.*, MS., ii. 155 et seq., besides business letters in other archives. Valdés, *Mem.*, MS., 7-9, has something to say of him, and also Osio, *Hist. Cal.*, MS., 62. From 1817 he was anxious to retire, but could not get his passport, though in 1826 he refused to take the oath of allegiance. In his last illness he went to Sta Bárbara, where he died at the house of Capt. Guerra in Nov. or Dec. 1834 and was buried in the vault of the mission church by P. Jimeno. *Sta B., Lib. Mis.*, MS., 37.

Buenaventura Fortuni, or more correctly Fortuny, as he usually wrote it, was born at Moster, Cataluña, in Feb. 1774, and took the habit at Reus Oct. 30, 1792. He left Cádiz in May 1803, and came to Cal. in 1806. His ministry was at S. José in 1806-25, S. Antonio in 1825-6, S. Francisco Solano in 1826-33, S. Luis Rey in 1833-6, and S. Buenaventura in 1837-40. His superiors pronounced him an able, zealous, and faithful missionary. *Autobiog. Autog. de los Padres*, MS.; *Sarría, Inf., 1817*, MS., 70-1; *Payeras, Inf., 1820*, MS., p. 139. Valdés, *Mem.*, MS., 9, describes the padre as of medium height and spare. He was a quiet unobtrusive man, careful in temporal management, moderate in his views and expressions, strict in religious duties, but indulgent to the Indians, and noted for his charitable disposition. In 1826 he refused to take the oath, but was respectful and obedient to the government. Like Uría he came to Sta Bárbara in his last days, and died at the residence of José Ant. Aguirre on Dec. 16, 1840. *St. Pap., Mis.*, MS., ix. 49. His remains were deposited in the mission vault on the 18th. *Sta B., Lib. Mis.*, MS., 38.

secularization the decline was not rapid, there being a gain in horses, a loss of only about 50 per cent in herds and flocks, and a succession of good crops at Santa Paula rancho down to the end of the decade, when there were still about 250 Indians in the community with perhaps as many more scattered in the district.[9] The records of secularization are very slight, but it was not effected until the spring of 1837 by Cárlos Carrillo as comisionado under appointment of the preceding year. Carrillo was called away by his contest for the governorship, and in 1838–40 Rafael Gonzalez was in charge as majordomo and ad-

[9] S. Buenaventura statistics of 1831–4. Decrease of pop. 726 to 626. Baptisms, 71; largest no., 21 in 1834; smallest, 12 in 1833. Deaths, 158; greatest no., 51 in 1832; smallest, 30 in 1834. Increase in large stock, 4,860 to 5,140; horses and mules, 360 to 640; decrease in sheep, 3,350 to 2,850. Largest crop, 2,925 bush. in 1834; smallest, 1,525 bush. in 1833; average, 2,352, of which 1,050 wheat, yield 6 fold; 600 barley, 18 fold; 525 corn, 31 fold; 178 beans, 14 fold.

Statistics of 1835–40. Baptisms, 126; marriages, 50. Feb. 28, 1837, credits $4,475, debts $4,215. *St. Pap. Miss.*, MS., vii. 67. 1838. Income, $10,496, expend. $9,543. Total receipts for cattle, liquors, manufactures, etc., $9,541; support of Ind. $2,316. Credits at end of year $13,925, debts $1,163. Income for Dec. $3.386, expend. $421. *Id.*, viii. 8–12. 1839. Receipts Jan.–March, $6,584, expend. $570. *Id.* Property in June, 5,587 animals, 180 hides, 409 arr. tallow, 532 fan. grain, $219 soap. *Id.*, vii. 4–5. Hartnell's inventory in July, 2,208 cattle, 1,670 sheep, 799 horses, 35 mules, 15 asses, 65 goats, 320 fan. wheat, 182 fan. corn, 30 fan. pease, 180 hides, 394 arr. tallow, 15 arr. lard, 5 bbls brandy, 13 bbls wine, 168 arr. iron, $219 soap. Debts about $3,000. Pop. 263 in community and 22 with license. *Diario*, MS., 77–8, 87–8. Acc. to *St. Pap., Miss.*, MS., viii. 1, the pop. was 457, probably including many scattered Ind. in the district. Inventory of Dec. *Id.*, viii. 9. Debts incurred May 1838 to June 1839, $465; credits $1,005. *Id.*, vii. 5. 1840. Receipts Aug. 1839 to July 31, 1840, $6,830; expend., $6,737. Debts Aug. 25th, $4,918. *Id.*, vi. 5–6; *Pico, Pap. Mis.*, 83. Debts Aug. 25th, $7,227. *Id.*, 47–51; *Vallejo, Doc.*, MS., xxxiii. 12. The chief creditors were Concepcion Argüello $1,000, P. Fortuni $1,983, Aguirre $1,843, Scott $779, and Thompson, $447. Inventory in Dec., 5,907 animals, other property about as in June. *St. Pap., Miss.*, MS., vii. 4–5. Receipts Sept. and Nov., $431, $735; expend., $402, $970. *Id.*, ix. 48–52.

Statistics of 1782–1834, the whole period of the mission's annals. Total of baptisms 3,876, of which 1,896 Ind. adults, 1,909 Ind. children, 4 and 67 de razon; annual average 54. Marriages 1,107, of which 11 gente de razon. Deaths, 3,216, of which 2,015 Ind. adults, 1,158 Ind. children, 22 and 21 de razon. Annual average 61; death rate 7.5 per cent of pop. Largest pop., 1,330 in 1816. Males slightly in excess of females, and children about 1-6 of the pop. Largest no. of cattle, 23,400 in 1816; horses 4,652 in 1814; mules 342 in 1813; asses, 2 each year; sheep, 13,144 in 1816; goats, 488 in 1790; swine, 200 in 1803, 1805; all kinds, 41,390 in 1816. Total product of wheat 148,855 bush., yield 18 fold; barley, 54,904 bush., 19 fold; maize, 51,214 bush., 84 fold; beans, 9,061 bush., 14 fold.

ministrator.[10] The great event of the period was the fight of March 1838, between Carrillo's supporters under Captain Castañeda and those of Alvarado under General Castro, the only battle of the war in which blood was shed.

Padre Blas Ordaz continued his ministry at Santa Inés till 1833, when Padre José Joaquin Jimeno came from the north, serving throughout the decade, with Marcos Antonio Saizar de Vitoria as associate in 1835–6, and Felipe Arroyo de la Cuesta in 1836–40.

[10] Summary of S. Buenaventura annals. 1831–5. Blank, except an occasional mention of this mission with others in various secularization plans not carried into effect, and the death of padres Suñer and Uría as recorded in an earlier note of this chapter. 1836. Cárlos Carrillo comisionado for secularization, appointed in June, the act being hastened by Gov. Chico's quarrel with the padres at Sta Inés and Sta Bárbara; but the formal transfer of the property by inventory did not apparently take place until February of the next year; and the records are very slight. *St. Pap. Miss. and Colon.*, MS., ii. 3723; *Id., Miss.*, vii. 67; *Vallejo, Doc.*, MS., xxxii. 24; this work, iv. p. 46; this vol., p. 426, 435. 1837. Alvarado and his northern forces at S. Buenaventura in Jan. on their way to Los Angeles. *Id.*, 494, 497. Carrillo received his appointment as gov. in Sept. or Oct. *Id.*, 534. 1838. Rafael Gonzalez in charge as majordomo from May. *St. Pap., Miss.*, MS., ix. 48–9. March, occupation of the mission by southern forces; battle between Castañeda's and Castro's armies. This vol., p. 549–55. Gonzalez, *Exper.*, MS., 35–6, claims to have received the mission in good condition, and to have delivered it 4 years later still prosperous, he having always been on excellent terms with the padre; but he says that much aid was given to the troops for which no return was ever made. 1839. Gonzalez mentioned as administrator this year and the next in many records. Hartnell's inspection was June 25th to July 1st. He found affairs in fairly good condition, crops looking well at Sta Paula, though much injured by squirrels at the mission. There was complaint that no clothing had been distributed since Carrillo's departure, and the admin. was authorized to buy $1,000 worth of effects on credit, the debt to be a preferred one; also to kill 200 cattle, in addtion to the regular monthly slaughter of 30. *Hartnell, Diario*, MS., 14, 77–8; *Arch. Miss.*, MS., ii. 905. July 3d, P. Fortuni complains to the visitador that the Ind. will not attend to prayers, alleging that he did not wish them to pray, and that the administrator, majordomo, and alcaldes will not oblige them. *Id.*, 907. In later years it was claimed that there was no distribution of clothing, etc., after Sept. 1839. *St. Pap., Mis.*, MS., 50. 1840. Hartnell's second visit was in Aug. The Ind. had no fault to find with Gonzalez, admitting that he cared well for them; still, for the sake of novelty, they desired his removal, and the appointment of Miguel or Vicente Pico; but H. finally made them understand the folly and injustice of such a demand. The Ind. were also very much alarmed at the danger of losing Sta Paula rancho, their only dependence for crops, and of which Manuel Jimeno was trying to get a grant. If they could not keep the rancho they desired to quit the community; and the padres, administrator, and neighbors all agreed that the Ind. were right. Hartnell thought so himself, though very friendly to Jimeno. *Diario*, MS., 15, 21–2. The rancho was not granted for several years. In Dec., for lack of a minister, the sacristan officiated at several burials. *S. Buen., Lib. Mis.*, MS., ii. 68.

Both Vitoria and Arroyo died at this mission.[11] In neophyte population the loss to 1834 was about 15 per cent, and from that time to 1840 about 12 per cent; but at the end of the decade only 180 of the 300 Indians were living in community.[12] Agricul-

[11] Felipe Arroyo de la Cuesta was born at the villa of Cubo, Castilla la Vieja, on April 30, 1780, becoming a Franciscan Aug. 3, 1796, at the chief convent of Búrgos. He sailed from Cádiz Sept. 2, 1804, and left the college of S. Fernando on Dec. 14, 1807, for Cal., where he arrived early in 1808. His missionary service was at S. Juan Bautista in 1808–33, at S. Miguel in 1833–4, at S. Luis Obispo in 1834–5, at Purísima in 1835–6, and at Sta Inés in 1836–40, though it was only at San Juan that his bodily infirmities permitted him to work. His superiors accredited him with great merit, ability, and zeal. *Autobiog. Autog. de los Padres*, MS.; *Sarría, Inf. de 1817*, MS., 64–5; *Payeras, Inf. de 1820*, MS., 137. From about 1813 he suffered almost continually from rheumatism, and was repeatedly at the point of death. In 1809 he said the first mass in the new church of Mission San José. In 1826, though maintaining his allegiance to the king of Spain, he took a modified oath to republicanism. Father Arroyo was a scholar and always a student, giving special attention to the languages of the Indians of the San Juan region, of which he had already prepared a grammar before 1817, which and the padre's skill in the native idioms are mentioned in Sarría's report of that year. His *Grammar of the Mutsun Language* and his *Vocabulary or Phrase-book* were published by Shea in New York, 1861; and the original MSS. were at one time in my possession. In *Larios, Vida*, MS., 35, I have a curious table or perpetual calendar apparently made by him. The biographic notice (by A. S. Taylor) in the introduction to the *Grammar* is very erroneous. Robinson, *Life in Cal.*, 108, describes him as closely confined to his chamber, and when tired of study he would have the children called in to play before him, calling them by such names as Cicero, Plato, Alexander, etc. All testify to his great learning and piety. Florencio Serrano, *Apuntes*, MS., 186–8, spent much time with the padre when he was at San Luis Obispo. At that time his legs were paralyzed, and he was moved about in a wheeled chair by attendants. He used to invent all kinds of pretexts for keeping Serrano at his side for days for the pleasure of conversation. Alluding to the difficulty of quitting the Californian service, he used to say:

> 'Si fueres á California
> Encomienda á Dios la vida
> En tu mano está la entrada
> Y en la de Dios la salida.'

Father Arroyo died at Sta Inés on Sept. 20, 1840, at the age of 60, and his body was buried on the 22d by P. Jimeno in the mission church on the gospel side near the presbytery. *Sta Inés, Lib. Mis.*, MS., 22–4. The burial notice containing a biog. sketch was translated with some additional notes and printed in the *S. F. Bulletin*, 1865, being republished in the *S. José Pioneer*, Feb. 22, 1877.

For a biographic notice of Padre Vitoria, see *Pioneer Register and Index*, vol. v. of this work.

[12] Sta Inés statistics 1831–4. Decrease of pop. 408 to 344. Baptisms 63. Deaths 109. Decrease in live-stock 7,590 to 7,460; gain in horses and mules 390 to 460; sheep 2,160 to 2,000. Largest crop 2,373 bush. in 1832; smallest 1,623 bush. in 1834; average 1,962 bush., of which 1,525 wheat, yield 10 fold; barley only produced in 1834 125 bush., 11 fold; corn 382 bush., 54 fold; beans 20 bush., 5 fold.

Statistics of 1835–40. Inventory of Aug. 1, 1836, of the property turned over to Covarrubias by P. Jimeno. Credits $1,892; buildings $945; furniture, tools, and goods in store $14,527; live-stock 8,040 cattle $24,850; 1,923

tural operations were always on a moderate scale, with constantly decreasing crops; but in live-stock the mission held its own down to the secularization, and afterward showed a considerable gain. The church property was valued at about $11,000; the inventory of other property was generally about $45,000, and the mission debt was reduced from $6,000 to $2,000; so that the establishment was more prosperous than any in the south. The mission was not secularized until 1836, when José M. Ramirez was made comisionado, being succeeded by José M. Covarrubias in 1836–7, Francisco Cota in 1837–40, and Miguel Cordero perhaps acting temporarily from October 1840. Except a few inventories and other statistics, there exist no records of events connected with secularization;[13] nor

sheep $1,469; 343 horses $886; 45 mules $540; 987 fruit trees $987; church $4,000 (48¾x9 varas, walls of adobe, 4 doors, 8 windows, sacristy 9x6, 3 doors, 1 window, tile roof, board ceiling, brick floor); ornaments $6,251, library of 66 volumes $188; total $56,437 (or $46,186 besides church property); debts $5,475; net assets $50,962. *St. Pap. Miss.*, vi. 27–8. Oct., $1,689 paid to Jas Scott. *Id.*, vii. 53. 1837. Jan. 27th, receipts $645, expend. $642. Feb. 6th, Covarrubias' general account, credits $55,619; debits $55,459. *Id.*, vii. 54. Feb. 6th, Covarrubias turns over to his successor property to the value of $44,772 with debts of $5,487. *Id.*, vi. 28. Dec. 31st, receipts for year $49,770, expend. $54,123. Property on hand (except church, etc.) $45,552, and debts $2,715. *Id.*, vi. 30–1. 1838. Dec. 31st, receipts $50,478, expend. $54,754. Inventory $47,362, debt $2,713, credits $1,533. *Id.*, vi. 29, 31. 1839. Monthly salaries, padre $83.34, prefect $41.65, worship $41.65, clerk $25, admin. $50, 2 majordomos $15, $12, watchman $10, servant $10, total $288.64. *Id.*, vi. 32. March, pop. 315. *Id.*, 31. July, Hartnell's inventory. 9,720 cattle, 2,180 sheep, 382 horses, 32 mules, 4 asses, 50 hogs, 796 fan. grain, 448 arr. tallow, 75 arr. lard, 87 hides, 50 arr. wool, 200 arr. iron, $30 soap, 1 bbl. brandy, etc. Pop. 183 souls. Planted 112 fan. grain. *Hartnell, Diario*, MS., 82, 90. Nov., 2,129 varas of cloth, 40 rebozos, 4 jackets, etc., distrib. among the Ind. *St. Pap. Miss.*, MS., vii. 17. 1840. Jan. 31st, 'administraciones' for a year, receipts $282, expend. $282. *Id.* Feb. 1st, inventory similar to Hartnell's, except that there are 2,720 (9,720 ?) cattle, and 1,268 fan. of grain. Debts $1,747. *Id.*, 16–20. Debt $2,079. *Pico, Pap. Mis.*, MS., 47–51.

Statistics of 1804–34, the whole period of the mission annals. Total of baptisms 1,372, of which 566 Ind. adults, 757 Ind. children, 1 and 48 gente de razon; annual average 45. Marriages 409, of which 9 de razon. Deaths 1,271, of which 736 Ind. adults, 519 Ind. children, 3 and 13 de razon; annual average 42; average death rate 7.56 per cent of pop. Largest pop. 770 in 1816. Females generally in excess of males, and children about ⅓ of the pop. Largest no. of cattle 7,300 in 1831 (but increased after 1834); horses 800 in 1816; mules 124 in 1822; sheep 6,000 in 1821; goats 130 in 1818; swine 250 in 1816; all kinds 12,320 animals in 1820. Total yield of wheat 63,250 bushels or 17 fold; barley (for 12 years only) 4,024 bush., 26 fold; maize 39,850 bush., 164 fold; beans 4,340 bush., 27 fold.

[13] Summary of Sta Inés events. 1831–5. Nothing to be noted. 1836.

are there any local occurrences of the decade requiring further notice than that contained in the appended items.

Padre Vitoria was the minister at Purísima until August 1835; Padre Arroyo de la Cuesta served here in 1835–6; and Padre Juan Moreno in 1834. Possibly Moreno was in charge part of the time in 1836–40, but I find no definite record for these years, and there was no regular minister. In neophyte population the mission nearly held its own down to 1834, when it had 407 souls, but at the end of the decade, the number had fallen to 120 in community, with perhaps as many more scattered in the region. The falling-off in crops and in live-stock was constant for the decade, except that there was a considerable increase of horses after the secularization, if the somewhat irregular statistics may be trusted.[14] The value

June, trouble between Gov. Chico and P. Jimeno, leading to secularization. This vol., p. 433–5, 426; iv. 45–6. José María Ramirez as comisionado, turning over the estate Aug. 1st to José M. Covarrubias as majordomo. *Vallejo, Doc.*, MS., xxxii. 24; *St. Pap. Miss. & Colon.*, MS., ii. 372; *Id., Miss.*, vi. 27. 1837. Jan., Covarrubias delivers the property to his successor Francisco Cota. *Id.*, 28–30. Feb., Cota complains that the no. of working horses and mules has been so reduced by supplies to the troops, that only 80 horses and 30 mules are left. *Id.*, vii. 53–4. Trapper horse-thieves at the mission in Oct. Vol. iv., p. 113. 1838. Nothing. 1839. Cota admin., Joaquin Villa and Miguel Valencia majordomos, José Linares llavero. *St. Pap. Miss.*, MS., vi. 32. April, Cota asks permission to spend $1,000 for clothing for the Ind., who have received none in two years, and also to slaughter 300 cattle; which is granted by Hartnell. *Id.*, ix. 7; *Vallejo, Doc.*, vii. 15; *Hartnell, Diario*, 2, 4. Hartnell's visit was on July 15th. He found the Ind. desirous of getting rid of their administrator, on whom and his dependents they claimed that all the mission revenue was spent; but H. reported Cota successful in paying off debts. *Diario*, MS., 82, 90. Aug., Gov. authorizes the transfer (probably temporary for repairs?) of the church to the weaving-room. *Dept. Rec.*, MS., x. 15. Dec., Anastasio Carrillo to Hartnell about the 300 cattle promised him, the padre prefecto consenting. Letter copied in *Vallejo, Hist. Cal.*, MS., iv. 83–5, to illustrate the methods of disposing of mission property. 1840. Aug. 5th, an anonymous letter in English warning Hartnell that the admin. is plundering the mission of all its property. *Arch. Mis.*, MS., ii. 1095. Sept. 10th, Hartnell's visit, only a fragment of the record. He found the Ind. much alarmed at reports that the gov. had given orders for mission cattle in favor of private individuals. *Hartnell, Diario*, MS., 93. Oct. 23d, Cota resigns, and Miguel Cordero takes charge as majordomo. *Dept. Rec.*, MS., xi. 44–5.

[14] Purísima statistics 1831–4. Decrease in pop. 413 to 407. Baptisms 88, largest no. 47 in 1834, smallest 10 in 1833. Deaths, 167, largest no. 50 in 1832, 1833, smallest 28 in 1834. Decrease in large stock 13,430 to 7,470;

of the Purísima estate in 1835 and for several years
thereafter was about $60,000, divided as follows:
church property $8,000, buildings $5,000, implements
and furniture $2,000, produce $11,000, lands $17,000,
and live-stock $17,000.[15] Domingo Carrillo, appointed

horses and mules increase 430 to 1,270; sheep 6,070 to 6,514. Largest crop
1,842 bush. in 1834; smallest 600 bush. in 1833; average 1,260 bush., of
which 830 wheat, yield 8 fold; 210 barley, 9 fold; 142 corn, 31 fold; 52
beans, 12 fold.

Statistics of 1835–40. Feb. 18, 1835. Inventory formed by the comisionado, and Wm G. Dana and Santiago Lugo as appraisers. Chief building with
21 rooms $4,300, 12 smaller buildings $1,205, furniture (tools, etc.) $2,001,
effects in store $6,255, grain and produce $4,821, church ornaments, etc.,
$4,944, church $400, library $655, 5 bells $1,000, 3 gardens $728, live-
stock (pertaining to church?) $201; total of church property $7,928; ranchos,
Sitio de Mision Vieja $373, S. do Jalama $784, Los Álamos $1,185, S An-
tonio $1,418, Sta Lucía $1,080, S. Pablo $1,060, Todos Santos $7,176,
Guadalupe $4,065; total of lands $17,141; live-stock $17,321. Credits
$3,613, total $62,058; debt $1,218; net assets $60,840. St. Pap. Mis., MS.,
v. 43–4. Aug. 18th, inventory of delivery from comisionado to majordomo,
excepting real estate and church property, $29,981, about the same as before,
credits $1,774, debt $1,371. Id., vi. 16. 1837. Inventory of March 25th
$23,653, credits $2,155, debt $2,155. Id., viii. 11. 1838. Inventory of de-
livery by Carrillo to Valenzuela, $27,394. Id., 2–3. Dec. 31st, receipts since
June 15th $4,427, expend. $2,441. 1839. Jan. and March, receipts $2,247,
$2,301, expend. $255, $190. Salaries of admin., majordomo de campo, and
llavero $982. No padre is mentioned. In Feb. over 600 sheep were
drowned in the floods. Pop. Feb. 28th 242. Id., 3–5. July 25th, Hartnell's
inventory. Pop. 122, many of them sick, at the mission and 47 free Ind. at
Álamos. 3,824 cattle, 1,532 (?) horses, 1,300 sheep, 89 mules, 1 burro, 3½ bbls
wine, 3½ bbls brandy, 60 arr. tallow, 22 arr. lard, 100 hides, 99 tanned skins,
210 fan. grain, etc. Planted 60 fan. wheat and barley. Crops looking well,
many wild cattle. Hartnell, Diario, MS., 23. Debt July 25th $3,696. Pico,
Pap. Mis., MS., 47–51.

Statistics of 1787–1834. Total of baptisms, 3,314, of which 1,740 Ind.
adults, 1,492 Ind. children, 4 and 78 de razon; annual average 70. Marriages 1,031, 5 being gente de razon. Deaths 2,711, of which 1,790 Ind.
adults, 902 Ind. children, 1 and 18 de razon; annual average 57. Largest
pop. 1,520 in 1804. Sexes about equal to 1800, females in excess in 1801–7,
and males later; children about ¼ of pop. Largest no. of cattle 13,000 in
1830; horses 1,454 in 1821; mules 300 in 1824; sheep 12,600 in 1820; goats
292 in 1791; all kinds 23,862 animals in 1821. Total product of wheat
9,522 bush. yield 11 fold; barley 9,306 bush., 17 fold; maize 28,255 bush.,
82 fold; beans 4,818 bush., 14 fold.

[15] Events at Purísima. 1831. Fears of an Ind. revolt. Dept. Rec., MS.,
ix. 7. 1832–3. No record except as this mission is mentioned in secularization plans never put in operation. 1834. Domingo Carrillo appointed comisionado in Nov. Slaughter of mission cattle rather vaguely recorded. This
vol., p. 346, 349–50. 1835. The place seems to have been called Pueblo de
los Berros. Guerra, Doc., MS., vii. 81; Dept. St. Pap., Ben., P. y J., MS.,
vi. 17. Secularization effected in Feb., and on Aug. 18th the comisionado
turned the estate over to his brother Joaquin Carrillo as maj. St. Pap. Miss.,
MS., vi. 16. Aug. 25th, Carrillo writes to gov. about the Lompoc rancho
where he is going to build, and is apparently using the mission effects and
Ind. rather freely for his private advantage. Dept. St. Pap., MS., iv. 48–9.
The rancho was granted two years later. The building of a new church was
contemplated this year, the old one being in a sad state, but nothing was

in 1834 as comisionado, effected the secularization
early in 1835; and his successors in the administration were Joaquin Carrillo in 1835–8, José María
Valenzuela in 1838–40, and Eugenio Ortega from
October of the latter year.

apparently accomplished. 1836–7. No record except an inventory already
given. 1838. June 15th, Carrillo surrenders the estate to José María Valenzuela. *St. Pap. Miss.*, MS., viii. 2, 4. 1839. Emigdio Ortega was majordomo de campo under Valenzuela, and Juan Salgado llavero. *Pico, Pap.
Mis.*, MS., 49. Visitador Hartnell's inspection was in July. The Ind. were
content with their administrator but wished to have a padre, Moreno preferred. At their request Salgado was removed; the killing of wild bulls was
authorized, also the slaughter of 300 cattle and purchase of $800 in clothing.
The 47 Ind. at Álamos were anxious to keep their lands, and J. A. de la
Guerra, the grantee, promised in writing not to molest them. *Hartnell,
Diario*, MS., 2, 3, 23–4, 42. 1840. No record of Hartnell's 2d visit. Oct.
23d, Eugenio Ortega succeeded Valenzuela in the administration. *Dept. Rec.*,
MS., xi. 45. Douglas, *Journal*, MS., 87, speaks of the mission as nearly in
ruins, and estimates exports at $2,000.

CHAPTER XXIV.

LOCAL ANNALS OF MONTEREY DISTRICT.

1831-1840.

Population—Visits and Descriptions—Summary and Index of Events —Military Record—Municipal Affairs and Administration of Justice—Prefecture—Criminal Record—Private Ranchos—Mission San Cárlos—San Luis Obispo—Padre Gil y Taboada—Statistics of Decline—San Miguel—Padre Juan Cabot—Population and Property—San Antonio—Secularization—Merçado's Complaints— Hartnell's Inspection—La Soledad—Padre Sarría—Inventories of Live-stock and Crops—San Juan Bautista or San Juan de Castro— Padres and Neophytes—Mission Estate—Emancipation of the Indians—Pueblo and Capital of the District—Santa Cruz, or Pueblo de Figueroa—Villa de Branciforte.

The population of gente de razon in the Monterey district, including Branciforte and seven missions, may be regarded, on authority that is tolerably satisfactory, as having increased from 1,100 at the beginning to 1,600 at the end of the decade. Of the latter number 700 lived at Monterey, 550 at the ranchos of the district, 250 at and about Branciforte, 50 at San Juan, and 50 at all the other missions.[1] There were perhaps 75 foreigners who may be re-

[1] The *Monterey, Padron, 1836*, MS., shows a pop. in the town of 255 men, 146 women, and 293 children, total 694, of whom about 30 Ind. and 42 foreigners; on 28 ranchos 206 men, 105 women, and 270 children, total 581, of whom 65 Ind. and 15 foreigners; total 1,180 gente de razon (including 57 foreigners) and 95 Ind. The same doc. with slight variations in *Vallejo, Doc.*, MS., xxxii. 10 et seq. In *Id.*, xxxi. 76, is a padron of 1834, showing 1,049 persons in 146 families or households, 43 being foreigners, 52 Ind., and 96 'militares.' In *Id.*, 250, is a list, apparently incomplete, of 145 voters, including 5 naturalized foreigners. For Branciforte we have nothing earlier than 1845, when a padron shows 294 Cal. and Mex., 56 foreigners, and 120 Ind. *Doc. Hist. Cal.*, MS., ii. 218. For S. Juan, Mofras gives a pop. of 100 in 1842.

(667)

garded as permanent settlers.   The ex-neophyte Indian population decreased from 3,500 to 1,740, of which
number about 1,020 lived in communities, or at least
near the ex-missions.   Many vessels anchored in this
port each year, as has been noted elsewhere in marine
lists and commercial annals, where the visits and adventures of different voyagers have received sufficient
attention; but several of these visitors have published
their observations, and of these I have deemed it well
to quote descriptive portions relating to Monterey,[2]

[2] Monterey, descriptions by visitors, town improvements, etc. 1834. A
voluntary contribution to be requested from each vessel for the construction
of a wharf. This vol., 380.   1835-8.   See view of Monterey in *Forbes' Cal.*
1834-5.   'Monterey, as far as my observation goes, is decidedly the pleasant-
est and most civilized-looking place in California.   In the centre of it is an
open square, surrounded by four lines of one-story buildings, with half a dozen
cannon in the centre, some mounted and others not.   This is the presidio or
fort, entirely open and unfortified...The houses, as everywhere else in Cal.,
are of one story, built of adobes...of a common dirt-color.   The floors are
generally of earth, the windows grated and without glass, and the doors,
which are seldom shut, open directly into the common room, there being no
entries.   Nearly all the houses are whitewashed on the outside.   The better
houses, too, have red tiles upon the roofs.   The Indians do all the hard work.
The men in Monterey appeared to me to be always on horseback.   Nothing
but the character of the people prevents Monterey from becoming a large
town.' *Dana's Two Years*, 89-93.   1836.   'The town is a scattered series of
houses, containing not more than 500 inhabitants, among whom are 15 or 20
foreigners, Americans and Englishmen, engaged in trade.' *Ruschenberger's
Narr.*, ii. 403-4.   June 1st, Gov. Chico orders the administrator of Sta Cruz
to cut and send him a tree 20 varas long for a flag-staff. *Savage, Doc.*, MS.,
i. 23.   1837.   'Monterey I found as much increased as S. Francisco had fallen
into ruin.   It was still, however, very miserable, and wanting in the military
air of 1827.   The adobe or mud-brick battery remained, and had been newly
bedaubed during the late ebullition of independence.'   The fortifications, of
which plans must not be taken, 'consisted of a mud wall of three sides, open
in the rear, with breastwork about three feet in height; with rotten platforms
for 7 guns, the discharge of which would annihilate their remains of car-
riages.'   But the author got few supplies, and was not in a good humor.
Belcher's Narr., i. 136.   'Tout se présente sous l'aspect le plus neuf, et tel
enfin que l'on peut imaginer qu'ont dû le voir les premiers découvreurs.   En
approchant de la pointe Vénus on commence cependant à distinguer par-
dessus les roches une éminence sur laquelle est érigé un mât de pavillon ou
l'on abore les couleurs nationales.   Tout à côté, est le corps-de-garde d'une
batterie à barbette de 8 canons, que l'on nomme le Castillo...Peu après avoir
aperçu la pointe du fort on découvrira le fond de l'anse on l'on verra d'abord
dans la partie de l'Est, le clocher de la chapelle du Presidio, ainsí que les
bâtiments qui en dépendent et qui sont tous renfermés dans la même en-
ceinte; puis successivement et à mesure que le bâtiment avancera, ou découvrira dans l'Ouest du Presidio des maisons éparses cà et là, sans aucun ordre;
elles forment, par leur réunion, ce que l'on nomme la ville de Monterey, sans
doute par déférence pour le siége du gouvernement; il semble inutile d'ajouter
qu'il n'y a aucun autre monument que l'église du Presidio.   Parmi ces maisons, dont le nombre s'élève tout au plus de 40 à 50, plusieurs sont blanchies
á la chaux, quelqus-únes ont un étage et une certaine apparence de conforta-

though the sum total of information thus gathered from Dana, Ruschenberger, Belcher, Petit-Thouars, Laplace, and others, is not very complete; nor is it supplemented to any satisfactory extent by local records on the material growth of the town. Events at the capital were for the most part of such a nature as to be naturally included in the political record of territorial affairs as summarized in chronologic order and indexed in the appended note.[3]   A few minor

bilité, mais la plupart sont de misérables cases couverte en joncs on en branches d'arbres; presque toutes n'ont ni cour, ni jardin.' Population not over 200, créoles, natives, Mexicans, Scotch, Irish, American, kanakas, and even a few French.   Many compliments for the women.   *Petit-Thouars, Voyage,* ii. 83-5, 110, 112.   1839.   'Ainsi par exemple Monterey, que le cour de Madrid avait traitée toujours en enfant gâté (!), qui est dans una magnifique situation, devant un bon mouillage, auprés de cantons fertiles, etc.   Monterey, dis-je n'avait fait presque aucun progrès depuis 25 années.   Elle comptait, il est vrai, quelques maisons, quelques familles de résidents étrangers de plus, mais elle manquait tout à fait de commerce et d'industrie.'   Yet the author was well treated and has much to say in praise of the gov. and people of the higher classes. *Laplace, Campagne,* vi. 304.   Alvarado, *Hist. Cal.,* MS., iv. 128-30, tells us that by his efforts a new cuartel was built for the soldiers—still standing in 1875—at a cost of $9,000, being the best building in Cal.   He also improved roads in the vicinity, building a bridge from the new cuartel to Hartnell's college, and another toward Capt. Cooper's house.   In *Vallejo, Doc.,* MS., vi. 119-23, 335, vii. 249, 404, is found corresp. of the year between Petronilo Rios, com. of the artillery, and Gen. Vallejo respecting improvements in the fortifications, on which work seems to have been done with very slight results.   1840.   Farnham restricts his descriptive matter to the mission, but the pictorial edition of his work (N. Y. 1857) gives on p. 69 what purports to be a view of Monterey, with a huge edifice on the summit of the hills in the distance.   'J. F. B. M.,' *Leaves from My Journal,* describes the new bridge mentioned above, for crossing which on horseback he was arrested and fined $2.   Nov. 12th, P. Gonzalez writes to ask of Vallejo the gift of the old presidio chapel to be used as a town church. *Vallejo, Doc.,* MS., xxxiii. 154.

[3] Summary and index of events at Monterey.   1831. Jan., arrival of Gov. Victoria, who takes the oath of office on the 31st, and has trouble with the ayunt. This vol., pp. 182, 187.   April–May, execution of Anastasio, Águila, and Sagarra for robbery, for which the gov. was blamed. *Id.,* 190-1.   Sept., military trial of Duarte, alcalde of S. José. *Id.,* 195.   Nov., departure of Gov. Victoria to meet the southern rebels. *Id.,* 205.   Dec., Monterey adheres to the S. Diego plan against Victoria. *Id.,* 212.

1832.   Jan.–Feb., Zamorano's pronunciamiento against the S. Diego plan, organization of the compañia extrangera, and Z.'s departure from the south. *Id.,* 220-4.   May–June, Ávila's revolt. *Id.,* 230.

1833.   Jan., arrival of Gov. Figueroa and his assumption of office; also coming of the Zacatecan friars; first printing in Cal. *Id.,* 240-2.   March, election for assembly and congress, repeated in Dec. *Id.,* 246.   April 27th–28th, public diversions, illuminations, bull-fight, ball, etc., to celebrate the peace of Zavaleta. *Dept. St. Pap.,* MS., iii. 114-15.   Weather record by Larkin, 1833-5. This vol., p. 357.   Nov., arrival of Capt. Walker's overland trappers, who pass the winter at Monterey. *Id.,* 390-2; iv. 434.

1834.   The 1st printing-press put in operation, by Zamorano & Co.   It

items are added, but such as require no general remarks.   Leading topics of interest were the troubles
with Governor Victoria in 1831, Zamorano's counter-
revolt and organization of the foreign company in

is not known exactly how the press came, but its products—7 little books and
over 100 documents—are preserved in my library.   The press was carried to
Sonoma by Gen. Vallejo in 1837, after Zamorano's departure, but subsequently returned to Monterey, where it was used by the Americans in 1846.
May–Nov., sessions of the diputacion. This vol., pp. 248–52.   May, scare at
reports of a southern conspiracy. *Id.*, 257.   Sept. 11th, arrival of a courier
from Mex. with orders to Figueroa. *Id.*, 271.   Sept. 12th, return of the gov.
from a tour in the north. *Id.*, 256.   Sept. 25th, arrival of the *Morelos* with
the colony from Mex. *Id.*, 268.   Oct. 14th, arrival of Híjar, and resulting
controversies with the gov. *Id.*, 272 et seq.   Oct. 16th, election of assembly
and member of congress. *Id.*, 258, 291.   Dec. 21st, wreck of the *Natalia. Id.*,
268.   Trouble between Angel Ramirez and Juan Bandini, lasting several
years. *Id.*, 370 et seq.   Hartnell and P. Short perhaps began their educational enterprise this year. *Id.*, 317.

1835.   March–April, ayunt. meets to approve the gov.'s acts in the colony
controversy.   Híjar and Padrés with other prisoners sail from Mex. on the
Rosa. Id., 287–8.   Larkin built a bowling alley at a cost of $438. *Larkin's
Accts.*, MS., ii. 311.   Aug.–Oct., sessions of the assembly. This vol., p. 291.
Sept. 29th–Oct. 2d, death of Gov. Figueroa and funeral ceremonies. *Id.*, 295.
Oct., etc., alarm at the prospect of losing the capital. *Id.*, 291–2.

1836.   April 25th, an earthquake shock at 5 A. M. *Gomez, Diario*, MS.
More shocks June 9–10. *Id.*   Heavy rains. *Vallejo, Doc.*, MS., xxxvi. 214.
May, arrival of Gov. Chico; election and meeting of dip. This vol., p. 421–6.
July, revolution against Chico, preceded by the Castañares-Herrera scandal,
and resulting in the governor's departure July 31st. *Id.*, 429–42.   Sept. 6th,
arrival of Gov. Gutierrez. *Id.*, 445.   Oct. visit of the U. S. man-of-war *Peacock.* Vol. iv. 141.   Oct.–Nov., Alvarado's revolt, overthrow and exile of Gutierrez. This vol., 455–64.   Nov., meeting and acts of the dip. or congress.
Id., 469–76.   Dec., Alvarado and his army march southward. *Id.*, 491.

1837.   Jan.–Feb., threatened movement against the new govt. *Id.*, 511–
13.   May–June, return of Alvarado and Castro; called south again by new
hostilities. *Id.*, 510–11, 522–3.   July, revolt of Ramirez and Peña against Alvarado; capture and recapture of the town; arrest of rebels. *Id.*, 523–6.   Oct.,
visit of the French man-of-war *Venus*, Petit-Thouars com.; news of Cárlos
Carrillo's appointment as gov. *Id.*, 534; vol. iv. 148.   Nov. 19th, wreck of
the *Com. Rodgers. Id.*, 103.   Dec., visit of the British exploring ship *Blossom*, Belcher com. *Id.*, 145–6.

1838.   June–July, Ind. robbers cause much trouble by their depredations
in the district. *Vallejo, Doc.*, MS., xxxii. 146.   Earthquakes. Vol. iv., p.
78, this work.   Aug. 13th the *Catalina*, arrives with news from Mex. favorable to Alvarado. This vol., p. 572.

1839.   Feb.–March, public reception to Alvarado; sessions of the assembly. *Id.*, 584 et seq.   May, elections for congress and junta. *Id.*, 589–90.
July, arrival of J. A. Sutter on the *Clementina*, iv. 127.   Aug., visit of the
French man-of-war *Artemise*, Laplace com. *Id.*, 154–5.   Marriage of the gov.,
and festivities at the capital. This vol., p. 593.   Oct., visit of the chief Solano
and his Indians from Sonoma. *Id.*, 598–9.

1840.   Feb.–May, sessions of the junta; Monterey declared the capital.
Id., 602–6.   March–April, arrest and exile of Graham and other foreigners.
Vol. iv. 1–41.   June, visit of the French *Danaide*, Rosamel, and U. S. *St
Louis*, Forrest. *Id.*, 35–7.   Nov. 30th, a Cal. earthquake reported in Mexico,
but nothing known of it in Cal. *Dept. St. Pap., Mont.*, MS., iv. 43; *Sta B.
Arch.*, MS., 21.

1832, the arrival of Governor Figueroa in 1833, the coming of the colony and the establishment of a printing-office in 1834, troubles with Híjar and Padrés and death of Figueroa in 1835, the coming and going of Chico and Alvarado's revolution in 1836, the Ramirez counter-revolt and the waiting for news of sourthern war and politics in 1837–8, military reform and the governor's marriage in 1839, and the exile of the foreigners to San Blas in 1840. Ordinary local happenings were beneath the dignity of a town so devoted to grand affairs of state.

The military organization was still kept up, but the records are even more fragmentary and confusing than in the past decade, so much so indeed—and naturally enough in connection with frequent changes in the comandancia general, revolutionary movements, calls on volunteer troops or soldiers from another district, and absence of the regular company in southern campaigns—that it is not worth while to attempt the presentment of details either in notes or text. Agustin Zamorano was captain of the company in 1831–6, and José Castro in 1839–40, but Captain José Antonio Muñoz was much of the time comandante of the post in 1833–6, and Lieut-colonel Gumesindo Flores in 1839–40. Gervasio Argüello, lieutenant of the company, was absent in Mexico, and Bernardo Navarrete was acting lieutenant in 1833–6. Rodrigo del Pliego was alférez, departing in 1831; Ignacio del Valle in 1832–6 and perhaps later; José Sanchez in 1832–4; José Antonio Pico from 1836; Rafael Pinto, Jacinto Rodriguez, and Joaquin de la Torre in 1839–40. One of these acted as habilitado. Sergeants named are José A. Solórzano, ayudante de plaza in 1832–3, Francisco Soto, Gabriel de la Torre, and Andrés Cervantes in 1835–6, and Manuel R. Castro in 1840. The company varied very irregularly from 20 to 50 men including inválidos, and the monthly pay-rolls from $570 to $900. There was generally an artillery force of five men under Sergeant José M. Me-

drano in 1831–2, and Petronilo Rios in 1839–40.   An
infantry detachment, the piquete de Hidalgo, numbering about 25 men, was commanded by Lieut Patricio
Estrada until his exile in 1836.[4]   Matters pertaining
to the custom-house, collection of revenues, and financial administration at the capital have been fully set
forth, including lists of officials, in the two chapters
devoted to commerce, finance, and maritime affairs for
the decade.

Matters pertaining to the local government and
the administration of justice are appended at some
length.[5]   The succession of municipal rulers was as

[4] Additional military items.   1831.   71 'militares' with 39 women and
children.   1832.   Hartnell and J. B. Espinosa commanding compañía extrangera.   Lieut Mariano Estrada, Alf. Juan Malarin, and Alf. Fran. Pacheco
called into service.   1833.   Cadet Fran. Araujo, ayudante de plaza.   1836.
José M. Cosío, id.   1837.   Ramon Estrada com. during Alvarado's absence.
José M. Villavicencio and Santiago Estrada also named as com.   References
for military items.   Dept. St. Pap., B. M., MS., lxvi. 17; lxxiii. 12; lxxiv.
4–5; lxxv. 8; lxxvi. 2, 10–11, 53, 111; lxxviii. 4, 7; lxxix. 70, 78, 81; lxxx.
4, 23–4; lxxxi. 23, 26, 44–7, 49; lxxxii. 56, 64–5; lxxxiii. 1, 3–5, 65; lxxxiv.
5; lxxxv. 6; lxxxviii. 31, 36; Vallejo, Doc., MS., i. 286, 291, 293; ii. 196; iii.
190; iv. 80–1; vi. 44–5, 119, 220, 334, 465; vii. 388; viii. 201, 407; xxii. 36;
xxv.–vi. passim; xxxii. 12–13, 58, 74, 103, 201; Pinto, Doc., MS., i. 8–13;
Dept. Rec., MS., ix. 47; xi. 33; S. José Arch., ii. 29; iv. 18; v, 23, 39; St. Pap.,
Sac., MS., xiii. 3–4, 7; xiv. 12–13, 44; Dept. St. Pap., iv. 70, 247; Savage,
Doc., MS., iv. 312; St. Pap., Miss., MS., v. 40; Soberanes, Doc., MS., 130–1,
258.

Dec. 1833.   List of live-stock and implements to be loaned by the missions
for 6 years to form ranchos nacionales for the Mont. and S. F'co companies.
Dept. St. Pap., Ben. C. & T., MS., ii. 79-81.   1834–5, receipts from Soledad
property as above to the amount of $1,513.   Dept. St. Pap., B. M., MS., lxxx.
11.   Nov. 2, 1834.   Gov. orders Simeon Castro and Trinidad Espinosa to leave
the lands held provisionally by them, the same being needed for the national
rancho.   Id., C. & T., iii. 14.   Oct. 1835, controversy between the comp. and
ayunt. for El Toro and S. Francisquito, the ayunt. having claimed the former
and ceded it to Estrada.   Dept. St. Pap., MS., iv. 60–6.

For matters connected with revenue and finance for 1831–5, see chap. xiii.
this vol., and for 1836–40, chap. iii. vol. iv.   The officials successively in
charge at Monterey as administrators of customs, sub-comisarios, and collector, were Joaquin Gomez 1831–2, Mariano Estrada 1832–3, Rafael Gonzalez
1833–4, Angel Ramirez and José M. Herrera 1834–6, Wm E. Hartnell 1837,
Antonio M. Osio, Eugenio Montenegro, and José Abrego 1838–40.   Lieut. P.
Narvaez was capt. of the port 1839–40.

[5] Monterey pueblo officials, municipal government, prefecture, administration of justice, and criminal record.   1831.   Alcalde Antonio Buelna; regidores, Antonio Castro, Juan Higuera, José María Castillo, and Joaquin Alvarado; síndico, José M. Aguilar; secretary, José Castro; depositario, Francisco Pacheco; jueces de campo, Faustino German and Agustin Martinez.
Alcalde auxiliar Salvador Espinosa.   Jan. 10th, appointment of comisionados
for missions of the district.   26th, police regulations in 4 art.   April 11th,
vote against buying a table-cloth and inkstand.   Nov. 27th, preparations for
election, the jurisdiction being divided into 4 manzanas, one including the

follows: Antonio Buelna, Salvador Espinosa, Marcelino Escobar, Manuel Jimeno Casarin, David Spence, José Ramon Estrada, Estévan Munrás, Simeon Cas-

ranchos. Full record of meetings in *Monterey, Actas del Ayunt.*, MS., 23–43. Felipe Arceo for being concerned in the death of Timoteo Lorenzana has to pay $25 to the widow. Gabriel Espinosa sentenced to work 2 months for Mariano Castro for taking his horse. *Mont. Arch.*, MS., vi. 1–2. April, J. M. Ramirez arraigned for death of Gomez. *Dept. Rec.*, MS., ix. 10. April-May, Atanasio, Aguilar, and Sagarra shot for stealing. Sept., several men ask for license to hunt wild cattle in the Gavilan Mts. *Dept. St. Pap., Ben.*, *P. y J.*, MS., iii. 21.

1832. Alcalde, Salvador Espinosa; regidores, Joaquin Alvarado, José M. Castillo, José Aguilar, and Santiago Moreno; síndico, Manuel Jimeno Casarin (excused as not being for 5 years a resident). Only the sess. of Jan. 1st for installation of the new ayunt., *Mont. Actas*, MS., 43–4, and the organization in Dec. for a new election, *Mont. Arch.*, MS., vii. 39, are recorded. In March, on account of non-payment of duties on brandy the school had to be closed.

1833. Alcalde, Marcelino Escobar; regidores, José Aguilar (or Ávila ?) Santiago Moreno, Pedro Castillo (succeeded in Aug. by Simeon Castro, who was unwilling to serve, but was required to do so), and Antonio Romero; síndico, Santiago Estrada; Francisco Perez Pacheco, treasurer; comisario de policía, 1st cuartel, José M. Águila, suplente Antonio de Sta Cruz; 2d cuartel, Ignacio Acedo, supl. Felipe Vasquez; capt. of the port, Juan Malarin. Munic. finance, balance Jan. 1st $68; receipts for year $892; expend, school $238; sec. ayunt. and dip. $325, porter $60, prisoners $188, office exp. of ayunt. $39, miscell. $128, síndico's percentage on receipts $26, Ind. working on the road $29, total $1,036. *Doc. Hist. Cal.*, MS., i. 77–8; *Mont. Arch.*, vii. 40–2. Jan. 4th–11th police regulations in 18 art. *Id.; Dept. St. Pap.*, MS., iii. 159–63; *Id., Mont.*, ii. 13–17. Jan. 10th, division of the town into 2 cuarteles, and appointment of police. *Id.*, 22. Jan. 27th, prosecution of Sergt Solórzano for entering the prison of a woman and causing scandal. *St. Pap. Sac.*, MS., x. 24. March, prisoners have nothing to eat, ayunt. asked for 1 meal per day. *Dept. St. Pap., Ben., P. & J.*, MS., iii. 87. April, a cabin boy of the *Catalina* sent to S. Blas to be tried for assault on the mate. *Id.*, *B. M.*, lxxix. 35–6. July, choice of a regidor to succeed Castillo, who went to S. F. as receptor. *Id., Ben., P. & J.*, v. 43. Sept., estimate of ayunt. expenses for a year $988. *Mont. Arch.*, MS., xvi. 44.

1834. Alcalde Manuel Jimeno Casarin; regidores, Simeon Castro, Antonio Romero, John B. Cooper, and José Joaquin Gomez (from July); síndico José Águila; sec. José M. Maldonado, and later José M. Mier y Teran; capt of the port Malarin. Jan., plans and estimates submitted for casas consistoriales. *Dept. St. Pap., Ben., P. & J.*, MS., vi. 49. Feb., police regulations. *Vallejo, Doc.*, MS., xxxi. 68. Liquor tax in March–April $215. *Dept. St. Pap., B. M.*, MS., lxxvi. 3. May, Marcos Juarez, a soldier, tried by mil. court for robbing the storehouse, and sentenced to 5 years' work at Sta Rosa on the northern frontier. *Id.*, lxxxviii. 22–3. June, Joaquin Alfaro and Gertrudis Garibay accused of murder of the soldier Encarnacion Hernandez. No result recorded. *Id.*, 9–18. A boy put in prison for rape on a child. *St. Pap. Sac.*, MS., xiv. 44. June 28th, boundaries fixed by gov. provisionally, so vaguely as to be of no value. *St. Pap., M. & C.*, MS., ii. 220. Nov., assembly grants a secretary to the ayunt. at $20 salary, the síndico having served. *Leg. Rec.*, ii. 210. A vagrant sentenced to 8 months of 'colonizacion en el territorio.' *Mont. Arch.*, MS., i. 32.

1835. Alcaldes David Spence and Rafael Gonzalez; regidores, John Cooper, Joaquin Gomez, Rafael Gomez, Wm Hartnell, Jesus Vallejo, and Salvador Espinosa. (Fran. P. Pacheco is mentioned in Oct.); síndico, Miguel

tro, and David Spence again.   In 1831–7 an ayuntamiento of one or two alcades, four or six regidores,
and a síndico, was elected each year to serve the

Ávila; sec. Francisco Castillo Negrete to June, José M. Maldonado from
June; alcaldes auxiliaries, Los Ortegas (?) John Gilroy, Pilarcitos Luis Mesa,
Buena Vista Santiago Estrada, Pájaro Antonio Castro, Soledad Nicolás Alviso,
S. Cárlos José Ant. Romero; juecos de policía, José Castañares and Antonio
de Sta Cruz; juez del monte, Santiago Duckworth.   Jueces de campo, Pilarcitos, Francisco Lugo; Alisal, Vicente Cantua; Guadalupe, Guadalupe Cantua; Carneros, Joaquin Soto; La Brea, Antonio German and Faustino German; Las Llagas, Cárlos Castro; Pájaro, Ramon Amez(quita); Monterey,
Felipe García; Laguna Seca, Teodoro Sanchez; Buena Vista, Mariano Estrada,
Salinas, José M. Boronda.   Majordomo of the ayunt., Geo. Allen.   Jan. 3d,
teacher cannot begin work for lack of furniture, etc.   Jan. 5th, police regul.
of the past year adopted.   10th, committee appt. to consider land grants, and
one on schools.   12th, building a jail.   17th, limits of the ejidos, from the
mouth of the river to Pilarcitos, to Laguna Seca, bounds of S. Cárlos to Cañada Honda and the sea.   24th, schools, contributions to be solicited; com. to
form a tariff on wood; regulation of bread; 31st, wood and timber tariff fixed.
Feb. 7th, proposition for a girls' school; a map of the town needed but very
hard to make; appeal to govt for arms to use against cattle-thieves; a record
book for town lots to be obtained; 14th, trouble with the síndico.   28th, J.
B. Alvarado chosen to solicit funds for the girls' school.   March 14th, one
real per day to be paid to a watchman for the prisoners on public works.
28th, a room rented for a sala capitular at $10 per month.   April–May, po-
litical and colony matters chiefly.   June 20th, the church transferred from
the military to municipal care.   July 11th, vote to grant the request of Los
Angeles for a copy of the reglamento as a model, but Angeles must pay the
expense of copying.   18th, action to oblige regular attendance at the 'normal
school.'   Slow progress on the buildings, as the prisoners were not properly
incited to work.   Aug. 1st, José Arana put in charge of the work and prisoners, his salary to be completed by a contribution.   Lumbermen must pay a
tax of 10 per cent on sales.   8th, et seq., land grants approved.   29th, vote
to pay $8 for an ox that died in the service of the ayunt.   Sept. 12th, orga-
nization of militia.   Oct. 3d, com. to provide for a separate burial place for
foreigners.   28th, tiles borrowed to save the unfinished building from ruin by
the rains.   Nov. 7th, serious complaints against the principal of the school
for neglect of his duties and failure to attend to religious instruction.   21st,
Romero the teacher defends himself.   Foreign cemetery selected.   Dec. 5th,
vigorous action to be taken against the horse-thieves, etc.   Town well to be
repaired.   Dec. 18th, extra session to consider the arrest by Capt. Muñoz of
the síndico.   The acts of the ayunt. are recorded in full in *Monterey, Actas del
Ayunt.*, MS., 46–249, it being of course impossible to present a satisfactory
résumé.   I have omitted repetitions of matters noticed here and elsewhere;
internal regulations, and leaves of absence to members; grants of town lands;
and action on about 20 grants of ranchos in the district.   Many of the items
given above are also noticed in other records.   Feb., gov. decides that $20 is
an excessive salary to the sec. *Mont. Arch.*, MS., ix. 3.   June, trial of Julian
Padilla for passing counterfeit onzas. *Id.*, ii. 3–6.   Aug. José de Jesus Berreyesa condemned to 5 years' presidio at Sta Rosa for stealing horses.   Oct.,
controversy between the military and munic. authorities for the possession of
the ranchos El Toro and S. Francisquito.   El Toro had belonged to the garrison, but the ayunt. obtained it (for ejidos) and granted it to Estrada. *Dept.
St. Pap.*, MS., iv. 60–6; *Leg. Rec.*, MS., ii. 224–5.   There is much in the
ayunt. records about the ejidos, but no definite results of discussion are apparent.   Dec., Eugenio Murillo sentenced to Texas for 10 years. *Dept. St.
Pap., Ben., P. & J.*, MS., iii. 47.

1836.   Alcaldes José Ramon Estrada and Marcelino Escobar; regidores

next; but for only 1831 and 1835 are the records of ayuntamiento sessions extant, those of the latter year being especially complete. In 1838 the governor,

Wm Hartnell, Teodoro Gonzalez, (also acting alcalde), Bonifacio Madariaga, and Gil Sanchez (to April); síndico, James Watson; sec., José M. Maldonado; Antonio Lara, alguacil. Jueces de campo Santiago Estrada, Trinidad Espinosa, Feliciano Espinosa, José Arceo, Guadalupe Cantua, Santiago Guat (Jas. Watt?); auxiliaries, Quentin Ortega, José M. Villavicencio, Luis Mesa. Comisarios de policía, José Madariaga, Francisco Soto, José Ábrego, José Pacomio; suplentes, José Sta Cruz, Nicanor Zamora, Gil Cano, Luis Placencia. Ayunt. records not extant. Jan., two couples sentenced to chain-gang and seclusion for illicit intercourse. One of the women was the wife of Cosme Peña. *Mont. Arch.*, MS., vi. 6–7. Two girls of the colony while bathing at Huerta Vieja were carried off by Carmeleño Ind., who were arrested and flogged. *Híjar, Cal.*, MS., 118–19. April, ayunt. allowed to use the assembly chamber temporarily. *Dept. St. Pap., Ben., P. & J.*, MS., iii. 31. Grant of a town lot to Louis Pombert. *Doc. Hist. Cal.*, MS., 1. 255. June, gov. decides that Maldonado may be sec. of ayunt. and assembly. *Leg. Rec.*, MS., iii. 22–3. Aug.–Oct., trial of Corporal Antonio Cadena, of the piquete de Hidalgo, for the murder of private Bárbaro Barragan of the artillery. He was sentenced to 10 years' presidio at Chapala; and a woman in the case to 2 years confinement at S. José mission. *Dept. St. Pap., Ben.*, MS., lxxxii. 29–54; lxxviii. 2–3.

1837. Alcaldes Estévan Munrás and perhaps Marcelino Escobar. Munrás is often mentioned as 2d alcalde, and Escobar is named once in Dec. The only regidores named are Simeon Castro and Bonifacio Madariaga. *Mont. Arch.*, MS., vi. 7; *Dept. St. Pap., Ang.*, MS., ii. 107. Juez de campo Eufemio Soto. Fragmentary police regulations in *Vallejo, Doc.*, MS., xxxii. 60.

1838. Alcaldes (or encargados de justicia) Simeon Castro and Feliciano Soberanes; secretary Florencio Serrano. Jan. 10th (or Aug. 10th) bando of police regulations. *Dept. St. Pap., Mont.*, MS., iii. 66–8; *Sta Cruz Arch.*, MS., 85–6.

1839. Prefect of 1st or Monterey district, with headquarters at S. Juan de Castro, José Castro appointed Feb. 28th, and installed, making a patriotic speech March 10th; salary $2,000. His secretary was José M. Covarrubias. Castro was required to give up the military command. During his temporary absence in May, Juan Ansar, the juez de paz at S. Juan, acted as prefect. *Dept. St. Pap.*, MS., iv. 247–8; xvii. 44; *Id., S. J.*, v. 21. 26, 56; *Id., Mont.*, iii. 78; iv. 4, 78, 81; *Id., Ang.*, x. 12–13; xii. 14; *Id., Ben., P. y J.*, iii. 2; *Id., C. & T.*, iv. 28; *Mont. Arch.*, MS., iv. 4; xvi. 28; *S. José Arch.*, MS., ii. 72; iii. 30–1; *Dept. Rec.*, MS., x. 7; *Unb. Doc.*, MS., 242; *Vallejo, Doc.*, MS., viii. 407; xxxii. 183; *Estudillo, Doc.*, MS., i. 255; *Gomez, Doc.*, MS., 39. Encargados de justicia Castro and Soberanes as before till April. Jueces de paz from May, David Spence and Estévan Munrás; secretary at $300, and collector at commission of 5 per cent, Manuel Castro, juez auxiliar Vicente Cantua. Feb. instructions to comisarios de policía. *Vallejo, Doc.*, MS., xxxii. 176. April, justices fined $20 by gov. for permitting a game of bagatelle on holy days. Fine for benefit of school. *Dept. St. Pap., Mont.*, MS., iv. 12. Alcalde Castro by order of the prefect decides to appoint jueces de paz at Mont., S. Cárlos, Salinas, Natividad or Alisal, S. Cayetano, Carneadero, and S. Luis Obispo ranchos. *Mont. Arch.*, MS., ix. 6. April 29th, elections to take place on May 1st. *Vallejo, Doc.*, MS., vi. 497.

1840. Prefect José Castro until his departure with the Graham exiles in May, after which José M. Villavicencio acted ad interim until August 20th when Tiburcio Castro, father of José, was appointed. Francisco Arce was secretary until Dec., when he was succeeded by Manuel Castañares. *Dept. Rec.*, MS., xi. 16–18, 31, 60; *Arch. Doc.*, MS., 19; *Dept. St. Pap., Mont.*,

having accepted the Mexican central system, abolished the town council and appointed an encargado to serve temporarily until the new organization could be effected; and accordingly in 1839–40 a juez de paz was at the head of affairs. Also in 1839 José Castro was made prefect of the first district with headquarters at San Juan, his father, Tiburcio Castro, succeeding him in 1840. Excepting the Castañares-Herrera cases, noted elsewhere in connection with the political troubles to which they contributed, the administration of justice at Monterey furnishes very little matter that is either interesting or instructive; nevertheless the criminal record with other details of municipal affairs are believed to be worth preserving. Private ranchos[6] mentioned in the records as having

MS., iii. 84; *Id., Ben. P. y J.*, iii. 13; *Mont. Arch.*, MS., ix. 30. Juez de paz David Spence and perhaps Estévan Munrás; juez auxiliar Joaquin Buelna at Pilarcitos; capt. of the port Pedro Narvaez. Simeon Castro is also named as alcalde. April 7th while the town was under martial law on account of the arrest of foreigners Diego Félix murdered his wife and her unborn child, for which crime he was shot by the governor's order within 12 hours. *Vallejo, Doc.*, MS., ix. 108; *Pinto, Apunt.*, MS., 45–9; *Castro, Rel.*, MS., 57–60. July, gov. organizes and instructs a patrol force to protect the district against Ind. and other robbers. *Dept. St. Pap., St. José*, MS., v. 58–60. Aug.–Sept., the jurisdiction of the juez defined as extending to Rio de Soledad, including Alisal, Sauzal, Espinosa's rancho, Bolsa Nueva, all the ranchos of the Salinas, Tucho, to the Carmelo boundary. *Dept. St. Pap., Mont.*, MS., iv. 23; *Mont. Arch.*, MS., ix. 26–7. Dec., owners of shops, etc. must keep a light before their doors till 10 P. M., even if the shop is closed. *Id.*, 30–1; *Dept. Rec.*, MS., xi. 29. Additional references for the list of town officials. *Mont. Arch.*, MS., i. 28; ii. 1, 3, 8, 12; iii. 2–4; v. 1; vi. 3–9, 24; vii. 40, 43, 62–6; ix. 3, 9, 25–7; xi. 12, 14; xvi. 16, 23; *Dept. St. Pap., Mont.*, MS., ii. 21–2; iv. 82; iii. 93; vi. 10, 28, 36, 38; *S. José Arch.*, MS., i. 46–7; ii. 50; iii. 40, 103; iv. 15, 18, 51; v. 32, 39–40; vi. 27, 38; *Dept. St. Pap.*, MS., iii. 95, 162, 167; iv. 249; xiv. 2; xvii. 2, 3; *Id., Ben., P. y J.*, iii. 30, 47–8, 79, 84, 88; vi. 37; *Id., Ben.*, ii. 3; vi. 74, 310; *St. Pap., Miss.*, MS., v. 40; *Id., Sac.*, xi. 69; xii. 10; xiv. 7, 13; *Id., Miss. & Col.*, ii. 229, 235, 353–6; *Leg. Rec.*, MS., i. 348; ii. 262; iii. 22–3; *Gomez, Doc.*, MS., 24–5, 33.

   [6] Ranchos of Monterey district, 1831–40. Those marked with a * were rejected by the land commission or U. S. courts. Aguajito, ½ l., granted in 1835 to Gregorio Tapia, who was the claimant. Aguajito (Sta Cruz Co.), 500 v., 1837, Miguel Villagrana, who was cl. Alisal, 1½ l., 1834, Feliciano Soberanez et al.; B. Bernal cl. In 1836 Soberanes and 37 other persons lived on the rancho. Alisal, ⅔ l., Wm. E. Hartnell, who was cl. Ánimas, or Sitio de la Brea (Sta Clara Co.), 24,000 acres, conf. in 1835 to Josefa Romero de Castro, who was cl. In 1836 she and her family, 16 persons, were living at Las Ánimas. At the same time Antonio German and 32 persons were living at La Brea. See also Cañada de S. Felipe y Las Ánimas. *Arias Rancho, 1 l., 1839, Francisco Arias; A. Canil et al. cl. Aptos (Sta Cruz Co.), 1 l., 1833, Rafael Castro, who was cl. Aromitas y Agua Caliente, 3 l., 1835, Juan M. Ánsar, who was cl. Arroyo de la Laguna (Sta Cruz Co.), 1840, Gil Sanchez;

been granted or occupied during the decade number
about 95, the population of which, at the end, as already noted, was about 550 souls, or about one third

J. and S. Williams cl. Arroyo de la Purísima, see Cañada Verde. Arroyo
del Rodeo (Sta Cruz Co.), 1¼ l., 1834, Fran. Rodriguez; J. Hames et al. cl.,
Arroyo Seco, 4 l., 1840, Joaquin de la Torre, who was cl. Ballena, see Rincon de Ballena. Bolsa Nueva y Moro Cojo, 8 l., 1825, 1836-7, 1844, Simeon
Castro; M. Antonia Pico de Castro, cl. Bolsa del Pájaro (Sta Cruz Co.), 2 l.,
1837, Sebastian Rodriguez, who was cl. Bolsa, see also S. Cayetano, S. Felipe, Escorpinas, and Chamisal. Brea, see Ánimas. Buena Esperanza, see
Encinal. Buenavista, 2 l., 1822-3, Santiago and José Mariano Estrada; Mariano Malarin, Attorney for Estrada, and David Spence cl. The Estrada
brothers with families, 34 persons, lived here in 1836. Butano (Sta Cruz Co.),
1 l., 1838, 1844, Ramona Sanchez; M. Rodriguez cl. Calabazas, see Cañada
de C. Cañada Honda, 1835, Angel Ramirez. Leg. Rec., MS., ii. 225; Mont.,
Actas del Ayunt., MS., 114. Not brought before the L. C. Cañada de S.
Felipe y las Ánimas, 1839, Thomas Bowen; C. M. Weber cl. Cañada de la
Segunda, 1 l., 1839, Lázaro Soto; A. Randall et al. cl. Cañada Verde, 1836,
mentioned by Janssens, Vida, MS., 67-8, as having been granted by Gov. Chico
to Francisco Castillo Negrete, but the grant was not completed on account of
the political troubles. Cañada Verde y Arroyo de la Purísima (Sta Cruz Co.), 2
l., 1838, José M. Alviso; J. A. Alviso cl.; Carbonera (Sta Cruz Co.), ½ l., 1838,
Wm Buckle, who was cl. Carneros, 1 l., 1834. David Littlejohn, whose heirs
were cl. * Chamizal, 1 l., 1835, Felipe Vasquez, whose heirs were cl. Approved by the ayunt. in 1835. Chamizal (Bolsa de), 1837, Francisco Quijada;
L. T. Burton cl. Chualar (Sta Rosa de), 2 l., 1839, Juan Malarin, whose executor was cl. Joaquin and Francisco Estrada with 2 servants lived on the
rancho in 1836. * Corral de Padilla, 2,000 v., 1836, Baldomero; M. Antonia
Pico de Castro cl. Corral de Tierra, 1836, Guadalupe Figueroa; H. D. Mc-
Cobb cl. Corralitos (Sta Cruz Co.) not yet granted, but occupied in 1836 by
Ignacio Coronel and family, 12 persons in all. Encinal y Buena Esperanza, 3
l., 1834, 1839, David Spence, who was cl. Vicente Félix as majordomo with
5 others living here in 1836. Escorpinas (Escarpinas or Escorpiones ?) 2 l.,
1837, Salvador Espinosa, who was cl. * Espíritu Santo (Loma), 1839, M.
del E. S. Carrillo, who was cl. Los Gatos, or Sta Rita, 1 l., 1820, 1837, José
Trinidad Espinosa, whose heirs were cl. Guadalupe, 1840, D. Olivera and
T. Arellanes, who were cl. Guadalupe or Llanito de los Correos, 2 l., 1833,
Juan Malarin, whose executor was cl.; occupied in 1836 by Guadalupe Cantua
as majordomo and 8 persons. Laguna, see Arroyo de la L. Laguna de las
Calabazas (Sta Cruz Co.), 2 l. 1833, Felipe Hernandez; C. Morse, cl. Laguna
Seca, 1½ l., 1834, C. M. de Munrás, who was cl.; occupied in 1836 by Teo-
doro Moreno as majordomo and 6 others. Laureles, 1½ l., 1839, J. M. Boronda et al., who were cl.; the grant of Cañada de Laureles to José Ant. Romero was approved by the ayunt. in 1835. Llagas, 6 l., 1834, Cárlos Castro;
Murphy cl. (Sta Clara Co.), Cárlos and Guillermo Castro with 11 other
persons lived on the rancho in 1836. Llano de Tequisquite, ½ l., 1835, J. M.
Sanchez, who was cl. Llano, see Buenavista. Llanito, see Guadalupe. Loma,
see Espíritu Santo. Milpitas, 1838, Ignacio Pastor, who was cl. Moro Cojo,
see Bolsa Nueva. Rancho Nacional, 2 l., 1839, Vicente Cantua who was cl.;
occupied in 1836 by Francisco Mesa as majordomo and 7 others. The Huerta
de la Nacion was asked for in 1835 by Capt. J. A. Muñoz, and approved by
the ayunt. Natividad, 2 l., 1837, Manuel Butron and Nicolás Alviso; Ramon
Butron et al. cl. M. Burton and others, 29 in all, lived on the rancho in 1836.
Noche Buena (Huerta de la Nacion ?), 1 l., 1835, José Ant. Muñoz; José and
Jaime de Puig Monmany (?) cl. Ojitos, see Poza. Pájaro, see Vega del Rio;
also Bolsa del P. Palo de Yesca, see Shoquel. Parage de Sanchez, 1½ l.,
1839, Francisco Lugo; Juana Briones de Lugo cl. Patrocinio (Alisal ?), occu-

of the total population of the district. Excepting, however, the padron of 1836, showing the names and numbers of inhabitants at that time, we have no sat-

pied in 1836 by Hartnell, P. Short, and 13 colegiales with servants, etc., 44 persons in all. Pescadero, 1 l. 1836, Fabian Baretto, who was cl. Pescadero or S. Antonio (Sta Cruz Co.), ¾ l., 1833, Juan José Gonzalez, who was cl. Piedra Blanca (S. Luis Obispo Co.), 1840, Jesus Pico, who was cl. Pilarcitos; expediente of Gabriel Espinosa in 1835. *Doc. Hist. Cal.*, MS., i. 485; grant of a tract to Luis Mesa approved by ayunt. in 1835; occupied in 1836 by José M. Arceo, Gregorio Tapia, and others, 40 in all; not before L. C. Pismo, 2 l., 1840, José Ortega; Isaac Sparks cl., in S. Luis Obispo Co. Potrero, see S. Cárlos; also S. Pedro. Poza de los Ositos, 4 l. 1839, Cárlos C. Espinosa, who was cl. Puente del Monte, see Rincon. Punta de Pinos, 2 l., 1833, 1844, José M. Armenta, José Ábrego; J. P. Leese cl. Purísima, see Cañada Verde. * Quien Sabe, 6 l., 1836, Fran. Castillo Negrete, who was cl. (S. Joaquin Co.) * Refugio (Sta Cruz Co.), 1839, María de los Angeles Castro et al.; J. L. Majors cl. *Rincon de la Ballena (Sta Cruz Co.), 1 l., 1839, José C. Bernal; S. Rodriguez cl. Rincon de la Puente (Punta?) del Monte, 7 l. 1836, Teodoro Gonzalez, who was cl. In 1835 the grant to Felipe Agulla was approved by the ayunt. Rincon, see Salinas, also S. Pedro. Rinconada del Zanjon, 1½ l., 1840, Eusebio Boronda, who was cl. Rosario, see S. Francisco. Rodeo, see Arroyo del R. Rosa Morada, see S. Joaquin. Sagrada familia, see Bolsas. Salinas, 1 l., 1836, Gabriel Espinosa, who was cl. Salinas (Rincon) ¼ l., 1833, Cristina Delgado; Ramon Estrada cl. In 1836 Salinas was occupied by José M. Boronda, Blas Martinez, and others, 78 persons in all. Salsipuedes (Sta Cruz Co.) 8 l., 1834, 1840, Manuel Jimeno Casarin; James Blair et al. cl. San Andrés (Sta Cruz Co.), 2 l., 1833, Joaquin Castro; G. Castro cl. S. Antonio, occupied in 1836 by José Ant. Castro and family, 15 persons. The identity of this rancho is uncertain. See also Pescadero. S. Bernabé, see S. Justo. S. Bernardo, 1 l., 1840, Vicente Cané, who was cl. S. Cárlos (Potrero), 1 l., 1837, Fructuoso; J. Gutierrez cl. S. Cayetano (Bolsa), 2 l., 1824, 1834, Ignacio Vallejo; J. J. Vallejo cl. In *Doc. Hist. Cal.*, MS., i. 123, are some papers relating to the Pico claim on this rancho. Jesus Vallejo and 15 persons occupied the rancho in 1836. S. Felipe, 3 l., 1836, F. D. Pacheco; F. P. Pacheco cl. S. Felipe (Bolsa) 2 l., 1840, F. D. Pacheco; F. P. Pacheco cl.; occupied in 1836 by Rafael de la Mota and 7 others. S. Francisco del Rosario, occupied in 1836 by Angel Castro and 13 other persons (perhaps Paicines granted to Castro in 1842). S. Francisquito, 2 l., 1835, Catalina M. de Munrás; José Ábrego cl. Occupied in 1836 by Juan Rosales as majordomo with family, etc., 9 persons. S. Gregorio (Sta Cruz Co.), 4 l., 1839, Antonio Buelna; E. Buelna et al. cl. S. Isidro, 1 l., 1833, Quintin Ortega, who was cl. (Sta Clara Co.) Occupied in 1836 by Ortega and 37 persons. S. Joaquin or Rosa Morada, 2 l., 1836, Cruz Cervantes, who was cl. *S. José y Sur Chiquito, 2 l., 1839, Marcelino Escobar; J. Castro cl. The grant of Sur Chiquito to Teodoro Gonzalez was approved by the ayunt. in 1835. S. Juan y Cajon de Sta Ana, 1837, Juan P. Ontiveros, who was cl. S. Justo, 4 l., 1839, José Castro; F. P. Pacheco cl. *S. Justo el Viejo y S. Bernabé, 6 l., 1836, Rafael Gonzalez; Ellen E. White et al. cl. S. Matías, occupied in 1836 by Joaquin Soto and family, 14 persons (not in L. C. cases under this name; Soto was granted El Piojo and Cañada de Carpentería later). S. Miguel, occupied in 1836 by Trinidad and Salvador Espinosa, 21 persons (the grant of Cañada de S. Miguel to José M. Andrade was approved by the ayunt. in 1835). *S. Pedro, Potrero y Rincon de (Sta Cruz Co.), 1838, José R. Buelna. *S. Vicente (Sta Cruz Co.), 2 l., 1839, Antonio Rodriguez, who was cl. S. Vincente, 2 l., 1835, Francisco Soto and S. Munrás; Concepcion Munrás et al. cl. (Las Pozas was approved to Soto in 1835 by the ayunt.) *Sta Ana y Sta Anita (S. Joaquin Co.), 6 l., 1836, Francisco Castillo Negrete; Josefa M. de C. N. cl. Sta Ana, see S.

isfactory statistics nor any record of events at the ranchos beyond the occasional mention of a few in connection with general annals of the territory.

Padre Ramon Abella remained in charge of Mission San Cárlos until 1833, when he was succeeded by the Zacatecan José María del Refugio Sagrado Suarez del Real. There is extant neither record of secularization or other events, nor statistical information for any part of the decade; but I append the few scattered items that can be found.[7] Seculariza-

Juan. Sta Cruz Co. ranchos, see Aguajito, Aptos, Arroyo de la Laguna, Arroyo del Rodeo, Bolsa del Pájaro, Butano, Cañada Verde, Carbonera, Corralitos, Laguna de Calabazas, Pescadero, Refugio, Rincon de la Ballena, Salsipuedes, S. Andrés, S. Gregorio, S. Pedro, S. Vincente, Sayante, and Shoquel. Sta Manuela, 1837, Francis Branch, who was cl. (S. Luis Obispo Co.) Sta Rita, see Los Gatos. Sta Rosa, see Chualar. Saucito, 1½ l., 1833, Graciano Manjares; J. Wilson et al. cl.; occupied by M. and fam., 8 persons, in 1836. Sauzal, 2 l., 1834, 1845, José Tiburcio Castro; J. P. Leese, cl.; occupied in 1836 by Martin Olivera and fam., 19 persons in all. *Sayante (Sta Cruz Co.), 3 l., 1833, Joaquin Buelna; N. Cathcart cl. Shoquel and Palo de Yesca (Sta Cruz Co.), 4 l., 1833-4, 1844. Martina Castro, who was cl. Sur, 2 l., 1834, J. B. Alvarado; J. B. R. Cooper cl. Sur Chiquito, see S. José. Toro, 1½ l., 1835, Ramon Estrada; C. Wolters cl.; much trouble about the right of the ayunt. to grant this rancho, which was claimed by the military company. Trinidad, occupied by Sebastian Rodriguez, etc., 40 persons in 1836 (not before L. C. under this name; but Rodriguez was granted 2 ranchos in Sta Cruz Co.) Tucho, occupied by Cruz Cervantes majordomo and 10 others in 1836; parts of the rancho granted after 1840; the grant to Manuel Boronda and Blas Martinez approved by ayunt. in 1835. Tularcitos, 6 l., 1834, Rafael Gomez, whose widow was cl. Vega del Rio del Pájaro, 8,000 acres, 1820. Ant. M. Castro; J. M. Ánzar cl.; not mentioned in this decade. Verjeles, 2 l., 1835, José Joaquin Gomez; J. C. Stokes cl.; occupied in 1836 by 14 persons, Eusebio Boronda being majordomo. Yesca, see Shoquel. Zanjones, 1½ l., 1839, Gabriel de la Torre; Mariano Malarin cl. Zanjon, see also Rinconada. Also the following ranchos without names: Antonio Romero, 1840; Jas Meadows cl. Francisco Perez Pacheco, 2 l., 1833, id. cl. *Hermenegildo, 500 v., 1835, Id. cl. Manuel Larios, 1 l., 1839; Id. cl. Mariano Castro, 1839; Rufina Castro cl. Estévan Espinosa, ¼ l., 1840; Henry Cocks cl. Ranchos approved by the ayunt. in 1835 and not mentioned above; Los Pajines, or Paicines, to Angel Castro; not named, near Soledad, to José Cantor; Chichiguas, near S. Juan B., to Rafael Gonzalez; not named, S. Luis Cbispo region, to Simeon Castro. See *Hoffman's Reports* and *Monterey, Actas del Ayunt.*, MS.

[7] San Cárlos events. 1831. Provisions of Echeandía's decree, or the Padrés plan, never carried into effect; Manuel Crespo being appointed comisionado; visit of Gov. Victoria; robbery of the mission storehouse by Aguilar and Sagarra. This vol., p. 183, 190, 305-7. 1832-3. No record except of the change of padres in the latter year. P. Duran favored the partial secularization. *Id.*, 319, 335. 1834. No record of secularization. July 8th, the assembly permits a moderate slaughter of cattle to pay debts. *Leg. Rec.*, MS., ii. 148. The majordomo forbidden by the gov. to punish Ind., some of them having complained of being beaten. *Dept. St. Pap., Ben.*,

tion was effected in 1834–5, Joaquin Gomez being comisionado, succeeded by José Antonio Romero as majordormo. There was but little mission property left in 1834, and none at all except the ruined buildings in 1840. The neophytes numbered about 150 at the time of secularization, and I suppose there were 30 left in Carmelo Valley at the end of the decade, with perhaps 50 more in private service in town or on the ranchos.

At San Luis Obispo, the southernmost mission of the district, Padre Gil y Taboada continued to serve as minister till his death at the end of 1833, in which

MS., v. 38–40. Joaquin Gomez was probably appointed comisionado this year. This vol., p. 354. 1835. José Ant. Romero administrator put in charge by Gomez, according to Torre, *Remin.*, MS., 37–8, who says that the Ind. rapidly got rid of their share of the live-stock, and that Romero stocked his own rancho with the mission cattle and sheep. July. Gov. Figueroa's plan to establish a mission rancho of 600 cattle, 1,000 sheep, and a few horses for the support of the padres and worship; but the president declined to permit the friars to take charge of such an establishment. This vol. p. 351; *St. Pap. Miss. and Colon.*, MS., ii. 334–5. July 31st, P. Real asks the gov. to order the majordomo to detail the horses for his ministerial duties as agreed on by the gov. and president. *Id.*, 339. 1836. Ruschenberger, *Narr.*, ii. 407, visited S. Cárlos, and describes the mission as in ruins and nearly abandoned; though he found 8 or 10 Ind. at work repairing the roof. 1837. Petit-Thouars, *Voyage*, ii. 113 et seq., gives a melancholy description of the prevalent dilapidation; but he found P. Real, who 'fit les honneurs de ses ruines,' and two or three families of Ind., who lived in the mission buildings, living on shell-fish and acorns. 1838. No record. 1839. Juan Rosales, juez de paz. Marcelino Escobar juez interino in March. March 11th, inventory of buildings, 25 rooms, apparently turned over by P. Real to Escobar, the padre's habitation and other rooms being reserved as church property. *Dept. St. Pap.*, MS., xvii. 5–6. April 10th, prefect to juez; an Ind. must return and live with his wife. *Doc. Hist. Cal.*, MS., i. 406. Oct. 5. Mission owes $160 to Escobar and Rafael Gonzalez. *Pico, Pap. Mis.*, MS., 47–51. Laplace, *Campagne*, vi. 294, gives a view of the mission as it was in this year. 1840. Nov. 11th, gov. orders the encargado to surrender to Jesus Molino some lands, house, etc., held by José Aguila. *Dept. Rec.*, MS., xi. 48. Farnham visited and described the forsaken buildings of 'San Carmelo.' According to the reglamento of this year, the govt was to continue to manage S. Cárlos 'according to circumstances.' Vol. iv., p. 60.

Statistics of S. Cárlos 1831–4, entirely lacking. Statistics of 1770–1834 (only estimates for the last four years). Total of baptisms, 3,957, of which 1,790 adult Ind.; 1,306 Ind. children; 17 and 838 de razon; annual average of Ind. 49. Total of marriages 1,065, of which 199 de razon. Deaths, 2,885, of which 1,365 Ind. adults; 1,137 Ind. children; 194 and 189 de razon; annual average 38; average death rate 8.17 per cent. of pop. Largest pop., 921 in 1794; sexes very nearly equal; children 1-3 to 1-5. Largest no. of cattle, 3,000 in 1819–21; horses, 1,024 in 1806; mules, 76 in 1786; sheep, 7,000 in 1805–12; goats, 400 in 1793; swine, 25 in 1783; all kinds, 9,749 animals in 1809. Total production of wheat, 43,120 bush., yield 10 fold; barley, 55,300 bush., 15 fold; maize, 23,700 bush., 56 fold; beans, 24,000 bush., 25 fold.

year Padre Ramon Abella came down from the north to take his place, remaining throughout the decade. Padre Felipe Arroyo de la Cuesta was Abella's associate in 1833–5.[8] The statistical record of San Luis is comparatively complete, and shows that down to 1834 the establishment lost but slightly in population, having 264 neophytes in that year; gained somewhat in live-stock, especially in sheep; but had little success in agricultural operations.[9] After the secu-

[8] Luis Gil y Taboada was one of the few Mexican Fernandinos, though of Spanish parentage and himself intensely Spanish in feeling. He was born at Guanajuato, May 1, 1773, becoming a Franciscan at Pueblito de Querétaro in 1792, joining the S. Fernando college in 1800, and being sent to Cal. in 1801. He served as a missionary at S. Francisco in 1801–2, 1804–5, 1819–20; at S. José in 1802–4, Sta Inés in 1806–10, Sta Bárbara in 1810–12, S. Gabriel in 1813–14, Purísima in 1815–17, S. Rafael in 1817–19, Sta Cruz in 1820–30, and S. Luis Obispo in 1820, 1830–3. His superiors gave him credit for more than average merit, noting the fact that he saved many souls by the Cæsarean operation, but he was often in bad health. *Autobiog. Autog. de los Padres*, MS.; *Sarría, Inf. sobre Frailes, 1817*, MS., 54–5; *Payeras Inf. de 1820*, MS., p. 137–8. In 1814 he blessed the corner-stone of the Los Angeles church; in 1816 he asked leave to retire, having more than fulfilled his contract with the king in 16 years of service, ' que le han parecido otros tantos siglos; in 1817 was the founder of S. Rafael, being thus the first to introduce christianity north of the bay; in 1821 he was asked to become pastor of Los Angeles, declining on account of ill health; again in 1825 and 1830 he tried hard to get a license for departure; and in 1833, while recognizing his destiny to die in the country, he declared that he was tired of mission affairs. It was at his own request and against the wishes of P. Jimeno that he was given charge of S. Luis. He was a man of much nervous energy and considerable executive ability, with a certain skill in medicine and surgery, and a knowledge of several Indian languages. To his neophytes he was indulgent and was well liked by them, being very free and familiar in his relations with them—somewhat too much so in the case of the women it is said, and it is charged that his infirmities of body were aggravated by syphilitic complications. In 1821 he was accused of improper intimacy with a married woman who often visited his room and was found in his bed by the husband under circumstances hardly explained by the padre's plea of services as amateur physician; but his superiors were inclined to regard him as innocent, though imprudent. *Arch. Arzob.*, MS., xii. 360–1. In Dec. 1833, at the rancho of Sta Margarita where he had gone to say mass for the Ind. occupied in planting, he was attacked by dysentery and vomiting of blood, and died on the 15th. He was buried next day in the mission church on the gospel side near the presbytery, by P. Juan Cabot. *Guerra, Doc.*, MS., i. 246–7.

[9] Statistics of S. Luis Obispo 1831–4. Decrease in pop. 283 to 264. Baptisms 26; 9 in 1831; 4 in 1832. Deaths 115; 38 in 1832; 19 in 1834. Increase in large stock 3,740 to 3,800; horses and mules 1,540 to 800; sheep 1,000 to 3,440. Largest crop 900 bush. in 1834; smallest 556 in 1833; average 745 bush., of which 490 wheat, yield 8 fold; 12 barley, 3 fold; 105 maize, 30 fold; 27 beans, 7 fold; and 115 of various grains, 30 fold.

Statistics of 1772–1834. Total of baptisms 2,657, of which 1,277 Ind. adults, 1,331 Ind. children, 49 children de razon; annual average 42. Total of marriages 775, of which 23 de razon; annual average 12. Total of deaths 2,318, of which 1,429 Ind. adults, 877 Ind. children, 4 and 8 de razon; annual

larization the number of neophytes was gradually reduced to 170 at the end of the decade; and live-stock
decreased about 50 per cent in the five years, only

average 32; average death rate 7.30 per cent. of pop. Largest pop. 852 in
1803. Males in excess to 1798, females later; children ⅓ to ⅔ and even less
at last. Largest no. of cattle 8,900 in 1818; horses 1,594 in 1799; mules 340
in 1830; asses 134 in 1817; sheep 11,000 in 1813; goats 515 in 1786; swine
210 in 1788; all kinds 20,820 animals in 1813. Total product of wheat
116,161 bush., yield 11 fold; barley 1,375 bush., 4 fold; maize 26,923 bush.,
104 fold; beans 3,595, 22 fold; miscell. grains 3,156 bush., 20 fold.

Statistics of 1835-40. Feb. 5, 1835, pop. 253. *St. Pap., Miss.*, MS., x. 9.
April 28, 1835, P. Abella gave letters of attorney to A. M. Ercilla to collect
of U. Sanchez, Mazatlan, $9,390 due the mission. *Guerra, Doc.*, MS., iii. 17.
Dec. 13, 1836. Inventory of the estate; buildings, goods, produce, tools, etc.
$13,458; live-stock $19,109; fábrica, $5,000, garden $6,858; Sta Margarita
rancho $4,039; 9 sitios of land $9,000; church and ornaments $7,257; library
and musical instruments $519; credits $5,257 (besides the $9,390 due from
Urbano Sanchez as above); total $70,769. Increase over inventory of 1835,
$7,657, besides $100 given to troops, $333 debts paid, and $1,285 in cloths
etc. to Ind., total gain $9,376. No debt mentioned. *St. Pap., Miss.*, MS.,
vii. 57-9. Jan. 1837, admin. ordered by Gen. Castro to deliver $1,200 in
produce, and there are other similar orders of smaller amounts. *Id.*, 65.
March 19th, credits $5,884; debts $776. *Id.*, 57. Jan. 1839, credits $343;
debts $2,304; inventory $61,163. *Id.*, 60-3. July 30th, Hartnell's inventory,
etc.; pop. 170; 1,684 cattle, 1,200 horses, 2,500 sheep, 16 mules; 157 hides,
53 arr. tallow, 21 arr. lard, 300 arr. iron, 100 arr. wool, 388 fan. grain, etc.
Id., 59-60; *Hartnell, Diario*, MS., 24. Debts to 5 persons $987. *Pico, Pap.,
Mis.*, MS., 47-51.

Record of events. 1831. Status under Echeandia's decree of no effect,
except that J. B. Alvarado was appointed comisionado, and a comisario apparently chosen. This vol. p. 306-7. 1833. Mules stolen by N. Mexicans.
Id., 396. Lat. and long. observed by Douglas. *Id.*, 404. Death of P. Gil.
Two neophytes robbed the church and shops, confessing the crime; but during the trial one died and the other escaped. *Dept. St. Pap., B. M.*, MS.,
lxxvi. 53-6. April, Isidro Ibarra reports to gov. that the N. Mex. sell liquor
to the Ind. and insult him. Needs a guard, else he will have to shoot somebody. *Id.*, lxxix. 28-9. 1834. Part of the colony here. This vol. p. 267.
S. Luis to be a parish of the 2d class under the reglamento. *Id.*, 384. 1835.
Secularization in Oct. by Manuel Jimeno as comisionado, Santiago Moreno
being at the same time appointed majordomo, or administrator. *St. Pap.,
Miss.*, MS., ix. 14-15. 1836. Manuel Trujillo, administrator until Dec. 13th,
when Moreno again takes charge (or perhaps Moreno had not accepted the
appointment in 1835, Trujillo taking his place). *Id.*, vii. 57, 61, 63. In Sept.
the Ind. had trouble with Trujillo and several of them went to Monterey to
lay their grievances before the govt in a long memorial written by P. Mercado
at S. Antonio and signed by them with crosses on Oct. 5th. The document
represented the neophytes as living in slavery, being grossly ill-treated,
starved, and overworked, naming several instances where women had died
for want of a little atole. Several Ind., however, came from S. Luis to testify that the charges were false; and finally the complainants themselves testified to the same effect. They said they had a very different complaint about
some cattle, which the padre advised them to lay before the govt. P. Abella
came with them to S. Antonio where P. Mercado wrote out their complaint,
as they supposed, and obtained their signatures. They were much surprised
to learn the nature of the document they had signed! *Carrillo (J.), Doc.*, MS.,
35-6, 39-45 (including the original memorial); *Dept. St. Pap., B. M.*, MS.,
lxxxii. 9-27. 1838. Moreno still in charge. Some of Castro's prisoners sent

horses showing an increase, and all the horses being stolen by New Mexican 'traders' in 1840. Most of the cattle however were wild, and only slight reliance was placed in agriculture. The inventory showed a valuation of about $70,000 in 1836, and $60,000 in 1839, after which there are indications that the loss was rapid. Secularization was effected in 1835 by Manuel Jimeno Casarin, whose successors as major-domos or administrators were Manuel Trujillo in 1835–6, Santiago Moreno in 1836–9, Juan P. Ayala in 1839–40, and Vicente Cané from November 1840.

At San Miguel, the next mission proceeding north-ward, Padre Juan Cabot remained at his post until his departure from California in 1835, and his succes-sor Juan Moreno until after 1840. Padre Arroyo de la Cuesta, of San Luis, spent much of his time here in 1833–5, as did Padre Abella in 1839-40.[10] Under

here. This vol., p. 555. June, P. Abella represents affairs as in a bad way; there are some gentiles that might be converted if there was any inducement in the shape of food and clothing. *Guerra, Doc.*, MS., vii. 55. Oct. 5th, admin. complains of the insolence of the native alcaldes. Needs a guard. *St. Pap., Mis.*, MS., ix. 74–5. Nov., complaints of robberies by Ind. and Eng-lishmen. *Vallejo, Doc.*, MS., v. 220. 1839. Moreno is succeeded in May by Juan P. Ayala. *St. Pap., Mis.*, MS., vii. 61; ix. 74–6; *Dept. Rec.*, x. 10. A. was also encargado de justicia. Victor Linares was made majordomo under Ayala in May, but removed in Oct. by Hartnell's advice to save his salary of $20 and the cost of supporting his large fam. H. in July found the Ind. very content, but fearful of losing the rancho which Sra Filomena Pico de Pombert had asked for. H. authorized the slaughter of 200 bulls for the purchase of clothing. *Id.*, x. 8; *Hartnell, Diario*, MS., 4, 25, 33, 46. S. Luis was the southern boundary of the 1st district. This vol., p. 585. 1840. Ayala was succeeded by Vicente Cané in Nov. *Dept. Rec.*, MS., xi. 46. Feb., 120 mares exchanged for 60 cattle. *Vallejo, Doc.*, MS., ix. 50. Death of Angel Ramirez at S. Luis. This vol., p. 587. April, stealing of 1,200 mis-sion horses by the Chaguanosos. Vol., iv. p. 77. Nov. 19th, gov. to encar-gado; Ind. must prepare to unite with those of S. Miguel (?). *Dept. Rec.*, MS., xi. 43. Sept. 11th, Hartnell's visit. He found the Ind. desirous of being left under the padre's care. *Diario*, MS., 93. Ávila, *Cosas de Cal.*, MS., 24–5, says that under Cané's care the mission went entirely to ruin. $6,000 was Douglas' estimate of exports from S. Luis and Purísima. Vol. iv. p. 80. In *Mellus' Diary*, MS., 6–7, is described a cave at the anchorage used by the dealers in hides and tallow.

[10] Juan Cabot, a brother of Padre Pedro Cabot, was born at Buñola, Isl. of Mallorca, in June 1781, becoming a Franciscan at Palma in 1796, coming to Mexico in 1804 and to Cal. in 1805. He served at Purísima in 1805–6, at S. Miguel in 1807–19, at S. Francisco in 1819–20, at Soledad in 1821–4, and again at S. Miguel in 1824–35. Rated by his superiors as a zealous mission-ary of medium capacity. *Autobiog. Autog. de los Padres*, MS., *Sarría, Inf. de 1817*, MS., 58–9; *Payeras Inf. 1820*, MS., 133–4. Robinson, *Life in Cal.*, 84, describes him as a tall, robust man with the rough frankness of a sailor, cele-

the ministrations of these friars the neophyte population fell off from 684 to 599 in 1834, and to 350 or
less in 1840.   There was a gain in cattle and not a
very marked loss in crops down to the date of secularization;[11] but later the falling-off was much more

brated for his good humor and hospitality.   Indeed he was known as 'el marinero' in contrast with his dignified brother Pedro, 'el caballero.'   In 1814
he made a tour among the gentile tribes of the Tulares, and his narrative appears in my list of authorities.   He tried unsuccessfully to get a license to
retire in 1819; in 1820–1 served as secretary to Prefect Payeras in his tour of
inspection; and in 1826 declined to take the oath to republicanism.   More
fortunate than his brother, Fray Juan at last secured his passport.   Dec. 20,
1834, Gov. Figueroa orders the payment of $400 to the friar, who after 30
years' service is about to return to his own country, proposing to embark on
the *California. Dept. St. Pap.*, B. M., MS., lxxix. 52.   He probably departed
early in 1835.   According to an article in the *S. F. Bulletin*, April 25, 1864,
Padre Cabot was heard of in Spain by Bishop Amat in 1856 and died a little
later.

[11] S. Miguel statistics of 1831–4.   Decrease of pop. 684 to 599.   Baptisms
152 (including 26 adults in 1834); largest no. 94 in 1834; smallest 12 in 1832.
Deaths 253; largest no. 87 in 1834; smallest 32 in 1832.   Increase in large
stock 4,960 to 5,140; horses, etc. 1,120 to 920; sheep, etc., 7,506 to 5,931.
Largest crop 2,044 bush. in 1832; smallest 1,087 bush. in 1831; average 1,638
bush., of which 715 bush. wheat, yield 6.4 fold; 480 barley, 11 fold; 168 maize,
32 fold; 37 beans, 8 fold; 135 miscell. grain, 21 fold.

Statistics of 1835–40.   Inventory of March 20, 1837; main buildings of
the mission cuadro $37,000; rancheria or Indians' houses, 74 rooms, of adobes
and tile roofs, $3,000; goods in warehouse, implements, furniture, and manu-
facturing outfit, $5,043; garden with 166 vines and fence, $584; ranchos, S.
Simeon, Sta Rosa, Paso de Robles, and Asuncion, with buildings $10,211;
vineyards of Aguage and Sta Isabel with 5,500 vines, $22,162; live-stock (in-
cluding $2,400 in wild cattle at La Estrella) $20,782; crops growing $387;
credits $906; total $82,806; debts $231. *St. Pap., Miss.*, MS., viii. 24–6.   Jan.
31, 1839, administrator's account for 1837–8; inventory on taking charge
$79,268 (why not $82,806?), additions to goods in store $6,092, supplied to
troops (?) $9,001, cellar $807, cattle $1,340, total charged $96,508; paid to
employés, etc., $4,748, supplies to neophytes of home products $4,381, id. foreign goods $2,030, house expenses $1,302, paid out for goods and produce
$4,469, live-stock purchased $3,457, total credited $20,588; balance, or present
valuation $75,919.   As will be noticed this account is not wholly intelligible.
By the end of June the valuation had been reduced to $74,763.   Salary list;
admin. $800, clerk $240, two majordomos each $144, total $1,328; credits in
Jan. $278; debts $947.   Population in Jan. 525 at the mission and 75 absent.
Id., 16–23.   Aug. 1839, Hartnell's census and inventory.   Pop. 361 souls;
990 cattle, 249 horses, 3,800 sheep, 28 mules, 52 asses, 46 goats, 44 swine, 700
fan. grain, etc. *Hartnell, Diario*, MS., 25; *St. Pap., Miss.*, MS., viii. 15.

Statistics of 1797–1834.   Total of baptisms 2,588, of which 1,285 Ind.
adults, 1,277 Ind. children, 26 children de razon; annual average of 67.
Total of deaths 2,038, of which 1,225 Ind. adults, 796 Ind. children, 6 and 11
de razon; annual average 53; average death rate 6.91 per cent of pop.   Largest
pop. 1,076 in 1814; sexes about equal to 1805, males in excess later; children
about ⅕.   Largest no. of cattle 10,558 in 1822; horses 1,560 in 1822; mules
140 in 1817, sheep 14,000 in 1820; goats 66 in 1834; swine 245 in 1813; asses
59 in 1818; all kinds 24,393 animals in 1822.   Total product of wheat 72,544
bush., yield 12 fold; barley 9,727 bush., 9 fold; maize 6,417 bush., 68 fold;
beans 646 bush., 7 fold; miscell. grains 1,344 bush., 15 fold.

Summary of events etc.   1831. Status under Echeandía's decree, José

rapid. The mission was secularized in 1836 by Ignacio Coronel; and Inocente García was the administrator in 1837–40. The inventory of transfer showed a valuation, not including church property, of $82,000, which in the middle of 1839 had been reduced to $75,000. There were several ranchos with buildings, and two large vineyards, none of the lands being granted to private ownership during the decade. The

Castro being appointed comisionado, and the Ind. manifesting a preference for the old system. Nothing done. This vol., p. 306–8. 1833. Jan., P. Cabot to gov., announcing election of native alcaldes and regidores. *Gomez, Doc.*, MS., 22. Feb., a large quantity of growing wheat destroyed by flood. *Vallejo, Doc.*, MS., xxxi. 4. Mrs Ord, *Occurrencias*, MS., 69, visiting the mission this year noted the prevalent prosperity and the large amount of property, there being a notable change for the worse at her next visit two years later. Lat. and long. as taken by Douglas. This vol., p. 404. 1836. June 30th, secularization considered in the diputacion. *Leg. Rec.*, MS., iii. 23. July 14th, Ignacio Coronel put in charge, probably as comisionado, at $600 salary. *Coronel, Doc.*, MS., 189. Sept. 30th, P. Moreno writes that on the coming of the admin. all property was distributed among the Ind. except the grain, and of that they carried off more than half. *Guerra, Doc.*, MS., vii. 4. Oct. 16th, P. Abella writes that P. Moreno refuses, very properly, to render accounts; and the govt seems disposed to bother the padres in every possible way. *Carrillo (J.), Doc.*, MS., 37. 1837. Inocente García takes possession as administrator by inventory. March 30th, Mariano Bonilla served as his clerk. *García, Hechos*, MS., 73–4, relates that on one occasion a party of men under Isaac Graham forced the doors of the monjería, after which G. abolished the institution, leaving each family to care for their women. G. says he raised large crops until he found it was of no use, as there was no market and there was more food than the Ind. could eat. He gives many details in a confused way about S. Miguel affairs. The Ind. were addicted to theft and could not be controlled. *Hechos*, 57 et seq. 1838. P. Moreno complains bitterly of his poverty and the disappearance of the mission property. *Guerra, Doc.*, MS., viii. 2–3. 1839. García still admin., but Bonilla acting in June–July. *Monterey, Arch.*, MS., ix. 12; *St. Pap., Miss.*, MS., x. 18. Hartnell's visit was early in Aug. His reports do not indicate a bad state of affairs, though there was a dispute pending about some blankets which the Ind. claimed not to have been distributed; and at their request he dismissed the majordomo at S. Simeon, Manuel Ortega. The Ind. wished to have no administrator and to be left with the padre—anything for a change. They were also afraid of losing their lands at S. Simeon, Asuncion, Paso de Robles, and Sta Rosa; but they were willing to spare La Estrella, Cholam, Güegüero, and Cáñamo. Orders were given to investigate the case of men said to be 'cuereando' or killing cattle for their hides on the mission lands; also permission for P. Moreno to cultivate the Huerta de Asuncion on his own account. In Nov. there were complaints from the admin. that the Ind. were running away, and from the padres that García was not obeying the visitador's instructions, flogging the Ind. excessively, and otherwise interfering with the padre's prerogatives. *Hartnell, Diario*, MS., 25–7, 34, 47–8, 83–4. Aug., a majordomo poisoned by two Ind., who were arrested for the murder. *St. Pap., Miss.*, MS., x. 18. Hartnell's instructions for the administrator, including repairs, concentration of industries, payment of debts, etc. *Id.*, viii. 17–20. 1840. No record. Hartnell was here in Sept. but says nothing of mission affairs. *Diario*, MS., 93.

Indians lived at the ranchos as well as at the mission proper, and were somewhat unmanageable at times, on account of their intimate relations with the Tulareño gentiles; yet though the padre complained of poverty and mismanagement, the absolute ruin of the establishment does not appear to have begun until after 1840.

Padre Pedro Cabot remained at San Antonio until 1834, and Padre Jesus María Vasquez del Mercado, one of the newly arrived Zacatecanos, succeeding Cabot in that year, remained till 1839, to be succeeded in his turn by Padre José de Jesus María Gutierrez. Down to 1834 the neophyte population was reduced by deaths from 681 to 567; and five years later Visitador Hartnell found 270 living at the mission and its adjoining ranchos, though as the number was reported as 520 in the same year, it is likely that in 1840, there were 500 Indians connected with the establishment, half of the number being scattered at some distance.[12]   Live-stock decreased about

[12] S. Antonio statistics 1831–4. Decrease in pop. 681 to 567. Baptisms 51; 17 in 1832, 9 in 1834. Deaths 184; 58 in 1833, 38 in 1832. Loss in large stock 5,000 to 2,540, horses and mules 1,000 to 540; gain in sheep 10,000 to 11,000. Largest crop 2,718 bush. in 1832; smallest 2,100 bush. in 1833; average 2,448 bush., of which 1,527 wheat, yield 10 fold; 555 barley, 15 fold; 168 maize, 50 fold; 36 beans, 19 fold; 159 miscel. grains, 38 fold.

Statistics of 1835–40. Sept. 10, 1835. Inventory of produce, implements, furniture, and goods, $7,883. *St. Pap., Miss.,* MS., vi. 16. April 27, 1836 (1835?). Inventory; credits (?) $18,642, buildings $11,197, vineyards, implements, furniture, and goods in store $22,671, ranchos (S. Carpóforo?, S. Bartolomé or Pleito, Tule, S. Lúcas, S. Benito, S. Bernabé, S. Miguelito, Ojitos, S. Timoteo, and S. Lorenzo) $32,834, live-stock $1,000; total $93,122, besides church property $7,617; but there should be deducted $16,886 for property distributed among the Ind. *St. Pap., Miss.,* v. 51–3. May 3, 1836, a minute and descriptive inventory of church property, total value $7,617. *Pico, Pap. Mis.,* MS., 17–25. Inventories of Sept. 7, 1836, deducting debts, $35,703; Dec. 30, 1836, $36,355; Sept. 1, 1837, $37,639, and without date $35,399 (apparently none of these including lands or buildings). *St. Pap. Miss.,* MS., viii. 27–29. General accounts, not intelligible, Sept. 10, 1835, on delivery to Ramirez, debit $15,587; credit $15,098, balance $489. Dec. 31, 1836, Andrade to Ábrego, dr. $35,703; cr. $38,892; gain $3,188. Sept. 1, 1837, Abrego to Villavicencio, dr. $36,121; cr. $41,477; gain $5,356. *Id.,* 38–9. 1839. Feb., salaries, $500 to padre, $500 to admin., and $180 each to two majordomos. *Id.,* 37. Pop. in Jan. acc. to Pico's report 520, including 53 absent. *Id.,* 36. Pico's accounts of Oct. 1838 to April 1840 show an excess of expenditures over receipts of $500. *Id.,* 33–7. Aug. 6, 1839. Hartnell's census and inventory; pop. 270; 1,462 cattle, 306 horses, 2,612 sheep, 15 mules, 9 swine; 130 hides, 240 fan. grain, 114 arr. tallow, 10 arr. lard, 100

50 per cent before 1834, except sheep, in which there
was a small gain; but by the end of the decade cattle
and horses had lost another 50 per cent, and sheep

arr. wool; crops in good condition. *Hartnell, Diario*, MS., 27; *St. Pap. Miss.*,
MS., viii. 30. Debts $499, including those to José M. Águila, clerk, and
Manuel Lopez, ex-llavero. *Pico, Pap. Mis.*, MS., 47–51.

Statistics of 1771–1834. Total of baptisms 4,456, of which 1,761 Ind.
adults, 2,587 Ind. children, 1 and 107 gente de razon; annual average 68.
Total of deaths 3,772, of which 2,000 Ind. adults, 1,763 Ind. children, 5 and
4 gente de razon; annual average 58; average death rate 7.66 per cent of pop.
Largest pop. 1,296 in 1805; males always in excess of females, notably so
after 1805; children ⅓ to ½ and in the last years ½. Largest no. of cattle 8,000
in 1828; horses 1,030 in 1831; mules 82 in 1832; sheep 11,500 in 1816; goats
293 in 1790; swine 150 in 1817; all kinds 20,118 in 1818. Total product of
wheat 99,713 bush., yield 10 fold; barley 12,097 bush., 11 fold; maize 19,-
591 bush., 85 fold; beans 2,514 bush., 15 fold; miscel. grains 4,500 bush., 21
fold.

Summary of events, etc. 1831. Status under Echeandía's decree, never
put in execution, Antonio Castro being appointed comisionado. This vol., p.
306–7. 1833. Duran favors partial secularization. *Id.*, 335. Lat. and
long. by Douglas. *Id.*, p. 404. 1834. Rumors of colony plots. *Id.*, 281. S.
Antonio to be a parish of the 2d class under the reglamento. *Id.*, 348. 1835.
Secularization by Manuel Crespo as comisionado in June, with Mariano Soberanes as majordomo till Sept., when he turned over the estate to José M.
Ramirez, R.'s appointment being on Aug. 16th. *Id.*, 353–4; *St. Pap. Miss.*,
MS., vi. 16; xi. 30–3; *Leg. Rec.*, MS., iii. 4, 8, 9. Florencio Serrano was
employed as teacher. June 22d, P. Mercado complains that all his efforts for
the good of the Ind. are rendered futile by the persons in authority, who
commit adultery openly and other excesses. The gov. orders an investigation. *St. Pap. Miss.*, MS., xi. 32–7. Aug. 12th, the debt of P. Pedro Cabot
to the mission, $808, was annulled on account of his poverty. *Vallejo, Doc.*,
MS., iii. 48–9. Ramirez declares that on his taking charge there was no
money, no cloth, no table furniture; the shops closed, only a few poor and
dying horses, very little other live-stock; the year's yield of hides and tallow
estimated at $1,500; and expenses over $2,500. *Dept. St. Pap., B. M.*, lxxxi.
73–4. Dec. 28th, P. Mercado writes to the gov. on the unjust and even inhuman treatment of the Ind., who are beaten and starved in defiance of the
laws under Ramirez' management. He also claims that their spiritual interests are neglected, because the admin. will not provide horses for the padre,
and the Ind. are allowed to live at S. Lorenzo and other distant points; moreover he cannot collect his pay as minister. *Id.*, 57; *Leg. Rec.*, MS., iii. 3–6.
Dec. 31st, Mercado's report to same general effect; heathenism gaining on
christianity; Ind. naked and starving, and two thirds of them absent in
quest of food not to be had at the mission. *S. Antonio, Doc. Sueltos*, MS.,
120–1. 1836. Ramirez succeeded by José María Andrade on Sept. 7th, and
the latter by José Ábrego on Dec. 30th. *St. Pap. Miss.*, MS., viii. 27, 29, 38.
P. Mercado continued his charges of mismanagement and cruelty against Ramirez, declaring that the Ind. had passed from their former condition of minors
under guardianship to that of slaves under inhuman and irresponsible masters. He cited several instances of excessive punishment. In March an investigation was ordered by the gov., José M. Cosio being the fiscal. Many
witnesses were examined, including Mercado, Ramirez, and several neophytes.
The testimony indicates that the padre, angry because the admin. could not
pay him all his salary, had greatly exaggerated his charges of cruelty; and
that Ramirez, a comparatively efficient manager, had resorted to the lash in
accordance with Figueroa's regulations, as the only means of controlling the
vicious and lazy Ind., whose complaints it suited the padre's purposes to en-

about 80 per cent. Evidently there were but slight traces of former prosperity; and matters were not mended by the interference of a quarrelsome friar and frequent changes in the administration. Manuel Crespo was the comisionado for secularization in 1835, and the successive administrators were Mariano Soberanes, José M. Ramirez, José M. Andrade, José Ábrego, José M. Villavicencio, and Jesus Pico ad int. Padre Mercado was loud and constant in his complaints and charges, especially against Ramirez, who was exonerated after a formal investigation; and the Indians were always discontented and unmanageable.

The venerable friar and ex-prefect Vicente Francisco Sarría died at Soledad in 1835; [13] and from that

courage. The result was the acquittal of Ramirez, with an earnest admonition to him and Mercado to work harmoniously for the good of the mission. *Dept. St. Pap., B. M.*, MS., lxxxi. 33, 48–78; *Leg. Rec.*, MS., ii. 7–12. Yet, as we have seen, a change of administrators was made in Sept. with a view to promote harmony. 1837. Ábrego was replaced by José M. Villavicencio on Sept. 1st. *St. Pap. Miss.*, MS., viii. 29. García, *Hechos*, MS., 72–3, relates that the Ind. rose against Ábrego, accusing him of sending off hides and tallow, and giving them nothing. Ábrego was besieged in his house, but released by García who came from S. Miguel with 30 men. There is nothing in the records about this affair; nor are there any of P. Mercado's complaints extant for this year. 1838. Villavicencio was succeeded on Oct. 15th by Jesus Pico, with José M. Aguilar as clerk. *St. Pap. Miss.*, MS., viii. 30–1; *Pico, Pap., Mis.*, MS., 48. 1839. Pico, *Acont.*, MS., 53–4, says he merely acted ad int. during the absence of Capt. Villavicencio in the south. He says the padre was arrogant and himself quick-tempered, and they quarrelled at first; but soon became friends and associates in cock-fighting and gambling. April–May, P. Mercado and Angel Ramirez arrested for plots against the govt. This vol., p. 586–7. Aug. 6th–7th. Hartnell found the mission accounts in a sad state of confusion, and the Ind. much discontented, complaining of harsh treatment, and that of all the produce sent away and the effects received they get nothing but threats and blows. They wished to live without any admin., and were very bitter against the incumbent. (Pico or Villavicencio? H. also names José Ant. Rodriguez as the man who gave up the administration to the incumbent.) Diego Félix was majordomo, and he made charges against the administrator. The Ind. also complained of a bad man de razon living at S. Bernabé, who had given venereal disease to many of the mission women. Hartnell's instructions required the admin. to expel all gente de razon not employed by the mission, and to seek a new majordomo with a smaller family. *Hartnell, Diario*, MS., 27–8, 34, 47–8, 51, 84; *St. Pap., Miss.*, MS., viii. 31–2. 1840. Vicente Moraga seems to have succeeded Pico in the temporary management under Villavicencio, who on June 20th orders M. not to deliver the property to Hartnell when he comes. He proposes to give up nothing till his own claims are paid. If his (V.'s) wife needs anything, she is to have it, if the mission has to be sold to pay for it! *Guerra, Doc.*, MS., ii. 192–3; *Vallejo, Doc.*, MS., xxxiii. 81. There is no record of the result. Aug. 5th, P. Gutierrez writes to Hartnell that the mission is advancing every day toward complete destruction. *Id.*, ix. 214.

[13] Vicente Francisco Sarría was a Biscayan, born in Nov. 1767, at S.

time the mission had no resident minister, Padre
Mercado of San Antonio having charge of its spiritual interests and making occasional visits from the

Estévan de Echabarris, near Bilbao, at which latter town he became a Franciscan in Nov. 1783, serving at his convent as lector de filosofía for laymen,
maestro de estudiantes, and lector de artes de religiosos. He left Cádiz in
June 1804, and after four years' service at the College of S. Fernando, he was
sent to California in 1809. His missionary service was at S. Cárlos in 1809–
29, and at Soledad in 1829–35; that is, these missions were his headquarters,
he being absent much of the time on official tours. *Autobiog. Autog. de los
Padres*, MS.; *Sarría, Inf. sobre Frailes, 1817*, MS., 76–7; *Payeras, Inf., 1820*,
MS., 134–5, in which latter report he is highly praised, as of the most distinguished merit and ability, fitted for the highest positions, and one who might
with advantage be entrusted with a needed manual for Franciscans. In 1813–19
Sarría held the office of comisario prefecto of the missions—the highest in the
province—and again filled the position in 1823–30, or perhaps a little longer,
being also president in 1823–5. In the discharge of his official duties he
proved himself as prelate the worthy successor of Serra, Lasuen, and Tapis,
and associate of Señan and Payeras. Readers of my chapters on mission annals are familiar with his acts and views and writings, which space does not
permit me to recapitulate here. In my list of authorities some half-a-dozen
of his more notable productions appear, among which is a curious volume of
manuscript sermons in his native Basque. He was a scholarly, dignified,
and amiable man; not prone to controversy, yet strong in argument, clear
and earnest in the expression of his opinions; less disposed to asceticism and
bigotry than some of the earlier Fernandinos, yet given at times to fasting and
mortification of the flesh; devoted to his faith and to his order; strict in the observance and enforcement of Franciscan rules, and conscientious in the performance of every duty; yet liberal in his views on ordinary matters, clear-headed in
business affairs, and well liked by all who came in contact with him. As
prefect, no Californian friar could have done better, since in the misfortunes of
his cloth he never lost either temper or courage. Declining as a loyal Spaniard to accept republicanism, P. Sarría was arrested in 1825, and his exile
ordered; but his arrest, which lasted about five years, was merely nominal,
and the order of exile, though never withdrawn and several times renewed,
was never enforced. In *S. Antonio, Doc. Sueltos*, MS., 83–4, is a letter to
the padre from his nephew in Spain, 1820, on family poverty and misfortunes.
After 1830, old and infirm, but still actively engaged in local missionary
duties, he lived quietly at Soledad, which he declined to leave in 1834 when
the northern missions were given up to the Zacatecanos, especially as no resident minister was assigned to this mission. Thus he was the last of the Fernandinos in the north, dying just before the secularization which put an end
to the Franciscan régime. He died suddenly, perhaps fell while saying mass
at the altar, on May 24, 1835, without receiving the final sacraments. Padre
Mercado declared that his 'muerte violenta' was due to 'escasez de alimentos.'
S. Antonio, Doc. Sueltos, MS., 120; and the tradition became somewhat prevalent that he died through neglect of the administrator. Mrs Ord heard this
version; see also *Mofras, Explor.*, i. 389–91; *E. C.*, in *Revista Cientif.*, i.
328; *Vallejo, Hist. Cal.*, MS., iv. 93. By these writers the death is dated
1838, and Mofras names the month as August. Vallejo says Sarría's death
was caused by neglect on the part of the Mexican friars. The truth is,
probably, that the aged friar, childishly insisting on remaining alone with his
Indians. overtasked his strength and shortened his life, circumstances rendering suitable care impossible. I do not credit Mercado's charges, or believe
that there was an administrator in Cal. who would have maltreated a missionary so widely known and loved. His body was carried to S. Antonio
and buried in the mission church, on the epistle side of the presbytery in the

autumn of 1834.   There was but slight loss in population or in live-stock down to 1834, though crops
were very small; but later Indians, animals, and property of all kinds rapidly disappeared.   The population
was about three hundred in 1834; and in 1840 it had
dwindled to about 70, with perhaps as many more
scattered in the district.[14]   The debt was large,

sepulchre nearest the wall, on May 27th. *S. Antonio, Extracto, Muerte de
Sarría*, MS.; translation in *Taylor's Discov. and Found.*, ii. no. 24, p. 199.
Padre Ambris was told that years later Sarría's body was found to be intact.

[14] Soledad statistics 1831-4.   Decrease in pop., 342 to about 300.   Baptisms, 140, rather strangely including more than half adults; 54 in 1833, 26 in
1831.   Deaths, 150; 50 in 1834, 26 in 1832.   Increase in large stock, 5,000 to
6,200; horses and mules decrease 1,000 to 200; sheep, 5,257 to 5,000.   Largest
crop, 1,890 bush. in 1832; smallest, 784 (?) in 1834; average 1,200, of which
777 wheat, yield 10 fold; 253 barley, 7 fold; 84 maize, 25 fold; 21 beans, 8
fold; 58 miscell. grain, 6 fold.
   Statistics of 1835-40.   June 30, 1835, delivered to govt for national rancho
in the past year, $1,513, and for the colony, $222. *Dept. St. Pap., B. M.*,
MS., lxxx. 11.   Inventory of Aug. 12, 1835; credits, $412; buildings, $1,764;
implements, furniture, effects, etc., $3,234; church property (church, $85,
ornaments, etc., $3,347, library of 51 vol., $186) $3,618; ranchos, with live-
stock and produce, $31,366; total, $47,297 (should be $40,394). *St. Pap.,
Miss.*, MS., v. 57.   Dec. 31, 1836, inventory without valuation, including
a vineyard with 5,000 vines; ranchos of S. Lorenzo, S. Vicente, and S. Fernando; 3,246 cattle, 32 horses, 2,400 sheep; credits, $556, debts $677. *Id.*,
viii. 39-41.   1837.   Salary list $1,240. *Id.*, 43.   Administrator's account
for the year, dr $2,792, cr $2,750, balance on hand $42. *Id.*, 46.   1838.
Admin. acct, dr $1,065, cr $929, on hand $136; also 1,306 animals, great and
small. *Id.*, 47.   Pop. Dec. 31st, 168 souls. *Id.*, 48.   1839.   Jan.-Aug.,
equal receipts and expend., no balance. *Id.*, 44-5.   Feb., credits $556, debts
$88. *Id.*, 46.   March, due to employés, $1,587. *Id.*, 77.   May, June, excess of receipts over expend., $54. *Id.*, ix. 73-4.   May. 544 cattle, 32
horses, 900 sheep. *Id.*, 74.   Aug. 8th, Hartnell's census and inventory; pop.,
78; 45 cattle, 25 horses, 865 sheep, 1 mule, 1 ass, 156 fan. barley. *Diario*,
MS., 28.   Nov., debts $1,297. *Pico, Pap. Mis.*, MS., 47-51.
   Statistics of 1791-1834.   Total of baptisms, 2,222, of which 1,235 Ind.
adults, 924 Ind. children, 63 children de razon; annual average 50.   Total of
marriages 682, of which 11 de razon.   Total of deaths 1,803, of which 1,207
Ind. adults, 574 Ind. children, 9 and 13 gente de razon; annual average 40;
average death rate 9 per cent. of pop.   Largest pop., 725 in 1805; males always in excess of females, sometimes greatly so; children from 1-3 to 1-10.
Largest no. of cattle, 6,599 in 1831; horses, 1,257 in 1821; mules, 80 in 1807;
sheep, 9,500 in 1808; swine, 90 in 1814; all kinds, 16,551 animals in 1821.
Total product of wheat 64,254 bush., yield 12 fold; barley 13,956 bush.,
16 fold; maize 18,240 bush., 90 fold; beans, 2,260 bush., 11 fold; miscell.
grains, 13,012 bush., 27 fold.
   Record of events, etc.   1831.   Status under Echeandía's decree, not carried out; Tiburcio Castro comisionado.   This vol., p. 306-7.   1833.   Election
of an Ind. ayuntamiento. *Arch. Arzob.*, MS., v. pt 1, p. 375.   1834.   The
padre reported destitute of means, and leading a hermit's life.   Soledad was
to be a parish of 2d class.   This vol., p. 348.   1835.   Secularization by
Nicolás Alviso, who was majordomo and perhaps comisionado; also alcalde
auxiliar.   1836.   José M. Águila succeeded Alviso at a date not given, and
on Dec. 31st was succeeded by Salvador Espinosa, salary $500; José Ant.

and there were left only 45 cattle, 25 horses, and 865 sheep, though the inventory of 1835 had shown an estate valued at $36,C00 besides the church property. Secularization was effected in 1835 by Nicolás Alviso, and the successive administrators were José M. Águila, Salvador Espinosa, and Vicente Cantúa. At the end of the decade the establishment was on the verge of dissolution, and I am not sure that the final order was not issued before the end of the last year.

At San Juan Bautista padres Felipe Arroyo de la Cuesta and Juan Moreno served together in 1831–2, and the latter remained till 1833, when Padre José Antonio Ánzar took his place. The regular statistical reports cease in 1832, when there were 916 Indians on the register. As no extraordinary cause of dispersion is known, there may have been 850 neophytes in 1834. The only subsequent record is to the effect that the number of Indians emancipated—and there is no allusion to any others—in 1835 was 63, presumably heads of families and possibly representing 250 souls, but probably much less. As an estimate, which is hardly more than a guess, there may have been 100 ex-neophytes in the immediate vicinity of the mission, and as many more scattered but not relapsed wholly to savagism in 1840.[15] Secu-

Gaxiola sec. $120 (later $180). José Rosas, majordomo, $120. 1837–9. Espinosa still in charge. 1839. Hartnell's visit was in Aug. He found the Ind. complaining of both Espinosa and Rosas, the former taking mission cattle for his rancho, and the latter spoiling the crops by his obstinate ignorance. They wanted to be free, under a kind of supervision by Águila, who had been well liked as administrator. *Hartnell, Diario*, MS., 28. Nov. 5th. Espinosa was succeeded by Vicente Cantúa. *St. Pap. Miss.*, MS., viii. 45. 1840. Cantúa still in charge; ordered in March to sell 6,000 tiles to buy food for the Ind. *Dept. Rec.*, MS., xi. 37.

[15] Statistics of S. Juan Bautista 1831–4. There are no records after 1832, so that the figures for 1834 are only estimates. Decrease in pop. 964 to 850. Baptisms 144. Deaths 304. Decrease in large stock 7,820 to 5,000; horses and mules 324 to 200; sheep 7,000 to 4,000. Average crop (2 years) 2,029 bush., of which 1,380 bush. wheat, yield 11 fold; 405 bush. barley, 10 fold; 150 bush. corn, 25 fold; 49 bush. beans, 11 fold; 43 bush. miscel. grains, 5 fold.

Statistics of 1835–40. Inventory of May 1835; land $5,120; live-stock, including 41 horses, $1,782; implements, effects, etc., $1,467; total $8,369, to be distributed among 63 emancipated Ind. *St. Pap. Miss.*, MS., x. 16. Inventory of church property; church $3,500 (?), ornaments, etc., $29,240 (?),

larization was effected in 1835 by Tiburcio Castro, who was administrator through 1836, no successor being named. The inventory of the change shows a

library, 182 vol., $591, 6 bells $1,060, furniture of the choir $453, total $44,844. *Id.*, vi. 10. June 6, 1835, paid to S. F. comp. since July 1834, $84, for the colony $435, besides $500 still due on colony account. *Id.*, viii. 48. Inventory of 1835 (no month named), buildings $36,000; implements, goods and furniture $7,774; church property (church, fully described, $35,000, ornaments, etc., $7,740, library $461, bells $1,060, choir furniture $1,643) $45,904; vineyards, lands, and buildings outside the mission $37,365; ranchos, probably including live-stock (S. Justo $1,300, Todos Santos $1,755, S. Felipe $16,052) $19,107; credits $1,040; cash $222; total $147,413; deducting amount distrib. to Ind. $8,439, and debt $250, balance $138,723. *Id.*, vi. 17–19. 1836. Jan. 1, 1837. Castro's general account for 1836; salaries (P. Ánzar $265, Admin. Castro $262, Maj. Castro and Rios $149 and $171) $847. Expenses of house, etc., $155; goods and produce supplied to Ind. $312; total $1,315. Product of garden and vineyard $150, slaughter $270, due from the ship *California* $357, cheeses left over $134, total $911. Balance of expend. over receipts $404. Cattle and horses branded 175; sheep sheared 2,024; crops 607 fan. Cattle on hand 869, sheep 4,120. Credits in March $338, debts $1650. *Id.*, viii. 49–51. Nothing for 1838–40.

Statistics of 1797–1834. Total of baptisms 4,100, of which 1,898 Ind. adults, 2,015 Ind. children, 2 and 195 gente de razon; annual average 103. Total of marriages 1,028, of which 53 de razon. Total of deaths 3,027, of which 1,708 Ind. adults, 1,203 Ind. children, 5 and 65 gente de razon; annual average 79; average death rate 9.35 per cent. Largest pop. 1,248 in 1823; sexes about equal to 1810, males largely in excess later; children ⅓ to ⅕. Largest no. of cattle 11,000 in 1820; horses 1,598 in 1806; mules 35 in 1805; sheep 13,000 in 1816; swine 99 in 1803; all kinds 23,789 animals in 1816. Total product of wheat 84,633 bush., yield 15 fold; barley 10,830 bush., 19 fold; maize 18,400 bush., 88 fold; beans 1,871 bush., 12 fold; miscell. grains 2,640 bush., 10 fold.

Summary of events, officials, etc., 1831. Status of S. Juan under Echeandía's decree, not carried out; Juan Higuera comisionado. This vol., p. 306–7. 1834. S. Juan and Sta Cruz to form a parish of 2d class under the reglamento. *Id.*, 348. 1835. Secularization, Tiburcio Castro being administrator, or majordomo, and perhaps comisionado, though José Castro may have held the latter position, and Antonio Buelna also signs an inventory. Angel Castro and Joaquin Rios were subordinate majordomos. Felipe Amesti and Rafael Gonzalez are named as alcaldes 1st and 2d of the new pueblo. *Doc. Hist. Cal.*, MS., i. 483; *Mont. Arch.*, MS., ii. 2. July 27th, the gov. has learned that the Ind. have taken more property than was assigned to them. This must be corrected. *St. Pap. Miss. & Col.*, MS., ii. 342–3. July 31st, Castro to gov. complaining that P. Ánzar had taken the best rooms in addition to 11 already held by him. The padre wishes the admin. and all the Ind. to devote themselves entirely to his service. *St. Pap. Miss.*, MS., x. 15. Alvarado, *Hist. Cal.*, MS., ii. 212–18, says that secularization was successful here and at S. Antonio, though nowhere else, the Ind. being entirely freed, though watched, and making tolerably good use of their freedom and property. 1836. S. Juan was the headquarters of Alvarado and the revolutionists while preparing to oust Gov. Gutierrez, this vol., p. 453–4; and after the revolution the place began to be called S. Juan de Castro, in honor of the general, though the name was perhaps not officially used for two or three years. *Id.*, 511. 1837. José María Sanchez juez de paz. Revolutionary plots and arrest of conspirators. *Id.*, 512. March, the Ind. attacked the rancho of José Sanchez, killing two ex-neophytes and wounding Sanchez himself. *Vallejo, Doc.*, MS., iv. 223. 1838. Ravages of the Ind., said to be fugitive christians accompanied by many gentiles, at Pacheco's

valuation of $93,000, besides church property to the amount of $46,000, and over $8,000 distributed to the Indians.   At the end of 1836, the mission estate had still about 900 cattle and 4,000 sheep, with a crop of 900 bushels, and a debt of $1,300.   These are the latest statistics extant.   Secularization appears to have been much more complete than at the establishments farther south, there being no traces of the community after 1836.   Constant depredations of savages with ex-neophyte allies from 1837 contributed to the work of ruin; but a little settlement of gente de razon sprang into existence, containing I suppose 50 inhabitants at the end of the decade; the name became San Juan de Castro; jueces de paz took charge of local affairs; and the town was honored by being made cabecera of the district in 1839, on the organization of the prefecture.

Padre Joaquin Jimeno continued his ministry at Santa Cruz till 1833, when he was succeeded by Padre Antonio Suarez del Real, who remained throughout the decade.   In 1834 the neophyte population had fallen from 320 to about 250, and apparently there was no very marked loss in live-stock or agriculture down to that time.[16]   Secularization was

rancho, where they killed Hipólito Mejía.   They also burned J. M. Sanchez's house, and S. pursuing wounded seven of them.   A few days later they attacked José Castro's rancho, and again visited Pacheco's, driving off horses and stealing all they could carry.   There was much correspondence about an exped. against the savages, but no results are known. Vol. iv. 75.   1839. Juan Miguel Ánzar juez de paz, with Antonio Castro as suplente.   For prefecture see annals of Monterey in this chapter, S. Juan de Castro being the head-town of the district.   April, buildings being prepared for the prefecture.   Castro proposes to establish a rancho nacional at S. Luis Gonzaga. *Leg. Rec.*, MS., iii. 87-92; *Vallejo, Doc.*, MS., vi. 491.   1840.   Ánzar still juez de paz, with Manuel Larios as suplente.   By Alvarado's regulation of March on missions, S. Juan was one of the establishments which the govt was to 'continue to regulate according to circumstances.' vol. iv. 60.   July, organization of a patrol against Ind. between S. Juan and S. Jose. *Dept. St. Pap.*, MS., v. 14; *Id., Mont.*, iii. 85-90.   Sept. 1st the S. Juan jurisdiction defined as extending from Natividad by Los Carneros and Pájaro to Las Llagas. *Mont. Arch.*, MS., ix. 26-7.

[16] Sta Cruz statistics 1831-2 (no figures for 1833-4).   Decrease in pop. 320 to 284; baptisms 17; deaths 54; marriages 11; increase in large stock 3,363 to 4,095; horses, etc., 363 to 495; sheep 4,827 to 5,211.   Crops 3,570 bush. in 1831; 1,710 bush. in 1832.

Statistics of 1834-40.   Debt in Sept. 1834, $4,979; credits $1,877. *St. Pap.*,

effected in 1834–5 by Ignacio del Valle as comisionado; and the value of the property when he turned
it over to Juan Gonzalez as administrator at the end

Miss., MS., ix. 71. Nov. 14th, sub-comisario acknowledges draft of Deppe
on the mission for $2,266. *Dept. St. Pap.*, *Ben. C. & T.*, MS., iii. 11–12.
Nov. 27th gov. orders prompt delivery of 13 blankets for troops. *Sta Cruz,
Rec.*, MS., 18. 1835. Inventory of Dec. 1st. Buildings $16,940, furniture,
etc., $478, implements, machinery, etc., $2,163, huerta with 1,210 vines and
1,024 fruit-trees $2,173, live-stock at the mission $1,051, id. with tools at the
ranchos (Matadero $5,104, Ánimas $1,125, Jano $1,050, Año Nuevo $10,302)
$17,581, effects in store-house $3,291, produce $5,176, credits $3,338, total
$52,191, debt $4,979, balance $47,212, besides church property as follows:
building $8,050, ornaments, bells, cannon, etc., $23,505, library of 152 vols.
$386, total $32,142 (another copy makes it $40,191). The live-stock noted
above consisted of 3,700 cattle, 500 horses, 2,900 sheep, 18 mules, 10 asses,
28 swine. The chief creditor was Virmond, and the chief debtor the
national treasury. The lands 2x11 l. and mostly fit only for grazing are not
valued. *Sta Cruz Rec.*, MS., 1–3; *St. Pap. Miss.*, v. 54; vi. 40; *Miscel. Hist.
Pap.*, MS., no. 15. A newspaper scrap of unknown origin, often reprinted,
makes the total $168,000, and lands $79,000. Property distributed among
the Ind. from Aug. 24, 1834, to Dec. 1, 1835, $10,576. *St. Pap. Miss.*, MS.,
ix. 66–7. December 11th, payment of $300 to Comisionado Valle for his ser-
vices. *Id.*, 69. April 22, 1837, live-stock 1,000 cattle, 460 horses, 2,000 sheep,
22 mules, 16 asses; 70 fan. grain; credits $3,040, debts $594, to Russ. Amer.
Co. and N. Spear. *Id.*, vii. 47–8; *Pico, Pap. Mis.*, MS., 47–51. March 11,
1839, receipts since beginning of 1838, from sale of hides $1,120; expend. for
salaries $1,465, besides cattle and horses delivered on order of govt. *St.
Pap. Miss.*, MS., ix. 72. Oct. 7th, Hartnell found 70 Ind., 36 cattle, 127
horses, and 1,026 sheep. *Diario*, MS., 44.

Statistics of 1791–1834. Total of baptisms 2,466, of which 1,277 Ind.
adults, 939 Ind. children, 6 and 244 de razon; annual average 50. Marriages
847, of which 63 de razon. Deaths 2,035, of which 1,359 Ind. adults, 574
Ind. child., 45 and 47 de razon; annual average 44; average death-rate 10.93
per cent of pop. Largest pop. 644 in 1798. Males always in excess of
females; children ⅓ to ⅕. Largest no. of cattle 3,700 in 1828; horses 900 in
1828; mules 92 in 1805; sheep 8,300 in 1826; swine 150 in 1818; all kinds
12,502 animals in 1827. Total product of wheat 69,900 bush., yield 18 fold;
barley 13,180 bush., 21 fold; maize 30,500 bush., 146 fold; beans 9,250 bush.,
57 fold; miscel. grains 7,600 bush., 28 fold.

Summary and index of events. 1831. Status under Echeandía's decree
not enforced. This vol., p. 306–7. Jan., P. Jimeno reports election of
neophyte alcalde and regidores approved by gov. *Sta Cruz Rec.*, MS., 13.
1833. Jimeno succeeded by Real as padre. Duran favors partial secularization. This vol., p. 335. Lat. and long. by Douglas. *Id.*, 404. Fortifications to prevent smuggling recommended by Capt. Gonzalez. *Dept. St. Pap.*,
MS., iii. 114. 1834. Ignacio del Valle as comisionado took charge on Aug.
24th, appointing Juan Gonzalez majordomo Oct. 31st. *St. Pap. Miss.*, MS.,
x. 6; ix. 66; *Sta Cruz Rec.*, MS., 12; *Valle Lo Pasado*, MS., 9-10. Valle
gave to the new pueblo the name Pueblo de Figueroa, which had been ordered
by the gov. in Jan., and also gave Spanish surnames to the ex-neophytes.
Sta Cruz and Branciforte were to form a parish of the 2d class. *St. Pap.
Miss.*, MS., 68, 71; this vol., p. 384. Sept. 15th, the padre, having given
up the mission, asks the gov. for house, etc., grain and other supplies for
himself and horses, the care of church and wine, Ind. assistants for worship,
a division of goods in store, and that the comisionado shall not prejudice
Ind. against the padre. *Id.*, x. 6. Oct. 24th, gov. orders com. to settle the
mission accounts at once. *Sta Cruz Rec.*, MS., 23. Oct. 31st, gov. approves
appt of majordomo at $40 inclusive of rations. *Id.*, 12. Nov., the padre in-

of 1835 was $47,000, exclusive of land and church property, besides $10,000 distributed to the Indians. There is no record of subsequent distributions or of how the estate disappeared; but in 1839 Hartnell found only 70 Indians—with perhaps as many more scattered in the district—and about one sixth of the live-stock of the former inventory. Francisco Soto succeeded Gonzalez in 1839, and possibly the juez de

sisted on having 10 rooms and the granary for a stable, but the gov. decided that he could have only the rooms actually needed, and that the granary could not be spared. *St. Pap. Miss.*, MS., ix. 70. Nov. 17th, Valle has selected a room for the ayunt., one for the secretary, and one for a school. *Id.*, 69. 1835. The governor's plan for a mission rancho for support of church not carried out. This vol., p. 351. May 21st, gov. calls for accounts of supplies to govt and to colony. *Sta Cruz Rec.*, MS., 4. June 13th, majordomo to pay padre $20 for freight of lumber. *Id.*, 4. Dec. 1st (or perhaps earlier) the property was turned over by Valle to Gonzalez as administrator, the secularization being deemed complete. Valle was paid $300 for his services. *Id.*, 20. Inventories of Dec. 1st as given elsewhere, Asísara, an ex-neophyte, in *Amador, Mem.*, MS., 90–113, spins a long yarn, perhaps true in some particulars, about P. Real's success in making away with much of the property secretly by night before Valle took charge, and of the process by which Valle, Soto, and Bolcof appropriated the rest. 1836. Spear's lighter running between Sta Cruz and S. F. vol. iv., p. 83. Forces recruited for Alvarado's army. This vol., p. 491. March, gov. orders that Ind. must comply with their church duties. *Sta Cruz Arch.*, MS., 6. 1837. The oath to support centralism in July. This vol., p. 529. 1839. Francisco Soto succeeded Gonzalez as administrator in Jan., and in Oct. was ordered to turn over the property to José Bolcof, the juez de paz. *Dept. Rec.*, MS., x. 3; *Dept. St. Pap. Mont.*, MS., iv. 18, but perhaps did not do so at once. In Sept. Hartnell found the few remaining Ind. clamorous for liberty and a final distribution of property. They particularly wished to retain El Refugio and the mission puerta, which the padre also desired. They were bitter against their administrator; and José Antonio Rodriguez desired the position. *Hartnell, Diario*, MS., 8, 44. The French voyager Laplace, *Campagne*, vi. 272–84, devotes several pages to a melancholy picture of the establishment in its state of ruin, poverty, and filth, as compared with its former somewhat exaggerated magnificence. He found the administrator a man of fine appearance and manners, and he found a pretty ranchera willing to sell vegetables at a fair price, but this 'California dove' was frightened away by the appearance of P. Real. 'Vraiment il y avait de quoi d'effaroncher; car il serait difficile de rencontrer un individu au regard plus cynique, à la physionomie plus effrontée, à l'air plus débruillé que ce padre Mexicain, avec sa figure brulée, ses grands yeux noir à fond jaune, son chef convert d'un chapeau à larges bords et à moitie défoncé, sa robe de franciscain, autrefois blanche, maintenant souillée de mille taches, sans capuchon et retrousée jusqu'à la ceinture afir de laisser toute liberté aux membres inférieurs; enfir avec une escopette en bandoulière qui achevait de donner à ce costume quelque chose de pittoresque.' 1840. No record of the man in charge. According to the reglamento the govt was to continue to manage this ex-mission according to circumstances. Vol. iv., p. 60. In Jan., there was an earthquake, and tidal wave, carrying off a large quantity of tiles and bringing down the church tower. *Id.*, 78; *Mont. Arch.*, MS., ix. 24. March, gov. orders admin. to give up to P. Real the garden and distillery with the houses adjoining the church. *Dept. Rec.*, MS., xi. 9.

paz José Bolcof took charge this year or the next.
The secularization of 1835 was considered more complete than at most other establishments, and the
Pueblo de Figueroa, distinct from the villa across the
river, came into existence on paper; but I find no indication of real pueblo organization, or that the status
of this ex-mission community differed in any respect
from that of others.

The population of the villa de Branciforte, given as
150 at the beginning, may be estimated at 250 at the
end of the decade, though there are no definite figures
for this period. In 1831–5 the villa seems to have
elected its own ayuntamiento of alcalde, two regidores,
and síndico; though I find nothing to authorize this
apparent independence from the civil authorities of
Monterey. In 1836–40, however, the subordination
to the latter was officially asserted, and an alcalde
auxiliar was annually appointed, or a juez de paz after
1839, the popular choice being usually approved by
the Monterey ayuntamiento and governor or prefect.
The successive municipal chiefs of Branciforte, the
list of subordinate officers being incomplete,[17] were

[17] Summary of Branciforte annals. 1831, Alcalde Joaquin Castro. 1832.
Alcalde Joaquin Buelna, regidor Manuel Villagrana, jueces de campo Rafael
Castro and Francisco Soria. Municipal receipts $36, expend. $26. *Dept. St.
Pap., Ben.*, MS., v. 80–1. 1833, Alcalde José Antonio Robles, regidor Juan
José Castro, deposed by the alcalde in June but reinstated by the gov. *Id.*,
P. & J., v. 40. Munic. receipts with $10 balance from 1832, $43, expend.
$42. *Dept. St. Pap.*, MS., iii. 131. Dec. 18th, 24th, elections of town officers
for next year. *Id.*, 127–31. 1834. Alcalde José Bolcof; regidores José María
Salazar (?) and José Teran; síndico Rafael Castro, secretary José de los Santos
Ávila. Jan. 6th, alcalde's instructions to jueces de campo. *Sta Cruz, Arch.*,
MS., 93–4. Jan. 22d, gov. approves alcalde's appointment of a monthly com-
mission of regidor and 4 citizens to visit the ranchos, prevent thefts of horses,
and catch runaway neophytes to work on the casas consistoriales. *Id.*, 83.
Expenses of the year $40, including a *baston de justicia* which cost $15. *Dept.
St. Pap., B. M.*, MS., lxxviii. 6–7. May 10th, the ayunt had imposed a tax
of $1 per vara of thickness on every tree felled and $1 on every otter skin, for
the payment of a teacher and of the secretary. *Leg. Rec.*, MS., ii. 62; *St.
Pap., M. & C.*, MS., ii. 237–8. June 12th, Zamorano reports that the civil
jurisdiction of Branciforte extends from the ranchos north of Sta Cruz to the
rancho of José Amesti, between the summit of the sierra and the shore. *Id.*,
218. June 28th, gov. provisionally fixes the limits of the jurisdiction as the
S. F. boundary in the north, the S. Andrés rancho of Joaquin Castro in the
south, between the sea and the summit. *Id.*, 220. 1835. Alcalde Alejandro
Rodriguez. Síndico Macedonio Lorenzana. Receipts $31, expend. $13. *Sta
Cruz, Arch.*, MS., 84. Dec. 28th, gov. tells alcalde that Branciforte, not having the pop. necessary for an ayunt., must be subject to the ayunt. of Mon-

Joaquin Castro, Joaquin Buelna, José Antonio Robles, José Bolcof, Alejandro Rodriguez, Rafael Castro, Antonio Rodriguez, Joaquin Buelna again, and José Bolcof. Municipal finances were in a healthful condition, or at least expenses were so kept down that there was usually a balance of more than a dollar in the treasury at the year's end. The *villanos* still did something to sustain their old reputation in the way of social irregularities and popular tumults; if they seem not to have sustained it fully, the fault is perhaps not theirs but that of the defective records. About 20 ranchos were granted in this region before 1840, a list of which with others in the Monterey district has been given in this chapter.

terey. He will appoint an auxiliary alcalde. *St. Pap., M. & C.*, MS., ii. 366. 1836. Alcalde auxiliar Rafael Castro. Miguel Villagrana was elected Jan. 19th, but objection was made that he could not read or write and that the election was irregular; therefore the ayunt. of Mont. after consulting the gov. appointed Castro. *Dept. St. Pap., Mont.*, MS., vi. 13–15. Síndico, Miguel Ramirez. (But Francisco Juarez is mentioned in Jan. *Sta Cruz Arch.*, MS., 84.) Secretary Joaquin Buelna appointed in March at $10 per month. *Dept. St. Pap.*, MS., iv. 99–107. April, alcalde complains of the actions of Gervasio Soto and wife; who, in revenge for being watched in accordance with orders from Mont., caught two buzzards and tied firebrands to the birds, thus setting a man's house on fire. *Mont. Arch.*, MS., ii. 6–7. P. Real also complains to the gov. of disorders resulting from ill-assorted marriages; Juan Pinto and his wife separated; Fran. Soria beating his family; and Gervasio Soto and family the cause of all the trouble. Soto should be banished in the interest of public tranquillity. *Id.*, 7–8. 1837, Alcalde auxiliar Antonio Rodriguez. *Unb. Doc.*, MS., 245–6. No other record for the year. 1838. Alcalde Joaquin Buelna; regidores Francisco Soria and Macedonio Lorenzana; juez de campo Miguel Villagrana. Election of Feb. 12th. *S. José, Arch.*, MS., iv. 34. There is no explanation of this election, or why regidores were chosen. Probably there is some error, and Buelna was simply appointed alcalde auxiliar, though the people were allowed to express their choice. Indeed, Buelna is called juez auxiliar in several doc. of the year. There was no change of system. Aug. 1st, Feliciano Soberanes, from Mont., informs Gen. Vallejo of Ind. outrages in the region. Eugenio Soto's body riddled with arrows was found hanging near Sta Cruz. *Vallejo, Doc.*, MS., v. 122. 1839. Alcalde or juez auxiliar Joaquin Buelna until July, when Prefect Castro appointed José Bolcof on the ground that Buelna had long held the place, and other citizens should have a chance to hold office. *Sta Cruz, Arch.*, MS., 50; *St. Pap., Sac.*, MS., xi. 3. Síndico Macedonio Lorenzana; sec. Manuel Rodriguez, perhaps both for the next year. *Mont. Arch.*, MS., ix. 18. Gil Sanchez tithe-collector. *Sta Cruz, Arch.*, MS., 29. Branciforte's quota of recruits called for in July was 15. This vol., p. 583. Munic. receipts for year $48, expend. $39. *Mont. Co., Arch.*, MS., 18. Tumult of April 16th, in which citizens revolted against the alcalde and resisted arrest by the prefect's forces, two being killed and several wounded. *Id.*, 588; *Dept. St. Pap., Ang.*, MS., v. 3–4. 1840. Juez de paz, José Bolcof. April, 4 recruits called for. *Sta Cruz, Arch.*, MS., 22. May, 10 foreigners in the jurisdiction, 4 being naturalized. *Dept. St. Pap.*, MS., xviii. 71–3. For account of the Graham affair, many of the exiles residing in this region, see chap. i. of vol. iv.

CHAPTER XXV.

LOCAL ANNALS OF SAN FRANCISCO DISTRICT.

1831-1840.

Gain in Population—Number of Inhabitants in California, North and
South—Summary of San Francisco Events—Military Affairs—
Company Transferred to Sonoma—Pueblo and Ayuntamiento—
Granting of Lots—Later Litigation—Growth of Yerba Buena—
Richardson, Leese, and Spear—Private Ranchos of the District—
San Francisco Mission—San Rafael—Padre Amorós' Map of Mis-
sion Lands—San Francisco Solano—Pueblo of Sonoma—General
Vallejo's Achievements in the Frontera del Norte—San José Mis-
sion—A Prosperous Establishment—Santa Clara—Padres Viader
and Moreno—Pueblo de San José de Guadalupe de Alvarado—
Population—Municipal Affairs and List of Officials—Summary of
Events.

The population of gente de razon at San Francisco,
given as 300 in 1830, may be regarded as 280, about
equally divided between the peninsula and contra
costa, in 1840, the departure of the soldiers having
more than counterbalanced the gain from other
sources. Adding 750 for San José and 200 for Sonoma and the northern frontier we have a total for
the district of 1,330, a gain from 840 during the decade.[1] The ex-neophyte Indian population had meanwhile decreased from 4,920 to 2,300, of which num-

---

[1] Data for estimating the district pop., except at S. José, for which we
have a regular padron, are very meagre. The size of the ayunt.—2 regidores
—in 1835 may indicate a pop. between 50 and 200 in the jurisdiction. Also
in 1835, the resident signers to a petition were 30 in the contra costa. In
1837 the militia company of S. F. jurisdiction—peninsula and contra costa—
numbered 86, which should be about ⅓ of the pop. And finally in 1842 a
padron shows 157 gente de razon on the peninsula. In the northern frontier
district there were in 1840 about 70 soldiers, cavalry and infantry, who with
their families and those of the few rancheros etc. cannot have represented a
pop. of less than 200, my estimate.

ber not over 1,250 were still living in the ex-mission communities. Combining the totals for San Francisco and Monterey districts we have for the population of northern California 2,930 and 4,040 Indians, against 1,940 and 8,400 Indians ten years earlier, and against 2,850 and 5,100 Indians in the south. Again combining the figures for north and south we have a total population for California in 1840 of 5,780 and 9,140 Indians, against 4,250 and 18,000 Indians in 1830. The foreign population as estimated elsewhere was 380, more than half of the number probably being included in the preceding figures.

But for the organization of a municipal government and the growth of a new settlement at Yerba Buena, to be noticed presently, there is nothing in the record of events at San Francisco that calls for further mention than is given in the appended summary.[2] Never

---

[2] Summary and index of San Francisco events. 1831. Possible visit of Gov. Victoria in March or April. This vol., p. 186. Execution of Rubio for murder in Aug., a famous case. *Id.*, 191–3. Plottings of Padrés and Vallejo, and exile of the former in Oct. *Id.*, 197, 200. Cáceres, the only Spaniard in the jurisdiction, ordered away. *Id.*, 401. Adhesion of S. F. to the S. Diego plan against Victoria in Dec. *Id.*, 212. Oysters said to have been discovered in the bay by Capt. John Bell. *S. F. Call.*, June 5, 1867. 1832. S. F. adheres to the new Zamorano plan, after a little trouble and a temporary suspension of Com. Sanchez in favor of Martinez. This vol., 223–4. Mutiny on the *Wm Thompson*, smuggling by the *Bolivar*, and otter hunting in the bay. *Id.*, 364–5, 374. 1833. Trouble between Vallejo and his soldiers. *Id.*, 248. Hard times, and Vallejo's troubles with the padres. *Id.*, 322. Smuggling and seizure of vessels. *Id.*, 365–6, 369, 393. Visit of Douglas, the Scotch botanist. *Id.*, 404. 1834. Election of an ayuntamiento. See note on munic. affairs, this chapter. 1835. Proposition of the U. S. to purchase S. F. Bay. *Id.*, 400. The colonist conspirators embarked on the *Rosa. Id.*, 286–8. Dana's descriptive matter. *Two Years*, 261 et seq., 439 et seq. 1836. The presidio for the most part abandoned, the company having been transferred to Sonoma. Note on mil. affairs, this chapter. The Russians had a license to build a warehouse, but did not utilize it. This vol., p. 426. Wreck of the *Peor es Nada* in Jan. Vol. iv. 105. Celebration of July 4th. See note on Yerba Buena, this chap. 1837. Organization of a militia company. Visit of Edwards from Oregon. iv. 86. Edwards found half-a-dozen families living at the ruined presidio, and he incorrectly attributed its ruin and desertion to the late revolution against Mexico. Capt. Hinckley arrested for smuggling. iv. 103. Visits of Belcher and a part of Petit-Thouars' expedition in Oct., the narratives containing nothing on the state of affairs, though scientific observations were made. In his memorial to the gov't on Aug. 17th, Gen. Vallejo had much to say of the advantages of S. F., with 8 towns, 17 haciendas, and 25 ranchos, with 125,000 head of cattle, etc., situated near the bay, and tributary to the port. *Vallejo, Esposicion*, MS., 13–14; *Id., Doc.*, MS., iv. 299. 1838. Gov. Carrillo closes the port in Jan. This vol., p. 345. Vallejo

since the foundation had life in the peninsula establishments been more monotonous and uneventful than in this decade.   Even the stirring scenes of the revolution and following sectional quarrels in 1836–8 had little effect on the tranquillity of San Francisco, except that a few of its citizens went abroad to serve in the patriot, or rebel, army, and the rest were kept busy in awaiting and discussing news from Monterey and the south.   Belcher, Petit-Thouars, and Laplace made some explorations in the bay without having any remarkable experiences or embodying much information in their published narratives respecting the state of affairs on shore.   A small fleet of traders anchored each year in the port, but matters connected with commerce, vessels, and revenue have been pretty fully recorded elsewhere in chapters specially devoted to those subjects at all the ports.[3]

The presidial cavalry company varied in 1831–4 from 40 to 30 men rank and file, besides six or eight inválidos, half of this force or more being absent on escolta duty at the missions of Santa Clara, San José, San Rafael, and Solano, and the effective force of the

here in Feb. trying to raise men for service in the war. *Id.*, 547.   May.   Return of S. F. troops under Sanchez from the south. *Id.*, 563.   Earthquake in June, doing some damage at the mission. iv. 78.   Oct.   A band of robbers plundered stores (at the presidio?). *Vallejo, Doc.*, v. 204.   1839.   Visit of John A. Sutter in July. Vol. iv., p. 127 et seq.   Visit of Laplace in Aug. *Id.*, 153.   According to *Dept. St. Pap.*, *Mont.*, MS., iv. 107, the military post was abandoned so that no salute was fired.   Laplace's narrative gives no definite information about the state of things at S. F., though there is no lack of philosophic reflections; and there is the same lack of information in the narrative of Belcher, whose visit was in Sept.   According to Davis, *Glimpses*, MS., 44, the winter was very severe and rainy.   1840.   Nothing to be noted in the record of events.

[3] For 1831–5 see chap. xiii. this vol.; for 1836–40, chap. iii. of vol. iv.   Antonio M. Osio in charge of the revenues, $2,419 in 8 months, in 1831.   Russian vessels at S. F. during the decade, see iv. p. 158–9, 163 et seq.   1833.   Bandini in congress unable to open S. F. as a full port.   Pedro del Castillo in charge of revenues as receptor in 1833–5.   Much complaint of smuggling, and need of a treasury officer.   No custom-house officer in 1836–8.   Wm A. Richardson captain of the port from 1836 or 1837.   Vessels, tonnage, and exports in 1837–9, Richardson's record vol. iv. p. 88–93.   Vallejo from this year made earnest but unsuccessful efforts to transfer the custom-house from Mont. to S. F.   1838.   Carrillo attempts to close the port as a southern war measure. 1839.   Francisco Guerrero appointed receptor of customs after Leese had been recommended but not approved.   His pay was 25 per cent of receipts.   Richardson got $60 per month.   1840.   Douglas' estimate of S. F. exports $80,000.

garrison being from 18 to ten soldiers. The nominal expense as per pay-rolls was from $10,000 to $9,000 per year. The officers of the company, each serving at times as commandant of the post, after the retirement of Lieut Martinez in September 1831 were alféreces Mariano G. Vallejo and José Sanchez, the former being absent as member of the diputacion and revolutionist in 1832 and the latter being succeeded by Dámaso Rodriguez at the end of 1833. The company sergeants were José Berreyesa in 1831, Pablo Pacheco in 1832–5, and Cayetano Juarez from 1833.[4]

[4] San Francisco military items. 1833. Efforts of Vallejo to collect tithes in cattle for the company; 170 head collected; gov. also calls on the missions for contributions of cattle for a rancho nacional. *Pinto, Doc.*, MS., i. 67; *Vallejo, Doc.*, MS., ii. 67, *Dept. St. Pap., B. M*, MS., lxxv, 1–2; *Id., Ben. C. & T.*, ii. 73–81. March 6th, $737 in goods sent by the comisario at Mont. *Vallejo, Doc.*, MS., xxii. 25. Vallejo's complaints of privations of his men. This vol., p. 322; but also demands for more soldiers and for a treasury official. *Doc.*, MS., ii. 25, 27; *St. Pap., M. & C.*, MS., ii. 315. 1834. Jan., gov. declines to permit escoltas to go to S. Francisco to receive what the missions will give for the rancho nacional. *Dept. St. Pap.*, MS., iii. 142. May 3d, Vallejo reports the presidio buildings in a ruinous condition since the rains, the fort being nearly destroyed. He demands immediate aid to save the war material, and gets authority to act and make estimates. *Id., B. M.*, lxxviii. 5–6. Later V. suggested the sale of the buildings to soldiers on pay account or to others in exchange for live-stock for the rancho; and he is authorized to so dispose of them, reserving barracks; but there is no further record. *Vallejo, Doc.*, MS., iii. 129; xxxi. 133. For the year 1833–4, the company received $3,574, leaving $5,191 still due. *Dept. St. Pap., B. M.*, MS., lxxx. 3. 1835. Receipts from Solano in supplies $422. *Pinto, Doc.*, MS., i. 151. Sept. 10th, V. authorized to receive 200 cattle as a loan for the rancho. *Vallejo, Doc.*, MS., iii. 73. Oct. 20th, V. says he has sent 600 cattle and some horses by Carquines to the frontier rancho. No profit to be expected for two years. *Id.*, 79. 1836. A party sent to S. Rafael for cattle for the rancho. *Id.*, 109. Feb. 29th, Vallejo to gov. recommends that the best buildings be appraised and turned over to soldiers on acct of their back pay. Others may be sold for cattle for the rancho. *Id.*, 97. 1837. Over $30,000 of back pay due the company. *Id., Esposicion*, 20. Jan., a new civic company organized at S. F. under Capt. Francisco Sanchez, lieutenants José Martinez and Joaquin Castro, alféreces Manuel Sanchez and Antonio M. Peralta, with 3 sergeants, 6 corporals, and 72 privates, 86 men in all. *Vallejo, Doc.*, MS., iv. 14, xxiv. 7. Armament and war material at the presidio, report of Joaquin Piña Jan. 7th; 8 iron guns—3 24-pounders—3 of which are useless; 8 brass guns, 1 useless; 994 balls; 4 muskets, 1 pistol, 1 machete, 37 musket balls, and a few trifles. *Id.*, xxiv. 4. 1838. Oct., Spear has 2 small guns for sale to Gen. V. *Id.*, v. 214. 1839. Capt. Sanchez named as com., also Prado Mesa. Aug., minister of war, says orders have been given for the protection of S. F. *Savage, Doc.*, MS., iv. 327. Dec., the Mex. govt., in accordance with V.'s suggestions, authorized the removal of the fortifications to Angel Island. *Vallejo, Doc.*, MS., vi. 217; viii. 352; *Dept. Rec.*, MS., x. 32–3. 1840. Funds sent from Mont. to Sonoma for the comp. to amount of $2,700, and $700 for the general. Also for S. F., $2,700 in July. *Dept. St. Pap., Ben.*, iii. 146–7, 152; *Id., C. & T.*, iv. 53. Pay-roll for 1840, $14,658. March 17th, Vallejo calls on gov. for aid, being

There was also in 1831–2 an artillery detachment of
eight men under the successive command of Petronilo
Rios, Lázaro Piña, and Antonio Mendez.   In 1835
the company was tranferred to Sonoma, where its
force was reduced to 20 in 1837, but raised to nearly 50
in 1839–40.   The officers, after Vallejo had been made
captain and general, were Alférez Rodriguez to 1838;
Sergeant Juan Prado Mesa, made alférez in 1837,
and acting as comandante in 1839–40; Antonio Peña,
sergeant in 1836 and alférez in 1837; and sergeants
Cayetano Juarez in 1836, Ignacio Pacheco in 1837,
Ignacio Higuera and Lázaro Piña in 1839, and Santos
Berreyesa in 1840.   After the transfer Alférez Rodriguez remained at the presidio in 1835 with two or
three men; and after that year San Francisco was
abandoned by the regular soldiers but for an occasional
visit by an inspecting officer; and the mission escoltas
were also recalled.   In 1837 a company of civic militia
numbering 86 men was organized under Captain Francisco Sanchez, who subsequently figured as commandant of the post.   It does not appear that these militiamen did anything more than 'hold themselves in
readiness' for the country's service, or that they ever
garrisoned the presidio, where, however, from two to
six men lived with their families in 1836–40, and
where as we shall see ayuntamiento meetings were
held in 1835–8.

Down to 1834 the military commandant had exercised political and judicial jurisdiction in the San
Francisco district, except at San José and Branciforte; but now an organization of civil government, in
the north as elsewhere, was demanded by the laws, by
the spirit of the times, and by Figueroa's plans.   The
change was the more necessary because of the proposed
transfer of the military establishment to the frontera
del norte.   Besides the soldiers soon to depart for

about to station a company at S. F. *Vallejo, Doc.*, MS., ix. 79, 81.   For company rosters and accounts see *Vallejo, Doc.*, MS., xxi.–vi.; *S. F. Cuentos de
la Comp.*, MS., xxii., xxiv.–v., besides many scattered items in other archives.

Sonoma there were on the peninsula and contra costa a few gente de razon, perhaps nearly 200 in all, whose civil needs required attention. Accordingly the governor, after some preliminary correspondence with Comandante Vallejo and the taking of a census, gave orders in November 1834 for the election of an ayuntamiento to govern the pueblo of San Francisco and the adjoining region down to Llagas Creek or the Pulgas rancho on the peninsula and the ranchos across the bay eastward. The town council was duly elected, and installed in January 1835, being regularly renewed at the beginning of each year until 1839. The successive alcaldes were Francisco de Haro, José Joaquin Estudillo, Ignacio Martinez, and Haro again for a second and third term. The records of ayuntamiento meetings are not extant, and not all the members in all years can be named; but we have sufficient original documents to show the existence of the municipal government and the nature of proceedings, a summary of which is as for other towns appended in a note.[5] Meetings and elections—the former not

[5] In connection with later litigation on the S. F. pueblo lands, each of the many documents in the archives pertaining in any way to municipal affairs in 1834–36 was cited, translated, and commented on over and over again by lawyers and judges in briefs and decisions, which also contain in various combinations testimony from other sources. All this matter is extant in print in many forms; and there are several general treatises that are quite satisfactory. For this reason, and because my space does not permit the minute chronologic summary and analysis that would be in a sense desirable, and as the comparatively few items of evidence brought to light by my researches do not radically modify the conclusions previously reached, I shall attempt only a brief outline of the leading points. For more details I refer the reader to *Dwinelle's Colonial Hist. S. F.; Halleck's Land Titles in San Francisco, Decisions, etc., with Notes and Comments, etc.*, S. F., 1860; *Randolph's Argument in Hart v. Burnett*, S. F., 1850; *Jones' Pueblo Question Solved*, S. F., 1860; *Wheeler's Land Titles;* and *Cal. Supreme Court Reports.*

1834. Feb.-June, preliminary corresp. between Gov. Figueroa and Comandante Vallejo on the limits of S. F. jurisdiction, census of population, and desirability of an ayuntamiento. The limits were defined temporarily by the gov. as including the S. F. mission lands to the Sta Cruz line on the coast, the Pulgas rancho, and across the bay the ranchos of Peralta and Castro and all north and east to the gentilidad. *St. Pap., M. & C.*, MS., ii. 217-20; *Dept. St. Pap.*, MS., iii. 141. Nov. 3d, action of the diputacion, sent by gov. to Vallejo on the 4th, ordering the election of an ayunt., of alcalde, two regidores, and sindico, to reside at the presidio, and assume the political and judicial functions formerly pertaining to the mil. comandante. *Dwinelle*, add. 35-6. Nov. 4th, gov. to Vallejo, authorizing him to establish municipal govt, and approving a line fixed by him from Pt Lobos to Rincon Pt as the pueblo

very numerous, presumably—were required to be
held, and were held, so far as the records show, at
the presidio, though some of the officials and most of
the citizens lived elsewhere, the presidio, as we have

boundary. *Vallejo, Doc.*, MS., ii. 316. This was the 'Zamorano document,'
shown to be spurious, as no such 'Vallejo line' was ever adopted for the purpose indicated, though the land commission accepted it as authentic. Janssens, *Vida*, MS., 48–9, claims to have brought the gov.'s order from Mont. to
S. F., and to have witnessed the installation of the ayunt. Dec. 7th, record
of primary election at the presidio; electors chosen; Ignacio Peralta, Francisco Sanchez, Fran. Soto. Joaquin Castro, José C. Sanchez, Fran. de Haro,
Manuel Sanchez, Juan Miranda, Antonio Castro, Marcos Briones, and Apolinario Miranda, the highest no. of votes being 27. *Dwinelle*, add. 36.

1835. Alcalde Fran. de Haro, secretary Fran. Sanchez, regidores and
síndico unknown. Jan. 22d, Haro to gov., announcing that the ayunt. has
begun its sessions, having appointed a sec. at $15, and Gregorio Briones as
alcalde auxiliar of the contra costa. Jan. 31st, gov. approves the appointments. *Dept. St. Pap., Mont.*, MS., iv. 91–2. This is more definite than
Dwinelle's references for same facts. Jan. 31st, gov. to Joaq. Estudillo,
comandante of S. F. de Asis (there is no other evidence that he held such a
position), acknowledging receipt on the 23d inst of a padron, and ordering
the election of an ayunt. of 4 members according to the pop. (50 to 200?).
Dwinelle, add. 37. This order is unintelligible on its face. Dwinelle dwells
on the use of the word *partido* in the former order and *pueblo* in this, and
claims that after the 'aggregate' ayunt. of the partido was organized, the
gov., learning the no. of inhab., ordered the organization of a new 'compo-
site' ayunt. for the pueblo, which superseded the 1st. This conclusion
seems to me to rest on very slight foundation; and I prefer to suppose there
is something wrong about the 2d order, especially in view of its date. I do
not think there was a new election, though such was possibly the case on
account of some informality in the 1st; and I regard the fine distinction made
by lawyers on both sides between a partido and pueblo ayunt. as imaginary.
May 30th, petition of 30 residents of the northern ranchos (Contra Costa and
Alameda counties) to be transferred from the jurisdiction of S. F. to that of
S. José, on account of the long distance by land and perilous voyage by sea
to the place of ayunt. meetings, also the lack of proper lodgings at S. F. presidio. This was referred to the dip., and then to the respective ayunt. in
Sept. That of S. José on Nov. 4th reported in favor of the change; and
that of S. F. on Dec. 20th against it on the ground that the complaints of the
petitioners were frivolous, as they came frequently to S. F. on private business, and the presidio lodgings had been thus far satisfactory. This seems
to have ended the matter, and no change was made. *St. Pap., M. & C.*, MS.,
ii. 361–4. June, a reply to a petition of the ayunt. on assigning ejidos and
propios is mentioned in an index, but is not extant. *Dwinelle*, add. 53. July,
gov. decides that the ayunt. has no right to grant Estudillo a house lot on
the beach with sowing lands at Yerba Buena. *Dept. St. Pap., Ben., P. & J.*,
MS., vi. 16. This may have been because the granting of lots away from
the presidio required consideration, because of the location 'on the beach,' or
of the extent of land desired; at any rate on Sept. 22d, as made known by
gov. to alcalde on Oct. 27th, the dip. decided that the ayunt. could grant lots
of 100 varas and 200 varas from the shore at Yerba Buena. Dec. 13th, primary election; electors Bartolo Bojorges, José C. Sanchez, Felipe Briones,
Gabriel Castro, Manuel Sanchez, Ignacio Peralta, Joaquin Estudillo, and
Candelario Valencia. Election held in the plaza of the pueblo of S. F. de
Asis—probably at the presidio as before. *Dwinelle*, add. 47. Final election
on Dec. 27th, no record except that Joaquin Castro was chosen regidor and
his election declared null by reason of his relationship to the síndico. *Dept.*

seen, being almost entirely abandoned after 1836. In May 1839, under the new system of prefectures, the ayuntamiento was abolished here as elsewhere, and a justice of the peace was appointed, Francisco Guer-

St. Pap., Ben., P. & J., MS., vi. 18. The other officers chosen were as follows.

1836. Alcalde José Joaquin Estudillo, who announces his election Jan. 1st. *Ib.* Regidores Gregorio Briones and José C. Sanchez. *Dwinelle*, 62. Sec. Fran. Sanchez; alcalde auxiliar on the frontier Nicolás Higuera. *Vallejo, Doc.*, MS., iii. 181. Other appointments were probably made on the frontier, which Vallejo refused to recognize, being sustained by the dip., which body in July decided that the region north of the bay was subject only to military authority. *Dept. St. Pap., Ben., P. & J.*, MS., iii. 39–41; *Leg. Rec.*, MS., iii. 18–19. This year lots at Yerba Buena were granted by the ayunt. to Wm A. Richardson and Jacob P. Leese. No record of elections for the next year.

1837. Alcalde Ignacio Martinez, 1st regidor, holding over, probably José C. Sanchez; síndico Blas Angelino, sec. probably Fran. Sanchez, capt. of the port Wm A. Richardson, alcalde auxiliar of Contra Costa Francisco Armijo. Three lots at Yerba Buena granted to John Fuller, Francisco Sanchez, and J. Feil. Dec. 3d, primary election; electors Fran. Guerrero, Fran. de Haro, Vicente Miramontes, Antonio M. Peralta, José Ant. Alviso, Juan Bernal, Leandro Galindo, José C. Bernal, and Domingo Sais; highest vote 29. Final election on Jan. 8, 1838, result as below. *Dwinelle*, add. 53–4. But according to *Halleck*, 123, Wm A. Richardson was first elected alcalde, declining to serve.

1838. Alcalde Fran. de Haro, 2d regidor Domingo Sais, síndico José Rodriguez, sec. perhaps still Sanchez, alcalde aux. at S. Mateo Gregorio Briones. *S. Jose Arch.*, MS., v. 34. Capt. of port, Richardson. Lots at Y. B. granted this year to Fran. Cáceres and Wm Gulnac. Sept., trouble between Leese and Hinckley and Spear, partly on account of disagreement about a lot. *Dept. St. Pap.*, MS., iv. 226–7; xvii. 56. The Ojo de Figueroa near the presidio granted to Apolinario Miranda by Com. Sanchez(?). M. had already a house there. *Dwinelle*, add. 54–5. Dec. 31st, alcalde sends a sumario for the murder of José Peralta by his relative José Ant. Galindo in Sept. *Dept. St. Pap., Ben.*, v. 280–2; *Id., P. & J.*, MS., vi. 18. Election on Dec. 31st with result as below. *Dept. St. Pap.*, MS., xvii. 56.

1839. Alcalde Vicente Miramontes (who did not accept or was not approved, Haro continuing to act), regidores Domingo Sais and Tiburcio Vasquez, síndico Fran. Cáceres. In May under the new system the ayunt. ceased to exist, and on the 15th Francisco Guerrero became juez de paz by the gov.'s temporary appointment. *Id., Mont*, iv. 97. Vicente Miramontes juez suplente from July. *Id.*, 103–4; John Fuller síndico from Aug.; Richardson capt. of port; José Ant. Alviso and John Coppinger from July 20th jueces at S. Francisquito and Corte Madera; Ignacio Higuera 'encargado' at Contra Costa till May, when Ignacio Peralta was appointed juez and S. Pablo de Contra Costa was thus formally separated from the jurisdiction of S. F. *Estudillo, Doc.*, MS., i. 257. Lots at Y. B. granted this year to Salv. Vallejo, José Peña, Wm S. Hinckley, and John C. Davis; and on one occasion the gov. was consulted about certain applications for lots. There was some trouble with Cayetano Juarez, who when appointed for some duty in the north declared that the frontera did not belong to the jurisdiction of S. F. The alcalde desired permission to send the prisoner Galindo to S. José for want of a jail and guard. In Feb. Dolores was made the cabecera of the partido, extending from Llagas Creek to Sonoma; but no sub-prefect was appointed at S. F. until after 1840, S. José being made temporarily the cabecera. *S. José Arch.*, MS., ii. 18. April 20th, Haro asks instructions about granting a lot at the mission. *Dwinelle*, add. 61. May 21st, gov. permits Leese

rero holding that position in 1839–40. At the same time the mission was made nominally head town of the partido, though there was as yet no sub-prefect here; the municipal chief transferred his office also to Dolores from the presidio, where, in theory at least, it had been before; and the contra costa ranchos were cut off from the jurisdiction of San Francisco and given a júez de paz of their own. Meanwhile the town authorities granted seventeen house lots at Yerba Buena in 1836–40, and three lots at the mission in 1840.

The subject of municipal government at San Francisco in these years assumed later an importance not dreamed of at the time, from the fact that a great town grew up on the peninsula. Local authorities continued to grant lots as a matter of course down to 1846 and later, and after the American occupation the question whether lands not so granted belonged to the city or to the United States came up for settlement. This is not the place to record the litigation in its many phases, but brief mention cannot be avoided. It was finally decided, after unlimited discussion extending through many years and several adverse decisions, by the land commission, California

to build at Visitacion. *Dept. Rec.*, MS., x. 12. May 26th, Guerrero publishes a bando of police regulations. *Dept. St. Pap., Mont.*, MS., iv. 100. July 15th, Guerrero makes known to the prefect the desire of citizens to settle at the mission, favored by himself as also by the prefect, and Nov. 30th by the gov., who authorizes the granting of lots at the mission, 50 varas in extent, the settlers to use for their cattle the surrounding lands except S. Mateo and the coast, but not to disturb the Ind. or embarrass the administrator as long as the community exists. *Id.*, v. 102; xvi. 24. Many other routine communications of the year from Guerrero to prefect in *Id.*, v. 92–110. Alvarado's idea, *Miscel. Hist. Pap.*, MS., no. 24, is that the above movement was merely a transfer of the juzgado, or municipal headquarters, from presidio to mission; and this, I think, was what was practically effected, there being no change of pueblo or thought of a new pueblo proper.

1840. Guerrero still juez de paz. Feb. 1st, accepts the continuation of appointment. Feb. 2d, writes to prefect on his proposed plan of Dolores so as to regulate the granting of lots which the gov. has authorized. He will make the church the centre, and will repair some of the ruined buildings which the vecinos have occupied for many years. He desires the administrator to give up or lend a room for a jail. Many other routine communications of the year. *Dept. St. Pap., Mont.*, MS., v. 110–13. Lots were granted this year at Yerba Buena to Leese, J. A. Vallejo, J. B. Cooper, J. Vioget (2); and at Dolores to L. Galindo, C. Valencia, and F. Gomez.

supreme court, and United States district court, that San Francisco in 1835–46 was a pueblo; that as such it was entitled by Spanish and Mexican law and usage to four leagues of land, and that the United States was under obligation to recognize the pueblo title.[6]

[6] The position of Jones and Randolph as representing the opposition, was that there was at S. F. no pueblo, in the sense of a corporate body owning or entitled to own lands. There were two pueblos in the sense of 'settlements,' each originally intended to become the nucleus of a town, and each having a certain territorial franchise or right to the use of certain lands—the presidio for military, and the mission for missionary purposes. The presidio might become the seat of a pueblo, civil community, or municipality, by the settlement of retired soldiers; but these soldiers settled elsewhere, and the presidio became merely an abandoned military post. The mission also might by secularization and the aggregation of settlers de razon to the ex-neophytes have become a pueblo, but did not, secularization proving a failure and the Ind. disappearing. The ayunt. established in 1835 was for the government of the whole partido, not specially for the pueblo, and its creation was not the creation of a Pueblo de S. Francisco. A third pueblo, or settlement, sprang up at Yerba Buena from 1835-6. As a matter of convenience, the govt at Monterey delegated to the partido ayunt. authority to grant lots at Yerba Buena, and later at Dolores, and such lots were legally granted. Each settlement might have obtained from the govt certain lands for propios, etc., but never did so. All the lots were granted either at Y. B. or at Dolores, never at the pueblo of S. F. The 'pueblo system' so much talked of was for the most part an invention of later times; or if not so, the 4 leagues of land to which a pueblo was entitled must be formally granted by the govt, or at least marked out officially, the U. S. being under no obligation to recognize a title that the Mex. govt might, under certain circumstances if applied to, have seen fit to concede.

As a matter of fact S. F. was a pueblo exactly like S. Diego, Sta Bárbara, and Monterey. Much confusion has been caused by the multiplicity of names applied to peninsula establishments, such as presidio, mission, pueblo, establecimiento, port, S. Francisco, S. F. de Asis, Dolores, Yerba Buena, etc., and most of it may be removed by noting that San Francisco de Asis was the legal and proper name from the first for all on the peninsula, the other terms being used to indicate localities at S. F., very much as Mission, Presidio, or North Beach are still used. In early times S. F. was a mission-military establishment intended eventually to become a town or pueblo of Spanish citizens, composed of ex-neophyte Ind., retired soldiers and their descendants, colonists or settlers from abroad, naturalized foreigners—any or all of these. The pueblo would begin to exist, in the familiar sense of the term, whenever there should be any residents besides soldiers and neophytes; in the legal sense when a local civil govt should be provided for them. Nature in this case fixed the natural bounds of the pueblo lands on three sides; in the distribution of lots the convenience of citizens would be limited only by needs, actual and prospective, of military defence and of Ind. yet to be released from neophytism. In 1834 S. F. was a pueblo in the ordinary sense; in 1835, by the organization of an ayunt., it became a pueblo in a strictly legal sense. Nothing more was required. An ayunt. without a pueblo could have no existence; though the jurisdiction of every ayunt. extends far beyond its pueblo. This pueblo was not the presidio, it was not the mission, it was San Francisco. The presidio was the place of meeting, and the natural centre, or starting point, of the pueblo; but the residents did not want lots there, preferring Yerba Buena cove. The ayunt. had the right under the laws to grant town lots; possibly would have granted them without consulting the

The decision was, I think, entirely in accordance with fact, law, and equity; though many abler men still hold the contrary opinion. Among the many champions of the respective sides in the controversy may be appropriately named Edmund Randolph and William Carey Jones against the pueblo title, and in favor of it Henry W. Halleck and John W. Dwinelle, the latter's *Colonial History of San Francisco* being the most extensive and satisfactory treatise on the subject. As is their wont, the lawyers succeeded in making of a comparatively simple matter a very complicated one; but their efforts were valuable contributions to local history.

The settlement of Yerba Buena, nucleus of the modern city, had its humble beginning in this decade, and contained in 1840 more than half-a-dozen structures. As we have seen, the name Yerba Buena had been transferred from the anchorage west to that south of Loma Alta, or Telegraph Hill, where several vessels had anchored before 1830, where a French trader had landed to build a boat, and where the construction of a guard-house had been ordered in 1827, there being no evidence that it was ever built.[7] At any rate in 1831–4 all was in a state of nature but for the presence of a party of foreign boat-builders for a time in 1831 or 1832.[8] Vessels were still per-

---

gov.—though it was customary in Cal. to ask his advice and opinion on the most trifling measures—at the presidio; was instructed by the govt that it had the right to grant lots at Yerba Buena; and later received like instructions respecting Dolores. Lots were granted at these two points, and would have been granted at other points within the probable pueblo limits had they been desired. The gov. and dip. had no powers in the granting of lands that could be delegated to an ayunt. They could inform the ayunt. as to its powers, and to a certain extent regulate their exercise. The right of the pueblo to its lands was recognized indirectly by the govt in several ways, even in the granting of ranchos which infringed on the conventional four leagues. There can be no doubt that at any time before 1846 the local authorities might have had four leagues of land formally set apart for the town. Whether their failure to do so forfeited the city's right under the U. S. was a question for the U. S. to settle; but having assumed the obligations of Mexico by relinquishing the pretension to insist on perfect titles in the case of private ranchos, the govt virtually conceded the pueblo title, and the courts could not do otherwise than confirm it.

[7] See vol. ii. p. 590.

[8] James W. Weeks, *Reminiscences*, MS., 68–72, states that himself, George

mitted to anchor here, though not without occasional objection.[9] In 1835 William A. Richardson became the first settler, erecting as a temporary dwelling a tent, or 'shanty of rough boards' as Dana saw it in December, replaced within a year or two by an adobe building. His lot was granted in 1836, and his building stood near the corner of what were later Dupont and Clay streets. His business was the collection of produce from points about the bay to make up the cargoes of trading vessels by the aid of Indian crews who navigated two or three old launches belonging to himself and the missions. His Indians had a temascal, or bath-house, at the foot of Sacramento street, the water front being the present Montgomery street.[10] In 1836 Jacob P. Leese, in partnership with Spear and Hinckley, obtained a lot and built a wooden structure for house and store near Richardson's, completing the building in time for a grand celebration on July 4th, at which assembled as guests—and prospective customers of the enterprising proprietor—all the residents for leagues around.[11] In 1837, or possibly the next year, Leese obtained through the influence of Governor Alvarado permis-

Ferguson, John Matthews, and perhaps one Brown, undertook to repair an old launch of Captain Richardson's, towing her to Y. B. for the purpose, and living there for several months. But they abandoned the launch after doing much work on her. W. makes the date 1832, but he also speaks of the execution of Rubio, which was in 1831.

[9] Dec. 3, 1833. Receptor to admin. at Mont., urging that vessels be obliged to anchor in sight of the presidio and not at Y. B. *Dept. St. Pap., B. M.*, MS., lxxv. 3. Davis, *Glimpses*, MS., 7, says that on his arrival at Y. B. in 1833 Candelario Miramontes had a potato-patch on what is now the plaza. From him D. borrowed a horse for trips to the mission and presidio, keeping him tethered near the shore.

[10] Authorities for the progress of Y. B. in these early years are *Hittell's Hist. S. F.*, 77 et seq.; *Soulé's Annals of S. F.*, 162 et seq.; *Tuthill's Hist. Cal.*, 289 et seq.; *Dana's Two Years*, 261-2; *Davis' Glimpses*, MS.; and a great variety of newspaper and other accounts. As to minute details there is no agreement. According to Hittell the Widow Briones lived in the North Beach region, building about 1836 an adobe house at the corner of Filbert and Powell streets. José Ramon Sanchez, *Notas*, MS., 16-17, says that in the presidio region, but distinct from the presidio buildings, were two houses, one, occupied by the Sra de Higuera, built of timber by the Russians; the other of adobe at the Ojo de agua del Polin.

[11] See in *Annals of S. F.*, 170, a view—not from a photograph taken on the spot—of the house and festivities.

sion to occupy a beach lot on Montgomery street near Commercial, where he erected a large and substantial frame structure.   In 1838 the trail to the mission was widened into a very rough wagon road; and Rosalía Leese began life as the first child born at Yerba Buena, on April 15th.

Leese dissolved his partnership with Spear and Hinckley this year, and Spear, after vain efforts to secure the store on the beach, obtained permission to occupy another lot a little farther north, at the corner of Clay and Montgomery, with a ship's house landed from the *Kent*.   Leese tried to prevent the success of this scheme, and even went so far as to offer to give his building, if its location was to be made the 'pretext for illegal concessions by the alcalde,' to the government for a custom-house;[12] but this offer was not accepted, or fulfilled, since the building was sold later to the Hudson's Bay Company.   Spear, however, built another store adjoining 'Kent Hall' probably before the end of 1840.[13]   As we have seen, seventeen building lots were granted before the end of the decade, and doubtless several small buildings were erected besides the six that I have mentioned; but I make no attempt here to identify them.[14]   In 1839

[12] Sept. 11, 1838, Leese to Alvarado. *Dept. St. Pap.*, MS., iv. 226–7.   The gov. was expected at Y. B. when the matter was to be settled.   Hinckley and Spear also sent the gov. a complaint against Leese. *Id.*, xvii. 56.   Evidently there was a bitter business quarrel.

[13] Davis, *Glimpses*, MS., 193 et seq., who was Spear's agent from 1838, says that John Perry, a naturalized Mex. citizen, got a grant of the lot and deeded it to Spear; but there is no record of any such grant.

[14] Sutter, *Pers. Remin.*, MS., 16–18, says that on his arrival besides Spear & Hinckley's store within 50 yards of his vessel at anchor, and Richardson's adobe on Dupont St, there was a little frame building belonging to John Fuller near Sacramento and Montgomery, Prudon's adobe on Montgomery near Telegraph Hill, and a few other small houses.   Davis, *Glimpses*, MS., 197–8, implies that the two-story wooden grist-mill on Clay between Montgomery and Kearny was put in operation in 1839–40, the machinery being brought from Callao for H. and S. on the *Corsair* in 1839.   The same writer, p. 18–19, 191–2, describes the celebration of July 4th in 1839, at Leese's house, and that in 1840, including a picnic at the Rincon and a ball at Richardson's.   April 11, 1839, Manuel Pedrorena to Capt. Fitch on the business prospects for F. at Y. B., where he is advised to open an establishment. There are four small launches running on the bay, and a new large one is expected for Leese.   Y. B. is the liveliest port of Cal. *Fitch, Doc.*, MS., 59. May 10th, Gov. Alvarado to Vallejo.   Intends building at Y. B. warehouses

Captain Jean Vioget was employed to make a survey and map of Yerba Buena. His survey, by which lots were granted from that date, and to which those already granted were made to conform, covered the tract now included by California and Pacific between Montgomery and Stockton streets. No names were given to the streets, and none of the blocks had exactly the position of later times. The population of this little village in 1840 was probably about 50 souls, including 16 foreigners.

I append a list of private ranchos granted before 1840,[15] including for convenience all in the northern

and a wharf, so as to deter the Russians from desiring to establish themselves there. The S. F. merchants want all the advantages but only build shanties, and don't even keep them in repair. *Vallejo, Doc.*, MS., vii. 32.

[15] Ranchos of S. Francisco district, including all from Sta Clara Co. northward. Those marked with a * were rejected by the L. C. or U. S. courts. Abrevadero, see Llano. Acalanes (Contra Costa), 1 league, granted to Candelario Valencia in 1834; Elam Brown claimant. Agua Caliente (Alameda), 2 l., 1839, Fulgencio Higuera, who was cl. Agua Caliente (Sonoma), 1840, Lázaro Piña; conf. in sections to J. Hooker, M. G. Vallejo, T. M. Leavenworth, and C. P. Stone. *Alameda, rancho not named, 1840, Guillermo Castro, who was cl. Alameda Co. ranchos, see Agua Caliente, Arroyo de Alameda, Pozitas, S. Antonio, S. Leandro, S. Lorenzo, Sta Rita, Valle de S. José. *Los Angeles Island (S. F. Bay), 1839, A. M. Osio, who was cl. Las Ánimas or La Brea (Sta Clara), 1802, 1834, Mariano Castro. In 1836 Josefa Romero de Castro and fam. and Antonio German and fam., 48 persons in all, were living at Las Ánimas and La Brea. See also*S. Felipe y Las Ánimas. *Arroyo de la Alameda (Sta Clara ?), 1,000 varas, 1840, Jesus Vallejo, who was cl. Arroyo de las Nueces y Bolbones (Contra Costa), 2 l., 1834, J. S. Pacheco, whose heirs were cl. *Arroyo de S. Antonio (Sonoma), 1840, Antonio Ortega; C. White cl. Arroyo Seco (Sacramento), 11 l., 1840, Teodosio Yorba; Andrés Pico cl. Ausaymas (Tuolumne), 2 l., 1836, F. P. Pacheco, who was cl. Baulinas, see Tamales. Bolbones, see Arroyo. Brea, see Ánimas. Buri Buri (S. F.) 1835, José Sanchez; José de la Cruz Sanchez cl. Camaritas (S. F.), 300 v., 1840, J. J. Noé; F. Vassault cl. Cañada del Corte de Madera (Sta Clara), 1833, D. Peralta and M. Martinez; D. C. Peralta cl. Cañada de Guadalupe (S. F.), a petition of Manuel Sanchez in Feb. 1835, in *Doc. Hist. Cal.*, MS., i. 482, not granted. Cañada de Herrera (Marin), ½ l., 1839, Domingo Sais, who was cl. Cañada de Pala (Sta Clara), 8,000 v., 1839, J. J. Bernal, who was cl. Cañada de S. Felipe y Las Ánimas (Sta Clara), 2 l., Thos. Bowen; C. M. Weber cl. Cañada de Raimundo (S. Mateo), 2½ l., 1840, John Coppinger, whose widow was cl. *Capay (Tehama), 5 l., 1835 (1845?), Josefa Soto; P. B. Reading cl. Los Carneros (Solano), 1836, Nicolás Higuera; C. E. Hart, Ed. Wilson et al. cl. Caymus (Napa), 2 l., 1836, Geo. Yount, who was cl. Coche, see Ojo de Agua. Contra Costa Co. ranchos, see Acalanes, Arroyo de Nueces, Laguna de Palos Colorados, Médanos, Mt Diablo, S. Pablo, S. Ramon. Corral de Tierra (S. Mateo), 1 l., 1839, Tiburcio Vasquez, who was cl. Corral de Tierra (S. F.), 1 l., 1839, F. G. Palomares, whose heirs were cl. Corte de Madera del Presidio (Marin), 1 l., 1834, John Reed, whose heirs were cl. Corte de Madera de Novato (Marin), 1 l., 1839, John Martin, who was cl. See also Cañada. Diablo, see Mt Diablo. Entre Napa (Napa), 1836, Nicolás Higuera; conf. (or in two cases rejected)

district or all above the Santa Clara valley, instead
of introducing in different parts of the chapter separate lists for San José, the peninsula, the contra

in 12 tracts to different men. Estéro Americano (Sonoma), 2 l., 1839, Ed.
M. McIntosh; Jasper O'Farrell cl. Esteros, see Rincon. Figueroa, see Ojo
de Agua. Gatos, see Rinconada. Guadalupe, see Cañada. Guilicos (So-
noma), 4 l., 1837, John Wilson, who was cl. Herrera, see Cañada. Isla de
Yeguas, see Mare Isl. Juntas, see S. Ramon. Juristac (Sta Clara), 1 l.,
1835, A. & F. German, who were cl. Laguna de la Merced (S. Mateo & S.
F.), 1½ l., 1835, José Ant. Galindo; Josefa de Haro et al. cl. Laguna de
Palos Colorados (Contra Costa), 3 l., 1835, 1841, Joaquin Moraga and Juan
Bernal cl. Laguna Seca (Sta Clara), 4 l., 1834, Juan Alvires; heirs of Wm
Fisher cl. Llagas, S. F. de las (Sta Clara), 6 l., 1834, Cárlos Castro;
Murphy cl.; 12 persons living here in 1836. *Llana del Abrevadero (Sta
Clara), 1822, Ant. Higuera et al. cl. Mare Island (Solano), 1840-1, Victor
Castro; Lissell & Aspinwall cl. Marin Co. ranchos, see Cañada de Herrera,
Corte de Madera, Nicasio, Novato, Pt Quintin, Pt Peyes, S. José, Sauza-
lito, Tamales. Médanos (Contra Costa), 2 l., 1839, José A. Mesa et al.; J.
D. Stevenson et al. cl. Mejanos (Médanos?) (Contra Costa), 4 l., 1835, José
Noriega; John Marsh cl. Merced, see Laguna. Milpitas (Sta Clara), 1 l.,
1835, José M. Alviso, who was cl. (Claim of Nicolás Berreyesa on a grant of
1834 rejected.) Molino (Sonoma), or Rio Ayoska, 10½ l., J. B. R. Cooper,
who was cl. Monte del Diablo (Contra Costa), 1834, 1844, Salvio Pacheco,
who was cl. Napa (Napa Co.), 1838, Salvador Vallejo, confirmed in 24 tracts
to dif. men, and two claims rejected. *Napa, 4 l., 1834, C. Brown et al.
Napa Co. ranchos, see also Carneros, Caymus, Entre Napa, Salvador's rancho.
*Nicasio (Marin), 20 l., T. Quilaguegui et al. (Ind.); J. B. Alvarado cl.
Novato (Marin), 2 l., 1839, Fernando Félix; B. Simmons, cl. See also Corte
de Madera. Nueces, see Arroyo. Ojo de Agua de la Coche (Sta Clara), 2 l.,
1835, Juan M. Hernandez; B. Murphy cl. Ojo de Agua de Figueroa (S. F.),
100 v., Apolinario Miranda, whose heirs were cl. Pala (Sta. Clara),
1 l., 1835, I. Higuera; E. White et al. cl. See also Cañada. Palos
Colorados, see Laguna. Petaluma (Sonoma), 10 l., 1834, 1843-4, M. G. Vallejo cl. Pinole (Contra Costa), probably occupied by Ignacio Martinez, to
whom it was granted later. Polka (Sta Clara), 1 l., 1833, Isabel Ortega; B.
Murphy, cl. Potrero Nuevo, see Rincon. Pozitas (Alameda), 2 l., 1839,
Salvio Pacheco; J. Noriega and R. Livermore, cl. Presidio, see Corte de
Madera. Pulgas (S. Mateo), 4 l., 1836 and earlier, Luis Argüello, whose
heirs were cl. Punta de Quintin (Marin), 2 l., 1840, J. B. R. Cooper; B. R.
Buckelew, cl. Punta de Reyes (Marin), 8 and 2 l., 1836, James R. Berry;
B. Phelps and A. Randall, cl. A suit between Berry and Osio in 1844 is re-
corded in Dept. St. Pap., Ben., P. and J., iv. 49-52. Purísima Concepcion
(Sta Clara), 1 l., 1840, José Gorgonio, et al.; Juana Briones cl. Quien Sabe,
see Sta Ana. Quintin, see Punta. Raimundo, see Cañada. Rincon de los
Esteros (Sta Clara), 1838, Ignacio Alviso; Ellen C. White, Fran. Berreyesa et
al., and Rafael Alviso, cl. Rincon de Salinas y Potrero Nuevo (S. F.), 1 l.,
1839. J. C. Bernal, who was cl. Rinconada de los Gatos (Sta Clara) 1½ l.,
1840, S. Peralta and J. Hernandez, who were cl. Rio Ayoska, see Molino.
Sacramento Co., see Arroyo Seco. Salinas, see Rincon. Salvador's Rancho,
(Napa), 520 acres, 1839, S. Vallejo; conf. in 4 tracts to dif. men. San An-
tonio (Alameda), 1820, Luis Peralta; conf. in 5 tracts to heirs, etc. San An-
tonio (Sta Clara), 1839, Juan Prado Mesa; Encarn. Mesa et al., and Wm. A.
Dana et al., cl. (Three claims on this grant rejected.) San Antonio, see
Arroyo. S. Felipe, see Las Ánimas. S. Francisco co. ranchos, see Angeles Isl.,
Camaritos, Cañada-de Guadalupe, Corral de Tierra, L. Merced, Ojo de Agua,
Rincon de Salinas, Yerba Buena Isl.; also pueblo lots before L. C. granted to
Bernal, Estudillo, Gulnac, Leese and Vallejo, Valencia. See also Llagas.

costa, and Sonoma, or the frontera del norte. These ranchos were about eighty in number; but the only ones about whose exact population during the decade anything is known were a few in Santa Clara which have already been mentioned as within the jurisdiction of Monterey.

At San Francisco mission, Padre Esténega, retiring to the south, was succeeded in 1833 by Padre Lorenzo Quijas, a Zacatecan; and the latter in 1834 by Padre José de Jesus María Gutierrez, who served to the end of 1839. The neophytes numbered 204 in

S. Francisquito (Sta Clara), 1839, Antonio Buelna; M. Concepcion V. de Rodriguez et al., cl. S. Isidro (Sta Clara), 1 l., 1833, Quintin Ortega, who was cl. 39 persons living here in 1836. S. José (Marin), 1½ l., 1840, Ignacio Pacheco, who was cl. S. Leandro (Alameda), occupied in 1838 by J. J. Estudillo, to whom it was granted later. There were boundary disputes between Estudillo and Guillermo Castro, who occupied the rancho of S. Lorenzo. *S. Mateo, 2 l., 1836, 1841, J. C. Sanchez, who was cl. S. Mateo co. ranchos, see Buri Buri, Cañada de Raimundo, Corral de Tierra, L. Merced, Pulgas, S. Mateo, S. Pedro. S. Miguel (Sonoma), 6 l., 1840, 1844, Mark West, whose heirs were cl. S. Pablo (Contra Costa), 4 l., 1834. Francisco Castro and heirs et al.; Joaquin I. Castro, cl.; rancho also called Cochiyunes. *Leg. Rec.*, MS., iii. 78. S. Pedro (S. Mateo), 2 l., 1839, Francisco Sanchez, who was cl. S. Ramon (Contra Costa), 2 l., 1833, Rafael Soto de Pacheco et al., who were cl. S. Ramon, 1 l. 1834, José M. Amador; Leo Norris, cl. S. Ramon (Alameda), 4 l., 1835, J. M. Amador, who was cl. S. Ramon or Las Juntas (Contra Costa), 2 l., 1833, Bartolo Pacheco and Mariano Castro; Domingo Peralta, cl. Sta Ana y Quien Sabe (Sta Clara), 7 l., 1839, Manuel Larios and J. M. Ánzar, who were cl. Sta Clara, see Rio. Sta Clara co. ranchos, see Ánimas, Arroyo de la Alameda, Cañada de Corte de Madera, Cañada de Pala, Cañ. de S. Felipe, Juristac, Laguna Seca, Llagas, Llano del Abrevadero, Milpitas, Ojo de Agua, Pala, Polka, Purísima, Rincon de Esteros, Rinconada de los Gatos, S. Antonio, S. Francisquito, S. Isidro, Sta Ana, Sta Teresa, Solis, Tularcitos, and Yerba Buena. Sta Rita (Alameda), 1839, J. D. Pacheco, who was cl. Sta Rosa (Sonoma?), 1831. Rafael Gomez. *Dept. Rec.*, MS., ix. 78 (not before L. C.), Sta Teresa (Sta Clara), 1 l., 1834, Joaquin Bernal; Agustin Bernal, cl. Sauzalito (Marin), 3 l., 1835, José Ant. Galindo; (perhaps regranted in 1838 to) W. A. Richardson, cl. Socayre, see Yerba Buena. Solis (Sta Clara), (1835?), Mariano Castro, whose heirs were cl. Solano co. ranchos, see Carneros, Entre Napa, Mare Isl., and Soscol. Sonoma co. ranchos, see Agua Caliente, Arroyo de S. Antonio, Estero Americano, Guilicos, Molino, Petaluma, S. Miguel, and Sta Rosa. Soscol (Solano), used as a rancho nacional. Tamales and Baulinas (Marin), 2 l., 1836, Rafael García. who was cl. See Punta de Reyes, also. Tehama co., see Capay. Tularcitos (Sta Clara), 1821, José Higuera, whose heirs were cl. Tuolumne co., see Ausaymas. Valle de S. José (Alameda), 1839, Antonio M. Pico; Ant. Suñol et al., cl. Visitacion (S. F.), 1839, applied for and occupied, granted later. See also Cañada de Guadalupe. Yeguas, see Mare Isl. Yerba Buena or Socayre (Sta Clara), 1833, A. Chabolla, who was cl. *Yerba Buena Isl. (S. F.), 1838, José Castro; J. S. Polack, cl.

1832, probably less than 150 in 1834, and at the end
of the decade there were left only 90 living at San
Mateo, with possibly 50 more scattered in the district.[16]   Crops were small, and records of farming op-

[16] S. Francisco mission statistics 1831-4. (No figures whatever for 1833-
4.) Decrease in pop. 219 to about 150 (204 in 1832). Baptisms 7 and 8 in
1831-2. Deaths 10 and 11 in 1831-2. Gain in large stock 5,132 to 6,018 in
1832, and 10,329 in 1835; horses, etc., 932 to 1,511 in 1835; sheep 2,000 to
4,250 in 1835. Crops 1,670 bush. in 1831, 1,036 bush. in 1832.

Statistics for 1835-40. Debt in Nov. 1834, $10,089. *St. Pap. Miss.*, MS.,
ix. 65. Inventory of July 28, 1835. Account books, etc., no valuation;
buildings minutely described, including 27 structures besides the principal
vivienda, $22,482; utensils and furniture $319; manufacturing apparatus
$233; goods and produce in storehouse $2,414; garden with fences and fruit-
trees $334; corral $335; farming tools $34; launch and boat $880; live-stock,
chiefly on the coast, 4,445 cattle, 691 horses, 2,125 sheep, 5 mules, 6 asses,
122 swine, $17,172; church property, buildings $9,057, ornaments, etc.,
$8,770, total $17,827; S. Mateo buildings and produce $2,753; lands, 5 leagues
at the mission, 3 l. at S. Mateo, 9 l. at the Parage de la Costa as estimated,
for there was no doc. to show extent and no survey, no value given; credits,
40 items, the largest being the estate of Luis Argüello, $402; Id. of Pablo de
Sala $416, and Joaquin Ortega $300, total $2542; grand total $67,227, less
$7,222 debts (13 items, largest A. B. Thompson $1,948, Virmond $2,668,
John C. Jones $1,183), balance $60,004. Original signed by Estudillo, Flores,
Valle, and Pedro Castillo in *Vallejo, Doc.*, MS., xxxi. 220; also in *St. Pap. Miss.*,
MS., vi. 19-21. Sept. 23, 1839. Hartnell found 89 Ind. all at S. Mateo; 758
cattle, 967 horses, 1,272 sheep, 34 mules, and 2 asses. *Hartnell, Diario*, MS.,
43. May 13, 1840, there were 320 cattle, 707 horses, 1,300 sheep, 40 mules,
and 8 asses, other remnants of property being of no value. *St. Pap. Miss.*,
MS., vii. 36-7, and debts amounting to $2,615. *Pico, Pap. Miss.*, MS., 47-
51.

Statistics of 1776-1832. Total of baptisms, 6,998, of which 3,715 Ind.
adults, 2,829 Ind. children, 454 children de razon; annual average 115.
Marriages 2,121, of which 85 de razon; average 37. Deaths 5,553, of which
3,464 Ind. adults, 1,900 Ind. children, 58 and 111 gente de razon; annual av-
arage 94; average death rate 12.4 per cent of pop. Largest pop. 1,252 in
1820; males always in excess; children ⅓ to ½. Largest no. of cattle 11,240
in 1808; horses 1,239 in 1831; mules 42 in 1813; sheep 11,324 in 1813; all
kinds 22,663 animals in 1805. Total product of wheat 114,480 bush., yield
10 fold; barley 59,500 bush., 9 fold; maize 16,900 bush., 51 fold; beans 19,-
380 bush., 25 fold; miscel. grains 19,053 bush., 24 fold.

Summary of events, etc. 1831. Status under Echeandía's decree, never
enforced. This vol., p. 306-7. 1833. Proposition before the dip. to fix
bounds of mission lands. *Id.*, 249. Reports in favor of secularization. *Id.*,
333, 335. 1834. Joaquin Estudillo appointed comisionado in Sept. *St. Pap.,
Miss.*, MS., ix. 62. May 10th, petition of the padre to dip. for a definition
of boundaries. *Leg. Rec.*, MS., ii. 63. Sept. 28th, Estudillo recommends the
discharge of one of the two majordomos to save expense. *St. Pap. Miss.*, MS.,
ix. 62. Oct., claim of a neófita, married to Robles of Branciforte, for 65
head of cattle left by her father and incorporated with the mission herds. P.
Abella testified that he knew nothing of the matter, and the gov. decided
that the woman was entitled to only her pro rata on the general distribution.
Dept. St. Pap., Ben., MS., v. 22-31, 85-92. 1835. Estudillo having some
trouble with the padre, Ignacio del Valle came up from Sta Cruz to take his
place or to aid him; and on July 28th, as per inventory already cited, the
estate was turned over to Gumesindo Flores as administrator. *Valle, Lo Pasado*, MS., 10; *Sta Cruz Arch.*, MS., 74; *St. Pap., Miss.*, MS., vi. 19. The

erations amount to nothing; but in live-stock there seems to have been a large gain down to the secularization in 1834–5. Joaquin Estudillo was the comisionado, aided by Ignacio del Valle; and the successive administrators were Gumesindo Flores in 1835–6, José de la Cruz Sanchez in 1836–40, and Tiburcio Vasquez from 1840. The inventory of the transfer in 1835 showed a total valuation of $60,000, or, for real estate and fixtures, land not being valued, $25,-800; church property $17,800; and available assets, chiefly live-stock, in excess of debts, $16,400. In 1840 the debt amounted to only $2,600, but the little remnant of cattle and sheep could not have been worth much more. If any property was ever divided among the Indians, there are no records to show it.

Padre Amorós died at San Rafael in 1832,[17] and

trouble between Estudillo and P. Gutierrez arose from a charge of the former that the latter had neglected his duties in administering the sacraments to the dying Indians. E. complained to the gov., at which Prefect García Diego was angry, deeming it an interference of secular officials in matters of ecclesiastical prerogative; but in Aug. he acknowledged Gutierrez' 'criminal negligence,' and promised to chide him. *Id.*, ix. 62–5; *Arch. Arzob.*, MS., v. pt. ii. 8, 11. 1836. José de la Cruz Sanchez in Dec. succeeded Flores, who resigned. *Vallejo, Doc.*, MS., iv. 47, 36. 1837. March 19th, Sanchez asks Vallejo to compel the padre to give up one of his 9 rooms. *Id.*, i. 27. July 1st, Vallejo sends 19 Ind. from Sonoma to aid in mission work; will probably send more. *Id.*, iv. 262. 1838. See a view of the mission in *Forbes' Cal.*, reproduced in *Annals of S. F.* 1839. Sanchez still in charge. Hartnell in Sept. found the accounts in such a condition as might be expected, the admin. not being able to read or write (?). The Ind. were discontented with hard work and no *ropa;* wanted to live in liberty under the care of Vicente Miramonte; feared that S. Mateo would be taken from them; desired also to keep the coast lands from Pilarcitos to Purísima; and some of them to have the Cañada de Guadalupe. *Hartnell, Diario*, MS., 7–8. This year, as we have seen, Dolores was made cabecera of the partido, and three lots were granted to citizens of S. F. pueblo. 1840. Sanchez was succeeded in May by Tiburcio Vasquez. *St. Pap., Miss.*, MS., vii. 36.

[17] Juan Amorós was a Catalan, born at Porrera Oct. 10, 1773. He became a Franciscan at Gerona in 1791 and was ordained in 1797. He came to Mexico in 1803, and to California in 1804, serving as a missionary at S. Cárlos in 1804–19, and S. Rafael in 1819–32. His superiors rated him as possessed of more than common ability, and well fitted for office or a professorship. *Autobiog. Autog. de los Padres*, MS.; *Sarría, Inf. de 1817*, MS., p. 32–3; *Payeras, Inf., 1820*, MS., 140. Padre Amorós was noted for the zeal with which he undertook every task whether temporal or spiritual. He was a successful business manager, a mechanic of more than ordinary skill, and a kind missionary well liked by his neophytes. He was always in good health, and never could find too much work to do. He strove to please all classes and engaged in no controversies. In 1817 he wrote a letter urging the extension of trade and especially the fair treatment of foreigners. He promised fidelity to the

the mission was in charge of Padre Esténega of San
Francisco until the Zacatecan José María Vasquez
del Mercado came in 1833, to be replaced in 1834 by
Padre José Lorenzo de la Concepcion Quijas, also a
Zacatecan, who from that year had charge of both
San Rafael and Solano, living at the former chiefly.
Statistics of the last years of this establishment as a
mission are for the most part wanting,[18] but the num-

Mex. republic and was praised even by Echeandía and José M. Estudillo.
The tradition is that once when the mission was attacked by savages he crossed
the bay to S. F. on a tule balsa with a woman and several children.   He died
at S. Rafael at 3 A. M. on July 14, 1832, and was buried in the church on the
16th by P. Fortuni, his predecessor at the mission, who had known him since
1792, and declared him to be a saint. *S. Rafael, Lib. Mis.*, MS., 12.

[18] S. Rafael statistics for 1831-2, extremely unreliable (no figures for
1833-4).   Decrease in pop. 970 to 300 (probably should be 700 or 900, though
possibly 300 only were at the mission when the report was made, or more
likely there is an error in the figures).   Baptisms 155 (including 110 adults?)
in 1831 and 15 in 1832.   Deaths 29 and 37 in 1831-2.   Increase in large stock
1,548 to 2,442 (?); horses and mules 448 to 372; sheep 1,852 to 3,000.   Crops
1,900 bush. in 1831, 1,776 bush. in 1832.

Statistics of 1834-40.   Inventory of Sept. 31, 1834.   Church property,
building, $192, ornamentos, etc., $777, library of 75 vols $108, total $1,077;
mission buildings $1,123; garden or orchard, $968; boats, etc., $500; live-
stock $4,339; Nicasio rancho $7,256; credits $170; total $18,474; debts $3,448;
balance $15,025. *St. Pap., Miss.*, MS., v. 58-9.   Dec., there were distributed
to 343 Ind. (doubtless males or heads of families, representing a pop. of at
least 500 souls) 1,291 sheep and 439 horses. *Id.*   Inventory of Nov. 30, 1836.
Manufacturing estab., produce, tools, and probably buildings, $1,434; live-
stock $1,385; orchard $891; rancho $6,644; credits $464; total $10,818;
debts $3,177; balance $7,641. *Id.*, vii. 55-6, 78-9.   Pop. in 1838, 365 souls.
Id., vi. 26.   Hartnell's inventory of Sept. 18, 1839.   Pop. 195 at the mission;
474 horses, 26 yoke of oxen, 3 mules (cattle and sheep torn off); 417 fan.
grain, 42 hides, 72 deer-skins, 60 arr. tallow. *Hartnell, Diario*, MS., 98.
Debt in 1840 to Spear, Célis, Aguirre, Scott, Shaw, John Reed, Tim. Murphy,
and Rotscheff, $1,967. *Pico, Pap., Miss.*, MS., 47-51.

Statistics of 1817-34.   Total of baptisms, 1873, of which 1,096 Ind.
adults, 768 Ind. children, 2 and 7 de razon; annual average 103.   Marriages 543,
of which 8 de razon.   Deaths 698, of which 458 Ind. adults, 239 Ind. children,
1 de razon; annual average 38; average death rate 6.09 per cent of pop.
Largest pop. 1,140 in 1828; sexes about equal, children ¦.   Largest no. of
cattle 2,120 (?) in 1832; horses 450 in 1831; mules 1-4; sheep 4,000 in 1822-3;
swine 30 in 1823; all kinds 5,508 animals in 1832.   Total product of wheat
17,905 bush. yield 8 fold; barley 12,339 bush., 9 fold; maize 3,657 bush., 40
fold; beans 1,360 bush., 13 fold; miscel. grains 412 bush., 8 fold.

Summary of events, etc.   1832.   The mission was attacked by savages,
against whom an expedition was sent out under Lázaro Piña. *Vallejo, Doc.*,
MS., i. 307.   1833.   Trouble between P. Mercado and Alf. Vallejo; the
friar's murderous slaughter of gentiles. This vol., p. 322-4.   1834.   Ignacio
Martinez takes charge as comisionado.   Oct. 1st, boundaries assigned to the
pueblo of S. Rafael; from Arroyo de las Ánimas, down Cañada de los Baulenes
to the shore, and on opposite or northern side the Cañada of the Arroyo de S.
Antonio to Los Tamales, and from Punta de Quintin to the mouth of S. Antonio
cr. along the bay shore. *St. Pap., Miss.*, MS., xi. 11, 19, with the map which is
here reproduced.   S. Rafael, Solano, S. José mission, and the colony were to

ber of neophytes in 1834 must have been about 500, a decrease of about 50 per cent since 1830; and in 1840 there were 190 Indians living in community with probably 150 scattered. The valuation in 1834 was $18,500, or deducting real estate and church property, $4,500 in excess of debts; two years later the debt seems to have considerably exceeded the available assets, though this fact is somewhat misleading as an indication of the actual state of affairs. A large por-

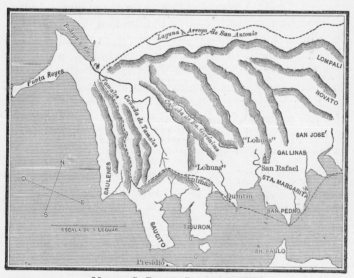

MAP OF S. RAFAEL LANDS IN 1834.

tion of the property was distributed at the secularization and is not included in the inventory of 1836. The Nicasio rancho was also granted to the ex-neo-

form a parish of 1st class. This vol., p. 348. 1835. Martinez in charge. May 1st, Vallejo acknowledges receipt of an order to put certain Ind. in possession of Nicasio, which is given them in full ownership, and their rights must be protected. *Vallejo, Doc.*, MS., iii. 29 (this grant was rejected by the L. C.) August 18th, gov. urges V. to attend to Figueroa's order of this date to take especial care of the S. F. Indians at S. Rafael, who had difficulty in moving their property (?) for lack of boats. *Id., Hist. Cal.*, iii. 70. Oct. 20th, V. complains that the padre (Quijas) resides at S. Rafael though paid by So-

phytes.   In 1837, as the Indians were not as a rule making good use of their liberty, and as political and other troubles rendered proper supervision impossible, the property was collected into a common fund, under General Vallejo's promise of redistribution when circumstances should be more favorable.   Ignacio Martinez was in charge as comisionado in 1834–6, followed by John Reed as administrator in 1836–7, and Timothy Murphy in 1837–40.   Hartnell in his first tour of 1839 found the Indians discontented, especially in view of constant encroachments on their lands.   They insisted on complete emancipation and the promised distribution of property, protesting in 1840 against the enforcement of Alvarado's reglamento, and being supported by Vallejo, who insisted that the mission had been completely secularized, and that his promises must be fulfilled.   After a controversy with Hartnell and the governor Vallejo's view of the matter in substance prevailed; and a distribution of the live-stock at least was ordered.

noma. *Id.*, *Doc.*, iii. 45.   1836.   Martinez turns over estate to John Reed on Nov. 30th. *St. Pap.*, *Miss.*, MS., vii. 55, 78.   1837.   Reed is succeeded by Timothy Murphy on April 21st. *Id.*, 78.   Visit of Edwards in March, *Diary*, MS., 14–17, who also visited Cooper's mill and the ranchos of Reed and Martin.   He gives little information, but notes that the Ind. were not making good use of the property that had been distributed.   Complaints of vagabond foreigners in the region. *Vallejo*, *Doc.*, MS., iv. 343.   1838.   Jan., José Talis, capt. of the Tamales, is permitted to leave S. Rafael with those of his tribe, on condition of sending a few men occasionally to hear mass, if any mass should be celebrated. *Id.*, v. 23.   1839.   Hartnell's visit was in Sept. He found the accounts in bad condition, as the admin. could not read or write.   The old Christians desired their liberty and the distrib. of property; and all complained that hardly any land remained to them.   They needed S. Anselmo, part of which was in possession of the Sainses and part asked for by Cooper; Las Gallinas desired by Berreyesa; and Arroyo de S. José cultivated last year by Murphy for the community, but now in possession of Pacheco; and Pt S. Pedro, which Murphy wants, and S. Gerónimo occupied by Rafael Cacho.   The neophyte Camilo had occupied Olompali since 1834, and was industrious and successful, but now the Mirandas were encroaching, and Camilo demanded a regular title to his land.   All complained that for two years no clothing had been distributed. *Hartnell*, *Diario*, MS., 7, 43, 52, 98.   1840. Jan.–May, controversy between Hartnell and Vallejo. This vol., 601; iv. 61. H. came to put the mission under the new reglamento, appointing Gregorio Briones as majordomo; but the Ind. were opposed to being returned to mission life; and H. finally agreed to favor Vallejo's plan of distributing the property after paying the debts. *St. Pap.*, *Miss.*, MS., xi. 12–17.   Oct. 13th, Vallejo to Murphy, orders him at once to distribute 3 cattle and one horse to each of the Ind. *Vallejo*, *Doc.*, MS., ix. 291.

Father Fortuni served at San Francisco Solano until 1833, when his place was taken by the Zacatecan, José de Jesus María Gutierrez, who in turn changed places in March 1834 with Padre Lorenzo Quijas of San Francisco. Quijas remained in charge of ex-mission and pueblo as acting curate throughout the decade, but resided for the most part at San Rafael. Though the neophyte population, as indicated by the reports, decreased from 760 to 650 in 1834 and 550 in 1835,[19] yet there was a gain in live-stock and but

[19] S. Francisco Solano statistics, 1831–4. Decrease in pop. 760 to 650. Baptisms 555, largest no. 232 (106 adults) in 1831; smallest 22 in 1833. Deaths 272, largest no. 106 in 1833, smallest 43 in 1834. Gain in large stock 2,729 to 6,015 (in 1833; no figures for 1834); horses and mules 729 to 1,164 (id.); sheep (id.) 4,000 to 7,114. Largest crop 3,260 bush. in 1832; smallest 2,347 bush. in 1833; average 2,750 bush., of which wheat 1,414, yield 10 fold; barley 917, 15 fold; corn 328, 62 fold; beans 36, 5 fold; miscel. grains 39, 7 fold.

Statistics of 1823–34. Total of baptisms (to 1835) 1,315, of which 641 Ind. adults, 671 Ind. children, 3 children de razon; annual average 101. Marriages (to 1833) 278, of which 1 de razon. Deaths 651, of which 462 Ind. adults, 187 Ind. chil., 1 and 1 de razon; annual average 54; average death-rate 7.8 per cent of pop. Largest pop. 996 in 1832; sexes nearly equal; children ⅓. Largest no. of cattle 4,849 in 1833; horses 1,148 in 1833; mules 18 in 1833; sheep 7,114 in 1833; swine 80 in 1826–7; all kinds 13,193 animals in 1833. Total product of wheat 13,450 bush., yield 9 fold; barley 5,970 bush., 15 fold, 3,270 bush., 62 fold; beans 306 bush., 7 fold; miscel. grains 640 bush., 13 fold.

Summary of events, and statistics 1835–40. Oct. 24, 1831. Part of the ranchería burned, a man and 4 women perishing. Vallejo, Doc., MS., i. 268. 1833. P. Gutierrez succeeds Fortuni. The padre interferes with settlements at Petaluma and Sta Rosa. This vol., p. 255. Padre complains of foreign 'hunters' at Suisun. Id., 392. Also 3 objectionable foreigners at the mission. Dept. St. Pap., MS., iii. 116. 1834. M. G. Vallejo in charge as comisionado of secularization in Oct.–Nov. This vol., p. 279, 294. This mission with S. Rafael and S. José was to form a parish of 1st class. Id., 348. Vallejo made an exped. to Solano in Jan. Vallejo, Doc., MS., xxxi. 58. 1835. Secularization by Comisionado Vallejo, who made Antonio Ortega majordomo. This vol., p. 346, 353–4. A census of June 4th shows a pop. of 549 souls. Vallejo, Doc., MS., iii. 33, 36, 54; xxiii. 9; xxxii. 2. Unfortunately the inventory sent at the same time to Mont. is not extant. March 3d, gov. to V., who must give the padre free use of furniture and utensils in addition to his regular allowance; may also furnish horses and boats for the padre's use. Id., iii. 11–12. June 4th, V. to gov., the Ind. chiefs constantly demand permission to go to their own lands, recognizing Sonoma as their head town, and V. has permitted it for fear of provoking hostility. Id., 37. Blotter of all V.'s commun. to gov. from June to Dec. Id., 35–47. June 27th, gov. uncertain about permitting the Ind. to live at their rancherías. Too much liberty is not good for them. Wants more suggestions. Id., 57. Supplies to colony down to June 20th, $421. Pinto, Doc., MS., i. 151. Aug. 2d, P. Quijas at S. Rafael to gov. complains that the Vallejos and Ortega have shown him great disrespect, besides refusing him beef; and that Ortega was immoral as well as insolent. He will not return unless Ortega is removed. St. Pap., M. & C., MS., ii. 345. Oct. 20th, Vallejo to gov. thinks if P. Quijas lives at

slight falling-off in crops; and the establishment must be regarded as having flourished down to the date of secularization, being one of the few missions in California which reached their highest population in the final decade, though this was natural enough in a new and frontier mission.   Mariano G. Vallejo was made comisionado in 1834, and in 1835–6, with Antonio Ortega as majordomo, completed the secularization. Movable property was distributed to the Indians, who were made entirely free, many of them retiring to their old rancherías.   A little later, however, in consequence of troubles with hostile gentiles, the ex-neophytes seem to have restored their live-stock to the care of General Vallejo, who used the property of the ex-mission for their benefit and protection, and for the general development of the northern settlement.   The general claimed that this was a legitimate use of the

S. Rafael, Solano should not have to pay his salary, which he has already claimed to be excessive ($1,500). *Vallejo, Doc.*, MS., iii. 45.   Dec. 15th, Vallejo resigns his position as comisionado, stating that 'mil circunstancias' have prevented the distribution of lands and other property. *Id.*, 47.   1836. Antonio Ortega acting administrator at $500, and Cayetano Juarez majordomo at $240.   Ignacio Acedo also an employé at $120.   Mission debts at end of year $1,138; credits $224.   Clothing, rations, etc., distributed to Ind. $4,191. *Id.*, xxiii. 26.   1837–8.   Pablo Ayala succeeded Ortega at a date not known; nor is anything known of his accounts.   Oct. 1837, padron of 185 Suisunes living at the ex-mission. *Arch., Mis.*, MS., ii. 844.   1839.   Salvador Vallejo was appointed on May 7th to succeed Ayala. *Dept. Rec.*, MS., x. 10. *Vallejo, Doc.*, vii. 16.   But the new administrator was not put in possession of the property; so he informed Hartnell in Sept. when H. came on his first tour of investigation, at the same time resigning. *Id.*, viii. 85.   Gen. Vallejo was then consulted, and on Sept. 9th wrote a letter of explanation.   He says that as comisionado he distributed all the live-stock (this does not agree with his statement of Dec. 15, 1835, given above, that the property had not been distributed, but possibly V.'s resignation was not accepted, and the distrib. took place in 1836), and the Indians were set entirely free.   But bitter hostility with the savages ensuing, the Ind. gathered anew about Vallejo, with many gentiles after treaties had been made, and gave up to him their stock, 2,000 cattle, 700 horses, and 6,000 sheep.   With this property he has cared for the Ind., paid expenses of worship, etc., besides indirectly developing the settlement of the north—a proper use for the mission funds.   Now there are 3,000 to 4,000 cattle, 500 horses, and 6,000 sheep (in March the gov. had ordered a loan of 3,000 sheep for 3 years from Sta Clara for the benefit of Solano. *Pico* (*Pio*), *Doc.*, MS., ii. 9.   What had become of these animals?) which, with the small vineyard and orchard, will be put at the visitador's disposal if he desires it. *Vallejo, Doc.*, MS., viii. 89.   But Hartnell did not deem it prudent to take charge of the estate under these circumstances. *Hartnell, Diario*, MS., 93–8.   And nothing appears on the subject in 1840 except that by the reglamento the govt was still to regulate Solano 'according to circumstances.' Vol. iv., p. 60.

estate; and he would have established a new mission in the north if the padres would have aided him. Doubtless his policy was a wise one, even if his position as guardian of the Indians in charge of their private property put by them in his care was not recognized by the laws. Moreover, there was a gain rather than a loss in live-stock. Thus the mission community had no real existence after 1836, though Pablo Ayala and Salvador Vallejo were nominally made administrators. The visitador made no innovations in 1839, and apparently none were made in 1840. I suppose there may have been 100 of the ex-neophytes living at Sonoma at the end of the decade, with perhaps 500 more in the region not relapsed into barbarism.

On the secularization of Solano a pueblo was founded at Sonoma in 1835. Besides the fact of the founding, the transfer of the San Francisco military company, the granting of several ranchos in the north, several campaigns against hostile Indians, and a few other matters fully treated elsewhere as indexed and supplemented with minor items in the appended note,[20] very little is really known in details of events and

[20] Summary and index of Sonoma events, etc. 1831. Sta Rosa granted to Rafael Gomez, as a check to the Russians, but never occupied under the grant. Vol. iv., p. 160, this work. 1832. In the instructions of the Mex. govt to Gov. Figueroa the colonization of the northern frontier is urged in view of probable encroachments of Russians and Americans; and a plan of Virmond to found a settlement at Sonoma is mentioned. *Figueroa, Instruc.*, MS., 35–7. 1833 et seq. Figueroa's efforts to effect the settlement of Sta Rosa and Petaluma. Founding and abandonment of Sta Anna y Farías. This vol., p. 246–7, 255–7, 272. Lat. and long. of Solano by Douglas. *Id.*, 404. 1834. Petaluma granted to Vallejo. Arrival of the colony. The governor's alleged Ind. campaign. *Id.*, 256–7, 360.

1835. Arrest and exile of the colony chiefs in March. *Id.*, 286 et seq. Founding of Sonoma by Vallejo, as comandante and director de colonizacion, at Figueroa's orders. *Id.*, 293–5. An exped. against the northern Ind. from Sonoma. *Id.*, 360. Dec. 3d, Com. Vallejo claims that there is no civil authority as yet and the district is therefore subject to his military rule. *Vallejo, Doc.*, MS., iii. 82. The four leagues of public lands were later confirmed by the land commission to the town on Vallejo's grant of June 24th. Also lots were confirmed to V. under the gov.'s grant of July 5th. *Hoffman's Repts.*

1836. Vallejo's campaigns against the Guapos and other hostile Ind.; his treaties of June; his excellent Ind. policy. Vol. iv., p. 70–2. The S. F. presidial company had been transferred the preceding year, except a few men who now came to Sonoma. The officers have already been named in this

progress at Sonoma and in the surrounding regions. The record is not more meagre perhaps than at several other places, but is remarkably so in view of

chap. See p. 702. The comp. was often called from this time caballería permanente de la frontera. There are extant many complaints from Vallejo that the force was insufficient to protect the frontier settlement and Mex. national interests against savages, Americans, and Russians. June, a scandal affecting one of the officers. *Bandini, Doc.*, MS., 40. Sept. 9th, circular of Vallejo on the misdeeds of James Doyle and his 11 foreign companions who are trying to 'purchase' houses of the Ind. *Castro, Doc.*, MS., i. 29; *Vallejo, Doc.*, MS., iii. 133. Nicolás Higuera was appointed alcalde auxiliar at Sonoma by the alcalde of S. F.; but Vallejo refused to recognize any civil authority, in which position he was sustained by the govt. *Id.*, iii. 99, 181.

1837. Gen. Vallejo's efforts to enlist and drill recruits; Capt. Salvador Vallejo made mil. comandante, the general going to Monterey Jan.–March. This vol., 511–12. June, campaign of Salv. Vallejo and Solano against the Yolos; capture of Zampay; treaty with Sotoyomes. Vol. iv., p. 72. Vallejo urges the employment of a competent surveyor in connection with the formalities of putting settlers in possession of lands; also recommends precautions against men who may desire ranchos only for speculation. *Vallejo, Doc.*, MS., iii. 125; iv. 99. Specimen of grant of a town lot by Vallejo. A house must be built within a year or the lot will be forfeited. *Id.*, iv. 5. July, Ramirez and other political prisoners from south of the bay sent to Sonoma. This vol., p. 525–6. The company's protest against centralism and the general's proffered resignation. *Id.*, 533. Dec. 26th, Vallejo to Carrillo on the progress made in the north through his efforts; desires to devote himself entirely to the frontier, rather than to be comandante general. *Vallejo, Doc.*, MS., iv. 365.

1838. Salvador Vallejo again in temporary command, and marches south. This vol., p. 547, 552. Southern political prisoners kept here June–Sept. *Id.*, 567. Various Ind. complications. Vol. iv., 72–3. Ravages of the smallpox. *Id.*, 73–4. An infantry company of 15–20 men is mentioned in *Vallejo, Doc.*, MS., xxiv.

1839. Salvador Vallejo was com. of the post, Alf. Prado Mesa and Alf. Lázaro Piña acting at times, and was also captain of the compañía de infantería organized the year before. This infantry company was composed of about 25 selected Indians who were, however, given Spanish names on the rosters. They were armed with muskets and their pay amounted to $1,390 this year. *Vallejo, Doc.*, MS., xxv. passim. The cavalry company was raised to over 40 men this year and the next. *Id.* Both general and captain urged the necessity of increasing the force, and complained of neglect on the part of the authorities at Monterey in the matter of supplying money. *Id.*, vi. 218; viii. 86. Artillery 10 guns, 9 of them brass, 2¼ to 8 lbs calibre. *Id.*, xxv. 63. Six of the guns bought with all their appurtenances by Gen. V. without aid from the govt. *Id.*, vii. 37. March, return of Gen. V. from the south, and his complaints of mismanagement by Capt. V. during his absence. The offences were of slight importance, but were deemed by so strict a disciplinarian worthy of reprimand. *Id.*, vi. 344–6. May, Gen. V. writes to Mex. govt explaining his operations at Sonoma in the past 5 years, and his success in founding a frontier settlement after great sacrifices and privations, and all without expense to the govt. But now his resources are nearly exhausted and he must have aid in order to ensure permanent success. *Id.*, vii. 26–8. Dec., court-martial of two deserters. *Soberanes, Doc.*, MS., 158–65. Oct., Solano's visit to Monterey. This vol., p. 589. Salvador was appointed juez de paz at Sonoma in Jan., taking the oath in May. Meanwhile in Feb.–March the people refused to attend an election on the plea that they were subject only to military authority, for which the alcalde (S. Vallejo ?) appears

General Vallejo's prominent position in all that concerned the frontera del norte and of the complete documentary record of other matters contained in the papers of his collection. Vallejo had many difficulties to contend with, but his zeal and energy in this cause were without parallel in California annals; and the credit due him is not impaired by the fact that the development of his own wealth was a leading incentive. His Indian policy was admirable, and in the native chief Solano he found an efficient aid. For the most part at his own expense he supported the regular presidial company, organized another of native warriors, kept the hostile tribes in check by war and diplomacy, protected the town and ranchos, and, in spite of the country's unfortunate political complications and lack of prosperity, established a feeling of security that in 1839 had drawn 25 families of settlers to the northern frontier. Could he have had the coöperation of the friars he would have founded new missions in the north and east. I have estimated the population of gente de razon, not including the Russians, north of the bay in 1840 at 200 souls. The establishments of Ross and New Helvetia during this period, having been treated in special chapters, require no further notice here.

Turning to the southern establishments of the district we find that Padre Narcisco Duran at San José

to have been fined $20. In June Gen. V. ordered the captain not to serve as juez, claiming that the gov. had no power to appoint a military officer to civil positions. *Mont. Arch.*, MS., ix. 10; *Dept. St. Pap.*, MS., xvii. 57; *Id., Ben. P. & J.*, iii. 26–9; *Id., Mont.*, iv. 96; *Doc. Hist. Cal.*, MS., i. 398. Vallejo's efforts to found a new line of frontier missions, particularly one at Sta Rosa. The friars could not be induced to undertake the task, and the gov. was not very warm in support of the measure. Vol. iv., p. 48; *Fernandez, Cosas*, MS., 88–90, with a letter of P. Quijas.

1840. Salv. Vallejo commandant; cavalry and infantry companies as before. In April there was a serious rising of the native infantry, who attacked the cavalry, and being repulsed joined the hostile chiefs of savage tribes. They were in turn attacked by Piña and Solano with a force of soldiers and friendly Ind., and were defeated with much loss. Subsequently two savage chiefs and 9 other Ind. were shot. Vallejo believed the rebels had an understanding with the Sacramento tribes. Vol. iv., p. 12, 74. Aug. 20th, order of Mex. govt to constitute the northern frontier into a comandancia militar. *Vallejo, Doc.*, MS., x. 223.

mission was succeeded in 1833 by the Zacatecan
Padre José María de Jesus Gonzalez Rubio, who remained throughout the decade.   This mission for the
whole decade was probably the most prosperous in
California both before and after secularization.   Its
highest population of 1,866 souls was reached in 1831,
and though the number fell to about 1,400 in 1834 [21]

[21] Statistics of S. José mission 1831–2 (no figures for 1833–4). ˙ Decrease of
pop. 1,745 to 1,456 (in 1833, but 1,886 in 1831).   Baptisms 366 (336 incl. 293
adults in 1831).   Marriages 129.   Deaths 398.   Increase of large stock 13,300
to 13,710, horses and mules 1,300 to 1,250; sheep remained at 13,000.   Crops
about 10,800 bush. each year.
   Statistics of 1835–40.   Statement of P. Gonzalez that the mission had
18,000 cattle, 15,000 sheep, 1,900 horses, and effects valued at 20,000.   *Taylor*,
in *Cal. Farmer*, June 1, 1860.   Inventory of Jan. 15, 1837.   Credits (chief
debtors Wm Gulnac $336, S. Rafael mission $1,236, the canónigo Fernandez
(!) $385, and dept. govt $6,117), $9,117.   Buildings, including corrals, etc.,
$10,700.   Utensils and furniture $240.   Manufacturing apparatus and material, also hides, tallow, lard, wagons, and 3,600 fan. of grain, $9,108.   Goods
in warehouse $17,810.   Orchard and vineyard at the mission, 6,000 vines,
about 600 fruit trees, $7,472; id., S. Cayetano, abt 600 trees, incl. 10 olive-
trees, $1,514.   Farming tools $282.   Live-stock, $18,000 cattle, 2,074 horses,
14,965 sheep, 30 mules, 15 asses, 77 swine, $98,977.   Boat $100.   Total valuation $156,325.   Debt (chief creditors J. A. Aguirre $402, Antonio Moreña
$377), $975.   Balance $155,350.   Original with autographs of J. J. Vallejo
and Padre Gonzalez, in *Vallejo, Doc.*, MS., xxxii. 64; also *St. Pap., Miss.*,
MS., vii. 49–51.   1837–8.   No records.   1839.   Pop. in Aug. according to Hartnell's count 589 souls. *Id.*, x. 12.   March 2d, gov. orders the loan of 3,000
sheep to the Solano establishment for 5 years. *Id.*, x. 14.   Aug. 28th, property available for trade or for distribution to the Ind. $30,000. *Id.*, vii. 48.
Sept. 1st, acct of supplies to govt and escolta (no period specified, possibly
since 1837) $16,809. *Id.*, 43.   1840.   Live-stock 20,000 cattle, 15,000 sheep,
1,120 horses, 15 mules, 150 swine, 2 asses.   Other property (enseres) $23,570.
Credits $3,452 (as to what had become of the acct of $6,000 against the govt
the reader may adopt any theory he likes except that it had been paid).   Debts
$4,434. *Id.*, 37–40; *Arce, Doc.*, MS., 28–9; *Pico, Pap., Mis.*, MS., 47–51.
   Statistics of 1797–1834.   Total of baptisms 6,737, of which 4,182 Ind.
adults, 2,488 Ind. children, 67 child. de razon; annual average 177.   Marriages
1,984, of which 4 de razon.   Deaths 5,109, of which 3,524 Ind. adults; 1,554
Ind. children, 4 and 27 de razon; annual average 134; average death rate 12.17
per cent of pop.   Largest pop. 1,886 in 1831; males always in excess of females;
children ¼ to ⅛.   Largest no. of cattle 18,000 in 1826; horses 1,425 in 1834;
mules 100 in 1830; sheep 20,000 in 1826; all kinds 35,600 in 1826.   Total
product of wheat 13,680 bush. yield 19 fold; barley 16,750 bush., 20 fold;
maize 17,290 bush., 80 fold; beans 3,790 bush., 25 fold; miscel. grains 8,800
bush., 33 fold.
   Summary of events, etc.   1831.   Status under Echeandía's plan not carried
out. This vol., p. 306–7.   1832.   P. Duran on the proposed reglamento. *Id.*,
316.   May 7th, Duran in great trouble because the Ind. die so fast.   They
seem 'mas frágiles que el vidrio.'   He has appointed 5 boys to report cases of
sickness, and has had them well flogged to make them attend to the duty,
yet now and then some Ind. slips out of the world without the sacraments.
S. José, Lib. Mis., MS., 27.   1833.   P. Gonzalez succeeds Duran, the latter reporting this mission in a condition for partial secularization. This vol., p. 318,
333.   S. J. was to be joined to Solano and S. Rafael as a parish of 1st class.

and to 580 in 1840—with probably 200 scattered in the district—yet crops were uniformly good, the yield being larger in proportion to the seed sown than elsewhere, and live-stock increased steadily to the end. Secularization was effected in 1836-7, Jesus Vallejo having charge as administrator until April 1840, when he was succeeded by José María Amador. The inventory made at the time of transfer showed a total valuation, not including lands or church property, of $155,000 over and above debts; and the fragmentary

Id., 348. 1834-5. No records. 1836. Secularization ordered; Jesus Vallejo takes partial possession as administrator in Dec. *Id.*, 426; iv. 47. 1837. Formal delivery of the property by P. Gutierrez to Vallejo by inventory as already cited, Jan. 15th. Feb. 13th, V. ordered to proceed to distribution of lots. *Vallejo, Doc.*, MS., xxxii. 71. Cattle delivered to Willamette co. Vol. iv. p. 86. 1838. June, mission damaged by an earthquake. *Id.*, 78. July 1st, specimen of grant of a lot by the admin. to V. Chologon, as per order of Feb. 13, 1837, as above. *Vallejo, Doc.*, MS., xxx. 94. 1839. Aug. 16th, J. Vallejo to the general, complaining that Alvarado and Jimeno at Monterey seem disposed to let the missions go to ruin. He wishes to save S. José, or if it can't be done to let it be ruined in charge of some other admin. *Id.*, iii. 40. Hartnell arrived on his tour of inspection Aug. 20th. He had expected some trouble with Vallejo, the nature of which is not explained, and had even been furnished with an order for troops from the pueblo under Antonio Buelna. But he was well received and was much pleased with the prosperous condition of the establishment at first sight, as he writes on the 21st, the Ind. being well clothed and the storehouse well filled. It seems that Don Jesus had either asked to be relieved, or it had been resolved to remove him, since H. asks the govt to select some suitable admin., as he cannot approve Cárlos Castro for the place. *Hartnell, Diario*, MS., 39-40; *S. José Arch.*, MS., iii. 34. Unfortunately the inventory is missing. Aug. 28th a series of instructions by Hartnell for the admin., which seem to imply that Vallejo had been somewhat too independent in his management, inclined to severe punishments, to private speculation, neglect of worship, and careless methods of keeping accounts. *St. Pap., Miss.*, MS., vii. 40-2; x. 13-14. Aug. 29th, H. to govt, has found the accounts in bad order as elsewhere, the Ind. discontented and destitute (a wonderful change in 8 days!), punishments too severe, majordomo brutal; administrator carries off property to his own rancho. *Id.*, x. 12. Vallejo was authorized in Sept. to spend $2,000 in goods for the Ind., but spent $2,800 before he got the permission, at which and other minor informalities Hartnell sent reprimands in Nov. Some blankets and other articles were ordered furnished to Soledad. *Vallejo, Doc.*, MS., viii. 175; *Hartnell, Diario*, MS., 50-1. 1840. Vallejo still in charge. According to the reglam. of March some of the property at this mission was to be distributed to the oldest Ind., and a clerk was to be put in charge of the estate. There is no record of Hartnell's visit in April, but his instructions to the majordomo and clerk on routine duties are dated April 23d. Vol. iv., p. 61. And on the same date the property was turned over to José María Amador as majordomo, the inventory being signed by José Antonio Estrada (doubtless the clerk) á ruego de Amador. *St. Pap., Miss.*, MS., vii. 37-8. Oct. 24th, order of govt to lend J. B. Alvarado 300 heifers and 25 bulls for 5 years! *Dept. Rec.*, xi. 46. Davis, *Glimpses*, MS., 28-9, mentions a slaughter of 2,000 cattle for their hides and tallow.

statistics of later years indicate no falling-off in any kind of property. This is the more remarkable as the wealth of San José made it a shining mark for government demands, and large amounts of live-stock and other property were loaned to private individuals and to other ex-missions. Don Jesus, though somewhat independent of supervision and informal in his methods, must be regarded as a very efficient manager. It is probable, however, that in 1840 the ebb of prosperity had begun and that the elements of approaching decadence were somewhat more apparent than is indicated by the imperfect records that have been preserved.

At Santa Clara Padre Viader concluded his missionary service of nearly 40 years in 1833, when he left the country. His successor was the Zacatecan prefect Padre Francisco García Diego who served to the end of 1835 with an associate from 1834 in the person of Padre Rafael de Jesus Moreno, after whose death in 1839 Padre Mercado took charge of the ex-mission.[22] Statistical reports by the missionaries

[22] José Viader was born at Gallines, Catalonia, on Aug. 27, 1765, and became a Franciscan at Barcelona in May 1788, sailing for Mexico in 1795, and starting from the college of S. Fernando for Cal. in Feb. 1796. His only missionary service was at Sta Clara from 1796 to 1833. His superiors accorded to him more than medium merit and ability both in temporal and spiritual affairs. *Autobiog. Autog. de los Padres*, MS.; *Sarría, Inf., 1817*, MS., 68–9; *Payeras, Inf., 1820*, MS., 138. Padre Viader was a large man of fine physique; somewhat reserved and stern in manner with strangers, but well liked by all acquaintances, with whom his manner was always frank and courteous; very strict in all matters pertaining to the faith and religious obervances, noted for the size of the crucifix hanging always with the rosary from his girdle; a diligent and effective man of business, devoted to the temporal prosperity of his mission, and not always impressed with the sanctity of the revenue laws. His diaries of two expeditions to the Rio de Merced and in search of sites for new missions in 1810 appear in my list of authorities. It is related than one night about 1814 while going to attend a dying neophyte he was attacked by three Ind. who tried to kill him but were instead overcome by his great physical strength, becoming subsequently the padre's faithful and useful allies. In 1818 he made a tour to S. F. and S. Rafael as secretary to the padre prefecto. In 1821 he was present at S. Juan Bautista at the laying of the corner-stone and dedication of the new church. In 1826 he declined to take the oath of allegiance. Swan in a newspaper sketch often reprinted mentions the valuable services attributed to Viader in connection with the drought of 1828–30, which he is said to have foretold. In early years he had desired to retire, but had consented to remain at the request of superiors and neophytes. Of his departure in 1833 on the coming of the

cease for the most part in 1832, when the neophyte
population had fallen to 1,125, being possibly 800 in
1834, and at the end of the decade about 290 with
probably 150 scattered in the district.[23] Down to

Zacatecanos we have no details; but in Oct. 1835 Virmond at Mex. wrote of
his safe arrival at Habana, whence he probably went to Spain.

Rafael de Jesus Moreno was a Mexican Franciscan of the Guadalupe college, Zacatecas, who came with the others in 1833 and served at Sta Clara
until 1839, being also president and vice-prefect of the Zacatecan friars in
1836–8. The fact that he was chosen for so responsible a position indicates
that he was a man of some ability, but otherwise no information direct or indirect about him appears in any records that I have seen. He died on June
8, 1839, at Mission San José where he had gone for his health a little earlier.
Manuel Jimeno wrote at the time that his illness was caused by a fit of anger,
and his death by a mercurial potion prescribed by an English doctor. He
was buried in San José mission church by P. Gonzalez on the 9th. *S. José, Lib.
Mis.*, MS., 29–30.

[23] Sta Clara statistics of 1831–2 (figures for 1833–4 missing). Decrease of
pop., 1,226 to 1,125 (800 in 1834 according to Hall and Gleeson); baptisms,
55; marriages, 34; deaths, 155. Increase in large stock, 9,766 to 10,705
(14,230 in 1834); horses and mules, 788 to 765 (1,230 in 1834); sheep, 8,000
to 9,500 (15,000 in 1834). Crops, 4,130 bush. in 1831; 5,580 bush. in 1832.

Statistics of 1835–40. Mission supplies to the escolta for 7 months to
April, 1835, $273. *Dept. St. Pap., Ben. C. & T.*, MS., iii. 89. To S. F. pre-
sidio, Jan.–Oct., $493. *Arch. Arzob.*, MS., v. pt ii. 7. 1837. Salary list.
Admin. $1,500, teacher $500, majordomo $192, tanner $240, clerk $240,
besides expenses of the padre and supplies to the com. of the escolta. *St.
Pap., Miss.*, MS., vii. 30–1. 1839. Receipts for year, including balance in
Jan., $23,385; expend., $10,607. *Id.*, 20–2. Sept. 2d property available for
trade or distribution, 5,620 cattle, 6,500 sheep, 353 horses, 30 swine, 1,686
fan. grain, 1,000 arr. dried meat, 500 arr. wool, 347 arr. tallow, 274 arr. lard,
415 hides, and other articles, no value given. *Id.*, 28–9; also in *Hartnell,
Diario*, MS., 29, where the number of Ind. is given as 291. Debt in March
$3,102, credits $3,947. Debt in Sept. $4,428. *St. Pap., Miss.*, MS., vii. 30.
The admin. bought of a ship $1,103 worth of goods for the Ind. without per-
mission, for which he was blamed. *Id.*, 33; *Hartnell, Diario*, MS., 52. 1840.
Receipts (not apparently incl. balance of Jan.) $12,537, expend. $2,507. *St.
Pap., Miss.*, MS., vii. 23–25. May 15th, inventory of property turned over
by Estrada to Alviso, 3,717 cattle, 218 horses, 4,867 sheep, 510 fan. grain,
20 arr. tallow, 20 arr. wool, and other miscel. articles, no value given; debts
$3,940. *Id.*, 33–6; *Pico, Pap. Mis.*, MS., 47–51. The chief creditors being
Mig. Pedrorena $1,496, J. A. Aguirre $1,379, and Thos Shaw $585.

Statistics of 1777–1834. Total of baptisms 8,640, of which 4,534 Ind.
adults, 3,177 Ind. children, 6 and 923 de razon; annual average 133. Marriages 2,548, of which 182 de razon. Deaths 6,950, of which 4,152 Ind.
adults, 2,329 Ind. children, 137 and 332 de razon; annual average 111; average death rate 12.63 per cent of pop. Largest pop. 1,541 (?) in 1795 (1,464 in
1827); males largely in excess of females; children ½ to 1/10. Largest no. of
cattle 14,500 in 1828; horses 2,800 in 1811; mules 45 in 1827; sheep 15,500 in
1828; goats 500 in 1786; swine 60 in 1820; all kinds, 30,936 animals in 1828.
Total product of wheat 175,800 bush., yield 17 fold; barley 21,270 bush.,
32 fold; maize 46,450 bush., 98 fold; beans 5,500 bush., 17 fold; miscel.
grains 11,400 bush., 21 fold.

Summary of events, etc. 1831. Visits of Gov. Victoria. This vol., p.
186–200. Status under Echeandía's decree not enforced. *Id.*, 306–7. Davis,
Glimpses, MS., 44., speaks of a slaughter of horses early in this decade.
1832. P. Viader accused of buying smuggled goods. This vol., 365. 1833.

1834 there was a gain in live-stock and the crops were large. Secularization was effected at the beginning of 1837 by Ramon Estrada, who served as administrator until May, 1840, when he was succeeded by Ignacio Alviso. The inventories of the transfer I have not been able to find; but lists of effects in 1839–40 show that two thirds of the cattle and sheep had disappeared, and apparently all other available property of any value. This had been one of the richest establishments, and its downfall had been remarkably rapid.

Viader left Cal. and was succeeded by PP. García Diego and Moreno. Juan Prado Mesa was com. of the escolta down to the time of secularization. Escolta involved in a revolt against Vallejo at S. F. *Id.*, 248. Aug. 7th, padre complains to alcalde that the neophytes go to the pueblo and get drunk with notable prejudice to their souls and bodies. *S. José, Arch.*, MS., i. 52. Lat. and long. by Douglas. This vol., 404. 1834. Sta Clara, with the pueblo, to form a parish of 1st class under the reglamento. This vol., p. 348. 1835. P. García Diego departs at end of the year. José Z. Fernandez, teacher, resigns in Sept. Many neophytes were given licenses of emancipation. *Id.*, 354. Specimen of March 9th, the Ind. being permitted to live at Solano. *Vallejo, Doc.*, MS., iii. 17. July. Sale of liquor forbidden. *Id.*, 61. Sept. P. Moreno to gov., says that if they go on granting licenses, the mission will soon have no gente. *Arch. Arzob.*, MS., v. pt. ii. 14. 1836. Order of secularization in Dec. José Ramon Estrada appointed comisionado. Vol. iv., p. 47. 1837. Estrada took possession early this year and became administrador as well as comisionado; but in some documents the admin. is called José Mariano Estrada. March 13th. Estrada to alcalde, says he came as admin. and not as executioner; is preparing a full report; something must be done to protect the poor Ind. The killing of 3 Ind. is referred to. *S. José Arch.*, MS., vi. 28. Vallejo's visit in March; interview with Alvarado in June; arrest of rebels. This vol., p. 513, 522, 525. Belcher, *Voy.*, i. 117, says: 'The mission is fast falling to decay, and scarcely common civility was shown to us.' 1838. Earthquake in June. Vol. iv., p. 78. 1839. The governor's marriage. This vol., iii. 593. José Peña, teacher. *Mont. Arch.*, MS., ix. 10. March–April. Order to send 3,000 sheep to Sonoma as a loan for 5 years, against which the Ind. protested, and the sheep were not sent. *St. Pap., Miss.*, MS., ix., 57–8; *Vallejo, Doc.*, MS., vi. 475. Two of the sprightliest Ind. delivered to the schr *California* by general's order. *Id.*, 356. July. Troubles with the Indians, several killed. Vol. iv., p. 75–6. In Sept. Hartnell found the Ind. discontented, clamorous for a new admin., complaining that they received no rations or clothing, though they seemed in good condition. They demanded that no more ranchos should be granted from mission lands, particularly the one asked for by Forbes, S. Miguel, and Paso de S. Francisquito asked for by Piña. H. thought the salary of $500 to a teacher for 6 or 8 small children should be saved. *Diario*, MS., 29–30. 1840. Estrada was succeeded in May by Ignacio Alviso. *St. Pap. Miss.*, vii. 33. Sebastian Peralta, majordomo. July. P. Mercado protests against an order to search his house and church, for music to celebrate the fiesta of independence. *Id.*, ix. 54–5. Nov. 16. No produce left except hides. All industries suspended. *Id.*, 53. Some of the arrested foreigners confined here. Vol. iv., p. 23.

The pueblo of San José de Guadalupe, also called San José de Alvarado after 1836 in honor of the governor, with the ranchos of its jurisdiction, increased in population from 540 at the beginning of the decade to 750 at the end.[24]   Both numbers probably included some Indians, and there are no means of determining the proportion of the population living on the ranchos which have been named in this chapter. Municipal affairs continued under the direction of an ayuntamiento of alcalde, two regidores, and a síndico, elected annually until 1839.   The successive alcaldes were Mariano Duarte, Ignacio Ceballos, Salvio Pacheco, Pedro Chabolla, Antonio M. Pico, José M. Alviso, Juan Alvires, and Dolores Pacheco.   Some details are appended.[25]   In 1839 the ayuntamiento

[24] A padron of 1831 shows a pop. of 524. *Hall's Hist. S. J.*, 118; *Sta Clara Co. Hist.*, *Atlas*, 9; and several newspaper articles.   In 1833-4 the census shows 602 souls, of which number, however, 171 were Indians; and it is not unlikely that a like no. in other padrones were Ind., though there is no indication of it.   The 602 did not include 7 families who it was thought might belong to S. F.   It should also be noticed that several large ranchos of what is now southern Sta Clara Co. were in the Monterey jurisdiction, and not included in these lists. *Dept. St. Pap., Ben., P. y J.*, MS., i. 46.   1836.   List of 123 men between the ages of 15 and 50, 7 being foreigners. *Vallejo, Doc.*, MS., xxiii. 22.   Feb. 1, 1840, pop. 939. *Dept. St. Pap., S. J.*, MS., vii. 18. 1841, pop. 936. *S. José, Padron*, MS.   This padron seems to include no Indians; but it does include the contra costa inhabitants, about 150 in number.   There is some doubt about my figures for 1830 (see vol. ii., p. 602), the pop. of 540 perhaps including Indians.

[25] Municipal government, list of officials, and criminal record of S. José. 1831.   Alcalde Mariano Duarte; regidores Leandro Flores, Antonio Rodriguez, and Fernando Félix; síndico José Luis Chabolla, secretary José Reyes Berreyesa, depositario Luis Peralta. *Dept. St. Pap., B. M.*, MS., lxxiii. 14– 19.   1832.   Alcalde Ignacio Ceballos; regidores (probably Félix or Rodriguez holding over) and Joaquin Higuera. *Castro, Doc.*, MS., i. 8; *S. J. Arch.*, MS., i. 41; ii. 55.   Sec. Salvio Pacheco. *Dept. St. Pap., S. J.*, MS., iv. 105.   Aug. José el Cantor to be sent to Mont.   Sept., the mail of the 22d of each month suspended, leaving that of the 11th. *Id.*, 105–6.

1833.   Alcalde Salvio Pacheco; regidores (Joaquin Higuera) and Máximo Martinez (Sebastian Peralta also called regidor); sec. José Berreyesa, juez de campo Francisco Palomares; Luis Peralta mentioned as juez de paz (?), Antonio M. Pico 'majordomo de propios.' *S. J. Arch.*, v. i.; vi. 10; *Dept. St. Pap., S. J.*, MS., iv. 132, 138.   Feb., guardia and jail to be repaired; meanwhile prisoners to be sent to Sta Clara.   No one to be allowed to cut down trees in the alameda.   March, ayunt. funds to be used for the purchase of powder and lead.   Dec. surplus funds (!) to be sent to the gov't at Mont. The number of regidores cannot be increased at present. *Id.*, 115–16, 140. Aug., lands *del fondo* to be given to the most industrious; not to be taken from owners, but the latter must cultivate or rent them. *Id.*, 121; *Id., Ben., P. & J.*, vi. 13.   Sept., the ayunt. has no power to compel vagrants to work for the public. *Id.*, 15.   Antonio Chabolla to be allowed to cultivate the

was dissolved here as elsewhere, and Dolores Pacheco served as juez de paz in 1839–40. The jurisdiction of the ayuntamiento extended after 1834 from the

Yerba Buena ejidos without prejudice to the common use of wood, water, etc. *Id.*, *S. J.*, iv. 137; *Doc. Hist. Cal.*, MS., i. 412.

1834. Alcalde Pedro Chabolla; regidores Máximo and Ignacio Martinez (the election of Tomás Pacheco being declared null), sec. Salvio Pacheco, and José Fernandez from July. *Dept. St. Pap.*, *S. J.*, MS., ix. 142, 146, 148, 155. Alcalde permitted by gov. to go to S. Rafael for 6 days; a regidor must be punished like any other man, and cannot leave town without permission. *Id.*, 148, 151. May 15th, municipal regulations issued by the alcalde. *Dept. St. Pap.*, MS., iii. 163–6. Citizens not to go in pursuit of horse thieves, except in company with troops. *Id.*, *S. J.*, iv. 143. June 12th, Sec. Zamorano reports that the civil and political jurisdiction of (por parte del) the pueblo of S. José has always been understood to extend 'from the Laguna rancho to Sta Clara, and on the other side comprising all the ranchos as far as the strait of Carquines, toward the villa de Branciforte as far as the summit of the sierra which divides them.' *St. Pap.*, *M. & C.*, MS., ii. 218. And on June 28th the gov. fixes the limits, not very clearly, as follows: 'The demarcation toward the pueblo of S. José Guadalupe will begin from the line fixed for that of S. F. at the rancho of the Castros' (S. Lorenzo and S. Leandro? but these ranchos not included) 'from the missions of Sta Clara and S. José and the said rancho and settlements (congregaciones) of the centre as far as la gentilidad toward the tulares, following the cordillera and the valley to the Laguna rancho, near the sierra of Sta Cruz, the summit of which will serve as dividing line between S. José and Branciforte.' *Id.*, 220.

1835. Alcalde Antonio María Pico; regidores (Ignacio Martinez) and Leandro Rochin, síndico Luis Chabolla, sec. José Berreyesa, depositario José Noriega. Jan. 15th, municipal and police regulations in 21 articles. *St. Pap. Sac.*, MS., xi. 23–9. Petition of inhab. of Contra Costa to be transferred from S. F. jurisdiction to that of S. José. This vol., p. 291.

1836. Alcalde José María Alviso; regidores (Leandro Rochin) and Nicolás Berreyesa, síndico Francisco Archuleta, sec. José Berreyesa. Record of elections Dec. 13, 21, 1835, in *Castro, Doc.*, MS., i. 23–5. March, padre complains that men at S. Ignacio rancho sell liquor to the Ind. *S. José, Arch.*, MS., i. 11. Sept. 10th, meeting of ayunt. to complain of the padres of S. José and Sta Clara who put obstacles in the way of justice and assumed authority not belonging to them; it was voted to call on the gov. to oblige the padres to give up to the court two Ind. offenders, Mateo and Estanislao. *St. Pap.*, *M. & C.*, MS., ii. 367–8. Only one prisoner in June. In Feb. the alcalde was excused from serving by the gov., but no successor is named. *Dept. St. Pap.*, *S. J.*, MS., iv. 113; v. 9.

1837. Alcalde Juan Alvires; regidores (Nicolás Berreyesa) and John Burton. Antonio Rodriguez is also mentioned in Nov. as alcalde (?). *Sta Cruz Arch.*, MS., 44. Burton acted as juez much of the year. Jan. 19th, municipal regulations published by the ayunt. *Vallejo, Doc.*, MS., xxxii. 68. Dec. 21st, nine citizens for all petitioned that no grants of land should be made until the pueblo lands could be marked out. A petition for the assigning of these lands was sent to the gov. on the 23d by the alcalde; and on the 24th the gov. authorized the ayunt. to appoint a commission to make a map. *Hall's Hist. S. J.*, 125 et seq.

1838. Alcalde Dolores Pacheco. No other member of the ayunt. named. In March the ayunt. appointed Guillermo Castro, Wm Gulnac, and Salvio Pacheco as comisionados to survey the pueblo lands, which they did with all due formalities, and the map and report were sent to the gov.; but there is no evidence of any subsequent confirmation. According to this survey, some of the original landmarks had been incorrectly placed. Full account of the

ranchos of San Leandro and Las Pulgas in the north, to Laguna Seca in the south, excluding all these ranchos, and from the summit of the Santa Cruz mountains eastward to the tulares. That of the juzgado from 1839 included also in a sense the contra costa ranchos up to Carquines strait, since the juez of that district was auxiliary to him of San José and not of San Francisco. San José was also made temporarily cabecera of the partido, but no sub-prefect was ap-

survey and lines adopted in *Hall's Hist. S. J.*, 125–32. Munic. receipts and expend., $326. *S. J. Arch.*, loose pap., 59.

1839. Alcalde José Noriega; regidores Tomás Pacheco and Wm Gulnac, síndico Diego Forbes, sec. José Z. Fernandez, comisario de policía Anastasio Cortés. In accordance with an order of June 15th, the ayunt. dissolved itself on the 18th; and Dolores Pacheco took charge of municipal affairs as juez de paz. *Dept. St. Pap., S. J.*, MS., v. 26; *Gomez, Doc.*, MS., 40. José Z. Fernandez was at the same time appointed juez de paz suplente, and in July Antonio Suñol was appointed síndico, or treasurer of the juzgado, and Pedro Mesa now or earlier was juez de campo. Jan. 29th. Prefect to gov. complains of the citizens who are accustomed to sign a threatening protest against any act of the ayunt. that does not please them, which does great harm. *S. J. Arch.*, MS., iii. 26. March. Record of elections; certain vocales who did not attend were fined $2 each; names of officers and primary electors given; elector de partido, José Fernandez, suplente Salvio Pacheco. *Id.*, vi. 54–6. March 14th. Ayunt. petitions gov. that S. Josè be made cabecera of the partido instead of San Francisco. Action on this matter was postponed; but in Sept. S. José was declared temporarily the cabecera. *Dept. St. Pap.*, MS., iv. 249; *Doc. Hist. Cal.*, MS., i. 398; *S. José Arch.*, MS., ii. 18. April. A soldier arrested and fined by the alcalde. Gen. Vallejo decides that he had no right to do it and the fine need not be paid. *Vallejo, Doc.*, MS., vi. 357. Prefect thinks two jueces de paz needed in town, and another if the contra costa ranchos are added to the jurisdiction. *S. J. Arch.*, MS. iii. 28. Capt. Salvio Pacheco of the civic guard was put under arrest for offensive expressions in a letter to Gen. Vallejo; but at the same time was required to go to Mont. as elector, being obliged to resume his state of arrest on return. *Vallejo, Doc.*, MS., vi. 493. May. Criminal proceedings against an Ind. girl and her accomplice for killing an Ind. at Milpitas. *Dept. St. Pap., S. J.*, vii. 13. Another against José J. Castro for killing Anastasio Cortés in a gambling quarrel. *Id.*, 17. June. Síndico's report of receipts and expend., $134. *S. J. Arch.*, loose pap., MS., 19; for next six mo., receipts $237, expend. $199. *Id.*, 17. July 30th. Police regulations. *S. J. Arch.*, MS., ii. 62.

1840. Juez de paz Dolores Pacheco, suplente José Z. Fernandez, síndico probably Suñol. In *Dept. St. Pap.*, MS., xvii. 49, is a report of Sec. Fernandez of an election of Dec. 19, 1839, of Antonio M. Pico and Félix Buelna as 1st and 2d alcalde (?). June 14th. Alcalde calls attention to the law that all but owners and servants living on ranchos must belong to the nearest town; therefore proprietors must dismiss all agregados under penalty of a fine of 30 reals. *Mont. Arch.*, MS., ix. 21. March 1st. Síndico's account, expenses $299, receipts in taxes and fines, $343. *S. J. Arch.*, loose pap., 22. May 2d. Juez sends (again?) to gov. the plan and expediente of the town ejidos. *S. J. Arch.*, MS., 36. June 4th. Sends list of foreigners in the jurisdiction. *Id.*, 39. July 4th. Gov. tells the juez of contra costa that he is auxiliary to the juez de partido of S. José. *Dept. Rec.*, xi. 17.

pointed till after 1840. The record of events in town for the decade is well nigh a blank, though I append the summary.[26] Of industrial progress we know nothing beyond the increase in population for the jurisdiction as already given, and the fact that the sum of $2,000 was spent on a church. No visitors during this period have furnished either descriptive matter or narratives of their visits. The people took but slight part in the revolutionary and sectional warfare of 1836–8; but raiding bands of Indian horse-thieves furnished constant material for excitement and semi-military ardor, most of the vecinos enrolling themselves in two companies of militia.

[26] Summary and index of events, etc. 1831. Part taken by S. José against Gov. Victoria; trial of Alcalde Duarte; adhesion to the S. Diego plan. This vol., p. 187–8, 194–5, 212. 1832. Slight part taken in the Zamorano revolt. *Id.*, 223–4. 1833. Expedition against the Moquelumnes Ind. *Id.*, 359, 394. 1835. Slight reference to exped. against Ind. horse-thieves. *S. José Arch.*, MS., i. 40; *Palomares, Mem.*, MS., 1–13. In June Padre Moreno informed the gov. that he was building a pueblo church with contributions from the citizens etc., and asked for the tithes for this purpose. Figueroa in reply sent a libranza of $30 as a personal contribution, and authorized the people to devote their tithes to the building fund, though the payment of tithes was no longer obligatory. There was some additional correspondence, and in 1838 Gen. Vallejo also authorized the use of the tithes; but it does not appear that any funds were obtained from this source until 1839, in which year $2,050 were received and expended. In 1840 Gov. Alvarado renewed the concession, and in July the work was still going on. *Arch., Arzob.*, MS., v. pt. ii. 9–10, 29; *Dept. St. Pap.*, v. 6; *Id., S. J.*, iv. 170; *Gomez, Doc.*, MS., 29, 38; *Vallejo, Doc.*, v. 206; xxxii. 353; xxxiii. 176; *S. J. Arch.*, MS., iii. 32, 36. 1836. Alvarado here preparing for revolution. This vol., p. 456. 1836–40. Ind. affairs, including one or more expeditions and raids in nearly every year. Vol. iv. 74–6. 1837. Recruiting a militia force. This vol., p. 511. Troubles connected with the arrest of A. M. Pico. *Id.*, 513–14, 523–7. Rumors of conspiracy in Nov. *Id.*, 573. There were two militia companies organized at S. José, each of 44 men, rank and file. The officers of the 1st were capt. Salvio Pacheco, lieut A. M. Pico and Guillermo Castro, alf. Tomás Pacheco and José M. Alviso Jr.; and of the 2d, Capt. José M. Alviso, lieut. Agustin Bernal and Ignacio Martinez, alf. Inocencio Romero and Fulgencio Higuera. Capt. Jesus Vallejo was mil. comandante. *Vallejo, Doc.*, MS., xxiv. 8, 9; *S. J. Arch.*, MS., vi. 26. The force was dissolved in 1840. *Dept. St. Pap., Ben., P. & J.*, MS., iii. 13. 1838. Earthquake in June, a house shaken down. Vol. iv. p. 78. Aug., Juan Carrasco found dead of hunger at Arroyo Mocho. *S. J. Arch.*, MS., v. 32. Nov., celebration of news of accession of Alvarado and Vallejo. This vol., p. 577. 1840. Arrest of foreigners. Vol. iv. p. 11. Ind. making trouble at Sutter's. *Id.*, 138. Douglas, *Journal*, MS., 88, estimates the exports of hides, tallow, and grain at $80,000.

CONTINUED ALPHABETICALLY FROM VOLUME II.

Fabbol, 1845, one of Frémont's men '45–7. iv. 583.   Fabregat (Narciso), 1819, Span. lieut of the Mazatlan cavalry, who served chiefly at Sta B., being often mentioned in the military records down to '30; being suspended for a time in '27–8 on account of his Span. birth, though he took the oath and gave no cause of suspicion; retired from mil. service in '33. ii. 254, 336, 361, 441, 533–4, 572–3, 575, 675; iii. 51–3. In '29 he was 67 years old, had been three times married, had a daughter in Sin. to whom he allowed one third of his pay, and two small children by his last wife. He became a trader at Sta B., and in '43 was grantee of the Catera or Pozitas rancho. iii. 655; iv. 642; ment. in '44. iv. 408. I have no later record than '45, but think the old lieut was murdered by robbers soon after '48.

Fages (Pedro), 1769, Span. lieut of Catalan volunteers, who accomp. the 1st exped. as com. of the forces that came by sea; mil. com. of Cal. July '70 to May '74, being capt. from '71; came back as gov. and com. gen. of Cal. Sept. '82 to April '91, being colonel from '89; in the city of Mex. '94, the date of his death not being known. See biog. i. 481–7; his *Voyage* and other writings, i. list of auth., 141, 396, 408, 443, 486; mention '69–74, including his explor. of S.F. Bay and his quarrels with P. Serra. i. 117, 119, 128, 131, 134, 136, 140–1, 147, 151, 153, 168–9, 171–2, 175–6, 178–9, 181–92, 195–6, 207, 210, 213, 215, 217–19, 223, 225–7, 229, 231–2, 245, 283–6, 290, 386, 671; ii. 44; ment. in '81–2, including his appt as gov. and operations on the Colorado. i. 363, 366–70, 373, 376, 378, 383–5; mention in 1783–90, gen. record, includ. family troubles. i. 387–408; mission affairs during his rule. i. 409–25; foreign relations and commerce. i. 426–49; occasional ment. in con. with local matters. i. 450–80; 1791–2, end of rule, departure, biog. i. 481–7; additional references. i. 492, 534, 583, 605, 609, 619, 625, 661–2, 666–7; ii. 44. Don Pedro was a central figure in early Californian annals; his character has been to me a most attractive one; but I refer the reader to i. 486–7, for my views on the subject.   Fagins (Lucius), 1847, owner of a S.F. lot.

Fairbanks (Henry), 1847, Co. A, Morm. Bat. (v. 469); at Payson, Utah, '82. F. (W.R.), 1848, nat. of Vt, who came by sea with his cousins, named Heyman, at the age of 10; in the mines to '55; 10 years in N.Y.; at Tomales '80 with wife, Belinda Scanlan, and 4 children. *Marin Co. Hist.*, 493.   Fairchild (Ephraim), 1847, prob. overl. immig. v. 556; blacksmith and wagon-maker, who worked at N. Helv. '47–9; at Sac. in '71.   F. (Wm H.), 1846, connected with the Mormon settlement on the Stanislaus in '46–7, though prob. not a Mormon; settled at Stockton '47; county surveyor and supervisor '78–9. Fairfax (D.M.), 1847, mid. on the *Columbus*, acting master of the *Erie*.   Fairfield (Levi), 1848, miner from whom Gov. Mason obtained specimens of gold. Fala (Francis), 1847, owner of lot at S.F.   Fales (Bounty), 1846–7, doubtful name, Cal. claims (v. 462).   Falker (Joseph K.), 1844, Amer. who got a pass for 1 year.   Falkner (E.R.), 1848, clerk of Starky, Junion, & Co. at S. F.   Fallet (1847), at N. Helv.   Fallon (Daniel), 1826, mr of the *Adam*. iii. 145.   F. (D.), 1846–7, in list of Cal. claims (v. 462).   F. (Jeremiah), 1847, owner of S.F. lot; also at S. José.

Fallon (Thomas), 1844, Canadian generally said to have come with Frémont, though there is some doubt in the matter. iv. 453; also said by the county histories to have lived for a time in Butte Co. The earliest original records of his presence are in Oct.–Nov. '45, when he was at Branciforte, age 26. In '46 he took part in enlisting men south of the bay to coöperate with the Bear filibusters. v. 137; and in July, being known as 'captain,' raised the U. S. flag at S. José. v. 245–6. Later in '46–7 he served in Co. F, Cal. Bat., enlisting at S. Juan in Oct. (v. 358); several times named in the *N. Helv. Diary* '46–7; in the list of Cal. claimants (v. 462); in '48–9 a successful miner; mayor of S. José in '51; absent in Texas '52–4; later a capitalist of S.F. and S. José, where he still lives in '85. His 1st wife, by whom he had 5 children, was, I think, a daughter of Michael Lodge, the Irish pioneer of '22. She obtained a divorce, as did the 2d wife; and in '84–5 the amorous old captain had to pay damages in a breach-of-promise suit.   F. (Wm O.), 1845, Irish trapper, known as 'Mountaineer,' 'Big,' or 'Le Gros' Fallon, who came from N. Mex. with a party of which little is known, and in Feb. '45 took part with the Calif. against Micheltorena in the south. iv. 495, 587. In Aug. he was at N. Helv. intending to start soon for the states; early in '46 he found Frémont's men in the S. Joaq. Val. v. 6; in June joined the Bears in the capture of Sonoma, and his signature appears in the original procl. of June 14th in my possession. v. 110, 114. He served prob. in Co. F, Cal. Bat. (v. 358), and had a Cal. claim of $50 for a mule (v. 462); was a member of the 4th Donner relief, and his diary, published in the *Star*, was the foundation of the absurd charges against Keseburg. v. 541–3. He went east with Gen. Kearny as guide. v. 452; and in the *S.F. Calif.* of Sept. 2, '48, we read that he had started alone from Ft Hall for Cal., and it was feared he had been killed by Ind.

Falls (Richard J.), 1846, nat. of N.Y.; sergt Co. C, 1st U.S. dragoons, who served under Kearny at S. Pascual, the S. Gabriel, and the Mesa '46–7. v. 347. He remained in Cal. after his disch., living on a Napa farm till '62, when he went east to serve in the war with distinction and wounds for 3 years, rising to the rank of colonel. Returning to Cal. he was in '69 an officer in the custom-house; and in '83–5 a sergt of police in S. F. His daughter, Ivy I. Falls, was appointed postmistress at Vallejo in '69.   Famin (Ign.), 1847, doubtful name of an Englishman at N. Helv.

Fannier (M.), 1846, doubtful name of the Cal. Bat. (v. 358).   Fanning (H.F.), 1847, resid. of Stockton. *Tinkham*.   F. (R.C.), 1846, Co. F, Cal. Bat. (v. 358); enlist at S. Juan, Oct.   Farías (José María), settler at Los Ang. '15. ii. 350; still there '39–48.   F. (Santiago), 1827, Scotchman, bapt. at S. Diego; prob. James 'McFerion,' q.v.   Farley (Anderson), 1846, Co. F, Cal. Bat. (v. 358); prob. an overl. immig., cl. for a Napa rancho '52.   F. (Geo.), 1847, Co. B, N.Y.Vol. (v. 499); at The Dalles, Or., '82.   F., 1846, said by Lancey to have come with Kearny; owner of a S.F. lot '47.   F. (John F.), 1847, Co. B, N.Y.Vol. (v. 499); died at Portland, Or., '69. *Hist. Or.*, i. 630.   F. (John G.), 1847, father of John F., Co. B, N.Y.Vol.; d. S.F. '49.   F. (Thos P.), 1847, Co. B, N.Y.Vol.; at Portland, Or., '82.   Farnesio (Francisco), 1805, priest from Manila, at Mont., sent to Mex. ii. 31, 160.

Farnham (Thos Jefferson), 1840, nat. of Me, who came overl. to Or. in '39, and to Cal. via Honolulu on the *Don Quixote*, returning east by S. Blas and across Mex., and writing books on Or., Mex., and Cal. as a result. See iii. 680; iv. 2, 4, 6–7, 10, 15–17, 25–8, 95, 103, 117, 120, 156–7, 192, 266. F. was a lawyer of some ability, and a writer of somewhat fertile imagination. His work on Cal. is criticised elsewhere in this work; here it must suffice to say that in all those parts resting on his own observations it is worthless trash, and in all that relates to the Californian people a tissue of falsehoods. He came back to Cal. in '47—perhaps in '46, as he took part in a public meeting at S.F. in June '47, v. 455—and died at S.F. in Sept. '48, age 42. He left a widow and 3 children in N.Y. The former, Eliza W. Farnham, came to Cal. by sea in '50, and in '56 published her *California Indoors and Out*, a pleasing picture of life on the Pacific coast. She was a woman bent on doing the world as much good as possible, and one of her hobbies was the bringing eastern girls to Cal. in quest of husbands. She died in '64 at the age of 49.   Farnsworth (J.B.), 1839, Engl. at Mont. acc. to newsp. item of '72.   F. (J.M.), 1846, doubtful memb. of the Mormon col. v. 547.   Farnum, 1848, mr of a

vessel at Sta Cruz and Mont.   Farr (Philip), 1847, Co. G, N.Y.Vol. (v. 499);
d. at Dutch Flat '83.

Farwell (Edward Augustus), 1842, Boston printer and sailor who came
from Honolulu with Capt. Cooper on the *California*, perhaps as mate, with
letters from Reynolds to Larkin, age 27. iv. 341. In '43 he was naturalized,
and in '44 got a grant of the Arroyo Chico rancho, Butte Co. iv. 670; I have
a letter of '45 from his brother Joseph R. in Bost. to the U.S. consul asking
for information about him. He went east overl. in '45, seeking relief from
weak eyes, returning in '48; was for a time in charge of Sutter's launch running on the Sac., and died at S. F. in Jan. '49.   F. (James), 1840, doubtful
name in Farnham's list of arrested foreigners. iv. 17.   Fatoute (Ezra), 1847,
Co. B, Morm. Bat. (v. 469); reënl.   Faucon (Edward H.), 1835, mr of the
Boston ships *Alert* and *Pilgrim* '35-7. iii. 381, 383; iv. 105, 141. Wm H.
Thomes informs me that Capt. F. is still living in Mass. '85.   Fauffer (Jo-
hann), 1847, musician of N.Y.Vol. (v.499); d. Wash. '64.   Faulkner (James
Y.), 1847, Co. G, N.Y.Vol. (v. 499); at S. José '50 and '74; S.F. '71; in Or. '78.

Fauntleroy (Daingerfield), 1844, nat. of Va, b. 1799; capt. of state militia
about 1838; purser U.S.N. from '33; on the *Savannah* '44-7. iv. 453. The
service that has made him best known in Cal. was as capt. of a comp. of volunteer dragoons to which was intrusted the preservation of order in the
Mont. district July-Sept. '46, F. commanding the garrison of S. Juan B. and
making an exped. against hostile Ind. v. 232, 247-8, 254, 293-4. Died at
Pensacola navy-yard in '53. His son W.H.F., in interviews and letters of
'77, being then in S.F., gave me information about his father's life.

Faura (José), 1798, Span. friar who served 12 years as missionary at S.
Luis Rey and S. Juan Cap. Biog. ii. 110; ment. i. 564, 577, 654, 657; ii. 110,
159-60.   Faust (John B.), 1847, owner of S.F. lot. v. 685; in May intending
to start from Sonoma with a party to explore Trinidad Bay; in March '48
digging wells at Benicia. v. 673; d. at the Yuba mines Aug. 18th.   Faustino, 1845, leader in a disturbance at Los Ang. iv. 523.   Fautrel, 1837, mr
of the *Nancy*. iv. 105.   Faxon (Wm. T.), 1840, Amer. trader who came by
sea and took charge of Larkin's store at Mont. '41. iv. 120. He went to Hon. in
'42 but returned in '44, his name frequently occurring in commercial corresp.
He left the country on the *California* in '46, and in a later letter Capt. Arther gave a very unfavorable report of his conduct on the voyage.

Febiger (Geo. Carson), 1846, lieut on the *Dale*, on land service at S.F.
F. (John C.), 1846, passed mid. on the *Dale;* at Wash. '78.   Feil (J.), 1837,
owner of S.F. lot. iii. 705; doubtful name.   Feliciano (Alejo), 1777, sirviente at S.F. i. 297.   Felipe, executed at Sta. B. '24.   F. (A.), 1848,
passp. from Hon.

Félix, see list in i. 735-6 of those who came before 1800.   Félix (Anastasio), at Los Ang. '46.   F. (Antonio), at Los Ang. '39, age 28.   F. (Antonio), soldier at S.F. '44, age 21.   F. (Diego), at Mont. '36, age 26, wife
María del Rosario, child Andrés; maj. at San Antonio '39. iii. 688; executed
for the murder of his wife '40. iii. 676.   F. (Dolores), alférez of cavalry at
Mont. '45. iv. 652. Still at Mont. '48.   F. (Domingo), murdered by his wife
and her paramour at Los Ang. '36, a crime that resulted in the 1st Cal. vigilance com. iii. 417-19, 631.   F. (Domingo), militia sergt at S.F. '37 and
later; owner of S.F. lot '43, and grantee of S. Mateo rancho '44. iv. 669, 671,
673, 676, 683; still at S.F. '55, a witness in the Santillan case.   F. (Doroteo),
settler at Los Ang. 1803. ii. 350.   F. (Fernando), regidor at S. José '31. iii.
729; at S. Mateo '35; grantee of Novato '39. iii. 712, and of Sanel '44. iv.
673; age 46 in '44; ment. by Revere. '46. ii. 297.   F. (Francisco), settler at
Los Ang. 1791. ii. 350.   F. (Hipólito), French, at Brancif. '45, age 27.   F.
(Ignacio), soldier at Sta. B. before '37.   F. (Jacoba), cl. of S. Fran. rancho.
iii. 633.   F. (Jesus), aux. alcalde at S. José '36. iii. 636.   F. (José), settler
at Los Ang. '13-19; ii. 349, 354.   F. (José), at S.F. and Son. '42-4, age 15-
20.   F. (José), juez de campo S. José. v. 662.   F. (José Antonio), killed
by Ind. about '24.   F. (José Antonio), at Los Ang. '46.   F. (Juan), soldier
at Sta. B. '32.   F. (Juan), at Los Ang. '39, age 57.   F. (Juan), killed by

Ind. at Refugio '45. iv. 642.   F. (Juan José), at Brancif. '28–45, age at latter date 45; wife Antonia Castro, child. Rafaela, Miguel b. '22, Leon '25, Angel '27, Antonio '32, Victoria '31, Josefa '39; juez de paz in '43. ii. 677; iv. 663. F. (Julian), at S. Mateo '35.   F. (Leonardo), soldier at S.F. '19–27; arrested at Mont. '37. iii. 525.   F. (Luciano), sentinel at S. Buen. '19. ii. 333; in revolt at Sta B. '29. iii. 78; at the Natividad fight '46; in 49 juez de policía at S. Luis Ob.   F. (Luis), soldier at S.F. '44, age 17.   F. (Luis), soldier at Sta B. '32–7, wife Secundina Cordero, 3 children.   F. (Manuel), in Los Ang. dist. '46–56.   F. (Nicolás), at Los Ang. '46.   F. (Rafael), at S. Mateo '35; S.F. militia '37; in '41 in S. José dist., age 44, wife Juana Amézquita, child. Ramon b. '28, Urbano '29, Macario '31, Julia '27, Sinforosa '34, Jose d. '40. F. (Rafael), soldier of S.F. comp. '39–42; detailed in '41 to accomp. capt. Castañeda to Mex.; grantee of Pescadero, S. Joaq., '43. iv. 672; ment. in '46. F. (Santiago), at S. Juan Cap. '46, age 30, wife Juana Riola, child. Juan, Andrea, Alonza, and Ascension.   F. (Tomás), soldier at Sta B. before '37. F. (Vicente), inválido corp. in charge of Los Ang. as comisionado much of the time 1785–1800. i. 347, 461, 479, 661; owner of the Félix rancho, 1802–16. ii. 111, 185, 353.   F. (Vicente), soldier at Sta B. before '37, wife Filomena Valenzuela; 5 children; in '36 maj. at Buena Esperanza rancho. iii. 677; widower, age 26, child. Casiana, Gerónimo, Juan, and José; grantee of Moro y Cayucos, S. Luis Ob., '42. iv. 655; in trouble with the auth. at S. Luis '47. Perhaps 2 or 3 men of this name.

Fellom (Caius Julius), 1845(?), Danish sailor, brother of Matthew, who came to Cal. in '52 and again in '62, and at S. José in '78 claimed to have touched at Sta B. before '46 on the whaler *Waverly. S. J. Pion.* Jul. 6, '78. F. (Matthew, or Felipe), 1821(?), Danish hatter and sailor, who landed from a whaler all the way from '21 to '24 acc. to dif. records. ii. 444, 526–7. He settled in the Gilroy region, and married after '34, when his age was 32. Felipe was prob. his baptismal name in Cal.; on Larkin's books '41–7; in '42 making soap at Gilroy's; in '46 juez at S. Juan B. v. 640. He is said to have become rich in lands and cattle, and to have died in '68 or '73.   Fellows (C.J.), 1845, doubtful arrival. iv. 587.   F. (Hiram W.), 1847, Co. C, Morm. Bat. (v. 469); reënl.   Fendero (Jesus), Mex. soldier of the piquete de Hidalgo at Mont. '36, age 29.   Fenley (Daniel), 1847, Co. A, N.Y.Vol. (v. 499).

Ferguson, 1846, doubtful memb. of the Mormon Col. v. 547.   F. (Adrian), 1835, at S. José; prob. Geo. A., q. v.   F. (Daniel), 1824, Irish shoemaker from N. Mex. ii. 526; iii. 156; joined the comp. extranjera at Mont. '32. iii. 221; in '36 a resid. of Los Ang., age 30, with a Cal. wife. He was one of the vigilantes (iii. 430); but failed to secure a lot; and in '39 or earlier came north, his name appearing on Larkin's books in '39–40. He was murdered in Salinas Val. '41 by Arana, the paramour of F.'s wife, Cármen Ruiz. iv. 280, 653.   F. (Geo. A.), 1831, Amer. sailor, cooper, and lumberman, who deserted from the *Fanny*, working at S. Rafael, S. F. iv. 708–9, Mont. in '33, and S. José from '34. iii. 405; arrested but not exiled in '40. iv. 17; in the contra costa '44; signed the S. José call to foreigners '45. iv. 599; lot at S.F. '47; perhaps had a store at Stockton '48; in '78–83 a resid. of Mayfield.   F. (James), 1847, sergt-maj. of Morm. Bat. v. 477, 483; in '58 adj.-gen. Utah; delivered a lecture in Liverpool '55.   F. (Jesse), 1828, Amer. trapper of Pattie's party, who remained in Cal., settling at Los Ang.; married a Rendon in '31; named in '36 as a trader, age 36; said to have died in L. Cal. a few years later. ii. 558; iii. 163, 178.   F. (J.C.), 1846, overl. immig., named by Bryant; Co. C, Cal. Bat., enlisting at S. Juan in Oct. (v. 358); Joseph F. had a Cal. claim (v. 462); Josiah F. was a witness in the Cal. claims and in the Frémont court-martial. v. 454. These may have been all the same man; but there was also a Ferguson at Sonoma in June before the arrival of the immig. v. 110, 128.   Fermor (Edward), 1847, Co. D, N.Y.Vol. (v. 499).

Fernandez (Antonio), regidor of Mont. '27–8. ii. 612.   F. (Diego), 1827, Span. trader on the *Waverly;* teacher at Sta B. '30. ii. 574; wife Brígida Navarro, 2 child.; widower in '36, age 51, 3 child.; maj. at Purísima '42. iv. 648.   F. (Dionisio), grantee with his bro. Máximo of land in Butte '46. v.

675.   F. (Francisco), 1825, Span. from the *Aquiles;* ordered away in '28-30. iii. 51.   F. (Gregorio), 1794, Span. friar, who served at S. Luis Ob. and Purísima, retiring 1805. Biog. ii. 123; ment. i. 547, 576, 675, 689; ii. 159-60.

Fernandez (José), 1817, Span. sailor who came from Peru with Rocquefeuil as a sailor on the *Bordelais,* and served in the S. F. comp. as soldier and corporal in '19-27, going with Argüello in '21 on the exped. to the north. ii. 232, 280, 446. In '28-9, like other Span., he was in some trouble with the Mex. auth. but was allowed to remain. iii. 51-2, 75; in '30 sec. of the ayunt. at S. José. iii. 730; in '39 partido elector. iii. 590, 731; in '44 síndico. iv. 685; in '46 juez de paz, capt. of defensores, serving in the south under Castro to Aug., and after U.S. occupation memb. of the council. v. 140, 295, 662, 664; in '49 2d alcalde. In later years he resided at Sta Clara, being a witness in the N. Almaden and many other cases. In '74 he dictated his recollections of early days, a most interesting narrative called *Cosas de California.* He died a year or two later, over 75 years of age. Capt. F. was a man who always merited the respect and esteem of those who knew him.

Fernandez (José María), 1796, Span. friar, who served at S. F., but was obliged to retire in '97, insane from the effects of a blow on the head. i. 712-13; also i. 577, 711.   F. (José Perez), see 'Perez Fernandez.'   F. (José Zenon), 1834, Mex. teacher who came in the H. & P. col., iii. 263, teaching for a short time at Sta Clara. iii. 728. In '39 he was sec. of the S. José ayunt. and suplente juez de paz. iii. 731; in '40-1 sec. of the junta and ad int. of the govt. iii. 604, 193; and grantee of Quito rancho, Sta Clara, in '41. iv. 672; in '42 juez de paz at Mont., administering justice in a way not quite satisfactory to Com. Jones, and going south with Jimeno Casarin as sec. iv. 39, 294, 653, 656; in '44 sec. of the assembly down to his death in Aug. iv. 410.   F. (Manuel), 1794, Span. friar who served at Sta Clara and Sta Cruz, retiring in 1798. Biog. i. 498; ment. i. 576-7, 618, 723.   F. (Mariano), artillery corporal at S.D. 1803-6. ii. 102-3.   F. (Mariano), of the custom-house guard at Mont. '45, perhaps the same.   F. (Máximo), grantee of rancho in Butte, and S. F. lot '46. v. 675, 684.   F. (Pedro), builder of 1st frame house at S. José '41. iv. 684.   F. (Sabás), Mex. corporal sent to Cal. for the Mont. comp. '37; employed at Sonoma as lieut in com. of an Ind. comp. iii. 511; iv. 72.   F. (Santiago), soldier of S.F. comp. '41.

Fernandez del Campo (José), 1828, Mex. lieut in com. of Cal. artill., stationed at Mont.; arrested by insurgents '29; died in '31. ii. 608, 674; iii. 68, 70, 89, 190, 239.   Fernandez de San Vicente (Agustin), 1822, Mex. priest and canónigo, sent to Cal. as commissioner by Iturbide to superintend the change of govt; skillful in politics and intrigue, a bon-vivant and gambler, whose character was not admired by the friars. He departed in '23, and a few years later was vicar at Sta Fé, N. Mex. ii. 457-70, 483, 496, 550, 591, 597, 631, 643-4, 661; iii. 11.   Fernando, neoph. grantee of Rincon del Alisal '44. Fernando, at Soledad '27. ii. 623.

Ferrelo (Bartolomé), 1542, piloto mayor in com. of one of Cabrillo's vessels in the discov. of Cal.; com. of the exped. after Cabrillo's death, continuing the voyage to the north. i. 77-81.   Ferrer (Antonio), 1825, on the *Asia.* iii. 26.   Ferrill (Thos J.), 1846, Fauntleroy's dragoons (v. 232, 247).   Fetzchoror (Christian), 1847, musician of N.Y. Vol. (v. 499).   Fetzer (John), 1846, Co. C, 1st U.S. dragoons (v. 336).

Fich (Henry), 1846, owner of S.F. lot; prob. Hen. D. 'Fitch,' q.v.   Fickett (S.H.), 1847, nat. of N.Y.; memb. of S. Joaq. pioneers '84.   Fidalgo (Salvador), 1790, Span. naval lieut, com. of the transports and explor. vessels *S. Cárlos* and *Princesa,* on the Cal. coast and at Nootka 1790-5. i. 444, 506, 509, 513, 517, 524, 523, 535, 543, list. of auth.; also *Hist. N. W. Coast,* index. Fiel (W.H.), 1846, Co. C, 1st U.S. dragoons, trans. from Co. K.; killed at S. Pascual. v. 346.   Field (B. Oscar), 1847, nat. of Penn., captured as a boy by Ind., and later interpreter and courier for the govt. Said to have come to Cal. '47; in Sac. Val. '48; at S.F. from '50. Died at S.F. '64. *Bulletin.*   F. (Daniel), 1847, Co. F, N.Y. Vol. (v. 499).   F. (John), 1847, ditto.   F. (Samuel), 1845, overl. immig., perhaps of the Grigsby-Ide party. iv. 579.

Fife (John), 1847, Co. C, Morm. Bat. (v. 469).   F. (Peter), 1847, Co. B, ditto.   F. (Wm), 1841, Scotch otter-hunter in Sta B. region from '45, and prob. several years earlier. iv. 279; v. 317; went to the mines '48, but resumed his hunting to '58 and later; murdered by a Sonoran at Sta B. in '66.   Fifer, see 'Pfeifer.'   Fifield (Ira), 1848, furnished specimens of gold to Gov. Mason; prob. same as following.   F. (Levi), 1847, Co. C, Morm. Bat. (v. 469); in Sutter's employ '47-8.

Figuer (Juan), 1772, Span. friar who served at S. Gabriel, San Luis Ob., and S. Diego, dying in 1784. Biog. i. 455; ment. i. 107, 192-3, 196, 272, 299, 316, 388, 457-9, 654, 106-7.   Figueroa (Felipe), soldier at Sta B. '32, wife Ignacia Lopez; still at Sta B. in '50.   F. (Francisco), 1833, Mex. capt. who came with his brother, the gov., and was appointed contador at Mont. in '34. iii. 236, 240, 378. In '36 he lived at Mont., age 32, wife María de Jesus Palomares, age 18, son Guadalupe b. '36; in '37 involved in the revolt against Alvarado. iii. 513, 523-6; from '39 in charge of his brother's Alamitos rancho near Los Ang. iii. 633, 637. In '44-6 he was a member of the assembly, being president of that body under Flores' administration, and taking some part against the U.S. iv. 361, 411, 495-6. 521; v. 37-8, 49-50, 264, 321-2. Don Francisco was city treasurer of Los Ang. in '50.   F. (Guadalupe), grantee of Corral de Tierra '36.

Figueroa (José), 1833, Mex. brigadier-gen. who had been com. gen. of Son. and Sin., and who was gov. and com. gen. of Cal. from Jan. 14, '33, to his death on Sept. 29, '35. See full account of his arrival, rule, and death, including his troubles with Hijar, Padrés, and Apalátegui, in iii. 234-98, espec. on biog. and character, 234, 296-7; also ment. i. 662; ii. 508, 594; iii. 16, 365, 414, 613, 633, 652, 669-71; acts and policy in mission and Ind. affairs. iii. 318, 321-36, 339-62, 620; commercial and financial affairs. iii. 368-80; the Russians. iv. 161-3. Figueroa is known as the best of California's Mex. governors, and in many respects merits his reputation. He was an intelligent man, of good intentions and liberal views; not a model in respect of private morality, and not always to be fully trusted; well versed in the arts of making friends and of gaining popularity by overcoming imaginary obstacles; was fortunate in the circumstances under which he was called to rule the country; and made no serious mistakes.   F. (Manuel), settler at Los Ang. in '79. i. 461.   Filibert (Francisco), 1825, Span. from the *Aquiles*, in list sent to Mex. '28; perhaps not sent away. iii. 51.

Finch (John), 1838, Engl. tinker and blacksmith who came to Mont. by sea, age 28. iv. 119. From '40 he lived at S.F., getting a lot, and keeping a saloon and bowling-alley at the cor. of Washington and Kearny streets. v. 683. He was more commonly known as John 'Tinker'; died Aug. 20, '47. Finch, 1847, mr of the *Com. Stockton*.   Findla (James), 1847, overl. immig. and carpenter from Mo., who worked at S.F. and became the owner of many town lots in '47-8. v. 556. Went to the mines in '48-9; later in the real estate business at S.F., where in '78 he dictated for my use his *Statement of Early Events*, and where I think he still lives in '85.   Findlay (John), 1847, Co. E, Morm. Bat. (v. 469).   F. (Wm), 1846, lieut and later capt. of Co. A, Cal. Bat. v. 361, 434; went east with Stockton or Kearny in '47. v. 454; at Wash. as a witness Jan. '48; perhaps the Wm Finlay at S. José '54 accredited to '45. *Annals of S.F.*, 822.

Fine (J. H.), 1846, nat. of Ky; claimant for Suisun rancho. iv. 674; died at Paso de Robles in '79, age 58.   F. (Quin?), 1847, blacksmith at Benicia; member of Sonoma council; died in '48. v. 668, 672-3.   Fink (Nicholas), 1836, German shoemaker who came to Los Ang. with a Mex. passp. of '35; age 30, and single in '40, when, having a shop in town, he was robbed and murdered, the 3 assassins being executed '41. iv. 118, 280, 629-30.

Finlay (Thomas), 1847, Co. D, Morm. Bat. (v. 469).   Finlayson (Duncan), 1833, agent of the H.B. Co., touched at S.F. on the *Dryad*. iii. 382, 404. Finley (Asa W.), 1846, overl. immig. with wife and 2 children; served under Aram at Sta Clara (v. 378); a farmer at S. José for 17 years; later in Linn Val., Kern Co., where he was in '79, having 2 sons, 3 married daughters, Mrs

Henry Pascoe, L. A. Beardsley, and J. P. Wilkes in Kern Co., and 2 daughters in Or. *Bakersfield Gazette.* Finley, 1844, a half-breed assistant of Laframboise. *Yolo Co. Hist.* F. (James), 1848, owner of lots at S.F. F. (John), 1847, Co. F, 3d U.S. artill. (v. 518). F. (John M.), 1848, of firm F., Johnson, & Co., traders at S.F. v. 680. F. (Richard), 1848, miner from Or., where he still lived in '82. Finley (S.), 1846, Cal. claim of $15 for a rifle (v. 462). Fippard (Chas), 1833, Engl. carpenter from the *Catalina*, who asked for a carta in '34, and was still at Mont. '35. iii. 409.

Fish (Wm), 1834, doubtful name in a Los Ang. list. Fisher, or Norris, 1818, negro of Bouchard's force, who rem. in Cal. There is no definite record of his later career, he being perhaps confounded in such vague allusions as exist with the following. ii. 248, 393. F., or Fisar, 1825, negro from Penn., who came to Sta B. on the *Sta Rosa;* in '29 at Los Ang., a farmer 35 years old, without religion, but of good conduct. iii. 29; ment. by Coronel, for whom he had worked, in '46–7; and perhaps by Foster in '48–9. It is possible, however, that this F. and the preceding were the same. F., 1846, of Cal. Bat., said to have been attacked by Ind. near Los Ang. in '47. *Frémont's Court-martial,* 233. F., 1847, mr of the *California.* v. 576. F., 1848, at Sutter's Fort from the quicksilver mines.

Fisher (Adam), 1843, named by Baldridge as a memb. of the Chiles-Walker immig. party. F. (Daniel), 1845, signer of the S. José call to foreigners. iv. 599. F. (Daniel), 1847, asst quartermaster in Stockton's Bat. Jan. v. 386. F. (F.), 1839, captain ment. in Larkin's accts as being at Mont. Aug. F. (Herman), 1848, German resid. of Sonoma Co. '73–7. *Son. Co. Hist.* F. (Joseph R.), 1846, one of the Mormon col., who rem. in Cal. v. 546. Fisher (Mary Ann), 1846, ditto; died in the faith at Mission S. José. v. 546. F. (Thomas M.), 1846, son of Wm, age 4, who settled in Sta Clara Co., married Anna Hanks in '61, and was still living, in '81, near Gilroy, with 5 children.

Fisher (Wm), 1845, nat. of Mass. who lived many years at Cape S. Lúcas, L. Cal., marrying Liberata Ceseña, trading on the coast, possibly visiting Upper Cal. earlier, but apparently coming for the 1st time in '45, when he got a S.F. lot, and is mentioned in Larkin's corresp. iv. 587, 669, 684. It was prob. on this visit that he purchased the Alvires, or Laguna Seca, rancho near S. José, for which his heirs were claimants in later years. iii. 712. In '46 he brought his family and settled at Laguna Seca, being also engaged in trade at S. José; it was on his rancho that Frémont encamped. v. 6, 660; in Dec. '46 memb. of council, v. 664, having declined the office of alcalde. v. 662. In '49 he sold his S. José business to Belden, and died in '50. His children were Mary C. wife of D. Murphy, Thos M., Cipriano W. (died), and Uloga Frico(?), as named in *Sta Clara Co. Hist.* The widow married Geo. H. Ball of N. Y. F. (Wm), 1825, mr of the *Recovery.* iii. 148. F. (Wm), 1830, at Los Ang. ii. 555. Fishpan(?), (John), 1846, Fauntleroy's dragoons (v. 232, 247). Fisk (Daniel), 1844, deserter from the *Warren.* Fiske (F.), 1841, mid. on the U.S. *St Louis.*

Fitch (Henry Delano), 1826, nat. of New Bedford, Mass., b. 1799, who came to Cal. as mr of Virmond's Mex. brig. *Maria Ester.* iii. 147, 176. In '27 he announced his intention of becoming a Mex. citizen; in '29 was baptized at S. Diego as Enrique Domingo Fitch; and was married at Valparaíso in July of the same year to Josefa Carrillo, daughter of Don Joaquin of S. Diego. For an account of his romantic clopement, return, and ecclesiastical trial, see iii. 140–4; ii. 551, 562, 569, 615. In '30–1 he was mr of the *Leonor,* iii. 49, 147, 383, his home being at S. Diego after his family troubles had been settled; in '32 already applying for lands north of S.F. bay. *Sup. Govt St. Pap.,* viii. 37; sons were born '30, '32, '34; naturalized in '33. He had a store at S. Diego; síndico in '35. iii. 615; com. de policía '36. iii. 616; afforded some aid —moistened powder, etc.—to the sureños in the political quarrels of '37–8. iii. 495, 553; in '39–40 presid. of election and juez de paz. iii. 614, 616–17. In '40 Capt. Fitch went to Hon. as sup. of the *California,* and at the Isl. bought of Peirce & Brewer for 2,500 hides a half-interest in the *Morse,* which he brought to Cal., renamed her the *Ninfa,* and made a trip to Mazatlan in

'41. iv. 102, 105, 209, 249, 567. Stearns, McKinley, and Temple were his partners in this venture, and Paty a little later. In '41 he was grantee of the Sotoyomi rancho, iv. 674; v. 297, 358, later Healdsburg, which was put in charge of his agents, as he still lived at S. Diego, being much of the time at sea. Receptor at S.D. '45-6; made a survey of town lands; juez de paz '46-7, grantee of lands at S.F., being also ment. in connection with various matters. iv. 345, 557, 620; v. 267, 317, 618-20, 659-60, 679. He died at S. Diego in '49, and was the last person buried on Presidio Hill. Capt. Fitch was one of the earliest, most prominent, and most popular of the early pioneers; straight-forward in his dealings, generous in disposition, frank and cheerful in man-ner, in physique a very tall man inclined to corpulency. Dana is the only man that has anything unfavorable to say of him, and it is hinted that D., a wild young sailor disposed to put on airs by reason of his education and high con-nections, was once rather summarily ejected from Don Enrique's house, when he and his companions applied for grog. I have hundreds of the captain's business and personal letters in the collections of Vallejo and Cooper, besides an immense vol. of the *Fitch, Doc. Hist. Cal.*, presented by his widow in '75. Doña Josefa—born at S. D. 1810, and baptized as María Ant. Natalia Elijia Carrillo, being called Josefa later because her godmother forgot the names, and thought that one of them was Josefa!—moved to the Healdsburg rancho soon after her husband's death, and was still living there in '80, dictating for my use in '75 a most interesting *Narracion*, besides presenting the doc. cited above, including her marriage certificate and the captain's naturalization pa-pers. There were 11 children, as follows: Henry E. b. '30, Fred. '32, Wm '34, Joseph '36, Josefa '37, John B. '39, Isabella '40, Charles '42, Michael '44, María Ant. Natalia '45, and Anita '48. The last two died in '50-4; Josefa became the wife of John Grant and a locally famous singer; Isabella married John Balash; Wm, in '75, had a vineyard on Russian River; John B. was a newspaper man, who visited my Library in '83.

Fitch, 1847, mr of the *Armalta*. v. 576.   F. (Worthington L.), 1847, Co. B, N.Y.Vol. (v. 499); d. S.F. '50.   Fitzhugh (John W.), 1848, immig. whose widow lived at Snelling in '77. *S. J. Pion.*   Fitzpatrick (John), 1836, Engl. on a Los Ang. list, age 40.   F. (Thos), well-known trapper and guide; possibly came to Cal. before '40; guide of Bartleson party '41 and Frémont '44, but did not come to Cal. then. iii. 392; iv. 268, 437.   Fitzsimmons (James), 1847, Co. G, N.Y.Vol. (v. 499).

Flaco (Juan), see John Brown.   Flandrew (J.B.), 1848, passp. from Hon. Flanning (H.T.), 1845, nat. of N.Y.; on the U.S. *Portsmouth;* later member of S. Joaq. pioneers. iv. 587.   Fleet (Wm H.), 1847, lot at S.F.   Fleetwood (Robert), 1847, Co. F, N.Y.Vol. (v. 499).   Flemming (James), 1829, Irish 'jack-at-all-trades,' age 40, working for Cooper at Mont. iii. 179; in '36 liv-ing with Larkin, age 52! often named in records of '36-8. In '41-4 he appears in the Sonoma and Bodega regions.   Fletcher, 1579, chaplain of Francis Drake's vessel, and author of a narrative of the voyage. i. 85 et seq.   F. (Philander), 1847, Co. D, Morm. Bat. (v. 469); reënl.   Fleury (Ernest de), 1848, the Baron de Lisle, a French traveller and officer in Mex. under Maxi-milian; said to have visited Cal. in '48; died in N.Y. '67. *Alta.*

Fling (Guy Freeman), 1826, nat. of Me, on the *Courier* '26-8. iii. 176. In '31 he came back from the Sandwich Islands to settle permanently, at the age of 34, getting a carta from Gov. Victoria, and in '32 joining the comp. extran-jera at Mont. iii. 221. From that time his name often appears on Larkin's books and other records. He worked at his trade as blacksmith at Mont., and in '36 at the Buenavista rancho, being then only 26 years old, acc. to the padron. In '40 he had a shop at Natividad, and is accredited by tradition with having refused to iron the foreign exiles, though John Chamberlain says this was not so, as Fling was absent at the time. iv. 28. I find no definite trace of him in '41-7, but he was prob. engaged in hunting, as he is said to have been with Geo. Yount in Napa Val., and to have spent much of his time among the Ind. He lived at Sonoma for some years; went to Napa about '50, and died in the county infirmary in '70, at the reputed age of 80 years.

Flint (Amos E.), 1847, Co. F, 3d U. S. artill. (v. 518).   F. (Isaac A.), 1845, overl. immig. perhaps of the Grigsby-Ide party, who prob. went back east with Clyman in '46. iv. 579; v. 526.   F. (Wm), 1846, doubtful member of the Mormon col. v. 547.   Flomboy (John), 1844, half-breed Ind. and overl. immig. of the Stevens party, acc. to Schallenberger and some of the county histories. iv. 445.   Flood (John), 1847, Co. A, N.Y.Vol. (v. 499); at S.F. '71-4.

Flores (Amando), 1836, Mex. convict; later one of Murrieta's band.   F. (Antonio), 1602, piloto of one of Vizcaino's vessels; died on the voy. i. 98, 104.   F. (Bernardo), settler at S.F. 1791-1800. i. 716.   F. (Francisco), 1791, surgeon of Malaspina's exped. i. 490.   F. (Francisco), soldier at mission S. José 1797-1800. i. 556.   F. (Gumesindo), 1834, Mex. capt. and brevet lieut-col, who came as a kind of political exile with the H. & P. col. iii. 263. In '35-6 maj. and admin. of S.F. iii. 354, 714-15; in '39-42, having been reinstated in his mil. rank, he was com. of the post at Mont. iii. 671; iv. 33, 652; in '42-6 com. at Sta B.; in '45 leader in an outbreak of the troops. iv. 541, 641; v. 317, 630. Capt. F. continued to reside at Sta B. until shot and killed in '60. His widow and daughter were still at Sta B. in '78.   F. (Hermene-gildo), killed 1794. i. 454.   F. (Isidro), soldier at S. Juan B. before 1800. i. 558.   F. (José Bern.), sirviente at Soledad 1791-1800. i. 499.

Flores (José María), 1842, Mex. capt. in the batallon fijo, who came with Micheltorena as secretary. iv. 289; in '44 named as instructor of the Sta B. defensores (?). iv. 407; but sent to Mex. as comisionado by the gov. to obtain aid. iv. 402, 414, 534, 564, 568. Returning in '45, he remained after Michel-torena's departure, and was the commissioner sent by Castro to treat with Stockton in Aug. iv. 513; v. 41, 268-9, 280. On the revolt of the Californians in Sept., Flores was made gov. and com. gen. from Oct., in this capacity directing all the operations of this final campaign of the war, and finally retreating to Sonora in Jan. '47. See v. 37-8, 309-25, 329-56, 365, 389-410, 563-5. In breaking his parole, Gen. Flores of course committed a most dishonorable act, though much may be said in defence of the general rising against the U.S. In other respects he acted with commendable energy, skill, and patriotism under difficult circumstances, meriting but little of the ridicule and abuse of which he has been the object. After leaving Cal. he served in the Mex. army, being in '49-50 sub-inspector, and in '51 et seq. com. gen. of the military colonies of the west; visiting Cal. in '50 to bring his family; but I think his wife, a daughter of A. V. Zamorano, did not leave Cal. He was at Mazatlan in '55, and is said to have died there in '66, Los Ang. Co. Hist., 24, though a colonel of the same name was serving in Michoacan in '67 against Maximilian.

Flores (José María), at S. José '25. ii. 605; in '41, age 48, wife Josefa Sepúlveda, child. Miguel b. '23, Sebastian '31, Cármen '27, José María '32, Juan B. '34, José '37, Paula '40, Fernando '41; juez de policía '43. iv. 685; in '46 juez de campo at S.F. v. 648.   F. (José María), soldier at Sta B. from 1788. F. (José María), grantee of Liebre rancho '46, also claimant in '53. v. 632. F. (José Miguel), maj. at S. Gabriel, 1791-6. i. 664.   F. (José S.), Mex. convict '29-34.   F. (Leandro), soldier in S. F. comp. '19-29; regidor at S. José '31. iii. 212, 729; in '41, age 42, wife Romana Martinez, child. José Ant. b. '33, María Ant. '16, María del Sac. '26, Refugio '34; in '43 juez del campo. iv. 685.   F. (M.), 1848, passp. from Hon.   F. (Manuel), artilleryman at Sta D. '24. ii. 592.   F. (Manuel), in Hidalgo piquete at Mont. '36   F (Miguel), son of José María, at S. José from '23 to '77, when he gave me his Recuerdos Históricos. v. 137.   F. (Teodosio), alcalde of S. José—and also of Mont?—in '20. ii. 378, 611; at S. José '41, age 52.   F. (Victoriano), sirviente at S.F. 1777. i. 297.   Florin (Joseph), 1833, Canadian gardener from Colombia at Los Ang. '36, '40, age 27, 31, and married. iii. 409. One record puts his arrival in '30.

Flügge (Chas W.), 1841, German of the Bartleson immig. party who went 1st to Or., but came down by land to Cal. before the end of the year. iv. 269, 276, 279. In '42-3 he was employed by Sutter, who had known him before, as clerk and adviser, F. being a man of many accomplishments and having some knowledge of law. He was sent by Sutter to conciliate Micheltorena. iv. 389; got a lot at S.F. iv. 669, 678; was naturalized at the end of '43; and in '44 was grantee of a rancho on Feather River. iv. 670-1. He opened a store at Los Ang.; used his influence for Sutter and Micheltorena. iv. 490; and at the end of '45 went to Honolulu, returning on the *Don Quixote* early in '46. He had a Cal. claim (v. 462), continuing in trade at Los Ang., and serving as a messenger from Flores to Stockton in Jan. '47. v. 387. He is mentioned with a wife (?) at N. Helv. in Sept. '47. *N. Helv. Diary*, 110; perhaps an error. At the end of '48 he left Cal., though McKinley, his partner, made efforts to prevent his departure, and is said to have gone to Germany with a considerable sum of money. Though admired for his accomplishments, he had quarrelled sooner or later with most of those who were intimate with him, showing divers eccentricities of conduct. In the winter of '51-2 he returned to Los Ang., secluding himself from old friends, acting strangely in other respects, and evidently insane. In Sept. '52 he wandered off into the country and was found dead some 12 miles from town. Flundin (Joseph), 1842, French steward of a hospital in Oakland '77, said to have visited S.F. in June '42. iv. 341; *S.J.Pion.* Flying (Andrew), 1847, Co. F, N. Y. Vol. (v. 499); at Sta B. '71-82.

Fogo (Manuel), 1825, Span. from the *Asia;* still in Cal. '30. iii. 27, 51-2. Foisy (M.G.), 1846, Or. pioneer of '44; a printer still in Or. '76, for whom it is claimed that he published (?) the *Californian* at Mont. *Hist. Or.*, i. 467. He may possibly have been a printer on that paper in '46 or '47, but prob. not. v. 293. Foley (Alfred), 1847, Co. E, N.Y.Vol. (v. 499). F. (Michael), 1846, Irish. of the Cal. Bat. (v. 358); owner of S.F. lot '47. v. 685; said to have been killed in a brawl at the mission a few years later. Folger (Edward F.), 1847, at S.F., agent, or perhaps partner, of Gelston & Co. F. (Wm D.), 1847, on roll of Soc. Cal. Pion. Follansbee (S.), 1846, doubtful newsp. ment. of a Shasta Co. pion. Follen (Julian), 1845, petitioner for land for a colony; perhaps not in Cal. iv. 571. Follett (Wm A.), 1847, Co. B, Morm. Bat. (v. 469); in Ariz. '81. F. (Wm T.), 1847, Co. E, Morm. Bat.; at St George, Utah, '82.

Folsom (Joseph Libbey), 1847, nat. of N. H., graduate of West Point in '40, and later instructor in that institution; came to Cal. as capt. U.S.A. and asst quartermaster in the N.Y.Vol.; and was chief of the Q.M. department station at S.F., being also collector of the port for a time in '47-9. v. 98, 503, 511-13, 650, 659-60, 673. Capt. F. invested all the money he could raise in town lots, which in a few years made him a rich man. During a trip to the east in '49 he was smart and lucky enough to find the heirs of Wm A. Leidesdorff and buy of them for a song their title to the immense Leidesdorff estate in S.F. He thus became one of the wealthiest men in Cal., owning large estates in the country, including the Amer. River rancho on which the town of Folsom now bears his name, as does Folsom Street in S.F. His reputation is that of a most enterprising man of business, an honorable gentleman of superior education and refinement, somewhat formal and haughty in manner. He died at Mission San José in '55 at the age of 38. F. (Wm H.), 1847, Co. H, N.Y.Vol. (v. 499); in N.Y. city '82.

Font (José), 1796, Span. lieut of Catalan volunteers, com. of the comp. after Alberni's death, also com. at S. Diego '99. Left Cal. with the Cal. Vol. 1803. i. 541, 647-8; ii. 5, 18-19, 78, 107, 153. F. (Pedro), 1775-6, Span. friar, prob. of the Querétaro Franciscans, who was chaplain of Anza's exped. to Cal., of which he left an important *Diario* and map. i. 258-60, 262-4, 267-9, 280-6, 330; ii. 44. Fontes (Pedro), sirviente at S.F. 1777. i. 297. Forbagh, 1847, at Benicia. v. 672; prob. 'Forbush,' q.v.

Forbes (Alexander), Scotch merchant of Tepic; author of the standard work on *California* pub. in '39. iv. 150-2. He had never visited Cal., though meditating a visit in '26. iii. 176. It is stated, however, that later, in '46-8, he came to Cal. in con. with the N. Almaden affairs; but I have no definite record of his presence. He has often been confounded by writers with James

A. Forbes.   F. (Eli B.), 1847, Co. E, N.Y.Vol. (v. 499); carpenter at Mont. '47-8.   F. (Hector M.), 1847, Co. D, N.Y.Vol. (v. 499).

Forbes (James Alex.), 1831, nat. of Scotland, who had lived for some years in Span. countries, prob. in Chili or Peru. The first that is definitely known of him is that in a trip to the isl. of the S. Amer. coast he was wrecked, picked up by the *Nelson* at or near the Galápagos, and transferred to the whaler *Fanny*, which brought him, rating as 4th mate, by way of the Marquesas to S.F. in Oct. '31, or possibly '30. iii. 405. In '32 he was acting as a kind of clerk or majordomo for P. Viader at Sta Clara; early in '33 asked for naturalization, which he obtained in April '34, and in July married Ana María, daughter of Juan C. Galindo, being then 27 years old, and having as witnesses Geo. Ferguson and Jas W. Weeks, who had come with him on the *Fanny*. For several years his name does not appear, but he was doubtless engaged in trade and farming at S. José, where from '36 he acted as agent for the H.B.Co., being elector in '38 and síndico in '39, trying in '40—to obtain a loan of mission sheep in comp. with Dr Marsh, signing bonds for some of the Bartleson immig., and, acc. to the padron of '41, having two sons, Cárlos b. '37, and Alejandro in '39. iii. 731; iv. 86, 117, 217-18, 275, 684. In '42 Forbes was appointed British vice-consul at Mont., assuming the office in Oct. '43, and performing some acts in his official capacity in the next few years, though not residing at Mont. iv. 384, 479, 563, 651. Grantee of the Potrero de Sta Clara '44. iv. 673; in '45-6 at S.F. in charge of the H.B.Co. property after Rae's death, having apparently used his influence against Sutter and Micheltorena, being involved in a controversy with Leidesdorff, and obtaining for himself and wife some beach lots in town. v. 486, 590-1, 649, 679-80. In '46 Larkin reported F. to the Wash. govt as a man of moderate property, whose private interests and official position clashed, but who wished the U. S. to have Cal. F. asserted at the time, and in later years, that he had nothing to do with schemes for an English protectorate, and it is certain that those schemes, as well as the vice-consul's agency, have been greatly exaggerated. v. 68, 70, 614. In the troubles of '46-7 he took but slight part. v. 298, 378, 380, 382. Gov. Mason declined to permit F., as vice-consul, to introduce goods free of duties. Don Diego was an intelligent man of good education, whose knowledge of Spanish gave him an advantage, though he never lost his broad Scotch accent, and whose record in early times was an excellent one, though many writers have exaggerated his prominence. After the U.S. occupation, he became interested in the New Almaden mines, and was involved in the complicated litigation that lasted for years, to the serious detriment of his financial hopes, of his reputation, and especially of his temper. In later years he led a life of retirement, nursing his intense, and perhaps not unfounded, bitterness against all that was American, and died at Oakland in '81, at the age of 77. His children, as named by his son in '85, were Cárlos H., residing at Los Ang. with 10 children, Martha (deceased), James Alex., Jr, Michael, Frederick, James Alonzo, Luis Felipe (deceased), María Clara, Juan Telésforo, Margaret, Francis H., and Alfred O. James Alex., Jr, was educated at Sta Clara college, has been state translator of the laws, and in '85 for some years has been employed as translator and keeper of the archives in the U.S. surveyor-general's office. Though not in charge when my search of the archives was made, he has afforded me aid on several points.

Forbes (John), 1833, Engl. on Larkin's books '33-5. iii. 409.   F. (Robert D.), 1025, mr of the *Nilo*. iii. 118. Visiting S.F. again in '70, he delivered a lecture which included reminiscences of '25; and in '78 he published his *Personal Reminiscences*, which describes both the visits and the lecture; still living at Milton, Mass., in '85.   F. (Wm), 1835, Engl. who worked for Larkin at Mont. '35-6. iii. 413; one of the exiles of '40. iv. 18; perhaps cl. for a Sonoma Co. rancho '52. iv. 671.   Forbush (Benj.), 1847, from Hon. on the *Euphemia;* at Benicia; perhaps Forbagh.   F. (Lorin), 1847, Co. C, Morm. Bat. (v. 469).

Ford (Henry L.), 1842-4, nat. of Vt or N.H., who prob. came by sea. He claimed to have come in '42; the 1st original record is a certificate of his U.S.

citizenship, dated at Mont. April 19, '44. iv. 341. He seems to have been one of Capt. Gantt's men in the Micheltorena campaign of '45 (v. 484), and was prominent among the Bears in '46, taking part in the stealing of Arce's horses and the capture of Sonoma. v. 78, 107, 110, 147. As lieut of the Bear army he commanded in the fight at Olompali, the only one of the revolt. v. 153, 164–9; went south with Frémont; returned with Maddox in Aug.; and later served in the final campaign as capt. of Co. B, Cal. Bat. v. 184, 282, 289, 361, 434. In '48 he settled in Tehama Co., where in '51 he married Susan Wilson, and in '56 was accidentally shot and killed at the age of 33. Ford's narrative of the *Bear Flag Revolt*, a MS. furnished to me by Rev. S. H. Willey, for whom it was written in '51, is noticed in v. 189. Not much is definitely known of Ford, but he appears to have been a good man of strong prejudices. F. (Henry). 1847, perhaps of N.Y.Vol. under another name.   F. (John), 1827, mr of the *Favorite*. iii. 147.   F. (Noah E.), 1847, in letter list at S.F. '47–8.   F. (Patrick), 1847, Co. E, N.Y.Vol. (v. 499); a deserter in '48; killed by Rogue Riv. Ind. '66.   Forero (Ramon), doubtful name in a S.F. list '35.

Forney (Peter), 1846, Co. C, 1st U.S. dragoons (v. 336).   Forrest (B.), 1841, clerk on the U.S. *St Louis*.   F. (French), 1840–1, com. of the U.S. *St Louis*. iv. 36–7, 106; commodore in Confed. navy '62.   F. (Richard), 1846, lieut on the *Portsmouth* and *Levant*.   F. (Sam.), 1848, lot at S.F.   Forrester (Geo. H. H.), 1847, Co. K, N.Y.Vol. (v. 499).   Forsgreen (John), 1847, Co. D, Morm. Bat. (v. 469).

Forster (John), 1833, nat. of England, who came to Guaymas in '31, and in '33 on the *Facio*—belonging to his uncle James Johnson—to Cal., returning to Sonora on the vessel as master, and coming back to Los Ang. by land the same year. iii. 365, 382, 389, 397, 509. He made other trips to Son. for his uncle, and in '36 announced his intention to remain permanently, claiming 7 years' residence in Mex. territory and 4 in Cal.; in '37 married Isidora, sister of Pio Pico; in '40–3 at S. Pedro as shipping agent, part of the time capt. of the port. iv. 322, 636. In '44 he settled at S. Juan Cap., purchasing the ex-mission estate in '45, and living there for 20 years. iv. 553, 558, 621, 627; grantee of rancho de la Nacion '45. iv. 621; juez de paz '45–7. iv. 627; v. 623–4; in '46 for a time in charge of S. Luis Rey, having trouble with Frémont, and aiding Gov. Pico to escape. v. 267, 278, 620; grantee of Trabuco. iv. 635; had a Cal. claim (v. 462); aided Stockton in the campaign of '47. v. 388. In '64 Forster bought the Sta Margarita rancho of Pio Pico, where he spent the rest of his life, dying in '84 at the age of 70. Don Juan was a man who was liked and respected by all who knew him, that is, by everybody in southern Cal. and hundreds more, a genial ranchero, famous for the hospitalities of his Sta Margarita home. He was for many years a man of immense wealth; formed several plans for colonization on a grand scale, which were never carried out; but was harassed in the later years by litigation and other troubles; and the estate was sold before his death. At his rancho in '74 he gave me a narrative of early experiences; and in '78 dictated his more complete *Pioneer Data*, giving also a few original papers. His wife died a short time before his death. In '46, acc. to the S. Juan padron, there were 6 children: Emerico and Dolores (perhaps error of copyist), Marcos Antonio b. '40, Francisco '42, Ana María '43, Juan Fernando '45. Francisco, or 'Chico,' killed by a woman at Los Angeles after '80. Mark Antony and John still live in S. Diego Co. '85. Two of Don Juan's brothers, Hugh and Thomas, came to Cal. after '48. Fort, see 'Ford.'   Forsyth (Thomas), 1834, Irish ship-carpenter who came on the *Leonor;* still at Mont. '37.

Fortuni (Buenaventura), 1806, Span. friar who served 34 years as a missionary in Cal., chiefly at S. José and Solano, dying at Sta B. in '40. Biog. iii. 659; ment. ii. 138, 159–60, 322, 375, 394, 505, 598–9, 623, 655; iii. 96, 318, 346, 622–3, 658, 660, 719; iv. 63, 66.   Fosdick (Jay), 1846, of the Donner party from Ill.; died in the mts. v. 530, 534, 537. His wife, Sarah Graves, survived, marrying Wm Ritchie in '48, and Samuel Spiers in '56; died near Watsonville in '71.

Foster, 1833, one of Hall J. Kelley's companions in the trip across Mex., whom K. denounces as a rascal, and who, as he learned, came to Mont. on a whaler, was ordered away, shipped on a man-of-war, and in trying to desert was drowned in the bay as a punishment for his sins. iii. 409; perhaps Chas or Ed. C. described as Amer. at Mont. in '34. F., 1846, of F. & Patterson, Cal. claim (v. 462). F. (Benj. F.), 1847, Co. C, N.Y.Vol. (v. 499); a printer and part proprietor of the *Californian* in '48; later foreman in the *Alta* office and connected with the *Standard* and other S. F. papers; making two trips to the Sandw. Isl. He went east and died at Portsmouth, N.H., in '65, at the age of 49.

Foster (Geo.), 1846, a Mo. immig. prob. of this year, who was killed at Natividad in Nov. v. 367. He was known as Captain Foster. Possibly came earlier, though those who imply this seem to confound him with another man. F. (James), 1841, mid. on the U. S. *St Louis*. F. (John), 1847, apparently sold lumber at Mont. F. (John R.), 1848, named by Lancey as a brother of the man killed at Natividad. F. (Joseph), 1846, Co. F, Cal. Bat. (v. 358), enlisting at S. Juan, Oct.; possibly identical with Geo. F. (Joseph), 1847, member of the 4th, and perhaps 1st, Donner relief. v. 538, 541; said to have been a sailor. F. (Joseph), 1846, Engl. who kept a saloon in S.F. '53-9; lost a leg in '49; died in '59. *Herald*; perhaps same as preceding F (Joseph E.), 1844, overl. immig. of the Stevens party. iv. 445, 453; named at N. Helv. '45-6; served in Co. B, Cal. Bat. (v. 358); prob. identical with one of the preceding F (Joseph R.), 1846, in the vicinity of Sta Cruz. F. (O. H.), 1846, Co. F, Cal. Bat. (v. 358).

Foster (Stephen Clark), 1847, nat. of Me, b. in '20; graduate of Yale in '40; teacher and medical student in Va, Ala, and La; physician in Mo.; trader in N. Mex. and Sonora; come to Cal. as interpreter with the Morm. Bat. v. 483. He was alcalde at Los Ang. in '48-9. v. 610, 626-7; memb. of the constit. convention in '49, also prefect; member of the Cal. senate '50-3; memb. of Los Ang. council '51, '58; mayor '54, '56. He married a Lugo, and is still living at Los Ang. in '85. He has written to some extent on pioneer topics for the newspapers. ii. 221, 292; and in '77 furnished for my use a fragment on *Los Angeles in '47-9*. He has had much to do with the Span. archives of the south, in familiarity with which he is excelled by few, if any. His official record in the early time, and so far as I know in later years, has been a good one. He was a man of remarkable natural abilities and of fine education. His prominent position in the past as a public man makes it necessary to add that in respect of morality and sobriety his conduct in later times is not exemplary. F. (Wm M.), 1846, surviving memb. of the Donner party, from Penn. with wife and infant son George, the latter dying in the mts. F. was also an active memb. of the 4th relief party. v. 531-5, 540-1. At N. Helv. '47; had a furniture store at S.F. '47-8. v. 678; later kept a store at the mines, giving his name to Foster's Bar. He died at S.F. in '74. His wife, Sarah A. C. Murphy, was living at Marysville with her brother in '80. F. (Wm S.), 1847, Co. A, N.Y.Vol. (v. 499).

Fourcade (Richard), 1841, named in Larkin's books '41-8; called also Albert R., and John R. Fouchade. iv. 279. Fourgeaud (G.), 1847, brother of Victor J., and overl. immig. at N. Helv.; owner of lot at S.F. F. (Victor J.), 1847, nat. of N.C., physician at St Louis, and overl. immig., with his wife, son, and brother. v. 556. He practised medicine at S.F. in '47-8, being a school trustee and otherwise prominent. v. 651, 656-7, 680; also owner of town lots, and author of an article on the *Prospects of Cal.* in the *Star* of '48. He moved later to Sac., but returned about '63, and died at S.F. in '75 at the age of 60. His widow died in '83, age 74. Fourri (François le), 1831, from N. Mex. in the Wolfskill party. iii. 387.

Fowler, 1846, Amer. of the Bear party murdered by the Californians near Sta Rosa in June. v. 110, 160-4. I cannot identify him; possibly Wm, Jr, of '44; called B. Fowler of '45; also George. F. (Henry), 1844, son of Wm, nat. of Ill. who came overl. to Or. in '43 and to Cal. in the Kelsey party with his father and brother. iv. 444-5. In '45 he worked for Sutter, asked for naturalization, and perhaps settled in Napa. With his father he purchased, later, a farm near Calistoga; and in '71 was a resident of Napa City.   F. (James E.), 1841, resid. of Sonoma Co. '51-77; nat. of N.Y. *Son. Co. Hist.*   F. (Jerusha), 1846, of the Mormon col. with 4 children. v. 546; rem. in Cal.   F. (John), 1843, overl. immig. who joined the Bears. v. 111; went south with Frémont, but returned with a broken arm in Nov. '46. This is his own statement in a narative of the *Bear Flag* given by him at Napa in '78. He may be a brother of Henry, or possibly the name may be John Henry. There was a J. W. Fowler in the Cal. Bat.   F. (John S.), 1847, nat. of N.J.; 2d alcalde at Sac. '48-9; died at Sac. '60, age 42.

Fowler (Wm), 1844, nat. of N.Y., from Ill. to Or. in '43, and to Cal. in the Kelsey party with 2 or more sons. iv. 444-5. He brought a letter of recommendation as a good catholic and 'carpenter from P. Dimers of the Walamet to P. Quijas. Worked for a time at Sonoma, after spending some time in Pope Valley; was at N. Helv. in '47, and finally with his son Henry bought a farm of Dr Bale near Calistoga, where at the age of 72 he married a 2d wife, and died in '65, at the age of 86.   F. (Wm, Jr), 1844, son of Wm, who came in the same party from Or., and worked as a carpenter at Sonoma, N. Helv., and S. Rafael. iv. 444-5. In Or. he married Rebecca Kelsey, who left him on arrival in Cal. Application was made to Larkin for a divorce, and despite his lack of authority to grant it, she was married by Sutter to another man. As I find no record of F. after '46, it is possible that he was the man killed with Cowie during the Bear revolt.   F. (Wm), immig. of the Bartleson party, '41, going to Or. iv. 269; perhaps the Wm named above.   F. (W.), 1843, mr of the *Diamond.* iv. 565.   Fowrklinot (Jacobo), 1844, otter-hunter at Los Ang., prob. 'Frankfort.'

Fox (J.), 1848, passp. from Honolulu.   Foxen (Benj.), 1826, Engl. sailor who came on the *Courier* and left that vessel in '28. iii. 176; ii. 573. He was baptized as Wm Domingo, though often called Julian; married Eduarda Osuna (or Olivera); was naturalized in '37, when he was 38 years old, and had 3 children, being in trade at Sta B. A few years later he became owner of the Tinaquaic rancho, iii. 656, where he spent the rest of his life, dying in '74 and leaving 10 children and a large estate. He was a rough and violent man, often in trouble with other rough men and with the authorities, being sentenced to 4 years in prison in '48 for killing Agustin Dávila. v. 611, 613; yet accredited with good qualities, such as bravery and honesty. His three daughters married respectively C. W. Goodchild, F. Wickenden, and John R. Stone. His son, Wm J.J., born in '33, was in '83 a ranchero in Sta B. Co. Portrait of Benj. and his wife in *Sta B. Co. Hist.*, 322.

Fraezher (Geo.), see 'Frazer.'   Framier (R.), 1846, Cal. Bat. (v. 358). France (Joseph), 1846, doubtful memb. of the Mormon col. v. 547.   Francis (Alex.), 1842, Florida Ind., deserter from the U. S. *Cyane* '43.   F. (Wm), 1847, lot at S.F.   Francisco, neoph. at S. Diego 1775. i. 253.   Francisco, 1818, negro of Bouchard's force captured at Mont. ii. 232.   Franco (Jose), convict settler 1797. i. 606.   F. (Juan José), a recruit who came with José de la Guerra y Noriega and J. J. de la Torre in 1801.   F. (Pablo), convict settler 1798; at Los Ang. '19. i. 606; ii. 354.   Franec (Wm), 1845, doubtful name of an Irishman at Branciforte, age 45, single.

Frank (Manuel), 1841, 1st frame house at S. José built for. iv. 684. Frankfort (Jacob), 1841, German tailor from N. Mex. in the Workman party. iv. 278-9; at Los Ang. '46; up and down the coast '47-8, making a trip to Hon. and back on the *Gen. Kearny* and *Eveline*, and obtaining a lot at S. F. Franz (Fred W.), 1845, at Mont. iv. 587; lot at S. F. '47.   Frapp, '32-40, doubtful name of a trapper chief. iii. 392.   Frare (Wm), 1844, Irish. who got a pass for 1 year; prob. same as 'Frere,' q.v.   Fraser, see 'Frazer.' Frawell (Ephraim P.), 1833, Phil. tailor who deserted from the whaler *Helvetius*, and worked at his trade at dif. points round S.F. bay. iii. 409. He was met by Wilkes at Mission S. José in '41; lived from '43 at S. José, where he died about '78; name also written 'Fravel.'   Frayer (Henry or Eugene), 1844, German who got a pass.

Frazer (Abner), 1845, Amer. carpenter from Or. in the McMahon-Clyman party, and returned to Or. in '46, where he still lived after '75. iv. 572, 526; written also 'Frazier.' F. (Alex.), 1827, signs as a witness at Mont. F. (Geo. W.), 1833, Amer. trapper with Walker's party. iii. 391; iv. 409. He is ment. in Mont. records of '34–5; in '40 exiled to S. Blas, but returned, obtaining cartas in '41–2, when he lived near Sta Cruz. iv. 18, 33; in '43 at Alviso's; in '45 signed the call to foreigners at S. José. iv. 599; applied for land at S. José '46; visited N. Helv. '45–8; at Stockton '47–8. Name also written 'Fraezher,' which was perhaps the correct form. F. (M.), 1836, lumberman at S. Rafael. iv. 118. F. (Thos), 1847, Co. D, Morm. Bat. (v. 469); in Sutter's employ '47–8; name prob. 'Frazier.' F. (Wm), 1845, Amer. farmer from Or. in the McM.-Clyman party; prob. went back '46 with Abner F., who was perhaps his brother. iv. 572–3, 526.

Frederick (J.), 1846, Co. F, Cal. Bat. (v. 358). Fredingburg (H.), 1848, passp. from Honolulu. Freeborn (John), 1847, Co. K, N. Y. Vol. (v. 499); passp. from Hon. '48. Freeman, 1837, mr of the *Indian*. iv. 104. F. (Duric), 1844, Amer. who obtained a carta at Mont. F. (Elijah), 1847, Morm. Bat. (v. 469); prob. not in Cal. F. (F.), Co. G, Cal. Bat. (v. 358), enlisting at S. José, Nov. F. (Isam), 1840, doubtful name of a naturalized foreigner at Sta B. F. (Richard), 1846, bought a house of Capt. Fitch at S. Diego. F. (Truman), 1844, Amer. age 25, in a S.F. padron. F. (W), 1848, passp. from Hon. Freer (Matthew), 1848, hanged at S. José for highway robbery and attempted murder. v. 663–4.

Frémont (John Charles), 1844, nat. of Ga, b. in '13, sometime teacher of mathematics and surveyor, lieut of top. engineers from '38, and husband of a daughter of Thos H. Benton from '41. He is in some respects the most famous of all the pioneers named in this register, and his Californian career was the foundation of his fame. Full details of that career will be found in other volumes of this work. His three exploring exped, of '42, '43–4, and '45, in the 2d and 3d of which he reached Cal., are described, with their results, in iv. 434–44, 452, 581–5, 679. Exploring and mapping regions before known only to trappers and immigrants, narrating his labors with modesty and full credit to those who preceded and accompanied him, he gained much credit at home and abroad for his skill in the field and for his reports. As the pioneer of scientific exploration in the far west, he deserves only praise. The ridicule of which he has been the object in this connection resulted mainly from the campaign of '56, in which his achievements as pathfinder were so magnified for effect in the east as to excite the jealousy of western pioneers, a feeling fomented by partisans for political purposes. Frémont's acts of Jan.–May '46 in Cal. are given in v. 1–29, 58–9, 644, 660. Being permitted by Gen. Castro to rest his men and animals in the S. Joaquin Valley for a continuation of his exploring trip to Or., he forfeited the privilege by marching his party into S. José and encamping for a week at Fisher's rancho; grossly insulted the alcalde who, in the discharge of his routine duties, served a legal notice on him; and finally marched over the Sta Cruz Mts and down the coast—for Oregon! When the authorities very properly ordered him to leave Cal., he fortified a position on Gavilan Peak and raised the U. S. flag. This was foolish bravado, as he realized after a day or two of reflection, in connection with Consul Larkin's advice and the sight of military preparations at San Juan; so he ran away in the night. The current version of Castro's broken promise and subsequent cowardly bluster is pure fiction, but it has long served its purpose—that of covering Frémont's folly. He was overtaken on the Or. frontier by despatches from Wash. which required him to remain in Cal. His part in the Bear revolt of June–July is recorded in v. 77–190. That most indefensible rising of the settlers, which interrupted negotiations for a pacific change of flag, would not have occurred but for F.'s promise of active support when needed; therefore he must be held responsible, not only for the bloodshed and bitterness of feeling that attended the conflict of '46–7, but for the much more disastrous state of affairs that, but for the sheerest good luck, must have resulted. His alleged motives were three fold: 1st, The welfare of Amer. settlers threatened with oppression and expulsion—a mere pretext, since the danger was wholly imagi-

nary, as F. and the leaders well knew, though a few settlers were led to believe it real; 2d, the necessity of prompt action to save Cal. from England—
an excuse invented later, which has had a success out of all proportion to its
merits, for had England entertained the idea of a protectorate the settlers' revolt would have afforded the best possible occasion for interference; and 3d,
the receipt of instructions from Wash. to seize the first opportunity to wrest
Cal. from Mex. In a statement of '85—a MS. furnished by Gen. and Mrs F.
to Dr Josiah Royce, and by the kindness of the latter added, with the authors'
consent, to my collection—he relies mainly on this 3d plea, and alleges positively, as he and his friends have always implied, that he received such instructions, guardedly expressed by Sec. Buchanan, and more openly by Benton
in a private letter. This is simply not true. I have the instructions sent from
Wash. in '45, both the original, signed by Buchanan, and the copy written
by Gillespie from memory on arrival, and they contain not a word to justify
any but conciliatory measures. The lieut disobeyed the letter and spirit of his
orders, unless deceived by Gillespie at Benton's instigation. His real motive
was a desire to make himself more prominent in the approaching occupation
by the U.S. than he could be if the whole matter were left to Larkin and the
naval officers. Doubtless he drew his inspiration largely from his brilliant
father-in-law. He saw several plausible avenues of escape from disgrace should
there be no war or should matters otherwise go wrong; but it is likely that
the young filibuster was far from anticipating the full measure of success that
good fortune was to give his deception. Once committed to the Bear cause,
he acted in most respects with commendable energy and consistency; yet it
must be stated that he meanly assumed for himself credit for the Bears' warlike acts, in which he took no active part; that never in his Cal. career was he
in the actual presence of an armed foe; that in his S. Rafael campaign, represented by him as a grand victory, he was completely outwitted by Joaq. de
la Torre; and that the murder of the Haro brothers and Berreyesa is an inef-
faceable stain on his record. This deed F. and his friends have chosen to ignore
as far as possible, alluding to it as a trivial occurrence incidental to a state of
war, falsely representing the Haros as spies, on whose bodies murderous instructions from Castro were found; and finally, F. has the assurance to refer
to it as the act of his Delawares out on a scout, unknown to him till later.
For his part in the conquest proper, from July '46 to Jan. '47, see v. 231,
246-53, 266-7, 283, 286-7, 290, 295, 302, 304-5, 357-60, 372-6, 385-410, 412,
617, 630, 634, 639. At Mont., though Com. Sloat would not adopt his views,
F. found in Stockton a filibuster after his own heart, willing to incorporate
the Gavilan episode and the Bear revolt in the sacred cause of the U.S. As
major of the Cal. battalion, he aided in the occupation of S. Diego and Los
Ang. in Aug., returning north as mil. com. of Cal. Later he reorganized the
battalion, and marched south to take part in the final campaign, concluded
by his treaty of Cahuenga in Jan. '47. In all this period the major and commodore merely overcame obstacles of their own creation, but the former effi-
ciently performed somewhat difficult duties, and merits but little of the blame
and derision heaped upon him for his methods of obtaining supplies, for his
disastrous crossing of the Sta Inés Mountain, and for his cautious approach
to Los Ang. His policy at Cahuenga deserves no more severe adjective than
the slangy one of 'cheeky.' Next we have his proceedings at the capital in
Jan.-May as gov. of Cal. by Stockton's appointment, and his connection with
the complicated controversies of the commodore and general, as related in v.
421-68. In general terms, it may be said of these quarrels that Kearny was in
the right, Stockton in the wrong, and Frémont first right, then wrong. Though
technically disobeying mil. orders, F. could not, consistently with the honor
that should prevail among filibusters as well as thieves, abandon the chief
who had fathered his cause and given him office; but at last his disobedience
was renewed in so offensive a form as to move Kearny to wrath and the fullest
exercise of his authority. Crossing the continent in disgrace, he was condemned by court-martial to dismissal from the army. v. 455-62. The verdict
was technically a just one, but the lieut-colonel refused to accept the presi-

dent's proffered pardon. He had just then no further use for the army; the trial had been a splendid advertisement; and the popular verdict had doubtless been in his favor. The evidence had been skilfully made to include as much as possible of such Cal. annals as could be made to appear flattering to the accused and unfavorable to his rivals; but if the accusers had had the wish and power to present all the facts in their true light, the popular hero's career might have been nipped in the bud. Something will be said in vol. vi. of his later career so far as it pertains to Cal.; of the rest my study has been comparatively superficial; yet I find no indication of qualities not clearly shown in the early record. In a 4th explor. exped. of '48 many of his men perished in the snow before reaching N. Mex., but the leader kept on and reached Cal. in '49. He accepted an appointment as commissioner of the boundary survey, but before beginning work was elected, in '50, to the U. S. senate from Cal., doing no harm during his brief term as senator, which expired in March '51. In '52, spending a year in Europe, he was once put in a London jail on charges growing out of his Cal. operations of '47. In '53-4 he made a 5th and last exploring tour across the continent between 38° and 39°. He had bought of ex-Gov. Alvarado in '46 the famous Mariposas estate, which now bade fair to make him the richest man in America; and in '56 he was nominated for the presidency by the republicans. He had no qualifications for the office, but it was hoped, with much reason, that his fame as 'pathfinder' and 'conqueror of Cal.' would make him an available candidate. At this period appeared many biographic sketches, notably those of Bigelow, Smucker, and Upham. Defeated by Buchanan, he lived a year or two in Cal., visited Europe, and in '61-2 served in the war as maj.-gen. of volunteers; but the govt not appreciating his military genius, he resigned, and devoted himself to grand schemes of speculation in connection with railroads, being temporarily the candidate of a few dissatisfied republicans for the presidency, and in '73 sentenced to fine and imprisonment for fraud by a French court. In '78, when reduced to extreme poverty, he was appointed gov. of Ariz., serving for a brief term, and subsequently resuming his speculations, which are always on the point of making him rich. In '85 he resides with his wife in N.Y. City, a venerable couple with several grown children. Frémont did more than any other to prevent or retard the conquest of Cal., yet his fame as 'conqueror' is the corner-stone of his greatness, and in all the structure there are few blocks more solid. He is to be regarded as an adventurer of marvellous good fortune, if it be good fortune for a man of moderate abilities to be made conspicuous before the world, or to enjoy opportunities that cannot be utilized. He was, moreover, intelligent, well educated, brilliant within certain limits, of gentlemanly manners, personally magnetic, full of enthusiasm. Abuse has done more for him than eulogy; and doubtless from his standpoint he has been a successful man.

French (Erasmus D.), 1846, Co. C, 1st U. S. dragoons (v. 336); nat of N. Y., educated as a physician, a miner '48-9, at S. José '50-8, then at Chico and the Coso mines; from '69 a farmer in S. Diego, where he still lived in '83, age 60, with his wife, C.S. Cowles. *S. Bern. Co. Hist.* F. (H.), 1847, lieut on the U.S. *Columbus.* F. (Wm), 1827, Amer. trader of Honolulu at Mont. in '27, '30; sup. of the *Europe* in '36-7, aiding Alvarado in his revolution. Very likely visited Cal. on other occasions. iii. 461; iv. 103, 141. Frere (Alex. W.), 1842, Amer. who got a carta, in '32 acc. to one record; named in Cal. till '44. iv. 341. Fresche (Francis), 1847, Co. G, N.Y.Vol. (v. 499); at S.F. '74. Freverdon (Wm), 1848, doubtful name of a lumberman at S. José. Frew (Alex.), 1828, trader on the coast; d. before '32.

Frias (Mariano), Mex. soldier at Mont. '33-6, age 33. Fricher (John), 1842, Amer. blacksmith at S.F., age 36. Frink (Chris. L.), 1848, at Mont. F. (Daniel), 1847, Co. K, N.Y.Vol. (v. 499); miner in El Dorado '48; made a trip to Chile and back; lumberman in Sonoma Co. '49-50; later owner of part of Nicasio rancho, Marin Co. iv. 672; justice of the peace and assoc. judge; memb. of legisl. '79; married in '52 to Pauline H. Reynolds; living '83 at Mountain View, Sta Clara Co., with 6 children. Portrait in *Sta Clara Co.*

Hist., 256.   Frisbie (Eleazer), 1847, sergt Co. H, N.Y.Vol. v. 504; kept a store at Sonoma '48–50; settled in Solano Co., and lived at Vallejo in '82 with his wife, Carrie E. Klink, and 7 children; a brother of John B.

Frisbie (John B.), 1847, capt. Co. H, N.Y.Vol. v. 504, 667; nat of N.Y., b. in '23; a lawyer, politician, and militia officer in N. Y. After leaving the mil. service Capt. F. was a candidate for lieut-gov. in '49; married a daughter of Gen. Vallejo; and became a prominent business man of the town of Vallejo, interested in the building of railroads, president of a bank, and a man of considerable wealth; in '60 sent the 1st cargo of wheat to Europe; a member of the legislature in '67. Losing his fortune just before 1880, he moved with his family to Mexico, where he still resides in '85, being engaged in mining operations. He furnished me his *Reminiscences,* containing information on Mex. as well as on early times in Cal. Portrait in *Solano Co. Hist.*, 48.   Friund (Henry J.), 1847, Co. D, N.Y.Vol. (v. 499); died before '82.   Froelich (Rosa), 1847, in Amador Co. from '54.   Frost (Lafayette N.), 1847, Co. A, Morm. Bat. (v. 469); d. S. Diego Sept.   Fructuoso, grantee of Potrero de S. Cárlos '37. iii. 678.   Frymire (Walter), 1846, Co. F, Cal. Bat. (v. 358).   Fuentes (José M.), grantee of Potrero '43. iv. 672.   Fuller (Hazel), 1832, Amer. blacksmith, deserter from the whaler *Friends;* still at Mont. '34. iii. 408.

Fuller (John Casimiro), 1823, Engl. sailor on the *Rover;* prob. made other visits; well known from about '27; on Larkin's books at Mont. from '33. He had been baptized at S. Blas, and married—apparently at Sta B—to Concepcion Ávila; in '36 at Mont. with wife and a daughter, born in '36 at the Sandwich Isl. In '37 he got a lot at S. F. iii. 705; v. 678; but also bought of Watson the Beltran house at Mont., retransferred 2 years later; moved to S. F. in '38; had a house there in '49. iii. 609, 678; being also síndico. iii. 705; worked for Dawson at Sonoma '39; in Farnham's list of arrested foreigners '40. iv. 17; naturalized '41, being also síndico. iv. 665; from 40 to 45 years old in '42, when he had 5 children, 2 of whom were Concepcion and Santiago. His name appears often in S.F. records to '47, when he took part in efforts for the relief of the Donner party, v. 539, and advertised that he would not be responsible for his wife's debts; and he seems to have died in '49. He was a butcher and cook well known to all the early traders; an alley in the city still bears his name; and his widow and children were still at S.F. in '63.

Fuller (Thos), 1831, Engl. carpenter, landed sick at Mont., and still there in '40, age 34. iii. 405.   F. (Wm M.), 1847, Co. F, N.Y.Vol. (v. 499); lot at S.F.; claimant in '53 for a Marin Co. rancho. iv. 674.   Fulma (Mores), 1846, came to S. José. *Hall.*   Funk (John), 1847, Co. B, N. Y. Vol. (v. 499); in Shasta Co. '74; doubtful name.   Furbush, 1847, came from Hon. on the *Euphemia;* prob. 'Forbush,' q.v.   Fuster (Vicente), 1773, Span. friar who served chiefly at S. Diego and S. Juan Cap., dying in 1800. See biog. i. 657; ment. i. 194–5, 250–3, 266–7, 300, 302, 377, 388, 425, 453, 575, 577; ii. 109–10.

Gabel (Ludovico), 1843, German sailor from Boston on the *Admittance,* under the name of Robt Foster, known as 'Bob the fisherman;' d. at Mont. '72, *Swan.*   Gabriel (Ralph), 1847, at S.F. to '70. *Alta.*   Gafan (Cárlos V.), 1837, mr of the *Veloz Asturiano.* iv. 106.   Gaitan (Cayetano), at Jamacha rancho '36. iii. 611.   G. (José M.), Mex. convict '29–35.   Gajiola (José Ant.), sec. of ayunt. at Mont. '29. ii. 612; clerk at Soledad '36. iii. 690–1; sec. at S. José '42–3. iv. 684.   G. (Valentin), alférez and habilitado at Mont. '45–6. iv. 652; v. 41.   Galbraith (Isaac), 1826, Amer. blacksmith and hunter who came with Jed. Smith's party and settled at San Gabriel. ii. 558; iii. 153, 155–6, 158, 160, 176; a crack shot, and a man of gigantic size and strength. I find no record of him after '29, when his age was 34.   Gale (Joseph), 1841–2, mr of the *State of Oregon.* iv. 568.   G. (Joseph), 1831, doubtful member of Young's party. iii. 388.

Gale (Wm Alden), 1810, Boston trader, who 1st visited Cal. as clerk on the *Albatross,* which did a large business in furs at the Farallones. ii. 93–4. In '22–3 he came back as sup. of the *Sachem,* the pioneer in the hide trade with Boston. ii. 474–5, 478, 492–3, 614. Again he returned in '25–7, still on the *Sachem*, taking back as wife Marcelina Estudillo, the 1st Cal. woman to visit the 'hub,' who seems never to have returned to Cal. iii. 24, 62, 118, 148. His next trip was on the *Brookline* in '29–30; and his last on the *Roxana* '32, when he remained on the coast as agent of Bryant & Sturgis's ships till '35, getting a carta in '33. iii. 137-8, 146, 381. He died in Mass. '11. He was a most popular trader, famous for the zeal with which he drove his bargains in broken Spanish. His most common nickname was Cuatro Ojos, by reason of his spectacles; but his name was also translated into Tormenta, 'a gale;' and he was sometimes called Cambalache, or 'barter.' Galente (Rafael), 1847, lot at S.F. Gali (Francisco), 1584, Span. voyager down the Cal. coast. i. 94–6. Galiano (Dionisio), 1792, Span. com. of the *Sutil* and *Mexicana* in an explor. exped. to Cal. and the N.W. Coast; killed at Trafalgar. i. 490. 506–9; see also *Hist. N. W. Coast*, i.

Galindo (Bautista), soldier at S.F. '37; at S. José '41, age 27, wife Alvisa (?) Moreno. G. (Crisóstomo), at S. José '41, age 67, wife Jacoba Bernal, child. Francisco b. '24, Antonio '26, José '29, Agustin '31, Juan '39. His daughter Ana María married J. A. Forbes; and the family home was at Milpitas; grantee and cl. of S. José mission land. v. 665. The full name was Juan C. See also José Jesus and Juan. G. (Eusebio), b. at S.F. 1802; soldier in S.F. comp. '28–9; ment. in '40. iv. 23; juez de paz at Sta Clara '45. iv. 683. Still at Sta Clara in '77, when he gave me some historical *Apuntes*. G. (Francisco), son of Crisóstomo or José Jesus; in Alameda Co. '78. G. (Francisco), Span. not required to quit Cal. in '30. iii. 52. G. (José), soldier of S.F. comp. '37–43. iv. 667. G. (José), soldier of S.F. comp. '38–9. G. (José Ant.), grantee of Laguna de la Merced and Sauzalito '35. iii. 712–13; corp. S.F. militia '37; killed José Peralta at S.F. in '38. G. (José de Jesus), died at Milpitas in '77, at the reputed age of 106; his son Francisco was then a resid. of Oakland; and his daughter Juana was the wife of José M. Alviso and later of José Uridias, still living in '77. José Jesus may have been Crisóstomo, q.v., whose age in '77 would have been 103. G. (Juan), corporal in S.F. comp. '19–29; very likely Juan Crisóstomo, q.v. G. (Leandro), regidor at S. José '22. ii. 604; militiaman and elector at S.F. '37. iii. 705; lot at S.F. mission '40. iv. 706; in '42 at S.F., age 55, wife Dominga Alaman, child. Seferino b. '30, María '33, Antonio '35, Francisco '38, Gregoria '39, Genaro '40, and Mariano '41; militia corporal '44; juez de campo and grantee of a lot '46. v. 648, 684. G. (Manuel), 1825, Span. officer on the *Constante*. iii. 26. G. (Nasario), son of Leandro; soldier, corp., and sergt of S.F. comp. '32–43. iii. 567, 667, 678; in '55 near mission S. José, age 40. G. (Nicolás), settler at S.F. 1791–1800. i. 716. G. (Rafael), soldier of S.F. comp. 1797–1800. i. 556; also '34–7, perhaps another man. Galista (José Ant.), Mex. clerk at Mont. '36, age 50, wife Andrea Jimeno, child. Darío b. '22 at Mont., Valentin '24, Domitila '27, José '29, Felipe '31, María G. '33, José Ant. '36.

Gallagher (John), 1847, Co. B, N.Y.Vol. (v. 499); an Irish farmer in Sonoma Co. '71–83, when he was at Bodega. Gallant (Victor), 1846, Co. E, Cal. Bat. (v. 358), enlist. at Sonoma, Oct. Gallardo (Anastasio), Mex. convict '29–35. G. (Félix), at Los Ang. '36. iii. 491; and '46. v. 312; 2 of the name in '46. G. (José Ant.), a settler at Brancif. 1797. i. 569. G. (Juan), soldier killed by Ind. at the Colorado 1781. i. 359–62. G. (Juan), Mex. shoemaker, and leader in the Apalátegui revolt of '35. iii. 282–6; still at Los Ang. to '46, when he was alcalde. iii. 504, 564; v. 50, 143, 625–6; claimant in '52 for land granted '38. G. (Rafael), at Los Ang. from '36; juez de paz '43. iv. 633; regidor '47. v. 626. G. (Simon), at Los Ang. '46. Gallego (Cárlos), settler on the Colorado, killed 1781. i. 359–62. G., trader forbidden to hold raffles 1798. i. 642. G. (Pablo), at Sonoma '44, age 35. Gallegos, drowned at Sta B. '30. ii. 576. Galusha (Elon A.), 1847, Co. F, N.Y.Vol. (v. 499); d. at Rochester, N.Y., before '83. Galway (James), 1847 (?), said to have come with his parents at the age of 5; page in the convention of '49; with Walker in Nic.; lieut in war of '61–5; editor of Sta Cruz *Journal;* d. in '70. *Sta Clara News*, Sept. 24, '70.

Gamble (Wm), 1841, a young naturalist sent out from Phil. by Nuttall to collect specimens; came from N. Mex. in the Workman party. iv. 278-9. Being financially crippled, he was employed by Com. Jones in '42 as clerk on the *Cyane*, and perhaps went away on that vessel; in '44 at Callao; said by Given to have ret. to Cal. about '49.   G. (Wm M.), 1845, mid. on the U. S. *Portsmouth*.   Gamon (José M.), 1844, mr of the *Trinidad*. iv. 569.   G. (Thos), 1826, at Mont.   Gándara (Pedro), apparently a clerk of Pedrorena '40-1.   Gann (Nicholas), 1847, overl. immig. with wife Ruth, to whom, in camp at Stockton, Oct., was born the 1st child in S. Joaq., named Wm; at Gilroy '79-82.   Gannon (Thos), 1847, Co. F, N. Y. Vol. (v. 499); d. Sta B. '55.   Gansevoort (Stanwix), 1845, mid. on U.S. *Portsmouth*.

Gantt (John), 1843, member of the Chiles-Walker immig. party. iv. 392-4, 400. In earlier times said to have been an officer in the U.S. army. Capt. G. commanded Sutter's force in Micheltorena's service '44-5; and after the campaign made a contract to attack Ind. horse-thieves for a share of the recovered animals. iv. 480, 485-6, 506-7, 516-17, 543.   In Sept. '46 Bryant found him ill at Dr Marsh's rancho, and it is likely that sickness prevented his taking part in the troubles of '46-7. In '47 he wrote from Sonoma asking an appointment as sub-Ind. agent, and from Yount's place in Napa, proposing to build a saw-mill on his 'mountain tract;' in '48 of firm G. & Hannah at Napa; in '49 mining on Feather River; died in Napa Val. later in '49.

Garaycoechea (José), at S. F. 1795. i. 700.   Garcés (Francisco T. H.), 1774, Span. friar of Querétaro college, and missionary in Sonora from '68; with Anza in his exped. to Cal. 1774-6; the 1st to explore the Tulare valley and the route from Mojave to S. Gabriel; later missionary at the Colorado pueblos, where he was killed by the Ind. in 1781. i. 221-3, 258-62, 273-8, 354-67, 573, and list of auth. ii. 43-4.

García (Anastasio), a desperado who killed Joaq. de la Torre and several other men in the Sta B. region '55.   G. (Anselmo), at S. José '47.   G. (Antonio), at Los Ang. '46.   G. (Bernardino), son of Francisco, age 19 in '41, when he enlisted in the S.F. comp. at Sonoma. iv. 667. He was the desperado, 'Four-fingered Jack,' who killed Cowie and Fowler in '46. v. 161-2; also ment. at Natividad. v. 370; Cal. claim of $1,375; I think he was hanged in later years.   G. (Bibiana Romero de), widow at J. José '41, age 21, child. José Ant. b. '34, Francisco '36.   G. (Bruno), settler at Los Ang. 1796. ii. 350. G. (Cárlos), ditto 1813.   G. (Cármen), Cal. claim $2,152 (v. 462).

García (Diego), 1787, Span. friar, who served chiefly at S.F. and retired in '97. Biog. i. 713; ment. i. 388, 474, 498-500, 575, 577.   G. (Dionisio), Mex. sold. at Mont. '36, age 37; owner of S. F. lots '39-46. v. 676, 682.   G. (Eugenio), soldier at Sta B. '32.   G. (Faustino), at Mont. '47.   G. (Felipe), Span. sold. of the Mont. comp. before 1780; had a garden at Mont. about 1815. ii. 209; his wife was Petra Lugo (or Rincon), and they had 20 children. G. (Felipe Santiago), regidor at Los Ang. 1789-90. i. 461; perhaps same as preceding.   G. (Felipe Santiago), son of preceding, b. at Mont. 1782; in '35, '46, juez de campo. iii. 674; v. 637; in '36 at Mont., wife Jacinta Fernandez, child. José de Jesus b. '22, Antonia '25, Manuel Estévan '27, Encarnacion '29. In '54 he gave Taylor, *Discov. and Founders*, ii. 25, his recollections; Cal. claim in '46 of $1,042 (v. 462); still living after '60.   G. (Felipe), in Los Ang. region '46, age 25.   G. (Francisco), maj. at Sta B. 1811-1820. ii. 364. G. (Francisco), Span. invalido of Sta B. comp. in '28-9, age 60. iii. 51.   G. (Francisco), soldier of S. F. '34-5.   G. (Francisco), Mex. at Mont. '36, age 34, wife Josefa Gonzalez, child. Bernabé b. '23, Pedro '25, José '26, Epitacio '28, Lugarda '30, Bonifacia '31, María Jesus '33, Micaela '34; grantee of ranchos in Mont. and Sta Clara '42, '45. iv. 655, 673; juez at S. Feliciano '45-6; iv. 625, 634, 637. Cal. claims of $14,625 and $2,170 in '46-7. (v. 462); still in Mont. Co. '50.   G. (Francisco), at Los Ang '46.   G. (Francisco), one of the Jack Powers gang hanged near S. Luis Ob. about '55; ment. in '46. v. 162; perhaps confounded with Bernardino.   G. (Gabriel), at the S. Pascual fight '46. v. 352; a soldier at Sta B. before '37.   G. (Hilarion), maj. at S. Diego '30. ii. 549; alférez at Sta B. '39-46. iii. 583; iv. 642; v. 35.

García (Inocente), son of Felipe, b. at Los Ang. 1791; soldier in Mont.

comp. from 1807, serving in the escolta of S. Miguel and Soledad; from '13 trader and soap-maker; maj. of S. Juan B. '22-3. ii. 624; ment. at Mont. '28-30. ii. 612; iii. 41; took part in Alvarado's revolt of '36, and in Ind. exped. of '37-9. iii. 457, 460, 469; iv. 75; admin. of S. Miguel '37-45. iii. 555, 587, 685; iv. 659; arrested by Frémont '46. v. 375-6. He went to the mines in '48; and for years supposed himself to be owner of a rancho near S. Luis Ob., but lost it. His wife was María del Cármen Ramirez, and there were many children. In '78 living at S. Luis in poverty, strong in body and mind, though 88 years old, and of good repute. He gave me his *Hechos Históricos*, a MS. full of interesting details of the old soldier's life and observations. ii. 232, 338-9, 386. In '85 I have not heard of his death.   G. (Jacinto), soldier at S.F. '27-40.   G. (Jesus), at Los Ang. '46.   G. (Joaq.), sent to Mex. '30. iii. 85.

García (José), 1800, Span. friar who served at S. Luis Rey, and retired in 1808. Biog. ii. 108; ment. i. 577; ii. 159-60.   G. (José), settler at Los Ang. 1808. ii. 350.   G. (José), soldier at S.F. '28-33.   G. (José), sent as prisoner to Sonora '37. iii. 638.   G. (José), came in '36 from S. Amer.; flogged for forgery at Mont. '37; clerk at S. José '41-2. iv. 684-5; ment. in '46. v. 321; said to have been killed at Natividad. v. 372.   G. (José Ant.), 1st death at Sta Clara. i. 306.   G. (José Ant.), petitioner for lands for N. Mex. colony '45. iv. 572, 635, 637.   G. (José Dolores), ment. at Sta B. '48, in con. with the Cañon Perdido. v. 588.   G. (José E.), son of José María, worked at Sta B. for Capt. Robbins '45; served under Carrillo and Flores '46. v. 400; took part in hiding the cannon in '48; and in '78 gave me his *Episodios*.   G. (José Manuel), lots at S.F. '39.   G. (José María), nat. of Sonora, of Span. parentage; síndico at Sta B. '31-2. iii. 653, 212; maj. and admin. of Sta B. '34-6. iii. 346, 353, 657-8; alcalde in '34. iii. 654. His wife was María Ant. Ayala.

G. (José Miguel), militiaman at S.F. '37; at S. José '41, age 21, wife Rafaela Miranda, child. Guadalupe b. '39.   G. (José Norberto), murdered at S. Juan B. '44. iv. 662.   G. (Juan), soldier at S.F. 1797-1800. i. 556.   G. (Juan), soldier at Mont. '36, age 26.   G. (Juan and Juan José), at Los Ang. '46. G. (Juan B.), soldier of S.F. comp. '34-42.   G. (Julian), at Los Ang. '46; S. Luis Ob. '58.   G. (Luis), at Brancif. '30. ii. 627; at S. José '41, age 28. G. (Luz), comisionado at Brancif. '15. ii. 390; inválido '28, wife Rosalía Vazquez, child. Rufino, Antonio, José María.

García (M.), grantee of S. Miguel rancho '46. v. 637.   G. (Manuel), 1822, mr of the *S.F. de Paula*. ii. 457, 474.   G. (Manuel), at Los Ang. '46.   G. (Marcelino), 1844, one of the Bat. fijo. iv. 289, 405; in '77 at Salinas City, where he gave me his *Apunte sobre Micheltorena*.   G. (Matias and Miguel), at Los Ang. '46.   G. (Máximo), soldier of the piquete de Hidalgo at Mont. '36, age 45.   G. (Miguel), grantee of S. Miguel '46.   G. (Norberto), at Salinas '36, age 35, wife María Victoria Gomez, child. María Francita b. '20, Rita '23, José '25, Juan José '28, Guadalupe '31, Teodora '34.   G. (Pascual), soldier at Sta B. before '37.   G. (Pascual), at La Brea '36, age 49, wife Juliana Sanchez.   G. (Pedro), 1842, lieut of the batallon fijo. iv. 389.   G. (Pedro Gonzalez), armorer and instructor 1792-5. i. 615, 684.   G. (Rafael), soldier of S.F. comp. '23-33; at S. Rafael '24. ii. 598; grantee of Tamales and Baulinas '36. iii. 713; grantee of land in Mendocino '44. iv. 672; raid on the Ind. '45. iv. 541, 679. He died in '66 in Marin Co., age 75.   G. (Rafael), at Los Ang. '46; soldier at Sta B. '32.   G. (Ramon), at S. José '41, age 27. G. (Reyes), in piquete de Hidalgo at Mont. '36.   G. (Rosalío), son of Felipe; went to Chili to avoid mil. service.   G. (Salvador), Span. sailor of the *Asia;* rem. in Cal. iii. 51-2.   G. (Tomás), soldier at Sta B. before '37.   G. (Trifion), grantee of Atascadero '42. iv. 655.

García Diego (Francisco), 1833, Mex. friar of the Zacatecanos, who served at Sta Clara to '35, being prefect of the northern missions, and in '41 came back as bishop of Cal., dying in '46. Biog. v. 632-3; ment. iii. 318-24, 328-36, 338, 347-8, 351-2, 726; iv. 63-5, 195-6, 219, 332-8, 372-4, 424-7, 519, 554, 565, 619, 640.   Gard (Chas and John), 1848, at Mont.   Gardner (Geo. W.), 1844, mr of the *Nantucket*. iv. 567.   G. (Wyman), 1840, at Mont. (?). G., 1848, worked for John Williams on Butte Cr.   Gareolo (Valentin), lieut in Cal. '45 (?). Garfias (Manuel), 1842, Mex. lieut in the batallon fijo '42–5. iv. 289; grantee of S. Pascual '43. iv. 635; rem. in Cal., and took part in the war against the U.S. '46–7, going to Mex. with Flores. iv. 513; v. 41, 49, 316, 391, 407. He came back to Cal., and was county treasurer of Los Ang. '50–1; in later years U.S. consul at Mazatlan, where he still lived, perhaps, in '77. G. (Salvador), Span. at S. José '41, age 41, wife Crecencia Cibrian, child. Salvador b. 31, Ascension '36, José Jesus, '34, Felicidad '29, Encarnacion '30, Cármen '38, Josefa '40. Garibay (Gertrudis), accused of murder at Mont. '34. iii. 673. Garner (Philip), 1847, Co. B, Morm. Bat. (v. 469). G. (R.), 1848, landed at Sta B. (?). G. (Wm A.), 1847, ditto, made bricks and dug a well at S. Diego.

Garner (Wm Robert), 1824, nat. of London, b. in 1803, who deserted from an English whaler at Sta B., the date being often given as '26. ii. 526. In '29 he was refused naturalization; in '31 married a daughter of Manuel Butron; in '32 joined the comp. extranjera at Mont. iii. 221. He was a lumberman, and appears on Larkin's books from '33; in '36–7 was a lieut of Graham's comp. in Alvarado's service. iii. 458–9, 512; and in '39 was naturalized, then living at S. Juan B. His part in the Graham affair of '40 is recorded in iv. 5–6, 10, 12, 21, 27, he being the man who revealed the plot of Graham and his associates. It is not quite clear whether he simply acted in good faith as a Mex. citizen, was prompted by hostility to G., or was entrapped by Castro into confession for self-protection. Continuing his lumber business for a few years, in '44–8 he kept a boarding-house at Mont., being also at times clerk, policeman, translator, auctioneer, and alcalde's sec., besides serving apparently in the campaign against Micheltorena. iv. 495; v. 637. He went to the mines with Colton, and with his sons made several mining trips, and then moved to S. Luis Ob., from which point, in '49, he made an exped. against the Ind. of the interior and was killed with 6 of his men. His son José C., b. about '32, in a letter of '75, gave me some information about his father; also to the S. José Pion. of '78, when he lived at S. José, as he does still, perhaps, in '85. In their anger at the affair of '40, Graham and his friends accused Garner not only of treachery in that matter, but of having been an Australian convict, murderer, and desperado; but in the absence of proofs, it is well to judge the man's character by his Cal. record, which is in every respect better than that of his accusers. He is said to have been of a good family, and was an intelligent man of some education. Garnica del 'Castillo,' q.v.

Garra, Ind. chief at Pauma '46. v. 567–8. Garraleta (Antonio), clerk at Sta B. mission '39. iii. 657. G. (José Ant.), lieut of the frontier comp., sometimes visiting S. Diego; killed in '41 by his wife. iv. 619. Garrick (Peter), 1834, Engl. carpenter at Mont. in Spear's service; written Garruk and Garrenk. Garriger (Solomon), 1846, Co. E, Cal. Bat. (v. 358), enlisting at N. Helv. Oct. Garter (David), 1848, doubtful name. Garue (Wm), 1834, nat. of Sto Domingo, from Hon.; cooper at Los Ang. '36. iii. 412.

Gasquet (Louis), 1845, French consul at Mont. '45–7. iv. 385, 587, 590; v. 34, 60, 232–3, 364. Gastelum (Francisco J.), at Los Ang. '39–45. Gaten (H.), 1846, Co. B, artill., Cal. Bat. (v. 358). Gautier (Julian), 1843, d. at Los Ang.; his widow at Sonoma, Dec. Gavitt (John), 1847, lot at S. F. Gay (Geo.), 1832, Engl. deserter from a whaler. iii. 408; went to Or. in '35, and came back in '37 in the cattle exped. iv. 85; see Hist. Or., i. 98.

Geddes (Paul), see Green (Talbot H.). Gehringer (Andrew), 1847, Co. H, N.Y.Vol. (v. 499); miner in '48–50; Sta Clara farmer '51–63; in '63–83 near Concord, Contra Costa. Geiger (Wm), 1841, N.Y. teacher, age 24, who came from Hon. on the Thos Perkins. iv. 104, 569; later in the year at N. Helv. Gelabert (Wm), 1846, Span. in U.S.N.; settled later at Stockton, where he died in '82, leaving a wife and 3 children. Gelston (Roland), 1847, mr of the Whiton, and a S. F. merchant of G. & Co. in '47–9; owner of town lot and building; in '53 claimant for lands in Sac. and S.F. v. 581, 676, 678, 683. Gendreau (François), 1844, Canadian in Sutter's employ '45–8; com. of an Ind. comp. in '46. iv. 453; v. 360. He, or his son Joseph, was in the 2d Donner relief '47. v. 540. His wife was a Walla Walla Ind., and their child was buried at S. José Mission in Dec. '44. His name is often written Gendran, Gendron, Geandreau, and even Jondro. **Genks**, 1846, named at N. Helv. **Genling** (Joaquin), doubtful name of a juez in Mont. dist. iv. 653. **Gennon** (John), 1847, named by Lancey as a member of Co. F, 3d U.S. artill. **Genoa y Aguirre** (Fermin), 1817-18, sup. of the *Hermosa Mexicana*. ii. 282-3, 424. **George** (J.), 1848, from Hon. on the *Julian*.

Gerardo (Rafael), maj. at Sta B. 1793-4. ii. 120. **Gerke** (Henry), 1847, German immig. at N. Helv. and S.F. in Oct. v. 556, lot-owner at S.F. '47-8. v. 656; later a well-known vineyardist in Tehama Co., where he still lived in '80. **German** (Antonio), juez de campo at La Brea and grantee of Juristac, iii. 674, 676, 711-12, being 50 years old in '36, wife María de la Luz Peña, child. Antonio b. '18, Juan '20, José '22, Luis '24. In early times he had been a soldier at Sta B. **G.** (Cayetano), at Los Ang. '46; cl. for the rancho in '53. **G.** (Faustino), brother of Antonio, at Mont. '26. ii. 612; juez de campo '31, '35. iii. 672, 674; grantee with Ant. of Juristac '35. iii. 712; in '36 at La Brea, age 48, wife María Ant. García, age 40. Faustino, like his brother, lost all his land under the manipulations of Amer. sharpers, and died in poverty at S. Juan in '83, at the age of 95, leaving his widow, aged 87, but no children. **G.** (John), 1847, Co. F, 3d U.S. artill. (v. 518). **G.** (Juan), vecino of S. Diego, killed in '26. ii. 549. **G.** (José de los Santos), son of Antonio, b. at Sta B. '23; in '78 at Tres Pinos, S. Benito Co., engaged in raising cattle with his brother Luis C. German. The two gave me their recollections of Californian *Sucesos*, which, on several points, have proved valuable material for history. iv. 359, 463; v. 167. **G.** (Manuel), soldier at Sta B. before '37; at Los Ang. '30-48. Gerónimo, Ind. alcalde at Soledad '26. ii. 623. **Gervasio** (José), soldier of S.F. comp. '37-42. **Gessen**, 1845, a German in the south. iv. 490. **Gettinger** (Peter), 1847, Co. F, 3d U.S. artill. (v. 518). **Geurron** (J.A.), 1846, Co. G, Cal. Bat. (v. 358). **Gholston** (Wm C.), 1846, Co. K, 1st dragoons; killed at S. Pascual. v. 346.

Gibbins, 1840, at Mont. **Gibbon** (L.), 1841, mid. on U.S. *St Louis*. **Gibbs** (John), 1845, overl. immig. of the Grigsby-Ide party. iv. 579, 587; of committee repres. the immig. before Castro. iv. 606; prob. of the Bears. v. 110; settled in Napa; at N. Helv. Nov. '47. **G.**, 1845, Amer. at Brancif., age 40. **Gibson**, 1842, purser with Com. Jones. iv. 308. **G.** (Horatio Gates), 1847-8 (?), lieut in 3d U.S. artill.; at S. Diego, S.F., and other points in Cal. to '61; colonel in war of '61-5; in '77 in com. of Fort Wardsworth, N. Y.; president of eastern assoc. of pioneers. I find no original record of such an officer before '49. **G.** (Joseph), 1831, Amer. trapper and tailor of 'Haquinsor' (Arkansas!), from N. Mex. with Jackson or Wolfskill. iii. 387, 405; at Los Ang. and S. Pedro '34-6; 44 years old in '36 and single. **G.** (Marion), 1845, Amer. farmer from Or. in the McM.-Clyman party. iv. 572, 587; in the mines with Job Dye '48; died at a date not recorded. **G.** (Samuel), 1845, Amer. immig. from Or., prob. in the McM.-Clyman party, and possibly identical with the preceding. iv. 578, 587. He took a prominent part in the proceedings of the Bears, being sergt. v. 110, 153, 163-4, 168; went south with Frémont, remaining with Gillespie at Los Ang. and S. Diego, ranking as capt. in the Cal. Bat., wounded at S. Pascual, and serving under Stockton in the final campaign. v. 326-7, 340, 343-7, 360, 386, 434. In '48 he mined on Feather River in partnership with G.P. Swift, and was drowned in the winter of '48-9. *Bidwell*. **G.** (Thos), 1847, Co. C, Morm. Bat. (v. 469).

Gifford (James), 1846, applicant for timber-land near S. Diego. **Gift** (Geo. W.), 1848, nat. of Tenn.; mid. on the U.S. *St Mary*; left navy in '52; banker at Sac. from '55; lieut in confed. navy from '61; newspaper man at S. Rafael and Napa till his death in '79, leaving a wife and 4 children. **Gil y Taboada** (Luis), 1801, Mex. friar of S. Fern. college, who served at many missions, being founder of S. Rafael, and died at S. Luis Ob. '33. Biog. iii. 680-1, ment. ii. 29, 121, 131, 135, 137, 159, 329-30, 337, 351, 355, 364, 366, 387, 394, 425, 562, 618, 623, 625, 627, 655. **Gilbert** (Albert), 1830, from N. Mex. to buy cattle; in trouble with the authorities; went to Hon. on the *Volunteer* in '32.

Gilbert (Edward), 1847, N.Y. printer, and lieut Co. H, N.Y.Vol. v. 504. He made a census of S.F. and wrote an article on the town published in the *Star.* v. 647, 656; was a candidate for alcalde, and declined the collectorship. v. 575, 652, 659; but seems to have acted as Collector Folsom's deputy. He took a prominent part from '48 in public affairs; was editor of the *Alta* from its beginning in Jan. '49. v. 659; was a member of the constit. convention; and in Nov. '49 was elected as the 1st congressman from Cal. One of his editorial articles drew out a letter which led him to challenge Gen. Jas W. Denver, by whom he was killed in a duel near Sac. in '52 at the age of 33. He was regarded as a man of unusual ability and promise.   G., 1848, at Mont.; of firm Newell, Brady, & G.   G. (James), 1845, at N.Helv. in Sutter's service '45-6.   G. (John), 1847, Co. D, Morm. Bat. (v. 469).   G. (Wm), 1846, said to have been steward on the U.S. *Savannah;* at Stockton '79.

Gilchrist (Edward), 1846, surgeon on the *Congress* and *Cyane;* justice of the peace at Mont.; acted as surg. of the Cal. Bat. v. 231, 361, 637-8.   Gildea (Wm B.), 1845, Amer. physician who came overl. in the Swasey-Todd party; died at N.Helv. Jan. '46. iv. 576, 580, 587.   Gili (Bartolomé), 1791, Span. friar, who served chiefly at S. Antonio and retired in '94. Biog. i. 689; ment. i. 496, 500, 523-4, 576, 597.   Gill (James), 1846, Co. F, Cal. Bat. (v. 358); enlisting at S. Juan Oct.; lot at S.F. '47.

Gillespie (Archibald H.), 1846, nat. of Penn. and lieut. of marines U.S.N., who was sent in Oct. '45 from Wash. to Cal. as a bearer of a duplicate of secret instructions to Larkin, with whom he was to coöperate, as was Frémont, in carrying out those instructions. He crossed Mex., destroying his official despatch after committing its contents to memory, and arrived at Mont. in April '46 on the *Cyane* via Honolulu, thence proceeding to the Oregon frontier to overtake Frémont. v. 24-9, 200, 636, 644. The original of his despatch is now in my possession, and also the copy written by him from memory at Mont. Frémont claims to have received a very different despatch, and there is a bare possibility that Gillespie deceived him. In the various events of May-July, G. took an active part, being made adjutant of the Cal. Bat. at its 1st organization. v. 79-80, 101-2, 127, 177, 184, 247, 252-3. Going south in July, he was left at Los Ang. in com. of the garrison, and by his unwise policy caused the people to revolt and drive him out in Oct. v. 286, 306-15, 319. Joining Stockton at S. Diego, he was sent with a reënforcement to meet Kearny, and was wounded in the fight at S. Pascual in Dec. v. 328-9, 340, 343-7. Ranking as major of the battalion, G. commanded a division of Stockton's army, and was again wounded at the S. Gabriel in Jan. '47. v. 360, 386, 391-5. Declining the secretaryship of state under Frémont, he was relieved from duty in Cal., and reported to Com. Biddle in May. v. 433, 437, 440, 445, 450. He went east overland with Stockton, and testified for Frémont at the court-martial; also in the Cal. claims investigation. v. 453-6. He seems to have returned overland to Cal. in '48, and to have spent much of his later life here, though for some years previous to '61 he was in Mex., perhaps as sec. of legation. He was never prominent after '49, having to a certain extent 'lost his grip' in the battle of life. He died at S.F. in '73, at the age of 60.

Gillespie (Chas V.), 1848, bro. of Arch. H., nat. of N. Y., who came on the *Eagle* from China with his family, a cargo of merchandise, and 2 Chinese servants. He advertised in the *Star* as a merchant and conveyancer; and was made notary public and judge of election. v. 648, 652, 680. He also made inquiries for a rancho, and wrote, 'One of my favorite projects is to introduce Chinese immigrants into this country.' He took a prominent part under Howard in settling the Leidesdorff estate. In '85 he still lives in S.F., where he has been well known as a lawyer and searcher of records. In '75 he contributed for my use a statement on the *Vigilance Committee* and other topics of early S.F. life; and later gave me some items about early buildings in the city. Mrs G. organized a sabbath-school in '48, and has since been prominent in church affairs. v. 657.   G. (James), 1828, mr of the *Telemachus.* iii. 149; a Mass. man who was lost with the same vessel near Mazatlan. *Forbes' Pers. Remin.*, 90.   G. (J.), 1848, mr of a vessel, or sup.   Gillingham (Henry),

1847, musician Co. I, N.Y.Vol. (v. 499); owner of S.F. lots '48.   Gilman (G. D.), 1848, from Honolulu; of firm Wetmore & G. at S.F. '48–9.

Gilroy (John), 1814, Scotch sailor, and the 1st foreigner to settle permanently in Cal., being left sick at Mont. by the *Isaac Todd*. ii. 204, 248, 272, 382, 393. His real name was John Cameron, but having run away from home as a minor, he changed it to avoid being arrested and sent back. His parents moved to England when John was very young; and indeed, he often claimed to be a native of Sunderland, Engl. In Sept. '14 he was baptized at S. Cárlos by P. Sarría as Juan Antonio María Gilroy. In '18 Capt. Guerra, at Sta B., sent to the viceroy his petition as an 'Amer. cooper' for permission to remain and marry in Cal., which was granted in '19; and in '21 he was married at S. Juan B. to María Clara de la Asuncion, daughter of Ignacio Ortega. The same year he accompanied Capt. Argüello in his famous exped. 'to the Columbia' as guide, or rather, interpreter, for Amer. intruders were to be met and talked to. ii. 444–5. The next we hear of him was in '33, when he obtained naturalization, producing certificates that he was a soap-maker and millwright of good character, with wife and 4 children, having also some livestock on the S. Isidro rancho. This rancho was granted the same year to the Ortegas; G. owned a league of it, on which he built an adobe house and spent the rest of his life. His name appears on Larkin's books from '34, when his age was given as 45. In '35 he was aux. alcalde at 'Los Ortegas.' iii. 674; by the padron of '36, age 40, wife age 28, child. Nicodemus b. '26, Miguel '28. iv. 117; age 46 in '40; not arrested in the Graham affair; often named in records of most years; said to have been sent to Frémont's Gavilan camp in '46. v. 18. In '51 for the 1st time Gilroy wrote to his family in England, and I have the original reply—presented by Valentin Alviso—of his brother Alex. Cameron, tanner, at Newton Heath, near Manchester, dated June 29, '52. Alex. is glad to learn that he has a brother living, for father, mother, and the other brothers are all dead. John Gilroy was an honest, good-natured old sailor-ranchero, well liked by everybody, much too fond of his grog and cards, careless and improvident, and as powerless in the hands of land-lawyers as were the natives themselves. He lost all his lands and cattle, but he lived to see his old rancho the site of a flourishing town, which bears his adopted name, Gilroy; and he died, as poor as when he landed in Cal. more than half a century before, in '69, at the age of about '75. I have no definite record of his sons since '48. 'Juanita' (McPherson) has given many items on G.'s early life, obtained from himself, in the *Sta Clara Argus* and other papers.   Gilt (Henry), 1840, at Brancif.; prob. 'Hill.'

Gines, executed at Purísima '24.   Gingery, 1847, in Sutter's employ '47–8; millwright and blacksmith.   Gios (José), sirv. S.F. 1777. i. 297.   Girard (A.), 1846, lieut in com. of Co. B, artill., Cal. Bat., v. 361, enlisting at S.F. Oct.   G. (Wm), 1846, came to S. José. *Hall.*   Giraudeau, 1841, French viniculturist at Los Ang.; named by Mofras.   Giribet (Miguel), 1785, Span. friar who served at S.F. and S. Luis Ob., retiring in 1800. Biog. i. 689; ment. i. 388, 422, 469, 473–4, 575, 577.   Gitt, 1847, a physician named in the *N. Helv. Diary* '47–8.

Given (Isaac L.), 1841, nat. of Ohio and civil engineer, who, on a visit to the Missouri River region in '40, heard of Cal., and failing to reach Independence in time to join the Bartleson party, went to Sta Fé, and with 4 of his comrades joined the Workman-Rowland party, or in a sense originated that party. v. 278–9. His 1st work in Cal. was to survey the Rowland rancho. In '42 he came north to apply for land for himself; explored the Sac. Val. with Capt. Merritt and others; visited Napa and Russian Riv.; and ret. to Mont. to get naturalization. Here he found letters from home which caused him to go east as clerk on the *Dale*. He came back in '49 by the Panamá route, worked as a surveyor at Sac., and was later engaged for many years in mining operations. His wife is Mary A. Thomes, sister of Rob. H. Thomes, a pioneer of '41. In '79–85 Maj. Given resides at Oakland, and his *Immigrant of '41* is a MS. narrative of much value and interest.   Given, 1847, mr of the *Mt Vernon*. v. 579.

Glande (Giovanni), 1827, Ital. trader still at Mont. '29, age 25. iii. 176. Gleason (James H.), 1846, trader at Mont. '46-9; owner of S.F. lot. He came from Hon. on the *Don Quixote*, and was agent for Paty & Co.; one record has it that he died in '60.   G. (John), 1848, roll of Soc. Cal. Pion.

Glein (Cárlos F.), 1844, German blacksmith who came from Mazatlan on the *California*, settling at S.F., obtaining naturalization and a town lot the same year, and having a blacksmith shop at the cor. of Montgom. and Pacific streets from '45 to '49 and later. iv. 453, 563, 669; v. 684; also owner of a Sonoma Co. rancho in '47; made a trip to Honolulu in '48. Later for many years a dealer in hardware in S.F., where he still lives in '85.   Gliddon (Geo. R.), 1846, sup. of the *Barnstable*, at S.F., Sonoma, Petaluma, and N. Helv. '46-8.   Glines (James H.), sergt-major of Morm. Bat. v. 477; did not come to Cal.   Gloria (Jacinto), at S. Juan Cap. 1776. i. 303.   Gloss (John), 1847. Co. C, N.Y.Vol. (v. 499).

Glover (Aquilla), 1846, memb. of 1st Donner relief. v. 538; owner of S.F. lots '47-8. v. 685.   G. (Wm), 1846, member of the Mormon colony with wife and 3 children. v. 546. He was the owner of S.F. lots, member of the town council and of the school committee in '47. v. 648, 656, 682; a mason and builder; also com. for settling the affairs of Brannan & Co.; a miner in '48, being one of those who furnished Gov. Mason specimens of gold. He went a little later with his family to Utah, where he still lives in '85 at Farmington. His *Mormons in Cal.* is an important source of information on its topic, and he has also sent me valuable items about early buildings in S.F.   G. (R. O.), 1841, purser on the U.S. *St Louis*.   Glynn (James), 1847, com. of the U.S. *Preble*. v. 580.

Goche (Wm), 1838, Fr. shoemaker from N. Mex., age 31, at Los Ang. '40. iv. 119.   Goddard (Nicodemus), 1824, Amer. shoemaker on the *Sachem*. v. 526; at Sta B. '40, age 31, single and catholic.   Godey (Alexis), 1844, nat. of Mo., of Fr. Canadian parentage, a hunter in Frémont's 2d, 3d, and 4th exped. iv. 437, 453, 583. He is named in connection with several of F.'s operations in '46. v. 4, 15, 22, 24; went south and remained with Gillespie, was for a time in charge at S. Luis Rey, and took part in the fight at S. Pascual, ranking as lieut in the Cal. Bat. v. 314, 347, 353, 360. He went east with his party but came back in '49; married a sister of A. F. Coronel, and became a farmer and sheep-raiser, like his old associate, Kit Carson. As late as '78 he was still living in southern Cal.   Gooway (J. M.), 1847, from Or. on the *Henry*.   Goff (Daniel), 1840, one of the exiles to S. Blas, who did not return. iv. 18.   Golden (Edward), 1847, Co. E, N.Y.Vol. (v. 499).   Goldsmith (Sam.), 1845, doubtful member of Frémont's party. iv. 583; said to have died in Valparaíso in '69, leaving a fortune. *Nev. Gazette.*   Goldwaite (Richard M.), 1847, Co. H, N.Y.Vol. (v. 499); at Albany, N.Y., in '82.   Golovnin (V. M.), 1818, Russian visitor and author of *Voy. of the Kamchatka.* ii. 251, 291, 317-18, 383, 416.

Gomez, killed at Mont. '31. iii. 673.   G. (Ambrosio), sec. of ayunt. at Mont. v. 636-7.   G. (Felipe), at S.F. '37-44; owner of S.F. lot '40. iii. 706; age 57 in '44.   G. (Felipe), son of Rafael, trader at Mont., and sometime postmaster, to '85.   G. (Francisco), 1769, Span. friar with the 1st division of the 1st exped.; one of the party discovering S.F. bay; at S. Diego and Mont. '70; retired in '71. Mention i. 127, 136, 140, 147, 151, 167, 175-6, 178.   G. (Francisco), at Sta Cruz 1794. i. 496.   G. (Francisco), Mex. teacher at Mont. '45.   G. (Guillermo), policeman at Mont. '46. v. 637.

Gomez (José Joaquin), 1830, Mex. trader who came on the *Leonor;* customs officer and comisario subalterno at Mont. '31-2. iii. 224-5, 376, 672; in '34 regidor and builder of the *Peor es Nada.* iii. 383, 673; in '35 regidor, comisionado to secularize S. Cárlos, and grantee of Los Verjeles. iii. 354, 673, 679, 680; in '36 member of the dip., being then 48 years old, having a wife and children in Mex. iii. 426, 454, 460, 469. From '40 his rancho of Verjeles is often mentioned, being on the way from Mont. to S. José; here Larkin was captured in '46, and the fight of Natividad was in the vicinity; he was also grantee of Tucho in '43. ii. 616; iv. 134, 212, 453, 656; v. 4, 14, 364. In '46

Don Joaquin was reported to the govt at Wash. by Larkin as a man of property and character, friendly to the U.S.; in '48 Los Verjeles was advertised for sale for the benefit of creditors. He had a son and a daughter, Dolores, who came to Cal. after his arrival. The latter married and died at Mont. after '78. G. (José María), soldier in S.F. comp. '19-26; killed by Ind. '29. iii. 110.

Gomez (José Miguel), 1842, Mex. priest who served as curate at Purísima in '42-4, and at S. Luis Ob. in '44-56; claimant for S. Simeon rancho. iv. 371, 421, 426, 647-8, 656-7, 659; v. 638-9.   G. (Juan), soldier of S.F. comp. '10. G. (Juan), 1834, mr of the *Natalia*, and of the *Leonidas* '36. iii. 265-7, 383; iv. 104.   G. (Juan), son of Rafael, resid. of Mont. and S.F. in '75-85, who gave me the privilege of copying a col. of his father's *Doc. Hist. Cal.*   G. (Manuel), Mex. sergt of artill. at S. F. and Mont. from '16; lieut from '19; left Cal. in '22. Biog. ii. 470; ment. ii. 225-32, 247, 263, 371, 422, 451, 454, 461.   G. (Nicolás), one of the mission guard at S. Juan Cap. 1776. i. 303. G. (Pedro), executed at Sta Cruz '47 for killing his wife. v. 641.   G. (Rafael), convict settler at S. José 1798-1808. i. 606, 638; ii. 192.

Gomez (Rafael), 1830, Mex. lawyer who came to Cal. as asesor, or legal adviser of the govt, a relation of Joaquin. ii. 607, 677; ii. 46, 54. As a supporter of Gov. Victoria, or rather by his legal opinions in the criminal cases of '31, he excited considerable opposition among the Californians, and tried to escape after V.'s downfall; but failed and was not molested. iii. 190-2, 195, 213, 660-1; grantee of Sta Rosa in '31. iii. 713, 721; iv. 160; supports Zamorano '32. iii. 222-3; action in P. Mercado's case '33. iii. 324; supports Figueroa '34. iii. 277; but resigned his office. He was grantee of Tularcitos in '34. iii. 679; regidor at Mont. '35. iii. 673; memb. of the dip. in '36, also appointed agent in Mex., but did not go. iii. 426, 454; being at this time 36 years old; wife Josefa Estrada, child. Felipe b. '33, María Isabel '34, Juan '35. His *Diario de Cosas Notables de '36* (erroneously accredited to his son in list of auth.) I have found to be a very useful document. iii. 422. A few years after '36, at his rancho of Tularcitos, he was accidentally killed by being entangled in the reata of a horse he was trying to drive away from his grain. Don Rafael was a man of good character and a lawyer of much ability, who came to Cal. in reality as a kind of political exile.   G. (Teodoro), soldier at Soledad 1791-1800. i. 499.   G. (Vicente), 1825. Mex. guerrillero chief in the war of independence; a fiend known as El Capador, who, however, behaved well enough in Cal. during his stay of a few months. iii. 16.

Gomez (Vicente Perfecto), 1842, son of José Joaquin and nat. of Guadalajara, who came to Cal. as a clerk with Gov. Micheltorena. In '44 he was, or at least claimed later to have been, the grantee of the Panocha Grande rancho. iv. 655, 672. This grant, rejected by the courts, was the foundation of the famous McGarragan claim to the New Idria quicksilver mines; and Don Vicente is the villain of Bret Harte's *Story of a Mine.* He was also the unsuccessful claimant for Tucho. iv. 656. In '45 he was sec. of the juzgado at Mont. iv. 653; aided Manuel Castro in Nov. '46. v. 366; had a Cal. claim of $11,500, of which $500 was paid (v. 462); and in '47-8 was for a time in charge of S. Antonio mission. v. 640. As a witness in later land litigation he met with some severe criticism, much of it doubtless undeserved; and though an intelligent clerk and good penman, knowing little English, he had a hard time in the later years to pay his grog bills. In '75-6 he worked for me in the Library and various archives, doing much faithful service.   Many were the stories he told of old times in Cal.; his fellow-laborers were instructed to write out his yarns; and the result is a large vol. of MS. called *Gomez, Lo Que Sabe*, full of interest, and by no means devoid of historic value. He died at Mont. in '84 at the age of about 60, a better man in several respects than he has been given credit for. He had no family.

Góngora (José Ant.), son of José M., b. 1778 at S. Antonio; ment. in '22. ii. 614; sergt of S. Diego comp. '25-8. ii. 543; in '42-3 juez at S. Diego. iv. 619-21.   G. (José María), soldier of S.D. comp. 1771; corp. of the guard at S. Antonio '73; sergt from '75; ment. in connection with Anza's exped. '76. i. 269-71, 287. In '79 Gov. Neve reported against his promotion; and in '82 he was retired as an inválido and went to Loreto. His wife was Rosalía Maximiana Verdugo, married in '76, died '79 at S. Antonio.   Gönnefgen (John A.), 1840, copy of his German passport of '24 made at Los Ang. by Fink '40.

Gonzalez, soldier poisoned at Sta B. 1796. i. 670.   G. (Alejo Ant.), of the S.D. guard. 1775. i. 250.   G. (Bernardo), settler at S. José 1791–1800. i. 716; wife Mónica, child. Petra and Antonia.   G. (Cirilo), sirv. at Sta Clara 1776. i. 306.   G. (Diego), 1781, Span. lieut in com. at Mont. '81–5, and S.F. '85–7; an incompetent officer, of bad conduct, sent to the frontier in '87 and dropped from the rolls in '93. i. 340–2, 466–70, 484, 678; ii. 44. G. (Dionisio), 1842, Mex. capt. of the batallon fijo with Micheltorena. Nothing is recorded of him in Cal. iv. 289.   G. (Felipe), at Brancif. '45, age 24, wife María Soria, child Antonio.   G. (Francisco), 1797, Span. friar who served at Sta Cruz and retired in 1805. i. 498, 577; ii. 154–5, 159–60.   G. (Francisco), settler at S. José 1791–1800; regidor in 1803. i. 716; ii. 134. G. (Francisco), soldier of S.F. comp. '19–24; also '37–40, perhaps another. G. (Francisco), corp. of the guard at Sta Inés '24. ii. 582.   G. (Francisco), at Brancif. '28–30, wife María Engracia, child. Felipe, Margarita, and Natividad. ii. 627.   G. (Fran.), at S. Felipe rancho, Mont., '36, age 30.   G. (Fran.), said to have been drowned '44–5.   G. (Francisco), Cal. claim of $15,850, '46–7 (v. 462).   G. (Jacinto), síndico at Sta B. '28. ii. 572.   G. (José), soldier of S.F. comp. '23–32.   G. (José Ant.), at Sta Clara 1776. i. 306.

Gonzalez (José María de Jesus), 1833, Mex. friar of the Guadalupe college at Zacatecas, a nat. of Guadalajara, b. in 1803, coming to Cal. with the other Zacatecanos in '33. He served at S. José mission '33–42, being president and vice-prefect of the northern missions in '38–43. iii. 318, 577, 593, 724; iv. 61, 64, 372, 680. From '43 he served at Sta B. iv. 426, 643. From '46 he was the bishop's vicar, and after the bishop's death the same year was governor of the diocese. v. 565, 634; thus being the chief ecclesiastical authority in Cal. until the coming of Bishop Alemany in '50, and later vicar; president of the Sta B. college of Franciscans '58–72; died at Sta B. in '75, the last survivor of the Cal. missionaries, a man respected and beloved by all from the beginning to the end of his career; one of the few Zacatecanos who in ability, missionary zeal, and purity of life were the equals of the Span. Fernandinos. Gonzalez Rubio was his full name.   G. (J. M. J.), com. de policía Sta Inés '35. iii. 291.   G. (Juan), at Brancif. '28, wife Eusebia Pinto.   G. (Juan), at Brancif. '30. ii. 627; maj. and admin. of Sta Cruz '34–9. iii. 346, 694–5; juez in '42. iv. 663; in '45, age 40, wife María Ana Rodriguez, both nat. of Cal., child. Ramona b. '23. Melanía '29, Francisca '30, Petra '33, Juana '35, Tomasa '38, Refugia '40, Rosa '36, Pedro '38, Gabriela '42.   G. (Juan José), soldier in S.F. comp. '23–33; grantee of Pescadero, Sta Cruz, '33. iii. 678. G. (Juan Pablo), officer in Mont. custom-house '27.

Gonzalez (Leandro), juez de campo at Sta B. '34; admin. and maj. of the mission '40–3. iii. 657–8; iv. 643; his wife was Josefa Guevara, with 4 child. before '37; still at Sta B. '50.   G. (Macedonio), Mex. half-breed alférez on the L. Cal. frontier from about '36; a famous Ind. fighter, who took some part with the sureños in the troubles of '37–40, being once arrested and sent to Sonoma. iii. 549, 606–7; iv. 68–9. In later years he lived in Cal., and was in S. Diego Co. '64, age over 70.   G. (Manuel), settler at S. José and S.F. from 1777; alcalde of S. José '85. v. 297, 312, 350, 478; wife Gertrudis Acebedo, child. Francisco, Romualdo, Antonia, in '93.   G. (Manuel), settler at Los Ang. '14. ii. 350.   G. (Manuel), at Sta B. '37. iii. 657; perhaps still there in '52.   G. (Manuel), executed at Mont. for murder '42. iv. 653–4, 686. G. (Mauricio), son of Rafael, appointed guarda of Mont. customs '29, but did not come from Mex. till '40. iii. 136; iv. 31; grantee of Cholam, S. Luis Ob. iv. 655; with Micheltorena in '45. iv. 511. In '77, living at Mont. with his wife, the daughter of Manuel Crespo, he gave me his *Memorias*, and a col. of *Papeles Originales*, that had belonged to his father; still living in '85.   G. (Miguel), 1825, Mex. capt. of artill., comandante de armas at Mont. '26–8, a bad fellow, if we credit the Californians, often in trouble, and finally sent away in '30. His daughter, Ildefonsa G. de Herrera, was more or less a famous character at Mont. iii. 39–41; also ii. 576, 605, 608, 610–11, 614, 624, 674; iii. 15, 44, 93, 121, 437. His full name was Gonzalez de Ávila.   G. (Pablo), of terna for contador '27. iii. 63.   G. (Pedro), 1791, surg. in Malaspina's exped. i. 490.

Gonzalez (Rafael), 1833, Mex. admin. of customs and sub-comisario at Mont. '33–4, having been appointed in '29, but coming to Cal. with Figueroa in '33, iii. 46, 136, 237–8, 240, 376–7, 437, 672. His *Diario* is an important record of '32–3. He had been a lieut in the war of independence, and was an ignorant man of good character. In '35 he was alcalde at Mont. iii. 673, 441; also governor's sec. iii. 463; and grantee of S. Justo, ii. 678, being then 10 years old, wife Cármen Sierra, a Mex. He was arrested in the troubles of '37. iii. 513; comandante de celadores at the custom-house '37–46. iv. 339, 97, 210, 357, 377, 431, 577; v. 570; member of the junta '39–43, being also delegate to the consejo general of '46. iii. 590, 604; iv. 294–5, 360, 460; v. 45, 61; grantee of S. Miguelito in '41, being cl. in '53. iv. 656; had a Cal. claim of $26,200. Larkin reported him as a man of property and influence. He died at Mont. in '68, at the age of 82. His *Doc. Hist. Cal.* were given me by his son Mauricio; his daughter, Ana G. de Castañares, was a woman with a will. iii. 437–8.   G. (Rafael), 2d alcalde at S. Juan B. '35. iii. 692.   G. (Rafael), son of Raf. Gerardo, b. at Sta B. in 1797, sold. of the Sta B. comp. '16–27. ii. 223, 235, 237–8, 337, 429, 508, 536. In '29–32 he was alcalde of Sta B., and again in '35 and '45. ii. 572; iii. 78, 212, 653 4; iv. 642; admin. and maj. of S. Buen. '38–42. iii. 660–1; iv. 644–5. His wife was Antonia Guevara, and there were 3 child. before '37. In '78 he was still living at Sta B., where he gave me an interesting narrative of his early *Experiencias*.   G. (Rafael G.), Mex. soldier before 1800; wife Tomasa Quinteros.   G. (Ramon T.), clerk of Célis at Los Ang. '40; at Sta Inés '44. iv. 426; perhaps at S. Luis Ob. '50.

Gonzalez (Teodoro), 1825, Mex. who lived at Mont. from his arrival; licensed to hunt otters '33. iii. 374; in '36 regidor and acting alcalde during the troubles with Gov. Chico. iii. 439, 675; grantee in '36 of Rincon de la Puente and Sur Chiquito. iii. 678; being then 30 years old, wife Guadalupe Villarnel de Rico, the mother of Francisco Rico. Alcalde in '37; at Buenavista '40; juez de paz '42–3; aux. de policía in '46. iii. 525; iv. 24, 637, 653–4, 656. He became a man of wealth and good standing in Cal.; and in '78, though his memory was failing with age, gave me some information about the *Revoluciones de Cal.* His death occurred a few years later. His sons Mariano and Alfredo were prominently connected with the Monterey and Salinas R. R., and in '85 reside in S.F. with their mother.   G. (Tiburcio), at Mont. '36, age 28, nat. of Cal., wife Cruz Espinosa, child. Ramona and José.   Gonzalvo (M.), 1848, passp. from Honolulu.

Goodhue, 1843, mate of the *Admittance*, died at sea on the passage home '45.   Goodsell (J.), 1846, on the *Cyane*, acting commandant's clerk.   Goodspeed (Galen), 1824, sailor and mate on the *Rover* '24–6.   Goodwell (James F.), 1847, Co. H, N.Y.Vol. (v. 499).   G. (James T.), 1847, Co. G, N.Y.Vol. Goodwin, 1847, mr of the *Eveline* from Hon., with wife. v. 578.   G. (Andrew), 1847, Co. A, Morm. Bat. (v. 469).   G. (Isaac), 1846, one of the Mormon col., with 6 children, his wife dying on the voyage. v. 546; nat. of Conn., and a mason who built a house for Larkin. Sent east to report to Brigham Young on Cal. prospects; interviewed in Utah '78 by Codman. *Round Trip*, 198–201. Goodyear (Andrew), 1847, nat. of Conn. and overl. immig.; at Benicia from '49; still living in '79.   G. (Miles), 1847, trapper and trader at Los Ang., with a Cal. claim of $1,800 (v. 462); a nat. of Conn. who died in '49; perhaps a brother of Andrew.   Goosebfh, 1800, mr of the *Coniach.* ii. 81.

Gordon, 1844, officer on H.B.M.S. *Modeste*.   G. (A. J.), 1846, nat. of Mo. and overl. immig.; prob. son of Joseph; perhaps the G. at N. Helv. from Benicia '47; in Sonoma Co. from '48; in Mendocino '77.   G. (Benj.), 1848, in the mines on Amer. Riv.; at S. José '50.   G. (B.H.), 1846, married a daughter of Ed. Pyle; father of John M. G. of Los Gatos in '80.   G. (Gilman), 1847, Co. A, Morm. Bat. (v. 469).   G. (G. van), 1846, nat. of Mich.; in S. Luis Ob. '66–83.   G. (Ira van), 1846, nat. of Penn. and overl. immig., prob.

with Harlan, whose daughter Rebecca he married in '41; one of Aram's men at Sta Clara; lot at S.F. '47; after several changes of residence and employment, became a farmer from '68 in S. Luis Ob., where he still lived '83. By some authorities he has been accredited to '43. iv. 393, 400. Either identical with or a brother of the preceding or following.   G. (John van), 1846, perhaps same as G., at N. Helv. May; not of '43. iv. 393, 400.   G. (John), 1845, com. of H.B.M.S. *America.* iv. 562.   G. (Jacob), 1846, overl. immig. with Young, v. 529, with family; perhaps went to Or.; perhaps one of the van G.'s.   G. (Joseph), 1846, overl. immig. ment. by Bryant; with fam.; perhaps went to Or. or back east. v. 528-9.   G. (Julian), 1844, in Sonoma dist. '44-6; age 45 in '46.   G. (Jemima), 1847, owner of S. F. lot.   G. (Nicholas), 1845, blacksmith at Mont. '45-8. iv. 587.   G. (Robert), 1846, came from Hon. on the *Elizabeth;* in '47-8 editor of the *Californian* at S.F., and judge of election. v. 650, 658; at Sac. '48-9, active in politics.

Gordon (Wm), 1841, nat. of Ohio, who became a Mex. citizen in N. Mex., where he married María Lucero, and came to Cal. in the Rowland-Workman party. iv. 277-9. In '42 came north to Sonoma, original passp. in my col.; and in '43 was grantee of Quesesosi rancho on Cache Cr., becoming the pioneer settler of Yolo Co. Here he lived till about '66, then moved to Cobb Valley, Lake Co., where he died in '76, at the age of 75. His wife died in '44, her sister being the wife of Cyrus Alexander; and in '55 G. married Elizabeth Corum. One of his daughters, Mrs Sarah Ingraham, died in Gordon Val. '68; another, Isabel, was the wife of Nathan Coombs. 'Uncle Billy' had been a trapper in his early years, and continued to be fond of the hunt in Cal.; a rough, uneducated, honest, and hospitable man. In '43-6 his place on Cache Cr. was a general rendezvous for settlers and hunters, and is oftener mentioned than any other place except Sutter's Fort and Sonoma. It was in the vicinity of the modern town of Frémont. Portrait *Yolo Co. Hist.*, 26; ment. iv. 573, 672; v. iii. 672.   Gorgonio, neoph. who killed his wife at S. Buen. '17. ii. 424.   G. (José), grantee of Purísima, Sta Clara, in '40. iii. 712. Gorgy (D.), doubtful name of a Russian owner of land near Bodega '37. ii. 638.

Gorman (Geo.), 1843, at Mont.   G. (John), 1831, Irish. from Hon. with a letter from P. Short. iii. 405; joined the comp. extranjera in '32. iii. 221; got a lot in '35; in '36 at Hartnell's rancho, age 50 and single.   Gormly (Martin F.), 1847, Co. F, N.Y.Vol. (v. 499); claimant for a Marin Co. rancho. iv. 674; mr of the *Bostonian,* and killed by explosion of the *Secretary* in '54. Goss, 1847, on the *Currency Lass* from Hon.

Gould, 1848, mr of the *Mary Frances.*   G. (John C.), 1847, Co. C, Morm. Bat. (v. 469).   G. (John R.), 1846, assisted in printing the Mont. *Californian.* v. 293.   G. (Samuel), 1847, Co. C, Morm. Bat. (v. 489).   Gouldin, 1847, doubtful name, Alameda Co. '55-78.   Goulet (G.), 1845, in Sutter's employ '45-6; and Geo. Goutler had a Cal. claim of $60 for shoeing horses (v. 462).   Gourville (Jean), 1836, Fr. laborer at Los Verjeles rancho, age 27. Goycoechea (Felipe), 1783, Mex. lieut and com. of the Sta B. comp. 1784-1802, being brevet capt. from 1797; habilitado gen. of Cal. in Mex. 1802-5; gov. of L. Cal. 1806-14, where he died at Loreto. A prominent and able officer. Biog. ii. 116-17; ment. i. list of auth., 396, 461-3, 464-6, 484, 501-2, 517, 521-2, 532, 537, 542, 573, 583, 588-94, 639; ii. 28, 30, 32-3, 36, 111, 154-6, 186, 188, 665, 669.

Grable (Benj.), 1841 (?), nat. of Ohio; d. S. Luis Ob. '76. iv. 279; date of arrival prob. a misprint in *Cal. Christ. Adv.*, Jul. 30, '76.   Grady (Thomas), 1846, Co. C, 1st U.S. dragoons (v. 336).   Graf (Joseph), 1848, overl. immig. with wife, who settled at Nicolaus; a teamster.   Graff (Geo. J.), 1847, Co. E, N. Y. Vol. (v. 499); at S.F. '74-82.   Grafton (Ed. C.), 1845, mid. on the U.S. *Portsmouth;* acting lieut Co. C, Stockton's bat. '46-7. v. 385.   Graham, 1848, from Or. with Martin; supposed to have been killed by Ind. the same year at Murderers bar.   G. (Chas K.), 1847, mid. on the U. S. *Columbus;* maj.-gen. in war of '61-5; surveyor of port of N. Y. '79.   G. (Geo.), 1847, Co. F, N.Y.Vol. (v. 499); passp. from Hon. '48.

Graham (Isaac), 1833-5, nat. of Ky, and for many years a trapper in the

great basin and N.Mex., whence he is generally said to have come to Cal. in
'33. iii. 388, 409. I have found no details of his arrival, which was very likely
in '34 or '35. In '36 he had a distillery and drinking-place at Natividad, and
from the loafers about his place, chiefly deserting sailors, raised a comp. of
'riflemen' to support Alvarado in his revolution, going south in that cause in
'37. See full details in iii. 454–9, 491, 524, 685. In '38 he was condemned to
8 months in the chain-gang for killing cattle on Gomez' rancho. *Mont. Arch.;*
and in '39 he and Naile tried to organize a comp. to cross the mts eastward.
In '40, with a dozen of his associates and enough other foreigners to make up
the number of 47, G. was sent to S. Blas on a charge of plotting against the
govt; but with 18 of the exiles came back the next year. iv. 2–41, 95, 116,
348. The current versions of this affair, as fully explained elsewhere, have but
a slight foundation in truth; the exiles were for the most part foreigners of
the worst class, who had come to Cal. in defiance of the laws; and while the
definite charges of conspiracy could not be proved, the arrest was only technical, and in the case of a few, an outrage, for which Gov. Alvarado was
willing that Mex. should pay damages. Statements that Alvarado broke his
promises to G., and that the prisoners were brutally treated, have no better
foundation than the absurd ravings of Farnham and the complaints of the
victims hungry for damages. After his return, G., with Majors and others,
bought the Sayante rancho near Sta Cruz, built a saw-mill, and engaged also
to some extent in tanning. His name appears constantly on Larkin's books.
He made desperate efforts to get damages from Mex. through the U. S. govt
for his exile; it is a popular tradition that he succeeded in getting $36,000,
and possibly he did in later years get a small sum, but I find no definite evidence to that effect. iv. 40–1. In '43 he offered his support and that of his
associates—without their knowledge—to Gov. Micheltorena, who declined at
first. iv. 356; but he finally went south with Sutter's force in defense of the
gov. in '44–5; iv. 472, 478, 483, 486, 507. In '45 he induced a young American woman to live with him, her mother making an effort through Consul
Larkin and the alcalde to oblige him to marry, but apparently without success; though G. claimed that she was his wife, and she so appears in the padron of '45, when G. was 46 years old. I have much of the original corresp. connected with the scandal. At this time 20 of G.'s foreign fellow-citizens signed
a petition to the prefect for his expulsion from the community, as a dissolute,
lawless, quarrelsome corruptor of the public peace and morals. I think the
woman left him in '49, about the time that some of his children by a former
marriage came to Cal. The case of Graham vs Roussillon in '46 was the 1st
tried by a jury in Cal. v. 289. After the U.S. occupation, G. continued to live
on his Sta Cruz rancho, for which he was the claimant. iv. 656; and died at
S. F. in '63 at the age of nearly 70. Two of his daughters, very respectable
people, live in Sta Cruz Co. '85; and his brother also resided in Cal. for many
years. Respecting Graham's character, much is said in my narrative of the
events of '40. But for the unmerited praise that has been so profusely accorded
him, and his own never-ending abuse of better men, it might be in doubtful
taste to dwell on the man's true character. In N. Mex. and on the plains,
where he was well known by Nidever, B. D. Wilson, Job Dye, and others, he
had the worst of reputations, amply justified by his career in Cal. At the best,
he was a loud-mouthed, unprincipled, profligate, and reckless man, whose only
good qualities seem to have been the personal bravery and prodigal hospitality of his class, with undoubted skill as a hunter, and a degree of industry.

Graham (John), 1791, Boston boy of Malaspina's exped. who died at Mont.,
called Groem. i. 491.   G. (John), 1841, lieut on the U.S. *St Louis.*   G. (Lawrence P.), 1848, brevet major 2d U. S. drag., in com. of a dragoon battalion
from Mex. arriving at the end of Dec.; mil. com. of the southern dist in '49.
v. 522, 618.   G. (Wm), 1841, doubtful name at S. José. *Bidwell.*   Grajera
(Antonio), Mex. lieut in com. of the S. Diego comp. 1793–9; capt. from '98;
conduct far from exemplary; left Cal. Jan. 1800, and died at sea 3 days after
sailing. Biog. i. 676; ment. i. 522, 532, 538, 543, 563, 588–94, 630, 634, 653,
656, 730.   Gralbatch (Wm), 1825, Engl. sailor and cooper who landed at

Mont. ii. 609; iii. 29. In '29 he kept a shop with Geo. Allen and applied for naturalization, age 26; a memb. of the comp. extranjera in '32. iii. 221; on Larkin's books from '33. In '36 he lived at S. Isidro rancho, being then single, but married before '40. I find no later record than Oct. '41; generally called Graybatch or Grayback, but I have his autographs.   Grambis (Fred.), 1847, chief musician N. Y. Vol. v. 503; d. before '82.   Grams (Philip), 1847, Co. K, N.Y.Vol. (v. 499); died at Milwaukee, Wis., '80.   Granados (Fran.), 1846, aux. de policía. Mont. v. 637.   Grant, 1844, off. on H.B.M.S. *Modeste*.   G. (B.), 1845, doubtful name of the Grigsby-Ide immig. party. iv. 579; prob. went to Or.   G. (James), 1825, Engl. waterman, age 25, protestant and single; in Mont. dist. '25–9. iii. 29.   G. (Thos), 1832, got a carta. iii. 408.

Graves (Franklin W.), 1846, member of the Donner party from Ill., accompanied by wife Elizabeth, 3 sons, and 6 daughters. The father, mother, and one son—Franklin W., Jr, age 5—died in the Sierra. v. 528, 530, 534, 537. Eight of the children survived. Jonathan B., age 7, and Elizabeth, Jr, died near Sutter's Fort in '47. v. 530, 534. Wm C. was, in '80–1, a blacksmith at Calistoga, and in '84 writes me from Merrimac, Plumas Co.; he also wrote for the newspapers a narrative of *Crossing the Plains in '46*. v. 530, 534, 536, 541. Eleanor married Wm McDonald in '49, and in '81 lived at Knight's Val., Sonoma, with 8 children. v. 530, 534. Mary Ann married Ed. Pyle in '47, and J. T. Clarke in '52, and in '81 lived at White River, Tulare, with 5 children. Lovina married John Cyrus in '56, and in '81 lived near Calistoga with 5 children. Nancy married R. W. Williamson in '55, and in '81 lived at Los Gatos, also with 5 children. A married daughter, also a survivor, was Mrs 'Fosdick,' q.v.   G. (Hiram), 1848, at S.F. acc. to his later testimony.

Gray (Andrew F. V.), 1846, lieut on the U.S. *Congress;* com. of the force sent by Stockton to Kearny's relief at S. Pascual; served as S.'s aide in the final campaign of '47; went east overland with despatches; and testified at the Frémont court-martial in Wash. v. 328, 350, 385, 420, 456.   G. (Alonzo), 1847, Co. D, N.Y.Vol. (v. 499).   G. (E.), 1847, mr of the *Antonita.* v. 576. G. (E. L.), 1846, from Hon. on the *Euphemia;* perhaps same as preceding. G. (G. R.), 1841, lieut on the U.S. *St Louis.*   G. (G.L.), 1847, at Hon. from Cal. twice, 1st on the *Currency Lass,* 2d on the *Gen. Kearny.*   G. (James A.), 1847, Co. D, N.Y.Vol. (v. 499); nat. of Penn.; and memb. of 1st Cal. legisl. '49–50; resid. at Salinas City '82.   G. (John B.), 1847, came from Va with letters from Fauntleroy and Minor to Larkin; at N.Helv. '48, interested in mines.   G. (L. C.), 1847, trader on the coast '47–8 from Honolulu on the *Gen. Kearny, Louise,* and *Undine;* owner of S.F. lot. v. 679; at Benicia '49– 50, and perhaps the S. C. Gray whose lecture in Benicia is published in the *Solano Co. Hist.*, 146; still living, I think, in '85.   G. (Robt), 1788, mr of the *Washington,* sighting the Cal. coast on his way north. i. 445, 499; see *Hist. N. W. Coast.*   G. (Wm), 1837, lumberman and militiaman at Sonoma.   G. (Wm D.), 1847, Co. K, N.Y.Vol. (v. 499).

Grayson (Andrew J.), 1846, nat. of La, and overl. immig.—being at the start in com. of a small party—with wife and child, living for a time in the Upper Sac. Val. v. 528. Active in raising men for the Cal. Bat., in which he ranked as lieut; but remained in the north, and took part in the campaign against Sanchez. v. 359, 361, 383. Mrs G. seems to have remained at Sonoma, where she is named as a witness in Jan. '47. In '47–8 G. obtained lots at Benicia and S.F., where he kept a little stationery shop in the City Hotel. v. 672, 680; also acting as Capt. Folsom's agent at Corte Madera, Marin Co., and soon founding—on paper—the town of Graysonville on the S. Joaq. Riv. In these days, though a gambler and associate of Lippincott, McDougal, and other like characters, he was regarded as a man of good abilities and character. In '50 he settled at S. José and gave his attention to the study of ornithology, in which branch, and as an artist, he became widely known to scientific men in all parts of the world. In '57 he went with his wife to Mex., and died at Mazatlan in '69 at the age of 50. His descrip. and paintings of Pac. coast birds have as yet, unfortunately, remained unpublished. His widow returned to Cal., married Dr G. B. Crane, and was still living at St Helena in '77, as she is, I think, in '85.   G. (Ned), 1846, at S. José '54. *Annals of S.F.*, 822; perhaps the preceding or his son.

Green (Alfred A.), 1847, Co. B, N.Y.Vol. v. 513, 610; a nat. of New Brunswick, who after a brief experience in the mines became a somewhat prominent lawyer at S.F., being at one time memb. of the legislature, and well known in connection with the pueblo land question, Santillan claim, and vigilance committee. In '78 he gave me a narrative of the *Adventures of a '47er*, containing many interesting details of early S.F. annals; still living in S F. '82, and I think in '85. There is some confusion in the records between him and H.A. Green, at Sonoma in '47-8.   G. (Alonzo), 1848 (?), doubtful date of a Sonora settler.   G. (Cambridge), 1832, one of Young's trappers, who killed a man named Anderson, and is said to have been imprisoned at Los Ang.; also had a brother in the same party. iii. 388.   G. (Daniel S. or C.), 1846, surgeon on the U. S. *Dale;* in confed. service '61-5.   G. (Ephraim), 1847, Co. B, Morm. Bat. (v. 469); at Sutter's and in the mines '48.   G. (Francis), 1836, Amer. age 40, in a Los Ang. list; perhaps at Sta Cruz '39.   G. (Geo. W.), 1829, on the *Brookline.* iii. 138-9; living in Mass. '72.   G. (Harry), 1848, named by Glover as a Mormon who went to Utah '49.   G. (Henry A.), 1844 (?), a lumberman and builder—possibly the G. at Sta Cruz '39—named in various records of '44-6 at Mont. and Sta Cruz. iv. 455; Cal. claim of $76 (v. 462). In '47 he was at Sonoma, being a member of the town council, v. 668, and employed in preparing material, under a contract with Larkin, for houses which were erected at Benicia in '48. v. 671-3. There was a Mrs G., perhaps his wife, at Sonoma in '47.   G. (H.F.A.), 1848, at Mont., acc. to consulate arch.   G. (Hugh W.), 1847, purser on the U. S. *Independence.* G. (Jacob), 1846, Swiss trapper at N. Helv. '46-7; Cal. claim $25 (v. 462); ment. by Ward in '48.   G. (J.L.), 1848, owner of a S.F. lot.   G. (James), 1847, doubtful member of N.Y.Vol. (v. 499); at S.F. '74.   G. (James), 1831, perhaps of Young's party. iii. 388.   G. (James M.), 1845, nat. of Conn., who came on a whaler. iv. 587; long a resid. of Hon., and mr of vessels running to Cal.; memb. of firm C. A. Williams & Co.; also ship-chandler at S. F.; died in Stockton insane asylum '68. Newspapers.   G. (John), 1847, Co. C, Morm. Bat. (v. 469).   G. (John D.), 1847, resid. at Sta Cruz, acc. to the county hist.   G. (Judson), 1846, overl. immig. with Steph. Cooper.   G. (Lewis), 1846 (?), at Los Ang. '59-76.   G. (Michael), 1846, Co. C, 1st U.S. dragoons (v. 336).   G. (T.C.), 1847, at N. Helv.

Green (Talbot H.), 1841, nat. of Penn., and overl. immig. of the Bartleson party. iv. 268, 270, 275, 279. Early in '42 he entered Larkin's service at Mont. as clerk; and in May '43 made a contract to carry on L.'s business for one year for $400 and 5 per cent of the profits. This arrangement was continued to the end of '45, and in Jan. '46 G. made a contract for 3 years to take the business, with $10,000 worth of goods, for one third of the profits. v. 55-6. I have much of his business corresp. In '44 he got a renewal of his passport, possibly naturalization; in '46 served on the 1st jury, v. 289, and was grantee of land near Mont. v. 637; and in '46-7 was collector of the port, having also a Cal. claim of $10,855, and obtaining a lot at S.F. v. 289, 433, 467, 570, 572. He made a trip to Mazatlan, and contributed items for the *Californian.* In '48 visited the mines. From Jan. '49 he was a member of the S.F. firm of Mellus & Howard, a prosperous and popular man of business, member of the town council, and taking an active part in political affairs. He married the widow Montgomery, of the Stevens immig. party of '44, by whom he had a son, in '85 state librarian at Sac., his mother, now Mrs Wallis, being a resident of Mayfield. In '51 Green, being then a prominent candidate for mayor, was recognized and denounced as Paul Geddes of Penn., a defaulting bank clerk, who had left a wife and children in the east. There is no agreement about the circumstances of the discovery. The charge proved true, but G. protested his innocence, and went east via Panamá for the avowed purpose of clearing his reputation, being escorted to the boat by a large company of prominent citizens. There are several confused versions of his later life. I have his letter to Larkin in '53, in which he expresses shame and penitence for the deception he had practised; says he has lost $3,200 from his trunk, and is 'penniless and destitute, with spirits broken and energy gone;' begs L., 'for God's sake,' to send him his share of the proceeds of the Cal. claims and other debts; confesses that he has deceived Thompson; but intends to buy a small farm in Tenn. Some day he will send a full history of his life. In '54 he visited Cal. and was seen by Wm F. White—whose *Grey's Picture of Pion. Times*, 124–31, contains a good account of G.'s life—and in '55 he writes to Larkin from N.Y. that he had settled with Mr H. (Howard ?); that Mr B. (Brannan) had settled the Penn. affair; and that he is about to start for Tenn. He is understood to have rejoined his 1st wife and to be still living in '85. In the *S. J. Pion.* of Apr. 21, '77, it is stated that G. had been for some time asst sec. of the U.S. senate, and that he visited Cal. in '76. Lieut Maddox accused Green of dishonorable conduct in '46–7, and there are some slight indications that his Penn. defalcation was not his only transgression; but his Cal. record, as a whole, was excellent.

Green (Theodore P.), 1846, lieut on the U.S. *Congress*.   G. (Wm), 1840, one of the S. Blas exiles, arrested in the south. iv. 14, 18.   G. (Wm G), 1847, Co. C, N.Y.Vol. (v. 499); d. S. Rafael '71.   Greenman (J. D.), 1848, passp. from Honolulu.   Greenock, 1846, ment. by Revere as the frontier settler on a journey from Napa Val. to Clear Lake. I think there may be some connection between this name and 'Guenoc,' that of a Lake Co. rancho granted in '45 to Geo. 'Rock.' Guenoc is still the name in use.

Greenwood (Caleb), 1844, trapper and mountaineer, who, with his two sons, Britain and John, by a Crow wife, guided the Stevens immig. party across the plains; and performed like service for other parties in '45–6, being sent to Ft Hall to divert the Or. immig. to Cal. They served in Sutter's force '45; Bryant met the old man in Lake Co. '46, when he claimed to be 83 years old; Britain was with the 2d Donner relief of '47, and lived in Mendocino Co. '84; S. S. Greenwood, apparently one of the 3, is said to have been a nat. of Nova Scotia, to have come with Frémont, and to have been justice of the peace and assessor at Sac., where he died in '78. John served in Co. E, Cal. Bat. (v. 358), and had a trading-post in Greenwood Val. '48. It is impossible to distinguish between the 3, or to locate any one of them at any definite time. iv. 445, 453–4, 486, 539, 575, 579.

Gregory (John), 1844, Engl. in Cal. '44–6; came back in '55; in Sonoma Co. '61–80 with wife and 3 child. *Son. Co. Hist.*, 691.   G. (Robert), 1846, Co. K, 1st U.S. drag., killed at S. Pascual. v. 346.   G. (Thos), 1848, at S. F. from Honolulu.   Gregson (James), 1845, Engl. who came to Phil. as a boy, and overl. to Cal. in the Grigsby-Ide party, with his wife, Elizabeth Marshall, and her two brothers, mother, and sister. v. 579, 587. In '45–8 he worked as a blacksmith for Sutter, serving in the Sac. garrison during the Bear revolt. v. 79; and later in Co. B, Cal. Bat. (v. 358), being perhaps at the Natividad fight, and taking part in the southern campaign of '46–7. Returning, he resumed work for Sutter, got a lot at S.F. v. 685, and was at work at the famous mill when gold was discovered. Mrs G. is mentioned in '47 as passenger on the 1st steamboat to Sac. v. 579. In '50–80 he lived in Green Val., Sonoma Co., with 9 children. His daughter, Annie, b. Sept. 3, '46, married Robert Reid of S. Luis Ob.; another, Mary Ellen, b. '48, married McChristian. Prob. still alive in '85. I have a MS. *Statement* from him. Portrait in *Son. Co. Hist.*, 509.   G. (Wm), 1834, Amer., age 29, in Spear's service at Mont.   Gremell, 1848, in list of letters, S.F.   Grems, 1821, mr of the *Sigloe* (?), at Sta B. ii. 440.   Grey (Wm), 1837, in S. F. militia.   G. (Louisa C.), 1848, wife of W.L.G., d. Stockton '79, age 31; named as 1st Amer. child born in Sonoma.

Grien (Carl), 1844, blacksmith at Mont.   Griffin, 1847, from Honolulu on the *Euphemia;* in '48 mr of the *Ariel.* v. 576.   G. (John S.), 1846, asst surg. U. S. A. from '40, prob. nat. of Ky, who came with Kearny from N. Mex., being present in the fights of S. Pascual, S. Gabriel, and the Mesa. v. 336–7, 385. His *Journal* of '46–7 is one of the best authorities extant, and is supplemented by his original *Doc. Hist. Cal.* in my collection. He was stationed at S.D. and Los Ang. in charge of the mil. hospital; visited the mines on leave of absence in '49, became interested with Vallejo and Frisbie in Napa lands, and was stationed at Benicia till '52, when he was transferred to the south; went east in '53, and in '54 resigned and settled at Los Ang., where he has since resided and practiced medicine down to '85.   G. (M.), 1847, at S. F. from Honolulu.   G. (Peter K.), 1844, Amer. at Mont., getting a pass for a year.   G. (Sam. P.), 1846, mid. on the U.S. *Savannah;* serving in garrison at S. José, v. 378, where he applied for land.

Griffith (Calvin C.), 1845, nat. of N.C., who came with his parents in the Grigsby-Ide party. iv. 579, 587. He served with the Bears, v. 110, and in the Cal. Bat. (v. 358), later becoming a miner and farmer. In '81 he lived at Rutherford, Napa Co., with his wife, Lydia Lensibaugh, mar. in '55, and 7 children. G. (F.G.), 1846, in Cal. Bat., and named in a list of Bears; perhaps a brother of Calvin.   G. (James A.), 1845, overl. immig. of Grigsby-Ide party, with wife, Elizabeth R., and one or more sons. Bonds given by Yount Nov. 19th. iv. 579, 587. The family settled in Napa Val.; Cal. claim of $1,000 for repairing barracks (v. 462); died in Sonoma '68.   G. (Jonathan), 1846, one of the Morm. Col. with wife and 2 children. v. 546; lot at S.F. '47; Mrs G. and son at Mont. '48. G. did not go to Utah.   G. (Thomas), 1846, doubtful name of a Bear; possibly a son of James A.   G. (Joseph), doubtful name of a trapper in S. Joaq. Val. in very early times. *Mont. Co. Hist.*, 29.

Grigsby (Franklin F.), 1845, Co. E, Cal. Bat. '46-7 (v. 358); prob. a son of John and immig. of '45.   G. (Granville W.), 1845, ditto.   G. (John), 1845, nat. of Tenn., came to Cal. from Mo. in the immig. party that bears his name, with his family. iv. 578-81, 587. He was one of the most active in fomenting the Bear revolt of '46; was for a few hours leader at Sonoma on June 14th; com. the guard that took the prisoners to N. Helv.; and after the U. S. occup. was in com. of the Sonoma garrison, being capt. of Co. B, Cal. Bat. v. 110, 114-19, 164, 168, 175, 184, 242-3, 296, 298. After the reorganization of the battalion in Nov. Capt. G. com. Co. E, in the southern campaign. v. 358-61. He had a Cal. claim (v. 462); and in '47 is mentioned in connection with political affairs at Sonoma. v. 433, 609. He settled in Napa, where he continued to live till about '72, when he went to Texas, and died in Mo. '76, at the age of 70. There is a strange lack of information about him and his family after '46. Two of the name, perhaps his sons, have been mentioned; his daughter was the wife of Wm Edgington; and he had a brother Jesse in Cal. I have copies of a small col. of *Grigsby Papers* furnished by the Sonoma Pion. Soc.   Grijalva (Juan Pablo), 1776, Mex. sergt with Anza's exped.; served at S.F. '76-86; alf. of S. Diego comp. '86-96; retired as lieut '96-1806, the date of his death. His daughters married Ant. Yorba and Pedro Peralta. Biog. ii. 104; ment. i. 258, 262-76, 286-7, 296-7, 359, 362, 452, 472-3, 547, 553, 647, 652-3, 663; ii. 57. G. (Luciano), at Los Ang. in '33.

Grimes (Eliab), 1838, nat. of Mass.; lieut on a privateer in the war of 1812; later for 20 years a well-known merchant of Honolulu, of firm E. & H. Grimes. iv. 141. In '38 he visited Cal. on the *Rasselas*, of which he was owner, and went to Boston. iv. 105, 117, 119. His next visit was on the schr *California* in '42, at which time he selected a rancho in the Sac. Val., which, after he had returned from a trip to Hon. on the *Fama*, was granted to him in '44. iv. 672. From this time Capt. G. may be regarded as a permanent resid. of S.F., though he made another trip to Hon. on the *Don Quixote* in '47. He had a lot and house, was a well-known trader, and was a memb. of the legisl. council in '47. v. 433, 653, 678, 680. G. & Sinclair had a Cal. claim for horses (v. 462). For some years he made 'Kent Hall' his home while in town, and kept there a case of extra fine liquors, which nothing would induce the old man to open for convivial purposes but a story that could arouse his interest; hence there was a continual rivalry in yarn-spinning among the younger merchants. As a boat was going up the Sac., after the gold excitement, the occupants were asked who was left at S.F., and 'nobody but old Grimes' was the reply; but 'old Grimes' died in Oct. '48, at the age of 69.   G. (Hiram), 1847, nephew and partner of Eliab at Honolulu; partner of Wm. H. Davis in '45-6; came to Cal. in Feb. '47 on the *Don Quixote;* and again on the *Euphemia* in July with his wife and child. Often named in S.F. annals of '48–9; claimant for several ranchos. iv. 672–3; still in Cal. '54. G. (A. J. and B.), 1847–8, doubtful mention; prob. confounded with the preceding.

Grimshaw (Wm Robinson), 1848, nat. of N.Y. city, b. in 1826 of Engl. parents; sailor on the *Isaac Walton*, and after arrival on the tender *Anita*, U.S.N.; also mr of the launch *Susanita*, on the trip up the Sac. v. 580. He worked as book-keeper for Brannan & Co. at Sac. in '48–9; and from Nov. '49 was partner of Wm Daylor in a store or Ind. trading-post on the Cosumnes. Daylor having died in '50, G. married his widow in '51, and continued to reside on the rancho, where in '72 he wrote for me his *Narrative*. This is not only an interesting sketch of his own life and adventures, but one of the best accounts extant of the events of '48–50 in the Sac. region. Still living in '80, with 7 children, Wm R., Jr, Thos W., Emma (Mrs W. D. Lawton of S.F.), George, Francis, Frederick, and Walter. Grinnell, 1848, from Hon. on the *Starling*. G. (Chas C.), 1847, Co. G, N.Y. Vol. (v. 499); d. before '82. Griswold (Theodore), 1847, at N.Helv.; lot at S.F.; named in '48.

Groem, 1791, see 'Graham.' i. 491. Groh (Jacob), 1847, Co. F, 3d artill. (v. 518). Grogan (Alex.), 1848, from Valparaíso with letter from Atherton; clerk for C. L. Ross at S.F. '48–9; still in S.F. after '80. Grove (Wm), 1848, lieut of S.F. guards. Grovecot, 1846, perhaps in Sta Clara. Grover (Sam.), 1816, Mass. sailor bapt. at S. Cárlos. ii. 276–7. Grow (Wm), 1847, sergt Co. H, N.Y.Vol. v. 504; at Yreka '78; at Deadwood, Dakota, '83. Guadalupe (José M.), soldier at S. Miguel 1797. i. 560. Guat (Santiago), 1836, juez de campo at Mont. iii. 678; prob. James 'Watt.' Guchapa, Ind. chief at S. Miguel 1804. ii. 150.

Guerra (Antonio María), son of José de la G. y N., b. '25; reg. and sec. of ayunt. '49; memb. of the Cal. senate in '53, several times mayor of Sta. B., holding other local offices; in the war of '61–5 a capt. of Cal. volunteers serving in Ariz. He is said to have been one of the ablest of the family; but in later years the loss of his palate and of his eyesight obliged him to lead a life of retirement. He never married, and died at Sta B. in '81 at the age of 56. G. (Bautista), 1831, from N. Mex. with Wolfskill. iii. 387. G. (Francisco), son of José de la G. y N., b. '18; acc. to the padron of '32 there were two Franciscos; from '43 member of the junta, elector at Sta B. '45, taking a somewhat prominent part in political and mil. affairs in '46–7, and involved in the imaginary Sta B. revolt of '48. iv. 361, 522, 540; v. 38–9, 404, 586. He took no pains to conceal his hostility to Amer., but after the change of flag was mayor of Sta B. for several years from '51. He inherited a rancho, but died poor in '78. His 1st wife was María Asuncion Sepúlveda, by whom he had Francisco, Jr (county assessor of Sta B. in '82), and María Antonia; the 2d wife was Concepcion Sepúlveda, sister of the 1st, and her children were Juan, Osbaldo, José, Hércules, Pablo, Aníbal, Anita (Mrs F. W. Thompson), Erlinda, Rosa, and Diana. There were also two natural children legitimated. G. (Joaquin), son of G. y N., b. '22; once sheriff; no family; d. before '70.

Guerra (José Antonio), son of G. y N., b. 1805; cadet in the Sta B. comp. '18–28. ii. 572, 576; accomp. his father to Mex. '19; síndico '29 and alcalde '33. ii. 572; iii. 654; elector in '34. From '35 a memb. of the dip., taking a prominent part in support of Alvarado's govt in '36–7. iii. 291, 426, 454–5, 461, 506; in '37–40 capt. of the port of Sta B., being made capt. by Vallejo, and at times acting as mil. com. iii. 583, 601–2, 651, 654; iv. 98; vocal of the dip., and grantee of Los Álamos '39. iii. 585, 655. Prop. for sub-prefect '41. iv. 641; admin. at Purísima '41–2. iv. 647–8; where there were serious charges against him by P. Abella and others. In '43 he was capt. of the port, and in '44 receptor. iv. 431–2, 640, 642; and in '44–6 a memb. of the assembly, being in '45 leader in an outbreak at Sta B. iv. 410, 497–8, 541, 559; v. 37–8, 142, 264, 280, 321–2. In '48 took part in the affair of the lost cannon at Sta B. v. 588. In later years he was several times sheriff of S. Luis Ob., holding that office—or his son—in '69. He had the whim of signing his name José Noriega, as he had no right to do. Don José Antonio's record was, in several respects, not of the best, though there is nothing very bad to be said of him.

His wife was María Concepcion Ortega, and his children—6 of them born before '40—were José Ant. J., Ramon (sheriff of S. Luis Ob.), Alejandro, Guillermo, Dolores, Catarina, Sola (?), Cristina, and Juana. G. (Juan J.), son of G. y N., b. about 1810, educ. in England; later at the Mont. school under Hartnell and P. Short; died in '33, unmarried; ment. i. 432. I have a long letter, in good English, written by him in '28 from Stonyhurst College, Engl. G. (Máximo), said to have been exiled in '29, and again in '39. iii. 78, 84-5, 580. G. (Miguel), son of G. y N., b. '23, wife Trinidad Ortega, child. Gaspar, Ulpiano, Leon, María (wife of Alex. S. Taylor), Josefa, Olimpia, Joaquina, and Paulina. Died at Sta B. in '78.

Guerra (Pablo), son of G. y N., b. '19, educated in Hartnell's school at Mont., where he is ment. in the padron of '36. His baptismal name was Pablo Andrés Antonio María Saturnino; and in '40 he is called Pablo Gaspar. From '38 he was vista, and from '42 contador and acting administrator of the Mont. custom-house. iii. 598; iv. 97, 309, 339, 353, 357, 364, 377, 431, 556, 570, 590; in '44 grantee of Nicasio rancho. iv. 672; in '45 elector de partido. iv. 515, 540, 651. In '46 Don Pablo was active against the Amer., trying to reconcile the hostile factions of his people, and favoring an Engl. protectorate. v. 43-4, 61, 68-9. On the raising of the U. S. flag he went south; served as Castro's commissioner to Stockton. v. 235, 268-9; and after Castro's departure returned to Mont., where he was arrested in Nov. on the outbreak of Flores' revolt, and kept a prisoner till Feb. '47. v. 363. He was alcalde of Sta B. in '47, and was suspected of complicity in a revolutionary movement in '48. v. 631, 586. His next public service was as memb. of the constit. convention in '49; and subsequently he was state senator for several terms, acting lieut-gov., U.S. marshal, and district judge from '64 to within a short time before his death, in '74. Don Pablo was by far the most prominent of the Guerra family, except his father; a man of good ability and education; of gentlemanly manners, though somewhat haughty and overbearing; a good speaker in Spanish and English; and one whose family name gave him an influence in the south greater than he could otherwise have acquired. It has been customary to eulogize him far beyond his merits; he was a politician of not the best type, trimming his sails adroitly to catch the breeze of popularity, and changing somewhat abruptly from secessionist to union man in the race for office; yet his record in office seems always to have been an honorable one. In private life also he is reported to have been liberal and honest, though health and property were largely sacrificed to his fondness for brandy and cards. He married Josefa Moreno in '47 at S. Cárlos; his children were Francisca (Mrs Dibblee), Delfina, Ernina, Paulina, and a son whose name I do not find.

Guerra y Noriega (José de la), 1801, nat. of Spain, b. Mar. 6, 1779, son of Juan José de la G. (died 1820) and María Teresa de Noriega (died 1815), both, and especially the mother, of old and distinguished Span. families. In boyhood he wished to be a friar, a freak that caused his parents much sorrow; but soon he went to Mex. to be a clerk in the store of his uncle, Pedro Noriega. In 1798 he left the store—much to the displeasure of Don Pedro, who afterwards relented and gave him much aid—and became asst in the office of Habilitado gen. Cárcaba, by whose influence he was enrolled as cadet in the army and attached to the S. Diego comp. Respecting this and most other parts of his life I have more original corresp. than I have room to utilize. In 1800 he was promoted to alférez of the Mont. comp., and came to Cal. on the *Concepcion* in Aug. 1801. At Mont. he was habilitado, and acting com. much of the time, in 1802-6, being mentioned in con. with many minor affairs. ii. 50, 78, 132-3, 135, 140, 150, 153, 155; having in 1804, with permission of the king, married Antonia, daughter of Raimundo Carrillo, with the condition that she and her children should not be entitled to montepio unless he were killed in battle. In 1806 he was promoted to lieut of the Sta B. comp., and sent to S. Diego as habilitado in 1806-9, being knocked down in a quarrel with Lieut Ruiz, which greatly alarmed his friends as likely to interfere with his rapid promotion. ii. 85, 99-100, 117, 540. From 1808 he received large consignments of goods from his uncle Pedro in Mex., the sale of which greatly improved his financial condition. ii. 186. In 1810 he was sent to Mex. as habilitado gen. of the Cals, but being arrested by insurgents at S. Blas, was unable to reach the capital, and returned to Cal. in '11, taking his position at Sta B., and continuing his commercial operations, though going to S. Diego again as habilitado in '13–15. ii. 98, 188–9, 197–8, 341, 419–21. From '15 he was com. at Sta B., taking part in the arrest of foreign smugglers, in defensive operations against Bouchard, having a quarrel with P. Señan, and being promoted to Capt. in '18. ii. 222–5, 235–42, 275, 284–5, 317, 332, 361, 382, 405, 416, 424. In '19 he was sent again to Mex. as repres. of the Cal. companies to obtain supplies, and prob. with a hope of getting an appointment as gov., returning in '20 after accomplishing very little, though all that was possible. ii. 260–2, 265, 354, 422. He was busied, besides his official duties, in '21–2 in obtaining ranchos, quarrelling with the friars on the subject, and getting a grant of Conejo in '22. ii. 441, 566, 569–70, 580. In '22 he was a candidate for gov., and but for his Span. birth and Canónigo Fernandez' consequent opposition, would have been chosen; being also favored by the friars for congressman. ii. 451, 453–4, 465–8. There is no truth in the statement of Wilkes, *U.S. Explor. Exped.*, v. 173, on this matter, and but little in that of Petit-Thouars, *Voy.*, ii. 90; though his disappointment may have had an influence on Don José's later policy between Mexicans and natives. Mention in '23–5, including his acts in suppressing the Ind. revolt of '24. ii. 495, 510, 530, 533, 536–7, 561, 576; iii. 27. He was elected dip. to congress in '27, and against the advice of many went to Mex. in '28, but was not given his seat, returned in '29, and was for some time, as a Span., nominally suspended from his command. ii. 570–1, 574–5, 676; iii. 33–4, 51–2, 61, 127; iv. 343. In '29–30 he bought a schr, perhaps had another built, and bought the cargo of a wrecked vessel. iii. 140, 146. He did not join the movement against Victoria in '31. iii. 205, 210; controlled the policy of Cárlos Carrillo in congress. iii. 214; and in all these years acted as a kind of treasurer and confidential adviser of the friars—síndico apostólico; accused in '34 of being engaged in a conspiracy against the govt. iii. 250, 257–8. In the sectional troubles of '36–8 Capt. G. was a firm supporter of Alvarado's cause, though personally a friend of Carrillo. Alvarado wished to make him com. gen., and did grant him the S. Julian or Nacional rancho. iii. 436, 492, 510, 533, 550, 582, 650–1. In '39 he made vain attempts to collect his back pay, being still com. at Sta B. iii. 584, 651; and having to his credit, including extra allowances, 51 years, 9 months, and 1 day of mil. service on May 10th. In '40 he asked for retirement because he could not get the $12,000 due him, nor the promotion to which he was entitled, and because of his ailments and age of 62. He finally retired from the mil. service on April 1, '42. Ment. in '40–2. iii. 655; iv. 199, 632, 640–1; ment. '44–6. iv. 403, 408, 530; v. 282. Though not friendly to the U. S., he kept quiet for the most part, and did not indulge in any offensive partisanship. In later years he was claimant for several ranchos. iv. 643, 655–6; living quietly at Sta B., and being a man of great wealth, most of which his sons managed to squander even before their father's death. He died in '58, leaving over 100 direct descendants. None of the pioneers here registered exerted for so long a period so wide and good an influence as Capt. de la Guerra. He was a man of excellent character and conduct throughout his career, though no great or brilliant achievements can be placed to his credit, though he had the advantage of rich and influential friends from the first, and though his Span. birth prevented his reaching the highest rank; yet his honest and efficient performance of each duty, his well-balanced judgment, his dignified conservatism, command admiration. At Sta B. he was known as the patriarch, to whom the people were wont to apply as a matter of course to settle their controversies; and he was famous for his charities. No man in Cal. ever came so near, by peaceful, legitimate means, absolute control of his district. He did not purchase popularity at the cost of independence, for many were his controversies, even with the friars, though their life-long friend and a devout churchman. The *Guerra, Doc. Hist. Cal.*, copies of which I was permitted to make by the kindness of Mr Dibblee, executor of the estate, are the most extensive and valuable family archives in Cal. except those of Vallejo. In person, Don José was short and stout, with a flat nose and an ugly face. His intimate friends in their letters were fond of applying nicknames. Gen. Cárcaba and the leading friars used such endearing epithets as *corcobado*, *chato maldito, chato flojo*, etc. On account of pride in his wife's family he had a fondness for her name, and was as often called Capt. Noriega as by his proper name; in the case of his sons this became ridiculous affectation. His wife, María Antonia Carrillo, died in '43. His 5 sons have been named in this list, being for the most part prominent citizens of good enough abilities and character, yet hardly what a union of the two best families of Cal. should have produced. The daughters, noted for beauty and intelligence, were 4, all of whom eventually married foreigners. Teresa de Jesus, b. 1809, married W. E. P. Hartnell, and still lives in '85, having furnished for my use valuable documents of the family archives and a *Narrative* of personal recollections. María de las Angustias, b. 1815, married Manuel Jimeno Casarin, and later Dr J. D. Ord; and she also is living in '85, her *Ocurrencias* being one of the best personal narratives in my collection. Ana María, b. '20, married Alfred Robinson and died in '55. María Antonia, b. '27, married Cesario Lataillade, and later Gaspar Oreña, a Span. with whom she still lives at Sta B. in '85.

Guerrero y Palomares (Francisco), 1834, Mex. who came from Tepic, I think, in the H. & P. colony, at the age of 23. iii. 263; but possibly in '28, as per Soc. Cal. Pion. rolls and Lancey. He perhaps obtained a S.F. mission lot in '36; was elector '37, '39. iii. 705, 590; receptor and admin. of customs from '39 to '44. iii. 700; iv. 98, 375, 431, 483, 670; in '39–41 juez de paz and alcalde. iii. 705–6; iv. 247, 665; grantee of several town lots and the rancho de los Putos. iv. 669, 673, 676, 682. In '42 he was 31 years old, wife Josefa de Haro, age 17, and one child; in '44 grantee of Corral de Tierra rancho; in '45–6 sub-prefect at S.F., being often mentioned in local annals of the north. iv. 667; v. 17, 129, 239, 241, 295, 455, 644, 648; in '49 again sub-prefect. He continued to reside at the mission, where in '51 he was murdered, and where his widow still lived in '80. A street in S.F. bears his name. Don Francisco seems to have been a kind-hearted, genial man, of much intelligence, and good character.   G. (José M.), at Los Ang. '46.   G. (José Vicente), ditto; síndico '41; 2d alcalde '48. v. 626.   G. (Joaquin), soldier killed on the Col. 1781. i. 363.   G. (Matias), teacher at Mont. about '15. ii. 427; sec. at S. José '24. ii. 605.   G. (Pedro), ment. in '29–31. iii. 68-9, 208.   Guescote (Fran.), armero at S.F. comp. '42; perhaps 'Westcot.'   Guest (John), 1846, passed mid. on U.S. *Congress*, and act. lieut on the *Warren;* capt. in Stockton's bat. v. 350, 386; commodore in '72; d. '79, in com. of Portsmouth navyyard.   Gueval (P.), 1848, passp. from Hon.   Guevara (Antonio), in revolt at Sta B.; sent to Mex. '29–30. iii. 78, 85.   G. (Canuto), at Sta B. before '37; wife Rafaela Lugo, 3 children.

Guibal (Eugene), 1847, Co. I, N.Y.Vol. (v. 499); in S. Joaquin '71–5; d. at Gilroy '83.   Guilcost (Wm), 1826, mr of the *María Teresa*. iii. 149.   Guild (H.M.), 1847, Co. B, N.Y.Vol. (v. 499); carpenter at Mont. '48.   Guile (Wm), 1847, musician Co. K, N.Y.Vol. (v. 499).   Guillen (Antonio), guard at S. Diego 1803. ii. 13.   G. (Isidoro), son of Eulalia Perez de G., sergt of Sta B. comp., made alf. in '39. iii. 583, 650; juez de paz at S. José '41–3. iv. 684–6.   Guillon (Chas F.B.), 1847, asst surg. on the U.S. *Columbus*.   Guirado (Bernardino), trader at Los Ang. from '39; supervisor in '58–9.   G. (Rafael), 1833, Mex. trader from Sonora, owner and sup. of the *Leonidas*, who settled at Los Ang., age 32; in '35–6 regidor. iii. 283, 635–6; in '39 clerk at S. Gabriel. iii. 645; owner of S. F. lot in '47. v. 684; coroner in '52; died at Los Ang. in '72.

Gulnac (Wm), 1833, nat. of N.Y., who had lived long in L. Cal., and who came on the *Volunteer*, via Honolulu, with his family, settling at S. José. iii. 409; iv. 86, 117. He was naturalized in '34; in '38 owner of S. F. land, and employed to survey S. José town lands. iii. 705, 730; in '39 regidor, and possibly arrested in '40. iii. 731; iv. 17, 120. In the padron of '41, age 40, wife Isabel Ceseña, child. José Ramon b. '26, Juan Pánfilo '31, Cárlos María '33,

Susana '34, Isabel '36, and Luisa '38. In '44-5 he joined Sutter's army, somewhat reluctantly, and was grantee of the French Camp rancho, sold to Weber. iv. 462, 486, 671, 674; signed the S. José call to foreigners in '45. iv. 599; on the 1st jury '48; and died in '51. Two of the sons, Cárlos and Juan, served with Fauntleroy's dragoons in '46 (v. 232, 247); and another, Pedro, is named in '43.   Gunn, see 'Gann.'

Gutche (Valentin), 1848, in Sutter's employ.   Guthrie, 1845, apparently one of Frémont's men. iv. 583.   G. (Alfred), 1847, Co. G, N.Y.Vol. (v. 499); doubtful; at S.F. '74.   G. (Dexter), 1846, overl. immig. from Ill., who lived in Napa Val. till his death by suicide in '81.   G. (R.), 1846, one of Fauntleroy's dragoons. v. 332, 347.   G. (Wm), 1847, Co. H, N.Y.Vol. (v. 499); at Coulterville '82.

Gutierrez, carpenter at S. Juan Cap. 1797. i. 658.   G. (Cirilo), at S. Juan Cap. '46, age 51, wife Ana M. Romero, child Pablo, b. '38.   G. (Fran.), sergt Catalan vol. 1796. i. 540.   G. (Fran.), 1825, Span. prob. from the *Asia*, iii. 27.   G. (Joaquin), soldier at Mont. '36, age 20; juez aux. Mont. dist '42. iv. 653; cl. for Potrero de S. Cárlos. '52. iii. 678.   G. (José M.), Mex. at Brancif. '45, age 40, wife Guadalupe.   G. (José de Jesus María), 1833, Mex. friar of the Zacatecanos, who served at Solano, S.F., and S. Antonio till '45, after which I find no record of him; prob. left Cal. iv. 680-1; iii. 318, 322, 353-4, 392, 399, 553, 660, 686-8, 713, 719.   G. (Juan), 1842, sub-lieut of the batallon fijo '42-5. iv. 289.   G. (Manuel), Span. who came to Cal. before 1790; on the Dominguez rancho, Los Ang. dist. from 1811. ii. 350, 353, 386; ment. '19. ii. 292; alcalde of Los Ang. '22-3. ii. 559; in '28-30, 80 years old, claiming exemption from expulsion as a Span. iii. 51-2.   G. (Manuel), Span. who came in '21, age 43 in '28, claimed exemption. iii. 51-2; had a vineyard at Los Ang.; alcalde at S. Pedro '36. iii. 635; at Sta Inés '42. iv. 646.

Gutierrez (Nicolás), 1833, Span. capt. in Mex. army, who came with Gov. Figueroa and was prom. the same year to lieut-col. He was comisionado for the secul. of S. Gabriel in '34-6; acting com. gen. Oct. 8, '35, to Jan. 2, '36, and from that date gefe pol. and com. gen. to May 3d; mil. com. in the south during Chico's rule; again gov. and com. gen. on Chico's departure from Sept. 6th to his own overthrow by Alvarado on Nov. 4, '36. See his rule and the revolution, iii. 445-66, with biog. 448; ment. iii. 236, 240, 258, 281, 284-5, 288, 298-300, 346, 414-20, 422, 431, 433, 442, 644-5; iv. 83, 102, 112, 141, 164. Gov. Gutierrez was an easy-going, faithful officer, of ordinary abilities and not very strict morals, the current charges against whom in justification of the revolt have but slight foundation in fact. Nothing is known of his later career.   G. (Octaviano), Mex. artill. corp. at Sta B. from '24. ii. 532; lieut in '39. iii. 583, 651; in '46 juez de paz, v. 635, and again in '49; claimant for the Laguna rancho '53. iv. 642.   G. (Pablo), Mex. grantee of rancho in Yuba Co. '44. iv. 671; in Sutter's employ '44-5; made plans with Bidwell to seek for gold on Bear Riv., but B. says he was captured and hanged by Castro in the Micheltorena campaign. Sutter tells a similar story; but I know nothing further of the matter.   G. (Romualdo), 1804, Span. friar who served at Sta Inés, and retired on account of ill health in 1806. Biog. ii. 29; ment. ii. 122, 159-60.   G. (Tomás), grantee of land at S. Juan Cap. '41. iv. 626; in '46 at S. Juan, age 63, wife María Ant. Cota, child. Luis b. '33, Ignacia '34, Francisco '37, Petra '39, Mariano '41, Ramona '45.   Guy (Omnes), 1842, Fr. sawyer at Sta Cruz who was naturalized in '44. iv. 341.   Guzman, settler at Brancif. 1797. i. 569.   G. (Laureano), 1842, fifer in the batallon fijo '42-5. iv. 289.   G. (Manuel), 1829, mex. convict, pardoned in '34.

Gwinn (Frank), 1841, blacksmith from N. Mex. in the Workman-Rowland party; went back the next year. iv. 278.   Gyzelaar (Henry), 1816, mr. of the *Lydia*, arrested at Sta B. ii. 275-8, 362-3, 382. In '18 he came back as mr of the *Clarion* with a warning against Bouchard. ii. 222, 291. In 22-3 he returned again as mr of the pioneer Boston trader *Sachem*, and remained in Cal., ii. 474-5, 478, 492-3, being drowned in '25 or '26 in trying to cross Russian River. iii. 29.

Haag (Fred.), 1847, Co. D, N.Y.Vol. (v. 499). Haan (Matthew J.), 1846, from Hon. on the *Elizabeth*; trader at Sonoma '47, in partnership with Fred. G. Blume, and later Victor Prudon; owner of S.F. lots. v. 680. Hace, 1831, perhaps of Young's trappers. iii. 388. Hacker (Wm), 1846, bugler Co. C, 1st U.S. dragoons (v. 336). Hackett (Pat.), 1847, Co. D, N.Y.Vol. (v. 499). Haenck (Tadeo), 1791, apothecary with Malaspina. i. 490. Hageman (Chas K.), 1847, Co. D, N.Y.Vol. (v. 499). Hagemeister, 1817, Russ. gov. of Alaska who visited Cal. on the *Kutusof* '17–18. ii. 216, 251, 283, 291, 315–18, 373, 383. Haggerty (John K.), 1847, Co. F, 3d U.S. artill. (v. 518); a miner in '48. Hägler (Henry), 1843, German ship-carpenter and mill-wright with Stephen Smith from Baltimore. iv. 395, 400. He worked at Bodega; in '47-8 in charge of the farm of his brother-in-law F. G. Blume; seems to have spent his life in Sonoma Co.; died at Bodega in '73. His name was perhaps Hegelar.

Haig (A.), 1822, mr of the *Snipe*. ii. 474. Haight (Jacob), 1846, artill. of Stockton's bat., killed at the S. Gabriel, Jan. '47. v. 395. H. (Sam. W.), 1847, sutler of N.Y.Vol. (v. 503); often named in commercial records of '47-8, being interested at Benicia; d. S.F. '56. Hails (R. C.), 1846, nat. of Tenn. and overl. immig.; several times memb. of the legisl. from Napa and Solano down to '78, when he was 62 years old. Haines (John), 1837, named in Larkin's books; in Sutter's employ '44; also ment. at N. Helv. '46. Hairbird (John), 1846, doubtful memb. of the Mormon col, v. 547.

Hale (Horatio), 1841, on the *Cowlitz;* of scientific corps U. S. ex. ex. IV. 218, 241–2, 246, 250. Haler (Lorenzo), 1845, one of Frémont's men in '48-9, and perhaps in '45. iv. 583; v. 453. Halee, 1842, doubtful name at S. F. Haley (John), 1828, Irish cooper at S. Pedro from an Engl. vessel; in '29-30 at S. Gab., age 34. ii. 558; written 'Geli.' Hall (Basil), 1847, owner of S.F. lot. v. 678. H. (Chas), 1832, Boston trader at Los Ang. '33-6; d. before '62. iii. 408. H. (James), 1826, mate on the *Rover*. H. (James), 1831 (?), mate of a trader, perhaps same as preceding; visited S.F. '81 from Me. H. (James), 1844, disabled Amer. sailor aided by the consul; sailed on the *Nantucket*. H. (James), 1848, at Mont., perhaps J. T. H. (J.T.), 1846, mr of the *Barnstable* and *Elizabeth* '46-8, perhaps 2 men. v. 576-7. H. (John), 1822, mr of the *Lady Blackwood*, author of notes on Cal. harbors. ii. 474; iv. 151. H. (John or Chas), 1847, Co. E, N.Y.Vol. (v. 499); for many years a miner in Nev., where he died in '77, leaving a widow and daughter. H. (John T.), 1847, mr of the *Malek Adhel*. H. (R.R.), 1847, boatswain on the *Columbus*. H. (Willard P.), 1847, memb. of congress from Mo., who came as guide (?) with the Morm. Bat. v. 483; served in Co. C, Cal. Bat. (v. 358); went east with Kearny. v. 452; and testified at Wash. in the Frémont court-martial. v. 456.

Halleck (Henry Wager), 1847, nat. of N.Y., graduate of West Point, and lieut of engineers U. S.A., who came with Co. F, 3d U. S. artill. to inspect Pacific coast fortifications. v. 518-20. Besides attending to his duties as engineer officer, being soon brevetted captain, he went down the coast to take part in the military operations at Mazatlan and in L. Cal.; prepared a report on Cal. land titles; and acted in '48-9 as govt secretary and auditor of revenues. In '49 he was an active and influential member of the constitutional convention; and in '50-4 acted as inspector of light-houses on the Pac. coast. Then he resigned his commission, and in '54-60 was a member of the law firm of Halleck, Peachy, & Billings in S.F., taking part as counsellor in many of the great land suits, acting as a kind of director of the New Almaden mines, acquiring a vast estate, and in '60-1 serving as major-gen. of militia. In '61 he went east and was commissioned major-gen.; commanded the dept. of Mo. in '61-2; was the highest mil. authority at Wash. as senior general, and later as chief of staff in '62-5; commanded for a time at Richmond; was in '65-9 com. of the dept. of the Pacific; and from '69 of the dept of the South until his death at Louisville, Ky, in '72, at the age of 56. No analysis of Gen. Halleck's character is called for here; his reputation is national, though he was essentially a Californian; and the positions held by him are sufficient to show his abilities. He was a cold-blooded, generally unpopular man; plodding rather than brilliant in all his efforts; arousing bitter enmity as well as profound admiration. He was the author of several professional works and translations, and his treatises on military, mining, and international law are regarded as of standard value. His wife was a daughter of John C. Hamilton, and survived him with a son. H., 1847, brother of H.W., said to have been in the Q.M. dept., and to have died at Mont. '48. It may be that there is an error in the date of death, and that this was Jabez Halleck, who was collector, harbor-master, and com. of deeds in '49.

Haller (John J.), 1847, owner of S.F. lot. Halloran (Luke), 1846, memb. of the Donner party, who died before reaching Cal. v. 531. Halls (John), 1847, surveyor at S.F., Mont., and N. Helv. '47-8. v. 683. Halpin (Michael), 1846, Irish bugler of Co. C, 1st U.S. dragoons (v. 336). Halsey, 1846, mr of the *Caroline*. v. 576.

Ham (Hiram), 1847, owner of S. F. lot. H. (R.S.), 1848, early settler and alcalde at Sonora. H. (Zacarias), 1831, with Wolfskill from N. Mex.; said to have been drowned in the Col. a little later. iii. 387. Hamel (Wm), 1847, Co. F, 3d U.S. artill. (v. 518); died in '84. *Swan*. Hamell (Dr), 1847, doubtful name at N. Helv. Hames (John), 1844 (?), named at Soquel. iv. 453; in '45 signed the S. José call to foreigners. iv. 599; ment. in '46. v. 641; memb. of Sta Cruz council '48. v. 642; alcalde in '49; claimant of Arroyo del Rodeo '53. iii. 677. Hamilton, 1847, of firm H. & Foster, Mont. H., 1845, one of Frémont's men. iv. 583. H. (Geo. W.), 1846, of Cal. Bat. (v. 358); lumber dealer at Mont. '48; at S. José '50. H. (James), 1847, Co. A, N.Y. Vol. (v. 499); d. at Jackson, Amador Co., '58. H. (J.R.), 1846, act. mid. on the *Dale;* lieut confed. navy '61-5. H. (Mary), 1846, one of the Mormon col., perhaps with family. v. 546; Mary Sparks was her daughter.

Hamlen (Mortimer J.), 1847, Co. E, N.Y.Vol. (v. 499). Hamley (Geo. W.), 1846, mr of the *Stonington*. v. 578, 580; bearer of despatches from Stockton to Frémont in Jan. '47. v. 401; and in Dec. witness at Wash., D.C.; in '53 cl. for Güejito rancho. v. 621. His name is written in many ways, but I have his autograph. Hammer (Robert), 1847, Co. G, N.Y.Vol. (v. 499); d. on Amer. Riv. '49. Hammond (Francis A.), 1847, from Hon. on the *Currency Lass;* kept a shoe-shop in S.F. '48. v. 685. H. (Thos C.), 1846, lieut Co. K, 1st U.S. dragoons. v. 336, 341, 343; died of his wounds at S. Pascual. v. 343-7. Hampton (Wade), 1841, Amer. gunsmith in Workman-Rowland party from N. Mex. iv. 278; at Los Ang. '42; returned via Mazatlan in '43, and was mysteriously killed on the way. *Given*.

Hance (Wm), 1838, Amer. sailor, who deserted from the *Sarah and Caroline*, perhaps in '36. iv. 118; arrested, but not exiled, in '40. iv. 17; got a pass in '41, being then a lumberman near Monterey. In '42 he signed an appeal on the sufferings of the arrested party; in '44 got his pass renewed, living at S. F., age 35. Hancock (Chas), 1847, Co. C, Morm. Bat. (v. 469). H. (Geo. W.), 1847, Co. C, ditto. H. (Levi W.), 1847, musician Co. E, Morm. Bat., being also poet, preacher, and spiritual director of the battalion. v. 477, 485, 488, 493-4; in Utah '82. Hand, 1841, mr of the *Hamilton*. iv. 566. H. (Chas S.), 1847, at Benicia '47-8. v. 673. H. (Patrick), 1847, sergt Co. F. 3d U.S. artill. v. 519. Handerick (James), 1847, owner of S.F. lots. v. 679. Handford, 1847, mr of the *Jóven Guipuzcoana*. Handley (Wm), 1837, mr of the *Loriot*. iv. 105. Hands, 1848, arrested at S. José. v. 662.

Hanks (Ephraim), 1847, Co. B, Morm. Bat. (v. 469). H. (Ebenezer), 1847, sergt ditto. v. 477. H. (Julian), 1845, mr of the *María Teresa*. v. 587, 579; perhaps came earlier; at S. José from '46, being member of the council. v. 664; in '49 memb. of the constit. convention, a nat. of Conn. age 37. He went later to L. Cal. Hanley (James), 1835-7, mr of the *Clementine*. iii. 382, 442; iv. 102. Hann (Wm), 1847, owner of S.F. lot. Hanna, 1848, mr of the *Lady Adams*. v. 579. Hannah (Dolphus), 1845, doubtful overl. immig. iv. 578. Hanner (Joseph), 1842, Amer. from N. Mex. at Los Ang. '42-3. Hannoah (Baptiste), 1848, d. at N. Helv. Hanns (H.), 1848, at Hon. from S.F. on the *Julian*. Hansen (Christian), 1840, mr of the *Catalina*

'40–2. iv. 192, 564; lieut in Mex. navy. Hanson (Geo. M.), 1846 (?), miner in early times, and later publisher of newspapers; perhaps an immig. of '46, died in Lake Co. '78. Hanton (Matthew O.), 1847, Co. G, N.Y. Vol. (v. 499). Harbin (James M.), 1846, overl. immig. (v. 526), who settled in Yolo '47, and about '57 at the springs in Lake that bear his name; sometimes accredited to '44. iv. 446; cl. for land in Napa and Yolo; d. Lake Co. '77. H. (Joshua), 1846, Co. E, Cal. Bat. (v. 358), enlisting at Son., Oct. H. (Matthew), 1844, son of J. M., and overl. immig. of the Stevens party. iv. 445, 453. He went south and was one of the prisoners at Chino. v. 313–14; later a resid. of Napa and Lake, and about '75 went to Mexico to engage in stock-raising. Harcourt (Geo.), 1846, Fauntleroy's dragoons (v. 232, 247); Co. G, Cal. Bat. (v. 358).

Hardcoop, 1846, Belgian of the Donner party, who died before reaching the Sierra. v. 531–2. Hardie (James A.), 1847, lieut 3d artill. U.S.A., major N.Y.Vol. v. 574; in com. of S.F. garrison '47–8. v. 513, 515, 649, 659; owner of town lots. In the war of '61–5 a brig.-gen.; d. Wash. '76. Harding, 1846, doubtful name at Los Ang. H., 1847, mr of the *Thos H. Benton.* H. (Francis), 1847, owner of S.F. lot. H. (James), 1846, Co. G, Cal. Bat. (v. 358). H. (Thomas), 1845, Amer. sailor of the *Tasso* and *Vandalia*, aided by the consul. v. 587. Hardmont (Wm), 1847, Co. I, N.Y. Vol. (v. 499), at S. José '50; d. before '82. Hardy, 1848, com. of the U.S. *Ohio.* v. 579. H. (Daniel), 1848, newspaper record. H. (H. C.), 1848, owner of S.F. lot.

Hardy (Thomas M.), 1843, Canadian who possibly came earlier or had been naturalized in some other Mex. province. iv. 400; grantee this year of Rio de Jesus María on the Sac. near mouth of Cache cr.; in '44 named in several records as carpenter and translator in Sonoma district, age 43. iv. 448; in '45–8 often named in *N. Helv. Diary* as visiting Sutter's Fort. I have an original letter in Span. of May '46. The Bear captors of Vallejo and Prudon spent the night at H.'s place. v. 120. He was unpopular with the settlers, perhaps because of his sympathy for the Mex. Had a Cal. claim for horses; in the gold mines May '48; and a little later in '48 or '49 he was drowned in Suisun Bay, perhaps accidentally. His property was sold by the public administrator, and as late as '70 the sons of John Hardy—claimed to be identical with Thos M.—were trying in the courts to overthrow the title of J. M. Harbin and other holders under the administrator's sale and U.S. patent to the rancho. H. (Thos), 1847, at Benicia; perhaps same as preceding. H. (Wm H.), 1845, landed at Sta Cruz from a whaler. v. 587; worked for Larkin and others as a carpenter and lumberman, building a schooner '46; of H. & Jenkins '48; still at Sta Cruz '80. Hare (Henry), 1836, Engl. clerk with Jas Watson at Mont., age 26, and single.

Hargrave (Wm), 1844, Amer. immig. from Or. in the Kelsey party. iv. 444–5, 453; settling in Napa as a hunter. He was prominent in the Bear revolt. v. 78–9, 95, 104, 110, 119; and later served in the south as lieut of Co. C, Cal. Bat. v. 361, 283. He is occasionally ment. in divers records of '45–8. In '78 he still lived in Napa, where he dictated for my use an interesting narrative of *California in '46.* Harlan (Geo.), 1846, overl. immig. from Ind. with wife—Elizabeth Duncan—2 sons, and 2 daughters. v. 528–30. He lived at S.F., and later in Contra Costa, dying in Sta Clara '50, and his wife in '48. H. (Elisha), 1846, son of Geo., in same party. H. (Joel), 1846, son of Geo., b. Ind. '28; in '49 married Minerva, daughter of Wm Fowler; lived at many dif. places, and from '82 in Amador Val., where he died in '72, leaving a widow and 7 children. Portrait in *Contra Costa Co. Hist.,* 78. Harlem (P. W.), 1846, Co. F, Cal. Bat. (v. 358). Harley (Henry), 1847, Co. D, N.Y.Vol. (v. 499); d. near Sac. after '70.

Harmand, see 'Harmon.' Harmes (Henry), 1847, owner of S. F. lot. H. (Wm), 1847, ditto. Harmon (De Witt J.), 1847, Co. I, N.Y.Vol. (v. 499); at Murphy's, Calav. Co., '71–4. H. (Ebenezer), 1847, Co. C, Morm. Bat. (v. 469). H. (Jacob), 1847, owner of lot at S.F. v. 685; in '48 had a garden at the mission, and a wife, Elenora, who obtained a divorce in '49. He died at S.F. '50, leaving a widow and 2 children, Mary Ann and Jacob. The widow married Michael Foley in '50, and died at Sta Clara '60. H. (Lorenzo F.), 1847, Co. C, Morm. Bat. (v. 469); reënl. H. (Oliver N.), 1847, Co. E, ditto; home missionary at Hoytsville, Utah, '82.

Harnden, 1847, mr of the *Naslednik*. v. 579. Harner (Joseph), 1843, Amer. tailor from N. Mex., who had a shop at Mont., where he worked at his trade, sold grog, and smuggled in a small way. Died in '44 of small-pox, leaving property worth about $2,000, of which the consul wrote to his mother, Dolly H. of Va. Harnes (Henry), 1847, Co. H, N.Y.Vol. (v. 499). Harness (Wm), 1846, at N. Helv. Jan.–March.

Haro (Francisco de), 1819, Mex. sub-lieut of the S. Blas infantry comp. in Cal. ii. 253, 371. In '21 accomp. Argüello on his trip to the north. ii. 445; and in '22–3 served as sec. of the govt and dip. ii. 461–3, 486, 676. In '24 2d in com. of the exped. against revolted neophytes. ii. 531–2; and the same year retired from mil. service. ii. 675 (error in ii. 585); elector de partido '27. ii. 584, 592; iii. 33; land grants in '29. ii. 595; iii. 75; suplente of the dip. '30–1. iii. 50, 187; vocal '33–4. iii. 246, 249–50. In '35 and '38 he was alcalde at S.F., and elector in '37. iii. 703–5; in '41–4 sec. of the juzgado, and owner of town lots. iv. 665–6, 669, 676, 683. In '42, age 50, apparently a widower (his wife had been a daughter of José Sanchez), child. Francisco and Ramon b. '27, Rosalía '28, Natividad '29, Prudencio '31, Carlota '33, Dolores '36, Jesus Felipe '40, Alonzo. The oldest daughter, Josefa, b. '25, was the wife of Fran. Guerrero, and cl. for the ranchos granted to her father and brothers. Rosalía became the wife of A. A. Andrews, and later of Chas Brown. iv. 669. In '46 Don Francisco was at times acting sub-prefect, inspector of election, and candidate for alcalde. v. 295, 648. He died in '48. His twin sons, Francisco and Ramon, were militiamen at S.F. in '43; were granted, or permitted to occupy, the Potrero in '44. iv. 673; Ramon, or 'Chico,' was involved in the Libbey assault of '45 (iv. 569); and both were murdered by Frémont's men at S. Rafael in June '46. v. 171–4. H. (Ignacio), at Sonoma '44, age 20.

Harper (Thos W.), 1847, Co. B, N.Y. Vol. (v. 499); d. Sta B. '56. Harran (Geo. and Joel), 1847, lots at S.F., prob. 'Harlan,' q.v. Harriens (David), 1826, mr of the *Cyrus;* also in '30. iii. 146. Harrington (John), 1847, Co. D, N.Y. Vol. (v. 499). Harris, 1847, in prison at N. Helv. for stealing horses. H., 1847, from Hon. on the *Currency Lass.* H. (Austin), 1848, passed mid. on the U.S. *Independence.* H. (Geo. Aug.), 1826, trader who had a quarrel with Dav. Spence. H. (Geo. C.), 1846, on the *Sarah Parker* acc. to *Swan.* H. (Henry), 1846, of the Mormon col., joining at Hon., and somewhat prominent by reason of his suit against Brannan. *Annals of S.F.*, 750. At S.F. '47–8; owner of town lots. v. 685. His wife was Mary ——, and their only child, Henry Wm, died in '48. H. (James), 1830, shipwrecked sailor of the *Danube;* still at Sta B. '36. iii. 180. H. (John), 1844, Engl. at Mont. H. (John D.), 1847, owner of S.F. lot. v. 685. H. (J. H.), 1848, subscribes for a ball at Mont. H. (Robert), 1847, captain's clerk on the *Columbus;* perhaps same as preceding. H. (Robert), 1847, Co. E, Morm. Bat. (v. 469). H. (Silas), 1847, Co. B, ditto; a Utah farmer '81; mail-carrier '48.

Harris (Stephen), 1847, Q. M. sergt N.Y. Vol. v. 503; with wife and 2 daughters. One of the latter died at S.F. in Aug.; the other was born on the voy., and christened Alta California at Rio Janeiro with much ceremony, v. 512, getting a S.F. lot in '48, as her father had in '47; candidate for council in '47. v. 650; still in Cal. '54. H. (Stephen A.), 1848, owner of S.F. lot; left Cal. in '50 and d. '67. His lot was claimed in '54 by Stephen, whose grantees held it from '64; and the heirs of Stephen A., in '70–9, were unable to recover the land in the courts. H. (Mrs S. E.), 1845, at Sonoma '77; maiden name not given. H. (Wm), 1844, Amer. sailor put ashore by the *Vandalia;* shipped by the consul on the *C. W. Morgan.* H. (Wm), 1846, Fauntleroy's dragoons (v. 232, 247). H. (Wm A.), 1847, asst surg. on the *Independence* '47–8.

Harrison (Ed. H.), 1847, Q.M. clerk of N.Y.Vol. and of the dept at S.F.; a prominent man from '48, school trustee, president of public meetings, owner of lots, and collector of the port. v. 575, 650–1, 656–7, 659, 678, 685; apparently of DeWitt & H., a well-known S.F. firm. H. (G.), 1847, mid. on the

U.S. *Columbus.* H. (Henry A.), 1848, had a store in S.F.; memb. of council '49; died in N. Y. '57. H. (H.H.), 1841, mid. on the U. S. *St Louis.* H. (Isaac), 1847, Co. E, Morm. Bat. (v. 469); at Sandy, Utah, '81. H. (Israel), 1847, Co. E, Morm. Bat. H. (N.B.), 1846, mid. and act. master of the U.S.*Portsmouth:* sent by Montgomery to Sloat with despatches. v. 228; at Mont. '48. H. (Thos), 1846, doubtful mention; a Mrs Russell is also said to have come in '46 with her father and mother named Harrison. Harron (James), 1847, Co. D, N. Y. Vol. (v. 499); at Sentinel, Fresno, '83. Harsh (Dan.), 1047, in Napa Val.

Hart, 1839, mr of the *Flibberty-gibbet.* iv. 103–4. H. (Henry L.), 1847, Co. A, N. Y. Vol. (v. 499); d. in L. Cal. '48. H. (James S.), 1847, Co. E, Morm. Bat. (v. 469); reënl. H. (Jerome), 1847, Co. G, N. Y. Vol. (v. 499); d. in Shasta '52. H. (John), 1829–30, mr of a vessel on the coast. H. (John), 1847, Co. D, ditto; at S.F. '71–4; d. before '82. H. (Joseph), 1846, Co. G, Cal. Bat. (v. 358); enlisted at S. José, Oct. Hartcell (David), 1847, Co. F, 3d U. S. artill. (v. 518). Hartman (Henry), 1847, owner of S.F. lot, who had a tin-shop in '48. v. 684. Hartnell (Horatio Nelson), see 'Hartwell.' H. (Jack), 1834, at Mont. H. (Wm A.), 1846, celador of Mont. custom-house. v. 570.

Hartnell (Wm Edward Petty), 1822, nat. of Lancashire, Engl., b. 1798, who, after a resid. of several years in S. Amer., came to Cal. on the *John Begg,* as member of the firm McCulloch, H., & Co., agents of Begg & Co, of Lima, and of the Brothertons in Liverpool and Edinburgh. This firm made a contract to take mission produce for 3 years from '23, and for some years did a large business. ii. 474–9, 564, 591, 603, 659; iii. 24, 28. In '24 he was baptized at S. Cárlos, the name Edward being added at that time (the 'Paty' of ii. 475 is prob. an error); and in '25 married María Teresa de la Guerra. iii. 27, 29. His business was prosperous down to '26, and some loans were made to the govt; but in '27–9 there came reverses that caused him to go to S. Amer. in '29 to close the partnership, leaving him with a heavy burden of debt. iii. 49, 57–8, 71, 118, 121–2, 127–8, 138, 147, 176. In '30 he was naturalized, and in '31 undertook the life of a ranchero at Alisal in partnership with the Soberanes. In '32 he com. the comp. extranjera at Monterey in support of Zamorano. iii. 221–5, 672; and in '33–6 acted as Cal. agent of the Russian comp. iv. 162–4; grantee in '34 of the Alisal, or Patrocinio, rancho, ii. 616, where with Father Short he established a kind of college, called sometimes Seminario de S. José. iii. 317, 670, 677–8. In '35–6 he was regidor. iii. 293, 673, 675; his children then being Guillermo Ant. b. '27, Adalberto '32, José '34, and Matilde '36, one or two having died and others perhaps not living at the college, where there were then 13 students. He was also collector of taxes and customs in '36–7, and employed to make a padron of the district. iii. 672; iv. 96, 116; but about this time the school was given up as unprofitable, and H. found it difficult to support his family. In '39–40 he served by Alvarado's appointment as visitador general of missions, at a salary of $2,000, his faithful efforts for reform being recorded, with his reports, in iii. 600-1, 620, 624–8, 645, 657–8, 661, 664, 666, 683, 685, 688, 691, 718, 720, 725, 728; iv. 9, 55–62, 194–5. Visited by Douglas '41. iv. 212; interpreter in '42 for Com. Jones' investig. of the Graham affair; in '43 an officer of customs, iv. 377, tithe collector, court clerk, and teacher; in '44, 1st officer, inspector, interpreter, and acting admin. of the custom-house, having also an interesting corresp. with Wyllie on plans of Engl. colonization. iv. 403, 430–1, 451–2, 654; ment. in '45. iv. 515, 559; being still in the custom-house '45–6, somewhat unfriendly to the U.S. until he lost all hope of an Engl. protectorate. v. 7, 9, 61, 235, 570. After the change of flag he was appointed by Stockton surveyor and appraiser of customs, being elected councillor, serving on the 1st jury, and making a trip to Honolulu in Dec. v. 289, 293, 637. In '47–50 H. was employed by the U.S. authorities as official interpreter and translator, v. 609, in which capacity he rendered most important services, both in connection with legal and land matters and the constit. convention. Later he was county assessor and held other positions, being claimant for two ranchos. iv. 643; iii.

676; dying in '54 at the age of 56. Hartnell was a man who enjoyed and merited the respect and friendship of all who knew him, being perfectly honest and straightforward in all his transactions, of most genial temperament, and too liberal for his own interests. In some directions he was a man of rare ability, being a master of the Spanish, French, and German languages besides his own. He was not a good business manager, lacking application, method, and energy, and being always in financial trouble; but in any clerical or subordinate capacity he was most reliable and efficient. In the later years he drank to excess. Besides the original records of the *Convention of '49* and the valuable *Diario del Visitador Gen. '39-40*, I have hundreds of his letters in various private archives; and indeed, his family doc. form more than one vol. of the Vallejo collection, which should bear his name. His correspondents were men of education and standing in many parts of the world. His widow still lives at Salinas in '85, at the age of 76, being still owner of the Alisal rancho. She gave me a personal *Narrativa*. There were 20 sons and 5 daughters acc. to her own statement. In '40 there had been 13, of whom 9 were living. Besides the 4 named above, I find the following in the *Sta B. Co. Hist.*: Juan, Uldarico, Pablo, Alvano (?), Nathaniel (died), George, Frank, Benjamin, Teresa, Anita, Magdalena, and Amelia. There was also an Estévan. Ramon (perhaps José) was majordomo at S. Juan in '40; Wm A. was customhouse guard in '45-6. Most of the sons seem to have inherited the father's weaknesses rather than his abilities; but several became respectable citizens.

Hartwell (Lorenzo Nelson), 1834, Amer. sailor from the *Catalina* at S. Diego. iii. 412; still there in '40, naturalized and married. Called generally Horatio and Lawrence Hartnell, but I have his authograph of '38.   H. (Wm), 1834, Engl., age 36, testifies in favor of John Reed.   Hartwig, 1847, a naturalist at N. Helv. in June.   Harvan (Wm), 1846, doubtful name at Los Ang.   Harvey (Thos), 1831, mate of the *Catalina*.

Hashagen, 1847, mr of the *Clementine*. v. 577.   Haschal (A. G.), 1846, one of the Mormon col. v. 546; lot at S.F. '47; did not go to Utah; perhaps 'Haskell.' Thales Haskell is also named.   Haskell (Geo.), 1847, Co. B, Morm. Bat. (v. 469).   H. (J. G.), 1847, owner of S.F. lot.   H. (John W.), 1847, Co. F, N.Y. Vol. (v. 499); d. Sta B. '78.   Hasking (Henry), 1847, at Hon. from S.F. on the *Julia*.   Haslitt (Geo.), 1845, perhaps one of Frémont's men. iv. 583, 587; in Sonoma Co. '74; a Cherokee Ind.   Hassard (J. G.), 1848, passp. from Hon.   Hassel (H.), 1848, ditto.   Hastie, 1848, from Hon. on the *Sagadahoc*.

Hastings (Lansford W.), 1843, nat. of Ohio, b. '19, a lawyer who com. a party crossing the plains to Or. '42, and came to Cal. '43 in com. of the immig. party that bears his name. iv. 389-92, 400, 444. His views were those of a filibuster, but he found that the time had not come for a successful movement; so he went back in '44, by sea and across Mex., to publish a worthless book called an *Emigrant's Guide*, and to attract settlers and prospective revolutionists by lectures and other methods. iv. 396-9, 355-6, 2, 6, 20, 26. In '45 he returned with another party overland to Cal. iv. 585-6; but in the spring of '46. after the settlers' revolt had been postponed, went with Clyman's party to Salt Lake in search of more immig., and thus missed the Bear movement. v. 526, 529; but returned in the autumn with Harlan's party, by H.'s new cutoff, which proved so fatal to the Donners, in time to serve as capt. of Co. F, Cal. Bat. v. 529-30, 359, 361. Before going east, however, he and Bidwell had laid out the new town of Sutterville, reported at the time to be intended for a Mormon town, v. 58; and indeed, H. was an agent for the Mormons in the secular phases of their enterprise. v. 548; selecting a site at Montezuma, Solano, where some time in '47-8 he built an adobe house, still standing in '80, and established a ferry across the S. Joaquin. v. 552. In '47-8 he also practised law at S.F., being the owner of town lots. v. 579, 645, 678, 681. In March –April '48 he was trying to recruit a battalion of volunteers to put down an imaginary revolt in the south; in May was elected school trustee at S.F.; in July married Charlotte Catherine, daughter of Hopeful Toler, at Sac., and in Sept. was appointed judge of the northern district. In '49 he was a member of the constit. convention, utilizing his geographical acquirements in the fixing of a boundary. He lived at or near Sac. till '57; then went to Arizona; came back on a visit in '64; and is said to have died in Brazil about '70. He was an intelligent, active man, never without some grand scheme on hand, not overburdened with conscientious scruples, but never getting caught in anything very disreputable. H. (Sam. J.), 1841, mr of the *Tasso* '41-4. iv. 569. Haswell (Robert), 1788, Engl. mate of the *Washington* in voy. to N. W. coast, the 1st Amer. vessel to enter Cal. waters. H. kept a diary which was furnished me by his daughter, Mrs John J. Clark, who died at Roxbury, Mass., in '83, at the age of 80.

Hatch (James B.), 1842, mr of the *Barnstable* '42-3, '44-5; possibly on the coast before. iv. 341, 563, 101; iii. 381; also mr of the *Loo Choo* in '47. v. 511. H. (J. W.), 1848 (?), killed accidentally at Napa '79. H. (Meltliah), 1847, Co. C, Morm. Bat. (v. 469); at Panguich, Utah, '82, H. (Orin), 1847, ditto, at Bountiful, Utah, '82. H. (Prince G.), 1847, in S.F. list of letters. H. (Sam. B.), 1843, at Sta Cruz. Hathaway (Humphrey), 1838, came on a vessel com. by Capt. Howland, and worked as a carpenter at Mont. On Larkin's books '38-43; in Farnham's list of arrests in '40; left Mont.—and his debts— on the *Rajah* in '43. iv. 17, 119. H. (James M.), 1847, Co. A, N.Y.Vol. (v. 499); d. Downieville '51. H. 1848, from Hon. on the *Sagadahoc.* Hatler (Alex.), 1847, owner of S.F. lots. v. 685. Hatton (Wm), 1826, on the *Rover.*

Hauff (Ernest), 1847, musician N.Y.Vol. (v 499); at S.F. '71-4; in Mendocino Co. '83. Haughty (Michael), 1847, Co. I, ditto. Haulstorn (Alex.), 1830, doubtful name in a business account. Haun (John S.), 1846(?), nat. of Mo.; in Sta Clara Co. '76; perhaps son of Wm. H. (Wm), 1846, settler at Sta Clara with wife, Lavinia Whisman, the latter still living in '80. Haust (Joseph), 1847, owner of S.F. lot. Havey (John), 1847, Co. D, N.Y.Vol. (v. 499); at West Point, Calaveras Co., '71-82.

Hawes (Horace), 1847, nat. of N. Y., who visited Cal. from Hon. on the *Angola,* en route to Tahiti, where he had been appointed U.S. consul. In '49 he came back and was prefect at S.F., where he spent the rest of his life as a prominent lawyer and legislator. He was the author of an important treatise on the Cal. mission cases, and of many other well-known briefs, political pamphlets, and speeches; also of the S.F. consolidation bill of '56 and registry law of '66; a member of the assembly for two terms, and of the state senate in '63-4. Hawes was a self-made man, a shrewd lawyer, a man of powerful mind, original in his views and methods, but full of conceit, suspicious by nature, always unpopular, and eccentric to the verge of insanity in his later years. He became a millionaire, and by his will of '71—the year of his death at the age of 58—left the bulk of his estate for the foundation of Mount Eagle University and a Chamber of Industry, making but a comfortable provision for his heirs and relations. But the heirs, in a suit that is one of the *causas célebres* of Cal., succeeded in breaking the will on the ground of the testator's insanity, and thus defeated his plans for the public good and his own permanent fame. His 2d wife, married in '58, was Catherine Coombs, who survived him with a son, Horace, who died in '84, and a daughter, Caroline, who married James, the son of Alfred Robinson, and is still living in '85.

Hawk (Nathan), 1847, Co. B, Morm. Bat. (v. 469); overland mail-carrier in '48, being employed by Brannan. H. (Wm), 1847, ditto; at Salt Lake City '81. Hawkhurst, 1837, perhaps one of the men employed to drive cattle to Or. iv. 85. Hawkins, 1848, lieut with Gen. Lane, Sta Fé to Or. via S. Diego. *Coutts.* H. (Benj.), 1847, Co. A, Morm. Bat. (v. 469); in S. F. letter list '48. H. (John A. or P.), 1847, perhaps of N.Y.Vol. under another name (v. 499); d. at S. F. H. (Sam.), 1845, doubtful name of an overl. immig. iv. 578. H. (Wm), 1830 (?), trapper of Ashley's comp., said to have hunted in the S. Joaquin Val. in very early times, and again in '52. *Mont. Co. Hist.,* 29. H. (Zacarias), 1845, doctor and overl. immig. prob. to Or., and not Cal. iv. 578. Hawley (Jos.), 1842, mr of the whaler *Hague* '42, '44; iv. 566. Haws (Alpheus P.), 1847, sergt Co. D, Morm. Bat. v. 477.

Hay, 1847, Scotchman, of H. & Dickson, S.F. traders at the 'Beehive' store '47–50; owner of town lots. v. 675, 684; left Cal. after '50.   H. (G.C.), 1848, treasurer of S.F.; called 'Dr'; perhaps same as preceding.   Hayden (Geo. W.), 1847, Co. D, N.Y.Vol. (v. 499).   Hayes, 1845, Amer. immig. from Or. in the McM.-Clyman party; prob. went back in '46; but may have been the H. wounded at Natividad. iv. 572; v. 526, 367.   H., 1848, at Mont. from Hon. on the *S. Francisco*.   H. (Elias), 1833, Amer. at Mont. '33–6; in '34–5 making shingles for Abel Stearns. iii. 409.   H. (Jacob), 1846, one of the Mormon col. v. 546; did not go to Utah; d. before '80; called also 'Hayse.' H. (James), 1846, at Mont. as a kind of policeman; in the Cal. Bat., wounded at Natividad in Nov. v. 367; also called John.   H. (Wm B.), 1847, mid. on the U.S. *Dale;* died at sea in '49.   Hayt (Elisha), 1848, doubtful name at Mont.; prob. 'Hyatt.'   Haywood (Philip H.), 1846, mid. on the *Independence;* lieut in Stockton's bat. '47. v. 386, 391–5.

Healy, 1845, on the *Sterling* at Mont.   Hearn (Thos), 1847, Co. E, N.Y. Vol. (v. 499).   Heartstene (H.T.), 1842, lieut U. S. N., sent east by Com. Jones with despatches. iv. 313.   Heath (Chas), 1843, nat. of N.Y., who got a carta in Oct., living at Sta Cruz. iv. 400, 356; ment. at N. Helv. '45–7; in '47 owner of S.F. lot, and builder of a ferry-boat at Benicia. v. 671, 673, 678. H. (Rich. W.), 1846 (?), came as quartermaster U.S.A., and later had a ferry on the Stanislaus. *Tinkham.*   H. (Russell), 1847, doubtful mention at S. Buen.   H. (W.), 1848, passp. from Hon.   Heathcoat, 1847, possibly of N. Y.Vol. under another name.   Heathcote (Theodore), 1846, sergt Co. C, 1st U.S. dragoons; in '48 ordnance sergt at Los Ang.

Heceta (Bruno), 1775, Span. capt. and com. of the *Santiago* in explor. voy. to Cal. and the N. W. coast. i. 241, 247–8, 280, 330.   Hecox (Adna A.), 1846, nat. of Mich., b. 1806, and overland immig. with wife, Margaret M. Hamer, and 3 children. v. 529. Remaining at Sta Clara during the winter— that is, 'taking an active part in the war with Mexicans'—he went to the Sta Cruz region, where he built a saw-mill, and worked as carpenter and builder; went to the mines for a short time in '48; alcalde at Sta Cruz '48–9. v. 642; later justice of the peace; county treasurer '61–3; from '70 in charge of the Sta Cruz light-house till his death, in '83. He was a methodist, and one of the first who preached protestant sermons in Cal. v. 641. His narr. of his early life, overl. trip, and experience in Cal., was published in the S. José *Pioneer* of '77, and was embodied by Willey in the *Sta Cruz Co. Hist.* His testimony on events connected with the 'war' in '46–7, like that of so many other immigrants, has little value. His widow survived him, with the follow- ing child.: Mrs M. E. Stampley of Carson, Nev., Mrs C. M. Brown of S.F., and Adna H. Hecox of S. Luis Ob., all pioneers of '46, and of those born in Cal. Mrs M. Longley of Sta Cruz, Mrs A. Rigg, Laura J., and Orville S. Por- trait of Adna A. in *Sta Cruz Hist.*, 44. He was an active and respectable man of business.   Hedges, 1844, mr of the *Monmouth*. iv. 567.

Heeney (Robert), 1846, marine on the U.S. *Dale;* one of Marston's men in the Sanchez campaign of '47; slightly wounded. v. 381.   Hefferman (Chas), 1847, Co. F, N. Y.Vol. (v. 499); in the mines '48; died at S.F. before '82. Heft (Geo.), 1816, sailor on the *Lydia*. ii. 275.   Hegarty (Peter), 1845, signer of the S. José call to foreigners. iv. 599; on the 1st S.José jury '48.   Hegel (Fred.), 1841, named in Larkin's accts '41–2. iv. 279; said to have been in the Bodega region '48–9; perhaps some confusion or relationship bet. him and 'Hägler;' also 'Hugel,' q.v.   Hehn (Henry), 1847, musician of N.Y.Vol. (v. 499).   Heil (Fred.), 1832, passp. at Mont.; perhaps 'Hegel ' or ' Hugel.' Heinrich (Chas), 1847, Co. B, N.Y.Vol. (v. 299); in the mines '48; later a trader at Sac., where he still lived in '82; nat. of Germany, b. '24; wife from '50, Sarah Neubauer.   Heinricks (Ed.), 1846, Co. C, 1st U.S. dragoons (v. 336). Heitleman, 1847, from Mazatlan with letters from Talbot & Co.

Heleno, grantee of Cosumnes rancho '44.   Helmstadler (James), 1847, Co. B, N.Y.Vol. (v. 499).   Hembkey (Conrad), 1846, Co. C, 1st U.S. dragoons (v. 336).   Hemen (James), 1828, Irish sailor, age 40, at Mont. '28–9.   Hem- enror (M. W.), 1846, doubtful name at Los Ang.   Hemerle (John), 1846, Co. C, 1st U.S. dragoons (v. 336).   Hempstead, 1847, mr of the *Corea*. v. 577.

Hempstead (Sidney C.), 1831, trader on the coast. Hen (Wm), 1846, doubtful name. *Hittell*, and Soc. Cal. Pion. roll. See ' Haun.' Henderson (And. J.), 1846, asst surg. on the U.S. *Portsmouth;* at N.Helv. and Sonoma in Bear times. v. 126, 128, 300; surg. of Stockton's bat. '47. v. 385. H. (Christian), 1846, Fauntleroy's dragoons (v. 232, 247). H. (James), 1842, lieut U.S.N. *Maxwell.* H. (Levin), 1846, sailor in navy, on sentry duty at Mont.; deserts with his escaping prisoners. H. (Moses), 1847, in S.F. letter list. H. (T.), 1848, passp. from Hon. H. (Wm,) 1826, mr of the *Olive Branch* '26-7. iii. 148, 154. H. (Wm), 1870, doubtful name in Farnham's list; perhaps 'Anderson,' q.v. H. (W. T.), 1848, nat. of Tenn., arr. S.F. June; perhaps same as T. above; in '50 slayer of Joaq. Murieta; in Fresno '80. Hendricks (Joseph), 1844, at Sonoma, age 54. H. (Wm), 1848, barber at S.F. v. 682. H. (Wm D.), 1847, Co. D, Morm. Bat. (v. 469); at Richmond, Utah, '82. Hendrickson (Henry), 1847, Co. D, N.Y.Vol. (v. 499); at Vallejo '74. H. (James), 1847, Co. C, Morm Bat. (v. 469). Hendy (James), 1846, marine on the *Congress,* wounded at the S. Gabriel, Jan. '47. v. 395. Henge (T.), 1848, passp. from Hon.

Hennet, 1829, mr of the *John Coleman.* iii. 147. Henriquez (Antonio), artisan at Sta Cruz, 1795. i. 496. H. (Abraham), 1847, Co. F, 3d U.S. artill. (v. 518). Henry (Dan.), 1847, Co. D, Morm. Bat. (v. 469); at Monte, Utah, '82. H. (Francis), 1844, Irish sailor of the *Vandalia,* arrested at Mont. H. (James), 1844, Scotch sailor on the *Vandalia;* prob. same as preceding. iv. 453. Known as ' Scotch Harry;' at Mont. and Sta Cruz '45-6; in Fallon's comp. at S. José; then served 2 years on the *Portsmouth* and *Cyane.* In '48 kept a shop at Mont.; in the mines '49-52; traveled 10 years in dif. parts of the world; went to Frazer River, and died in the Sonoma Co. hospital '76. His narr. was pub. in the Stockton *Indep.* of July 14, '76, but no reliance can be put in details. H. (James), 1847, Co. E, N.Y.Vol. (v. 499). H. (Robert), 1847, owner of S.F. lot. v. 683. Henschel (H. L), 1848, German custom-house broker in S.F. from '52 to '68, the year of his death; left a wife and two daughters. Henshaw (Geo.), 1841, overl. immig. of the Bartleson party, who went back in '42. iv. 266, 270, 275. H. (Hiram), 1846, doubtful name in list of Cal. claimants (v. 462).

Hensley (Samuel J.), 1843, nat. of Ky, and overl. immig. of the Chiles-Walker party. iv. 392, 394, 400. He had been a trapper and had spent some years in N. Mex. In '44 he was naturalized, got a grant of the Agua de Nieves rancho, iv. 670, and entered Sutter's service as supercargo of the launch; signing the order for Weber's arrest. iv. 483. He served as commissary in Sutter's army during the Micheltorena campaign. iv. 485-7, 517. Returning to the north, he took charge of Hock farm and attended to Sutter's general business, being often named in the *N. Helv. Diary.* In '46 he was prominent in fomenting the Bear revolt. v. 80, 104, 127-8, 170; was capt., and later major, of the Cal. Bat. in the south. v. 309, 328, 356, 360, 386, 391-5, 435; had a Cal. claim (v. 462); and a S.F. lot. v. 685. Going east with Stockton in '47, he testified at the Frémont court-martial. v. 454, 456; but returned to Cal. in '48, and after a brief experience in the mines opened a store at Sac. in partnership with Reading. From '50 he engaged in navigation of the Sac. river, and a little later was one of the founders of the Cal. Steam Nav. Co., of which he became president. His residence for many years was at S. José, and he died at Warm Springs, Alameda Co., in '66, at the age of 49. Of his career and that of his fellow-filibusters in '46 enough is said elsewhere; otherwise Maj. Hensley's record is that of an honest and successful man of business, of strong will and well-balanced mind, generous, temperate, and brave. His wife was Helen, daughter of E. O. Crosby, who survived him with a son and daughter. Henysey (James), 1842, Scotch sawyer in a S.F. list.

Herbert (Thos), 1842, Engl. lumberman at S.F., age 33. Herd (Henry), 1834, Amer. in Mont. dist. '34-7. iii. 412. Heredia (Bernardo), settler at S. José from 1791; in '95 owner of Chupadero rancho; in 1803 regidor at S. José. i. 683, 716; ii. 134. Herman (Jacob), 1845, overl. immig. iv. 578, 587; lived at S.F. mission '46-9 with a family; d. before '55. Hermosillo (Nicolás), leader of a revolt at Los Ang. and S. Diego '46. v. 308, 329.

Hernandez (Antonio), saddler instructor 1792-6. i, 615, 684.   H. (Antonio), soldier in S.F. comp. '19-35.   H. (Cornelio), at S. José '49, a soapmaker.   H. (Domingo), a Mex. convict whose term expired in '35.   H. (Dom.), nat. of Cal. and a noted desperado and murderer from '45-6; sentenced to be hanged on one occasion, but saved by the breaking of the rope, only to be hanged by vigilantes in later years. Some of his brothers and sisters are said to have been criminals; but there is little definite information about any of them.   H. (Encarnacion), soldier murdered at Mont. '34. iii. 673.   H. (Felipe), convict settler of 1798; alcalde of Branciforte 1805; grantee of Laguna de Calabazas '33. i. 606; ii. 156; iii. 677.   H. (José), convict settler of 1798, pardoned 1803, grantee of Rinconada de los Gatos '40. i. 606; ii. 156; iii. 712.   H. (Juan), convict settler of 1798. i. 606.   H. (Juan), regidor at S. José '22; stabbed by Mojica. ii. 604-5.   H. (Juan Ant.), at S. José '41, age 58.   H. (Juan María), Mex. at S. José '41, age 65, wife Francisca Lorenzana, child. Pedro b. '20, José Jesus '25; grantee of Ojo de Agua '35. iii. 712.   H. (Juana), poisoned her husband '43. iv. 364.   H. (Mariano), at S. José '41, age 29, wife Rosario Bernal, child. Fernando b. '37, María '38, and 2 others; grantee of Puerto in '44. iv. 672.   H. (Santiago), soldier of S.F. comp. '39-43. iv. 667.   H. (Simon), soldier in the Hidalgo piquete at Mont. '36, age 32.   H. (Tomasa), Cal. claim $100 (v. 462).   Hernano (Antonio), ment. of his lawsuit '47. v. 663.

Herrera (Dolores), 1840, nat. of N. Mex., at S. Luis Ob. to '83.   H. (Ignacio), took church asylum '30. ii. 660.   H. (José), corp. of S.F. comp. prom. to sergt 1811 for bravery in Ind. exped. ii. 91. Still sergt '20-4.   H. (José María), 1825, Mex. sub-comisario at Mont., who was involved in controversies with Gov. Echeandía and was sent to Mex. for alleged complicity in the Solis revolt. ii. 551, 607, 614, 648; iii. 14, 33, 38, 59-85, 117, 125, 159. In '34 he came back in the same capacity with the H. & P. colony; was in new troubles arising from the amours of his wife, Ildefonsa Gonzalez; and was again exiled in '36 because he refused to support the Alvarado govt. iii. 261-7, 377, 436-9, 672; iv. 96. See also biog. ment. in iii. 466. He was a man of much ability and good education, to whom the Californians, without much apparent reason, give a bad character. In '36 he was 33 years old, and had 2 children at Mont., Vicente b. '33, and Eulalia b. '35.   H. (José M.), regidor at Los Ang. '36-8; age 33 in '39; served under Castro '47. iii. 481, 509, 564-5, 636; v. 363.   H. (Tomás), grantee of S. Juan Cap. del Camote '46. v. 637; still a ranchero in S. Luis Ob. '60, having held several local offices after '48.   H. (Trineo), Mex. at S. Miguel rancho, Mont., '36, age 28, wife Antonia García, child Teresa b. 32.

Herriot (Adam), 1846, at Sta Cruz.   Herron (James C.), 1845, mid. on the U.S. *Portsmouth*.   H. (Walter), 1846, one of the Donner party from Ill. v. 530, 532. He came in advance over the mts with Reed; served in the Cal. Bat., Co. B; got a S.F. lot in '47, and aided O'Farrell as a surveyor at Stockton; but I find no later record of him.   Hersey (Stephen), 1832, mr of the *Newcastle*. iii. 383.   Herven (Jon.), 1840, doubtful name of Farnham's list. iv. 17.   Hescock (Isaac), 1845, doubtful name of an Amer. in the Brancif. padron, age 65, in the family of Isabel Patterson (?).   Hess, 1845, at N. Helv., prob. overl. immig. of Grigsby-Ide party. iv. 578-80. His daughter Nancy married John Chamberlain in Jan. '46, and all the fam. went to Or.

Hetherington (Wm E.), 1847, Co. D, N.Y.Vol. (v. 499).   Hense (Sam. E.), 1846, sailor in the navy; in Amador Co. '52-79, the date of his death.   Hewen (Jon.), 1840, in Farnham's list.   Hewes, 1847, mr of the *Iris*. v. 578.   Hewitt (A.), 1846, Co. F, Cal. Bat. (v. 358); perhaps at N. Helv. '48; see also 'Huet' of '45.   H. (Geo.), 1839, Amer. sailor and otter-hunter in Sta B. dist. '39-41. iv. 119, 24.   Hewlett (Palmer B.), 1847, lieut Co. I, N.Y.Vol. v. 504; later militia gen.; in Sonoma Co. '71-82.   Heydenrich (Wm), 1847, Co. D, N.Y.Vol. (v. 499).   Heyerman (A.), 1847 (?), doctor said to have left the *Clementine;* at N. Helv. May '48, on his way to the mines; also said to have lived at Petaluma from '45 (?) to '52, and to have returned in '73.   Heyland (John), 1847, Co. A, N.Y.Vol. (v. 499).   Heyward (James), 1847,

nephew of Com. Shubrick, at Mont. with letters to Larkin; returned to Hon olulu '48.   Heywood (Chas), 1847, lieut on the U.S. *Independence*.

Hibler (Geo.), 1845, Amer. immig. from Or. in McM.-Clyman party. iv. 572, 526; prob. went back in '46.   Hickenlooper (Wm F.), 1847, Co. A, Morm. Bat. (v. 469); reënl.   Hickey, 1818, com. of an Engl. vessel at Mont. ii. 291.   Hickman (Thos), 1842(?), German butcher in Alameda '70–8. iv. 341. Hickmot (John), 1847, Co. E, Morm. Bat. (v. 469).   Hicks (Harry), 1833, Amer. in Mont. dist. '33–5; also called George. iii. 409.   H. (Henry), 1839, negro cook on the *California*.   H. (Joseph), 1833, Amer. tailor on the *Leonor;* at Sta B. '36; perhaps same as Harry. iii. 409.   H. (Joseph), 1846, one of the Mormon col. who remained in Cal.; owner of S.F. lot '47; died before '80. v. 546, 678.   H. (Joseph Henry), 1841, built a house for Prudon at Sonoma; prob. same as Harry and Joseph of '33.   H. (Wm), 1843, nat. of Tenn., overl. immig. from Mo. in Walker-Chiles party. iv. 392, 400; at Sutter's Fort '47; claimed a land grant on the Cosumnes, iv. 671, where the town of Hicksville was named for him, and where he died in '84, at the age of 67. His wife was a Mrs Wilson, who died a few years before him.   Hicky, 1847, at N. Helv.; prob. Hicks.   Hidalgo (Miguel), at Mont. and Los Ang. '35. iii. 285.

Higares (Francisco), 1833, named as a Dutch shoemaker from the U.S. at Los Ang. in '36, age 29. iii. 409.   Higgins, 1846, in Pt Reyes region. *Marin Co, Hist.*   H., 1848, from Australia with his family. *El Dorado Co. Hist.* H., 1848, with Buttum in the mines.   H., 1848, deserter arrested at S. José. v. 663.   H. (Edward), 1847, at work on Larkin's house at Benicia '48. v. 673.   H. (Edward), 1846, act. lieut U.S.N., and capt. Stockton's bat. '46–7; later capt. in merchant marine N.Y., and officer in confed. navy; in '75 agent of P.M.S.S.Co. at S.F., where he died in that year. v. 386.   H. (Isaac), 1848, in S.F. letter list.   H. (James), 1841, mid. on the U.S. *St Louis*.   H. (James), 1830, one of Young's party. iii. 174.   H. (John), 1830, Irish trapper of Young's party from N. Mex., where he had been naturalized. iii. 180, 388. At Sta B. in '36, age 39, and single, being often a companion of Nidever in hunting tours. From '37 named on Larkin's books at Mont.; in '40 a lumberman on Carmelo Creek, where he was arrested and sent to S. Blas. iv. 18, 23; never came back.   H. (Nelson), 1847, capt. Co. D, Morm. Bat. v. 477; with wife and 4 children, but did not reach Cal. v. 477, 482.   H. (N.D.), 1847, servant to officer of Morm. Bat. (v. 469).   H. (Silas G.), 1847, Co. C, N.Y.Vol. (v. 499).   H. (W.D.), 1848, passp. from Hon.

Higuera, ment. in 1793–1808. i. 617, 640; ii. 192.   H. in Mont. revolt '37. iii. 525.   H. (Antonino), in S. José district '41, age 38, wife Josefa Alviso, 5 children named, but all called Alviso in the padron. The date of this man's death, in '46, is the turning-point in litigation for the Livermore rancho now in progress '85. Some papers of my col. bearing on the case—in which Antonino's name seems to have been rather clumsily forged before the papers came into my hands—were introduced as evidence.   H. (Antonio), soldier of S.F. comp. '19–22; at S. Mateo '35.   H. (Bernarda Soto de), widow at S. José '41, age 52, child. Joaquin b. '15, José Ant. '18, Ramona '22, Juan María '25, Dominga '32, Encarnacion '36.   H. (Bernardo), in Los Ang. dist. '19–43; grantee of Rincon de los Bueyes. ii. 355, 565; iv. 635.   H. (Dolores), arrested at Los Ang. '45. iv. 541.   H. (Doroteo), at Los Ang. '46.   H. (Estévan), soldier of S.F. comp. '19–30; militiaman '37.   H. (Francisco), soldier of S.F. comp. '19–24; elector '27; drowned in '30. ii. 592, 594.   H. (Fran.), soldier of S.F. comp. '37–42.   H. (Fran.), son of Bernardo; at S. Pascual '46. v. 352; claimant of Rincon de Bueyes '52. iv. 635.   H. (Fulgencio), son of José; soldier of S.F. comp. '19–30; alf. of militia at S. José '37. iii. 732; grantee of Agua Caliente, Alam. Co., '39. iii. 711; in '41 living at his rancho, age 42, wife Clara Pacheco, child. Albino b. '24, Tomás '26, Narciso '29, Gabriel '31, José Jesus '32, Fernando '35, Leandro '37, Francisca '22, María L. '27, María de los Ang. '36.   H. (Gregorio), at Los Ang. '39, prob. son of Bernardo, age 29.

Higuera (Ignacio), settler at S. José 1790; majordomo in 1805, killed by Ind., but ment. in 1807. i. 478; ii. 34, 135.   H. (Ignacio), soldier of S.F.

comp. '30–40; at Sonoma in '44, age 33. H. (Ignacio), soldier of S.F. comp. '35–6; sergt '39–40. iii. 702; encargado of the contra costa '39. iii. 705. H. (Ignacio), soldier of Mont. comp. '36, age 24. H. (Ignacio), maj. at Sta B. 1799–1801. ii. 120. H. (Ignacio), soldier at Sta B. before '37. H. (Jerónimo), at S. José '41, age 23, wife Rosario Félix, one child. H. (Joaquin), settler at Los Ang. 1790; alcalde in 1800. i. 461, 661; ii. 349. H. (Joaquin), regidor, alcalde, and juez de campo at S. José at dif. times '20–46. ii. 378, 604–5; iii. 729; iv. 662, 684; Cal. claim '46–7 (v. 462); claimant for Pala, Sta Clara Co., '52.

Higuera (José), soldier of S.F. comp. '19–41; perhaps the man who settled in Napa. H., at S. José '41, age 66, wife Ramona García, child. Florencio b. '36, Encarnacion '18 (?), Miguel '37, Rita '40. H. (José), grantee of Tularcitos and Llano del Abrevadero '21–2, and of Pala '35. ii. 594, 664, 712–13; Antonia H. et al. were claimants. H. (José), perhaps the same; the distrib. of his estate took place in March '46, and I have the orig. expediente in *Pico* (*Ramon*), *Doc. Hist. Cal.*, i. 107–24, which shows the following heirs: Fulgencio, Valentin, Mariano, 5 minors whose guardian was Mariano (prob. their father by a daughter of José), Mrs Robert Livermore, wife of Lázaro H., Florentino Archuleta, and Antonio Mesa, each receiving 133 cattle, 88 vines, and 10 fruit-trees. It was in these papers that the name of Antonino was fraudulently introduced, as noted above. H. (José), ment. in '46. v. 235. H. (José Ant.), son of Manuel; at S. José '41, age 52, wife Ambrosia Pacheco, child. Ricardo b. '22, Juan '24, Miguel '26, Leonardo '27, Isidro '29, Fernando '33, and Encarnacion '31. H. (José María), at Salinas rancho '36, age 50, wife María de Jesus Cota, child. Juan b. '14, Tomás '18, Pilar '19, Blas '21, José '26, Encarnacion '28, Gertrudis '31, Manuel '33, and Luisa '35.

Higuera (Juan), in '31 comisionado of S. Juan B., and regidor of Mont. iii. 212, 307, 672, 692; juez aux. '42. iv. 653; at S. José '50. H. (Juan), of Sta Cruz, killed at Los Ang. '45. iv. 492. H. (Juan), at Los Ang. '39, age 45. H. (Juan José), soldier at S. José mission 1797–1800. i. 556. H. (Juan José), juez at S. Juan B. '42. iv. 661. H. (Juan José), at Los Ang. '19, '25. ii. 354; iii. 7. H. (Lázaro), at N. Helv. '47; his wife was an Higuera, daughter of José. H. (Leonardo), in Los Ang. revolt '46. v. 308; Cal. claim of $12,072 (v. 462); age 37 in '39. H. (Manuel), soldier and settler at S. José and S. Juan B. before 1800. i. 477, 558; in 1793 named in S. José padron as a soldier, wife Antonia Arredondo, child. Ignacia, Ana María, Gabriela, José Joaquin, and José Ant. H. (Manuel), inválido of S.F. comp. '19–29, perhaps the same. H. (Manuel), at S. José '41; age 32, wife María N. Mesa, child. Antonio M. b. '30, José Jesus '32, José Balfino '37, José María '40, Argentina '34, María Ant. '36. H. (Manuel), at Los Ang. '46. H. (Mariano), at Los Ang. '39–46. H. (Mariano), at S. José '41, age 26, wife María Antonia Higuera, child. Emilio b. '39, José '41, Rosario '32, María Ascension '34, Inés '38. H. (Marta Frias de), cl. of Entre Napa rancho.

Higuera (Nicolás), soldier of S.F. comp. '19–23; alcalde on the frontier and grantee of Entre Napa and Carneros ranchos '36. iii. 705, 711, 722; at N. Helv. '48. H. (Policarpo), soldier at Sta B. before '37. H. (Salvador), soldier and settler at Sta Cruz and S. José 1791–1800. i. 495, 556, 716. H. (Secundino), at Los Ang. '46. H. (Tomás), soldier of S.F. comp. '30–2. H. (Valentin), resid. of Sta Clara region from '41, grantee of Pescadero rancho '43. iv. 672; juez de paz, suplente, '46, at S. José '46. v. 662; died '79, age 70. Híjar (Cárlos N.), 1834, nephew of José M., with whom he came in the colony in '34, and again in '45; and in '77, then a resident of S. José, gave me his recollections of *California in '34.* H. (José María), 1834, a wealthy and influential Mex. of Jalisco who joined J. M. Padrés and others in organizing the Cal. colony that bears their name. He also got an appointment as gov.; but Gov. Figueroa refused to recognize his title, the colony was a failure, and H. was sent to Mex. in '35 on a charge of conspiracy, which was but very slightly founded in fact. iii. 259–69, 272–91, 344–5, 383, 613, 652, 670. Nothing is known of his experience in Mex.; but in '45 he was sent back to Cal. as a commissioner of the govt to prepare for resisting the U.S. He died at Los Ang. very soon after his arrival. iv. 526-31, 631. He was an honorable man of many accomplishments and frail health, with little fitness or fondness for political wrangles.   Hilgers (Gerard), 1846, at Mont.; owner of S.F. lot '47.

Hill, 1848, called major at Mont.   H., 1847, at N. Helv.; brother of Tom Hill, Delaware Ind.   H., 1848, mr of the *Rhone*. v. 580.   H. (Daniel Antonio), 1823, nat. of Mass., who came from Hon. on the *Rover*, and settled at Sta B. ii. 495, 573; iv. 117. He was baptized by P. Ripoll in '25, iii. 29, being then 26 years old; and soon married Rafaela Ortega, being naturalized in '29. Robinson, *Life in Cal.*, 89, describes him as 'a sort of factotum for the whole town, carpenter or mason by turns as his services were needed.' In '36 he had 6 children. In '45 he leased the Sta B. mission. iv. 553, 558, 644; in '46 was the grantee of La Goleta rancho, having some trouble with the Flores govt. v. 317, 330, 632, 644; regidor in '49; went east in '60 on a visit; and died at Sta B. in '65. A son, Ramon J., was assemblyman and court interpreter, dying in '84. One of his daughters married Dr Nicholas Den, and another, Susana, married T. W. More in '53.   H. (Henry de Jesus), 1840, German who got a pass. in June; perhaps Jos. Henry.   H. (Henry), 1847, owner of S.F. lot; nat. of Va, and memb. of the constit. convention in '49.   H. (John), 1846, sailor of the navy, on sentry duty at Mont.; deserts with his prisoners. H. (John), 1847, later policeman.   H. (John E.), 1847, Co. D, N.Y.Vol. (v. 499.); d. at Pendleton, Or., '82.   H. (Joseph Henry), 1834, German from Mex. in the H. & P. col. iii. 412; at Sta Cruz '42-3.   H. (Thos), 1845, Delaware Ind. in Frémont's party, who distinguished himself by bravery on several occasions. iv. 583; v. 367, 371, 400.   H. (Thos J.), 1847, Co. A, N. Y. Vol. (v. 499); at S.F. '71-82.   H. (Wm Luther), 1831, nat. of N.Y. and partner of Louis Bouchet in a Los Ang. vineyard; died this year, making his will on the *Catalina* in July. There was a property of $406 for his father, Peter Hill. iii. 405.   Hilton (Benj.), 1847, Co. D, N. Y. Vol. (v. 499); d. Mont. '47.   H. (Gilman), 1845, one of the men lost on the *Warren's* launch. iv. 587; v. 384.   Hilts, 1848, mate of the *Isaac Walton* from N.Y. *Grimshaw.*

Hina (Jack), 1847, owner of S.F. lot.   Hinckley, 1847, mr of the *Alice*. v. 576.   H., 1848, mr of the *Starling*. v. 400.   H., 1848, from Hon. on the *Currency Lass*.   H. (Azra E.), 1837, Co. B, Morm. Bat. (v. 469); a Utah farmer '81.   H. (F. G.), 1842, in Dwinelle's list; wife Susana Suart (?); doubtless a confused ref. to Capt. Wm S.   H. (Sam. A.), 1844, Amer. who rec'd naturalization in June. iv. 453.   H. (Thomas), 1831-2, mr or sup. of the *Crusader*. iii. 382. He was a brother of Wm S., a partner of Henry A. Peirce at Honolulu, and died in Cent. America on his voy. home.   H. (Wm Crawley), 1847, nat. of Mass., from Valparaíso on the *Georgiana;* mr of the *Providence* in '47-8, to Tahiti, Hon., Mazatlan, then up the Sac. from Sta Cruz with a cargo of goods, converting the vessel temporarily into a country store; at S.F. from '49 to '72, when he gave me an autobiog. sketch. v. 580.

Hinckley (Wm Sturgis), 1830, nat. of Mass., nephew of Wm Sturgis, for several years a trader at Honolulu, and mr of the *Volunteer*, going to the U. S. iii. 85, 149, 170, 179. In '33-4 he came again as sup. of the *Don Quixote*, and in '34-5 mr of the *Avon*. iii. 381-2. After rendering aid to Alvarado in his revolution of '36, for which he was poetically and otherwise sharply criticised by Mexicans, his vessel having been wrecked, apparently, he went to Hon. on the *Quixote*. iii. 466-1, 487; iv. 82, 103, 116, 141. In '37-8 he was mr of the *Diana* or *Kamamalu*, being arrested at S.F. for smuggling, still a confidential friend of the gov., and from this time interested in business with Nathan Spear and Leese at S.F., obtaining and occupying a lot on Montgomery St. iii. 549, 699, 705, 709-10; iv. 699. In '39 he was mr and owner of the *Corsair*, being again in trouble with the revenue authorities, also grantee of town lot. iii. 705; iv. 103, 130; v. 681. In '42, dating his permanent residence from '40, he was naturalized and married; in '44 was alcalde, getting more lots. iv. 666, 676, 679, 683; in '45-6 capt. of the port, having much controversy with Leidesdorff and Forbes, escaping arrest by Frémont's men as a Mex. official by death in June '46, at the age of 39. iv. 593, 666; v. 3, 131, 136, 178, 649, 681. His

1st wife went east in '37, iv. 101, and died in Mass. '40; his 2d wife was Susana, daughter of Ignacio Martinez, who, after H.'s death, married Wm M. Smith in '48. I have no record of children. Capt. Hinckley was a handsome, jovial, intelligent man, immensely popular with the natives, somewhat reckless in the use of his tongue when under the influence of liquor. If there was anything he liked better than contraband trade it was probably practical joking. Some of his jokes, like the one of Christmas night at S. Juan in '37, are not exactly adapted to print; and for others space is lacking; but I may note how, in an interview with Gov. Alvarado on matters of state, he disposed of an over-inquisitive secretary who came in too often to snuff the candle, by filling the snuffers with powder; also how Gen. Vallejo avenged himself for some prank by mounting H. on a bear-hunting horse at Sonoma. The horse made it very lively for the mariner, who returned on foot with tales of encounters with grizzlies not wholly credited by the listeners.   Hinds (R. B.), 1837-9, surgeon in Belcher's exped.; author of *Regions of Vegetation, Botany* and *Zoölogy* of the exped. iv. 143-6.   Hinton, see 'Hoornbeck.'   Hintz (Herman), 1847, owner of S.F. lot.

Hipwood (Thos), 1847, sergt Co. F, N. Y. Vol. v. 504; killed in L. Cal. '48.   Hitchcock, 1844, guide of the Stevens immig. party. iv. 475-6. Acc. to Schallenberger he had no family, the boy generally called H., Jr, being Patterson. Mrs P. of that party with 3 children was apparently H.'s daughter. He claimed to have visited Cal. 11 years before, and had possibly been one of Walker's party in '33.   H. (Isaac), 1847, Co. F, 3d U. S. artill. (v. 518); in the mines '49; in Salinas Val. '77-80; d. at Sta Rita, from an accident, in '81, at the age of 64.   H. (John C.), 1847, Co. E, N. Y. Vol. (v. 499).   H. (R. B.), 1845, lieut on the U. S. *Savannah*.   H. (Rufus), 1848, overl. immig., who kept a boarding-house at N.Helv. in '48, with son and 2 daughters; later kept a hotel on the Amer. Riv. and at Green Springs, where H. and wife died of small-pox. One of the daughters, Mrs Lappeus, was in Or. '72; the other dead.   Hitt (Calvin), 1848, Co. H, N.Y.Vol. (v. 499); at Winona, Minn., '82.

Hoar (John A.), 1843 (?), prob. error in a list of pioneers; in S. F. '54. Hoarde (John), 1833, said to have been a member of Walker's party. iii. 391.   Hoban (Chas F.), 1847, nat. of N. Y., from Honolulu on the *Com. Shubrick;* Brannan's clerk at Mormon Isl. '49; d. S.F. '63, age 43.   Hobson (Joseph), 1848, nat. of Md, perhaps came on the *Lady Adams* from Callao; memb. of constit. conven. in '49.   H. (Wm L.), 1847, from Valparaíso with letters from Atherton; at Hon. as sup. of the *María Helena;* of S. F. guard '49.   Hodges (Hiram B.), mr of the *Monmouth.*   Hoen (Francis), 1845, overl. immig. of the Swasey-Todd party. iv. 576, 587; for a time in Sutter's employ; in '46 owner of S.F. lots and candidate for treasurer. v. 295, 684-5; kept a cigar-store; still in S.F. '54.

Hoeppner (Andrew), 1844, German long in Russian employ at Sitka, where he married a half-breed wife. The exact date and manner of his coming to Cal. are not known, but he was here in '45. iv. 453. Lived at Yerba Buena and Sonoma '45-9; a musician and man of many accomplishments, besides defeating Vioget in an eating-match, as Davis relates. In '47 he had great expectations from his warm springs of Annenthal, near Sonoma, as advertised in the *Star.* v. 667. Markof visited him in '45 and Sherman in '47. In '48 he was 2d alcalde at Sonoma. v. 668; and is named at N. Helv. on his way to the gold mines. About '49 he left his wife and went to Hon. and Chile, where he is said to have died about '55.   Hoffheins (Jacob), 1847, Co. B, Morm. Bat. (v. 469).   Hoffman (Chas), 1847, perhaps of N.Y.Vol. under another name. H. (Geo. W.), 1847, Co. A, N.Y.Vol. (v. 499).   H. (Henry), 1847, Co. F, 3d U.S. artill. (v. 528).   H. (Henry A.), 1847, ditto; corporal. v. 519.   Hoffstetter (John J.), 1847, died at N. Helv.; property sold at auction.   Hoit (John), 1846, Co. G, Cal. Bat. (v. 358).

Holbrook (Washington), 1848, sup. of the *Sabine;* came back on the *Elizabeth* from Hon.; negotiates for lot at S.F. v. 681.   Holdaway (Shadrach), 1847, Co. C, Morm. Bat. (v. 469); at Provo. Utah, '82.   Holden (Dr), 1848, with Gen. Lane from N. Mex. for Or.; in S. Diego region Dec.   H. (W. S.),

1848, passp. from Hon. Holland (F. S.), 1847, at Benicia. v. 673. H. (J.), 1847, in S.F. letter list. Hollingsworth (John McHenry), 1847, lieut Co. I, N.Y.Vol. v. 504; memb. of the constit. conven. '49; at Georgetown, D. C., '74-82. H. (Z.), 1846, an overl. immig. with Russell, at Sonoma; killed by Ind. in the mines '48; left a family in Solano, consisting of Harriet (later Mrs Anderson), John D., Hezekiah S., Joseph B., Wm T., and Sarah E. (later Mrs Duncan). Holloway (Adam), 1847, doubtful date; veteran of the Mex. war; at S. José '52-79; brewer and chief of fire dept; left a family at his death in '79; also accredited to '46. H. (M.), 1846, came to Sta Clara Co. (?). Holly (Gray), 1834, named in Larkin's accts. Holman (James D.), 1848, left Cal. a week after the discov. of gold; d. at Portland, Or., '82. H. 1847, lieut of Morm. Bat. (?); prob. 'Holmes.'

Holmes, 1848, Conn. mechanic in the mines. H., 1841; surgeon of U.S. ex. ex. (?). H. (H. P.), 1846, in Sonoma Co. '52-77; doubtful date of arrival. H. (John Andrew Christian), 1827, Boston trader, sup. and mr of the *Franklin*, *Maria Ester*, and *Catalina* '27-32. iii. 147-8, 176-7, 381. He died in March '32 between Acapulco and Callao. His wife Rachel came from Hon. to Cal. the same year to meet him, but only to hear of his death; and she soon married Thos O. Larkin, a fellow-passenger on the *Newcastle.* iii. 408. H. (Jonathan), 1847, Co. D, Morm. Bat., and presid. of a party on the return in '48, after working as shoemaker at N. Helv. v. 496. Holstein (W.), 1845, mr of the *Maria.* iv. 567. Holt (John), 1846, veteran of 1812, sailor in the navy, in Stockton's bat., at S. Gabriel '72, age 81. *Los Ang. Express.* H. (Wm), 1847, Co. C, Morm. Bat. (v. 469). Holton (Benj. D.), 1847, Co. F, 3d U.S. artill. (v. 518). Hommitch (John), 1847, Co. K, N.Y.Vol. (v. 499). Honey (Wm), 1847, owner of S.F. lot.

Hood (Frisbie), 1848, negro steward on the *Isaac Walton;* at Mokelumne Hill '52. *Grimshaw.* H. (Wm), 1846, Scotch carpenter at S.F. '47-8, of H. & Wilson; owner of lots and a house. v. 650, 684-5; in Sonoma Co. '50-77. Hook (Henry), 1831, writes to Cooper from Sta Fé; connected with the *Globe*, and had apparently been in Cal. H. (Solomon), 1846, one of the Donner party who survived; a son of Mrs Elizabeth Donner. v. 530, 534. W. C. Graves tells me he saw H. in Lake Co. in '63-4. H. (Wm), 1846, brother of Sol., who died in the Sierra. v. 530, 534. Hooker, 1841, sec. of Sir Geo. Simpson. Hooker (Wm), 1840, sent to Mont. from Branciforte; written 'Guca.' Hooper (Simon), 1840, Co. C, 1st U.S. dragoons (v. 336). H. (Wm M.), 1833, from Boston, with a letter from Childs to Larkin. iii. 409; went to Hon. in '45, and returned in '48; prob. the same who advertised as a merchant at S. F. '48-9; of the firm Cross, Hobson & Co. Hoornbeck (A. T.D.), 1848, known as Francis Hinton; died at S. Luis Rey '70. Hoover (Westley), 1846, overl. immig. with a family, who settled at S. José, where he served on the 1st jury in '48. v. 529. H., 1846, at N. Helv. in charge of a launch in Feb.; Sutter mentions him as a scientific man who superintended his farm for several years, and who was thought to be living at Sta Clara in '76; perhaps Westley, though he could not have been an immig. of '46.

Hope (Alex. W.), 1848, nat. of Va, who had been surg. in U.S.A.; at Los Ang. '48-56, where he died; memb. of 1st Cal. senate. H. (Gerard), 1834, Irish hatter of H. & Day at Mont. '34-6, age 30. iii. 412. H. (John), 1833, named in Larkin's accts '33-4; perhaps the same. Hoppe (Jacob D.), 1846, nat. of Md, and overl. immig.; owner of town lots, proprietor and editor of the *Californian*, and candidate for alcalde in '47-8. v. 652, 658, 685; projector of the new town of Halo Chemuck. v. 674; went to the mines, was a memb. of the constit. convention of '49, and settled at S. José, where he made a fortune in trade and lost it by speculation. Claimant of Ulistac rancho. v. 674; killed by the explosion of the *Jenny Lind* in '53, at the age of about 40. He was an enterprising and popular man, against whom nothing appears.

Hopper (Chas), 1841, nat. of N. C., a hunter who came with the Bartleson party, but went back as guide with part of the comp. in '42. iv. 270-1, 275-6, 279, 342. In '47 he came back overl. to Cal. with his family, v. 556, and bought a Napa farm, where he spent the rest of his life, dying in '80, at the age of 81, and leaving 5 children. *Hopper's Narrative* in my col. was written from conversations with H. by R. T. Montgomery in '71. Portrait in *Menefee's Hist. Sketch-book*, 128.   H. (James), 184, in Sta Clara Val. '60. *Hittell.*   H. (John), 1848, on 1st S. José jury.   H. (Thomas), 1847, nat. of Mo., and overl. immig. with his wife, Minerva Young; in Sta Cruz region '47-8; in the mines '48-9. From '49 at dif. places in Sonoma Co., being in '80 a rich landowner with 7 children. Portrait in *Sonoma Co. Hist.*, 384.   H. (Wm), 1847, Co. G, N.Y. Vol. (v. 499); d. Los Ang. '47.

Horden (Stephen), 1844, doubtful name of an Amer. in S.F. list.   Horn (Wm), 1846, settler in Sta Clara Val. with fam.; Cal. claim (v. 462).   Horndell (Joseph), 1847, Co. B, N.Y. Vol. (v. 499); at St Louis, Mo., '82.   Horner (John M.), 1846, one of the Mormon col. from N. J. with wife. v. 546; settled as a farmer at mission S. José, with a variation of mining experience in '48. In partnership with his brother, who came in '49-50; he took a prominent part in the early annals of Alameda Co. By agriculture, trade in farm produce, and land speculations, the Horners became rich and extended their operations to the peninsula of S.F., where their name is preserved in Horner's Addition. They lost their property in '54, and from that time lived on their Alameda farm till '80, when they went to the Sandwich Islands.   Horra (Antonio de la Concepcion), 1796, Span. friar who served at S. Miguel for a very brief term, and was sent away by Pres. Lasuen in '97 on a charge of insanity. In Mex. he made a long report against the Cal. friars, and the investigation of his charges formed one of the causas célebres of mission annals. i. 560-1, 567, 587-97.   Horry (Irwin), 1847, owner of S.F. lot.   H. (James), 1848, servant of Brooks' party in the mines; killed by Ind. in Bear Valley.   Horsely (Joseph), 1833, at Mont. '33-4; also called Horseman.   Horton, 1847, mr of the *Triad.* v. 580.   H. (Wm), 1840, in Farnham's list of arrested foreigners. iv. 17.   Hoseir (E.), 1848, in S.F. letter list.   Hoskins (Henry), 1847, Co. E, Morm. Bat. (v. 469.)   Hotchkiss (H.), 1848, passp. from Hon.

Houck (James), 1845, Amer. immig. from Or. in the McM.-Clyman party. iv. 572; about 10 days after arrival at Sutter's Fort he was charged with an attempt at rape, and nothing more is known of him.   Hough (H.), 1845, purser's clerk on the *Savannah.*   Houghtailing, 1847, at Hon. from S.F. Houghton (Sherman O.), 1847, sergt of Co. A, N.Y. Vol. v. 503. A nat. of N. Y., who became a prominent lawyer of Sta Clara Co., being mayor of S. José, county recorder, and member of congress '71-5. His 1st wife was Mary M. Donner, who died in '60 leaving one daughter, Mary M.; the 2d wife was Eliza P. Donner, who still lived in '85 with 7 children, Eliza P., Sherman O., Clara H., Chas D., Francis J., Stanley W., and Herbert S. (died '76). Portrait of S. O. H. in *Sta Clara Co. Hist.*, 32.   Houptman (Wm), 1840, German who got passports in '40 and '44, the former in Mex., so that he may have come later. iv. 120.   House (James), 1844, at Sonoma, age 50.   H. (Joseph), 1846, came to S. José. *Hall.*   Houston (Thos B. or T.), 1846, act. mid. on the U. S. *Dale;* died '63, as lieut. at Naples.

How (Oliver H.), 1847, Co. C, N.Y. Vol. (v. 499).   Howard (Wm), 1848, Swedish sailor on the U.S. *St Mary*, who quit the service at S.F., went to the mines, and in '50 settled in Sonoma Co., where he still lived in '80, at a R.R. station bearing his name; wife from '55 Caroline Kolmer of '46; 9 children. Portrait in *Sonoma Co. Hist.*, 296.   H. (Wm Davis Merry), 1839, nat. of Boston, sent to sea by his mother with a view to needed discipline, who came to Cal. as a cabin-boy on the *California.* iv. 117, 119; and worked for a while as clerk for Stearns at Los Ang. He went east in '40, and came back in '42 as sup. of the *California.* At Honolulu, on the way, he married Mary Warren, adopted daughter of Capt. Grimes, a native of Hon. and daughter of Wm Warren, q.v., who was returning on the vessel from Boston, where she had been educated. In '43-5 H. acted as sup. of the *Vandalia* and *California.* iv. 564, 569, 640; and in '45 opened a store at S.F. with Henry Mellus, buying the H.B. Co. establishment. In '46-9 Mellus & H. were the leading firm in town, and after the gold excitement did an immense business, having branches at Sac. in charge of Brannan, and at S. José under Belden's care, both being partners in the interior business, as was Talbot H. Green in the city. The firm was dissolved in '50, and H. retired a rich man. See mention of H. in various minor matters, he being a member of the council, and admin. of the Leidesdorff estate. v. 240, 321, 359, 539, 648–52, 678; cl. for the S. Mateo rancho. v. 660. After a visit to the east in '53 his health failed, and he died in '56, at the age of about 37. Howard was a large man, of fine personal appearance; jovial, generous, and humorous; fond of practical jokes, late suppers, and private theatricals; but always attentive to business. He had no political ambitions, but was fond of helping his friends into office. Among all the pioneer traders of S.F. there was probably no better man, nor more deservedly popular. A street in the city bears his name. His 1st wife died in '49, leaving one child, who died; and his 2d wife, Agnes Poett, married in '49, survived him, marrying his brother George, and later a man named Bowie. A son by the 2d wife was still living in '80.

Howe (Elisha W.), 1848, nat of R. I., who came by sea and went to the mines; in S. Luis Ob. '50–83; married Gabriela Estudillo, and had 6 children. H. (Franklin), 1846, Co. C, 1st U.S. dragoons (v. 336).   H. (Henry), 1848, in Sonoma, as he stated later.   Howell, 1848, from Honolulu.   H. (Chas), 1848, mining at Rose Bar.   H. (Isaac), 1846, nat. of N.Y., and overl. immig., settling in Napa Co. with his family. In '69 he moved to S. Luis Ob., where he died in '78, at the age of 80; known as Father Howell; left a widow and 7 children, one or more of whom came with him in '46. A son is ment. at N. Helv. in '48; the widow died in '83, also aged 80; two of the sons were John and Joseph.   H. (John), 1846, Cal. Bat. (v. 358); at Sonoma and N. Helv. '47–8; perhaps son of Isaac.   H. (T.C.D.), 1847, Co. E, Morm. Bat. (v. 469); in '82 a farmer at Clifton. Id.   H. (Wm), 1847, Co. E, Morm. Bat. (v. 469).   Howes (Horan), 1847, Soc. Cal. Pion. roll.   Howland (Henry S.), 1837, mr of the *Com. Rodgers* '37–8. iv. 103.   H. (Wm), 1848, sailor on *I. Walton*.

Hoxie, 1847, mr of the *S. Boston*. v. 550.   Hoyer (Cornelius), 1842, mr of the *Fama* '42–3, and perhaps '41; at Hon. '36. iv. 141, 565; passp. from Hon. '48.   Hoyt (Aug. A.), 1846, Fauntleroy's dragoons (v. 232, 247); Co. F, Cal. Bat. (v. 358).   H. (C.), 1847, at Mont. '47–8.   H. (Daniel C.), 1847, Co. K, N.Y. Vol. (v. 499).   H. (Henry P.), 1847, Co. A, Morm. Bat. (v. 469); d. on the return journey.   H. (R.C.M.), 1846, leased land and house at Mont.; Taber & H., hotel-keepers at Mont. '47–8; at S. José '50.

Hubbard, 1845, apparently one of Frémont's men; v. 453, 583, 587, at N. Helv. Feb. '46; in F.'s exped. of '48, when he died.   H. (Charles), 1834, German and naturalized Mex.; mr of the *Peor es Nada* '34–5, and of the Soledad '43. iii. 383, 412; iv. 568.   H. (Geo. C.), 1847, lieut Co. K, N.Y. Vol. v. 504; a printer; memb. of legisl. '49; d. in Ill. before '60.   H. (John E.), 1848, nat. of Chile, who came with his parents to S.F. at the age of 6; liquor-dealer at Vallejo '79. *Solano Co. Hist.*   H. (T. W.), 1845, nat. of N.Y.; came at age of 5; messenger in assembly '55.   H. (W. H.), 1847, rented a house at Sonoma.   Hubbell (Ezekiel), 1801, mr of the *Enterprise*. ii. 2. Huber (Henry), 1841, overl. immig. of the Bartleson party. iv. 270, 275, 279; grantee of Honcut rancho '45, for which he was an unsuccessful claimant in '53. iv. 671; ment. at Sutter's Fort '46; owner of lots at S.F. '47–8. v. 676. I think he is the man who for 15 years or more, down to '85, has kept a well-known liquor-store at S.F.   Hubert (Nicholas), 1844, deserter from the *Warren*.   Huchas (Heinrich), 1847, musician N.Y. Vol. (v. 499).

Huddart (John M.), 1847, lieut Co. F, N.Y. Vol. v. 504; d. at the Sandw. Isl. before '60.   Hudgekison (David), 1847, contract to haul lumber at N. Helv. Dec.   Hudson (A. J.), 1845, at S. Luis Ob. '68–83. *S. Luis Ob. Co. Hist.*, 388.   H. (Benj.), 1847, Co. K, N.Y. Vol. (v. 499).   H. (David), 1845, nat. of Mo., b. '20, overl. immig. of the Grigsby-Ide party, iv. 578, 587, with his brother, Wm, and sister, Mrs York; settled in Napa Val., where—but for his service with the Bears, v. 110, later in the Cal. Bat. (v. 356), and a brief mining experience in the mines '48—he lived till '73. Then he moved to a farm in Coyote Val., Lake Co., where he lived in '81 with wife—Francis

Griffith, married in '47—and 6 children, Rodney J. b. '50, Lavonia, Elbert, Ella, Ada, Bertha (died), and Robert L. Prob. still alive in '85. In '72, at Calistoga, he wrote his *Autobiography* for me. Portrait in *Lake Co. Hist.*, 188. Six of his brothers and sisters came to Cal., sooner or later. H. (Edward), 1847, owner of S.F. lot. v. 682; still in S.F. '52, a carpenter. H. (Hiram), 1847, laborer and watchman at Mont. H. (James T.), 1845, a trader at S. Pedro. H. (John T.), 1805–6, mr of the *Tamana.* ii. 24. H. (Martin), 1848, nat. of Va, brother of David, and overl. immig. with wife and 5 children; settled in Guilicos Val., Son. Co., '48–9 and lived there until his death in '71, at the age of 64. His widow, Elizabeth McAlroy, and 7 children were living in '80. The sons who came in '48, and were still living in '80, were Michael E, John W., David A., and Matthew T. H. (Thos), 1844, said to have come to Sta Clara Val. iv. 453; at Mont. '45; in '46–7 of Co. B, Cal. Bat. (v. 358), serving also a courier in Oct. '46; at Mont. '47–8. H. (T. F.), 1848, settler in Sonoma Co.; at Sta Rosa '77. H. (Wilford), 1847, Co. A, Morm. Bat. (v. 469); at Sutter's Fort in '48 when gold was discovered. H. (Wm), 1845, brother of David, overl. immig. of the Grigsby Ide party, apparently with a family. iv. 579, 587; at Sta Rosa from '46, in which year his daughter Mary, later Mrs McCormick, was born. His wife is credited with having furnished some material for the famous Bear flag. v. 148. He died in '66, leaving a large family. H. (Wm L.), 1841, com. of the U.S. *Peacock* in U.S. ex. ex. iv. 241.

Hudspeth (Benj. M. or N.), 1846, lieut, and later capt., Co. A, Cal. Bat. v. 361. I find nothing more about him. H. (James M.), 1843, nat. of Ala, who crossed the plains to Or. in '42, and came to Cal. in the Hastings party. iv. 390, 400. He worked for Stephen Smith at Bodega for a while. iv. 396; and subsequently visited various parts of Cal., working as a lumberman at Sauzalito, and hunting in the Sac. Val.; served, perhaps, as a 2d lieut of Gantt's comp. during the Micheltorena war of '44–5; and in the spring of '46 went east to the Salt Lake region with Hastings and Clyman to aid in diverting immig. and prospective filibusters from Or. to Cal. v. 526, 529. He returned in the autumn, v. 530, and served as lieut of Co. F, Cal. Bat., in '46–7. v. 361, 435. After the war he bought land in Sonoma, and worked with O'Farrell as surveyor at Benicia—where he owned a lot, v. 672, as also at S. F., v. 679—Napa, and other places; in the mines '49–50; later a farmer in Sonoma Co.; memb. of legislature '52–5; and still living in '85, at the age of 63. His wife, from '54, was Matilda Fuller, and he had no children. Portrait in *Son. Co. Hist.*, 160.

Huefner (Wm), 1847, Co. C, N. Y. Vol. (v. 499); ment. at Sonoma, where he took part in theatrical performances, and at N. Helv.; resid. of S. F. and for a long time marshal of the pioneer society to '82; but I think died before '85. Huerstel (Laurent), 1844 (?), in S.F. '81, said to have arrived in '44. Soc. Cal. Pion. roll. iv. 453. Huet, 1845, Amer. farmer from Or. in McM.-Clyman party, who prob. went back in '46. iv. 572, 526; perhaps 'Hewitt.' Huff (Columbus), 1847, Co. F, 3d U.S. artill. (v. 518); in Napa '48.

Hugel (Fred.), 1837, German who had been in Cal. 5 years when applying for a pass in '42. iv. 118; at Sutter's Fort '46; in '47 bought land of Rufus in Son. Co.; perhaps 'Hegel,' q.v. Hugenin (Dan. C.), 1846, mid. on the U. S. *Portsmouth;* lost on the *Warren's* launch. iv. 587; v. 384. Hughes (H. M.), 1839 (?), in Sonoma Co. '74–7. H. (John), 1847, Co. D, N. Y. Vol. (v. 499). H. (Wm), 1845, one of Frémont's men. iv. 583; Cal. claim '46–7 (v. 462). He was a nephew of Cyrus Alexander, and also in the exped. of '48. H. (Wm), 1847, Co. F, N.Y.Vol. (v. 499). H. (Wm O.), 1836, on Larkin's books '36–7; perhaps 'Hewes.' Huguee, 1845, mr of the *Medicis.* iv. 567. Huie (Geo. W.), 1847, physician said to have come with Lieut Thompson of the U.S.N.; joined by his family '49 at S. F.; at Petaluma '53–68, and later at S.F., where he died in '77.

Hulett (Sylvester), 1847, lieut Co. D, Morm. Bat. v. 477; in '82 at Manti, Utah. Hull, 1844, mr of the *Georgia.* iv. 566. H. (Isaac), 1848, passp. from Hon. H. (Joseph), 1848, nat. of Ohio, who came to Or. in '45, and to

Cal. on the discov. of gold; joined by his family '49; from '50 on a Sac. farm, where he still lived in '80 with wife and 4 children. H. (Joseph B.), 1843, com. of the U.S. *Warren* '43-7; in com. at S.F. '46-7, succeeding Montgomery. iv. 569; v. 284, 289, 380, 434, 539, 581, 649, 659.

Humphrey, 1840, at Mont.; Larkin urged to use his influence to start him for home. H. (Benj. F.), 1847, Co. E, N.Y.Vol. (v. 499). H. (Geo. L.), 1847, Co. H, N.Y.Vol. (v. 499); at Coulterville '74. H. (Isaac), 1848, nat. of Ga, at Sutter's Fort when gold was discovered; having been a miner in Ga, he hastened to the mill, made a rocker, and thus became the pioneer in a new industry. Ment. in *N. Helv. Diary* in April. Died at Victoria in '67. H. (Wm), 1847, Co. G, N.Y.Vol. (v. 499); at Coulterville '71-4; perhaps confounded with Geo. L. H. (W.), 1848, passp. from Hon. Humphries, 1840, mr of the *Columbia* '40-1. iv. 102-3, 564. H. (Stephen), 1848, in S.F. list.

Hunnewell (James), 1830, a well-known Boston trader in business at Hon. for some years. The only evidence I have that he ever came to Cal. is a letter of Oct. '30, in which he hopes to visit the country 'again;' but in '33 he was in Mass. and intended to stay there. He died in '69. He may have visited Cal. before '20. Hunsacker (Abraham), 1847, Co. D, Morm. Bat. (v. 469); later sergt; in '82 a bishop at Brigham City, Utah. H. (Daniel), 1847, overl. immig. from Mo. with his family; ment. at N. Helv. in Aug. with news of approaching immigration. v. 556. Settled at Benicia, and later in Contra Costa, where he was treasurer of the county. Of his sons who came in '47, Harrison K. was at one time deputy sheriff of Contra Costa; James C. was sheriff, and lost on the *Brother Jonathan;* and Nicholas, also sheriff, was a miner at Park's Bar in '48, and a resid. of S. Diego '74.

Hunt, 1813, agent of Astor's fur company, on the *Pedler.* ii. 271. H. (Gilbert), 1847, Co. A, Morm. Bat. (v. 469). H. (Jefferson), 1847, capt. Co. A, Morm. Bat., and also preacher. v. 477-80, 488, 493; had a project for raising a new battalion. v. 496. He was accomp. by his wife and 4 sons, Hiram, John, Joseph, and Martial; and three daughters, Jane, Harriet, and Mary; but it is doubtful if all the family came to Cal. In later years Capt. H. came back to Cal. and represented S. Bernardino in the legisl. of '55. H. (Martial), 1847, son of Capt. H., Co. A, Morm. Bat.; in '81 at Snowflake, Ariz. H. (Timothy Dwight), 1841, protestant clergyman who came from Honolulu in Nov., and was employed for a time as city chaplain. In '55 he was in Cal. as the agent of the Amer. Home Miss. Soc. v. 657.

Hunter (Barry), 1846, doubtful name in a Los Ang. list. H. (Benj. F.), 1846, lieut on the U.S. *Portsmouth;* at N.Helv. June. v. 102; acting capt. of Co. C, Stockton's bat. '46-7. v. 385. H. (Edward), 1847, Co. B, Morm. Bat. (v. 469); in '82 a bishop in Utah. H. (Jesse D.), 1847, nat. of Ky, and capt. Co. B, Morm. Bat. v. 477; in com. of S. Diego garrison. v. 488, 617. Ind. agent for southern Cal. at S. Luis Rey from Aug. v. 492, 568, 621-2. His wife died at S.D. in '47. v. 490. He remained in Cal., went to the mines in '48, but returned to the south to act again as Ind. agent. He died at Los Ang. in '77, at the age of 73, leaving 7 grown children with families. H. (Wm), 1847, musician of Morm. Bat., Co. B. (v. 469). Huntington (Dimick B.), 1847, Co. D, Morm. Bat. (v. 499); at Salt Lake City '55. Huntley (Ezra), 1847, Co. K, N.Y. Vol. (v. 499). Huntsman (Isaiah), 1847, Co. B, Morm. Bat. (v. 469); in Utah '81.

Huppertz (Gerard), 1834, succeeded Sill & Co. as baker at Sta B. Hurst, 1847, at N. Helv. from S.F., Oct. Hurtado (Joaquin), 1791, piloto in Malaspina's exped. i. 490. Huse (Sam. E.), 1846, gunner on the U.S. *Congress*, and in com. of a gun in Stockton's campaign of '46-7; in Amador Co. from '51; died at Yount in '79. Hutcheon (Walter), 1847, Co. E, N.Y.Vol. (v. 499); d. Brooklyn, N.Y., '80. Hutcheson, 1848, sentenced to corporal punishment by court-martial. Hutchins, 1846, mr of the whaler *Columbus.* Hutchinson (G.N.), 1846, in the U.S.N.; drowned in '78 at Vallejo, where he was mr of the navy-yard yacht *Freda*, and had lived for 20 years.

Hutchinson (Jacob A.), 1846, overl. immig. with family, who in '49 settled on the Cosumnes River, and soon started on a prospecting tour, from

which he never returned.   H. (Jacob A., Jr), 1847, son of the preceding;
living on the Cosumnes with family in '80; perhaps date of arrival should be
'46, or that of his father '47. The H. brothers are named as having bought
Isbel's claim in S. Joaq. '48.   H. (Joseph), 1846, Fauntleroy's dragoons (v.
232, 247).   H. (Wm A.), 1848, advertised for a lost rifle at S.F.   Hütt-
mann (Francis), 1847, mr and sup. of the *Matilda, Primavera*, and *Callao* in
'47–8; made advances of money to Frémont, about which there was much
trouble later. v. 441, 465–6, 576.   Hutton (James D.), 1847, surveyor of
pueblo lands at S. José; appointed official surveyor of the southern dept, but
the appointment was withdrawn on account of charges in connection with his
S. José work. v. 665.   Huxley (J. Mead), 1847, Co. A, N.Y.Vol. (v. 499);
at S.F. '54; officer in the war of '61–5; died before '82.

Hyatt (Elisha), 1846, one of the Mormon col. with wife and son. v. 546;
excommunicated at S. F.; and in Oct. at Mont., making tubs, etc.   Hyde
(Geo.), 1846, nat. of Penn., who came on the U.S. *Congress* as Com. Stockton's
sec. For a time, in Aug., he was alcalde at S. José. v. 294–5, 662; then came
to S.F., where he was 2d alcalde with Bartlett, and 1st alcalde from June '47
to March '48, having much trouble in his administration of the office, as fully
explained in v. 648–52, 680. There seems to have been but slight foundation
for the many and bitter charges against him. He was a lawyer, of good abilities and character. He was somewhat prominent in city politics in '49 and
the few years following; and has resided in S. F. ever since to '85, being in
the real estate business. In '78 he gave me a valuable statement of *Historical
Facts*, including not only his own controversies, but many other points of interest connected with early S.F. annals.   Hyde (Wm), 1847, sergt Co. B,
Morm. Bat., being also an elder and preacher, and a capt. of 50 on the return.
v. 477, 488, 490–1, 493.

To be Continued at the End of Vol. IV.